D0883211

Calendar
of
Literary
Facts

Calendar
of
Literary
Facts

**A Daily and Yearly Guide
to Noteworthy Events in
World Literature from 1450
to the present.**

Samuel J. Rogal, Editor
Illinois Valley Community College

Gale Research Inc. • DETROIT • LONDON

Samuel J. Rogal

Gale Research, Inc.

Jelena Krstovic, *Project Coordinator*

Mary Beth Trimper, *Production Manager*
Marilyn Jackman, *External Production Associate*

Arthur Chartow, *Art Director*
Cynthia D. Baldwin, *Graphic Designer*
C. J. Jonik, *Keyliner*
Bernadette M. Gornie, *Graphic Designer*

Laura Bryant, *Production Supervisor*
Louise Gagné, *Internal Production Associate*
Yolanda Y. Latham, *Internal Production Assistant*

The paper used in this publication meets the minimum requirements
of American National Standard for Information Sciences—Permanence
Paper for Printed Library Materials, ANSI Z39.48-1984.   ∞™

ISBN 0-8103-2943-3

Library of Congress Cataloging in Publication Data

Rogal, Samuel J.
    A calendar of literary facts : a daily guide to noteworthy events in world literature from 1450 through 1989 / Samuel J. Rogal.
        p.   cm.
    Includes index.
    ISBN 0-8103-2943-3 : $45.00
    1. Literary calendars.   I. Title
PN6075.R64   1991   90–14039
809'.002'02--dc20   CIP

Printed in the United States of America

Published in the United States by Gale Research Inc.
Published simultaneously in the United Kingdom
by Gale Research International Limited
(An affiliated company of Gale Research Inc.)

CONTENTS

PREFACE

The Calendar of Literary Facts is designed to address a deceptively simple need: to answer the questions of *who wrote what when.* Within a single volume, this ready-reference tool provides information on more than two thousand writers and their works. Encompassing the years 1450 to 1989, the *Calendar* opens the doors to all significant literary eras and to the literature of all nationalities. Year by year, it provides the reader (whether he or she is a serious student or a casual inquirer) with biographical summary, literary precis, and historical notation relative to *who wrote what when.* For those who seek information on more specific dates in literary history, the *Calendar* guides its patrons through 366 days of essential facts associated with the literati of the world.

Specifically, readers can turn to the *Calendar* to answer the following types of questions:

- the births and deaths of authors

- the nationalities of authors

- the publication dates of titles

- the literary forms and plots of specific works

- significant titles that commonly identify certain authors

- the chronology of a particular author's works and their chronological relationship to publications by other writers

In addition, the *Calendar* will answer questions concerning dates of significant newspapers, periodicals, journals, translations, editions of important writers' works, and the establishment of literary and selected cultural institutions, societies, and organizations.

The *Calendar* is the perfect source for the reader who wants answers to specific questions on authors, publications, and literary events. It stands ready to assist students and general readers in determining all that occurred on a specific date or year in literary history. This volume brings together within a single source a variety and quantity of literary information heretofore available only upon several library shelves (or the shelves of several libraries).

However, a word of advice and a statement of intent need to be expressed here. First, do not expect that this one volume contains a reference to *every* work ever inscribed by man or woman upon a sheet of paper, or that it identifies every man or woman who has ever written or has published a work of prose, poetry, or drama. Such a state of comprehensiveness may never be achieved, with or without the research capacity or technology of the present age. Thus, "representativeness" has served as the guiding principle for this work. Second, the *Calendar* should *never* be embraced as a substitute or expedient for the complete and careful reading of the primary source. Rather, it should serve to whet the appetite, to stimulate the imagination and to lead the reader to the primary source–the poem, the play, the essay, the novel, the short story, or whatever it is that arouses his or her interest. If this source can indeed promote reading and inquiry—can promote the urge to read and inquire—then it will, in turn, prove a useful and significant contribution to the genre of reference literature.

Acknowledgments

There require expressions of thanks and sincere appreciation to a number of individuals and groups who contributed significantly to the publication of this project: the staff of Jacobs Library, Illinois Valley Community College (Evelyn Moyle, Carol Bird, Mary Ann Kirzeder, Sandra Korter, Sherri Popurella, Melva Richards, Tari Sangston, and Jan Voglesang), who extended to me every courtesy and cooperation (and even bent the rules and regulations concerning borrowing privileges far beyond the regions of normal reason and organization); Janine Joerger of the secretarial staff at Illinois Valley Community College; Chris Nasso and Jelena Krstovic of Gale Research, Inc.—the former having suggested and offered the project to me, while the latter served as the in-house editorial contact; my wife Susan and sons Geoffrey and James who, as always, endured, tolerated, and supported my efforts.

July 1990

Samuel J. Rogal
Division of Humanities and Fine Arts
Illinois Valley Community College
Oglesby, Illinois

LIST OF SOURCES

In addition to the various editions of primary source materials, the following general reference sources have been consulted for the preparation of this volume:

Allibone, Samuel Austin. *A Critical Dictionary of English Literature and British and American Authors.* 3 vols. Philadelphia: J.B. Lippincott and Co., 1872.

Auge, Claude, and Paul Auge. *Nouveau Petit Larouse.* Paris: Librarie Larouse, 1937.

Beaty, Jerome, and J. Paul Hunter, eds. *New Worlds of Literature.* New York: W.W. Norton and Co., 1989.

Becka, Jiri, ed. *Dictionary of Oriental Literatures, Volume III: West Asia and North Africa.* London: George Allen and Unwin, 1974.

Behrens, C.B.A. *The Ancien Regime.* London: Thames and Hudson, 1967.

Block, Maxine, *et al.*, eds. *Current Biography.* New York: The H.W. Wilson Co., 1940–1990.

Bohn, Henry G. *A Catalogue of Books.* 2 vols. 1841. Reprint. New York: AMS Press, 1964.

Bruccoli, Matthew J. and Richard Layman, gen. eds. *Dictionary of Literary Biography.* 100 vols. Detroit: Gale Research, 1978-1990.

Castillo y Tuazon, Teofilo del, and Benaventura S. Medine, Jr. *Philippine Literature: From Ancient Times to the Present.* Quezon City, Philippines: Teofilo del Castillo, 1972.

Chase William D., and Helen M. Chase. *Chase's Annual Events.* 30th ed. Chicago and New York: Contemporary Books, 1986.

Colby, Vineta, ed. *World Authors, 1975–1980.* New York: The H.W. Wilson Co., 1985.

Donovan, Dianne, ed. *Tribune Books (The Chicago Tribune* Sunday Supplement). 23 October 1988–17 June 1990.

Drabble, Margaret, ed. *The Oxford Companion to English Literature.* 5th ed. Oxford: Oxford University Press, 1985.

Durand, Maurice M., and Nguyen Tran Huan. *An Introduction to Vietnamese Literature. Translated* by D.M. Hawke. New York: Columbia University Press, 1985.

Fargher, Richard. *Life and Letters in France: The Eighteenth Century.* New York: Charles Scribner's Sons, 1970.

Fitzsimmons, Thomas, ed. and trans. *Japanese Poetry Now*. Introduction by Kenneth Rexroth. New York: Schocken Books, 1972.

Gassner, John, and Edward Quinn eds. *The Reader's Encyclopedia of World Drama*. New York: Thomas Y. Crowell Co., 1969.

Giles, Herbert A. *A History of Chinese Literature*. New York and London: D. Appleton and Co., 1931.

Godwin, Parke. *The Cyclopaedia of Biography: A Record of the Lives of Eminent Persons*. New York: G.P. Putnam's Sons, 1884.

Grun, Bernard. *The Timetables of History*. New York: Simon and Schuster, 1975.

Hart, James D. *The Oxford Companion to American Literature*. 5th ed. New York: Oxford University Press, 1983.

Herbert, A.S. *Historical Catalogue of Printed Editions of the English Bible, 1525–1961*. London: The British and Foreign Bible Society; New York: The American Bible Society, 1968.

Herdeck, Donald E. *African Authors*. Washington, D.C.: Black Orpheus Press, 1973.

——————. *Caribbean Writers: A Bio-Bibliographical Critical Encyclopedia*. Washington, D.C.: Three Continents Press, 1979.

Hoffman, Daniel, ed. *Harvard Guide to Contemporary American Writing*. Cambridge, Mass.: The Belknap Press, 1979.

Johnson, Allen, *et al.*, eds. *Dictionary of American Biography*. 10 vols. and supplements. New York: Charles Scribner's Sons, 1885–1990.

Kepos, Paula, *et al.*, eds. *Twentieth-Century Literary Criticism*. 37 vols. Detroit: Gale Research, 1978-1990.

Konishi, Jin'ichi. *A History of Japanese Literature*. Translated by Aileen Gatten and Nicholas Teele. Edited by Earl Miner. 2 vols. Princeton, N.J.: Princeton University Press, 1984–1986.

Kravitz, Nathaniel. *Three Thousand Years of Hebrew Literature*. Chicago: The Swallow Press, 1972.

Kunitz, Stanley J., and Vineta Colby, eds. *European Authors, 1000–1900*. New York: The H.W. Wilson Co., 1967.

——————. *Twentieth Century Authors. First Supplement*. New York: The H.W. Wilson Co., 1955.

Kunitz, Stanley J. and Howard Haycraft, eds. *Twentieth Century Authors*. New York: The H.W. Wilson Co., 1942.

Levey, Judith S., and Agnes Greenhall, eds. *The Concise Columbia Encyclopedia*. New York: Columbia University Press, 1983.

Matuz, Roger, *et al.*, eds. *Contemporary Literary Criticism.* 61 vols. Detroit: Gale Research, 1973-1990.

Mullane, Janet, *et al.*, eds. *Nineteenth-Century Literature Criticism.* 28 vols. Detroit: Gale Research, 1981-1990.

O'Brien, Geoffrey, ed. *The Reader's Catalogue.* New York: Jason Epstein, 1989.

Packard, Lawrence Bradford. *The Age of Louis XIV.* Hinsdale, Illinois: The Dryden Press, 1957.

Parrington, Vernon Louis. *Main Currents in American Thought.* 3 vols. New York: Harcourt, Brace, and Co., 1927.

Person, James, Jr., *et al.*, eds. *Literature Criticism from 1400 to 1800.* 14 vols. Detroit: Gale Research, 1984-1990.

Pickering, James H., ed. *Fiction 100: An Anthology of Short Stories.* 5th ed. New York: Macmillan Publishing Co., 1988.

Rogal, Samuel J. *A Chronological Outline of British Literature.* Westport, Conn.: Greenwood Press, 1980.

_____. *A Chronological Outline of American Literature.* New York: Greenwood Press, 1987.

Sadiq, Muhammad. *A History of Urdu Literature.* 2d ed., rev. Delhi, India: Oxford University Press, 1984.

Seymour-Smith, Martin. *Funk and Wagnall's Guide to Modern World Literature.* New York: Funk and Wagnalls, 1973.

Spiller, Robert E., *et al. Literary History of the United States: History.* 3rd ed., rev. London and New York: The Macmillan Co., 1963.

Steinberg, S.H., ed. *Cassell's Encyclopaedia of World Literature.* 2 vols. New York: Funk and Wagnalls, 1954.

Stephen, Leslie, Sir Sidney Lee, *et al.*, eds. *The Dictionary of National Biography.* 31 vols. and supplements. London: Oxford University Press, 1885–1985.

Thorne, J.O., ed. *Chambers's Biographical Dictionary.* New York: St. Martin's Press, 1962.

Trager, James, ed. *The People's Chronology.* New York: Holt, Rinehart, and Winston, 1979.

Trosky, Susan, *et al.*, eds. *Contemporary Authors.* Vols. 1-131. Detroit: Gale Research, 1962-1990.

Turner, Roland, *et al. The Annual Obituary.* 9 vols. New York: St. Martin's Press, 1980–1988.

Urdang, Laurence, *et al.*, eds. *Holidays and Anniversaries of the World.* Detroit: Gale Research, 1985.

Vinson, James, ed. *Great Writers of the English Language: Poets*. New York: St. Martin's Press, 1979.

Wakeman, John, ed. *World Authors, 1950–1970*. New York: The H.W. Wilson Co., 1980.

_____. *World Authors, 1970–1975*. New York: The H.W. Wilson Co., 1980.

World Literature Today: A Literary Quarterly of the University of Oklahoma. Vols. 60–63, 1986–1989.

Zbavitel, Dusan, ed. *Dictionary of Oriental Literatures, Volume II: South and South-East Asia*. London: George Allen and Unwin, 1974.

JANUARY

1

BIRTHS

1484. Ulrich (Huldreich) Zwingli (d. 11 October 1531). Swiss theologian and essayist

1768. Maria Edgeworth (d. 22 May 1849). Irish writer of fiction

1819. Arthur Hugh Clough (d. 13 November 1861). English poet and essayist

1834. Ludovic Halevy (d. 8 May 1908). French playwright and writer of fiction

1839. Ouida (pseudonym of Marie Louise de la ,Ramee; d. 25 January 1908). English writer of fiction

1854. Sir James George Frazer (d. 7 May 1941). Scottish anthropologist and essayist

1879. Edward Morgan Forster (d. 6 June 1970). English writer of fiction and critical essayist

1897. Catherine Shober Drinker Bowen (d. 1 November 1973). American writer of fictional biography

1911. Audrey Wurdemann (d. 18 May 1960). American poet

1919. Jerome David Salinger. American writer of fiction

1922. John Brick (d. 15 October 1973). American historical novelist

DEATHS

1612. Sir Thomas Bodley (b. 1 March 1545). English scholar

1730. Samuel Sewall (b. 28 March 1652). English-born American essayist and diarist

1811. Christopher Friedrich Nicolai (b. 18 March 1733). German critical essayist and writer of fiction

1885. Peter Christian Asbjornsen (b. 15 January 1812). Norwegian folklorist

1934. Jakob Wassermann (b. 10 March 1873. German writer of fiction.

2

BIRTHS

1752. Philip Morin Freneau (d. 18 December 1832). American journalist, essayist, poet, and writer of narrative

1831. Justin Winsor (d. 22 October 1897). American librarian and historian

1865. William Lyon Phelps (d. 21 August 1943). American literary scholar and essayist

1866. George Gilbert Murray (d. 20 May 1957). English classical scholar and translator

1920. Isaac Asimov. Russian-born American writer of science fiction and popular science prose nonfiction

DEATHS

1783. Johann Jakob Bodmer (b. 19 July 1698). Swiss historian, essayist, critic, and poet

1801. Johann Kaspar Lavater (b. 15 November 1741). Swiss theologian and poet

1831. Barthold Georg Niebuhr (b. 27 August 1776). German biographer and historian

1890. George Henry Boker (b. 6 October 1823). American poet and playwright

1920. Paul Auguste Marie Adam (b. 7 December 1862). French writer of fiction

1924. Sabine Baring-Gould (b. 28 January 1834). English writer of fiction, poet, and writer of miscellaneous prose nonfiction

1927. Asher Ginzberg (b. 5 August 1856). Russian essayist and editor

1948. Vicente Huidobro (b. 10 January 1893). Chilean poet, writer of fiction, and literary theorist

3

BIRTHS

1698. Pietro Antonio Domenico Bonaventura Metastasio (d. 12 April 1782). Italian poet, playwright, and opera librettist

1886. John Gould Fletcher (d. 10 April 1950). American poet and essayist

1892. John Ronald Reuel Tolkien (d. 2 September 1973). South African-born English writer of fiction, poet, critical essayist, and scholar

DEATHS

1875. Pierre Athanase Larousse (b. 23 October 1817). French lexicographer, encyclopaedist, and essayist

1882. William Harrison Ainsworth (b. 4 February 1805). English writer of fiction and poet

1915. James Elroy Flecker (b. 5 November 1884). English poet and playwright

1923. Jaroslav Hasek (b. 30 April 1883). Czech writer of fiction and satirist

1980. Joy Friederike Voctoria Adamson (b. 20 January 1920). Austrian writer of prose nonfiction and memoirist

4

BIRTHS

1643. Sir Isaac Newton (d. 20 March 1727). English scientist, mathematician, essayist, and philosopher

1785. Jakob Ludwig Karl Grimm (d. 20 September 1863). German folklorist and philologist

1796. Henry George Bohn (d. 22 August 1884). English publisher, bookseller, and bibliographer

1813. Sir Isaac Pitman (d. 12 January 1897). English educator, essayist, and establisher of a system of shorthand

1874. Thornton Waldo Burgess (d. 6 June 1965). American writer of fiction for children

1878. Alfred Edgar Coppard (d. 13 January 1957). English writer of fiction and poet

1883. Max Forrester Eastman (d. 25 March 1969). American essayist and literary critic

DEATHS

1786. Moses Mendelssohn (b. 6 September 1729). German philosopher and essayist

1852. Jan Kollar (b. 29 July 1793). Czech poet and Slavonic scholar

1941. Henri Bergson (b. 18 October 1859). French philosopher and essayist

1960. Albert Camus (b. 7 November 1913). Algerian-born French philosopher, writer of fiction, poet, playwright, and journalist

1965. Thomas Stearns Eliot (b. 26 September 1888). American-born English poet, essayist, and playwright

1974. Charles Vincent Emerson Starrett (b. 26 October 1886). Canadian-born essayist, poet, and writer of miscellaneous prose nonfiction

1982. Margaret Culkin Banning (b. 18 March 1891). American writer of fiction and miscellaneous prose nonfiction

1986. Christopher William Bradshaw Isherwood (b. 26 August 1904). English writer of fiction and translator

5

BIRTHS

1846. Rudolph Christoph Eucken (d. 14 September 1926). German philosopher and essayist

1921. Friedrich Durrenmatt. Swiss playwright and writer of fiction

1926. William Dewitt Snodgrass. American poet

DEATHS

1867. Alexander Smith (b. 31 December 1830). Scottish poet and essayist

1913. Sir Edmund William Gosse (b. 21 September 1849). English writer of fiction, critical essayist, biographer, and literary historian

1987. Jean Margaret Wemyss Laurence (b. 18 July 1926). Canadian writer of fiction and essayist

6

BIRTHS

1706. Benjamin Franklin (d. 17 April 1790). American philosopher, scientist, and writer of miscellaneous prose tracts

1878. Carl August Sandburg (d. 22 July 1967). American poet and biographer

1883. Khalil Gibran (d. 10 April 1931). Lebanese poet and writer of fiction

1915. Allan Wilson Watts (d. 16 November 1973). English-born philosopher and essayist

1931. Edgar Lawrence Doctorow. American writer of fiction

DEATHS

1840. Frances Burnèy (b. 13 June 1752). English writer of fiction and diarist

1849. David Hartley Coleridge (b. 19 September 1796). English poet

1882. Richard Henry Dana, Jr. (b. 1 August 1815). American writer of prose narrative and essayist

1944. Ida Minerva Tarbell (b. 5 November 1857). American essayist and biographer·

1963. Stark Young (b. 11 October 1881). American writer of fiction and critical essayist

1981. Archibald Joseph Cronin (b. 19 July 1896). American writer of popular historical fiction

7

BIRTHS

1873. Charles Pierre Peguy (d. 5 September 1914). French poet, publisher, and essayist

1901(?). Zora Neale Hurston (d. 28 January 1960). American writer of fiction

DEATHS

1623. Pietro Sarpi (b. 14 August 1552). Italian ecclesiastical historian

1673. Margaret Cavendish, Duchess of Newcastle (b. ? 1623). English poet

1715. Francois de Salignac de la Mothe Fenelon (b. 6 August 1651). French essayist, compiler of fables and maxims, historian, and satirist

1758. Allan Ramsay (b. 15 October 1685). Scottish poet

1846. Nikolay Yazykov (b. 16 March 1803). Russian poet

1931. Edward Channing (b. 15 June 1856). American educator and historian

1972. John Berryman (b. 25 October 1914). American poet and essayist

1986. Juan Rulfo (b. ? 1918). Mexican writer of fiction and writer of nonfiction narrative

8

BIRTHS

1601. Baltasar Gracian y Morales (d. 6 December 1658). Spanish moralist, humanist, and essayist

1728. Thomas Warton the younger (d. 21 May 1790). English poet, editor, and literary historian

1792. Lowell Mason (d. 11 August 1872). American poet, hymnodist, and music educator

1824. William Wilkie Collins (d. 23 September 1889). English writer of fiction and playwright

1862. Frank Nelson Doubleday (d. 30 January 1934). American publisher and editor

DEATHS

1775. John Baskerville (b. 28 January 1706). English printer and bookseller

1896. Paul Verlaine (b. 30 March 1844). French poet

1972. Kenneth Patchen (b. 13 December 1911). American poet

1980. Lawrence Lovell Schoonover (b. 6 March 1906). American writer of historical fiction

9

BIRTHS

1857. Henry Blake Fuller (d. 28 July 1929). American writer of fiction and playwright

1873. Hayyim Nahman Bialik (d. 4 July 1934). Ukrainian Hebrew poet and writer of fiction

1881. Lascelles Abercrombie (d. 27 October 1938). English poet and critical essayist

Giovanni Papini (d. ? 1956). Italian writer of fiction, poet, and literary critic

1900. Richard Halliburton (d. 23[?] March 1939). American adventurer and writer of travel narrative

1904. Louis Kronenberger, Jr. (d. 30 April 1980). American drama critic, essayist, and writer of fiction

1908. Simone Lucie Ernestine Marie Bertrand de Beauvoir (d. 14 April 1986). French philosopher, writer of fiction, playwright, and critical essayist

DEATHS

1757. Bernard Le Bovier de Fontenelle (b. 11 February 1757). French essayist and popularizer of science

1908. Wilhelm Busch (b. 15 April 1832). German poet, satirist, and comic illustrator

1923. Katherine Mansfield (pseudonym of Kathleen Mansfield Beauchamp; b. 14 October 1888). New Zealand-born English writer of fiction

1924. Basil Lanneau Gildersleeve (b. 23 October 1831). American philologist and classical scholar

1930. Edward William Bok (b. 9 October 1863). Dutch-born American editor, historian, and autobiographer

1946. Countee Cullen (b. 30 May 1903). American poet, writer of fiction, and playwright

10

BIRTHS

1814. Aubrey Thomas De Vere (d. 21 January 1902). Irish-born English poet and critical essayist

1834. John Emerich Edward Dalberg Acton (d. 19 June 1902). English historian

1882. Aleksei Nikolaevich Tolstoi (d. 23 February 1945). Russian writer of fiction and historical narrative

1887. John Robinson Jeffers (d. 20 January 1962). American poet

1893. Vicente Huidobro (d. 2 January 1948). Chilean poet, writer of fiction, and literary theorist

1896. Worth Tuttle Hedden (d. 14 September 1985). American writer of fiction

DEATHS

1778. Carl Linnaeus (b. 23 May 1707). Swedish botanist and writer of scientific prose tracts

1855. Mary Russell Mitford (b. 16 December 1787). English writer of fiction and playwright

1863. Lyman Beecher (b. 12 October 1775). American theologian and essayist

1951. Harry Sinclair Lewis (b. 7 February 1885). American writer of fiction

1957. Gabriela Mistral (pseudonym of Lucila Godoy Alcayaga; b. 7 April 1889). Chilean poet

     Laura Ingalls Wilder (b. 7 February 1867). American writer of autobiographical fiction and narratives for children

1961. Samuel Dashiell Hammett (b. 27 May 1894). American writer of detective and mystery fiction

1970. Charles Olson (b. 27 December 1910). American critical essayist, poet, and playwright

1986. Jaroslav Seifert (b. 23 September 1901). Czech poet

11

BIRTHS

1789. John Payne Collier (d. 17 September 1883). English essayist and literary critic

1839. Eugenio Maria de Hostos (d. 11 August 1903). Chilean philosopher, sociologist, and essayist

1842. William James (d. 26 August 1910). American psychologist and essayist

1897. Bernard Augustine De Voto (d. 13 November 1955). American critical essayist, literary historian, and writer of fiction

1903. Alan Stewart Paton (d. 12 April 1988). South African writer of fiction

1905. Helen Howe (d. 1 February 1975). American writer of fiction

     Manfred Bennington Lee (d. 3 September 1971). American writer of detective and mystery fiction

DEATHS

1753. Sir Hans Sloan (b. 16 April 1660). English physician, scientist, essayist, and bibliophile

1817. Timothy Dwight (b. 14 May 1752). American poet, essayist, and writer of travel narrative

1843. Francis Scott Key (b. 1 August 1779). American poet and essayist

1896. Joao de Deus Ramos (b. 8 March 1830). Portuguese poet

1928. Thomas Hardy (b. 2 June 1840). English poet and writer of fiction

1972. Padraic Colum (b. 8 December 1881). Irish poet, playwright, and critical essayist

12

BIRTHS

1588. John Winthrop (d. 26 March 1649). English-born American colonial essayist and historian

1628. Charles Perrault (d. 16 May 1703). French poet, essayist, historian, and writer of fiction ("fairy tales")

1729. Edmund Burke (d. 9 July 1797). Irish-born English philosopher and political essayist

1746. Johann Heinrich Pestalozzi (d. 17 February 1827). Swiss educational philosopher, essayist, and writer of fiction

1751. Jakob Michael Reinhold Lenz (d. 24 May 1792). German playwright, poet, and essayist

1876. John Griffith (Jack) London (d. 22 November 1916). American writer of fiction and essayist

1878. Ferenc Molnar (d. 1 April 1952). Hungarian-born playwright and writer of fiction

DEATHS

1829. Karl Wilhelm Friedrich von Schlegel (b. 10 March 1772). German critical essayist and literary historian

1897. Sir Isaac Pitman (b. 4 January 1813). English educator, essayist, and establisher of a system of shorthand

1960. Nevil Shute (originally Nevil Shute Norway; b. 17 January 1899). English writer of popular fiction

1965. Lorraine Vivian Hansberry (b. 19 May 1930). American playwright

1976. Agatha Mary Clarissa Christie (b. 15 September 1890). English writer of mystery and detective fiction

13

BIRTHS

1749. Friedrich Muller (d. 23 April 1825). German poet and painter

1834. Horatio Alger, Jr. (d. 18 July 1899). American writer of juvenile fiction.

1901. Alfred Bertram Guthrie, Jr. American writer of fiction

DEATHS

1867. Victor Cousin (b. 28 November 1792). French philosopher and essayist

1941. James Joyce (b. 2 February 1882). Irish writer of fiction and poet

1945. Margaretta Wade Campbell Deland (b. 28 February 1857). American writer of fiction and poet

1957. Alfred Edgar Coppard (b. 4 January 1878). English writer of fiction and poet

1984. Justin Brooks Atkinson (b. 28 November 1894). American drama critic, essayist, and biographer

1989. Sterling Allen Brown (b. 1 May 1901). American poet and literary critic

14

BIRTHS

1818. Zacharias Topelius (d. 12 March 1898). Swedish poet, playwright, and writer of fiction

1875. Albert Schweitzer (d. 4 September 1965). Alsatian theologian, musician, medical missionary, and essayist

1882. Hendrik Willem Van Loon (d. 11 March 1944). Dutch-born American popular historian and biographer

1886. Hugh Lofting (d. 26 September 1947). English-born American writer of children's fiction

1896. John Roderigo Dos Passos (d. 28 September 1970). American writer of fiction, biographer, and writer of travel narrative

1925. Yukio Mishima (originally Kimitake Hiraoka; d. 25 November 1970). Japanese writer of fiction

1926. Thomas Tryon. American writer of fiction and actor

DEATHS

1753. George Berkeley (b. 12 March 1865). Irish-born theologian, philosopher, essayist, and poet

1831. Henry Mackenzie (d. 25 August 1745). Scottish writer of fiction, essayist, and periodical editor

1898. Lewis Carroll (pseudonym of Charles Lutwidge Dodgson; b. 27 January 1832). English mathematician, writer of children's fiction, poet, and classical scholar

1924. Arne Evenson Garborg (b. 25 January 1851). Norwegian writer of fiction, playwright, theologian, and linguistic reformer

1943. Laura Elizabeth Richards (b. 27 February 1850). American writer of fiction and biographer

1977. Anais Nin (b. 21 February 1903). French-born American writer of fiction, literary critic, and diarist

1980. Robert Ardrey (b. 16 October 1908). American anthropologist and essayist

15

BIRTHS

1622. Jean Baptiste Moliere (originally Jean-Baptiste Poquelin; d. 17 February 1673). French comic playwright and actor

1791. Franz Grillparzer (d. 21 January 1872). Austrian poet, playwright, and writer of fiction

1795. Aleksandr Sergeievich Griboyedov (d. 11 February 1829). Russian verse-dramatist

1798. Thomas Crofton Croker (d. 8 August 1854). Irish antiquary and writer of fiction

1812. Peter Christian Asbjornsen (d. 1 January 1885). Norwegian folklorist

1891. Osip Emilievich Mandelstam (d. 28 December 1938). Polish-born Russian poet

1929. Martin Luther King, Jr. (d. 4 April 1968). American social reformer and essayist

1933. Ernest James Gaines. American writer of fiction

DEATHS

1893. Frances Anne (Fanny) Kemble (b. 27 November 1809). English actress, poet, and memoirist

1934. Hermann Bahr (b. 19 July 1863). Austrian essayist and playwright

1945. Mary Ursula Bethell (b. 6 October 1874). English-born New Zealand poet

16

BIRTHS

1697(?). Richard Savage (d. 1 August 1743). English poet and playwright

1741. Hester Lynch Thrale Piozzi (d. 2 May 1821). English biographer and writer of prose narrative

1749. Vittorio Alfieri (d. 8 October 1803). Italian poet and playwright

1874. Robert William Service (d. 11 September 1958). American writer of verse

1901. Laura Riding (pseudonym of Laura Reichenthal; also Laura Riding Jackson). American critical essayist, writer of fiction, and poet.

1912. Nigel Forbes Dennis. English writer of fiction, playwright, journalist, and critical essayist

DEATHS

1599. Edmund Spenser (b. 1522?). English-born Irish poet

1794. Edward Gibbon (b. 27 April 1737). English essayist and historian

1985. Robert Stuart Fitzgerald (b. ? 1910). American poet, translator, essayist, and academician

17

BIRTHS

1600. Pedro Calderon de la Barca (d. 25 May 1681). Spanish playwright

1771. Charles Brockden Brown (d. 22 [?] February 1810). American essayist and writer of fiction

1820. Anne Bronte (d. 28 May 1849). English writer of fiction and poet

1860. Anton Pavlovich Chekhov (d. 2 July 1904). Russian writer of fiction and playwright

1886. Arthur Annesley Ronald Firbank (d. 12 May 1926). English writer of fiction, playwright, and poet

1899. Nevil Shute (originally Nevil Shute Norway; d. 12 January 1960). English writer of popular fiction

1914. William Edgar Stafford. American poet and critical essayist

DEATHS

1823. Friedrich Ludwig Zacharias Werner (b. 18 November 1768). German playwright

1891. George Bancroft (b. 3 October 1800). American historian and essayist

1972. Betty Wehner Smith (b. 15 December 1906). American playwright and writer of fiction

18

BIRTHS

1689. Charles Louis de Secondat, Baron de Montesquieu (d. 10 February 1755). French social and political philosopher and essayist

1779. Peter Mark Roget (d. 12 September 1869). English scholar, physician, and linguist

1840. Henry Austin Dobson (d. 2 September 1921). English poet, essayist, and biographer

1867. Ruben Dario (pseudonym of Felix Ruben Garcia Sarmiento; d. 6 February 1916). Nicaraguan poet and literary critic

1882. Alan Alexander Milne (d. 31 January 1956). English essayist and writer of verse and fiction for children

1912. William Sansom (d. 20 April 1976). English writer of fiction

DEATHS

1547. Pietro Bembo (b. 20 May 1470). Italian poet, essayist, and grammarian

1908. Edmund Clarence Stedman (b. 8 October 1833). American poet and essayist

1936. Joseph Rudyard Kipling (b. 30 December 1865). English poet and writer of fiction

1977. Carl Zuckmayer (b. 22 December 1896). German playwright, poet, and writer of fiction

1986. Nancy Wilson Ross (b. 22 November 1907). American fiction writer and philosopher

19

BIRTHS

1737. Jacques Henri Bernardin de Saint-Pierre (d. 21 January 1814). French writer of fiction and travel narrative and essayist

1749. Isaiah Thomas (d. 4 April 1831). American printer, publisher, and historian of the print trade

1798. Isidore Auguste Marie Francois Comte (d. 5 September 1857). French philosopher, sociologist, and essayist

1809. Edgar Allan Poe (d. 7 October 1859). American writer of fiction, poet, and critical essayist

1835. Thomas Hood the younger (d. 20 November 1874). English humorist

1850. Augustine Birrell (d. 20 November 1933). English literary essayist and biographer

1887. Alexander Humphreys Woollcott (d. 23 January 1943). American literary critic and essayist

1921. Patricia Highsmith. English writer of fiction

DEATHS

1576. Hans Sachs (b. 5 November 1494). German poet and playwright

1729. William Congreve (b. 10 February 1670). English playwright and poet

1848. Isaac D'Israeli (b. 17 May 1766). English critical essayist and writer of fiction

1874. August Heinrich Hoffman von Fallersleven (b. 2 April 1798). German poet, philologist, and antiquarian

20

BIRTHS

1804. Marie Joseph Eugene Sue (d. 3 August 1857). French writer of fiction

1806. Nathaniel Parker Willis (d. 20 January 1867). American writer of fiction, playwright, and poet

1873. Johannes Vilhelm Jensen (d. 25 November 1950). Danish writer of fiction, essayist, and poet

1920. Joy Friederike Victoria Adamson (d. 3 January 1980). Austrian writer of prose nonfiction and memoirist

DEATHS

1779. David Garrick (b. 19 February 1717). English actor, playwright, and poet

1813. Christoph Martin Wieland (b. 5 September 1733). German essayist, translator, poet, and writer of fiction

1850. Adam Gottlieb Oehlenschleger (b. 14 November 1779). Danish poet and playwright

1859. Bettina Elisabeth von Arnim (b. 4 April 1785). German social-political essayist and memoirist

1867. Nathaniel Parker Willis (b. 20 January 1806). American writer of fiction, playwright, and poet

1900. Richard Doddridge Blackmore (b. 7 June 1825). English writer of fiction

1926. Charles Montagu Doughty (b. 19 August 1843). English writer of travel narrative, poet, and playwright

1933. George Augustus Moore (b. 24 February 1852). Irish-born English writer of fiction

1955. Robert Peter Tristram Coffin (b. 18 March 1892). American poet, writer of fiction, biographer, and writer of miscellaneous prose nonfiction

1962. John Robinson Jeffers (b. 19 January 1887). American poet

1974. Edmund Charles Blunden (b. 1 November 1896). English poet and biographer

1978. Gilbert Arthur Highet (b. 22 June 1906). American literary scholar and essayist

21

BIRTHS

1823. Imre Madach (d. 5 October 1864). Hungarian poet and playwright

1867. Ludwig Thoma (d. 26 August 1921). German humorist, satirist, essayist, playwright, and poet

1904. Richard Palmer Blackmur (d. 2 February 1965). American poet and literary critic

1918. Frederick Guy Butler. South African poet and playwright

DEATHS

1609. Joseph Justus Scaliger (b. 4 August 1540). French-born scholar and editor

1683. Anthony Ashley Cooper, first Earl of Shaftesbury (b. ? 1621). English parliamentarian, and essayist.

1814. Jacques Henri Bernardin de Saint-Pierre (b. 19 January 1737). French writer of fiction and travel narrative and essayist

1815. Matthias Claudius (b. 15 August 1740). German poet and essayist

1831. Ludwig Achim von Arnim (b. 26 January 1781). German writer of fiction

1859. Henry Hallam (b. 9 July 1777). English historian

1870. Alexander Ivanovich Herzen (b. 6 April 1812). Russian philosopher and essayist

1872. Franz Grillparzer (b. 15 January 1791). Austrian poet, playwright, and writer of fiction

1900. John Ruskin (b. 8 February 1819). English art critic and social theorist

1902. Aubrey Thomas De Vere (b. 10 January 1814). Irish-born English poet and critical essayist

1924. Vladimir Ilyich Lenin (b. 4 May 1870). Russian political philosopher, revolutionary, and essayist

1932. Giles Lytton Strachey (b. 1 March 1880). English biographer, essayist, and literary historian

1943. Eric Mowbray Knight (b. 10 April 1897). English-born American writer of fiction for children

1950. George Orwell (pseudonym of Eric Arthur Blair; b. 25 June 1903). English writer of fiction and nonfiction narrative and essayist

22

BIRTHS

1561. Sir Francis Bacon (d. 9 April 1626). English philosopher and essayist

1592. Pierre Gassendi (d. 24 October 1655). French philosopher, essayist, mathematician, and biographer

1729. Gotthold Ephraim Lessing (d. 15 February 1781). German playwright, translator, essayist, and poet

1788. George Gordon, Lord Byron (d. 19 April 1824). English poet and writer of verse drama

1849. Johan August Strindberg (d. 14 May 1912). Swedish playwright, writer of fiction, and essayist

1861. Maurice Henry Hewlett (d. 15 June 1923). English writer of fiction, poet, and essayist

1882. Louis Pergaud (d. 8 April 1915). French writer of fiction

1894. Charles Langbridge Morgan (d. 6 February 1958). English writer of fiction, playwright, and poet

1937. Joseph Aloysius Wambaugh, Jr. American writer of fiction

DEATHS

1942. Xiao Hong (b. ? 1911). Chinese writer of fiction and poet

1945. Arthur Symonds (b. 28 February 1865). Welsh-born English cultural essayist and poet

23

BIRTHS

1783. Stendhal (pseudonym of Marie Henri Beyle; d. 23 March 1842). French writer of fiction and biographer

1813. Jacobine Camilla Wergeland Collet (d. 6 March 1895). Norwegian writer of fiction

1861. Katherine Tynan (d. 2 April 1931). Irish poet and writer of fiction

1904. Louis Zukofsky (d. 12 May 1978). American poet, critical essayist, and translator

DEATHS

1744. Giovanni Battista Vico (b. 23 June 1688). Italian historical philosopher and essayist

1854. Robert Montgomery Bird (b. 5 February 1806). American playwright and writer of fiction

1866. Thomas Love Peacock (b. 18 October 1785). English writer of fiction and poet

1875. Charles Kingsley (b. 12 June 1819). English writer of fiction, poet, playwright, and essayist

1888. Eugene Marin Labiche (b. 5 May 1815). French playwright

1893. Phillips Brooks (b. 13 December 1835). American theologian, essayist, and hymnodist

1943. Alexander Humphreys Woollcott (b. 19 January 1887). American literary critic and essayist

24

BIRTHS

1732. Pierre Augustin Caron de Beaumarchais (d. 18 May 1799). French playwright and memoirist

1776. Ernst Theodor Wilhelm Hoffman (d. 15 June 1822). German essayist, music critic, writer of fiction, and caricaturist

1862. Edith Newbold Jones Wharton (d. 11 August 1937). American writer of fiction and poet

1888. Vicki Baum (d. 29 August 1960). Austrian-born American writer of fiction and playwright

DEATHS

1894. Constance Fenimore Woolson (b. 5 March 1840). American writer of fiction and poet

1965. Winston Spencer Churchill (b. 30 November 1874). English historian, biographer, essayist, writer of prose nonfiction narrative, and statesman

1986. Lafayette Ronald Hubbard (b. 13 March 1911). American writer of science fiction and essayist

25

BIRTHS

1627. Robert Boyle (d. 30 December 1691). English scientist, philosopher, and essayist

1746. Stephanie Felicitie du Crest de Saint Aubin, Comtesse de Genlis (d. 31 December 1830). French playwright, writer of fiction, and memoirist

1759. Robert Burns (d. 21 July 1796). Scottish poet

1851. Arne Evenson Garborg (d. 14 January 1924). Norwegian writer of fiction, playwright, theologian, and linguistic reformer

1874. William Somerset Maugham (d. 15 December 1965). English writer of fiction and playwright

1882. Adeline Virginia Woolf (d. 28 March 1941). English writer of fiction and critical essayist

1926. Elie Kedouri. Iraqi-born English historian and essayist

DEATHS

1640. Robert Burton (b. 8 February 1577). English essayist and satirist

1878. John Doran (b. 11 March 1807). English writer of miscellaneous prose nonfiction and translator

1908. Ouida (pseudonym of Marie Louise de la Ramee; b. 1 January 1839). English writer of fiction

1968. Arthur Ivor Winters (b. 17 October 1900). American poet and critical essayist

26

BIRTHS

1468. Guillaume Bude (d. 23 August 1540). French scholar, philosopher, philologist, and writer on jurisprudence

1715. Claude Adrien Helvetius (d. 26 December 1771). French philosopher, encyclopaedist, and essayist

1781. Ludwig Achim von Arnim (d. 21 January 1831). German writer of fiction

1831. Mary Elizabeth Mapes Dodge (d. 21 August 1905). American writer of fiction, poet, and writer of stories for children

DEATHS

1849. Thomas Lovell Bedoes (b. 20 July 1803). English poet and playwright

1850. Francis Jeffrey (b. 23 October 1773). Scottish essayist and reviewer

1864. Vuk Stefanovic Karadzic (b. 26 October 1787). Yugoslavian (Serbian) poet, philologist, and translator

1871. George Ticknor (b. 1 August 1791). American literary and historical scholar

1948. John Avery Lomax (b. 23 September 1867). American ballad anthologist

27

BIRTHS

1568. William Alabaster (d. 28 April 1640). English theologian, poet, and essayist

1775. Friedrich Wilhelm Joseph von Schelling (d. 20 August 1854). German philosopher and essayist

1814. Giovanni Prati (d. 9 May 1884). Italian lyric and narrative poet

1832. Lewis Carroll (pseudonym of Charles Lutwidge Dodgson; d. 14 January 1898). English mathematician, writer of children's fiction, poet, and classical scholar

1836. Leopold Sacher-Masoch (d. 9 March 1895). Austrian writer of fiction and lawyer

1891. Ilya Grigoryevich Ehrenburg (d. 1 September 1967). Soviet Russian novelist

DEATHS

1844. Jean Charles Emmanuel Nodier (b. 29 April 1780). French poet, literary critic, and writer of fiction

1922. Giovanni Verga (b. 2 September 1840). Italian writer of fiction

28

BIRTHS

1706. John Baskerville (d. 8 January 1775). English printer and bookseller

1719. Johann Elias Schlagel (d. 13 August 1749). German playwright and critical essayist

1834. Sabine Baring-Gould (d. 2 January 1924). English writer of fiction, poet, and writer of miscellaneous prose nonfiction

1853. Jose Marti (d. 19 May 1895). Cuban poet and revolutionary

1873. Sidonie Gabrielle Colette (d. 3 August 1954). French writer of fiction

1933. Susan Sontag. American essayist and writer of fiction

DEATHS

1754. Baron Ludwig Holberg (b. 3 December 1684). Danish poet, playwright, and philosopher

1859. William Hickling Prescott (b. 4 May 1796). American historian

1861. Henri Murger (b. 24 March 1822). French writer of fiction and poet

1918. John McCrae (b. 30 November 1872). Canadian poet and physician

1928. Vicente Blasco Ibanez (b. 29 January 1867). Spanish writer of fiction

1939. William Butler Yeats (b. 13 June 1865). Irish poet, playwright, and essayist

1947. Morris Raphael Cohen (b. 25 July 1880) Russian-born American philosopher and essayist

1960. Zora Neale Hurston (b. 7 January 1901?). American writer of fiction

29

BIRTHS

1688. Emanuel Swedenborg (d. 29 March 1772). Swedish religious mystic, scientist, mathematician, philosopher, and essayist

1737. Thomas Paine (d. 8 June 1809). English-born American political philosopher and essayist

1866. Romain Rolland (d. 30 December 1944). French music historian, biographer, playwright, writer of fiction, and essayist

1867. Vicente Blaso Ibanez (d. 28 January 1928). Spanish writer of fiction

1874. Owen Davis (d. ? 1956). American poet and playwright

1892. Reinhard Johannes Sorge (d. 20 July 1916). German poet

1923. Sidney (Paddy) Chayefsky (d. 1 August 1981). American playwright and filmwriter

1925. Michael Crichton. American writer of fiction

DEATHS

1814. Johann Gottlieb Fichte (b. 19 May 1762). German philosopher, nationalist, and essayist

1860. Ernst Moritz Arndt (b. 26 December 1769). German poet, essayist, and writer of travel narrative

1864. Lucy Aiken (b. 6 November 1781). English historian, biographer, and writer of books for children

1888. Edward Lear (b. 12 May 1812). English writer of "nonsense" verse

1910. Edouard Rod (b. 31 March 1857). Swiss writer of fiction

1912. Herman Joachim Bang (b. 20 April 1857). Danish writer of fiction

1933. Sara Teasdale (b. 8 August 1884). American poet

1944. William Allen White (b. 10 February 1868). American journalist, editor, essayist, biographer, and social historian

1956. Henry Louis Mencken (b. 12 September 1880). American satirist, essayist, journalist, and reviewer

1963. Robert Lee Frost (b. 26 March 1874). American poet

1970. Basil Henry Liddell Hart (b. 31 October 1895). English historian, military scientist, and encyclopaedist

1974. Herbert Ernest Bates (b. 16 May 1905). English writer of fiction

1984. Frances Goodrich (b. ? 1891). American playwright

30

BIRTHS

1775. Walter Savage Landor (d. 17 September 1864). English poet, playwright, and writer of fictional prose dialogues

1912. Barbara Wertheim Tuchman (d. 6 February 1989). American popular historian

DEATHS

1869. William Carleton (b. 4 March 1794). Irish writer of fiction

1888. Asa Gray (b. 18 November 1810). American scientist, evolutionist, and essayist

Mary Howitt (b. 12 March 1799). English writer of fiction, poet, and writer of miscellaneous prose nonfiction

1909. Martha Farquharson Finley (b. 26 April 1828). American writer of moral and religious fiction for children

1934. Frank Nelson Doubleday (b. 8 January 1862). American publisher and editor

31

BIRTHS

1734. Michel-Guillaume-Jean de Crevecoeur (d. 12 November 1813). French-born American writer of travel narrative and essayist

1830. Victor-Henri Rochefort (d. 20 June 1914). French journalist, politician, and political essayist

1872. Zane Grey (d. 23 October 1939). American writer of fiction

1905. John Henry O'Hara (d. 11 April 1970). American writer of fiction and playwright

1915. Thomas Merton (d. 10 December 1968). American writer of nonfiction narrative prose, essayist, and poet

1923. Norman Mailer. American writer of fiction and miscellaneous prose nonfiction

DEATHS

1854. Silvio Pellico (b. 25 June 1789). Italian writer of fiction, poet, and essayist

1866. Friedrich Ruckert (b. 16 May 1788). German poet

1892. Charles Haddon Spurgeon (b. 19 June 1834). English theological and Biblical writer

1925. George Washington Cable (b. 12 October 1844). American writer of fiction

1933. John Galsworthy (b. 14 August 1867). English writer of fiction and playwright

1944. Hippolyte Jean Giraudoux (b. 29 October 1882). French poet, writer of fiction, and playwright

1956. Alan Alexander Milne (b. 18 January 1882). English essayist and writer of verse and fiction for children

1961. Dorothy Thompson (b. 9 July 1894). American journalist and essayist

FEBRUARY

1

BIRTHS

1552. Sir Edward Coke (d. 3 September 1634). English jurist and commentator upon jurisprudence

1801. Maximilien Paul Emile Littre (d. 2 June 1881). French philosopher, lexicographer, essayist, and language historian

1811. Arthur Henry Hallam (d. 15 September 1833). English poet and essayist

1825. Francis James Child (d. 11 September 1896). American literary scholar, academician, and ballad anthologizer

1874. Hugo von Hofmannsthall (d. 15 July 1919). Austrian poet, opera librettist, and playwright

1887. Charles Bernard Nordhoff (d. 11 April 1947). American writer of fiction

1902. James Langston Hughes (d. 22 May 1967). American writer of fiction, poet, playwright, and writer of autobiographical narrative

1904. Sidney Joseph Perelman (d. 17 October 1979). American social satirist, essayist, and comic playwright

1918. Sarah Muriel Spark. Scottish-born writer of fiction, poet, playwright, essayist, and biographer

1933. Reynolds Price. American writer of fiction, essayist, and poet

DEATHS

1650. Rene Descartes (b. 31 March 1596). French philosopher, mathematician, and essayist

1851. Mary Wollstonecraft Shelley (b. 30 August 1797). English writer of fiction, biographer, and writer of travel narrative

1878. George Cruikshank (b. 27 September 1792). English illustrator and caricaturist of contemporary fiction

1975. Helen Howe (b. 11 January 1905). American writer of fiction

2

BIRTHS

1745. Hannah More (d. 7 September 1833). English writer of fiction, playwright, and poet

1882. James Joyce (d. 13 January 1941). Irish writer of fiction and poet

1886. William Rose Benet (d. 4 May 1950). American poet, writer of verse novels, anthologist, and critical essayist

1899. Rebecca Caudill (d. 2 October 1985). American writer of fiction, children's writer, and poet

1905. Ayn Rand (d. 6 March 1982). Russian-born American writer of fiction, playwright, and essayist

1923. James Lafayette Dickey. American poet and critical essayist

DEATHS

1826. Anthelme Brillat-Savarin (b. 1 April 1755). French gastronome and legal essayist

1957. Valery Nicolas Larbaud (b. 29 August 1881). French traveler, scholar, translator, and writer of fiction

1965. Richard Palmer Blackmur (b. 21 January 1904). American poet and literary critic

1970. Bertrand Arthur William Russell (b. 18 May 1872). English philosopher and essayist

1987. Alistair Stuart MacLean (b. 28 April 1922). Scottish writer of fiction and poet

3

BIRTHS

1735. Count Ignacy Krasicki (d. 14 March 1801). Polish poet and writer of miscellaneous prose

1826. Walter Bagehot (d. 24 March 1877). English essayist

1842. Sidney Lanier (d. 7 September 1881). American writer of fiction, poet, and essayist

1874. Gertrude Stein (d. 27 July 1946). American writer of fiction, poet, and writer of miscellaneous prose nonfiction

1907. James Albert Michener. American writer of fiction and writer of miscellaneous prose nonfiction

1909. Simone Weil (d. 24 August 1943). French philosopher and essayist

DEATHS

1806. Nicolas-Edme Restiff de la Bretonne (b. 23 October 1734). French writer of fiction and essayist

1832. George Crabbe (b. 24 December 1754). English poet and writer of fiction

1875. Everhardus Johannes Potgieter (b. 17 June 1808). Dutch poet, essayist, literary critic, and editor

4

BIRTHS

1805. William Harrison Ainsworth (d. 3 January 1882). English writer of fiction and poet

1904. McKinlay Kantor (d. 11 October 1977). American writer of historical fiction

DEATHS

1746. Robert Blair (b. ? 1699). Scottish-born didactic poet

1970. Louise Bogan (b. 11 August 1897). American poet

1978. Bergan Evans (b. 19 September 1904). American linguist, lexicographer, grammarian, and essayist

5

BIRTHS

1505. Gilig Tschudi (d. 28 February 1572). Swiss Roman Catholic historian

1806. Robert Montgomery Bird (d. 23 January 1854). American playwright and writer of fiction

1848. Joris Karl Huysmans (originally Charles Marie George Huysmans; d. 12 May 1907). Dutch-born French writer of fiction and art critic

1914. William Seward Burroughs. American writer of fiction and autobiographical narrative

DEATHS

1881. Thomas Carlyle (b. 4 December 1795). Scottish essayist, historian, literary critic, and translator

1892. Emilie Flygare-Carlen (b. 8 August 1807). Swedish writer of fiction

1947. Hans Fallada (pseudonym of Rudolf Ditzen; b. 21 July 1893). German writer of fiction

1972. Marianne Craig Moore (b. 15 November 1887). American poet

6

BIRTHS

1564. Christopher Marlowe (d. 30 May 1593). English poet and playwright

1778. Ugo Foscolo (d. 10 October 1827). Italian poet

1833. Jose Maria de Perada (d. 1 March 1906). Spanish writer of fiction

1894. Eric Honeywood Partridge (d. 1 June 1979). English lexicographer, linguist, and essayist

DEATHS

1793. Carlo Goldoni (b. 25 February 1707). Italian playwright

1804. Joseph Priestley (b. 13 March 1733). English essayist, theologian, and scientist

1916. Ruben Dario (pseudonym of Felix Ruben Garcia Sarmiento; b. 18 January 1867). Nicaraguan poet and critical essayist

1958. Charles Langbridge Morgan (b. 22 January 1894). English writer of fiction, playwright, and poet

1988. Marghanita Laski (b. 24 October 1915). English writer of fiction, playwright, and essayist

1989. Barbara Wertheim Tuchman (b. 30 January 1912). American popular historian

7

BIRTHS

1478. Sir Thomas More (d. 6 July 1535). English writer of nonfiction, essayist, critic, and historian

1806. Charles Fenno Hoffman (d. 7 June 1884). American writer of fiction, writer of narrative prose nonfiction, poet, and editor

1811. Gilbert Abbott a'Beckett (d. 30 August 1856). English humorist, editor, and playwright

1812. Charles John Huffham Dickens (d. 9 June 1870). English writer of fiction

1837. Sir James Augustus Henry Murray (d. 26 July 1915). English philologist, essayist, and lexicographer

1867. Laura Ingalls Wilder (d. 10 January 1957). American writer of autobiographical fiction and narratives for children

1885. Harry Sinclair Lewis (d. 10 January 1951). American writer of fiction

DEATHS

1529. Baldissare Castiglione (b. 6 December 1478). Italian poet and essayist

1823. Ann Ward Radcliffe (b. 9 July 1764). English writer of fiction

1862. Francisco Martinez de la Rosa (b. 10 March 1787). Spanish playwright, poet, and historian

1873. Joseph Sheridan Le Fanu (b. 28 August 1814). Irish writer of fiction and poet

8

BIRTHS

1577. Robert Burton (d. 25 January 1640). English essayist and satirist

1612. Samuel Butler (d. 25 September 1680). English poet and writer of prose character sketches

1819. John Ruskin (d. 21 January 1900). English art critic and social theorist

1828. Jules Verne (d. 24 March 1905). French writer of fiction

1878. Martin Buber (d. 13 June 1965). Austrian Jewish theologian, philosopher, and essayist

1911. Elizabeth Bishop (d. 6 October 1979). American poet

DEATHS

1921. Prince Peter Alexeyevich Kropotkin (b. 26 November 1842). Russian geographer, essayist, and memoirist

Barrett Wendell (b. 23 August 1855). American literary historian

9

BIRTHS

1863. Anthony Hope (pseudonym of Anthony Hope Hawkins; d. 8 July 1933). English writer of fiction and playwright

1866. George Ade (d. 16 May 1944). American writer of fables, satirist, and playwright

1874. Amy Lawrence Lowell (d. 12 May 1925). American poet, playwright, writer of fiction, and essayist

1923. Brendan Francis Behan (d. 20 March 1964). Irish playwright

1931. Thomas Bernhard. Austrian writer of fiction, playwright, and poet

1940. John M. Coetzee. South African writer of fiction

1944. Alice Walker. American writer of fiction and poet

DEATHS

1881. Fyodor Mikhailovich Dostoyevsky (b. 11 November 1821). Russian writer of fiction

1903. Sir Charles Gavan Duffy (b. 12 April 1816). Irish poet

1906. Paul Lawrence Dunbar (b. 27 July 1872). American poet, playwright, and writer of fiction

1940. William Edward Dodd (b. 21 October 1869). American historian and diplomat

1952. Norman Douglas (b. 8 December 1868). English writer of fiction and miscellaneous prose nonfiction

1979. John Orley Allen Tate (b. 19 November 1899). American poet, biographer, essayist, and writer of fiction

10

BIRTHS

1670. William Congreve (d. 19 January 1729). English playwright and poet

1775. Charles Lamb (d. 27 December 1834). English essayist and poet

1868. William Allen White (d. 29 January 1944). American journalist, editor, essayist, biographer, and social historian

1890. Boris Leonidovich Pasternak (d. 30 May 1960). Russian poet, writer of fiction, and translator

1892. Ivo Andric (d. 13 March 1975). Yugoslav writer of fiction

1898. Bertolt Brecht (d. 11 August 1956). German playwright and poet

1927. Jakov Lind (originally Heinz Landwirth). German writer of fiction

DEATHS

1686. William Dugdale (b. 12 September 1605). English antiquarian and historian

1755. Charles Louis Secondat, Baron de Montesquieu (b. 18 January 1689). French social and political philosopher and essayist

1762. Motoori Norinaga (b. 21 June 1730). Japanese scholar, poet, and essayist

1837. Aleksandr Sergeyevich Pushkin (b. 6 June 1799). Russian poet, writer of fiction, and playwright

1868. Sir David Brewster (b. 11 December 1781). Scottish essayist and scientist

1874. Jules Michelet (b. 21 August 1798). French historian and writer of prose tracts on nature

1932. Richard Horatio Edgar Wallace (b. 1 April 1875). English writer of fiction and playwright

1944. Israel Joshua Singer (b. 30 November 1893). Polish-born Yiddish writer of fiction

1956. Leonora von Stosch Speyer (b. 7 November 1872), American poet

11

BIRTHS

1657. Bernard Le Bovier de Fontenelle (d. 9 January 1757). French essayist and philosopher of science

1780. Karoline Gunderode (d. 26 July 1806). German poet

1802. Lydia Maria Frances Child (d. 20 October 1880). American reformist, essayist, and writer of didactic fiction

1872. Edward Johnston (d. 26 November 1944). English essayist and calligrapher

1912. Roy Broadbent Fuller. English poet, writer of fiction and memoirist

1917. Sidney Sheldon. American writer of fiction

1937. Anders Bodelsen. Danish writer of fiction

DEATHS

1763. William Shenstone (b. 13 November 1714). English poet and writer of miscellaneous prose nonfiction

1829. Aleksandr Sergeivich Griboedov (b. 15 January 1795). Russian poet and playwright

1844. Shunsui Tamenaga (pseudonym of Sasaki Sadataka; b. ? 1789). Japanese writer of fiction

1940. John Buchan (b. 26 August 1875). Scottish writer of fiction, biographer, and historian

1949. Axel Martin Fredrik Munthe (b. 31 October 1857). Swedish psychiatrist and memoirist

1963. Sylvia Plath (b. 27 October 1932). American writer of fiction, poet, and writer of miscellaneous nonfiction prose

1968. Howard Lindsay (b. 29 March 1889). American playwright

1978. Harry Edmund Martinson (b. 6 May 1904). Swedish poet and writer of fiction

1981. Ketti Hartley Frings (b. ? 1920). American playwright

12

BIRTHS

1567. Thomas Campion (d. 1 March 1620). English poet, essayist, musician, and physician

1663. Cotton Mather (d. 13 February 1728). American theologian, essayist, poet, and psalmist

1809. Charles Robert Darwin (d. 19 April 1882). English scientist, evolutionist, essayist, and writer of travel narrative

1828. George Meredith (d. 18 May 1909). English writer of fiction, poet, and essayist

1912. Ronald Frederick Delderfield (d. 24 June 1972). English writer of fiction, essayist, and playwright

1923. Alan Dugan. American poet

DEATHS

1804. Immanuel Kant (b. 22 April 1724). German philosopher and essayist

1980. Muriel Rukeyser (b. 15 December 1913). American poet and critical essayist

1984. Julio Cortazar (b. 26 August 1914). Argentinian writer of fiction

1985. Emil Lengyel (b. 26 April 1895). Hungarian-born historian

13

BIRTHS

1674. Claude Prosper Jolyot de Crebillon, pere (d. 17 June 1762). French playwright

1703. Robert Dodsley (d. 23 September 1764). English poet, playwright, publisher, and anthologizer

1886. Ricardo Guiraldes (d. 11 November 1927). Argentinian writer of fiction and poet

1903. Georges Joseph Christian Simenon (d. 4 September 1989). Belgian writer of detective and mystery fiction

DEATHS

1571. Benvenuto Cellini (b. 3 November 1500). Italian artist, craftsman, and writer of autobiographical narrative

1653. Georg Rodolf Weckherin (b. 15 September 1584). German poet and translator

1728. Cotton Mather (b. 12 February 1663). American theologian, essayist, poet, and psalmodist

1837. Mariano Jose de Larra y Sanchez de Castro (b. 24 March 1809). Spanish poet, satirist, and political essayist

1951. Lloyd Cassel Douglas (b. 27 August 1877). American writer of fiction

1984. Roland Herbert Bainton (b. 30 March 1894). American theologian, biographer, and essayist

14

BIRTHS

1707. Claude Prosper Jolyot de Crebillon, fils (d. 12 April 1777). French writer of fiction

1766. Thomas Robert Malthus (d. 29 December 1834). English economist and essayist

1768. Ivan Andrevich Krylov (d. 21 November 1844). Russian writer of fables

1856. Frank Harris (originally James Thomas Harris; d. 26 August 1931). Irish-born American writer of fiction, critical essayist, and writer of autobiographical narrative

1864. Israel Zangwill (d. 1 August 1926). English writer of fiction, playwright, and poet

1882. George Jean Nathan (d. 8 April 1958). American satirist, playwright, essayist, and reviewer

DEATHS

1780. Sir William Blackstone (b. 10 July 1723). English essayist and commentator upon jurisprudence

1808. John Dickinson (b. 8 November 1732). American lawyer, essayist, and poet

1975. Julian Sorell Huxley (b. 22 June 1887). English biologist, poet, and essayist

Pelham Grenville Wodehouse (b. 15 October 1881). English humorist, satirist, and writer of fiction

1980. Clifford Odets (b. 18 July 1906). American playwright

15

BIRTHS

1497. Philipp Melanchthon (d. 19 April 1560). German theologian and essayist

1571. Michael Praetorius (d. 15 February 1621). German music historian, essayist, and composer

1748. Jeremy Bentham (d. 6 June 1831). English essayist on jurisprudence and Utilitarian ethics

1861. Alfred North Whitehead (d. 20 December 1947). English mathematician, idealistic philosopher, and essayist

1880. Joseph Hergesheimer (d. 25 April 1954). American writer of fiction

DEATHS

1621. Michael Praetorius (b. 15 February 1571). German composer, music historian, and essayist

1709. John Philips (b. 30 December 1676). English poet

1781. Gotthold Ephraim Lessing (b. 22 January 1729). German translator, essayist, playwright, and poet

1888. Petroleum V. Nasby (pseudonym of David Ross Locke; b. 20 September 1833). American humorist, writer of fiction, essayist, and journalist

1905. Lewis Wallace (b. 10 April 1827). American writer of fiction and poet

16

BIRTHS

1831. Nikolai Semyanovich Leskov (d. 5 March 1895). Russian writer of fiction

1838. Henry Brooks Adams (d. 27 March 1918). American essayist, reviewer, writer of fiction, historian, and memoirist

1850. Octave Mirbeau (d. 16 February 1917). French writer of fiction and playwright

1876. George Macaulay Trevelyan (d. 21 July 1962). English historian

1886. Van Wyck Brooks (d. 2 May 1963). American literary historian, critical essayist, and biographer

1901. Mario Andrew Pei (d. 2 March 1978). Italian-born American philologist and language historian

DEATHS

1687. Charles Cotton (b. 28 April 1630). English writer of dialogues, satirist, and poet

1907. Giosue Carducci (b. 27 July 1835). Italian poet

1911. Alice Morse Earle (b. 27 April 1853). American social and religious historian

1917. Octave Mirbeau (b. 16 February 1850). French writer of fiction and playwright

1936. James Harvey Robinson (b. 29 June 1863). American intellectual historian

17

BIRTHS

1879. Dorothy Canfield Fisher (d. 9 November 1958). American writer of fiction

1929. Chaim Potok. American writer of fiction

DEATHS

1673. Jean Baptiste Moliere (originally Jean-Baptiste Poquelin; b. 17 February 1673). French comic playwright and actor

1796. James Macpherson (b. 27 October 1736). Scottish poet

1827. Johann Heinrich Pestalozzi (b. 12 January 1746). Swiss educational philosopher, essayist, and writer of fiction

1856. Heinrich Heine (b. 13 December 1797). German poet and essayist

1884. Charles Stewart Calverley (b. 22 December 1831). English poet

1913. Joaquin Miller (pseudonym of Cincinnatus Hiner Miller; b. 10 March 1839). American poet and playwright

1970. Schmuel Yosef Halevi Agnon (b. 16 July 1888). Polish-born Israeli writer of fiction

1984. Jesse Hilton Stuart (b. 8 August 1907). American poet and writer of fiction

1986. Jiddu Krishnamurti (b. 22 May 1895). Indian-born religious philosopher and essayist

18

BIRTHS

1609. Edward Hyde, Earl of Clarendon (d. 9 December 1674). English historian and biographer

1836. Ramakrishna (pseudonym of Sri Ramakrishna Paramahansa; d. 16 August 1886). Indian (Hindu) mystic, philosopher, and essayist

1849. Alexander Lange Kielland (d. 16 June 1907). Norwegian writer of fiction and playwright

1854. Sholem Aleichem (pseudonym of Solomon J. Rabinowitz; d. 13 May 1916). Ukrainian-born Yiddish writer of fiction

1896. Andre Breton (d. 28 September 1966). French critical essayist and poet

1909. Wallace Earle Stegner. American writer of fiction

1926. Archie Randolph Ammons. American poet

1929. Len Deighton. English writer of fiction and miscellaneous prose nonfiction

1931. Toni Morrison. American writer of fiction and editor

DEATHS

1546. Martin Luther (b. 10 November 1483). German theologian, essayist, and poet

1564. Michelangelo Buonarotti (b. 6 March 1475). Italian artist and poet

1925. James Lane Allen (b. 21 December 1849). American writer of fiction

1942. Albert Payson Terhune (b. 12 December 1872). American writer of fiction and prose nonfiction

1982. Dame Ngaio Edith Marsh (b. 23 April 1899). English writer of detective and mystery fiction

1983. Pierre Stephen Robert Payne (b. 4 December 1911). English-born American essayist, biographer, and linguist

19

BIRTHS

1473. Niclaus Copernicus (d. 24 May 1543). Polish-born German astronomer, physician, and essayist

1717. David Garrick (d. 20 January 1779). English actor, playwright, and poet

1903. Kay Boyle. American writer of fiction and poet

1917. Carson McCullers (born Lula Carson Smith; d. 29 September 1967). American writer of fiction and playwright

DEATHS

1837. Georg Buchner (b. 17 October 1813). German playwright

1887. Eduard Douwes Dekker (b. 2 March 1820). Dutch writer of fiction and writer of verse drama

1951. Andre Paul Guillaume Gide (b. 22 November 1869). French writer of fiction, poet, playwright, critical essayist, biographer, and translator

1952. Knut Hamsun (pseudonym of Knut Pedersen; b. 4 August 1859). Norwegian writer of fiction

20

BIRTHS

1749. Ching-jen Huang (d. 25 May 1783). Chinese poet

1912. Pierre Francois Marie-Louis Boulle. French writer of fiction

1942. Hugo Williams. English poet and writer of travel narrative

DEATHS

1861. Eugene Scribe (b. 24 December 1791). French playwright

1895. Frederick Douglass (b. ? February 1817). American writer of autobiographical prose narrative

1916. Klas P. Arnoldson (b. 27 October 1844). Swedish political essayist

1959. Laurence Housmen (b. 18 July 1865). English playwright and writer of fiction

21

BIRTHS

1801. John Henry Cardinal Newman (d. 11 August 1890). English essayist and poet

1821. Charles Scribner the elder (d. 26 August 1871). American publisher and editor

1903. Anais Nin (d. 14 January 1977). French-born American writer of fiction, literary critic, and diarist

1907. Wystan Hugh Auden (d. 28 September 1973). English-born poet, playwright, and critical essayist

DEATHS

1595. Robert Southwell (b. ? 1561). English theologian and writer of devotional verse

1677. Baruch Spinoza (b. 24 November 1632). Dutch Jewish philosopher and essayist

1818. David Humphreys (b. 10 July 1752). American poet, essayist, and playwright

1852. Nikolai Vasilyevich Gogol (b. 31 March 1809). Russian writer of fiction and playwright

1857. Dionysius Solomos (b. 8 April 1798). Greek poet

1862. Justinius Andreas Christian Kerner (b. 18 September 1786). German poet

1984. Mikhail Aleksandrovich Sholokhov (b. 24 May 1905). Soviet Russian writer of fiction

22

BIRTHS

1788. Arthur Schopenhauer (d. 21 September 1860). German philosopher and essayist

1801. William Barnes (d. 7 October 1886). English writer of dialect verse

1819. James Russell Lowell (d. 12 August 1891). American poet, essayist, humorist, and political satirist

1886. Hugo Ball (d. 14 September 1927). German poet and theologian

1892. Edna St. Vincent Millay. (d. 19 October 1950). American poet, writer of verse drama, and writer of narrative sketches

1900. Sean O'Faolain. Irish writer of fiction

1903. Morley Edward Callaghan. Canadian writer of fiction, journalist, and playwright

1925. Edward St. John Gorey. American writer of prose narrative and illustrator

1938. Ishmael Scott Reed. American writer of fiction, poet, and essayist

DEATHS

1674. Jean Chapelain (b. 4 December 1595). French poet and critical essayist

1797. Karl Friedrich Hieronymous Munchhausen, Baron von Munchhausen (b. 11 May 1720). German writer of fantasy fiction

1816. Adam Ferguson (b. 20 June 1743). Scottish philosopher and historian

1875. Sir Charles Lyell (b. 14 November 1797). Scottish scientist, antiquary, essayist, and writer of prose narrative

1904. Sir Leslie Stephen (b. 28 November 1832). English literary critic biographer, essayist, and literary historian

1810. Charles Brockden Brown (b. 17 January 1771). American writer of fiction and essayist

1845. Sydney Smith (b. 3 June 1771). English satirist and writer of sermon literature

1973. Elizabeth Dorothea Cole Bowen (b. 7 June 1899). Irish-born English writer of fiction

1978. Phyllis McGinley (b. 21 March 1905). American poet and essayist

1980. Oskar Kokoschka (b. 1 March 1886). Austrian expressionist artist and writer

1987. Glenway Westcott (b. 11 April 1901). American writer of fiction and poet

23

BIRTHS

1633. Samuel Pepys (d. 26 May 1703). English diarist

1868. William Edward Burghardt Dubois (d. 27 August 1963). American writer of fiction, essayist, writer of autobiographical narrative, and poet

1879. Norman Lindsay (d. 29 November 1969). Australian writer of fiction and artist

1883. Karl Theodor Jaspers (d. 26 February 1969). German philosopher and essayist

1899. Erich Kastner (d. 29 July 1974). German writer of fiction, poet, and playwright

1904. William Lawrence Shirer. American essayist journalist and writer of fiction

DEATHS

1792. Sir Joshua Reynolds (b. 16 July 1723). English philosopher, essayist, and painter

1821. John Keats (b. 31 October 1795). English poet

1851. Johanna Baillie (b. 11 September 1762). Scottish playwright and poet

1900. Ernest Christopher Dowson (b. 2 August 1867). English lyric poet

1924. Thomas Woodrow Wilson (b. 28 December 1856). American statesman, academician, and historian

1942. Stefan Zweig (b. 28 November 1881). Austrian biographer and writer of fiction

1945. Aleksei Nikolaevich Tolstoi (b. 10 January 1882). Russian writer of fiction and historical narrative

1955. Paul Louis-Marie Claudel (b. 6 August 1868). French poet, essayist, and playwright

1968. Fannie Hurst (b. 18 October 1889). American writer of fiction

1984. Jessamyn West (b. 18 July 1902). American writer of fiction and essayist

24

BIRTHS

1463. Giovanni Pico della Mirandola (d. 17 November 1494). Italian humanist and essayist

1786. Wilhelm Karl Grimm (d. 16 December 1859). German folklorist, philologist, and collector of tales for children

1844. William Clark Russell (d. 8 November 1911). American-born English writer of fiction and poet

1852. George Augustus Moore (d. 20 January 1933). Irish-born writer of fiction

1887. Mary Ellen Chase (d. 28 July 1973). American writer of fiction and literary and Biblical scholar

DEATHS

1825. Thomas Bowdler (b. 11 July 1754). Scottish literary scholar, editor, and expurgator

1862. Bernhard Severin Ingemann (b. 28 May 1789). Danish poet and writer of fiction

1950. Irving Bacheller (b. 26 September 1859). American writer of fiction

1974. Margaret Leech (b. 7 November 1893). American historical writer and novelist

1976. Harry Allen Smith (b. 19 December 1907). American humorist and essayist

1980. Robert Hayden (pseudonym of Asa Bundy Sheffey; b. 4 August 1913). American poet

25

BIRTHS

1707. Carlo Goldoni (d. 6 February 1793). Italian playwright

1866. Benedetto Croce (d. 20 November 1952). Italian philosopher, essayist, historian, and politician

1907. Mary Coyle Chase (d. 23 October 1981). American playwright

1908. Frank Gill Slaughter. American writer of fiction

1917. Anthony Burgess (born John Anthony Burgess Wilson). English writer of fiction

1945. Shivadhar Srinivasa Naipaul (d. 13 August 1985). Trinidadian journalist, essayist, and writer of fiction

DEATHS

1638. Sir Robert Ayton (b. ? 1569). Scottish poet

1852. Thomas Moore (b. 28 May 1779). Irish poet, satirist, and writer of fiction

1964. Grace De Repentigny Metalious (b. 8 September 1924). American writer of popular fiction

1983. Thomas Lanier (Tennessee) Williams (b. 26 March 1911). American playwright and writer of fiction

26

BIRTHS

1564. Christopher Marlowe (d. 1 June 1593). English poet and playwright

1802. Victor Marie Hugo (d. 22 May 1885). French poet and writer of fiction

1893. Ivor Armstrong Richards (d. 7 September 1979). English literary critic

1913. George Granville Barker. English poet

1929. Chaim Icyk Bermant. Lithuanian-born English writer of fiction

DEATHS

1821. Joseph Marie de Maistre (b. 1 April 1753). French philosopher and essayist

1954. William Ralph Inge (b. 6 June 1860). English theologian, essayist, and writer of sermon literature

1969. Karl Theodor Jaspers (b. 23 February 1883). German philosopher and essayist

27

BIRTHS

1807. Henry Wadsworth Longfellow (d. 24 March 1882). American poet

1850. Laura Elizabeth Richards (d. 14 January 1943). American writer of fiction and biographer

1861. Rudolph Steiner (d. 30 March 1925). Austrian social philosopher and essayist

1904. James Thomas Farrell (d. 22 August 1979). American writer of fiction, essayist, and poet

1910. Peter De Vries. American writer of fiction

1912. Lawrence George Durrell. English writer of fiction, poet, and writer of travel narrative

1913. Irwin Shaw (d. 16 May 1984). American playwright and writer of fiction

DEATHS

1706. John Evelyn (b. 31 October 1620). English diarist and writer of miscellaneous prose non-fiction

1735. John Arbuthnot (b. 29 April 1667). English pamphleteer and satirist

1859. Freidrich Bleek (b. 4 July 1793). German Biblical scholar and essayist

1887. Edward Rowland Sill (b. 29 April 1841). American poet

1977. Edward Dahlberg (b. 22 July 1900). American writer of fiction and poet

1984. Richmond Alexander Lattimore (b. 6 May 1906). American literary scholar and poet

28

BIRTHS

1533. Michel Eyquem de Montaigne (d. 13 September 1592). French essayist and translator

1814. William Henry Giles Kingston (d. 5 August 1880). English writer of fiction for boys and writer of travel narrative

1823. Joseph Ernest Renan (d. 2 October 1892). French philologist, historian, and essayist

1857. Margaretta Wade Campbell Deland (d. 13 January 1945). American writer of fiction and poet

1865. Arthur Symons (d. 22 January 1945). Welsh-born English critical essayist and poet

1894. Ben Hecht (d. 18 April 1964). American playwright and writer of fiction

1909. Stephen Harold Spender. English poet, critical essayist, and translator

DEATHS

1572. Gilig Tschudi (b. 5 February 1505). Swiss Roman Catholic historian

1866. Count Henryk Rzewuski (b. 3 May 1791). Polish writer of fiction

1869. Alphonse Marie Louis Prat de Lamartine (b. 21 October 1790). French poet, historian, and essayist

1916. Henry James (b. 15 April 1843). American-born English writer of fiction, essayist, and writer of narrative

1959. Maxwell Anderson (b. 15 December 1888). American playwright and writer of verse drama

1968. Laurence Stallings (b. 25 November 1894). American writer of fiction and playwright

1986. Laura Zametkin Hobson (b. 19 June 1900). American writer of fiction

1989. Richard Willard Armour (b. 15 July 1906). American poet and literary scholar

29

BIRTHS

1692. John Byrom (d. 26 September 1763). English poet, hymnodist, translator, and essayist

1900. George Seferis (pseudonym of Georgios Stylinaou Sepheriades; d. 20 September 1971). Greek poet and translator

1902. John Ernst Steinbeck (d. 20 December 1968). American writer of fiction

1908. Victor Wolfgang von Hagen. German historian

MARCH

1

BIRTHS

1701. Johann Jakob Breitinger (d. 13 December 1776). Swiss literary critic, theorist, and essayist

1782. Thomas Hart Benton (d. 10 April 1858). American painter and writer of autobiographical prose narrative

1837. William Dean Howells (d. 11 May 1920). American writer of autobiographical narrative, biographer, essayist, writer of fiction, playwright, and writer of verse drama

Georg Moritz Ebers (d. 7 August 1898). German Egyptologist, essayist, and writer of historical fiction

1863. Fedor Sologub (pseudonym of Fedor Kuzmich Teternikov; d. ? 1927). Russian poet, playwright, and writer of fiction

1880. Giles Lytton Strachey (d. 21 January 1932). English biographer, essayist, and literary historian

1886. Oskar Kokoschka (d. 22 February 1980). Austrian expressionist artist and writer

1892. Ryunosuke Akutagawa (d. 24 July 1927). Japanese writer of fiction

1900. Basil Bunting (d. 17 April 1985). English poet

1914. Ralph Waldo Ellison. American writer of fiction and essayist

1917. Robert Traill Spence Lowell, Jr. (d. 12 September 1977). American poet, essayist, and translator

1920. Howard Nemerov. American poet, writer of fiction, and satirist

1921. Richard Purdy Wilbur. American poet and essayist

DEATHS

1620. Thomas Campion (b. 12 February 1567). English poet, essayist, musician, and physician

1633. George Herbert (b. 3 April 1593). English poet and religious prose writer

1734. Roger North (b. 3 September 1653). English lawyer, historian, and biographer

1906. Jose Maria de Perada (b. 6 February 1833). Spanish writer of fiction

1938. Gabriele D'Annunzio (b. 12 March 1863). Italian poet, writer of fiction, playwright, and journalist

2

BIRTHS

1545. Sir Thomas Bodley (d. 1 January 1612). English scholar

1817. Janos Arany (d. 22 October 1882). Hungarian poet, satirist, and translator

1820. Eduard Douwes Dekker (d. 19 February 1887). Dutch writer of fiction and writer of verse drama

1829. Carl Schurz (d. 14 May 1906). German-born American journalist and biographer

1904. Theodore [Dr.] Suess Geisel. American writer of fantasy fiction for children

1905. Geoffrey Edward Harvey Grigson (d. 25 November 1985). English poet and essayist

1931. Thomas (Tom) Kennerly Wolfe, Jr. American essayist and illustrator

1942. John Winslow Irving. American writer of fiction

DEATHS

1788. Salomon Gessner (b. 1 April 1730). Swiss pastoral poet

1791. John Benjamin Wesley (b. 17 June 1703). English churchman, poet, essayist, memoirist, and writer of sermon literature

1797. Horace Walpole, fourth Earl of Orford (b. 24 September 1717). English essayist and writer of fiction

1824. Susanna Rowson (born Susanna Haswell; b. ? 1762.). English-born American writer of fiction

1895. John Stuart Blackie (b. 28 July 1809). Scottish classical scholar

1916. Carmen Sylva (pseudonym of Elisabeth, Queen of Romania; b. 29 December 1843). German-born Romanian poet and translator

1918. Hubert Howe Bancroft (b. 5 May 1832). American historian

1930. David Herbert Lawrence (b. 11 September 1885). English writer of fiction, poet, and essayist

1978. Mario Andrew Pei (b. 16 February 1901). Italian-born American philologist and language historian

3

BIRTHS

1652. Thomas Otway (d. 10 April 1685). English playwright and poet

1756. William Godwin (d. 7 April 1836). English political essayist and writer of fiction

1793. Karl Anton Postl (d. 26 May 1864). Austrian writer of fiction

1863. Arthur Llewellyn Jones Machen (d. 15 December 1947). Welsh-born English writer of fiction and verse

1920. Ronald William Fordham Searle. English illustrator and essayist

1926. Sir Sidney Lee (b. 5 December 1859). English critical essayist, editor, and biographer

1983. Arthur Koestler (b. 5 September 1905). Hungarian-born English literary, historical, and scientific essayist, as well as writer of fiction

4

BIRTHS

1745. Charles Dibdin (d. 25 July 1814). English playwright and poet

1782. Johann Rudolf Wyss (d. 21 March 1830). Swiss writer of fiction, essayist, and philosopher

1794. William Carleton (d. 30 January 1869). Irish writer of fiction

1798. Sigurdur Erikson Breidifjord (d. 21 July 1846). Icelandic poet

1881. Theodore Sigismund Stribling (d. 10 July 1965). American writer of fiction

1904. Ding Ling (d. 4 March 1986). Chinese writer of fiction

1928. Alan Sillitoe. English poet, writer of fiction, and essayist

DEATHS

1832. Jean Francois Champollion (b. 23 December 1790). French archaeologist, linguist, and essayist

1888. Amos Bronson Alcott (b. 29 November 1779). American educational philosopher, essayist, and poet

1937. Paul Elmer More (b. 12 December 1864). American critical and literary essayist

1940. Hannibal Hamlin Garland (b. 16 September 1860). American writer of fiction, essayist, and writer of autobiographical narrative

1963. William Carlos Williams (b. 17 September 1883). American poet, essayist, and playwright

1986. Ding Ling (b. 4 March 1904). Chinese writer of fiction

5

BIRTHS

1817. Sir Austin Henry Layard (d. 5 July 1894). English writer of travel narrative and archaeologist

1840. Constance Fenimore Woolson (d. 24 January 1894). American writer of fiction and poet

1852. Lady Isabella Augusta Gregory (d. 22 May 1932). Irish playwright, translator, and folklorist

1853. Howard Pyle (d. 9 November 1911). American writer of books for children, illustrator, and painter

1870. Benjamin Franklin (Frank) Norris (d. 25 October 1902). American writer of fiction and essayist

1919. Paul Darcy Boles (d. 4 May 1984). American writer of fiction

DEATHS

1883. Karl Heinrich Marx (b. 5 May 1818). German philosopher, essayist, historian, and journalist

1893. Hippolyte Adolphe Taine (b. 21 April 1828). French critical essayist, historian, and philosopher

1895. Nikolai Semyanovich Leskov (b. 16 February 1831). Russian writer of fiction

1944. Max Jacob (b. 11 July 1876). French poet

1950. Edgar Lee Masters (b. 23 August 1869). American poet, playwright, and writer of fiction

1971. Allan Nevins (b. 20 May 1890). American historian and biographer

6

BIRTHS

1475. Michelangelo Buonarroti (d. 18 February 1564). Italian artist and poet

1483. Francesco Guicciardini (d. 22 May 1540). Italian historian

1492. Juan Luis Vives (d. 6 May 1540). Spanish philosopher, humanist, and essayist

1606. Edmund Waller (d. 21 October 1687). English poet

1619. Savinien de Cyrano de Bergerac (d. 28 July 1655). French adventurer and prose writer

1806. Elizabeth Barrett Browning (d. 29 June 1861). English poet

1834. George Louis Palmella Busson du Maurier (d. 8 October 1896). French-born English writer of fiction

1885. Ringgold Wilmer Lardner (d. 25 September 1933). American journalist, humorist, writer of fiction, and poet

1906. Lawrence Lovell Schoonover (d. 8 January 1980). American writer of historical fiction

1909. Obafemi Awolowo (d. ? 1987). Nigerian politician and political essayist

DEATHS

1616. Francis Beaumont (b. ? 1584).

1672. Richard Barnfield (b. 13[?] June 1574). English pastoral poet and sonneteer

1867. Artemus Ward (pseudonym of Charles Farrar Browne; b. 26 April 1834). American essayist and humorist

1888. Louisa May Alcott (b. 29 November 1832). American writer of fiction and narrative nonfiction prose

1895. Jacobine Camilla Wergeland Collett (b. 23 January 1813). Norwegian writer of fiction

1967. Zoltan Kodaly (b. 16 December 1882). Hungarian composer, musician, and essayist

1973. Pearl Sydenstricker Buck (b. 26 June 1892). American writer of fiction, essayist, and biographer

1982. Ayn Rand (b. 2 February 1905). Russian-born American writer of fiction, playwright, and essayist

7

BIRTHS

1785. Alesandro Francesco Tommasso Antonio de Manzoni (d. 28 April 1873). Italian writer of fiction and poet

1903. William York Tindall (d. 8 September 1981). American critical essayist

1924. Kobo Abe. Japanese writer of fiction, poet, and playwright

DEATHS

1911. Antonio Fogazzaro (b. 25 March 1842). Italian writer of fiction, poet, and playwright

1940. Edwin Charles Markham (b. 23 April 1852). American poet

1957. Percy Wyndham Lewis (b. 18 November 1882). American-born English artist, writer of fiction, and critical essayist

1967. Alice Babette Toklas (b. 30 April 1877). American memoirist and writer of miscellaneous prose nonfiction

8

BIRTHS

1753. William Roscoe (d. 30 June 1831). English biographer and poet

1830. Joao de Deus Ramos (d. 11 January 1896). Portuguese poet

1859. Kenneth Grahame (d. 6 July 1932). Scottish-born English essayist, writer of autobiographical narrative, and writer of fiction for children

1899. Eric Robert Russell Linklater (d. 7 November 1974). Scottish writer of fiction, playwright, and poet

1917. Leslie Aaron Fiedler. American academician, critical essayist, and writer of fiction

DEATHS

1817. Anna Maria Lenngren (b. 18 June 1754). Swedish satirical poet

1868. Jon Thoroddsen (b. 5 October 1819). Icelandic writer of fiction and poet

1941. Sherwood Berton Anderson (b. 13 September 1876). American writer of fiction, poet, writer of nonfiction narrative, and essayist

1976. Doris Miles Disney (b. 22 December 1907). American writer of fiction

9

BIRTHS

1749. Gabriel Honore Rigueti Mirabeau (d. 2 April 1791). French politician and essayist

1762. William Cobbett (d. 18 June 1835). English political and social reformist writer

1814. Toras Grigorievich Shevchenko (d. 10 March 1861). Ukrainian poet and essayist

1883. Umberto Sabro (pseudonym of Umberto Poli; d. 25 August 1957). Italian poet

1892. Victoria Mary Sackville-West (d. 2 June 1962). English poet and writer of fiction

1905. Peter Courtney Quennell. English poet, biographer, historian, and editor

1907. Mircea Eliade (d. 22 April 1986). Romanian-born religious scholar and philosopher

1918. Frank Morrison (Mickey) Spillane. American writer of detective fiction

1924. Herbert Gold. American writer of fiction

DEATHS

1825. Anna Laetitia Aiken Barbauld (b. 20 June 1743). English essayist, editor, writer of prose pieces for children, poet, and translator

1895. Leopold von Sacher-Masoch (b. 27 January 1836). Austrian lawyer and writer of fiction

1918. Frank Wedekind (b. 24 July 1864). German playwright and essayist

10

BIRTHS

1672. Sir Richard Steele (d. 1 September 1729). Irish-born English essayist, poet, and playwright

1772. Karl Wilhelm Friedrich von Schlegel (d. 12 January 1829). German critical essayist and literary historian

1787. Francisco Martinez de la Rosa (d. 7 February 1862). Spanish playwright, poet, and historian

1788. Joseph Karl Eichendorff (d. 26 November 1857). German poet, writer of fiction, and critical essayist

1791. Angel Saavedra (pseudonym of Ramirez de Baquedano; d. 22 June 1865). Spanish poet and playwright

1833. Pedro Antonio de Alarcon (d. 20 July 1891). Spanish diarist, poet, writer of travel narrative, and writer of fiction

1839. Joaquin Miller (pseudonym of Cincinnatus Hiner Miller; d. 17 February 1913). American poet and playwright

1873. Jakob Wassermann (d. 1 January 1934). German writer of fiction

DEATHS

1861. Taras Girgorievich Shevchenko (b. 9 March 1814). Ukrainian poet and essayist

1872. Guissepe Mazzini (b. 22 June 1805). Italian patriot. diarist, and political essayist

1943. Robert Laurence Binyon (b. 10 August 1869). English poet, playwright, translator, and art critic

1944. Irvin Shrewsbury Cobb (b. 23 June 1876). American journalist, writer of fiction, and humorist

1966. Frank O'Connor (pseudonym of Michael O'Donovan; b. 17 September 1903). Irish writer of fiction

11

BIRTHS

1544. Torquato Tasso (d. 25 April 1595). Italian poet, playwright, and essayist

1754. Juan Melendez Valdes (d. 24 May 1817). Spanish lyric poet

1807. John Doran (d. 25 January 1878). English writer of miscellaneous prose nonfiction and translator

1920. Dennis Joseph Enright. English poet, writer of prose fiction for children, critical essayist, and editor

DEATHS

1711. Nicolas Boileau-Despreaux (b. 1 November 1636). French critical essayist and satirist

1944. Hendrik Van Loon (b. 14 January 1882). Dutch-born American popular historian and biographer

1970. Erle Stanley Gardner (b. 17 July 1889). American writer of detective and mystery fiction

1980. Gladys Leonae Bagg Taber (b. 12 April 1899). American writer of fiction and miscellaneous prose nonfiction

1982. Horace Victor Gregory (b. 10 April 1898). American poet and translator

12

BIRTHS

1626. John Aubrey (d. ? June 1697). English antiquarian and biographer

1685. George Berkeley (d. 14 January 1753). Irish-born English theologian, philosopher, essayist, and poet

1799. Mary Howitt (d. 30 January 1888). English writer of fiction, poet, and writer of miscellaneous prose nonfiction

1858. Adolph Simon Ochs (d. 8 April 1935). American newspaper publisher and promoter of *The Dictionary of American Biography*

1863. Gabriele d'Annunzio (d. 1 March 1938). Italian poet, playwright, writer of fiction, and journalist

1922. Jean Louis-Lebrid de (Jack) Kerouac (d. 21 October 1969). American "Beat" writer of fiction and poet

DEATHS

1898. Zacharias Topelius (b. 14 January 1818). Swedish poet, playwright, and writer of fiction

1928. Edward Franklin Albee. American playwright

13

BIRTHS

1616. Joseph Beaumont (d. 25 September 1699). English epic poet

1733. Joseph Priestley (d. 6 February 1804). English theologian, scientist, historian, and essayist

1869. Ramon Menedez Pidal (d. 14 November 1968). Spanish literary historian and critical essayist

1884. Hugh Seymour Walpole (d. 1 June 1941). English writer of fiction

1892. Janet Flanner (d. 7 November 1978). American journalist and writer of fiction

1911. Lafayette Ronald Hubbard (d. 24 January 1986). American writer of science fiction and essayist

DEATHS

1695. Jean de La Fontaine (b. 8 July 1621). French poet

1877. Charles Cowden Clarke (b. 15 December 1787). English Shakespearean scholar, editor, and critical essayist

1895. Louise Otto (b. 26 March 1819). German essayist and writer of fiction

1930. Mary Eleanor Wilkins Freeman (b. 31 October 1852). American writer of fiction

1939. Lucien Levy-Bruhl (b. 10 April 1857). French philosopher, anthropologist, sociologist, and essayist

1941. Elizabeth Madox Roberts (b. 30 October 1881). English writer of fiction and poet

1943. Stephen Vincent Benet (b. 22 July 1898). American poet, writer of fiction, and librettist

1957. John Middleton Murry (b. 6 August 1899). English literary essayist and biographer

1975. Ivo Andric (b. 10 February 1892). Yugoslav writer of fiction

14

BIRTHS

1837. Charles Ammi Cutter (d. 6 September 1903). American librarian and essayist

1875. Isadore Gilbert Mudge (d. 17 May 1957). American librarian, essayist, and bibliographer

1879. Albert Einstein (d. 18 April 1955). German-born American mathematician, physicist, and essayist

1919. Max Shulman (d. 28 August 1988). American writer of fiction and humorist

1925. John Barrington Wain. English poet, essayist, and writer of fiction

DEATHS

1801. Count Ignacy Krasicki (b. 3 February 1735). Polish poet and writer of miscellaneous prose

1803. Friedrich Gottlieb Klopstock (b. 2 July 1724). German poet

1932. Frederick Jackson Turner (b. 14 November 1861). American historian

15

BIRTHS

1794. Friedrich Christian Diez (d. 29 May 1876). German philologist and essayist

1830. Paul Johann Ludwig von Heyse (d. 2 April 1914). German writer of fiction, poet, playwright, and translator

1867. Lionel Pigot Johnson (d. 4 October 1902). English critical essayist and poet

1918. Richard David Ellmann (d. 12 May 1987). American literary scholar and critical essayist

DEATHS

1673. Salvatore Rosa (b. 21 June 1615). Italian satirical poet

1942. Rachel Lyman Field (b. 19 September 1894). American writer of fiction and literature for children

1983. Dame Rebecca West (pseudonym of Cicily Isabella Fairfield; b. 25 December 1892). English writer of fiction, essayist, and reviewer

16

BIRTHS

1581. Pieter Corneliazoon Hooft (d. 21 May 1647). Dutch poet, humanist, and essayist

1585. Gerbrand Adrianenszoon Bredero (d. 23 August 1618). Dutch poet and playwright

1634. Marie-Madeleine de La Fayette (d. 23 May 1693). French writer of fiction

1803. Nikolay Yazykov (d. 7 January 1846). Russian poet

1825. Camillo Castello Branco (d. 1 June 1890). Portuguese writer of fiction

1839. Rene Francois Armand Sully Prudhomme (d. 7 September 1907). French poet, philosopher, essayist, and diarist

1868. Maksim Gorki (pseudonym of Aleksei Maksimovich Peshkov; d. 14 June 1936). Russian writer of fiction

1878. Emile Cammaerts (d. 2 November 1953). Belgian poet

DEATHS

1680. Francois, duc de La Rouchfaucauld (b. 15 December 1613). French memoirist; writer of prose nonfiction narrative and of maxims

1864. Robert Smith Surtees (b. 17 May 1803). English writer of fiction and of miscellaneous prose nonfiction

1892. Edward Augustus Freeman (b. 2 August 1823). English historian

1898. Aubrey Vincent Beardsley (b. 21 August 1872). English illustrator, editor, and writer of erotic fiction

1940. Selma Lagerlof (b. 20 November 1858). Swedish writer of fiction and fairy tales

1970. Arthur Adamov (b. 23 August 1908). French playwright, essayist, and translator

1977. Cecil Woodham-Smith (b. ? 1896). English biographer and historian

17

BIRTHS

1846. Catherine (Kate) Greenaway (d. 6 November 1901). English artist and illustrator of books for children

1884. Frank Howard Buck (d. 25 March 1950). American explorer and author of adventure fiction and narrative

1898. Ella Winter (d. 5 August 1980). Australian-born American journalist and essayist

DEATHS

1635. Thomas Randolph (b. 15 June 1605). English playwright and poet

1715. Gilbert Burnett (b. 18 September 1643). Scottish-born historian

1741. Jean-Baptiste Rousseau (b. 6 April 1671). French poet

1781. Johannes Ewald (b. 18 November 1743). Danish poet and playwright

1860. Anna Brownell Murphy Jameson (b. 17 May 1794). Irish-born English writer of miscellaneous prose nonfiction and diarist

1871. Robert Chambers (b. 10 July 1802). Scottish poet, essayist, and publisher

1986. Bernard Malamud (b. 26 April 1914). American writer of fiction

18

BIRTHS

1733. Christoph Friedrich Nicolai (d. 1 January 1811). German critical essayist and writer of fiction

1813. Christian Friedrich Hebbel (d. 13 December 1863). German playwright, poet, essayist, and writer of fiction

1830. Numa Denis Fustel de Coulanges (d. 12 September 1889). French historian and essayist

1842. Stephane Mallarme (d. 9 September 1898). French poet, translator, and essayist

1891. Margaret Culkin Banning (d. 4 January 1982). American writer of fiction and miscellaneous prose nonfiction

1892. Robert Peter Tristram Coffin (d. 20 January 1955). American poet, writer of fiction, biographer, and writer of miscellaneous prose nonfiction

1893. Wilfrid Owen (d. 4 November 1918). English poet

1915. Richard Thomas Condon. American writer of fiction

1932. John Hoyer Updike. American writer of fiction, playwright, and poet

DEATHS

1768. Laurence Sterne (b. 24 November 1713). English writer of fiction, nonfiction prose narrative, and sermon literature

1812. John Horne Tooke (b. 25 June 1736). English philologist and essayist

1876. Ferdinand Hermann Freiligrath (b. 17 June 1810). German poet

1916. Stopford Augustus Brooke (b. 14 November 1832). Irish-born English essayist, biographer, poet, and literary historian

1956. Louis Bromfield (b. 27 December 1896). American writer of fiction

1983. Sarah Catherine Marshall (b. 27 September 1914). American biographer and writer of prose nonfiction

19

BIRTHS

1589. William Bradford (d. 9 May 1657). English-born colonial American historian and writer of narrative

1721. Tobias George Smollett (d. 17 September 1771). Scottish-born English writer of fiction, poet, travel anthologist, literary editor, and historian

1727. Ferdinand Berthoud (d. 20 June 1807). Swiss-born French essayist, horologist, and clockmaker

1821. Sir Richard Francis Burton (d. 20 October 1890). English explorer, anthropologist, writer of nonfiction narrative, essayist, and translator

1824. William Allingham (d. 18 November 1889). Irish poet

1858. K'ang Yu-wei (d. 31 March 1927). Chinese scholar and political reformer

1899. Berry Jiles Fleming (d. 15 September 1989). American writer of fiction

1915. Helen Yglesias. American writer of fiction and memoirist

1916. Irving Wallace. (d. 29 June 1990). American writer of fiction

1928. Hans Kung. Swiss-born German Catholic theologian and essayist

1933. Philip Roth. American writer of fiction

DEATHS

1884. Elias Lonnrot (b. 9 April 1802). Finnish literary scholar, folklorist, and lexicographer

1887. Jozef Ignacy Krascewski (b. 28 July 1812). Polish writer of historical fiction and poet

1907. Thomas Bailey Aldrich (b. 11 November 1836). American writer of fiction, poet, and periodicals editor

1930. Arthur James Balfour (b. 25 July 1848). Scottish philosopher and essayist

1950. Edgar Rice Burroughs (b. 1 September 1875). American writer of adventure and fantasy fiction

1974. Austin Clarke (b. 9 May 1896). Irish poet, playwright, and verse dramatist

1978. Faith Cuthrell Baldwin (b. 1 October 1893). American writer of popular fiction and poet

20

BIRTHS

1770. Johann Friedrich Holderlin (d. 7 June 1843). German poet, writer of fiction, and writer of verse drama

1811. Ned Buntline (pseudonym of Edward Zane Carroll Judson; d. 16 July 1886). American writer of popular fiction and playwright

1828. Henrik Ibsen (d. 23 May 1906). Norwegian playwright and poet

1892. Max Brand (pseudonym of Frederick Faust; d. 16 May 1944). American writer of popular adventure fiction

1907. John Hugh MacLennan. Canadian writer of fiction

1909. Kathryn Forbes (pseudonym of Kathryn Anderson McLean; d. 15 May 1966). American writer of fiction

DEATHS

1727. Sir Isaac Newton (b. 4 January 1643). English scientist, mathematician, essayist, and philosopher

1875. John Mitchell (b. 3 November 1815). Irish writer of miscellaneous prose nonfiction

1936. Robert Montine Cunninghame Graham (b. 24 May 1852). Scottish writer of fiction and writer of travel narrative

1964. Brendan Francis Behan (b. 9 February 1923). Irish playwright

21

BIRTHS

1763. Jean Paul Friedrich Richter (d. 14 November 1825). German writer of fiction and humorist

1905. Phyllis McGinley (d. 22 February 1978). American poet, essayist, and writer of children's fiction

1926. John Robert Fowles. English writer of fiction

DEATHS

1556. Thomas Cranmer (b. 2 July 1489). English churchman and theological essayist

1640. Thomas Carew (b. ? 1595). English poet and playwright

1830. Johann Rudolf Wyss (b. 4 March 1782). Swiss writer of fiction, essayist, and philosopher

1843. Robert Southey (b. 12 August 1774). English poet, essayist, and biographer

22

BIRTHS

1908. Louis Dearborn L'Amour (d. 10 June 1988). American writer of Western adventure fiction

1910. Nicholas John Turney Monsarrat (d. 7 August 1979). English writer of fiction

DEATHS

1758. Jonathan Edwards (b. 5 October 1703). American theologian, essayist, and writer of sermon literature

1832. Johann Wolfgang von Goethe (b. 28 August 1749). German poet, playwright, essayist, and writer of fiction

1986. Harriette Simpson Arnow (b. 7 July 1908). American writer of fiction

23

BIRTHS

1881. Roger Martin du Gard (d. 22 August 1958). French writer of fiction and playwright

1899. Louis Adamic (d. 4 September 1951). Yugoslavian-born American writer of autobiographical narrative, writer of fiction, and essayist

DEATHS

1842. Stendahl (pseudonym of Marie Henri Beyle; b. 23 January 1783). French writer of fiction and biographer

1939. Richard Halliburton (b. 9 January 1900). American adventurer and writer of travel narrative

1960. Franklin Pierce Adams (b. 15 November 1881). American essayist, poet, and journalist

1968. Edwin Greene O'Connor (b. 29 July 1918). American writer of fiction

24

BIRTHS

1754. Joel Barlow (d. 24 December 1812). American poet and essayist

1809. Mariano Jose de Larra y Sanchez de Castro (d. 13 February 1837). Spanish poet, satirist, and political essayist

1822. Henri Murger (d. 28 January 1861). French writer of fiction and poet

1834. William Morris (d. 6 October 1896). English poet, essayist, writer of short fiction, and translator

1855. Olive Emilie Albertina Schreiner (d. 11 December 1920). South African writer of fiction

1906. Dwight Macdonald (d. 19 December 1982). American essayist, biographer, and memoirist

1919. Lawrence Monsanto Ferlinghetti, American poet, writer of fiction, and playwright

1935. Peter Bichsel. Swiss writer of fiction

DEATHS

1773. Philip Dormer Stanhope, fourth Earl of Chesterfield (b. 22 September 1694). English epistolary essayist and writer of political tracts

1877. Walter Bagehot (b. 3 February 1826). English essayist

1882. Henry Wadsworth Longfellow (b. 27 February 1807). American poet

1904. Edwin Arnold (b. 10 June 1832). English poet, journalist, and Oriental scholar

1905. Jules Verne (b. 8 February 1828). French writer of science fiction

1909. John Millington Synge (b. 16 April 1871). Irish playwright, poet, and translator

25

BIRTHS

1842. Antonio Fogazzaro (d. 7 March 1911). Italian writer of fiction, poet, and playwright

1881. Mary Gladys Webb (d. 8 October 1927). English writer of fiction

1916. Gabriel Fielding (d. 27 November 1986). English-born writer of fiction and poet

1925. Mary Flannery O'Connor (d. 3 August 1964). American writer of fiction

1939. Toni Cade Bambara. American writer of fiction

DEATHS

1458. Inigo Lopex de Mendoza (b. 19 August 1398). Spanish poet and statesman

1794. Marie-Jean Antoine Nicolas Caritat, Marquis de Condorcet (b. 17 September 1743). French mathematician, essayist, and encyclopaedist

1914. Frederic Mistral (b. 8 September 1830). French poet and lexicographer

1937. John Drinkwater (b. 1 June 1882). English poet, playwright, and critical essayist

1950. Frank Howard Buck (b. 17 March 1884). American explorer and writer of adventure fiction and narrative

1969. Max Forrester Eastman (b. 4 January 1883). American essayist and critic

1980. Roland Barthes (b. 12 November 1915). French critical essayist and theorist

26

BIRTHS

1819. Louise Otto (d. 13 March 1895). German feminist writer

1838. William Edward Hartpole Lecky (d. 22 October 1903). Irish historian and essayist

1850. Edward Bellamy (d. 22 May 1899). American writer of fiction and political essayist

1859. Alfred Edward Housman (d. 30 April 1936). English poet, critical essayist, and classical scholar

1874. Robert Lee Frost (d. 29 January 1963). American poet

1904. Joseph Campbell (d. 31 October 1987). American scholar, mythologist, and critical essayist

1911. Thomas Lanier (Tennessee) Williams (d. 25 February 1983). American playwright and writer of fiction

1930. Gregory Nunzio Corso. American "Beat" poet and writer of fiction

1942. Erica Mann Jong. American writer of fiction and poet

DEATHS

1649. John Winthrop (b. 12 January 1588). English-born colonial American essayist and historian

1892. Walt Whitman (b. 31 May 1819). American poet, writer of fiction, and essayist

1959. Raymond Thornton Chandler (b. 23 July 1888). American writer of detective and mystery fiction

1973. Sir Noel Pierce Coward (b. 16 December 1899). English playwright, poet, and writer of fiction and autobiographical narrative

1976. Lin Yu-T'ang (b. 10 October 1895). Chinese-born essayist and philosopher

1979. Jean Stafford (b. 1 July 1915). American writer of fiction

27

BIRTHS

1797. Alfred Victor, Comte de Vigny (d. 17 September 1863). French poet, playwright, and writer of fiction

1900. Edward Charles Wagenknecht. American literary critic and essayist

1914. Budd Wilson Schulberg. American writer of fiction and essayist

1923. Louis Aston Marantz Simpson. Jamaican-born poet, writer of fiction, and critical essayist

DEATHS

1772. Emmanuel Swedenborg (b. 29 January 1688). Swedish religious mystic, scientist, mathematician, philosopher, and essayist

1869. James Harper (b. 13 April 1795). American publisher and editor

1918. Henry Brooks Adams (b. 16 February 1838). American essayist, reviewer, writer of fiction, historian, and memoirist

1931. Enoch Arnold Bennett (b. 27 May 1867). English writer of fiction

1981. Mao Dun (pseudonym of Shan Yan-bing; b. 4 July 1896). Chinese writer of fiction

1989. Malcolm Cowley (b. 24 August 1898). American poet, critical essayist, and writer of nonfiction narrative

28

BIRTHS

1592. Johannes Amos Comenius (d. 4 November 1670). Czech educational reformer, essayist, and writer of books for children

1652. Samuel Sewall (d. 1 January 1730). English-born colonial American essayist and diarist

1674. William Byrd II (d. 26 August 1744). colonial American historian, diarist, and writer of nonfiction narrative

1702. Ignacio de Luzan (d. 19 May 1754). Spanish critical essayist and poet

1817. Francesco De Sanctis (d. 19 December 1883). Italian literary critic and essayist

1909. Nelson Algren (d. 9 May 1981). American writer of fiction

DEATHS

1848. Steen Steensen Blicher (b. 11 October 1782). Danish poet, writer of fiction, and translator

1929. Katherine Lee Bates (b. 12 August 1859). American poet, critical essayist, and writer of books for children

1941. Adeline Virginia Woolf (b. 25 January 1882). English writer of fiction and critical essayist

1944. Stephen Butler Leacock (b. 30 December 1869). English-born Canadian humorist, essayist, and writer of fiction

1957. Christopher Darlington Morley (b. 5 May 1890). American writer of fiction, playwright, and poet

29

BIRTHS

1889. Howard Lindsay (d. 11 February 1968). American playwright

DEATHS

1788. Charles Wesley (b. 18 December 1707). English religious poet and hymnodist

1921. John Burroughs (b. 3 April 1837). American naturalist, essayist, and writer of literary critical commentary

1957. Arthur Joyce Lunel Cary (b. 7 December 1888). Irish writer of fiction, essayist, and poet

30

BIRTHS

1820. Anna Sewell (d. 25 April 1878). English writer of prose fiction for children

1842. John Fiske (d. 4 July 1901). American philosopher and historian

1844. Paul Verlaine (d. 8 January 1896). French poet

1880. Sean O'Casey (pseudonym of John Casey; d. 18 September 1964). Irish playwright and writer of autobiographical narrative

1894. Roland Herbert Bainton (d. 13 February 1984). American theologian, biographer, and essayist

1895. Jean Giono (d. ? 1970). French writer of fiction

DEATHS

1840. George Brian (Beau) Brummell (b. 7 June 1778). English wit and gentleman of fashion

1910. Jean Moreas (pseudonym of Yannis Papadiamantopoulos; b. 15 April 1856). Greek-born French poet

1925. Rudolph Steiner (b. 27 February 1861). Austrian social philosopher, spiritualist, and essayist

1967. Jean Toomer (b. 26 December 1894). American writer of fiction, poet, and playwright

1984. Luigi Giorgio Barzini the younger (b. 21 December 1908). Italian cultural historian

1986. John Anthony Ciardi (b. 24 June 1916). American poet, literary critic, and translator

31

BIRTHS

1596. Rene Descartes (d. 1 February 1650). French philosopher, mathematician, and essayist

1621. Andrew Marvell (d. 18 August 1678). English poet, satirist, and essayist

1809. Edward Fitzgerald (d. 14 June 1883). English poet, translator, biographer and writer of epistles

Nikolai Vasilyevich Gogol (d. 21 February 1852). Russian writer of fiction and playwright

1838. Leon Dierx (d. 11 June 1912). French poet

1844. Andrew Lang (d. 20 July 1912). Scottish poet, writer of fiction, literary historian, biographer, and essayist

1857. Edouard Rod (d. 29 January 1910). Swiss writer of fiction

1887. St. John Perse (pseudonym of Marie-Rene-Auguste Alexis Saint-Leger Leger; d. 20 September 1975). French poet

1895. Vardis Alvero Fisher (d. 9 July 1968). American writer of fiction and poet

1912. William Julius Lederer. American writer of fiction and prose nonfiction

1914. Octavio Paz. Mexican poet and critical essayist

DEATHS

1631. John Donne (b. ? 1572). English poet, essayist, and writer of sermon literature

1855. Charlotte Bronte (b. 21 April 1816). English writer of fiction and poet

1904. Otto von Bohtlingk (b. 11 June 1815). German Sanskrit scholar, Oriental linguist, and essayist

1927. K'ang Yu-wei (b. 19 March 1858). Chinese scholar and political reformer

1981. Enid Algerine Bagnold, Lady Jones (b. 27 October 1889). English writer of fiction and playwright

1983. Christina Ellen Stead (b. 17 July 1902). Australian writer of fiction

APRIL

1

BIRTHS

1616. Charles de Marguetel de Saint-Denis de Saint-Evremond (d. 20 September 1703). French satirist and essayist

1647. John Wilmot, Earl of Rochester (d. 26 July 1680). English poet

1697. Abbe Antoine Francois Prevost (d. 23 December 1763). French writer of fiction and periodical essayist

1730. Solomon Gessner (d. 2 March 1788). Swiss pastoral poet

1753. Joseph Marie de Maistre (d. 26 February 1821). French philosopher and essayist

1755. Anthelme Brillat-Savarin (d. 2 February 1826). French gastronome and legal essayist

1868. Edmond Rostand (d. 2 December 1918). French poet and playwright

1875. Richard Horatio Edgar Wallace (d. 10 February 1932). English writer of fiction and playwright

1922. William Manchester. American journalist, biographer, popular historian, and writer of fiction

1931. Rolf Hochhuth. German playwright

DEATHS

1872. John Frederick Denison Maurice (b. 29 August 1805). English theologian, writer of fiction, and essayist

1952. Ferenc Molnar (b. 12 January 1878). Hungarian-born playwright and writer of fiction

1966. Brian O'Nolan (pseudonym of Brian O'Nuallain; b. 5 October 1911). Irish writer of fiction and playwright

2

BIRTHS

1725. Giovanni Jacopo Casanova de Seingalt (d. 4 June 1798). Italian adventurer and memoirist

1798. August Heinrich Hoffmann von Fallersleben (d. 19 January 1874). German poet, philologist, and antiquarian

1805. Hans Christian Andersen (d. 4 August 1875). Danish writer of fiction, poet, satirist, and composer of fairy tales

1840. Emile Zola (d. 28 September 1902). French writer of fiction and journalist

1927. Kenneth Peacock Tynan (d. 26 July 1980). English drama critic and essayist

1928. Cheikh Hamidou Kane. Senegalese writer of fiction

DEATHS

1780. Etienne Bonnot de Mabley de Condillac (b. 30 September 1714). French philosopher and essayist

1791. Gabriel Honore Rigueti Mirabeau (b. 9 March 1749). French politician and essayist

1914. Paul Johann Ludwig von Heyse (b. 15 March 1830). German writer of fiction, poet, playwright, and translator

1931. Katherine Tynan (b. 23 January 1861). Irish poet and writer of fiction

1966. Cecil Scott Forester (pseudonym of Cecil Lewis Troughton Smith; b. 27 August 1899). English writer of adventure and historical fiction

3

BIRTHS

1593. George Herbert (d. 1 March 1633). English poet and writer of religious prose

1783. Washington Irving (d. 28 November 1859). American journalist, satirical essayist, writer of fiction, playwright, popular biographer and historian, and writer of narrative nonfiction

1822. Edward Everett Hale (d. 10 June 1909). American cleric, writer of fiction, and historian

1837. John Burroughs (d. 29 March 1921). American naturalist, essayist, and writer of literary critical commentary

DEATHS

1854. Christopher North (pseudonym of John Wilson; b. 19 May 1785). Scottish essayist and poet

4

BIRTHS

1785. Bettina Elisabeth von Arnim (d. 20 January 1859). German social and political essayist and memoirist

1793. Jean Francois Casimir Delavigne (d. 11 December 1843). French playwright, satirist, and lyric poet

1818. Mayne Reid (d. 22 October 1883). English-born American writer of fiction

1846. Isidore Lucien Ducasse, Le Comte de Lautreamont (d. 24 November 1870). Uruguayan-born French prose-poet and writer of surrealist verse

1895. Helen Dore Boylston (d. 30 September 1984). American writer of fiction for young girls

1896. Robert Emmet Sherwood (d. 14 November 1955). American playwright, writer of fiction, and biographer

1913. Jerome Weidman. American writer of fiction and playwright

1914. Marguerite Donnadieu Duras. French writer of fiction, playwright, essayist, and journalist

1928. Maya Angelou (pseudonym of Marguerite Ann Johnson). American memorist and poet

DEATHS

1604. Thomas Churchyard (b. ? 1520). English poet and miscellaneous nonfiction prose writer

1765. Mikhail Vasilievich Lomonosov (b. 8 November 1711). Russian philologist, poet, essayist, and scientist

1774. Oliver Goldsmith (b. 10 November 1730?). Irish-born English writer of fiction, playwright, poet, and essayist

1806. Count Carlo Gozzi (b. 13 December 1720). Italian playwright and poet

1831. Isaiah Thomas (b. 19 January 1749). American printer, publisher, and historian of the print trade

1944. John Peale Bishop (b. 21 May 1892). American poet, writer of fiction, and essayist

1966. Evelyn Arthur St. John Waugh (b. 28 October 1903). English writer of fiction, journalist, diarist, and writer of travel narrative

1968. Martin Luther King, Jr. (d. 15 January 1929). American social reformer and essayist

1969. Romulo Gallegos Freire (b. 2 August 1884). Venezuelan writer of fiction

5

BIRTHS

1588. Thomas Hobbes (d. 4 December 1679). English philosopher, essayist, translator, and literary critic

1801. Vincenzo Gioberti (d. 26 October 1852). Italian philosopher, political theorist, and essayist

1834. Frank Richard Stockton (d. 20 April 1902). American writer of fiction

1835. Vitczslav Halek (d. 8 October 1874). Czech poet, writer of fiction, and playwright

1837. Algernon Charles Swinburne (d. 10 April 1909). English poet, playwright, writer of fiction, and critical essayist

1856. Booker Taliafero Washington (d. 14 November 1915). American educational leader, historian, writer of narrative, and essayist

1904. Richard Ghormley Eberhart. American poet and playwright

1908. Mary Welsh Hemingway (d. 26 November 1986). American journalist and essayist

1920. Arthur Hailey. American writer of popular fiction

DEATHS

1933. Earl Derr Biggers (b. 26 August 1884). American journalist and writer of detective and mystery fiction

1961. Henry Seidel Canby (b. 6 September 1878). American literary and social critic, historian, and critical biographer

6

BIRTHS

1671. Jean-Baptiste Rousseau (d. 17 March 1741). French poet

1773. James Mill (d. 23 June 1836). Scottish philosopher, historian, and essayist

1785. John Pierpont (d. 27 August 1866). American poet and essayist

1812. Alexander Ivanovich Herzen (d. 21 January 1870). Russian philosopher and essayist

1818. Aasmund Olavssen Vinje (d. 30 July 1870). Norwegian poet and critical essayist

1866. Joseph Lincoln Steffens (d. 9 August 1936). American reform journalist, editor, essayist, and writer of autobiographical narrative

1903. Charles Reginald Jackson (d. 21 September 1968). American writer of fiction

1935. John Pepper Clark. Nigerian poet, playwright, and critical essayist

DEATHS

1695. Richard Busby (b. 22 September 1606). English schoolmaster, tutor to the likes of John Locke, John Dryden, Matthew Prior, Francis Atterbury

1860. James Kirke Paulding (b. 22 August 1778). American poet, writer of fiction, and playwright

1935. Edward Arlington Robinson (b. 22 December 1869). American poet and playwright

7

BIRTHS

1770. William Wordsworth (d. 23 April 1850). English poet and essayist

1772. Francois Marie Charles Fourier (d. 10 October 1837). French social theorist and essayist

1780. William Ellery Channing the elder (d. 2 October 1842). American theologian, essayist, and writer of sermon literature

1889. Gabriela Mistral (pseudonym of Lucila Godoy Alcayaga; d. 10 January 1957). Chilean poet

1931. Donald Barthelme (d. 23 July 1989). American writer of fiction

DEATHS

1668. Sir William D'Avenant (b. ? February 1606). English playwright, poet, and writer of songs

1836. William Godwin (b. 3 March 1756). English political essayist and writer of fiction

1850. William Lisle Bowles (b. 24 September 1762). English poet and essayist

1915. Francis Hopkinson Smith (b. 23 October 1838). American writer of travel narrative, fiction writer, and illustrator

1975. Sir Sarvepalli Radhakrishnan (b. 5 September 1858). Indian philosopher and essayist

1987. Rudolph John Frederick Lehmann (b. 2 June 1907). English poet and biographer

8

BIRTHS

1585. Phineas Fletcher (d. ? 1650). English poet

1798. Dionysius Solomos (d. 21 February 1857). Greek poet

1859. Edmund Gustav Albrecht Husserl (d. 26 April 1938). Austrian-born German philosopher and essayist

1886. Margaret Ayer Barnes (d. ? October 1967). American writer of fiction and playwright

1898. Cecil Maurice Bowra (d. 4 July 1971). English literary scholar and essayist

DEATHS

1835. Karl Wilhelm von Humboldt (b. 22 June 1767). German statesman and philologist

1885. Richard Grant White (b. 23 May 1821). American critical essayist

1894. Bankim Chandra Chatterjee (b. 27 June 1838). Indian writer of fiction, essayist, and poet

1915. Louis Pergaud (b. 22 January 1882). French writer of fiction

1931. Erik Axel Karlfeldt (b. 20 July 1864). Swedish poet

1935. Adolph Simon Ochs (b. 12 March 1858). American newspaper publisher and a principal sponsor of *The Dictionary of American Biography*

1958. George Jean Nathan (b. 14 February 1882). American playwright, satirist, essayist, and reviewer

9

BIRTHS

1802. Elias Lonnrot (d. 19 March 1884). Finnish literary scholar, folklorist, and lexicographer

1821. Charles Pierre Baudelaire (d. 31 August 1867). French symbolist poet

DEATHS

1626. Sir Francis Bacon (b. 22 January 1561). English philosopher and essayist

1852. John Howard Payne (b. 9 June 1791). American playwright and drama journalist

1882. Dante Gabriel Rossetti (born Gabriel Charles Dante Rossetti; b. 12 May 1828). English poet and translator

1909. Francis Marion Crawford (b. 2 August 1854). American writer of fiction and playwright

1968. Zofia Kossak (pseudonym of Zofia Kossak-szucka; b. ? 1890). Polish writer of historical fiction

10

BIRTHS

1583. Hugo Grotius (also Huig van Groot; d. 28 August 1645). Dutch jurist, statesman and legal essayist

1778. William Hazlitt (d. 18 September 1830). English essayist

1827. Lewis Wallace (d. 15 February 1905). American writer of fiction and poet

1847. Joseph Pulitzer (d. 29 October 1911). Hungarian-born American newspaper publisher and sponsor of awards in literature, journalism, drama, and music

1857. Lucien Levy-Bruhl (d. 13 March 1939). French philosopher, anthropologist, sociologist, and essayist

1867. AE (pseudonym of George William Russell; d. 17 July 1935). Irish poet and essayist

1897. Eric Mowbray Knight (d. 21 January 1943). English-born American writer of fiction for children

1898. Horace Victor Gregory (d. 11 March 1982). American poet and translator

1934. David Halberstam. American journalist; social, political, economic critical commentator

1941. Paul Theroux. American writer of fiction

DEATHS

1685. Thomas Otway (b. 3 March 1652). English playwright and poet

1858. Thomas Hart Benton (b. 1 March 1782). American painter and writer of autobiographical prose narrative

1893. John Addington Symonds (b. 5 October 1840). English poet, historian, and biographer

1909. Algernon Charles Swinburne (b. 5 April 1837). English poet, playwright, writer of fiction, and critical essayist

1931. Khalil Gibran (b. 6 January 1883). Lebanese poet and writer of fiction

1945. Carl Lotus Becker (b. 7 September 1873). American historian

1950. John Gould Fletcher (b. 3 January 1886). American poet and essayist

1955. Pierre Teilhard de Chardin (b. 1 May 1881). French scientist, theologian, philosopher, and essayist

11

BIRTHS

1492. Margaret of Navarre (d. 21 December 1549). French poet, epistolary essayist, playwright, and writer of dialogues

1722. Christopher Smart (d. 21 May 1771). English poet

1901. Glenway Westcott (d. 22 February 1987). American writer of fiction and poet

DEATHS

1839. John Galt (b. 2 May 1779). Scottish writer of fiction

1884. Charles Reade (b. 8 June 1814). English writer of fiction and playwright

1916. Richard Harding Davis (b. 17 April 1864). American journalist, writer of fiction, playwright, and writer of narrative

1932. Gamaliel Bradford (b. 9 October 1863). American historian and biographer

1944. Albert Auguste Gabriel Hanataux (b. 19 November 1853). French diplomat and historian

1947. Charles Bernard Nordhoff (b. 1 February 1887). American writer of fiction

1970. John Henry O'Hara (b. 31 January 1905). American writer of fiction and playwright

1981. Caroline Gordon (b. 6 October 1895). American writer of fiction and essayist

1987. Erskine Preston Caldwell (b. 17 December 1903). American writer of fiction and of narrative nonfiction

Primo Levi (b. 31 July 1919). Italian memoirist, writer of fiction, poet, and essayist

12

BIRTHS

1539. Garcilaso de la Vega (d. ? 1616). Peruvian historian

1726. Charles Burney (d. 12 April 1814). English musician, musicologist, and music historian

1816. Sir Charles Gavan Duffy (d. 9 February 1903). Irish poet

1823. Alexander Nikolaevich Ostrovsky (d. 14 June 1886). Russian playwright

1899. Gladys Leonae Bagg Taber (d. 11 March 1980). American writer of fiction and of miscellaneous prose nonfiction

1932. Jack Gelber. American playwright and writer of fiction

1939. Alan Ayckbourn. English playwright

DEATHS

1704. Jacques Benigne Bosseut (b. 27 September 1627). French theologian, writer of sermon literature, historian, and essayist

1777. Claude Prosper de Jolyot de Crebillon (b. 14 February 1707). French writer of fiction

1782. Pietro Antonio Domenico Bonaventura Metastasio (b. 3 January 1698). Italian poet, playwright, and opera librettist

1814. Charles Burney (b. 12 April 1726). English musician, musicologist, and music historian

1988. Alan Stewart Paton (b. 11 January 1903). South African writer of fiction

13

BIRTHS

1729. Thomas Percy (d. 30 September 1811). English poet and antiquarian

1739. Christian Friedrich Daniel Schubart (d. 10 October 1791). German poet and satirist

1795. James Harper (d. 27 March 1869). American publisher and editor

1906. Samuel Barclay Beckett (d. 22 December 1989). Irish-born French playwright, essayist, writer of fiction, and poet

1909. Eudora Welty. American writer of fiction and essayist

1922. John Gerard Braine (d. 23 October 1986). English writer of fiction and playwright

1939. Seamus Heaney. Irish poet

14

BIRTHS

1879. James Branch Cabell (d. 5 May 1958). American writer of fiction, essayist, and poet

1889. Arnold Joseph Toynbee (d. 22 October 1975). English historian and economist

1935. Erich von Daniken. Swiss writer of fiction and of prose nonfiction

DEATHS

1859. Lady Sydney Owenson Morgan (b. 25 December 1776). Irish writer of fiction

1917. Ludwick Lazanz Zamenhof (b. 15 December 1859). Polish linguist and language innovator

1930. Vladimir Vladimirovich Mayakovsky (b. 19 July 1893). Soviet Russian poet and playwright

1964. Rachel Carson (b. 27 May 1907). American scientist and essayist

1986. Simone Lucie Ernestine Marie Bertrand de Beauvoir (b. 9 January 1908). French philosopher, writer of fiction, essayist, and playwright

15

BIRTHS

1452. Leonardo da Vinci (d. 2 May 1519). Italian artist, craftsman, scientist, musician, and essayist

1569. Sir John Davies (d. 7 December 1626). English poet

1814. John Lathrop Motley (d. 29 May 1877). American historian and writer of fiction

1817. Benjamin Jowett (d. 1 October 1893). English classical scholar, translator, and essayist

1832. Wilhelm Busch (d. 9 June 1908). German poet, satirist, and comic illustrator

1843. Henry James (d. 28 February 1916). American-born writer of fiction, essayist, writer of narrative, and playwright

1856. Jean Moreas (pseudonym of Yannis Papadiamantopoulos; d. 30 March 1910). Greek-born French poet

1861. William Bliss Carman (d. 8 June 1929). Canadian-born American poet and essayist

DEATHS

1888. Mathew Arnold (b. 24 December 1822). English poet and critical essayist

1912. William Thomas Stead (b. 5 July 1849). English journalist and writer of miscellaneous prose nonfiction

1937. Oscar Bloch (b. 8 May 1877). French linguist and essayist

1980. Jean-Paul Charles Aymard Sartre (b. 21 June 1905). French philosopher, playwright, writer of fiction, essayist, and journalist

1984. William Empson (b. 27 September 1906). English poet and critical essayist

1986. Jean Genet (b. 19 December 1910). French playwright, writer of fiction, and poet

16

BIRTHS

1660. Sir Hans Sloane (d. 11 January 1753). English physician, scientist, essayist, and bibliophile

1661. Charles Montagu, first Earl of Halifax (d. 19 May 1715). English poet

1800. William Chambers (d. 20 May 1883). Scottish historian, antiquary, and publisher

1844. Anatole France (pseudonym of Anatole Francois Thibault; d. 13 October 1924). French writer of fiction, critical essayist, and satirist

1850. Herbert Baxter Adams (d. 30 July 1901). American artist and essayist

1871. John Millington Synge (d. 24 March 1909). Irish playwright, poet, and translator

1922. Kingsley William Amis. English writer of fiction, poet, and anthologizer

DEATHS

1689. Aphra Johnson Behn (b. 1640?). English playwright and writer of fiction

1788. George Louis Leclerk du Buffon (b. 7 September 1707). French scientist, naturalist historian, and essayist

1930. Jose Carlos Mariategui (b. 14 June 1895). Peruvian social reformer and essayist

1968. Edna Ferber (b. 15 August 1885). American writer of fiction, playwright, and essayist

1972. Kawabata Yasunari (b. 11 June 1899). Japanese writer of fiction

17

BIRTHS

1586. John Ford (d. ? 1640). English poet and playwright

1622. Henry Vaughan (d. 23 April 1695). English poet

1732. George Colman the elder (d. 14 August 1794). English playwright

1806. William Gilmore Simms (d. 11 June 1870). American writer of fiction, poet, historian, biographer, and editor

1816. Samuel Austin Allibone (d. 2 September 1889). American librarian, encyclopaedist, and compiler of literary and historical reference works

1864. Richard Harding Davis (d. 11 April 1916). American journalist, writer of fiction, playwright, essayist, and writer of narrative

1870. Ray Stannard Baker (d. 12 July 1946). American essayist and historian

1885. Isak Dinesen (pseudonym of Baroness Karen Blixen (d. ? 1962). Danish writer of Gothic fiction and of autobiographical narrative

1897. Thornton Niven Wilder (d. 7 December 1975). American writer of fiction and playwright

1904. Edward Chodorov (d. 9 October 1988). American playwright

DEATHS

1790. Benjamin Franklin (b. 6 January 1706). American philosopher, scientist, and writer of miscellaneous prose tracts

1904. Samuel Smiles (b. 23 December 1812). Scottish social and educational reformer, essayist, and biographer

1985. Basil Bunting (b. 1 March 1900). English poet

18

BIRTHS

1759. Thomas Thorild (d. 1 October 1808). Swedish poet, philosopher, and critical essayist

1817. George Henry Lewes (d. 28 November 1878). English writer of miscellaneous prose nonfiction, editor, critical essayist, biographer, writer of fiction, and playwright

1842. Anthero de Quental (d. 11 September 1891). Portuguese poet and critical essayist

DEATHS

1556. Luigi Alamanni (b. 28 October 1495). Italian poet

1802. Erasmus Darwin (b. 12 December 1731). English physician, poet, philosopher, scientist, and essayist

1905. Don Juan Valera y Alcala (b. 18 October 1824). Spanish writer of fiction and critical essayist

1940. Thomas Beer (b. 22 November 1889). American essayist and writer of fiction

1955. Albert Einstein (b. 14 March 1879). German-born mathematician, physicist, and essayist

1964. Ben Hecht (b. 28 February 1894). American playwright and writer of fiction

1978. Frank Raymond Leavis (b. 14 July 1895). English literary critic

19

BIRTHS

1772. David Ricardo (d. 11 September 1823). English political economist and essayist

1832. Jóse Echegaray y Eizaguirre (d. 14 September 1916). Spanish prose and verse dramatist

1900. Richard Arthur Warren Hughes (d. 28 April 1976). English writer of fiction, playwright, and poet

DEATHS

1560. Philipp Melanchthon (b. 15 February 1497). German theologian and essayist

1627. Sir John Beaumont (b. ? 1582). English poet

1813. Benjamin Rush (b. 24 December 1745). American physician, statesman, and writer of medical tracts

1824. George Gordon, Lord Byron (b. 22 January 1788). English poet and writer of verse drama

1881. Benjamin Disraeli (b. 21 December 1804). English statesman, poet, essayist, and writer of fiction

1882. Charles Robert Darwin (b. 12 February 1809). English scientist, evolutionist, essayist, and writer of travel narrative

1951. Ludwig Josef Johann Wittgenstein (b. 26 April 1889). Austrian-born philosopher and essayist

1989. Daphne Du Maurier (b. 13 May 1907). English writer of popular fiction

20

BIRTHS

1492. Pietro Aretino (d. 21 October 1556). Italian poet and writer of verse drama

1793. David Laing (d. 18 October 1878). Scottish antiquarian and essayist

1807. Louis Jacques Napoleon Bertrand (d. 29 April 1841). French writer of prose poems

1813. Henry Theodore Tuckerman (d. 17 December 1871). American essayist and poet

1857. Herman Joachim Bang (d. 29 January 1912). Danish writer of fiction

1868. Charles Maurras (d. 16 November 1952). French essayist

DEATHS

1558. Johann Bugenhagen (b. 24 June 1485). German theologian, religious reformer, essayist, and Biblical translator

1795. Johan Henrik Kellgren (b. 1 December 1751). Swedish poet

1902. Frank Richard Stockton (b. 5 April 1834). American writer of fiction

1976. William Sansom (b. 18 January 1912). English writer of fiction

1982. Archibald MacLeish (b. 7 May 1892). American poet, playwright, and essayist

21

BIRTHS

1488. Ulrich von Hutten (d. ? September 1523). German humanist, essayist, and scholar

1818. Josh Billings (pseudonym of Henry Wheeler Shaw; d. 14 October 1885). American humorist

1816. Charlotte Bronte (d. 31 March 1855). English writer of fiction and poet

1828. Hippolyte Adolphe Taine (d. 5 March 1893). French critical essayist, historian, and philosopher

1838. John Muir (d. 24 December 1914). American naturalist, explorer, and writer of nonfiction prose narrative

1907. Dorothy Baker (d. 17 June 1968). American writer of fiction

DEATHS

1699. Jean Racine (b. 22 December 1639). French dramatic poet

1910. Mark Twain (pseudonym of Samuel Langhorne Clemens; b. 30 November 1835). American humorist, writer of fiction, essayist, and writer of prose narrative

1930. Robert Seymour Bridges (b. 27 October 1844). English poet, playwright, and critical essayist

1946. John Maynard Keynes (b. 5 July 1883). English economist and essayist

1956. Charles Gordon MacArthur (b. 5 November 1895). American playwright

22

BIRTHS

1707. Henry Fielding (d. 8 October 1754). English writer of fiction, playwright, satirist, journalist, essayist, and writer of travel narrative

1724. Immanuel Kant (d. 12 February 1804). German philosopher and essayist

1766. Anne Louise Germaine Necker de Stael (d. 14 July 1817). French playwright, poet, essayist, and writer of fiction

1816. Philip James Bailey (d. 6 September 1902). English poet

1873. Ellen Anderson Gholson Glasgow (d. 21 November 1945). American writer of fiction and essayist

1876. Ole Edvart Rolvaag (d. 5 November 1931). Norwegian-born American writer of fiction and of prose narrative nonfiction

1887. James Norman Hall (d. 5 July 1951). American writer of fiction, poet, essayist, and writer of prose nonfiction narrative

1899. Vladimir Vladimirovich Nabokov (d. 2 July 1977). Russian-born writer of fiction, poet, essayist, playwright, biographer, and translator

1939. Jason Miller. American playwright

DEATHS

1672. Georg Stiernhielm (b. 7 August 1578). Swedish poet, scholar, and essayist

1839. Thomas Haynes Bayly (b. 13 October 1797). English poet, writer of fiction, and playwright

1901. William Stubbs (b. 21 June 1825). English historian

1924. Edith Nesbit (b. 15 August 1858). English writer of fiction, poet, and writer of short fiction for children

1957. Ignatius Roy Dunnachie Campbell (b. 20 October 1901). South African poet and essayist

1986. Mircea Eliade (b. 9 March 1907). Romanian-born religious scholar and philosopher

23

BIRTHS

1484. Julius Caesar Scaliger (d. 21 October 1558). Italian-born French scholar, poet, essayist, and translator

1564. William Shakespeare (d. 23 April 1616). English poet and playwright

1708. Freidrich von Hegedorn (d. 28 October 1754). German poet

1720. Elijah Ben Solomon (d. 17 October 1797). Lithuanian-born Hebrew theologian and essayist

1852. Edwin Charles Markham (d. 7 March 1940). American poet

1853. Thomas Nelson Page (d. 1 November 1922). American writer of fiction and poet

1899. Dame Ngaio Edith Marsh (d. 18 February 1982). English writer of detective and mystery fiction

1902. Halldor Kiljan Laxness. Icelandic writer of fiction, poet, and playwright

1918. Margaret Kirkland Avison. Canadian poet

1926. James Patrick Donleavy. American-born Irish writer of fiction and playwright

DEATHS

1616. Miguel de Cervantes Saavedra (b. 29 September 1547). Spanish writer of fiction, playwright, and poet

William Shakespeare (b. 23 April 1564). English poet and playwright

1695. Henry Vaughan (b. 17 April 1622). English poet

1825. Friedrich Muller (b. 13 January 1749). German poet and painter

1850. William Wordsworth (b. 7 April 1770). English poet and essayist

1889. Jules Amedee Barbey D'Aurevilly (b. 2 November 1808). French writer of fiction and essayist

1915. Rupert Chawner Brooke (b. 3 August 1887). English poet, playwright, and essayist

24

BIRTHS

1703. Jose Francisco de Isla (d. 2 November 1781). Spanish writer of fiction, satirist, and translator

1719. Guiseppe Marc'antonio Baretti (d. 5 May 1789). Italian critical essayist, lexicographer, and writer of travel narrative

1766. Robert Baily Thomas (d. 19 May 1846). American journalist and founder of *The Farmer's Almanack*

1815. Anthony Trollope (d. 6 December 1882). English writer of fiction

1845. Karl Friedrich Georg Spitteler (d. 29 December 1924). Swiss poet and writer of fiction

1905. Robert Penn Warren (d. 15 September 1989). American writer of fiction, poet, and critical essayist

DEATHS

1530. Jacopo Sannazaro (b. 28 July 1458). Italian poet and humanist

1879. Sarah Josepha Buell Hale (b. 24 October 1788). American writer of fiction, poet, and writer of verse and fiction for children

1926. Ellen Karoline Sofia Key (b. 11 December 1849). Swedish social reformer, feminist, and essayist

1936. Finley Peter Dunne (b. 10 July 1867). American journalist, editor, and humorist

1947. Willa Sibert Cather (b. 7 December 1873). American writer of fiction, poet, and essayist

25

BIRTHS

1873. Walter de la Mare (d. 22 June 1956). English poet, writer of fiction, and critical essayist

1905. Fredson Thayer Bowers. American literary scholar and textual critic

1930. Paul Mazursky. American director and playwright

DEATHS

1472. Leon Battista Alberti (b. 14 February 1401). Italian architect and architectural historian

1595. Torquato Tasso (b. 11 March 1544). Italian poet, playwright, and essayist

1800. William Cowper (b. 15 November 1721). English poet

1812. Edmund Malone (b. 4 October 1741). Irish-born essayist, textual editor, and literary scholar

1853. William Beaumont (b. 21 November 1785). American physician, scientist, and essayist

1878. Anna Sewell (b. 30 March 1820). English writer of prose fiction for children

1954. Joseph Hergesheimer (b. 15 February 1880). American writer of fiction

26

BIRTHS

1711. David Hume (d. 25 August 1776). Scottish philosopher, essayist, writer of dialogue, and historian

1828. Martha Farquharson Finley (d. 30 January 1909). Writer of fiction for children

1834. Artemus Ward (pseudonym of Charles Farrar Browne; d. 6 March 1867). American humorist and essayist

1889. Ludwig Josef Johann Wittgenstein (d. 19 April 1951). Austrian-born English philosopher and essayist

1893. Anita Loos (d. 18 August 1981). American writer of fiction and satirist

1895. Emil Levgyel (d. 12 February 1985). Hungarian-born historian

1898. Vicente Aleixandre y Merlo (d. 14 December 1984). Spanish poet

1914. Bernard Malamud (d. 18 March 1986). American writer of fiction

1916. Morris Langlo West. Australian writer of fiction

1930. Bruce Jay Friedman. American writer of fiction, playwright, and humorist

DEATHS

1859. Alexis Charles Henri Clerel de Tocqueville (b. 29 July 1805). French historian and diarist

1876. Frantisek Palacky (b. 14 June 1798). Czech historian and politician

1910. Bjornstjerne Bjornson (b. 8 December 1832). Norwegian writer of fiction and playwright

1938. Edmund Gustav Albrecht Husserl (b. 8 April 1859). Austrian-born German philosopher and essayist

27

BIRTHS

1737. Edward Gibbon (d. 16 January 1794). English essayist and historian

1744. Nikolay Ivanovich Novikov (d. 31 July 1818). Russian essayist and publisher

1759. Mary Wollstonecraft Godwin (d. 10 September 1797). English essayist and writer of fiction

1840. Edward Whymper (d. 16 September 1911). English artist and writer of travel narrative

1853. Alice Morse Erle (d. 16 February 1911). American social and religious historian

1898. Ludwig Bemelmans (d. 1 October 1962). Austrian-born writer of miscellaneous prose nonfiction, illustrator, humorist, writer of fiction and of travel narrative

1904. Cecil Day-Lewis (d. 22 May 1972). English poet, writer of fiction, and critical essayist

DEATHS

1794. Sir William Jones (b. 28 September 1746). English Oriental scholar and philologist

1859. John Mitford (b. 31 August 1781). English poet

1882. Ralph Waldo Emerson (b. 25 May 1803). English poet and essayist

1932. Harold Hart Crane (b. 21 July 1899). American poet

28

BIRTHS

1630. Charles Cotton (d. 16 February 1687). English poet and translator

1665. Pier Iacopo Martello (d. 10 May 1727). Italian poet and playwright

1922. Alistair Stuart MacLean (d. 2 February 1987). Scottish writer of fiction and poet

1926. Nell Harper Lee. American writer of fiction

1931. Vincent Chukwuemeka Ike. Nigerian writer of fiction

DEATHS

1640. William Alabaster (b. 27 January 1568). English theologian, poet, and essayist

1873. Alessandro Francesco Tommaso Antonio de Manzoni (b. 7 March 1785). Italian writer of fiction and poet

1896. Heinrich Gotthard von Treitschke (b. 15 September 1834). German historian

1973. Jacques Maritain (b. 18 November 1882). French Catholic philosopher, art critic, and writer of miscellanous prose nonfiction

1976. Richard Arthur Warren Hughes (b. 19 April 1900). English writer of fiction, playwright, and poet

29

BIRTHS

1667. John Arbuthnot (d. 27 February 1735). English pamphleteer and satirist

1780. Jean Charles Emmanuel Nodier (d. 27 January 1844). French poet, critic, and writer of fiction

1841. Edward Rowland Sill (d. 27 February 1887). American poet

1933. Rod McKuen. American poet, writer of songs, and writer of prose nonfiction narrative

DEATHS

1658. John Cleveland (b. 20 June 1613). English poet and satirist

1841. Louis Jacques Napoleon Bertrand (b. 20 April 1807). French writer of prose poems

1937. William Hooker Gillette (b. 24 July 1855). American playwright

30

BIRTHS

1877. Alice Babette Toklas (d. 7 March 1967). American memoirist and writer of miscellaneous prose nonfiction

1883. Jaroslav Hasek (d. 3 January 1923). Czech satirist and writer of fiction

1888. John Crowe Ransom (d. 3 July 1974). American poet and critical essayist

DEATHS

1841. Peter Andreas Heiberg (b. 16 November 1758). Danish dramatic poet

1854. James Montgomery (b. 4 November 1771). Scottish poet

1895. Gustav Freytag (b. 13 July 1816). German writer of fiction and playwright

1936. Alfred Edward Housman (b. 26 March 1859). English poet

1943. Jens Otto Harry Jespersen (b. 16 July 1860). Danish philologist, grammarian, and language innovator

1980. Louis Kronenberger, Jr. (b. 9 January 1904). American drama critic, essayist, and writer of fiction

MAY

1

BIRTHS

1672. Joseph Addison (d. 17 June 1719). English essayist, poet, and playwright

1828. Adelardo Lopez de Ayala y Herrera (d. 30 December 1879). Spanish poet, playwright, and statesman

1881. Pierre Teilhard de Chardin (d. 10 April 1955). French scientist, theologian, philosopher, and essayist

1900. Ignazio Silone (d. ? 1978). Italian writer of fiction and political essayist

1901. Sterling Allen Brown (d. 13 January 1989). American poet and critical essayist

1923. Joseph Heller. American writer of fiction

DEATHS

1700. John Dryden (b. 9 August 1631). English poet, playwright, and essayist

1968. Sir Harold George Nicolson (b. 21 November 1886). English literary biographer

1981. Vern Sneider (b. 6 October 1916). American playwright and writer of fiction

2

BIRTHS

1551. William Camden (d. 9 November 1623). English antiquary and historian

1779. John Galt (d. 11 April 1839). Scottish writer of fiction

1837. Henry Martyn Robert (d. 11 May 1923). American parliamentarian

1859. Jerome Klapka Jerome (d. ? 1927). English humorist, writer of fiction, and playwright

1860. Theodor Herzel (d. 3 July 1904). Hungarian-born essayist, playwright, and pamphleteer on behalf of Zionist causes

1865. William Clyde Fitch (d. ? 1909). American playwright

1905. Charlotte Armstrong (d. 18 July 1969). American writer of mystery fiction

DEATHS

1519. Leonardo da Vinci (b. 15 April 1452). Italian painter, sculptor, architect, engineer, and essayist

1831. Hester Lynch Thrale Piozzi (b. 16 January 1741). English biographer and writer of narrative nonfiction

1826. Antoni Malczewski (b. 3 June 1793). Polish poet

1844. William Bedford (b. 1 October 1760). English writer of fiction and travel narrative

1857. Louis Charles Alfred de Musset (b. 11 December 1810). French poet and playwright

1905. Jose Maria Heredia (b. 31 December 1842). Cuban-born French poet

1963. Van Wyck Brooks (b. 16 February 1886). American critical essayist, biographer, and writer of nonfiction narrative

3

BIRTHS

1469. Niccolo di Bernardo Machiavelli (d. 21 June 1527). Italian statesman, historian, and essayist

1791. Count Henryk Rzewuski (d. 28 February 1866). Polish writer of fiction

1848. Francisco Teixeira de Queiroz (d. ? 1919). Portuguese writer of fiction

1912. Eleanor May Sarton. Belgian-born American writer of fiction, poet, playwright, and writer of autobiographical narrative

1913. William Motter Inge (d. 10 June 1973). American playwright and writer of fiction

DEATHS

1845. Thomas Hood the elder (b. 23 May 1799). English poet

4

BIRTHS

1796. William Hickling Prescott (d. 28 January 1859). American historian

1825. Thomas Henry Huxley (d. 29 June 1895). English scientist and essayist

1870. Vladimir Ilyich Lenin (d. 21 January 1924). Russian revolutionary and essayist

1928. Thomas Kinsella. Irish poet

DEATHS

1667. Isaac Barrow (b. 16 June 1630). English mathematician and essayist

1873. William Holmes McGuffey (b. 23 September 1800). American educational philosopher, philologist, and writer of schoolbooks

1950. William Rose Benet (b. 2 February 1886). American poet, playwright, writer of fiction, and essayist

1969. Sir Francis Osbert Sacheverell Sitwell (b. 6 December 1892). English poet, playwright, writer of fiction, and writer of miscellaneous prose nonfiction

1984. Paul Darcy Boles (b. 5 March 1919). American writer of fiction

5

BIRTHS

1813. Soren Aaby Kierkegaard (d. 11 November 1855). Danish theologian, philosopher, and essayist

1815. Eugene Marin Labiche (d. 23 January 1888). French playwright

1818. Karl Heinrich Marx (d. 14 March 1883). German philosopher, essayist, historian, and journalist

1832. Hubert Howe Bancroft (d. 2 March 1918). American historian

1846. Henryk Sienkiewicz (d. 15 November 1916). Polish writer of fiction and writer of stories for children

1890. Christopher Darlington Morley (d. 28 March 1957). American writer of fiction, playwright, and poet

1897. Kenneth Duva Burke. American critical essayist, poet, and writer of fiction

DEATHS

1789. Guiseppe Marc'antonio Baretti (b. 24 April 1719). Italian critical essayist, lexicographer, and writer of travel narrative

1881. Franz Felix Adalbert Kuhn (b. 19 November 1812). German philologist and folklorist

1887. James Grant (b. 1 August 1822). Scottish writer of fiction

1902. Francis Brett Harte (b. 25 August 1836). American writer of fiction, poet, satirist, playwright, and periodicals editor

1958. James Branch Cabell (b. 14 April 1879). American writer of fiction, essayist, and poet

6

BIRTHS

1856. Sigmund Freud (d. 23 September 1939). Austrian psychologist and essayist

1881. Gregorio Martinez Sierra (d. ? 1947). Spanish writer of fiction and playwright

1902. Harry Lewis Golden (d. 2 October 1981). American journalist, essayist, humorist, and popular historian

1904. Harry Edmund Martinson (d. 11 February 1978). Swedish poet and writer of fiction

1906. Richmond Alexander Lattimore (d. 27 February 1984). American literary scholar and poet

1914. Randall Jarrell (d. 14 October 1965). American poet, playwright, writer of fiction, and critical essayist

1915. Theodore Harold White (d. 15 May 1986). American journalist, writer of narrative, and political commentator

1939. Margaret Drabble. English writer of fiction, literary scholar, and compiler of literary reference work

DEATHS

1640. Juan Luis Vives (b. 6 March 1492). Spanish philosopher, humanist, and essayist

1638. Cornelius Jansen (b. 28 October 1585). Dutch theologian and essayist

1859. Friedrich Heinrich Alexander von Humboldt (b. 14 September 1769). German naturalist, traveler, essayist, and geographer

1862. Henry David Thoreau (b. 12 July 1817). American essayist, diarist, writer of personal narrative, and poet

1919. Lyman Frank Baum (b. 15 May 1856). American journalist, playwright, and writer of stories for children

1949. Maurice Maeterlinck (b. 29 August 1862). Belgian playwright, poet, and writer of philosophical essays

1965. Edgar Austin Mittelholzer (b. 16 December 1909). Guyanaian writer of fiction

7

BIRTHS

1812. Robert Browning (d. 12 December 1889). English poet and playwright

1851. Adolf von Harnack (d. 10 June 1930). German theologian, essayist, and literary and theological historian

1861. Rabindranath Tagore (d. 7 August 1941). Indian poet, philosopher, playwright, and essayist

1867. Wladyslaw Stanislaw Reymont (d. 5 December 1925). Polish writer of fiction

1892. Archibald MacLeish (d. 20 April 1982). American poet, playwright, and critical essayist

DEATHS

1852. Matthias Alexander Castren (b. 2 December 1813). Finnish philologist, linguist, and essayist

1915. Elbert Hubbard (b. 19 June 1856). American writer of fiction, publisher, and writer of descriptive and narrative essays

1941. Sir James George Frazer (b. 1 January 1854). Scottish anthropologist, folklorist, mythologist, and essayist

8

BIRTHS

1668. Alain Rene LeSage (d. 17 November 1747). French writer of fiction and playwright

1828. Jean Henri Dunant (d. 30 October 1910). Swiss philanthropist and essayist

1877. Oscar Bloch (d. 15 April 1937). French linguist and essayist

1885. Thomas Bertram Costain (d. 8 October 1965). Canadian-born American periodicals editor and writer of popular historical fiction

1895. Edmund Wilson (d. 12 June 1972). American journalist, literary critical essayist, and poet

1920. Sloan Wilson. American writer of fiction

1930. Gary Sherman Snyder. American poet

1937. Thomas Pynchon. American writer of fiction

1940. Peter Bradford Benchley. American writer of travel narrative and of fiction

DEATHS

1873. John Stuart Mill (b. 20 May 1806). English essayist

1880. Gustav Flaubert (d. 12 December 1821). French writer of fiction

1908. Ludovic Halevy (b. 1 January 1834). French playwright and writer of fiction

1936. Oswald Spengler (b. 29 May 1880). German historian

1967. Elmer Leopold Rice (pseudonym of Elmer Leopold Reizenstein; b. 28 September 1892). American playwright and writer of fiction

1988. Robert Anson Heinlein (b. 7 July 1907). American writer of science and fantasy fiction, and of fiction for children

9

BIRTHS

1773. Jean Charles Carlo Leonard Simondi de Sismondi (d. 25 June 1842). Italian historian, economist, critical essayist, and writer of fiction

1860. Sir James Matthew Barrie (d. 19 June 1937). Scottish writer of fiction and playwright

1883. Jose Ortega y Gasset (d. 18 October 1955). Spanish humanist and critical and literary essayist

1896. Austin Clarke (d. 19 March 1974). Irish poet, playwright, and verse dramatist

1920. Richard George Adams. English writer of fiction

DEATHS

1657. William Bradford (b. 19 March 1589). English-born colonial American historian and writer of narrative

1805. Johann Christoph Friedrich von Schiller (b. 10 November 1759). German playwright, poet, and historian

1860. Samuel Griswold Goodrich (b. 19 August 1793). American publisher, poet, writer of fiction, and essayist

1884. Giovanni Prati (b. 27 January 1814). Italian lyric and narrative poet

1911. Thomas Wentworth Storrow Higginson (b. 22 December 1823). American writer of nonfiction narrative and of fiction, essayist, biographer, and poet

1936. Mary Johnston (b. 21 November 1870). American writer of fiction

1977. James Jones (b. 6 November 1921). American writer of fiction

1981. Nelson Algren (b. 28 March 1909). American writer of fiction and poet

10

BIRTHS

1758. George Vancouver (d. 10 May 1798). English explorer and writer of prose nonfiction narrative

1886. Karl Barth (d. 9 December 1968). Swiss theologian, Biblical commentator, and essayist

1898. Ariel Durant (d. 22 October 1981). American essayist and writer on the history of ideas

DEATHS

1727. Pier Iacopo Martello (b. 28 April 1665). Italian poet and playwright

1798. George Vancouver (b. 10 May 1758). English explorer and writer of prose nonfiction narrative

1829. Thomas Young (b. 13 June 1773). English scientist, philologist, Egyptologist, and essayist

1876. George Sand (pseudonym of Amandine Aurore Lucie Dupin; b. 1 July 1804). French writer of fiction and playwright

1904. Henry Morton Stanley (b. 29 June 1841). Welsh writer of travel narrative

1982. Peter Weiss (b. 8 November 1916). German-born Swedish playwright

11

BIRTHS

1720. Karl Friedrich Hieronymous Munchhausen, Baron von Munchhausen (d. 22 February 1797). German writer of fantasy fiction

1916. Camile Jose Cela. Spanish writer of fiction

1930. Edward Brathwaite. Barbadian poet and playwright

DEATHS

1696. Jean de la Bruyere (b. 16 August 1645). French writer of maxims and of dialogues, and translator

1886. Isidore Kalish (b. 15 November 1816). American Jewish theologian and essayist

1920. William Dean Howells (b. 1 March 1837). American writer of autobiographical narrative, biographer, essayist, writer of fiction, playwright, and writer of verse drama

1923. Henry Martyn Robert (b. 2 May 1837). American parliamentarian and writer of guides to meetings

1927. Sir Sidney Colvin (b. 18 June 1845). English art and literary critic, academician, and museum director

1975. Paul McClelland Angle (b. 25 December 1900). American historian

12

BIRTHS

1812. Edward Lear (d. 29 January 1888). English writer of "nonsense" verse and of miscellaneous prose nonfiction

1828. Dante Gabriel Rossetti (born Gabriel Charles Dante Rossetti; d. 9 April 1882). English poet and translator

1857. William Archibald Dunning (d. 25 August 1922). American historian, essayist, and academician

1891. Sir Francis Meredith Wilfred Meynell (d. 9 July 1975). English poet and publisher

1894. Marguerite Steen (d. 4 August 1975). English writer of historical fiction

1902. Philip Wylie (d. 15 October 1971). American writer of fiction and essayist

1907. Leslie Charteris. English writer of mystery and detective fiction

1933. Andrei Andreyevich Voznesensky. Russian poet

1938. Andrei Alekseyevich Amalrik. Russian playwright and writer of narrative

1939. Rosellen Brown. American poet and writer of fiction

DEATHS

1634. George Chapman (b. ? 1560). English playwright, poet, and translator

1845. August Wilhelm von Schlegel (b. 8 September 1767). German poet, critical essayist, and translator

1859. Sergei Timofeyevitch Aksakov (b. 1 October 1791). Russian writer of fiction

1903. Richard Henry Stoddard (b. 2 July 1825). American poet and critical essayist

1907. Joris Karl Huysmans (born Charles Marie George Huysmans; b. 5 February 1848). Dutch-born French writer of fiction and art critic

1913. Frederich Huch (b. 19 June 1873). German writer of fiction

1925. Amy Lawrence Lowell (b. 9 February 1874). American poet, playwright, writer of fiction, and critical essayist

1926. Arthur Annesley Ronald Firbank (b. 17 January 1886). English writer of fiction, playwright, and poet

1944. Arthur Thomas Quiller-Couch (b. 21 November 1863). English essayist, scholar, biographer, and writer of fiction

1967. John Masefield (b. 1 June 1878). English poet, playwright, writer of fiction and of miscellaneous prose nonfiction

1970. Nelly Leonie Sachs (b. 10 December 1891). German poet and playwright

1978. Louis Zukofsky (b. 23 January 1904). American poet, critical essayist, and translator

1987. Richard David Ellmann (b. 15 March 1918). American critical scholar and literary essayist

13

BIRTHS

1840. Louis Marie Alphonse Daudet (d. 17 December 1897). French writer of fiction

1907. Daphne Du Maurier (d. 19 April 1989). English writer of popular fiction

DEATHS

1704. Louis Bourdaloue (b. 20 August 1632). French pulpit orator, rhetorician, philosopher, and theologian

1916. Sholem Aleichem (pseudonym of Solomon J. Rabinowitz; b. 18 February 1859). Ukrainian-born Yiddish writer of fiction

1937. Thomas James Wise (b. 7 October 1859). English bibliophile, literary forger, and pamphleteer

14

BIRTHS

1752. Timothy Dwight (d. 11 January 1817). American poet, essayist, and writer of travel narrative

1853. Thomas Henry Hall Caine (d. 31 August 1931). English writer of fiction and biographical narrative

DEATHS

1894. Henry Morley (b. 15 September 1822). English essayist and biographer

1906. Carl Schurz (b. 2 March 1829). German-born American journalist, writer of narrative, and biographer

1912. Johann August Strindberg (b. 22 January 1849). Swedish playwright, writer of fiction, and critical essayist

1925. Sir Henry Rider Haggard (b. 22 June 1856). English writer of adventure fiction

1931. David Belasco (b. 25 July 1853). American actor and playwright

1979. Jean Rhys (pseudonym of Ella Gwendolen Rees Williams; b. 24 August 1890). West

Indian-born English writer of fiction and translator

15

BIRTHS

1687. Thomas Prince (d. 22 October 1785). American historian

1856. Lyman Frank Baum (d. 6 May 1919). American journalist, playwright, and writer of fiction for children

1862. Arthur Schnitzler (d. 21 October 1931). Austrian playwright and writer of fiction

1890. Katherine Anne Porter (d. 18 September 1980). American writer of fiction, essayist, and translator

1926. Peter Levin Shaffer. English playwright

DEATHS

1773. Alban Butler (b. 24 October 1710). English religious biographer

1886. Emily Dickinson (b. 10 December 1830). American poet

1966. Kathryn Forbes (pseudonym of Kathryn Anderson McLean; b. 20 March 1909). American writer of fiction

1976. Samuel Eliot Morison (b. 9 July 1887). American historian and biographer

1986. Theodore Harold White (b. 6 May 1915). American journalist, writer of narrative, and political commentator

16

BIRTHS

1788. Friedrich Ruckert (d. 31 January 1866). German poet

1816. Friedrich Wilhelm Christian Gerstacker (d. 31 May 1872). German writer of fiction

1886. Douglas Southall Freeman (d. 13 June 1953). American historian and biographer

1905. Herbert Ernest Bates (d. 29 January 1974). English writer of fiction

1912. Studs Louis Terkel. American writer of narrative, biographer, playwright, and oral historian

DEATHS

1703. Charles Perrault (b. 12 January 1628). French poet, essayist, historian, and writer of fiction ("fairy tales")

1818. Matthew Gregory Lewis (b. 9 July 1775). English writer of gothic fiction, playwright, and poet

1835. Felicia Dorothea Hemans (b. 25 September 1793). English poet and hymnodist

1944. George Ade (b. 9 February 1866). American playwright and satirist

Max Brand (pseudonym of Frederick Faust; b. 20 March 1892). American writer of adventure and Western fiction

1955. James Agee (b. 27 November 1909). American poet, writer of autobiographical fiction, and reviewer

1984. Irwin Shaw (b. 27 February 1913). American writer of fiction and playwright

17

BIRTHS

1766. Isaac D'Israeli (d. 19 January 1848). English critical essayist and writer of fiction

1794. Anna Brownell Murphy Jameson (d. 17 March 1860). Irish-born English writer of miscellaneous prose nonfiction and diarist

1803. Robert Smith Surtees (d. 16 March 1864). English writer of fiction and miscellaneous prose nonfiction

1845. Mosen Jacinto Verdaguer (d. 10 June 1902). Spanish (Catalan) poet

1873. Henri Barbusse (d. 30 August 1935). French poet and writer of fiction

Dorothy Richardson (d. 17 June 1957). English writer of fiction

1905. John Patrick (born John Patrick Goggan). American playwright

1908. Mark Schorer (d. 15 August 1977). American literary essayist and biographer

DEATHS

1729. Samuel Clarke (b. 11 October 1671). English philosopher, textual editor, and essayist

1879. Charles Theodore Henri DeCoster (b. 20 August 1827). Belgian writer of fiction

1957. Isadore Gilbert Mudge (b. 14 March 1875). American librarian and bibliographer

18

BIRTHS

1692. Joseph Butler (d. 16 June 1752). English moral philosopher, essayist, and writer of sermon literature

1814. Mikhail Aleksandrovitch Bakunin (d. 13 July 1876). Russian revolutionary and essayist

1872. Bertrand Arthur William Russell (d. 2 February 1970). English philosopher, mathematician, nonconformist, and essayist

1921. Patrick Dennis (pseudonym of Edward Everett Tanner III; d. 6 November 1976). American writer of popular fiction

DEATHS

1799. Pierre Augustin Caron de Beaumarchais (b. 24 January 1732). French playwright and memoirist

1909. George Meredith (b. 12 February 1828). English writer of fiction, poet, and essayist

1949. James Truslow Adams (b. 18 October 1878). American historian

1960. Audrey Wurdeman (b. 1 January 1911). American poet

1981. William Saroyan (b. 31 August 1908). American writer of fiction, poet, playwright, and essayist

19

BIRTHS

1762. Johann Gottlieb Fichte (d. 29 January 1814). German philosopher, nationalist, and essayist

1785. Christopher North (pseudonym of John Wilson; d. 3 April 1854). Scottish essayist and poet

1921. Yusuf Idris. Egyptian writer of fiction and playwright

1930. Lorraine Vivian Hansberry (d. 12 January 1965). American playwright

DEATHS

1715. Charles Montagu, first Earl of Halifax (b. 16 April 1661). English poet

1754. Ignacio de Luzan (b. 28 March 1702). Spanish critical essayist and poet

1795. James Boswell (b. 29 October 1740). Scottish biographer, diarist, writer of travel narrative, and poet

1846. Robert Baily Thomas (b. 24 April 1766). American journalist and founder of *The Farmer's Almanack*

1864. Nathaniel Hawthorne (b. 4 July 1804). American writer of fiction, essayist, and reviewer

1895. Jose Marti (b. 28 January 1853). Cuban poet and revolutionary

1898. William Ewart Gladstone (b. 29 December 1809). English statesman, classical literary scholar, and historical essayist

1912. Boleslaw Prus (pseudonym of Aleksander Glowacki; b. 20 August 1847). Polish writer of fiction

1935. Thomas Edward Lawrence (b. 15 August 1888). English writer of autobiographical narrative and commentator upon the Arab world

1942. Arthur Edward Waite (b. 2 October 1857). American-born poet and writer of prose nonfiction

1946. Newton Booth Tarkington (b. 29 July 1869). American writer of fiction

1971. Frederic Ogden Nash (b. 19 August 1902). American writer of light verse, playwright, and writer of juvenile literature

1984. Sir John Betjeman (b. 28 August 1906). English poet and architectural historian

20

BIRTHS

1470. Pietro Bembo (d. 18 January 1547). Italian poet, essayist, and grammarian

1799. Honore de Balzac (d. 18 August 1850). French writer of fiction

1806. John Stuart Mill (d. 8 May 1873). English essayist

1882. Sigrid Undset (d. 10 June 1949). Norwegian writer of fiction

1890. Allan Nevins (d. 5 March 1971). American historian and biographer

DEATHS

1847. Mary Ann Lamb (b. 3 December 1764). English essayist and writer of fiction for children

1864. John Clare (b. 13 July 1793). English poet

1883. William Chambers (b. 16 April 1800). Scottish historian, antiquarian, and publisher

1940. Werner von Heidenstam (b. 6 July 1859). Swedish poet and writer of miscellaneous prose nonfiction

1956. Henry Maximilian Beerbohm (b. 24 August 1872.). English critical essayist and caricaturist

1957. George Gilbert Murray (b. 2 January 1866). English classical scholar and translator

21

BIRTHS

1688. Alexander Pope (d. 30 May 1744). English poet, satirist, and writer of critical essays

1817. Rudolf Hermann Lotze (d. 1 July 1881). German idealist philosopher and essayist

1892. John Peale Bishop (d. 4 April 1944). American poet and writer of fiction

1912. John Cheever (d. 18 June 1982). American writer of fiction

1916. Harold Robbins. American writer of fiction

1926. Robert White Creeley. American poet, writer of fiction, and essayist

DEATHS

1639. Tommaso Campanella (b. 5 September 1568). Italian philosopher, essayist, and poet

1647. Pieter Corneliszoon Hooft (b. 16 March 1581). Dutch poet, humanist, and essayist

1690. John Eliot (b. 5 August 1604). English-born colonial American linguist and Biblical translator

1771. Christopher Smart (b. 11 April 1722). English poet and playwright

1790. Thomas Warton the younger (b. 8 January 1728). English poet, editor, and literary historian

1901. Abel Bergaigne (b. 31 August 1838). French linguist, philologist, and Sanskrit scholar

1921. Emilia Pardo Bazan (b. 16 September 1852). Spanish writer of fiction and essayist

1949. Klaus Mann (b. 18 November 1906). German-born writer of fiction, essayist, and playwright

1980. Julian Parks Boyd (b. 3 November 1903). American historian and editor

1983. Eric Hoffer (b. 25 July 1902). American social and political essayist

22

BIRTHS

1859. Sir Arthur Conan Doyle (d. 30 July 1930). Scottish-born English writer of detective and mystery fiction, political pamphleteer, and historian

1895. Jiddu Krishnamurthi (d. 17 February 1986). Indian-born religious philosopher and essayist

1914. Vance Oakley Packard. American social and political commentator and essayist

DEATHS

1540. Francesco Guicciardini (b. 6 March 1483). Italian analytical historian

1826. Nikolai Mikhaylovich Karamzin (b. 12 December 1766). Russian historian and writer of fiction

1849. Maria Edgeworth (b. 1 January 1768). Irish writer of fiction

1885. Victor Marie Hugo (b. 26 February 1802). French writer of fiction, poet, playwright, and critical essayist

1899. Edward Bellamy (b. 26 March 1850). American writer of fiction and political theorist

1932. Lady Isabella Augusta Persse Gregory (b. 5 March 1852). Irish playwright, folklorist, translator, and theater historian

1939. Ernst Toller (b. 1 December 1893). German playwright

1948. Claude McKay (born Festus Claudius McKay; b. 15 September 1890). Jamaican-born American poet and writer of fiction

1967. James Langston Hughes (b. 1 February 1902). American poet, playwright, writer of fiction and of autobiographical narrative

1970. Joseph Wood Krutch (b. 25 November 1893). American literary and intellectual critic and writer of miscellaneous prose nonfiction

1972. Cecil Day-Lewis (b. 27 April 1904). Irish-born poet, writer of fiction, and critical essayist

23

BIRTHS

1707. Carl Linnaeus (d. 10 January 1778). Swedish natural scientist, physician, and essayist

1729. Giuseppe Parini (d. 15 August 1799). Italian poet

1799. Thomas Hood the elder (d. 3 May 1845). English poet

1810. Sarah Margaret Fuller, Marchioness Ossoli (d. 19 July 1850). American-born essayist and periodicals editor

1821. Richard Grant White (d. 8 April 1885). American literary essayist

1842. Maria Wasilowska Konopnicka (d. 8 October 1910). Polish poet and writer of fiction

1891. Par Fabian Lagerkvist (d. 11 July 1974). Swedish expressionist poet, writer of fiction, and playwright

1914. Barbara Mary Ward, Baroness Jackson of Lodsworth (d. 31 May 1981). English economist and writer of miscellaneous prose

DEATHS

1693. Marie-Madeleine de La Fayette (b. 16 March 1634). French writer of fiction

1825. Mason Locke Weems (b. 11 October 1759). American churchman, bookseller, biographer, and moral essayist

1870. Mark Lemon (b. 30 November 1809). English playwright and journalist

1886. Leopold von Ranke (b. 21 December 1795). German historian

1906. Henrik Ibsen (b. 20 March 1828). Norwegian playwright and poet

1923. Henry Bradley (b. 3 December 1845). English philologist, lexicographer, and editor

1947. Charles Ferdinand Ramuz (b. 24 September 1878). French-Swiss writer of fiction

24

BIRTHS

1810. Abraham Geiger (d. 23 October 1874). German Jewish scholar and Biblical historian

1852. Robert Bontine Cunninghame Graham (d. 20 March 1936). Scottish writer of fiction and of travel narrative

1855. Arthur Wing Pinero (d. 23 November 1934). English playwright

1878. Harry Emerson Fosdick (d. 5 October 1969). American theologian, essayist, and writer of sermon literature

1891. William F. Albright (d. 19 September 1971). American Oriental and Biblical scholar, anthropologist, and essayist

1905. Mikhail Aleksandrovich Sholokhov (d. 21 February 1984). Soviet Russian writer of fiction

1932. Arnold Wesker. English playwright, essayist, and writer of fiction

1940. Joseph Brodsky. Russian-born American poet

DEATHS

1543. Nicolaus Copernicus (b. 19 February 1473). Polish-born German astronomer, physician, and essayist

1792. Jakob Michael Reinhold Lenz (b. 12 January 1751). German playwright and poet

1817. Juan Melendez Valdes (b. 11 March 1754). Spanish lyric poet

1932. John Back McMaster (b. 29 June 1852). American historian and literary biographer

25

BIRTHS

1803. Edward George Earle Bulwer-Lytton (d. 18 June 1873). English writer of fiction, poet, and playwright

Ralph Waldo Emerson (d. 27 April 1882). English essayist and poet

1818. Jakob Christoph Burckhardt (d. 8 August 1897). Swiss historian and art critic

1908. Theodore Huebner Roethke (d. 1 August 1963). American poet and writer of prose and verse for children

1938. Raymond Carver (d. 2 August 1988). American poet and writer of fiction

DEATHS

1681. Pedro Calderon de la Barca (b. 17 January 1600). Spanish playwright

1783. Ching-jen Huang (b. 20 February 1789). Chinese poet

1805. William Paley (b. 30 August 1743). English philosopher and theologian

1862. Johann Nepomuk Edward Ambrosius Nestroy (b. 7 December 1801). Austrian playwright and theatre director

1946. Ernest Rhys (b. 17 July 1859). English writer of fiction

26

BIRTHS

1689. Lady Mary Wortley Pierrepont Montagu (d. 21 August 1762). English poet, writer of epistolary travel narrative, and essayist

1822. Edmond Louis Antoine Huot de Goncourt (d. 16 July 1896). French artist, writer of fiction, and memoirist

1863. Shailer Mathews (d. 23 October 1941). American theologian, educator, and essayist

1931. Sven Axel Herman Delblanc. Swedish writer of fiction, playwright, and essayist

DEATHS

1703. Samuel Pepys (b. 23 February 1633). English diarist

1845. Jonas Hallgrummsson (b. 16 November 1807). Icelandic poet, scientist, and linguist

1848. Vissarion Grigorevich Belinski (b. 30 May 1811). Russian philosopher and critical essayist

1864. Karl Anton Postl (b. 3 March 1793). Austrian writer of fiction

1976. Martin Heidegger (b. 26 September 1889). German philosopher and essayist

27

BIRTHS

1819. Julia Ward Howe (d. 17 October 1910). American poet, essayist, and biographer

1867. Enoch Arnold Bennett (d. 27 March 1931). English writer of fiction

1894. Samuel Dashiel Hammett (d. 10 January 1961). American writer of detective and mystery fiction

1907. Rachel Carson (d. 14 April 1964). American scientist, essayist, and environmentalist

1915. Herman Wouk. American writer of fiction and playwright

1930. John Simmons Barth. American writer of fiction

1934. Harlan Jay Ellison. American writer of science and fantasy fiction and drama

DEATHS

1564. John Calvin (d. 10 July 1509). French theologian, religious reformer, and essayist

1867. Thomas Bulfinch (b. 15 July 1796). American historical writer and literary historian

28

BIRTHS

1779. Thomas Moore (d. 25 February 1852). Irish poet, playwright, writer of fiction, textual editor, and writer of miscellaneous prose nonfiction

1789. Bernhard Severin Ingemann (d. 24 February 1862). Danish poet and writer of fiction

1908. Ian Lancaster Fleming (d. 12 August 1964). English journalist and writer of adventure and espionage fiction

1912. Patrick Victor Martindale White. English-born Australian writer of fiction

1916. Walker Percy. American writer of fiction and essayist

1919. May Swenson. American poet

1932. Stephen Birmingham. American social and cultural historian

DEATHS

1688. Abbe Antoine Furetiere (b. 28 December 1619). French scholar and lexicographer

1843. Noah Webster (b. 16 October 1758). American philologist, lexicographer, essayist, and periodicals editor

1849. Anne Bronte (b. 17 January 1820). English writer of fiction and poet

1878. Lord John Russell (b. 18 August 1792). English political essayist

1900. Sir George Grove (b. 13 August 1800). English musicologist, Biblical scholar, periodicals editor, and music encyclopaedist

29

BIRTHS

1821. Frederick Locker-Lampson (d. 30 May 1895). English poet

1874. Gilbert Keith Chesterton (d. 14 June 1936). English essayist, writer of fiction, and poet

1880. Oswald Spengler (d. 8 May 1936). German historian

1912. Pamela Hansford Johnson (d. 18 June 1981). English critical essayist and writer of fiction

1935. Andre Brink. South African writer of fiction

DEATHS

1876. Friedrich Christian Diez (b. 15 March 1794). German Romance philologist, linguist, and essayist

1877. John Latrop Motley (b. 15 April 1814). American historian and writer of fiction

1888. Gisli Brynfulfsson (b. 3 September 1827). Icelandic Romantic poet

1911. Sir William Schwenck Gilbert (b. 18 November 1836). English writer of comic verse, satirist, and light opera librettist

1958. Juan Ramon Jimenez (b. 24 December 1881). Spanish lyric poet

1970. John Gunther (b. 30 August 1901). American journalist and writer of social and political documentary nonfiction

30

BIRTHS

1811. Vissarion Grigorevich Belinski (d. 26 May 1848). Russian philosopher and critical essayist

1835. Alfred Austin (d. 2 June 1913). English poet, playwright, writer of fiction, and critical essayist

1901. Cornelia Otis Skinner (d. 9 July 1979). American playwright, writer of autobiographical narrative, and actress

1903. Countee Cullen (born Countee L. Porter; d. 9 January 1946). American poet, writer of fiction, essayist, and playwright

1912. Julian Gustave Symons. English writer of fiction, poet, biographer, and critical essayist

DEATHS

1593. Christopher Marlowe (b. 6 February 1564). English poet and playwright (see also 26 February and 1 June)

1744. Alexander Pope (b. 21 May 1688). English poet, satirist, textual editor, and critical essayist

1778. Francois Marie Arouet de Voltaire (b. 21 November 1694). French satirist, poet, essayist, historian, playwright, writer of fiction, and philosopher

1895. Frederick Locker-Lampson (b. 29 May 1821). English poet

1918. Georgi Valentinovich Plekhanov (b. 11 December 1856). Russian revolutionary, periodicals editor, essayist, and commentator upon Marxist theory

1951. Hermann Broch (b. 1 November 1886). German writer of fiction

1960. Boris Leonidovich Pasternak (b. 10 February 1890). Russian lyric poet, writer of fiction, and translator of Shakespeare

1969. Inglis Fletcher (b. ? 1888). American writer of historical fiction

31

BIRTHS

1819. Walt(er) Whitman (d. 26 March 1892). American poet, writer of fiction, and essayist

1895. George Rippey Stewart (d. 22 August 1980). American writer of fiction, poet, and writer of miscellaneous nonfiction prose

1909. Gladys Schmitt (d. 30 October 1972). American writer of historical fiction

DEATHS

1872. Friedrich Wilhelm Christian Gertsacker (b. 16 May 1816). German writer of fiction

1908. Louis-Honore Frechette (b. 16 November 1839). French-Canadian poet, playwright, and writer of miscellaneous prose

1963. Edith Hamilton (b. 12 August 1867). American literary scholar and mythologist

1981. Barbara Mary Ward, Baroness Jackson of Lodsworth (b. 23 May 1914). English economist and writer of miscellaneous prose

1989. Owen Lattimore (b. 29 July 1900). American writer of travel narrative, historian, and political essayist

JUNE

1

BIRTHS

1878. John Edward Masefield (d. 12 May 1967). English poet, playwright, writer of fiction, and writer of miscellaneous prose nonfiction

1882. John Drinkwater (d. 15 March 1937). English poet, playwright, critical essayist, and actor

DEATHS

1593. Christopher Marlowe (b. 26 February 1564). English poet and playwright (see also 6 February and 30 May)

1890. Camillo Castello Branco (b. 16 March 1825). Portuguese writer of fiction

1941. Hugh Seymour Walpole (b. 13 March 1884). English writer of fiction

1968. Witter Bynner (b. 10 August 1881). American poet and playwright

Helen Adams Keller (b. 27 June 1880). American writer of autobiographical narrative

1971. Reinhold Niebuhr (b. 21 June 1892). American theologian, philosopher, and essayist

1979. Eric Honeywood Partridge (b. 6 February 1894). English lexicographer, linguist, and essayist

1983. Anna Seghers (b. 19 November 1900). East German writer of fiction

2

BIRTHS

1740. Donatian Alphonse Francois de Sade (d. 2 December 1814). French writer of erotic fiction

1811. Henry James the elder (d. 18 December 1882). American writer of religious, social, and theological prose nonfiction

1840. Thomas Hardy (d. 11 January 1928). English poet and writer of fiction

1857. Karl Adolf Gjellerup (d. 11 October 1919). Danish poet and writer of fiction

1899. Edwin Way Teale (d. 18 October 1980). American writer of nonfiction prose concerning nature

1907. Rudolph John Frederick Lehmann (d. 7 April 1987). English poet and biographer

1915. Lester Del Ray (pseudonym of Ramon Alvarez del Ray). American writer of science fiction

DEATHS

1881. Maximilien Paul Emile Littre (b. 1 February 1801). French lexicographer, philosopher, language historian, translator, and essayist

1913. Alfred Austin (b. 30 May 1835). English poet, playwright, writer of fiction, and critical essayist

1961. George Simon Kaufman (b. 16 November 1889). American journalist and playwright

1962. Victoria Mary Sackville-West (b. 9 March 1892). English poet and writer of fiction

3

BIRTHS

1771. Sydney Smith (d. 22 February 1845). English satirist and writer of sermon literature

1780. William Hone (d. 6 November 1842). English bookseller, satirist, pamphleteer, and critical essayist

1793. Antoni Malkczewski (d. 2 May 1826). Polish poet

1926. Allen Ginsberg. American poet, playwright, and writer of miscellaneous prose nonfiction

DEATHS

1780. Thomas Hutchinson (b. 9 September 1711). Colonial American government administrator, essayist, and historian

1853. Cesare Balbo (b. 21 November 1789). Italian statesman, literary biographer, and historical essayist

1872. Charles James Lever (b. 31 August 1806). Irish writer of fiction

1882. James Thomson (b. 23 'November 1834). Scottish-born poet and essayist

1924. Franz Kafka (b. 3 July 1883). Czech-born Austrian writer of existentialist fiction and essayist

1964. Frans Eemil Sillanpaa (b. 16 September 1888). Finnish writer of fiction

4

BIRTHS

1718. Aleksandr Petrovich Sumarokov (d. 1 September 1777). Russian playwright, poet, and theatre manager

1744. Jeremy Belknap (d. 20 June 1798). American theologian, historian, biographer, and essayist

DEATHS

1798. Giovanni Jacopo Casanova de Seingalt (b. 2 April 1725). Italian adventurer and memoirist

1849. Marguerite Power Farmer Gardiner, Countess of Blessington (b. 1 September 1789). English diarist and writer of fiction

1945. Georg Kaiser (b. 25 November 1878). German expressionist playwright

1973. Arna Wendell Bontemps (b. 13 October 1902). American writer of fiction

5

BIRTHS

1723. Adam Smith (d. 17 July 1790). Scottish economist, philosopher, and essayist

1867. Paul Jean Toulet (d. 6 September 1920). French poet and writer of fiction

1883. John Maynard Keynes (d. 21 April 1946). English economist and essayist

1887. Ruth Fulton Benedict (d. 17 September 1948). American cultural anthropologist and essayist

1899. Federico Garcia Lorca (d. ? August 1936). Spanish poet and playwright

1920. Cornelius John Ryan (d. 23 November 1974). American journalist and writer of fiction

DEATHS

1900. Stephen Townley Crane (b. 1 November 1871). American writer of fiction and journalist

1910. O. Henry (pseudonym of William Sidney Porter; b. 11 September 1862). American writer of fiction

1921. Georges Leone Jules Marie Feydeau (b. 8 December 1862). French playwright

6

BIRTHS

1606. Pierre Corneille (d. 30 September 1684). French playwright, poet, and verse translator

1799. Aleksandr Sergeyevich Pushkin (d. 10 February 1837). Russian poet and writer of fiction in verse and prose

1804. Louis Antoine Godey (d. 29 November 1878). American publisher and periodicals editor

1860. William Ralph Inge (d. 26 February 1954). English theologian, essayist, and diarist

1875. Thomas Mann (d. 12 August 1955). German writer of fiction and critical essayist

1925. Maxine Winokur Kumin. American writer of fiction, poet, and essayist

DEATHS

1831. Jeremy Bentham (b. 15 February 1748). English essayist on jurisprudence and utilitarian ethics

1947. James Evershed Agate (b. 9 September 1877). English essayist and writer of fiction

1961. Carl Gustav Jung (b. 26 July 1875). Swiss psychiatrist, psychologist, essayist, and periodicals editor

1965. Thornton Waldo Burgess (b. 4 January 1874). American writer of nature and animal books for children

1970. Edward Morgan Forster (b. 1 January 1879). English writer of fiction and critical essayist

1982. Kenneth Rexroth (b. 22 December 1905). American poet, playwright, and essayist

7

BIRTHS

1778. George Brian (Beau) Brummell (d. 30 March 1840). English wit and gentleman of fashion

1825. Richard Doddridge Blackmore (d. 20 January 1900). English writer of fiction

1899. Elizabeth Dorthea Cole Bowen (d. 22 February 1973). Irish-born English writer of fiction

1943. Nikki Giovanni (born Yolande Cornelia Giovanni). American poet and essayist

DEATHS

1843. Johann Christian Friedrich Holderlin (b. 20 March 1770). German poet and writer of fiction

1848. Vissarion Grigorievich Belinski (b. 12 July 1811). Russian literary critic, literary historian, editor, and journalist

1910. Goldwin Smith (b. 13 August 1823). English historian and essayist

1967. Dorothy Rothschild Parker (b. 22 August 1893). American writer of fiction, literary critic, poet, and playwright

1980. Henry Valentine Miller (b. 26 December 1891). American-born writer of autobiographical narrative, fiction, and prose nonfiction

8

BIRTHS

1814. Charles Reade (d. 11 April 1884). English writer of fiction and playwright

1903. Marguerite Yourcenar (pseudonym of Marguerite de Crayencour; d. 17 December 1987). Belgian-born writer of fiction, poet, essayist, playwright, and translator

DEATHS

1768. Johann Joachim Winckelmann (b. 9 December 1717). German classical archaeologist and essayist

1809. Thomas Paine (d. 29 January 1737). English-born political philosopher and essayist

1889. Gerard Manley Hopkins (b. 28 July 1844). English poet

1929. William Bliss Carman (b. 15 April 1861). Canadian poet, playwright, and essayist

1946. Gerhart Hauptmann (b. 15 November 1862). German playwright and writer of fiction

9

BIRTHS

1791. John Howard Payne (d. 9 April 1852). American playwright and writer of verse drama

1893. Samuel Nathaniel Behrman (d. 9 September 1973). American playwright

1903. Marcia Davenport. American writer of fiction and music critic

1905. David Cornel DeJong (d. 5 September 1967). Dutch-born writer of fiction

DEATHS

1826. Jedediah Morse (b. 23 August 1861). American theologian, periodicals editor, geographer, historian, and essayist

1870. Charles John Huffham Dickens (b. 7 February 1812). English writer of fiction

1901. Walter Besant (b. 14 August 1836). English biographer, essayist, writer of fiction, and playwright

1973. John Creasey (b. 17 September 1908). English writer of detective and mystery fiction

1974. Miguel Angel Asturias (b. 19 October 1899). Guatemalan writer of fiction and poet

10

BIRTHS

1832. Edwin Arnold (d. 24 March 1904). English poet, journalist, and Oriental scholar

1863. Louis Couperus (d. 16 July 1923). Dutch writer of fiction and essayist

1911. Sir Terence Mervyn Rattigan (d. 30 November 1977). English playwright

1915. Saul Bellow. Canadian-born American writer of fiction and playwright

1928. Maurice Bernard Sendak. American writer and illustrator of fiction for children

DEATHS

1552. Alexander Barclay (b. ? 1475). Scottish poet, scholar, theologian, and translator

1705. Michael Wigglesworth (b. 18 October 1631). English-born colonial American churchman, poet, and writer of verse essays

1865. Lydia Howard Huntley Sigourney (b. 1 September 1791). American poet and hymnodist

1901. Robert William Buchanan (b. 18 August 1841). Scottish poet, writer of fiction, and playwright

1902. Mosen Jacinto Verdaguer (b. 17 May 1845). Spanish (Catalan) poet

1909. Edward Everett Hale (b. 3 April 1822). American clergyman, writer of fiction, and historian

1930. Adolf von Harnack (b. 7 May 1851). German theologian, essayist, and theological historian

1949. Sigrid Undset (b. 20 May 1882). Norwegian writer of fiction

1973. William Motter Inge (b. 3 May 1913). American playwright and writer of fiction

1980. Aloysius Michel Sullivan (b. 9 August 1896). American poet and periodical editor

1988. Louis Dearborn L'Amour (b. 22 March 1908). American writer of Western and adventure fiction

11

BIRTHS

1572(?). Ben(jamin) Johnson (d. 6 August 1637). English poet and playwright

1603. Sir Kenelm Digby (d. 11 June 1665). English narrative writer and essayist

1815. Otto von Bohtlingk (d. 31 March 1904). German Sanskrit scholar, essayist, and textual editor

1899. Kawabata Yasunari (d. 16 April 1972). Japanese writer of fiction

1912. Mary Lavin. American writer of fiction

1920. Irving Howe. American literary scholar, critic, and essayist

1925. William Clark Styron. American writer of fiction, playwright, and essayist

DEATHS

1665. Sir Kenelm Digby (b. 11 June 1603). English narrative writer and essayist

1793. William Robertson (b. 19 September 1721). Scottish historian

1870. William Gilmore Simms (b. 17 April 1806). American writer of fiction, poet, historian, biographer, and editor

1884. Charles Fenno Hoffman (b. 7 February 1806). American writer of fiction, writer of narrative prose nonfiction, poet, and editor

1903. William Ernest Henley (b. 23 August 1849). English poet and playwright

1912. Leon Dierx (b. 31 March 1838). French poet

12

BIRTHS

1802. Harriet Martineau (d. 27 June 1876). English religious essayist, writer of fiction, biographer, writer of fiction for children, and historian

1819. Charles Kingsley (d. 23 January 1875). English writer of fiction, poet, playwright, and essayist

1892. Djuna Chappell Barnes (d. 18 June 1982). American writer of fiction, playwright, and poet

1929. Anne Frank (d. ? March 1945). Dutch Holocaust diarist

DEATHS

1759. William Collins (b. 25 December 1721). English poet

1842. Thomas Arnold (b. 13 June 1795). English educational reformer, essayist, and historian

1852. Xavier de Maistre (b. 8 November 1763). French writer of fiction and of personal meditations

1878. William Cullen Bryant (b. 3 November 1794). American poet, essayist, literary editor, and translator

1966. William Ernest Hocking (b. 10 August 1873). American Idealist philosopher and essayist

1968. Sir Herbert Edward Read (b. 4 December 1893). English essayist and intellectual critic

1972. Edmund Wilson (b. 8 May 1895). American journalist, literary critical essayist, and poet

13

BIRTHS

1574. Richard Barnfield (d. 6 March 1627). English poet

1752. Frances Burney (d. 6 January 1840). English writer of fiction and diarist

1773. Thomas Young (d. 10 May 1829). English scientist, Egyptologist, philologist, and essayist

1795. Thomas Arnold (d. 12 June 1842). English educational reformer, essayist, and historian

1865. William Butler Yeats (d. 28 January 1939). Irish poet, playwright, essayist, writer of fiction and of miscellaneous prose nonfiction

1893. Dorothy Leigh Sayers (d. 17 December 1957). English writer of mystery and detective fiction and translator

1894. Mark Albert Van Doren (d. 10 December 1972). American poet, writer of fiction, critical essayist, and editor of literary anthologies and texts

DEATHS

1953. Douglas Southall Freeman (b. 16 May 1886). American historian and biographer

1965. Martin Buber (b. 8 February 1878). Austrian-born theologian, philosopher, and essayist

14

BIRTHS

1798. Frantisek Palacky (d. 26 April 1876). Czech historian and politician

1811. Harriet Elizabeth Beecher Stowe (d. 1 July 1896). American writer of fiction and of narrative prose nonfiction, and religious poet

1820. John Bartlett (d. 3 December 1905). American bookseller and compiler of references on quotations

1895. Jose Carlos Mariategui (d. 16 April 1930). Peruvian social reformer and essayist

1907. Rene Emile Char (d. ? 1988). French poet

1933. Jerzy Nikoden Kosinski. Polish-born (Russian educated) American writer of fiction and of miscellaneous prose nonfiction

DEATHS

1837. Giacomo Leopardi (b. 29 June 1798). Italian poet, essayist, and writer of dialogues

1883. Edward Fitzgerald (b. 31 March 1809). English poet, translator, biographer, and writer of epistles

1886. Alexander Nikolaevich Ostrovsky (b. 12 April 1823). Russian playwright

1936. Gilbert Keith Chesterton (b. 29 May 1874). English essayist, writer of fiction, and poet

Maksim Gorki (pseudonym of Aleksei Maksimovich Peshkov; b. 16 March 1868). Russian writer of fiction

1948. Gertrude Franklin Atherton (b. 30 October 1857). American-born writer of fiction, poet, writer of autobiographical narrative, essayist, and writer of miscellaneous prose nonfiction

1968. Salvatore Quasimodo (b. 20 August 1901). Italian poet and translator

1986. Jorge Luis Borges (b. 25 August 1899). Argentinian writer of fiction, essayist, poet, translator, and writer of miscellaneous prose nonfiction

15

BIRTHS

1605. Thomas Randolf (d. 17 March 1635). English playwright and poet

1856. Edward Channing (d. 7 January 1931). American educator and historian

DEATHS

1844. Thomas Campbell (b. 27 July 1777). Scottish poet and biographer

1923. Maurice Henry Hewlett (b. 22 January 1861). English writer of fiction, poet, and essayist

16

BIRTHS

1514. Sir John Cheke (d. 13 September 1557). English classical scholar, translator, and essayist

1630. Isaac Barrow (d. 4 May 1667). English mathematician and essayist

1920. John Howard Griffin (d. 9 September 1980). American writer of narrative and miscellaneous prose nonfiction, and musicologist

1937. Erich Segal. American writer of fiction, classical scholar, and essayist

1938. Joyce Carol Oates. American writer of fiction and critical essayist

DEATHS

1752. Joseph Butler (b. 18 May 1692). English moral philosopher, essayist, and writer of sermon literature

1907. Alexander Lange Kielland (b. 18 February 1849). Norwegian writer of fiction and playwright

1929. Vernon Louis Parrington (b. 3 August 1871). American literary scholar and cultural historian

1940. DuBose Heyward (b. 31 August 1885). American poet, writer of fiction, and playwright

1943. Albert Bushnell Hart (b. 1 July 1854). American historian, editor, and essayist

1948. Holbrook Jackson (b. 31 December 1874). English essayist and literary historian

17

BIRTHS

1703. John Benjamin Wesley (d. 2 March 1791). English religious reformer, poet, diarist, essayist, and writer of miscellaneous prose nonfiction

1810. Ferdinand Hermann Freiligrath (d. 18 March 1876). German poet

1808. Everhardus Johannes Potgieter (d. 3 February 1875). Dutch poet, essayist, literary critic, and editor

Henrik Arnold Wergeland (d. 12 July 1845). Norwegian lyric and nationalist poet, and playwright

1871. James Weldon Johnson (d. 26 June 1933). American civil rights advocate, politician, poet, and writer of miscellaneous prose

1880. Carl Van Vechten (d. 21 December 1964). American essayist and writer of fiction

1914. John Richard Hersey. American writer of fiction, of historical narrative, and of miscellaneous prose nonfiction

1917. Gwendolyn Elizabeth Brooks. American poet and writer of fiction and of miscellaneous prose nonfiction

DEATHS

1719. Joseph Addison (b. 1 May 1672). English essayist, poet, and playwright

1762. Prosper Jolyat de Crebillon, pere (b. 13 February 1674). French playwright

1845. Richard Harris Barham (b. 6 December 1788). English humorist, lyric poet, and writer of burlesque metrical tales

1947. Maxwell Evarts Perkins (b. 20 September 1884). American literary editor

1957. Dorothy Richardson (b. 17 May 1873). English writer of fiction

1963. John Cowper Powys (b. 8 October 1872). English essayist, writer of fiction, and poet

1968. Dorothy Baker (b. 21 April 1907). American writer of fiction

1983. Elisabeth Seifert (b. 19 June 1897). American writer of fiction

1988. Miguel Pinero (b. 19 December 1946). Puerto Rican-born poet and playwright

18

BIRTHS

1754. Anna Maria Lenngren (d. 8 March 1817). Swedish satirical poet

1845. Sir Sidney Colvin (d. 11 May 1927). English art and literary critic, academician, and museum director

1871. Leonid Nikolayevich Andreyev (d. ? 1919). Russian writer of fiction

1896. Philip Barry (d. 3 December 1949). American playwright

1903. Raymond Radiguet (d. 12 December 1923). French poet and writer of fiction

DEATHS

1835. William Cobbett (b. 9 March 1762). English political and social reform writer

1871. George Grote (b. 17 November 1794). English historian, politician, classical scholar, and essayist

1873. Edward George Earle Bulwer-Lytton (b. 25 May 1803). English writer of fiction, poet, and playwright

1902. Samuel Butler (b. 4 December 1835). English writer of fiction, painter, and writer of miscellaneous prose nonfiction

1928. Donn Byrne (b. 20 November 1889). Irish-born writer of fiction

1981. Pamela Hansford Johnson (b. 29 May 1912). English critical essayist and writer of fiction

1982. Djuna Chappell Barnes (b. 12 June 1892). American writer of fiction, playwright, and poet

John Cheever (b. 21 May 1912). American writer of fiction

Granville Hicks (b. 9 September 1901). American historical and critical essayist, and writer of fiction and of miscellaneous prose nonfiction

19

BIRTHS

1623. Blaise Pascal (d. 19 August 1662). French mathematician, scientist, theologian, pamphleteer, and essayist

1764. Sir John Barrow (d. 23 November 1848). English writer of travel narrative

1834. Charles Haddon Spurgeon (d. 31 January 1892). English theological essayist and Biblical commentator

1856. Elbert Hubbard (d. 7 May 1915). American writer of fiction, publisher, and writer of descriptive and narrative essays

1861. Jose Mercado Rizal (d. 30 December 1896). Philippine writer of fiction, physician, and revolutionary

1878. Edmond Jaloux (d. 22 September 1949). French essayist and writer of fiction

1880. Johann Sigurjonsson (d. 31 August 1919). Icelandic playwright and poet

1897. Elizabeth Seifert (d. 17 June 1983). American writer of fiction

1900. Laura Zametkin Hobson (d. 28 February 1986). American writer of fiction

1947. Ahmed Salman Rushdie. Indian writer of fiction

DEATHS

1902. John Emerich Edward Dalberg Acton (b. 10 January 1834). English historian

1937. Sir James Matthew Barrie (b. 9 May 1860). Scottish writer of fiction and playwright

1982. Richard Lockridge (b. 26 September 1898). American writer of detective and mystery fiction

20

BIRTHS

1613. John Cleveland (d. 29 April 1658). English poet and satirist

1743. Adam Ferguson (d. 22 February 1816). Scottish philosopher and historian

Anna Laetitia Aiken Barbauld (d. 9 March 1825). English essayist, textual editor, writer of prose pieces for children, poet, and translator

1786. Marceline Desbordes-Valmore (d. 23 July 1859). French poet

1793. Count Alexander Fredro (d. 15 July 1876). Polish playwright and poet

1858. Charles Waddell Chesnutt (d. 15 November 1932). American writer of fiction and biographer

1905. Lillian Hellman (d. 30 June 1984). American playwright and memoirist

1910. Josephine Winslow Johnson. American writer of fiction and of miscellaneous prose nonfiction

DEATHS

1798. Jeremy Belknap (b. 4 June 1744). American theologian, historian, biographer, and essayist

1807. Ferdinand Berthoud (b. 19 March 1727). French-born essayist, horologist, and clockmaker

1870. Jules Alfred Huot de Goncourt (b. 17 December 1830). French writer of fiction and historian

1876. John Neal (b. 25 August 1793). American writer of fiction, poet, and essayist

1971. James Ramsay Ullman (b. 24 November 1907). American writer of fiction and of miscellaneous prose nonfiction

1990. Levin Kipnis (b. ? 1894). Ukrainian-born Israeli writer of fiction and of verse for children

21

BIRTHS

1615. Salvatore Rosa (d. 15 March 1673). Italian satirical poet

1639. Increase Mather (d. 23 August 1723). Colonial American theologian, essayist, historian, and biographer

1676. Anthony Collins (d. 13 December 1729). English materialistic philosopher and essayist

1730. Motoori Norinaga (d. 10 February 1762). Japanese scholar, poet, and essayist

1792. Ferdinand Christian Bauer (d. 2 December 1860). German theologian and essayist

1813. William Edmonstone Aytoun (d. 4 August 1865). Scottish poet and writer of fiction

1825. William Stubbs (d. 22 April 1901). English historian

1892. Reinhold Niebuhr (d. 1 June 1971). American theologian, philosopher, and essayist

1905. Jean-Paul Charles Aymard Sartre (d. 15 April 1980). French philosopher, playwright, essayist, biographer, journalist, and writer of short fiction

1910. Alexandr Trifonovich Tvardovsky (d. 17 December 1971). Russian poet and editor

1912. Mary Therese McCarthy (d. 25 October 1989). American writer of fiction

1935. Francoise Sagan (born Francoise Quoirez). French writer of fiction

DEATHS

1527. Niccolo Bernardo Machiavelli (b. 3 May 1469). Italian statesman, historian, and essayist

1529. John Skelton (b. ? 1460?). English poet and satirist

1788. Johann Georg Hamann (b. 27 August 1730). German theologian, philosopher, and essayist

1990. Cedric Belfrage (b. ? 1905). English journalist, editor, essayist, and translator

22

BIRTHS

1748. Thomas Day (d. 28 September 1789). English writer of didactic fiction for children, poet, and writer of miscellaneous prose

1767. Karl William von Humboldt (d. 8 April 1835). German statesman and philologist

1805. Giuseppe Mazzini (d. 10 March 1872). Italian patriot, diarist, and political essayist

1844. Harriet Mulford Stone Lothrop (d. 2 August 1924). American writer of fiction for children

1846. Julian Hawthorne (d. 14 July 1934). American writer of fiction

1856. Sir Henry Rider Haggard (d. 14 May 1925). English writer of adventure fiction

1887. Julian Sorell Huxley (d. 14 February 1975). English biologist, poet, and essayist

1888. Alan Seeger (d. 4 July 1916). American poet

1898. Erich Maria Remarque (d. 25 September 1970). German-born writer of fiction

1906. Gilbert Arthur Highet (d. 20 January 1978). American literary scholar and essayist

1907. Ann Spencer Morrow Lindbergh. American writer of narrative, essayist, poet, writer of fiction, and memoirist

DEATHS

1865. Angel Saavedra (pseudonym of Ramirez de Baquedano; b. 10 March 1791). Spanish poet and playwright

1923. Morris Rosenfeld (pseudonym of Moshe Jacob Alter; b. 28 December 1862). Polish-born American Yiddish poet and periodicals editor

1956. Walter de la Mare (b. 25 April 1873). English poet, writer of fiction, and critical essayist

1988. Rose Franken (b. 28 December 1895). American playwright and writer of fiction

23

BIRTHS

1668. Giovanni Battista Vico (d. 23 January 1744). Italian historical philosopher and essayist

1876. Irvin Shrewsbury Cobb (d. 10 March 1944). American journalist, writer of fiction, and humorist

1910. Jean Marie Lucien Pierre Anouilh (d. 3 October 1987). French playwright, editor, translator, and writer of fiction

DEATHS

1770. Mark Akenside (b. 9 November 1721). English poet and essayist

1836. James Mill (b. 6 April 1773). Scottish philosopher, historian, and essayist

1956. Michael Arlen (b. 16 November 1895). English writer of fiction

24

BIRTHS

1485. Johann Bugenhagen (d. 20 April 1558). German theologian, religious reformer, essayist, and Biblical translator

1542. Juan de Yepis y Alvarez (St. John of the Cross; d. 24 December 1591). Spanish aesthete and lyric and mystical poet

1842. Ambrose Gwinnet Bierce (d. ? 1914). American writer of fiction, poet, essayist, journalist, and humorist

1915. Norman Cousins. American essayist and periodicals editor

1916. John Anthony Ciardi (d. 30 March 1986). American poet and literary critic

DEATHS

1729. Edward Taylor (b. ? 1642?). English-born American poet, diarist, and writer of sermon literature

1909. Sarah Orne Jewett (b. 3 September 1849). American writer of fiction and poet

1972. Ronald Frederick Delderfield (b. 12 February 1912). English writer of fiction, essayist, and playwright

25

BIRTHS

1736. John Horne Tooke (d. 18 March 1812). English essayist

1789. Silvio Pellico (d. 31 January 1854). Italian writer of fiction, poet, and essayist

1903. George Orwell (pseudonym of Eric Arthur Blair; d. 21 January 1950). English writer of fiction, essayist, and writer of prose nonfiction narrative

DEATHS

1822. Ernst Theodor Wilhelm Hoffmann (b. 24 January 1776). German essayist, music critic, writer of fiction, and caricaturist

1842. Jean Charles Carlo Leonard Simondi de Sismondi (b. 9 May 1773). Italian historian, economist, critical essayist, and writer of fiction

26

BIRTHS

1865. Bernhard Berensen (d. 6 October 1959). Lithuanian-born American art critic and art historian

1891. Sidney Coe Howard (d. 23 August 1939). American playwright

1892. Pearl Sydenstricker Buck (d. 6 March 1973). American writer of fiction, essayist, and biographer

1930. Slawomir Mrozek. Polish satirical playwright

1931. Colin Henry Wilson. English writer of fiction and essayist

DEATHS

1666. Sir Richard Fanshawe (b. ? June 1608). English poet and translator

1711. Wang Shih-Chen (b. 19 October 1634). Chinese poet

1793. Gilbert White (b. 18 July 1720). English naturalist, diarist, and naturalist historian

1918. Peter Rosegger (pseudonym of Petri Kettenfeier; b. 31 July 1843). Austrian writer of fiction

1933. James Weldon Johnson (b. 17 June 1871). American civil rights advocate, politician, poet, and writer of miscellaneous prose

1939. Ford Madox Ford (pseudonym of Ford Hermann Hueffer; b. 17 December 1873). English writer of fiction, critical essayist, periodicals editor, and writer of autobiographical narrative

1961. Kenneth Flexner Fearing (b. 28 July 1902). American writer of fiction and poet

27

BIRTHS

1817. Marie Louise von Francois (d. 23 September 1893). German writer of fiction

1838. Bankim Chandra Chatterjee (d. 8 April 1894). Indian writer of fiction, essayist, and poet

1850. Lafcadio Hearn (d. 26 September 1904). Ionian Islands-born American writer of fiction and of narrative prose nonfiction

Ivan Vazov (d. 22 September 1921). Bulgarian poet, playwright, essayist, and writer of fiction

1880. Helen Adams Keller (d. 1 June 1968). American writer of autobiographical prose narrative

1926. Frank O'Hara (d. 25 July 1966). American poet

1929. Peter Maas. American writer of fiction

DEATHS

1574. Giorgio Vasari (b. 30 July 1511). Italian art historian, biographer, and critical essayist

1650. Jean de Rotrou (b. 21 August 1609). French playwright

1876. Harriet Martineau (b. 12 June 1802). English religious essayist, writer of fiction, biographer, writer of fiction for children, and historian

1957. Clarence Malcolm Lowry (b. 28 July 1909). English writer of fiction and poet

1980. Carey McWilliams (b. 13 December 1905). American periodicals editor and social critic

1989. Alfred Jules Ayer (b. 29 October 1910). English philosopher and essayist

28

BIRTHS

1712. Jean-Jacques Rousseau (d. 2 July 1778). Swiss-born French political philosopher, educationist, essayist, poet, writer of fiction and of autobiographical prose narrative

1867. Luigi Pirandello (d. 10 December 1936). Italian playwright, writer of fiction, critical essayist, and poet

1887. Floyd Dell (d. 23 July 1969). American writer of fiction and playwright

1905. Ashley Montagu (pseudonym of Montague Francis). English–born anthropologist and essayist

1909. Eric Ambler. English writer of espionage fiction

DEATHS

1904. Daniel Decatur Emmett (b. 29 October 1815). American writer of verse and popular songs

1929. Edward Carpenter (b. 29 August 1844). English poet and essayist

1958. Alfred Noyes (b. 16 September 1880). English poet

29

BIRTHS

1798. Giacomo Leopardi (d. 14 June 1837). Italian poet, essayist, and writer of dialogues

1841. Henry Morton Stanley (d. 10 May 1904). Welsh writer of travel narrative

1852. John Bach McMaster (d. 24 May 1932). American historian and literary biographer

1863. James Harvey Robinson (d. 16 February 1936). American intellectual historian

1900. Antoine de St. Exupery (d. 31 July 1944). French writer of fiction and of nonfiction narrative prose

1926. James Keir Baxter (d. 22 October 1972). New Zealand poet, playwright, and critical essayist

DEATHS

1861. Elizabeth Barrett Browning (b. 6 March 1806). English poet and essayist

1895. Thomas Henry Huxley (b. 4 May 1825). English scientist and essayist

1990. Irving Wallace (b. 19 March 1916). American writer of fiction

30

BIRTHS

1674. Nicholas Rowe (b. 6 December 1718). English playwright and poet

1884. Georges Duhamel (d. ? 1966). French poet, writer of fiction, and essayist

1911. Czeslaw Milosz. Lithuanian-born Polish poet, writer of fiction, and essayist

DEATHS

1831. William Roscoe (b. 8 March 1753). English biographer and poet

1914. Victor-Henri Rochefort (b. 31 January 1831). French journalist, politician, and political essayist

1917. William Winter (b. 15 July 1836). American essayist, poet, and drama and theatre historian

1965. Robert Chester Ruark (b. 29 December 1915). American journalist and writer of fiction

1973. Nancy Freeman Mitford (b. 28 November 1904). English writer of fiction, biographer, and essayist

1984. Lillian Hellman (b. 20 June 1905). American playwright and memoirist

JULY

1

BIRTHS

1646. Gottfried Wilhelm von Leibnitz (d. 14 November 1716). German philosopher, mathematician, theologian, and essayist

1804. George Sand (pseudonym of Amandine Aurore Lucie Dupin; d. 10 May 1876). French writer of fiction and playwright

1854. Albert Bushness Hart (d. 16 June 1943). American historian, editor, and essayist

1876. Susan Keating Glaspell (d. 27 July 1948). American playwright and writer of fiction

1892. James Mallahan Cain (d. 27 October 1977). American writer of fiction

1915. Jean Stafford (d. 26 March 1979). American writer of fiction

DEATHS

1881. Rudolf Hermann Lotze (b. 21 May 1817). German idealist philosopher and essayist

1896. Harriet Elizabeth Beecher Stowe (b. 14 June 1811). American writer of fiction and of narrative prose nonfiction, and religious poet

1980. Charles Percy Snow (b. 15 October 1905). English scientist, writer of fiction, and critical essayist

2

BIRTHS

1489. Thomas Cranmer (d. 21 March 1556). English churchman and theological essayist

1724. Friedrich Gottlieb Klopstock (d. 14 March 1803). German poet

1825. Richard Henry Stoddard (d. 12 May 1903). American poet and critical essayist

1877. Hermann Hesse (d. 9 August 1962). German writer of fiction and poet

DEATHS

1566. Nostradamus (born Michel de Notredame; b. 14 December 1503). French astrologer, physician, poet, and essayist

1778. Jean-Jacques Rousseau (b. 28 June 1712). Swiss-born French political philosopher, educationist, essayist, poet, writer of fiction and of autobiographical prose narrative

1904. Anton Pavlovich Chekhov (b. 17 January 1860). Russian writer of fiction and playwright

1961. Ernest Miller Hemingway (b. 21 July 1899). American writer of fiction

1977. Vladimir Vladimirovich Nabokov (b. 22 April 1899). Russian-born writer of fiction, poet, essayist, playwright, biographer, and translator

3

BIRTHS

1883. Franz Kafka (d. 3 June 1924). Czech-born Austrian writer of existentialist fiction and essayist

1937. Thomas (Tom) Stoppard. Czech-born (raised in Singapore) English playwright and writer of fiction

DEATHS

1582. James Crichton (b. 19 August 1560). Scottish adventurer, scholar, linguist, poet, and essayist

1904. Theodor Herzl (b. 2 May 1860). Hungarian-born essayist, playwright, and pamphleteer on behalf of Zionist causes

1908. Joel Chandler Harris (b. 9 December 1848). American journalist and writer of regional and dialect fiction

1970. Frances Parkinson Keyes (b. 21 July 1885). American writer of fiction

1974. John Crowe Ransom (b. 30 April 1888). American poet and critical essayist

4

BIRTHS

1610. Paul Scarron (d. 6 October 1660). French poet, playwright, and writer of fiction

1793. Friedrich Bleek (d. 27 February 1859). German Biblical scholar and essayist

1804. Nathaniel Hawthorne (d. 19 May 1864). American writer of fiction, essayist, and reviewer

1870. Sazanami Iwaya (pseudonym of Iwaya Sueo; d. 5 September 1933). Japanese writer of children's fiction

1896. Mao Dun (pseudonym of Shen Yan-bing; d. 27 March 1981). Chinese writer of fiction and essayist

1905. Lionel Trilling (d. 5 November 1975). American journalist, critical essayist, and writer of fiction

1927. Neil Simon. American playwright

DEATHS

1761. Samuel Richardson (b. 31 July 1689). English writer of epistolary fiction, printer, and moral essayist

1848. Francois-Rene Vicomte de Chateaubriand (b. 4 September 1768). French writer of travel narrative, political essayist, memoirist, and writer of prose epics

1888. Hans Theodor Woldsen Storm (b. 14 September 1817). German writer of fiction and poet

1901. John Fiske (b. 30 March 1842). American philosopher and historian

1916. Alan Seeger (b. 22 June 1888). American poet

1934. Hayyim Nahman Bialik (b. 9 January 1873). Ukrainian Hebrew poet and writer of fiction

1971. Cecil Maurice Bowra (b. 8 April 1898). English literary scholar and essayist

1974. Georgette Heyer (b. 16 August 1902). English writer of historical fiction

5

BIRTHS

1803. George Henry Borrow (d. 26 July 1881). Scottish-born English writer of travel narrative and fiction

1849. William Thomas Stead (d. 15 April 1912). English journalist and writer of miscellaneous prose nonfiction

1889. Jean Maurice Eugene Clement Cocteau (d. 11 October 1963). French playwright, poet, writer of fiction, and critical essayist

DEATHS

1894. Sir Austin Henry Layard (b. 5 March 1817). English writer of travel narrative and archaeologist

1899. Richard Congreve (b. 14 September 1818). English essayist

1908. Jonas Lauritz Idemil Lie (b. 6 November 1833). Norwegian writer of fiction, playwright, and poet

1935. Oliver Herford (b. 18 December 1863). English-born American poet and humorist

1951. James Norman Hall (b. 22 April 1887). American writer of fiction, poet, essayist, and writer of prose nonfiction narrative

6

BIRTHS

1859. Werner von Heidenstam (d. 20 May 1940). Swedish poet and writer of miscellaneous prose nonfiction

1866. Helen Beatrix Potter (d. 22 December 1943). English writer of children's fiction and memoirist

1879. Dezso Szabo (d. ? 1945). Hungarian writer of fiction

DEATHS

1533. Ludovico Ariosto (b. 8 September 1474). Italian Latin poet

1535. Sir Thomas More (b. 7 February 1478). English writer of speculative prose nonfiction, essayist, critic, and historian

1893. Guy de Maupassant (b. 5 August 1850). French writer of fiction

1932. Kenneth Grahame (b. 8 March 1859). Scottish-born English essayist and writer of autobiographical narrative

1962. William Faulkner (b. 25 September 1897). American writer of fiction

7

BIRTHS

1586. Thomas Hooker (d. 19 July 1647). English-born colonial American clergyman, essayist, and writer of sermon literature

1798. Robert Gilfillan (d. 4 December 1850). Scottish poet

1884. Lion Feuchtwanger (d. ? 1958). German writer of fiction and playwright

1907. Robert Anson Heinlein (d. 8 May 1988). American writer of science and fantasy fiction, and of fiction for children

1908. Harriette Simpson Arnow (d. 22 March 1986). American writer of fiction

DEATHS

1816. Richard Brinsley Sheridan (b. 30 October 1751). English playwright, theatre manager, and poet

8

BIRTHS

1478. Giangiorgio Trissino (d. 8 December 1550). Italian linguist, philologist, and essayist

1621. Jean de La Fontaine (d. 13 March 1695). French poet

1790. Fitz-Greene Halleck (d. 19 November 1867). American poet

1887. Hermann Rauschning (d. ? 1982). German statesman and writer of anti-fascist essays and tracts

1892. Richard Edward Godfrey Aldington (d. 27 July 1962). English poet, writer of fiction, and biographer

1898. Alexander (Alec) Raban Waugh (d. 3 September 1981). English writer of fiction and of travel and autobiographical narrative

1913. Walter Francis Kerr. American drama critic, playwright, and critical essayist

1917. James Farl Powers. American writer of fiction and playwright

1925. Vincent Thomas Buckley. Australian poet and essayist

1929. Shirley Ann Grau. American writer of fiction

DEATHS

1822. Percy Bysshe Shelley (b. 4 August 1792). English poet, writer of verse drama and of fiction, and essayist

1933. Anthony Hope (born Anthony Hope Hopkines; b. 9 February 1863). English writer of fiction and playwright

9

BIRTHS

1764. Ann Ward Radcliffe (d. 7 February 1823). English writer of fiction

1775. Matthew Gregory Lewis (d. 16 May 1818). English writer of gothic fiction, poet, and playwright

1777. Henry Hallam (d. 21 January 1859). English historian

1887. Samuel Eliot Morison (d. 15 May 1976). American historian and biographer

1894. Dorothy Thompson (d. 31 January 1961). American journalist and essayist

1936. June Meyer Jordan. American poet, writer of fiction, and essayist

DEATHS

1797. Edmund Burke (b. 12 January 1729). Irish-born philosopher and political essayist

1843. Washington Allston (b. 5 November 1779). American writer of fiction, poet, and essayist

1975. Sir Francis Meredith Wilfred Meynell (b. 12 May 1891). English poet and publisher

1977. Loren Corey Eiseley (b. 3 September 1907). American anthropologist and essayist

1979. Cornelia Otis Skinner (b. 30 May 1901). American playwright, writer of autobiographical narrative, and actress

1981. Meyer Levin (b. 8 October 1905). American writer of fiction and of miscellaneous prose nonfiction

10

BIRTHS

1509. John Calvin (d. 27 May 1564). French-born theologian, religious reformer, and essayist

1723. Sir William Blackstone (d. 14 February 1780). English essayist and commentator upon jurisprudence

1752. David Humphreys (d. 21 February 1818). American poet, essayist, and playwright

1792. Frederick Marryat (d. 9 August 1848). English writer of fiction

1793. William Maginn (d. 21 August 1842). Irish-born satirist and writer of fiction

1802. Robert Chambers (d. 17 March 1871). Scottish poet, essayist, and publisher

1834. Jan Neruda (d. 22 August 1891). Czech poet, writer of prose fiction and nonfiction, and playwright

1867. Finley Peter Dunne (d. 24 April 1936). American journalist, editor, and humorist

1871. Marcel Proust (d. 18 November 1822). French writer of fiction and critical essayist

1885. Mary O'Hara (d. 15 October 1980). American writer of fiction

1915. Saul Bellow. Canadian-born American writer of fiction, playwright, and writer of narrative nonfiction

1923. Jean Collins Kerr. American playwright and writer of autobiographical narrative.

DEATHS

1863. Clement Clarke Moore (b. 15 July 1779). American poet

1957. Sholem Asch (b. 1 November 1880). Polish-born writer of fiction and of drama in Yiddish

1965. Theodore Sigismund Stribling (b. 4 March 1881). American writer of fiction

11

BIRTHS

1723. Jean Francois Marmontel (d. 31 December 1799). French writer of fiction and playwright

1754. Thomas Bowdler (d. 24 February 1825). Scottish literary scholar, editor, and expurgator

1876. Max Jacob (d. 5 March 1944). French poet

1899. Elwyn Brooks White (d. 1 October 1985). American essayist, writer of fiction for adults and children, humorist, and language stylist

DEATHS

1966. Delmore Schwartz (b. 8 December 1913). American poet, playwright, essayist, and writer of fiction

1974. Par Fabian Lagerkvist (b. 23 May 1891). Swedish expressionist poet, writer of fiction, and playwright

1983. Ross MacDonald (pseudonym of Kenneth Millar; b. 13 December 1915). American writer of detective fiction and essayist

12

BIRTHS

1602. Edward Benlowes (d. 18 December 1676). English poet

1811. Vissarion Grigorievich Belinski (d. 7 June 1848). Russian literary critic, literary historian, editor, and journalist

1817. Henry David Thoreau (d. 6 May 1862). American essayist, diarist, writer of personal narrative, and poet

1828. Nikolay Gavrilovich Chernyshevski (d. 17 October 1889). Russian critical essayist and writer of fiction

1850. Kate O'Flaherty Chopin (d. 22 August 1904). American writer of fiction

1868. Stefan George (d. 4 December 1933). German poet

1904. Pablo Neruda (pseudonym of Neftali Ricardo Reyes Basualto; d. 23 September 1973). Chilean poet and diplomat

DEATHS

1536. Desiderius Erasmus (b. 26 October 1466). Dutch humanist, essayist, Biblical translator and commentator, and satirist

1845. Henrik Arnold Wergeland (b. 17 June 1808). Norwegian lyric and nationalist poet and playwright

1874. Fritz Reuter (b. 7 November 1810). German writer of fiction and poet

1946. Ray Stannard Baker (b. 12 April 1870). American essayist and historian

13

BIRTHS

1793. John Clare (d. 20 May 1864). English poet

1816. Gustav Freytag (d. 30 April 1895). German writer of fiction and playwright

1869. Mikhail Osipovich Gerschenzon (d. ? 1925). Russian essayist and philosopher

1934. Wole Soyinka (born Akinwande Oluwole Soyinka). Nigerian playwright, poet, writer of fiction, and critical essayist

DEATHS

1876. Mikhail Aleksandrovich Bakunin (b. 18 May 1814). Russian revolutionary and essayist

1954. Henry Grantland Rice (b. 1 November 1880). American journalist, sportswriter, and essayist

14

BIRTHS

1743. Gavriil Romanovich Derzhavin (d. 21 July 1816). Russian poet and government minister

1794. John Gibson Lockhart (d. 25 November 1854). Scottish encyclopedist, translator, essayist, writer of fiction, textual editor, and biographer

1816. Joseph Arthur Gobineau (d. 13 October 1882). French Orientalist scholar, philosopher, and essayist

1869. Owen Wister (d. 21 July 1938). American writer of fiction and biographer

1895. Frank Raymond Leavis (d. 18 April 1978). English literary critic

1903. Irving Stone (d. 26 August 1989). American writer of popular historical and biographical fiction

1904. Isaac Bashevis Singer. Polish-born writer of fiction, memoirist, playwright, and translator

1923. James Purdy. American writer of fiction, playwright, and poet

1940. Susan Howatch. English writer of historical fiction

DEATHS

1817. Anne Louise Germaine Necker de Stael (b. 22 April 1766). French playwright, poet, essayist, and writer of fiction

1934. Julian Hawthorne (b. 22 June 1846). American writer of fiction

1954. Jacinto Benavente y Martinez (b. 12 August 1866). Spanish playwright, poet, and writer of fiction

15

BIRTHS

1779. Clement Clarke Moore (d. 10 July 1863). American poet

1796. Thomas Bulfinch (d. 27 May 1867). American historical and literary scholar and mythologist

1836. William Winter (d. 30 June 1917). American essayist, poet, and drama and theatre historian

1903. Walter Dumaux Edmonds. American writer of historical fiction and of prose fiction for children

1906. Richard Willard Armour (d. 28 February 1989). American poet and literary scholar

1913. Hammond Innes. English writer of fiction

1919. Iris Jean Murdoch. Irish-born English writer of fiction, playwright, and writer of philosophical prose tracts

DEATHS

1876. Count Alexander Fredro (b. 20 June 1793). Polish playwright and poet

1890. Gottfried Keller (b. 19 July 1819). Swiss poet and writer of fiction

1919. Hugo von Hoffmannsthal (b. 1 February 1874). Austrian poet, playwright, and opera librettist

1933. Irving Babbitt (b. 2 August 1865). American literary and intellectual scholar and essayist

1976. Paul Willliam Gallico (b. 26 July 1897). American journalist and writer of fiction

1977. William Alexander Gerhardi (b. 21 November 1895). Russian-born English writer of fiction

16

BIRTHS

1723. Sir Joshua Reynolds (d. 23 February 1792). English philosopher, essayist, and painter

1773. Josef Jungmann (d. 14 November 1847). Czech philologist, critical essayist, poet, and lexicographer

DEATHS

1857. Pierre Jean de Beranger (b. 19 August 1780). French poet

1860. Jens Otto Harry Jespersen (d. 30 April 1943). Danish philologist, grammarian, and language innovator

1886. Ned Buntline (pseudonym of Edward Zane Carroll Johnson; b. 20 March 1811). American writer of popular fiction (the "dime novel") and playwright

1896. Edmond Louis Antoine Huot de Goncourt (b. 26 May 1822). French artist, writer of fiction, and memoirist

1923. Louis Couperus (b. 10 June 1863). Dutch writer of fiction and essayist

1953. Hilaire Belloc (born Joseph Hilary Pierre Belloc; b. 27 July 1870). French-born English essayist, writer of fiction, biographer, poet, and writer of travel narrative

1960. John Phillips Marquand (b. 10 November 1893). American writer of fiction and satirist

1985. Heinrich Theodor Boll (b. 21 December 1917). German writer of fiction, essayist, playwright, and translator

17

BIRTHS

1674. Isaac Watts (d. 24 November 1748). English clergyman, poet, hymnodist, and essayist

1810. Martin Farquhar Tupper (d. 8 December 1889). English poet, essayist, and playwright

1859. Ernest Rhys (d. 25 May 1946). English writer of fiction

1862. Oscar Ivan Levertin (d. 22 September 1906). Swedish poet, writer of fiction, and essayist

1888. Shmuel Yosef Halevi Agnon (d. 17 February 1970). Polish-born Israeli writer of fiction

1889. Erle Stanley Gardner (d. 11 March 1970). American writer of detective and mystery fiction

1902. Christina Ellen Stead (d. 31 March 1983). Australian writer of fiction

DEATHS

1790. Adam Smith (b. 5 June 1723). Scottish philosopher, economist, and essayist

1878. Aleardo Aleardi (b. 4 November 1812). Italian lyric poet

1894. Charles Marie Rene Leconte de Lisle (b. 22 October 1818). French poet and translator

1935. AE (pseudonym of George William Russell; b. 10 April 1867). Irish poet and essayist

1985. Susanne Katherina Knauth Langer (b. 20 December 1895). American philosopher and essayist

18

BIRTHS

1504. Heinrich Bullinger (d. 17 September 1575). Swiss theological reformer and essayist

1720. Gilbert White (d. 26 June 1793). English naturalist, diarist, and naturalist historian

1811. William Makepeace Thackeray (d. 24 December 1863). English writer of fiction

1865. Laurence Housman (d. 20 February 1959). English playwright and writer of fiction

1902. Nathalie Sarraute. French writer of fiction and critical essayist

Jessamyn West (d. 23 February 1984). American writer of fiction and essayist

1906. Clifford Odets (d. 14 February 1980). American playwright

1926. Jean Margaret Weymyss Laurence (d. 5 January 1987). Canadian writer of fiction and essayist

1933. Yevgeny Aleksandrovich Yevtushenko. Soviet Russian poet, writer of fiction, playwright, and essayist

DEATHS

1817. Jane Austen (b. 16 December 1775). English writer of fiction

1881. Arthur Penrhyn Stanley (b. 13 December 1815). English theologian, historian, biographer, and essayist

1899. Horatio Alger, Jr. (b. 13 January 1834). American writer of juvenile fiction for boys

1950. Carl Clinton Van Doren (b. 10 September 1885). American periodicals and textual editor, biographer, and critical essayist

1966. Konrad Heiden (b. 7 August 1901). German-born historian

1969. Charlotte Armstrong (b. 2 May 1905). American writer of mystery fiction

19

BIRTHS

1698. Johann Jakob Bodmer (d. 2 January 1783). Swiss historian, essayist, critic, and poet

1769. Louis Benoit Picard (d. 31 December 1828). French playwright and writer of fiction

1819. Gottfried Keller (d. 15 July 1890). Swiss poet and writer of fiction

1863. Hermann Bahr (d. 15 January 1934). Austrian essayist and playwright

1893. Vladimir Vladimirovich Mayakovsky (d. 14 April 1930). Soviet Russian poet and playwright

1896. Archibald Joseph Cronin (d. 6 January 1981). American writer of popular historical fiction

1898. Herbert Marcuse (d. 29 July 1979). German-born American philosopher and essayist

1938. Dom(inick) Frank Moraes. Indian poet and writer of miscellaneous prose nonfiction

DEATHS

1647. Thomas Hooker (b. 7 July 1586). English-born colonial American clergyman, essayist, and writer of sermon literature

1850. Sarah Margaret Fuller, Marchioness Ossoli (b. 23 May 1810). American-born essayist and periodicals editor

1972. Sara (Sally) Mahala Redway Smith Benson (b. 3 September 1900). American writer of fiction

20

BIRTHS

1591. Anne Hutchinson (d. ? August 1643). English-born colonial American memoirist

1803. Thomas Love Beddoes (d. 26 January 1849). English poet and playwright

1838. George Otto Trevelyan (d. 17 August 1928). English historian and biographer

1864. Erik Axel Karlfeldt (d. 8 April 1931). Swedish poet

1924. Thomas Berger. American writer of comic fiction

DEATHS

1891. Pedro Antonio de Alarcon (b. 10 March 1833). Spanish diarist, poet, writer of travel narrative, and writer of fiction

1912. Andrew Lang (b. 31 March 1844). Scottish poet, writer of fiction, literary historian, biographer, and essayist

1916. Reinhard Johannes Sorge (b. 29 January 1892). German poet

1945. Paul Ambroise Toussaint Jules Valery (b. 30 October 1871). French poet and writer of philosophical and speculative prose nonfiction

1950. Robert Smythe Hichens (b. 14 November 1864). English writer of fiction

1978. Gerald Warner Brace (b. 23 September 1901). American writer of fiction

21

BIRTHS

1664. Matthew Prior (d. 18 September 1721). English poet, essayist, and diplomat

1821. Visilio Alexandri (d. 22 August 1890). Romanian poet and patriot

1885. Frances Parkinson Keyes (d. 3 July 1970). American writer of fiction

1893. Hans Fallada (pseudonym of Rudolf Ditzen; d. 5 February 1947). German writer of fiction

1899. Harold Hart Crane (d. 27 April 1932). American poet

Ernest Miller Hemingway (d. 2 July 1961). American writer of fiction

1911. Herbert Marshall McLuhan (d. 31 December 1980). Canadian communications theorist, educator, literary scholar, and essayist

1933. John Champlin Gardner, Jr. (d. 14 September 1982). American writer of fiction, literary scholar, and critical essayist

DEATHS

1796. Robert Burns (b. 25 January 1759). Scottish poet

1816. Gavriil Romanovich Derzhavin (b. 14 July 1743). Russian poet and government minister

1846. Sigurdur Erikson Breidifjord (b. 4 March 1798). Icelandic poet

1899. Robert Green Ingersoll (b. 11 August 1833). American agnostic and essayist

1932. Rene Bazin (b. 20 December 1853). French writer of fiction

1938. Owen Wister (b. 14 July 1869). American writer of fiction and biographer

1957. Kenneth Lewis Roberts (b. 8 December 1885). American writer of historical fiction

1962. George Macaulay Trevelyan (b. 16 February 1876). English historian

22

BIRTHS

1621. Anthony Ashley Cooper, first Earl of Shaftesbury (d. 21 January 1683). English parliamentarian, essayist, and subject of contemporary poems and plays

1846. Alfred Percival Graves (d. 27 December 1931). Irish poet

1849. Emma Lazarus (d. 19 November 1887). American poet and translator

1898. Stephen Vincent Benet (d. 13 March 1943). American poet, writer of fiction, and librettist

1900. Edward Dahlberg (d. 27 February 1977). American writer of fiction and poet

DEATHS

1916. James Whitcomb Riley (b. 7 October 1849). American poet and writer of fiction

1967. Carl August Sandburg (b. 6 January 1878). American poet and biographer

23

BIRTHS

1823. Coventry Kersey Dighton Patmore (d. 26 November 1896). English poet and essayist

1886. Salvador de Madariaga y Rojo (d. 14 December 1978). Spanish philosopher and historian

1888. Raymond Thornton Chandler (d. 26 March 1959). American writer of detective and mystery fiction

1919. Davis Alexander Grubb (d. 24 July 1980). American writer of fiction

1926. Ludvik Vaculik. Czech writer of fiction

1944. Lisa Alther. American writer of fiction

DEATHS

1859. Marceline Desbardes-Valmore (b. 20 June 1786). French poet

1969. Floyd Dell (b. 28 June 1887). American writer of fiction and playwright

1989. Donald Barthelme (b. 7 April 1931). American writer of fiction

24

BIRTHS

1738. Elisabeth Wolff-Bekker (d. 5 November 1804). Dutch writer of fiction, essayist, poet, and translator

1802. Alexandre Davy de la Pailleterie Dumas, pere (d. 5 December 1870). French writer of fiction, playwright, historian, essayist, writer of travel narrative, and translator

1855. William Hooker Gillette (d. 29 April 1937). American playwright

1857. Henrik Pontippidan (d. 21 August 1943). Danish writer of fiction

1864. Frank Wedekind (d. 9 March 1918). German playwright and essayist

1895. Robert Ranke Graves (d. 7 December 1985). English poet, playwright, writer of fiction, and essayist

1916. John Dann MacDonald (d. 28 December 1986). American writer of mystery, detective, and fantasy fiction

DEATHS

1927. Ryunosuke Akutagawa (b. 1 March 1892). Japanese writer of fiction

1980. Davis Alexander Grubb (b. 23 July 1919). American writer of fiction

25

BIRTHS

1814. Charles Dibdin (d. 4 March 1745). English playwright and poet

1848. Arthur James Balfour (d. 19 March 1930). Scottish philosopher and essayist

1853. David Belasco (d. 14 May 1931). American actor and playwright

1880. Morris Raphael Cohen (d. 28 January 1947). Russian-born American philosopher and essayist

1902. Eric Hoffer (d. 21 May 1983). American social and political essayist

1905. Elias Canetti. Bulgarian-born German writer of fiction, playwright, critical essayist, and writer of autobiographical nonfiction narrative

DEATHS

1794. Andre-Marie Chenier (b. 20 October 1762). French poet and political pamphleteer

1834. Samuel Taylor Coleridge (b. 21 October 1772). English poet, writer of verse drama, and essayist

1966. Frank O'Hara (b. 27 June 1926). American poet

1969. Witold Gambrowicz (b. 4 August 1904). Polish writer of fiction and playwright

1972. Ruth McKenny (b. 18 November 1911). American writer of fiction

26

BIRTHS

1856. George Bernard Shaw (d. 4 November 1950). Irish-born playwright, writer of fiction, and essayist

1875. Carl Gustav Jung (d. 6 June 1961). Swiss psychiatrist, psychologist, essayist, and periodicals editor

1885. Andre Maurois (d. 9 October 1967). French literary biographer, historian, and writer of fiction

1894. Aldous Leonard Huxley (d. 22 November 1963). English writer of fiction, poet, and essayist

1897. Paul William Gallico (d. 15 July 1976). American journalist and writer of fiction

DEATHS

1680. John Wilmot, Earl of Rochester (b. 1 April 1647). English poet

1806. Karoline von Gunerode (b. 11 February 1780). German poet

1881. George Henry Borrow (b. 5 July 1803). Scottish-born English writer of travel narrative and fiction

1915. Sir James Augustus Murray (b. 7 February 1837). English philologist, essayist, and lexicographer

1965. Eugene Burdick (b. 12 December 1918). American writer of fiction and political theorist and essayist

1980. Kenneth Peacock Tynan (b. 2 April 1927). English drama critic and essayist

1987. James (Jim) Bishop (b. 21 November 1907). American journalist and writer of historical narrative

27

BIRTHS

1777. Thomas Campbell (d. 15 June 1844). Scottish poet and biographer

1824. Alexandre Dumas, fils (d. 27 November 1895). French playwright, writer of fiction, poet, and essayist

1835. Giosue Carducci (d. 16 February 1907). Italian poet

1870. Hilaire Belloc (born Joseph Hilary Pierre Belloc; d. 16 July 1953). French-born English essayist, writer of fiction, biographer, poet, and writer of travel narrative

1872. Paul Lawrence Dunbar (d. 9 February 1906). American poet, playwright, writer of fiction, and essayist

DEATHS

1841. Mikhail Yurievich Lermontov (b. 15 October 1814). Russian poet, writer of fiction, and verse dramatist

1946. Gertrude Stein (b. 3 February 1874). American writer of fiction, poet, and writer of miscellaneous prose nonfiction

1948. Susan Keating Glaspell (b. 1 July 1876). American playwright and writer of fiction

1962. Richard Edward Godfrey Aldington (b. 8 July 1892). English poet, writer of fiction, and biographer

28

BIRTHS

1458. Jacopo Sannazaro (d. 24 April 1530). Italian poet and humanist

1804. Ludwig Andreas Feuerbach (d. 13 September 1872). German philosopher and essayist

1809. John Stuart Blackie (d. 2 March 1895). Scottish classical scholar and essayist

1812. Jozef Ignacy Kraszewski (d. 19 March 1887). Polish writer of historical fiction and poet

1844. Gerard Manley Hopkins (d. 8 June 1889). English poet

1902. Kenneth Flexner Fearing (d. 26 June 1961). American writer of fiction and poet

1909. Clarence Malcolm Lowry (d. 27 June 1957). English writer of fiction and poet

1927. John Lawrence Ashbery. American poet, playwright, writer of fiction, editor, and translator

DEATHS

1631. Guillen de Castro y Bellvis (b. 4 November 1569). Spanish playwright

1655. Savinien de Cyrano de Bergerac (b. 6 March 1619). French adventurer and prose writer

1842. Clemens Brentano (b. 8 September 1778). German poet, playwright, and writer of fiction

1929. Henry Blake Fuller (b. 9 January 1857. American writer of fiction and playwright

1973. Mary Ellen Chase (b. 24 February 1887). American writer of fiction and literary and Biblical scholar

29

BIRTHS

1793. Jan Kollar (d. 4 January 1852). Czech poet and Slovonic scholar

1796. Christian Winther (d. 20 December 1876). Danish Romantic poet

1805. Alexis Charles Henri Clerel de Tocqueville (d. 26 April 1859). French historian and diarist

1869. Newton Booth Tarkington (d. 19 May 1946). American writer of fiction

1878. Donald Robert Perry Marquis (d. 29 December 1937). American journalist, social and political satirist, humorist, poet, and playwright

1900. Eyvind Johnson. Swedish writer of fiction

Owen Lattimore (d. 31 May 1989). American writer of travel narrative, historian, and political essayist

1905. Stanley Jasspon Kunitz. American poet and compiler of literary biographical reference works

1909. Chester Bomar Himes (d. 12 November 1984). American writer of fiction and essayist

1918. Edwin Greene O'Connor (d. 23 March 1968). American writer of fiction

DEATHS

1856. Karl Havlicek (pseudonym of Havel Borousky; b. 31 October 1821). Czech literary critic, journalist, and poet

1974. Erich Kastner (b. 23 February 1899). German writer of fiction, poet, and playwright

1979. Herbert Marcuse (b. 19 July 1898). German-born American philosopher and essayist

30

BIRTHS

1511. Giorgio Vasari (d. 27 June 1574). Italian art historian, biographer, and critical essayist

1818. Emily Jane Bronte (d. 19 December 1848). English writer of fiction, poet, and essayist

1857. Thorstein Bunde Veblen (d. 3 August 1919). American sociologist, social theorist, and essayist

DEATHS

1771. Thomas Gray (b. 26 December 1716). English poet

1784. Denis Diderot (b. 5 October 1713). French philosopher, essayist, encyclopedist, writer of fiction, playwright, satirist, and art critic

1870. Aasmund Olavssen Vinje (b. 6 April 1818). Norwegian poet and critical essayist

1894. Walter Horatio Pater (b. 4 August 1839). English critical essayist, historian, writer of fiction, and philosophical biographer

1901. Herbert Baxter Adams (b. 16 April 1850). American artist and essayist

1918. Alfred Joyce Kilmer (b. 6 December 1886). American poet, journalist, and critical essayist

1930. Sir Arthur Conan Doyle (b. 22 May 1859). Scottish-born writer of detective and mystery fiction, political pamphleteer, and historian

31

BIRTHS

1689. Samuel Richardson (d. 4 July 1761). English writer of epistolary fiction, moral essayist, and printer

1843. Peter Rosegger (pseudonym of Petri Kettenfeier; d. 26 June 1918). Austrian writer of fiction

1919. Primo Levi (d. 11 April 1987). Italian memoirist, writer of fiction, poet, and essayist

DEATHS

1818. Nikolay Ivanovich Novikov (b. 27 April 1744). Russian essayist and publisher

1921. Edgar Evertson Saltus (b. 8 October 1855). American writer of fiction

1944. Antoine Marie Roger de St. Exupery (b. 29 June 1900). French writer of fiction and of nonfiction narrative

AUGUST

1

BIRTHS

1779. Francis Scott Key (d. 11 January 1843). American poet and essayist

1791. George Ticknor (d. 26 January. 1871). American literary and historical scholar and essayist

1815. Richard Henry Dana, Jr. (d. 6 January 1882). American writer of prose narrative and essayist

1819. Herman Melville (d. 28 September 1891). American writer of fiction, poet, and writer of narrative nonfiction

1822. James Grant (d. 5 May 1887). Scottish writer of fiction

DEATHS

1743. Richard Savage (b. 16 January 1697?). English poet and playwright

1821. Elizabeth Inchbald (b. 15 October 1753). English writer of fiction and playwright

1926. Israel Zangwill (b. 14 February 1864). English writer of fiction, playwright, and poet

1963. Theodore Huebner Roethke (b. 25 May 1908). American poet

1981. Sidney (Paddy) Chayefsky (b. 29 January 1923). American playwright and filmwriter

2

BIRTHS

1823. Edward Augustus Freeman (d. 16 March 1892). English historian

1854. Francis Marion Crawford (d. 9 April 1909). American writer of fiction and playwright

1865. Irving Babbitt (d. 15 July 1933). American literary and intellectual scholar and essayist

Dmitry Sergeyevich Merezhkovsky (d. ? 1941). Russian poet and essayist

1867. Ernest Christopher Dowson (d. 23 February 1900). English lyrical poet, playwright, writer of fiction, and translator

1884. Romulo Gallegos Freire (d. 4 April 1969). Venezuelan writer of fiction

1920. Lonnie William Coleman (d. 13 August 1982). American writer of fiction

1924. James Baldwin (d. 1 December 1987). American writer of fiction, writer of autobiographical narrative nonfiction, essayist, and playwright

1946. Kenji Nakagami. Japanese writer of fiction

DEATHS

1924. Harriet Mulford Stone Lothrop (b. 22 June 1844). American writer of fiction for children

1955. Wallace Stevens (b. 2 October 1879). American poet, playwright, and essayist

1963. Oliver Hazard Perry Lafarge (b. 19 December 1901). American writer of fiction, essayist, and historian of the Native American

1980. Donald Ogden Stewart (b. 30 November 1894). American writer of humorous fiction and narrative, and playwright

1988. Raymond Carver (b. 15 May 1938). American poet and writer of fiction

3

BIRTHS

1871. Vernon Louis Parrington (d. 16 June 1929). American literary and intellectual historian and scholar

1887. Rupert Chawner Brooke (d. 23 April 1915). English poet, playwright, and critical essayist

1909. Walter Van Tilberg Clark (d. 11 November 1971). American writer of fiction and poet

1920. Phyllis Dorothy James. English writer of mystery and crime fiction

1921. Hayden Carruth. American poet, writer of fiction, essayist, and reviewer

1924. Leon Marcus Uris. American writer of contemporary historical fiction

DEATHS

1805. Christopher Anstey (b. 31 October 1724). English writer of humorous and colloquial verse

1857. Marie Joseph Eugene Sue (b. 20 January 1804). French writer of fiction

1919. Thorstein Bunde Veblen (b. 30 July 1857). American sociologist, social theorist, and essayist

1924. Joseph Conrad (born Teodor Josef Konrad Korzeniowski; b. 3 December 1857). Polish-born (Russian Ukraine) English writer of fiction

1948. Albert Frederick Pollard (b. 16 December 1869). English historian and biographer

1954. Sidonie Gabrielle Colette (b. 28 January 1873). French writer of fiction

1964. Mary Flannery O'Connor (b. 25 March 1925). American writer of fiction

1972. Paul Goodman (b. 9 September 1911). American writer of fiction, playwright, and poet

4

BIRTHS

1540. Joseph Justus Scaliger (d. 21 January 1609). French-born scholar and editor

1792. Percy Bysshe Shelley (d. 8 July 1822). English poet, playwright, and writer of fiction and of miscellaneous prose nonfiction

1839. Walter Horatio Pater (d. 30 July 1894). English essayist, intellectual historian, and writer of biographical fiction

1841. William Henry Hudson (d. 18 August 1922). Argentinian-born (of American parents) English writer of fiction, essayist, naturalist, and writer of narrative nonfiction

1859. Knut Hamsun (pseudonym of Knut Pedersen; d. 19 February 1952). Norwegian writer of fiction

1904. Witold Gambrowicz (d. 25 July 1969). Polish writer of fiction and playwright

1913. Robert Hayden (pseudonym of Asa Bundy Sheffey; d. 24 February 1980). American poet

Jerome Weidman. American writer of fiction and playwright

DEATHS

1865. William Edmonstone Aytoun (b. 21 June 1813). Scottish poet and writer of fiction

1875. Hans Christian Andersen (b. 2 April 1805). Danish writer of fiction, poet, satirist, and composer of fairy tales

1975. Marguerite Steen (b. 12 May 1894). English writer of historical fiction

5

BIRTHS

1604. John Eliot (d. 21 May 1690). English-born colonial American linguist and Biblical translator

1850. Guy de Maupassant (d. 6 July 1893). French writer of fiction

1856. Asher Ginzberg (d. 2 January 1927). Russian essayist and periodicals editor

1876. Mary Ritter Beard (d. 14 August 1958). American social historian

1889. Conrad Potter Aiken (d. 17 August 1973). American poet, playwright, writer of fiction, essayist, reviewer, and editor

1916. Peter Robert Edwin Viereck. American intellectual and cultural historian, poet, and writer of verse drama

DEATHS

1880. William Henry Giles Kingston (b. 28 February 1814). English writer of fiction for boys and writer of travel narrative

1895. Friedrich Engels (b. 28 November 1820). German-born political and economic philosopher, essayist, and translator

1959. Edgar Albert Guest (b. 20 August 1881). American writer of popular verse

1980. Ella Winter (b. 17 March 1898). Australian-born American journalist and essayist

6

BIRTHS

1638. Nicolas de Malebranche (d. 13 October 1715). French philosopher, theologian, psychologist, and essayist

1651. Francois Salignac de la Mothe Fenelon (d. 7 January 1715). French essayist, compiler of fables and maxims, historian, and satirist

1809. Alfred Lord Tennyson (d. 6 October 1892). English poet and playwright

1868. Paul Louis-Marie Claudel (d. 23 February 1955). French poet, essayist, and playwright.

1889. John Middleton Murry (d. 13 March 1957). English literary essayist and biographer

1916. Richard Hofstadter (d. 24 October 1970). American intellectual historian

DEATHS

1637. Ben(jamin) Jonson (b. 11 June 1572?). English poet and playwright

7

BIRTHS

1533. Alonso de Ercilla y Zuniga (d. 29 November 1594). Spanish epic poet

1578. Georg Stiernhielm (d. 22 April 1672). Swedish poet, scholar, and essayist

1901. Konrad Heiden (d. 18 July 1966). German-born historian

DEATHS

1898. Georg Moritz Ebers (b. 1 March 1837). German Egyptologist, essayist, and writer of historical fiction

1941. Rabindranath Tagore (b. 7 May 1861). Indian poet, philosopher, playwright, and essayist

1979. Nicholas John Turney Monsarrat (b. 22 March 1910). English writer of fiction

8

BIRTHS

1694. Francis Hutchinson (d. 1 November 1746). Irish philosophical essayist

1807. Emilie Flygare-Carlen (d. 5 February 1892). Swedish writer of fiction

1884. Sara Teasdale (d. 29 January 1933). American poet

1896. Marjorie Kinnan Rawlings (d. 14 December 1953). American writer of fiction and journalist

1907. Jesse Hilton Stuart (d. 17 February 1984). American poet and writer of fiction

1922. Philip Arthur Larkin (d. 2 December 1985). English poet, writer of fiction, and diarist

DEATHS

1854. Thomas Croften Croker (b. 15 January 1798). Irish writer of fiction and antiquary

1873. Fyodor Ivanovich Tyuchev (b. 1803). Russian lyric poet

1897. Jakob Christoph Burckhardt (b. 25 May 1818). Swiss historian and art critic

1965. Shirley Hardie Jackson (b. 14 December 1919). American writer of fiction, playwright, and writer of personal narrative nonfiction

9

BIRTHS

1593. Izaak Walton (d. 15 December 1683). English biographer and essayist

1631. John Dryden (d. 1 May 1700). English poet, playwright, and critical essayist

1653. John Oldham (d. 7 December 1683). English poet

1884. Kenneth Scott Latourette (d. 26 August 1968). American Church historian

1896. Aloysius Michael Sullivan (d. 10 June 1980). American poet and periodicals editor

1908. Zhou Libo (d. 25 September 1979). Chinese writer of fiction

DEATHS

1848. Frederick Marryat (b. 10 July 1792). English writer of fiction

1921. Aleksandr Aleksandrovich Blok (b. 28 November 1880). Russian poet and writer of verse drama

1936. Joseph Lincoln Steffans (b. 6 April 1866). American reform journalist, editor, essayist, and writer of autobiographical narrative

1958. Louis Golding (b. 19 November 1895). English writer of fiction

1962. Hermann Hesse (b. 2 July 1877). German writer of fiction and poet

1978. James Gould Cozzens (b. 19 August 1903). American writer of fiction

1983. Robert Greenhalgh Albion (b. 15 August 1896). American maritime historian

10

BIRTHS

1869. Robert Laurence Binyon (d. 10 March 1843). English poet, playwright, and critical essayist

1873. William Ernest Hocking (d. 12 June 1966). American Idealist philosopher and essayist

1878. Alfred Doblin (d. ? 1957). German writer of fiction

1881. Witter Bynner (d. 1 June 1968). American poet and playwright

DEATHS

1857. John Wilson Croker (b. 20 December 1780). Irish-born historian, textual editor, essayist, and literary scholar

1876. Edward William Lane (b. 17 September 1801). English Arabic scholar and essayist

1961. Julia Mood Peterkin (b. 31 October 1880). American writer of fiction

11

BIRTHS

1821. Octave Feuillet (d. 29 December 1890). French writer of fiction, playwright, and librarian

1833. Robert Green Ingersoll (d. 21 July 1899). American agnostic and essayist

1884. Panait Istrati (d. ? 1935?). Romanian writer of fiction

1892. Hugh Macdiarmid (pseudonym of Christopher Murray Grieve; d. 9 September 1978). Scottish poet, writer of miscellaneous prose nonfiction, and textual editor

1897. Louise Bogan (d. 4 February 1970). American poet

1913. Angus Frank Johnstone Wilson. South African-born English writer of fiction, critical essayist, and biographer

1921. Alex Palmer Haley. American biographer, journalist, and writer of fictionalized historical and biographical narrative

1932. Fernando Arrabal. Spanish writer of fiction, playwright, and memoirist

DEATHS

1872. Lowell Mason (b. 8 January 1792). American poet, hymnodist, and music educator

1890. John Henry Cardinàl Newman (b. 21 February 1801). English essayist and poet

1903. Eugenio Maria de Hostos (b. 11 January 1839). Chilean philosopher, sociologist, and essayist

1937. Edith Newbold Jones Wharton (b. 24 January 1862). American writer of fiction and poet

1956. Bertolt Brecht (b. 10 February 1898). German playwright and poet

12

BIRTHS

1774. Robert Southey (d. 21 March 1843). English poet, essayist, and biographer

1859. Katherine Lee Bates (d. 28 March 1929). American poet, essayist, and writer of books for children

1866. Jacinto Benavente y Martinez (d. 14 July 1954). Spanish poet, playwright, and writer of fiction

1867. Edith Hamilton (d. 31 May 1963). American literary scholar and mythologist

1876. Mary Roberts Rinehart (d. 22 September 1958). American writer of mystery and crime fiction

1884. Frank Arthur Swinnerton (d. 6 November 1982). English writer of fiction and essayist

1912. Jorge Amado. Brazilian writer of fiction

DEATHS

1827. William Blake (b. 28 November 1757). English poet and engraver

1885. Helen Maria Hunt Jackson (b. 15 October 1830). American poet and writer of travel narrative, books for children, and fiction

1891. James Russell Lowell (b. 22 February 1819). American poet, playwright, essayist, and textual editor

1955. Thomas Mann (b. 6 June 1875). German writer of fiction and critical essayist

1964. Ian Lancaster Fleming (b. 28 May 1908). English writer of espionage and adventure fiction, and journalist

13

BIRTHS

1802. Nikolaus Lenau (pseudonym of Nicolaus Franz Niembsch; d. 22 August 1850). Austrian poet

1820. Sir George Grove (d. 28 May 1900). English musicologist, Biblical scholar, periodicals editor, and music encyclopedist

1823. Goldwin Smith (d. 7 June 1910). English historian and essayist

1884. Jo. Van Ammers-Kuller (d.?). Dutch writer of fiction

DEATHS

1749. Johann Elias Schlegel (b. 28 January 1719). German playwright and critical essayist

1881. Edward John Trelawney (b. 13 November 1792). English writer of fiction and of biographical prose narrative

1934. Mary Hunter Austin (b. 9 September 1868). American writer of fiction and essayist

1946. Herbert George Wells (b. 21 September 1866). English writer of fiction, essayist, historian, and writer of autobiographical narrative

1982. Lonnie William Coleman (b. 2 August 1920). American writer of fiction

1985. Shivadhar Srinivasa Naipaul (b. 25 February 1945). Trinidadian journalist, essayist, and writer of fiction

14

BIRTHS

1552 Pietro Sarpi (d. 7 January 1623). Italian ecclesiastical historian

1836. Walter Besant (d. 9 June 1901). English biographer, essayist, writer of fiction, and playwright

1860. Ernest Thompson Seton (d. 23 October 1946). English-born American writer of fiction for boys

1863. Ernest Lawrence Thayer (d. 21 August 1940). American poet and writer of comic ballads ("Casey at the Bat")

1867. John Galsworthy (d. 31 January 1933). English writer of fiction and playwright

1931. Frederic Michael Raphael. English writer of fiction and critical essayist

DEATHS

1778. Augustus Montagu Toplady (b. 4 November 1740). English poet, hymnodist, and Church pamphleteer

1794. George Colman the elder (b. 17 April 1732). English playwright

1937. Herman Cyril McNeile (b. 28 September 1888). English writer of crime, adventure, and detective fiction

1958. Mary Ritter Beard (b. 5 August 1876). American social historian

1969. Leonard Sidney Woolf (b. 25 November 1880). English writer of miscellaneous prose nonfiction

1984. John Boynton Priestley (b. 13 September 1894). English writer of fiction, playwright, and writer of miscellaneous prose nonfiction

15

BIRTHS

1740. Matthias Claudius (d. 21 January 1815). German poet and essayist

1771. Sir Walter Scott (d. 21 September 1832). Scottish writer of fiction, poet, playwright, biographer, essayist, and textual editor

1785. Thomas DeQuincey (d. 8 December 1859). English essayist

1858. Edith Nesbit (d. 22 April 1924). English writer of fiction, poet, and writer of stories for children

1885. Edna Ferber (d. 16 April 1968). American writer of fiction, essayist, and playwright

1888. Thomas Edward Lawrence (d. 19 May 1935). English adventurer, writer of autobiographical narrative, and commentator upon the Arab world

1896. Robert Greenhalgh Albion (d. 9 August 1983). American maritime historian

1924. Robert Oxton Bolt. English playwright

DEATHS

1779. Giuseppe Parini (b. 23 May 1729). Italian poet

1977. Mark Schorer (b. 17 May 1908). American literary essayist, scholar, and biographer

16

BIRTHS

1645. Jean de La Bruyere (d. 11 May 1696). French writer of maxims and of dialogues, and translator

1658. Sir Ralph Thoresby (d. 16 October 1725). English antiquarian writer

1766. Carolina Oliphant, Baroness Nairne (d. 27 October 1845). Scottish poet

1794. Jean Henri Merle d'Aubigne (d. 21 October 1872). French ecclesiastical historian and essayist

1830. Diego Barros Arana (d. 4 November 1907). Chilean historian, educator, and essayist

1860. Jules LaForgue (d. 20 August 1887). French poet and essayist

1902. Georgette Heyer (d. 4 July 1974). English writer of historical fiction

1909. Marchette Gaylord Chute. American biographer and literary historian

DEATHS

1886. Ramakrishna (born Sri Ramakrishna Paramahansa; b. 18 February 1836). Indian (Hindu) mystic, philosopher, and essayist

1936. Grazia Cosima Deledda (b. 27 September 1875). Italian writer of fiction, poet, and playwright

1949. Margaret Mitchell (b. 8 November 1900). American writer of fiction

1973. Richard Tregaskis (b. 28 November 1916). American journalist and writer of fiction

1980. Gwen Bristow (b. 16 September 1903). American writer of fiction

1987. Charles Harris Wesley (b. 2 December 1891). American historian

17

BIRTHS

1801. Fredrika Bremer (d. 31 December 1865). Swedish writer of fiction and social reformer

1819. Jon Arnason (d. 4 September 1888). Icelandic folklorist and compiler of folk legends

1840. Wilfrid Scawen Blunt (d. 12 September 1922). English poet, playwright, and historical commentator

1847. Alice Christiana Gertrude Thompson Meynell (d. 27 November 1922). English essayist and poet

1868. Geneva Grace Stratton-Porter (d. 6 December 1924). American writer of fiction for girls

1871. Jesse Lynch Williams (d. 14 September 1929). American writer of fiction and playwright

1925. John Clendennin Burne Hawkes, Jr. American writer of fiction and playwright

1932. Vidiadhar Surajpresad Naipaul. Trinidadian-born English writer of fiction, writer of travel narrative, and political essayist

DEATHS

1928. George Otto Trevelyan (b. 20 July 1838). English historian and biographer

1973. Conrad Potter Aiken (b. 5 August 1889). American poet, writer of fiction, essayist, reviewer, and editor

18

BIRTHS

1564. Frederigo Borromeo (d. 22 September 1631). Italian churchman, scholar, essayist, and librarian

1792. Lord John Russell (d. 28 May 1878). English political essayist

1807. Charles Francis Adams (d. 21 November 1886). American diplomat, essayist, biographer, and textual editor

1841. Robert William Buchanan (d. 10 June 1901). Scottish poet, writer of fiction, and playwright

1922. Alain Robbe-Grillet. French writer of fiction, essayist, and filmwriter

1925. Brian Wilson Aldiss. English writer of science and fantasy fiction and critical essayist

DEATHS

1563. Etienne de la Boetie (b. 1 November 1530). French poet, translator, and essayist

1678. Andrew Marvell (b. 31 March 1621). English poet, satirist, and essayist

1803. James Beattie (b. 25 October 1735). Scottish poet, essayist, and textual editor

1850. Honore de Balzac (b. 20 May 1799). French writer of fiction

1870. John Pendleton Kennedy (b. 25 October 1795). American writer of fiction

1922. William Henry Hudson (b. 4 August 1841). Argentinian-born (of American parents) English writer of fiction, essayist, naturalist, and writer of narrative nonfiction

1981. Anita Loos (b. 26 April 1893). American writer of fiction and satirist

19

BIRTHS

1560. James Crichton (d. 3 July 1582). Scottish adventurer, scholar, linguist, essayist, and poet

1780. Pierre Jean de Beranger (d. 16 July 1857). French poet

1793. Samuel Griswold Goodrich (d. 9 May 1860). American publisher of didactic fiction for children, poet, writer of nonfiction narrative, and publisher

1843. Charles Montagu Doughty (d. 20 January 1926). English writer of travel narrative, poet, and playwright

1902. Frederick Ogden Nash (d. 19 May 1971). American writer of verse, playwright, and writer of miscellaneous nonfiction prose

1903. James Gould Cozzens (d. 9 August 1978). American writer of fiction

DEATHS

1662. Blaise Pascal (b. 19 June 1623). French mathematician, scientist, theologian, pamphleteer, and essayist

1823. Robert Bloomfield (b. 3 December 1766). English poet and playwright

1889. Jean Marie Mathias Philippe Auguste, Comte de Villiers de L'Isle-Adam (b. 7 November 1838). French writer of symbolist fiction, playwright, and satirist

1971. Henry Fitzgerald Heard (b. 6 October 1889). English essayist

20

BIRTHS

1625. Thomas Corneille (d. 8 December 1709). French poet, essayist, and playwright

1632. Louis Bourdaloue (d. 13 May 1704). French pulpit orator, rhetorician, philosopher, theologian, and essayist

1749. Aleksandr Nikolayevich Radischev (d. 12 September 1802). Russian poet, critic, and political reformer

1827. Charles Theodore Henri De Coster (d. 17 May 1879). Belgian writer of fiction

1847. Boleslaw Prus (pseudonym of Alexander Glowacki; d. 19 May 1912). Polish writer of fiction

1881. Edgar Albert Guest (d. 5 August 1959). American writer of popular verse

1886. Paul Johannes Tillich (d. 22 October 1965). German Protestant theologian, philosopher, and essayist

1901. Salvatore Quasimodo (d. 14 June 1968). Italian poet

1921. Jacqueline Susann (d. 21 September 1974). American writer of popular fiction

DEATHS

1639. Martin Opitz von Boberfeld (b. 23 December 1597). German poet and translator

1854. Friedrich Wilhelm Joseph von Schelling (b. 27 January 1775). German philosopher and essayist

1887. Jules LaForgue (b. 16 August 1860). French poet and essayist

21

BIRTHS

1609. Jean de Rotrou (d. 27 June 1650). French playwright

1798. Jules Michelet (d. 10 February 1874). French historian and writer of prose tracts on nature

1872. Aubrey Vincent Beardsley (d. 16 March 1898). English illustrator, editor, and writer of erotic fiction

1896. Roark Bradford (d. 13 November 1938). American humorist and writer of fiction.

1929. X. J. Kennedy (born Joseph Charles Kennedy). American writer of light verse, critical essayist, and anthologizer

DEATHS

1649. Richard Crashaw (b. ? 1612?). English poet and translator

1723. Dimitri Kantemir (b. 26 October 1673). Moldavian historian and essayist

1762. Lady Mary Wortley Montagu (b. 26 May 1689). English poet, writer of epistolary travel narrative, and essayist

1905. Mary Elizabeth Dodge (b. 26 January 1831). American writer of fiction, poet, and writer of stories for children

1940. Ernest Lawrence Thayer (b. 14 August 1863). American poet and writer of comic ballads ("Casey at the Bat")

Leon Davidovich Trotsky (b. 26 October 1879). Russian political philosopher, historian, essayist, biographer, critic, and diarist

1943. William Lyon Phelps (b. 2 January 1865). American literary scholar and essayist

Henrik Pontippidan (b. 24 July 1857). Danish writer of fiction

22

BIRTHS

1778. James Kirke Paulding (d. 6 April 1860). American poet, writer of fiction, and playwright

1800. Edward Bouverie Pusey (d. 14 September 1882). American theological essayist

1852. Alfredo Oriani (d. 18 October 1909). Italian critical theorist and essayist

1893. Dorothy Rothschild Parker (d. 7 June 1967). American writer of fiction, literary critic, poet, and playwright

1920. Ray Douglas Bradbury. American writer of fantasy and science fiction, and poet

DEATHS

1850. Nikolaus Lenau (originally Nicolaus Franz Niembach; b. 13 August 1802). Austrian poet

1884. Henry George Bohn (b. 4 January 1796). English publisher, bookseller, and bibliographer

1890. Vasile Alexandri (b. 21 July 1821). Romanian poet and playwright

1891. Jan Neruda (b. 10 July 1834). Czech poet, writer of prose fiction and nonfiction, and playwright

1904. Kate O'Flaherty Chopin (b. 12 July 1850). American writer of fiction

1958. Roger Martin du Gard (b. 23 March 1881). French writer of fiction and playwright

1979. James Thomas Farrell (b. 27 February 1904). American writer of fiction, essayist, and poet

1980. George Rippey Stewart (b. 31 May 1895). American writer of fiction, poet, and writer of miscellaneous prose nonfiction

23

BIRTHS

1761. Jedediah Morse (d. 9 June 1826). American theologian, periodicals editor, geographer, historian, and essayist

1849. William Ernest Henley (d. 11 June 1903). English poet and playwright

1855. Barrett Wendell (d. 8 February 1921). American literary historian

1869. Edgar Lee Masters (d. 5 March 1950). American poet, playwright, and writer of fiction

1908. Arthur Adamov (d. 16 March 1970). French playwright, essayist, and translator

DEATHS

1540. Guillaume Bude (b. 26 January 1468). French scholar, philosopher, philologist, and writer on jurisprudence

1618. Gebrand Adriaenszoon Bredero (b. 16 March 1585). Dutch poet and playwright

1628. George Villiers, second Duke of Buckingham (b. 28 August 1592). English poet and playwright

1723. Increase Mather (b. 21 June 1639). Colonial American theologian, essayist, historian, and biographer

1939. Sidney Coe Howard (b. 26 June 1891). American playwright

24

BIRTHS

1591. Robert Herrick (d. ? October 1674). English poet

1817. Alexey Konstantinovich Tolstoy (d. 28 September 1875). Russian playwright, lyrical poet, and writer of fiction

1872. Henry Maximilian Beerbohm (d. 20 May 1956). English critical essayist and caricaturist

1890. Jean Rhys (pseudonym of Ella Gwendolyn Rees Williams; d. 14 May 1979). West Indian-born English writer of fiction and translator

1898. Malcolm Cowley (d. 27 March 1989). American poet, critical essayist, and writer of prose nonfiction narrative

1902. Fernand Paul Braudel (d. 28 November 1985). French historian

DEATHS

1666. Francisco Manuel de Melo (b. 23 November 1608). Portuguese critical essayist, historian, and poet

1841. Theodore Edward Hook (b. 22 September 1788). English writer of fiction, playwright, and biographer

1923. Kate Douglas Wiggin (b. 28 September 1856). American writer of fiction for adults and for children

1943. Simone Weill (b. 3 February 1909). French philosopher and essayist

1985. Morris (Morrie) Ryskind (b. 20 October 1895). American comic playwright

25

BIRTHS

1744. Johann Gottfried von Herder (d. 18 December 1803). German critical essayist, translator, and poet

1745. Henry Mackenzie (d. 14 January 1831). Scottish writer of fiction, essayist, and periodical editor

1793. John Neal (d. 20 June 1876). American writer of fiction, poet, and essayist

1836. Francis Brett Harte (d. 5 May 1902). American writer of fiction, poet, satirist, playwright, and periodicals editor

1899. Jorge Luis Borges (d. 14 June 1986). Argentinian writer of fiction, essayist, poet, translator, and writer of miscellaneous prose nonfiction

1921. Brian Moore. Irish-born writer of fiction

DEATHS

1770. Thomas Chatterton (b. 20 November 1752). English poet, essayist, playwright, and literary "forger"

1776. David Hume (b. 26 April 1711). Scottish philosopher, essayist, writer of dialogues, and historian

1800. Elizabeth Montagu (b. 2 October 1720). English essayist

1860. Johan Ludvig Heiberg (b. 14 December 1791). Danish critical essayist, playwright, and poet

1867. Michael Faraday (b. 22 September 1791). English scientist, theorist, and essayist

1900. Friedrich Wilhelm Neitzsche (b. 15 October 1844). German philosopher, critic, and essayist

1922. William Archibald Dunning (b. 12 May 1857). American historian, essayist, and academician

1957. Umberto Saba (pseudonym of Umberto Poli; b. 9 March 1883). Italian poet

26

BIRTHS

1863. Alfred Edward Newton (d. 29 September 1940). American bibliophile and essayist

1875. John Buchan (d. 11 February 1940). Scottish writer of fiction, biographer, and historian

1880. Guillaume Apollinaire (d. 10 November 1918). French poet, writer of fiction, and essayist

1884. Earl Derr Biggers (d. 5 April 1933). American journalist and writer of detective and mystery fiction

1885. Jules Romains (originally Louis Farigoule; d. ? 1972). French writer of fiction, poet, and playwright

1904. Christopher Isherwood (d. 4 January 1986). English writer of fiction and translator

1914. Julio Cortazar (d. 12 February 1984). Argentinian writer of fiction

1929. Kateb Yacine. Algerian writer of fiction, playwright, and poet

DEATHS

1744. William Byrd II (b. 28 March 1674). Colonial American historian, diarist, and writer of nonfiction narrative

1813. Karl Theodor Korner (b. 23 September 1791). German poet

1871. Charles Scribner (b. 21 February 1821). American publisher and periodicals editor

1884. Antonio Garcia Gutierrez (b. 5 October 1813). Spanish poet, playwright, scientist, and essayist

1910. William James (b. 11 January 1842). American psychologist and essayist

1931. Frank Harris (originally James Thomas Harris; b. 14 February 1856). Irish-born American writer of fiction, critical essayist, and writer of autobiographical narrative

1945. Franz Werfel (b. 10 September 1890). Austrian poet, playwright, and writer of fiction

1979. Mika Toimi Waltari (b. 18 September 1908). Finnish writer of fiction, poet, and playwright

1984. Truman Capote (b. 30 September 1924). American writer of fiction, essayist, and writer of miscellaneous prose

1989. Irving Stone (b. 14 July 1903). American writer of popular fictionalized biography

27

BIRTHS

1730. Johann Georg Hamann (d. 21 June 1788). German theologian, philosopher and essayist

1770. Georg Wilhelm Friedrich Hegel (d. 14 November 1831). German Idealist philosopher and essayist

1776. Barthold Georg Niebuhr (d. 2 January 1831). German biographer and historian

1865. James Henry Breasted (d. 2 December 1935). American Egyptologist, archaeologist, historian, academician, and essayist

1871. Theodore Herman Albert Dreiser (d. 28 December 1945). American writer of fiction, journalist, essayist, poet, and playwright

1877. Lloyd Cassel Douglas (d. 13 February 1951). American writer of fiction

1899. Cecil Scott Forester (originally Cecil Lewis Troughton Smith; d. 2 April 1966). English writer of adventure and historical fiction

1904. Norah Robinson Lofts (d. 10 September 1983). English writer of fiction

1929. Ira Levin. American writer of fiction and playwright

1932. Antonia Packenham Fraser. English biographer and writer of fiction

DEATHS

1635. Lope Felix de Vega Carpio (b. 25 November 1562). Spanish playwright and poet

1748. James Thomson (b. 11 September 1700). Scottish-born poet and playwright

1866. John Pierpont (b. 6 April 1785). American poet and essayist

1963. William Edward Burghardt Dubois (b. 23 February 1868). American writer of fiction, essayist, writer of autobiographical narrative, and poet

28

BIRTHS

1481. Francisco de Sa de Miranda (d. ? 1558). Portuguese poet and writer of verse comedies and prose epistles

1592. George Villiers, second Duke of Buckingham (d. 23 August 1628). English poet and playwright

1749. Johann Wolfgang von Goethe (d. 22 March 1832). German playwright, poet, essayist, and writer of fiction

1814. Joseph Sheridan LeFanu (d. 7 February 1873). Irish writer of fiction and poet

1828. Leo Lev Nikolayevich Tolstoi (d. 20 November 1910). Russian writer of fiction, essayist, and playwright

1906. Sir John Betjeman (d. 19 May 1984). English poet and architectural historian

1913. William Robertson Davies. Canadian writer of fiction and playwright

DEATHS

1645. Hugo Grotius (also Huig van Groot; b. 10 April 1583). Dutch jurist, statesman, and legal essayist

1757. David Hartley (b. 29 August 1705). English philosopher and essayist

1859. James Henry Leigh Hunt (b. 19 October 1784). English essayist, poet, and playwright

1978. Bruce Catton (b. 9 October 1899). American historian

Francis Van Wick Mason (b. 11 November 1901). American writer of fiction

1988. Max Shulman (b. 14 March 1919). American writer of fiction and humorist

29

BIRTHS

1632. John Locke (d. 28 October 1704). English philosopher and essayist

1705. David Hartley (d. 28 August 1757). English philosopher and essayist

1805. John Frederick Denison Maurice (d. 1 April 1872). English theologian, writer of fiction, and essayist

1809. Oliver Wendell Holmes the elder (d. 7 October 1894). American physician, essayist, and poet

1844. Edward Carpenter (d. 28 June 1929). English poet and essayist

1862. Maurice Maeterlinck (d. 6 May 1949). Belgian playwright, poet, and writer of philosophical essays

1881. Valery Nicolas Larbaud (d. 2 February 1957). French traveler, scholar, and writer of fiction

1929. Thom(son) William Gunn. English poet

DEATHS

1960. Vicki Baum (b. 24 January 1888). Austrian-born American writer of fiction and playwright

30

BIRTHS

1743. William Paley (d. 25 May 1805). English philosopher and theologian

1797. Mary Wollstonecraft Shelley (d. 1 February 1851). English writer of fiction, biographer, and writer of travel narrative

1811. Pierre Jules Theophile Gautier (d. 23 October 1872). French poet, essayist, and writer of fiction

1901. John Gunther (d. 29 May 1870). American journalist and writer of social and political documentary nonfiction

DEATHS

1856. Gilbert Abbot a' Beckett (b. 7 February 1811). English humorist, editor, and playwright

1935. Henri Barbusse (b. 17 May 1873). French poet and writer of fiction

1985. Janet Miriam Taylor Caldwell (b. 7 September 1900). English-born American writer of historical fiction

31

BIRTHS

1781. John Mitford (d. 27 April 1859). English poet

1806. Charles James Lever (d. 3 June 1872). Irish writer of fiction

1838. Abel Bergaigne (d. 21 May 1901). French linguist, philologist, and Sanskrit scholar

1885. DuBose Heyward (d. 16 June 1940). American poet, writer of fiction, and playwright

1908. William Saroyan (d. 18 May 1981). American writer of fiction, poet, playwright, and essayist

DEATHS

1688. John Bunyan (b. 28 November 1628). English writer of prose allegory and of prose nonfiction, and poet

1867. Charles Pierre Baudelaire (b. 9 April 1821). French symbolist poet

1919. Johann Sigurjonsson (b. 19 June 1880). Icelandic playwright and poet

1931. Thomas Henry Hall Caine (b. 14 May 1853). English writer of fiction and biographical narrative

1946. Harley Granville-Barker (b. 25 November 1877). English actor, director-producer, essayist, and drama scholar

SEPTEMBER

1

BIRTHS

1789. Marguerite Power Farmer Gardiner, Countess of Blessington (d. 4 June 1849). English diarist and writer of fiction

1791. Lydia Howard Huntley Sigourney (d. 10 June 1865). American poet and hymnodist

1875. Edgar Rice Burroughs (d. 19 March 1950). American writer of adventure and fantasy fiction

1877. Rex Ellingwood Beach (d. 7 December 1949). American writer of fiction and of miscellaneous prose nonfiction

DEATHS

1729. Sir Richard Steele (b. 10[?] March 1672). Irish-born English essayist, playwright, and poet

1777. Aleksandr Petrovich Sumarokov (b. 4 June 1718). Russian playwright, poet, and theatre manager

1943. William Wymark Jacobs (b. 8 September 1863). English writer of fiction

1948. Charles Austin Beard (b. 27 November 1874). American historian and essayist

1967. Ilya Grigoryevich Ehrenburg (b. 27 January 1891). Soviet Russian writer of fiction

Siegfried Lorraine Sassoon (b. 8 September 1886). English poet, playwright, writer of fiction, and memoirist

1970. Francois Mauriac (b. 11 October 1885). French writer of fiction, playwright, and critical essayist

2

BIRTHS

1840. Giovanni Verga (d. 27 January 1922). Italian writer of fiction

1850. Eugene Field (d. 4 November 1895). American journalist, essayist, and writer of verse

1852. Paul Charles Joseph Bourget (d. 25 December 1935). French writer of fiction, playwright, and essayist

1864. Miguel de Unamuno y Jugo (d. 31 December 1936). Spanish poet, essayist, philosopher, historian, and writer of fiction and travel narrative

1912. David Daiches. Scottish-born literary critic and scholar

1917. Cleveland Amory. American journalist and critical essayist

1918. Allen Stuart Drury. American writer of fiction, journalist, and writer of travel narrative

DEATHS

1872. Nikolai Frederick Severin Grundtvig (b. 8 September 1783). Danish poet, historian, and linguist

1889. Samuel Austin Allibone (b. 17 April 1816). American librarian, encyclopedist, and compiler of literary and historical reference works

1921. Henry Austin Dobson (b. 18 January 1840). English poet, essayist, and biographer

1962. Edward Estlin Cummings (b. 14 October 1894). American writer of verse, playwright, and writer of fiction

1973. J. R. R. Tolkien (b. 3 January 1892). South African-born English writer of fiction, poet, critical essayist, and scholar

3

BIRTHS

1653. Roger North (d. 1 March 1734). English lawyer, historian, and biographer

1827. Gisli Brynjulfsson (d. 29 May 1888). Icelandic Romantic poet

1849. Sarah Orne Jewett (d. 24 June 1909). American writer of fiction and poet

1900. Sara (Sally) Mahala Redway Smith Benson (d. 19 July 1972). American writer of fiction

1906. Lawrence Clark Powell. American academic librarian, bibliophile, literary biographer, and essayist

1907. Loren Corey Eisley (d. 9 July 1977). American anthropologist and essayist

1926. Alison Lurie. American writer of fiction and essayist

DEATHS

1634. Sir Edward Coke (b. 1 February 1552). English jurist and commentator upon jurisprudence

1874. Hans Conon von der Gabelentz (b. 13 October 1807). German linguist, essayist, and scholar of the Melanesian languages

1883. Ivan Sergeyevich Turgenev (b. 9 November 1818). Russian writer of fiction

1963. Frederick Louis MacNeice (b. 12 September 1907). Irish-born poet, playwright, writer of radio drama and fiction, and essayist

1971. Manfred Bennington Lee (b. 11 January 1905). American writer of detective and mystery fiction

1981. Alexander (Alec) Raban Waugh (b. 8 July 1898). English writer of fiction and of travel and autobiographical narrative

1982. Frederic Dannay (b. 20 October 1905). American writer of mystery and detective fiction

4

BIRTHS

1768. Francois-Rene Vicomte de Chateaubriand (d. 4 July 1848). French writer of travel narrative, political essayist, memoirist, and writer of prose epics

1905. Mary Renault (originally Mary Challans; d. 13 December 1983). English writer of historical fiction

1908. Richard Nathaniel Wright (d. 5 December 1960). American writer of fiction and of autobiographical narrative, and essayist

DEATHS

1888. Jon Arnason (b. 17 August 1819). Icelandic folklorist and compiler of folk legends

1951. Louis Adamic (b. 23 March 1899). Yugoslavian-born American writer of autobiographical narrative, writer of fiction, and essayist

1965. Albert Schweitzer (b. 14 January 1875). Alsatian theologian, musician, medical missionary, and essayist

1984. Harnett Thomas Kane (b. 8 November 1910). American writer of fiction

1989. Georges Joseph Christian Simenon (b. 13 February 1903). Belgian writer of detective and mystery fiction

5

BIRTHS

1568. Tommaso Campanella (d. 21 May 1639). Italian philosopher, essayist, and poet

1596. James Shirley (d. ? October 1666). English playwright and poet

1733. Christoph Martin Weiland (d. 29 January 1813). German essayist, translator, poet, and writer of fiction

1831. Victorien Sardou (d. 8 November 1908). French playwright

1888. Sir Sarvepalli Radhakrishnan (d. 7 April 1975). Indian philosopher and essayist

1905. Arthur Koestler (d. 3 March 1983). Hungarian-born English literary, historical, and scientific essayist, and writer of fiction

1916. Frank Garvin Yerby. American writer of fiction

DEATHS

1808. John Home (b. 21 September 1722). Scottish clergyman, playwright, poet, and historian

1857. Isidore Auguste Marie Francois Comte (b. 19 January 1798). French philosopher, sociologist, and essayist

1914. Charles Pierre Peguy (b. 7 January 1873). French poet, publisher, and essayist

1933. Sazanami Iwaya (pseudonym of Iwaya Sueo; b. 4 July 1870). Japanese writer of fiction for children

1967. David Cornel De Jong (b. 9 June 1905). Dutch-born writer of fiction

6

BIRTHS

1711. Heinrich Melchoir Muhlenberg (d. 7 October 1787). German-born colonial American theologian and essayist

1729. Moses Mendelssohn (d. 4 January 1786). German philosopher and essayist

1795. Frances Wright (d. 13 December 1852). Scottish-born essayist, playwright, writer of fiction, and advocate of social reform

1869. Felix Salten (d. 8 October 1945). Austrian writer of fiction

1878. Henry Seidel Canby (d. 5 April 1961). American literary and social critic, historian, and critical biographer

1900. Julien Hartridge Green. French-born writer of fiction

DEATHS

1902. Philip James Bailey (b. 22 April 1916). English poet

1903. Charles Ammi Cutter (b. 14 March 1837). American librarian and essayist

1920. Paul Jean Toulet (b. 5 June 1867). French poet and writer of fiction

7

BIRTHS

1799. Georges Louis Leclerc du Buffon (d. 16 April 1788). French scientist, naturalist historian, and essayist

1873. Carl Lotus Becker (d. 10 April 1945). American historian

1885. Elinor Hoyt Wylie (d. 16 December 1928). American poet and writer of fiction

1887. Dame Edith Sitwell (d. 9 December 1964). English poet, playwright, writer of fiction, and critical essayist

1900. Janet Miriam Taylor Caldwell (d. 30 August 1985). English-born American writer of historical fiction

1909. Elia Kazan. Turkish-born writer of fiction and film director

1950. David Bradley. American writer of fiction

DEATHS

1779. John Armstrong (b. ? 1709). Scottish-born poet, playwright, essayist, and physician

1833. Hannah More (b. 2 February 1745). English writer of fiction, playwright, and poet

1881. Sidney Lanier (b. 3 February 1842). American writer of fiction, poet, and essayist

1891. Heinrich Graetz (b. 31 October 1817). German Jewish historian

1892. John Greenleaf Whittier (b. 17 December 1803). American poet and writer of prose sketches and narratives

1907. Rene Francois Armand Sully Prudhomme (b. 16 March 1839). French poet, philosopher, essayist, and diarist

1939. Kyoka Izumi (pseudonym of Izumi Kyotaro; b. 4 November 1873). Japanese writer of fiction

1962. Isak Dinesen (pseudonym of Karen Blixen; b. 17 October 1885). Danish writer of fiction

1970. Donald Baxter Macmillan (b. 10 November 1874). American explorer and writer of nonfiction prose narrative

1979. Ivor Armstrong Richards (b. 26 February 1893). English literary critic and essayist

8

BIRTHS

1474. Ludovico Ariosto (d. 6 July 1533). Italian Latin poet

1767. August Wilhelm von Schlegel (d. 12 May 1845). German poet, critical essayist, and translator

1778. Clemens Brentano (d. 28 July 1842). German poet, playwright, and writer of fiction

1783. Nikolai Frederick Severin Grundtvig (d. 2 September 1872). Danish poet, historian, and linguist

1830. Frederic Mistral (d. 25 March 1914). French Provencal poet and lexicographer

1863. William Wymark Jacobs (d. 1 September 1943). English writer of fiction

1886. Siegfried Lorraine Sassoon (d. 1 September 1967). English poet, playwright, writer of fiction, and memoirist

1924. Grace De Repentigny Metalious (d. 25 February 1864). American writer of popular fiction

1947. Ann Beattie. American writer of fiction

DEATHS

1645. Francisco Gomez Quevedo y Villegas (b. 17 September 1580). Spanish religious and political essayist, poet, playwright, and writer of fiction

1981. William York Tindall (b. 7 March 1903). American critical essayist

9

BIRTHS

1711. Thomas Hutchinson (d. 3 June 1780). Colonial American government administrator, essayist, and historian

1868. Mary Hunter Austin (d. 13 August 1934). American writer of fiction and essayist

1877. James Evershed Agate (d. 6 June 1947). English essayist and writer of fiction

1878. Adelaide Cropsey (d. 8 October 1914). American poet

1900. James Hilton (d. 20 December 1954). English writer of fiction and filmwriter

1901. Granville Hicks (d. 18 June 1982). American essayist, historical and critical commentator, and writer of fiction and of miscellaneous prose nonfiction

1908. Cesare Pavese (d. ? 1950). Italian writer of fiction, translator, poet, and essayist

1911. Paul Goodman (d. 3 August 1972). American writer of fiction, playwright, and poet

DEATHS

1898. Stephane Mallarme (b. 18 March 1842). French poet, translator, and essayist

1973. Samuel Nathaniel Behrman (b. 9 June 1893). American playwright

1978. Hugh Macdiarmid (pseudonym of Christopher Murray Grieve; b. 11 August 1892). Scottish poet, writer of miscellaneous prose nonfiction, and textual editor

1980. John Howard Griffin (b. 16 June 1920). American writer of narrative and miscellaneous prose nonfiction and musicologist

10

BIRTHS

1771. Mungo Park (d. ? 1806). Scottish physician, explorer, and writer of travel narrative

1835. William Torrey Harris (d. 5 November 1909). American philosopher, educator, essayist, and literary critic

1885. Carl Clinton Van Doren (d. 18 July 1950). American periodicals and textual editor, biographer, and critical essayist

1886. Hilda Doolittle (wrote under the pseudonym "H.D."; d. 28 September 1961). American poet, playwright, and writer of fiction

1890. Franz Werfel (d. 26 August 1945). Austrian poet, playwright, and writer of fiction

1912. William Oliver Everson (sometimes wrote under the pseudonym of "Brother Antoninus"). American poet

DEATHS

1797. Mary Wollstonecraft Godwin (b. 27 April 1759). English essayist and writer of fiction

1845. Joseph Story (b. 18 September 1779). American lawyer, politician, essayist, and commentator upon jurisprudence

1883. Hendrik Conscience (b. 3 December 1812). Flemish writer of fiction

1980. Virginia Kirkus (b. 7 December 1893). American literary critic, essayist, and reviewer

1983. Norah Robinson Loftis (b. 27 August 1904). English writer of fiction

11

BIRTHS

1524. Pierre de Ronsard (d. 27 December 1585). French poet and critical essayist

1700. James Thomson (d. 27 August 1748). Scottish-born poet and playwright

1762. Johanna Baillie (d. 23 February 1851). Scottish playwright and poet

1862. O. Henry (pseudonym of William Sidney Porter; d. 5 June 1910). American writer of fiction

1885. David Herbert Lawrence (d. 2 March 1930). English writer of fiction, poet, and essayist

1917. Jessica Mitford. English-born American writer of nonfiction prose commentaries upon American political and social institutions

DEATHS

1823. David Ricardo (b. 19 April 1772). English political economist and essayist

1844. Basil Hall (b. 31 December 1788). Scottish writer of travel narrative

1891. Anthero de Quental (b. 18 April 1842). Portuguese poet and critical essayist

1896. Francis James Child (b. 1 February 1825). American literary scholar, academician (Harvard), and ballad anthologizer

1958. Robert William Service (b. 16 January 1874). American writer of verse

1976. Carl Carmer (b. 16 October 1893). American folklorist and essayist

12

BIRTHS

1605. William Dugdale (d. 10 February 1686). English antiquary and historian

1829. Charles Dudley Warner (d. 20 October 1900). American lawyer, periodicals editor, essayist, biographer, and literary and intellectual historian

1855. Fiona Macleod (pseudonym of William Sharp; d. 14 December 1905). Scottish essayist, poet, writer of fiction, biographer, and composer of mystic Celtic tales and romances

1880. Henry Louis Mencken (d. 29 January 1956). American journalist, reviewer, essayist, satirist, and language historian

1907. Louis MacNeice (d. 3 September 1963). Irish-born poet, playwright, writer of radio drama and of fiction, and essayist

DEATHS

1660. Jacob Cats (b. 10 November 1577). Dutch diplomat, lawyer, poet, and writer of autobiographical prose narrative

1802. Aleksandr Nikolayevich Radischev (b. 20 August 1749). Russian poet, critic, and political reformer

1869. Peter Mark Roget (b. 18 January 1779). English scholar, physician, and linguist

1889. Numa Denis Fustel de Coulanges (b. 18 March 1830). French historian and essayist

1922. Wilfrid Scawen Blunt (b. 17 August 1840). English poet, playwright, and historical commentator

1977. Robert Traill Spence Lowell, Jr. (b. 1 March 1917). American poet, essayist, and translator

1981. Eugenio Montale (b. 21 October 1896). Italian poet, writer of fiction, and translator

13

BIRTHS

1876. Sherwood Anderson (d. 8 March 1941). American writer of fiction, poet, writer of nonfiction prose narrative, and essayist

1894. John Boynton Priestley (d. 14 August 1984). English writer of fiction, playwright, and writer of miscellaneous prose nonfiction

1916. John Malcolm Brinnin. Canadian-born American poet and literary critical essayist

Roald Dahl. English writer of fiction and of literature for children

DEATHS

1557. Sir John Cheke (b. 16 June 1514). English classical scholar, translator, and essayist

1592. Michel Eyquem de Montaigne (b. 28 February 1533). French essayist and translator

1629. Johannes Buxtorf the elder (b. 25 December 1564). German Hebraic scholar, essayist, and lexicographer

1872. Ludwig Andreas Feuerbach (b. 28 July 1804). German philosopher and essayist

1874. Francois Pierre Guillhaume Guizot (b. 4 October 1787). French historian, diplomat, essayist, and literary and historical textual editor

1939. Olav Duun (b. 21 November 1876). Norwegian writer of fiction

14

BIRTHS

1769. Friedrich Heinrich Alexander von Humboldt (d. 6 May 1859). German naturalist, traveler, essayist, and geographer

1791. Franz Bopp (d. 23 October 1867). German philologist, linguist, and essayist

1817. Hans Theodor Woldsen Storm (d. 4 July 1888). German writer of fiction and poet

1818. Richard Congreve (d. 5 July 1899). English essayist

1926. Michel Marie Francois Butor. French writer of fiction

1934. Katherine Murray (Kate) Millett. American writer of autobiographical narrative and social activist and commentator

DEATHS

1638. John Harvard (b. 26 November 1607). English-born colonial American clergyman and bibliophile

1851. James Fenimore Cooper (b. 15 September 1789). American writer of fiction, essayist, social critic, historian, and biographer

1882. Edward Bouverie Pusey (b. 14 September 1800). English theological essayist

1916. Jose Echegaray y Eizaguirre (b. 19 April 1832). Spanish prose and verse dramatist

Josiah Royce (b. 20 November 1855). American philosopher and essayist

1926. Rudolph Christoph Eucken (b. 5 January 1846). German philosopher and essayist

1927. Hugo Ball (b. 22 February 1886). German poet and theologian

1929. Jesse Lynch Williams (b. 17 August 1871). American writer of fiction and playwright

1982. John Champlin Gardner, Jr. (b. 21 July 1933). American writer of fiction and literary scholar and critic

1985. Worth Tuttle Hedden (b. 10 January 1896). American writer of fiction

15

BIRTHS

1584. Georg Rodolf Weckherin (d. 13 February 1653). German poet and translator

1765. Manuel Maria Barbosa du Bocage (d. 21 December 1805). Portuguese lyric poet

1789. James Fenimore Cooper (d. 14 September 1851). American writer of fiction, essayist, social critic, historian and biographer

1822. Henry Morley (d. 14 May 1894). English essayist and biographer

1834. Heinrich Gotthard von Treitschke (d. 28 April 1896). German historian

1889. Robert Chalres Benchley (d. 21 November 1945). American drama critic, essayist, humorist, and actor

1890. Agatha Mary Clarissa Christie (d. 12 January 1976). English writer of mystery and detective fiction

Claude McKay (born Festus Claudius McKay; d. 22 May 1948). Jamaican-born poet and writer of fiction

DEATHS

1833. Arthur Henry Hallam (b. 1 February 1811). English poet and essayist

1938. Thomas Clayton Wolfe (b. 3 October 1900). American writer of fiction, playwright, and essayist

1989. Berry Giles Fleming (b. 19 March 1899). American writer of fiction

Robert Penn Warren (b. 24 April 1905). American poet, writer of fiction, and critical essayist

16

BIRTHS

1678. Henry St. John, Viscount Bolingbroke (d. 12 December 1751). English diplomat, essayist, historian, and philosopher

1685. John Gay (d. 4 December 1732). English poet, playwright, and essayist

1823. Francis Parkman (d. 8 November 1893). American historian, essayist, and writer of travel narrative

1852. Emilia Pardo Bazan (d. 12 May 1921). Spanish writer of fiction and essayist

1860. Hannibal Hamlin Garland (d. 4 March 1940). American writer of fiction, essayist, and writer of autobiographical narrative

1880. Alfred Noyes (d. 28 June 1958). English poet

1883. Thomas Ernest Hulme (d. 28 September 1917). English critical essayist and poet

1888. Frans Eemil Sillanpaa (d. 3 June 1964). Finnish writer of fiction

1903. Gwen Bristow (d. 16 August 1980). American writer of fiction

1926. John Knowles. American writer of fiction

1939. Breyton Breytenbach. South African poet and essayist

DEATHS

1672. Anne Dudley Bradstreet (b. ? 1612). English-born colonial American poet

1845. Thomas Osborne Davis (b. 14 October 1814). Irish poet and political essayist

1892. Judah Loeb ben Asher Gordon (b. 7 December 1830). Russian-born Hebrew poet and satirist

1911. Edward Whymper (b. 27 April 1840). English artist and writer of travel narrative

17

BIRTHS

1580. Francisco Gomez de Quevedo y Villegas (d. 8 September 1645). Spanish religious and political essayist, poet, playwright, and writer of fiction

1743. Marie-Jean Antoine Nicolas Caritat, Marquis de Condorcet (d. 25[?] March 1794). French mathematician, essayist, and encyclopaedist

1801. Edward William Lane (d. 10 August 1876). English Arabic scholar and essayist

1869. Christian Louis Lange (d. 11 December 1938). Norwegian historian and essayist

1883. William Carlos Williams (d. 4 March 1963). American poet, essayist, and playwright

1903. Frank O'Connor (originally Michael O'Donovan; d. 10 March 1966). Irish writer of fiction

1905. Feng Zhi. Chinese lyric poet and literary scholar

1908. John Creasey (d. 9 June 1973). English writer of detective fiction

1916. Mary Florence Elinor Stewart. English writer of romance and suspense fiction

1935. Ken(neth) Elton Kesey. American writer of fiction

DEATHS

1575. Heinrich Bullinger (b. 18 July 1504). Swiss theological reformer and essayist

1771. Tobias George Smollett (b. 19 March 1721). Scottish-born writer of fiction, poet, travel anthologist, literary editor, and historian

1863. Alfred Victor, Comte de Vigny (b. 27 March 1797). French poet, playwright, and writer of fiction

1864. Walter Savage Landor (b. 30 January 1775). English poet, playwright, and writer of fictional-critical dialogues in prose

1883. John Payne Collier (b. 11 January 1789). English essayist and literary critic

1948. Ruth Fulton Benedict (b. 5 June 1887). American cultural anthropologist and essayist

18

BIRTHS

1643. Gilbert Burnett (d. 17 March 1715). Scottish-born historian

1709. Samuel Johnson (d. 13 December 1784). English poet, writer of fiction and verse drama, essayist, biographer, textual editor, and lexicographer

1779. Joseph Story (d. 10 September 1845). American lawyer, politician, essayist, and commentator upon jurisprudence

1786. Justinus Andreas Christian Kerner (d. 21 February 1862). German poet

1908. Miko Toimi Waltari (d. 26 August 1979). Finnish writer of fiction, poet, and playwright

DEATHS

1721. Matthew Prior (b. 21 July 1664). English poet, essayist, and diplomat

1775. Andrew Foulis (b. 23 November 1712). Scottish bookseller, printer, and textual editor

1830. William Hazlitt (b. 10 April 1778). English essayist

1890. Dion Boucicault (originally Dionysius Lardner Bourisquot; b. 26 December 1820). Irish-born playwright

1905. George MacDonald (b. 10 December 1824). Scottish writer of fiction, poet, and writer of literature for children

1964. James Frank Dobie (b. 26 September 1888). American folklorist, essayist, and textual editor

Sean O'Casey (originally John Casey; b. 30 March 1880). Irish playwright and writer of autobiographical narrative

1980. Katherine Anne Porter (b. 15 May 1890). American writer of fiction, essayist, and translator

19

BIRTHS

1655. Jan Luyts (d. ?). Dutch scholar, physicist, mathematician, astronomer, geographer, and essayist

1721. William Robertson (d. 11 June 1793). Scottish historian

1796. David Hartley Coleridge (d. 6 January 1849). English poet

1894. Rachel Lyman Field (d. 15 March 1942). American writer of fiction and of literature for children

1904. Bergen Evans (d. 4 February 1978). American linguist, lexicographer, grammarian, and essayist

1911. William Gerald Golding. English writer of fiction, poet, and playwright

1915. Oscar Handlin. American historian and essayist

DEATHS

1971. William Foxwell Albright (b. 24 May 1891). American Oriental and Biblical scholar, anthropologist, and essayist

1985. Italo Calvino (b. 15 October 1923). Italian writer of fiction, essayist, and translator

20

BIRTHS

1833. Petroleum V. Nasby (pseudonym of David Ross Locke; d. 15 February 1888). American humorist, essayist, writer of fiction, and journalist

1878. Upton Beall Sinclair (d. 25 November 1968). American writer of fiction, advocate of social reform, essayist, and pamphleteer

1884. Maxwell Evarts Perkins (d. 17 June 1947). American literary editor

1928. Donald Andrew Hall, Jr. American poet, essayist, and anthologist

DEATHS

1703. Charles de Marguetel de Saint-Denis de Saint-Evremond (b. 1 April 1616). French essayist and satirist

1863. Jakob Ludwig Karl Grimm (b. 4 January 1785). German folklorist and philologist

1898. Theodor Fontane (b. 30 December 1819). German writer of fiction and poet

1971. George Seferis (pseudonym of Georgios Stylianou Sepheriades; b. 29 February 1900). Greek poet and translator

1975. St. John Perse (pseudonym of Marie-Rene-Auguste Alexis Saint-Leger Leger; b. 31 March 1887). French poet

21

BIRTHS

1722. John Home (d. 5 September 1808). Scottish clergyman, playwright, poet, and historian

1792. Johann Peter Eckermann (d. 3 December 1854). German critical essayist, textual editor, and writer of prose nonfiction narrative

1849. Sir Edmund William Gosse (d. 5 January 1913). English writer of fiction, critical essayist, biographer, and literary historian

1866. Herbert George Wells (d. 13 August 1946). English writer of fiction, essayist, historian, and writer of autobiographical narrative

1947. Stephen King. American writer of horror and fantasy fiction

DEATHS

1832. Sir Walter Scott (b. 15 August 1771). Scottish writer of fiction, poet, playwright, biographer, and textual editor

1860. Arthur Schopenhauer (b. 22 February 1788). German philosopher and essayist

1921. Ivan Vazov (b. 27 June 1850). Bulgarian poet, playwright, essayist, and writer of fiction

1968. Charles Reginald Jackson (b. 6 April 1903). American writer of fiction

1973. William Charles Franklin Plomer (b. 10 December 1963). English writer of fiction

1974. Jacqueline Susann (b. 20 August 1921). American writer of popular fiction

22

BIRTHS

1606. Richard Busby (d. 6 April 1695). English schoolmaster and tutor to such writers as

John Locke, Matthew Prior, John Dryden, and Francis Atterbury

1694. Philip Dormer Stanhope, fourth Earl of Chesterfield (d. 24 March 1773). English epistolary essayist and writer of political tracts

1788. Theodore Edward Hook (d. 24 August 1841). English writer of fiction, playwright, and biographer

1791. Michael Farraday (d. 25 August 1867). English scientist, theorist, and essayist

1895. Babette Deutsch (d. 13 November 1982). American poet, essayist, and translator

DEATHS

1631. Frederigo Borromeo (b. 18 August 1564). Italian churchman, scholar, essayist, and librarian

1906. Oscar Ivan Levertin (b. 17 July 1862). Swedish poet, writer of fiction, and essayist

1914. Alain Fournier (b. 3 October 1886). French writer of fiction

1949. Edmond Jaloux (b. 19 June 1878). French essayist and writer of fiction

1958. Mary Roberts Rinehart (b. 12 August 1876). American writer of mystery and crime fiction

23

BIRTHS

1728. Mercy Otis Warren (d. 19 October 1814). American playwright, political satirist, historian, and writer of fiction

1791. Karl Theodor Korner (d. 26 August 1813). German poet

1800. William Holmes McGuffey (d. 4 May 1873). American educational philosopher, philologist, and writer of schoolbooks

1867. John Avery Lomax (d. 26 January 1948). American ballad anthologist

1889. Walter Lippman (d. 14 December 1974). American journalist and political essayist

1901. Gerald Warner Brace (d. 20 July 1978). American writer of fiction

Jaroslav Seifert (d. 10 January 1986). Czech poet

DEATHS

1738. Hermann Boerhaave (b. 31 December 1688). Dutch physician, botonist, scientific theorist and historian, and essayist

1764. Robert Dodsley (b. 13 February 1703). English poet, playwright, publisher, and literary anthologizer

1870. Prosper Merimee (b. 28 September 1803). French writer of fiction, archaeological and historical essayist, playwright, poet, literary critic, and translator

1889. William Wilkie Collins (b. 8 January 1824). English writer of fiction and playwright

1923. John Morley (b. 24 December 1838). English critical essayist and biographer

1939. Sigmund Freud (b. 6 May 1856). Austrian psychologist and essayist

1943. Elinor Sutherland Glyn (b. 17 October 1864). English writer of fiction

1973. Pablo Neruda (pseudonym of Neftali Ricardo Reyes Basualto; b. 12 July 1904). Chilean poet and diplomat

24

BIRTHS

1717. Horace Walpole, fourth Earl of Orford (d. 2 March 1797). English essayist and writer of fiction

1762. William Lisle Bowles (d. 7 April 1850). English poet and essayist

1878. Charles Ferdinand Ramuz (d. 23 May 1947). French-Swiss writer of fiction

1890. Alan Patrick Herbert (d. 11 November 1971). English writer of fiction and essayist

1896. Francis Scott Key Fitzgerald (d. 21 December 1940). American writer of fiction, essayist, and playwright

1912. Robert Lewis Taylor. American writer of fiction, journalist, and biographer

1934. John Brunner. English writer of science and fantasy fiction

25

BIRTHS

1793. Felicia Dorothea Hemans (d. 16 May 1835). English poet

1881. Lu Hsun (pseudonym of Chou Shujen; d. 19 October 1936). Chinese writer of fiction and essayist

1897. William Faulkner (d. 6 July 1962). American writer of fiction

DEATHS

1680. Samuel Butler (b. 8 February 1612). English poet and writer of prose character sketches

1689. Joseph Beaumont (b. 13 March 1616). English epic poet

1808. Richard Porson (b. 25 December 1759). English classical scholar and essayist

1893. Marie Louise von Francois (b. 27 June 1817). German writer of fiction

1933. Ringgold Wilmer Lardner (b. 6 March 1885). American journalist, humorist, writer of fiction, and poet

1970. Erich Maria Remarque (b. 22 June 1898). German-born writer of fiction

1979. Zhou Libo (b. 9 August 1908). Chinese writer of fiction

1987. Emlyn Williams (b. 26 November 1905). Welsh playwright and actor

26

BIRTHS

1547. Mateo Aleman (d. ? 1614). Spanish writer of fiction

1859. Irving Bachellor (d. 24 February 1950). American writer of fiction

1888. James Frank Dobie (d. 18 September 1964). American folklorist, essayist, and textual editor

1888. Thomas Stearns Eliot (d. 4 January 1965). American-born poet, playwright, and critical essayist

1889. Martin Heidegger (d. 26 May 1976). German philosopher and essayist

1898. Richard Lockridge (d. 19 June 1982). American writer of detective and mystery fiction

DEATHS

1763. John Byrom (b. 29 February 1692). English poet, hymnodist, translator, and essayist

1904. Lafcadio Hearn (b. 27 June 1850). Ionian Islands-born American writer of fiction and narrative prose nonfiction

1947. Hugh Lofting (b. 14 January 1896). English-born American writer of fiction for children

1952. George Santayana (born Jorge Ruiz de Santayana y Borrias; b. 16 December 1863). Spanish-born American essayist, poet, intellectual and cultural philosopher, writer of fiction, and Biblical commentator

1973. Samuel Flagg Bemis (b. 20 October 1891). American diplomatic historian

27

BIRTHS

1627. Jacques Benigne Bosseut (d. 12 April 1704). French theologian, writer of sermon literature, historian, and essayist

1772. Sandor Kisfaludy (d. 28 October 1844). Hungarian poet

1792. George Cruikshank (d. 1 February 1878). English illustrator and caricaturist of contemporary fiction

1875. Grazia Cosima Deledda (d. 16 August 1936). Italian writer of fiction, poet, and playwright

1906. William Empson (d. 15 April 1984). English poet and critical essayist

1914. Sarah Catherine Marshall (d. 18 March 1983). American biographer and writer of prose nonfiction

1917. Louis Stanton Auchincloss. American writer of fiction, essayist, literary critic, and biographer

DEATHS

1886. John Esten Cooke (b. 3 November 1830). American writer of fiction and biographer

28

BIRTHS

1746. Sir William Jones (d. 27 April 1794). English Oriental scholar, philologist, and essayist

1803. Prosper Merimee (d. 23 September 1870). French writer of fiction, archeological and historical essayist, playwright, poet, literary critic, and translator

1856. Kate Douglas Wiggin (d. 24 August 1923). American writer of fiction for adults and for children

1888. Herman Cyril McNeile (d. 14 August 1937). English writer of crime, detective, and adventure fiction

1892. Elmer Leopold Rice (born Elmer Leopold Reizenstein; d. 8 May 1967). American playwright and writer of fiction

DEATHS

1789. Thomas Day (b. 22 June 1748). English writer of didactic fiction for children, poet, and writer of miscellaneous prose

1875. Alexey Konstantinovich Tolstoy (b. 24 August 1817). Russian playwright, lyrical poet, and writer of fiction

1891. Herman Melville (b. 1 August 1819). American writer of fiction, poet, and writer of narrative nonfiction prose

1902. Emile Zola (b. 2 April 1840). French writer of fiction and journalist

1917. Thomas Ernest Hulme (b. 16 September 1883). English critical essayist and poet

1961. Hilda Doolittle (wrote under pseudonym of "H.D."; b. 10 September 1886). American poet, playwright, and writer of fiction

1966. Andre Breton (b. 18 February 1896). French critical essayist and poet

1970. John Roderigo Dos Passos (b. 14 January 1896). American writer of fiction, biographer, and writer of travel narrative

1973. Wystan Hugh Auden (b. 21 February 1907). English-born poet, playwright, and critical essayist

1981. Eugenio Montale (b. 12 October 1896). Italian poet and critical essayist

29

BIRTHS

1547. Miguel de Cervantes Saavedra (d. 23 April 1616). Spanish writer of fiction, playwright, and poet

1810. Elizabeth Cleghorn Gaskell (d. 12 November 1865). English writer of fiction

1897. Herbert Sebastian Agar (d. 24 November 1980). American historian, literary critic, and political essayist

1940. Alfred Edward Newton (b. 26 August 1863). American bibliophile and essayist

1967. Carson McCullers (pseudonym of Lula Carson Smith; b. 19 February 1917). American writer of fiction and playwright

30

BIRTHS

1714. Etienne Bonnot de Condillac (d. 2 April 1780). French philosopher and essayist

1857. Herman Sudermann (d. 22 November 1928). German playwright

1907. Joseph Kramm. American playwright

1924. Truman Capote (d. 26 August 1984). American writer of fiction, essayist, and miscellaneous prose

1927. William Stanley Merwin. American poet and playwright

DEATHS

1628. Sir Fulke Greville, first Baron Brooke (b. 3 October 1554). English poet, playwright, and biographer

1684. Pierre Corneille (b. 6 June 1606). French playwright, poet, and verse translator

1811. Thomas Percy (b. 13 April 1729). English poet and antiquarian

1984. Helen Dore Boylston (b. 4 April 1895). American writer of fiction for young girls

1985. Helen Clark MacInnes (b. 7 October 1907). Scottish-born American writer of fiction, filmwriter, and playwright

OCTOBER

1

BIRTHS

1760. William Beckford (d. 2 May 1844). English writer of fiction and travel narrative

1791. Sergei Timofeyevitch Aksakov (d. 12 May 1859). Russian writer of fiction

1885. Louis Untermeyer (d. 18 December 1977). American poet, translator, biographer, anthologist, critical essayist, and writer of prose fiction

1893. Faith Cuthrell Baldwin (d. 19 March 1978). American writer of popular fiction and poet

1914. Daniel Joseph Boorstin. American historian, essayist, and librarian

DEATHS

1499. Marsilio Ficino (b. 19 October 1433). Italian philosopher, theologican, and essayist

1808. Thomas Thorild (b. 18 April 1759). Swedish poet, philosopher, and critical essayist

1873. Emile Gaboriau (b. 9 November 1832). French writer of fiction

1893. Benjamin Jowett (b. 15 April 1817). English classical scholar, translator, and essayist

1962. Ludwig Bemelmans (b. 27 April 1898). Austrian-born writer of miscellaneous prose nonfiction, illustrator, humorist, writer of fiction and of travel narrative, and writer of literature for children

1985. Elwyn Brooks White (b. 11 July 1899). American essayist, writer of fiction for adults and children, humorist, and language stylist

2

BIRTHS

1720. Elizabeth Montagu (d. 25 August 1800). English essayist

1857. Arthur Edward Waite (d. 19 May 1942). American-born poet and writer of prose nonfiction

1879. Wallace Stevens (d. 2 August 1955). American poet, playwright, and essayist

1901. Ignatius Roy Dunnachie Campbell (d. 22 April 1957). South African poet and essayist

1904. Henry Graham Greene. English writer of fiction and playwright

DEATHS

1842. William Ellery Channing (b. 7 April 1780). American theologian, essayist, and writer of sermon literature

1892. Joseph Ernest Renan (b. 28 February 1823). French philologist, historian, and essayist

1905. Jose Maria de Heredia (b. 22 November 1842). Cuban-born French poet

1981. Harry Lewis Golden (b. 6 May 1902). American journalist, essayist, humorist, and popular historian

1985. Rebecca Caudill (b. 2 February 1899). American writer of fiction, writer of prose fiction for children, and poet

3

BIRTHS

1554. Sir Fulke Grevill, first Baron Brooke (d. 30 September 1628). English poet, playwright, and biographer

1800. George Bancroft (d. 17 January 1891). American historian and essayist

1809. Alexey Vasilyevich Koltsov (d. 19 October 1842). Russian lyric poet

1886. Alain Fournier (d. 22 September 1914). French writer of fiction

1895. Sergei Aleksandrovich Esenin (d. 27 December 1925). Soviet Russian imagist poet

1897. Louis Marie Antoine Alfred Aragon (d. 24 December 1982). French poet and writer of fiction

1900. Thomas Clayton Wolfe (d. 15 September 1938). American writer of fiction, playwright, and essayist

1925. Gore Vidal. American writer of fiction, television playwright, satirist, and essayist

DEATHS

1972. Gladys Schmitt (b. 31 May 1909). American writer of historical fiction

1987. Jean Marie Lucien Pierre Anouilh (b. 23 June 1910). French playwright, editor, translator, and writer of fiction

4

BIRTHS

1741. Edmond Malone (d. 25 April 1812). Irish-born essayist, textual editor, and literary scholar

1787. Francois Pierre Guillaume Guizot (d. 13 September 1874). French historian, diplomat, essayist, and literary and historical textual editor

1797. Jeremias Gotthelf (d. 22 October 1854). Swiss clergyman and writer of fiction

1884. Alfred Damon Runyon (d. 10 December 1946). American journalist, sportswriter, and writer of fiction

1914. Brendan Gill. American journalist and essayist

DEATHS

1874. Barry Cornwall (pseudonym of Bryan Waller Procter; b. 21 November 1787). English poet and biographer

1902. Lionel Pigot Johnson (b. 15 March 1867). English critical essayist and poet

1974. Anne Harvey Sexton (b. 9 November 1928). American poet, playwright, and writer of books for children

1982. Howard Oliver Sackler (b. 19 December 1929). American playwright

5

BIRTHS

1703. Jonathan Edwards (d. 22 March 1758). Colonial American theologian, essayist, and writer of sermon literature

1713. Denis Diderot (d. 30 July 1784). French philosopher, essayist, encyclopaedist, writer of fiction, playwright, satirist, and art critic

1813. Antonio Garcia Gutierrez (d. 26 August 1884). Spanish poet, playwright, scientist, and essayist

1819. Jon Thoroddsen (d. 8 March 1868). Icelandic writer of fiction and poet

1840. John Addington Symonds (d. 10 April 1893). English poet, historian, and biographer

1911. Brian O'Nolan (born Brian O'Nuallain; d. 1 April 1966). Irish writer of fiction and playwright

1936. Vaclav Havel. Czech playwright, poet, and political leader

DEATHS

1864. Imre Madach (b. 21 January 1823). Hungarian poet and playwright

1969. Harry Emerson Fosdick (b. 24 May 1878). American theologian, essayist, and writer of sermon literature

6

BIRTHS

1823. George Henry Boker (d. 2 January 1890). American playwright and poet

1874. Mary Ursula Bethell (d. 15 January 1945). English-born New Zealand poet

1889. Henry FitzGerald Heard (d. 19 August 1971). English essayist

1895. Caroline Gordon (d. 11 April 1981). American writer of fiction and essayist

1916. Vern(on) John Sneider (d. 1 May 1981). American playwright and writer of fiction

DEATHS

1660. Paul Scarron (b. 4 July 1610). French poet, playwright, and writer of fiction

1892. Alfred Lord Tennyson (b. 6 August 1809). English poet and playwright

1896. William Morris (b. 24 March 1834). English poet, essayist, writer of short fiction, and translator

1907. David Masson (b. 2 December 1822). Scottish biographer and writer of miscellaneous prose nonfiction

1959. Bernhard Berenson (b. 26 June 1865). Lithuanian-born American art critic and art historian

1979. Elizabeth Bishop (b. 8 February 1911). American poet

7

BIRTHS

1629. Chu I-tsun (d. 14 November 1709). Chinese poet and scholar

1849. James Whitcomb Riley (d. 22 July 1916). American poet and writer of fiction

1859. Thomas James Wise (d. 13 May 1937). English bibliophile, literary forger, and pamphleteer

1907. Helen Clark MacInnes (d. 30 September 1985). Scottish-born American writer of fiction, filmwriter, and playwright

1927. Juan Benet Goitia. Spanish writer of fiction and essayist

1934. LeRoi Averelt Jones (also wrote under the name of Imamu Amiri Baraka). American poet, playwright, writer of fiction, and essayist

DEATHS

1577. George Gascoigne (b. ? 1539). English poet, playwright, writer of fiction, and essayist

1787. Heinrich Melchoir Muhlenberg (b. 6 September 1711). German-born colonial American theologian and essayist

1849. Edgar Allan Poe (b. 19 January 1809). American poet, writer of fiction, and critical essayist

1886. William Barnes (b. 22 February 1801). English dialect poet, playwright, and writer of miscellaneous prose nonfiction

1894. Oliver Wendell Holmes the elder (b. 29 August 1809). American physician, essayist, and poet

1932. Christopher John Brennan (b. 1 November 1870). Australian poet, playwright, and translator

1979. Wilmarth Sheldon Lewis (b. 14 November 1895). American bibliophile, literary scholar, textual editor, and essayist

8

BIRTHS

1619. Philipp von Zesen (d. 13 November 1689). German writer of fiction, lyric poet, and language reformer

1833. Edmund Clarence Stedman (d. 18 January 1908). American poet and essayist

1855. Edgar Evertson Saltus (d. 31 July 1921). American writer of fiction

1872. John Cowper Powys (d. 17 June 1963). English essayist, writer of fiction, and poet

1905. Meyer Levin (d. 9 July 1981). American writer of fiction and of miscellaneous prose nonfiction

DEATHS

1754. Henry Fielding (b. 22 April 1707). English writer of fiction, playwright, satirist, journalist, essayist, and writer of travel narrative

1803. Vittorio Alfieri (b. 16 January 1749). Italian poet and playwright

1874. Vitezslav Halek (b. 5 April 1835). Czech poet, writer of fiction, and playwright

1896. George Louis Palmella Busson du Maurier (b. 6 March 1834). French-born English writer of fiction

1910. Maria Wasilowska Konopnicka (b. 23 May 1842). Polish poet and writer of fiction

1914. Adelaide Crapsey (b. 9 September 1878). American poet

1927. Mary Gladys Webb (b. 25 March 1881). English writer of fiction

1945. Felix Salten (b. 6 September 1869). Austrian writer of fiction

1965. Thomas Bertram Costain (b. 8 May 1885). Canadian-born American periodicals editor and writer of popular historical fiction

9

BIRTHS

1863. Edward William Bok (d. 9 January 1930). Dutch-born American historian, editor, and autobiographer

Gamaliel Bradford (d. 11 April 1932). American historian and biographer

1899. Bruce Catton (d. 28 August 1978). American historian

1906. Leopold Sedar Senghor. Senegalese poet and political leader

DEATHS

1729. Sir Richard Blackmore (b. ? 1653). English physician, poet, historian, and writer of medical tracts

1967. Andre Maurois (b. 26 July 1885). French literary historian, biographer, and writer of fiction

1988. Edward Chodorov (b. 17 April 1904). American playwright

10

BIRTHS

1560. Jacobus Arminius (originally Jacob Harmensen; d. 19 October 1609). Dutch theologian and essayist

1780. John Abercrombie (d. 14 November 1844). Scottish philosopher and essayist

1802. Hugh Miller (d. 23 December 1856). Scottish writer of miscellaneous prose nonfiction

1834. Aleksis Kivi (pseudonym of Aleksis Stenvall; d. 31 December 1872). Finnish poet, playwright, and writer of fiction

1895. Lin Yu-T'ang (d. 26 March 1976). Chinese-born essayist and philosopher

1924. James Dumaresq Clavell. English-born American writer of fiction and filmwriter

1930. Harold Pinter. English poet, playwright, and filmwriter

DEATHS

1791. Christian Friedrich Daniel Schubart (b. 13 April 1739). German poet and satirist

1827. Ugo Foscolo (b. 6 February 1778). Italian poet

1837. Francois Maria Fourier (b. 7 April 1772). French social theorist and essayist

11

BIRTHS

1671. Samuel Clarke (d. 7 May 1729). English philosopher, textual editor, and essayist

1759. Mason Locke Weems (d. 23 May 1825). American churchman, bookseller, biographer, and moral essayist

1782. Steen Steensen Blicher (d. 28 March 1848). Danish poet, writer of fiction, and translator

1881. Stark Young (d. 6 January 1963). American writer of fiction and critical essayist

1885. Francois Mauriac (d. 1 September 1970). French writer of fiction, playwright, and critical essayist

DEATHS

1531. Ulrich (Huldreich) Zwingli (b. 1 January 1484). Swiss theologian and essayist

1919. Karl Adolf Gjellerup (b. 2 June 1857). Danish poet and writer of fiction

1963. Jean Maurice Eugene Clement Cocteau (b. 5 July 1889). French playwright, poet, writer of fiction, and critical essayist

1977. McKinlay Kantor (b. 4 February 1904). American writer of historical fiction

12

BIRTHS

1775. Lyman Beecher (d. 19 January 1863). American theologian and essayist

1844. George Washington Cable (d. 31 January 1925). American writer of fiction

1896. Eugenio Montale (d. 28 September 1981). Italian poet and critical essayist

1908. Paul Hamilton Engle. American poet, writer of fiction, and academician

1910. Robert Stuart Fitzgerald (d. 16 January 1985). American poet, translator, critical essayist, and academician

1927. Charles Gordone. American playwright

13

BIRTHS

1797. Thomas Haynes Bayly (d. 22 April 1839). English poet, writer of fiction, and playwright

1807. Hans Conon von der Gabelentz (d. 3 September 1874). German linguist, essayist, and scholar of the Melanesian languages

1890. Conrad Michael Richter (d. 30 October 1968). American writer of fiction

1902. Arna Wendell Bontemps (d. 4 June 1973). American writer of fiction

1910. Ernest Kellogg Gann. American writer of fiction and memoirist

1925. Frank Daniel Gilroy. American playwright and writer of fiction

DEATHS

1715. Nicolas de Malebranche (b. 6 August 1638). French philosopher, theologian, psychologist, and essayist

1869. Charles Augustin Sainte-Beauve (b. 23 December 1804). French critical essayist

1882. Joseph Arthur Gobineau (b. 14 July 1816). French Orientalist scholar, philosopher, and essayist

1924. Anatole France (born Anatole Francois Thibault; b. 16 April 1844). French writer of fiction, critical essayist, and satirist

14

BIRTHS

1814. Thomas Osborne Davis (d. 16 September 1845). Irish poet and political essayist

1888. Katherine Mansfield (born Kathleen Mansfield Beauchamp; d. 9 January 1923). New Zealand-born writer of fiction

1894. E. E. Cummings (d. 2 September 1962). American writer of innovative typographical verse, playwright, and writer of fiction

1906. Hannah Arendt (d. 4 December 1975). German-born American political theorist, essayist, academician, and scholar

DEATHS

1619. Samuel Daniel (b. ? 1562[?]). English poet, playwright, critical essayist, translator, and historian

1885. Josh Billings (pseudonym of Henry Wheeler Shaw; b. 21 April 1818). American humorist

1965. Randall Jarrell (b. 6 May 1914). American poet, playwright, writer of fiction, critical essayist, and writer of books for children

15

BIRTHS

1685. Allan Ramsay (d. 7 January 1758). Scottish poet

1753. Elizabeth Inchbald (d. 1 August 1821). English writer of fiction and playwright

1814. Mikhail Yurievich Lermontov (d. 27 July 1841). Russian poet, writer of fiction, and verse dramatist

1830. Helen Maria Hunt Jackson (d. 12 August 1885). American poet and writer of travel narrative, books for children, and fiction

1844. Friedrich Nietzsche (d. 25 August 1900). German philosopher, critic, and essayist

1881. Pelham Grenville Wodehouse (d. 14 February 1975). English humorist, satirist, and writer of fiction

1905. Charles Percy Snow (d. 1 July 1980). English scientist, writer of fiction, and critical essayist

1908. John Kenneth Galbraith. American economist, essayist, academician, and diplomat

1917. Arthur Meier Schlesinger, Jr. American historian and biographer

1920. Mario Puzo. American writer of popular fiction

1923. Italo Calvino (d. 19 September 1985). Italian writer of fiction, essayist, and translator

1926. Evan Hunter. American writer of popular fiction

DEATHS

1865. Andres Bello (b. 29 November 1781). Chilean poet, scholar, and statesman

1973. John Brick (b. 1 January 1922). American historical novelist

1980. Mary O'Hara (b. 10 July 1885). American writer of fiction

16

BIRTHS

1708. Albrecht von Haller (d. 12 December 1777). Swiss scientist, poet, and scientific bibliographer

1758. Noah Webster (d. 28 May 1843). American philologist, lexicographer, essayist, and periodicals editor

1854. Oscar Fingall O'Flahertie Wills Wilde (d. 3 November 1900). Irish playwright, poet, writer of fiction, essayist, and literary critic

1888. Eugene Gladstone O'Neill (d. 27 November 1953). American playwright and poet

1893. Carl Carmer (d. 11 September 1976). American folklorist and essayist

1906. Cleanth Brooks. American literary critic and essayist

1908. Robert Ardrey (d. 14 January 1980). American anthropologist and essayist

1927. Gunter Wilhelm Grass. German writer of fiction, essayist, poet, playwright, and film-writer

DEATHS

1725. Sir Ralph Thoresby (b. 16 August 1658). English antiquarian and essayist

17

BIRTHS

1711. Jupiter Hammon (d. ? 1790). American poet

1813. Georg Buchner (d. 19 February 1837). German playwright

1864. Elinor Sutherland Glyn (d. 23 September 1943). English writer of fiction

1885. Isak Dinesen (pseudonym of Karen Blixen; d. 7 September 1962). Danish writer of fiction

1900. Arthur Yvor Winters (d. 25 January 1968). American poet and critical essayist

1903. Nathanael West (pseudonym of Nathan Wallenstein Weinstein; d. 22 December 1940). American writer of fiction and film-writer

1915. Arthur Miller. American playwright, writer of fiction, and essayist

1930. James (Jimmy) Breslin. American journalist and writer of fiction

DEATHS

1586. Sir Philip Sidney (b. 30 November 1554). English poet, writer of fiction, and essayist

1797. Elijah Ben Solomon (b. 23 April 1720). Lithuanian-born Hebrew theologian and essayist

1836. George Colman the younger (b. 21 October 1862). English playwright

1889. Nikolay Gavrolovich Chernyshevsky (b. 12 July 1828). Russian critical essayist and writer of fiction

1910. Julia Ward Howe (b. 27 May 1819). American poet, essayist, and biographer

1979. Sidney Joseph Perelman (b. 1 February 1904). American social satirist, essayist, and comic playwright

18

BIRTHS

1631. Michael Wigglesworth (d. 19 June 1705). English-born colonial American churchman, poet, and writer of verse essays

1785. Thomas Love Peacock (d. 23 January 1866). English writer of fiction and poet

1809. Thomas Holley Chivers (d. 18 December 1858). American poet, playwright, and biographer

1824. Juan Valera y Alcala Galiano (d. 18 April 1905). Spanish writer of fiction and critical essayist

1859. Henri Bergson (d. 4 Jaunary 1941). French philosopher and essayist

1878. James Truslow Adams (d. 18 May 1949). American historian and essayist

1889. Fannie Hurst (d. 23 February 1968). American writer of fiction

1896. Harold Lenoir Davis (d. 31 October 1960). American poet and writer of fiction

1906. Sidney Kingsley. American playwright

DEATHS

1878. David Laing (b. 20 April 1793). Scottish antiquarian and essayist

1909. Alfredo Oriani (b. 22 August 1852). Italian critical theorist and essayist

1955. Jose Ortego y Gasset (b. 9 May 1883). Spanish humanist and literary and critical essayist

1980. Edwin May Teale (b. 2 June 1899). American writer of nonfiction prose relative to nature

1936. Lu Hsun (pseudonym of Chou Shujen; b. 25 September 1881). Chinese writer of fiction and essayist

1950. Edna St. Vincent Millay (b. 22 February 1892). American poet, playwright, and translator

19

BIRTHS

1433. Marsilio Ficino (d. 1 October 1499). Italian philosopher, theologian, and essayist

1605. Sir Thomas Browne (d. 19 October 1682). English physician and noral essayist

1634. Wang Shih-Chen (d. 26 June 1711). Chinese poet

1784. James Henry Leigh Hunt (d. 28 August 1859). English essayist, poet, and playwright

1895. Lewis Mumford. American critical essayist

1899. Miguel Angel Asturias (d. 9 June 1974). Guatemalan writer of fiction and poet

1931. John LeCarre (pseudonym of David John Moore Cornwell). English writer of adventure and espionage fiction

DEATHS

1609. Jacobus Arminius (born Jacob Harmensen; b. 10 October 1560). Dutch theologian and essayist

1682. Sir Thomas Browne (b. 19 October 1605). English physician and moral essayist

1745. Jonathan Swift (b. 30 November 1667). Irish-born essayist, satirist, political pamphleteer, poet, and writer of fiction

1814. Mercy Otis Warren (b. 23 September 1728). American playwright, political satirist, historian, and writer of fiction

1842. Alexey Vasilyevich Koltsov (b. 3 October 1809). Russian lyric poet

1909. Cesare Lombroso (b. 18 November 1836). Italian criminologist, phychiatrist, theorist, and essayist

1920. John Reed (b. 22 October 1887). American poet, journalist, and political commentator upon contemporary events

20

BIRTHS

1762. Andre-Marie Chenier (d. 25 July 1794). French poet and political pamphleteer

1854. Jean Nicolas Arthur Rimbaud (d. 10 November 1891). Belgian writer of prose and verse poems

1891. Samuel Flagg Bemis (d. 26 September 1973). American diplomatic historian

1895. Morris (Morrie) Ryskind (d. 24 August 1985). American comic playwright

1905. Frederic Dannay (d. 3 September 1982). American writer of mystery and detective fiction

1932. Michael Thomas McClure. American poet, playwright, and writer of fiction.

DEATHS

1880. Lydia Maria Frances Child (b. 11 February 1802). American reform advocate, essayist, and writer of didactic fiction

1890. Sir Richard Francis Burton (b. 19 March 1821). English explorer, anthropologist, writer of nonfiction narrative, essayist, and translator

1900. Charles Dudley Warner (b. 12 September 1829). American lawyer, periodicals editor, essayist, biographer, and literary and intellectual historian

21

BIRTHS

1762. George Colman the younger (d. 17 October 1836). English playwright

1772. Samuel Taylor Coleridge (b. 25 July 1834). English poet, playwright, and critical essayist

1790. Alphonse-Marie-Louis de Prat de Lamartine (d. 28 February 1869). French poet, historian, and essayist

1845. Will(iam) McKendree Carleton (d. ? 1912). American poet

1869. William Edward Dodd (d. 9 February 1940). American historian, essayist, and diplomat

1896. Eugenio Montale (d. 12 September 1981). Italian poet, writer of fiction, and translator

DEATHS

1556. Pietro Aretino (b. 20 April 1492). Italian poet and writer of verse drama

1558. Julius Caesar Scaliger (b. 23 April 1484). Italian-born French scholar, poet, essayist, and translator

1687. Edmund Waller (b. 6 March 1606). English poet, playwright, biographer, and parliamentarian

1872. Jean Henri Merle d'Aubigne (b. 16 August 1794). French ecclesiastical historian and essayist

1873. Johan Sebastian Welhaven (b. 22 December 1807). Norwegian poet and critical essayist

1931. Arthur Schnitzler (b. 15 May 1862). Austrian playwright and writer of fiction

1969. Jean Louis-Lebrid de (Jack) Kerouac (b. 12 March 1922). American "Beat" writer of fiction and poet

22

BIRTHS

1740. Sir Philip Francis the younger (d. 23 December 1818). English political essayist

1818. Charles Marie Rene Leconte de Lisle (d. 17 July 1894). French poet and translator

1870. Ivan Alexeyevich Bunin (d. 8 November 1953). Russian poet and writer of fiction

1887. John Reed (d. 19 October 1920). American poet, journalist, and political commentator upon contemporary world events

1919. Doris May Taylor Lessing. Persian-born, Rhodesian-raised English writer of fiction

DEATHS

1565. Jean Grolier de Servieres (b. ? 1479). French bibliophile, bibliographer, and librarian

1758. Thomas Prince (b. 15 May 1687). American historian and essayist

1854. Jeremias Gotthelf (b. 4 October 1797). Swiss clergyman and writer of fiction

1882. Janos Arany (b. 2 March 1817). Hungarian poet, satirist, and translator

1883. Thomas Mayne Reid (b. 4 April 1818). English-born American writer of fiction

1897. Justin Winsor (b. 2 January 1831). American librarian, historian, and essayist

1903. William Edward Hartpole Lecky (b. 26 March 1838). Irish historian and essayist

1965. Paul Johannes Tillich (b. 20 August 1886). German Protestant theologian, philosopher, and essayist

1972. James Keir Baxter (b. 29 June 1926). New Zealand poet, playwright, and writer of miscellaneous prose nonfiction

1975. Arnold Joseph Toynbee (b. 14 April 1889). English historian, economist, and essayist

1982. Richard Franklin Hugo (b. 21 December 1923). American poet

23

BIRTHS

1734. Nicolas-Edme Restiff de la Bretonne (d. 3 February 1806). French writer of fiction and essayist

1773. Francis Jeffrey (d. 26 January 1850). Scottish essayist and reviewer

1817. Pierre-Athanase Larousse (d. 3 January 1875). French lexicographer, encyclopaedist, and essayist

1831. Basil Lanneau Gildersleeve (d. 9 January 1924). American philologist, classical scholar, and essayist

1838. Francis Hopkinson Smith (d. 7 April 1915). American writer of travel narrative and of fiction and illustrator

1942. John Michael Crichton. American writer of fiction

DEATHS

1867. Franz Bopp (b. 14 September 1791). German philologist, linguist, and essayist

1872. Pierre Jule Theophile Gautier (b. 30 August 1811). French poet, essayist, and writer of fiction

1874. Abraham Geiger (b. 24 May 1810). German Jewish scholar, Biblical historian, and essayist

1939. Zane Grey (b. 31 January 1872). American writer of fiction

1941. Shailer Mathews (b. 26 May 1863). American theologian, educator, and essayist

1946. Ernest Thompson Seton (b. 14 August 1860). English-born American writer of fiction for boys

1981. Mary Coyle Chase (b. 25 October 1907). American playwright and writer of literature for children

1986. John Gerard Braine (b. 13 April 1922). English writer of fiction and playwright

24

BIRTHS

1710. Alban Butler (d. 15 May 1773). English religious biographer

1788. Sarah Joseph Buell Hale (d. 30 April 1879). American essayist, periodicals editor, advocate of education reform, writer of fiction, poet, and biographer

1904. Moss Hart (d. 20 December 1961). American playwright and librettist

1915. Marghanita Laski (d. 6 February 1988). English writer of fiction, playwright, and essayist

1923. Denise Levertov. English-born American poet, writer of fiction, and essayist

1930. Elaine Feinstein. English poet, writer of fiction, and translator

DEATHS

1601. Tycho Brahe (b. 14 December 1546). Danish astronomer and essayist

1655. Pierre Gassendi (b. 22 January 1592). French philosopher, mathematician, essayist, and biographer

1970. Richard Hofstadter (b. 6 August 1916). American intellectual historian

25

BIRTHS

1735. James Beattie (d. 18 August 1803). Scottish poet and essayist

1759. Henri Benjamin Constant de Rebecque (d. 8 December 1830). French political philosopher, essayist, and writer of fiction

1795. John Pendleton Kennedy (d. 18 August 1870). American writer of fiction

1800. Thomas Babington Macaulay (d. 28 December 1859). English political philosopher, essayist, historian, biographer, literary critic, and poet

1902. Henry Steele Commager. American historian, essayist, biographer, and academician

1907. Mary Coyle Chase (d. 23 October 1981). American playwright and writer of literature for children

1914. John Berryman (d. 7 January 1971). American poet, writer of fiction, and biographer

DEATHS

1902. Benjamin Franklin (Frank) Norris (b. 5 March 1870). American writer of fiction and essayist

1971. Philip Wylie (b. 12 May 1902). American writer of fiction and essayist

1981. Ariel Durant (b. 10 May 1898). American essayist and writer on the history of ideas

1989. Mary Therese McCarthy (b. 21 June 1912). American writer of fiction

26

BIRTHS

1466. Desiderius Erasmus (d. 12 July 1536). Dutch humanist, essayist, Biblical translator and commentator, and satirist

1673. Dimitrie Kantemir (d. 21 August 1723). Moldavian historian and essayist

1787. Vuk Stefanovic Karadzic (d. 26 January 1864). Yugoslavian (Serbian) poet, philologist, essayist, translator, and anthologist

1879. Leon Davidovich Trotsky (d. 21 August 1940). Russian political philosopher, historian, essayist, biographer, and diarist

1886. Charles Vincent Emerson Starrett (d. 4 January 1974). Canadian-born American essayist, poet, and writer of miscellaneous prose nonfiction

1930. John Arden. English playwright and writer of fiction

DEATHS

1852. Vincenzo Gioberti (b. 5 April 1801). Italian philosopher, political theorist, and essayist

1890. Carlo Collodi (originally Carlo Lorenzini; b. 24 November 1826). Italian journalist and writer of fiction for children (*Pinocchio*)

1957. Nikos Kazantzakis (b. 2 December 1885). Greek writer of fiction

27

BIRTHS

1736. James Macpherson (d. 17 February 1796). Scottish poet, historian, and translator of the classics

1844. Klas P. Arnoldson (d. 20 February 1916). Swedish political essayist

1844. Robert Seymour Bridges (d. 21 April 1930). English poet, playwright, and critical essayist

1889. Enid Algerine Bagnold, Lady Jones (d. 31 March 1981). English writer of fiction and playwright

1914. Dylan Marlais Thomas (d. 9 November 1953). Welsh poet, playwright, writer for radio and films, writer of fiction, and miscellaneous prose writer

1932. Sylvia Plath (d. 11 February 1963). American poet, playwright, and writer of fiction

DEATHS

1553. Michael Servetus (b. ? 1511). Spanish-born theologian, physician, and essayist

1845. Carolina Oliphant, Baroness Nairne (b. 16 August 1766). Scottish poet

1938. Lascelles Abercrombie (b. 9 January 1881). English poet and critical essayist

1975. Rex Todhunter Stout (b. 1 December 1886). American writer of detective and mystery fiction

1977. James Mallahan Cain (b. 1 July 1892). American writer of fiction

28

BIRTHS

1495. Luigi Alamanni (d. 18 April 1556). Italian poet

1585. Cornelius Jansen (d. 6 May 1638). Dutch theologian and essayist

1903. Evelyn Arthur St. John Waugh (d. 10 April 1966). English writer of fiction

1904. George Bubb Dangerfield (d. 27 December 1986). American historian and essayist

1939. Armah (George) Ayi Kwei. Ghanaian writer of fiction and poet

DEATHS

1704. John Locke (b. 29 August 1632). English philosopher and essayist

1754. Friedrich von Hagedorn (b. 23 April 1708). German poet

1844. Sandor Kisfaludy (b. 27 September 1772). Hungarian poet

29

BIRTHS

1740. James Boswell (d. 19 May 1795). Scottish-born biographer, memoirist, writer of travel narrative, and poet

1815. Daniel Decatur Emmett (d. 28 June 1904). American writer of verse and popular songs ("Dixie")

1882. Hippolyte Jean Giraudoux (d. 31 January 1944). French poet, writer of fiction, and playwright

1910. Alfred Jules Ayer (d. 27 June 1989). English philosopher and essayist

DEATHS

1618. Sir Walter Ralegh (b. ? 1552). English poet and writer of miscellaneous prose nonfiction

1911. Joseph Pulitzer (b. 10 April 1847). Hungarian-born American newspaper publisher and sponsor of awards in literature, journalism, drama, and music

1924. Frances Eliza Hodgson Burnett (b. 24 November 1849). English-born American writer of fiction, playwright, and writer of literature for children

1958. Zoe Akins (b. 30 October 1886). American playwright and writer of fiction

30

BIRTHS

1751. Richard Brinsley Sheridan (d. 7 July 1816). English playwright, poet, and theatre manager

1857. Gertrude Franklin Atherton (d. 14 June 1948). American writer of fiction, poet, writer of autobiographical narrative, essayist, and writer of miscellaneous prose nonfiction

1871. Paul Ambroise Toussaint Jules Valery (d. 20 July 1945). French poet and writer of philosophical and speculative prose nonfiction

1881. Elizabeth Madox Roberts (d. 13 March 1941). English writer of fiction and poet

1885. Ezra Weston Loomis Pound (d. 1 November 1972). American-born poet and essayist

1886. Zoe Akins (d. 29 October 1958). American playwright and writer of fiction

1941. Larry Alfred Woiwode. American writer of fiction and poet.

DEATHS

1842. Allan Cunningham (b. 7 December 1784). Scottish poet, writer of fiction, textual editor, essayist, biographer, and anthologist

1910. Jean Henri Dunant (b. 8 May 1828). Swiss philanthropist and essayist

1919. Ella Wheeler Wilcox (b. 5 November 1850). American poet and writer of fiction

1956. Pio Baroja y Nessi (b. 28 December 1872). Spanish writer of fiction

1968. Conrad Michael Richter (b. 13 October 1890). American writer of fiction

31

BIRTHS

1620. John Evelyn (d. 27 February 1706). English diarist and writer of miscellaneous prose nonfiction

1724. Christopher Anstey (d. 3 August 1805). English writer of humorous and colloquial verse

1795. John Keats (d. 23 February 1821). English poet

1817. Heinrich Graetz (d. 7 September 1891). German Jewish historian and essayist

1821. Karl Havlicek (pseudonym of Havel Borousky; d. 29 July 1856). Czech literary critic, journalist, and poet

1852. Mary Eleanor Wilkins Freeman (d. 13 March 1930). American writer of fiction

1857. Axel Martin Fredrik Munthe (d. 11 February 1949). Swedish psychiatrist, essayist, and memoirist

1880. Julia Mood Peterkin (d. 10 August 1961). American writer of fiction

1895. Basil Henry Liddell Hart (d. 29 January 1970). English historian, military scientist, essayist, and encyclopaedist

1925. Robert (Robin) Lowell Moore, Jr. American writer of fiction

DEATHS

1556. Johannes Sleidanus (pseudonym of Johannes Philippi; b. ? 1506). German historian, essayist, biographer, and diplomat

1960. Harold Lenoir Davis (b. 18 October 1896). American poet and writer of fiction

1987. Joseph Campbell (b. 26 March 1904). American scholar, mythologist, and critical essayist

NOVEMBER

1

BIRTHS

1530. Etienne de la Boetie (d. 18 August 1563). French poet, translator, and essayist

1636. Nicolas Boileau-Despreaux (d. 11 March 1711[?]). French critical essayist and satirist

1870. Christopher John Brennan (d. 7 October 1932). Australian poet and playwright

1871. Stephen Townley Crane (d. 5 June 1900). American writer of fiction and journalist

1880. Sholem Asch (d. 10 July 1957). Polish-born writer of fiction and of drama in Yiddish

Henry Grantland Rice (d. 13 July 1954). American journalist, sportswriter, and essayist

1886. Hermann Broch (d. 30 May 1951). German writer of fiction

1896. Edmund Charles Blunden (d. 20 January 1974). English poet, playwright, writer of fiction, biographer, and critical essayist

1921. Ilse Aichinger. Austrian writer of fiction, poet, and playwright

DEATHS

1746. Francis Hutcheson (b. 8 August 1694). Irish philosophical essayist

1903. Theodor Mommsen (b. 30 November 1817). German historian, textual editor, and essayist

1922. Thomas Nelson Page (b. 23 April 1853). American writer of fiction and poet

1972. Ezra Weston Loomis Pound (b. 30 October 1885). American-born poet and writer of miscellaneous prose nonfiction

1973. Catherine Shober Drinker Bowen (b. 1 January 1897). American fictional biographer

2

BIRTHS

1808. Jules Amedee Barbey D'Aurevilly (d. 23 April 1889). French writer of fiction and essayist

1883. Martin Archer Flavin (d. 27 December 1967). American writer of fiction and playwright

DEATHS

1781. Jose Francisco de Isla (b. 24 April 1703). Spanish writer of fiction, translator, and satirist

1846. Esaias Tegner (b. 13 November 1782). Swedish poet

1953. Emile Cammaerts (b. 16 March 1878). Belgian poet

3

BIRTHS

1500. Benvenuto Cellini (d. 13 February 1571). Italian artist, craftsman, and writer of autobiographical narrative

1794. William Cullen Bryant (d. 12 June 1878). American poet, essayist, translator, textual editor, and anthologist

1815. John Mitchell (d. 20 March 1875). Irish writer of miscellaneous prose nonfiction

1830. John Esten Cooke (d. 27 September 1886). American writer of fiction and biographer

1901. Andre Malraux (d. 23 November 1976). French writer of social fiction; essayist on such subjects as art history, archaeology, and anthropology; and government minister

1903. Julian Parks Boyd (d. 21 May 1980). American historian, essayist, and editor

DEATHS

1900. Oscar Fingall O'Flahertie Wills Wilde (b. 16 October 1854). Irish-born playwright, writer of fiction, essayist, and poet

4

BIRTHS

1569. Guillen de Castro y Bellvis (d. 28 July 1631). Spanish playwright

1740. Augustus Montagu Toplady (d. 14 August 1778). English churchman, poet, hymnodist, and pamphleteer

1771. James Montgomery (d. 30 April 1854). Scottish poet

1812. Aleardo Aleardi (d. 17 July 1878). Italian lyric poet

1862. Eden Phillpotts (d. 29 December 1960). Indian-born English writer of fiction, poet, and playwright

1873. Kyoka Izumi (pseudonym of Izumi Kyotaro; d. 7 September 1939). Japanese writer of fiction

1906. Sterling North (d. 22 December 1974). American writer of fiction, poet, essayist, and biographer

1850. Ella Wheeler Wilcox (d. 30 October 1919). American poet and writer of fiction

1857. Ida Minerva Tarbell (d. 6 January 1944). American essayist, biographer, and advocate of social and economic reform

1884. James Elroy Flecker (d. 3 January 1915). English poet and playwright

1885. William James Durant (d. 7 November 1981). American essayist, intellectual historian, and writer on the history of Western ideas

1895. Charles Gordon MacArthur (d. 21 April 1956). American playwright

1937. Geoffrey Ansell Wolff. American biographer and writer of fiction

DEATHS

1670. Johannes Amos Comenius (b. 28 March 1592). Czech educational reformer, essayist, and writer of books for children

1764. Charles Churchill (b. ? February 1732). English poet and satirist

1895. Eugene Field (b. 2 September 1850). American journalist, essayist, and writer of verse

1907. Diego Barros Arana (b. 16 August 1830). Chilean historian, educator, and essayist

1918. Wilfrid Edward Salter Owen (b. 18 March 1893). English poet

1950. George Bernard Shaw (b. 26 July 1856). Irish-born playwright, writer of fiction, and critical essayist

1961. James Grover Thurber (b. 8 December 1894). American writer of fiction, essayist, and humorist

DEATHS

1804. Elisabeth Wolff-Bekker (b. 24 July 1738). Dutch writer of fiction, poet, essayist, and translator

1909. William Torrey Harris (b. 10 September 1835). American philosopher, essayist, educator, and literary critic

1931. Ole Edvart Rolvaag (b. 22 April 1876). Norwegian-born American writer of fiction and of prose narrative nonfiction

1975. Lionel Trilling (b. 4 July 1905). American journalist, critical essayist, and writer of fiction

6

BIRTHS

1671. Colley Cibber (d. 11 December 1757). English poet, playwright, memoirist, and theatre manager

1781. Lucy Aiken (d. 29 January 1864). English historian, biographer, and writer of books for children

1833. Jonas Lauritz Idemil Lie (d. 5 July 1908). Norwegian writer of fiction, playwright, and poet

1866. Jens Johannes Jorgensen (d. ? 1956). Danish writer of fiction, poet, and essayist

5

BIRTHS

1494. Hans Sachs (d. 19 January 1576). German poet and playwright

1558. Thomas Kyd (d. ? December 1594). English playwright

1779. Washington Allston (d. 9 July 1843). American writer of fiction, poet, and essayist

1921. James Jones (d. 9 May 1977). American writer of fiction

DEATHS

1836. Karel Hynek Macha (b. 16 November 1810). Czech poet and writer of fiction

1842. William Hone (b. 3 June 1780). English bookseller, pamphleteer, and critical essayist

1901. Catherine (Kate) Greenaway (b. 17 March 1846). English artist and illustrator of books for children

1941. Maurice Le Blanc (b. 11 December 1864). French writer of fiction and playwright

1976. Patrick Dennis (pseudonym of Edward Everett Tanner III; b. 18 May 1921). American writer of popular fiction

1982. Frank Arthur Swinnerton (b. 12 August 1884). English writer of fiction and essayist

7

BIRTHS

1810. Fritz Reuter (d. 12 July 1874). German writer of fiction and poet

1811. Karel Jaromir Erben (d. 21 November 1870). Czech poet, scholar, and essayist

1838. Jean Marie Mathias Philippe Auguste, Comte de Villiers de L'Isle-Adam (d. 19 August 1889). French writer of symbolist fiction, playwright, and satirist

1872. Leonora von Stosch Speyer (d. 10 February 1956). American poet

1893. Margaret Leech (d. 24 February 1974). American historical essayist and writer of fiction

1897. Ruth Pitter. English poet

1913. Albert Camus (d. 4 January 1960). French philosopher, writer of fiction, poet, playwright, and journalist

1924. Wolf Mankowitz. American playwright

1929. Benny Allan Andersen. Danish poet and writer of fiction

DEATHS

1974. Eric Robert Russell Linklater (b. 8 March 1899). Scottish writer of fiction, playwright, and poet

1978. Janet Flanner (b. 13 March 1892). American journalist and writer of fiction

1981. William James Durant (b. 5 November 1885). American essayist, intellectual historian, and commentator upon the history of Western ideas

8

BIRTHS

1711. Mikhail Vasilievich Lomonosov (d. 4 April 1765). Russian philologist, poet, essayist, and scientist

1732. John Dickinson (d. 14 February 1808). American lawyer, essayist, and poet

1763. Xavier de Maistre (d. 12 June 1852). French writer of fiction and writer of personal meditations

1900. Margaret Mitchell (d. 16 August 1949). American writer of fiction

1908. Wallace Fowlie. American poet and essayist

1910. Harnett Thomas Kane (d. 4 September 1984). American writer of fiction

1916. Peter Weiss (d. 10 May 1982). Swedish experimental playwright

DEATHS

1674. John Milton (b. 9 December 1608). English poet, essayist, and verse dramatist

1893. Francis Parkman (b. 16 September 1823). American historian, essayist, and writer of travel narrative

1908. Victorian Sardou (b. 5 September 1831). French playwright

1911. William Clark Russell (b. 24 February 1844). American-born English writer of fiction and poet

1953. Ivan Alexeyevich Bunin (b. 22 October 1870). Russian poet and writer of fiction

9

BIRTHS

1721. Mark Akenside (d. 23 June 1770). English poet and essayist

1818. Ivan Sergeyevich Turgenev (d. 3 September 1883). Russian writer of fiction

1832. Emile Gaboriau (d. 1 October 1873). French writer of fiction

1928. Anne Sexton (originally Ann Gray Harvey; d. 4 October 1974). American poet, playwright, and writer of books for children

1934. Carl Edward Sagan. American astronomer, popularizer of scientific information, and essayist

DEATHS

1623. William Camden (b. 2 May 1551). English antiquary, historian, and essayist

1911. Howard Pyle (b. 5 March 1853). American writer of books for children, illustrator, and painter

1953. Dylan Marlais Thomas. (b. 27 October 1914). Welsh poet, playwright, writer of plays for films and radio, writer of fiction, and writer of miscellaneous prose nonfiction

1958. Dorothy Canfield Fisher (b. 17 February 1879). American writer of fiction

10

BIRTHS

1483. Martin Luther (d. 18 February 1546). German theologian, essayist, and poet

1577. Jacob Cats (d. 12 September 1660). Dutch diplomat, lawyer, poet, and writer of autobiographical prose narrative

1730(?). Oliver Goldsmith (d. 4 April 1774). Irish-born writer of fiction, playwright, poet, and essayist

1759. Johann Christoph Friedrich Schiller (d. 9 May 1805). German playwright, poet, and historian

1874. Donald Baxter Macmillan (d. 7 September 1970). American explorer and writer of prose nonfiction narrative

1879. Nicholas Vachel Lindsay (d. 5 December 1931). American poet and writer of miscellaneous nonfiction prose narrative

1887. Arnold Zweig (d. 26 November 1968). German writer of fiction, playwright, and essayist

1893. John Phillips Marquand (d. 16 July 1960). American writer of fiction and satirist

1913. Karl Jay Shapiro. American poet, playwright, writer of fiction, essayist, and biographer

DEATHS

1891. Jean Nicolas Arthur Rimbaud (b. 20 October 1854). Belgian writer of prose and verse poems

1918. Guillaume Apollinaire (b. 26 August 1880). French poet, writer of fiction, and essayist

11

BIRTHS

1821. Fyodor Mikhailovich Dostoyevsky (d. 9 February 1881). Russian writer of fiction

1836. Thomas Bailey Aldrich (d. 19 March 1907). American writer of fiction, poet, and periodicals editor

1901. Francis Van Wyck Mason (d. 28 August 1978). American writer of fiction

1914. Howard Melvin Fast. American writer of historical fiction, biography, playwright, and writer of fiction for children

1922. Kurt Vonnegut, Jr. American writer of fiction, essayist, filmwriter, and reviewer

1928. Carlos Fuentes. Mexican writer of fiction, playwright, essayist, and filmwriter

DEATHS

1751. Julien Offroy de Lamettrie (b. 25 December 1709). French materialist philosopher, essayist, and satirist

1855. Soren Aaby Kierkegaard (b. 5 May 1813). Danish theologian, philosopher, and essayist

1927. Ricardo Guiraldes (b. 13 February 1886). Argintinian writer of fiction and poet

1971. Walter Van Tilberg Clark (b. 3 August 1909). American writer of fiction and poet

    Alan Patrick Herbert (b. 24 September 1890). English writer of fiction and essayist

1980. Andrei Alekseyevich Amalrik (b. 12 May 1938). Russian playwright and writer of narrative nonfiction prose

12

BIRTHS

1615. Richard Baxter (d. 8 December 1691). English writer of theological prose tracts

1651. Sor Juana Ines de la Cruz (d. ? 1695). Spanish poet and playwright

1769. Amelia Briggs Opie (d. 2 December 1853). English writer of fiction and poet

1906. George Dillon (d. ? May 1968). American poet

1915. Roland Barthes (d. 25 March 1980). French critical essayist and theorist

DEATHS

1813. Michael-Guillaume-Jean de Crevecoeur (b. 3 January 1734). French-born American writer of travel narrative and essayist

1865. Elizabeth Cleghorn Gaskell (b. 29 September 1810). English writer of fiction

1984. Chester Bomar Himes (b. 29 July 1909). American writer of fiction and essayist

13

BIRTHS

1714. William Shenstone (d. 11 February 1763). English poet and writer of miscellaneous prose nonfiction

1782. Esaias Tegner (d. 2 November 1846). Swedish poet

1792. Edward John Trelawney (d. 13 August 1881). English writer of fiction and of biographical prose narrative

1850. Robert Louis Balfour Stevenson (d. 3 December 1894). Scottish playwright, writer of fiction, poet, writer of travel narrative, and essayist

DEATHS

1689. Philipp von Zesen (b. 8 October 1619). German writer of fiction, lyric poet, and language reformer

1861. Arthur Hugh Clough (b. 1 January 1819). English poet and essayist

1907. Francis Thompson (b. 16 December 1859). English poet, biographer, and critical essayist

1915. Nathaniel Goddard Benchley (d. 14 December 1981). American writer of fiction and of children's literature

1916. Saki (pseudonym of Hector Hugh Munro; b. 18 December 1870). Burmese-born English writer of fiction, journalist, and political satirist

1948. Roark Bradford (b. 21 August 1896). American humorist and writer of fiction

1955. Bernard Augustine De Voto (b. 11 January 1897). American critical essayist, literary historian, and writer of fiction

1982. Babette Deutsch (b. 22 September 1895). American poet, essayist, and translator

14

BIRTHS

1779. Adam Gottlob Oehlenschlager (d. 20 January 1850). Danish poet and playwright

1797. Sir Charles Lyell (d. 22 February 1875). Scottish scientist, antiquary, essayist, and writer of prose narrative

1832. Stopford Augustus Brooke (d. 18 March 1916). Irish-born essayist, biographer, poet, and literary historian

1861. Frederick Jackson Turner (d. 14 March 1932). American historian and essayist

1864. Robert Smythe Hichens (d. 20 July 1950). English writer of fiction

1895. Wilmarth Sheldon Lewis (d. 7 October 1979). American bibliophile, literary scholar, textual editor, and essayist

DEATHS

1709. Chu I-tsun (b. 7 October 1629). Chinese poet, scholar, and essayist

1716. Gottfried Wilhelm Leibnitz (b. 1 July 1646). German philosopher, theologian, mathematician, and essayist

1825. Jean Paul Friedrich Richter (b. 21 March 1763). German writer of fiction and humorist

1831. Georg Wilhelm Friedrich Hegel (b. 27 August 1770). German Idealist philosopher and essayist

1844. John Abercrombie (b. 10 October 1780). Scottish philosopher and essayist

1847. Josef Jungmann (b. 16 July 1773). Czech philologist, critical essayist, poet, and lexicographer

1915. Booker Taliaferro Washington (b. 5 April 1856). American educational leader, historian, writer of prose nonfiction narrative, and essayist

1955. Robert Emmet Sherwood (b. 4 April 1896). American playwright, writer of fiction, and biographer

1968. Ramon Menendez Pidal (b. 13 March 1869). Spanish literary historian and critical essayist

15

BIRTHS

1731. William Cowper (d. 25 April 1800). English poet and memoirist

1741. Johann Kaspar Lavater (d. 2 January 1801). Swiss theologian, essayist, and poet

1816. Isidore Kalish (d. 11 May 1886). American Jewish theologian and essayist

1862. Gerhart Hauptmann (d. 8 June 1946). German playwright and writer of fiction

1881. Franklin Pierce Adams (d. 23 March 1960). American essayist, poet, and journalist

1887. Marianne Craig Moore (d. 5 February 1972). American poet

1938. Chen Jo-Hsi. Chinese-born Canadian writer of fiction

DEATHS

1630. Johannes Kepler (b. 27 December 1571). German astronomer, physicist and essayist

1916. Henryk Sienkiewicz (b. 5 May 1846). Polish writer of fiction and writer of stories for children

1932. Charles Waddell Chesnutt (b. 20 June 1858). American writer of fiction and biographer

1978. Margaret Mead (b. 16 December 1901). American anthropologist, essayist, and writer of autobiographical narrative

16

BIRTHS

1758. Peter Andreas Heiberg (d. 30 April 1841). Danish writer of dramatic verse

1807. Jonas Hallgrummsson (d. 26 May 1845). Icelandic poet, scientist, essayist, and linguist

1810. Karel Hymek Macha (d. 6 November 1836). Czech poet and writer of fiction

1839. Louis-Honore Frechette (d. 31 May 1908). French-Canadian poet, playwright, and writer of miscellaneous prose

1889. George Simon Kaufman (d. 2 June 1961). American journalist and playwright

1890. George Henry Seldes. American writer of fiction

1895. Michael Arlen (d. 23 June 1956). English writer of fiction

1930. Albert Chinualumogu Achebe. Nigerian writer of fiction, poet, essayist, and writer of books for children

DEATHS

1952. Charles Maurras (b. 20 April 1868). French essayist and rightist political journalist

1973. Alan Wilson Watts (b. 6 January 1915). English-born philosopher and essayist

17

DEATHS

1794. George Grote (d. 18 June 1871). English historian, classical scholar, politician, and essayist

1876. Cornelia James Cannon (d. ? 1969). American writer of fiction and essayist

1939. Auberon Alexander Waugh. English writer of fiction and essayist

DEATHS

1494. Giovanni Pico della Mirandola (b. 24 February 1463). Italian humanist and essayist

1747. Alain Rene Lesage (b. 8 May 1668). French writer of fiction and playwright

1926. George Sterling (b. 1 December 1869). American poet

18

BIRTHS

1647. Pierre Bayle (d. 28 December 1706). French philosopher, critic, essayist, periodicals editor, and encyclopaedist

1743. Johannes Ewald (d. 17 March 1781). Danish poet and playwright

1768. Freidrich Ludwig Zacharias Werner (d. 17 January 1823). German playwright

1810. Asa Gray (d. 30 January 1888). American scientist, evolutionist, and essayist

1836. Cesare Lombroso (d. 19 October 1909). Italian criminologist, psychiatrist, theorist, and essayist

Sir William Schwenck Gilbert (d. 29 May 1911). English writer of comic verse, satirist, and light opera librettist

1874. Clarence Shepard Day, Jr. (d. 28 December 1935). American essayist, writer of autobiographical prose narrative, and satirist

1882. Percy Wyndham Lewis (d. 7 March 1957). American-born English artist, writer of fiction, and critical essayist

Jacques Maritain (d. 28 April 1973). French Catholic philosopher, essayist, art critic, and writer of miscellaneous prose nonfiction

1906. Klaus Mann (d. 21 May 1949). German-born writer of fiction, essayist, and playwright

1911. Ruth McKenny (d. 25 July 1972). American writer of fiction

1939. Margaret Eleanor Atwood. Canadian poet, writer of fiction, and anthologist

DEATHS

1889. William Allingham (b. 19 March 1824). Irish-born poet

1922. Marcel Proust (b. 10 July 1871). French writer of fiction and critical essayist

1952. Paul Eluard (pseudonym of Eugene Grindal; b. 14 December 1895). French surrealist poet

19

BIRTHS

1812. Franz Felix Adalbert Kuhn (d. 5 May 1881). German philologist, folklorist, and essayist

1853. Albert Auguste Gabriel Hanataux (d. 11 April 1944). French diplomat, historian, and essayist

1894. Phyllis Eleanor Bentley (d. ? 1977). English writer of fiction

1895. Louis Golding (d. 9 August 1958). English writer of fiction

1899. John Orley Allen Tate (d. 9 February 1979). American poet, biographer, essayist, and writer of fiction

1900. Anna Seghers (d. 1 June 1983). German writer of fiction

DEATHS

1867. Fitz-Greene Halleck (b. 8 July 1790). American poet

1887. Emma Lazarus (b. 22 July 1849). American poet and translator

20

BIRTHS

1752. Thomas Chatterton (d. 25 August 1770). English poet, essayist, playwright, and "literary forger"

1855. Josiah Royce (d. 14 September 1916). American philosopher and essayist

1858. Selma Lagerlof (d. 16 March 1940). Swedish writer of fiction and fairy tales

1889. Donn Byrne (d. 18 June 1928). Irish-born writer of fiction

1923. Nadine Gordimer. South African writer of fiction and critical essayist

DEATHS

1874. Thomas Hood the younger (b. 19 January 1835). English humorist, illustrator, writer of fiction, poet, and writer of books for children

1910. Lev Nikolayevich Tolstoi (b. 28 August 1828). Russian writer of fiction, essayist, and playwright

1933. Augustine Birrell (b. 19 January 1850). English literary essayist and biographer

1952. Benedetto Croce (b. 25 February 1866). Italian philosopher, essayist, historian, and politician

21

BIRTHS

1495. John Bale (d. ? November 1563). English playwright, historian, and essayist

1694. Francois Marie Arouet de Voltaire (d. 30 May 1778). French satirist, poet, essayist, historian, playwright, writer of fiction, and philosopher

1785. William Beaumont (d. 25 April 1853). American physician, scientist, and essayist

1787. Barry Cornwall (pseudonym of Bryan Waller Procter; d. 4 October 1874). English poet and biographer

1789. Cesare Balbo (d. 3 June 1853). Italian statesman, literary biographer, and historical essayist

1863. Arthur Thomas Quiller-Couch (d. 12 May 1944). English essayist, scholar, biographer, and writer of fiction

1870. Mary Johnston (d. 9 May 1936). American writer of fiction

1876. Olav Duun (d. 13 September 1939). Norwegian writer of fiction

1886. Sir Harold George Nicholson (d. 1 May 1968). English literary biographer

1895. William Alexander Gerhardi (d. 15 July 1977). Russian-born English writer of fiction

1904. Isaac Bashevis Singer. Polish-born American writer of Yiddish fiction, memoirist, playwright, journalist, and translator

1907. James (Jim) Bishop (d. 26 July 1987). American journalist and writer of historical narrative

DEATHS

1844. Ivan Andreyevich Krylov (b. 14 February 1768). Russian writer of fables

1870. Karel Jaromir Erben (b. 7 November 1811). Czech poet, scholar, and essayist

1886. Charles Francis Adams (b. 18 August 1807). American diplomat, biographer, essayist, and textual editor

1945. Robert Charles Benchley (b. 15 September 1889). American drama critic, essayist, humorist, and actor

Ellen Anderson Gholson Glasgow (b. 22 April 1873). American writer of fiction and essayist

22

BIRTHS

1819. George Eliot (pseudonym of Mary Ann Evans; d. 22 December 1880). English writer of fiction, translator, periodicals editor, and poet

1842. Jose Maria de Heredia (d. 2 October 1905). Cuban-born French poet

1857. George Robert Gissing (d. 28 December 1903). English writer of fiction, biographer, and essayist

1869. Andre Paul Guillaume Gide (d. 19 February 1951). French writer of fiction, poet, playwright, critical essayist, biographer, and translator

1889. Thomas Beer (d. 18 April 1940). American essayist and writer of fiction

1907. Nancy Wilson Ross (d. 18 January 1986). American writer of fiction and Oriental philosopher

DEATHS

1916. John Griffith (Jack) London. American writer of fiction and essayist

1924. Herman Hierjermans (b. 3 December 1864). Dutch playwright and writer of fiction

1928. Herman Sudermann (b. 30 September 1857). German playwright

1963. Aldous Leonard Huxley (b. 26 July 1894). English writer of fiction, poet, and essayist

Clive Hamilton Staples Lewis (b. 29 November 1898). English literary scholar, critical essayist, and writer of fiction

23

BIRTHS

1608. Francisco Manuael de Melo (d. 24 August 1666). Portuguese critical essayist, historian, and poet

1712. Andrew Foulis (d. 18 September 1775). Scottish bookseller, printer, and textual editor

1834. James Thomson (d. 3 June 1882). Scottish-born poet and essayist

DEATHS

1848. Sir John Barrow (b. 19 June 1764). English writer of travel narrative

1934. Arthur Wing Pinero (b. 24 May 1855). English playwright

1974. Cornelius John Ryan (b. 5 June 1920). American journalist and writer of fiction

1976. Andre Malraux (b. 3 November 1901). French writer of social fiction; essayist on such subjects as art history, archaeology, and anthropology; and government minister

24

BIRTHS

1632. Baruch de Spinoza (d. 21 February 1677). Dutch Jewish philosopher and essayist

1713. Laurence Sterne (d. 18 March 1768). English writer of fiction, nonfiction prose narrative, and sermon literature

1826. Carlo Collodi (pseudonym of Carlo Lorenzini; d. 26 October 1890). Italian journalist and writer of fiction for children (*Pinocchio*).

1828. George Augustus Henry Sala (d. 8 December 1895). English writer of fiction

1849. Frances Eliza Hodgson Burnett (d. 29 October 1924). English-born American writer of fiction, playwright, and writer of literature for children

1907. James Ramsay Ullman (d. 20 June 1971). American writer of fiction and of miscellaneous prose nonfiction

1912. Garson Kanin. American playwright, writer of fiction, and memoirist

1925. William Frank Buckley, Jr. American journalist, essayist, periodicals editor, and writer of fiction

DEATHS

1748. Isaac Watts (b. 17 July 1674). English poet, hymnodist, and essayist

1870. Isidore Lucien Ducasse, Comte de Lautreamont (b. 4 April 1846). Uruguayan-born French prose-poet and writer of surrealist verse

1980. Herbert Sebastian Agar (b. 29 September 1897). American historian, literary critic, and political essayist

25

BIRTHS

1562. Lope Felix de Vega (d. 27 August 1635). Spanish playwright and poet

1877. Harley Granville-Barker (d. 31 August 1946). English actor, producer, director, and drama scholar

1878. Georg Kaiser (d. 4 June 1945). German expressionist playwright

1880. Leonard Sidney Woolf (d. 14 August 1969). English writer of fiction and of miscellaneous prose nonfiction

1893. Joseph Wood Krutch (d. 22 May 1970). American literary and intellectual critic and writer of miscellaneous prose nonfiction

1894. Lawrence Stallings (d. 28 February 1968). American writer of fiction and playwright

1904. Ba Jin (pseudonym of Le Fei-Kan). Chinese writer of fiction, essayist, and translator

DEATHS

1854. John Gibson Lockhart (b. 14 July 1794). Scottish encyclopaedist, translator, essayist, writer of fiction, textual editor, and biographer

1950. Johannes Vilhelm Jensen (b. 29 January 1873). Danish writer of fiction, essayist, and poet

1968. Upton Beale Sinclair (b. 20 September 1878). American writer of fiction, advocate of social reform, essayist, and pamphleteer

1970. Yukio Mishima (pseudonym of Kimitake Hiraoka; b. 14 January 1925). Japanese writer of fiction

1985. Geoffrey Edward Harvey Grigson (b. 2 March 1905). English poet and essayist

26

BIRTHS

1607. John Harvard (d. 14 September 1638). English-born colonial American bibliophile, clergyman, and essayist

1842. Prince Peter Alexeyevich Kropotkin (d. 28 February 1921). Russian theorist of anarchism, geographer, essayist, and memoirist

1905. Emlyn Williams (d. 25 September 1987). Welsh playwright and actor

1912. Eugene Ionesco. Romanian-born French playwright, essayist, filmwriter, and writer of fiction

DEATHS

1855. Adam Bernard Mickiewicz (b. 27 December 1798). Polish poet, diplomat, and librarian

1857. Joseph Karl Eichendorff (b. 10 March 1788). German poet, writer of fiction, and critical essayist

1896. Coventry Kersey Dighton Patmore (b. 23 July 1823). English poet and essayist

1944. Edward Johnston (b. 11 February 1872). English essayist and calligrapher

1968. Arnold Zweig (b. 10 November 1887). German writer of fiction, playwright, and essayist

1986. Mary Welsh Hemingway (b. 5 April 1908). American journalist and essayist

27

BIRTHS

1809. Frances Anne (Fanny) Kemble (d. 15 January 1893). English actress, poet, and memoirist

1874. Charles Austin Beard (d. 1 September 1948). American historian and essayist

1909. James Agee (d. 16 May 1955). American poet, writer of autobiographical fiction, and reviewer

DEATHS

1895. Alexandre Dumas fils (b. 27 July 1824). French playwright, writer of fiction, poet, and essayist

1922. Alice Christiana Gertrude Thompson Meynell (b. 17 August 1847). English essayist and poet

1953. Eugene Gladstone O'Neill (b. 16 October 1888). American playwright and poet

    Theodore Francis Powys (b. 20 December 1875). English writer of fiction

1986. Gabriel Fielding (b. 25 March 1916). English-born writer of fiction and poet

28

BIRTHS

1628. John Bunyan (d. 31 August 1688). English writer of prose allegory and of prose nonfiction, and poet

1757. William Blake (d. 12 August 1827). English poet, artist, and printmaker

1792. Victor Cousin (d. 13 January 1867). French philosopher and essayist

1820. Friedrich Engels (d. 5 August 1895). German political and economic philosopher and essayist

1832. Sir Leslie Stephen (d. 22 February 1904). English literary critic, biographer, essayist, and literary historian

1880. Aleksandr Aleksandrovich Blok (d. 9 August 1921). Russian poet and writer of verse drama

1881. Stefan Zweig (d. 23 February 1942). Austrian biographer and writer of fiction

1894. Justin Brooks Atkinson (d. 13 January 1984). American theatre critic and essayist

1904. Nancy Freeman Mitford (d. 30 June 1973). English writer of fiction, biographer, and essayist

1907. Alberto Moravia (pseudonym of Albert Pincherle). Italian writer of fiction, essayist, literary critic, playwright, and translator

1916. Richard Tregaskis (d. 16 August 1973). American journalist and writer of fiction

DEATHS

1859. Washington Irving (b. 3 April 1783). American journalist, satirical essayist, writer of fiction, playwright, popular biographer and historian, and writer of narrative nonfiction

1878. George Henry Lewes (b. 18 April 1817). English writer of miscellaneous prose nonfiction, editor, critical essayist, biographer, writer of fiction, playwright, and literary adviser

1985. Fernand Paul Braudel (b. 24 August 1902). French historian

29

BIRTHS

1781. Andres Bello (d. 15 October 1865). Chilean poet, scholar, and statesman

1799. Amos Bronson Alcott (d. 4 March 1888). American educational philosopher, essayist, and poet

1818. William Ellery Channing (d. 23 December 1901). American poet, essayist, biographer, and textual editor

1832. Louisa May Alcott (d. 6 March 1888). American writer of fiction and of narrative nonfiction prose

1834. George Holmes Howison (d. 31 December 1916). American mathematician, philosopher, and essayist

1898. Clive Hamilton Staples Lewis (d. 22 November 1963). English writer of fiction, critical essayist, allegorist, and literary scholar

1918. Madeleine L'Engle. American writer of fiction for children

1934. William (Willie) Morris. American periodicals editor, writer of fiction, and writer of miscellaneous prose nonfiction

DEATHS

1594. Alonso de Encilla y Zuniga (b. 7 August 1533). Spanish epic poet

1878. Louis Antoine Godey (b. 6 June 1804). American publisher and periodical editor

1969. Norman Lindsay (b. 23 February 1879). Australian writer of fiction and artist

30

BIRTHS

1554. Sir Philip Sidney (d. 17 October 1586). English poet and essayist

1667. Jonathan Swift (d. 19 October 1745). Irish-born satirist, poet, essayist, and writer of fiction

1809. Mark Lemon (d. 23 May 1870). English playwright and journalist

1817. Theodor Mommsen (d. 1 November 1903). German historian, textual editor, and essayist

1835. Mark Twain (pseudonym of Samuel Langhorne Clemens; d. 21 April 1910). American humorist, writer of fiction, essayist, and writer of prose nonfiction narrative

1872. John McCrae (d. 28 January 1918). Canadian poet and physican

1874. Winston Spencer Churchill (d. 24 January 1965). English historian, biographer, essayist, writer of prose nonfiction narrative, and statesman

1893. Israel Joshua Singer (d. 10 February 1944). Polish-born Yiddish writer of fiction

1894. Donald Ogden Stewart (d. 2 August 1980). American playwright and writer of humorous fiction and narrative

1907. Jacques Martin Barzun. French-born American historian, critical essayist, and textual editor

DEATHS

1654. John Selden (b. 16 December 1584). English antiquary and essayist

1977. Sir Terence Merwyn Rattigan (b. 10 June 1911). English playwright

1983. Richard Llewellyn (b. 8 December 1906). Welsh writer of fiction and playwright

DECEMBER

1

BIRTHS

1751. Johan Henrik Kellgren (d. 29 April 1795). Swedish poet

1869. George Sterling (d. 17 November 1926). American poet

1886. Rex Todhunter Stout (d. 27 October 1975). American writer of detective and mystery fiction

1893. Ernst Toller (d. 22 May 1939). German playwright

DEATHS

1987. James Baldwin (b. 2 August 1924). American writer of fiction, writer of autobiographical narrative nonfiction, essayist, and playwright

2

BIRTHS

1813. Mattias Alexander Castren (d. 7 May 1852). Finnish philologist, ethnographic researcher, and essayist

1822. David Masson (d. 6 October 1907). Scottish biographer and miscellaneous prose nonfiction writer

1885. Nikos Kazantzakis (d. 26 October 1957). Greek writer of fiction

1891. Charles Harris Wesley (d. 16 August 1987). American historian and essayist

DEATHS

1745. Jisho Ando (pseudonym of Ando Hachizaemon; b. ? 1658). Japanese writer of fiction

1814. Donatien Alphonse Francois de Sade (b. 2 June 1740). French writer of erotic fiction

1853. Amelia Briggs Opie (b. 12 November 1769). English poet and writer of fiction

1860. Ferdinand Christian Bauer (b. 21 June 1792). German theologian and essayist

1918. Edmond Rostand (b. 1 April 1868). French poet and playwright

1935. James Henry Breasted (b. 27 August 1865). American Egyptologist, archaeologist, historian, academician, and essayist

1985. Philip Arthur Larkin (b. 8 August 1922). English poet and writer of fiction

3

BIRTHS

1684. Baron Ludvig Holberg (d. 28 January 1754). Danish poet, playwright, philosopher, and essayist

1764. Mary Ann Lamb (d. 20 May 1847). English essayist and writer of fiction for children

1766. Robert Bloomfield (d. 19 August 1823). English poet and playwright

1812. Hendrik Conscience (d. 10 September 1883). Flemish writer of fiction

1845. Henry Bradley (d. 23 May 1923). English philologist, lexicographer, essayist, and editor

1857. Joseph Conrad (born Teodor Josef Konrad Korzeniowski; d. 3 August 1924). Polish-born (Russian Ukraine) English writer of fiction

1864. Herman Heijermans (d. 22 November 1924). Dutch playwright and writer of fiction

DEATHS

1854. Johann Peter Eckermann (b. 21 September 1792). German critical essayist, textual editor, and writer of prose nonfiction narrative

1894. Robert Louis Balfour Stevenson (b. 13 November 1850). Scottish playwright, writer of fiction, poet, writer of travel narrative, and essayist

1905. John Bartlett (b. 14 June 1820). American bookseller and compiler of references on quotations

1949. Philip Barry (b. 18 June 1896). American playwright

4

BIRTHS

1585. John Cotton (d. 23 December 1652). English-born colonial American clergyman, theologian, essayist, and writer of catechism for children

1595. Jean Champlain (d. 22 February 1674). French poet and critical essayist

1795. Thomas Carlyle (d. 5 February 1881). Scottish essayist, historian, literary critic, and translator

1835. Samuel Butler (d. 18 June 1902). English writer of fiction, painter, and writer of miscellaneous prose nonfiction

1875. Rainer Maria Rilke (d. 29 December 1926). German poet, writer of fiction, playwright, and biographer

1893. Sir Herbert Edward Read (d. 12 June 1968). English essayist and intellectual critic

1911. Pierre Stephen Robert Payne (d. 18 February 1983). English-born American essayist, biographer, and linguist

DEATHS

1679. Thomas Hobbes (b. 5 April 1588). English philosopher, essayist, translator, and literary critic

1732. John Gay (d. 16 September 1685). English poet, playwright, and essayist

1850. Robert Gilfillan (b. 7 July 1798). Scottish poet

1933. Stefan George (b. 12 July 1868). German poet

1975. Hannah Arendt (b. 14 October 1906). German-born American political theorist, essayist, academician, and scholar

5

BIRTHS

1803. Fyodor Ivanovich Tyutchev (d. 8 August 1873). Russian lyric poet

1830. Christina Georgina Rossetti (d. 29 December 1894). English poet, playwright, and writer of fiction

1859. Sir Sidney Lee (d. 3 March 1926). English critical essayist, editor, and biographer

1934. Joan Didion. American writer of fiction and essayist

DEATHS

1870. Alexandre Davy de la Pailleterie Dumas, pere (b. 24 July 1802). French writer of fiction, playwright, historian, essayist, writer of travel narrative, and translator

1925. Wladyslaw Stanislaw Reymont (b. 7 May 1867). Polish writer of fiction

1931. Nicholas Vachel Lindsay (b. 10 November 1879). American poet and writer of miscellaneous prose narrative

1960. Richard Nathaniel Wright (b. 4 September 1908). American writer of fiction, essayist, and writer of autobiographical narrative

6

BIRTHS

1478. Baldassare Castiglione (d. 7 February 1529). Italian poet and essayist

1788. Richard Harris Barham (d. 17 June 1845). English humorist, lyric poet, and writer of burlesque metrical tales

1886. Alfred Joyce Kilmer (d. 30 July 1918). American poet, journalist, and critical essayist

1892. Sir Francis Osbert Sacheverell Sitwell (d. 4 May 1969). English poet, playwright, and writer of fiction and miscellaneous prose nonfiction

DEATHS

1658. Baltasar Gracian y Morales (b. 8 January 1601). Spanish moralist, humanist, and essayist

1718. Nicholas Rowe (b. 30 June 1674). English playwright and poet

1882. Anthony Trollope (b. 24 April 1815). English writer of fiction

1924. Geneva Grace Stratton-Porter (b. 17 August 1868). American writer of fiction for girls

7

BIRTHS

1784. Allan Cunningham (d. 30 October 1842). Scottish poet, writer of fiction, textual editor, essayist, biographer, and anthologist

1801. Johann Nepomuk Edward Ambrosius Nestroy (d. 25 May 1862). Austrian playwright and theatre manager

1830. Judah Loeb ben Asher Gordon (d. 16 September 1892). Russian-born Hebrew poet and satirist

1862. Paul Auguste Marie Adam (d. 2 January 1920). French writer of fiction

1873. Willa Siebert Cather (d. 24 April 1947). American writer of fiction, poet, and essayist

1888. Arthur Joyce Lunel Cary (d. 29 March 1957). Irish writer of fiction, essayist, and poet

1893. Virginia Kirkus (d. 10 September 1980). American essayist, literary critic, and reviewer

1928. Avram Noam Chomsky. American linguist, essayist, and political activist

DEATHS

1626. Sir John Davies (b. 15[?] April 1569). English poet

1683. John Oldham (b. 9 August 1653). English poet

1949. Rex Ellingwood Beach (b. 1 September 1877). American writer of fiction and miscellaneous prose nonfiction

1975. Thornton Niven Wilder (b. 17 April 1897). American writer of fiction and playwright

1985. Robert Ranke Graves (b. 24 July 1895). English poet, playwright, writer of fiction, critical essayist, biographer, and writer of miscellaneous prose (including works for children)

8

BIRTHS

1832. Bjornstjerne Bjornson (d. 26 April 1810). Norwegian writer of fiction and playwright

1862. George Leone Jules Marie Feydeau (d. 5 June 1921). French playwright

1868. Norman Douglas (d. 9 February 1952). English writer of fiction and of miscellaneous prose nonfiction

1881. Padraic Colum (d. 11 January 1972). Irish poet, playwright, writer of fiction, and writer of miscellaneous prose (including works for children)

1885. Kenneth Lewis Roberts (d. 21 July 1957). American writer of historical fiction

1889. Hervey Allen (d. 28 December 1949). American writer of fiction, poet, and biographer

1894. James Grover Thurber (d. 4 November 1961). American writer of fiction, humorist, essayist, and writer of humorous prose sketches

1906. Richard Llewellyn (d. 30 November 1983). Welsh writer of fiction and playwright

1913. Delmore Schwartz (d. 11 July 1966). American poet, playwright, essayist, and writer of fiction

DEATHS

1550. Giangiorgio Trissino (b. 8 July 1478). Italian linguist, philologist, and essayist

1691. Richard Baxter (b. 12 November 1615). English writer of religious prose tracts

1709. Thomas Corneille (b. 20 August 1625). French poet, essayist, and playwright

1830. Henri Benjamin Constant de Rebeque (b. 25 October 1759). French political philosopher, essayist, and writer of fiction

1859. Thomas DeQuincey (b. 15 August 1785). English essayist

1889. Martin Farquhar Tupper (b. 17 July 1810). English poet, essayist, and playwright

1895. George Augustus Henry Sala (b. 24 November 1828). English writer of fiction

9

BIRTHS

1608. John Milton (d. 8 November 1674). English poet, playwright, and essayist

1717. Johann Joachim Wincklemann (d. 8 June 1768). German classical archaeologist and essayist

1848. Joel Chandler Harris (d. 3 July 1908). American journalist and writer of regional and dialect fiction

1930. Michael J. Arlen. American essayist

1936. Avraham Ben Yehoshua. Israeli essayist, playwright, and writer of fiction

DEATHS

1674. Edward Hyde, Earl of Clarendon (b. 18 February 1609). English historian and biographer

1964. Dame Edith Sitwell (b. 7 September 1887). English poet, playwright, writer of fiction, critical essayist, and writer of miscellaneous prose nonfiction

1968. Karl Barth (b. 10 May 1886). Swiss theologian, Biblical commentator, and essayist

10

BIRTHS

1824. George Macdonald (d. 18 September 1905). Scottish writer of fiction, poet, and writer of literature for children

1830. Emily Elizabeth Dickinson (d. 15 May 1886). American poet

1851. Melvil Dewey (d. 26 December 1931). American librarian, essayist, and originator of the catalogue classification system that bears his name

1891. Nelly Leonie Sachs (d. 12 May 1970). German poet and playwright

1903. William Charles Franklin Plomer (d. 21 September 1923). English writer of fiction

1907. Rumer Godden. Anglo-Indian writer of fiction

DEATHS

1936. Luigi Pirandello (b. 28 June 1867). Italian playwright, writer of fiction, critical essayist, and poet

1946. Alfred Damon Runyon (b. 6 October 1884). American journalist, sportswriter, and writer of fiction

1968. Thomas Merton (b. 31 January 1915). American writer of nonfiction narrative prose, essayist, and poet

1972. Mark Albert Van Doren (b. 13 June 1894). American poet, writer of fiction, critical essayist, and editor of literary anthologies and texts

11

BIRTHS

1781. Sir David Brewster (d. 10 February 1868). Scottish essayist and scientist

1801. Christian Dietrich Grabbe (d. 12 September 1836). German playwright

1810. Louis Charles Alfred de Musset (d. 1 May 1857). French poet and playwright

1849. Ellen Karoline Sofia Key (d. 24 April 1926). Swedish social reformer, feminist, and essayist

1856. Georgi Valentinovich Plekhanov (d. 30 May 1918). Russian revolutionary, periodicals editor, political essayist, and commentator upon Marxist theory

1864. Maurice LeBlanc (d. 6 November 1941). French writer of fiction and playwright

1918. Alexandr Isayevich Solzhenitsyn. Russian writer of fiction, essayist, memoirist, and writer of documentary

1935. Reza Baraheni. Iranian poet, writer of fiction, and essayist

DEATHS

1757. Colley Cibber (b. 6 December 1671). English poet, playwright, autobiographer, actor, and theatre manager

1843. Jean Francois Casimir Delavigne (b. 4 April 1793). French playwright, satirist, and lyric poet

1920. Olive Emilie Albertina Schriener (b. 24 March 1855). South African writer of fiction

1938. Christian Louis Lange (b. 17 September 1869). Norwegian historian and essayist

12

BIRTHS

1731. Erasmus Darwin (d. 18 April 1902). English physician, poet, philosopher, scientist, and essayist

1766. Nikolai Mikhaylovich Karamzin (d. 22 May 1826). Russian historian, essayist, and writer of fiction

1821. Gustav Flaubert (d. 8 May 1880). French writer of fiction

1864. Paul Elmer More (d. 4 March 1937). American critical and literary essayist

1872. Albert Payson Terhune (d. 18 February 1942). American writer of fiction and of prose nonfiction

1918. Eugene Burdick (d. 26 July 1965). American writer of fiction, political theorist, and essayist

1929. John James Osborne. English playwright

DEATHS

1751. Henry St. John, Viscount Bolingbroke (b. 16 September 1678). English diplomat, essayist, historian, and philosopher

1777. Albrecht von Haller (b. 16 October 1708). Swiss scientist, essayist, poet, and scientific bibliographer

1889. Robert Browning (b. 7 May 1812). English poet, playwright, essayist, and biographer

1923. Raymond Radiguet (b. 18 June 1903). French poet and writer of fiction

13

BIRTHS

1720. Count Carlo Gozzi (d. 4 April 1806). Italian playwright and poet

1797. Heinrich Heine (d. 17 February 1856). German poet and essayist

1815. Arthur Penrhyn Stanley (d. 18 July 1881). English historian, biographer, and literary essayist

1835. Phillips Brooks (d. 23 January 1893). American theologian, essayist, and hymnodist

1890. Marcus Cook Connelly (d. 21 December 1980). American playwright, journalist, and writer of fiction

1905. Carey McWilliams (d. 27 June 1980). American periodicals editor and social critic

1911. Kenneth Patchen (d. 8 January 1972). American poet

1914. Alan Louis Charles Bullock. American political historian, essayist, and biographer

1915. Ross MacDonald (pseudonym of Kenneth Millar; d. 11 July 1983). American writer of detective fiction and essayist

DEATHS

1729. Anthony Collins (b. 21 June 1676). English materialistic philosopher and essayist

1776. Johann Jakob Breitinger (b. 1 March 1701). Swiss literary critic, theorist, and essayist

1784. Samuel Johnson (b. 18 September 1709). English poet, essayist, journalist, writer of fiction and of travel narrative, biographer, lexicographer, and playwright

1852. Frances Wright (b. 6 September 1795). Scottish-born essayist, playwright, writer of fiction, and advocate of social reform

1863. Christian Friedrich Hebbel (b. 18 March 1813). German playwright, poet, essayist, and writer of fiction

1957. Michael Sadleir (b. 25 December 1888). English biographer and writer of fiction

1983. Mary Renault (pseudonym of Mary Challans; b. 4 September 1905). English writer of historical fiction

14

BIRTHS

1503. Nostradamus (born Michel de Notredame; d. 2 July 1566). French astrologer, physician, poet, and essayist

1546. Tycho Brahe (d. 24 October 1601). Danish astronomer and essayist

1791. Johan Ludvig Heiberg (d. 25 August 1860). Danish critical essayist, playwright, and poet

1895. Paul Eluard (pseudonym of Eugene Grindal; d. 18 November 1952). French surrealist poet

1919. Shirley Hardie Jackson (d. 8 August 1965). American writer of fiction, playwright, and writer of personal narrative nonfiction

DEATHS

1905. Fiona Macleod (pseudonym of William Sharp; b. 12 September 1855). Scottish essayist, poet, writer of fiction, biographer, and composer of mystic Celtic tales and romances

1953. Marjorie Kinnan Rawlings (b. 8 August 1896). American writer of fiction and journalist

1974. Walter Lippman (b. 23 September 1889). American political essayist and journalist

1978. Salvador de Madariaga y Rojo (b. 23 July 1886). Spanish philosopher, historian, and essayist

1981. Nathaniel Goddard Benchley (b. 13 November 1915). American writer of fiction and of literature for children

1984. Vicente Aleixandre y Merlo (b. 26 April 1898). Spanish poet

15

BIRTHS

1613. Francois, duc de La Rochefoucauld (d. 16 March 1680). French memoirist; writer of prose nonfiction narrative and of maxims

1787. Charles Coweden Clarke (d. 13 March 1877). English Shakespearean scholar, editor, and critical essayist

1859. Ludwik Lejzer Zamenhof (d. 14 April 1917). Polish linguist, essayist, and creator of Esperanto

1888. Maxwell Anderson (d. 28 February 1959). American playwright and writer of verse drama

1904. Betty Smith (d. 17 January 1972). American writer of fiction

1913. Muriel Rukeyser (d. 12 February 1980). American poet and critical essayist

1941. Lemuel Adolphus Johnson. Sierra Leonean poet and essayist

DEATHS

1683. Izaak Walton (b. 9 August 1593). English biographer and essayist

1938. Thomas Clayton Wolfe (b. 3 October 1900). American writer of fiction, playwright, and essayist

1947. Arthur Llewellyn Jones Machen (b. 3 March 1863). Welsh-born English writer of fiction and poet

1965. William Somerset Maugham (b. 25 January 1874). English writer of fiction and playwright

16

BIRTHS

1584. John Selden (d. 30 November 1654). English antiquarian and essayist

1775. Jane Austen (d. 18 July 1817). English writer of fiction

1787. Mary Russell Mitford (d. 10 January 1855). English writer of fiction and playwright

1859. Francis Thompson (d. 13 November 1907). English poet, biographer, and critical essayist

1863. George Santayana (born Jorge Ruiz de Santayana y Borras; d. 26 September 1952). Spanish-born American essayist, poet, philosopher, writer of fiction, and Biblical commentator

1869. Albert Frederick Pollard (d. 3 August 1948). English historian, essayist, and biographer

1882. Zoltan Kodaly (d. 6 March 1967). Hungarian composer and essayist

1899. Sir Noel Pierce Coward (d. 26 March 1973). English playwright, poet, and writer of fiction and of autobiographical narrative

1901. Margaret Mead (d. 15 November 1978). American anthropologist, essayist, and writer of autobiographical prose narrative

1909. Edgar Austin Mittelholzer (d. 6 May 1965). Guyanaian writer of fiction

1917. Arthur Charles Clarke. English writer of science and fantasy fiction

1921. Tamas Aczel. Hungarian poet and writer of fiction

DEATHS

1859. Wilhelm Karl Grimm (b. 24 February 1786). German folklorist, philologist, and collector of tales for children

1928. Elinor Hoyt Wylie (b. 7 September 1885). American poet and writer of fiction

17

BIRTHS

1807. John Greenleaf Whittier (d. 7 September 1892). American poet and writer of miscellaneous prose nonfiction

1830. Jules Alfred Huot de Goncourt (d. 20 June 1870). French writer of fiction, historian, and essayist

1873. Ford Madox Ford (pseudonym of Ford Hermann Hueffer; d. 26 June 1939). English writer of fiction, critical essayist, periodicals editor, and writer of autobiographical narrative

1903. Erskin Preston Caldwell (d. 11 April 1987). American writer of fiction and of prose narrative nonfiction

DEATHS

1871. Henry Theodore Tuckerman (b. 20 April 1813). American essayist and poet

1897. Louis Marie Alphonse Daudet (b. 13 May 1840). French writer of fiction

1957. Dorothy Leigh Sayers (b. 13 June 1893). English writer of mystery and detective fiction, scholar, and translator

1971. Alexander Trifonovich Tvardovsky (b. 21 June 1910). Russian poet and periodicals editor

1987. Marguerite Yourcenar (originally Marguerite de Crayencour; b. 8 June 1903). Belgian-born French writer of fiction, poet, essayist, playwright, and translator

18

BIRTHS

1707. Charles Wesley (d. 29 March 1788). English religious reformer, poet, and hymnodist

1863. Oliver Herford (d. 5 July 1935). English-born American poet and humorist

1870. Saki (pseudonym of Hector Hugh Munro; d. 13 November 1916). Burmese-born English writer of fiction, journalist, and political satirist

1907. Christopher Harris Fry. English verse dramatist, filmwriter, and translator

DEATHS

1676. Edward Benlowes (b. 12 July 1602). English poet

1803. Johann Gottfried von Herder (b. 25 August 1744). German critical essayist, translator, and poet

1832. Philip Morin Freneau (b. 2 January 1752). American journalist, essayist, poet, and writer of prose narrative

1858. Thomas Halley Chivers (b. 18 October 1809). American poet, playwright, and biographer

1882. Henry James the elder (b. 2 June 1811). American writer of religious, social, and theological prose nonfiction

1977. Louis Untermeyer (b. 1 October 1885). American poet, translator, biographer, anthologist, critical essayist, and writer of prose fiction

19

BIRTHS

1861. Italo Svevo (pseudonym of Ettore Schmitz; d. 13 September 1928). Italian writer of fiction

1901. Oliver Hazard Perry Lafarge (d. 2 August 1963). American writer of fiction, essayist, and historian of the Native American

1907. Harry Allen Smith (d. 24 February 1976). American humorist and essayist

1910. Jean Genet (d. 15 April 1986). French playwright, writer of fiction, and poet

1929. Howard Oliver Sackler (d. 4 October 1982). American playwright

1946. Miguel Pinero (d. 17 June 1988). Puerto Rican-born poet and playwright

DEATHS

1848. Emily Jane Bronte (b. 30 July 1818). English writer of fiction and poet

1883. Francesco De Sanctis (b. 28 March 1817). Italian literary critic and essayist

1982. Dwight MacDonald (b. 24 March 1906). American essayist, biographer, and memoirist

20

BIRTHS

1780. John Wilson Croker (d. 10 August 1857). Irish-born historian, essayist, and literary scholar

1853. Rene Bazin (d. 21 July 1932). French writer of fiction

1875. Theodore Francis Powys (d. 27 November 1953). English writer of fiction

1895. Susanne Katherina Knauth Langer (d. 17 July 1985). American philosopher and essayist

1911. Hortense Calisher. American writer of fiction

DEATHS

1954. James Hilton (b. 9 September 1900). English writer of fiction and filmwriter

1961. Moss Hart (b. 24 October 1904). American playwright and librettist

1968. John Ernst Steinbeck (b. 29 February 1902). American writer of fiction

21

BIRTHS

1795. Leopold von Ranke (d. 23 May 1886). German historian and essayist

1804. Benjamin Disraeli (d. 19 April 1881). English statesman, poet, essayist, and writer of fiction

1849. James Lane Allen (d. 18 February 1925). American writer of fiction

1905. Anthony Dymoke Powell. English writer of fiction and memoirist

1908. Luigi Giorgio Barzini the younger (d. 30 March 1984). Italian cultural historian and essayist

1917. Heinrich Theodor Boll (d. 16 July 1985). German writer of fiction, essayist, playwright, and translator

1923. Richard Franklin Hugo (22 October 1982). American poet

DEATHS

1549. Margaret of Navarre (b. 11 April 1492). French poet, epistolary essayist, playwright, and writer of dialogues

1805. Manuel Maria Barbosa du Bocage (b. 15 September 1765). Portuguese lyric poet

1842. William Maginn (b. 10 July 1793). Irish-born satirist and writer of fiction

1940. Francis Scott Key Fitzgerald (b. 24 September 1896). American writer of fiction, essayist, and playwright

1964. Carl Van Vechten (b. 17 June 1880). American essayist and writer of fiction

1980. Marcus Cook Connelly (b. 13 December 1890). American playwright, journalist, and writer of fiction

22

BIRTHS

1639. Jean Racine (d. 21 April 1699). French dramatic poet

1823. Thomas Wentworth Storrow Higginson (d. 9 May 1911). American writer of nonfiction narrative and of fiction, essayist, biographer, and poet

1831. Charles Stuart Calverley (d. 17 February 1884). English poet

1869. Edward Arlington Robinson (d. 6 April 1935). American poet and playwright

1905. Kenneth Rexroth (d. 6 June 1982). American poet, playwright, and essayist

1907. Doris Miles Disney (d. 8 March 1976). American writer of fiction

DEATHS

1880. George Eliot (pseudonym of Mary Ann Evans; b. 22 November 1819). English writer of fiction, translator, periodicals editor, and poet

1940. Nathanael West (originally Nathan Wallenstein Weinstein; b. 17 October 1903). American writer of fiction and filmwriter

1943. Helen Beatrix Potter (b. 6 July 1866). English writer of fiction for children and memoirist

1974. Sterling North (b. 4 November 1906). American writer of fiction, poet, essayist, and biographer

1989. Samuel Barclay Beckett (b. 13 April 1906). Irish-born playwright, essayist, writer of fiction, and poet

23

BIRTHS

1597. Martin Opitz von Boberfeld (d. 20 August 1639). German poet and translator

1783. Giovanni Berchet (d. 23 December 1851). Italian poet, translator, and critical essayist

1790. Jean Francois Champollion (d. 4 March 1832). French archaeologist, linguist, and essayist

1804. Charles Augustin Sainte-Beuve (d. 13 October 1869). French critical essayist

1812. Samuel Smiles (d. 17 April 1904). Scottish social and educational reformer, essayist, and biographer

1922. Calder Baynard Willingham, Jr. American writer of fiction, playwright, and filmwriter

1926. Robert Elwood Bly. American poet, anthologist, and translator

DEATHS

1652. John Cotton (b. 4 December 1585). English-born colonial American clergyman, theologian, essayist, and writer of catechism for children

1763. Abbe Antoine Francois Prevost (b. 1 April 1697). French writer of fiction and periodical essayist

1818. Sir Philip Francis the younger (b. 22 October 1740). English political essayist

1851. Giovanni Berchet (b. 23 December 1783). Italian poet, translator, and critical essayist

1856. Hugh Miller (b. 10 October 1802). Scottish writer of miscellaneous prose nonfiction

1901. William Ellery Channing (b. 29 November 1818). American poet, essayist, biographer, and textual editor

24

BIRTHS

1745. Benjamin Rush (d. 19 April 1813). American physician, statesman, and writer of medical tracts

1754. George Crabbe (d. 3 February 1832). English poet and writer of sermon literature

1791. Augustin Eugene Scribe (d. 20 February 1861). French playwright

1822. Matthew Arnold (d. 15 April 1888). English poet, playwright, and essayist

1838. John Morley (d. 23 September 1923). English critical essayist and biographer

1881. Juan Ramon Jimenez (d. 29 May 1958). Spanish lyric poet

DEATHS

1591. Juan de Yepis y Alvarez (also known as St. John of the Cross; b. 24 June 1542). Spanish lyrical and mystical poet

1812. Joel Barlow (b. 24 March 1754). American poet, essayist, and historian

1863. William Makepeace Thackeray (b. 18 July 1811). English writer of fiction

1914. John Muir (b. 21 April 1838). American naturalist, explorer, and writer of nonfiction prose narrative

1982. Louis Marie Antoine Alfred Aragon (b. 3 October 1897). French poet and writer of fiction

25

BIRTHS

1564. Johannes Buxtorf the elder (d. 13 September 1629). German Hebraic scholar, essayist, and lexicographer

1709. Julien Offroy de Lamettrie (d. 11 November 1751). French materialist philosopher, essayist, and satirist

1721. William Collins (d. 12 June 1759). English poet

1759. Richard Porson (d. 25 September 1808). English classical scholar and essayist

1776. Lady Sydney Owenson Morgan (d. 14 April 1859). Irish writer of fiction

1888. Michael Sadleir (d. 13 December 1957). English biographer and writer of fiction

1892. Dame Rebecca West (pseudonym of Cicily Isabel Fairfield; d. 15 March 1983). English writer of fiction, essayist, and reviewer

1900. Paul McClelland Angle (d. 11 May 1975). American historian and essayist

1931. Carlos Castaneda. Brazilian-born American anthropologist, essayist, and writer of narrative prose nonfiction

DEATHS

1935. Paul Charles Joseph Bourget (d. 2 September 1852). French writer of fiction, playwright, and essayist

26

BIRTHS

1716. Thomas Gray (b. 30 July 1771). English poet

1769. Ernst Moritz Arndt (d. 29 January 1860). German poet, essayist, and writer of travel narrative

1820. Dion Boucicault (born Dionysius Lardner Bourisquot; d. 11 September 1890). Irish-born playwright

1891. Henry Valentine Miller (d. 7 June 1980). American-born writer of autobiographical narrative, fiction, and prose nonfiction

1894. Jean Toomer (d. 30 March 1967). American writer of fiction, poet, and playwright

DEATHS

1771. Claude Adrien Helvetius (b. 26 January 1715). French philosopher, encyclopaedist, and essayist

1921. Ludwig Thoma (b. 21 January 1867). German humorist, satirist, essayist, playwright, and poet

1931. Melvil Dewey (b. 10 December 1851). American librarian, essayist, and originator of the catalogue classification system that bears his name

1968. Kenneth Scott Latourette (b. 9 August 1884). American church historian and essayist

27

BIRTHS

1571. Johannes Kepler (d. 15 November 1630). German astronomer, physicist, and essayist

1798. Adam Bernard Mickiewicz (d. 26 November 1855). Polish poet, diplomat, and librarian

1896. Louis Bromfield (d. 18 March 1956). American writer of fiction

Carl Zuckmayer (d. 18 January 1977). German playwright, poet, and writer of fiction

1910. Charles Olson (d. 10 January 1970). American critical essayist, poet, and playwright

DEATHS

1585. Pierre de Ronsard (b. 11 September 1524). French poet and critical essayist

1834. Charles Lamb (b. 10 February 1775). English essayist and poet

1925. Sergei Aleksandrovich Esenin (b. 3 October 1895). Russian poet

1931. Alfred Percival Graves (b. 22 July 1846). Irish poet

1967. Martin Archer Flavin (b. 2 November 1883). American writer of fiction and playwright

1986. George Bubb Dangerfield (b. 28 October 1904). American historian and essayist

28

BIRTHS

1619. Abbe Antoine Furetiere (d. 14 May 1688). French poet, linguist, and lexicographer

1856. Thomas Woodrow Wilson (d. 23 February 1924). American statesman, essayist, and historian

1862. Morris Rosenfeld (pseudonym of Moshe Jacob Alter; d. 22 June 1923). Polish-born American Yiddish poet and periodicals editor

1872. Pio Baroja y Nessi (d. 30 October 1956). Spanish writer of fiction

1895. Rose Franken (d. 22 June 1988). American playwright and writer of fiction

DEATHS

1706. Pierre Bayle (b. 18 November 1647). French philosopher, critic, essayist, periodicals editor, and encyclopaedist

1859. Thomas Babington Macaulay (b. 25 October 1800). English political philosopher, essayist, historian, biographer, literary critic, and poet

1903. George Robert Gissing (b. 22 November 1857). English writer of fiction, biographer, and essayist

1935. Clarence Shepard Day (b. 18 November 1874). American essayist, writer of autobiographical prose narrative, and satirist

1938. Osip Emilievich Mandelstam (b. 15 January 1891). Polish-born Russian poet

1945. Theodore Herman Albert Dreiser (b. 27 August 1871). American writer of fiction, journalist, essayist, poet, and playwright

1986. John Dann MacDonald (b. 24 July 1916). American writer of mystery, detective, and fantasy fiction

29

BIRTHS

1809. William Ewart Gladstone (d. 19 May 1898). English statesman, classical literary scholar, and historical essayist

1843. Carmen Sylva (pseudonym of Elisabeth, Queen of Romania; d. 2 March 1916). German-born Romanian poet and translator

1915. Robert Chester Ruark (d. 30 June 1965). American journalist and writer of fiction

DEATHS

1834. Thomas Robert Malthus (b. 14 February 1766). English economist and essayist

1890. Octave Feuillet (b. 11 August 1821). French writer of fiction, playwright, and librarian

1894. Christina Georgina Rossetti (b. 5 December 1830). English poet, playwright, and writer of fiction

1924. Carl Friedrich Georg Spitteler (b. 24 April 1845). Swiss poet and writer of fiction

1926. Rainer Maria Rilke (b. 4 December 1875). German poet, writer of fiction, playwright, and biographer

1937. Donald Robert Perry Marquis (b. 29 July 1878). American journalist, social and political satirist, humorist, poet, and playwright

1960. Eden Phillpotts (b. 4 November 1862). Indian-born English writer of fiction, poet, and playwright

30

BIRTHS

1676. John Philips (d. 15 February 1709). English poet

1819. Theodor Fontane (d. 20 September 1898). German writer of fiction and poet

1865. Joseph Rudyard Kipling (d. 18 January 1936). Indian-born English poet and writer of fiction

1869. Stephen Butler Leacock (d. 28 March 1944). English-born Canadian humorist, essayist, and writer of fiction

1910. Paul Frederic Bowles. American writer of fiction

DEATHS

1691. Robert Boyle (b. 25 January 1627). English scientist, philosopher, and essayist

1876. Christian Winther (b. 29 July 1796). Danish Romantic poet

1879. Adelardo Lopez Ayala y Herrera (b. 1 May 1828). Spanish poet, playwright, and statesman

1896. Jose Mercado Rizal (b. 19 June 1861). Philippine writer of fiction, physician, and revolutionary

1944. Romain Rolland (b. 29 January 1866). French music historian, biographer, playwright, writer of fiction, and essayist

1947. Alfred North Whitehead (b. 15 February 1861). English mathematician, idealistic philosopher, and essayist

31

BIRTHS

1668. Hermann Boerhaave (d. 23 September 1738). Dutch physician, botanist, scientific theorist and historian, and essayist

1788. Basil Hall (d. 11 September 1844). Scottish writer of travel narrative

1830. Alexander Smith (d. 5 January 1867). Scottish poet and essayist

1842. Jose Maria Heredia (d. 2 May 1905). Cuban-born French poet

1874. Holbrook Jackson (d. 16 June 1948). English essayist and literary historian

DEATHS

1799. Jean Francois Marmontel (b. 11 July 1723). French writer of fiction and playwright

1828. Louis Benoit Picard (b. 19 July 1769). French playwright and writer of fiction

1830. Stephanie Felicitie de Crest de Saint Aubin, Comtesse de Genlis (b. 25 January 1746). French playwright, writer of fiction, and memoirist

1865. Frederika Bremer (b. 17 August 1801). Swedish writer of fiction and advocate of social reform

1872. Aleksis Kivi (pseudonym of Aleksis Stenvall: b. 10 October 1834). Finnish poet, playwright, and writer of fiction

1916. George Holmes Howison (b. 29 November 1834). American mathematician, philosopher, and essayist

1936. Miguel de Unamuno y Jugo (b. 2 September 1864). Spanish poet, essayist, philosopher, historian, and writer of fiction and travel narrative

1980. Herbert Marshall McLuhan (b. 21 July 1911). Canadian communications theorist, educator, literary scholar, and essayist

1450

BIRTHS

Aldus Manutius (d. 1515). Italian teacher, scholar, printer, publisher, and editor; he will establish an academy at Venice for the study of Greek and Latin and begin to edit and print grammars and important classical texts; his Roman, Greek, and italic types will influence the design of printers' letters, and he will popularize small formats for scholarly volumes.

DEATHS

Alain Chartier (b. 1385?). French writer and secretary to Charles VI and Charles VII; his work is noted for its themes of escapism from war, the mourning for lost lovers, and the debate over whether the people or the nobility are to blame for the ills of France; he also wrote ballades and lyrics.

Thomas Hoccleve (b. 1370?). English poet; he composed a verse adaptation of Aegidius on the duties of a ruler (with a eulogy on Geoffrey Chaucer), an autobiographical piece containing a petition for salary, and two verse tales.

PUBLICATIONS

Vaettaeve, *Guttilaya*—a narrative poem by the Sinhalese monk; the piece relates the tale of an ungrateful pupil who vied with his master in a musical contest; written in a fairly simple but highly melodious style, the story holds the attention of the reader.

EVENTS

Johannes Gutenberg and Johannes Fust print the Constance Mass Book (*Missale Speciale Constantiense*).

Pope Nicholas V, a liberal patron of scholars, rejuvenates the Vatican Library, Rome; the collection dates from the fourth century.

1451

BIRTHS

Franchino Gafori (d. 1522). Italian priest, music scholar, and prose writer; he will serve as *maestro di cappella* at Monticello and Bergamo, then become attached to the cathedral at Milan; he will write eleven major prose tracts on music theory, composition, and application.

1452

EVENTS

Dutch and German printers begin to employ metal plates for the printing process.

1453

BIRTHS

Kamaloddin Shir Ali Benai (d. 1512). Persian poet of Central Asia; in his didactic verse, he will condemn immorality and evil, emphasizing the importance of training and education; he will also write historical works in prose and verse.

Shin Thilawuntha (d. 1520). Burmese poet and monk; he will write poetic expositions of Buddhism, riddles, and a variety of prose (the earliest known transcribed upon a palm leaf).

Shin Urramagyaw (d. 1542). Burmese poet and monk; only a single nine-stanza poem will remain extant of his works; however, that piece of devotional poetry, with its sensitive observation and personification, will prove sufficient to earn him a high literary reputation.

EVENTS

Johannes Gutenberg, with his financier and partner, Johannes Fust, begins the printing of the 42-line Mazarin Bible, at Mainz; until 1455.

Cosimo de' Medici welcomes to his palazzo at Florence Greek scholars fleeing Constantinople; that city has just fallen to the Ottoman Empire.

1454

BIRTHS

Angelo Ambrogini Politian (d. 1494). Italian humanist; by age seventeen, he will have written Latin and Greek epigrams and begun a translation of the *Illiad* into Latin hexameters; he will become professor of Greek and Latin at Florence, translate works of, Latin and Greek writers, publish an edition of Justinian, write a secular drama in Latin, and produce a miscellany of prose and verse.

EVENTS

Johannes Gutenberg produces papal Indulgences bearing printed data.

Various printers at Mainz (including Johannes Gutenberg and his partner, Johannes Fust) introduce movable type.

1455

BIRTHS

Johann Reuchlin (d. 1522). German humanist and Hebrew scholar; he will write a Latin dictionary, study Hebrew under a noted Italian Jewish court physician, and promote Greek studies in Germany; he will also publish a Greek grammar, edit a series of polemical pamphlets concerning the controversy over the destruction of Hebrew books, and write a satirical drama.

PUBLICATIONS

Padmanabh, *Kanhadade Prabandha*—a long poem by a Brahmin poet about whom little is known; the piece consists of 353 two-line verses in various metres, in addition to two prose passages; relates the herioc struggle of Raja Kanhadade of Jalaur against the repeated attacks of the Sultan of Delhi, Alauddin; the poet weaves a romantic love theme into that struggle; the language of the piece is the Old Western Rajasthani of the fifteenth century.

1456

BIRTHS

Jacopo Sannazaro (d. 1530). Italian poet and prose writer; he will become an influential poet of the Renaissance because of his ability to interweave poetry and prose and to define and popularize the pastoral romance; he will also write Latin verse and an ambitious epic on the birth of Christ that blends Christian and classical themes and styles.

PUBLICATIONS

François Villon, *La Petit Testament*—a poem by the French versifier; comprises forty octosyllabic octaves, a number of which concern the poet's activities with the criminal organization known as "Brotherhood of the Coquille."

EVENTS

Johannes Gutenberg, German printer, publishes his noted Bible (The Gutenberg Bible) after five years of work; the project consists of two volumes, folio, and two columns of forty-two lines each per page; the question of whether Gutenberg did the actual printing remains unanswered.

1457

BIRTHS

Sebastian Brant (d. 1521). German poet and humanist; he will study and lecture at Basel, then return to his native Strasbourg; he will gain a significant literary reputation from a satire on the follies and vices of his times, an excellent example of didactic verse.

1458

DEATHS

Inigo Lopez de Mendoza, Marquis de Santillana (b. 1398). Spanish scholar and poet; influenced by the poetry of Dante and Petrarch, he introduced their styles and methods into Spanish literature; the first Spanish poet to write sonnets, his best work came in the form of short pieces ("serranillas"); he also wrote a prose tract upon the literature of his own times.

1459

BIRTHS

Conradus Celtis (d. 1508). German poet; he will write in Latin, creating odes, love poems, and epigrams; he will also write a prose history of the city of Nuremberg.

Cem Sultan (d. 1492). Turkish poet and younger son of Sultan Mehmed II; he will become a capable statesman, as well as a learned and accomplished versifier, writing a romantic epic and poetic accounts of his travels while in exile in France and Italy; his life as an adventurer will serve as a source for Turkish and Bulgarian novels and plays.

1460

BIRTHS

William Dunbar (d. 1529?). Scottish poet; he will become secretary to various embassies; his hymns, satires, and political allegories will merit occasional placement beside similar pieces by Geoffrey Chaucer, Edmund Spenser, and William Cowper.

John Skelton (d. 1529). English poet; he will attempt translations and elegies, but his poetic talent will sustain itself in satirical vernacular pieces overflowing with grotesque language and imagery and unrestrained jocularity.

1461

PUBLICATIONS

François Villon, *Le Grand Testament*—a lyric poem by the French writer; one hundred and seventy-three stanzas in length, it contains a number of ballads and other verse forms; including a series of facetious bequests to family, friends, and (especially) enemies; written after his arrest at Meung-sur-Loire for an unidentified crime, his death sentence having been overturned because of a public holiday.

1463

BIRTHS

Pico della Mirandola (d. 1494). Italian philosopher; he will study at the principal universities of France and Italy; his writings will combine both mysticism and recondite knowledge, taking the form of Latin epistles, elegies, sonnets, and treatises; he will emphasize the theme of free will.

DEATHS

François Villon (b. 1431). French poet; he injected vitality into outworn medieval verse forms such as the ballade and the rondeau; with stark realism, he dispassionately observed himself and the life around him, combining penetration, unsentimental, and ironic poetic comment with a decided longing for forgiveness; he is never heard from again after his banishment from Paris in January of this year for theft and brawling.

PUBLICATIONS

Matteo Maria Boiardo, *Carmina de Laudibus Estensium*— a collection of songs by the Italian poet, probably his earliest work; written shortly after his marriage to the daughter of the Count of Norellara and strongly imitative of the ancients.

EVENTS

Cosimo de' Medici, duke of Florence, appoints the Italian Platonist Marsilio Ficino president of an academy at Florence for the diffusion of Platonic doctrines.

1464

DEATHS

Nicolaus of Cusa (b. 1401). German Roman Catholic prelate and philosopher; his prose tracts advanced the notion that the pope is subordinate to councils; he also denounced perverted scholasticism and, as a teacher of scientific theory, taught that the earth went around the sun.

1465

BIRTHS

Hector Boece (d. 1536). Scottish historian; he will become a professor of philosophy and presider at Aberdeen; he will publish, in Latin, biographical sketches of the bishops of Mortlach and Aberdeen, in addition to a history of Scotland.

William Dunbar (d. 1530?). Scottish poet and Franciscan missionary to England; he will write perhaps the most positive poetic allegory in English literature, rich in imagination and color; his poetry will also reflect his piety and sense of devotion; he will achieve, in addition, note for his ability as a satirist.

Fernando de Rojas (d. 1541?). Spanish writer of fiction; he will achieve literary recognition for a single dramatic novel of passion and will rise among the masters of late fifteenth-century Spanish literature.

EVENTS

The first printed texts of music begin to appear.

1466

BIRTHS

Desiderius Erasmus (d. 1536). Dutch humanist; he will become one of the most significant figures of the Renaissance, teaching throughout Europe and influencing European letters; he will edit the Latin and Greek classics and the writings of the Church Fathers; he will also produce a Latin translation of the New Testament from the Greek and his original satirical works will appear in Latin; he will combine extensive learning with a fine style, incorporating humor, moderation, and tolerance.

EVENTS

Johann Mentel prints, at Strassbourg, the first German Bible.

1467

BIRTHS

John Bourchier, Lord Berners (d. 1533). English statesman, writer, and translator; he will translate works by Jean Froissart (1337?-1410?) and Antonio de Guevara (1490-1545).

Guillaume Bude (d. 1540). French scholar; he will publish prose tracts on philology, philosophy, and jurisprudence (mostly in Latin); he will become royal librarian and found the royal collection at Fontainebleau (predecessor to the Bibliotheque Nationale); at his suggestion Francis I will establish the Collège de France.

EVENTS

The appearance of the earliest ballad about William Tell, the Swiss patriot of Burglen, in

Uri, who was reported to have been the savior of his native district from the tyranny of Austria; however, the tale of "the master shot" extends beyond the supposed incident of 1307, becoming incorporated into Aryan, Samoyede, and Turkish folklore.

1468

BIRTHS

Elija Levita (d. 1549). Italian Hebrew grammarian and linguistic scholar; he will write a Hebrew grammar, but reject offers from foreign princes to serve at their universities; he will then comment on Hebrew orthography and vowels, while compiling a Talmudic dictionary of difficult words; he will also write, in Yiddish, a book of romances based upon Italian models.

Shin Maha Rahtathara (d. 1530). Burmese poet and monk; he will write poems in four-syllable lines, most of them focusing upon the life and religious doctrines of Buddha; those pieces, reflecting a deep understanding of human life, will significantly influence later writers.

DEATHS

Johannes Gutenberg (b. 1397). German printer, regarded as the inventor of printing; credited with printing the *Fragment of the Last Judgment,* twenty editions of the Latin school grammar of Aelius Donatus (360 a.d.?), and the 42-line Mazarin Bible of 1452-1455.

PUBLICATIONS

Moulana Abdorrahman Jami, *Haft Aurang* (Seven Thrones)—a collection of seven poetic idylls ("masnavi") by the Persian poet and essayist; allegorical in nature, the poems serve as an extension of the writer's almost life-long study of Sufism, or Muslim mysticism; although the pieces may actually be derivative, the poet's language and recreation of Sufist themes provide sufficient degrees of originality; to 1485.

1469

BIRTHS

Juan de la Encina (d. 1529). Spanish playwright and poet; he will also become musical director in Pope Leo X's chapel at Rome; in addition to a poetic account of his pilgrimage to Jerusalem, he will create fourteen dramatic poems, half secular and half religious; in 1492, his secular plays will be the first of their kind to be acted in Spain.

Jean (John) Fisher (d. 1535). English churchman and prose writer; he will become Bishop of Rochester, the first Lady Margaret Professor of Divinity at Cambridge, and chancellor and bishop of that university; his tracts will advance the "new learning" and advocate internal reforms in the Church; he will, however, resist the Lutheran schism and denounce the divorce of King Henry VIII.

Niccolo di Bernardo Machiavelli (d. 1527). Italian essayist, playwright, historian, and biographer; he will become the most complex and controversial political figure of the Renaissance; his literary-political-philosophical reputation will rest upon his manual for the preservation of autocratic leadership, which maintains that only strength from within can protect the state from outside forces that seek to destroy it.

John Major (d. 1550). English scholar; he will lecture on scholastic logic and theology at Glasgow and St. Andrews, and then at Paris; he will publish commentaries upon Peter Lombard and a history of England and Scotland in Latin advocating a union of the two nations.

1470

BIRTHS

Pietro Bembo (d. 1547). Italian poet and churchman; he will attempt to restore a high literary style to Italian poetry; he will also write a formal treatise on Italian prose, a piece that introduced a new period of Italian grammar.

Bernardo Dovizi, Cardinal Bibiena (d. 1520). Italian poet, playwright, and churchman; he will rise from humble origins, principally through help from Pope Leo X; a number of his comic dramas will become popular during his day.

Badroddin Helali (d. 1529). Persian poet of Central Asia; he will compose long poems that are both mystical and didactic; a number of his shorter poetic pieces will continue to be sung to folk tunes (with instrumental accompaniment) well into the twentieth century.

Gil Vicente (d. 1536). Portuguese actor and playwright; he will be termed the founder of the Portuguese theater, writing both farces and morality pieces, the latter inspired by the humanism of Desiderius Erasmus and the playwright's own criticism of the Catholic clergy; his dramatic work will remain within the medieval dramatic and literary traditions.

DEATHS

Naghash Mkrtitch (b. 1393?). Armenian poet, painter, and priest; he relied upon his own experiences for subjects for his poetry; introduced to Armenian poetry the theme of the pilgrim seeking protection and subsistence in foreign lands, usually dying homesick and impoverished; his lyrics assumed traditional Armenian folk forms.

PUBLICATIONS

Sir Thomas Malory, *Le Morte d'Arthur*—the Arthurian romance cycle by the English writer; completed during his imprisonment and printed by William Caxton in 1485; a compilation of highly diverse narrative materials, originating at various times and among various nations; the best and most complete treatment of Arthur and his knights, as well as the most significant contribution to early English prose; the most dramatic incident focuses upon the death of the aged Arthur (from which the work gains its title) and a review of his past life and deeds.

EVENTS

Three German printers establish the first French print shop at the Sorbonne, Paris.

Nicolas Jensen, a French printer, establishes a shop at Venice for the printing and publishing of books; he will be the first to employ purely Roman letters in his texts.

1471

DEATHS

Thomas á Kempis (b. 1380?). German Augustinian priest and writer; he composed sermons, ascetical treatises, pious biographies, letters, and hymns; his major work traces the gradual progress of the soul toward Christian perfection; although generally termed mystical, his tracts gained popularity and achieved influence because of their directness and simplicity; he managed to give religious teachings a universal appeal.

Sir Thomas Malory (b. ?). English prose romance writer; through his adaptation of the Arthurian legends *(Le Morte d'Arthur),* he gave epic unity to the whole mass of French Arthurian romance; his work will exercise a decided influence upon such English poets as Alfred Lord Tennyson and Algernon Charles Swinburne.

PUBLICATIONS

Sir John Fortesque, *A Declaration upon Certayne Wrytinges*—a prose tract by the English jurist; essentially a recantation of the writer's Lancastrian political views during the War of the Roses; to 1473.

1472

BIRTHS

Wang Yang-min (d. 1528). Chinese philosopher and prose writer.

EVENTS

The *Divina Commedia* (1314?-1321?) of Dante Alighieri first printed at Foligno, in Perugia (central Italy).

1473

BIRTHS

Nicolas Copernicus (d. 1543). Polish-born astronomer and physician; he will complete, twelve years prior to his death, a treatise summarizing his studies and observations and proving the sun to be the center of the universe; that tract will be published while the author lies on his death bed; he will become the founder of modern astronomy.

1474

BIRTHS

Ludovico Ariosto (d. 1533). Italian poet, playwright, and satirist; he will become one of the most significant poets of the Italian Renaissance, masterfully blending narrative and almost flawless poetic technique with graceful linguistic expression; he will rely upon both classical and medieval literary and philosophical traditions.

Gavin Douglas (d. 1522). Scottish poet; he will become Bishop of Dunkeld; his literary efforts will include allegorical poems and a translation of the *Aeneid;* he will receive credit for being the earliest translator of the classics into English.

1475

BIRTHS

Alexander Barclay (d. 1552). Scottish-born poet, scholar, and churchman; he will translate works from the German, French, and Latin, as well as compose original eclogues.

EVENTS

The English printer William Caxton, having spent from 1469 to 1471 translating *The Re-cuyell* [Collection] *of the Historys of Troye* from the French, prints the work on a press at Bruges, with assistance from his pupil, Colard Mansion, who was also a calligrapher.

1476

DEATHS

Sir John Fortesque (b. 1394?). English jurist and constitutional lawyer; he will write Latin treatises on the differences between absolute and constitutional monarchies and on the English legal system, as well as English-language tracts on monarchy and governance in England.

PUBLICATIONS

Moulana Abdorrahman Jami, *Nafahat al-Uns* (Breaths of Familiarity)—the principal prose work of the Persian poet and critic; a collection of 616 biographies of noteworthy scholars, saints, and poets, all of whom are considered mystical writers; to 1478.

EVENTS

William Caxton returns to his native England from Bruges and, toward the end of the year, becomes the first English printer to employ movable type; he establishes a press under the sign of the Red Pail near the court at Westminster; he has acquired the patronage of King Edward IV.

1477

EVENTS

William Caxton, English printer and translator, having established a press at Westminster, issues his first dated book from that press: *The Dictes or Sayengis of the Philosophres;* he has employed type fonts brought from Bruges.

1478

BIRTHS

Sir Thomas More (d. 1535). English statesman and prose writer; he will primarily write in Latin; his major prose piece presents a picture of the ideal state founded on reason; he will also write devotions, philosophical tracts, poems, prayers, and meditations; his works will be published in English in 1557.

Giangiorgio Trissino (d. 1550). Italian poet and papal diplomat; his major work will be in the form of an epic on the deliverance of Italy from the Goths; he will also write a tragedy in imitation of Euripides.

Baldassare Castiglione (d. 1529). Italian statesman and writer; he will make a major contribution to the Renaissance ideal of aristocracy by writing a treatise on etiquette, social problems, and intellectual accomplishments; he will influence the literature of England (especially the Earl of Surrey, Thomas Wyatt, Sir Philip Sidney, and Edmund Spenser).

EVENTS

The English printer William Caxton produces the first printed edition of Geoffrey Chaucer's *The Canterbury Tales* (1387-1400).

1479

PUBLICATIONS

Moulana Abdorrahman Jami, *Salaman u Absal* (Salaman and Absal)—an allegorical prose tale by the Persian poet and critic; based upon an Hellenistic romance involving a youth who becomes the passionate lover of his nurse; an allegory of how the soul can become independent of sensual lusts; in the end, the despairing lovers cast themselves into a fire and only Salaman emerges from the flames, proving that he has been liberated from bondage to Absal.

EVENTS

Establishment of a printing press at St. Albans, in Hertfordshire, shortly after William Caxton had begun to print at Westminster; until 1486.

1480

BIRTHS

Antonio de Guevara (d. 1545). Spanish historian and prose writer; he will become Bishop of Mondonedo and historiographer to Charles V; his exalted prose style will anticipate the euphuism of John Lyly; his principal literary contribution will be a volume on Marcus Aurelius.

Surdas (d. ?). Hindi poet of India; his lyrics will reveal a compelling mastery of rhythm and a natural grace of language; his themes will become variations on the devotion to Krishna.

DEATHS

Aloys da Cadamosto (b. 1432?). Italian explorer and resident of Venice; he wrote narratives about his voyages for Prince Henry of Portugal, the most noted a journey to the Canary Islands as far as the mouth of the Gambia River.

PUBLICATIONS

Moulana Abdorrahman Jami, *Shawahidu'n-Nubuwwat* (Evidences of Prophethood)—a prose essay by the Perisan poet and critic; essentially a study of the prophet Mohammed.

EVENTS

The birth of the German wandering magician Johann Faust; he will become the prototype for works by Christopher Marlowe, Johann Wolfgang von Goethe, and others.

1481

PUBLICATIONS

Moulana Abdorrahman Jami, *al-Durrah al-Fakhirah* (The Precious Pearl)—a treatise on contemporary philosophy and mysticism by the Persian writer; composed at the direction of the Ottoman sultan Mohammed II.

EVENTS

William Caxton, English printer at Westminster, translates and prints a Flemish version of the satirical bestiary *Roman de Renart* (Reynard the Fox); the fox symbolizes the man who, under the guise of various characters, preys upon and deludes society; upon being brought to justice, he escapes through his cunning; the most notable version of the story in English appears in Geoffrey Chaucer's *Canterbury Tales,* in "The Nun's Priest's Tale."

1483

BIRTHS

Muhammad Zahiruddin Babur (d. 1530). Afghan warrior, ruler, poet, essayist, and calligrapher; his autobiography will represent the most skilled example of prose in the Turki (or Chaghatay) language; he will write descriptions of landscapes, people, and animals with clarity and directness; he will also translate mystical-didactic prose pieces.

Johann Mayer von Eck (d. 1543). German Catholic theologian; he will become professor of theology at Ingolstadt; his written tracts will serve to advance his struggle against the Protestant Reformation and Martin Luther.

Martin Luther (d. 1546). German cleric, theologian, and leader of the Reformation; his literary endeavors will include a translation of Scriptures, hymns, and prose tracts designed to advance his evangelical doctrine; his prose and poetry will help to set the literary standards of the modern German language.

PUBLICATIONS

Matteo Maria Boiardo, *Orlando Inamorato*—an epic poem by the Italian poet and playwright; concerns Charlemagne's campaigns against pagan adversaries, Orlando's love for Angelica, and the love of Ruggero for Bradamante; the piece succeeded in uniting two strains of epic romance: the Carolingian style

(valor and patriotism) and the Arthurian mode (chivalrous love adventure); three volumes to 1495; left unfinished at the poet's death, but completed and revised by others (notably Francesco Berni [1497-1535]).

Moulana Abdorrahman Jami, *Yusuf u Zulaikha* (Joseph and Zulaikha)—a poem by the Persian versifier and essayist; based upon the story of Joseph and Potiphar's wife as told in the Koran, the work treats the themes of pure and impure love; the heroine's fleshly love becomes transformed, in time, into a spiritual adoration; she weds Joseph and devotes herself to religion: the life of the soul thus triumphs over the life of the flesh.

1484

BIRTHS

Julius Caesar Scaliger (d. 1558). Italian philologist and physician who will eventually reside in France; he will write commentaries upon and develop new critical theories about the works of Cicero, Hippocrates, Theophrastus, and Aristotle; his treatise on poetics will heighten interest in Virgil and Seneca as classical models.

DEATHS

Luigi Pulci (b. 1432). Italian poet at Florence; noted principally for a burlesque epic of chivalric romance that is valuable as a specimen of the early Tuscan dialect; he also wrote long fiction and humorous sonnets.

PUBLICATIONS

Shin Maha Rahtathara, *Bhuridat Lingagyi*—a poetry collection by the Burmese poet; the four-syllable-line poems constitute the oldest examples on record of the "pyo" form: verses religious in theme and didactic in tone, narrating episodes from the life of Buddha; elaborate descriptions and praise of Buddha, the king, and the royal capital; stanzas average between thirty and thirty-five lines, each poem containing 200-300 stanzas.

1485

BIRTHS

Matteo Bandello (d. 1562). Italian writer of fiction and poetry, as well as Bishop of Agen; he will compose 215 tales, all of interest as social histories of the period; he will also prove a source for such playwrights as William Shakespeare and Philip Massinger.

Beatus Rhenatus (d. 1547). German humanist and Biblical scholar; he will produce editions of the classics, the Church Fathers, and Desiderius Erasmus; he will also compose tracts against the revolutionary character of the Reformation.

DEATHS

Rudolphus Agricola (or Roelof Huysmann; b. 1443). Dutch humanist and the most prominent scholar of the "new learning" in Germany; also a distinguished musician and painter; his writing reflects his interest in all aspects of learning; dies at Heidelberg.

PUBLICATIONS

Moulana Abdorrahman Jami, *Silsilatu' dh-Dhahab* (Chain of Gold)—a collection of verse idylls by the Persian poet and prose writer; discusses the unity of God and the teachings of the Prophet.

——————— , *Khirad-nama-yti Iskandari* (The Wisdom of Alexander)—another series of Persian verse idylls; highly moralistic in tone and language, the work traces the ancient legends related to Alexander the Great.

1486

BIRTHS

Heinrich Cornelius Agrippa von Nettesheim (d. 1535). German philosopher, physician, and diplomat; his early tracts will antagonize the

Church and the Emperor, principally because of his defense of witchcraft and consideration of occult philosophy.

PUBLICATIONS

Ali Behhaqi Hoseym Vaeze Kashefi, *Sayahat-nameye Hateme Tai* (The Travels of Hateme Tai)—a collection of fairy tales by the Persian poet; all of the pieces concern the adventures of the legendary title hero.

EVENTS

Publication of *The Book of St. Albans,* a collection of treatises on hawking, hunting, and heraldry; the last work published by the press at St. Albans, which had been established in 1479, shortly after William Caxton opened his printing shops at Westminster.

1487

BIRTHS

Francesco Guicciardini (d. 1540). Italian historian, jurist, and law professor; he will hold a number of diplomatic positions; he will write an analytical history of Italy, covering the period 1494 through 1532.

PUBLICATIONS

Alaoddoule Bakhtishah Samarqandi Doulat-shah, *Tazkerat Osh-sho-Ara* (The Record of Poets)—a literary history by the Persian scholar; provides biographical sketches of the Persian poets, from the beginnings to the writer's own time, and includes examples of their work; a number of the biographies will be translated into European languages.

1488

BIRTHS

Miles Coverdale (d. 1568). English clergyman, biblical translator, and religious writer; at

Antwerp, he will translate the Bible and Apocrypha from the German and Latin, as well as from William Tyndale's version; he will also oversee the publication of the "Great Bible"; his collected works, including translations of theological tracts and German hymns, will be published in 1844-1846.

Ulrich von Hutten (d. 1523). German humanist, poet, and satirist; he will attack the ignorance of the monks, argue against the Roman Church, and author a set of dialogues in opposition to the papal party in Germany.

DEATHS

Bernardo Pulci (b. 1438). Italian poet of Florence; he wrote an elegy on the death of Simonetta, mistress of Julian de' Medici, and has received credit for the first translation of Virgil's *Eclogues*.

1489

BIRTHS

Thomas Cranmer (d. 1556). English churchman, politician, and religious writer; he will become Archbishop of Canterbury; he will promote the translation of the Bible and the service book, while his own forty-two pieces of original composition will consist largely of prefaces and doctrinal tracts.

Madhavadeva (d. 1596). Indo-Iranian religious poet; he will write devotional songs that will be well received by the masses; he will combine beauty of expression with profound spiritual ideas; he will also compose free renderings of Sanskrit devotional verse.

Sebastian Munster (d. 1552). German theologian, cosmographer, linguist, and Biblical scholar; he will publish a Hebrew Bible and a series of Chaldee grammars; he will also produce a noteworthy prose tract on cosmography.

1490

BIRTHS

Vittoria Colonna (d. 1547). Italian poet; after the death of her husband, she will find solace in writing verse; she will become friends with Michaelangelo, Ludovico Ariosto, and Baldassare Castiglione; her poems will reach publication in 1538, at Parma.

Sir Thomas Elyot (d. 1546). English prose writer, translator, and lexicographer; he will write tracts on education and politics that reveal a definite Platonic influence; his translations will contribute significantly to popularizing the classics in England.

Hugh Latimer (d. 1555). English churchman and writer of sermons; his prose will gain merit for its simple vernacular style and vivid illustrations.

Sir David Lindsay (d. 1555). Scottish poet; his verse will reflect social and political conditions at the Scottish court, particularly the state of his own career; he will also write historical romances and moral satires in verse.

Giovanni Francesco Straparola (d. 1557?). Italian writer of fiction; he will publish a collection of seventy-four stories in the fashion of Boccaccio; those will be translated into English in 1894.

Marco Girolamo Vida (d. 1560?). Italian Latin poet who will become Bishop of Alba; he will write Latin orations and dialogues; his poems will concern such subjects as religion, prosody, silk culture, and chess.

EVENTS

Production of the Corpus Christi play at Eger, Bohemia.

Beginning of the development of serious dramatic activity in Spain.

1491

BIRTHS

Bach Van (pseudonym of Nguyen Binh Khiem; d. 1587). Vietnamese poet; he will dominate his nation's literature in the sixteenth century, writing over one hundred poems reflecting a gentle, resigned philosophy based upon the ephemeral quality of the world and a return to nature; he will come under the influence of Chinese culture, principally Confucianism and Taoism.

Teofilo Folengo (d. 1544). Italian Benedictine poet; he will become the most important of the Macaronic poets, a group of writers who combined Italian and Latin words to form an artificial language.

Ignatius Loyola (d. 1556). Spanish soldier and churchman, he will found an order to be known as the Jesuits; he will develop an interest in education and missionary work, writing prose tracts and manuals focusing upon those areas; he will be canonized in 1622.

DEATHS

William Caxton (b. 1421?). English printer; the first to issue books printed in English; produced approximately one hundred volumes, a third of those his own translations from the French.

PUBLICATIONS

Moulana Abdorrahman Jami, *Khatimat al-Hayat*—a collection of verse by the Persian poet; noted for their mathematical refinement, the lyrical poems are primarily concerned with the theme of love; ornate in language and substance.

1492

BIRTHS

Pietro Aretino (d. 1556). Italian poet; he will exercise his wit and sharp literary tongue in the writing of sonnets and dramatic comedies and tragedies; his favor among Church leaders and nobles will fluctuate radically.

Margaret of Navarre (d. 1549). Queen of Navarre and writer, she will, in her royal position, encourage agriculture, the arts, and learning; she will write poems, Boccaccio-like tales, prose epistles, and dialogues.

Juan Luis Vives (d. 1540). Spanish humanist and philosopher; he will edit works by and pen commentaries upon Aristotle, in addition to composing a learned prose tract on education.

DEATHS

Cem Sultan (b. 1459). Turkish poet; fled to France and Italy after an attempt to seize the throne of his father (Sultan Mehmud II); wrote lyrics, romantic epics, and poetic accounts of his reactions to his European travels; appears to have been poisoned.

Moulana Abdorrahman Jami (b. 1414). Persian poet and prose writer; spent most of his life at the court of Herat; considered the last significant classical Persian poet who excelled in every form of poetry, from lyric to epic; he also wrote on theology, poetics, rhetoric, grammar, and letter writing.

PUBLICATIONS

Diego San Pedro, *La Carcel de Amor* (The Prison of Love)—one of the earliest Spanish novels focusing upon the subject of courtly-love; contains the elements of the lady who epitomizes feudal social virtue and the lover who remains true in spite of cruelty and scorn.

EVENTS

The emergence of the profession of book publisher, combining the three major elements: type founder, printer, and bookseller.

Elio Antonio Nebrija, Spanish linguist and philologist, publishes his Latin-Spanish dictionary.

Johann Reuchlin, German humanist, begins his study of Hebrew in Cesena, Italy, under a noted physician and Biblical scholar, Obadiah Sforno; Sforno recommended to Reuchlin by Cardinal Domenico Grimani.

1493

BIRTHS

François de Bonivard (d. 1570). Swiss theologian, clergyman, and statesman; he will endure four years of prison at Chillon and thus serve as a source for Lord Byron's nineteenth-century poem; he will write an important historical text.

Paracelsus (Theophrastus Bombastus von Hohenheim; d. 1541). Swiss medical practitioner whose writing will reflect his interest in alchemy and mysticism; nonetheless, he will advance theories in pharmacy and therapeutics and encourage medical research and experimentation.

Olaus Petrie (d. 1552). Swedish writer and statesman; he will compose, in addition to his memoirs, a mystery play and a number of tracts on theology and politics.

PUBLICATIONS

Alishir Navai, *Mizan ul-Auzan* (Scales of Poetic Metres)—a study of prosody by the Afghan classical writer and scholar; the writer refers to the literary language of his time as "Chaghatay"; praises the charm of the syllabic folk verse of the Old Uzbek literary traditions.

Hartmann Schedel, *The Nuremberg Chronicle*—an illustrated outline of world history by the German historian and scholar; chronicles events from the Creation to the present; published in Latin and German.

EVENTS

Richard Pynson, Normandy-born English printer, issues his first dated volume: *Dialogue of Dives and Pauper* (in Latin), by Henry Parker, a Carmelite monk of Doncaster, Yorkshire.

1494

BIRTHS

François Rabelais (d. 1553). French satirist, scholar, and translator; his work will reflect the language and the wit of a profound thinker possessed of a remarkably original voice and highly creative literary style; he will influence writers from the eighteenth through the twentieth centuries and will develop to prefection the form of the prose narrative.

DEATHS

Matteo Maria Bioardo (b. 1441). Italian poet and playwright; his literary fame will come to

rest upon a long narrative poem recasting the romances of Charlemagne into ottavo rima; he attempted to unite the spirit of chivalry with the spirit of the Renaissance; he also wrote Latin eclogues and sonnets.

Pico della Mirandola (b. 1463). Italian philosopher; he wrote bewildering tracts that combined mysticism with recondite knowledge; he also wrote Latin epistles, elegies, and a series of Italian sonnets.

Angelo Ambrogini Politan (b. 1454). Italian humanist and student of ancient languages; translated the *Iliad* into Latin hexameters; professor of Greek and Latin at Florence; died at Florence.

PUBLICATIONS

Sebastian Brant, *Das Narrenschiff* (The Ship of Fools)—a satire by the German poet and humanist; attacks the follies and vices of his times; what the piece lacks in poetic quality it compensates for with sound moral teachings; published at Basel and translated into English in 1509.

John Lydgate, *Fall of Princes*—a poem by the English versifier, written between 1430 and 1438; based upon Giovanni Boccaccio's *De Casibus Virorum Illustrium,* an encyclopaedic work in Latin; the poem extends to 36,000 lines in rhyme royal.

Shin Maha Rahtathara, *Bhuridat Zatpaung Pyo*—a "classical" verse narrative by the Burmese poet and monk; religious in theme and didactic in tone; narrates episodes from the life of Buddha; written in a simple style with four-syllable lines, 30-35 stanzas (depending upon the version).

EVENTS

Aemilius Paulus of Verona appointed historiographer royal to King Charles VIII of France.

1495

BIRTHS

John Bale (d. 1563). English playwright and churchman; he will write Latin biographical catalogues of British writers, morality plays in verse, and a drama about John the Baptist that will become one of the masterpieces of the Elizabethan stage.

Hans Sachs (d. 1576). German poet and playwright; he will write in excess of six thousand poems and plays, part in support of Martin Luther and the Reformation, part as commentary upon the life and manners of his age; he will employ vigorous language, good sense, homely morality, and fresh humor.

DEATHS

Alaoddoule Bakhishah Samarqandi Doulatshah (b. ?). Persian literary historian; he specialized in biographies, a number of which underwent European translations.

PUBLICATIONS

Peter Dorland van Diest, *Den Spieghel der Salicheit van Elckerlijc* (Everyman)—a Dutch morality play and the source for the English *Everyman*; Death comes to Everyman in the midst of his rejoicing and tells him that his time has come; in searching for a companion to accompany him to his accounting before God, Everyman discovers that only Virtue will serve as his guide to the grave.

EVENTS

Lytell Geste of Robyn Hoode, the first detailed history of the fabled forest character, published; the writer places Robin Hood in southwest Yorkshire.

Aldus Manutius, Italian printer at Venice, begins his series of printed editions of the Greek and Latin classics (known as "Aldine editions"); 908 works published through 1597.

1496

BIRTHS

Clement Marot (d. 1544). French poet; he will write witty satires, translate and paraphrase

Psalms, and produce verse in practically every known form, from elegies to epigrams; his bent toward satire will bring him political enemies and cause him to move about Europe.

PUBLICATIONS

Juan del Encina, *Cancionero*—a one-act play by the Spanish poet and dramatist; performed during the Easter season in the drawing room of the Duke of Alba's palace at Salamanca; a form of secular prologue to a typical liturgical drama revealing the playwright's tendency to transfer the focus of Church drama from Christ to Venus.

Franchino Gafori, *Practica Musice*—a prose tract by the Italian churchman and music theorist, published at Milan in Latin; concerned principally with musical composition; further editions in 1497, 1502, and 1512.

Hoseyn Vaeze Kashefi, *Aklake Mohseni* (The Morals of the Beneficent)—forty chapters of prose and verse by the Persian writer; dedicated to Abu 1-Mohsen, the son of Hoseyn Bayqara; the author's most important literary effort.

Shin Maha Rahtathara, *Tada uti Mawgun*—a collection of verse by the Burmese poet and monk; considered a model by subsequent Burmese composers of panegyric poems; abounds in descriptions of human qualities, and thus has a popular appeal.

Johann Reuchlin, *Sergius*—a dramatic comedy in Latin by the German writer; through his humanistic dialogue, the playwright attacks the hypocrisy of priests and monks.

EVENTS

John Colet, English religious philosopher and disciple of Savonarola, returns to England from Italy; at Oxford he lectures on the Epistles of St. Paul; his principles of Pauline interpretation stand in opposition to those of the scholastic theologians.

Marino Sanudo begins his *Diarii* of Venetian life and politics; completed in 1535, but the work was not published until the end of the nineteenth century.

1497

BIRTHS

John Heywood (d. 1580?). English playwright and poet; he will gain his literary reputation from the writing of interludes, short plays that became an integral aspect of Elizabethan theater; as products of the medieval tradition, his plays will be especially noted for their lack of moralizing.

Philipp Melanchthon (d. 1560). German scholar, humanist, and religious reformer; he will form an association with Martin Luther and will present the first systematic exploitation of the principles of the Reformation, clarifying the new gospel for the benefit of those outside of the movement.

William Tyndale (d. 1536). English writer, translator, churchman, and biblical scholar; he will advance the influence of the "new learning" through his translations of Scriptures and his tracts defending the English Reformation; he will be arrested for heresy because of his involvement in the case of Thomas More.

EVENTS

Conradus Celtis, German Latin poet, founds the Sodalitas Danubiana, a center for humanistic studies in Vienna emphasizing the humanities disciplines, a conscious return to classical ideals and forms, and rejection of medieval religious authority.

1498

BIRTHS

Nawade I (d. 1588?). Burmese poet, courtier, and soldier; he will introduce a number of new themes and forms into Burmese poetry, relying upon his military and political experiences for subject and substance; he will produce more than three hundred short poems of four-syllable lines ("yadu").

PUBLICATIONS

Hinrek van Alkmaar, *Reinke de Vos* (Reynard the Fox)—an animal epic by the Dutch poet; actually a satire on contemporary political and social conditions; derived from the French satirical fables ("bestiaries") collected under the title *Roman de Renart* (c. 1200).

Philippe de Comines, *Memoires*—autobiographical notes by the French statesman and historian; focus principally upon his political relationships with Louis XI of France and his son and successor, Charles VIII; the work constitutes the earliest French example of history as distinguished from the chronicle.

Alishir Navai, *Char Divan* (Four Divans)—a volume of lyric poems by the Afghan writer; the pieces contain fresh descriptions of nature and a variety of philosophical meditations.

Johann Reuchlin, *Henno*—a satiric comedy in Latin by the German humanist and Hebraist; the essentially pedagogical play attacks the Obscurantists, those medieval Latin scholars opposed to the "new learning"; actors declaim lines, rather than portray them; five acts, each with two scenes, and a chorus at the end.

EVENTS

Desiderius Erasmus, Dutch humanist, makes his first visit to England, coming from Rotterdam to live and teach at Oxford; to 1500.

Aldus Manutius, Italian printer and type designer at Venice, prints the comedies of Aristophanes and edits a five-volume folio edition of the works of Aristotle.

1499

BIRTHS

Sebastian Franck (d. 1543). German humanist and religious writer; he will differ with Martin Luther on the issue of moral reform versus dogma; he will author moral treatises and a universal German history.

DEATHS

Marcilio Ficino (b. 1433). Italian Platonist philosopher and scholar; his prose will reflect his theological system, a mixture of seemingly incongruous views.

PUBLICATIONS

Willibald Pirkheimer, *Bellus Helveticum* (The Swiss War)—a history of the Swiss war against the German King Maximilian I in 1499, which led to the separation of Switzerland from the German Empire; includes the Swiss writer's autobiography.

Fernando de Rojas, *La Comedia de Calisto y Melibea*—a play by the Spanish poet and dramatist; the interest of the piece focuses not upon the title characters and their love affair, but upon the old hag Celestina, a procuress, witch, and cosmetics vendor; the drama exists as a moral warning to lovers who defy their ladies and ignore the treachery and avarice of their servants, in whom they tend to confide; the writer expanded the sixteen acts into a later version of twenty-one acts and termed it a tragicomedy.

John Skelton, *The Bowge of Court*—an allegorical poem in seven-line stanzas by the English writer; satirizes the court of King Henry VII; the word "bowge" (from the French "bouche") refers to the availability of free board at the King's table (or freeloading at royal expense).

1500

BIRTHS

Benvenuto Cellini (d. 1571). Italian autobiographer, essayist, and poet; he will compose a significant autobiographical history; that work will exist as a chronicle of violent passions in conflict with a reverence for beauty; twentieth-century scholars will describe him as "a magnificent Renaissance man . . . [who] will live forever" both in his own works and in the works of others.

Wu Ch'eng-en (d. 1582?). Chinese novelist, poet, and essayist; his major literary effort will be a novel of one hundred chapters focusing upon a monkey, who represents a calm awareness of and harmony with the environment; in addition, he will become an intelligent and witty scholar.

DEATHS

John Alcock (b. 1430). English scholar, essayist, and churchman; became Bishop of Ely and founded Jesus College, Cambridge, and participated in the dissolution of the nunneries; his prose works describe those activities.

PUBLICATIONS

Hieronymous Brunschwig, *Liber de Arti Distellandi*—a tract by the German naturalist and physician; the first treatise on herbal medicine.

Desiderius Erasmus, *Adagia* (Adages)—a collection of proverbs by the Dutch humanist; gathered principally from Greek and Latin authors, with the addition of witty and detailed comments from the Dutch writer; one of the first literary products of the so-called "new learning" and a significant source throughout the sixteenth century; published at Paris, with an enlarged edition published at Vienna in 1508.

John Lydgate, *The Siege of Thebes*—a long poem by the English verse writer; written as early as 1420, but not published until this year; essentially a liberal translation from a French prose version of the *Roman de Thebes*.

EVENTS

The first black-lead pencils produced in England.

Mariken van Nieumeghen (Mary of Nijmegen), a miracle play and the most significant example of Middle Dutch drama, has its first production at Amsterdam; the title character enters into a pact with the Devil, but the Virgin Mary rescues her.

Aldus Manutius, Italian printer and type designer, founds an academy for the study of Greek classics in Venice; there he will design and produce italic type.

The first edition of *Till Eulenspiegel*, a collection of German or Flemish satirical tales, published at Lubeck, in Schleswig-Holstein.

1501

DEATHS

Alishir Navai (b. 1441). Afghan scholar and writer; he wrote tracts on linguistics, attempting to prove that the Turkish language could be as literary as Persian or Arabic; he also wrote literary histories and romantic, philosophical, and didactic poetry.

PUBLICATIONS

Conradus Celtis, *Ludus Dianae*—an allegorical verse drama by the German humanist and writer; written in Latin.

Gavin Douglas, *The Palice of Honour*—a poem by the Scottish cleric and writer; termed a "dream allegory" and written in the vernacular, which the poet described as "Scottis"; concerns the life of a virtuous man.

Desiderius Erasmus, *Enchiridion Militis Christiani*—a Latin prose piece by the Dutch humanist; a manual of simple Christian piety; translated into English by William Tyndale.

EVENTS

Between 1445 and 1501, more than one thousand European printing offices have produced approximately 35,000 separate titles for a total of approximately ten million copies.

Conradus Celtis, German Latin poet and historian, discovers at Nuremberg manuscripts of six Terentian comedies in Latin by Hroswitha of Gandersheim (932?-1002), a German Benedictine nun.

A papal bull orders the burning of all books identified as being opposed to the Roman Catholic Church.

1502

PUBLICATIONS

Conradus Celtis, *Amores*—a Latin poem by the German writer; concerns humanistic love, rather than physical attraction or emotional involvement.

EVENTS

Ambrogio Calepino, an Italian Augustinian monk, compiles his *Cornucopiae*, a polyglot dictionary.

Margaret Beaufort, Countess of Richmond and Derby and mother of King Henry VII, establishes professorships in divinity at Oxford and Cambridge.

1503

BIRTHS

Diego Hurtado de Mendoza (d. 1575). Spanish poet, prose writer, and statesman; he will write a general history of the Italian-Spanish wars that will reveal the elegance of his prose style.

Garcilaso de la Vega (d. 1565). Spanish soldier and poet; he will introduce the Petrarchan sonnet into Spanish poetry, as well as compose odes in imitation of Virgil.

Sir Thomas Wyatt (d. 1542). English poet; his verse will be influenced significantly by the Italian love poets; he will write the earliest sonnets in English, as well as a number of lyrics, rondeaux, satires, and Psalm paraphrases.

DEATHS

Mehmed Hamdullah Hamdi (b. 1449). Turkish poet; his verse reflects his bitter feelings concerning his poverty and his inability to gain the appreciation of those in political power; he wrote poems on the story of Joseph and the wife of Potiphar.

PUBLICATIONS

William Dunbar, "The Thrissil and the Rois"—a poem by the Scottish writer in rhyme royal; a political and allegorical prothalamium celebrating the marriage of James IV of Scotland (the thistle) and Margaret Tudor (the rose).

EVENTS

The publication of the first English translation of *De Imitatione Christi* (The Imitation of

Christ) by Thomas á Kempis, the German Augustinian monk and mystic; the work traces the gradual progress of the soul toward Christian perfection, a state of detachment from the world and union with God.

1504

BIRTHS

Giambattista Cinzio Giraldi (d. 1573). Italian writer and philosopher; he will hold the chair of rhetoric at Pavia, write nine plays in imitation of Seneca, and produce the first modern classical tragedy performed in Italy; his collection of tales will provide William Shakespeare with models for at least two plays.

Nicholas Udall (d. 1556). English playwright; he will translate Erasmus, the Great Bible, and biblical commentaries; he will write one of the most humorous dramatic comedies produced in England during the middle of the sixteenth century.

PUBLICATIONS

Hoseyn Vaeze Kashefi, *Anvare Soheyli (The Shining Star Canopus)*—the best-known work of the Persian poet and prose writer; a prose version of an older collection of moralistic, humorous, and erotic verse fables; written in a highly artificial style.

Jacopo Sannazaro, *Arcadia*—a work in poetry and prose, written in the Italian vernacular and imitative of the classics; the narrator has come to Arcadia from Naples, seeking solace from an unhappy romance; the pastoral, idyllic statet is represented as both innocent and objectionable; bountiful natural beauty, and the joys it provides, are set against the narrator's immoderate grief and the threat of disorder.

1505

BIRTHS

Matthew Parker (d. 1575). English churchman, scholar, and writer; he will organize the li-

brary of Corpus Christi College, Cambridge, become Archbishop of Canterbury, and supervise the production of "the Bishops' Bible."

Mikolaj Rej (d. 1569). Polish writer and playwright; he will be labeled the "Father of Polish literature," principally because of his insistence upon writing in the vernacular Polish language; his dramatic dialogues will elevate the form to a respected position in Renaissance Polish literature.

Aegidius Tschudi (d. 1572). Swiss historian; his chronicle of Swiss history will remain a standard work until the late eighteenth century; he will assume an active role on the Catholic side during the Reformation.

DEATHS

Hoseyn Vaeze Kashefi (b.   ?). Persian poet, theologian, and astrologer; he wrote eight volumes on astrology as well as legendary fairy tales, didactic poems, and at least forty pieces of prose on a variety of moral issues.

Jallaladdin Abdarrahman as-Suyuti (b. 1445). Egyptian encyclopaedist and scholar; one of the most prolific writers of Islam, his works range from studies on grammar and philology to examinations of sexology and pornography.

PUBLICATIONS

Jakob Wimpfeling, *Epitome Rerum Germanicarum*—a German history in Latin by the German writer; noted for its reliance upon original sources, rather than the works of earlier historians.

1506

BIRTHS

George Buchanan (d. 1582). Scottish poet, essayist, historian, and playwright; he will become an accomplished writer of Latin verse and eventually exercise a significant influence on the transition of the drama from the medieval period to the modern age; his Latin paraphrase of the Psalms will endure for more than a century.

John Leland (d. 1552). English historian; he will become the earliest of modern English antiquaries, touring England and publishing records of his travels and discoveries.

PUBLICATIONS

William Dunbar, *The Dance of the Sevin Deidly Synnis*—a poem by the Scottish writer; in a trance, the poet sees the fiend Mahoun, who calls a dance to be performed by a group of spiritual outcasts who have never confessed their sins; the writer describes the dancers with extreme vigor.

EVENTS

Johann Reuchlin, German humanist and Hebraist, publishes his *Rudimenta Linguae Hebraicae,* a combination Hebrew grammar and dictionary.

1507

BIRTHS

Annibale Caro (d. 1566). Italian poet and prose writer; he will serve as secretary to a number of cardinals in Rome; he will earn literary recognition for his translations from the Greek and Latin, particularly the *Aeneid.*

PUBLICATIONS

Aloys da Cadamosto, *La Prima Navagazione per l'Oceano alle Terre de'Negri della Bassa Ethiopia*—a travel narrative by the Italian navigator in the employ of Prince Henry of Portugal; posthumously published after the writer's death in 1480; describes explorations in the Canary Islands as far as the mouth of the Gambia River.

EVENTS

Polydore Vergil, Italian historian, appointed historiographer to Henry VII of England.

Martin Waldseemuller, German cartographer, in his *Cosmographiae Introductio* (a map), labels the New World "America" after the Italian explorer Amerigo Vespucci.

1508

DEATHS

Don Isaac Abravanel (b. 1437). Spanish Jewish philosopher, scholar, and statesman; settled in Venice after the expulsion of the Jews from Spain; his writings take the form of biblical exegesis, religious philosophy, and apologetics; his biblical commentaries reflect his knowledge of political and social history.

Conradus Celtis (b. 1459). German poet who wrote principally in Latin; known for his odes, lyrics, and epigrams; he also produced a prose history of Nuremburg.

PUBLICATIONS

Ludovico Ariosto, *La Cassaria* (The Coffer)—a dramatic comedy by the Italian writer, originally written in prose, but revised (1531) in verse; follows the classical structures of Plautus and Terence; the play is set on the Greek island of Metellinus, although the characters and dialogue reflect contemporary life.

Guillaume Bude, *Annotationes in Pandectas*—a prose tract by the French scholar of philosophy and jurisprudence; essentially a series of interpretations of Roman law.

Garcia Rodriguez de Montalvo, *Amadis de Gaula*—a romantic narrative by the Spanish writer; a revision of a fourteenth-century verse narrative on chivalry.

EVENTS

Girolomo Aleandro, Italian humanist and churchman, begins to teach Greek at the University of Paris.

The *Historia Regum Britanniae* of Geoffrey of Monmouth, a history of the British kings whose accuracy has been questioned, published at Paris.

The Maying or Disport of Chaucer, the first book printed in Scotland, published.

1509

DEATHS

Phillippe de Comines (b. 1445). French statesman and historian; one of the most trusted advisors of King Louis XI of France; his memoirs and letters describe his relationships with Louis XI and Charles VIII; his historical writings exist as the earliest French examples of "history," as opposed to "chronicle."

Necati Bey. Turkish court poet and Ottoman official; he wrote Turkish versions of well-known Arabic and Persian poems; his original lyric poems rely upon the Kastamonu dialect and descriptions of nature.

PUBLICATIONS

Alexander Barclay, *The Ship of Fools*—a long poem by the Scottish-born writer and churchman; a liberal translation of the *Narrenschiff* (published at Basel in 1494) of Sebastian Brandt (1458-1521); concerns the shipping off of an assortment of fools from their native habitats to the Land of Fools; the writer introduces his subjects by social class and humorously exposes their follies; Barclay "anglicizes" Brandt's original.

Desiderius Erasmus, *Encomium Moriae* (The Praise of Folly)—a satire by the Dutch humanist, written at the suggestion of Sir Thomas More; primarily ridicules theologians, Church officials, and the nobility; written in Latin.

EVENTS

During the persecution of the Jews in Germany, Johann Pfefferkorn receives authority from Emperor Maximilian I to confiscate and burn all Jewish books (except the Old Testament), including the Talmud; the humanist and Hebraist Johann Reuchlin opposes the action and instigates a controversy between the Dominicans of Cologne and the independent thinkers throughout Germany.

1510

BIRTHS

Bernard Palissy (d. 1589). French Huguenot potter and glass painter; his written work will principally consist of narratives relating his artistic and political experiences; a complete edition of those will be published in 1880.

Lope de Rueda (d. 1565). Spanish playwright and actor; he will write comic dramas in the Italian style, in addition to humorous pastoral dialogues and short burlesques (as interlude pieces).

DEATHS

Johannes Geiler von Kaiserberg (b. 1445). German preacher at Strasbourg Cathedral and theologian; in addition to his sermons, he wrote earnest, witty, and original devotional works advocating Church reform.

PUBLICATIONS

Everyman—an English morality play of unknown authorship, 921 lines in length; derived from a Dutch counterpart, *Elckerlijk*; summoned by Death in the last hour of his life, Everyman discovers that none of his friends (Fellowship, Kindred, Cousin, Goods) will or can accompany him; only Good Deeds, whom he has neglected in the past, will serve as his guide.

Sir Thomas More, *Life of Johan Picus, Erle of Mirandula*—a biography by the English statesman, printed at London by Wynkyn de Worde; a liberal translation of a fifteenth-century biography of Pico della Mirandola (1463-1494), the Italian philosopher, poet, and theologian who advanced the notion of free will.

1511

BIRTHS

Johannes Secundus (Jan Evaraerts; d. 1536). Dutch poet; he will study and write in Latin;

his principal works will be composed while serving the archbishop of Toledo, the bishop of Utrecht, and the Holy Roman Emperor.

Michael Servitus (d. 1553). Spanish theologian, physician, and writer; he will, in his most noted tract, deny the Trinity; his medical treatises will advance his theory of the pulminary circulation of the blood.

PUBLICATIONS

Shin Thilawuntha, *Parayana Wuthtu*—a prose tract by the Burmese monk, poet, and essayist; one of the earliest known pieces of prose written on palm leaf; a combination narrative and historical chronicle.

EVENTS

Desiderius Erasmus, Dutch humanist, appointed Lady Maragaret reader in Greek at Cambridge; until 1514.

1512

BIRTHS

Giorgio Vasari (d. 1574). Italian architect, painter, and writer; he will write entertaining biographies of artists that will become the principal source of knowledge about Renaissance art history.

DEATHS

Kamaloddin Shir Ali Benai (b. 1453). Persian poet of central Asia; his didactic verse condemns immorality and evil; the works identify the importance of training and education; he also wrote historical works in prose and verse; he loses his life when an Iranian army captures Qarshi, where he resided.

PUBLICATIONS

Nicolas Copernicus, *Commentariolus*—a tract by the Polish-German scientist and philosopher; the writer sets forth his belief that the

earth and the other planets revolve around the sun; a preface to the *De Revolutionibus* of 1530.

EVENTS

Gavin Douglas, Scottish poet and churchman, translates the *Aeneid*, with a prologue, into what he terms "the Scotis"; the writer becomes the earliest identifiable translator of the classics into English.

1513

PUBLICATIONS

Bernardo Dovizi, Cardinal Bibiena, *La Calandria*—a comic play by the Italian churchman and playwright; an extremely popular piece among his secular contemporaries.

John Lydgate, *Troy Book*—a poem consisting of five books and written in ten-syllable couplets, by the English churchman and versifier; written between 1412 and 1420, but published over sixty years after the poet's death; relates the history of Troy and introduces the story of the Trojan settlement of England by Brutus, the great grandson of Aeneas; written at the request of Prince Henry (later King Henry V).

Niccolo Machiavelli, *Il Principe* (The Prince)—a treatise on statecraft by the Italian writer; presents the idealistic views of an acute observer of the contemporary political scene who envisions an Italian savior who will expel all foreign usurpers; lessons from Roman history should apply to the present; acquisition and application of power may necessitate unethical methods, but the circumstances may allow their employment.

——————, *Comedia di Callimaco: E di Lucretia*—a play by the Italian writer; despite its premise—that humans are flawed and given to self-centeredness—the piece proved quite popular; after the third edition, it assumes the title *La Mandragola*.

John Skelton, "Ballade of the Scottysshe Kynge"—a poem by the English versifier; a spirited celebration of the battle of Flodden Field (Northumberland) where, on 9 September 1513, the forces of the Earl of Surrey defeated James VI of Scotland.

Gil Vicente, *Auto de la Sibilla Cassandra* (Act of the Sibyl Cassandra)—a dramatic devotional piece by the Portuguese actor and playwright; the sibyl foresees the birth of the Messiah and refuses to marry her suitor, Solomon; thus, remaining a virgin, she can qualify to give birth to the Christ; in the end, the divinely appointed Mary and the Child appear.

1514

BIRTHS

Andreas Vesalius (d. 1564). Belgian anatomist; he will significantly advance the study of biology through his tracts describing the bones and the nervous system; he will also challenge the Aristotelian doctrine that the heart, as opposed to the brain and the nervous system, serves as the physical correlative of personality.

EVENTS

Septem Horae Canonicae, the first volume printed in Arabic type, published in Rome.

1515

BIRTHS

Roger Ascham (d. 1568). English humanist and educator; he will write a tract in defense of archery and a lengthy essay promoting the virtues of a classical education.

DEATHS

Aldus Manutius (b. 1450). Italian printer at Venice; he published (as the Aldine editions) reprints and editions of the Greek and Roman classics, as well as works by Italian writers; his son and grandson will continue the project, printing a total of 908 works.

PUBLICATIONS

Desiderius Erasmus, *Institutio Principis Christiani* (The Education of a Christian Prince)—a prose tract, in Latin, by the Dutch humanist; records the writer's impressions during his visits to England and France.

Giangiorgio Trissino, *Sofonisba*—a tragedy in imitation of Euripides by the Italian playwright; reportedly the first play written in blank verse.

EVENTS

Johann Grieninger, Strasbourg printer, issues an edition of the stories and verse of the fourteenth-century German peasant clown, Till Eulenspiegel.

The Lateran Council's decree, *De Impressione Liborun,* forbids the printing of books without permission from the Roman Catholic authorities.

Mutianus Rufus, Ulrich von Hutten, and others publish their *Epistolae Obscurorum Virorum*; a satire on scholarship, written in dog-Latin, by German humanists in support of Johann Reuchlin, a German Hebraist who had been engaged in a controversy over several attempts to burn all Jewish books.

1516

BIRTHS

Konrad von Gessner (d. 1565). Swiss naturalist and prose writer; he will become known as a significant classical bibliographer and naturalist cataloguer; he will also write tracts on medicine, mineralogy, and philology.

Juan Latino (d. 1606). Guinean-born Spanish poet and Latin scholar; he will emerge from slavery to become a professor at the University of Granada and a friend of Don Juan of Austria; he will compose a poem celebrating the latter's victory over the Turks at Lepanto.

PUBLICATIONS

Pietro Martier d'Anghiera (or Peter Martyr), *De Rebus Oceanicus et Novo Orbe* (The New

World)—a prose tract by the Italian-born historian and churchman; the first published account of the discovery of America in 1492.

Ludovico Ariosto, *Orlando Furioso di Ludovico Ariosto da Ferrara*—a poem by the Italian poet and playwright; a subtly ironic epic romance combining tales of chivalry, adventure, and magic; known for the multiplicity and variety of its action and the vast number of characters; forty cantos (first edition) in ottava rima; revised in 1521 and 1532; an English edition in 1591.

Sir Thomas More, *Utopia*—a speculative political essay by the English statesman and writer, composed in Latin and published at Louvain; Desiderius Erasmus supervised the printing; concerns the search for the best possible form of government; considers such ideas as communism, a national system of education extended to men and women, and religious toleration; a French edition in 1530, an English translation in 1551, and further editions in German, Italian, and Spanish.

John Skelton, *Magnyfycence*—a morality play by the English poet; Magnificence is represented by a prince, who is ruined by misguided generosity and bad counselors; in the end, Goodhope, Perseverance, and other virtues restore him.

Gil Vicente, *Auto de la Barca* (The Ship of Hell)—a morality play by the Portuguese playwright and actor; concerns persons of various social classes attempting to gain admission into a vessel bound for Heaven.

EVENTS

Desiderius Erasmus, Dutch humanist, publishes his annotated New Testament of both Greek and Latin texts.

Sir Anthony Fitzherbert, English jurist, publishes his *Le Graunde Abridgement*; a digest of important legal cases from the reigns of Richard II, Edward I, Edward II, and Henry III down to Henry VII; further editions through 1577.

Garcia de Resende, Spanish writer, compiles his *Cancioneiro Geral*, an anthology of Portuguese and Spanish verse.

1517

BIRTHS

Pierre Belon (d. 1564). French naturalist and traveler; he will write valuable prose tracts on trees, herbs, birds, and fishes.

Henry Howard, Earl of Surrey (d. 1547). English poet; his love poems will serve as manifestations of courtly love verse from the Middle Ages; his Petrarchan sonnets will complement his lyrics, elegies, Psalm paraphrases, and translations; he will produce, in blank verse, the first English translations of Books Two and Four of Virgil's *Aeneid*.

PUBLICATIONS

Teofilo Folengo, *Opus Maccaronicum*—a collection of satiric poems in Latin by the Italian Benedictine writer; ridicules contemporary romantic epics for their ornamentation and affectation.

Johann Reuchlin, *De Arte Cabbalistica*—prose tract by the German humanist and linguistic scholar; attempts to explain the documents and the principles of medieval Hebrew mysticism.

John Skelton, *The Tunnynge of Elynour Rummyng*—a comic poem by the English versifier; a description of contemporary English low life containing a fair share of coarse humor; the title character, an alewife, concocts brew for mixed tavern company, who throng to consume it.

Bartolome de Torres Naharro, *Propalladia* (The First Fruits of Pallas)—a collection of seven comedies by the Spanish humanist and playwright, published at Naples; in the preface, the writer sets forth his theory of drama: five acts, six to twelve characters, and a distinction between plays representing real life and those written entirely from the imagination.

EVENTS

Emperor Maximilian I crowns Ulrich von Hutten, German humanist, as "King of Poets."

1518

BIRTHS

Andrea Palladio (d. 1581). Italian architect; his treatise on Roman architecture will greatly influence the English architects of the seventeenth and eighteenth centuries, particularly Inigo Jones (1573-1652) and Sir Christopher Wren (1632-1723).

DEATHS

Kabir (b. ?). Indian poet and Hindu secular reformer; his verse will have a significant impact on the founders of Sikhism; his devotional poetry reflects the traditions of Vaisnava, reinforced by Muslim Sufi mysticism.

PUBLICATIONS

Martin Luther, *Eyn Sermon von Ablass und Gnade* (A Sermon on Indulgence and Grace)—a sermon by the German religious reformer, a complement to the *95 Thesen* of 1517; he states with conviction his continuing dissatisfaction with the Church of Rome; questions the validity of papal authority.

Gil Vicente, *Auto de la Barca do Purgatorio* (The Ship of Purgatory)—a morality play by the Portuguese actor and playwright; concerns souls attempting to attain salvation and includes a court of justice, complete with a prosecutor (Satan) and a judge (the Angel of Heaven).

EVENTS

Philip Melanchton, German religious reformer, appointed professor of Greek at the University of Wittenberg, specifically to work on an edition of Aristotle; he will abandon that project after coming under the influence of Martin Luther; he will then devise the educational program to implement the Lutheran Reformation.

Adam Riese, German mathematician, publishes his first book on practical arithmetic.

1519

PUBLICATIONS

Desiderius Erasmus, *Colloquia*— tract by the Dutch humanist and priest; the writer confronts the abuses of the Church with audacity and incisiveness; may well have prepared the world for the reforms of Luther (with whom he eventually came into conflict); the work enlarged in subsequent editions.

John Skelton, *Colyn Clout*—a satirical poem by the English writer, directed against ecclesiastical abuses; in the form of a complaint by the title character, a vagabond; the piece influenced Edmund Spenser's "Colin Clout come home againe" (1595), an allegorical pastoral poem.

Timanna, *Parijatapahananamu*—a narrative poem by the Indian (Teluguan) court poet; relates the predicament of the god Krishna, which results from the jealousy between his two wives; the title was taken from the name of a flower, which proves to be the cause of the jealousy and the problems that follow.

Gil Vicente, *Auto de la Barca de la Gloria* (Act of the Ship of Glory)—a morality play by the Portuguese actor and playwright; concerns souls trying to attain salvation; highly lyrical in tone and language.

1520

BIRTHS

Jacques de Cujas (d. 1590). French jurist; he will become professor of jurisprudence at Bourges and gain a reputation for being able to formulate extremely difficult hypotheses; a ten-volume French edition of his works will be published in 1658.

Mattias Flacius Illyricus (d. 1575). Lutheran theologian, born in Albania; he will hold professorships in Hebrew and religion at Wittenberg and Jena; he will write a general Church history and tracts defending his belief in original sin.

Jorge de Montemayor (d. 1561). Spanish poet and novelist; his pastoral romances, written in the Castilian dialect, will influence seventeenth-century English pastoral poets.

DEATHS

Bernardo Dovizi, Cardinal Bibiena (b. 1470?). Italian churchman and writer of comedies that were extremely popular in his native country; dies from poison.

Shin Thilawuntha (b. 1453). Burmese monk and poet; the major portion of his verse explains Buddhism; composed riddles in verse.

PUBLICATIONS

Martin Luther, *An den Christlichen Adel Deutscher Nation: Von des Christlichen Standes Besserung* (Address to the Nobility of the German Nation)—an essay by the German religious reformer; a direct appeal to the civil authorities to resist the exercises of secular power by the Roman Church; the writer seeks to undermine the Pope's claim to spiritual authority; he sets forth proposals for practical reforms, including a significant decrease in German contributions to the Church treasury and the abolition of celibacy for the clergy.

EVENTS

King Francis I (reigned 1515-1547) establishes, at Fontainebleau, the Royal Library of France.

1521

BIRTHS

Richard Eden (d. 1576). English traveler, prose writer, and translator; he will contribute informative narratives relating to navigation and exploration and translate such works from Spanish and German adventurers.

DEATHS

Sebastian Brant (b. 1457?). German poet, satirist, and humanist; noted for his didactic sat-

ire on the follies and vices of his times; translations of his verse into English appeared as early as 1509.

Abdollah Hatefi (b. 1445?). Persian poet of central Asia; wrote love poetry, as well as didactic and historical verse narratives; especially noted for his poems on the bloody and violent campaigns of the fourteenth-century conqueror Timur.

PUBLICATIONS

Niccolo Machiavelli, *Libro della Arte della Guerra* (The Art of War)—a prose tract by the Italian writer and political philosopher; essentially a treatise on military science and tactics, although the writer does not completely ignore the political implications of war; an English edition in 1560.

John Major, *A History of Greater Britain, both England and Scotland*—an historical survey by the Scottish scholar; written in Latin, the work advances the notion of a union between England and Scotland (which will not occur until 1707).

Philip Melanchthon, *Loci Communes*—a prose tract by the German scholar, humanist, and religious reformer; the first systematic presentation of the principles of the Reformation; attempts to clarify the new gospel to those outside the movement and to explicate Lutheran dogma.

John Skelton, "Speke, Parrot"—a satiric poem by the English writer, the first of his two major poetic attacks upon Cardinal Thomas Wolsey; the writer emphasizes what he believes to be the evils resulting from the Cardinal's political dominance.

EVENTS

Alexander Barclay, Scottish poet, scholar, and churchman, publishes *The Introductory To Write and To Pronounce French.*

1522

BIRTHS

Joachim du Bellay (d. 1560). French poet and prose writer; he will become, after Pierre de

Ronsard, the most important member of the Pleiade school; he will advocate the rejection of medieval linguistic traditions and the return to classical and Italian literary models; he will write collections of Italian sonnets, inspired by his diplomatic visits to Rome.

DEATHS

Gavin Douglas (b. 1475). Scottish churchman and poet; he wrote moral and historical allegories in verse and translated Latin classics; dies at London from the plague and is buried at the Church of the Savoy.

Farid (b. ?). Muslim Panjabi poet; wrote 130 poems and four hymns, all important Muslim contributions to the Sikh scriptures; they also serve as the oldest examples of Muslim Panjabi verse; his couplets focused upon the transitory state of youth and worldly success, exhorting readers to trust only in God.

Franchino Gafori (b. 1451). Italian priest and music scholar; wrote practical and theoretical prose tracts, published between 1480 and 1520; copies of his works exist in the British Museum; dies at Milan.

Johann Reuchlin (b. 1455). German humanist and Hebraic scholar; became the principal promoter of Greek studies in Germany and spoke out against the destruction of all Jewish books; edited various Greek texts; published a Greek grammar, a series of polemical pamphlets, and satirical drama.

PUBLICATIONS

Johann Pauli, *Schimpf und Ernst*—a collection of humorous short stories and anecdotes by the German writer.

John Skelton, "Why come ye nat to courte"—a satirical poem by the English writer; contains attacks upon Cardinal Thomas Wolsey (1475?-1530) describing the evil consequences of his dominating political position; results in the poet having to seek sanctuary at Westminster.

EVENTS

Alessandro Alessandri, Italian scholar, publishes *Dies Geniales,* a nonsequential encyclopaedia.

Martin Luther completes his translation of the New Testament at Wittenberg; printed by Hans Lufft.

The Polyglot Bible (Latin, Greek, Hebrew, and Aramaic) published at the University of Alcala.

1523

DEATHS

Ulrich von Hutten (b. 1488). German humanist and poet; his literary reputation will suffer because of his political entanglements, which caused him to act impetuosly; known for a number of social dialogues and satiric poems; the exact location of his grave, on the island of Ufnau in the Lake of Zurich, was discovered in 1958.

PUBLICATIONS

Hans Sachs, *Die Wittenbergische Nachtigall*—an allegorical tale in verse by the German poet and playwright; celebrates the Reformation and sings the praises of Martin Luther.

John Skelton, *The Garlande of Laurell*—a poem by the English university laureate; a self-glorifying allegorical piece describing the crowning of the writer among the great poets of the world.

EVENTS

John Bourchier, Lord Berners, English statesman and translator, translates into English the *Chroniques* (Chronicles) of Jean Froissart; to 1525.

Anthony Fitzherbert, prominent English jurist, publishes his *The Boke of Husbandrie,* the first work in the English language entirely devoted to agriculture.

Hans Holbein the younger, German painter, paints the portrait of Desiderius Erasmus.

1524

BIRTHS

Luiz Vaz de Camoens (d. 1580). Portuguese poet; he will become the most significant poet of his nation; his highly regarded sonnets and lyrics will not be published until after his death; his epic poems will focus upon his own adventures and rely on segments of Portuguese history.

Pierre de Ronsard (d. 1585). French poet and critic; he will gain recognition as his nation's most significant Pindaric poet, being celebrated in his day as the Prince of Poets; scholars and commentators will consider his work the epitome of French Renaissance poetics and a major force in the advancement of the French language.

PUBLICATIONS

Petrus Apianus of Ingolstadt, *Cosmogaphia*— a lengthy treatise by the German mathematician, astronomer, and prose writer; considered the first textbook on theoretical geography; contains a discussion on comets.

EVENTS

Pietro Aretino, Italian poet, expelled from Rome for publication of his sixteen "shameless" sonnets, *Sonetti Lussuriosi.*

Jan Wynkyn de Worde, Dutch-born printer and pupil of William Caxton, publishes in London a translation of the *Gesta Romanorum,* a collection of tales in Latin that was first printed in 1472.

————————, in publishing Robert Wakefield's *Oratorio,* inserts Italic type for the first time in England.

1525

BIRTHS

George Gascoigne (d. 1577). English poet and playwright; he will gain literary recognition for his nondramatic satiric pieces, the earliest formal verse satires in English, as well as for one of the earliest English treatises on prosody; he will also write the earliest extant prose comedy in English and will develop what has come to be known as "tragicomedy"; estimates of his year of birth range from 1525 to as late as 1534 and 1542.

Louise Labe (d. 1566). French poet; she will gain as much notice for her physical beauty as for her verse; she will be known by the epithet "La Belle Cordiere," the result of her marriage to a wealthy rope manufacturer of Lyons.

Thomas Wilson (d. 1581). English statesman and prose writer; he will urge the importance of writing upon English themes and subjects in the English language and will also advise writers to avoid affectation and Latin.

PUBLICATIONS

Pietro Bembo, *Prose della Volgar Lingua*—a prose tract that, as its title illustrates, advocates reliance upon common but proper native language; the earliest example of popular Italian writing.

Gil Vicente, *Juiz da Beira* (The Judge from Beira)—a dramatic satire by the Portuguese actor and playwright; ridicules the actions of a magistrate who does not understand the laws he must uphold and interpret.

Juan Luis Vives, *De Subventione Pauperum*—a prose tract by the Spanish philosopher and humanist; the writer demands that the state provide assistance to the poor.

1526

BIRTHS

Wang Shih-cheng (d. 1593). Chinese scholar, statesman, and novelist; he will receive credit for composing one of the earliest novels in Chinese literature.

PUBLICATIONS

Hector Boece, *Historia Gentis Scotorum* (History of Scotland)—a general history by the

Scottish historian, written in Latin; although the writer appears to have relied on his imagination for significant portions of the work, his contemporaries approved of the piece, which earned the historian a royal pension and a benefice.

Shin Maha Rahtathara, *Kogan Pyo*—a collection of poems by the Burmese monk and versifier, written in the Burmese classical verse form of four-syllable lines; religious in theme and didactic in tone; contains narratives of Buddha's life and elaborate praise for his words and deeds.

Jacopo Sannazaro, *De Partu Virginis*—a Latin epic by the Italian poet and prose writer; an attempt to write a Virgilian epic poem on a Christian theme (the Annunciation and the birth of Christ); written in Latin hexameters and replete with mythological allusion and references to pagan deities; the piece has been consistently criticized for its merging of classical and Christian motifs.

——————, *Eclogae Piscatoriae* (Piscatory Eclogues)—a collection by the Italian poet; Latin imitations of classical forms, but substituting fishermen for the usual shepherds; prompted a critical debate among eighteenth-century English writers, who could not understand how anyone could exchange the countryside and its traditional shepherds for the sea and its fishermen.

EVENTS

Francisco sa de Miranda, Portuguese poet, founds the Italianate (or Petrarchan) school of literature in Portugal.

Peter Schoeffer the younger prints, at Worms, 3000 copies (octavo) of William Tyndale's translation of the New Testament; the translation represents a combination of Tyndale's own scholarship with the previous efforts of Martin Luther and Desiderius Erasmus.

1527

BIRTHS

Mahmud Abdulbaki Baki (d. 1600). Turkish poet and jurist; he will translate Arabic legal treatises into Turkish and compose original tracts on the law; his lyric poetry will be considered the height of classical Turkish literature; his verses are meditations on life, many praising wine and beauty.

Remy Belleau (d. 1577). French poet and translator of Anacreon; he will compose a variety of descriptive prose and verse, including a collection of poems on precious stones.

DEATHS

Niccolo Machiavelli (b. 1469). Italian essayist and historian; his controversial manual on political conduct remains a key document in the study of political history, and his theories have become common terms in the lexicon of political thought; he also demonstrated a high degree of literary and rhetorical competence.

PUBLICATIONS

Marco Girolamo Vida, *De Arte Poetica*—a tract on poetic theory by the Italian churchman and Latin poet; advances purely classical critical concepts of prosody.

EVENTS

Hans Holbein the younger, German painter, completes his portrait of Sir Thomas More and his family.

1528

DEATHS

Wang Yang-ming (b. 1472). Chinese philosopher and prose writer.

PUBLICATIONS

Baldassare Castiglione, *Il Cortegiano* (The Courtier)—a prose dialogue by the Italian humanist and writer; delineates the qualifications of the ideal courtier, both ethical and intellectual; also focuses upon such areas as the military, sporting activities, and cultural endeavors; the work will influence considerably the English court poets of the sixteenth century; and English translation in 1561 by Sir Thomas Hoby (1530-1566).

Desiderius Erasmus, *Ciceronianus*—a satire on Latin scholarship by the Dutch humanist; attacks those humanists who set style above substance.

Sir Thomas More, *Dialogue*—the first controversial book in English by the English statesman; directed against William Tyndale's commentary on the divorce of King Henry VIII.

EVENTS

Johannes Agricola (1494-1566), German religious reformer and principal court preacher at Berlin, publishes his collection of German proverbs, a volume that will assure him a lasting place in German literary history; to 1529.

1529

BIRTHS

Etienne Pasquier (d. 1615). French religious writer; he will rise in the judiciary system by pleading against the Jesuits in their parliament; his prose works will reflect his hatred of that Roman Catholic society.

Francisco Patrizi (d. 1597). Italian writer; he will become a respected historian and philosopher.

DEATHS

Baldassare Castiglione (b. 1478). Italian diplomat and court officer; he gained his literary-historical reputation from the composition of a manual for courtiers, as well as from his Italian and Latin poems; his letters contributed to the political and intellectual history of his times.

Juan de la Encina (b. 1469). Spanish poet and playwright; musical director in Pope Leo X's chapel at Rome and prior of Leon, Spain; he wrote a poetic account of his pilgrimage to Jerusalem, as well as fourteen religious and secular dramatic poems.

Badroddin Helali (b. 1470?). Persian poet of Central Asia; wrote lengthy didactic-mystical poems; his shorter pieces were sung to folk tunes; executed on the grounds that he was a Shiite.

John Skelton (b. 1460?). English satirical poet; his satirical vernacular verses contained an abundance of grotesque language and imagery; he attacked the corruption of the Church and its archbishop; an edition of his poems will not appear until 1568.

PUBLICATIONS

Antonio de Guevara, *El Relos de Principes*—a tract by the Spanish religious writer and rhetorician; focuses upon the education of Spanish princes.

Shin Maha Rahtathara, *Thanwara Pyo*—a classical poem by the Burmese versifier; weaves pure human interest into descriptions and praise of Buddha's life.

EVENTS

Kunst und Recht Alchamei Buchlein, a manual of alchemy, published at Worms.

1530

BIRTHS

Jean Bodin (d. 1596). French social and political philosopher; as a lawyer, he will become dismayed by the chaos resulting from the conflicts between Roman Catholics and Huguenots; his prose work will argue that the well-ordered state requires religious toleration and a sovereign monarch; his theories will contribute to the notion of the modern nation-state.

Jan Kochanowski (d. 1584). Polish poet; he will write elegies, epigrams, verse, and translations of the Psalms.

DEATHS

Muhammad Zahiruddin Babur (b. 1483). Afghan essayist, poet, caligrapher, and warrior-ruler; he wrote an autobiography and composed prose descriptions of landscapes, people, and animals; his poetry demonstrates instances of humor, but its language is always pure, simple, and fresh.

William Dunbar (b. 1465?). Scottish poet; he wrote political allegories and poetic conversations; influenced by François Rabelais, he demonstrates considerable humor, satiric power, and poetic imagination.

Shin Maha Rahtathara (b. 1468). Burmese poet and monk; he wrote his verse in four-syllable lines, relying upon Buddhist themes and appealing to ordinary people.

Jacopo Sannazaro (b. 1456?). Italian court poet; his major work is a combination of prose and verse that influenced the poetry of Sir Philip Sidney; he also wrote sonnets and canzoni.

PUBLICATIONS

Philip Melancthon, *Apologia*—a prose tract by the German humanist and theologian; amplifies the theology of the Augsburg Confession.

——————— , *Confessio Augustana* (The Augsburg Confession)—the Lutheran confession of faith presented to Emperor Charles V at the Diet of Augsburg; in carefully moderate language, the tract presents the principles of Lutheran doctrine and reviews abuses for which the reformers (particularly Martin Luther) seek remedy; the original text remains a standard of faith in Lutheran churches; revised in 1540.

Hans Sachs, *Das Schlaraffenland*—a collection of humorous anecdotes told in doggerel verse by the German poet and dramatist; satirical good humor does not obscure the moral purpose of the work.

Jacopo Sannazaro, *Sonetti e Canzoni*—a collection of verse by the Italian court poet; known for its unique blending of Christian and classical themes and styles.

EVENTS

Claude Garamond, French type designer and manufacturer, created Imprimeur de Roi by King Francis I.

William Tyndale, English translator and biblical scholar, translates the Pentateuch; his work is considered an extremely accurate text.

1531

BIRTHS

Azariah ben Moses Dei Rossi (d. 1578). Italian-born Hebrew scholar and physician; he will become versed in Hebrew, Latin, and Italian literatures, while studying medicine, archaeology, history, Greek and Roman antiquities, and philosophy; his writings will reflect his broad knowledge and education and his independent thinking in the field of religion.

PUBLICATIONS

Clement Marot, *Adolescence Clementine*—a collection of verse by the French poet, focusing upon his early experiences and observations; a number of the pieces concern the poet's trip to Italy with the Duke of Alencon.

EVENTS

Desiderius Erasmus, the Dutch humanist, publishes the first complete edition of the works of Aristotle.

William Tyndale, English scholar and translator, publishes his translation of the Book of Jonah.

1532

BIRTHS

Tulsidas (d. 1623). Brahmin Hindi poet; his devotional poems will achieve significance in medieval Hindi literature; he will write principally in the vernacular.

PUBLICATIONS

François Rabelais, *Les Horribles et Espouvantables Faictz et Prouesses du Tres Renomme Pantagruel Roy de Dipsodes Filz* *du Grand Geant Gargantua* (Pantagruel, King of the Dipsodes, with His Heroic Acts and Prowesses)—a satire by the French writer, translator, and editor; denounced by the Sorbonne for its obscenity; essentially a bawdy piece that will become a classic of racy humor, the work came forth under the pen name "Alcofribis Nasier," an anagram of the writer's name.

EVENTS

The *Works* of Geoffrey Chaucer published posthumously; *The Testament of Cresseid*, by Robert Henryson, included in error, a mistake not corrected until 1721.

Robert Estienne, French printer to King Francis I, publishes his *Thesaurus Linguae Latinae*, the first Latin-English dictionary.

1533

BIRTHS

Alonso de Ercilla y Zuniga (d. 1594). Spanish poet; his major piece will focus upon the Araucanian Indians of Chile and their conquest by the Spaniards; the piece will be considered the finest epic of the Spanish Golden Age.

Isaak Luria (d. 1572). Jerusalem-born Palestinian mystic and philosopher; he will lead an important school of mysticism combining Messianism with older doctrines; he will also be concerned with the nature of and the connection between early redemption and cosmic restoration.

Michel Eyquen de Montaigne (d. 1592). French essayist, diarist, and translator; he will develop the essay as a valid literary genre; he will produce his first two books of essays during his retirement; those pieces will demonstrate the maturation of the writer's thought from a study of himself to a more general study of humankind and nature.

DEATHS

Ludovico Ariosto (b. 1474). Italian poet; an artist of noble personal appearance and ami-

able character who wrote comedies, satires, sonnets, and poems in Latin; the sonnets in particular reveal the poet's genius.

John Bourchier, Lord Berners (b. 1467). English statesman, writer, and translator; primarily, he translated works by Jean Froissart and Antonio de Guevara.

Seyh Mahmud Lamii (b. ?). Turkish prose writer and poet; twenty-four volumes of his works survive, the prose pieces mainly translations or paraphrases of Persian and Arabic texts; wrote nine allegorical epics in praise of earnest submission to the will of Allah.

PUBLICATIONS

George Buchanan, *Rudimenta Grammatices*—a manual of Latin prosody by the Scottish essayist, poet, playwright, and historian; well received by the writer's contemporaries.

EVENTS

Allerhand Farben und Mancherley Weyse Dunten zu Bereyten, a manual for the production of paints and inks for printing, published at Augsburg.

1534

BIRTHS

Hernando de Herrera (d. 1597). Spanish poet; he will be known for his lyrics; his love poems will express extremely tender sentiments, while his odes will attain a grandeur foreshadowing the poetic diction of John Milton; he will also write a prose history of the 1572 war in Cyprus.

PUBLICATIONS

Sir Thomas More, *Dialogue of Comfort against Tribulation*—reflections by the English statesman and prose writer; written during the first days of the writer's imprisonment in the Tower of London for opposing Henry VIII's divorce from Catherine and for refusing to impugn the authority of the Pope.

François Rabelais, *La Vie Inestimable du Grand Gargantua, Pere de Pantagruel* (The Inestimable Life of the Great Gargantua, Father of Pantagruel)—a satire by the French comic writer, editor, and translator; the writer's attempt to recreate the myth of Gargantua; also presents his idealized conception of a new world order, meant to promote responsible, active participation in God's community on earth.

EVENTS

Sebastian Munster produces the first German edition of the Hebrew Bible, to 1535; includes a literal Latin version and notes; relied upon by Miles Coverdale for the Old Testament of his Great Bible (1539).

1535

BIRTHS

Ulisse Aldrovandi (d. 1605). Italian naturalist and prose writer; he will hold the chairs of Botany and Natural History at Padua; for over forty years he will study and publish on the subjects of birds, insects, and mollusca.

DEATHS

Jean (John) Fisher (b. 1469). English churchman, writer, and Bishop of Rochester; advocated reformation of the Church from within and strongly resisted the Lutheran schism; tried for denial of the King's supremacy and ultimately beheaded.

Sir Thomas More (b. 1478). English statesman and one of the most eminent humanists of the Renaissance; initiated modern English historical writing, which became distinct for both its literary quality and factual accuracy; known principally for his Latin treatise on the ideal existence; beheaded for high treason after refusing to recognize Henry VIII as head of the Church.

Heinrich Cornelius Agrippa von Nettesheim (b. 1486). German philosopher and physician; his prose tracts antagonized both Crown and Church because of their emphasis upon the occult, their defense of witches, and their Lutheran leanings; dies at Grenoble.

EVENTS

The Golden Book of Marcus Aurelius, John Bourchier, Lord Berners's translation of *El Relox de Principes* by Antonio de Guevara, is published.

Miles Coverdale, English cleric and translator, publishes the complete English Bible; rather than a translation from the original text, the work constitutes parts of Martin Luther's version (1534), the Zurich Bible, the Vulgate version (1382-1388), and William Tyndale's translation (1530); a second edition in 1537.

Marino Sanudo publishes his *Diarii,* begun in 1496; it serves as a source for the history and daily life of early sixteenth-century Venice.

1536

BIRTHS

Shah Abdul-karim of Bulrri (d. 1624). Sindhi mystic poet; he will write over ninety short verses in popular Indian metre and rhythm; those pieces will rely for substance upon folk tales and the daily lives of villagers and fishermen.

Thomas Sackville, first Earl of Dorset (d. 1608). English poet and parliamentarian; he will write tragedies in blank verse and various occasional poems.

DEATHS

Hector Boece (b. 1465). Scottish historian and professor of philosophy at Paris; appointed to preside over the new university at Aberdeen; published Latin biographies of bishops and a not always accurate history of Scotland (also in Latin).

Desiderius Erasmus (b. 1466). Dutch humanist who spent time in France, Switzerland, and England; his prose works exhibited the supreme type of cultivated common sense applied to human affairs; he contributed, more than any other person of his age, to the revival of learning.

Johannes Secundus (Jan Evaraerts; b. 1511). Dutch Latin poet; served as secretary to the archbishop of Toledo, the bishop of Utrecht, and the Emperor Charles V; his collection of Latin poems is noted for its elegant style and has been translated into most European languages.

William Tyndale (b. 1495?). English cleric and translator; although he wrote a number of polemical tracts and short moral allegories, he will be remembered most as the first to translate the New Testament into English from the Greek text; strangled and then burned at the stake in Antwerp.

Garcilaso de la Vega (b. 1503). Spanish poet and soldier; introduced the Petrarchan sonnet into Spanish poetry and wrote odes in imitation of Virgil; dies at Nice of a wound received near Frejus during the wars of Charles V.

Gil Vicente (b. 1470). Portuguese actor and playwright; he wrote 44 plays: 16 in Portuguese, 11 in Spanish, and 17 in both languages; his work is characterized by psychological insight, lyricism, and a predominantly comic spirit.

PUBLICATIONS

Sir Thomas Elyot, *The Castle of Helth*—an instructional treatise by the English writer and diplomat; considered an important manual of health.

Reginald Pole, *Pro Ecclesiasticae Defensione*—a tract by the English Catholic cleric in defense of the Church against the schism of Henry VIII and the suppression of the monasteries.

1537

PUBLICATIONS

Robert Recorde, *Introductions for To Lerne To Recken with the Pen*—a treatise and introductory text by the English mathematician and astronomer; focuses upon the practice of arithmetic.

EVENTS

Publication, at Venice, of a four-volume edition of Cicero's *Opera Omnia*.

John Rogers, English Reformed churchman, publishes a translation of the Bible under the pseudonym "John Matthew"; thus, the work comes to be known as "Matthew's Bible."

1538

BIRTHS

Caesar Baronius (d. 1607). Italian church historian; his historical work will attempt to defend the Roman Church against Protestant criticism; he will become Vatican librarian.

Giovanni Battista Guarini (d. 1612). Italian poet and diplomat; he will write a pastoral play in imitation of Torquato Tasso; his literary reputation will come to rest upon that piece.

Abdurrahman Mushfiqi (d. 1588). Persian poet of Central Asia (Bukhara and Samarkand); his poetry will describe the sufferings of the masses from the mistreatment of unscrupulous rulers; he will also write popular poetry based upon folk legends.

PUBLICATIONS

Elijah Levita, *Masoret Ha-Masoret*—a general linguistic reference work in two parts by the Italian Hebrew grammarian and scholar; an explanation of the various phases of biblical spelling of words in accordance with the marginal notes of the Masoretes; advances the theory that the Hebrew vowels had been invented and introduced in post-Talmudic times, contradicting the general belief that those vowels came from biblical times.

EVENTS

Sir Thomas Elyot, English writer and diplomat, publishes his *Dictionarium, Latin and English;* the first occasion on which the word "dictionary" appears in the title of a book.

Clement Marot, French poet and satirist, begins to translate the Psalms into French; they will soon be sung to secular airs; in 1541, these pieces will be condemned by the Sorbonne, forcing the poet to flee to Geneva.

1539

BIRTHS

Jose de Acosta (d. 1600). Peruvian Jesuit cleric and writer; he will publish one of the earliest histories of the West Indies.

Sah Hussain (d. 1593). Panjabi poet; he will write short mystical lyrics designed to be sung by religious minstrels; he will develop his imagery from the activities of common people; he will not aspire to intellectual or cultural refinement in his poetry.

Philippe van Marnix, Heer van Sainte Adelgonde (d. 1598). Flemish diplomat and writer; after retiring from public life, he will compose patriotic songs, metrical versions of the Psalms, a prose translation of the Bible, and a prose satire.

PUBLICATIONS

Martin Luther, *Von den Conciliis und Kirchen* (On the Councils and Churches)—an essay by the German theologian and religious reformer; a work of profound historical and theological scholarship written to discredit the historical claims of the Papacy; presents the writer's clearest and most systematic definition of the relationship between the empirical Church and the hidden (or "invisible") Church; a English edition in 1847.

EVENTS

Publication of "The Great Bible" under the sponsorship of King Henry VII of England; supervised by Archbishop Thomas Cranmer and printed under the direction of Miles Coverdale; the printing was begun in Paris and completed at London.

Richard Taverner, English religious scholar, translator, and writer, publishes *Proverbs or Adagies,* a translation of Desiderius Erasmus's *Adagia* (revised edition of 1515).

———————— completes his revision of the "Matthew's Bible" of 1537.

1540

BIRTHS

Akhund Darweza (d. 1639). Afghan divine and prose writer; he will compile, in Persian and Pashto, a compendium of his orthodox Muslim faith and his opposition to current teachings he considered heretical.

Pierre de Bourdeilles, Seigneur de Brantome (d. 1614). French narrative and descriptive writer; his memoirs will provide detailed accounts of life at the court of Valois, combining literary quality with historical interest.

Joseph Justus Scaliger (d. 1609). French scholar and editor; he will publish editions of Catullus, Tibullus, Propertius, Eusebius, and Manilius; he will become the founder of modern chronology and set standards for literary and historical scholarship.

DEATHS

Guillaume Bude (b.1467). French philologist, philosopher, and jurist; royal librarian and founder of the royal collection at Fontainebleau.

Francesco Guicciardini (b. 1487?). Italian historian and professor of law at Florence; he wrote a dispassionate and analytical history of Italy for the period 1492-1532.

Juan Luis Vives (b. 1492). Spanish philosopher and humanist; edited St. Augustine and commented upon Aristotle; wrote a treatise on education and anticipated the inductive methods of Sir Francis Bacon.

PUBLICATIONS

Sir David Lindsay, *Ane Pleasant Satyre of the Thrie Estaitis*—a morality play in verse by the Scottish poet; various poetic metres: eight-line and six-line stanzas and couplets; an interesting image of contemporary Scottish life.

EVENTS

Paul Fagius, a student of Elijah Levita, establishes a Hebrew printing press at Isny, near

Constance; there he will publish a Talmudic dictionary of 712 difficult words, with explanations in German.

King Henry VIII of England establishes regius professorships at Oxford and Cambridge in Greek, Hebrew, divinity, civil law, and physic.

1541

BIRTHS

Pierre Charron (d. 1603). French theologian; his major "theological" prose tract will assume a skeptical attitude toward all forms of religion; his work will open the way for Deism, free thought, and the secularization of morals.

David ben Solomon Gans (d. 1613). Westphalian-born scholar of rabbinical literature; he will be the first to attempt to write a history of the Jewish people in the Hebrew language; he will also write tracts on mathematics and astronomy, coming into contact with Johannes Kepler and Tycho Brahe.

DEATHS

Paracelsus (Theophrastus Bombastus von Hohenheim; b. 1493). Swedish alchemist, physician, and mystic; his works, written in German and Latin, are records of his contributions to science: he introduced new chemical compounds, advanced the studies of pharmacy and therapeutics, and encouraged research and experimentation.

Fernando de Rojas (b. 1465). Spanish novelist; his dramatic novel of passion is considered a masterpiece of Spanish literature.

PUBLICATIONS

Giambattista Cinzio Giraldi, *Orbecche*—a dramatic tragedy by the Italian writer and scholar; although strongly imitative of Seneca, the play has merit in its own right as the first modern tragedy along classical lines to be performed in Italy; the piece also enuciates for the first time the principles of unity of action and time.

1542

DEATHS

Sebastian Franck (b. 1499). German humanist and moral reformer; he published a tract against drunkenness and attempted to filter his ideas on religious toleration through a universal German history; published one of the earliest collections of German proverbs.

Shin Urramagyaw (b. 1453). Burmese monk and poet; his literary reputation rests on his only extant work, a nine-stanza devotional poem noted for its sensitive observation and personification of nature.

Sir Thomas Wyatt (b. 1503). English courtier and poet; noted for his short, graceful verses, as well as for his satires; his work was not published until 1557; dies of a fever contracted while on a diplomatic mission for King Henry VIII.

1543

BIRTHS

Thomas Deloney (d. 1607?). English writer and silk-weaver; he will write popular broadside ballads on the defeat of the Spanish Armada (1588) and a number of fictional pieces emphasizing hard work and self-advancement.

DEATHS

Nicolas Copernicus (b. 1473). Polish-German astronomer, prose writer, and translator; he has become known as the founder of modern astronomy; in addition to his noted treatise proving the sun to be the center of the universe, he wrote a tract on trigonometry and translated into Latin the epistles of Theophylactus Simocatta.

Johann Mayer von Eck (b. 1483?). German Catholic theologian and professor of theology at Ingolstadt; his prose tracts passionately denounce the Reformation and declare Martin Luther a heretic.

PUBLICATIONS

Andreas Vesalius, *De humani Corporis Fabrica* (The Composition of the Human Body)—a detailed treatise by the Belgian anatomist; the piece will significantly advance the science of biology because of its excellent descriptions of bones and the nervous system; supplemented with drawings of muscle dissections by Jan Stephen van Calcar, a pupil of Titian; the piece was condemned by the medical establishment of the day (the Galenists), and the Inquisition sentenced the writer to death for body snatching and dissecting the human body; that sentence was commuted.

Nicolas Copernicus, *De Revolutionibus Orbium Coelstium*—a treatise by the Polish-German astronomer, written in 1530, but not published until the day of the writer's death; defies Church doctrine that the earth exists as the center of the universe; establishes, instead, the theory that the earth rotates daily on its axis and, with other planets, revolves in orbit around the sun.

EVENTS

Pope Paul III issues an *Index Librorum Prohibitorum,* a list of forbidden books; this list predates the first "official" Index of 1564.

1544

BIRTHS

Guillaume du Bartas (d. 1590). French poet and soldier; as a poet, he will be less appreciated in France than in England and Scotland; he will publish an epic on the creation of the world, which will have some influence on the epics of Edmund Spenser and John Milton.

Torquato Tasso (d. 1595). Italian prose writer, poet, and playwright; he will become perhaps the most significant poet of the Italian Renaissance, particularly for his epic poem on the capture of Jerusalem by Christians during the first Crusade; he will also become the key figure in the transition of European literature from the Renaissance to the seventeenth century.

DEATHS

Teofilo Folengo (b. 1491). Italian poet; one of the Macaronic poets, writers who created an artificial language by combining Italian and Latin words; often wrote under the name "Merlinus Coccaius."

Clement Marot (b. 1496). French poet, satirist, and psalm translator; he wrote elegies, epistles, ballads, rondeaux, sonnets, madrigals, epigrams, and nonsense verse; dies at Turin.

PUBLICATIONS

Matteo Bandello, *Canzoniere* (Songs)—a collection of lyric poems by the Italian churchman and writer of short fiction.

Sebastian Munster, *Cosmographia Generalis* (Introduction to Cosmography)—a prose tract by the German theologian and cosmographer; attempts a general description of the universe.

1545

BIRTHS

Robert Garnier (d. 1590). French playwright; he will become the most talented tragic playwright in sixteenth-century France; the form and content of his dramas will be derived from French humanist theory, which was based upon Senecan models: five acts, chorus, sententia (aphorism/maxim), and stichomythia (dialogue in alternate lines); the formula will be strengthened, however, by the writer's acute dramatic sense and extremely sensitive lyric voice.

Gines Perez de Hita (d. 1619). Spanish soldier and narrative writer; he will write a popular semiromantic history of the civil wars in Granada during 1569-1570.

DEATHS

Antonio de Guevara (b. 1490). Spanish writer and churchman; wrote a collection of popular and familiar letters, as well as a volume on Marcus Aurelius; the latter work employs an ornate style that anticipates the euphuism of John Lyly; the writer served as historiographer to Charles V, Holy Roman Emperor.

PUBLICATIONS

Roger Ascham, *Toxophilus*—a treatise by the English classical scholar, teacher, and diplomat; written in dialogue form, it focuses upon the general subject of archery; urges the importance of physical training in education, and condemns gambling (to which the writer appeared addicted).

Konrad von Gesner, *Bibliotheca Universalis*—a reference work by the Swiss naturalist; contains the titles of all of the books then known in Hebrew, Greek, and Latin; critiques and summaries accompany each title; complete version published in 1549.

EVENTS

Claude Garamond, French designer and manufacturer of printing types, designs his antique typography, unique in being fashioned as metal type, not simply as imitations of handwriting.

1546

BIRTHS

Tycho Brahe (d. 1601). Danish astronomer; his written work will document his planetary observations and his refusal to accept fully the Copernican system; the complete edition of his writings will appear in Prague in 1611.

DEATHS

Sir Thomas Elyot (b.1490?). English statesman and prose writer; he wrote perhaps the earliest treatise in English on moral philosophy, while his translations helped popularize the classics in England.

Martin Luther (b. 1483). German theologian, translator, and hymn writer; his disputations signaled the beginning of a European religious reform that would lead to the establish-

ment of Protestantism; his prose tracts stood as the foundation of his Reformation theology; his sermons, lectures, and hymns exist as extensions of and complements to those tracts; he practically dominated the literary activity of sixteenth-century Germany: 450 essays, 3000 sermons, 2600 letters (in Latin or German).

PUBLICATIONS

Pietro Aretino, *Orazia*—a tragic drama in verse by the Italian poet, prose writer, and playwright; one of the few pieces outside the writer's characteristically satiric mode.

EVENTS

John Heywood, English narrative writer and playwright, publishes his collection of proverbs and epigrams.

Publication of the first complete book in the Welsh language, *Yny Lhyvyr Mwnn.*

1547

BIRTHS

Mateo Aleman (d. 1615?). Spanish novelist; he will lead a turbulent life including jail terms for debt; after the publication of his most noted picaresque novel, he will settle in Mexico.

Miguel de Cervantes Saavedra (d. 1616). Spanish novelist, poet, and playwright; he will write pastoral romances in prose and verse; his masterpiece, *Don Quixote*, featuring a hero who has placed all of his faith in an outdated set of ideals, will prove a significant influence upon the development of the novel; his literary efforts will demonstrate independence from tradition and artifice.

Shaikh Abul-Faiz Faizi (d. 1595). Indo-Persian poet; he will write in a simple, traditional style representing a synthesis of the Indian and Iranian ideals regarding substance, form, and language.

Johann Fischart (d. 1590). German satirist; his work will reveal the influence of François Rabelais; he will attack such groups as corrupt clergy and fanciful astrologers.

Justus Lipsius (d. 1606). Brussels-born Flemish humanist; he will become a significant classical scholar, and his writings will reveal his fluctuating religious beliefs; he will gain a literary reputation from his editions of Tacitus and Seneca.

Aldus Manutius the younger (d. 1597). Italian printer; he will follow his grandfather and father in publishing excellent (typographically and textually) editions of the Greek and Roman classics, as well as the significant writers of Italy.

DEATHS

Pietro Bembo (b. 1470). Italian churchman and poet; restored the so-called "good" style to both Latin and Italian literature; he also attempted to purify Italian grammar.

Vittoria Colonna (b. 1490?). Italian poet, daughter of the constable of Naples and wife of Condottiere Pescara, friend of Michaelangelo; she published a collection of her poems at Parma in 1538.

Henry Howard, Earl of Surrey (b. 1516?). English courtier and poet; his love poems are a late manifestation of the courtly love of the Middle Ages and bear the influence of Petrarch; the poems were not published until ten years after his death; beheaded in late January on charges of high treason.

Beatus Rhenatus (b. 1485). German humanist; he produced numerous editions of the classics and works by the Church Fathers; he also edited the works of Desiderius Erasmus.

PUBLICATIONS

Pierre de Ronsard, "Ode de Pierre de Ronsard à Jacques Peletier, des Beautez qu'il Voudroit en S'amie"—the first piece published by the French poet; reflects the influence upon the twenty-three year old writer of Jacques Peletier, secretary to the Bishop of Le Mans and a distinguished poet, philosopher, physician, and mathematician.

Giangiorgio Trissino, *L'Italia Liberata dai Goti* (The Deliverance of Italy from the Goths)—an epic poem by the Italian papal diplomat and poet; principally concerns events during the third century a.d.

EVENTS

The Council of Edward VI of England publishes the first Book of Homilies.

French replaces Latin as the official language of the French authorities.

1548

BIRTHS

Giordano Bruno (d. 1600). Italian philosopher, known as a speculative thinker; his religious skepticism will lead him to Geneva, then on to London and Oxford; he will influence both Baruch Spinoza and Gottfried Wilhelm Leibniz.

Francisco Suarez (d. 1617). Spanish Jesuit theologian and scholastic philosopher; his thought will foreshadow the modern doctrine of international law, and he will condemn the divine right of kings theory.

PUBLICATIONS

John Bale, *Illustrum Majoris Britanniae Scriptorum Summarium*— a collection of historical and biographical sketches by the English playwright, churchman, and historian; an attempt to survey five centuries of English, Scottish, Irish, and Welsh writers; the work generally reflects the Anglican cleric's anti-Catholic sentiments.

Ignatius Loyola, *Exercitia* (Spiritual Exercises)—a manual by the Spanish Catholic churchman and founder of the society of the Jesuits; a guide to devotion and rules for meditation and prayer; important toward the training of Jesuits.

1549

DEATHS

Elija Levita (b. 1468). Italian Hebrew grammarian; taught Cardinal Egidius of Viterbo, Paul Fagius, and Sebastian Munster; he published Hebrew grammars to assist Christians in learning the literature of the Old Testament.

Margaret of Navarre (b. 1492). Queen of Navarre; she encouraged architecture, the arts, and learning in general; she wrote epistles, poems, dialogues, and at least two plays.

PUBLICATIONS

Joachim du Bellay, *Defense et Illustration de la Langue Francais*—a tract by the French poet and prose writer; the manifesto of the Pleiade poets; advocates the rejection of medieval linguistic traditions and a return to classical and Italian models; accompanied by illustrations in the form of a set of Petrarchan sonnets.

Friedrich Dedekind, *Grobianus*—a satiric piece by the German writer; an attack upon the coarseness of the times.

Thomas Sternhold and John Hopkins, *The Whole Booke of Psalmes*—a collection by the English poets of the Old Testament Psalms, paraphrased and formed into English poetic metre; the work marks the beginning of English psalmody which would, in turn, develop into English congregational hymnody.

Sir Thomas Wyatt, *Certayne Psalmes drawen into Englyshe Meter*—the first published works of the English poet, published seventeen years after his death; the pieces exemplify the lyricism generally associated with the writer's poetry.

EVENTS

The first version of *The Book of Common Prayer* published; intended to meet the popular need for devotional aids and the demand for the vernacular in Church services; much of the work is credited to Thomas Cranmer, Archbishop of Canterbury, who supervised its production.

1550

BIRTHS

Juan de la Cueva (d. 1610). Spanish poet and playwright; he will gain attention for his de-

velopment of new metrical forms and his introduction of historical material into the Spanish drama.

Vicente de Espinel (d. 1624). Spanish soldier and writer; his narratives will be based upon his own adventures in Italy and France; he will publish a volume of original verse and a translation of Homer.

Thomas Sanchez (d. 1610). Spanish Jesuit and prose writer; his major tract will examine the legal, moral, and religious issues arising from the institution of marriage.

DEATHS

John Major (b. 1469?). Scottish theologian and historian; lectured on scholastic logic at Oxford, Cambridge, and Paris; he wrote prodigiously on English and Scottish history, among other topics; provost of St. Salvator's College, St. Andrews.

Giangiorgio Trissini (b. 1478). Italian poet and papal diplomat; wrote an epic poem on the deliverance of Italy from the Goths, as well as a dramatic tragedy on Sophonisba.

PUBLICATIONS

Olaus Petrie, *Tobia Commedia* (The Comedy of Tobias)—a play by the Swedish statesman, religious reformer, and writer; a religious drama, identified as the oldest preserved Swedish stage play.

Giovanni Francesco Straparola, *Tradeci Piacevoli Notti* (Facetious Nights)—a collection of seventy-four stories by the Italian writer; modeled in form and style after the Decamaron (1358) of Giovanni Boccaccio; to 1553.

Giorgio Vasari, *Le Vite de' Piu Eccellente Architetti, Pittori e Sculptori Italiani* (The Lives of the Most Eminent Italian Architects, Painters, and Sculptors)—a collection of essays and sketches by the Italian art historian; despite the factual errors in the early pieces, the work remains a model of art criticism and intellectual biography.

1551

BIRTHS

William Camden (d. 1623). English scholar, antiquary, and historian; he will undertake a survey of the British Isles, the publication of which will establish his literary reputation; he will also publish a list of the epitaphs in Westminster Abbey, a collection of the writings of early English historians, a narrative of the trial of the Gunpowder plotters, and the annals of the reign of Elizabeth I.

DEATHS

Qadi Qadan (b.   ?). Sindhi mystic poet and religious scholar; his short mystical verses in the Sindhi (Indo-Iranian) language remain popular.

PUBLICATIONS

Konrad von Gesner, *Historia Animalium*—a prose volume by the Swiss naturalist; an attempt to collect all the information known at that time concerning every animal; to 1558.

Thomas Wilson, *Rule of Reason*—a prose tract on logic by the English statesman and rhetorician; further editions through 1580; interestingly, the writer identifies Nicholas Udall's *Ralph Roister Doister* as the oldest original comedy in English.

EVENTS

Ralph Robinson, translates into English from the original Latin Thomas More's *Utopia* (1516).

1552

BIRTHS

Alberico Gentili (d. 1608). Italian jurist and philosopher; his prose tracts will focus upon international law and politics; he will spend the last twenty-eight years of his life in England, lecturing at Oxford.

Sir Walter Raleigh (d. 1618). English soldier, courtier, adventurer, poet, novelist, and essayist; his short poems will become especially popular when set to music; he will study science and write a voluminous history of the world.

Pietro Sarpi (d. 1626). Italian philosopher and theologian; he will write a history of the Tri-

dentine Council, argue with the Pope on the issue of clerical immunities, and advocate freedom of thought and a republican form of government.

Edmund Spenser (d. 1599). English poet; he will be recognized by contemporaries as the foremost poet of his age; his major work will be an allegorical epic relating his moral vision of the world; his poetic treatment of moral concerns and his nine-line stanza form will prove lasting contributions to Western world literature.

DEATHS

John Leland (d. 1506?). English antiquary and historical commentator; he gathered records of antiquity in cathedrals, colleges, abbeys, and priories throughout England; his papers lie in the Bodleian Library and British Museum.

Sebastian Munster (b. 1489). German theologian and cosmographer; taught Hebrew and theology at Heidelberg; published a Hebrew translation of the Bible, as well as Hebrew and Chaldee grammars.

Olaus Petri (b. 1493). Swedish theologian and writer; author of a mystery play, hymns, controversial prose tracts, and memoirs; contributed significantly to the Reformation in Sweden.

PUBLICATIONS

Etienne Jodelle, *Cleopatre Captive*—a play by the French poet and dramatist, the first classical French tragedy; limited to 1615 lines (Acts 1 and 4 in alexandrines, the rest in decasyllabic verse); a dramatization of the principal character's faults; an attempt to recapture in the modern age the dignity of classical literature.

Michel de Nostradamus, *Centuries*—a book of rhymed prophecies by the French astrologer; expressed in obscure and enigmatic language; most noted for its foretelling of the manner of King Henry II's death in 1559; to 1558.

Pierre de Ronsard, *Les Amours de P. de Ronsard Vandomoys, Ensemble son Bocage*—a collection of sonnets by the French poet, inspired by his passionate love for a Florentine banker's daughter, Cassandre de Salviati; the poems are generally Petrarchan in form, sensual and elaborate; focus is upon conventional themes: unrequited love, solitude during a lover's absence, erotic longing; revised and expanded editions in 1553, 1557, 1560, and 1578.

EVENTS

Publication of the second issue of the Book of Common Prayer (see 1549).

Books on geography and astronomy destroyed in England because of the common belief that they are infected with "magic."

1553

BIRTHS

Richard Hakluyt (d. 1616). English geographer, traveler, and prose writer; he will gather and publish accounts of his and others' voyages and discoveries; those narratives will help promote discovery and colonization, particularly in North America.

Jacques Auguste de Thou (d.1617). French statesman and historian; he will publish a Latin history of his own times, as well as author Latin verse, personal reflections, and commentaries on his contributions to parliament.

DEATHS

François Rabelais (b. 1494?). French satirist; his comedy and satire show him to be a profound thinker and a master of wit and language; he gained recognition for his experimentation with language and development of the prose narrative form.

Michael Servetus (b. 1511). Spanish theologian, physician, and prose writer; his principal works explain the reasons for his denial of the Trinity; upon the orders of John Calvin, he dies upon the stake at Geneva, accused of heresy.

PUBLICATIONS

Nicholas Udall, *Ralph Roister Doister*—the earliest known English comic play; written in short rhymed doggerel; the title character, a swaggering simpleton, courts a widow who is engaged to an absent merchant named Gawin Goodlucke; both substance and form bear the unmistakable influences of Terence and Plautus.

1554

BIRTHS

Stephen Gosson (d. 1624). English playwright and poet; he will achieve recognition for his pastorals, his attack upon poets and playwrights of the day, and his minor literary feud with Sir Philip Sidney.

John Lyly (d. 1606). English playwright and prose writer; in a two-part work of fiction, he will attempt to establish an ideal prose style characterized by artificiality and convolution; his plays will introduce prose as a vehicle for comic dialogue.

Sir Philip Sidney (d. 1586). English poet; he will write the first renowned pastoral poem in English, a significant sonnet sequence, and a critical essay that will influence early seventeenth-century English poets.

PUBLICATIONS

Matteo Bandello, *Le Novelle*—a collection of 214 short stories and tales by the Italian writer, most of them racy prose romances; translated into English (from a French translation) by Geoffrey Fenton as *Certaine Tragicall Discourses* (1567); the work will serve as a source for a number of pre-Shakespearean playwrights.

1555

BIRTHS

Johann Arndt (d. 1621). German devotional writer; his reputation, theological and literary, will come to rest upon a tract that attempts to explicate true Christianity, a document that will be translated into almost every European language.

Francois de Malherbe (d. 1628). French poet, critic, and translator; he will strive to establish a critical criteria for versification and to preserve the purity of the French language; he will also labor to purge French poetry of linguistic and stylistic affectation.

DEATHS

Hugh Latimer (b. 1490?). English Protestant martyr, university preacher, and writer of sermons; in his later years, he devoted his time to "teaching, preaching, exhorting, writing, correcting, and reforming"; burned at the stake opposite Balliol College.

Sir David Lindsay (b. 1490?). Scottish poet; his coarse verses were extremely popular among Scots for their humor, common sense and worldliness; many believe his poems accòmplished more for the cause of the Reformation in Scotland than all the sermons of John Knox.

PUBLICATIONS

Pierre de Ronsard, *Les Hymnes de P. de Ronsard a Tresillustre et Reverendissime Odet, Cardinal de Chastillon*—a collection by the French poet containing three major pieces: "Les Daimons," "Hymne de la Mort," and "Hymne de la Philosophie' " addresses and panegyrics to friends and patrons on philosophic and scientific subjects.

EVENTS

Publication of a dictionary of the Aztec language.

Richard Eden, English translator and traveler, translates Peter Martyr's 1516 Italian work, *De Rebus Oceanicis et Novo Orbe*, as *Decades of the Newe Worlde or West India*; the translation will stimulate English interest in America.

gal commentaries in Arabic; he will primarily examine issues relating to the slave trade, but he will also manage to collect legends.

Orfi (d. 1591). Persian-born Indian poet; his poems will become the most passionate pieces of Persian verse—difficult to read, but nonetheless conveying his extreme despair; he will influence Turkish poetry, and with his powerful imagery, inspire the poets of India.

DEATHS

Pietro Aretino (b. 1492). Italian poet and satirist; his poetic works include five witty comedies and a single tragedy; his death was reportedly caused by laughing heartily about one of his sisters' adventures, then falling from a stool and suffering a fatal injury.

Thomas Cranmer (b. 1489). Archbishop of Canterbury and author of over forty doctrinal prose tracts; he supervised the production of the first prayer book of Edward VI; edited the first book of homilies; the principal author of the English liturgy.

St. Ignatius Loyola (b. 1491). Spanish soldier and ecclesiastic; earned literary recognition principally for his spiritual exercises designed for the training of Jesuits; beatified in 1609 and canonized in 1622.

Nicholas Udall (b. 1504). English playwright; his dramatic work, inspired by Plautus and Terence, will, in turn, influence the English dramatists of the early seventeenth century.

PUBLICATIONS

Juan de Avila, *Audi, Filia*—an ascetic Christian text by the Spanish writer and preacher.

Hans Sachs, *Der Paur Egfeur* (Under the Pressure or Care of Poverty)—a form of poetic folk-play by the German poet and playwright; dramatizes anecdotes and incidents of everyday life in a Fastnachtsspiel, to be produced each year at Shrovetide.

1556

1557

BIRTHS

Ahmad al-Tinbukhti Baba (d. 1627). Mali linguistic scholar; he will write his tracts and le-

DEATHS

Giovanni Francesco Straparola (b. 1490?) Italian writer of fiction; his collection of seventy-four stories appears in the form and style of Giovanni Boccaccio's *Decameron* (1358).

PUBLICATIONS

Robert Recorde, *Whetstone of Wit*—an important treatise by the English mathematician and physician; concerns the science of algebra and introduces the sign " = ".

EVENTS

The stage production of *The Sack-Full of Newes,* the first English play to be censored.

The Stationers' Company incorporated by royal charter; no person not a member of the Company can print, for sale in the Kingdom, a volume unless authorized by special privilege or patent; every member required to enter into the register of the Company the name of the volume desired to be printed.

Forty poems by Henry Howard, Earl of Surrey (1517?-1547), and a collection of rondeaux, lyrics, and satires by Sir Thomas Wyatt, published for the first time in Richard Tottel's Miscellany.

Richard Tottel, London publisher, translates *De Legibus et Consuetudinibus Angliae* (On the Laws and Customs of England), a treatise by the English judge and ecclesiastic, Henry de Bracton.

1558

DEATHS

Julius Caesar Scaliger (b. 1484). Italian philologist and physician who resided and worked in France; he analyzed the rhetorical methods of Cicero and criticized the classical studies of his predecessors; he earned recognition in the fields of literature and science for his commentaries on the medical and botanical works of Hippocrates, Theophrastus, and Aristotle.

PUBLICATIONS

Margaret of Navarre, *Heptameron*—a volume of short fictional narratives by the Queen of Navarre and the mother of King Henry IV;

modeled upon the *Decameron* of Giovanni Boccaccio (completed 1358).

Abdurrahman Mushfiqi, *Diviani Mutaibat* (Collection of Satires)—a collection of approximately 1500 short poems by the Central Asian-Persian poet; the simple subjects and language made the work exceedingly popular.

EVENTS

Publication of the *Sefer Zohar* (Book of Splendor), a thirteenth-century cabalistic work of Jewish mysticism; four distinct interpretations of the Torah emphasizing the "inner meaning" of that work.

1559

BIRTHS

George Chapman (d. 1634). English poet, translator, and playwright; he will gain a reputation as a classical scholar with his translation of Homer and write tragedies and comedies for the stage.

PUBLICATIONS

Mattias Flacius, *Ecclesiastica Historica*—a church history by the German Lutheran theologian and linguist; a general chronology of the Church by centuries, with special reference to the rise and growth of the Antichrist; the work reflects the writer's erudition.

Jorge de Montemayor, *La Diana*—a pastoral romance by the Spanish novelist and poet.

EVENTS

Elizabeth I authorizes the publication of the second and revised *Book of Common Prayer* ("the Elizabethan Prayer Book") of Edward VI (1552); contains changes so that it will appear less offensive to the Roman Catholics.

1560

BIRTHS

Qutb Shah Muhammad Quli (d.1611). Urdu poet who developed secular motifs for his work; he will compose in excess of 100,000 couplets on such subjects as love, the Indian seasons, Hindu and Muslim festivals, and fruits and vegetables; his erotic poetry will express love of woman in the guise of mystical love of God.

DEATHS

Joachim du Bellay (b. 1522). French poet and prose writer; advocated the rejection of medieval language traditions and a return to classical and Italian models; his poetry took the form of the Petrachan sonnet.

Philip Melanchthon (b. 1497). German theological reformer and writer; he produced the first significant Protestant work on dogmatic theology and composed the Augsburg Confession of 1530; professor of Greek at Wittenberg and a colleague of Martin Luther.

Marco Girolomo Vida (b. 1490?). Italian Latin poet, known as "the Christian Virgil"; he wrote Latin orations and dialogues, a religious epic, and poems on such diverse and curious subjects as silk-culture and chess.

PUBLICATIONS

Pierre de Ronsard, *Les Oeuvres de P. de Ronsard, Gentilhomme Vandomois* (Songs and Sonnets of Pierre de Ronsard, Gentleman of Vendomois)—the first collected edition of the French poet's works; brought the writer both recognition and favor; further editions (revised) 1567, 1571, 1572-1573, 1578, 1584, and 1587.

Wang Shih-cheng, *Ch'in, P'ing Mei*—a novel by the Chinese scholar and statesman, perhaps the first classic Chinese work of fiction; the title is taken from the names of the three principal female characters; a covert satire, often employing ambiguous language, upon the morals of the court of the Emperor K'ang Hsi.

significantly to the discipline of philosophy through his application of the inductive method; modern science will embrace that approach as a replacement for the *a priori* method of medieval scholasticism; he will also be known for a highly ornate prose style.

Luis de Gongora y Argote (d. 1627). Spanish poet and a major figure of the Golden Age; he will write sonnets, ballads, and lengthy pastorals, he will be known for his complex and artificial style, which relies upon metaphor, Latinate vocabulary, and classical and mythological allusions.

DEATHS

Jorge de Montemayor (b. 1520?). Spanish poet and novelist of Portuguese descent; he wrote pastoral romances in Castilian that influenced such English writers as Sir Philip Sidney.

PUBLICATIONS

Julius Caesar Scaliger, *Poetics*—a prose tract by the Italian-born physician, essayist, and philologist; published posthumously; the writer extols the critical principles of Virgil and Seneca; the piece displays the writer's encyclopaedic knowledge and acute observation, and he at times emerges as arrogant and vain.

EVENTS

Sir Thomas Hoby, English scholar, translates into English *Il Cortegiano* (The Book of the Courtier, 1528), by Baldassare Castiglione.

Thomas Norton, English parliamentarian, lawyer, and poet, translates into English the *Christianae Religionis Institutio* (Institution of the Christian Religion, 1536) of John Calvin.

John Stowe (1525-1605), English historian and antiquary, publishes his edition of *The Workes of Geoffrey Chaucer.*

1561

1562

BIRTHS

Francis Bacon (d. 1626). English philosopher, statesman, and essayist; he will contribute

BIRTHS

Samuel Daniel (d. 1619). English poet and playwright; he will write lyrics, narratives, masques, classical tragedies, and pastoral comedies; his well-crafted verses will contribute significantly to the literary success of his dramas.

Lope Felix de Vega Capio (d. 1635). Spanish dramatist, poet, and novelist; he will become the founder of modern Spanish drama, writing approximately 1800 short plays (five hundred of which still exist); those dramatic pieces will succeed because of their relative brevity, startling turns of plot, and attention to themes of interest to the common people, such as honor, justice, and the conflict between the peasants and the nobility.

DEATHS

Matteo Bandello (b. 1485?). Italian churchman and writer of short fiction; his 214 *novelle* (tales), published between 1554 and 1573, complement the social histories of the period; they will provide source material and themes for such playwrights as William Shakespeare and Philip Massinger.

PUBLICATIONS

Torquato Tasso, *Il Rinaldo*—the Italian writer's first published work; an epic poem relating the title hero's quest for fame; an attempt to reconcile certain Aristotelian requirements of unity with the design of the traditional epic romance; the piece achieved popular success.

EVENTS

The Whole Booke of Psalmes, a collection of verse paraphrases edited by Thomas Sternhold and John Hopkins added to the *Book of Common Prayer* of the Church of England.

1563

BIRTHS

Michael Drayton (d. 1631). English poet; he will write metrical passages from the Scriptures and eclogues; he will be known for the

sheer beauty of his pastoral descriptions in verse, which gave creative life to what might otherwise be considered dull subjects.

DEATHS

John Bale (b. 1495). English Protestant churchman and playwright; his literary contributions will primarily consist of Latin biographical catalogues of British writers and plays that provided the transition from the interlude to the complete historical drama.

PUBLICATIONS

George Ferrers and William Baldwin (editors), *A Mirrour for Magistrates*—a poetic work in which a variety of noted individuals, chiefly subjects from English history, relate their downfalls; twenty tragic narratives; further editions in 1574, 1578, 1587, and 1610; will serve as source material for Edmund Spenser, William Shakespeare, Samuel Daniel, and Michael Drayton.

Johann Wier, *De Praestigiis Daemonum et Icantationabus ac Veneficiis*—a prose tract by the Belgian physician and sometimes religious writer; condemns the folly and cruelty of current witchcraft trials; the writer maintains that witches simply exist as manifestations of miserable people with distorted minds; the work naturally aroused the ire of the Church.

EVENTS

The first printing presses established in Russia.

1564

BIRTHS

Christopher Marlowe (d. 1593). English playwright and poet; he will inaugurate the age of Elizabethan drama with the first love tragedy in English and such innovations as the grand historical hero, racial and ethnic stereotypical heroes, a distinctive form of blank verse used to convey intense dramatic moments, and unique dramatic diction.

William Shakespeare (d. 1616). English playwright and poet; the most notable literary
figure of the Elizabethan Age; among his
many contributions to literature will be his
use of complex versification and rhythm to
reflect a character's state of mind and his
ability to create histories and tragedies in
which characterization and realistic elements
harmoniously blend; his comedies will move
from simple farce to idyllic romance; the enduring appeal of his plays will lie in his recognition of the complexity of moral questions
and his talent for conveying these ideas to an
audience through the richness of his language.

DEATHS

Pierre Belon (b. 1517). French naturalist and
traveler; author of important treatises on
trees, herbs, birds, and fishes; murdered by
robbers while gathering herbs in the Bois de
Boulogne.

Andreas Vesalius (b. 1514). Belgian anatomist;
his prose works will significantly advance the
science of biology through their detailed descriptions of bones and the nervous system.

PUBLICATIONS

George Buchanan, *Psalmorum Dauidis Para-*
phrasis Poetica (Paraphrases of the Psalms of
David)—a skillful metrical paraphrase of the
Old Testament Psalms by the Scottish poet
and prose writer; the work remains a standard model for scholastic and academic Latin
translation exercises; originally published at
Paris; translated into English in 1754.

EVENTS

The *Index Librorum Prohibitorum,* a list of
books "forbidden" by the Roman Catholic
Church, published after receiving papal approval; the Index will continue to be compiled until 1948; the Second Vatican Council
(1962-1965) will declare it inoperative, beginning in 1966.

The Whole Psalmes of David in English Meter,
the first psalm book for the Church of
Scotland, printed in Edinburgh by Robert
Lekprevick; the psalms are not accompanied
by paraphrases or hymns.

1565

BIRTHS

Taqi Auhadi (d. 1630). Indo-Persian poet; he
will write epic poems, eleven lyrics, and a
number of satiric pieces attacking his contemporaries; he will also collect over 3100 biographies of Persian poets, with samples of their
work.

Allessandro Tassoni (d. 1635). Italian poet
who will flourish under the patronage of several princes; he will gain extensive literary
and scientific knowledge, but his literary reputation will rest on a single heroic-comic
poem.

DEATHS

Konrad von Gesner (b. 1516). Swiss naturalist;
professor of Greek at Lausanne and professor
of physics and natural history at Zurich; published seventy-two titles, while another eighteen remained in manuscript; known for his
bibliography of Greek, Latin, and Hebrew
titles.

Lope de Rueda (b. 1510). Spanish playwright; a
pioneer of Spanish drama, he wrote comedies
in the Italian style, short humorous pastoral
dialogues, and at least ten burlesques.

PUBLICATIONS

Pierre de Ronsard, *Elegies, Mascarades et*
Bergerie—a collection of occasional verse by
the French poet and critic; the major piece
is an ambitious court pastoral dedicated to
Queen Elizabeth of England.

Giambattista Cinzio Giraldi, *Ecatommiti*—a
collection of moral and love tales by the Italian writer and natural philosopher; the volume was eventually translated into Spanish
and French; provided William Shakespeare
with the plots for *Measure for Measure* and *Oth-*
ello.

Bernardino Telesio, *De Rerum Natura*—a
prose tract by the Italian philosopher and scientist; foreshadows the empirical scientific
method.

EVENTS

Thomas Cooper, English churchman and Latin scholar, publishes his *Thesaurus Linguae Romanae et Brittannicae,* a compendium from earlier Latin and German dictionaries; it becomes a favorite reference work for Queen Elizabeth, and thus earns the compiler a number of preferments.

Arthur Golding, English translator and poet, translates the first four books of Ovid's *Metamorphoses;* that particular translation known to William Shakespeare.

Pencils first manufactured in England.

Torquato Tasso, Italian poet and playwright, appointed court poet at Ferrara by Duke Alphonso II d'Este.

1566

DEATHS

Annibale Caro (b. 1507). Italian poet and prose writer; he will become secretary to a succession of cardinals; dies at Rome.

Louise Labe (b. 1525?). French poet; called "La Belle Cordiere," she disguised herself as a knight and fought at the siege of Perpignan.

PUBLICATIONS

Jean Bodin, *Methodus ad Facilem Historiarum Cognitionem* (The Methods of History)—a prose tract by the French political philosopher; a significant contribution to historiography.

George Gascoigne, *The Supposes*—a translation, by the English poet and playwright, of Ludovico Ariosto's *Gli Suppositi;* the earliest extant prose comedy in English and a fast moving and skillfully plotted farce; the source of a subplot in William Shakespeare's *The Taming of the Shrew.*

EVENTS

William Aldington translates *The Golden Ass,* by the Latin satirist Lucius Apuleius.

Notizie Scritte, A manuscript newsletter and one of the earliest forerunners of true newspapers, begins to be published in Venice.

William Painter, English translator and schoolmaster, publishes his *Palace of Pleasure;* an anthology of stories by such writers as Giovanni Boccaccio, Matteo Bandello, and Margaret of Navarre; the collection will become a source for a number of Elizabethan dramatists, including William Shakespeare.

1567

BIRTHS

Thomas Nashe (d. 1601). English essayist and writer of fiction; he will gain a literary reputation from his prose satires and pieces of spirited romantic adventure; his work will serve as the forerunner of the English picaresque adventure novel.

Honore d'Urfe (d. 1625). French writer of fiction; his pastoral romance will be regarded as the first French novel.

PUBLICATIONS

Francesco Guicciardini, *Storia d'Italia*—a dispassionate analytical history of Italy by the Italian historian and diplomat; published posthumously; covers the period from 1494 to 1532.

EVENTS

Edward Hake, English theologian and historian, translates *The Imitation of Christ* of Thomas a'Kempis.

1568

BIRTHS

Tommaso Campanella (d. 1639). Italian philosopher, prose writer, and poet; he will compose over fifty tracts, principally in Latin and imitative of Plato's political writings; he will also experiment with the sonnet form, and these poems will be translated into English in 1878 by John Addington Symonds.

DEATHS

Roger Ascham (b. 1515). English humanist and classical scholar; he wrote in a simple style, perhaps best represented by his noted treatise on classical education.

Miles Coverdale (b. 1488). English biblical scholar; a number of fine phrases from his translation of the Bible found their way into the King James version.

PUBLICATIONS

Roger Ascham, *The Scholemaster*—a prose tract by the English classical scholar, published shortly after his death; concerns the education of boys of position, both at school and afterwards; criticizes the prevailing discipline at educational institutions; written in an exceedingly simple prose style.

EVENTS

Matthew Parker, Archbishop of Canterbury, completes his edition of "the Bishops' Bible," begun in 1563; an effort to counteract the popularity of the Calvinistic Geneva Bible of 1560.

The first translation of the Bible into Czech.

The first modern "eisteddfod" for Welsh music and literature held at Caerwys.

Richard Grafton, English printer and historian, publishes his *Abridgement of the Chronicles of England.*

1569

BIRTHS

Giambattista Marini (d. 1625). Italian poet; he will become ducal secretary at Turin and compose his finest poetry at the court of France; his work will be marked by florid hyperbole and exaggerated imagery.

DEATHS

Miklaj Rej (b. 1505). Polish Calvinist poet and playwright; the so-called "Father of Polish literature"; the first prominent writer in the vernacular Polish language; exercised his talent in the dramatic dialogue.

Sankaradeva (b. 1449). Assamese (Indo-Iranian) poet; he authored approximately thirty volumes, designed for the uneducated, outlining his plans for religious and social reform; he also wrote hymns, doctrinal poems, epics, and plays.

PUBLICATIONS

Alonso de Ercilla y Zuniga, *La Araucana*— perhaps the finest epic poem of the Spanish "Golden Age" of literature; concerns the conquest of the Araucanian Indians of Chile, in which the poet himself participated; to 1589.

1570

BIRTHS

Thomas Dekker (d. 1632?). English playwright and prose writer; his prose work will present a satiric but generally accurate picture of Jacobean London; the characters of his plays will reflect his sympathy for the outcasts of society.

Shekh Ahmad Malaye Jizri (d. 1640). Kurdish poet; he will become court poet to the ruler of Jazirat; his lyric poems, rich in imagery, will transmit a variety of philosophical ideas.

Thomas Middleton (d. 1627). English playwright and poet; he will write satirical comedies; his so-called "city comedies" will be termed "amoral" for their vicious and contemptible characters; he will maintain that the satirist can establish moral standards by portraying vice.

DEATHS

Francois de Bonivard (b. 1493). Swiss churchman, politician, and historian; his imprisonment in the Chillon Castle (1532-1536) will become a source for a poem by Lord Byron; he wrote an important chronicle of his life and times.

PUBLICATIONS

Andrea Palladio, *I Quattro Libri dell' Architettura* (The Four Books of Architecture)—a major work by the Italian Renaissance architect; contains his own measured drawings of Roman architecture, his plans, and a treatise based upon the Roman writer Vitruvius; the work significantly influenced the writer's successors, particularly Inigo Jones (1573-1652) and Christopher Wren (1632-1723).

EVENTS

Jean Antoine de Baif, French poet, founds the Academie de Poesie et de Musique, Paris; De Baif attempted to introduce blank verse into French poetry and also experimented with combinations of music and verse.

Lodovico Castelvetro demands the introduction of Aristotelian principles into contemporary Italian drama.

1571

BIRTHS

Leon de Modena (d. 1648). Italian Jewish teacher, poet, and translator; his work will attack traditional Judaism, yet defend the theological essence of that religion; he will attempt to prove the invalidity of a number of Jewish laws and demand liturgical and social reforms; he will write a history of ancient Israel in Italian.

Tirso de Molina (d. 1648). Spanish playwright; he will gain recognition for his characterization, short interludes, and masterful treatment of the Don Juan legend.

DEATHS

Benvenuto Cellini (b. 1500). Italian essayist, poet, and autobiographer; acclaimed by his contemporaries for his artistry but his literary

reputation rests almost entirely upon his autobiography; that work represents the various dimensions of the Italian Renaissance.

PUBLICATIONS

Hugh Latimer, *Fruitefull Sermons*—a collection of sermons by the English churchman and preacher; the addresses have been praised for their simple vernacular style and clarity.

Azariah ben Moses dei Rossi, *Me'or Enayim* (Light of Eyes)—a prose narrative by the Italian Jewish scholar and physician; contains an interesting description of the earthquake of 1571 at Ferrara, in which two hundred persons perished; also contains a survey of the history of the Jewish people at the time of the Second Commonwealth, records the origins of the Hebrew settlements in Egypt, and describes the Bar Kochba revolt against the Romans.

Events

The Bibliotheca Laurenziana, Florence, opens its doors to the public.

1572

BIRTHS

John Donne (d. 1631). English churchman and the most significant of the metaphysical poets; his poetry will reveal a religious faith in the medieval order shaken by growing scientific and philosophic doubt; his love sonnets and religious and philosophical verse will be characterized by a striking blend of passion and reason.

Ben Jonson (d. 1637). English poet and playwright; his drama will be characterized by biting satire and intriguing plots; he will seek to teach moral improvement by exaggerating the foibles and the passions of his characters.

DEATHS

Isaak ben Solomon Luria (b. 1533). Jerusalem-born Jewish mystic writer; settling in Palestine, he led an important school of mysticism that combined Messianism with older doctrines; his written work concerns the nature of and connection between earthly redemption and cosmic restoration.

Aegidius Tschudi (b. 1505). Swiss historian; an active Roman Catholic during the Reformation; his history of Switzerland remained for a considerable period of time a standard reference.

Yahya Bey. Turkish poet; he composed lyrics, meditations on the meaning of life, and mystic erotic verse; he also wrote five epic poems in fresh, simple language.

PUBLICATIONS

Luis de Camoens, *Os Lusiados* (The Lusitanians)—an epic poem by the Portuguese versifier; ten cantos modeled upon Virgil's *Aeneid;* recounts in ottava rimo Vasco Da Gama's discovery (1498) of the sea route to the Indies; the work accomplishes for the Portuguese language what Geoffrey Chaucer achieved for English through his *Canterbury Tales*, and thus it exists as Portugal's national epic.

Matthew Parker, *De Antiquitate Britannicae Ecclesiae* (The History of the English Church)—a history of the Anglican Church by the Archbishop of Canterbury; reportedly the first book privately printed in England; completed in 1574.

Pierre de Ronsard, *Les Quatre Premiers Livres de la Franciade*—an unfinished epic poem by the French poet and critic; an account of the French nation's Trojan ancestry; evidences the poet's debt to Greek forms.

EVENTS

Henri Etienne, French-born classical scholar and printer at Geneva, publishes his *Thesaurus Linguae Graecae.*

Archbishop Matthew Parker founds the Society of Antiquaries; the group is suppressed in 1603 at the accession of King James I; refounded in January 1717.

1573

BIRTHS

Mathurin Regnier (d 1613). French versifier; he will write satires, epistles, elegies, odes,

songs, and epigrams; his work will be characterized by a polished technique, vigor, and originality; most importantly, he will provide a lively picture of the Paris of his own times.

DEATHS

Giambattista Cinzio Giraldi (b. 1504). Italian writer and professor of natural philosophy and belles lettres at Florence; wrote nine plays in imitation of Seneca, as well as a collection of short pieces of fiction; his tales provided William Shakespeare with the sources for at least two of his plays.

PUBLICATIONS

Johann Fischart, *Der Flohatz*—a verse satire by the German writer and humorist; an outrageously comic and original poem on the follies of women.

Juan Latino, *Austrias*—a Latin poem by the Guinean poet and scholar; composed after the Battle of Lepanto (7 October 1571), a naval engagement between Christians and Turks; celebrates Don Juan's victory over the Turks.

1574

BIRTHS

Brahman (pseudonym of Chandar Bhan; d. 1662). Indo-Persian poet, prose writer, and translator; his prose narratives will be partly autobiographical, and he will translate philosophical documents about Hindu beliefs and customs.

Thomas Heywood (d. 1641). English playwright; his dramatic compositions, written in a simple and direct style, rely upon good humor and express the tastes of the masses for whom he wrote; he will develop the ability to portray the emotional life of his characters.

DEATHS

Giorgio Vasari (b. 1511). Italian art historian and biographer; his lives of painters, sculptors, and architects contain some factual inaccuracies, but they nonetheless remain models of art criticism and biography.

PUBLICATIONS

Ulissi Aldrovandus, *Antidotarii Bononiensis Epitome*—a treatise on drugs and their healing powers by the celebrated Italian natural historian; also describes his superb collection of plants and minerals gathered during his travels.

Jean Bodin, *Discours sur les Causes de l'Extreme Cherte en France* (A Discourse on the Causes of Extremely High Payments and Prices in France)—a prose tract by the French political philosopher concerning luxury and affluence; the writer deems the subject important as it relates to the development of the modern nation-state.

Tulsidas, *Ramcaritmanas* (The Holy Lake of the Deed of Rama)—a poem by the Hindi verse writer, considered the most significant achievement of medieval Hindi literature and still the most influential single scripture among the Hindus of Northern India; urges devotion to Rama (an incarnation of Visnu) as the best means for salvation; Rama and his wife Sita serve as ideals of human conduct for the devotee.

EVENTS

Justus Lipsius, Flemish classical scholar, edits the *Annales* of Publius Tacitus (55-120), a history of the Julian line from Tiberius to Nero (14-68); the work published by the French printer and bookseller of Antwerp, Christophe Plantin.

1575

BIRTHS

Giovanni Battista Basile (d. 1632). Italian folklorist and editor; he will compile an important collection of Neopolitan folk tales.

John Marston (d. 1634). English playwright; he will contribute both honesty and intensity to Jacobean drama, portraying the deception and hypocrisy existing in the world; he will have a profound influence upon John Webster and William Shakespeare.

Cyril Tourneur (d. 1626). English playwright; his tragedies will depict his reaction to the religious skepticism of the early seventeenth century; he will eventually inject comic scenes and engaging villains into his dramatic tragedies.

DEATHS

Mattias Flacius Illyricus (b. 1520). Albanian-born Lutheran theologian and writer; he wrote church history and tracts defending the idea of original sin.

Diego Hurtado de Mendoza (b. 1503). Spanish diplomat, statesman, political commentator, and poet.

Matthew Parker (b. 1505?). English churchman, librarian, and scholar; prepared the earliest editions of Gildas, Asser, Ælfric, and Matthew Paris; his Church history may well have been the first book privately printed in England (1572).

PUBLICATIONS

Johann Fischart, *Geschichtsklitterung*—a satire by the German writer, essentially an adaptation of Francois Rabelais' *Gargantua* (1534); he sets serious and nonsensical ideas side by side in an attempt to attack the social and religious corruption of his day.

Gammer Gurton's Needle—the second English comedy in verse, first acted in 1566; the authorship of the piece is unknown; a farce focusing upon the loss and eventual discovery of the needle essential to mending the clothes of Hodge, Gammer Gurton's hired man; Hodge finds the needle in the seat of his breeches.

Torquato Tasso, *La Gierusalemme Liberata* (Jerusalem Delivered)—a religious epic poem by the Italian poet and playwright; historical characters from the First Crusade prepare to face martyrdom to save the Christians from the beleaguered holy city; the "authorized version" not published until 1581; the first English translation in 1594.

EVENTS

Matthew Parker, Archbishop of Canterbury, bequeaths his collection of historical documents to Corpus Christi College, Cambridge.

1576

DEATHS

Richard Eden (b. 1521?). English translator and narrative writer; his translations, compilations, original accounts of voyages to the New World, and treatises on navigation were the earliest means of disseminating information about recent discoveries; a precursor of the more famous English geographer Richard Hakluyt.

Hans Sachs (b. 1495). German poet and playwright; wrote in excess of 6300 religious and secular poems; he also composed innumerable Fastnachsspiele; the principal character in Richard Wagner's *Die Meistersinger* (1868).

PUBLICATIONS

Jean Bodin, *Les Six Livres de la Republique* (Six Books of the Commonwealth)—a prose tract by the French political philosopher; maintains that property and the family form the basis of society, and thus a limited monarchy appears the best possible form of government; however, under no circumstances must citizens rebel against their ruler; one prince may, nonetheless, interfere on behalf of another's oppressed subjects; essentially an attempt to revive the system of Aristotle and apply it to modern politics.

Johann Fischart, *Das Gluckhafft Schiff von Zurich*—a satirical verse narrative by the German comic writer; concerns the journey, by ship, from Zurich to Strassbourg.

EVENTS

Henry III of France (reigned 1575-1589) establishes, at Paris, the Academie du Palais.

1577

BIRTHS

Robert Burton (d. 1640). English churchman and scholar; his significant treatise on the so-called "medical" aspects of melancholy, with its countless commentaries upon learning and his own life and study, will have a profound influence upon such writers as John Milton, Samuel Johnson, Laurence Sterne, Lord Byron, and Charles Lamb.

DEATHS

Remy Belleau (b. 1527?). French poet and translator; he composed delicately descriptive prose and verse.

George Gascoigne (b. 1525?). English playwright and poet; noted for his formal verse satires, fiction, and tracts upon prosody; also known for his innovative adaptations of Greek drama and tragicomedies.

PUBLICATIONS

Richard Eden, *The History of Travel in the East and West Indies*—a travel narrative by the English writer and compiler of travel literature; contains accounts of early maritime enterprise, and records of the writer's own voyages; the work was completed by Richard Willes and published a year after Eden's death in 1576.

William Harrison, *An Historical Description of the Island of Britain*—a prose account by the English churchman, historian, and prose writer; a valuable record of the life, manners, and customs of sixteenth-century Britain; compiled principally from the manuscripts of the English antiquarian John Leland (1506?-1552).

EVENTS

William Allot publishes his *Thesaurus Bibliorum,* an early form of concordance.

Jakob Andreae, chancellor of Tuebingen, and Martin Chemnitz, ducal librarian at Konigsberg, draft the Lutheran Book of Concord (*Concordia*), containing the confessional writings of the Lutheran Church; Andreae's official German edition will appear in 1580, with a Latin edition in 1584.

Raphael Holinshed, English translator and historian, publishes his *Chronicles;* a work by several authors, it forms the first authoritative account in English of English history in its entirety; the expanded edition of 1587 will be the one consulted by William Shakespeare and other Elizabethan playwrights for their "historical" plays about England, Scotland, Ireland, and Wales.

1578

BIRTHS

Natshinnaung (d. 1613). Burmese poet; his short poems will focus upon his imperial ambitions and convey the beauties of the woman he adored; he will sometimes subordinate the expression of his personal passion and plight to the concerns of poetic form.

DEATHS

Azariah ben Moses dei Rossi (b. 1531). Italian Jewish historian and physician; he wrote in Hebrew, Latin, and Italian, and his prose work reflects his wide knowledge of history and philosophy; he also wrote liturgical poems.

PUBLICATIONS

Guillaume de Salluste, Sieur de Bartas, *La Semaine* (The Week)—a religious epic poem by the French soldier and versifier; concerns the creation of the world; translated into English (1592-1599) by Joshua Sylvester (1563?-1618), a London merchant; the piece had a decided influence upon Edmund Spenser, John Donne, and John Milton.

Jacques de Cujas, *D'Interpreter le Droit Romain* (Commentaries on Roman Law)—a prose tract by the eminent French jurist and scholar; reveals his ability to expound upon difficult historical and legal questions.

John Lyly, *Euphues: The Anatomy of Wit*—the first part of a prose romance by the English writer; the title character, a young Athenian, visits Naples, where he meets a traveling companion, Philautus; the two argue over affairs of love, but mend their differences; Euphues pens a pamphlet of advice to lovers; the thin plot serves merely as a means for discoursing upon the general topic of love.

Pierre de Ronsard, *Sonets pour Helene* (Sonnets for Helen)— a collection by the eminent French lyric poet; conveys a sense of rich simplicity and restrained but sincere emotion; Petrarchan in form and substance, but contains elements of the poet's own creative expression: complex rhyme, picturesque imagery, and classical allusions and metaphors; written between 1570 and 1574 and first published in the fourth revised edition (1578) of the poet's complete works.

1579

BIRTHS

Samuel Coster (d. 1665). Dutch playwright and rhetorician; life's common activities will be the source for his farces.

John Fletcher (d. 1625). English playwright; he will succeed William Shakespeare as the principal dramatist of the King's Men; he will write satire, masque romance, and pure tragedy; collaborations with Francis Beaumont, Philip Massinger, Ben Jonson, and George Chapman will achieve both popularity and literary recognition.

Luis Velez de Guevara (d. 1644). Spanish playwright and novelist; his drama will imitate that of Lope de Vega and his fiction will influence the work of Alain Rene Le Sage.

PUBLICATIONS

Stephen Gosson, *The Schoole of Abuse*—a prose tract by the English minor playwright and churchman; an attack in "pleasant invective" against the theater, both poets and actors; most probably the motivation for Sir Philip Sidney's *Apologie for Poetrie.*

Edmund Spenser, *The Shepheards Calender*—the earliest important work by the English poet; twelve eclogues, one for each month of the year, each in a different metre; the first and last pieces consist of "complaints" by the poet, with the remaining ten being dialogues among shepherds: four on the subject of love, one in praise of the Queen, four in the form of religious or moral allegories, one a description of a singing contest, and one a lament upon the current contempt for poetry.

EVENTS

Lives of the Noble Grecians and Romans, by the Greek biographer Plutarch, published in an English translation from the French of Jacques Amyot by the English translator Sir Thomas North; he will add additional lives in 1595; North's effort will provide a source for Elizabethan playwrights, most notably William Shakespeare.

1580

BIRTHS

Daniel Heinsius (d. 1655). Dutch classical scholar and poet; he will edit the Latin classics and publish his own Latin poems and orations; his principal work will be an edition of Aristotle's *Poetics.*

Francisco Gomez Quevedo y Villegas (d. 1645). Spanish poet and political writer; he will write occasional sonnets and verse satires, a picaresque novel, devotional prose, and tracts on the monarchy.

John Smith (d. 1631). English soldier, adventurer, and colonist in America; his prose narratives will be considered important by cultural and literary historians.

John Webster (d. 1634). English playwright; his tragedies will penetrate the darkest and most horrid aspects of human personality and existence; his hero-villains will achieve a considerable degree of strength, despite their evil ways.

DEATHS

John Heywood (b. 1497?). English playwright; he primarily published dramatic interludes, replacing allegories of moral instruction with human comedies utilizing contemporary stock characters; his pieces emphasize and debate, rather than plot and action.

Luis Vaz de Camoens (b. 1524). Portuguese poet, identified as his nation's most significant writer of verse; through his poetry and reliance upon his native language, he became the interpreter of the deepest aspirations of the Portuguese people; he dies, at Lisbon, in poverty and obscurity.

PUBLICATIONS

Jean Bodin, *Demonomanie de Sorciers* (The Demonism of Witches)—a prose tract by the French social and political philosopher; sets forth the writer's arguments against witchcraft in what are for him surprisingly traditional terms.

Johann Fischart, *Das Jesuitenhutlein*—a satire by the German humorist, one of his attacks against corrupt clergy; in this instance, he strikes out against the Jesuits.

Jan Kochanowski, *Threny*—a series of verse laments by the Polish Poet; the pieces may be compared with the elegies of the eighteenth- and nineteenth-century English poets.

John Lyly, *Euphues and His England*—the second part of the prose romance by the English writer; relates the adventures of the title character in England and focuses upon the live affairs of his companion, Philautus; describes the institutions of England, including the men and women of the nobility and the monarchy.

Michel de Montaigne, *Le Essais*—the major work of the French writer; he emerges as a person of insatiable intellectual curiosity searching after wisdom, tolerance, and morality; he comes to recognize the fallibility of human reason and the relativity of human science; essentially, people must discover their own natures before they can live with one another in peace and dignity; revised editions in 1582, 1588, 1595.

Francois de la Noue, *24 Discours Politiques et Militaires* (Twenty-Four Discourses on Politics and the Military)—a collection of essays by the French-Calvinist soldier and prose writer; presents a Huguenot point of view upon the French wars of religion.

Torquato Tasso, *Aminta*—a pastoral drama by the Italian writer, written as early as 1573; the piece has been identified as the purest pastoral idyll since Virgil and Theocritus; concerns the love of the shepherd Aminta for the reluctant Sylvia; includes scenes of rescue, flight, peril, and marriage; most effective because of the moving and lyrical descriptions of the lovers' various states of mind.

EVENTS

John Stow, English historian and antiquary, publishes *The Chronicles of England,* later to be known as *The Annales of England;* further edition in 1592.

1581

BIRTHS

Peter Corneliszoon Hooft (d. 1647). Dutch historian, playwright, and poet; his principal historical work will document the Dutch war against Spain; French and Italian culture will exercise a considerable influence upon his literary development.

Juan Ruiz de Alarcon y Mendoza (d. 1639). Spanish playwright; he will be known for his heroic tragedies and comedies of character; his scant literary productions will not gain recognition until well after his death.

DEATHS

Andrea Palladio (b. 1518). Italian architect; his prose tracts explicated his architectural philosophy and complemented his own plans.

Thomas Wilson (b. 1525?). English scholar, statesman, and rhetorician; he urged Englishmen to write about English matters and concerns in English, avoiding linguistic affectation and Latinisms.

PUBLICATIONS

Lancelot Popeliniere, *Primier Livre de l'Idee de l'Histoire Accomplice* (The Principal Records of the Ideas and Accomplishments of History)—a tract on contemporary history by the French historian.

1582

DEATHS

George Buchanan (b. 1506). Scottish poet, essayist, playwright, and historian; wrote Latin verse skillfully and, as a playwright, helped to initiate the transition of the drama from the medieval age to the modern; he also achieved recognition for his Latin paraphrase of the Psalms.

Wu Ch'eng-en (b. 1500?). Chinese writer of fiction, poetry, and nonfiction; he has been identified as the writer of an allegorical novel that has been termed the most significant work of Chinese fiction.

PUBLICATIONS

George Buchanan, *Rerum Scoticarum Historia, Auctore Georgio Buchanano* (The History of Scotland)—a prose work by the Scottish poet and prose writer; an attempt to explicate the annals of his native country for educated Europeans.

Richard Hakluyt, *Divers Voyages Touching the Discovery of America*—a narrative by the English explorer and geographer; this important anthology of English explorations gained him the chaplaincy of the English embassy to Paris.

EVENTS

A new Gregorian calendar devised by the late Neopolitan astronomer and physician Aloysius Lilius (Luigi Lilio Ghiraldi) instituted by Pope Gregory XIII; the Pope abolishes the ancient Julian calendar, thus changing the vernal equinox from 11 March to 21 March.

Roman Catholic scholars at Rheims and Douai, in France, publish a translation of the New Testament.

The Utrecht Library, Netherlands, founded.

1583

BIRTHS

Hugo Grotius (d. 1645). Dutch jurist, humanist, and essayist; he will compose the first definitive text upon international law, drawing his sources from the Bible and classical history; he will argue that natural law prescribes rules of conduct for nations, as well as for individuals.

PUBLICATIONS

Robert Garnier, *Les Juifves* (The Jewish Women)—a tragedy by the French playwright; depicts the sufferings of people who have turned their minds and hearts away from God; derived from humanist theory and modeled after Seneca.

Fray Luis Ponce de Leon, *De Los Nombres de Cristo* (The Names of Christ)—a Platonic discussion by the Spanish monk, scholar, and poet; concerns the issue of the nature of Christ.

———— , *La Perfecta Casada* (The Perfect Wife)—a handbook on the duties of a wife.

Joseph Justus Scaliger, *Opus de Emendatione Temporum*—a scholarly work by the French-born man of learning; a reconstruction of the lost chronicle of Eusebius that will become the foundation of modern chronology.

EVENTS

Thomas Thomas appointed the first printer for the Cambridge University Press; the appointment opposed by the Stationers' Company of London as an infringement of its privileges and responsibilities.

1584

BIRTHS

Francis Beaumont (d. 1616). English playwright; his literary reputation will derive from his association with John Fletcher; the two will produce at least six plays directed toward an aristocratic audience with an acquired taste for masque-like romances, brittle satire, and a new form known as the "tragicomedy."

John Cotton (d. 1652). English-born clergyman who will settle in Massachusetts; his published works will include catechisms, forms of prayer, and tracts against those civil authorities who would determine religious issues.

Lucilio Vanini (d. 1619). Italian Catholic philosopher and free thinker; his teaching will reflect his pantheism; as an author, he will be known more for his vanity and audacity than for his knowledge or originality.

DEATHS

Jan Kochanowski (b. 1530). Polish poet; known for his elegies, epigrams, Latin verses, and translations of the Psalms; served as secretary to King Sigismund Augustus.

PUBLICATIONS

Giordano Bruno, *Spaccio della Bestia Trionfante* (On the Infinite Universe and Worlds)—a tract by the Italian Dominican philosopher; draws heavily from the Hermetic gnosticism and other works on magic and the occult; thus, he bases his defense of Copernicus not upon mathematics, but upon animist and religious grounds; there exists a variety of possible modes for viewing the world, and therefore we cannot postulate absolute truth.

John Lyly, *Alexander and Campaspe*—an early play by the English playwright and prose writer; focuses upon the story of Alexander the Great and his unsuccessful pursuit of the love of his captive, Campaspe.

———— , *Sapho And Phao*—a dramatized debate between the opposing principles of love and chastity; concludes with an elaborate compliment to Queen Elizabeth.

EVENTS

Accademia dei Scienze, Lettere, ed Arti founded at Lucca.

1585

BIRTHS

Gerbrand Adriaenszoon Bredero (d. 1618). Dutch poet and playwright; he will be the first Dutch master of dramatic comedy, writing pieces that depict life in Amsterdam.

Uriel Acosta (d. 1640). Portuguese Jewish scholar and prose writer; he will, upon moving to Amsterdam, discover how shallow stands the relationship between modern Judaism and Mosaic law; he will attempt to examine the Pharisaic traditions, only to be excommunicated for charges of atheism.

Jean Chapelain (d. 1674). French writer; he will gain recognition for his learning and achieve some degree of acceptance as a poet and a critic; he will also become an original member of the Academie Francaise.

DEATHS

Pierre de Ronsard (b. 1524?). French poet and critic; considered the most significant lyric poet of the French Renaissance; he sought to create a national literature to rival that of Renaissance Italy; he wrote songs, elegies, sonnets, and philosophical and scientific poems.

PUBLICATIONS

Miguel de Cervantes Saavedra, *La Galatea*—a pastoral romance by the Spanish novelist, playwright, and poet; an exercise in the attempt to master the pastoral romance form.

Pimgali Suranna, *Kalapurnodayamu*—a comedy of errors by the Telugu (Indian) poet; a celestial troublemaker creates impersonations of two heavenly lovers; the counterfeit of each falls in love with the true form of the other.

EVENTS

William Shakespeare leaves Stratford-upon-Avon for London.

1586

DEATHS

Sir Philip Sidney (b. 1551). English poet and courtier; his poetry represented the models of Renaissance chivalry: verse idylls, pastorals, sonnet sequences; he also wrote a prose tract in defense of poetry.

PUBLICATIONS

Caesar Baronius, *Annales Ecclesiastici*—a work by the Italian church historian describing the rise and development of the Roman Catholic church; attempted to prove that the Church of Rome stood identical with the Christian church of the first century; to 1607.

Edmund Spenser, *Astrophel*—a pastoral elegy by the English poet; written upon the death of Sir Philip Sidney, who had been mortally wounded that year at Zutphen.

William Webbe, *A Discourse of English Poetrie*—an account, by the student of English literature, of the characteristics of English poets, from Geoffrey Chaucer to the middle of the sixteenth century; the piece also promotes the new fashion of English hexameters.

EVENTS

William Camden, English antiquarian and historian, publishes his *Britannia,* a county-by-county guidebook with historical and geographical information.

1587

BIRTHS

Johann Valentin Andreae (d. 1654). German theologian and prose writer; he will be regarded as the founder of the Rosicrucian Society, and his writing will both explicate and defend the principals of that organization.

Joost van den Vondel (d. 1679). Dutch poet; he will be considered his nation's most significant poet; he will primarily write satirical verse directed against the sectarian disputes of his time; he will also write highly baroque Christian drama; his work in both genres will reveal a powerful imagination.

DEATHS

Bach Van (pseudonym of Nguyen Binh Khiem; b. 1491). Vietnamese poet who dominated his nation's literature during the sixteenth century; his poetry is the product of Chinese culture, particularly Confucianism and Taoism; thus, the reader observes a gentle, resigned philosophy based upon a return to Nature.

PUBLICATIONS

Robert Greene, *Euphues, His Censure of Philautus*—a prose pamphlet by the English hack writer; a continuation of John Lyly's 1578 prose romance, *Euphues;* illustrates clearly the major objection to his work by contemporaries: London printers appeared only too willing "to pay him deare for for the very dregs of his wit."

EVENTS

Isaac Casaubon, French humanist, edits the works of the Greek geographer Strabo.

Rederijckkunst, a Dutch manual on rhetoric, published at Amsterdam.

1588

BIRTHS

Ivan Gundulic (d. 1638). Croatian poet; he will publish an epic poem on the Polish wars against the Turks; his verse will be an early instance of the effort to promote Slavic nationalism.

Thomas Hobbes (d. 1679). English philosopher and essayist; he will develop a materialistic and highly pessimistic philosophy; his major work will present a bleak picture of humankind functioning in a state of pure nature, ready to surrender their natural rights and to submit to the absolute authority of a sovereign.

Marin Mersenne (d. 1648). French mathematician, musician, and philosopher; a friend of Rene Descartes, he will devote considerable time writing in defense of the orthodoxy of Cartesian philosophy.

DEATHS

Abdurrahman Mushfiqi (b. 1538). Central Asian-Persian poet, regarded as the last occa-sional poet of quality within central Asia; his best work describes the sufferings of the masses, blaming those misfortunes upon governors who failed to consider the welfare of the people.

Nawade I (b. 1498). Burmese courtier, soldier, and poet; his verses introduced fresh forms and themes based upon his political and military experiences; wrote more than three hundred poems.

PUBLICATIONS

Thomas Stapleton, *Tres Thomae*—a controversial Roman Catholic prose tract by the English theologian; concerns "three Thomases": the New Testament apostle, the Archbishop of Canterbury, and St. Thomas More.

EVENTS

The Czech translation of the New Testament by Jan Blahoslav becomes incorporated into the Kralice Bible.

Timothy Bright, Yorkshire physician and clergyman, publishes his *An Arte of Shorte, Swifte, and Secrete Writing by Character,* a manual of shorthand; thus, the invention of the modern method of shorthand.

William Morgan, Bishop of Llandaff, translates the Holy Bible into Welsh; the volume published in London.

The Vatican Library opens at Rome.

1589

BIRTHS

Honorat de Bueil Racan (d. 1670). French poet; he will become a disciple of Francois de Malherbe, write a pastoral play, and become an original member of the Academie Francaise.

Teimuraz I (d. 1663). Georgian (Turko-Persian) monarch and poet; his poetry will follow traditional Persian models and reveal a growing mood of hopelessness and despair at the ill will among peoples of the world; his long poems will evidence strong patriotic sentiment.

DEATHS

Bernard Palissy (b. 1510?). French artist and writer on art and pottery; his prose tracts will cover natural history, physics, and agriculture and will include accounts of his experiences at the Tuileries; died in the Bastille of Bucy.

PUBLICATIONS

Amador Arrais, *Dialogues de Dom Frei Amador Arraiz*—a tract by the Portuguese writer and philosopher; conversations upon moral and religious themes.

Justus Lipsius, *Politicorum sive Civilis Doctrinae*—a prose tract on civil and political doctrine by the Flemish humanist, reflecting his first-hand knowledge of the various Protestant denominations.

Edmund Spenser, *The Faerie Queene*—an epic poem by the English writer; the first three books were submitted to the publisher in November of this year, while the second three books appeared in 1596; the poem serves as an allergorical treatment of moral virtues, written in the nine-line stanza form that bears the poet's name; designed to demonstrate the ideal courtier (or gentleman) in action; the stanza form itself proved a substantial influence upon the poetry of such writers as James Thomson, John Keats, Percy Bysshe Shelley, and Lord Byron.

EVENTS

The Kiev Academy founded during the reign and under the sponsorship of Boris Fyodorovich Godunov; promotes literature and the arts in general.

1590

BIRTHS

Uriel da Costa (d. 1647). Portuguese-born Dutch Jewish writer; he will write in support of his opinion that Jews labored unnecessarily under burdens imposed upon them by regulations and ordinances extraneous to the orig-inal Torah; he will write his autobiography in Latin, declaring his opposition to the Talmud and the Mosaic laws.

Talib 'Amuli (d. 1627). Indo-Persian poet laureate of the Emperor Jahangir; his lyrics will abound in unusual parallels and delicate metaphors, praising the prophet Mohammad or the court dignitaries; his natural poetic style will stand in sharp contrast to the highly ornamental devices used by his contemporaries.

Theophile de Viau (d. 1626). French poet; he will write love poetry distinguished by its naturalness; his work will be considered impious and obscene.

DEATHS

Jacques de Cujas (b. 1520?). French jurist and legal writer; professor of jurisprudence at Bourges and Turin; his prose tracts evidence his ability to expound upon difficult legal questions.

Guillaume de Salluste du Bartas (b. 1544). French soldier, diplomat, and poet; his poetic works are generally religious, and his poetic account of the Creation will have a profound influence on John Milton's *Paradise Lost;* he dies of wounds received at the Battle of Ivry.

Johann Fischart (b. 1547?). German satirist; his pieces lash out, with inexhaustible humor, at the corruptions of the clergy, the fancies of the astrologers, and the general follies of the times; he also wrote spiritual songs.

Robert Ganier (b. 1545). French playwright; known for his work in the early development of the French tragicomedy.

PUBLICATIONS

Jose de Acosta, *Historia Natural y Moral de las Indias*—a history of the West Indies by the Peruvian Jesuit; a fairly thorough account given the paucity of accurate source materials.

Giovanni Battista Guarini, *Il Pastor Fido* (The Faithful Shepherd)—a pastoral tragicomedy in five acts by the Italian poet and playwright; written in blank verse, interspersed with chorus and dance; set in Arcadia, the piece relates a complicated love story; it enjoyed success throughout the seventeenth century, influencing the European pastoral drama that would become so popular during that period.

Christopher Marlowe, *Tamburlaine the Great*—a drama in blank verse by the English poet and playwright; the title character is an ambitious, cruel, and ruthless shepherd/usurper; nonetheless, the Mongolian conqueror is celebrated as the victorious superman who rescues Christian Europe from the heathen Turks.

Sir Philip Sidney, *The Arcadia*—a prose romance by the English writer, with a pastoral eclogue at the end of each book; begun as early as 1580, but not published until almost four years after the writer's death; an intricate love story written in melodious, elaborate prose, a style that relies heavily upon the artificial conceits of the age; its value as literature primarily rests on its contribution to the development of English prose rhythm.

EVENTS

Gasparo Balbi sixteenth-century Venetian merchant and traveler, publishes his *Viaggio all'India Orientali;* the piece narrates his journey from Aleppo to India, during which he visited Baghdad, Basra, Goa, Cochin, and Pegu; thus, the work is the first by a European to offer an account of India beyond the River Ganges; a Latin translation printed at Frankfort-am-Main in 1594.

1591

BIRTHS

Joseph Solomon Delmedigo (d. 1655). Jewish theologian, physician, and philosopher; born on Crete, educated in Italy, lived in Holland and Germany, died in Prague; he will compose numerous scientific tracts on mathematics, astronomy, logic, metaphysics, and optics; he will also attempt to harmonize faith with philosophy.

Robert Herrick (d. 1674). English poet; a reliance upon Latin models and themes will earn him the epithet England's most "pagan" poet, but that will not detract from his reputation as the most significant among the Cavalier versifiers; his lyrics will be highly praised for their simplicity and sensuousness.

DEATHS

Orfi (b. 1556?). Persian poet who migrated to India in 1585; in his poetry, he developed new combinations of words, fresh metaphors, and original subjects; he dies suddenly at Lahore.

PUBLICATIONS

John Lyly, *Endimion, the Man in the Moone*—an allegorical prose play by the English writer; a slight plot moves forward by means of such devices as a forty-year forced sleep and the breaking of a spell with a kiss; the allegory perhaps relates to the rivalry between Queen Elizabeth and Mary Queen of Scots, as well as Elizabeth's relationship with Lord Leicester.

Sir Walter Raleigh, *A Report of the Truth of the Fight about the Isles of the Azores*—a prose narrative by the English courtier, poet, and soldier-adventurer; relates the famous encounter of Sir Richard Grenville (1541?-1591) with the Spanish fleet; that naval commander, in the *Revenge*, fought fifteen Spanish ships off Flores; he was mortally wounded in that engagement.

William Shakespeare, *The Comedy of Errors*—a dramatic comedy by the English poet and playwright; concerns the arrival in Ephesus of a Syracusan merchant in search of his son, who had left Syracuse five years earlier to seek his mother, twin brother, and slave's twin brother; the errors occur because of mistaken identity among the twins.

——————, *Titus Andronicus*—a dramatic tragedy by the English playwright; Titus, upon returning to Rome after victory over the Goths, assents to a religious sacrifice of Queen Tamora's oldest son; through political intrigue and complicated matrimonial arrangements, Tamora plots revenge upon Titus; then follow death, illicit romance, and the emergence of the surviving offspring; the earliest and most violent of the playwright's tragedies.

Sir Philip Sidney, *Astrophel and Stella*—a series of sonnets by the English poet in which he expresses his love for Penelope Devereux, daughter of the first Earl of Essex; published posthumously; the 108 poems were written about 1582 and are modeled on the Italian sonnet; two editions within this year.

Edmund Spenser, *Complaints, Containing Sundrie Small Poems of the Worlds Vanitie*—a miscellany volume produced by the English poet's publisher to take advantage of the recent success of *The Faerie Queene;* includes the poet's minor verse and juvenilia, as well as "The Ruines of Time," an elegy on Sir Philip Sidney.

——————, *Daphnaida*—an elegy by the English poet on Douglas Howard, daughter of Lord Byndon and the wife of Sir Arthur Gorges (1557-1625), courtier and poet.

1592

BIRTHS

Johann Amos Comenius (d. 1670). Czech-born Moravian churchman, educator, and essayist; he will advocate relating education to everyday life by systematizing all knowledge, teaching in the vernacular rather than Latin, and establishing a universal system of education that would include opportunities for women.

Pierre Gassendi (d. 1655). French philosopher and mathematician; he will examine the Aristotelian system and become an early critic of the new philosophy of Rene Descarte; he will write on Epicurus, become friends with Johann Kepler and Galileo, and publish biographies of Tycho Brahe, Copernicus, and Regiomontanus.

DEATHS

Michel de Montaigne (b. 1533). French essayist, diariest, and translator; he developed the essay as a distinct literary genre, raising it to the level of art; his prose covers an enormous variety of subjects concerning human experience and observation, and his rambling but intimate style creates a relationship between writer and reader; thus, "I am a man, and nothing human is alien to me" serves as the guide to both the sound and the sense of his written work.

Nahapet Khutchak (b. ?). Armenian poet; he wrote, in both Armenian and Turkish, hundreds of quatrains on nature, love, pilgrimage, and philosophy; scholars often compare his poetry with that of Omar Khayyam.

PUBLICATIONS

David ben Solomon Gans, *Zemah David* (The Plant of David)—an historical piece by the Westphalian-born Jewish writer, considered the first attempt to write a history of the Jewish people in the Hebrew language; the writer also conducts a general review of history, relying on the works of prominent European historians.

John Lyly, *Midas*—a prose play by the English essayist and playwright; focuses upon the legend of Midas, King of Phrygia, who underscores the theme of the piece: the nature of kingship as it applies to and functions within Elizabethan England.

Thomas Nashe, *Pierce Pennilesse, His Supplication to the Divell*—a prose satire and fantasy by the English writer; a humorous complaint to Satan becomes the vehicle by which the writer discusses the vices of the day, particularly excessive drinking; he describes and catalogues the various types of drunkards; he also undertakes an analysis of spirits as part of his attack upon certain astrologers of the time.

Thomas Sanchez, *De Sacramento Matrimonii*—a prose tract by the Spanish Jesuit; concerns the legal, moral, and theological questions arising from the institution of marriage; because it was a comprehensive discussion of both moral and canonical aspects of matrimony, it enjoyed considerable respect throughout the seventeenth century as an authoritative tract on the subject.

William Shakespeare, *Richard III*—a historical drama by the English poet and playwright, the longest of his history plays and his first popular success; the piece concerns the tragic outcome of the attempt by Richard of York, Duke of Gloucester to ascend the throne of England; the title character will do anything to achieve his end; the playwright fully develops the character of Richard, causing him to dominate the rhetorical, poetic, and theatrical aspects of the play; the political and moral events of the past must pose important lessons for the present.

Wu Ch'eng-en, *Hsi-yu Chi* (The Journey to the West)—a novel by the Chinese writer, begun as early as 1570, but not published until this year; a work of one hundred chapters that develops the biography of the principal character, his attainment of celestiality, and his long pilgrimage, which constitutes the essence of the work; the writer incorporates into his lengthy narrative Taoist, Buddist, and Confucian teachings; the most revered and popular narrative work in all of Chinese literature; a four-volume English translation in 1977-1983.

EVENTS

Philip Henslowe, manager of the Rose Playhouse, Bankside, London, begins his diary; the work is noted for its observations and comments upon a host of minor actors and playwrights; the "diary" is actually a memorandum account book maintained by the manager until 1603; a scholarly edition published in 1961.

1593

BIRTHS

George Herbert (d. 1633). English metaphysical poet and Anglican churchman; he will write devotional poems and will also devise a prose piece to dispense plain, prudent, and useful rules to the country parson.

Izaak Walton (d. 1683). English prose writer; he will achieve literary recognition for his treatise upon fishing, a picture of peace and simple virtue; he will also write significant biographies of the poets John Donne and George Herbert.

DEATHS

Sah Husain (b. 1539). Panjabi poet and mystic, known for his love of singing and dancing; wrote short mystical lyrics designed to be sung by religious minstrels; his poems are characterized by imagery drawn from the activities of spinning and weaving.

Christopher Marlowe (b. 1564). English poet and playwright, the most significant of William Shakespeare's predecessors; Shakespeare's early work will reveal the influence of his tragedies; fatally stabbed in May of this year, at age twenty-nine, in a tavern brawl at Deptford.

Wang Shih-chang (b. 1526). Chinese scholar and statesman; he has been identified as the author of the earliest Chinese novel (c. 1560).

PUBLICATIONS

Pierre Charron, *Les Trois Verites* (The Three Truths)—a theological treatise by the French skeptic; a vindication of Catholicism.

Thomas Nashe, *Christes Teares over Jerusalem*—a tract by the English prose writer, who assumes the role of a religious reformer; applies Christ's prophecy of the fall of Jerusalem as a warning to the sinful citizens of London; he then analyzes the vices of contemporary society.

William Shakespeare, *The Taming of the Shrew*—a comedy by the English poet and playwright; after the introduction of the drunken tinker, Christopher Sly, the plot turns to a wealthy young man on a wife-hunting expedition; he finds a young shrew and tames her into obedience; a comment upon marriage and the nature of human personality and identity.

——————, *Venus and Adonis*—a poem by the English playwright; Venus woos Adonis, but cannot win his love; in the end, she attempts to dissuade him from hunting a boar; she fails, and the animal kills Adonis; the story receives additional substance and dimension from lengthy dialogue, vivid natural description, and pronounced didacticism.

1594

BIRTHS

Jean-Louis Guez de Balzac (d. 1654). French historiographer and essayist; he will attempt to popularize Latin writers; he will also strive to replace the disjointed prose of the sixteenth century with an orderly style with which to express abstraction, rhythm, and balance.

DEATHS

Alonso de Ercilla y Zuniga (b. 1553). Spanish poet; his major epic poem taken from the Spanish expedition against the Araucanians in Chile; Miguel Cervantes placed the work among the finest Italian epics.

Thomas Kyd (b. 1558). English playwright; he gained considerable popularity and recognition as a writer of tragedies; imprisoned on a charge of atheism, he eventually dies in extreme poverty.

PUBLICATIONS

Diego Bernardez, *Varias Rimas ao Bom Jesus*—a series of religious poems by the Portuguese pastoral poet; written after his imprisonment by the Moors at the battle of Alcazarquiver.

George Chapman, *The Shadow of Night*—a long, obscure poem by the English playwright, his earliest known composition; published at London in two parts; expresses in terms of exaggeration and affection the poet's darkest moods; thus, chaos appears better than creation, and night comes forward as his goddess.

Thomas Kyd, *The Spanish Tragedy*—written by the English playwright as early as 1588, but not published until this year; one of the most popular and influential Elizabethan plays; the theme of vengeance is carried out through an old man's grief and madness; contains visually sensational scenes, including a play-within-a-play.

Christopher Marlowe, *Edward II*—a dramatic tragedy by the English playwright, published posthumously; emphasizes the personal decline and suffering of a man who must govern; two parallel tragedies exist here: Edward falls from his own weakness and inability to exercise royal power and Mortimer declines in moral stature as he rises in political power; the work exercised considerable influence over William Shakespeare, particularly in *Richard II*.

Pierre Matthieu, *Histoire des Derniers Troubles de France* (The History of the Vilest Disturbances of France)—a general historical narrative by the French historiographer and jurist; focuses upon events prior to the reign of Henry IV (1575-1589).

Thomas Nashe, *The Unfortunate Traveller; or the Life of Jack Wilton*—a prose tale of adventure by the English writer, the first of its kind in England; the title character, a page in the court of Henry VIII, lives by his wits, taking advantage of everyone he can; he also travels about Europe, meeting famous persons and encountering tragedy, rape, murder, torture, and execution; depressed by what he has seen, Wilton eventually converts to a better way of life.

William Shakespeare, *Love's Labour's Lost*—a comedy by the English poet and playwright; the King of Navarre attempts to transform his court into a Platonic-style academy for three years; during that period, four courtiers vow to abstain from associating with women; in the simplest of terms, the piece exists as an attack upon those who believe they can separate learning from life.

——————, *The Rape of Lucrece*—a long poem by the English playwright that proved especially popular (six editions through 1616); based upon the theme that a good woman would rather die than abandon her chastity.

——————, *The Two Gentlemen of Verona*—a comedy by the English playwright; the title characters take their leave of each other: one seeks honor, the other love; a complex love entanglement follows, complete with travel, schemes, and disguise; a meeting in the forest finally disentangles all; reconcilication and forgiveness dominate this, the playwright's initial romantic comedy.

Torquato Tasso, *Discorsi del Poema Eroico* (Discourses on the Heroic Poem)—a prose tract by the Italian poet and essayist, a revision of an earlier (1587) critical work on the art of poetry; contains the writer's mature theories of epic poetry, anchored firmly to Aristotle, Horace, and Virgil, whom he sought to follow in terms of unity, style, and form, while not straying too far from the notions of the medieval romance.

1595

BIRTHS

Biharilal (d. 1664). Hindi poet; his work will reveal an ability to fuse various literary traditions and will also strongly reflect the thriving cultural environment of the middle Mughal period; he will draw his themes from the devotional and erotic traditions of Indian literature.

Jean Desmarets Saint-Sorlen (d. 1676). French poet and critic; the first chancellor and cofounder of the Academie Francaise; he will become involved in the critical controversy pitting the ancients against the moderns.

Matthias Casimire Sarbiewski (d. 1640). Polish Jesuit poet; he will write odes in Latin; he will become known as "the Christian Horace" and will revise the breviary hymns under Pope Urban VIII; his polished Latin verses will have an influence on English vernacular poetry of the late seventeenth and early eighteenth centuries.

DEATHS

Shaikh Abul-Faiz Faizi (b. 1547). Indo-Persian poet and poet-laureate of the Emperor Akbar; editor of numerous Persian versions of Sanskrit literary works.

Torquato Tasso (b. 1544). Italian poet, prose writer, and playwright; considered the most significant poet of the Italian Renaissance; known for his major epic poem describing the capture of Jerusalem by Christian forces during the first Crusade; a key transitional figure between the literatures of the Renaissance and the neoclassical period.

PUBLICATIONS

George Chapman, *Ovid's Banquet of Sense*—a poem by the English playwright and versifier; provides an allegorical account of Ovid's courtship of Corinna.

Gines Perez de Hita, *La Guerres Civiles de Grenade* (The Civil Wars of Grenada)—a semiromantic history by the Spanish prose writer and soldier; concerns the Moorish wars of 1569-1570, in which he participated; a second part published in 1604; republished in Madrid, 1913-1915.

William Shakespeare, *A Midsummer Night's Dream*—a comedy by the English poet and playwright; concerns the approaching wedding of Theseus, Duke of Athens, and Hippolyta, Queen of the Amazons; the major plot, however, centers on the matrimonial matching and mismatching of two young Athenian couples; parental authority, Athenian law, and supernatural influences provide the necessary romantic and comic complications; essentially, the piece reveals the conflicts between the magical world of romance and reality and reason.

—————, *The Tragedy of King Richard the Second*—a historical play by the English playwright, depicting the last two years of the monarch's life; charges of treasonous conduct, financial mismanagement, and the loss of his nobles' allegiance force the king to abdicate;

he is eventually poisoned by a misguided agent of the new monarch; the playwright combines ideas of Tudor government with the tragedy surrounding one's fall from power; in the end, the title character does gain insight into his role as man and monarch, and he dies with some degree of dignity.

—————, *Romeo and Juliet*—a tragedy by the English writer; in Verona, the Montagues and the Capulets bear an ancient grudge against one another; the secret marriage of the title characters, a Montague and a Capulet, leads only to their deaths; in the end, the surviving family members realize the tragic results of their feud; the ideas and the action of the play develop the theme of the relationship between fate and free will.

Sir Philip Sidney, *The Apologie for Poetrie; or, Defence of Poesie*—a prose tract by the English writer, written as early as 1580 and published posthumously; examines the art of poetry and undertakes a critical discussion of its state in England; considers the essential nature of poetry, the art of imitation, the classifications of poetry, the relationship of poetry to history and philosophy, objections to the genre, poetic principles, and the special relationship of prosody with the English language.

Edmund Spenser, *Amoretti*—a series of eighty-eight sonnets by the English poet; may represent his experiences while courting Elizabeth Boyle, the woman he eventually marries.

—————, *Colin Clouts Come Home Againe*—an allegorical pastoral by the English poet; describes, in allegorical form, the visit of Sir Walter Ralegh to the poet in Ireland, where he induces him to come to England to see the Queen; contains a description of the sea voyage, of the Queen and her court, and of political intrigue in general.

—————, *Epithalamion*—a hymn by the English poet, thought to be a celebration of his marriage to Elizabeth Boyle in 1594; admired for the sheer beauty of its composition; recent scholarship has connected its twenty-four stanzas to the hours of Midsummer Day.

EVENTS

Andrew Maunsell, London bookseller and publisher of various pieces of antiCatholic literature, publishes his *Catalogue of English Printed Books;* Part I (123 pages) and Part II (27 pages) focus upon divinity, mathematics, and medicine; Part III, promised but never printed, was to list titles relative to rhetoric, history, poetry, and politics; one of the earliest attempts to record and catalogue English publications.

1596

BIRTHS

Abdulrahman as-Sadi (d. 1656). Mali scholar, historian, and collector of legends and tales; he will seek to anthologize the stories and legends of his native Timbuktu prior to its invasion by the Moroccans in the early seventeenth century; in the process, he will create a valuable compendium of African history and culture; he will write his major works in Arabic.

Rene Descartes (d. 1650). French philosopher, mathematician, and scientist; he will become the so-called "father" of modern philosophy, his work regarded as the transition between scholasticism and all the major philosophical schools to follow him; he will always be remembered for his noted assertion, "Cogito, ergo sum" (I think, therefore I am).

Constantijn Huygens (d. 1687). Dutch poet and humanist; he will gain praise for his descriptive and satirical poems, receiving knighthood from both French and English monarchs.

DEATHS

Jean Bodin (b. 1530?). French political philosopher; in opposition to prevailing Protestant thought, he held that under no circumstances can citizens justify rebellion against their leaders; however, he maintained that one prince may intervene on behalf of the oppressed subjects of another.

Madhavadeva (b. 1489). Indo-Iranian (Assamese) religious poet; his devotional poems became popular among the people because of their musicality; also noted for his profound spiritual ideas.

PUBLICATIONS

Sir Walter Raleigh, *The Discovery of the Empyre of Guiana*—a narrative by the English soldier, adventurer, and poet; provides a detailed account of his initial expedition, in 1595, to the American continent.

William Shakespeare, *King John*—a history play by the English poet and playwright; focuses upon the later part of the monarch's reign, particularly the determination of his mother, Eleanor of Aquitaine, to maintain her son's royal power; he allies himself with Philip Faulconbridge, invades France, achieves a hollow victory, and dies in agony after having been poisoned by a monk; the true hero of the piece, the bastard Philip Faulconbridge, represents the spirit of the English nation that remains loyal even to a weak and worthless monarch.

———————, *The Merchant of Venice*—a comedy by the English playwright; the plot arises out of a bond between the merchant, Antonio, and a Jewish usurer; the former wishes to finance his young friend Bassanio in an expedition to Belmont, there to court and marry the wealthy and beautiful Portia; love, shipwreck, legal and monetary squabbles, disguise, and general confusion follow; the playwright artfully combines plot, character development, setting, and poetry.

Edmund Spenser, *Fowre Hymnes*—poems by the English writer, composed "in the greener times of my youth," probably at Cambridge; contains "An Hymne in Honour of Love," " . . . Beautie," " . . . Heavenly Love," and " . . . Heavenly Beautie"; the pieces are informed by the poet's Christian thought, combined with Platonic elements generally adaptable to Christian belief.

———————, *Prothalamion*—a poem by the English writer in honor of the double marriage of Elizabeth and Katherine Somerset, daughters of the Earl of Worcester, to Henry Gilford and William Peter; demonstrates the degree to which the poet had refined his stanza form; concerns the ceremonial visit of the two prospective brides to Essex House, not long before their weddings.

EVENTS

The English poet and courtier Sir John Harington designs the first water closet and installs it at the Queen's Palace, Richmond; that act will not, however, save him from banishment from the court as a result of his satire, *Matamorphosis of Ajax* (1596).

1597

BIRTHS

Fatehabad Aloal (d. 1673?). Bengali poet who will write under the patronage of court officials; he will principally compose Bengali verse translations and adaptations of Hindi and Persian compositions; his lengthy poetic narratives will be strongly religious.

Martin Opitz (d. 1639). German poet who will spend considerable time courting royal patronage; he will write didactic poetry and translate works by Sophocles and Seneca.

DEATHS

Hernando de Herrera (b. 1534?). Spanish lyric poet and cleric; his love poems are remembered for their tender feelings, while his odes sometimes rise to the grandeur of John Milton; he also wrote history and translated from the Latin.

Aldus Manutius (b. 1547). Venetian printer, the first to produce Greek books; he produced beautiful fonts of Greek and Latin type and became the first printer to rely upon Italics on a large scale; he issued no less than 908 works under his imprint.

Francisco Patrizi (b. 1529). Italian historian and philosopher.

PUBLICATIONS

Francis Bacon, *The Essays, or Counsels, Civill and Morall*—a collection of prose by the English essayist; reflections, generalizations, and extracts from various writers, brought together as counsel for the successful conduct of life and the management of human affairs; three editions published during the writer's lifetime (1597, 1612, 1625).

William Shakespeare, *Henry IV, Part One*—a history play by the English poet and playwright; concerns the troubles upon England's frontier and the difficulties encountered by the monarch in carrying out his pilgrimage to the Holy Land; the dissipation of his son does little to relieve the King's problems, for the former has been taken in by the principal wastrel of the land, Sir John Falstaff; the playwright manages a skillful and unique dramatic blending of history and comedy; the major characters manage to combine both positive and negative qualities; thus, Prince Hal emerges as both useless and noble, Falstaff, although a fat rogue, loves life, and Hotspur's pride is not without merit because of his dedication to chivalry.

——————— , *Henry IV, Part Two*—a continuation of *Henry IV, Part One;* resumes the narrative of the Percy rebellion; the Prince reconciles with his father on his deathbed; the King provides his son with advice on the proper method of government, and the piece closes with the coronation of Hal as King Henry V; the play also brings to an end the influence of Sir John Falstaff, whom the newly crowned monarch publicly rejects in favor of rational and serious governance.

1598

BIRTHS

Thomas Carew (d. 1639). English poet; he will publish his initial volume of verse at age twenty; he will learn from his friends Ben Jonson and John Donne to write polished lyrics in the Cavalier tradition.

Vincent Voiture (d. 1648). French poet and writer of epistles; he will become an original member of the Academie Francaise and enjoy the favor of Cardinal Richelieu and King Louis XIII; his sonnets and social verse, although not published until 1650, will delight French court society.

DEATHS

Philippe de Marnix, Baron de St. Aldegonde (b. 1538). Flemish statesman and prose writer; wrote patriotic songs, prose satires, a metrical translation of the Psalms, and a portion of a prose translation of the Bible.

PUBLICATIONS

George Chapman, *The Blind Beggar of Alexandria*—the earliest known play by the English poet and dramatist; a tragicomedy in which a ruler manipulates an entire series of episodes by rapidly changing disguises.

Ben Jonson, *Every Man in His Humour*—a comedy by the English poet and playwright in which he sets forth in the prologue his theory of drama; a crowd of riotous but harmless gallants descends upon the house of a merchant; a series of moral misinterpretations, mischievous antics, and attempts at disguise follow; a shrewd and kindly justice finally manages to resolve the misunderstandings; as with its 1599 sequel, the comedy focuses upon individuals controlled by a single "humor."

William Shakespeare, *The Merry Wives of Windsor*—a comedy by the English poet and playwright; concerns Sir John Falstaff, the impoverished, old, stout lecher; he attempts to gain financial profit from the simultaneous courtship of two women, both wives of wealthy Windsor citizens; the ladies discover his plans and devise intrigues of their own; the piece exists as the one attempt by the playwright to illustrate contemporary English rural life; thus, it became extremely popular.

——————, *Much Ado about Nothing*—another comedy by the English dramatist; a young lord rejects his bride at the altar because he has been convinced, wrongly, of her lack of chastity and fidelity; sharp-tongued battles of wit color the events of the love-comedy game that follows.

Lope de Vega, *Arcadia*—a novel by the Spanish dramatist and poet; a story set in a highly ornamental but pastoral setting; concerns the prenuptial vagaries of the Duke of Alva; written before the Duke's marriage in July 1590, but not published until eight years later.

——————, *La Dragontea*—an epic poem by the Spanish writer; in ten cantos, the poet conducts a shout of exultation over the death of Sir Francis Drake; the poet's first signed publication.

EVENTS

George Chapman, English playwright and poet, publishes his partial translation of Homer's *Iliad.*

John Florio, English scholar, publishes his *A World of Wordes, an Italian-English Dictionary.*

Francis Meres, English scholar and churchman, publishes his *Palladis Tamia, or Wit's Treasure;*

an anthology of maxims and quotations from 125 English writers, from Chaucer to his own time.

John Stowe, English chronicler and antiquary, publishes his *A Survey of London;* a detailed work containing information on the city and its customs; further edition in 1603; expanded in 1720 by the ecclesiastical historian John Strype; a scholarly edition in 1908.

1599

BIRTHS

Meric Casaubon (d.1671). Swiss-born Anglican cleric, who will study at Oxford and live near Canterbury; he will edit the works of Marcus Aurelius and will write tracts vindicating the reputation of his father, who suffered (as royal librarian at Paris) for his Protestant beliefs.

DEATHS

Edmund Spenser (b. 1552?). English poet and author of one of the principal epics in all of English literature; known for the harmonies of his verse, his poetic diction, and the sincerity of his Christian feeling; his lasting reputation largely rests on the depth of his moral vision and the nine-line stanza form he invented to convey that vision to his audience.

PUBLICATIONS

Mateo Aleman, *Guzman de Alfarache*—a picaresque novel by the Spanish writer; completed in 1604; its subtitle, "The Spanish Rogue," sets the theme and tone of the piece.

Ben Jonson, *Every Man Out of His Humour*—a satirical comedy by the English poet and playwright; the writer ridicules absurd characters and the fashions of his day; because of their various vocations and points of view, the courtier, the student, the father, and the knight all find themselves "out of their humour."

Christopher Marlowe, "The Passionate Shepherd to His Love"—a poem by the English playwright and poet, consisting of six four-line stanzas; a pastoral lyric of invitation, certainly the most famous of Elizabethan songs; a number of poets have written replies to this piece, which opens, "Come live with me and be my love, / And we will all the pleasures prove. . . . "

William Shakespeare, *As You Like It*—a dramatic comedy by the English poet and playwright; principally a dramatic adaptation of Thomas Lodge's pastoral novel, *Rosalynde* (1590); Rosalind and Orlando fall in love at first sight and both must flee their homes; independently they seek shelter; then follow disguise, the actions of malcontents, love affairs among the country folk, the male disguise of the heroine, a wedding of four couples, and reconciliation between villains and their relatives; the playwright combines comedy with elements of the pastoral drama and explores the issue of appearance versus reality; he attempts to seek the formula for the total well being of humankind.

——————, *Henry V*—a history play by the English dramatist; focuses upon the claim of Henry V of England to the throne of France; the English defeat the French at the battle of Agincourt; at the peace treaty, the victorious English monarch also wins the hand of Princess Katherine; in his title character, the playwright develops the image of the ideal monarch, isolating him from former companions who would only destroy him; also a military play demonstrating how the monarch can unite the diverse elements within his kingdom and gain a truly national victory.

——————, *Julius Caesar*—a tragedy by the English dramatist; the plot revolves around the assassination of the Roman leader because of the fear that he might want to become king; Brutus, the real hero of the piece, and thus the victim of this tragedy, stands (and falls) as the supreme political idealist; the complexity of the piece arises from its ambiguous purpose: character analysis or politics?

1600

BIRTHS

Hermann Busenbaum (d. 1688). German Jesuit theologian and essayist; his treatise on moral theology will become a standard authority in Jesuit seminaries, although several of his propositions will be condemned by papal decree.

Pedro Calderon de la Barca (d. 1681). Spanish poet and playwright; he will become the most significant dramatist to write in Spanish and the author of over two hundred full-length plays; he will also write more than seventy one-act sacramental dramas (known as "autos") and at least one extremely powerful religious poem; he will rise to a literary stature equal to that of William Shakespeare in England and Jean Racine in France.

DEATHS

Jose de Acosta (b. 1539). Peruvian Jesuit historian and essayist; known for his thorough and accurate history of the West Indies.

Mahmud Abdulbaki Baki (b. 1527?). Turkish poet and jurist; his lyric poetry is considered the height of classical Turkish literature; individual pieces praise wine and beauty and form meditations on life.

Giordano Bruno (b. 1548). Italian philosopher and speculative thinker; his philosophy reflected his Aristotelian views and encompasses a number of influences: pantheism, Copernican astronomy, Neoplatonism, stoicism, epicureanism; arrested by the officers of the Inquisition and burned in Rome after a trial of seven years.

PUBLICATIONS

Ben Jonson, *Cynthia's Revels*—a comedy by the English poet and dramatist; a satire of court types, with the title character representing Queen Elizabeth; contains (4:3) the song of Hesperus, "Queen and huntress, chaste and fair," one of the writer's most beautiful lyric poems.

Christopher Marlowe, *The Massacre at Paris*—a play by the English dramatist and poet; based upon the French civil wars that had only recently come to an end; the central character, the Duke of Guise, is a true Machiavellian villain, gaining power as he commits a series of political evils; much of the piece concerns the St. Bartholomew's Day Massacre (1572); in the end, the Duke falls, showing himself to be a complete fool.

William Shakespeare, *Hamlet*—a tragedy by the English playwright and poet; the young prince of Denmark learns from his father's ghost that his father was murdered by his own brother, Claudius; Claudius has married Hamlet's mother and now controls the kingdom; the prince sets out to avenge his father's murder, but in the process causes the deaths of a number of people, some innocent, some guilty; he, himself, becomes victim; the first of the playwright's significant dramatic tragedies; also a penetrating psychological analysis of a single character.

—————, *Twelfth Night, or, What You Will*—a dramatic comedy by the English playwright; a young woman, separated from her brother in a shipwreck, arrives in Illyria, disguised as a boy; she enters the service of the duke, but also falls in love with him; a surrogate lover and the arrival of the lost brother (her identical twin) cause further complications; in the end, however, the four lovers are properly paired; the last of the playwright's romantic comedies, it is also his most musical production; the piece also benefits from a number of "low-comedy" characters.

1601

BIRTHS

Baltasar Gracian (d. 1658). Spanish essayist, novelist, and philosopher; his work will be principally didactic, concerning itself with Jesuit ideology and practical ethics; he will strive to teach the reader how to adapt means to ends, how to purge the mind of irrational illusions, and how to become master of oneself and one's own destiny.

DEATHS

Tycho Brahe (b. 1546). Danish astronomer; although technically not a member of the literati, he did publish his observations and theories, which exercised considerable influence upon philosophers and poets prior to the time of Sir Isaac Newton; he dies near Prague while residing with the Emperor Rudolph II.

Thomas Nashe (b. 1567). English playwright and satirist; possessed a ready talent for vituperation, which often found its way into his works; authored one of the earliest pieces of picaresque fiction; died amidst the poverty in which he had always lived.

PUBLICATIONS

Pierre Charron, *De la Sagesse* (Treatise on Wisdom)—a prose tract by the French theologian; establishes a system of stoic philosophy, especially embracing a skeptical attitude toward all forms of religion; the piece opens the way for the secularization of morals, for Deism, and for free thought in general.

Ben Jonson, *The Poetaster*—a satirical comedy by the English poet and playwright that focuses upon the wars among the London playwrights and London theaters; the writer not too carefully hides his burlesque within the court of Caesar Augustus; thus, for example, "a light vomit" is administered to Crispinus (John Marston) to rid him of his long words.

EVENTS

Bento Teixeira Pinto writes his *Prosopopeya*, recognized as the first Brazilian epic.

1602

BIRTHS

Mirza Mohammad 'Ali Saeb (d. 1678). Persian poet; his poetry will bear certain similarities to that of the English metaphysicals, notably Andrew Marvell and George Herbert; he will rely upon words of nontraditional and often contradictory association to elevate the reader to a high level of poetic and linguistic consciousness; his work will also serve as an important link in Persian poetry between the early Iraqi style and the later Indian verse forms.

PUBLICATIONS

Lope de Vega, *La Hermosura de Anglica* (The Beauty of England)—an epic poem by the Spanish playwright and poet, his first work of any length; written at sea in 1588, when the poet accompanied the Spanish Armada in its attempted invasion of England.

EVENTS

The Ambrosian Library, Milan, founded; the institution will open its doors in 1609; established by Cardinal Federigo Borromeo, Archbishop of Milan, it will become one of the earliest libraries open to the public.

Sir Thomas Bodley, English diplomat and bibliophile, establishes the Bodleian Library at Oxford University.

Konrad Kircher publishes a concordance to the Septuagint.

John Willis publishes, at London, his *The Arte of Stenographie or Short Writing by Spelling Characterie;* one of the earliest examples of a shorthand alphabet; thirteen editions to 1644; a Latin edition in 1618.

1603

DEATHS

Pierre Charron (b. 1541). French theologian; his prose tracts attack Church institutions and reveal a generally skeptical attitude toward all forms of religion; a friend of Michel de Montaigne.

PUBLICATIONS

Johannes Althusias, *Politica Methodice Digesta* (A Digest of Political Systems)—a tract by the German professor of law and political philosophy; he states boldly that monarchs exist as nothing more than magistrates, that sovereignty belongs to the people, and, therefore, as a natural consequence, people may change and even banish their rulers.

Ben Jonson, *Sejanus, His Fall*—a dramatic tragedy by the English poet and playwright; concerns the rise of the Roman Sejanus, the confident of the emperor Tiberius; his all-consuming lust for power leads to his fall and eventual execution; the piece may well be described as a tragic satire upon the political type.

William Shakespeare, *All's Well That Ends Well*—a comedy by the English poet and playwright; concerns the orphan daughter of a distinguished physician, now the ward of a countess; she falls in love with the countess's

son; the two manage a union only after considerable travel, trial, and intrigue; termed a "dark comedy" because of its emphasis upon sex and its satire of various character types.

EVENTS

The Accademia dei Lincei founded at Rome.

1604

BIRTHS

Manasseh ben Israel (d. 1657). Dutch writer, publisher, diplomat, and Talmudic scholar; he will establish the first Hebrew printing press in Holland; he will write his own works—historical studies and commentaries—in Hebrew, Latin, Spanish, Portuguese, and English.

Jean Mairet (d. 1686). French playwright; he will write pastoral tragicomedies, but his later pieces will be marked by a technique that essentially rejects the classical unities; he will, in the end, combine farce with tragedy.

PUBLICATIONS

Christopher Marlowe, *The Tragical History of the Life and Death of Doctor Faustus*—a play by the English poet and dramatist; the only one of the writer's dramatic pieces to have a specific "Christian" setting and to concern theological issues; portrays the damnation of the human soul with great tragic power; evokes terror, pity, and a sense of human loss; establishes clearly the conflict between submission to divine will and belief in one's ability to control Nature.

William Shakespeare, *Measure for Measure*—a dramatic comedy by the English poet and playwright; a duke assumes the guise of a friar and moves about among his people so that he may test the ability of a "stand-in" to govern his city; he attempts to control and regulate the morals and sexual practices of his subjects, which sets in motion the usual comic and complex actions, reactions, separations, and reconciliations; a combination tragedy and comedy of intrigue; goes forward upon the premise that sex is the basis for a healthy state as long as law and morality are maintained.

——————— , *The Tragedy of Othello, Moor of Venice*—a clearly psychological drama by the English playwright; in the simplest terms, jealousy and treachery bring an end to the major characters; the piece focuses upon domestic issues: love, lust, and hate exist outside of any political environment; the title hero may indeed by an experienced soldier and governor, but he lacks experience in love and doubts his qualities as a husband and lover; more than anything, he fears the ruin of his good name, which makes him easy prey for the base insinuations of others.

Jacques Auguste de Thou, *Historia Sui Temporis*—a significant work of historical commentary by the French historian and diplomat; a chronicle in Latin of his own times; eleven volumes to 1614; eventually placed upon the Index of the Roman Catholic Church.

EVENTS

The *Adi Granth* (Original Book), the Sikh scriptures written in the Gurmukhi script, completed; contains approximately 6000 hymns and poems by various writers; various versions published throughout the eighteenth century; a four-volume English translation in 1962.

Robert Cawdrey, English scholar and writer, publishes his *A Table Alphabetical.*

James I of England appoints a commission to retranslate the Old and New Testaments; Sir Henry Savile, William Bedwell, and Lancelot Andrewes are among the 450 scholars selected for the task.

1605

DEATHS

Ulisse Aldrovandi (b. 1535). Italian naturalist and physician; imprisoned at Rome as a heretic; published significant prose tracts on birds, insects, and mollusca, published between 1599 and 1642.

PUBLICATIONS

Francis Bacon, *The Advancement of Learning*—a prose tract by the English philosopher, written in English (instead of the usual Latin); considers the various methods of advancing knowledge and the defects of current practices; discusses and analyzes the various divisions of knowledge: history, poetry, and philosophy.

Miguel de Cervantes Saavedra, *El Ingenioso Hidalgo Don Quixote de la Mancha* (The History of the Valorous and Wittie Knight-Errant, Don Quixote of the Mancha)—a satirical romance by the Spanish writer, the second part of which appeared in 1615; on the surface, the piece appears to be a burlesque of the romances of chivalry; however, in developing the character of his hero, the writer transferred his attention to a criticism of life; in the end, he created an amiable character, essentially a rational man, who nonetheless has his wits shaken by his irrational devotion to romantic tales; he then imagines himself called upon to roam the world in search of adventure.

Ben Jonson, John Marston, George Chapman, *Eastward hoe!*—a comedy by the three English playwrights; the piece casts considerable light upon the London of the day and provides a sympathetic picture of city tradesmen; the plot focuses upon the contrasting careers of virtuous and idle apprentices.

Justus Lipsius, *Monita Exempla Politica*—a political and philosophical treatise by the Flemish humanist and scholar; focuses principally upon the organization of the state.

William Shakespeare, *King Lear*—a dramatic tragedy by the English poet and playwright; the principal plot concerns the aged and egocentric Lear as he attempts to divide his kingdom among his three daughters; each will receive according to the degree that she describes her love for him; beneath that plot runs the conspiracy of Edmund, the bastard son of the Earl of Gloucester, against his brother Edgar; Edgar must, therefore, flee his home; certainly the most serious of the playwright's dramatic pieces, particularly because it considers such issues as the relationship between parent and child, between sibling and sibling, and between human beings in general; finally, one needs to consider both the social and political levels upon which the tragedy exists.

——————, *Macbeth*—a tragedy by the English dramatist; concerns the personal and political ambitions of the title character, whose motivation comes as much from his wife as from himself; murder, revenge, and madness abound, given additional depth and substance by the intervention of subconscious influences; the playwright creates a tragic hero with whom the audience can form a relationship: an essentially good man, but a weak individual; he ultimately destroys himself through his own fear; the strength of the piece lies in the character contrasts of Macbeth (weakness) and Lady Macbeth (strength of will).

EVENTS

Angelo Rosco founds the Biblioteca Anglica, the first public library in Rome.

Abraham Verkoeven, Antwerp printer, begins publication of the world's first newspaper, *Nieuwe Tijdenghen.*

1606

BIRTHS

Pierre Corneille (d. 1684). French playwright; his early dramas will ingenuously develop intricate and extravagant plots; eventually, he will master the classical tragedy and become proficient as a writer of comedy.

Tukaram (d. 1649). Indo-Iranian poet who wrote in the Marathi language; from his low social position, and under impoverished conditions, he will write poetry that influences the common people; will compose religious hymns characterized by an intensity of feeling, spontaneity, and delicate charm; his secular poetry will reflect the cruelty inflicted upon him by social superiors and his loathing of the ways of the world.

Edmund Waller (d. 1687). English poet; his poems will revive the heroic couplet form and evidence a technically correct and highly polished craft; he will be known as the poet who refused to tolerate, in his verse, "any line that did not contain some motive to virtue."

DEATHS

Juan Latino (b. 1516?). Guinea-born poet and Latin scholar, brought to Spain as a child of twelve; professor of classics at the University of Granada; his poetry displays refined wit and language and vigorously rejects racial stereotypes.

Justus Lipsius (b. 1547). Flemish humanist and classical scholar; held professorships at Louvain, Jena, and Leyden; known for his thorough and scholarly editions of Tacitus and Seneca.

John Lyly (b. 1554). English dramatist and writer of fiction; his fiction relies heavily upon similes drawn from fabulous stories concerning the properties of animals, plants, and minerals and often indulges in antithesis.

PUBLICATIONS

Johann Arndt, *Wahres Christentum* (True Christianity)—a semimystic tract by the German Lutheran divine; rejecting the penal theory of the Atonement, the writer dwells upon the work of Christ within the hearts of human beings.

Ben Jonson, *Volpone, or the Fox*—a comedy by the English poet and playwright; recounts the story of Volpone, a wealthy Venetian who, pretending to be dying, attempts to dupe a group of greedy townsmen; each attempts to inherit the old man's fortune; the piece has all the markings of a morality play, but the characters of Volpone and his servant, Mosca, transform it to the level of pure comedy.

William Shakespeare, *Antony and Cleopatra*—a dramatic tragedy by the English poet and playwright; depicts Antony under the spell of Cleopatra, giving himself over to a life of idleness and completely ignoring his administrative responsibilities; in the end, he battles with Octavius Caesar, suffering defeat because he cannot develop a proper strategy; death comes to both the Roman general and his young Egyptian mistress; the piece portrays the struggle between personal desire and public responsibility; from a less romantic view, it also serves as a commentary upon middle-aged romance.

EVENTS

Joseph Justus Scaliger, French scholar and editor, completes the publication of his *Thesau-*

rus Temporum, a chronology of ancient times and a reconstruction of the lost chronicle of Eusebius.

1607

BIRTHS

Paul Gerhardt (d. 1676). German poet and hymnodist; he will be banished from the assistant pastorship of St. Nicholas Church, Berlin, and become pastor at Lubben; in an age of splendor and ornamentation, he will write hymns known for their sincerity and simple, direct style.

Francisco de Rojas Zorilla (d. 1648). Spanish playwright; he will achieve recognition for his neo-Senecan tragedies, the majority of which are set within a Baroque pastoral world; his plots will influence the work of French dramatists later in the century.

Madeleine de Scudery (d. 1701). French novelist and essayist; she will become one of the best known and most influential writers of romance tales in Europe during the seventeenth century; a refined and well-educated woman, she will establish salons in Paris for the promotion of literature and culture.

DEATHS

Caesar Baronius (b. 1538). Italian church historian; wrote the first critical history of the Church; also served as the Vatican librarian.

Thomas Deloney (b. 1543). English balladist and writer of fiction; his fiction is known for its lively dialogue and characterization; his work marks one of the major starting points for the development of the English novel.

PUBLICATIONS

Francis Beaumont, *The Knight of the Burning Pestle*—a comedy by the English playwright, modeled on Miguel de Cervantes's *Don Quixote* (1605); a delightful burlesque of the historical romances popular upon the Elizabethan stage; however, the playwright takes equal aim at the audiences who flocked to those productions; the piece also contains a play-within-a-play.

George Chapman, *Bussy D'Ambois*—a historical dramatic tragedy by the English playwright and poet; based upon the career of a French courtier, duelist, and lover, who is murdered by the husband of his mistress; the title character may be viewed from at least two perspectives: (1) the errant sinner who falls from power because of his own excesses or (2) the ideal hero from another time who can exist free from those restrictions that serve to impede one's search for true heroism; the playwright's most significant literary achievement.

William Shakespeare, *Coriolanus*—a dramatic tragedy by the English poet and playwright; concerns the election of Caius Marcius, a proud, aloof patrician, to the consulship and his immediate fall from power; after capturing Corioli, the capital of the Volscians, he assumes the name of the title character; his pride and anger lead to his banishment and eventual death; the playwright produces a totally unattractive "hero," unstable both politically and emotionally, and thus incapable of governing; the reader-viewer must wrestle with the play on two levels: the study of political unrest and the analysis of character.

——————, *Timon of Athens*—a tragedy by the English dramatist; relates the story of a wealthy Athenian nobleman who lavishly entertains his friends and freely showers them with gifts; eventually, he exhausts his fortune; his "friends" refuse him financial assistance; he discovers gold and distributes it to those who would commit harm to Athens; the piece ends with the "reported" death of the title character, which has led scholars to believe that the playwright never completed the project.

Cyril Tournier, *The Revenger's Tragedy*—a dramatic tragedy by the English playwright, published anonymously; in avenging the murder of his beloved, Vindice sets in motion a series of brutal horrors; murder, betrayal, and lust surround the characters; the piece appears to underscore the contemptibleness of human nature, but draws literary and emotional strength from its intense portrayal of human evil.

Honore d'Urfe, *Astree*—a pastoral romance by the French writer, often considered the first French novel; presents the ideal of polite and distinguished living, wherein men and women appear as shepherds; the title character believes her lover to be unfaithful, which causes him to throw himself into a river; however, he does not drown, and, after several trials and adventures, manages a reunion with his lover.

EVENTS

John Cowell, English jurist and regius professor of civil law at King's College, Cambridge, publishes his *Interpreter,* a glossary of the legal meanings of words; chief justice Sir Edward Coke will attack the work for its controversial interpretations of the monarchy; thus, Parliament will order the book to be burned by the common hangman.

1608

BIRTHS

John Milton (d. 1674). English poet and essayist; his prose pamphlets will support the Presbyterian struggle for reform within the Church of England; he will write one of the most significant epic poems in all of Western world literature in an effort to explain Satan's rebellion against God and the expulsion of Adam and Eve from the Garden of Eden (*Paradise Lost*); he will also write nearly two dozen English and Italian sonnets.

DEATHS

Alberico Gentili (b. 1552). Italian writer on international law and politics; spent the last twenty-eight years of his life in England after having been exiled as a heretic.

Thomas Sackville, first Earl of Dorset (b. 1536). English poet and diplomat; wrote perhaps the earliest tragedy in the English language; his poetry came to be recognized for its pure and eloquent style, as well as for the forcefulness of its thought.

PUBLICATIONS

George Chapman, *The Conspiracy and Tragedy of Charles, Duke of Byron*—a two-part dramatic tragedy by the English poet and playwright; the writer takes theme and substance from French history; depicts the fall of a heroic spirit; the hero, a brave soldier, has fought successfully for and has been re-warded by his king, Henry IV of France; however, his strong ambitions clash with his political loyalties.

William Shakespeare, *Pericles, Prince of Tyre*—a dramatic romance by the English poet and playwright; the title character, a suitor of the daughter of the king of Antioch, must solve a riddle before he can win the lady's hand; the riddle uncovers incest, which leads to war, death, marriage, abandonment of children, discovery of long-lost identities, and the recovery of lost relationships; an attempt to reconcile the traditional conflicts between tragedy and comedy; the first of the playwright's dramatic romances.

John Smith, *A True Relation of Occurrences and Accidents in Virginia*—a prose piece by the English settler of colonial America; the writer's first published work; actually a letter that he sent from Virginia to a friend in England; contains his most noted adventure, his capture in Virginia by the Indians under Powhatan; however, the writer (at this time) does not include his rescue by Pocahontas.

John Webster, *The White Devil*—a dramatic tragedy by the English playwright; based upon an actual murder in Italy that occurred during the latter part of the sixteenth century; focuses upon an adulterous affair between the Duke of Bracciano and Vittoria Carombona, who plan the murders of their respective spouses; the theme of the piece transcends its complex but spirited plot and underscores the issues of pride, passion, and death; grandeur combines with villainy, courage with cynicism; in this piece, the playwright may well have risen to a Shakespearean level of dramatic art and poetry.

1609

BIRTHS

Paul Fleming (d. 1640). German lyric poet; as a member of the Duke of Holstein's embassy to Persia, he will observe a variety of unusual sights that will find their way into his secular poetry; his poems will be noted for their melody and versification.

Katib Celebi Haci Halifa (d. 1657). Turkish scholar, poet, and essayist; his poetry will be overshadowed by his scholarly efforts, particularly his biographical encyclopaedia of famous men and his history of the Turkish navy.

Jean de Rotrou (d. 1650). French playwright; he will form plays from ideas given to him by Cardinal Richelieu, following the Spanish romantic style; his best work will be composed when he adheres to the rules of classical drama.

Sir John Suckling (d. 1642). English poet; he will be known for creating poetry spontaneously out of immediate intuition and immediate language of thought; however, he will also gain a reputation as one able to control poetic tone and emotion.

DEATHS

Judah Low ben Bezalel (b. ?). Czech-Jewish philosopher, scientist, and mathematician; he wrote tracts on the laws and guidelines for moral conduct set forth in the Talmud; lived and died in Prague.

Joseph Justus Scaliger (b. 1540). French-born writer, perhaps the most significant scholar of the Renaissance; the founder of historical criticism; revolutionized ancient chronology by insisting upon the recognition of historical material relating to the Jews, Persians, Babylonians, and Egyptians; most noted for his critical editions of classical writers.

PUBLICATIONS

Hugo Grotius, *Mere Liberum* (The Freedom of the Sea)—an early prose tract by the Dutch jurist, statesman, and essayist; argues for freedom of the seas for all nations; asserts that the major resource of the sea, the fish, exists in an inexhaustible supply.

Ben Jonson, *Epicoene, or the Silent Woman*—a comedy by the English poet and playwright; recounts the trials of Morose, a gentleman inordinately sensitive to noise; he attempts to find a woman with equal sensitivity, but manages to become involved with a total shrew (the title character); that "woman" turns out to be a boy, disguised for the part by Morose's nephew in an attempt to preserve his inheritance; the piece represents the playwright's comic vision, attacking those who deviate from the normal course of life.

William Shakespeare, *Cymbeline*—a romantic drama by the English poet and playwright, adapted from legendary material of early Britain; King Cymbeline banishes his son-in-law to Italy so as to sever his daughter's secret marriage to the man; attempted seduction through wager and war between Britain and Rome create the necessary confusion prior to final reconciliation; above it all stand the themes of death and rebirth, father-daughter relationships, and the attainment of self-identity; one may also take full advantage of the pure beauty of the playwright's lyric poetry.

——————— , *Sonnets*—the principal poetry collection by the English playwright; the majority of the sonnets were written between 1593 and 1596 and trace the course of the writer's affection for a young patron of rank and beauty (William Lord Herbert, Earl of Pembroke? or Henry Wriothesley, Earl of Southampton?); each sonnet is fourteen lines and is based on the following rhyme scheme: a b a b c d c d e f e f g g.

Mulla Vajhi, *Qutb-o-Mushtari* (Polar Star and Jupiter)—a romantic poem by the Urdu writer and court poet; relates the adventures of a prince in love with an unknown Bengali princess; the poet also glorifies the charms of his native Deccan, south of the Narbada River (in India).

John Webster and Thomas Heywood (?), *Appius and Virginia*—an English tragic play set in classical Rome; the piece emphasizes the classical virtues of decorum and simplicity; based upon the story of Virginia, the daughter of the centurion Lucius Virginius, and Appius Claudius, who became enamored of her.

EVENTS

Aller Furnemmen und Gedenckwurdigen Historien begins publication at Strasbourg; one of the world's earliest newspapers.

Aviso Relation oder Zeitung begins weekly publication at Wolfenbuttel, Lower Saxony; one of the earliest newspapers to appear on a regular basis.

The Rheims-Douai version of the Old Testament published; complete publication by 1610.

1610

BIRTHS

Francois Eudes de Mezeray (d. 1683). French popular historian and essayist; he will author a comprehensive history of France.

Paul Scarron (d. 1660). French poet and satirist; the element of the burlesque will dominate his sonnets, madrigals, and poetic epistles; he will write a significant realistic novel.

DEATHS

Juan de la Cueva (b. 1550?). Spanish poet and playwright; known particularly for his employment of new metrical forms and for his introduction of historical material into the drama.

Thomas Sanchez (b. 1550). Spanish Jesuit moralist; his tract on the legal, moral, and religious questions concerning marriage was an authoritative work on the subject throughout the remainder of the seventeenth century.

PUBLICATIONS

Ben Jonson, *The Alchemist*—a dramatic comedy by the English poet and playwright; an assortment of dupes receive the full treatment by two gifted confidence men who convince them that they can transform base metals into gold; the knaves and fools, representing a cross section of London society, bring their valuables to the two alchemists; after being unexpectedly exposed, the two men manage to escape, leaving their profits behind; the piece has gained fame for its perfect plot, rapidity of action, and expressive verse.

William Shakespeare, *The Winter's Tale*—a romantic drama by the English poet and playwright; the complicated plot concerns the relationships between two men who are friends, the wife of one, and their children; friendship, jealousy, attempted murder, escape, love, marriage, and social differences all have play here; in the end, the triumph of time and patience stands as the theme of the piece; time, or seasonal movement, becomes the benevolent force that contributes significantly to life's natural processes.

Lope de Vega, *Peribanez*—a play by the Spanish poet and dramatist depicting fifteenth-century peasants driven to murder their tyrannical lord in defense of their honor; the title character is a peasant whose social status has been raised by his lord so that he can seduce his new bride; thus, he has been honored so that he can, in turn, be dishonored; however, social and moral justice prevail.

EVENTS

The Academy of Poetry founded at Padua.

The Stationers' Company, London, begins to send a copy of every book printed in England to the Bodleian Library, Oxford University.

1611

BIRTHS

Dervis Muhammed Zilli Evliya Celebi (d. 1682). Turkish travel writer; his work will not only provide narratives of travel and military campaigns, but will also offer the writer's personal observations on Turkish culture, folklore, geography, and language.

DEATHS

Qutb Shah Muhammad Quili (b. 1560?). The first Dakkhini Urdu secular poet and the fourth ruler of the Shiite Qutbshahi dynasty (1580-1611); wrote over 100,000 simple but sweet couplets on such subjects as love, the Indian seasons, and Hindu and Muslim festivals.

PUBLICATIONS

Francis Beaumont and John Fletcher, *The Maid's Tragedy*—a dramatic tragedy by the English playwrights; focuses upon the frustrated love of Amintor and Aspatia, the king having broken their engagement and forced Amintor to marry another; then, Amintor's wife reveals herself as the king's mistress; death, murder, and suicide result; the success of the piece rests not on its plot or characterization, but on dramatic individual scenes and carefully crafted poetry.

George Chapman, *May Day*—a comedy by the English playwright; a translation from the Italian *comedia erudita* of Alessandro Piccolomini; the piece goes forward on the cheerful but unrelenting gulling of foolish persons.

John Donne, *An Anatomy of the World: The First Anniversary*—an elegiac lament by the English writer, written in 1611; offers praise and consolation to Sir Robert Drury, the poet's patron, for the death of his daughter, Elizabeth (17 December 1610); the term "anniversarie" signifies the yearly celebration of the death of a saint; thus, one would offer prayers for the souls of the dead.

Etienne Pasquier, *Les Recherches de France* (Inquiries Respecting France)—another of the French writer's anti-Jesuit tracts, passionately denouncing what he believed to have been an overly ambitious and powerful order.

William Shakespeare, *The Tempest*—a romantic drama by the English poet and playwright; the writer's last significant dramatic effort; the play takes place upon an island amidst an atmosphere of mystery and enchantment; its real and fantastic characters carry out the various thematic relationships between art and nature, appearance and reality, and immortality and death; it may even be seen as a grand allegory upon the various facts of human existence.

EVENTS

The Authorized Version of the English Bible published; the result of the conference at Hampton Court convened in 1604 by King James I of England; a compromise between the High Church and Low Church parties of the Church of England; also known as "the King James Version."

The English poet and playwright George Chapman publishes his poetic translation of the *Iliad;* set in rhyming, fourteen-syllable lines; a specimen had been published in 1598.

1612

BIRTHS

Anne Bradstreet (d. 1672). English-born colonial American poet; she will become the first noted American poet, one whose work will represent true Puritanism; scholars will claim that her lyrics will remain unsurpassed by any American woman poet until the appearance of Emily Dickinson's poems.

Samuel Butler (d. 1680). English poet and satirist; he will gain immediate popularity, and a

place in the history of English poetry, through his burlesque of Puritanism.

Richard Crashaw (d. 1649). English religious poet; his reputation as a writer will be gained from the thirty-three poems of the *Carmen Deo Nostro;* he will rejoice in the ecstatic vision of the long-sought joy of mystical death; he will also establish himself as the poet of confident and unquestioning faith.

Ku Chiang (d. 1681). One of the foremost Chinese scholars of the seventeenth century; he will write commentary upon the classics of Chinese literature, historical studies, topographical descriptions, and poems.

DEATHS

Giovanni Battista Guarini (b. 1538). Italian playwright, poet, and diplomat; his pastoral plays generally imitated those of Torquato Tasso; known for interspersing his blank verse with chorus and dance.

Muhammad Hussain Naziri Nishapuri (b. ?). Indo-Persian poet whose work represented the ornate Indian style; composed abstract philosophical pieces within the context of his own sense of contemplative mysticism; his lyrics are difficult to read because of their heavy reliance upon sophisticated metaphors and deep pathos.

PUBLICATIONS

Francis Beaumont and John Fletcher, *Cupid's Revenge*—a tragedy by the English playwrights; essentially based upon *The Arcadia,* a prose romance by Sir Philip Sidney.

George Chapman, *The Widow's Tears*—a tragicomedy by the English poet and playwright; an exercise in philosophical preoccupation; a bitter, profound, and searching examination of the superficiality of human pretension.

Samuel Coster, *Teeuwis de Boer* (Teeuwis the Peasant)—a comedy by the Dutch playwright; adapted from an old folk song; a farce about a peasant hero who seduces his master's wife and tricks them both.

John Donne, *The Progresse of the Soule: The Second Anniversary*—a metaphysical poem by the English writer; the poet adopts the doctrine of metempsychosis and traces the migration of the soul of Eve's apple through the bodies of various heretics; begun as early as 1601, but left uncompleted.

William Shakespeare, *Henry VIII*— a chronicle play by the English dramatist and poet, concerned with the period 1510-1533; develops the dominant figure of Cardinal Thomas Wolsey (1475?-1530) and his political intrigues and manipulations; although criticized for its loose structure and organization, the play gains strength from its theme of the providential designs of history; the forces of history (or divine will) overshadow the triumphs, defeats, and ambitions of human beings.

EVENTS

The Academia della Crusca publishes the Italian *Vocabolario*, an early attempt at language control and regulation.

1613

BIRTHS

Khushhal Khan Khatak (d. 1689). Afghan national poet; his lyrics and odes will be based on his experiences as a huntsman, soldier, patriot, moralist, and philanderer; he will contribute fresh descriptions of Nature while at the same time borrowing from national folk songs.

Francois de La Rochefoucauld (d. 1680). French moral and political writer; he will strive to analyze the human character and such traits as vanity, pride, and self-love.

DEATHS

David ben Solomon Gans (d. 1541). Westphalian-born scholar of rabbinical and Talmudic literature; considered the first historian to attempt a record of Jewish history in Hebrew; he also contributed to the literatures of the physical sciences and mathematics; dies at Prague.

Natshinnaung (b. 1578). Burmese poet and monarch; his poems focus upon his unfortunate political career and his equally unsuccessful experiences in love; executed for treason.

Mathurun Regnier (b. 1573). French satirist; author of sixteen satires, three epistles, five elegies, and a small quantity of odes, epigrams, and songs; his poetry presents a lively and accurate description of Paris during the reign of Henry IV (1553-1610).

PUBLICATIONS

Miguel de Cervantes Saavedra, *Novelas Exemplares* (Exemplary Stories)—volume of short fiction by the Spanish novelist and playwright; a collection of new as well as older material; a number of the earlier pieces anticipated the style and theme of *Don Quixote*.

George Chapman, *The Revenge of Bussy D'Amboise*—a dramatic tragedy by the English poet and playwright in which he explores the implications of stoicism in the face of evil; first performed by the Children of the Queen's Revels between 1609 and 1612; contains the playwright's definition of tragedy: he terms such plays "natural fictions" that provide material instruction, elegant and "sententious excitation to virtue," and overall moral purpose.

Francisco Suarez, *Defensio Catholicae Fidei Contra Anglicanae Sectae Errores*—a prose tract by the Spanish-Jewish Jesuit theologian and philosopher; condemns as extravagant the divine right of kings theories of James I of England.

Lope de Vega, *Fuenteovejuna*—one of the several dramatic pieces by the Spanish playwright concerned with the efforts of the peasantry to correct the evils done to them by perverse members of the ruling class; thus, a rebellious "comendador" rapes several peasant women and the villages of Fuenteovejuna, motivated by mutual love, rise and kill the rapist; then, under torture, they further display their unity by refusing to reveal the name of the killer; unable to execute anyone, the king pardons the entire village and incorporates it into his own immediate domain.

EVENTS

Sir Thomas Bodley, English diplomat and scholar, dies, leaving the bulk of his fortune to Oxford University and to the Bodleian

Library; he had opened the library in 1602 and endowed it with land and real estate in 1609.

1614

BIRTHS

Hallgrimur Petursson (d. 1674). Icelandic hymn writer and poet; he will create spiritual hymns that will endure as meaningful instruments of public worship; he will contribute significantly to Icelandic literature, language, and culture; he will also write verse satire and humorous and occasional poems.

DEATHS

Pierre de Bourdeilles Brantome (b. 1540?). French writer and courtier; his memoirs, which provide detailed illustrations of life at the court at Valois, are considered historically and artistically significant.

PUBLICATIONS

Ben Jonson, *Bartholomew Fair*—a dramatic comedy by the English poet and playwright about the annual fair on 24 August at Smithfield, a London suburb; focuses upon an assortment of people drawn to the event: Puritans, country squires, wives, lovers, suitors, rogues, and commoners; the characters undergo a variety of experiences designed to rid them of their foolishness or enhance their fortunes; essentially a satire, but also a celebration of joyous participation in social festivity.

Sir Walter Raleigh, *The History of the World*—a work by the English adventurer and poet, written for Prince Henry; focuses upon the history of the Jews, early Egyptian history, Greek mythology, and Greco-Roman times from the beginnings to 130 B.C.; also attempts to demonstrate the judgment of God upon the wicked.

John Webster, *The Duchess of Malfi*—a tragedy by the English playwright; concerns the disastrous consequences of the marriage of a widowed duchess to her steward, a union viewed by the bride's brothers as a disgrace to their family; thus, the brothers cause the death of their sister, her new husband, and her children; in focusing upon the suffering of the heroine and the elaborate schemes of the villains, the playwright explores the nature of life, evil, and death; horror and wonder are the vehicles upon which the play moves forward.

1615

BIRTHS

Richard Baxter (d. 1691). English Nonconformist churchman and prose writer; his work will reveal him as a moderate who sided only half-heartedly with Parliament against the King; although a prolific writer who accurately recorded his theological and political thoughts, he never carefully pursued any conscious literary aims.

Muhammad Dara Shikoh (d. 1658). Indo-Persian mystic poet and prose writer; he will write biographies of mystics and tracts outlining how to achieve ultimate spiritual fulfillment; his poetry will be essentially lyrical.

DEATHS

Mateo Aleman (b. 1547). Spanish novelist whose fame rests upon his picaresque fiction; spent the last seven years of his life in Mexico.

Etienne Pasquier (b. 1529). French anti-Jesuit writer; his prose tracts delineate his legal arguments against the power of the Church.

Nuruddin Muhammad Tahir Zuhuri (b. ?). Indo-Persian poet and prose writer; wrote in the flowery style characteristic of Persian prose; his poems and essays abound in metaphors derived from the Indian musical tradition; also praised sultans and analyzed court artists and their methods.

PUBLICATIONS

Miguel de Cervantes Saavedra, *Pedro de Urdemalas* (Pedro, the Artful Dodger)—a three-act play by the Spanish writer; centers upon the title character, a rogue; the first of eight plays published under the title *Ocho Comedias y Ocho Entremeses.*

EVENTS

The Huguenot-inspired historical survey *Histoire Universelle, 1550-1601* by the French scholar Theodore Agrippa D'Aubigne is burned in Paris by the common hangman.

William Camden, English scholar, antiquary, and historian, publishes his *Annales Anglicarum; or, Annals of the Reign of Elizabeth to 1588;* a second part printed posthumously in 1627; English translations in 1625, 1628, 1635.

George Chapman, the English poet, completes and publishes his translation of Homer's *Odyssey* in rhyming, ten-syllable lines.

The *Frankfurter Oberpostamts-Zeitung,* founded by Egenolph Emmel, begins publication as a newspaper; until 1886.

1616

BIRTHS

Andreas Gryphius (d. 1664). Silesian-born German poet and playwright; he will master seven languages and be influenced by William Shakespeare, Seneca, Jan van Hout, and Joost van den Vondel; will treat such subjects in his tragedies as the joys of Christianity and the nature of worldly vanity; character development will be subordinate to theme.

DEATHS

Francis Beaumont (b. 1584?). English playwright; provided delightful burlesques of the historical romances so popular upon the Elizabethan stage; attacked in his plays the London audiences who flocked to see his work.

Miguel de Cervantes Saavedra (b. 1547). Spanish novelist, poet, and playwright; his *Don Quixote* will elevate him to a position among the most significant writers of the Western world, although many agree the piece is one of the most carelessly written of all great books.

Richard Hakluyt (b. 1553?). English geographer and voyager; introduced globes into English schools as an instructional aid; his narratives of voyages were a major contribution to the development of travel literature in England.

William Shakespeare (b. 1564). English poet and playwright; the most significant playwright in world literature; also one of the foremost poets of the English language.

PUBLICATIONS

Johann Valentin Andrea, *Chymische Hochzeit Christiani Rosenenkreuz*—a prose tract by the German theologian and principal founder of the Rosicrucians; relates the story of the Christian Rosenkreutz, who founded a secret society devoted to the study of the hidden elements of nature that formed an esoteric version of Christianity; the tract led to the establishment of societies with alchemistic tendencies, but some scholars claim that the work was actually meant as a satire.

Ben Jonson, *The Devil Is an Ass*—a comedy by the English poet and playwright; ridicules the projectors and the monopolists, exposing the pretend demoniacs and witch hunters of the times; an agent of Satan, who has been allowed to practice his iniquity on earth for a single day, finds himself no match for his human counterparts; his adventure ends, eventually, in Newgate Prison.

——————— , *The Forest*—a collection of short poems, odes, epistles, and songs by the English writer; contains two of his most noted verses, "Drink to me only with thine eyes" and "Come, my Celia, let us prove."

John Smith, *A Description of New England*—the longest and most influential prose work by the English-born leader of the earliest colonial American settlements; captures the essence of his tact and energy in dealing with the Indians and helping the colonists to survive; although not always thoroughly reliable, the narrative was interesting and entertaining reading for those outside of colonial New England.

1617

BIRTHS

Chu Yung-Shen (d. 1689). Chinese writer; he will author philosophical commentaries but will gain his greatest literary recognition with his volume of maxims; "To know what ought to be known, and to do what ought to be done, that is enough. There is no time for anything else" is an example.

Peter Folger (d. 1690). Benjamin Franklin's grandfather and an occasional writer; he will write "folksy" poetry and, in prose tracts, argue for human liberties; he will maintain that God has sponsored the colonists' wars against the Indians to punish the religious and social prejudices of New Englanders.

DEATHS

Francisco Suarez (b. 1548). Spanish-Jewish philosopher and theologian; concerned himself with developing a doctrine of international law and condemned as extravagant the divine right of kings theory.

Jacques Augustus de Thou (b. 1553). French historian and statesman; authored a Latin history of his own times, commentaries upon his own life, and Latin verse.

PUBLICATIONS

John Calvin, *Collected Works*—the first edition of the works of the French Protestant theologian; twelve volumes, published posthumously at Geneva.

Theophile de Viau, *Pyrame et Thisbe*—a poetic tragedy by the French versifier; contains much love poetry distinguished by its natural style and clear language.

EVENTS

Samuel Coster founds the Duytsche Academie at Amsterdam.

James I of England appoints Ben Jonson Poet Laureate of England; Johnson actually gains the position through a pension granted to him by the King.

Martin Opitz, Silesian-born German poet, establishes the Fruchtbringende Gesellschaft, a literary society, at Weimar.

1618

BIRTHS

Abraham Cowley (d. 1667). English poet who will begin to write verse at ten years of age;

his anacreontics and Pindaric odes will provide models for the poets of the eighteenth century; his familiar prose essays will be written in the language of everyday speech, rather than in the balanced, elaborate style that was typical of the poetic prose of the seventeenth century.

Richard Lovelace (d. 1658). English poet; he will not only write poetry, but will excel in music, art, statesmanship, and the military; for him, poetry will exist as a gentlemanly pastime; thus, he will spend little time revising, preferring to allow his rough and obscure lines to be published as written.

Augustin Moreto y Cabana (d. 1664). Spanish playwright; he will gain a reputation as a competent comic writer among the followers of Pedro Calderon de la Barca; he will secularize the Spanish drama almost to the point of irreverence.

Hayashi Shumsai (d. 1680). Japanese historian and chronicler.

DEATHS

Gerbrand Adriaanszoon Bredero (b. 1585). Dutch playwright; he will become the most significant writer of Dutch comedy; his popular language and style will also be seen in his lyric poetry, both religious and love poems; he will write the first romantic Dutch plays.

Sir Walter Raleigh (b. 1552). English courtier, navigator, and writer; he composed poems, political essays, and philosophical tracts; executed for treason.

PUBLICATIONS

John Fletcher, *The Loyal Subject*—a drama by the English playwright; focuses upon the Duke of Muscovy's jealousy toward his late father's loyal general; the Duke dismisses the general and replaces him with an incompetent flatterer; then follows, in fast order, disguise, ambitious assault for power, love, war, and torture; in the end, repentance and love reign supreme.

Ben Jonson, *Pleasure Reconciled to Virtue*—a play by the English poet and dramatist; most significant as a source for John Milton's *Comus.*

EVENTS

Marquise Catherine de Vivonne de Rambouillet, Italian-born French noblewoman, begins her literary salon in Paris; she exercises considerable influence upon the cultural and intellectual life of the city.

1619

BIRTHS

Savinien Cyrano de Bergerac (d. 1655). French writer and adventurer; despite his participation in over a thousand duels, he will find time to write a variety of vigorous, witty, and inventive works of prose and poetry, most notably plays and novels; the hero of a play by Edmond Rostand in 1897.

DEATHS

Gines Perez de Hita (b. 1544). Spanish writer and soldier; his semiromantic histories reflect his experiences in the Moorish war of 1569-1570.

Lucilio Vanini (b. 1585). Italian Catholic philosopher and freethinker; an exponent of extreme pantheism; his prose works reveal his vanity and audacity, more than his learning; executed at Toulouse: strangled and burned, after first having his tongue cut out.

PUBLICATIONS

Johan Valentin Andreae, *Christianopolis*—a tract by the German theologian and Protestant court chaplain at Stuttgart; describes the history of the founding of the Rosicrucian society.

Johannes Kepler, *Harmonice Mundi* (The Harmony of the World)—a prose tract by the German astronomer; pronounces "Kepler's Third Law": the square of a planet's periodic time becomes proportional to the cube of its mean distance from the sun; a source for Newton.

Honorat de Buel de Racan, *Le Bergeries*—a pastoral play in verse by the French poet;

composed in the manner of his mentor, Francois de Malherbe.

Pietro Sarpi, *Istoria de Concilio Tridentino*—a history of the Council of Trent by the Italian philosopher, linguist, and mathematician; written after he had been excommunicated; published in London; although based upon accurate materials, the work lacks objectivity; the writer represents the Council (1545-1563) as a conspiracy against the church.

1620

BIRTHS

Miklos Zrinyi (d. 1664). Hungarian poet and patriot.

PUBLICATIONS

Francis Bacon, *Instauratio Magna: Novum Organum Scientiarum*—a treatise by the English philosopher and essayist; he will proclaim a new system for learning, setting forth a preliminary arrangement of the actual field of human learning in relation to potential knowledge; points a new direction for learning, encouraging experiments in a variety of academic disciplines.

EVENTS

Johann Heinrich Alstedius, German philosopher and Protestant churchman, publishes his *Encyclopaedia Septem Tomis Distincta.*

1621

BIRTHS

Johann Jakob Christoffel von Grimmelshausen (d. 1676). German novelist, satirist, and essayist; will be termed the most significant writer of fiction in seventeenth-century Germany; will exert a lasting influence on the development of German fiction through his ability to combine the picaresque, romantic, and realistic forms.

Jean de La Fontaine (d. 1695). French poet; his frivolity and dissipation will not detract from the beauty of his language; his wit and acumen will make his charming and simple fables popular with children and adults.

Andrew Marvell (d. 1678). English poet; he will rise to significance as a poet of the pre-Restoration because of his wit and delicacy of language; a genuine enjoyment of Nature and of gardens will characterize his poetry.

DEATHS

Johann Arndt (b. 1555). German Lutheran cleric and partial mystic; he attacked the penal theory of the Atonement and dwelt on the work of Christ in the heart of humankind.

PUBLICATIONS

Robert Burton, *The Anatomy of Melancholy*—a tract by the English prose writer; in the simplest terms, the piece is a medical work establishing melancholy as an inbred malady affecting every human being; however, the writer expands the work to cover the many other facts of human existence, from politics to social custom to other aspects of bodily and mental health; essentially a storehouse of miscellaneous learning.

EVENTS

The first of the news-sheets from foreign sources and on foreign topics appears in London; these "corantos" exist as half-sheets in folio, printed on both sides of the paper; an example of a title: *Corante; or, Newes from Italy, Germany, Hungaria, Polonia, France and Dutchland.*

1622

BIRTHS

Jean Baptiste Moliere (d. 1673). French playwright; his genius and originality will result from his abandonment of romanesque comedy to concentrate on farce; he will produce not only great dramatic literature, but also great theater; he will also work to develop character types.

PUBLICATIONS

Francis Bacon, *The History of Henry VII*—a biographical, critical, and historical work by the English statesman and philosopher; a scholarly work written in a direct style.

Alessandro Tassoni, *La Secchia Rapita* (The Rape of the Bucket)—a mock heroic poem by the Italian versifier and scientist; his literary reputation rests solely upon this piece.

EVENTS

Camilo Baldo publishes his strange but interesting tract, *How To Perceive from a Letter the Nature and Character of the Person Who Wrote It.*

Ignatius Loyola, founder of the Jesuit order and writer of tracts on education and missionary work is canonized.

The Papal Chancellery adopts 1 January as the beginning of the year, replacing 25 March.

The *Weekeley Newes,* London, begins publication; this marks the beginning of the English newspaper.

1623

BIRTHS

Blaise Pascal (d. 1662). French mathematician, physician, theologian, and philosopher; he will offer profound insights into religious truths, maintaining a skeptical attitude toward rationalist thought and theology.

Benedict (Baruch) Spinoza (d. 1677). Dutch-Jewish philosopher; he will develop a system that relates to pantheism; he will identify mind and matter, the finite and the infinite, transforming them into manifestations of one universal or absolute being; these he will conceive as Substance, or God, or the Whole; he will also develop the basic principle of life as self-love; thus, the love of God becomes the highest ideal of humankind.

DEATHS

Tulsidas (b. 1532?). Hindi Brahmin poet; through his poetry, he will urge devotion to Rama, viewed as an incarnation of Visnu, as the best means toward salvation.

PUBLICATIONS

Francis Bacon, *De Augmentis Scientiarum*—a Latin prose tract by the English philosopher, essayist, and statesman; an enlarged edition of the *Advancement of Learning* (1605); the last phase of the writer's attempt to replace the system of Aristotle with a new system of philosophy based upon a right interpretation of Nature.

William Drummond, *The Cypresse Grove*—a prose tract by the Scottish-born poet; a philosophical meditation upon death.

John Webster, *The Devil's Law Case*—a tragicomedy of intrigue by the English playwright; focuses upon a hero-villain, Romelio, whose Machiavellian manipulations gain dignity by the strength and resolve of his own character.

EVENTS

The Bibliotheca Palatine transferred from Heidelberg to Rome.

Matthias Casimire Sarbiewski, Polish Jesuit poet termed "the Polish Horace" because of his Latin odes on moral subjects, crowned laureate in Rome by Pope Urban VIII.

The first Shakespeare folio published.

1624

BIRTHS

Arnold Guelincx (d. 1669). Belgian philosopher; he will become professor of philosophy at Leyden; the interaction of mind and body, he will maintain, results from a preordained divine arrangement, not totally unrelated to the independence of two synchronized clocks.

Angelus Silesius (d. 1677). German philosophical poet who will become a Catholic priest; a controversial mysticism will dominate his poetry; born Johann Scheffler, the son of a Lutheran Polish noble.

DEATHS

Shah Abdul-karim of Bulrri (b. 1536). The first Indo-Iranian mystic poet to write in the Sindhi language; wrote ninety-three short verses in popular Indian meters and rhythms; the substance of his work taken from Sindhi folk tales.

Vicente de Espinel (b. 1550). Spanish poet and writer of fiction; may well have been the originator of the ten-line octosyllabic stanza, while, in music, he added the fifth string to the guitar.

Stephen Gosson (b. 1554). English pastoral playwright and Anglican cleric; an advocate of Puritan censorship, he attacked, in his plays, poets and actors whom he believed challenged religion and morality.

PUBLICATIONS

John Fletcher, *Rule a Wife and Have a Wife*— a comedy by the English playwright; concerns a rich heiress from Seville who desires to marry solely so she can exercise her amorous proclivities; she must, therefore, marry a fool; there also exists a subplot, in which the heiress's servant beguiles a conceited suitor into marrying her by posing as the owner of her absent mistress's house.

Martin Opitz, *Das Buch von der Deutschen Poeterey* (The Book on German Poetry)—the most significant literary contribution by the leader of the Silesian school of German poetry; attempts to restore German poetry to its purest origins.

John Smith, *The General History of Virginia, New England, and the Summer Isles*—the longest and most influential prose work by the English adventurer and colonial American leader; written both to record the settlement of North America and to promote the lands that he had explored; the work confirmed the European ideal of America as the land of freedom, happiness, and wealth.

1625

DEATHS

John Fletcher (b. 1579). English playwright; succeeded William Shakespeare (1612?) as principal dramatist of the King's Men; in collaboration with Francis Beaumont, he transferred English drama from the province of the common people to the court, to an aristocratic audience who had acquired theatrical tastes for masque romances and sharp satire.

Giambattista Marini (b. 1569). Italian poet who wrote his best verse at the court of France; known for his florid hyperbole and exaggerated imagery.

Honore d'Urfe (b. 1567). French writer; author of a pastoral romance regarded as the first French novel; dies at Villefranche-sur-mer during the war between Savoy and Genoa.

John Webster (b. 1580?). English playwright; his tragedies achieved for him a literary and theatrical reputation second only to that of William Shakespeare; he has always received negative criticism for his excessive reliance upon horror.

PUBLICATIONS

John Fletcher, *The Woman's Prize; or, the Tamer Tamed*—a drama by the English playwright, actually a sequel to William Shakespeare's *Taming of the Shrew;* produced on the stage as early as 1611; a popular comedy.

Ghavvasi, *Qissa-e Saifu'l-Muluk va Badi'u'l-Jamal*—a romantic poem by the Urdu versifier; 14,000 lines, narrating the love of the Egyptian prince Saifu'l-muluk for the Chinese princess Badi'u'l-jamal; adapted from a story in the "Arabian Nights."

Hugo Grotius, *De Jura Belli et Pacis*—a tract on international law by the Dutch jurist and statesman; he appeals to natural law and the social contact as the bases for rational principles upon which a system of laws could be formulated; the piece begins the science and discipline of international law.

Ben Jonson, *A Staple of News*—a comedy by the English playwright; the writer satirizes the credulity of his times while at the same time describing the employment and abuse of wealth; the title takes its name from an office established for the collection, sorting, and dissemination of news and gossip; the plot revolves about the actions of a number of characters personifying the problems of wealth (Lady Pecunia, Pennyboy, etc.).

Kaciyappa Civaccariyar, *Kantapuranam*—a long poem by the Indian (Tamil) versifier, based upon the Sanskrit work *Skandapurana;* an ambitious piece of more than ten thousand stanzas.

John Milton, "On the Death of a Fair Infant Dying of a Cough"—an elegy by the English poet, written when he was only seventeen years of age; directed to the daughter of the poet's sister, born on 12 January of this year, and buried ten days later: "O fairest flower no sooner blown but blasted, / Soft silken Primrose fading timelessly, / Summer's chief honour if thou hadst outlasted / Bleak winter's force that made thy blossom dry. . . . "

Joost van den Vondel, *Palamedes of Vermoorde Onnoselheit* (Palamedes, or Murdered Innocence)—a dramatic piece by the Dutch poet and playwright; set against the background of a Greek fable; the writer defends religious freedom within the context of the significant religious and political struggle that had resulted in the death, on false charges of treason, of Sir Jan van Olden Barneveldt (1547-1619), Dutch statesman and lawyer; to prevent a civil war, Barneveldt had proposed an ecclesiastical assembly to administer a system of toleration.

Edmund Waller, "His Majesty's Escape at St. Andere"—a poem by the English versifier, written before he had reached the age of twenty; complimentary to Prince Charles and his escape from shipwreck at Santander; in heroic couplets, the work is one of the finest examples of a form that prevailed in English poetry for the next two centuries.

EVENTS

Martin Opitz, German poet who earned a reputation by writing to and for German princes, crowned poet laureate in Vienna.

1626

BIRTHS

Marie de Rabutin-Chantal, Madame de Sevigne (d. 1696). French writer of letters; her work will provide a detailed history of her own times; these same letters will reveal a religious woman without superstition, a woman who gained considerable knowledge from her reading and conversations.

DEATHS

Francis Bacon (b. 1561). English philosopher, statesman, and essayist; a writer of English prose and a student of human nature, he championed the scientific method of induction, conducted scholarly research, and translated and paraphrased Holy Scriptures.

Pietro Sarpi (b. 1552). Italian philosopher, linguist, and mathematician; an advocate of freedom of thought; excommunicated from the Church and seriously wounded by assassins.

Cyril Tourneur (b. 1575?). English playwright and poet; best known for his dramatic tragedies, pieces containing excellent comic scenes, engaging villains, and contrasting philosophical positions.

Theophile de Viau (b. 1590). French poet; his love poetry is distinguished by its naturalness; dies at Paris, banished for life for the impiety and obscenity of his verse.

PUBLICATIONS

Francis Bacon, *The New Atlantis*—a treatise on political philosophy by the English essayist; an unfinished work that assumes the form of a fable; an account of a visit to an imaginary island and the social conditions existing there; located on the island is "Solomon's House," a college of natural philosophy dedicated to the study of the works and creatures of God.

EVENTS

George Sandys, English writer, traveler, and treasurer of the Virginia Company, produces the first translation of a classic work in colonial America; Ovid's *Metamorphoses*.

1627

BIRTHS

Jacques Benigne Bossuet (d. 1704). French churchman, sermonizer, and essayist; he will achieve a literary reputation from his attempts to approach history from a philosoph-

ical point of view; he will also challenge the mystic philosophers and historians.

Dorothy Osborne (d. 1695). English traveler, writer, and wife of Sir William Temple (1628-1699); she will become known in English literature because of her correspondence with her future husband (1652-1654), not published until 1888.

DEATHS

Ahmad al-Timbukhti Baba (b. 1556). Mali-born essayist and writer of legal commentaries, a number of which still apply to the judicial structure in West Africa; he attempted to expose the inhumanity of slavery and the slave trade, identifying the flawed reasoning behind religious sanction for such practice.

Don Luis de Gongora y Argote (b. 1561). Spanish lyric poet; his sonnets, lyrics, odes, ballads, and songs are marked by an extravagant, artificial style; his long poems tend toward the pedantic.

Talbib 'Amuli (b. 1590). Indo-Persian poet; poet-laureate under the Emperor Jahangir; wrote panegyrics in praise of the prophet Muhammad, as well as of court dignitaries.

PUBLICATIONS

Ivan Gundulic, *Osman*—an epic poem by the Croatian poet; concerns the Polish wars against the Turks; demonstrates an early sense of Slavic nationalism, as well as the influence of ancient Slavic song.

John Milton, "At a Vacation Exercise in the College"—a poem by the then nineteen-year-old poet, a part of the entertainment at the beginning of the long vacation (July 1628); the piece develops the thesis that occasional indulgence in sporting activities is compatible with academic studies.

Francisco Gomez de Quevedo y Villegas, *Vida del Buscon Pablos* (The Life of Buscon)—a picaresque novel by the Spanish writer; English translations in 1657 and 1707.

——————— , *Las Suenos* (Visions)—biting satiric portraits by the Spanish writer; focuses upon members of all classes of society; essentially a burlesque of Hell, Judgment Day, and the world in general.

EVENTS

Gabriel Naude, librarian for Cardinal Richelieu and Cardinal Mazarin in Paris, publishes his *Avis pour Dresser une Bibliotheque,* an early tract on librarianship.

Lope Felix de Vega Carpio, Spanish poet and playwright, elevated to doctor of theology by Pope Urban VIII.

1628

BIRTHS

John Bunyan (d. 1688). English prose writer; his allegories will reflect his own religious experiences and commitment; despite the spiritual nature of his narratives, he will recount "fictional" events with an accurate eye for detail, combining morality with authenticity; indeed, because of his realism and psychological insight, he will anticipate the modern novel.

Charles Perrault (d. 1703). French poet, essayist, biographer, and writer of fairy tales; such works as "Sleeping Beauty," "Little Red Riding Hood," and "Cinderella" will become standard works of children's literature throughout the world.

DEATHS

Francois de Malherbe (b. 1555). French poet, critic, and translator; he established principles of versification while attempting to preserve the purity of his native language; his contemporaries viewed him as the principal figure in the struggle to save French verse from those who would debase it and to rid it of ornate, baroque elements.

PUBLICATIONS

Juan Ruiz de Alarcon, *La Verdad Sospechosa* (Truth under Suspicion)—a comedy by the Mexican-born Spanish playwright; written according to the Aristotelian rules; the piece will become the model for Pierre Corneille's *Le Menteur* (1642); urbane ridicule of a man having but a single peccadillo.

Johann Amos Comenius, *Informatorium der Mitterschul*—a tract by the Czech educational reformer and Moravian churchman; focuses upon the need for primary education; until 1631.

1629

PUBLICATIONS

Pedro Calderon de la Barca, *La Dama Duende* (The Phantom Lady)—a play by the Spanish poet and playwright, classified as "cape and sword" drama; the idea of appearance and reality has a major role in this play containing a web of shadowy complications and mischievous deceptions; focuses upon Dona Angela, a young widow confined to her brothers' house, but who escapes to see the world; a libertine brother, incest, superstition, and phantom appearances compete to transform the rules of honor into the rules of love, producing disastrous and deathly results.

John Ford, *The Lover's Melancholy*—the first major dramatic effort by the English playwright; based upon Robert Burton's *Anatomy of Melancholy* (1621); a dramatized analysis of melancholy woven into an elaborate and complex tale of romance and disguise; evidences the influence of the later plays of William Shakespeare.

Philip Massinger, *The Roman Actor*—a tragedy by the English playwright; based upon the life of the Emperor Domitian, as related by Suetonius and Dio Cassius; the emperor forcibly abducts the wife of a Roman senator; the new empress, however, falls in love with Paris, an actor; Domitian kills Paris, but suffers death by the empress, who has conspired with a number of his enemies.

John Milton, *On the Morning of Christ's Nativity*—an ode by the English poet and essayist; concerns the triumph of the infant Christ over the gods of paganism; the development of that theme in stanzas 16 through 25 anticipates the poet's lengthy discussion of the pagan deities in the first book of *Paradise Lost.*

EVENTS

Thomas Hobbes, the English philosopher, publishes his translation of Thucydides' history of the Peloponnesian War.

1630

DEATHS

Taqi Auhadi (b. 1565). Indo-Persian poet, essayist, and critic; best known for panegyrics and satires of his contemporaries; his most significant effort is a collection of 3186 biographies of Persian poets, with samples from their work.

PUBLICATIONS

Anders Christiensen Arrebo, *Hexaemeron*—a religious poem by the Danish clergyman and Bishop of Trondheim; a monumental epic in the vernacular concerning the six days of Creation; one of the earliest contributions to the history of "modern" Danish literature.

Pierre Corneille, *Melite, ou les Fausses Lettres* (Melite, or the False Letters)—a comedy by the French poet and playwright; an early dramatic effort that evidenced the twenty-four-year-old writer's understanding of the new trend toward depicting social improprieties; first performed in 1629.

John Milton, "On Shakespeare"—a short poem by the English writer, then twenty-two years old; sixteen lines in heroic couplets; develops the idea of Shakespeare as a national monument without a tomb, as well as the notion of the Elizabethan playwright as a child of Nature, rather than of art.

Tirso de Molina, *El Burlador de Sevilla y Convidado de Piedra* (The Deceiver of Seville and the Stone Guest)—a drama by the Spanish playwright in which he creates the great modern myth of "Don Juan"; after seducing both shepherdesses and noble ladies of the court, the protagonist finds himself dragged to Hell by the agent of God, the statue of a man he has killed; as one who takes the name of God in vain, the "hero" commits the crime of having excessive confidence in God's mercy; thus, when the monument of his death unexpectedly arrives, he finds himself unprepared for his end.

1631

BIRTHS

John Dryden (d. 1700). English poet, dramatist, and essayist; his diverse writings will come to represent the complexity and full literary range of the seventeenth century; he will personify the effort toward refinement of art and life during the so-called "classical" period.

Urian Oakes (d. 1681). Massachusetts poet and churchman; his poetry will reflect a certain degree of art and grace, complementing the elegance and fluency of his Latin; although he will not become a great poet, his verse will reach a sufficiently high point in the history of colonial American letters.

Michael Wigglesworth (d. 1705). English-born colonial American poet, minister, and physician; his verse will reflect the essence of American Puritanism; for substance, he will look to Puritan dogma, attempting to console the lot of humankind by transforming the principles of that dogma into poetic song.

DEATHS

John Donne (b. 1573). English poet; his creative work can be placed into three distinct periods marked by passion and cynicism, anguished meditation and flattery of great persons, and general acceptance of life marred only by occasional moments of theological and artistic doubt.

John Smith (b. 1580). English adventurer, Virginia colonist, and descriptive writer; his narratives and descriptions have contributed significantly to the early history and literature of colonial America; he dies in London.

PUBLICATIONS

Evilya Celebi (Dervis Muhammed Zilli), *Tarihi Seyyah* (Chronicle of a Traveler)—a description of travels and campaigns by the Turkish adventurer; the writer also provides a number of observations on culture, folklore, geography, and linguistic practices; he further describes remarkable buildings, beautiful cities, and exciting landscapes; focuses upon parts of Turkey, Hungary, and northern Africa.

George Chapman, *Caesar and Pompey*—a dramatic tragedy by the English poet and playwright; written between 1599 and 1607, performed in 1613, but not published until this year; focuses upon the deep differences between Caesar and Pompey and events leading to the battle of Pharsalus (48 B.C.); relates the murder of Pompey and the suicide of Cato, the real hero of the piece; the thesis concerns the hero's classic statement, "Only a just man is a free man."

EVENTS

Theophraste Renaudot, French Protestant physician, founds, at Paris, the *Gazette de France,* reportedly the first newspaper in France.

1632

BIRTHS

John Locke (d. 1704). He will become one of the principal founders of philosophical liberalism; he will, in an intolerant age, advance and codify liberal principles, particularly empiricist epistemology; in the end, he will insist upon recognizing the natural morality of presocial human beings.

Jean Mabillon (d. 1707). French Benedictine monk and historian, an erudite and discerning scholar; he will produce some twenty folio works, including editions of St. Bernard of Clairvaux (1090-1153) and a variety of important liturgical documents.

Samuel von Puffendorf (d. 1694). German writer on jurisprudence; he will become professor of the law of nations at Heidelberg and expose the absurdities in the constitution of the Germanic empire; he will also receive appointment as Swedish historiographer.

Benedictus (Baruch) de Spinoza (d. 1677). Dutch philosopher; his works will be divorced from religious dogma, yet informed by religious faith; he rarely wrote for the general public, considering his philosophy so complex as to be comprehensible only to a small number of intellectuals.

DEATHS

Giovanni Battista Basile (b. 1575). Italian poet; compiler of Neopolitan fairy tales; his most significant collection, *Pentamerone,* published at Naples in 1637.

PUBLICATIONS

Ben Jonson, *The Magnetic Lady, or Humours Reconciled*—a dramatic comedy by the English playwright and poet; concerns Lady Loadstone, the "Magnetic Lady," who draws to her side an odd assortment of guests; various intrigues comprise the plot, most of which focuses upon Lady Loadstone's supposed niece, Placentia, and the girl's uncle, Sir Moth Interest.

John Milton, *Il Penseroso*—a poem by the English writer that, by its title (in poor Italian), refers to deep contemplation; an invocation to the goddess Melancholy, asking that she bring Peace, Quiet, Leisure, and Contemplation; the poet further describes the pleasures of the studious and meditative life encompassing drama (particularly tragedy), epic poetry, and music.

——————, *L'Allegro*—an English poem meaning "the cheerful man"; an invocation to the goddess Mirth, in which the poet asks that he be allowed to live with her amid the delights of rustic scenes, then accompany her to towered cities and the "busy hum of men"; *Il Penseroso* and *L'Allegro* are companion pieces.

EVENTS

John Davies, a native of Wales and scholar of Jesus College and Lincoln College, Oxford, publishes his Welsh dictionary under the title *Antiquae Linguae Britannicae, nunc Vulgo Dictae Cambro-Britannicae, et Linguae, Dictionarium Duplex; Accesserunt Adagia Britannica.*

The True Tale of Robin Hood, a poetic version of the legendary outlaw's exploits, published.

The second Shakespeare folio published.

1633

BIRTHS

Samuel Pepys (d. 1703). English diarist and government official; his name and literary reputation will rest upon his shorthand diary (1660-1669), the highlights of which concern three principal disasters of the age: the great plague, the great fire of London, and the Dutch fleet sailing up the Thames River.

DEATHS

George Herbert (b. 1593). English cleric and poet; he represents, both in his life and literary labors, the Laudian party's (headed by Archbishop William Laud [1573-1645]) challenge to the Puritan movement; the themes of Christian humility and unwearying service pervade his poetry.

PUBLICATIONS

Abraham Cowley, *Poetical Blossomes*—a collection by the English poet, including "Pyramus and Thisbe," written when the poet was ten, and "Constantia and Philetus" written when he was twelve.

George Herbert, *The Temple*—a collection of 160 religious poems by the English versifier, published in the year of his death; the pieces tend to be characterized by quaint and ingenious imagery, with occasional extravagant conceits and sublime expression.

Ben Jonson, *A Tale of a Tub*—a comedy by the English playwright and poet, the last play that he staged; the play takes place on St. Valentine's Day, focusing upon attempts by various suitors to marry Awdrey, the daughter of Tobie Turfe, the high constable of Kentish Town; however, her father wishes her to marry John Clay, a title maker; a series of adventures and antics finally end in Awdrey's marriage to Squire Tub.

Christopher Marlowe, *The Jew of Malta*—a drama in blank verse by the English poet and playwright; first produced on the stage in 1592(?), but not published until this year; the governor of Malta determines that the island's tribute to Turkey will be paid by the Jews; Barnabas, a rich Jew, refuses to pay; the governor impounds the man's wealth and turns his house into a nunnery; then follow revenge, slaughter, betrayal, and attempts at destruction; Barnabas meets his death from one of his own devices.

John Milton, *A'rcades*—a dramatic entertainment by the English writer; the short piece consists of a song by nymphs and shepherds, an address by the Genius of the Wood in praise of music, and two other songs, by the Genius and the chorus; written for and presented to the Countess-Dowager of Derby at Harefield.

1634

BIRTHS

Marie Madelaine de La Fayette (d. 1693). French novelist, essayist, historian, and biographer; she will develop psychological analysis in the French novel with works exploring complex moral questions and the inner conflicts experienced by her characters.

DEATHS

George Chapman (b. 1559?). English playwright, poet, and translator; his poetry and drama reflect a spirit at odds with life, but one nonetheless capable of conveying its significance; his pessimism anticipates the English Romantics of the early nineteenth century; recognized as much for his translations of Homer as for his original work.

PUBLICATIONS

Jean Mairet, *Sophonisbe*—a tragedy by the French playwright; considered one of the first "regular" French classical tragediès because of its reliance upon the three unities; demonstrates the writer's true sense of the tragic in the portrait of the two lovers crushed by the political force to which they refuse to yield; designed according to the writer's commitment to the principles of simple and swift action.

John Milton, *Comus, a Masque*—a dramatic piece by the English writer, presented for the celebration of the Earl of Bridgewater's entry to the presidency of Wales and the Marches; focuses upon the actions and influence of the title character, a pagan god (invented by the writer), son of Bacchus and Circe, who waylays travelers and tempts them to drink a magic liquor, which changes their appearances into those of wild beasts.

1635

BIRTHS

Hijri Ashraf Khan Khatak (d. 1693). Afghan (Pashtu) poet; melancholy will dominate his verse, brought on by his twelve-year political imprisonment in India.

Philippe Quinault (d. 1688). French playwright and poet and a member of the Academie Francaise; his characters will display extreme tenderness, and he will possess a strong sense of "theater"; he will rise to become one of the best poets of the seventeenth century.

DEATHS

Nef'i (b. ?). Turkish poet; he made a number of enemies with his satires; in harsh language, he relentlessly exposed the flaws of lawyers, courtiers, mullahs, wandering dervishes, and popular saints; a master of flowery insults; executed for insulting one of the viziers.

Alessandro Tassoni (b. 1565). Italian poet in the service of several princes; a man of extensive literary and scientific knowledge; most prominent for his heroic poems.

Lope Felix de Vega Capio (b. 1562). Spanish playwright and poet; a master of flowing, musical, and graceful verse; his dramas appealed to audiences because of their excitement and boundless invention; he combined striking dramatic situations with ingenious complications.

PUBLICATIONS

Pedro Calderon de la Barca, *La Vida es Sueno* (Life Is a Dream)—a metaphysical problem play by the Spanish dramatist; the situation involves Prince Segismundo, who has been imprisoned in a wasteland tower since infancy by his father, Basilio, King of Poland; the king had wished to forestall the prophecy (pronounced at birth) that Segismundo would usurp the throne and become a tyrant; a series of wild actions appears to prove the prophecy, but in the end, the prince learns from experience, exerts his own free will, and counteracts the agents of fate.

Vincenzo Kornaros, *I Thysia tou Avraam* (The Sacrifice of Abraham)—the first mystery drama in modern Greek; although structurally modelled upon Luigi Groto's *La Isach* (1586), the piece surpasses its source because of the quality of its poetry and the humanity of its theme; 1154 lines in rhymed meter, without scene and act divisions; the playwright humanizes the Old Testament Yahweh and develops Abraham as a distraught father rather than as a steeled Hebrew patriarch; the title character struggles with the conflicts created by his fatherly love for Isaäc and his desire to obey God.

Mulla Vajhi, *Sab Ras* (All Sentiments)—a poem by the Urdu writer and court poet, in rhythmical rhyming prose; a free translation of an earlier Persian allegory; explains various philosophical, ethical, and mystical problems by personifying the parts of the human body and their qualities; the first work of literary prose in the Urdu language.

EVENTS

The Academie Francaise founded by Armand Jean Duplessis, Cardinal Richelieu; it will establish the rules of grammar and determine proper language usage; it will also function to rid the French language of its impurities.

Guilio Alenio, a Jesuit priest of Brescia who zealously propagated Christianity in China, publishes the first life of Christ in Chinese.

1636

BIRTHS

Nicolas Boileau-Despreaux (d. 1711). French poet and critic; he will gain recognition as one of the most prominent French poets of his time; he will write witty and brilliant satires and epistles and humorous mock-epics; he will also gain a reputation as an advocate of neoclassical literary theory; earned the title "the Legislator of Parnassus."

Joseph Glanvill (d. 1680). English philosopher; he will have difficulty finding a middle ground between the Aristotelian philosophy dominant at Oxford and the Puritan dogma prevailing outside that university.

PUBLICATIONS

Pierre Corneille, *L'Illusion Comique* (The

Comic Illusion)—a comic drama by the French playwright and poet; one of the better pieces representing French comedy prior to the rise of Moliere.

Peter Heylyn, *The History of the Sabbath*—a prose pamphlet by the Church of England controversialist and advocate of High Church policy and doctrine; the piece was written at the direct command of King Charles II to counter Puritan influence.

Philip Massinger, *The Great Duke of Florence*—a romantic comedy by the English playwright; the complicated plot arises out of the actions of Giovanni, nephew of the widowed Duke of Florence; the young man has, for three years, been entrusted to a tutor, Charomonte, at whose house the pupil has fallen in love with his daughter, Lydia; suddenly, Giovanni must return to his uncle's court and the old man falls in love with his nephew's intended; however, the piece comes to an end when the Duke remembers his vow never to remarry, which permits Giovanni and Lydia to wed.

EVENTS

George Sandys, English poet and traveler, publishes his verse *Paraphrase upon the Psalmes of David,* one of the earliest works of its kind to achieve literary distinction; in the next year, Henry Lawes, epistler of the Chapel Royal, London, set those paraphrases to music; however, the work will never become popular for private or public worship.

1637

DEATHS

Bhai Gurdas Bhalla (b. ?). Indian (Punjabi) poet; wrote approximately forty heroic poems, a number of which contained rhymed stanzas of vivid and homely imagery.

Ben Jonson (b. 1572). English playwright and poet; as a dramatist, he tended to avoid romantic comedy and to focus instead upon realistic themes; he possessed a number of anti-Puritan prejudices which helped him to create many eccentric but humorous characters.

PUBLICATIONS

Pedro Calderon de la Barca, *El Magico Prodigioso* (The Wonder-Working Magician)—a popular religious drama by the Spanish poet and playwright.

Pierre Corneille, *Le Cid*—a tragicomedy by the French playwright; narrates the adventures of Rodrigue and Chimene; they love each other (and, in fact, have been destined for each other), but must separate because of a quarrel between their fathers; the playwright created a young man who was demanding, active, and heroic, one passionately attracted by honor and glory; for him, love cannot exist without those qualities; throughout, those traits complicate the love affair.

Rene Descartes, *Discours de la Methode*—a tract by the French scientist and philosopher; establishes the Cartesian principle of basing metaphysical demonstrations upon mathematical certitude, rather than upon scholastic subtleties; one must doubt everything automatically before arriving at a clear, simple, and unquestionable idea.

John Milton, *Lycidas*—a poem by the English writer; a pastoral elegy on the death of the poet's friend, Edward King, who drowned while crossing from Chester Bay to Dublin; the work casts criticism upon the English Church and, at the same time, sounds a personal note of concern about the poet's own forthcoming ocean voyage.

John Suckling, *Aglaura*—a play by the English poet and playwright; contains two fifth acts: one decidedly tragic, the other less so; includes the memorable lyric "Why so pale and wan, fond lover? / Prithee, why so pale?"

——————, *Session of the Poets*—a work by the English writer in which a number of his literary contemporaries, including Ben Jonson, Thomas Carew, and William D'Avenant, vie for laurels, essentially a piece of contemporary literary criticism.

EVENTS

Sir William D'Avenant, English playwright and poet, appointed Poet Laureate of England, succeeding Ben Jonson; until 1688.

Japan prohibits the importation of foreign books.

1638

BIRTHS

Edmonde Boursault (d. 1701). French comic playwright; although lacking a formal education, he will acquire a thorough knowledge of the French language; his plays will reflect a moving spirit but modest learning.

Nicolas Malebranche (d. 1715). French philosopher; he will pronounce the intervention of God necessary to bridge the gulf between entities so unlike as the human soul and the human body.

DEATHS

Ivan Gundulic (b. 1588). Croatian poet; his work promoted an early form of Slavic nationalism.

PUBLICATIONS

Abraham Cowley, *Love's Riddle*—a pastoral drama by the English poet, written when he was fifteen; if nothing else, the piece demonstrates the writer's precocity.

———————— **,*Naufragium Jocular*—**a Latin comedy by the then-juvenile English writer; an excellent example of a schoolboy exercise.

Sir John Suckling, *The Gobblins*—a comedy by the English poet and playwright; principally known for its extensive borrowing from William Shakespeare's *The Tempest;* the goblins are thieves who disguise themselves as devils and behave like Robin Hood and his merry men.

Joost van den Vondel, *Gysbreght van Aemstel*—a historical drama by the Dutch poet and playwright, based upon the history of Amsterdam; the piece symbolizes the decline of earthly grandeur, as opposed to the eternal significance of such values as humility and obedience to God's commands; the playwright also draws material from classical antiquity, the Middle Ages (Catholicism), and contemporary affairs.

1639

BIRTHS

Jean Racine (d. 1699). French poet and playwright; he will be remembered for his originality in not relying upon the dramatic conventions of his day; instead, his drew upon his own experiences and sufferings; thus, the behavior of his characters will parallel his own life and nature; finally, his tragedies will mark the high point of French classical theatre.

Makhfi Zebu'n-nisa (d. 1702). Indo-Persian mystic poet; her works will at times be extremely pessimistic and reveal her hatred of the cold Islamic orthodoxy of her parents.

DEATHS

Akund Darweza (b. 1540?). Afghan divine and exponent of Muslim orthodoxy; wrote a large quantity of religious prose in Persian.

Juan Ruiz de Alarcon y Mendoza (b. 1580?). Mexican-born Spanish playwright; wrote brilliant heroic tragedies and character comedies; became a model for such dramatists as Pierre Corneille.

Tommaso Campanella (b. 1568). Italian philosopher; he wrote over fifty Latin prose tracts, as well as a number of sonnets; after being confined for twenty-seven years as a theological and political heretic in a Neopolitan dungeon, where he suffered through seven trials upon the rack, he dies in the Dominican monastery of St. Honore, near Paris.

Thomas Carew (b. 1598?). English poet and a disciple of Ben Jonson; wrote a number of graceful songs and lyrics.

Martin Opitz (b. 1597). Silesian-born German poet; his poems tend to lack imagination and feeling, and are characterized instead by coldness, formality, and didacticism; dies at Danzig of the plague.

PUBLICATIONS

George Chapman, *The Tragedy of Chabot, Admiral of France*—a play by the English dramatist, completed about 1613, but not published until five years after his death; his final play; he turned to the recent history of France to present the destruction of an isolated but heroic man; emphasizes the title character's profound sense of virtue.

Ghavvasi, *Tuti-Nama* (Tales of a Parrot)—a poem by the Urdu epic poet; derived from a Persian rendering of a twelfth-century Sanskrit collection of tales and anecdotes.

Constantijn Huygens, *Daghwerck*—a verse collection by the Dutch humanist and poet; expresses in graceful and ornamental language the poet's love for his wife.

EVENTS

The Academie Francaise compiles and begins the initial publication of its dictionary of the French language; the project not completely published until 1694.

The first printing press in North America begins operation at Cambridge, Massachusetts; Stephen Daye prints a broadside, *Oath of a Free-Man,* a legal tract.

William Pierce publishes his *An Almanac for New England for the Year 1639.*

1640

BIRTHS

Aphra Behn (d. 1689). English poet, playwright, and novelist; she will become, according to certain accounts, the first professional woman writer; she will lead a notoriously bohemian existence for the times; she will also create the forerunner of the philosophical novel.

Claude Fleury (d. 1723). French church historian; he will tutor various princes of the French court and will write the first complete history of the French Church.

P'u Sung-ling (d. 1715). Chinese writer of fiction, poetry, and nonfiction; he will rise to become a monumental figure in Chinese literature, principally for his collections of supernatural and satiric folktales; his vernacular fiction focusing upon family life will place him above his contemporaries because of its superior plot construction.

William Wycherley (d. 1716). English playwright; perhaps the most expert dramatist of the Restoration, principally because of his brilliant wit and satire; however, he will also be the most vicious and licentious of the writers for the Restoration stage.

DEATHS

Uriel d'Acosta (b. 1585). Portuguese-born Dutch-Jewish philosopher; his literary works underscore his identity as a tragic figure: restive, rebellious, dissatisfied, and contradictory; after suffering excommunication and submitting to a humiliating penance, he shoots himself.

Robert Burton (b. 1577). English writer and mathematician; his most noted contribution to literature, his study of melancholy, is marked by keen irony, often gloomy humor, and rationality; he dies by his own hand.

Paul Fleming (b. 1609). German lyric poet; wrote a considerable body of poetry describing the strange sights he viewed while traveling throughout Persia; his poems are noted for their melody and versification.

Shekh Ahmud Malaye Jizri (b. 1570?). Kurdish poet who wrote in the obscure Kurmanji dialect; his lyric poems contain rich imagery and philosophical ideas.

Matthias Casimire Sarbiewski (b. 1595). Polish Jesuit poet; wrote Latin verse on moral issues and religious subjects; his major work consists of twenty-seven odes and seven epigrams, all in rhymed verse; a significant influence upon the poetry of Henry Vaughan and the congregational hymns of Isaac Watts.

PUBLICATIONS

Pierre Corneille, *Cinna, ou Le Clemence d'Augustine* (Cinna, or the Clemency of Augustus)—a dramatic tragedy by the French playwright; remembered because of its dramatic portrait of Auguste, who is initially presented as a tyrant, but who, in the end, is admirable for rising above his desire for revenge.

——————, *Polyeucte*—a tragedy by the French playwright; set in Armenia during the third century; the title hero, a convert to Christianity, breaks the idols in a pagan temple, for which his cowardly father-in-law imprisons him; the hero's martyrdom causes others to convert and convinces a Roman warrior to attempt to stop the persecution of Christians; there is a gradual spiritual reconciliation of the characters.

——————, *Horace* (Horatio)—a tragedy, set during the period of a war between Rome and Alba Longa; the action of the piece is based upon Horace and his father's absolute and passionate patriotism; they both destroy the values of the champions of Alba Longa.

Ben Jonson, *Timber, or Discoveries Made upon Men and Matter*—a collection of notes, extracts, and reflections on miscellaneous subjects by the English playwright and poet; the pieces vary in length from single sentences to complete essays, the majority of which have been adapted from Latin writers; published almost three years after the writer's death.

——————, *Underwoods*—a collection of minor poems by the English writer; includes pieces written to William Shakespeare and Mary Herbert, Countess of Pembroke and the sister of Sir Philip Sidney.

Joost van den Vondel, *Joseph in Egypten*—a drama by the Dutch playwright and poet; considers the biblical episode of Joseph and Potiphar's wife, and explores the nature of good and evil.

EVENTS

John Cotton, Richard Mather, John Elyot, and Thomas Weld produce *The Whole Book of Psalms Faithfully Translated into English Metre*, commonly referred to as "The Bay Psalm Book"; the first book in English to be printed in America; a metrical version of the Psalms that could be sung by all in attendance at Puritan worship services.

1641

DEATHS

Thomas Heywood (b. 1574?). English playwright, musician, and writer of epigrams; his several short plays and interludes contain individual characters representative of various social classes; his work forms a transitional link between the old morality plays and the modern drama.

Sarah Copia Sullam (b. ?). Italian (Venetian) poet; her sonnets reveal a sensitive Jewess proclaiming her great faith in God; according to an unidentified admirer, she "revelled in the realm of beauty, and crystallized her enthusiasms in graceful, sweet, maidenly verses."

PUBLICATIONS

Abraham Cowley, *The Cutter of Coleman Street*—a comedy by the English writer directed against the Puritans; originally entitled *The Guardians* and written for the occasion of King Charles' visit to Cambridge.

Madeleine de Scudery, *Ibrahim; ou, L'Illustre Bassa* (Ibrahim; or, the Illustrious Bassa)—the French writer's first novel published under the pseudonym Georges de Scudery; in four volumes; she attempts to link her subplots to the main action of the piece, which focuses upon the marriage of Justiniano and Isabella.

Luis Valez de Guevara, *El Diablo Cojuelo*—a picaresque novel by the Spanish writer and playwright; the piece gained additional recognition when it was adapted by Rene Lesage in 1707 under the title *Le Diable Boiteux* (The Devil upon Two Sticks).

EVENTS

The Heads of Severall Proceedings in the Present Parliament begins publication in London; the first weekly periodical of domestic news; three numbers published in November.

1642

BIRTHS

Yusuf Nabi (d. 1712). Turkish poet; his work will display his knowledge of both Persian and Arabic, as well as an attraction for proverbs; new proverbs in apt similes will be especially popular with readers of his verse.

Sir Isaac Newton (d. 1727). English scientist, mathematician, and philosopher; his scientific experiments will lead to the conclusion .that rays of light that differ in color differ also in refrangibility; he will also develop a theory of gravity; both discoveries will have profound effects upon the philosophers, poets, and fiction writers of his day.

Saikaku Ihara (d. 1693). Japanese poet and writer of fiction.

Benjamin Tompson (d. 1714). Massachusetts physician and teacher; he will become acknowledged as the first native-born colonial American poet; his satiric verse will earn him some degree of literary recognition.

Christian Weise (d. 1702). German educator, prose writer, and playwright; his educational career will inform the style and subject of his plays; he will regard his literary efforts as pedagogical instruments.

DEATHS

Sir John Suckling (b. 1609). English poet and playwright; considered the epitome of the court poet, known for the casual grace of his verses in both language and rhythm; he reportedly invented the game of cribbage.

PUBLICATIONS

Sir Thomas Browne, *Religio Medici*—a tract by the English physician and writer, published without his consent; written as early as 1635; a confession of Christian faith and a miscellany of opinions on religious subjects; the writer also included two prayers in verse.

Thomas Hobbes, *De Cive*—a tract by the English philosopher that details his views on government; in Latin, preceding the English text of 1651 entitled *Philosophical Rudiments concerning Government and Society;* focuses upon the nature of civil society as it arises out of the actions and desires of individual citizens.

1643

BIRTHS

Gilbert Burnet (d. 1715). Scottish-born essayist, historian, and churchman; he will become bishop of Salisbury; he will gain a literary reputation for a history of the Reformation and a chronicle of his own times.

PUBLICATIONS

Francois Eudes de Mezeray, *Histoire de France*—the principal historical work by the French historian, presents the country's history from the beginnings to 1598; three volumes to 1651.

John Milton, *The Doctrine and Discipline of Divorce*—a prose tract by the English writer, published anonymously; attacks custom as the cause of reaction in the Church; the writer outlines "the bad consequences of abolishing or condemning as sin, that which the law of God allows, and Christ abolished not."

Roger Williams, *A Key to the Language of America*—a dictionary of the language of the Narragansett Indians by the London-born New England divine; the work also contains a series of verses celebrating the virtues of the Indians in contrast to civilized Europeans; the verses combine moralizing with an idealized concept of the noble savage.

EVENTS

Christiana Almanack, the first Norwegian printed book, published.

Mercurius Aulicus, a Cavalier news-sheet, begins Sunday publication at Oxford.

Mercurius Britannicus, Communicating the Affaires of Great Britaine. For the Better Informed of the People begins publication as a Roundhead news-sheet; until 1646.

1644

BIRTHS

Basho (pseudonym of Matsuo Munefusa; d. 1694). Japanese poet who will contribute significantly to the development of the "haiku"; he will create the "Basho style," through which the reader will realize the simultaneous expression of experience and emotion.

Abdulqadir Bedil (d. 1721). Persian-born Indian poet; he will develop into a philosopher-poet whose verse will focus upon fundamental human problems; not content with purely Islamic answers, he will rely upon a combination of Hindu philosophy and his own nonconformist views.

DEATHS

Luis Valez de Guevara (b. 1579). Spanish novelist and playwright who patterned his style after that of Lope de Vega.

PUBLICATIONS

Pedro Calderon de la Barca, *El Alcalde de Zalamea* (The Mayor of Zalamea)—a historical drama by the Spanish playwright, based upon an actual incident during the campaign of Philip II to annex the throne of Portugal in 1578; features quarrels, abduction, rape, and insults; the theme of the piece centers on the principal character's statement of his personal cause: "My life and property I render / To the King; but honor is / The heritage of my soul, / And my soul belongs to God alone."

Pierre Corneille, *Rodogune*—a tragedy by the French playwright; Cleopatre, queen of Syria, believes that her glory lies in seeking revenge upon Rodogune, her former husband's second wife; however, both of her sons, to whom she entrusts the foul deed, love their assigned victim, which means that the queen must kill them; in the end, she also manages to poison herself; the queen's monstrosity, the title character's strength, and the sons' tortured generosity create melodrama and powerful tragedy.

John Milton, *Areopagitica: a Speech . . . for the Liberty of Unlicensed Printing to the Parliament of England*—a prose tract (technically a discourse) by the English writer; attacks the licensing of publications and all those who advocate it; licensing, he maintains, deters learning; expression must not be restricted: "Give me the liberty to know, to utter, and to argue freely, according to conscience, above all liberties."

Roger Williams, *The Bloody Tenet of Persecution for the Cause of Conscience*—a prose tract by the English-born New England divine, perhaps his most noted piece; an attack upon the "soul killing" nature of religious conformity, opposed by the writer because it conflicted with his doctrine of "liberty for cause of conscience"; the work set in motion a ten-year controversy with the Rev. John Cotton, who supported prosecution of those holding "dangerous" religious opinions.

EVENTS

Pegnitzischer Blumenorden, a German poetical society, founded at Nuremberg.

1645

BIRTHS

Jean de La Bruyere (d. 1696). French writer and translator; he will gain a literary reputation for his translation of Theophrastus and character portraits of his own contemporaries; he will be known more as a writer than a thinker.

Carlos de Siguenza y Gongora (d. 1700). Mexican chronicler, historian, essayist, biographer, and poet; he will write prolifically on a wide variety of secular subjects, and the Church will discourage the publication of his works; he will achieve recognition for his ability to record historical and narrative facts in an artful manner.

DEATHS

Hugo Grotius (b. 1583). Dutch jurist, statesman, and prose writer; his work on natural law appealed to and influenced such philosophers as Thomas Hobbes and John Locke.

Francisco Gomez Quevedo y Villegas (b. 1580). Spanish essayist and poet; a prolific poet, he wrote principally for his friends and for his own amusement, and thus mainly produced occasional pieces; his nonfiction is mostly political and devotional.

PUBLICATIONS

Hermann Busenbaum, *Medulla Theologiae Moralis*—a tract by the German Jesuit theologian in which he preaches the philosophy of the means justifying the end; contains sections on regicide, for which it will be publicly licly condemned and copies of it burned; however, the work will become a standard authority in Jesuit seminaries.

John Milton, *Tetrachordon*—the third and best known of the English writer's prose pamphlets on divorce; concerns four sets of passages from Genesis, Deuteronomy, St. Matthew, and First Corinthians.

Paul Scarron, *Les Trois Dorothees* (The Three Dorothys)—the second of two comedies by the French playwright, novelist, and poet; written for the clown Jodelet; heroic comedy whose humor derives from the gluttony, cowardice, and clumsy wiles of the comic fool.

Edmund Waller, "Go, Lovely Rose!"—a poem by the English versifier, representative of the effortless clarity of his love poetry:

> Small is the worth
> Of beauty from the light retired;
>   Bid her come forth,
> Suffer herself to be desired,
> And not blush so to be admired.

EVENTS

Ordinarie-Post-Tidende begins publication as a news-sheet in Stockholm.

The Philosophical Society of London founded; its activities will be interrupted by the civil wars and the Commonwealth period; two years after the restoration of Charles I, the organization will resume under the title of the Royal Society (1662).

1646

BIRTHS

Glueckel of Hameln (d. 1724). German-Jewish writer; she will write seven books of memoirs in Yiddish, the only language at her command.

Gottfried Wilhelm Leibniz (d. 1716). German philosopher and mathematician; he will become one of the great intellects of the world, conceiving a universal linguistic calculus and pioneering a modern symbolic logic.

PUBLICATIONS

John Cotton, *Milk for Babes, Drawn Out of the Breasts of Both Testaments*—a popular catechism for children by the English-born New England Puritan clergyman.

Richard Crashaw, *Steps to the Temple*—the principle poetic effort by the English writer; a collection of religious pieces demonstrating devotional ecstasy; the collection evidences the influence of Giambattista Marino (1569-1625) and the Spanish mystic poets.

Jean Rotrou, *Le Veritable Saint Genest*—a dramatic tragedy by the French playwright; set during a wedding at the court of the Emperor Diocletian; an actor, Genest, performs a tragedy based upon the martyrdom of Adrian; the actor, in the course of the "play," undergoes a miraculous vision and receives divine grace; the emperor imprisons and executes him.

Sir John Suckling, *Brennoralt*—a tragedy by the English poet, published after his death; reflects upon the disloyalty of the Scots, here disguised as Lithuanians; a major character, a colonel, assumes one of the writer's particularly melancholy moods.

——————, *Fragmenta Aurea*—a collection by the English poet, published four years after his death; consists of poems, plays, letters, and prose tracts; the most noted piece is "Ballad upon a Wedding."

1647

BIRTHS

Archil (d. 1713). Russian poet who will become king of two east Georgian kingdoms; his poetry will attempt to transcend Persian models by taking a didactic pose and exposing the vanity of human endeavor.

Pierre Bayle (d. 1706). French philosopher and critic; his work will discuss speculative themes in a detached and comprehensive manner; that very detachment will form the basis for his skepticism.

Anne Therese Lambert (d. 1733). French writer and patron of Paris art and culture; upon the death of her husband and the inheritance of his fortune, she will sponsor literature and learning; her narratives and memoirs will not be collected and published until after her death.

John Wilmot, Earl of Rochester (d. 1680). English poet and satirist; he will earn as much notoriety for his lavish lifestyle and vulgar language as for his poetry; his verse satires will mark him as one of the earliest of the Augustan poets.

1648

DEATHS

Uriel da Costa (b. 1590). Portuguese-born Dutch writer; earned the disfavor of his own people for opposing the Talmud and embracing the Bible; later, he completely rejected the Mosaic laws.

Pieter Corneliszoon Hooft (b. 1581). Dutch historian, poet, and playwright; his historical work documents the revolt of the Dutch against Spain; for more than a half-century, he exerted a significant influence on the Dutch drama.

PUBLICATIONS

Abraham Cowley, *The Mistress*—a poetic love cycle by the English writer; conflict arises between the illusions and follies of the lover and his mistress on the one hand, and reason and humor on the other; although not intended to do so, these conflicting forces create a comedy of situation.

Robert Herrick, *Noble Numbers; or, His Pious Pieces*—a collection of poems by the English versifier; all of the pieces concern sacred subjects: absolution, mercy, love, the Holy Spirit, and thanksgiving.

Nathaniel Ward, *The Simple Cobbler of Aggawamm in America*—a satire by the English-born New England Congregational minister; an intolerant plea for Puritan orthodoxy; a didactic piece, despite its linguistic gimmicks; printed in London, it went through four editions within three months.

EVENTS

The first newspaper advertisement, to announce publication of *The Divine Right of Church Government*, appears in the London sheet *Perfect Occurrences of Every Dai Journall in Parliament.*

BIRTHS

Peter Dass (d. 1708). Norwegian poet.

DEATHS

Marin Mersenne (b. 1588). French philosopher, mathematician, musician, and scientist; a friend of Rene Descartes, his written work defends the orthodoxy of Cartesian philosophy.

Leon de Modena (b. 1571). Italian rabbi, Talmudic scholar, teacher, and poet; he both attacked and defended traditional Juadaism, demanding synagogue reform; wrote a history of ancient Israel in Italian.

Tirso de Molina (pseudonym of Gabriel Tellez; b. 1584). Spanish playwright; wrote comedies and interludes; excelled in the portrayal of character, particularly of spirited women.

Francisco de Rojas Zorrilla (b. 1607). Spanish novelist; his fiction combines drama with passion.

Vincent Voiture (b. 1598). French poet and letter writer; an original member of the Academie Francaise; wrote sonnets and social poems.

PUBLICATIONS

Brahman, *Chahar Chaman* (Four Meadows)—the principal prose work of the Indo-Persian poet and essayist; partly autobiographical, the work describes festivities at the Moghul court, episodes from the life of the Emperor Shahjahan, and sets forth religious and moral principles.

John Cotton, *The Way of the Congregational Churches Cleared*—a prose tract by the English-born New England clergyman, ponderous in style and subject; attempts to trace the pedigree of the New England Independents and to explain the results of their strict discipline.

Robert Herrick, *Hesperides*—the principal work of the English poet; a collection of some 1200 poems, most of them written in Devonshire; "The Argument of His Book" reveals the range of the volume:

> I sing of brooks, of blossoms, birds and
>   bowers,
> Of April, May, of June, and July flowers.
> I sing of Maypoles, hock carts, wassails,
>   wakes,
> Of bridegrooms, brides, and of their
>   bridal cakes.
> I write of youth, of love, and have access
> By these to sing of cleanly wantonness.

Paul Scarron, *Le Roman Comique*—the one picaresque novel by the French playwright, novelist, and poet; focuses upon provincial life and theatrical road companies; a reaction to what the writer viewed as the overly elegant and artificial fiction of Madeleine de Scudery and Honore d'Urfe; to 1657.

Madeleine de Scudery, *Artamene; ou, Le Grand Cyrus* (Artemenes; or, the Grand Cyrus)—a novel by the French writer of romances, ten volumes written under the pseudonym George Scudery; relies heavily upon character portraits of the writer's friends and acquaintances from the royal court and the Paris salons; to 1653.

1649

DEATHS

Richard Crashaw (b. 1612?). English religious poet; his poetry reflects mixed traditions: Roman Catholic, Italian, and Counter-Reformation; his poetry, largely based upon contemporary Italian models, will eventually achieve a high level of artistry.

John Winthrop (b. 1588). English-born Massachusetts governor and prose writer; his literary reputation will come to rest upon his journal, which he began in 1630 and continued until his death; the events recorded therein reflect his strong Puritan beliefs, based upon the Calvinist notion that all human beings are corrupted by the sin of Adam.

PUBLICATIONS

Rene Descartes, *Les Passions de l'Ame* (The Passions of the Soul)—the principal ethical work of the French philosopher, mathemati-

cian, and scientist; one of the writer's attempts to deduce the existence of God as theguarantor of the reality of the perceptible world.

John Dryden, "Upon the Death of the Lord Hastings"—the English writer's first published poem, written when he was seventeen; Lord Hastings, the poet's classmate at Westminster School, has recently died at the age of nineteen; the piece contains its fill of classical erudition and scholarly pedantry, and its rhyme tends to be imperfect; thus:

> Who should be one rich draught become
>   whate'er
> Seneca, Cato, Numa, Caesar, were,
> Learned, virtuous, pious, great, and have
>   by this
> An universal metempsychosis!

Andreas Gryphius, *Carolus Stuardus, oder Ermordete Majestat* (Charles Stuart, or Majesty Murdered)—a tragic drama by the German (Silesian) playwright and poet; the result of the murder of Charles I of England; the title character becomes the ideal of the Christian martyr, while the dramatist simply groups the remaining characters into categories of "good" or "bad"; the crime against the Crown of England becomes a crime against God.

Richard Lovelace, "To Althea, from Prison" —a poem by the English lyricist, written from the Gatehouse prison, to which he had been confined by the Puritan government: "Stone walls do not a prison make, / Nor iron bars a cage; / Minds innocent and quiet take / That for an hermitage."

————————, **"To Lucasta, Going to the Wars"**—a poem to the writer's fiancee, Lucy Sacheverell: "I could not love thee, Dear, so much, / Loved I not honour more."

John Milton, *The Tenure of Kings and Magistrates*—an essay by the English writer; proceeds on the thesis that the great Protestant reformers of the past had justified tyrannicide; attacks custom as opposed to reason, and illustrates well the writer's contempt for legal jargon; defines the term "tyrant" and discusses what the people may do against one.

EVENTS

In Great Britain, English becomes the language of all legal documents, replacing Latin.

1650

BIRTHS

Abdulgadir Khan Khatak (d. 1720?). Afghan religious poet and translator; his collected poetry will be strongly mystic.

Abdurrahman Mohammand (d. 1720?). Afghan religious poet; his poetry will reflect his piety of love of God; he will become perhaps the most popular among Afghan (or Pashto) poets.

Ahmade Khani (d. 1707). Kurdish poet who will write in the Kurmanji dialect; will arouse the consciousness of his people by providing artistic form to Kurdish folk literature, demonstrating that the Kurdish language could produce literature of the highest quality and value.

Alauddin Sabit (d. 1713). Turkish poet and jurist; the humor of his poetry will be radical and will at times be judged immoral; he will also achieve humorous and absurd effects through the incorrect use of proverbs, causing unclear and ambiguous interpretations.

Jam Durak (d. 1706). Iranian (Baluchi) lyric poet; he will introduce art poetry into Baluchi literature, replacing folk ballads and romances; his melodious love lyrics will have a source in his deep emotional experiences.

DEATHS

Rene Descartes (b. 1596). French philosopher, mathematician, and scientist; termed the "father" of modern philosophy; his tracts provided the transition between scholasticism and all of the philosophical schools that followed him; the founder of analytic geometry.

Jean de Rotrou (b. 1609). French playwright; focuses in his tragedies on the forces that motivate heroic acts and passionate self-examination; one of the most vigorous representatives of the initial period of French classical theater; dies of the plague at his native town of Dreux.

PUBLICATIONS

Richard Baxter, *The Saints Everlasting Rest; or, a Treatise of the Blessed State of the Saints in Their Enjoyment of God in Glory*—a tract by the English Presbyterian divine; one of the principal works of evangelical doctrine that deeply affected religious life in England and America.

Thomas Hobbes, *The Elements of Law*—a prose tract by the English philosopher, written as early as 1640; the writer defends the monarch's prerogative on psychological grounds; he refuses to accept the theological notion of Divine Right.

EVENTS

Giles Menage, French lexicographer, publishes his *Dictionnaire Etymologique;* a new edition will come forth in 1670.

1651

BIRTHS

Juana Ines de la Cruz (d. 1695). Mexican poet, playwright, and essayist; remembered as a poet, but her literary talent is best seen in her plays, mostly short pieces meant to function as introductions or interludes; her poetry displays her complex personality, combining wisdom with passion.

Francois de Salignac Fenelon (d. 1715). French mystic writer and Roman Catholic cleric; he will gain literary recognition for his admirable imaginary prose and his astute critical tracts.

DEATHS

Abu Talib Kalim Kashani (b. ?). Indo-Persian poet laureate; his lyrics record his observations on the life and customs of his people; wrote in simple language, with Indian vernacular expressions.

PUBLICATIONS

Thomas Hobbes, *The Leviathan, or the Matter, Form, and Power of a Commonwealth, Ecclesiastical and Civil*—a treatise on political philosophy by the English philosopher;

sets forth the notion, in opposition to Aristotle, that man does not naturally exist as a social being; man does not recognize the claims of the community upon him, nor does he share in its prosperity; instead, man exists as a purely selfish creature in search of his own advantage and resisting the claims of others; such an attitude results in contention, enmity, and war.

EVENTS

The European book trade begins at this time to establish the distinction, and therefore the division, between "publisher" and "printer" (or, between producer and craftsman).

The French Parliament orders the close of the library of the minister of France, Cardinal Jules Mazarin; however, he will regain those volumes, as well as his power, within two years; upon his death, that magnificent collection will be turned over to the College Mazarin.

1652

DEATHS

John Cotton (b. 1585). English clergyman with Puritan views who fled to Boston, Massachusetts; there he wrote sermons, prayers, catechism, and a defense of the civil authorities in religious matters.

Nathaniel Ward (b. 1578). English churchman, who subsequently held a New England Pastorate; he helped to frame the first legal code in New England and wrote satires of religious toleration.

PUBLICATIONS

Jean-Louis Guez de Balzac, *Socrate Chretien* (The Christian Socrates)—a series of religious dialogues by the French writer and historiographer; successful because of its elegant prose style: orderly, capable of expressing abstractions, rhythmic, and balanced.

Shunsai Hayashi, *O-Dai-Ichi-Ran*—a general history of Japan by the Japanese historian.

George Herbert, *A Priest to the Temple*—the principal prose work by the English poet and essayist; contains plain, prudent, and practical rules for the country parson; set forth with sincere and ardent piety; not published until almost twenty years after the writer's death.

Roger Williams, *The Bloudy Tenet Yet More Bloudy*—a prose tract by the New England apostle of civil and religious freedom; one of the series of responses to John Cotton concerning the prosecution of those holding "dangerous opinions."

1653

BIRTHS

Monzaemon Chikamatsu (d. 1725). Japanese playwright; he will become his nation's principal dramatist by establishing drama on a thoroughly new ground, reaching out to new forms and, at the same time, altering what he borrowed from traditional models; he will combine sensational journalism with a highly conscious and sophisticated technique.

PUBLICATIONS

Jean Baptiste Moliere, *L'Etourdi* (The Blunderer)—an example of fashionable high comedy by the French playwright; proved successful because it rose to the high literary standards expected of the genre.

Izaak Walton, *The Compleat Angler, or the Contemplative Man's Recreation*—a discourse on fishing by the English writer; five editions through 1676; assumes the form of a discourse between the writer (a fisherman), a fowler, and a hunter; each expounds on his own recreation; the writer then instructs others on the proper mode of catching various types of freshwater fish and on preparing them for table; interestingly enough, the writer knew little of his subject, relying upon sources and second-hand information.

EVENTS

Humphrey Chetham, Manchester merchant and cloth manufacturer, manages before his death to found Chetham's Library, Manchester.

tan, Syrian, Arabic, Persian, Ethiopian, Greek, and Latin; six volumes to 1657.

1654

DEATHS

Johann Valentin Andrea (b. 1586). German theologian and Lutheran pastor, long regarded as the founder of the Rosicrucians.

Jean Louis Guez de Balzac (b. 1594). French writer and historiographer royal; achieved a fair literary reputation by popularizing Latin writers.

PUBLICATIONS

Muhammad Dara Shikoh, *Majma u'l-Bahrain* (Mingling of Two Oceans)—a prose volume by the Indo-Persian mystic poet and writer; a comparative study of Hinduism and Islam.

Augustin Moreto y Cabana, *El Desden con el Desden* (Disdain Turned against Disdain)—a dramatic comedy by the Spanish playwright; presents a frigid blue-stocking who converts into a willing lover after discovering that she has been as much disdained as she had disdained her suitors; the playwright secularizes the Spanish drama to the point of irreverence.

Madeleine de Scudery, *Clelie: Histoire Romaine*—a novel by the French writer of fiction and nonfiction; ten volumes to 1660; one of the most popular and widely translated novels of the seventeenth century.

Joost van den Vondel, *Lucifer*—an example of Sophoclean drama by the Dutch playwright; termed a masterpiece of lyrical religious drama; recalls, in terms of style, feeling, and majesty of language, John Milton's *Paradise Lost.*

EVENTS

Johann Amos Commenius, Czech educational reformer, publishes at Nuremberg his *Orbis Sensualium Pictus,* the first picture book for children.

Brian Walton, English divine, publishes his edition of the *London Polyglott Bible;* includes nine languages—Hebrew, Chaldee, Samari-

1655

BIRTHS

Johann Beer (d. 1700). German novelist, poet, diarist, essayist, and composer; he will be regarded as an experimentalist whose novels will appear inventive, humorous, and realistic in contrast to the traditional examples of German baroque fiction; he will be praised by twentieth-century scholars for his talent for realistic fiction.

Bernard de Montfaucon (d. 1741). French critic and writer of antiquarian tracts; after military service, he will enter a Benedictine monastery and author what will become a standard prose pamphlet on classical archaeology.

Jean Francois Regnard (d. 1709). French comic playwright; he will write, in consort with others, numerous farces for the Italian players and the fair theaters; he will earn recognition as a dramatist who strove to make his audiences laugh.

Christian Thomasius (d. 1728). German rationalist philosopher and international jurist; he will, in his lectures and prose tracts, attempt to break away from traditional pedantry and antiquated terminology.

DEATHS

Savinien Cyrano de Bergerac (b. 1619). French writer; although his work, especially his poetry, tends to be crude, he was witty, inventive, and energetic.

Joseph Solomon Delmedgio (b. 1591). Italian rabbi, physician, and philosopher; he stood between two theological and philosophical worlds: traditional Judaism and free-thinking science; composed numerous works on scientific subjects.

Pierre Gassendi (b. 1592). French mathematician and philosopher; wrote on Epicurus and became an early critic of the new philosophy of Rene Descartes.

Daniel Heinsius (b. 1641). Dutch classical scholar; edited Latin classics and published Latin poems and orations.

PUBLICATIONS

John Milton, *Pro Se Defensio* (John Milton's Defense . . . of the Notorious Book Entitled "Cry of the King's Blood")—the English Puritan's reply to Alexander More's *Fides Publica* (1654), which censured the injustice of an attack upon one of Oliver Cromwell's adherents; defends the employment of grosslanguage and personal vilification against the enemies of righteousness.

EVENTS

The first regular newspaper (so called) begins to be published in Berlin.

1656

DEATHS

Abdulrahman as-Sadi (b. 1596). Mali folklorist, historian, scholar, and diplomat; his stories and legends capture the shock and horror of the Mauridic conquest of Timbuktu (or Mali) in the late sixteenth century; he also reflects on the decay and despair evident throughout the once proud empire of Songhai.

PUBLICATIONS

Menasseh ben Israel, *Vindiciae Judaeorium*— a prose tract by the Dutch-born Jewish diplomat and scholar; a reply to English attacks upon Oliver Cromwell's readmission of Jews into England.

Jean Chapelain, *La Pucelle d'Orleans* (The Maid of Orleans)—an "unreadable" epic by the French poet and critic, in twenty-four books; the piece was attacked by Nicolas Boileau.

Abraham Cowley, *Miscellanies*—a collection by the English poet; includes, as the principal piece, four books of the "Davideis," an epic poem in decasyllabic couplets on the biblical history of King David.

Blaise Pascal, *Lettres Provincales*—eighteen brilliant prose pamphlets by the French mathematician, theologian, and writer; an at-

tack upon the Jesuits and their meaningless jargon, false doctrines, and moral laxity; its rhetorical structure was a model for the prose of Francois Marie Voltaire.

Abdulrahman as-Sadi, *Ta'rikh al-Sudan* (Legends and Tales)—a collection by the Mali scholar and historian; an immensely valuable encylopaedia of almost one thousand years of African history and culture; written in Arabic, but subsequently translated into French and German.

1657

BIRTHS

Bernard le Bovier de Fontenelle (d. 1757). French writer who will become involved in the various arguments over the ancients and the moderns in literature; he will side with the moderns and attack the ancient Greeks and their French imitators; dies at Paris in his one hundredth year, after attempting to write virtually every form of literature.

DEATHS

Katib Celebi Haci Halifa (b. 1609). Turkish scholar, poet, and encyclopaedist; his poetry tends to be overshadowed by his scholarly efforts in history, astronomy, geography, theology, and law.

Manasseh ben Israel (b. 1604). Dutch-Jewish teacher and scholar; a linguist and Talmudist, he was also a printer and publisher; his writing focuses on the Messianic era, describing the sufferings of the Jewish people and their displacement.

William Bradford (b. 1590). English-born Separatist leader who came to America aboard the *Mayflower* and who signed the *Mayflower Compact;* gained literary recognition for his history of Plymouth Plantation, which he began in 1630.

PUBLICATIONS

Savinien Cyrano de Bergerac, *Histoire Comique des Etats de la Lune et du Soleil*—a work by the French writer and adventurer, displaying his characteristic invention, vigor, and wit; focuses upon a pretended journey to the moon; published posthumously.

Andreas Gryphius, *Absurda Comica, oder Herr Peter Squentz* (The Absurda Comica, or Master Peter Squentz)—a comic play by the German (Silesian) playwright, based upon the "Pyramus and Thisbe" scene in William Shakespeare's *A Midsummer Night's Dream;* the piece at times approaches slapstick, but it is somewhat salvaged by its wordplay, personification through the comic mishandling of the "high style," and displays of false erudition.

Angelus Silesius, *Heilige Seelenlust* (The Holy Heart and Soul)—a mystical and controversial poem by the Polish-born German Protestant physician who converted to Roman Catholicism.

EVENTS

The first (so-called) "fountain pens" manufactured in Paris.

Le Sieur Saunier publishes in Paris his *L'Encyclopedie des Beaux Espirits;* believed to be the first reference book with the word "encyclopaedia" in the title.

1658

BIRTHS

Abbe Charles Irenee Castel Saint-Pierre (d. 1743). French writer; he will author tracts upon political economy and philosophy, advocating the principles of the physiocratic school.

DEATHS

Muhammad Dara Shikoh (b. 1615). Indo-Persian mystic poet and prose writer; authored biographies of mystic writers, tracts on the means by which ultimate spiritual fulfillment could be achieved, and comparative studies of Hinduism and Islam.

Balthasar Gracian (b. 1601). Spanish philosopher, didactic writer, and novelist; his work is rooted in Jesuit ideology and propounds a system of practical ethics; attempted to guide readers so that they learned to adapt means to ends.

Richard Lovelace (b. 1618). English Cavalier lyric poet; known for his smooth rhythms and sophisticated subject matter; a number of his songs and sonnets have been set to music by more than a half-dozen composers; many of the pieces are self-moralizing.

PUBLICATIONS

Thomas Hobbes, *De Homine*—a tract by the English philosopher that serves as the completion of his formal philosophic statement; concerns human nature.

John Milton, Sonnet 23: "Methought I saw my late espoused Saint"—a poem by the English writer, directed to one of his first two wives; a blind widower's grief manifests itself in a dream; the lost wife appears to the poet, dressed as one of those who (as in Revelation 7:14) "have washed their robes and made them white in the blood of the Lamb."

EVENTS

The Whole Duty of Man, a devotional work of uncertain authorship, published in London; analyzes and discusses in detail humankind's duties to God and one another. It will remain popular for more than a century following its publication.

1659

PUBLICATIONS

John Milton, *Considerations Touching the Likeliest Means To Remove Hirelings Out of the Church*—a prose essay by the English writer; a contribution to the raging public debate over the form English government should assume following the recent death of Oliver Cromwell; a logical and well thought out piece about the issue of an established church supported by tithes through a constitutional form of taxation.

————— , *A Treatise of Civil Power in Ecclesiastical Causes*—a tract by the English writer, a companion piece to his *Considerations;* the writer discusses the effects of compulsion, or state restraint in matters of religion and general speculation.

Jean Baptiste Moliere, *Le Depit Amoureux* (The Amorous Quarrel)—an example of fashionable high comedy by the French playwright, containing a number of fashionable conventions: the substitution of one child for another, a girl playing the role of a man, imbroglios, and parallelism between masters and servants involved in love quarrels.

——————, *Le Precieuses Ridicules* (The Affected Ladies)—the French playwright's first stage success, a one-act farce; a negative reaction to the excesses of fashion.

Joost van den Vondel, *Jeptha of Offerbelofte* (Jephthah, or the Promised Sacrifice)—a tragedy by the Dutch poet and playwright that offers a portrait of religious pride; the title character refuses to abandon what he considers his promise to God, in spite of the priest's willingness to absolve him of it.

EVENTS

John Macock and **Thomas Newcome,** London printers, begin publication of *Mercurius Publicus,* a news sheet devoted to the publication of Parliamentary reports; until 1663.

The Prussian State Library, Berlin, founded.

William Somner, master of St. John's Hospital, Canterbury, and auditor of Christ Church, Canterbury, publishes his *Dictionarium Saxonica-Latina-Anglicum, cum Grammatica et Glossario Ælfrici;* printed at Oxford.

1660

BIRTHS

Daniel Defoe (d. 1731). English poet, essayist, novelist, and journalist; his works of fiction, personal memoirs to be considered as fact, will gain wide recognition; as a prose stylist, he will be known as a straightforward and vivid writer with a concern for detail.

DEATHS

Paul Scarron (b. 1610). French writer and cleric; he produced sonnets, madrigals, songs,

epistles, and satires; influenced Rene Le Sage, Daniel Defoe, Henry Fielding, and Tobias George Smollet; paralyzed after 1638.

PUBLICATIONS

Pierre Corneille, *La Toison d'Or* (The Golden Fleece)—a tragedy by the French playwright and poet; a spectacular "machine tragedy" that astounded spectators.

John Dryden, *Astrea Redux*—a poem by the English writer upon the occasion of the restoration of Charles II to the throne of England: "At home the hateful names of parties cease, / And factious souls are wearied into peace, / The discontented now are only they / Whose crimes before did your just cause betray."

John Milton, *The Ready and Easy Way to Establish a Free Commonwealth*—a prose tract by the English poet and essayist; written hastily after General George Monk entered London in February 1660 and betrayed his wavering attachment to republican principles before the "Rump" Parliament; the writer urges the general to support a republican government in the form of a perpetual grand council.

EVENTS

James Howell, English writer, traveler, and parliamentarian, publishes his *Lexicon Tetraglotten,* an English-French-Italian-Spanish dictionary; a revision of an earlier work (1611) by the English lexicographer Randle Cotgrave.

Friedrich Staedtler establishes a pencil factory in Nuremberg.

1661

BIRTHS

Florent Carton Dancourt (d. 1725). French playwright; his plays will depict the stupidity of the peasantry and the follies of the bourgeoisie; he will create characters who morally corrupt themselves or one another; thus, his comedies will contain a host of seducers, gamblers, and social climbers.

Anne Finch, Countess of Winchelsea (d. 1720). English poet; her work will be known for its treatment of pleasant and occasional themes, although a tendency toward melancholy will also be significantly represented.

DEATHS

Said Sarmad Kashani (b. ?). Indo-Persian mystical poet; his several hundred quatrains of verse are pantheistic, as the poet attempted to find a middle ground between Islam and Hinduism; condemned to death for heresy.

PUBLICATIONS

Abraham Cowley, *The Advancement of Experimental Philosophy*—a prose pamphlet by the English poet and essayist; patterned after Francis Bacon's essay *The Advancement of Learning* (1605); advocates the establishment of a "Philosophical College"; the pamphlet was influential in the founding of the Royal Society.

John Evelyn, *Fumifugium, or the Inconvenience of the Air and Smoke of London Dissipated*—a prose pamphlet by the English diarist; suggests decreasing the smog of London by removing the noisy trades of brewers, dyers, and soap boilers to the outskirts of the city; the planting of fragrant trees, shrubs, and flowers would follow.

Jean Baptiste Moliere, *L'Ecole des Maris* (The School for Husbands)—a successful three-act comedy by the French playwright.

EVENTS

John Eliot, English-born missionary to the Indians of colonial America, translates the New Testament into the language of the Massachuset Indians; the first edition of Scriptures to be published in America.

Kongelige Bibliothek founded at Copenhagen.

1662

DEATHS

Brahman (pseudonym of Chandar Bhan; b. 1574). Indo-Persian poet, prose writer, and translator; his work, which is partly autobiographical, concerns life at the Mughal court and expounds upon his religious and moral principles.

Blaise Pascal (b. 1623). French mathematician, physicist, theologian, and writer; his major literary efforts attacked the Jesuits, attempted to develop profound religious truths, and expressed a skeptical attitude toward rationalist thought and theology.

PUBLICATIONS

John Evelyn, *Sculptura; or, the History and Art of Chalcography and Engraving in Copper*—a tract by the English diarist, termed by one biographer as a "dull, difficult book"; essentially a compilation of artists' names; the writer's purpose was to promote the new art of engraving in mezzotint; the work inspired individuals of means to begin to collect prints.

Marie Madelaine de La Fayette, *La Princesse de Montpensier*—the first novel by the French writer; describes the plight of an unhappily married woman in love with another man, the exiled counte de Guiche; in the end, the heroine obeys the conventions of her times and remains faithful to her husband.

Jean Baptiste Moliere, *L'Ecole des Femmes* (The School for Wives)—a comedy by the French playwright in which he added depth to the traditional farce and simple comedy; a young man attempts to woo a girl away from an elderly man; conflict arises out of the opposition between the tyranny and possessiveness of Arnolphe and the instinctive passion of Agnes; the double identity of Arnolphe leads to comic confusion.

Benedictus (Baruch) Spinoza, *Tractatus de Intellectus Emendatione* (A Short Treatise on the Correction of the Understanding)—an essay by the Dutch philosopher, not discovered until a century after his death; the writer outlines his aim of discovering a true good, a phenomenon he identified as "a joy continuous and supreme to all eternity."

Michael Wigglesworth, *The Day of Doom*—a poem by the English-born colonial American writer; a Puritan epic of 244 eight-line stanzas; describes the last judgment about which the poet had dreamed; a dramatization of God's sudden appearance among wicked men, His summons of the living and the dead to judgment, His extension of grace to all who had received the Gospel, and His punishment of the damned; became popular as a theological guide to and confirmation of Puritan dogma.

EVENTS

Academia Leopoldina established at Vienna by the Holy Roman emperor, Leopold I.

The final revision of the original *Book of Common Prayer* published; it will stand as the guide to worship service in the Church of England until it is further revised in 1927.

Poor Robin, a facetious almanac, published; contains bawdy anecdotes and picaresque narratives; intended to expose the lower reaches of London life.

The Royal Society for the Improvement of Knowledge, London, receives a charter from King Charles II.

1663

BIRTHS

Cotton Mather (d. 1728). New England churchman and writer; he will be ordained minister of the Second Church of Boston and will become one of the few eighteenth-century Americans to gain election to the Royal Society of London; the major portion of his writing will aim to reinvigorate the waning Puritanism of his time.

Anselm von Ziegler (d. 1696). German novelist.

DEATHS

Teimuraz I (b. 1589). Georgian (Persian) king and poet; king of Kakheri (1606-1616 and 1623-1632); his poetry will be based on traditional Persian models; it will focus upon love, carefree mirth, and drinking parties, but will be set against a background of hopeless despair and will lament the ill-will among people in the world.

PUBLICATIONS

Samuel Butler, *Hudibras*—a satire in octosyllabic couplets by the English poet; in three parts, each containing three cantos (part 1, 1663; part 2, 1664; part 3, 1678); a mock-heroic ridiculing the hypocrisy and self-seeking of Presbyterians and Independents, patterned after Miguel Cervantes Saavedra's *Don Quixote;* a pedantic Presbyterian is accompanied on a quest by his Independent squire; the name of the title comes from Edmund Spenser's *Faerie Queene.*

Andreas Gryphius, *Horribilicribrifax*—a satirical comedy by the German (Silesian) lyric poet and playwright; focuses upon the state of affairs in Germany after the Thirty Years' War (1618-1648); written in 1650, but not published until 1663.

EVENTS

James Clifford, canon of St. Paul's Cathedral, London, and curate of St. Gregory's parish church, publishes in London *The Divine Services and Anthems Usually Sung in the Cathedrals and Collegiate Choirs of the Church of England;* the first collection of anthems with words.

Jean Baptiste Colbert, French statesman and patron of industry, commerce, art, science, and literature, founds the Academie des Inscriptions et Belles Lettres at Paris.

John Eliott, English-born missionary to New England, translates the Old Testament into the language of the Massachuset Indians.

Europaische Zeitung, a news-sheet, begins publication in Copenhagen.

Roger L'Estrange, English journalist and writer of political pamphlets, begins publication of *The Intelligencer;* until 1666; in this same year, L'Estrange receives appointment as surveyor of printing presses and licenser of the English press; he also begins publication of another news-sheet, *The News* (also to 1666).

The third folio of William Shakespeare's works published.

1664

BIRTHS

Gian Vincenzo Gravina (d. 1718). Italian jurist and literary figure; he will become professor of civil and canon law at Rome, as well as one of the founders of the Arcadian academy; his numerous prose tracts will reflect his deep love of learning.

Matthew Prior (d. 1721). English poet and diplomat; he will become a master practitioner of what Joseph Addison termed "the easy way of writing": neat, colloquial, and epigrammatic verse; he will also write well-respected light and occasional verse mock-lyrics.

DEATHS

Biharilal (b. 1595). Hindi poet; his poems are a brilliant fusion of numerous Hindi literary traditions and express the composite culture of his time more than the works of any other Hindi poet.

Andreas Gryphius (b. 1616). The most significant German lyric poet and playwright of the baroque period; his lyrics express a deep melancholy, while his dramas focus principally upon the issue of martyrdom; indirectly influenced by William Shakespeare and Joost van den Vondel.

Miklos Zrinyi (b. 1620). Hungarian poet and patriot.

PUBLICATIONS

Anne Bradstreet, *Meditations Divine and Moral*—a collection of aphorisms by the colonial American poet, composed for her son; marked by the writer's sincerity and simple style.

John Dryden, *The Rival Ladies*—an early play by the English writer; not particularly important except that it serves as an example of how rhymed couplets could function effectively in dramatic verse.

Jean Baptiste Moliere, *Le Marriage Force* (The Forced Marriage)—a comedy-ballet by the French playwright; written for King Louis XIV of France.

——————— , *Tartuffe*—a comedy by the French playwright; the title character is a sensual parasite, a pious man attracted to a friend's wife; based upon the relationship between two men: one appears ready to sacrifice, without restrictions, his family to the religious ideals of another; the other is a hypocrite who appears content to trick his friend; the writer attacks, through the instrument of comedy, both hypocrisy and excessive piety.

Jean Racine, *La Thebiade, ou les Freres Ennemis* (The Thebans, or the Enemy Brothers)—the fourth tragedy by the French poet and playwright; essentially a failure as a dramatic production because of its well-worn subject, one having been presented to the French audience since the Renaissance; contained contemporary political digressions, but even those came forward in outmoded theatrical fashion.

1665

DEATHS

Samuel Coster (b. 1579). Dutch playwright; relied upon old folk songs for source material; created a farce out of everyday life without depending upon foreign models.

PUBLICATIONS

Pierre de Brantome *Vies des Dames Galantes* (Lives of Gallant Women)—a portion of the memoirs of the French courtier and writer; provides a detailed picture of the French court at Valois; focuses upon scandalous affairs, yet such sensationalism does not contribute to an inaccurate record of contemporary events; published posthumously.

John Dryden, *The Indian Emperor*—a heroic play by the English poet and playwright; concerns the conquest of Mexico by Hernando Cortez, the love of the daughter of the emperor Montezuma for Cortez, and the death of both father and daughter; the piece was extremely popular.

Jean de La Fontaine, *Contes et Nouvelles en Vers* (Tales and Novels in Verse)—humorous poetic tales by the French poet; based largely upon works written by Ludovico Ariosto (1474-1533), the Italian epic and lyric poet, and Giovanni Boccaccio (1313-1375), Italian poet and story teller.

Francois de La Rochefoucauld, *Reflexions, ou Sentences et Maximes Morales*—a collection of several hundred lucid and polished moral maxims by the French writer and courtier; express the writer's pessimistic view that selfishness motivates human behavior.

Jean Baptiste Moliere, *Dom Juan ou Le Festin de Pierre* (Don Juan, or the Stone Guest)—a comedy in prose by the French playwright; identified as free-form "machine comedy"; the playwright surrounds the title character with great ambiguity; Dom Juan is both disgusting and attractive; he appears indifferent to divine and human values (excepting, perhaps, courage) and is in constant conflict with his valet, Sganarelle, who simultaneously hates and adores his master.

Jean Racine, *Alexandre Le Grande* (Alexander the Great)—a tragedy by the French playwright and poet; combined the tenderness and heroism then characteristic of the romanesque tragedy.

EVENTS

Jacques Godefroy edits and publishes the *Codex Theodosianus,* which was written in 435 by Theodosius II and which summoned the Council of Ephesus.

Journal des Savantes, the first purely literary periodical, begins publication at Paris.

Henry Muddiman, the most noted seventeenth-century journalist, begins publication of *The Oxford Gazette,* the first "real" newspaper to be published in England; succeeded by *The London Gazette.*

The Philosophical Transactions of the Royal Society of London begins publication; the first permanent scientific journal.

1666

PUBLICATIONS

Jakob Bidermann, *Ludi Theatrales Sacri*—a collection of Latin religious plays by the German writer; published posthumously.

John Bunyan, *Grace Abounding to the Chief of Sinners, or the Brief Relation of the Exceeding Mercy of God in Christ to His Poor Servant John Bunyan*—a homiletic narrative by the English religious writer; a spiritual autobiography in which the writer describes his birth, his wicked childhood and youth, his various escapes from death, the perils of his military service, and his gradual awakening to religion; the piece contains accounts of the writer's spiritual experiences, temptations,

and call to the ministry; a tone of intense fervor and sincerity dominates the work.

————————, *The Holy City, or the New Jerusalem*—a prose work by the English writer, inspired by a passage from *Revelation.*

Johann Jakob Christoffel von Grimmelshausen, *Der Keusche Joseph* (The Chaste Joseph)—a novel by the German satirist and romance writer, modeled on the Old Testament story of Joseph; noted for its compelling, colloquial prose style.

Jean Baptiste Moliere, *Le Misanthrope*—a comedy by the French playwright and poet; concerns the absolute incompatability of two extremely different people: one appears totally exclusive, while the second is gregarious and eager for compliments; the playwright develops a portrait of egotistic and self-satisfied society with pretensions to sincerity.

EVENTS

The printing of the first Bible in the Armenian language.

1667

BIRTHS

Jonathan Swift (d. 1745). Irish-born prose writer and poet, perhaps the most significant prose satirist of the eighteenth century; he will end his life's work back in his native Ireland, which he outwardly will seem to detest; however, he will strenuously campaign for Irish liberties and, in the end, emerge as a national and literary hero.

DEATHS

Abraham Cowley (b. 1618). English poet; considered in his own time the most significant of his nation's versifiers; he developed the couplet as a vehicle for narrative verse.

PUBLICATIONS

John Dryden, *Annus Mirabilis*—a poem by the English writer, written in quatrains; the first two hundred of those concern the sea fight between the British and the Dutch at Bergen on 3 August 1665, the indecisive four days of battle between the two fleets in June 1666, and the British victory over the Dutch fleet off the North Foreland on 25 July 1666; the poet then devotes an additional one hundred quatrains to the Great Fire of London on 2-7 September 1666.

John Milton, *Paradise Lost*—certainly one of the most significant epic poems in any language; the English poet's thesis is contained in his statement that he wishes to "assert Eternal Providence, / And justify the ways of God to men"; the structure is ambitious but clearly balanced: the adventures of Satan balance with the history of mankind, the entry of Satan into Paradise parallels the description of the loss of Paradise, the destructive war in heaven stands in opposition (and in balance) to the description of the Creation and the problems human beings experience in attempting to understand that great act; the epic combines the best of the traditional aspects of that form with the most original and innovative approaches to it.

Samuel Puffendorf, *De Statu Republicae Germanicae* (The State of the German Empire)—a prose tract by the German writer on history and jurisprudence; attacks the Hapsburgs and exposes the absurdities of the constitution of the Germanic empire.

Jean Racine, *Andromaque*—a dramatic tragedy by the French playwright; concerns a complicated love relationship between Oreste, Hermione, Pyrrhus, and Andromaque; ends on a note of pure tragic fate: Hermione has Pyrrhus killed by Oreste, and then commits suicide; Oreste loses his mind, while Andromaque endures agonizing struggles.

1668

BIRTHS

Alain-Rene Lesage (d. 1747). French novelist, playwright, and translator; he will be termed the "father" of the French picaresque novel and will be the first French writer to produce the popular "roman de moeurs" (the novel of manners); he will influence such English writers as Henry Fielding and Tobias George Smollett.

Giovanni Battista Vico (d. 1744). Italian philosopher; he will engage himself in the studies of literature, history, and philosophy, receiving appointment as professor of rhetoric at Naples; he will influence German Romantic historians.

DEATHS

Sir William D'Avenant (b. 1608). English poet and playwright; succeeded Ben Jonson as Poet Laureate of England; he has gained a literary reputation as the most important transitional figure between the theater prior to its closing in 1642 and the theater of the Restoration; he anticipated the heroic themes of Restoration drama.

PUBLICATIONS

John Dryden, *Essay of Dramatick Poesie*—a tract by the English writer in the form of a conversation between four interlocutors, one of whom is the writer himself; the setting is a boating trip upon the River Thames on the very day (3 June 1665) of the engagement between the British and the Dutch fleets; however, the principal topic of conversation focuses upon the comparative merits of French and English drama; the writer defends rhyme in drama and Shakespeare's plays.

Jean de La Fontaine, *Fables; Choises Mises en Vers* (Selected Fables in Verse)—twelve books of verse fables by the French poet; contains approximately 230 fables drawn largely from Aesop; although the pieces appeal to children, they are sophisticated satires and serious commentaries upon French society.

Jean Baptiste Moliere, *L'Avare* (The Miser)—a comic drama in prose by the French playwright, based upon the rivalry between a father and his son for the same young woman; further complications arise from a secret love between the father's daughter and his steward; the playwright creates suspense through the dramatization of the father's incurable avarice.

Jean Racine, *Les Plaideurs* (The Litigants)—the only comedy written by the French playwright and poet; the piece is inferior to his tragedies; satirizes French law courts.

EVENTS

John Dryden appointed Poet Laureate of England, succeeding Sir William D'Avenant; the first poet to hold that office through official appointment of the English sovereign; to 1688.

1669

DEATHS

Arnold Guelincx (b. 1625). Belgian philosopher and professor at the University of Leyden; a leading exponent of the philosophy of Rene Descartes; originated the doctrine of "Occasionalism" as an answer to the philosophical objections to the Cartesian antithesis of mind and body.

Augustin Moreto y Cabana (b. 1618). Spanish playwright; in his comedies, the fool tends to manipulate the action by devising tricks to bring about a happy ending.

PUBLICATIONS

Johann Jakob Christoffel von Grimmelshausen, *Der Abenteurliche Simplicissimus. Teutsch, das Hist: Die Beschreibun dess Lebens Eines Seltzamen Vaganten, Gennant Melchio Sternfels von Fuchsheim*—(Simplicissmus, the Vagabond; That Is, The Life of a Strange Adventurer Named Melchio Sternfels von Fuchsheim)—the first great German novel and a pioneer effort in the history and development of German fiction; a picaresque piece about the Thirty Years' War (1618-1648); concerns the adventures of a youth who becomes a soldier, jester, bourgeois citizen, robber, pilgrim, slave, and hermit; has gained recognition as a satire, rich in characterization and theme.

John Dryden, *Tyrannic Love; or, the Royal Martyr*—a heroic play in rhymed couplets by the English writer; focuses upon a Roman emperor, Maximin, who falls in love with a Christian princess of Alexandria, Catharine; Catharine converts the emperor's wife to Christianity, and the emperor orders the execution of both women; one of the emperor's officers kills him; an unconvincing plot detracts from the many well-written passages.

Jean Racine, *Britannicus*—a dramatic tragedy by the French playwright; concerns the young emperor Neron, who strives to escape his mother's domination and grows to hate his half brother, Britannicus; the brothers love the same woman, Junie, who loves only Britannicus; Britannicus dies by poison at his brother's hand; the playwright shows how criminal instincts can be unleashed by jealousy.

1670

BIRTHS

William Congreve (d. 1729). English playwright; he will become the most significant of the English writers who attempted the comedy of manners; he will be particularly known for his witty dialogue.

Bernard Mandeville (d. 1733). Dutch-born English poet and satirist; he will gain both social and literary recognition for his notion that "private vices are public benefits"; for him, at the bottom of every virtue lurks some degree of selfishness.

DEATHS

Johann Amos Comenius (b. 1592). Czech educational reformer who wished to bring education in closer connection to everyday life; he advocated systematizing all knowledge, teaching in the vernacular rather than in Latin, and establishing a universal system of education with opportunities for women.

Honorat de Bueil Racan (b. 1589). French poet; became a disciple of Francois de Malherbe (1555-1628); wrote pastoral poetry and a pastoral play in verse; an original member of the Academie Francaise.

PUBLICATIONS

Jean Baptiste Moliere, *Le Bourgeois Gentilhomme* (The Would-Be Gentleman)—a comedy-ballet in prose by the French playwright; the son of a rich merchant dreams of being a gentleman and attempts to imitate the aristocracy in his outward appearance and manner; that resolve is further complicated by a love affair; a farcical portrait of an egotist willing to sacrifice everything to his illusions; the playwright further satirizes a society in which the bourgeoisie aspire to nobility, while penniless nobility practice fraud.

Blaise Pascal, *Pensees*—a tract by the French scientist, theologian, and philosopher, published posthumously; proceeds upon the thesis that all persons, by nature, hate one another; evil springs from zealous religious conviction, and human beings are the most feeble, yet thoughtful, creatures of Nature.

Jean Racine, *Berenice*—a tragedy by the French playwright; the Roman emperor Titus falls in love with Berenice, the queen of Palestine; for political and selfish reasons, Titus leaves his lover; Antiochus, king of Commagene, also loves Berenice; concerns the distress experienced by the three characters; such an impossible love situation can only lead to the separation of all parties involved.

Benedictus (Baruch) Spinoza, *Tractatus Theologico-Politicus* (A Treatise Partly Theological and Partly Political)—an anonymous prose tract by the Dutch philosopher; attempts to demonstrate that the Bible does not support the intolerance of religious authorities and their interference in civil and political affairs; intended to liberate philosophers from ecclesiastical proscription.

EVENTS

John Dryden appointed Historiographer Royal by Charles II, in addition to his office of Poet Laureate; until 1688.

John Ray, one of England's best-known naturalists, publishes *A Collection of English Proverbs.*

1671

BIRTHS

Colley Cibber (d. 1757). English playwright and poet; he will be attached almost his entire dramatic career (as actor, playwright, and manager) to the Theatre Royal, in Drury Lane, London; he will make the English stage more respectable and receive appointment as Poet Laureate of England.

Anthony Ashley Cooper, third Earl of Shaftesbury (d. 1713). English philosopher; al-

though he will be attacked as a deist in England, he will gain the attention of such prominent literary figures as Leibnitz, Voltaire, Diderot, Lessing, and Herder.

DEATHS

Meric Casaubon (b. 1599). Swiss-born humanist and writer; studied near Oxford and, upon his death, held the office of rector of Ickham, near Canterbury; gained a reputation as a Latin scholar and an editor of the works of Marcus Aurelius.

PUBLICATIONS

John Milton, *Paradise Regained*—an epic poem in four books by the English writer; a sequel to *Paradise Lost* (1667) focusing exclusively upon the temptation of Christ in the wilderness; Adam and Eve lost Paradise because they yielded to Satan's temptation; the regaining of Paradise came about by the resistance of the Son of God to the temptation of the same spirit; the poet represents Satan as a cunning, smooth, and totally dissembling creature, a "Spirit unfortunate."

——————, *Samson Agonistes*—a tragedy by the English poet; concerns the final phase in the life of Samson (Judges 16), blind and imprisoned by the Philistines; thus, there exist certain similarities between the poet and his hero.

Jean Baptiste Moliere, *Les Fourberies de Scapin* (The Cheats of Scapin)—a prose comedy by the French playwright, set in Naples; a valet helps two young men trick their fathers to obtain money and their consent to marry girls of their own choice; the title character of the piece comes into conflicts with two tyrannical and obstinate old men.

William Wycherley, *Love in a Wood*—the first play by the English dramatist, which secured for him the favor of the Duchess of Cleveland, mistress to King Charles II; a comedy of intrigue set in St. James's Park, London.

EVENTS

The first edition of the Bible in the Arabic language printed in Rome.

1672

BIRTHS

Joseph Addison (d. 1719). English essayist, poet, and playwright; his literary reputation will rest on his periodical essays; as a critic, he will aim not for profundity, but for reason and good taste.

Lodovico Antonio Muratori (d. 1750). Italian historian; he will gain appointments as Ambrosian librarian at Milan and ducal librarian and archivist at Modena.

Sir Richard Steele (d. 1729). Irish-born essayist and playwright; his periodical essays, along with those of Joseph Addison, will express bourgeois sentiment and morality, in contrast to the aristocratic ethos of the Restoration; in the comments and the characters of the *Spectator* papers, one may well discover the beginnings of the domestic novel.

DEATHS

Anne Bradstreet (b. 1612). The first notable American poet; an authentic Puritan voice shines through her works with simplicity and force; Cotton Mather termed her poetry "a grateful entertainment unto the ingenious."

PUBLICATIONS

John Milton, *Artis Logicae Plenior Institutio*— a prose tract by the English writer; attempts to clarify the system of Peter Ramus (1515-1572), the French humanist; the Protestant universities had welcomed the educational ideals of Ramus in opposition to the traditional logic of Aristotle, which they believed had been too tightly embraced by Catholicism.

Jean Baptiste Moliere, *Les Femmes Savantes* (The Learned Ladies)—a comedy by the French playwright, known for the psychological complexity of its characters; involves a series of complicated love affairs among characters in the household of Chrysale, a Parisian bourgeois.

Jean Racine, *Bajazet*—a tragedy of guile and lies by the French playwright, set in a seventeenth-century Constantinople seraglio; love and blackmail evolve into murder, assassination, and suicide.

EVENTS

Oxford University grants to John Fell, dean of Christ Church, Oxford, and bishop of Oxford, the responsibility for printing and publishing books under the imprint of the University.

Jean Donneau de Vize begins publication, at Paris, of *Le Mercure Galant,* a literary journal intended for light reading.

1673

DEATHS

Fatehabad Alaol (b. 1597?). Bengali poet; he wrote verse translations or adaptations, in Bengali, of Hindi and Persian compositions.

Jean Baptiste Moliere (b. 1622). French playwright; his originality derived from his move away from romanesque comedy toward farce; he created plays significant both as literature and popular entertainment; he developed the comedy of character. Died from a lung ailment.

PUBLICATIONS

Petrovich Avvakum, *Zhitie* (Life)—purportedly the first Russian autobiography; written by the Archpriest of Russia.

John Dryden, *Amboyna*—a dramatic tragedy in prose and blank verse by the English poet and playwright; designed to raise the spirits of the English against the Dutch by reviving the story of the massacre of a number of Englishmen at Amboyna, in the Moluccas, by the Dutch in 1623.

——————— , *Marriage a la Mode*—a comedy by the English playwright, produced in 1672; contains a heroic plot concerning the love of Leonidas for Palmyra, and an opposing comic plot, focusing upon the cynical and libertine behavior to two other couples; the second plot is a satiric commentary on Restoration society.

John Milton, *Of True Religion, Heresy, Toleration, and the Growth of Popery*—a prose tract by the English poet and essayist; an attempt to bring the Protestant sects together and to induce them to be tolerant toward differences in the nonessential points of doctrine; does not encourage violence against Papists, but openly advocates the suppression of their public worship.

Jean Racine, *Mithridate*—a dramatic tragedy by the French playwright, set in 64 B.C.; concerns Pharnace, a traitor and ally of the Romans, and his brother Xiphares; both vie for the love of Monime, betrothed to Mithridate, their father, whom they believe to be dead; although certainly a heroic figure, Mithridate is an old man and the victim of a degrading passion from which he can be freed only by death.

William Wycherley, *The Gentleman Dancing-Master*—a comedy by the English playwright, considered the most entertaining of his plays; concerns social affectation, particularly imitation of French and Spanish manners; a series of diverting scenes contribute to the comic turmoil; in the end, and in spite of all the carryings on, the two lovers manage to unite.

EVENTS

Robert Clavell publishes, at London, his *Catalogue of All the Books Printed in England Since the Dreadful Fire of London in 1666.*

1674

BIRTHS

Justus Bohmer (d. 1749). German political philosopher and jurist.

Prosper Jolyot de Crebillon (d. 1762). French playwright; he will write nine tragedies performed between 1705 and 1726, in addition to two later pieces (1748, 1754); he will seek to inject new life and vigor into dramatic tragedy by rejecting the traditions of his age and extending tragic terror to the limits of horror, selecting the bloodiest and most criminal situations.

DEATHS

Jean Chapelain (b. 1585). Learned and industrious French poet and critic, and an original member of the Academie Francaise.

Robert Herrick (b. 1591). English poet; often referred to as the most pagan of English poets since his verse emphasized youth and love in Greco-Roman settings.

John Milton (b. 1608). English Puritan poet and prose essayist; blind from 1652; he produced perhaps the most significant epic in the English langauge, while his less ambitious sonnets (twenty-three in all) are among the best written.

Hallgrimur Petursson (b. 1614). Icelandic hymn writer and poet; remembered for a collection of fifty devotional lyric poems derived from the story of the passion of Christ; his death resulted from leprosy.

PUBLICATIONS

Giambattista Basile, *Il Pentamerone*—a collection of fifty Neapolitan folk tales by the Italian writer and folklorist; published posthumously at Naples.

Nicolas Boileau-Despreaux, *L'Art Poetique* (The Art of Poetry)—a didactic and satirical poem by the French poet and critic, focusing upon literary taste; in four cantos the poet presents his idea of good writing, citing examples of inferior poetry and defending his own sense of taste; praises classical standards for poetry and thus exists as the manifesto of French neoclassical criticism.

——————, *Le Lutrin*—a mock heroic epic, the first four cantos appearing in 1674 and the last two in 1683; depicts a ludicrous quarrel over the placement of a lectern ("lutrin") in the Sainte Chapelle; satirizes the faults and weaknesses of clerics, including ignorance, sloth, and gluttony.

Nicholas Malebranche, *De la Recherche de la Verite* (On the Search after Truth)—a treatise by the French philosopher; combines a psychological investigation of the causes of error with a mystic idealism ("the vision of all things in God"); the intervention of God is necessary to bridge the gulf between such extremely unlike entities as the human soul and body.

Jean Racine, *Iphegenie en Aulide*—a tragedy by the French playwright and poet, based upon the unfinished tragedy of Euripides; for the French dramatist, the piece was a way to revive the noble art of pathos in Greek tragedy.

EVENTS

Louis Moreri, French scholar and preacher, publishes his *Le Grand Dictionnaire Historique*, the first encyclopaedic reference work on history; in 1675 the compiler will go from Lyons to Paris to work on the expansion of his dictionary; twenty editions through 1759; first English edition in 1694.

1675

BIRTHS

Arai Hakuseki (d. 1725). Japanese scholar, writer, and historian.

Francesco Scipione Maffei (d. 1755). Italian playwright; he will contribute significantly to the development of modern Italian tragedy and comedy while challenging the alleged superiority of the French stage.

Louis de Rouvroy de Saint-Simon (d. 1755). French courtier; he will gain a respectable literary reputation from his *Memoirs* of 1752, detailed accounts of life at court between 1695 and 1723.

PUBLICATIONS

William Wycherley, *The Country Wife*—a comedy by the English playwright in which a libertine feigns impotence to disarm the suspicions of various husbands; the writer directs his witty satire at the hypocrisy of supposedly virtuous women who can easily and willingly be seduced; he shocked contemporary spectators with his uproarious and licentious humor.

EVENTS

Andrew Clark, printer at Aldersgate Street, London, begins publication of news-sheet, *The City Mercury; or, Advertisements concerning Trade;* fourteen numbers, November-February 1675-1676.

1676

DEATHS

Jean Sieur de Saint-Sorlen Desmarets (b. 1595). French poet and critic; first chancellor and a cofounder of the Academie Francaise; also a protagonist in the ancients versus moderns literary controversy.

Paul Gerhardt (b. 1607). German hymn writer; assistant pastor of St. Nicholas, Berlin (1657-1666); pastor at Lubben (1669-1676); wrote sincere and simple hymns, considered unique for the baroque period; ranks with Martin Luther as the most gifted and popular hymnodist of the Lutheran Church.

Johann Jakob Christoffel von Grimmelshausen (b. 1621?). German novelist, essayist, satirist, and writer of romances; considered the most significant novelist of seventeenth-century Germany; his ability to combine the picaresque, romantic, and realistic narrative forms was a lasting influence upon the development of European fiction.

PUBLICATIONS

John Dryden, *Aureng-Zebe*—a dramatic tragedy by the English writer, his last play in rhymed couplets before adopting blank verse; remotely based upon contemporary events, in which Aureng-Zebe usurped the throne of the empire of India from his father, Shah Jehan, and brothers; the playwright redirects that plot to an attempt to take from Aureng-Zebe his fiancee, Indamora, herself a captive queen; however, the couple thwarts that attempt; the theme of the piece focuses on how anarchy and impotence can threaten the emotional, moral, and political fabric of human existence.

Peter Folger, *A Looking-Glass for the Times*—a poem by the New-England grandfather of Benjamin Franklin, in ballad form; maintains the necessity of religious liberty and claims that God brought the Indian wars upon the Massachusetts people as punishment for their religious intolerance: "The sin of persecution / Such laws established; / By which laws they have gone so far / As blood hath touched blood"; reprinted as late as 1763.

Benjamin Tompson, *New Englands Crisis; or, a Brief Narrative of New Englands Lamentable Estate at Present*—a satire in heroic couplets by the Massachusetts physician and teacher; the poet holds up the past as a wiser and holier time than the present; in the so-called good old days people resided "Under thatch'd huts, without the cry of rent, / And the best sauce to every dish—content. . . . "

1677

DEATHS

Angelus Silesius (b. Johann Scheffler, 1624). German philosophical poet and mystic writer; a Protestant physician who became a Roman Catholic priest.

Benedictus (Baruch) de Spinoza (b. 1632). Dutch philosopher who profoundly influenced generations of Western intellectuals and writers; formulated an essentially monastic conception of existence and a deterministic understanding of the relationship between God, humanity, and the cosmos; according to his system, the divine will gives purpose to and flows through all life.

PUBLICATIONS

Aphra Behn, *The Rover, or the Banished Cavaliers*—a play in two parts by the English writer, the second published in 1681; concerns the amorous adventures in Naples and Madrid of a band of English cavaliers during the exile of Charles II (1648-1660); the hero of the piece may well have been modelled after John Wilmot, Earl of Rochester; another model for the libertine Willmore may have been the playwright's lover, John Hoyle, lawyer and son of the regicide Thomas Hoyle.

John Dryden, *The State of Innocence, and Fall of Man*—a play by the English writer; a dramatic version of John Milton's *Paradise Lost;* a rhyming play (or opera) in which the playwright experimented with verse, triplets and Alexandrines embellishing traditional patterns.

Urian Oakes, *Elegy upon the Death of the Reverend Mr. Thomas Shepard*—a poem by the colonial American writer; the subject, a Massachusetts minister, had died in December

1677 at the age of forty-two; the piece contains fifty-two six-lined stanzas; it gains its beauty and its strength from the poet's authentic imaginative vision:

> Away, loose-reined careers of poetry;
> The celebrated Sisters may be gone;
> We need no mourning women's elegy,
> No forced, affected, artificial tone;
> > Great and good Shepard's dead! Ah! this alone
> > Will set our eyes abroach, dissolve a stone.

Jean Racine, *Phedre*—a tragedy by the French poet and playwright; the title character is the daughter of Minos and Pasiphae and a descendant of the sun; she yearns for the love of Hippolyte, her husband's son; all characters assume, to some degree, guilt for the death of the heroine, although her continual agony dominates her tragedy; her moral consciousness and superhuman efforts of will are powerless against the curse that weighs upon her and her race.

William Wycherley, *The Plain Dealer*—a dramatic comedy by the English playwright; focuses upon Manly, the misanthropic "plain dealer" who is disgusted by the insincerity and disloyalty of humankind; despite its obvious hilarity, the piece displays the writer's personal bitterness and at moments crosses the line between comedy and tragedy.

EVENTS

Johann Jacob Hofmann publishes his *Lexicon Universale,* a volume that focuses upon the sciences and the arts.

1678

DEATHS

Andrew Marvell (b. 1621). English poet of the pre-Restoration period known for his witty and delicate language; the poet's respect for Nature and enjoyment of gardens are clearly evident in his works; a master of the eight-syllable couplet; an incompetent physician was responsible for his death.

Mary White Rowlandson (b. 1635?). American narrative writer, wife of a Massachusetts clergyman and mother of four children; composed one of the earliest Indian captivity narratives, a seventeeth-century adventure-thriller set on the colonial American frontier.

Mirza Mohammad Ali Saeb (b. 1602). Persian poet who spent six years in India; he became poet laureate to Shah Abbas II of Persia; reportedly composed more than 300,000 verses, incorporating fresh metaphors and similes and ignoring traditional poetic techniques; used language and subjects of everyday life and relied upon idiom.

PUBLICATIONS

Aphra Behn, *Oroonoko, or the History of the Royal Slave*—a novel by the British writer of fiction and drama; concerns the grandson and heir of an African king, who obtains the love of the beautiful Imoinda, daughter of the king's general (and loved by the king himself); the first expression in English literature of sympathy for the oppressed Africans, reflecting the writer's own experiences in Surinam; reworked into a dramatic tragedy of the same title by Thomas Southerne in 1695.

Anne Bradstreet, *Poems* (2nd ed.)—a posthumously published collection of revised and new pieces by the colonial American Puritan poet; simple lyric poetry demonstrating the spiritual struggles of a Christian who must confront her own doubt and skepticism; expresses the writer's struggles with her inherited Puritan conscience.

John Bunyan, *The Pilgrim's Progress, from This World to That Which Is To Come*—an allegory by the English writer, three editions to 1679; assumes the form of a dream by the author; Part One describes Christian's pilgrimage from the Slough of Despond to the Celestial City; Part Two relates the journey of Christian's wife and her children on the same pilgrimage; a universal classic in part because of its beautiful and simple language.

John Dryden, *All for Love, or, the World Well Lost*—a historical dramatic tragedy by the English writer, in blank verse; focuses upon the story of Antony and Cleopatra, but limits that narrative to the last phase of Antony's career; the Roman military leader, besieged in Alexandria, struggles with Ventidius (his general), Dolabella (his friend), Octavia (his wife), and Cleopatra (his lover); all vie for the Roman's soul; in the end, Antony falls on his own sword and Cleopatra dies by inflicting an asp upon her arm.

Marie Madeleine Pioche de la Vergne, Comtesse de la Fayette, *La Princesse de Cleves* (The Princess of Cleves)—a novel by the French writer depicting the world of King Louis XIV; treats personal and political maneuvers with timeless sophistication and artistry; the heroine obeys the dictates of society and religion and remains true to her husband; the writer disguises her intent by setting the novel in the sixteenth century, but even then she cannot hide (nor does she try to) the hypocrisy of the royal court of Louis XIV.

1679

DEATHS

Thomas Hobbes (b. 1588). English philosopher; obsessed by the civil disorder of his day; the basis of his metaphysics focused upon the motion of bodies, attraction and repulsion of the human will; considered good and evil inconsistent terms applied haphazardly by different persons to what attracted or repelled them; thus life exists as a conflict between everyman and everyman.

Joost van den Vondel (b. 1587). Perhaps the most renowned Dutch poet; wrote satirical verses upon the sectarian disputes of the time; developed a wide taste for and knowledge of the Greco-Roman classics.

PUBLICATIONS

John Dryden, *Troilus and Cressida*—a play by the English dramatist and poet; referred to by critics as a pot boiler which might better have been left unwritten; Chaucer, Shakespeare, and Henryson had attempted translations before the Restoration writer (and with no better success).

P'u Sung-ling, *Liao-chai Chih-i* (Strange Stories from a Chinese Studio)—an entertaining collection of supernatural and satiric folk tales by the Chinese writer of fiction and poetry; contains numerous short narratives in a highly allusive and traditional style; circulated in manuscript for almost eighty years before it reached publication.

John Wilmot, Earl of Rochester, *A Satyr against Reason and Mankind*—a poem by the

English "rake," written sometime in March 1676 and published as a broadside; the poet develops, in a highly individual manner, commonplace themes reflecting his free thought, an attitude that prevailed during the seventeenth century: the unreliability of speculative reasoning, the superiority of unerring animal instinct as opposed to fallible human reason, and the contrast between the so-called innocent warfare of animals as they fight to survive and the pride and treachery of human beings.

EVENTS

Elias Ashmole, English antiquary and lawyer, founds at Oxford the Ashmolean Museum, principally housing his own collection of curiosities.

1680

BIRTHS

Philippe (Nericault) Destouches (d. 1754). French playwright and author of at least seventeen comedies; he will develop plays hostile to the skeptical ideas emerging at the outset of the Enlightenment; thus, he will write high-minded, moralistic comedies.

DEATHS

Samuel Butler (b. 1612). English satirist; died of consumption and buried in the churchyard of St. Paul's, Convent Garden, London; his political satires secured the favor of the monarchy and were popular among those who did not adhere to English Puritanism.

Francois de La Rouchefoucauld (b. 1613). French philosophical essayist and moralist; a remorseless analyst of the human character; investigated self-love in its most elusive forms and under its most ingenious disguises.

John Wilmot, Earl of Rochester (b. 1647). English courtier and poet; his debauchery and buffoonery did not detract from the excellence of his letters, satires, bacchanalian and amatory songs, and obscene and licentious verses.

Hayashi Shunsai (b. 1618). Japanese historian and chronicler.

PUBLICATIONS

Abdulqadir Bedil, *Chahar 'Unsur* (The Four Elements)—a tract in prose and verse by the Persian-Indian poet; contains many of the poet's philosophical ideas, autobiographical details, and reminiscenses; until 1694.

John Bunyan, *The Life and Death of Mr. Badman*—an allegory by the English Dissenter; assumes the form of a dialogue in which Mr. Wiseman relates the life of Mr. Badman, recently deceased; Mr. Attentive comments upon that life; as entertainment and moral the work assumes a place within the history of the English novel.

Carlos de Siguenza y Gongora, *Glorias de Queretaro en la Nuevo Congregacion Eclesiastica de Maria Santissima de Guadalupe* (The Glories of Queretaro)—a chronicle by the Mexican historian, essayist, and poet; records the founding of the Church of the Virgin of Guadalupe in Queretaro; a significant work in the cultural history of New Spain.

EVENTS

Mercurius Librarius, or a Faithful Account of All Books and Pamphlets begins publication; identified as the first English literary periodical; essentially a catalogue of books issued, published either weekly or fort-nightly.

Cesar-Pierre Richet publishes his *Dictionnaire Francaise.*

1681

DEATHS

Pedro Calderon de la Barca (b. 1600). Considered Spain's finest dramatist; wrote with perfect fidelity to the thought and manners of his age; scholars have traditionally placed him in a select group with Homer, Dante, and Shakespeare; wrote seventy-two "autos sacramentales" (outdoor plays) for the festival of Corpus Christi, in addition to 118 other dramatic pieces.

Ku Chiang (b. 1612). Chinese scholar and writer; after the downfall of the Ming dynasty, he changed his name to "Ku Yen-wu" and wandered about the country in disguise; wrote classical, historical, and topographical works, as well as poetry.

Urian Oakes (b. 1631?). English-born Massachusetts poet, clergyman, and president of Harvard College; a gifted preacher who delivered commencement sermons in Latin, he wrote at least one poem significant to the history of colonial American literature.

PUBLICATIONS

Jacques-Benigne Bossuet, *Discours sur l'Histoire Universelle*—a historical tract by the French churchman and sermonizer, written for his pupil, the Dauphin of France; scholars have tended to regard the work as the first attempt at a philosophy of history; also constitutes a summary of history in which the writer traces divine intervention at each stage.

John Dryden, *Absalom and Achitophel*—a poem by the English writer, composed toward the end of the Whigs' heated opposition to Charles II; the Earl of Shaftesbury had introduced a bill into the House of Lords to exclude Charles' Catholic brother, James, Duke of York, from succession, favoring, instead, the King's illegitimate Protestant son, the Duke of Monmouth; the bill failed and Shaftesbury found himself imprisoned for high treason; the poet relies upon biblical parallels to political persons and events; thus, the David-Absalom-Achitophel relationship to the King's problems; in the end, "Once more the God-like David was Restor'd, / And willing Nations knew their Lawfull Lord."

———————— , *The Spanish Fryar*—a verse comedy by the English writer, clearly an attack upon Papists; thus, Elvira, with the aid of a friar, carries on an intrigue with Lorenzo, who turns out to be her brother; the poetic variations of the work are considered superior to its plot and characterization.

Jean Mabillon, *De re Diplomatica*—a prose tract by the French Benedictine monk, editor, and historian; the piece promotes the study of historical documents as a foundation for historical criticism.

Andrew Marvell, "The Garden"—a posthumously published poem by the English writer; anticipates the nineteenth-century Romantics by allowing nature to serve as a projection of the poet's own feelings, thus providing an escape into "other worlds and other seas"; nature exists as a source of human joy and as a means to identify humankind's often limited understanding and purpose.

———————— , **"To His Coy Mistress"**—another posthumously published poem; based upon the traditional shepherd-lover's complaint; proposes that the young woman yield her virtue, rationalized by the idea that intense sexual pleasure can hide death and its "deserts of vast eternity" from the consciousness.

Carlos de Siguenza y Gongora, *Manifesto Philosophico Contra los Cometas Despojados del Imperio que Tenian Sobre los Timidos* (Philosophical Manifest against Comets Stripped of Their Dominion over the Mind)—a prose pamphlet by the Mexican historian and essayist; the writer admits his ignorance of the true cause and nature of comets, yet he asserts that people ought not to fear them superstitiously as omens of evil; the work caused disputes among the principal astronomers of the day.

EVENTS

The Academy of Sciences, at Moscow, founded.

Sir Roger L'Estrange, English journalist and political pamphleteer, begins publication of his anti-Whig journal *The Observator;* he attacks, in addition to the Whigs, Titus Oates and all Dissenters; followed a question and answer format; until 1687.

1682

DEATHS

Evilya Celebi (b. Dervis Muhammad Zilli, 1611). Turkish writer of descriptive and travel narratives; recorded numerous accounts of diplomatic journeys and military campaigns in Europe, Asia, and Africa; many of his pieces did not see publication until the 1890s, 1929, and 1936.

PUBLICATIONS

Aphra Behn, *The City Heiress*—a dramatic comedy by the English playwright and novelist; the complicated plot involves an old knight who marries, by accident, his nephew's mistress; may be seen in terms of the writer's anti-Whig contributions to the English stage during the period of the Popish Plot and as a satire directed against the Earl of Shaftesbury.

John Bunyan, *The Holy War*—an allegory by the English Dissenter partially drawn from his experience as a soldier during the Parliamentary War (1644-1646); concerns the means by which Diabolus schemes to gain control of the city of Mansoul, the metropolis of the universe; in the end, Emmanuel defeats Diabolus.

John Dryden; *Mac Flecknoe; or, A Satyr upon the True-Blew-Protestant Poet, T.S.*—a poetic satire by the English writer, directed against the English dramatist and poet Thomas Shadwell (1642?-1692); Flecknoe, an Irish versifier, passes to Shadwell the rights to dullness; after receiving his crown in a London suburb, Shadwell assumes rights to the province of stupidity: "In prose and verse, was owned, without dispute, / Thro' all the realms of Nonsense, absolute."

————— , *The Medal*—a poem by the English writer on the occasion of a commemorative medal being struck for the Earl of Shaftesbury: "Five days he sate for every cast and look; / Four more than God to finish Adam took. / But who can tell what essence angels are, / Or how long Heaven was making Lucifer?"

————— , *Religio Laici, or a Layman's Faith*—a poetic statement by the English writer of his religious beliefs (three years later he would convert to Roman Catholicism); he relies upon the authority of the Church's traditional interpretation of Hebrew Scripture against the excesses of personal guidance; in the preface, the writer offers a prose explication of Church authority in such matters.

Saikaku Ihara, *Koshuku Ichidai Otoko* (The Life of an Amorous Man)—a Japanese novel traditional for its time: the action moves naturally, complemented by description; the novelist tends to place the individual (or major character) within a large social group.

EVENTS

Acta Eruditorum, the first scholarly journal, begins publication at Leipzig; written entirely in Latin; until 1776.

1683

BIRTHS

Edward Young (d. 1765). English poet; his literary productions, though slight, will be witty and brilliant; his sparkling satires will be eclipsed by those of Alexander Pope.

DEATHS

Izaac Walton (b. 1593). English essayist and writer of moral reflections and dialogues; also known for his biographies; he will always be remembered for his tract on fishing.

Roger Williams (b. 1603?). English-born colonial American Puritan tract writer; known as the apostle of Toleration and as the founder of the Rhode Island colony; his prose works tended to reflect the strain of anarchy that became an essential part of the American tradition.

PUBLICATIONS

Johann Beer, *Die Kurtzweiligen Sommer-Tage* (Tales of Summer)—a multi-part novel by the German writer; also known as the "Willenhag romances," since Wolfgang von Willenhag serves as the narrator and protagonist; more than 1600 pages of prose, with over two hundred characters.

Edmund Boursault, *Le Mercure Galand*—a satirical comedy by the French poet and playwright; typical of his dramatic productions in that it represents his modest learning and forgiving spirit.

Juana Ines de la Cruz, *Los Emperos de Una Casa* (The Determinations of a House)—a play by the Mexican poet and dramatist; considered a splendid example of baroque rhetoric; the playwright successfully followed the formula of comedy that dominated the Spanish "Golden Age": delicate complexity, unusual characterization, and subtle humor.

John Dryden and Nathaniel Lee, *The Duke of Guise*—a play by the two English writers; Dryden wrote the initial scene, the entire fourth act, and the larger portion of act five; Lee composed the remainder; draws a historical parallel between the League in France and the Covenant in England during the height of the controversy over the successor to Charles II; thus, an analogy of the Duke of Monmouth's return to London with the entry of the Duke of Guise into Paris.

Bernard le Bovyer de Fontenelle, *Dialogues des Mortes*—an essay in dialogue form by the French writer; an imitation of Lucan attacking authoritarianism.

EVENTS

Publication (appoximately) of *The New England Primer,* a small textbook containing short verses, hymns, prayers, and rhyming alphabets; designed to provide "Spiritual Milk for American Babes"; first published in Boston; a reported five million copies published and sold prior to the American Revolution.

1684

BIRTHS

Ludvig Holberg (d. 1754). Danish and Norwegian playwright, historian, novelist, poet, and essayist; he will become known as the "father" of Scandinavian literature for shaping the literary traditions of Denmark and Norway; he will contribute significantly to the creation of a national Danish drama.

DEATHS

Pierre Corneille (b. 1606). French playwright and poet; considered equal to the best dramatists of his age; ultimately affirmed his independence within the limits of classical doctrine; thus, for him, theater was a spectacular art meant to astound the audience.

PUBLICATIONS

Carlos de Siguenza y Gongora, *Parayso Occidental, Plantado y Cultivado por la Liberal*

Benefica Mano des los muy Catholicos (Occidental Paradise)—a combination history and biography by the Mexican writer; a history of the Royal Convent of Jesus Mary in Mexico City, combined with biographies of a number of the prominent nuns within that institution; historically significant as a chronicle of the colonial culture of New Spain.

EVENTS

Pierre Bayle, French philosopher and critic, publishes at Rotterdam his literary review, *Nouvelles de la Republique des Lettres;* one of the most successful attempts at a popular journal of literary criticism.

The Japanese poet Saikaku Ihara composes 23,500 verses in a single day and night at the Sumiyoshi Shrine is Osaka; the scribes could not record them all, and thus merely kept track of the number of verses.

1685

BIRTHS

George Berkeley (d. 1753). Irish-born churchman, philosopher, and essayist; his idea of subjective idealism denies the existence of matter independent of perception; the observing mind of God makes possible the continued apparent existence of material objects.

John Gay (d. 1732). English poet, dramatist, and satirist; he will achieve literary recognition, but will be known more for his ability to attract literary patronage and significant sums through subscriptions to his poems and plays.

Sulkhan Saba (d. 1725). Georgian Russian writer and diplomat; he will achieve recognition for his linguistic and lexicographical projects, in addition to his travel narratives and discussions on European civilization.

PUBLICATIONS

John Dryden, *Albion and Albanius*—the first of two operas by the English writer; he strived to harmonize language and rhythm; for the music, the poet secured the services of a French musician who had come to England in 1665, Louis Grabut; the failure of the piece may be equally blamed upon the dramatist and the musician.

——————, *Threnodia Augustalis*—a Pindaric ode by the English writer focusing upon the death of King Charles II, who had perished a month earlier: "Thus long my grief has kept me dumb: / Sure there's a lethargy in mighty woe, / Tears stand congealed and cannot flow, / And the sad soul retires into her inmost room."

Edmund Waller, *Of Divine Love*—didactic poem by the English versifier, in six cantos.

EVENTS

Cesar de Rochefort publishes his *Dictionnaire General et Curieux.*

The fourth Shakespeare folio edition published.

1686

BIRTHS

John Balguy (b. 1686). English Protestant theologian and pamphleteer; most of his literary efforts will attack the Deists, primarily the followers of Lord Shaftesbury.

DEATHS

Jean Mairet (b. 1604). French tragic playwright and poet; wrote pastoral tragicomedies; employed a free technique, rejecting the unity of time and properties; intertwined farce with tragedy.

PUBLICATIONS

Monzaemon Chikamatsu, *Shusse Kagekiyo* (Successful Kagekiyo)—a puppet play by the Japanese dramatist; performed in Tokyo and considered the first "new" puppet play, one of serious literary value, as opposed to sheer entertainment.

John Dryden, *To the Pious Memory of the Accomplished Young Lady Mrs. Anne Killigrew,*

Excellent in the Two Sister-Arts of Poesie, and Painting. An Ode—a poem by the English laureate, proclaimed by Samuel Johnson as the finest of its form in the English language; Anne Killigrew (1600-1685) was the daughter of Dr. Henry Killigrew, master of the Savoy Hospital, and the niece of Thomas Killigrew, one of the owner-managers of the London Theatre Royal (for whom the poet wrote a number of plays); she herself contributed odes to English letters: "Her *Arethusian* Stream remains unsoil'd, / Unmixt with Foreign Filth, and undefil'd, / Her Wit was more than Man, her Innocence a Child!"

Bernard de Fontenelle, *Entretiens sur le Pluralite des Mondes* (Conversations on the Plurality of Worlds)—an essay by the French miscellaneous writer; popularizes the cosmological theories of Rene Descartes (1596-1650); also discusses Copernican astronomy and scientific principles; however, the essayist does so under the guise of a conversation with an attractive young marquise walking by moonlight through the park in her country estate.

——————, *L'Histoire des Oracles*—an essay by the French writer in which he attacks credulity and superstition.

Saikaku Ihara, *Koshoku Gonin Onna* (Five Women Who Choose Love)—a realistic Japanese novel.

——————, *Koshoku Ichidai Onna* (A Woman Who Devoted Her Entire Life to Love-making)—another realistic novel by the Japanese writer.

Edmund Waller, *Of the Last Verses Written in His Book*—a poem by the English versifier; described as "a poised and fluent production" that illustrates the poet's graceful manipulation of the heroic couplet: "Leaving the old, both worlds at once they view, / That stand upon the threshold of the new."

EVENTS

The German pietist and educator August Hermann Francke begins at Leipzig his *Collegium Philobiblicum,* a tract promoting the study of the Bible.

Jean Le Clerc, Swiss Reformed theologian, begins publication of his twenty-five volume *Bibliotheque Universelle et Historique;* until 1693.

1687

DEATHS

Constantijn Huygens (b. 1596). Dutch humanist and poet; his descriptive and satirical verse was highly esteemed, and he was knighted by both English and French monarchs.

Edmund Waller (b. 1606). English poet; wrote one of the earliest examples of the true heroic couplet, a form that prevailed in English poetry for nearly two centuries; generally, his verse displayed what critics have long labeled "polished simplicity."

PUBLICATIONS

John Dryden, *The Hind and the Panther*—a poem by the English writer, partially the result of his conversion to Roman Catholicism in 1685; narrates the rivalry among the religious sects, which are represented by different beasts; thus, the Church of Rome is the Hind, while the Church of England is the Panther.

——————, *Song for St. Cecilia's Day*—a poem by the English writer; the piece established a new form of imitative harmony; the poet's verse became, in a phrase, a linguistic orchestra; dedicated to the patroness of music, commemorated on 22 November; the music for the piece was originally composed by the court musician Giovanni Baptista Draghi.

Francois de la Mothe Fenelon, *Traite de l'Education des Filles* (Treatise on the Education of Women)—a prose tract by the French cleric and prose writer; written after he had become director of an institution for female converts to the Catholic faith; thus the piece has a clear but limited purpose and scope, although it does consider the psychological aspects of female education.

Sir Isaac Newton, *Philosophiae Naturalis Principia Mathematica* (Mathematical Principles of Natural Philosophy)—a tract by the English Physicist and mathematician in which he demonstrates his principle of universal gravitation, explaining both the motions of heavenly bodies and the falling of bodies upon earth; focuses upon dynamics, motion, and fluid mechanics, as well as upon the phenomena of tides.

Samuel Freiherr von Puffendorf, *De Habitu Religionis Christianae Vitam Civilem* (Of the Relation between Church and State)—a prose tract by the German professor of natural and international law; he maintains that while moral law derives from revelation and civil law from the positive enactments of the State, natural law derives from the instincts of society; thus natural law is based on human reason.

1688

BIRTHS

Pierre Carlet de Chamblain de Marivaux (d. 1763). French playwright, novelist, poet, essayist, and journalist; he will achieve recognition as an innovative European dramatist and novelist; he will influence the evolving genre of the novel, particularly with his treatment of the individual psyche and of everyday French life.

Alexander Pope (d. 1744)—the most significant poet of eighteenth-century England; he will become a master craftsman and the most brilliant of all English verse satirists; he will also define the doctrine of classicism.

Giovanni Battista Vico (d. 1744).—Italian philosopher who studied law; he will devote his energies to literature, history, and philosophy; he will receive the appointment as professor of rhetoric at Naples, while his historicism will influence the German Romantics.

DEATHS

John Bunyan (b. 1628). English Dissenter; a master of plain and beautiful English prose whose realism and psychological insight formed the basis of the modern English novel.

Hermann Busenbaum (b. 1600). German Jesuit theologian; upon his death he held the seat as rector of the Jesuit college of Munster; his theological propositions failed to be accepted by Church authorities.

Philippe Quinault (b. 1635). French poet and playwright; wrote comedies and libretti for the operas of the Italian-born French composer, Giovanni Battista Lully (1632-1687).

PUBLICATIONS

Jacques-Benigne Bossuet, *Histoire des Variations des Eglises Protestantes*—a historical tract by the French preacher and bishop; somewhat of a classic of French ecclesiastical history, although its antiProtestant sentiment cannot be ignored; the writer demonstrates admirable learning and rhetorical skill.

John Dryden, *Britannia Rediviva; a Poem on the Birth of the Prince*—a poem by the English essayist, dramatist, and poet; written on the occasion of the birth of an heir to King James II (reigned 1685-1688); the piece hailed the extension of a dynasty that the people of England deplored.

Jean de La Bruyere, *Les Caracteres de Theophrast, Traduits du Grec, avec les Caracteres et les Moeurs de ce Siecle* (Theophrastus, Translated from the Greek, with the Manners of the Present Age)—the portraits and aphorisms of the French moralist expose the arrogance and stupidity of the French ruling class; the writer cries out against the prevailing social injustice; according to Francois Marie Voltaire, the "rapid and nervous style of the piece struck the public at once; and the allusions to living persons, which abound through its pages, completed its success."

Bernard de Fontenelle, *Digression sur les Anciens et les Modernes*—a tract by the French writer defending the evolution of the arts; the writer sides with the moderns, attacking the ancient Greeks and their French imitators; he is in turn attacked by Nicolas Boileau, Jean Racine, Jean Baptiste Rousseau, and Jean de La Bruyere.

1689

BIRTHS

Charles de Secondat Montesquieu (d. 1755). French philosopher and jurist who will earn an appointment to the Academie Francaise; he will advocate the separation and balance of powers within governments as a means of guaranteeing the freedom of the individual.

Alexis Piron (d. 1773). French poet and playwright; he will compose dramatic pieces for the French comic opera.

Samuel Richardson (d. 1761). English novelist; he will develop and refine the epistolary novel as a method of suggesting authenticity during a period when readers were highly suspicious of pure fiction; his voluminous correspondence will be equal to his fiction in literary quality.

DEATHS

Aphra Behn (b. 1640). English writer; identified as the first professional English woman of letters; her poetry and drama appeared well suited to the coarse cultural and stylistic requisites of the Restoration; her remains will lie among the "great" in Westminster Abbey.

Chu Yung-Shun (b. 1617). Chinese writer; the author of maxims and commentaries upon the "Great Learning" and the "Doctrine upon the Mean"; three days prior to his death, he struggled into the ancestral hall where, before the family tablets, he called forth the spirits of his forefathers to witness that he had never dishonored them through his literary works.

Khushhal Khan Khatak (b. 1613). Afghan national poet; he expressed personal sentiments in a series of odes and lyrics, a number of which he wrote in prison and exile; his descriptions of nature are unique in their freshness.

PUBLICATIONS

John Locke, *Letters on Toleration*—essays by the English philosopher, issued between 1689 and 1692; adovcates religious independence and toleration, with the exception of Roman Catholicism and atheism; advances the idea that each individual is the product of different sense impressions; thus, each will possess a different religious viewpoint, and each viewpoint will prove morally "correct."

Cotton Mather, *Memorable Providence Relating to Witchcraft and Possessions*—a narrative by the New England divine; an early analysis of a victim of witchcraft the writer took into his home.

Jean Racine, *Esther*—a tragic drama by the French poet and playwright; drawn from the New Testament; the playwright was persuaded by Francoise de Maintenon (1635-1719), the second wife of Louis XIV, to write the piece for performance at her school at Saint-Cyr.

EVENTS

Sir George Mackenzie of Rosehaugh, Scottish lawyer, King's advocate, and parliamentarian, founds the Advocates' Library at Edinburgh; by 1925, the institution will become the National Library of Scotland, and thus will receive a copy of every work published in Great Britain.

Thomas Shadwell, English playwright and poet, receives appointment as Poet Laureate of England, succeeding John Dryden; to 1692.

1690

DEATHS

Peter Folger (b. 1617). Colonial American poet and grandfather of Benjamin Franklin, as well as a surveyor, lay missionary, and schoolmaster; disseminated his views on religious toleration through his verse.

PUBLICATIONS

John Dryden, *Amphitryon*—a comedy by the English poet and playwright, adapted from the comedies of Plautus and Jean Baptiste Moliere on the story of the Theban prince; a comedy of errors focusing on the complications that arise from the arrival at Amphitryon's palace of two sets of twins.

——————, *Don Sebastian*—a tragicomedy by the English writer; based upon the legend of Sebastian, King of Portugal, and his survival following the battle of Alcazar; the playwright avails himself of the opportunity to chastise the English clergy; the dramatist's most complicated dramatic treatment of a number of important political, sexual, and religious themes.

John Locke, *An Essay concerning Human Understanding*—a philosophical tract by the English prose writer; a fifth edition in 1706; an examination of the nature of knowledge, calculated to guide the reader to a proper application of human understanding; the field of knowledge is limited and must be supplemented by faith; accepts the possibility of rational demonstration of moral principles and the existence of God, as well as the scholastic doctrine of substance; denies innate ideas and demonstrates that all knowledge derives from sense, or sensation.

——————, *Two Treatises on Government*—prose tracts by the English philosopher designed to combat the theory of the divine right of kings and to justify the Glorious Revolution of 1688; the government, by means of the legislature, has the fiduciary power to act for specific ends; however, the people remain the supreme power and may remove or alter the legislative branch if they find that it acts contrary to the trust assigned to it.

Juana Ines de la Cruz, *El Divino Narciso* (The Divine Narcissus)—a long play by the Mexican poet, playwright, and essayist; partially based upon the legend of Echo and Narcissus; a sacramental play that moves forward upon a simple allegory about a pagan lover; the writer transforms that story to revolve around the life and passion of Christ; the piece may well be the height of the writer's literary achievement.

Carlos de Siguenza y Gongora, *Infortunios que Alonso Ramirez Natural de la Cuidad de S. Juan de Puerto Rico* (The Misadventures of Alonso Ramirez)—a chronicle by the Mexican historian, essayist, biographer, and poet of the perilous journeys of a Puerto Rican adventurer; concerns a boy who leaves home to make his fortune, enduring the vagrant life and numerous adventures upon land and sea, including capture by English pirates; often referred to as a picaresque novel, although the piece is completely factual; a fine example of the blending of historical fact with literary artistry.

EVENTS

The Academia dell' Arcadia founded in Rome.

The London publisher and bookseller John Dunton founds *The Athenian Gazette,* a penny weekly newssheet designed to resolve "all the most Nice and Curious Questions"; continues until 1696 and changes its name to *The Athenian Mercury;* first English periodical to answer readers' letters.

Oxford University assumes ownership of the books and printing equipment of Dr. John Fell, dean of Christ Church, Oxford, and bishop of Oxford; in 1672, the University had granted Fell the privilege of printing its books; from this date, the printing of the University's books has come under the management of its Delegates.

the *Gentleman's Journal,* said to be the forerunner of the modern popular magazine; contains news of the month, poetry, and miscellaneous prose; until 1694.

Elkanah Settle, English heroic playwright, drama critic, and hack poet, receives the appointment as City Poet of London, a position he will hold until at least 1717.

1691

PUBLICATIONS

John Dryden, *King Arthur*—a dramatic opera by the English poet and playwright, with music by Henry Purcell (1659-1695); music is relied on only during the climactic scenes; the "air" (or "aria") serves as a substitute for the dramatic (or heroic) declamation, and music, rather than figures of speech, produce the desired intensity; the effect appeared to be an increase in the formality of the production; the playwright wrote the piece in blank verse, dedicating it to Purcell and admitting (in the dedication) that in certain instances he sacrificed the quality of the verse for the sake of the composer.

Claude Fleury, *Histoire Ecclesiastique*—a significant work of scholarship by the French historian; the first complete church history; twenty volumes, not completed until 1723; the writer carried the project forward to the year 1714; other scholars took on the project after his death in 1723 until 1778.

Gottfried Wilhelm Leibniz, *Protogaea*—a tract on geology by the German philosopher and mathematician.

Jean Racine, *Athaliah* (Athalie)—a tragedy, with chorus, by the French playwright and poet; the title character murders her own grandchildren, worships Baal, usurps a throne, attempts to seize the King of Judah, and dies at the hands of the Levites; a tragedy devoid of love but dominated by the presence of God; the playwright draws a sharp contrast between the raptures of faith and the violence of tragic action.

EVENTS

Peter Anthony Motteux, French-born English editor and translator, begins publication of

1692

BIRTHS

Carlo Innocenzo Frugoni (d. 1768). Italian poet; he will become quite popular at Parma, especially after he gains appointment as court poet there; he will use a wide variety of forms and subjects and write in an elegant style.

Pierre Claude Nivelle de La Chaussee (d. 1754). French dramatist; he will enjoy popularity for his sentimental plays that will influence Voltaire.

PUBLICATIONS

William Congreve, *Incognita*—a mediocre work of fiction by the English playwright, composed before he turned his attention and skill to drama; nonetheless, the piece (published under a pseudonym) reveals the young writer's craftsmanship and sharp wit.

Juana Ines de la Cruz, "Respuesta Sor Filotea de la Cruz"—an autobiographical essay by the Mexican writer; a response to a letter from the bishop of Mexico, who attacked her habit of secular study; the writer defends her desire for knowledge and the direction of her adult life; argues for the right of women to an education and the liberty of the individual to pursue a broad spectrum of knowledge; one of the finest prose essays produced in New Spain.

Florent Carton Dancourt, *Les Bourgeoises a la Mode* (The Fashionable Bourgeois Ladies)—a comedy by the French playwright and actor; a highly cynical, but lively and gay, piece; contains numerous parallels with the comedies of Jean Baptiste Moliere.

John Dryden, *Eleonora: a Panegyrical Poem to the Memory of the Countess of Abingdon*—an elegy by the English poet and dramatist, composed (for a rather high fee) in honor of one whom the poet had never seen; a catalogue of female Christian virtues.

Jonathan Swift, "Ode to the Athenian Society"—one of the earliest attempts at poetry by the Irish-born writer; concerns the schemes by the English publisher John Dunton (1659-1733) to establish a society to encourage and promote fanciful investigations; the piece lacks the irony, humor, and imaginative force that will characterize the satirist's later works.

EVENTS

Johann Konrad Amman publishes his *Der Redende Stumme* (The Silent Reader), a manual of language for deaf mutes.

Sir Roger L'Estrange, English political pamphleteer, linguist, and translator, publishes in London his translation and edition of *Aesop's Fables.*

Nahum Tate, Irish-born dramatist, poet, and psalmodist, appointed Poet Laureate of England, succeeding Thomas Shadwell; until 1715.

foolish and amusing plot; thus, the piece succeeds more as stage entertainment than as literature.

John Locke, *Thoughts Concerning Education*— a tract by the English philosopher, written from Holland as advice to a friend on raising his son; maintains that education should include the health and diet of the individual; "That which every gentleman (that takes any care of his education) desires for his son, besides the estate he leaves him, is contained . . . in these four things, virtue, wisdom, breeding, and learning."

Cotton Mather, *The Wonders of the Invisible World*—a prose tract by the colonial New England cleric; written after a special court had been convened (June 1692) to try the accused in an alleged outbreak of witchcraft in Salem (Massachusetts) Village; attempts to reconstruct the proceedings and defend the trials, ultimately hoping to prevent serious religious backsliding among the members of his congregation: " . . . those interests of the gospel, which were the errand of our fathers into these ends of the earth, have been too much neglected and postponed. . . . "

1694

1693

DEATHS

Ashraf Khan Khatak (b. 1635). Afghan poet and political figure; his pen name, "Hijri," means "exile."

Marie Madelaine de La Fayette (b. 1634). French novelist, biographer, essayist, and historian; important to the history of the development of fiction because she redirected the novel from the overly wordy heroic adventure tale to a concise, realistic, and psychologically complex portrait of human character.

PUBLICATIONS

William Congreve, *The Old Bachelor*—the first of the English playwright's dramatic comedies, containing a host of amusing and foolish characters; various disguises and romantic intrigues help to sustain an equally

BIRTHS

Philip Dormer Stanhope, fourth Earl of Chesterfield (d. 1773). English statesman, orator, and writer; he will become a close friend of Jonathan Swift, Alexander Pope, and Viscount Bolingbroke; his literary fame will come from two sources: the letters to his natural son and godson and his quarrel with Samuel Johnson over the issue of literary patronage.

Johann Lorenz von Mosheim (d. 1755). German theological writer; he will become professor of theology at Helmstedt and Gottingen; the English historian Edward Gibbon will assess his work as "full, rational, correct, and moderate."

Francois Marie Voltaire (d. 1778). French writer and the most notable intellectual figure representing the eighteenth-century enlightenment; he will develop a hatred of judicial arbitrariness, combined with an enthusiastic admiration for English liberalism; he will also be a primary influence upon eighteenth-century French politics leading to the 1789 revolution.

DEATHS

Basho (pseudonym of Matsuo Munefusa; b. 1644). Japanese poet; his verses have helped to popularize the form of haiku poetry; actually composed stanzas of "haikai no renga," a sequence of lined verses created by more than one poet.

Samuel von Puffendorf (b. 1632). German writer on jurisprudence; as historiographer of Sweden, he published a history of his nation from the wars of Gustavus Adolphus (1594-1632) to the death of Queen Christina (1689).

PUBLICATIONS

William Congreve, *The Double Dealer*—the second comedy by the English playwright; a satire on the heartless sexual morals of late seventeenth-century Londoners; the piece failed to please the theater's best customers since it attacked them directly.

John Dryden, *Love Triumphant*—the last dramatic comedy by the English poet, essayist, and playwright; the most noteworthy part appears to be the prologue, wherein the writer sets down his last will and testament, bequeathing his dramatic talents to the critics and the dandies; thus, for instance, "He leaves his manners to the roaring boys, / Who come in drunk, and fill the house with noise. / He leaves to the dire criticks of his wit / His silence and contempt of all they writ."

EVENTS

The first edition of the *Dictionnaire de l-'Academie Francais*, 2 volumes, published at Paris; a clear attempt to determine proper usage and to regulate the written and spoken language.

1695

BIRTHS

Johann Christian Gunther (d. 1723). German poet; he will achieve modest literary recognition for his love lyrics.

DEATHS

Juana Ines de la Cruz (b. 1651?). Mexican poet, dramatist, and essayist; made a great contribution to seventeenth-century Hispanic culture as a writer and intellectual figure; best known for her love lyrics and a single long poem; several scholars have identified her as possibly the best female poet of the seventeenth century.

Jean de La Fontaine (b. 1621). French poet; a significant, brilliant, and original writer; wrote sophisticated satires and serious commentary upon French society, as well as poems with classical themes.

Dorothy Osborne Temple (b. 1627). English traveler and letter writer; wife of Sir William Temple (1628-1699), English diplomat, essayist, and patron of Jonathan Swift.

PUBLICATIONS

William Congreve, *Love for Love*—a comedy by the English playwright; the complicated plot focuses upon a spendthrift's attempts to win the love of a lady and to maintain his inheritance, despite his father's efforts to redirect it to another son; successful because of its repartee and cast of amusing characters.

John Locke, *Reasonableness of Christianity*—a prose tract by the English philosopher, aimed specifically at a reunion of the churches of England and Rome; the writer maintains that, since human understanding cannot comprehend all reality, knowledge must be supplemented by religious faith, without resort to creed.

1696

BIRTHS

Henry Home, Lord Kames (d. 1782). Scottish philosopher; he will devote his interests to the historical study of law, especially to the differences between the English and Scottish systems; he will also focus upon the psychological study of the law; finally, he will attempt to write a history of the human species as it progressed from the savage state to its highest point in civilization.

St. Alfonso Maria de Liguori (d. 1787). Italian bishop whose written works will embrace divinity, casuistry, exegesis, history, canon law, hagiography, asceticism, and poetry; he will forsake the study of common law and take holy orders.

DEATHS

Jean de La Bruyere (b. 1645). French prose writer and translator; known more for his ability to write than to think profoundly.

Marie de Rabutin-Chantal Sevigne (b. 1626). French writer and courtier; her letters record the history of the times in explicit detail; those epistles also reveal her wide learning and common sense.

Anselm von Ziegler (b. 1663). German novelist.

PUBLICATIONS

Jean-Francois Regnard, *Le Jouriur* (The Gamester)—a dramatic farce by the French playwright, written for the Italian players and the fair theaters at Paris; deception is practiced for the purpose of obtaining money and arranging marriages.

Christian Reuter, *Schelmuffskye Reisebeschreibung* (The Rogue's Travel Book)—an adventure novel by the German writer.

EVENTS

The *Biliotheca Hispana Vitus* of Nicolas Antonio, Spanish historian, published posthumously.

London coffee-house keeper Edward Lloyd, who operates a shop in Lombard Street, begins publication of *Lloyd's News,* a thrice-weekly news-sheet.

William Nicolson, English antiquary and clergyman and Bishop of Carlisle and Derry, publishes *The English Historical Library,* containing English, Scottish, and Irish works; three volumes to 1669.

Nahum Tate, Irish-born Poet Laureate of England and dramatist, and Nicholas Brady, Anglican clergyman (and also born in Ireland), publish *The Psalms of David in Metre;* known as the "Authorized Version" of the Psalms, the volume emerged as the initial step

leading to the development of English hymnody and congregational song.

1697

BIRTHS

Abbe Antoine Francois Prevost (d. 1763). French novelist, essayist, poet, and literary critic; he will contribute significantly to the literature of his nation, particularly with his criticisms and translations of English writers and his major piece of popular fiction, which will eventually become an opera, a ballet, and even a motion picture.

DEATHS

Sirhindi Nasir Ali. Persian poet; a gifted lyricist, he influenced Persian poetry in India during the eighteenth and nineteenth centuries; the patient reader will recognize the beauty of the lyrics despite the complicated rhetorical structure.

PUBLICATIONS

Pierre Bayle, *Dictionnaire Historique et Critique*—a two-volume work by the French philosopher and critic, published at Rotterdam; objective and comprehensive, the volumes discuss the literary and philosophic controversies of the day; nonetheless, the writer cannot hide his preference for orthodoxy; the work exercised considerable influence upon Enlightenment philosophy, particularly in terms of its advocacy of the Cartesian principle of clear and distinct ideas.

William Congreve, *The Mourning Bride*—the only attempt at tragedy by the English playwright; concerns the discovery of a secret marriage and attempts to murder the husband and punish the bride; the sponsor of those deeds, the bride's father, and a secret lover of the husband fall accidental victims to the plot, and the end sees the reunion of husband and wife; the London audience of the day held the piece in high esteem, as did, later, Samuel Johnson; also known for two lasting quotations: "Music has charms to soothe a savage beast" and "Heaven has no rage, like love to hatred turned, / Nor hell a fury, like a woman scorned."

Daniel Defoe, *An Essay upon Projects*—the first long essay by the English miscellaneous writer; views the laws applying to debtors as unreasonable and inhuman; thus, the debtor can never help himself; the writer proposes a court of inquiry that would hear and try cases of debt, determine their causes, and attempt to resolve disputes between debtors and creditors.

John Dryden, *Alexander's Feast; or, the Power of Music: An Ode, in Honor of St. Cecelia's Day*—perhaps the finest poem by the English writer, composed to celebrate the power of music; the story of Alexander the Great, sitting by the side of his Thais, being moved by the music of Timotheus to think of nothing but wine, women, and war; according to the poet himself, the organ of St. Cecelia enlarges the theme of the poem in the same manner and scope as heaven enlarges the earth; in 1736, George Frederick Handel set the poem to music.

Charles Perrault, *Histoires ou Comtes du Temps Passe, avec des Moralities: Contes de Ma Mere l'Oye* (Histories, or Tales of Past Times: Mother Goose Tales)—a collection of fairy tales by the French writer and poet, written (or at least completed) in 1695; includes "Sleeping Beauty," "Little Red Riding Hood," "Bluebeard," "The Master Cat; or, Puss in Boots," "The Fairies," "Cinderella, or the Little Glass Slipper," "Ricky with the Tuft," and "Tom Thumb, or, Hop o' My Thumb"; the writer combines traditional (oral and written) folk tales with scenes and elements of contemporary life at the French court.

EVENTS

Edward Bernard, critic, linguist, and Savilian Professor of Astronomy at Oxford, and Humfry Wanley, assistant at the Bodleian Library, Oxford, publish their *Catalogi Librorum Manuscriptorum Angliae et Hiberniae* (A Library Catalogue of English and Irish Manuscripts); a catalogue of the Bodleian manuscripts begun and supervised by Bernard, assisted by Wanley, the published work records volumes available at places other than Oxford; comprises one of the major achievements of the Oxford Saxonists since it inspired further research by Old English and medieval scholars.

1698

BIRTHS

Johann Jakob Bodmer (d. 1783). Swiss historian and poet; he will be appointed to a chair of history at Zurich; the study of classical writers will convince him of the tastelessness of contemporary German literature.

Pietro Metastasio (d. 1782). Italian poet; his literary reputation will rest on his masques and opera libretti; he will become one of the most representative of the Italian Arcadian poets—and will, at the age of thirty-one, gain appointment as court poet at Vienna.

PUBLICATIONS

Cotton Mather, *Eleutheria; or, an Idea of the Reformation of England*—a tract by the New England Puritan theologian; the subject concerns the attainment of the utopian ideal of religious freedom through religious reform; if nothing else, the piece demonstrates the writer's knowledge of English history and sources.

Madeleine de Scudery, *Conversations Nouvelles sur Divers Sujets* (Conversations upon Several Subjects)—a series of dialogues by the French romance writer; the conversations originated from actual discussions between the writer friends who frequented her Paris salon; in published form, the pieces propose to assist young people in acquiring social grace and high moral standards; these same conversations also found their way into her more celebrated novels and romantic tales.

EVENTS

Dr. Thomas Bray, London divine and philanthropist, founds the Society for Promoting Christian Knowledge (SPCK); its initial aims included the promotion and establishment of charity schools in England and Wales and the distribution of Bibles and religious tracts in Britain and abroad.

Cardinal Casanatense founds, in Rome, the Bibliotheca Casanatense.

Francis Daniel Pastorius, German-born American Quaker, publishes his *A New Primer of English*, an early attempt to stabilize and standardize the language.

1699

DEATHS

Jean Racine (b. 1639). French dramatist and poet; he is considered the dramatist best able to create tragic pathos; however, a number of scholars, fascinated by the tender sweetness of his rhythms and the perfection and flexibility of his cadence, hold him in even higher esteem as a poet.

PUBLICATIONS

John Dryden, *Fables, Ancient and Modern*—verse paraphrases by the English poet and dramatist of tales from Geoffrey Chaucer, Giovanni Boccaccio, and Publius Ovidius Naso (Ovid); the writer's last literary effort before his death in May 1700; the preface to the collection outlines the writer's last thoughts on the art of translation, which occupied so much of his literary career, and contains an excellent critical comparason of Homer, Ovid, Boccaccio, and Chaucer.

Francois de Salignac Fenelon, *Telemaque*—a masked satire by the French cleric and writer, directed at the court of Louis XIV; however, the work should be principally considered as a graceful narrative of the imaginary adventures of Telemachus; despite its satire, the cleric wrote the piece for the instruction of his pupil.

Anthony Ashley Cooper, third Earl of Shaftesbury, *Enquiry Concerning Virtue*—an essay by the English philosopher, published surreptitiously by John Toland during the writer's absence in Holland; the writer's first, and perhaps only, attempt at systematic philosophy.

EVENTS

Peter the Great, Emperor of Russia, decrees that the New Year in Russia will begin on 1 January, rather than on 1 September.

1700

BIRTHS

Johann Christoph Gottsched (d. 1766). German essayist and playwright; at Leipzig, he will become professor of philosophy and poetry and of logic and metaphysics; he will attempt to improve the literary quality of the German language and strive to reform German drama.

James Thomson (d. 1748). Scottish-born poet; recognized by William Wordsworth as the first poet since John Milton to present new images of Nature, but many succeeding Romantics and Victorians reacted negatively to what they considered his highly artificial poetic diction.

DEATHS

Johann Beer (b. 1655). German novelist, poet, diarist, essayist, and musical composer; a prose experimentalist whose fiction combines humor, invention, and realism; tended, generally, to disregard the traditions of German prose fiction, fusing the picaresque with courtly narrative forms.

John Dryden (b. 1631). English poet, dramatist, and essayist; a key transitional figure between the Metaphysical school of John Donne and the neoclassicism of the early seventeenth century; he set the stage for the Age of Reason and became the major literary figure of the Restoration.

Carlos de Siguenza y Gongora (b. 1645). Mexican poet, biographer, essayist, historian, and chronicler; one of the leading intellectuals of colonial New Spain, known particularly for his scholarship and literary versatility; appointed to the chair of mathematics and astrology at the Royal University of Mexico.

PUBLICATIONS

William Congreve, *The Way of the World*—a play by the English poet and comic dramatist; a comedy of manners focusing upon the courtship of Mirabell and Millamant and attempts to circumvent those opposed to it; an overly melodramatic plot does not detract from the play's brilliant dialogue; the playwright establishes conflicts between genuine wit (Mirabell) and pretentious wit (Witwoud) and between hearty crudity (Sir Wilfull Witwoud) and affectation (Lady Wishfort).

George Farquhar, *The Constant Couple; or A Trip to the Jubilee*—a fairly coarse, farcical drama by the Irish-born playwright; the piece owes its theatrical success to the character of Sir Harry Wildair, a carefree gentleman of little substance who affects humor and nonchalance.

Charles Perrault, *Les Hommes Illustres qui ont Paru en France Pendant ce Siecle* (Characters Historical and Panegyrical of the Greatest Men Who Have Appeared in France during the Last Century)—a two-volume biographical work by the French writer, begun in 1696; written in support of the progress and invention of the modern age; contains one hundred biographical sketches of the most important figures in France during the seventeenth century; attempts to demonstrate that modern culture existed in a golden age equal to or surpassing the civilizations of ancient Greece and Rome; nearly all professions are represented in the collection, and the writer's assessment of the individuals' contributions to cultural and intellectual history are generally accurate.

Matthew Prior, *Carmen Seculare for the Year 1700. To the King*—a long poem by the English versifier and diplomat, dedicated to William III; according to Samuel Johnson in his *Life of Prior,* the poet, in this piece, "exhausts all his powers of celebration. I mean not to accuse him of flattery: he probably thought all that he writ, and retained as much veracity as can be properly extracted from a poet professedly ecomiastic."

EVENTS

The Earl of Bellmont, governor of New York, established a reading room that by 1754 will become the New York Society Library.

The German Protestant states, by order of the Diet of Regensburg, adopt the Gregorian calendar of 1582.

Mian Abul-Hassan composes the first religious treatise in Sindhi verse; concerns 130 questions of ritual practice in Islam.

Leading London Whigs, including Sir Richard Steele, Joseph Addison, William Congreve,

Sir Samuel Garth, John Vanbrugh, and Jacob Tonson, found the Kit-Cat Club, which meets at the house of Christopher Katt, a pastry cook of Shire Lane, north of Temple Bar; the club takes its name from Katt's mutton pies ("kit-cats"); later, the group meets at Tonson's house in Barn Elms; Sir Godfrey Kneller will paint each member's portrait, and those paintings now hang in the National Portrait Gallery.

Frederick I founds the Academy of Sciences in Berlin; its first president will be Gottfried Wilhelm Leibnitz.

Samuel Sewall, New England intellectual and diarist, publishes *The Selling of Joseph,* the earliest American protest against the practice of slavery.

1701

BIRTHS

Wu Ching-tzu (d. 1754). Chinese novelist, poet, and essayist; he will write a single novel that will be widely acknowledged as the most important work of social satire composed in China; he will criticize feudalism, primitive religious superstitions, self-serving moral ideologies, and various aspects of the culture of eighteenth-century China.

DEATHS

Edmonde Boursault (b. 1638). French writer who, without a formal education, nonetheless managed to acquire a thorough knowledge of the French language; wrote several comedies for the stage.

Madeleine de Scudery (b. 1607). French novelist and essayist; perhaps the most recognized writer of romance tales in Europe during the seventeenth century; her fiction portrays the polite and genteel life of the literary and intellectual salons of Paris.

PUBLICATIONS

Daniel Defoe, *The True-Born Englishman*—a satirical poem by the English writer; attempts to attack the popular prejudice against a king of foreign birth, in this instance, the settlement of the crown of England from the last of the Stuarts (Anne) upon the House of Hanover (George I).

Arai Hakuseki, *Hankampu*—a chronicle by the Japanese historian relating the history and deeds of the diamyo, the feudal lords of Japan.

Sir Richard Steele, *The Christian Hero*—an essay by the English playwright and prose writer, composed after a period of dissipation; the writer sets out to prove (to himself, as well as to his readers) that "no principles but those of religion are sufficient to make a great man."

——————, *The Funeral; or, Grief a-la-Mode*—the beginning of the English writer's career as a dramatist; the piece succeeded because of its lively dialogue and pure comic amusement; a departure from the conventions of Restoration drama, the play depicts virtue and vice in their true contexts.

Jonathan Swift, *Discourse of the Contests and Dissensions in Athens and Rome*—a tract by the Irish-born essayist and satirist; on one level, the piece deals with the 1701 impeachment of the Whig lords from Parliament; on a more philosophical and theoretical level, it concerns abstract questions relating to political power and its management.

EVENTS

Jeremy Collier, English Nonjuring bishop and scholar, publishes *The Great Historical, Geographical, Genealogical, and Political Dictionary of Great Britain;* 2 volumes, volume 3 appeared in 1705, volume 4 in 1721; a translation from the French, with considerable addition, of *Le Grand Dictionnaire Historique* (1674) by Louis Moreri, a scholar and preacher at Lyons.

Father Francisco Ximenes begins to translate the *Popul Vah,* the sacred national book of the Quiche Indians of Guatemala; to 1721.

1702

BIRTHS

Ignacio de Luzan Claramunt de Suelves y Gurra (d. 1754). Spanish literary critic and essayist.

Yokai Yagu (d. 1783). Japanese poet; he will become one of the most significant literary figures of eighteenth-century Japan.

DEATHS

Moses Germanus (pseudonym of Johann Peter Spaeth; b. ?). Italian-born Dutch-German writer who converted to Judaism from Roman Catholicism; composed five tracts in German and Latin defending Judaism and describing how he arrived at his religious conversion.

Makhfi Zebun-nisa (b. 1639). Indo-Persian mystic poet; her work is pessimistic in tone, manifesting her convincing feeling of the suffering of the human soul.

Christian Weise (b. 1642). German educator and writer of pedagogic plays reflecting the German Enlightenment and the rise of the German middle class.

PUBLICATIONS

Daniel Defoe, *The Shortest Way with Dissenters*—a pamphlet by the English novelist and miscellaneous writer; Defoe, himself a Dissenter, ironically demands the total suppression of Protestant religious dissent; that suppression will substantiate the absurdity of Anglican ecclesiastical intolerance; the writer, as a result of this piece, was fined, imprisoned, and pilloried.

Cotton Mather, *Magnalia Christi Americana* (The Great Works of Christ in America)—a prose tract by the colonial American divine containing a history of the settlement of New England; also includes biographies of significant persons, a history of Harvard College, reports on the churches of New England and their controversies, and a description of so-called divine providences; begun as early as 1693 and completed (in manuscript) in 1696: "I write the wonders of the Christian religion, flying from the deprivations of Europe to the American strand, and assisted by the holy Author of that religion. . . . "

EVENTS

The Daily Courant, the first English daily newspaper, begins publication; contains foreign news, most of it translated from foreign newspapers; until 1735.

Moskovskya Vredomosti (Moscow Gazette) begins publication as a regular newspaper.

1703

BIRTHS

Henry Brooke (d. 1783). Irish novelist, playwright, poet, essayist, fabulist, and translator; he will become a prolific and versatile writer whose work will reflect a variety of eighteenth-century beliefs and theories, particularly the educational ideals of Jean-Jacques Rousseau and the scientific discoveries of Copernicus, Galileo, and Sir Isaac Newton.

Jonathan Edwards (d. 1758). Colonial American theologian, metaphysician, and sermon writer; among the earliest of the original thinkers in America, despite the inflexibility of his theological and moral beliefs; his faith will be developed along mystical and logical lines.

DEATHS

Charles Perrault (b. 1628). French poet, essayist, biographer, and writer of fairy tales; created enduring fairy tales, but is also widely recognized for his poetry and voluminous philosophical dialogues celebrating the culture of France during the reign of Louis XIV (1661-1715).

Samuel Pepys (b. 1633). English Admiralty official and the one name synonymous with the term "diary"; his narratives provide graphic, accurate, and lively reconstructions of daily life and political intrigue during the period following the restoration of Charles II to the throne of England.

PUBLICATIONS

Monzaemon Chikamatsu, *Sonezaki Shinju* (The Love Suicide at Sonezaki)—a domestic tragedy by the Japanese dramatist; the first of several plays based upon actual incidents; focuses upon love affairs among Japan's grow-ing middle class; the episodes tend to be highly idealized.

Daniel Defoe, "Hymn to the Pillory"—a mock-Pindaric ode by the English writer, composed during his detention at Newgate Prison for the publication of his *The Shortest Way with Dissenters* (1702); thus the bitterness:

> But who can judge of crimes by punishment,
> Where parties rule, and law's subservient?
> Justice with change of interest learns to bow,
> And what was merit once is murther now:
> Actions receive their tincture from the times,
> And, as they change, are virtues made or crimes.

Sir Richard Steele, *The Lying Lover*—the second dramatic piece by the English essayist and playwright, adapted from Pierre Corneille's *Le Menteur* (The Liar, 1645); a theatrical failure that ran for only six nights.

EVENTS

Sir Isaac Newton elected president of the Royal Society of London; he will maintain that office until his death.

Publication of the *Universal, Historical, Geographical, Chronological and Classical Dictionary*; the first A to Z reference work.

1704

BIRTHS

Charles Pinot Duclos (d. 1772). French moralist, novelist, essayist, scholar, and historian; he will achieve recognition as a social psychologist who accurately observed and analyzed the customs of his age; he will be considered one of Europe's leading historians and essayists and will rival such of his contemporaries as Francois Marie Voltaire and Jean-Jacques Rousseau.

DEATHS

Jacques Benigne Bossuet (b. 1627). French churchman and controversialist and the most noteworthy pulpit orator in the nation; his reputation as a preacher spread throughout the country; reportedly the first scholar to attempt a comprehensive history of philosophy.

John Locke (b. 1632). English philosopher and the principal founder of philosophical liberalism and English empiricism; believed that contracting into civil society by surrendering personal power to a ruler and magistrates was the most efficient method of securing natural morality.

PUBLICATIONS

Joseph Addison, *The Campaign*—a commissioned poem by the English political essayist, poet, and dramatist; celebrates the victory of John Churchill, Duke of Marlborough, at Blenheim during the War of the Spanish Succession:

> Ten thousand wonders op'ning to my
> view
> Shine forth at once; sieges and storms
> appear,
> And wars and conquests fill th' important
> year,
> Rivers of blood I see, and hills of slain,
> An Iliad rising out of One campaign.

Raimondo Montecuccili, *Memorie del Generale Principe di Montecuccoli*—the posthumously published memoirs of the Italian-Austrian general, who distinguished himself during the Thirty Years' War against the Turks and against the French on the Rhine River (1664, 1672-1675).

Jean Francois Regnard, *Les Folies Amoureuses*—a comedy of manners by the French playwright; in verse and performed at the Comedie Francaise; deception is used for purposes of obtaining money and contriving a marriage.

Jonathan Swift, *The Battle of the Books*—a prose satire by the Irish-born churchman and writer; treats the issue of the ancients versus the moderns with satirical humor; the battle originates from a request by the moderns that the ancients evacuate the higher of the two peaks of Mount Parnassus, which they have always occupied; the ancients appear to have the advantage, but, at the end of a parley, the issue remains virtually undecided.

————— , *A Tale of a Tub*—another prose satire by the Anglo-Irish writer; directed against the Roman Catholic Church—its

bulls, dispensations, and doctrine of transubstantiation; however, the writer does not totally ignore the weaknesses of Protestant Dissent and the Church of England.

EVENTS

John Campbell, the postmaster at Boston, begins to submit to colonial New England governors a hand-written account of local and foreign news; he entitles his project *The Boston News-Letter;* the sheet then becomes more sophisticated, at least in form, and becomes the "official" organ of the city government; to 1776.

The earliest subscription library in Berlin begins to circulate books.

The Jesuits at Trevoux, the ancient capital and the principal city of Dombes, France, publish their *Dictionnaire de Trevoux,* a glossary of terms relating to the arts and sciences.

Isaac Newton, English scientist and mathematician, publishes his *Optics,* a defense of the emission theory of light; his research on the subject had begun as early as 1672.

Daniel Defoe begins his periodical under the title *A Review of the Affairs of France; and of All Europe*; a nonpartisan political newspaper, but an organ of the commercial interests of England; appears three times per week, almost entirely from Defoe's own hand; significant for its information on domestic and foreign affairs of the day; until 1713.

Vossische Zeitung begins publication as a newspaper in Berlin; until 1933.

1705

DEATHS

Michael Wigglesworth (b. 1631). English-born colonial American poet, minister, and physician; his poems served as theological guides to and confirmations of New England Puritan theology and dogma.

PUBLICATIONS

Colley Cibber, *The Careless Husband*—a major piece of comic drama by the English playwright, poet, and actor; focuses upon witty intrigues among the aristocracy, a subject common since the Restoration and the new sentimentalism; according to one critic, the play "helped to fix standards of gentility and politeness which were profoundly to influence comic writing throughout most of the eighteenth century."

Prosper Jolyot de Crebillon, *Idomenee* (Idomeneus)—the first dramatic tragedy by the French playwright, a popular success; concerns the king of Crete, an ally of the Greeks in the Trojan War; through a promise, he sacrifices his son to Poseidon; the Cretans expel him from his kingdom because of that act of inhumanity.

Bernard Mandeville, *The Grumbling Hive; or, Knaves Turned Honest*—a satire in octosyllabic verse by the Dutch-born satirist and physician; the predecessor to his more noted *Fable of the Bees* (1714).

Sir Richard Steele, *The Tender Husband*—an example of pure comedy by the English playwright and informal essayist; comic situations complement scenes of sentimental reconciliation; the piece was exceedingly successful on stage.

Christian Thomasius, *Fundamenta Juris Naturalis et Gentium*—a legal tract by the German rationalist philosopher and international jurist; denounces traditional pedantry and medieval legal terminology; argues for eradication of trial by witchcraft and torture.

1706

BIRTHS

Benjamin Franklin (d. 1790). American statesman, scientist, philosopher, and writer; he will rise to become the intellectual and cultural epitome of America; indeed, he will epitomize the late eighteenth-century Enlightenment.

DEATHS

Pierre Bayle (b. 1647). French philosopher and critic; wrote on behalf of religious toleration; became a skeptic and significantly influenced

the literature and philosophy of the coming age of Enlightenment.

Jam Durrak (b. 1650?). Iranian poet and founder of Baluchi lyric poetry; introduced art poetry into Baluchi literature, which had previously consisted only of folk ballads and romances.

John Evelyn (b. 1620). English diarist and writer upon a variety of scientific and humanistic subjects; he owes his literary reputation to his diary, which rivals and complements that of his contemporary, Samuel Pepys.

Ahmade Khani (b. 1650). Turkish (or Kurdish) poet who wrote in the Kurmanji dialect; spokesman for patriots, he wrote poetry to arouse the consciousness of his people; also attempted to provide artistic form to Kurdish folk literature.

PUBLICATIONS

Daniel Defoe, *The True Relation of the Apparition of One Mrs. Veal*—a vivid account of a current ghost story by the English writer.

George Farquhar, *The Recruiting Officer*—a comedy by the English playwright based upon his own experiences in Shrewsbury while serving with the English army; the piece became one of the stock comedies of the London theater during the eighteenth century; concerns the humorous aspects of military recruiting in a country town; "Captain Plume" makes love to the women of the town so that he can acquire their lovers as recruits; the vividness of the playwright's first-hand account more than compensates for the slight plot.

EVENTS

John Morphew, London bookseller, publishes the first evening newspaper in London, *The Evening Post. With the Historical Account;* until 1740.

1707

BIRTHS

George Louis Leclerc Buffon (d. 1788). French naturalist and historian of science; he will translate Newton and become one of the prominent philosophes; under his guidance, the Jardin du Roi will become a center of research during the Enlightenment.

Claude Prosper Jolyot de Crebillon (d. 1777). French novelist, playwright, and short story writer; son of Prosper Jolyot de Crebillon (1674-1762); his popular satirical fiction, focusing on the psychology of sexuality, will be the cause of his exile.

Henry Fielding (d. 1754). English novelist; he will write successful burlesques and parodies; in opposition to the conventional moral hero, he will develop the fictional model of the good natured man.

Carlo Goldoni (d. 1793). Italian playwright, librettist, and autobiographer; he will gain a reputation for introducing elements of realism and naturalism to the Italian stage, thus becoming known as the "Italian Moliere."

Moses Hayyim Luzzatto (d. 1747). Italian-born Jewish poet and playwright; he will be regarded by literary historians as the father of modern Hebrew literature; he will compose several poetic dramas that, although unadaptable to the stage, will be significant as literature.

DEATHS

George Farquhar (b. 1677). Irish-born playwright; certainly the most significant comic dramatist of the late seventeenth and early eighteenth centuries, principally because of his ability to inject variety and character into the form; he dies almost penniless.

Jean Mabillon (b. 1632). French Benedictine monk who edited the works of St. Bernard, Abbot of Clairvaux (1090-1153), wrote a history of the Benedictine order (1668-1702), and composed a number of important liturgical documents.

PUBLICATIONS

Prosper Jolyot de Crebillon, *Atree et Thyeste* (Atreus and Thyseus)—a dramatic tragedy by the French playwright; in another attempt to demonstrate the true sense of the tragic, the writer presents his characters as victims of a monstrous fate that blinds them and forces them toward the innocent commission of heinous acts.

George Farquhar, *The Beaux' Strategem*—perhaps the best of the Irish-born playwright's comedies, written two months before his death; the piece is set in Litchfield, a provincial English town, rather than in London; the characters possess youth and high spirits and give to the play a freshness never before seen on the London stage; emphasizes the concept of rational freedom.

Alain-Rene Lesage, *Crispin, Rival de Son Maitre* (Crispin, His Master's Rival)—a one-act comedy by the French novelist and playwright; a crafty valet passes himself off as his master in order to obtain a dowry; the writer's incisiveness and cynical tone give the piece originality.

——————, *Le Diable Boiteux* (The Devil upon Two Sticks)—a picaresque novel by the French writer, set in Spain but satirizing French customs; blends elements of supernaturalism and realism, satire and melodrama.

EVENTS

Edward Lhuyd, an eminent antiquary and linguist and a graduate of Jesus College, Oxford, publishes at Oxford his tract on the Celtic language, *Archaeologia Britannica*; contains eleven sections, including comparative etymology, vocabulary of the original languages of Britain and Ireland, an Irish-English dictionary, and a catalogue of Irish manuscripts.

1708

BIRTHS

Olaf von Dalin (d. 1763). Swedish historian, poet, and journalist; he will become the most significant figure of the Swedish Enlightenment; he will rely upon folk material in satirizing relationships between the Swedish people and their monarchs.

Albrecht von Haller (d. 1777). Swiss poet, anatomist, botanist, and physiologist; he will write three political romances, a number of scientific bibliographies, and poems that combine description, didacticism, and lyricism.

DEATHS

Petter Dass (b. 1648). Norwegian poet.

PUBLICATIONS

Prosper Jolyot de Crebillon, *Electra*—one of nine tragedies by the French playwright; highly melodramatic, this version of the classical Greek tragedy responds to the growing public taste for strong emotion by depicting horror and atrocity.

John Gay, *Wine*—a burlesque in verse by the English writer; denies that people who drink water can become successful writers.

Bernard Montfaucon, *Paleographica Graeca* (Greek Paleography)—another work by the French Benedictine monk, critic, and antiquary focusing upon Greco-Roman antiquity.

Jean Francois Regnard, *Le Legataire Universel* (The Residuary Legatee)—a verse comedy by the French playwright, written for the Comedie Francaise; focuses upon the theme of obtaining money by deceitful means.

Jonathan Swift, *An Argument* [against] . . . *the Abolishing of Christianity in England*—a prose pamphlet by the Irish-born satirist; an ironic piece directed against the Whigs and all those who favored the repeal of the Test Act of 1673, a statute intended to strengthen the Anglican establishment by requiring officeholders to sign an oath of allegiance; thus, "If Christianity were once abolished, how could the Free Thinkers, the Strong Reasoners, and the Men of profound Learning, be able to find another Subject so calculated in all Points whereupon to display their Abilities."

EVENTS

The Professorship of Poetry established at Oxford University.

1709

BIRTHS

John Cleland (d. 1789). English traveler, novelist, playwright, and philologist; he will gain literary notoriety for *Fanny Hill*, which will be considered an indecent novel; the work will earn a fortune for his publisher but almost nothing for him.

Charles Colle (d. 1783). French satirist and playwright.

Samuel Johnson (d. 1784) English lexicographer, poet, essayist, and editor; he will become the most significant intellectual figure of eighteenth-century London, gathering about him the principal wits and literati of his day; the mid-eighteenth century in England will be known as "the Age of Johnson."

Julien Offray de La Mettrie (d. 1751). French philosopher; his work on materialism will cause political controversy, forcing him to take refuge in Leyden and Berlin.

DEATHS

Jean Francois Regnard (b. 1655). French comic dramatist; he wrote successful plays for the Theatre Francaise; his death was caused by a dose of horse medicine that he drank to ease a case of indigestion.

Abraham a Sancta Clara (b. 1644). Austrian satirist and pulpit orator who spent most of his life in Vienna.

PUBLICATIONS

George Berkeley, *Essay towards a New Theory of Vision*—a prose tract by the Irish churchman and philosopher explicating his early system of philosophy; concerns the independence of the ideas derived from sight and from feeling (or the senses) and their arbitrary connection that, nonetheless, remains constant.

Alexander Pope, *Pastorals*—a group of poems by the English writer, composed sometime during his youth; the poet's interest focuses more upon form and technique than upon substance, thus yielding four graceful pieces in the Virgilian manner representing the notion that the aim of the poet should be "correctness."

Jonathan Swift, "A Description of a City Shower"—a poem by the Irish-born satirist and churchman, who at the time thought it was the best piece he had written; illustrates well his ability to use poetry to shock his readers into seeing the real world in which they live:

> Now from all Parts the swelling Kennels flow,
> And bear their Trophies with them as they go:
> Filths of all Hues and Odors seem to tell,

What Streets they sail'd from, by the Sight and Smell.

—————, **"A Description of the Morning"**—a companion piece to "A Description of a City Shower," written six months earlier; again, the poet directs the reader to the less attractive aspects of daily life: "Now Betty from her Master's Bed had flown, / And softly stole to discompose her own."

EVENTS

The English Parliament passes the Copyright Act of 1709: "An Act for the encouragement of Learning, by vesting the copies of printed books in the authors or purchasers of such copies during the times therein mentioned" (fourteen years for books not yet published, twenty-one years for books already in print).

Nicholas Rowe, playwright, poet, and first editor and authoritative biographer of William Shakespeare, publishes the first edition of Shakespeare's works; contains criticism and illustrations; published in six octavo volumes; second edition in 1714.

Richard Steele begins publication of *The Tatler,* a thrice-weekly literary paper; the author assumed the character of "Isaac Bickerstaffe"; Joseph Addison, Jonathan Swift, and Alexander Pope are among the principal contributors; until January 1711, when Addison and Steele begin *The Spectator.*

1710

PUBLICATIONS

George Berkeley, *Of the Principles of Human Knowledge*—a prose tract by the Irish churchman and philosopher; sets forth the notion that all objects capable of being discerned by the senses exist as natural and real, as distinct from being perceived by the human understanding.

Gottfried Wilhelm Leibnitz, *Theodicee*—a prose piece by the German philosopher and mathematician, written to gain both popular and princely favor; contends that God created the best of all possible worlds; Francois Marie Voltaire satirized the German writer's optimism in his philosophical tale *Candide* (1759).

Alain Rene Le Sage, *Turcaret; ou, Le Financier* (Turcaret; or, The Financer)—a comedy by the French novelist and playwright; depicts the comic spirit at the end of the reign of Louis XIV (1638-1715; 1661-1715); "joyous theatricalism" that serves as a vehicle for the playwright's sharp and cynical social satire.

Cotton Mather, *Bonifacius; or, Essays To Do Good*— a prose collection by the colonial American divine and philosopher; moral and "homespun" lessons in simple expository prose; Benjamin Franklin was impressed by the work.

Jonathan Swift, *Journal to Stella*—a series of letters by the Irish-born churchman and satirist to Esther Johnson and her friend Rebecca Dingley; written between 1710 and 1713 (published in 1766, 1768, and 1948); recounts the details of the writer's daily activities in London, particularly his associations with Tory ministers.

EVENTS

Henry St. John, Viscount Bolingbroke, English philosopher and political essayist, begins publication of *The Examiner*, a Tory periodical later under the control of Jonathan Swift; politically antagonistic toward Richard Steele's *Guardian* and Joseph Addison's *Whig Examiner*; to 1711.

Joseph Addison begins his literary and political periodical, *The Whig Examiner*; publishes only five numbers between September and October.

1711

BIRTHS

David Hume (d. 1776). Scottish philosopher and historian; he will become the most noted British empiricist; he will substantiate the empiricism of John Locke and George Berkeley.

DEATHS

Mian Abdul-Hassan (b. ?). Religious poet who resided in the northwest of India and wrote in the Sindhi language; he wrote the first religious treatise in Sindhi verse, which discussed 130 questions of ritual practice in Islam.

Nicolas Boileau-Despreaux (b. 1636). French critical writer; wrote several critical dissertations, a collection of epigrams, a translation of Longinus, and a series of letters; he exerted his greatest influence through his criticism.

PUBLICATIONS

Prosper Jolyot de Crebillon, *Rhadamiste et Zenobie* (Rhadamisthus and Zenobia)—a dramatic tragedy by the French playwright; a reaction against the gallantry of contemporary tragedies, the piece contains horror, crime, and violence.

Alexander Pope, *Essay on Criticism*—an anonymously published work in heroic couplets, written when the poet was twenty-one; sets forth rules of critical and poetic taste; critics must be guided by the ancients, and those who are not are ridiculed by the poet.

Anthony Ashley Cooper, third Earl of Shaftesbury, *Characteristics of Men, Manners, Opinions, Times*—a prose collection by the English essayist and philosopher; contains his most important prose pieces—"Inquiry Concerning Virtue" (1698), "Letter Concerning Enthusiasm" (1708), "Sensus Communis: An Essay on the Freedom of Wit and Humour" (1709), "Moralists" (1709), and "Soliloquy, or Advice to an Author" (1710)—and a number of miscellaneous reflections; revised in 1713.

Jonathan Swift, *The Conduct of the Allies*—a political pamphlet by the Irish-born prose satirist; an extremely popular work, it went into six editions and sold 11,000 copies within two months; an appeal for an end to the War of the Spanish Succession: ". . . what have we been Fighting for all this while? The Answer is ready; We have been Fighting for the Ruin of the Publick Interest, and the Advancement of a Private."

EVENTS

Richard Steele and Joseph Addison begin writing and editing *The Spectator,* the most noted eighteenth-century English literary periodical; it appears daily, with Addison and Steele as the principal contributors; other writers include Alexander Pope, Thomas Tickell, Eustace Budgell, Ambrose Philips, and Laurence

Eusden; the essays, principally concerned with manners, morals, and literature, attempted to "enliven morality with wit, and to temper wit with morality"; from March 1711 to December 1712; revived briefly by Addison in 1714.

1712

BIRTHS

Jean-Jacques Rousseau (d. 1778). Swiss-born French philosopher, educationist, and essayist; he will eventually conceive of the idea of man as a freeborn creature who exists everywhere in chains; that notion gives birth to his insistence, which planted the seeds of the French Revolution, that humankind must be forced into freedom; his ideas will influence such German philosophers as Immanuel Kant and Georg Friedrich Hegel.

DEATHS

Yusuf Nabi (b. 1642). Turkish poet and court scribe; he relied upon proverbs to reach his readers; also wrote poems celebrating Turkish military victories.

PUBLICATIONS

Pierre Carlet de Marivaux, *Le Pere Prudent et Equitable* (The Fair and Wise Father)—the first publication of the French playwright and novelist and his earliest creative effort; a one-act comedy written between 1709 and 1711.

Alexander Pope, *The Rape of the Lock*—a satire by the English poet; two cantos published this year and an enlarged five-canto version in 1714; supplies an unforgettable picture of Augustan high life set against heroic backgrounds worthy of Homer, Virgil, and John Milton; the mock epic proceeds upon the simple theme of the opening lines: "What dire offense from amorous causes springs, / What mighty contests rise from trivial things."

—————, **"The Messiah"**—a sacred eclogue by the English poet, published in Joseph Addison and Richard Steele's *The Spectator;* the piece embodies in verse the Messianic prophecies of Isaiah:

The seas shall waste, the skies in smoke
decay
Rocks fall to dust, and mountains melt
away;
But fixed his word, his saving power remains;
Thy realm for ever lasts, thy own Messiah
reigns!

EVENTS

**Academie des Sciences, Belles Lettres, et
Arts** founded at Bourdeaux, France.

Biblioteca Nacional, established at Madrid,
Spain.

The English Parliament passes the first Stamp
Act on newspapers and pamphlets; the
shrewd English printers find loopholes in the
Act and enjoy immunity from the tax for the
next thirteen years (until the Stamp Act of
1725).

1713

BIRTHS

Denis Diderot (d. 1784). French writer and encyclopaedist; he will enlist nearly all of the
important French writers of the day for his
gigantic encyclopaedic project, a scholarly instrument compiled on behalf of the French
philosophes; he will also write dramas, novels,
and satirical and philosophic prose tracts.

Laurence Sterne (d. 1768). English novelist; he
will make a significant contribution to the development of the English novel, widening its
scope and loosening its structure.

DEATHS

Archil (b. 1647). Georgian-Russian king and
poet; objected to the reliance upon Persian
poetic models; promoted the ideal of the
Georgian nobleman: physical valor combined
with cultivated learning.

Anthony Ashley Cooper, third Earl of Shaftesbury (b. 1671). English philosopher; attacked
by his contemporaries for being a deist; believed that man possessed a moral sense and

that everything in the world existed in its best
possible state.

Alauddin Sabit (b. 1650?). Yugoslavian-born
Turkish poet; wrote short, humorous pieces,
in addition to a number of so-called immoral
verse narratives; he achieved humorous and
sometimes absurd effects by misusing well-
known proverbs.

PUBLICATIONS

Joseph Addison, *Cato*—a dramatic tragedy by
the English essayist, poet, and playwright;
concerns the last phase of the life of the republican Marcus Porcius Cato, who was besieged in Utica by Caesar in 46 B.C.; betrayal,
love, and a rivalry resolved by death follow;
the piece was immediately popular because
Cato's last stand for liberty paralleled the failing health of England's Queen Anne and the
question of royal succession.

John Gay, *Rural Sports*—a poem by the English
writer, modeled after Alexander Pope's *Windsor Forest*; appeared in Sir Richard Steele's
Guardian; strictly follows the georgic form.

Alexander Pope, *Ode for Music on St. Cecelia's Day*—one of the English Augustan poet's few attempts at lyric poetry.

———————— , *Windsor Forest*—a pastoral poem
that combines descriptions of the English
countryside and field sports with historical,
literary, and political references; celebrates
the Treaty of Utrecht and the end of the War
of the Spanish Succession (1702-1713).

Abbe Charles Irenee Castel Saint Pierre,
Projet pour la Paix Perpetuelle (A Plan for
Perpetual Peace)—a tract by the French
writer, especially optimistic in tone and substance toward a new age; proposes a project
for peace and morality through legislation;
combines reforms for everyone and everything with the idea of the grandest pleasures
for the largest numbers, as long as rich men
invest their wealth in productive industry.

Jonathan Swift, *Cadenus and Vanessa*—a poem
by the Irish-born satirist, essayist, and churchman, written for Esther Vanhomrigh (Vanessa) and published after her death; a narrative of the poet's relationship with Vanessa
and an apology for his conduct toward her;
mock-classical in form.

**Anne Finch, Countess of Winchelsea, "To the
Nightengale"**—a poem by the English writer,
in octosyllables; transcends the bounds of sim-

ple and direct description and achieves legitimate poetic image: "And still the unhappy poet's breast, / Like thine, when best he sings, is placed / against a thorn."

EVENTS

Roger Cotes, English mathematician, Plumian Professor of Astronomy and Natural Philosophy at Cambridge, and a Fellow of the Royal Society, revises Sir Isaac Newton's *Principia* for a second edition.

Sir Richard Steele begins *The Guardian*, publishing from March through October; contributors include Joseph Addison, George Berkeley, Alexander Pope, and John Gay; succeeded by *The Englishman* (to 1714), which was more political in content.

Alexander Pope, Jonathan Swift, John Gay, Thomas Parnell, William Congreve, and Francis Atterbury are among the founding members of the Martinus Scriblerus Club, a London literary group that set out to ridicule false taste in learning.

Daniel Defoe founds his London trade journal, *The Mercatur; or, Commerce Retrieved*; to 1714.

1714

BIRTHS

Emmerich de Vattel (d. 1767). Swiss jurist and essayist; he will attempt to demonstrate the relationship between natural law and politics.

DEATHS

Benjamin Tompson (b. 1642). Boston physician and teacher; known as the first native-born colonial American poet; his work generally combined satire and historical narrative.

PUBLICATIONS

John Gay, *The Shepherd's Week*—a series of six pastoral poems by the English playwright and versifier; he presents shepherds and milkmaids not in their usual classical pastoral settings, but against a background of grotesque reality.

Gottfried Wilhelm Leibnitz, *Monodalogie*—a tract by the German philosopher and mathematician, one of the principal philosophical instruments of the German Enlightenment; uses his philosophical theories to support the claim that a divine plan made this world the best of all possible planets in the universe.

Bernard Mandeville, *The Fable of the Bees; or, Private Vices, Publick Benefits*—a verse satire, with prose commentary, by the Dutch-born English physician and satirist; designed to illustrate the essential vileness of human nature.

Sir Richard Steele, *The Crisis*—a political pamphlet by the English essayist and playwright; promoted the Hanoverian succession to the English throne and prompts an answer by Jonathan Swift (see below); led to the writer's expulsion from Parliament.

Jonathan Swift, *The Public Spirit of the Whigs*—a political tract by the Irish writer and cleric; written to counter the idea of a Hanoverian succession as set forth in Sir Richard Steele's *The Crisis* (see above).

EVENTS

Joseph Addison, without Richard Steele, revives *The Spectator*, which has not been published since December 1712; it proves to be inferior in literary quality to its predecessor.

Sir Richard Steele begins writing and publishing *The Lover*, a literary periodical intended to counter Joseph Addison's revived *Spectator*.

1715

BIRTHS

Etienne Bonnot de Mably de Condillac (d. 1780). French philosopher; he will found the school of Sensationalism and promote the idea that all knowledge should be based upon the senses.

Christian Furchtegott Gellert (d. 1769). German poet and moralist; he will become a prolific writer of stories and fables and be decidedly influenced by the English novelist Samuel Richardson.

Claude Adrien Helvetius (d. 1771). French philosopher; he will become one of the Encyclopaedists and associate with the foremost French philosophers of his day.

Ewald Christian von Kleist (d. 1759). German poet; he will write idylls, moral treatises, and a military romance.

DEATHS

Francois de Salignac de la Mothe Fenelon (b. 1651). French writer and churchman who spoke for orthodoxy.

Nicolas Malebranche (b. 1638). French philosopher; combined psychological investigation with mystic idealism.

PUBLICATIONS

Joseph Addison, *The Drummer*—a comic play by the English essayist, poet, and playwright; the main character, Sir Joseph Truman, who has supposedly been killed at war, returns home unexpectedly after a year of captivity; he rousts the suitors of Lady Truman, one of whom has disguised himself as a ghostly drummer to advance his amorous cause; succeeds more for its literary merit is than for its theatrical effects.

John Gay, *What D'Ye Call It*—a satirical farce by the English playwright and poet; a total mockery of sentimentality, both on the stage and in life.

Alaine Rene Le Sage, *L'Histoire de Gil Blas de Santillana* (Gil Blas)—a picaresque novel by the French writer; four volumes to 1735; a rambling romance, unusual for its realism and attention to detail; it will have a major influence upon the realistic novels of the late eighteenth and early nineteenth centuries.

EVENTS

Joseph Addison begins his political periodical, *The Freeholder*; to 1716.

Alexander Pope publishes the first volume of his translation of Homer's *Iliad*; in heroic couplets; to 1720.

Nicholas Rowe, dramatist and poet, appointed Poet Laureate of England, succeeding Nahum Tate; to 1718.

1716

BIRTHS

Jean-Jacques Barthelemy (d. 1795). French cleric and antiquarian writer; he will achieve some degree of literary recognition for his reconstructions of ancient travel narratives.

Thomas Gray (d. 1771). English poet; for his odes, he will be recognized as one of the most significant poets of eighteenth-century England and a precursor of nineteenth-century Romanticism.

Ts'ao Chan (d. 1764). Chinese novelist.

DEATHS

Gottfried Wilhelm Leibnitz (b. 1646). German philosopher and mathematician, one of the finest intellects of the Western world; conceived of a universal linguistic calculus incorporating all existing knowledge, which would render argument obsolete and replace it by a process of calculation.

William Wycherley (b. 1641). English dramatist; a major force in the comic drama of the Restoration and perhaps the most dexterous playwright of that age.

PUBLICATIONS

John Gay, *Trivia; or, The Art of Walking the Streets of London*—a poem in three books by the English writer; the poet guides his reader through the streets of London by day and by night, providing instruction upon the most trivial details, such as clothing and the weather; the reader confronts a host of characters: ballad-singers, chairmen, footmen, bullies, criminals, etc.; an important and convenient source of information on the life and customs of eighteenth-century London.

Arai Hakuseki, *Ori-Taku-Shiba*—the Japanese writer's autobiography.

EVENTS

Diario di Roma, the first newspaper in Italy, begins publication in Rome.

Fenix Renascida, an anthology of Portuguese poetry, published in Lisbon.

Mercurius Politicus, a monthly political periodical, begins publication in London; until 1720.

1717

BIRTHS

Horace Walpole (d. 1797). English writer and bibliophile; his literary reputation will come to rest principally upon his correspondence, which includes discussions of politics, foreign affairs, literature, and art, as well as outright gossip.

Johann Joachim Winckelmann (d. 1768). German archaeologist and essayist; he will write treatises on ancient art and architecture and will be appointed librarian to a cardinal at Rome.

PUBLICATIONS

Henry St. John, Viscount Bolingbroke, *A Letter to Sir William Windham*—the first important contribution to political literature by the English writer and philosopher; an attempt to vindicate his conduct during the period 1710-1715 and to persuade Tories to renounce all attempts at Jacobite restoration; provides details of the disastrous Jacobite uprising of 1715; written in 1717, but not published until 1753.

Alexander Pope, *Eloisa to Abelard*—poem by the Augustan satirist demonstrating a type of Shakespearean dramatic power; the heroine is an intellectual woman in love with the absent Abelard; Abelard has been cruelly mutilated, while Eloisa, a nun, has pledged to forget the world.

————, *Elegy to the Memory of an Unfortunate Lady*—a poem constructed upon three distinct elements: the writer's own inadequacies as a cripple, the longings of hopeless love, and the deceptions arising from love.

EVENTS

John Baskett, Oxford printer and bookseller, publishes a magnificent edition of the Holy Bible; printed in large type with beautiful engravings and artistic initial letters; unfortunately, the work contains a host of typographical errors and thus is called "a Baskett-ful of Errors"; also known as the "Vinegar Bible," from the misprint "The parable of the vinegar" (for "vineyard").

1718

BIRTHS

Maria Gaetana Agnesi (d. 1799). Italian linguist, philosopher, mathematician, and theologian; she will become professor of mathematics at Bologna.

DEATHS

Gian Vincenzo Gravina (b. 1664). Italian jurist and writer on jurisprudence; appointed professor of civil and canon law at Rome and a founder of the Arcadian Academy.

PUBLICATIONS

Matthew Prior, *Alma; or, The Progress of the Mind*—a dialogue by the English poet; three cantos, in the meter and style of Samuel Butler's *Hudibras* (1663-1678); based upon the theme of the progress of the soul upward, from the legs in childhood to the head in maturity; the poet also addresses the issue of the vanity of worldly concerns.

————, *Solomon on the Vanity of the World*—a long soliloquy by the English poet, in three books and heroic couplets; he again takes up the theme of the vanity of worldly concerns.

Francois Marie Voltaire, *Oedipe*—a dramatic tragedy by the French philosopher, playwright, novelist, and poet, composed during his eleven months' imprisonment in the Bastille; follows closely the original classical version.

EVENTS

The Accademia de Scienze, Lettre, ed Arti founded at Palermo, Italy.

Laurence Eusden appointed Poet Laureate of England, succeeding Nicholas Rowe; to 1730; Alexander Pope reacted with, "Know, Eusden thirsts no more for sack or praise, / He sleeps among the dull of ancient days"; the classical translator Thomas Cooke later commented, "Eusden, a Lawrel'd Bard, by Fortune rais'd, / By very few been read, by fewer prais'd. . . . "

The Leeds Mercury begins publication; contains news and editorial matter gleaned from London newspapers.

Philibert-Joseph Le Roux publishes his *Dictionnaire Comique, Satyrique, Critique, Burlesque, Libre, et Proverbial*; a survey of comic literature.

Cotton Mather publishes his *Psalterium Americanum. The Book of Psalms in a Translation Exactly Conformed unto the Original, but in Blank Verse*; the New England divine wishes to provide the churches of the American colonies with a Psalm version free "of the human frailty that found delight in jingling rhymes".

Lady Mary Wortley Montagu, English writer, publishes her *Innoculation against Smallpox,* reporting upon a workable method for treatment and prevention which she learned from the Turks during her visit to Constantinople.

The Society of Antiquaries reestablished in London; the original institution, dating from 1572, had been suppressed by James I at the outset of his reign (1685).

1719

BIRTHS

Johann Wilhelm Ludwig Gleim (d. 1803). German poet; his literary reputation will rest on the war poems he wrote during the age of Frederick the Great (1740-1786).

Michel Jean Sedaine (d. 1797). French playwright and poet; his plays will conform to the requirement of Denis Diderot's theory of drama: simple plot, imminent catastrophe resolved by an act of virtue, and silent tableaus.

DEATHS

Joseph Addison (b. 1672). English essayist, playwright, and poet; in terms of the informal or light essay, he had no equal; rather than attempting to be profound, he cast his pen in the direction of sobriety and good sense, with a prose style reflecting the grace and subtlety of his humor; his death was caused by dropsic asthma.

PUBLICATIONS

Daniel Defoe, *The Life and Adventures of Robinson Crusoe*—a novel by the English writer, based upon the actual experiences of a Scottish sailor, Alexander Selkirk, who was stranded upon the island of Juan Fernandez in 1704 and who survived a solitary life for four years and four months; Crusoe undergoes a psychological experience as Defoe probes the issue of humankind's ability to confront nature; Crusoe represents the triumph of early eighteenth-century mercantilism over the economic primitivism of former ages.

Ludvig Holberg, *Peder Paars*—a mock-epic poem by the Danish poet, playwright, and philosopher; he ridicules the pedantic stiffness and stupidity of contemporary life and thought; written under the pseudonym "Hans Mikkelsen"; to 1720.

Edward Young, *Busiris, King of Egypt*—a play by the English poet, a verse tragedy of violence and ungoverned passion.

——————— , *A Paraphrase on a Part of the Book of Job*—an attempt by the English poet to filter the Book of Job through his own poetic imagination; the result may be best observed in these lines by Walter Savage Landor:

> *A Paraphrase on Job we see*
> *By Young: it loads the shelf:*
> *He who can read one half must be*
> *Patient as Job himself.*

EVENTS

Andrew Bradford founds at Philadelphia *The American Weekly Mercury,* a newspaper heavily dependent upon extracts from English periodicals; Benjamin Franklin is a principal contributor; to 1746.

James Franklin begins publication of *The Boston Gazette,* the second newspaper in the American colonies; supported by the conservatives in New England, principally Cotton and Increase Mather; James Franklin will leave the paper in 1721; until 1741.

1720

BIRTHS

Charles Bonnet (d. 1793). Swiss philosopher and naturalist; his failing eyesight will force him to abandon his scientific research and focus upon philosophy; he will become critical of vitalistic theories and challenge the notion that the nonexistence of the soul can never be proved.

Carlo Gozzi (d. 1806). Italian playwright; he will write popular comedies and dramatic fairy tales and found what has come to be known as the "theater of the fabulous."

DEATHS

Abdulqadir Khan Khatak (b. 1650). Afghan poet and translator; he gained a reputation for translating literary works from Persian into his native Pashto.

Abdurrahman Mohmand (b. 1650?). Afghan religious poet; his poetry reflected his piety and love of God; he rose to become the most popular of the poets writing in his native Pashto.

PUBLICATIONS

Daniel Defoe, *The Adventures of Captain Singleton*—a novel by the English writer; concerns an adventurer who has been at sea from infancy and who possesses no sense of virtue or religion; dissolute, he engages in mutiny and piracy; he ultimately achieves wealth and marries the sister of a shipmate.

——————, *Memoirs of a Cavalier*—an English novel that introduces the writer's only gentleman-hero, Col. Andrew Newport; focuses upon Newport's adventures during the Thirty Years' War at Vienna, Magdeburg, and Lutzen; then moves on to the Bishops' War in Scotland and the English civil war, particularly the battles at Edgehill and Naseby.

Monzaemon Chikamatsu, *Shinju Ten no Amijimi* (The Love Suicides at Amijimi)—the most noted of the Japanese playwright's domestic tragedies, originally performed in the puppet theater at Osaka; centers on the fatal infatuation of two lovers; a weak-willed hero sacrifices his wife and family to his love of a courtesan; the heroine appears more courageous and determined to die than does her male companion, which heightens the final, ceremonious death scene in an isolated spot in the countryside.

Pierre Carlet de Marivaux, *Arlequin Poli par l'Amour* (Harlequin Refined by Love)—a dramatic comedy about love by the French playwright; derived from the Italian *commedia dell' arte,* in which comedy is improvised rather than written into the dialogue.

Bernard de Montfaucon, *L'Antiquite Explique et Representee en Figures*—the most important treatise by the celebrated French critic and antiquary; explains and describes the significant monuments of the classical world; ten volumes, containing over nine hundred plates; to 1724.

EVENTS

A German religious sect known as the Dunkers established the Ephrata Cloister near Philadelphia; women members copy and illuminate the society's hymnbooks; in 1730, Benjamin Franklin will publish the first Ephrata hymnal.

1721

BIRTHS

William Collins (d. 1759). English poet noted for his odes; his "Ode on the Superstitions of the Highlands" will foreshadow English Romanticism of the early nineteenth century.

Tobias George Smollett (d. 1771). Scottish-born novelist; his adventurous narratives will provide the eighteenth-century reader with a welcome break from the social novels of the times.

DEATHS

Abdulqadir Bedil (b. 1644). Persian-born Indian poet and philosopher; his collected works number sixteen volumes and contain some 147,000 lines of poetry; he had an enormous influence on the development of poetry in Afghanistan and the Central Asian Soviet Republics.

Matthew Prior (b. 1664). English poet and diplomat; carved himself a niche in English literary history with his light, occasional verses, and charming poetic addresses to the children of nobility.

PUBLICATIONS

Monzaemon Chikamatsu, *Onnagoroshi Abura Jigoku* (The Woman Killer and the Hell of Oil)—one of several "love-suicide" plays by the Japanese dramatist; a domestic drama of exceptional power and trauma; especially notable for the writer's skill at suggesting the bustle of crowds in the early scenes.

Cotton Mather, *The Christian Philosopher*—a prose tract by the New England divine; delineates the arguments for Christianity to be found in the natural world.

Charles Montesquieu, *Lettres Persanes* (Persian Letters)—a work of fiction by the French philosopher and jurist, his first literary success; two Persian visitors to Paris satirize French society; from the capital they proceed through the rest of the country.

Edward Young, *The Revenge, a Tragedy*—a drama by the English poet fashioned after Shakespeare's *Othello*; a prisoner devises revenge upon his captor, who has humiliated him; the captor, his wife, and his friend all meet untimely ends.

EVENTS

James Franklin, Boston printer, begins publication of *The New England Courant,* a combination newspaper and literary journal; attempts to be entertaining, amusing, and instructive; Benjamin Franklin anonymously contributes his first literary efforts to his brother's paper; until 1726.

Benjamin Franklin and the Scottish-born physician William Douglass form a literary circle and contribute to James Franklin's Boston periodical, *The New England Courant*; Cotton and Increase Mather label the group the "Hell-Fire Club," comparing it to reactionary London social and political clubs, although the Franklins and Dr. Douglass oppose radical points of view.

Johann Theodor Jablonski, of Danzig, publishes his *Allgemeines Lexikon,* the first short encyclopaedia.

1722

BIRTHS

Christopher Smart (d. 1771). English poet; his satiric, irreverent works will evidence a strong wit; his eccentric behavior and periods of insanity will detract from his literary reputation.

Joseph Warton (d. 1800). English poet and essayist; he will gain more recognition for his translations of the classics and his critical essays on poetry than for his own verse.

PUBLICATIONS

Daniel Defoe, *The History and Remarkable Life of the Truly Honourable Col. Jacque, Commonly Call'd Col. Jack*—a novel of adventure by the English writer in which he incorporates a number of his ideas upon human nature and society; the hero, though born a gentleman, was apprenticed to a pickpocket and spent twenty-six years as a thief; eventually kidnapped and taken to Virginia, the title character acquires knowledge not through academic learning but through experiencing the world; in the end, on the battlefield, he learns about the most important aspect of human existence: moral courage.

——————— , *The Fortunes and Misfortunes of the Famous Moll Flanders*—a novel by the English writer, supposedly written from the title character's own memoirs; Moll, born in Newgate Prison, spends the first sixty years of her life as a social undesirable; she has a variety of husbands and spends twelve years as a prostitute, twelve years as a thief, and eight years as a transported felon in Virginia; finally she gains wealth and position and atones for her past; Moll travels the only road open to her in a society that permits children to be born in prison.

——————, *A Journal of the Plague Year*—another work of fiction by the English writer, although factual in many details; the narrative of a "resident" of London during the Great Plague of 1664-1665, graphically describing the spread of the disease and the terror of the city's inhabitants.

Sir Richard Steele, *The Conscious Lovers*—a dramatic comedy by the English essayist and playwright, his last play and certainly his most popular piece for the stage; presents the writer's view on dueling and the "proper" attitude of men toward women; a young heir foresakes his intended (and wealthy) bride for a destitute orphan, who turns out to be her long lost sister.

EVENTS

The English Parliament forbids journalists to report parliamentary debates.

Thomas Guy, bookseller in London and Oxford, purchases land opposite St. Thomas Hospital, London; he then subscribes £300,000 for the founding of a new institution to be known as Guy's Hospital.

French painter Hyacinthe Rigaud publishes his *Grand Tour,* a handbook for travelers.

1723

BIRTHS

Sir William Blackstone (d. 1780). English jurist and commentator on the law; he will write the most influential exposition of English law in point of style and accuracy.

Paul Heinrich Dietrich d'Holbach (d. 1789). German-born French philosopher; he will advance the notion that self-interest is the principal motivation of all human beings.

Sir Joshua Reynolds (d. 1792). English portrait painter, essayist, and critic; he will become the first president of the Royal Academy; his cultivated literary style will be matched by the high quality of his art.

DEATHS

Claude Fleury (b. 1640). French church historian; his lifelong project on ecclesiastical history, although incomplete at his death, constitutes the first comprehensive work of its type and scope.

Johann Christian Gunther (b. 1695). Silesian-born German poet; wrote love lyrics known for their sensitivity.

Increase Mather (b. 1639). English-born American divine; published no less than 136 works, including a statement on miracles and a history of the Indian wars.

PUBLICATIONS

Ludovico Antonio Muratori, *Rerum Italicarum Scriptores*—a collection of medieval Italian historical material by the Italian librarian and archivist; 28 volumes to 1751.

Matthew Prior, *Down-Hall, a Ballad*—a poem by the English diplomat and verse writer; a lively account of a journey to Essex:

> But I sing Exploits, that have lately been
> done
> By Two British Heroes, call'd Matthew
> and John:
> And how they rid Friendly from fine
> London-Towne,
> Fair Essex to see, and a Place they call
> DOWN.

Francois Marie Voltaire, *La Henriade*—an epic poem by the French satirist, novelist, and historian; focuses upon the career of Henry IV (1553-1610), King of France and Navarre; the authorities refused to sanction publication of the poem because the writer promoted Protestantism and religious toleration; thus, the poem was surreptitiously printed at Rouen and smuggled into Paris under the title *La Ligue; ou, Henry le Grand.*

EVENTS

T'u Shu Chi Ch'eng published; a Chinese encyclopaedia, amply illustrated, consisting of 1628 volumes of approximately 200 pages each.

1724

BIRTHS

Immanuel Kant (d. 1804). German philosopher; he will be regarded as the most significant contributor to philosophical idealism; his philosophical inquiries will remain of permanent interest, especially his treatment of questions relating to God, freedom, and immortality.

Friedrich Gottlieb Klopstock (d. 1803). German religious poet; he will write patriotic odes and religious epics.

DEATHS

Glueckel of Hameln (b. 1646). German-born Jewish writer; she composed seven books of memoirs in Yiddish.

PUBLICATIONS

Daniel Defoe, *Roxana; or, The Unfortunate Mistress*—a work of fiction by the English writer, purportedly the autobiography of Mlle. Beleau, the beautiful daughter of French Protestant refugees; coming to England, she marries a London brewer, then dissipates his property and leaves him and their five children; after a life of wickedness and travel, she remarries; she ends her days in debtors prison, filled with remorse.

——————, *A Tour through the Whole Island of Great Britain*—a prose narrative by the English writer, perhaps one of the most accurate descriptions of Great Britain during the early eighteenth century; the work shows the writer's talent for acute observation, and it served as a model of travel literature for his contemporaries; three volumes to 1726.

Bernard le Bovyer de Fontenelle, *De l'Origine des Fables* (The Origin of Myths)—a critical essay and historical study by the French writer; he explores the psychological and intellectual origins of mythology; refutes superstitions and other popular beliefs.

Cotton Mather, *Parentator*—a biography by the New England divine of his father, Increase Mather, who was known for his association with Harvard College, his participation in the Salem witchcraft trials, and his sermons and religious prose tracts.

Jonathan Swift, *The Drapier's Letters*—a series of four epistolary essays by the Irish satirist and cleric; a response to a patent granted to the Duchess of Kendal for supplying copper coins

for circulation in Ireland; the writer assumes the persona of a Dublin draper who prophesies ruin for Ireland if the coins circulate; as a result, the English abandon the scheme.

EVENTS

Thomas Longman purchases, from the estate of William Taylor, a bookselling business at the Ship and Black Swan, Paternoster Row, London; thus begins the history of one of the most noted publishing firms in England: Longmans, Green and Company.

Oxford and Cambridge Universities both establish chairs in modern history and languages.

1725

BIRTHS

Giovanni Jacopo Casanova (d. 1798). Italian adventurer and rogue; his memoirs will not be published until forty years after his death.

DEATHS

Monzaemon Chikamatsu (b. 1653). Japanese playwright who flourished after the creative period of the "noh" plays, three centuries earlier; his literary style has been described as an extraordinary combination of sensationalism and sophistication; still recognized as one of the world's leading dramatists.

Florent Carton Dancourt (b. 1661). French dramatist, actor, and court favorite; he depicted the stupidity of the peasants and the follies of the bourgeoisie.

Arai Hakuseki (b. 1675). Japanese essayist and historian, prominent among the prose writers of the nation's so-called modern era.

Sulkhan Saba (b. 1685). Georgian Russian writer and diplomat; a prominent lexicographer, travel writer, and compiler of fables and moral exhortations from both Oriental and European sources.

PUBLICATIONS

Benjamin Franklin, *A Dissertation upon Liberty and Necessity, Pleasure and Pain*—a pamphlet by the then nineteen-year-old American printer, written while working in a London printing house; intended as a refutation of an optimistic religious tract by William Wollaston (1659-1724), *Religion in Nature* (1724); according to Alexander Pope, the young American set out to prove that whatever exists is right; the writer burned all but three or four copies, proving, perhaps, the theology would not become his principal concern.

Giovanni Battista Vico, *Principi di Una Scienza Nuova d' Intorno alla Commune* (Principles of the New Science)—a tract by the Italian philosopher in which he attempts to discover and organize laws common to the evolution of all societies; argues that the historical method is no less exact than the scientific; postulates evolutionary cycles in civilization corresponding to mental development.

Edward Young, *The Universal Passion; or, The Love of Fame*—a series of satires by the English poet and cleric; witty and brilliant, they were very popular until they were eclipsed by the satiric poems of Alexander Pope: "Why slumbers Pope, who leads the tuneful Train, / Now hears that Virtue, which he loves, complain?"

EVENTS

Nathaniel Ames begins compiling at Boston his *Astronomical Diary and Almanack;* it will achieve a circulation of 60,000 copies and will serve as one of the models for Benjamin Franklin's *Poor Richard's Almanack;* until 1764.

William Bradford, Philadelphia and New York printer, begins publication of *The New York Gazette*; the first newspaper in New York City; contains current events; until 1744.

Alexander Pope publishes his edition of Shakespeare, which will lead to a confrontation with Lewis Theobald, the "hero" of Pope's *Dunciad* of 1728; Pope also publishes his translation of Homer's *Odyssey* (to 1726), which will be financially lucrative.

The correspondence of Marie de Rabutin-Chantal, Madame de Sevigne, published; the letters, written to her daughter beginning in 1671, describe in detail the life at court in Paris.

1726

BIRTHS

Louise Florence d'Epinay (d. 1783). French writer; she will write essays, memoirs, and correspondence, but will be known more for her association with Jean-Jacques Rousseau.

DEATHS

Sir John Vanbrugh (b. 1664). English playwright and architect; his plays were a significant contribution to the Restoration comedy of manners; he also gained a considerable reputation for designing and constructing immense baroque structures, including Castle Howard and Blenheim Palace.

PUBLICATIONS

Cotton Mather, *Manuductio ad Ministerium* (Directions for a Candidate of the Ministry)—a manual for theological students by the New England divine; contains proposals for the reformation of divinity studies, the writer's general views on literature, and his suggestions for the attainment of a proper literary style.

Johann Lorenz von Mosheim, *Institutiones Historiae Ecclesiasticae* (The History of Ecclesiastical Institutions)—a prose tract by the German theologian; the work evidenced unprecedented objectivity and depth, causing the writer to be judged as the first modern ecclesiastical historian.

Jonathan Swift, *Gulliver's Travels*—a prose satire by the Irish writer, perhaps the most significant contribution to the form in all of English literary history; although it conveys, particularly in the second, third, and fourth parts, the despair and pessimism of the writer, it appeals to both young and old because it is a powerful satire on humanity and human institutions, as well as a fascinating piece of travel literature; the writer takes his persona, the surgeon Lemuel Gulliver, through Lilliput, Brobdingnag, Laputa, Balnibarbi, and the land of the Houyhnhnms and Yahoos.

James Thomson, "Winter"—the first section of the Scottish-born poet's *The Seasons;* sets forth the relationship between humankind and the elements during the harshest of seasons: rain, wind, snow; the visit of the redbreast; a man perishing in a snow drift while his family anxiously awaits him; wolves descending from the mountain; winter evenings in a city and in a village.

EVENTS

Nicholas Amherst, English Whig poet, founds *The Craftsman,* a London political periodical; he adopts the name "Caleb d'Anvers"; contributors include Henry St. John, Viscount Bolingbroke, and Henry Pulteney; primarily intended to oppose the ministry of Sir Robert Walpole (the "man of craft"); until 1736(?).

1727

BIRTHS

Jean Andre Deluc (d. 1817). Swiss scientist and religious writer; he will claim that biblical creation is consistent with scientific thought.

Anne Robert Jacques Turgot (d. 1781). French economist and statesman; will promote improvements for the poor, particularly in terms of their working conditions; his call for reforms will alienate him from the privileged classes; his work will anticipate that of Adam Smith (1723-1790), the Scottish economist and philosopher.

DEATHS

Sir Isaac Newton (b. 1642). English scientific philosopher and mathematician and president of the Royal Society; buried in Westminster Abbey; considered by a number of scholars to be the most significant contributor to the history of science, especially in terms of his discovery of the laws of universal gravitation.

PUBLICATIONS

John Balguy, *The Foundation of Moral Goodness; or, A Further Inquiry into the Original*
of Our Idea of Virtue—a prose tract by the English scholar and divine; a response to *An Inquiry into the Original of Our Ideas of Beauty and Virtue* (1725), by the Irish Presbyterian, Francis Hutcheson (1694-1747).

Philippe Destouches, *Le Philosophe Marie* (The Married Philosophe)—a high-minded and didactic comic drama by the French playwright; attacks the vulgarity of the comedies written by his contemporaries.

John Gay, *Fables*—a collection by the English dramatist and poet, according to some the best examples in English of the genre; each fable is a short narrative in octosyllables carefully directing the reader to an obvious and conventional moral; a second series in 1738; over sixty editions to 1800; "Accept, young Prince [William, Duke of Cumberland], the moral lay, / And in these tales mankind survey; / With early virtues plant your breast, / The specious arts of vice detest."

Moses Hayyim Luzzatto, *Migda Oz* (Tower of Victory)—a romantic, allegorical drama in Hebrew by the Italian-born Hebrew poet and playwright; the writer idealizes nature, the simple pastoral life, innocence, integrity, and moral purity.

Francesco Scipione Maffei, *Istoria Diplomatica* (The History of Diplomacy)—a prose work by the Italian playwright and historian; fairly comprehensive in scope and objective in tone.

James Thomson, "Summer"—the second part of *The Seasons,* the poet's major effort; describes the progress of a summer's day: haymaking, sheep shearing, bathing; includes an ode upon Great Britain and two mythological narrative episodes: the tragedy of Celadon and Amelia and the excitement of Damon as he observes Musidora bathe.

EVENTS

Benjamin Franklin founds at Philadelphia The Junto Club, a social and debating society limited to a dozen of his friends; became an important influence upon the culture of the city and established a subscription library; until 1767(?).

The first marriage notice to appear in a newspaper published in the Manchester, England, *News-Letter, Containing the Freshest Advices, Both Foreign and Domestick.*

William Parks, lawyer and author of legal tracts, publishes and edits *The Maryland Ga-*

zette, the first newspaper in the Maryland colony; contains essays on political and constitutional issues; until 1839.

Samuel Kneeland founds *The New England Weekly Journal*, the fourth newspaper to be published regularly in Boston; contains essays, letters, and poems; includes contributions by Mather Byles, Alexander Pope, and Thomas Prince; until 1741.

1728

BIRTHS

Thomas Warton the younger (d. 1790). English poet and literary historian; he will become Poet Laureate of England and Camden Professor of History and Professor of Poetry at Oxford.

DEATHS

Cotton Mather (b. 1663). Colonial American divine and writer; author of approximately 380 volumes, a number of which helped to spark New England religious fury and bigotry.

Christian Thomasius (b. 1655). German rationalist philosopher and noted jurist; professor of jurisprudence at Halle and the first member of his profession to lecture to students in German, rather than in Latin; opposed witchcraft and trial by torture.

PUBLICATIONS

John Gay, *The Beggar's Opera*—a musical play by the English dramatist and satirist, known generally as a Newgate pastoral; the piece focuses upon a love intrigue among thieves, both inside and outside of prison: Polly and Lucy are rival claimants for the affection of Macheath who, in the end, manages to escape from prison.

Anne Therese Lambert, *Avis d'une Mere a sa Fille et a Son Fils*—an essay by the French writer and literary patron; recommends a university education for women.

Alexander Pope, *The Dunciad. In Three Books*—a satirical poem by the English writer, perhaps the most significant piece of satire in

verse written during the eighteenth century; inspired by Lewis Theobald's criticism of Pope's edition of Shakespeare in his *Shakespeare Restored* (1726); Theobald becomes the "hero" of this satire (to be replaced by Colley Cibber in the 1742 version); however, the satirist directs his mock epic against dulness in general and attacks all those writers of poetry, prose, and drama who have contributed to the catastrophic decline in literary standards.

Abbe Antoine Francois Prevost, *Memoirs et Adventures d'un Homme de Qualities* (Memories and Adventures of a Man of Quality)—a semiautobiographical work by the French novelist and cleric, drawing on the writer's own travels and adventures through England, Holland, and Germany; vols. 1-4 in 1728 and vols. 5-7 in 1731.

James Thomson, "Spring"—the third part of the English poet's poem in blank verse, *The Seasons*; describes the influence of the season upon inanimate objects and humans; known especially for its charming depiction of the fertility of the season: "At last, / The clouds consign their treasures to the fields; / And, softly shaking on the dimpled pool / Prelusive drops, let all their moisture flow, / In large effusions, o'er the freshened world."

EVENTS

The first publication of *The Autobiography of Benvenuto Cellini*, begun in 1558; provides a vivid picture of city life in sixteenth-century Italy; Cellini (1501-1571), a goldsmith, sculptor, and engraver, worked under the patronage of Cosimo de' Medici.

Ephraim Chambers, English encyclopaedist, publishes his *Cyclopaedia, or, An Universal Dictionary of Arts and Sciences*; two folio volumes; a French translation will inspire the grand *Encyclopedie* of Denis Diderot, issued between 1751 and 1765.

Samuel Keimer, English-born printer who established a shop at Philadelphia and employed Benjamin Franklin, begins publication of *The Universal Instructor and Pennsylvania Gazette* to rival a proposed newspaper by his former employee; Franklin ultimately purchased Keimer's paper and operated it until 1766; publishes news and informal essays, as well as weather reports and political cartoons; until 1815.

1729

BIRTHS

Edmund Burke (d. 1797). Irish-born statesman, parliamentarian, political philosopher; he will become one of the foremost political thinkers and writers in England, combining a knowledge of events with great passion and imagination.

Gotthold Ephraim Lessing (d. 1781). German playwright and essayist; he will become a leading exponent of religious tolerance and one of Europe's greatest critics; he will free German literature from the limitations of French conventionalism.

Moses Mendelssohn (d. 1786). German philosopher; he will become a student of the English Augustans, including John Locke, Anthony Ashley Cooper, Earl of Shaftesbury, and Alexander Pope, and ponder Deism and metaphysics.

Guiseppe Parini (d. 1799). Italian poet; he will become professor of belles lettres, eloquence, and the fine arts at Milan; he will gain fame as both a satirist and lyric poet.

DEATHS

William Congreve (b. 1670). English playwright and poet; one of the most significant English writers of the comedy of manners and a master of witty dialogue; died from injuries received when his carriage overturned; buried in Westminster Abbey.

Richard Steele (b. 1672). English essayist and dramatist; wrote social comedies intended to make Christians comfortable with eighteenth-century society; his prose and drama both tend to be motivated by Whig sentiments.

PUBLICATIONS

John Gay, *Polly*—a musical by the English playwright, prohibited by Lord Chamberlain from being presented upon the stage until 1777; a sequel to *The Beggar's Opera* (1728); Polly Peacham comes to the West Indies to seek Macheath; after being trapped in the household of a planter, she escapes, engages in an Indian rebellion, and marries an Indian prince.

Alexander Pope, *The Dunciad Variorum with the Prolegomena of Scriblerus*—a variant of the English satirist's most significant poetic achievement; the volume contains an assortment of burlesque critical commentary; the names of the dunces, in previous versions indicated only by initials, now printed in full.

Jonathan Swift, *A Modest Proposal for Preventing the Children of Poor People in Ireland from Becoming a Burden to Their Parents or Country, and for Making Them Beneficial to the Public*—a satirical prose tract by the Irish cleric and writer; irony pervades the work and the writer's rigorous logic produces shocking arguments that force the reader into agreement before the vulgar solutions appear; throughout, he hides behind a veil of benevolent humanitarianism; reduced to its simplest thesis, the piece proclaims that the English have been engaged in a logical plan to devour the Irish.

EVENTS

The Academia de Buenas Letras established in Barcelona, Spain.

Andrew Motte translates the *Philosophiae Naturalis Principia Mathematica* (1687) of Sir Isaac Newton into English.

1730

BIRTHS

Oliver Goldsmith (d. 1774). Irish-born poet, playwright, novelist, and informal essayist; his great desire for fame will cause him to attempt many types of literature, resulting in a body of work of inconsistent quality.

Johann Georg Hamann (d. 1788). German philosopher and theologian; his prose will focus upon the symbolical and the oracular and will be richly suggestive in tone and thought.

DEATHS

Ahmed Nedim. Turkish poet who lost his life in a political uprising at Istanbul; although a scholar and a translator, his poetry was fresh and simple, resembling folk songs.

1731

PUBLICATIONS

Henry Fielding, *Tom Thumb, a Tragedy*—a dramatic farce by the English writer, one of the most successful of his plays; an attack against the grand tragedies then in fashion upon the London stage; the text contains many absurd scholarly notes that heighten the burlesque; another version appeared in 1731 under the title *The Tragedy of Tragedies; or, The Life and Death of Tom Thumb the Great.*

Pierre Carlet de Marivaux, *Le Jeu de l'Amour et du Hasard* (The Game of Love and Chance)—a prose comedy by the French playwright; fast-paced comic drama in which the psychological action goes forward without serious interruption; humor exists because the characters are either unaware of, or choose to ignore, the strong emotions conveyed by their language; the premise concerns the progress of the characters' love and their inability to recognize their feelings; the piece ends in a double marriage.

James Thomson, "Autumn"—the last book in *The Seasons,* a four-part poem in blank verse by the Scottish-born poet; he provides a vivid picture of shooting and hunting, condemning those so-called sports for their barbarity; then follow descriptions of the reaping of the fruits of the earth, the arrival of the fog, the migration of birds, and the mirth of the country folk after harvest.

EVENTS

Colley Cibber, actor, theater manager, playwright, and poet, appointed Poet Laureate of England, succeeding Laurence Eusden; he will produce birthday odes to the English monarch and, in so doing, incur the wrath of his contemporaries, particularly Alexander Pope; until 1757.

The Grub Street Journal begins publication as a weekly London literary magazine; satirical in substance and tone, it will attack *The Gentleman's Magazine, The Bee,* Lewis Theobald, Colley Cibber, Laurence Eusden, and Edmund Curll; scholars suspect that, because of the objects of those attacks, Alexander Pope played no small role as a contributor.

BIRTHS

William Cowper (d. 1800). English poet; he will become the nonclerical poet of the eighteenth-century evangelical revival, expressing for and impressing upon the new English middle class the humanitarian ideals of a new era.

Ramon da la Cruz (d. 1794). Spanish dramatist; he will compose over 450 one-act comedies about middle-class and lower middle-class life, while at the same time striving to develop a purely Spanish drama.

Girolamo Tiraboschi (d. 1794). Italian scholar and literary historian; he will become professor of rhetoric at Milan and the librarian to the Duke of Modena.

DEATHS

Abdulhamid Mohmand. Pakistani romantic poet; a writer of polished, learned, and subtle verse; also a translator of romantic fiction from the Persian.

Daniel Defoe (b. 1660). English essayist, poet, and novelist; anticipated practically every form of modern fiction, at the same time writing upon a host of political and social issues, a number of which caused him personal and financial problems.

PUBLICATIONS

Alexander Pope, *Epistle to Richard Boyle, Earl of Burlington. Of the Use of Riches*—a poem by the English satirist occasioned by the publication of his friend Burlington's first volume of designs of ancient Roman buildings (1730); the poet focuses upon the larger issues of taste and wealth, which, he believes, can lead to prodigality; thus, "'Tis strange, the miser should his cares employ / To gain those riches he can ne'er enjoy: / It is less strange, the prodigal should waste / His wealth to purchase what he ne'er can taste."

Pierre Carlet de Marivaux, *La Vie de Marianne* (The Life of Marianne)—a novel by the

French writer, continued through 1741, but never finished; marked by an affected and so-called precious style that came to be known as "Marivaudage"; the heroine is a beautiful, intelligent, and penniless girl of sixteen who manages to marry her way into aristocratic circles.

Abbe Antoine Francois Prevost, *Histoire des Grieux et de Manon Lescaut*—a novel by the French Jesuit writer; the story of an aristocrat who abandons everything in his passion for a satanic woman; condemned by contemporaries as immoral, although the piece set the tone for romantic fiction; its strength derives from its mixture of simplicity, reality, and truth both in substance and language.

Francois Marie Voltaire, *Histoire de Charles XII*—a combination biography and historical account by the French writer and philosopher; concerns the King of Sweden (1682-1718), whose wars exhausted his nation and caused its demise as a European political power; despite errors of fact, the work remains among the better biographies of the Swedish monarch.

EVENTS

Benjamin Franklin establishes a subscription library in Philadelphia.

Edward Cave, London publisher and bookseller, founds *The Gentleman's Magazine* under the pseudonym "Sylvanus Urban"; a monthly, it furnishes news, parliamentary reports, statistics, maps, and essays; Samuel Johnson was a regular contributor between 1739 and 1744; until 1914.

Jeremiah Gridley, Boston lawyer and soon-to-be attorney general of Massachusetts, publishes and edits *The Weekly Rehearsal*; contains informal essays and political news; until 1735.

1732

BIRTHS

Johann Christoph Adelung (d. 1806). German linguist and lexicographer; he will hold the office of chief librarian of Dresden and will publish an important dictionary of grammar and criticism.

Pierre Augustin Caron de Beaumarchais (d. 1799). French playwright who will become one of his nations most significant comic dramatists; his legal problems involving libel and ownership of plays will earn him a reputation as a champion of popular rights in opposition to the corrupt tribunals of the *ancien regime*.

DEATHS

John Gay (b. 1685). English poet, dramatist, and writer; consorted with John Arbuthnot, Alexander Pope, Jonathan Swift, and other Tories in satirizing the ministry of Robert Walpole; buried in Westminster Abbey.

PUBLICATIONS

George Berkeley, *Alciphron; or, The Minute Philosopher*—a treatise by the Irish-born divine and philosopher; composed during the writer's visit to America; seven dialogues comparatively heedless of the Socratic method of formal interrogation; the "minute philosophers" are those "free-thinkers" who have rejected the ancient methods of philosophy in favor of new views of religion and morality; the writer groups them in the same category as atheists, libertines, and metaphysicians.

Destouches (pseudonym of Philippe Nericault), *Le Glorieux* (The Conceited Count)—a moralistic comedy by the French playwright, highly imitative of Moliere; the work is considered the writer's masterpiece.

Francois Marie Voltaire, *Zaire* (Zara)—a dramatic tragedy by the French philosopher, dramatist, and poet; based upon Shakespeare's *Othello*, but also considers the issue of religious intolerance; may most concisely be described as a Turkish tale of fated love that exhibits all the formality and artificiality characteristic of the genre.

EVENTS

The London Magazine begins publication as a rival to *The Gentleman's Magazine*; to 1785; it never achieves the popularity or the quality of its early nineteenth-century successor (1820-1829).

The Dilettanti Society established as a London dining society by men of wealth and position who had traveled to Italy; initially, it devoted its efforts to encouraging the fine arts, but later, the members transferred their interests to classical archaeology; according to Horace Walpole, "The nominal qualification for the Dilettanti is having been in Italy and the real one being drunk; the two chiefs are Lord Middlesex and Sir Francis Dashwood who were seldom sober the whole time they were in Italy"; during the eighteenth century, the club sponsored the publication of a number of books about Greece.

Johann Heinrich Zedler, German bookseller, begins publication of his *Grosses, Vollstandiges Universal Lexikon* (Large and Complete Universal Lexicon); sixty-four volumes to 1750.

1733

BIRTHS

Christoph Friedrich Nicolai (d. 1811). German writer, bookseller, and publisher; he will gain recognition for his criticism, satires, anecdotes, and autobiography.

Christoph Martin Wieland (d. 1813). German translator, novelist, poet, and playwright; he will write innovative works in several genres and become popular among readers in fashionable society.

DEATHS

Anne Therese Lambert (b. 1647). French writer and patron of literature through her Paris salon; her essays and journals remained unpublished during her lifetime.

Bernard Mandeville (b. 1670). Dutch-born English satirist; he was condemned by the grand juries and openly attacked by jurists for maintaining that private vices were public benefits.

PUBLICATIONS

Benjamin Franklin, *Poor Richard's Almanack*—a general reference book and guide by the Philadelphia printer; its supposed author, "Richard Saunders," may well be the first truly fictional character in American literature; it contains the usual prophecies and forecasts found in a host of similar almanacs, but it gained literary recognition for its creator's marginal sayings, concocted from a variety of literary and popular sources; the work will become one of the most influential publications in American history; Franklin will sell the *Almanack* in 1758, although it will continue until 1796.

Alexander Pope, *Epistle to Allen, Lord Bathurst. Of the Use of Riches*—a poem by the English satirist, focusing upon the problem of avarice; concerned with the "money-grubbing" vices of middle-class capitalism; the poet poses the moral question of whether money has been good or harmful for society: " . . . gold but sent to keep the fools in play / For some to keep, and some to throw away."

——————— , *Essay on Man*—a philosophic essay in verse by the English poet, one of the most significant poems of the eighteenth century; unique in English literature because of its attempt to unite philosophy and poetry without relying upon a fictional vehicle; the poem focuses not upon the visible universe, but the intelligible universe manifested in the visible; to 1734.

——————— , *The First Satire of the Second Book of Horace Imitated. To Mr. Fortescue*—a poetic dialogue dedicated to William Fortescue, lawyer, Whig parliamentarian, and the poet's friend; the poet goes out of his way to declare that his motive is not malice, but rather sincere concern for the public good; he speaks through a public character who, as a man of tolerance and virtue, opposes the activities of others when they actually deserve such challenge, not because he feels vindictive: "Satire's my weapon, but I'm too discreet / To run amuck, and tilt at all I meet; / I only wear it in a land of hectors, / Thieves, supercargoes, sharpers, and directors."

Francois Marie Voltaire, *La Mort de Cesar* (The Death of Caesar)—a dramatic tragedy by the French philosopher, historian, and playwright; written almost strictly according to the classic rules of form and modeled after Shakespeare and Joseph Addison (*Cato*).

EVENTS

Latin removed as the official language of the English law courts.

John Peter Zenger, German-born printer and journalist, begins publication of *The New York Gazette*; it will come under attack from the colonial government, causing Zenger's imprisonment and subsequent trial for libel; he will emerge victorious and return to the editorship of the paper; until 1752.

1734

BIRTHS

Akinari Ueda (d. 1809). Japanese novelist; he will become one of the earliest of the "modern" writers of fiction in his native language.

PUBLICATIONS

George Berkeley, *The Analyst*—a prose piece by the Irish-born churchman and philosopher; criticizes the new theories in mathematics, particularly Sir Isaac Newton's theory of fluxions; his point of view is theological and philosophical rather than scientific.

Jonathan Edwards, *A Divine and Supernatural Light*—a sermon by the colonial New England divine, delivered in 1733; asserts that although the experience of regeneration and the resulting sense of divine beauty may be understood by human reason, humans may acquire regeneration and divine beauty only through the grace of God; based upon *Matthew* 16:17.

Charles-Louis Montesquieu, *Considerations sur le Causes de la Grandeur des Romains et de leur Decadence* (Considerations of the Causes of the Grandeur and Decadence of the Romans)—a prose essay by the French jurist and philosopher, perhaps his most skilfully crafted piece; claims that the ancient Roman world had a population larger than eighteenth-century Europe; from that point, argues against luxury; in addition, the writer draws parallels between the societies of classical antiquity and modern France.

Alexander Pope, *Epistle to Cobham*—a political poem by the English satirist; dedicated to Sir Richard Temple, Viscount Cobham (1675-1749), the most recent of the Whig outcasts and one of the most passionate of patriots;

the poet relies heavily upon the essays of Montaigne and sets forth a lively exposition of the difficulty of assessing the human character: "Oft in the Passions, wild rotation tost, / Our spring of action to ourselves is lost:"

James Thomson, *Liberty*—a poem by the Scottish-born writer that marks his entry into politics; dedicated to Frederick, Prince of Wales, then a leader in the opposition to the ministry of Sir Robert Walpole; in five books, to 1735.

Francois Marie Voltaire, *Lettres Anglaises ou Philosophiques* (Philosophical Letters Concerning the English Nation)—epistolary essays by the French philosopher and writer exalting the English constitution and discussing the nature and form of representative government; the work will initiate an interest in English philosophy and science, particularly the works of Sir Isaac Newton and John Locke.

EVENTS

George Sale, English Oriental scholar and lawyer, translates the Koran from the standard Arabic to English.

Lewis Theobald, Shakespearean scholar, poet, essayist, and dramatist, publishes his edition of the works of Shakespeare; the work is considered superior to that of his rival, Alexander Pope (1725); well over three hundred of his editorial changes continue to be accepted by scholars; regarded as a pioneer effort in the field of Shakespearean studies.

1735

BIRTHS

Michel-Guillaume Jean de Crevecoeur (also known as J. Hector St. John de Crevecoeur; d. 1813). French-born American writer and agriculturist; he will write epistolary essays and pieces describing rural life in the American colonies.

Johann Karl August Musaus (d. 1787). German prose satirist; he will write popular German folktales, leading people to believe that these stories originated from actual oral narratives.

PUBLICATIONS

George Berkeley, *The Querist*—a volume of questions and answers posed by the Irish-born philosopher and divine; focuses upon issues of social and economic reform, particularly in Ireland.

Henry St. John, Viscount Bolingbroke, *A Dissertation upon Parties*—one of the English political philosopher's attacks upon the Whig government of Robert Walpole and Charles Townshend; calls for setting aside party differences and governing the nation in a manner consistent with its consitution.

Samuel Johnson, *Voyage to Abyssinia*—an anonymously published English translation and abridgement (from the French by way of the Portuguese) by the then relatively young and totally unknown English writer; the work was written by Father Jeronimo Lobo (1593-1678), a Portuguese Jesuit who served as superintendent of missions in Abyssinia (1625-1634); a French translation of his *Voyage Historique d'Abissinie* appeared in 1728.

Pierre Carlet de Marivaux, *Le Paysan Parvenu* (The Upstart Peasant)—a novel by the French writer; the central character Jacob rises from farmer's son to financier, passing through lower middle-class surroundings in which the grocer keeps his distance from the ex-footman, and the daughter of a farmer turned shopkeeper attempts to act as a lady in front of a man whose father continues to plow the fields; eventually, Jacob learns how to pass himself off as a gentleman; to 1736.

Alexander Pope, "Epistle II. To a Lady," from *Epistles to Several Persons*—a poem by the English Augustan writer, derived from Juvenal's sixth satire on women and Nicolas Boileau's sixth satire on the same subject; a portrait gallery of various prominent females of the day, unified by the metaphor of painting; the poem progresses in intensity, from simple depictions of the female temperament to profound images in which women represent the various poses of the world: "Nothing so true as what you once let fall, / 'Most women have no characters at all.' / Matter too soft a lasting mark to bear, / And best distinguished by black, brown, or fair."

——————, *An Epistle to Dr. Arbuthnot*—a poem addressed to the poet's lifelong friend, Dr. John Arbuthnot (1667-1735), at the time near death; the first section of the piece establishes a literary context, emphasizing the frustrations of the poet who finds himself constantly under attack from second-rate critics and third-rate rivals; the second section assumes a more moralistic tone, explaining the degrees to which the poet must stoop whenever he attempts to offer his services to the public.

EVENTS

The Boston Evening Post begins publication, succeeding *The Weekly Rehearsal;* contains local news and short notes; one of the more literary newspapers in colonial America, reprinting English poems and essays; until 1775.

The Calves' Head Club, a London group formed at the end of the seventeenth century to ridicule Charles I, suppressed by the government.

The Old and New Testaments translated from Greek to Lithuanian.

John Rich, manager of Covent Garden Theatre, London, founds The Sublime Society of Beef Steaks; the members meet and dine at a room in the theater; David Garrick, although not a member, is a frequent guest at the Club's functions.

John Peter Zenger, the publisher of *The New York Weekly Journal,* concludes his year-long legal battle over a libel suit brought by the governor's party; his imprisonment by the governor of New York and eventual vindication by a jury are a victory for freedom of the press, as well as for liberty of speech.

1736

BIRTHS

Charles Augustin de Cuolomb (d. 1806). French physicist and philosopher; he will be remembered most for his works on electricity, magnetism, and friction.

James Macpherson (d. 1796). Scottish poet and translator of the Ossian poems, the questionable authenticity of which will cause a controversy and detract from his reputation as a scholar and poet.

PUBLICATIONS

Henry St. John, Viscount Bolingbroke, *A Letter on the Spirit of Patriotism*—a political treatise by the English philosopher, addressed to Baron George Lyttleton (1709-1773), chancellor of the exchequer and friend of Alexander Pope and Henry Fielding; the writer's final views upon politics; the misfortunes of the nation have resulted from a lack of opposition to the corruption of the Whig ministry; reforms should ensue so that the government does not become absolute.

Henry Fielding, *Pasquin*—a satirical comedy by the English writer; focuses upon various religious and political practices, including the abuses of electioneering; the satire was so successful that it caused the government to promote the Licensing Act; the piece is also a play about plays and thus an artistic effort about art.

Francois Marie Voltaire, *Les Americans*—a comedy by the French playwright and philosopher; lively in terms of dramatic effect, but not a major literary work.

EVENTS

The Virginia Gazette, the first newspaper published in the Virginia colony, founded at Williamsburg; noted for its essays focusing upon life in London; until 1773.

1737

BIRTHS

Edward Gibbon (d. 1794). English historian; a visit to Rome when he is twenty-seven will motivate him to produce one of the classic works of history written in English; he will prove that creativity is an important aspect of the historian's craft.

Thomas Paine (d. 1809). Radical and Deist who will divide his time between England, France, and America.

Jacques Henri Bernardin de Saint-Pierre (d. 1814). French essayist and novelist; he will come under the influence of Jean Jacques Rousseau and will spend considerable time writing utopian cricitism; he will become a favorite of Louis Napoleon.

PUBLICATIONS

Jonathan Edwards, *A Faithful Narrative of the Surprising Work of God*—a sermon by the New England divine; a defense of the Great Awakening, the evangelical revival that caused considerable division among the Protestant establishment in colonial America.

Henry Fielding, *The Historical Register for the Year 1736*—a political satire by the English novelist and comic playwright; an attack upon the administration of Robert Walpole; the piece so enraged the government that the minister retaliated by passing the Licensing Act of 1737.

Ignazio de Luzan Claramunt de Suelves y Gurrea, *Poetica*—a prose tract by the Spanish writer; sets forth the classic rules for Spanish literary composition.

Pierre Carlet de Marivaux, *Les Fausses Confidences* (False Confessions)—a comedy by the French playwright, novelist, and essayist; another of the series of dramas focusing upon the discovery of love and its ultimate effects.

Alexander Pope, *The First Epistle of the Second Book of Horace. To Augustus*—a poem by the English satirist, partly an apology for poetry; follows Horace pleading the cause of the living Roman poets against the "taste of the town" and against the emporor himself, who had little use for poets and instead encouraged playwrights; thus the writer's plea to George II:

> While you, great patron of mankind! sustain
> The balanced world, and open all the main;
> Your country, chief, in arms abroad defend,
> At home, with morals, arts, and laws amend;
> How shall the Muse, from such a monarch, steal
> An hour, and not defraud the public weal?

EVENTS

Alexander Cruden, Scottish-born London bookseller, publishes his *Concordance of the Holy Scriptures,* dedicated to Queen Caroline, who dies just a few days later.

1738

BIRTHS

Cesare Beccaria-Bonesana (d. 1794). Italian political and philanthropic writer; he will denounce capital punishment and torture, advocating prevention of crime by education; he will receive appointments as professor of political philosophy at Milan and as a member of the board for the reform of the Italian judicial code.

PUBLICATIONS

Olof von Dalin, *The Envious Man*—a dramatic tragedy by the Swedish poet, historian, playwright, and journalist; the writer's liberal and humanitarian tendencies are evident in his treatment of the principal political and social issues of the day.

Samuel Johnson, *London: A Poem*—a piece that established the writer's reputation as a poet within the Augustan mode; an exercise in the then highly fashionable mode of poetry known as "imitation," the work is an English version of a familiar Latin form; reflects the poet's hostility toward London: he appears lonely, insecure, and shocked at the heartless city he views.

Lodovico Antonio Muratori, *Antiquitates Italic* (Italian Antiquities)—a six-volume work by the Italian historian, completed in 1742; contains what is known as the "Muratorian Fragment," a work originating from the New Testament books and apparently written by an unknown contemporary of St. Irenaeus (140?-202), one of the Christian fathers of the Greek church.

Alexander Pope, "**One Thousand Seven Hundred and Thirty Eight. A Dialogue Something Like Horace**"—a poem in imitation of the second satire of Horace, after the manner of Jonathan Swift; perhaps better known as the first dialogue of the *Epilogue to the Satires:*

> . . . if Satire knows its Time and Place,
> You still may lash the Greatest—in Disgrace:
> For Merit will by turns forsake them all;

Would you know when? exactly when they fall.

EVENTS

Louis Francois Roubillac, Parisian-born sculptor who came to London shortly before 1738, finishes his bust of Alexander Pope.

1739

BIRTHS

Christian Friedrich Daniel Schubart (d. 1791). German poet; he will write satirical and religious verse and have a decided influence upon Johann Friedrich Schiller.

PUBLICATIONS

David Hume, *A Treatise on Human Nature*—a tract by the Scottish philosopher that may best be understood in terms of the writer's own summary: ". . . objects bear to each other the relations of contiguity and succession; that like objects may be observed in several instances to have like relations; and that all this is independent of, and antecedent to, the operation of the understanding."

Samuel Johnson, *A Complete Vindication of the Licensers of the Stage*—a pamphlet by the English essayist; a defense of the Stage Licensing Act of 1737 and of freedom of the press; the government had, in March 1739, prohibited the production of Henry Brooke's *Gustavus Vasa*, an allegorical attack upon the ministry of Robert Walpole and the policies of King George II.

—————, *Marmor Norfolciense; or, An Essay on the Ancient Prophetical Inscription*—another satirical pamphlet, on the subject of the "Norfolk Marble"; reportedly, the large stone had been claimed from the earth in Norfolk (the home county of Robert Walpole) and bore an old Latin inscription inflammatory to both minister and King; published anonymously.

Jonathan Swift, *Verses on the Death of Dr. S[wift], D.S.P.D. Occasioned by Reading a Maxim in Rochefoucault*—a poem by the

Irish satirist, then Dean of St. Patrick's, Dublin (D.S.P D.); composed in 1731; planned as a humorous farewell to friends and enemies alike, the work records the author's own impressions of himself and his work.

James Thomson, *Edward and Eleanore*—a tragedy by the Scottish poet; the piece is also a thinly disguised attack upon the government.

EVENTS

The Champion, a thrice-weekly literary periodical, begins publication in London; Henry Fielding is a principal contributor; the essays focus upon an imaginary family known as the Vinegars; until 1741.

John Mottley, a minor English playwright and biographer, publishes *Joe Miller's Jests; or, The Wits Vade Mecum; being a Collection of the Most Brilliant Jests, the Polite Repartees, the Most Elegant Bon-Mots, the Most Pleasant Short Stories in the English Language;* the volume contains 247 original jokes; the compiler borrowed the name from Joseph Miller, a Drury Lane actor and humorist; the term "Joe Miller" will become associated with a stale joke.

1740

BIRTHS

James Boswell (d. 1795). Scottish lawyer, journalist, and biographer; his *Life of Samuel Johnson* will be one of the most important biographies in the English language; the discovery of his papers in Scotland during the twentieth century will also reveal him to be an important journalist and diarist of the Hanoverian period.

Matthias Claudius (d. 1815). German poet and prose writer; he will be a major force in the return to simplicity and directness in lyric poetry; he will also write a large quantity of prose essays appealing to popular tastes.

Donatien Alphonse Francois, Marquis de Sade (d. 1814). French writer of scandalous romances; his literary efforts will be overshadowed by their creator's reputation for cruel and licentious sexual behavior.

PUBLICATIONS

Colley Cibber, *An Apology for the Life of Mr. Colley Cibber, Comedian*—a multi-volume autobiography by the London actor, theater manager, playwright, and poet; known for its portraits of the principal actors and actresses of the day, including Thomas Betterton, Mrs. Anne Bracegirdle, Robert Nokes, and Anne Oldfield.

Olof von Dalin, *Tale of the Horse*—the prose masterpiece of the Swedish historian, poet, and journalist; the writer relies upon folk material to satirize the relations between the Swedish people and the monarchy.

Pierre Carlet de Marivaux, *L'Epreuve* (The Test)—a comedy in prose by the French playwright, novelist, and essayist; the affected style of the work is known to drama historians as "Marivaudage."

Samuel Richardson, *Pamela; or, Virtue Rewarded*—the first work of fiction by the English novelist and the initial example of what has come to be known as the modern English novel of character; epistolary in form; the narrative concerns a young servant girl who must defend herself against attacks upon her virtue; in the second part (1741), she endures the burden of a profligate husband.

Louis de Rouvroy, Duc de Saint-Simon, *Memoires*—autobiographical accounts by the French courtier, begun as early as 1723 and published at intervals between 1740 and 1752; contains lively, detailed descriptions of life at the French court between 1695 and 1723; in 1761, the French minister of state, Etienne Francois Choiseul-Amboise, impounded the work for the French foreign office; a final edition of forty-three volumes appeared between 1879 and 1930.

James Thomson and David Mallet, *Alfred*—a dramatic masque by the two Scottish writers, composed for the Prince of Wales; the most significant part of the work may be found in a song by a bard in the second act, written by Thomson and beginning,

> When Britain first, at Heaven's command,
> Arose from out the azure main,
> This was the charter of the land,
> And guardian angels sung this strain—
> "Rule, Britannia, rule the waves;
> Britons never will be slaves."

1741

BIRTHS

Pierre Ambroise Francois Choderlos de Laclos (d. 1803)—French novelist and politician; he will spend almost his entire life in the military; influenced by Jean Jacques Rousseau and Samuel Richardson, he will be best remembered for his epistolary novel *Les liaisons dangereuses.*

DEATHS

Bernard de Montfaucon (b. 1655). French critic and antiquary; after a career in the military, he became a Benedictine monk; wrote important treatises on classical archaeology.

PUBLICATIONS

John Arbuthnot and Alexander Pope, *Memoirs of Martinus Scriblerus*—a satirical piece, primarily written by the two eighteenth-century English writers and directed against false tastes in learning; the education of the hero focuses upon the ancients, but he becomes a critic, a physician, and a philosopher—all of which go against the purest of neoclassic ideals.

Jonathan Edwards, *Sinners in the Hands of an Angry God*—a sermon by the American divine; describes the impending and awesome wrath of an inscrutable and arbitrary God; intended to eradicate the religious complacency of the preacher's congregation at Ensfield, Connecticut, and to make the wicked recognize their sin and danger: "The devil stands ready to fall upon them, and seize them as his own, at what moment God shall permit him."

Henry Fielding, *An Apology for the Life of Mrs. Shamela Andrews*—the English novelist's reaction to Samuel Richardson's *Pamela* (1740); events and characters remain as in the source of the parody, except that the heroine (Pamela/Shamela) comes forth as a calculating, immoral hussy.

David Hume, *Essays Moral and Political*—a collection by the Scottish philosopher; until 1742; contemporary commentators considered the volumes rhetorically elegant but without philosophical substance; nonetheless, the work was successful.

Alexander Pope, *Works*—a collection by the English poet, satirist, and prose writer; includes correspondence with Jonathan Swift and *The Memoirs of Martinus Scriblerus.*

Francois Marie Voltaire, *Le Fantisme Mahomet le Prophete* (Mahomet the Prophet)—a drama by the French philosopher and playwright, drawn from national history and created under the influence of William Shakespeare; demonstrates the writer's skill for theatrical construction, particularly for creating powerful and spectacular effects.

EVENTS

John Webbe begins at Philadelphia publication of *The American Magazine*; only three issues were printed, but it deserves recognition as the first magazine published in the American colonies.

Benjamin Franklin publishes and edits at Philadelphia *The General Magazine; or, An Historical Chronicle for All the British Plantations in America*; the second colonial American periodical, concerned mainly with political and military news; issued three days after John Webb's *American Magazine,* it lasted for only six months (January to June).

Baron von Borck, the Prussian ambassador to London, publishes a German translation of *Julius Caesar* in alexandrine verse; the first printed text of a German translation of a Shakespearean play; German critics then began to rail against what they considered Shakespeare's flagrant disregard of the classical rules and unities; nonetheless, those same critics admired the English playwright's seemingly natural powers of characterization.

1742

BIRTHS

Georg Christoph Lichtenberg (d. 1799). German satirist and physicist; he will travel to England, meet David Garrick, and write witty commentaries on the plates and sketches of William Hogarth.

PUBLICATIONS

William Collins, *Persian Eclogues*—a set of pastorals by the English poet, written and published during his undergraduate years; conventional eighteenth-century pastorals, strongly influenced by Alexander Pope; in spite of the title, the pieces contain little that can be termed "Oriental"; instead, the poet follows the conventional dramatic structure of morning, noon, evening, and night; however, the young student did manage a combination of pastoral convention and Oriental setting: "Thus sung the swain, and eastern legends say / The maids of Bagdat verified the lay: / Dear to the plains, the Virtues came along, / The shepherds loved, and Selim blessed the song."

Claude Prosper Jolyot de Crebillon, *Le Sopha, Conte Moral* (The Shah, a Moral Tale)—a novel by the son of a prominent French dramatist; generally considered indecent; Madame de Pompadour, mistress of Louis XV, was so offended by the piece that the writer was banished from Paris for five years.

Henry Fielding, *The History of the Adventures of Joseph Andrews and His Friend Mr. Abraham Adams*—a novel by the English writer, begun as a parody of Samuel Richardson's *Pamela* (1740); as the Richardson novel concerned the efforts of Pamela Andrews to escape the advances of her master, this work relates the adventures of her brother, Joseph Andrews, in his attempts to defend his virtue; however, the novel also focuses upon Parson Adams, a simple and good hearted but fairly ridiculous curate in the employ of Sir Thomas Booby.

Thomas Gray, "Ode to Adversity"—an ode (sometimes referred to and even entitled a "hymn") by the English poet; a mature and positive confrontation of the evils of adult life; emphasizes that suffering may lead to wisdom and various social virtues.

——————, **"Ode on a Distant Prospect of Eton College"**—poem that idealizes the poet's schooldays; contrasts the joys of childhood and the suffering of adult life; Eton assumes a state of Miltonic innocence, a form of Eden prior to the fall; the literary value of the piece derives from the poet's creation of a new form by combining the topographical poem with the subjective ode.

——————, **"Ode on the Spring"**—a piece in which the retired poet contemplates the frivolity of the world while at the same time denouncing his own moral complacency; finally, he contrasts the industry of the modern world with the contemplative life: "Still is the toiling hand of Care; / The panting herds repose. / Yet hark, how through the peopled air / The busy murmur glows!"

Edward Young, *The Complaint; or, Night Thoughts on Life, Death, and Immortality*—a didactic poem by the English writer, consisting of 10,000 lines of blank verse in nine books; until 1745; the poet reflects on life's vicissitudes, death, and immortality; he then encourages a transformation from infidelism to faith and virtue; he concludes with a vision of the "last day" and of eternity, surveying the wonders of the firmament at night.

EVENTS

Etienne Fourmont, French scholar of Chinese literature and language, publishes his *Grammatica Sinaica* (Chinese Grammar).

Charles Viner, English writer on the law, publishes the first volumes of his legal encyclopaedia under the title *A General Abridgement of Law and Equity, Alphabetically Digested under Proper Titles, with Notes and References to the Whole;* 23 volumes to 1753; the writer has spent more than a half century on this project.

1743

BIRTHS

Marie Jean Antoine Nicolas Caritat, Marquis de Condorcet (d. 1794). French mathematician and pamphleteer; he will win seats in the Academy of Sciences and the French Academy and take an active part in the completion of Diderot's *Encyclopedie*.

Gavril Romanovich Derzhavin (d. 1816). Russian poet; after a brief army career, he will become secretary of state, imperial treasurer, and minister of justice; his poetry will reveal him to be an innovator in the age of classicism.

Johannes Ewald (d. 1781). Danish lyric poet and playwright; he will compose the Danish national anthem ("King Christian stood by the lofty mast") and become the founder of Danish tragic drama.

Johann David Wyss (d. 1818). Swiss writer; he will author a children's classic based upon Daniel Defoe's *Robinson Crusoe*.

PUBLICATIONS

Henry Fielding, *A Journey from This World to the Next*—a lively satirical account of the journey of the writer's spirit on a stage coach; he rides in company with the spirits of other recently dead persons; they all seek admittance to Elysium.

——————, *The Life of Jonathan Wild the Great*—a satirical novel by the English writer, intended to expose the true meaning and rewards of greatness as distinct from goodness; the narrative focuses upon the career of a consummate rogue from baptism to death on the gallows; the exposure of the hero's trickery brings an abrupt end to his greatness.

Alexander Pope, The Dunciad in Four Books—a satirical poem by one of the most significant eighteenth-century English poets; the satire attacks, generally, the problem of Dulness, tracing the course of all of the writers who have earned the right to receive condemnation and to be held high in redicule; in this final version, the poet and playwright Colley Cibber (!671-1757) has replaced Lewis Theobald (1688-1744) as king of the dunces.

Francois Marie Voltaire, *Merope*—a dramatic tragedy by the French writer and philosopher, written within the confines of classical tradition; a vehicle for the writer's philosophical ideals, particularly his belief in religious tolerance.

EVENTS

Benjamin Franklin founds the American Philosophical Society at Philadelphia; one of the earliest informal discussion groups in colonial America intended to promote literature and science.

William Bradford founds *The Pennsylvania Journal and Weekly Advertiser*; until 1797; opposes the Stamp Act and competes with Benjamin Franklin's Philadelphia newspaper, *The Pennsylvania Gazette*.

1744

BIRTHS

Johann Gottfried von Herder (d. 1803). German critic and poet, important for his contributions to the Sturm und Drang and Romantic movements; he will maintain that the verses of the people are the truest poetry.

DEATHS

Alexander Pope (b. 1688). English poet, critic, satirist, translator, and editor; the most significant figure of the Augustan Age of English literature.

Giovanni Battista Vico (b. 1668). Italian jurist and philosopher; Professor of Rhetoric at Naples; exercised a profound influence upon the German Romantics.

PUBLICATIONS

Mather Byles, *Poems on Several Occasions*—a collection by the American Puritan minister and nephew of Cotton Mather; the pieces evidence an undue reliance upon Alexander Pope, and an unchurchly respect for trivial and frivolous subjects; the work provided him with a high degree of provincial notoriety, but did little to establish a literary reputation.

Benjamin Franklin, *An Account of the New Invented Pennsylvania Fire Places*—if nothing else, this piece by the American sage describes what will become an American institution: the "Franklin stove," another of his practical inventions.

Samuel Johnson, *The Life of Richard Savage*—a biographical and critical essay by the English writer; a romantic account of the minor poet and playwright, who was a friend of Johnson.

Ludovico Antonio Muratori, *Annali d'Italia* (The Annals of Italy)—a detailed history of Italy, published in twelve volumes through 1749; known for its almost microscopic detail.

Jonathan Swift, *Sermons*—a collection of orations by the Irish-born satirist and cleric, only four of which were published in 1744;

marked by the writer's characteristic combination of energy, reason, and common sense.

Joseph Warton, *The Enthusiast; or, The Lover of Nature*—a poem by the English versifier and critic; a survey, in Miltonic blank verse, of the poetic themes popular in the 1740s: the cult of wild nature and the preference for primitive life over civilization; this preference, as the title of the piece implies, is an amateur enthusiasm rather than a profound conviction.

EVENTS

Robert Dodsley, London poet and bookseller, publishes his *Select Collection of Old Plays* in twelve volumes; an important contribution to the history of the drama.

Eliza Haywood, English novelist and playwright, publishes the literary journal *The Female Spectator*; until 1746.

The future national anthem of Great Britain, "God Save the King," appears anonymously in a collection entitled *Harmonia Anglicana:* "God save our Lord the King / Long live our noble King, / God save the King!"

The London publisher and bookseller John Newbery opens a bookshop and publishing house at the Bible and Sun, St. Paul's Churchyard; he begins to publish literary newspapers and wishes to specialize in books for children, which he issues in cheap form; the Newbery Medal, established in 1922, will honor significant writers of books for children.

Samuel Baker Sotheby founds at York Street, Covent Garden, London, the first sale room in Great Britain exclusively for books, manuscripts, and prints.

The publication in London of *Tommy Thumb's Pretty Song Book,* a collection of nursery rhymes that includes "London Bridge," "Hickory, dickory dock," and "Little Tommy Tucker."

deistic science and modern invention, both of which had begun to challenge orthodoxy and good manners; his work will be considered immoral by some nineteenth-century critics, but middle and late twentieth-century literary scholars will praise him for his important contributions to the history of English literature.

PUBLICATIONS

Samuel Johnson, *Miscellaneous Observations on the Tragedy of Macbeth*—an anonymously published critical tract by the English writer; a specimen of the edition of Shakespeare that he would publish twenty years later.

James Thomson, *Tancred and Sigismunda*—a dramatic tragedy by the Scottish poet; concerns the heir to the kingdom of Sicily, who is lured into accepting, with his throne, a bride he does not love; in so doing, he must abandon his true love, Sigismunda; she, in turn, marries another man, who stabs her before fighting with Tancred.

EVENTS

Sir Francis Dashwood founds a convivial social club known as Franciscans, or The Hell-Fire Club; the group meets at Medmenham Abbey, a ruined Cistercian abbey on the Thames embankment near Marlow; George Bubb Doddington, a politician and political diarist, and John Wilkes, Parliamentarian and political writer, are among its most noted members; not to be confused with the London ruffians and vandals of the same name who emerged early in the eighteenth century.

Dr. Alexander Hamilton, Scottish-born Maryland physician, and Jonas Green, the editor of *The Maryland Gazette,* found the Tuesday Club of Annapolis; a forum for colonial intellectuals and literati.

1746

BIRTHS

Stephanie Felicite Ducrest de St. Aubin, Comtesse de Genlis (d. 1830). French writer; she will compose four volumes of plays and nearly one hundred volumes of historical romance.

1745

DEATHS

Jonathan Swift (b. 1667). Irish-born satirist; he directed his sharp attacks against the vogue of

Johann Wilhelm Heinse (d. 1803). German poet and writer of romances.

PUBLICATIONS

Denis Diderot, *Pensees Philosophiques* (Philosophical Thoughts)—a philosophical treatise by the French dramatist, critic, and philosopher; claims that extreme passion, elevating the soul to grand objectives, is the source of sublimity in life, literature, painting, and sculpture; burned by the Parliament of Paris in 1746.

Jonathan Edwards, *A Treatise Concerning Religious Affections*—a tract by the American clergyman focusing upon the psychology of religion; discusses the problem of human destiny and the issue of emotion in religion; true religion constitutes holy love and divine affection, and thus the union of man and God would be achieved through the mysteries of the heart.

Christian Furchtegott Gellert, *Fabelen und Erzahlungen* (Fables and Stories)—a collection of stories by the German moralist and writer; each of the pieces reveals the influence of the English novelist Samuel Richardson, particularly his *Pamela* (1740-1741).

Tobias George Smollett, *The Tears of Scotland*—a rare poem by the Scottish novelist, written after the battle of Culloden, near Inverness, where the Duke of Cumberland defeated the forces of the Young Pretender, thus ending the Jacobite uprising of 1745; inspired by the rumored English atrocities after the battle: "Mourn, hapless Caledonia, mourn / Thy banish'd peace, thy laurels torn! / Thy sons, for valour long renown'd, / Lie slaughter'd on their native ground. . . . "

Joseph Warton, "Ode to Fancy"—a poem by the English critic and versifier; the most noteworthy piece in his 1746 collection *Odes on Various Subjects;* its thesis may be determined by the final lines: "With native beauties win applause, / Beyond cold critic's studied laws: / O let each Muse's fame increase, / O bid BRITANNIA rival GREECE!"

EVENTS

Eliza Haywood, English actress, novelist, and playwright, is instrumental in establising *The Parrot,* a London literary and miscellaneous periodical; it lasts only through the year.

1747

BIRTHS

Gottfried August Burger (d. 1794). German lyric poet; he will be influenced by Shakespeare and will become one of Germany's favorite poets; yet, he will have to earn a living through translations and hackwork.

Gyorgy Bessenyei (d. 1811). Hungarian lyric poet and playwright; he will become a major figure of the Hungarian Enlightenment, especially in his proposal for the establishment of a Hungarian Learned Society.

DEATHS

Alain Rene Lesage (b. 1668). French novelist and playwright; though he often borrowed ideas, incidents, and tales from other authors he was the first writer to perceive the possibilities inherent in the picaresque novel, and he developed an original literary style.

Moses Hayyim Luzzatto (b. 1707). Italian Jewish writer and mystic who wrote both in Hebrew and Italian; a leader of the renaissance of Hebrew literature.

PUBLICATIONS

William Collins, *Odes on Several Descriptive and Allegoric Subjects*—a collection by the English poet, who destroyed all of the unsold copies; includes "Ode to Pity," "Ode to Fear," "Ode to Simplicity," "Ode on the Poetical Character," "Ode, Written in the Beginning of the Year 1746," "Ode to Mercy," "Ode to Liberty," "Ode, to a Lady on the Death of Colonel Ross in the Action of Fontenoy," "Ode to Evening," "Ode to Peace," and "The Passions. An Ode for Music."

Christian Furchtegott Gellert, *Die Kranke Frau* (The Sick Woman)—a comedy by the German poet, playwright, and moralist; a popular favorite among contemporary audiences because of its realistic portrayal of the eighteenth-century Saxon middle class; represents the dramatist's commitment to the bourgeois enlightenment.

Thomas Gray, "Ode on the Death of a Favourite Cat, Drowned in a Tub of Goldfishes"—a poem written in response to a request by Horace Walpole for an epitaph on one of his cats, who had recently drowned in a goldfish bowl at his house in Arlington Street, London: "Her conscious tale her joy declared; / The fair round face, the snowy beard, / The velvet of her paws, / Her coat that with the tortoise vies, / Her ears of jet and emerald eyes. . . ."

Samuel Johnson, *Plan of a Dictionary of the English Language*—an essay by the English writer, written at the insistence of his publishers and dedicated to his literary patron, Philip Dormer Stanhope, Earl of Chesterfield; a prospectus for the *Dictionary* that would appear in 1755; the writer outlines his ideas on language purity, linguistic accuracy, literary quality, and grammatical form.

Samuel Richardson, *Clarissa Harlow*—an epistolary novel by the English writer; two volumes published in 1747, five more in 1748; concerns the moral dilemmas that can arise from a love affair between a lady of good family (Clarissa) and an attractive but unscrupulous suitor (Robert Lovelace); Clarissa dies of shame, while Lovelace duels with her cousin.

Francois Marie Voltaire, *Zadig*—a philosophical tale by the French writer and philosopher, composed for the amusement of the Duchesse de Maine, with whom he had taken refuge; displays the writer's interest in Orientalism.

EVENTS

The Accademia dei Granelleschi founded at Venice, in part through the efforts of Carlo Gozzi, an Italian playwright; its objective is to preserve the Italian literary language against any introduction of popular or realistic elements.

The Biblioteca Nazionale founded at Florence, Italy.

The National Library founded in Warsaw, Poland.

William Warburton, Anglican preacher at Lincoln's Inn, publishes his edition of the works of Shakespeare; in eight volumes, based on Alexander Pope's edition of 1725; although criticized for its lack of scholarship, the work was nonetheless popular.

1748

BIRTHS

Emmanuel Joseph Sieyes (d. 1836). French statesman, cleric, and pamphleteer; his essays will reflect his fluctuating political beliefs.

DEATHS

John Balguy (b. 1686). English Anglican theologian; his pamphlets and essays focus upon redemption and the relationship between beauty and virtue; he burned most of his sermons so that his son, Thomas Balguy (1716-1795), would have to rely upon his own thought.

James Thomson (b. 1700). Scottish poet; his focus upon Nature and its harmony with the new science helped pave the way for Romanticism.

PUBLICATIONS

John Cleland, *Fanny Hill: Memoirs of a Woman of Pleasure*—a novel by the English writer and journalist, published in two volumes, 1748-1749; a graphic examination of sexuality, the piece was suppressed as pornography in 1749, and an unexpurgated edition was seized by the London police in 1963.

Carlo Goldoni, *La Vedova Scaltra* (The Crafty Widow)—the Italian playwright's first dramatic success; he provides his audience with a precise indication of the dramatic reform he intended to institute: to replace the mannered and vulgar theater in verse with realistic plays in prose; the piece mirrors actual life in Venetian society.

David Hume, *Philosophical Essays Concerning Human Understanding*—prose tracts by the Scottish essayist, philosopher, and historian; challenges John Locke's assumption of a solid inner self; concerning the issue of causation, cause rests upon nothing more than the memory of one phenomenon following another.

Friedrich Klopstock, *Der Messias* (The Messiah)—a religious epic by the German poet, inspired by John Milton's *Paradise Lost;* the opening three cantos published this year, the remaining portions in 1773.

Charles Louis Montesquieu, *De l'Espirit des Lois* (The Spirit of the Laws)—a pioneering sociological work by the French writer and philosopher; demonstrates the interrelation of economical, geographical, political, religious, and social forces of history; published anonymously and placed on the Roman Catholic *Index Librorum Prohibitorum,* although it passed through twenty-two editions in two years; popular because the writer held up the English constitution as the model for all European documents of government.

Tobias George Smollett, *The Adventures of Roderick Random*—The first significant novel by the Scottish writer; a series of episodes related with spirit and energy by the selfish and unprincipled hero; the novelist draws from his own experience a graphic picture of the life of a sailor in the Royal Navy; he also introduces the reader to a corps of interesting characters: Strap, Tom Bowling, Melinda Goosetrap, Narcissa, and Don Roderigo, Roderick's wealthy father.

James Thomson, *The Castle of Indolence*—a poem in Spenserian stanzas by the Scottish writer, begun as early as 1733; comprised of two cantos: the first describes the castle of the wizard Indolence, into which he entices the weary pilgrims of the earth, and the second relates the conquest of the wizard and the destruction of his castle by the knights of Arms and Industry; various real-life characters, including the poet himself, appear at strategic places throughout the piece.

EVENTS

A subscription library opens in Charleston, South Carolina.

Robert Dodsley, English publisher, bookseller, and writer, publishes his *A Collection of Poems by Several Hands;* the series continues until 1758, and then again in 1775; it functions as the classical and influential statement of mid-eighteenth-century taste.

Marie Therese Rodet Geoffrin, French patron of literature, opens a salon in Paris; it becomes a meeting place for Parisian artists and writers, particularly the philosophes.

1749

BIRTHS

Vittorio Alfieri (d. 1803). Italian poet and dramatist; he will publish twenty-one tragedies and six comedies; in addition, his canon will include sixteen satires and a number of lyrical poems.

Lorenzo Da Ponte (born Emmanuele Conegliano; d. 1838). Italian poet who will become professor of rhetoric at Treviso; he will move on to Vienna, where he will write the libretti for several operas of Wolfgang Amadeus Mozart.

Johann Wolfgang von Goethe (d. 1832). German poet, dramatist, scientist, and court official; he will emerge as one of the most significant influences on the literature of the Western world; by the middle of the twentieth century, he will have become a symbol of German liberalism, standing firmly in opposition to the emerging Prussian militarism and nationalism.

Honore Gabriel Riqueti, Comte de Mirabeau (d. 1791)—French orator, essayist, and diplomat; his essays will reflect his fiery spirit and eloquence; an astute politician who contributed significantly to the early phase of the French Revolution.

PUBLICATIONS

Henry St. John, Viscount Bolingbroke, *The Idea of a Patriot King*—a treatise by the English philosopher and essayist; determines that the institution of monarchy has been degraded by tyranny, amibition, and vanity; monarchy must be limited to preserve liberty, but liberty without government exists as sheer tyranny; a constitution should come into being, and the role of the patriot king must be to uphold and protect that document.

William Collins, *An Ode on the Popular Superstitions of the Highlands of Scotland, Considered as the Subject of Poetry*—a piece by the English poet addressed to John Home (1722-1808), a Scottish cleric and playwright who was preparing to leave England for his native country; the diction features many pure Scotticisms: "Nor e'er of me one hapless thought renew, / While I lay weltering on the osiered shore, / Drowned by the Kaelpoe's wrath, nor e'er shall aid / thee more" (11.135-138).

Denis Diderot, *Lettres sur les Aveugles a l'Usage de Ceux qui Voient*—a collection of philosophical essays by the French political philosopher; begins to outline his rejection of the idea of a universe operating according to fixed and regular laws; the whole of nature exists as a process of turbulent change and modification of matter.

Jonathan Edwards, *An Account of the Life of the Late Reverend Mr. David Brainerd*—a biographical tract by the New England cleric, emphasizing the piety of his subject; Brainerd, a Connecticut-born missionary, labored among the American Indians; he published a journal in 1746.

Henry Fielding, *Tom Jones, a Foundling*—a novel by the English writer consisting of eighteen books, each one preceded by an introduction on a general topic related to the theme; in a sense, a parody of Samuel Richardson's *Pamela* since the hero serves as the male opposite of that heroine; essentially, the novelist focuses upon the age-old question of right versus wrong; before his eventual commitment to right, young Jones engages in a number of high-spirited escapades that the writer's audience recognized as societal evils.

Samuel Johnson, *Irene*—a tragic drama by the London author; written in blank verse and performed in 1736; concerns a Greek slave who falls in love with an emperor but becomes a victim of her weakness.

——————, *The Vanity of Human Wishes*—an English poem in imitation of the tenth satire of Juvenal; the poet considers such objects of human ambition as power, learning, military glory, and physical beauty.

Jean-Jacques Rousseau, *Discours dur les Arts et Sciences*—an essay by the French writer and philosopher; glorifies the savage state, while identifying civilized society as the source of moral corruption; the piece earns for its creator a prize at the Academy Dijon.

EVENTS

The Danish newspaper *Berlingske Tidende* begins publication.

The London bookseller and publisher Ralph Griffiths founds *The Monthly Review,* a critical journal; Oliver Goldsmith contributes regularly; a rival to *The Critical Review;* until 1845.

Gacobbo Rodriguez Pereire, Spanish-born inventor of a sign language for deaf mutes, presents a pupil before the Paris Academy of Sciences; ten years from this date, he will become a member of the Royal Society.

1750

BIRTHS

Lodovico Antonio Muratori (b. 1672). Italian historian; he will be attacked by the Jesuits for teaching heresies, but Pope Benedict XIV (1675-1758) will claim that he is deserving of papal protection.

PUBLICATIONS

William Collins, *Ode on the Music of the Grecian Theatre*—a work by the English poet, most of which has been lost; in the words of the poet, he intended to introduce "the various characters with which the chorus was concerned (as Oedipus, Medea, Electra, Orestes) . . ."; the classical tragedies serve as models.

Carol Goldoni, *Il Teatro Comico* (The Comic Theater)—a dramatic comedy by the Italian playwright, one of the sixteen comedies that he had promised to provide the public within the course of a single season; a realistic play based on direct observation of daily life.

——————, *La Bottega del Caffe* (The Coffee House)—another of the Italian playwright's realistic domestic comedies offering a picture of bourgeois life.

Thomas Gray, "Elegy Written in a Country Church-Yard"—a popular piece by the English poet; pirated, imitated, quoted, parodied, and translated into Latin and Greek; a pastoral elegy infused with elements of the gothic; written in quatrains of ten-syllable lines; in a reflective and melancholy mood, the poet records thoughts called to mind by the sight of tombs: he compares the humble dead with those who pursued and achieved greatness; in the end, "The Paths of Glory lead but to the Grave."

Samuel Johnson, *The Rambler*—a series of periodical essays by the London wit; he produced an issue every Tuesday and Friday, from 20 March 1750 through 17 March 1752, a total of 208 papers; the essays take various forms and address a wide range of topics; some analyze moral issues, others such "practical" issues as criticism and authorship; still others are brief oriental tales or satirical character sketches of snobs, modish ladies, and naive young gentlemen.

Julien Offroy de La Mettrie, *Anti-Seneque, System d'Epicure*—a tract by the French physician and philosopher in which he maintains that the only pleasures in life come from the senses; thus, life should be spent enjoying those pleasures; the soul ceases to exist with the death of the body.

EVENTS

The Benedictine monks of St.-Maur edit the *Dictionnaire de l'Art de Verifier les Dates des Faits Historique*.

Frederick the Great of Prussia publishes his *Oeuvres du Philosophe de Sans-Souci* (The Works of a Free and Easy-Going Philosopher).

1751

BIRTHS

Jakob Michael Reinhold Lenz (d. 1792). German essayist and playwright; he will become a fervent admirer of Shakespeare and a principal writer of the Sturm und Drang (Storm and Stress) movement.

Richard Brinsley Sheridan (d. 1816). Irish-born playwright; his emphasis upon what came to be known as "high Georgian comedy" will succeed in creating an atmosphere of general good will and well being upon the London stage; depicted the ridiculousness of human nature and society.

Johann Heinrich Voss (d. 1826). German poet and translator; he will gain a reputation for his translations of Shakespeare and of classical works, including those of Horace, Hesiod, and Theocritus.

DEATHS

Henry St. John, first Viscount Bolingbroke (b. 1678). English statesman, philosopher, and essayist; his prose reflects the influence of Machiavelli and the classical republican tradition; he insisted on the importance of cultivating the virtues of prudence and eloquence and a form of democratic Toryism anticipating Disraeli.

Julien Offray de La Mettrie (b. 1709). French philosopher and satirist; pursued the study of materialism.

PUBLICATIONS

Henry Fielding, *Amelia*—a novel by the English writer, the last of his major fictional works; throughout most of the piece, the author attacks various social evils, such as debtors and debtors prisons; virtue and physical courage confront poverty, but misery and suffering continue to abound; however, the novel does contain a number of pleasant and benevolent minor characters.

Benjamin Franklin, *Experiments and Observations in Electricity*—the results of the American sage's contributions to science, continued until 1754; develops the distinction between positive and negative electricity, proving the identical natures of lightning and electricity; further suggests that buildings be protected by lightning conductors.

David Hume, *Enquiry concerning the Principles of Morals*—a tract by the Scottish philosopher intended to correct and complete the philosophies of John Locke and George Berkeley.

Tobias George Smollett, *The Adventures of Peregrine Pickle*—a novel by the Scottish writer; the hero is a scoundrel and swashbuckler who is endowed with courage and wit; focuses on the hero's adventures in England and on the Continent and contains a number of amusing secondary characters; the novelist also attacks the social, literary, and political conditions of the time.

EVENTS

Denis Diderot publishes at Paris the initial volume of his *L'Encyclopedie*, a thirty-five volume work of universal knowledge, carried forth until 1776; the most representative monument of the Enlightenment.

The Halifax Gazette, the first newspaper in Canada, begins publication.

Gotthold Ephraim Lessing, German playwright and scholar, travels from Leipzig to Berlin and joins the *Vossiche Zietung* as literary critic.

William Warburton, English prelate and scholar, publishes his edition of *The Works of Alexander Pope*; he had been appointed the Twickenham poet's literary executor in 1744.

1752

BIRTHS

Frances (Fanny) Burney (d. 1840). English novelist and diarist; her early fiction will be praised by Samuel Johnson, Edmund Burke, and Sir Joshua Reynolds; her later work will keenly portray domestic scenes and anticipate the novels of Jane Austen.

Thomas Chatterton (d. 1770). English "boy" poet; he will "discover" a series of pseudo-antique poems and convince a number of eminent members of the literary establishment of their authenticity; the "Rowley" controversy remained in the public mind for the next eighty years.

Philip Freneau (d. 1832). American poet and sailor; he will become America's first professional journalist and a propagandist for the American Revolution and Jeffersonian democracy; his literary fame will come to rest upon a small quantity of lyrical poems.

Friedrich Maximilian von Klinger (d. 1831). German playwright and novelist; the term "Sturm und Drang" (Storm and Stress) will come from one of his plays.

PUBLICATIONS

David Hume, *Political Discourses*—essays by the Scottish philosopher; French translations secured for him some degree of recognition upon the European continent; focuses principally upon economic considerations.

EVENTS

John Hawksworth, London editor and essayist, founds *The Adventurer*, a London literary periodical; Samuel Johnson and Joseph Warton are among the principal contributors; until 1754.

Great Britain and her colonies adopt the Gregorian calendar of 1582; eleven days between that and the Old Style Julian calendar of 46 B.C.; Thursday, 14 September follows Wednesday, 2 September.

Henry Fielding, the English novelist, begins, under the pseudonym "Sir Alexander Drawcansir," the periodical *Covent Garden Journal*; contains essays on literature and manners; issued twice each week.

The Public Advertiser (originally *The London Daily Post and General Advertiser*) begins publication as a London newspaper; contains the noted "Letters of Junius" as well as domestic and foreign news, and letters from political writers; until 1798.

1753

BIRTHS

Jean Jacques Regis de Cambaceres (d. 1824). French statesman and essayist; he will become Duke of Parma and arch-chancellor of the French empire; his legal writings will provide the basis for the Napoleonic codes.

Lazare Nicolas Marguerite Carnot (d. 1823). French politician; in addition to his political maneuverings and "achievements" during the Revolution, he will write tracts on mathematics, military tactics, politics, and political philosophy.

Joseph Marie de Maistre (d. 1821). French diplomat and political philosopher; his prose tracts will, above everything, maintain that the Pope is the source and center of all earthly authority; he will advance the idea of an ordered theocracy as the only protection from social and religious anarchy.

Phillis Wheatley (d. 1784). African-born black poet; she will train herself to write poetry in the style of Alexander Pope, and her work will be praised by the most prominent literary figures of eighteenth-century England.

DEATHS

George Berkeley, Bishop of Cloyne (b. 1685). Irish philosopher and divine; an ardent seeker of solutions to Irish social problems; his philosophy profoundly influenced Immanuel Kant and Thomas Reid, as well as the principal Scottish psychologists.

PUBLICATIONS

Carlo Goldoni, *La Locandiera* (The Mistress of the Inn)—a comedy by the Italian playwright; Mirandolina, the protagonist, operates an inn in Florence, where people of different temperaments and social classes gather; the middle-class Mirandolina practices simple wisdom, which counters the decadent and pretentious nobility and the rich bourgeois snobs.

Samuel Richardson, *The History of Sir Charles Grandison*—epistolary novel; begins with Harriet Byron, a beautiful and accomplished lady, who comes to London and attracts a number of admirers, particularly Sir Hargrave Pollexfen and Sir Charles Grandison, the latter of whom she eventually marries; interestingly, the novelist takes the aristocracy as his subject, a society he knew relatively little about.

Christopher Smart, *Hilliad*—a satiric poem by the English eccentric directed against John Hill, a quack physician; based upon *The Dunciad* of Alexander Pope and composed with the assistance of Arthur Murphy, a journalist, actor, and playwright.

Tobias George Smollett, *The Adventures of Ferdinand, Count Fathom*—a novel by the Scottish writer; the story of Fathom, a villain who assumes a noble title without any right to it, Fathom lacks honor and decency and his story is one of fraud and seduction; in the end, he is imprisoned, but the novelist saves him from his due fate by having him undergo an insincere repentance.

EVENTS

The government acquires the old Montagu House, London, to house the library and curiosity collection of the Scottish-born physician, Sir Hans Sloane; the 50,000 volumes and 3,560 manuscripts form the basis of the British Museum; George II grants the institution a Royal Foundation charter.

The London bookseller, publisher, and writer Robert Dodsley and the playwright Edward Moore begin publication of *The World*; the London literary periodical will feature such writers as Horace Walpole and Philip Dormer Stanhope, fourth Earl of Chesterfield; until 1756.

1754

BIRTHS

Louis Gabriel Ambroise Bonald (d. 1840). French writer; he will advocate the system of monarchy and prophesy the return of the Bourbons; Napoleon I will appoint him minister of instruction.

George Crabbe (d. 1832). English poet; he will depict the humble and middle classes of English rural and village society.

DEATHS

Henry Fielding (b. 1707). English novelist and burlesque writer; wrote novels of life and manners that appealed to common readers; a conscientious artist who calculated practically every fictional detail.

Ludvig Holberg (b. 1684). Danish poet, playwright, and philosopher; wrote satirical poems ridiculing the pedantic stiffness and stupidity of contemporary thought and life.

Pierre Claude Nivelle de La Chaussee (b. 1692). French playwright; his dramas, though sentimental, were popular; critics labeled his work "La Comedie Larmoyante" (sentimental, or weeping, comedy).

Ignacio de Luzan Claramunt de Suelves y Gurrea (b. 1702). Spanish literary critic.

Philippe Destouches (pseudonym of Philippe Nericault; b. 1680). French playwright, noted for his seventeen comedies; hostile to the skeptical ideas at the beginning of the Enlightenment, he wrote high-minded and moralistic comic dramas.

PUBLICATIONS

Jonathan Edwards, *A Careful and Strict Enquiry into the Prevailing Notions of Freedom of the Will*—a treatise by the New England theologian and cleric, directed at certain contemporary heresies; an essay on human liberty; morality is an emotional and impulsive process, not as a rational exercise.

Salomon Gessner, *Daphnis*—a sentimental, pastoral eclogue by the Swiss poet.

Thomas Gray, *Progress of Poetry. A Pindaric Ode*—a response by the English poet to the contemporary cult of the Sublime; outlines the various sources of poetry, all of which provide life and lustre to the quiet, majestic progress of the genre; poetry enriches every subject with a pomp of diction; poetry rushes forward upon the conflict of tumultuous passions: "In climes beyond the solar road, / Where shaggy forms o're ice-built mountains roam, / The Muse has broke the twilight-gloom / To clear the shiv'ring Native's dull abode."

David Hume, *History of Great Britain*—an expanded history by the Scottish philosopher, completed in 1761; attempts to trace the steps by which Britain had arrived at its current system of government; despite what some consider its Tory bias and superficial scholarship, the work continues to be recognized as the first English history of significance; long regarded as the "standard" history of Great Britain.

Jean Jacques Rousseau, *Discours sur l'Origine de l'Inegalitie Parmi les Hommes* (Discourse on the Inequalities of Men)—a tract by the French philosopher and political theorist; emphasizes the natural goodness of man and the corrupting influences of institutionalized life; people need to enter into a social contract among themselves and to establish governmental and educational systems to correct the inequalities brought about by the rise of civilization.

Thomas Warton the younger, "Observations of *The Faerie Queene* **of Spenser"**—an essay by the English poet and scholar that demonstrates the superiority of his scholarship over his critical powers; the writer's admiration for Spenser comes into sharp conflict with his respect for the rules of neoclassical poetry.

EVENTS

The Select Society, an association of eminent and educated Scottish men of letters, begins to meet at Edinburgh, principally to discuss philosophical issues; David Hume and William Robertson, a Presbyterian minister and historian, are among the members.

1755

BIRTHS

Jean Baptiste de Cloots (d. 1794). Swiss-born French writer and humanist; he will travel through Europe under the name "Anacharsis" to promote his idea of a single family of nations; his published work will attack Christianity and promote Mohammedism.

Philibert-Louis Debucourt (d. 1832). French poet and illustrator; his subjects and themes will be drawn from classical antiquity.

DEATHS

Francesco Scipione Maffei (b. 1675). Italian playwright who principally wrote in verse; revived Italian tragedies from past ages; then went on to challenge the alleged superiority of French drama.

Charles Montesquieu (b. 1689). French philosopher and jurist; known for his satires and political-philosophical tracts; denounced the abuses of the French monarchical system, yet advocated a benevolent form of monarchy; completely blind at the time of his death.

Johann Lorenz Mosheim (b. 1694). German theologian and historian; presented a rational, moderate view of ecclesiastical history.

Louis de Rouvroy, Duc de Saint-Simon (b. 1675). French diplomat and statesman, known for his graphic and accurate descriptions of French court life between 1695 and 1723; dies bankrupt.

PUBLICATIONS

Benjamin Franklin, *Observations concerning the Increase of Mankind, Peopling of Countries* [etc.]—a tract by the colonial American sage advancing the idea that population levels depend upon subsistence; a civilization will grow as long as it maintains its supplies; thus, the people of America must, in the near future, outnumber the population of the British Isles, which will lead to a reorganization of the British Empire in terms of its overseas colonies; the piece further expresses the writer's faith in human progress, attacking the notion of inevitable poverty and limited growth.

Samuel Johnson, *A Dictionary of the English Language*—one of the major literary and linguistic projects of the eighteenth century; the London intellect attempts to fix the English language by adhering to the nation's own literary traditions; the three-volume work is noted not only for the freshness of its definitions, but also for the lexicographer's reliance upon literary quotations to illustrate usage.

Gotthold Ephraim Lessing, *Miss Sara Sampson*—a domestic tragedy by the German playwright influenced by George Lillo's *The London Merchant* (1731); while the dramatist carefully observes the unities of time and place, the ideals of virtue and vice are not presented as unconditional opposites; he presents the passions, the true subject of the play, as potentially destructive to the social order; for the first time in German drama, a middle-class character appears as a subject worthy of bearing the dignity of tragedy.

Francois Marie Voltaire, *La Pucelle d'Orleans* (The Maid of Orleans)—a mock-epic poem by the French philosopher and writer; an attack upon Joan of Arc, a subject generally considered sacred.

EVENTS

The Boston Gazette (second series) begins publication; it will become a leading mouthpiece in the movement for independence from England; John Adams and Thomas Hutchinson become principal contributors; until 1798.

The first *Edinburgh Review* appears in the Scottish capital, but only two numbers are published; Adam Smith is one of the contributors; the noted literary quarterly of the same title will not appear for another forty-seven years.

Richard Beckford, a London merchant, founds *The Monitor*, a weekly political newspaper in support of Whig interests; John Wilkes becomes a principal contributor; not to be confused with the thrice-weekly literary sheet of the same title that was founded in 1713.

1756

BIRTHS

Willem Bilderdijk (d. 1831). Dutch poet and philologist; in form, his works will range from light verse to serious epic.

PUBLICATIONS

Edmund Burke, *A Philosophical Enquiry into the Origin of Our Ideas of the Sublime and Beautiful*—a tract by the Irish-born philosopher and Parliamentarian; advances the notion that anything capable of exciting the ideas of pain and danger exists as a source of the sublime; beauty, that property which causes love (but not desire), consists only in the narrowest senses of smoothness, straitness, and brightness; the essayist also discusses the effects of distress upon the human psyche.

————— , *A Vindication of Natural Society*—an ironic response to the indictment of revealed religion set forth by Henry St. John, Viscount Bolingbroke (1678–1751), who had identified the "unfortunate" results of human creeds; the response examines such forms of artificial society as despotism, aristocracy, and democracy, demonstrating that all may result in tyranny; evils may well result from artificial laws and the division of society into rich and poor.

Francois Marie Voltaire, "Disastre de Lisbonne" (The Disaster of Lisbon)—a pessimistic poem by the writer and moralist concerning the Lisbon earthquake of 1755, which destroyed a number of the city's old buildings and architectural treasures.

Joseph Warton, *Essay on the Genius and Writings of Pope*—a two-volume critical essay by the English poet and critic, the second volume of which was not published until 1782; a work comprising fourteen sections and almost five hundred pages; examines Alexander Pope's poems in chronological order; the writer focuses upon the "correct school" of poetry and attempts to differentiate between the man of wit, the man of sense, and the true poet; distinguishes between the sublime and the pathetic in poetry.

EVENTS

Archibald Hamilton, Edinburgh printer, begins publication of *The Critical Review*, a rival journal to *The Monthly Review*; Tobias George Smollett is the first editor (1756–1759); until 1817.

Samuel Johnson establishes and contributes to *The Literary Magazine; or, Universal Review*, a periodical published in London.

1757

BIRTHS

William Blake (d. 1827). English poet, engraver, painter, and mystic; he will produce some of the purest lyrics in the English language; he will detest rationalism and materialism and express his passionate belief in the freedom of the imagination.

Royall Tyler (d. 1826). American poet, novelist, and playwright; he will write the first comic drama by an American to be performed by professional actors; he will introduce one of the most popular themes of early American drama: the contrast between native honesty and foreign hypocrisy.

DEATHS

Colley Cibber (b. 1671). English actor, theater manager, playwright, and poet; became Poet Laureate of England in 1730, an event that aroused the anger and jealousy of Alexander Pope.

Bernard le Bovier de Fontenelle (b. 1657). French writer; sided with the moderns in the century-old quarrel between ancients and moderns; assailed the Greeks and their French imitators; died at Paris in his one hundredth year, having attempted a wide variety of literary genres and forms.

PUBLICATIONS

Denis Diderot, *Le Fils Naturel; ou, Les Epreuves de la Vertu* (The Natural Son; or, The Proofs of Virtue)—a drama by the French philosopher, essayist, critic, and playwright, first acted at the Comedie Francaise in 1761; criticized for being overly sentimental and contrived.

——————, *Entretiens sur le "Fils Natural"* (Conversations on *The Natural Son*)—an essayin which the playwright views the theater

as a means of achieving social reform; his dramatic theory is rooted in humanity's natural goodness and emotional response to suffering.

Thomas Gray, *The Bard*—a Pindaric ode by the English poet; based on the story that Edward I, who reigned from 1272 to 1307, ordered all Welsh bards who fell into his hands put to death; thus comes forth a lamentation by a Welsh bard and his curse on Edward's progeny and race; the bard then sings of the glory that will come to the Tudors and the poets of that age.

David Hume, *The Natural History of Religion*—a tract by the Scottish philosopher promulgating the thesis that there exists evidence of design in the universe; however, while one may possibly infer from design the existence of the intelligence of God, one cannot infer the goodness of God; therefore, the cause or causes of order in the universe may well bear some remote analogy to human intelligence.

EVENTS

William Bradford, who will become the official printer for the first Continental Congress, publishes at Philadelphia *The American Magazine and Monthly Chronicle*, a political journal; advocates the establishment of an independent American nation; until 1758.

The Swiss poet and literary critic Johann Jakob Bodmer edits at Zurich *Das Nibelungenlied*, a German epic by a poet of the early thirteenth century; it recounts the story of Siegfried; the text will become the basis for an operatic tetralogy by Richard Wagner: *Das Rheingold* (1853-1854), *Die Walkure* (1854-1856), *Siegfried* (1856-1869), and *Gotterdammerung* (1874).

Benjamin Franklin goes to England, attempting to secure for the American colonies more independence; he will remain there until 1775.

King George II presents to the British Museum, London, the Royal Library of 10,500 volumes; those works represent collections of British monarchs from Henry VIII to Charles II; from this time, the Museum will receive a copy of every book registered at Stationers' Hall (or, every book published under "copyright").

Horace Walpole establishes near Twickenham, about ten miles from London, the Strawberry Hill Press, a private enterprise; he will print his own writings and the collected *Odes* of Thomas Gray, among other works.

William Whitehead, poet and playwright, appointed Poet Laureate of England, succeeding Colley Cibber; until 1785.

1758

BIRTHS

Noah Webster (d. 1843). American lexicographer; he will write grammar and spelling texts, as well as a monumental dictionary in an attempt to create and standardize a truly American form of English.

DEATHS

Jonathan Edwards (b. 1793). American theologian and metaphysician; although his Calvinist beliefs appear terribly rigid, he continues to rank among the most original American metaphysical thinkers.

PUBLICATIONS

Denis Diderot, *Le Pere de Famille* (The Father of the Family)—a dramatic comedy by the French playwright that demonstrates his faith in the dramatic viability of bourgeois, domestic subjects; this theory displays the influence of the English advocate of middle-class domestic comedy and tragedy, George Lillo (1693-1739).

Jonathan Edwards, *The Great Christian Doctrine of Original Sin Defended*—an essay by the American theologian attempting to discover the cause of evil and to determine its origins; proclaims the originality of sin as a property of the species; God had ordained a system that allowed sin, and therefore, sin will necessarily come to pass; however, since sin exists as the responsibility of man (man must necessarily commit it), God's punishment of sinners (and of sin) remains just.

Salomon Gessner, *Der Tod Abels* (The Death of Abel)—on one hand, a biblical play by the Swedish pastoral poet and playwright; on the other, an idyllic, heroic prose poem.

Oliver Goldsmith, *The Memoirs of a Protestant, Condemned to the Galleys of France for His Religion*—a translation by the Irish-born writer under the pseudonym "James Willington"; a narrative written by Jean Marteilhe, a victim of the revocation of the Edict of Nantes, the 1598 decree defining the rights of French Protestants.

Claude Adrien Helvetius, *De l'Espirit*—a tract by the French philosopher in which he extends the sensationist psychology of John Locke to the areas of ethics and sociology; advocates a utilitarianism with atheistic and materialistic applications; endeavors to prove that sensation exists as the source of all intellectual activity; the tract was denounced by the Sorbonne and condemned by the parliament of Paris to be publicly burned; yet, the piece was very popular, and it was translated into the principal languages of Europe.

Samuel Johnson, *The Idler*—a series of essays by the London sage originally contributed to *The Universal Chronicle; or, Weekly Gazette*, between 15 April 1758 and 7 April 1760; the essays focus upon events of the day, as the writer attempts to "update" (as it were) the familiar essays of Joseph Addison and Sir Richard Steele; characterized by simple diction and short sentences; literary historians will praise the essays as a repository of some of the finest proverbial wisdom in the English language.

Emmerich de Vattel, *Le Droit des Gens* (The Law of the Nations)—a tract by the Swiss jurist attempting to systemize the doctrines of Hugo Grotius (1583-1645), Samuel Freiherr von Puffendorf (1632-1694), and Johann Christian von Wolff (1679-1754).

Horace Walpole, *A Catalogue of the Royal and Noble Authors of England*—a collection of anecdotes about the principal writers of England; the work became extremely popular.

EVENTS

Robert Dodsley, English poet and bookseller, publishes *The Annual Register*, a review of events from the previous year; in addition to a catalogue of events, the *Register* included poetry and literary criticism; Edmund Burke served as the editor for a number of years; the most comprehensive of all extant periodicals, it continues to be published.

James Franklin, Jr., a nephew of Benjamin Franklin, founds *The Newport* [Rhode Island] *Mercury*; ceased publication in 1928; one of the earliest colonial American newspapers.

1759

BIRTHS

William Beckford (d. 1844). English novelist and travel writer; he will write a gloomy oriental tale of wild imagination that continues to be discussed and admired by critics.

Robert Burns (d. 1796). Scottish poet; he will write a significant number of beautiful, tender, and passionate verses and songs, most of them easily adapted to old Scottish airs; he will become an unromantic love poet within the folk tradition.

Johann Christoph Friedrich von Schiller (d. 1805). German playwright, poet, and historian; he will become one of the most significant figures in all of German literature, perhaps second only to Johann Wolfgang von Goethe.

Mary Wollstonecraft [Godwin] (d. 1797). Anglo-Irish feminist writer, born in London; she will be remembered for writing one of the earliest tracts advocating the equality of the sexes.

DEATHS

William Collins (b. 1721). English poet; his fame rests upon his odes, which received little notice during the poet's own lifetime; dies of a mental disorder and in total obscurity.

Ewald Christian von Kleist (b. 1715). German poet; mortally wounded at the battle of Kunersdorf.

PUBLICATIONS

Oliver Goldsmith, *An Enquiry into the Present State of Polite Learning*—a tract by the Irish-born writer; examines the causes of the decline of polite learning from ancient times to the present day; particularly in France, Holland, Germany, and England; literary decay in England is caused by pedantry, solemnity, artificiality, restriction, and ignorance; the English universities have contributed to the decline of learning.

Samuel Johnson, *Rasselas, Prince of Abyssinia*—a didactic novel by the English writer, based upon the theme that life must be endured, never enjoyed; composed in the evenings of a single week to enable the writer to defray the expenses of his mother's funeral and to pay her debts.

Gotthold Ephraim Lessing, *Briefe, die Neueste Literatur Betreffend* (Letters Concerning the Most Recent Literature)—a series of essays by the German playwright, to 1764; concerns a variety of literary topics, but particularly attacks the slavish adherence to French dramatic models as practiced by Johann Christoph Gottsched (1700-1766), the rationalist critic and teacher; instead, the German poets and dramatists ought to look to Shakespeare (as but one example).

Francois Marie Voltaire, *Candide*—a short French novel, considered a satirical masterpiece; describes in detail the Lisbon earthquake of 1755 and reflects upon the idea that the ultimate reasons for actions and events are unknowable; ridicules Leibnizian optimism because of the predicament of humankind; elaborates a rational protection against the basic evils of life.

Edward Young, *Conjectures on Original Composition. In a Letter to the Author of Sir Charles Grandison*—an essay by the English poet addressed to his friend, the English novelist Samuel Richardson; one of the last contributions to the ancients versus the moderns controversy; the writer traces his "modernist" position to a reading of Longinus's *On the Sublime*.

EVENTS

Oliver Goldsmith, the Irish-born poet, essayist, and novelist, publishes *The Bee*, a literary periodical that runs during October and November; in it appear the editor's own "Elegy on Mrs. Mary Blaizes," "A City Night Piece," and "The Fame Machine."

John Newbery, London publisher and bookseller, establishes *The British Magazine*; Tobias George Smollett serves as the editor, while Oliver Goldsmith becomes a major contributor.

The British Museum, located in Montagu House in the London district of Bloomsbury, opens its library and collection of curiosities.

John Newbery (see above) begins publication of *The Public Ledger*; Oliver Goldsmith publishes his "Chinese Letters" (*The Citizen of the World*) here.

1760

BIRTHS

Johann Peter Hebel (d. 1826). German poet.

Arnold Hermann Ludwig Heeren (d. 1842). German historian; he will become professor of history and philosophy at Gottingen; his economic interpretation of history will foreshadow works by Karl Marx and Friedrich Engels.

Claude Joseph Rouget de Lisle (d. 1836). French army officer and poet; he will gain fame for composing the French national anthem, "La Marseillaise."

Claude Henri de Saint-Simon (d. 1825). French political writer and politician; he will found French socialism; his prose will offer a positive reorganization of society following the French Revolution, as opposed to the destruction brought on by that event.

PUBLICATIONS

Benjamin Franklin, *The Interest of Great Britain Considered with Regard to Her Colonies*—a tract by the colonial American statesman; argues that the change in the balance of population between England and her colonies demands a reorganization of the British Empire; mainly focuses upon events in Canada.

Carlo Goldoni, *I Rusteghi* (The Boors)— another of the Italian playwright's comedies intended to depict eighteenth-century bourgeois consciousness, mentality, and morality; he attempts to strip his characters of their social masks and expose them for what they actually are: boorish!

Oliver Goldsmith, "The Adventures of a Strolling Player"—an essay by the Irish-born writer, originally published in *The British Magazine* during the editorship of Tobias George Smollett; the narrator has been, for the past sixteen years, "Merry Andrew" in a puppet show; he relates the rules of the strolling players and the circumstances under which they must perform; the piece was reprinted in the writer's 1765 collection of *Essays*.

James Macpherson, *Fragments of Ancient Poetry Collected in the Highlands of Scotland, and Translated from the Gaelic or Erse Language*—a collection of primitive poetry from the Highlands of Scotland, supposedly found and translated by the Scottish poet; the poems, according to the poet and his sponsors, pointed to the existence of a great primitive epic, which he would "uncover" and publish two years later; this volume and the epics that follow initiate a controversy concerning their authenticity between English writers, including Samuel Johnson, who termed them forgeries, and Scottish scholars, among them John Home and Hugh Blair, who defended them as authentic.

Tobias George Smollett, *Sir Launcelot Greaves*—a novel by the Scottish author written for periodical publication; an imitation of Miguel de Cervantes Saavedra's satirical romance, *Don Quixote de la Mancha* (1605, 1615), it brings a knight-errant in armor to eighteenth-century England and Scotland; the piece also contains prison scenes drawn from the novelist's own experiences; reveals the usual burlesque and stylistic freedom and variety associated with the writer.

Laurence Sterne, *The Life and Opinions of Tristram Shandy, Gentleman*—a novel by the cleric from Yorkshire; the title of the work is misleading for it tells little of the life and even less of the opinions of Shandy, who enters rather late in the "narrative"; instead, the writer presents a grand and extremely complicated criticism of humanity, setting illusion in conflict with reality; the chaos of the piece is intended as an attack upon the superficial order of eighteenth-century life, especially as depicted in the prominent fiction of the time; nine books, through 1767.

EVENTS

Edmond Hoyle, London writer on card games termed the "Father of Whist," publishes his manual entitled *Laws of Whist*; the volume and its revisions are the authority on the game until they are superseded in 1864.

1761

BIRTHS

August Friedrich Ferdinand von Kotzebue (d. 1819). German playwright; he will quarrel with Johann Wolfgang von Goethe and satirize the leaders of German Romanticism; he will write more than two hundred dramas.

DEATHS

Samuel Richardson (b. 1689). English novelist and printer; known for his epistolary novels that support the highest, and therefore the most restrictive, moral principles; attempted to inject authenticity into fiction and to elevate the genre to a position of greater respect.

PUBLICATIONS

Edward Gibbon, *Essai sur l'Etude de la Litterature* (Essay on the Study of Literature)—the first published work by the English historian, valuable as an early indication of the writer's method, which would be more fully developed in later works; relates familiar texts to historical circumstances, allowing for an understanding of the work and the times in which it was composed; readers must understand the history, laws, and religion of a generation if they are to fully appreciate its literature.

Carlo Goldoni, *La Trilogia della Vileggiatura* (Trilogy on Holidays in the Country)—three comedies by the Italian playwright; each sets forth in detail, and with considerable technical mastery, specific issues relating to various levels of Italian society; in each piece can be seen the beginnings of what came to be known as the modern bourgeois theatre.

Thomas Gray, *The Descent of Odin. An Ode*—a Gothic poem by the English writer, based upon a legend from the tenth or twelfth century; Balder, son of Odin, chief of the gods of Northern mythology, dreams of attempts upon his life; his mother extracts an oath from all creatures and bodies not to bring harm to him, but forgets about the mistletoe, which turns out to be the instrument of Balder's death; prior to Balder's death, Odin

visits the underworld to learn of his son's fate, an occasion that constitutes the major portion of the poem.

————————, *The Fatal Sisters. An Ode*—another of the English poet's pieces concerned with Old Norse mythology; based upon a legend from the eleventh century about a battle that occurred on Christmas day; twelve gigantic figures resembling women sit about a loom, weaving and singing a "dreadful" song; afterward, they tear the web they have woven into twelve pieces; each takes a piece, then six gallop to the north, six to the south: "Horror covers all the heath, / Clouds of carnage blot the sun. / Sisters, weave the web of death; / Sisters, cease. The work is done."

Jean-Jacques Rousseau, *Julie; ou, La Nouvelle Heloise* (Julie; or, The New Heloise)—an epistolary novel by the French writer, his greatest popular success; criticizes contemporary manners and ideas as it tells the story of the passionate love of the tutor of St. Preux and his pupil, Julie; the two separate, Julie marries Baron Wolmar, and all three share virtuous lives within the confines of the Baron's country estate; settles upon the question of a return to Nature as that environment relates to the sexes and to the family.

EVENTS

The first English edition of Voltaire's works published in London: *Voltaire's Works, with Notes Historical and Critical by Dr. Smollett, and Others*; 37 volumes to 1774.

1762

BIRTHS

Marie Andre Chenier (d. 1794). French poet; he will write a number of idyls of merit and produce some ambitious, but incomplete, poems in imitation of Lucretius.

Johann Gottlieb Fichte (d. 1814). German philosopher; he will receive a professorial appointment at Jena and there propose modifications to the Kantian system; his work will contain the rudiments of existentialist ideas that were later developed by Martin Heidegger (1889-1976) and Jean-Paul Sartre (1905-1980).

DEATHS

Prosper Jolyot de Crebillon the elder (b. 1674). French playwright; sought to inject new vigor into the dramatic tragedy by promoting graphic scenes of terror and horror; served as Royal censor, arousing the hostility of Voltaire.

PUBLICATIONS

Denis Diderot, *Le Neveu de Rameau* (Rameau's Nephew)—an amusing character sketch by the French writer; assumes the form of an imaginary conversation between the author and a parasite; he exposes the follies of society with sardonic humor and piercing insight; the title of the piece comes from Louis Sebastien Mercier (1740-1814), the nephew of Jean Philippe Rameau (1683-1764), a French composer of operas and ballets.

Carlo Goldoni, *Le Baruffe Chiozzotte* (The Squabbles at Chioggia)—a comedy by the Italian playwright; concerns jealousies and misunderstandings among the fishermen of Chioggia, a town at the extreme south of the Venetian lagoon, where Goldoni was co-adjutor in 1729; significant as one of the first works of the "modern" European theater, the subject matter focuses upon the lives of the townspeople, and the play is written in their dialect.

Oliver Goldsmith, *The Citizen of the World*—a collection of epistolary essays by the Irish-born writer; supposedly letters written by and to Lien Chi Altangi, a Chinese resident of London; appeared as "Chinese Letters" in *The Public Ledger* during 1760; republished as *The Citizen of the World*; a series of whimsical and satiric comments upon English customs and peculiarities, as well as upon literary matters.

Henry Home, Lord Kames, *Elements of Criticism*—a prose tract by the Scottish jurist, psychologist, and essayist; explores the psychology of readers' responses to literature.

James Macpherson, *Fingal, an Ancient Epic Poem, in Six Books; together with Several Other Poems, Composed by Ossian the Son of Fingal, Translated from the Gaelic Language*—either authentic translations from the Gaelic or products of the Scottish poet's imagination spiced with misreadings and misinterpretations of several original ballads; the central figure, Fingal, rights wrongs and defends the oppressed; the Scots "translator" combines Fingal and Cuthulin (the Irish Cuchulain), although legend maintains the two were centuries apart, and transposes the Irish Finn into a Scot.

Jean Jacques Rousseau, *Emile; ou, Traite de l'Education* (Emile; or, A Treatise on Education)—a significant work on education by the French political philosopher and essayist, composed in the form of a novel; not only do the writer's views on monarchy and governmental institutions outrage the authorities, but his negative attitudes toward natural religion, alien to both Protestants and Catholics, force him to flee to Motiers, in Neuchatel, to seek protection from Frederick the Great.

———————, *Du Contrat Social; ou, Principes du Droit Politique* (Social Contract)—the French writer attempts to solve the problem set forth in his opening sentence. "Man is born free; and everywhere he is in chains"; maintains that human beings are essentially good, and equal in the state or nature; however, the introduction of property, agriculture, science, and commerce corrupts everyone; people must enter into a social contract among themselves, establishing governments and educational systems to correct the inequalities brought about by the rise of civilization; an expression of the writer's opposition to monarchism.

Edward Young, *Resignation*—the last lengthy piece by the English poet; written at the request of Mrs. Elizabeth Montagu (1720-1800), the English writer and society leader, for the widow of Admiral Edwin Boscawen (1711-1761); the first section focuses on the need for people to resign themselves, cheerfully and absolutely, to the will of God; the second part is an address to Voltaire, from one dying man to another, as it were: "To mend the moments of your heart, / How great is my delight / Gently to wind your morals up, / And set your hand aright!"

EVENTS

Tobias George Smollett, the Scottish novelist, begins publication of *The Briton,* a weekly periodical in support of John Stuart, Third Earl of Bute; prime minister from May 1762 to April 1763; the periodical supports the fundamental principle of the Bute ministry: the supremacy of the royal prerogative.

John Wilkes, English Parliamentarian and literary wit, begins publication of *The North Briton,* a weekly periodical in opposition to Tobias George Smollett's *The Briton* (see above) and to the ministry of Lord Bute; Charles Churchill, a political satirist, is a major contributor; the government will suppress the periodical within the year.

The Sorbonne Library opens in Paris.

Christoph Martin Wieland, the German writer and scholar, begins translating into German seventeen Shakespearean plays (until 1766); he thus gives to his nation the first German translations of the English playwright.

1763

BIRTHS

Johann Paul Friedrich Richter (d. 1825). German novelist and humorist; he will gain recognition for his fictional satires, particularly those translated into English by Thomas Carlyle; often known simply as "Jean Paul."

DEATHS

Olof von Dalin (b. 1708). Swedish historian, poet, satirist, and journalist; a significant figure of the Swedish Enlightenment.

Pierre Marivaux (b. 1688). French playwright, novelist, and essayist; a member of the Academie Francaise; his plays are known for their swiftly moving dialogue; his prose comedies of one, three, and five acts focusing upon social problems of the day were very popular.

Abbe Antoine Francois Prevost (b. 1697). Prolific French novelist; Samuel Richardson translated a number of his works; his best fiction focuses upon serious psychological issues and problems.

William Shenstone (b. 1714). English poet; his ballads were praised by such important authors as Samuel Johnson and Thomas Gray.

PUBLICATIONS

James Macpherson, *Temora*—an epic poem in eight books by the Scottish poet, supposedly a translation of Ossian from the Gaelic; the title has its origin in the name of the palace of the kings of Ulster; concerns the murder of a young king, Carnac, and the arrival of Fingal to reestablish the dynasty; a bloody battle ensues, and Fingal, who loses a son in the fighting, slays the leader of the rebel forces.

Guiseppe Parini, *Il Giorno*—a sequence of poems by the eminent Italian lyricist, not completely published until 1803, four years after his death; known for its elegant style.

Thomas Percy, *Five Pieces of Runic Poetry Translated from the Icelandic Language*—a collection by the English antiquary and translator intended to save Icelandic poetry from neglect; includes the "Incantation of Hervor" and the "Death-Song of Ragnar Lodbrog"; will have a significant influence on the study of ancient Norse among English scholars.

Christopher Smart, *A Song to David*—a poem by the English writer reflecting his commitment to Freemasonry; focuses upon the biblical presentation of David, the reformed sinner, as the architect of Solomon's temple; James Boswell termed the piece "a very curious composition, being a strange mixture of *dun obscure* and glowing genius . . . "; written during the period of the poet's confinement for insanity in St. Luke's Hospital, London.

EVENTS

Twenty-three-year-old James Boswell, the Scottish lawyer, meets Samuel Johnson in London; the literary and intellectual sage of eighteenth-century London advises the young Scot to maintain a journal, and those notes will form the basis of Boswell's biography of Johnson.

1764

BIRTHS

Marie Joseph Chenier (d. 1811). French satirist and dramatist; an ardent Republican and legislator, his political sentiments will be reflected in his writings.

Ann Ward Radcliffe (d. 1823). English Romantic novelist who will earn the praise of Sir Walter Scott and influence such writers as Lord Byron, Percy Bysshe Shelley, and Charlotte Bronte.

DEATHS

Ts'ao Chan (b. 1716). Chinese novelist.

PUBLICATIONS

Cesare Beccaria-Bonesana, *Dei Delitti e Delle Pene* (On Crimes and Punishment)—an anonymous tract by the Italian political and philanthropic writer; denounces capital punishment and torture, while advocating the prevention of crime through education; the piece will have widespread influence on the punishment and prevention of crime.

Charles Bonnet, *Contemplation de la Nature*—an essay by the Swiss philosopher and naturalist; criticizes the vitalistic theories claiming that the nonexistence of the soul can never by proved; promulgates a catastrophic theory of evolution.

Ts'ao Chan, *The Dream of the Red Chamber*—the one significant Chinese novel of manners, describing the glory and then the decline of the great Chia family; frequent references to the supernatural world; the author died before finishing the piece.

Thomas Chatterton, *Apostate Will*—a satiric piece by the English poet, then only twelve years of age; concerns a man who professes Methodism for the purpose of obtaining grain, only to forsake his new-found religion for the same reason.

Oliver Goldsmith, *The Traveller; or, A Prospect of Society*—a poem by the Irish-born writer, the first work to bear his name; welcomed by contemporaries as a return to the Augustan tradition of English poetry, absent since the death of Alexander Pope (1744), the work is written in a favorite Augustan form, the Horatian verse-epistle; also an example of the English topographical poem, the piece is a panoramic survey of various nations, with emphasis upon their moral characters; reflects the poet's interest in the virtues of simple, rugged people in contrast to the decadent sophistication of civilized life.

Francois Marie Voltaire, *Dictionnaire Philosophique* (Philosophical Dictionary)—a distillation of the French writer's political and religious views; underscores his distrust of existing institutions and his contempt for authority.

Horace Walpole, *The Castle of Otranto*—a Gothic novel by the English man of letters, written as an attack against the "tameness" of English fiction; according to Sir Walter Scott, the piece was unique because of "the wild interest of the story" and because it was "the first modern attempt to found a tale of amusing fiction upon the basis of the ancient romances of chivalry."

Thomas Warton the younger, *The Oxford Sausage*—a volume of poetry edited by the English writer, perhaps the most noted among the miscellanies of English university verse.

Johann Joachim Winckelmann, *Geschichte der Kunst des Alterthums* (The History of Ancient Art)—a history of art by the German archaeologist and librarian, including critical discussion of specific monuments and pieces of sculpture; considered a very significant work at the time of its publication.

EVENTS

French engraver and type founder Pierre Simon Fournier publishes his *Manuel Typographique*, 2 vols.; sets forth the first system for naming and measuring sizes of type.

The Hartford Courant begins publication in Hartford, Connecticut; the oldest continuously published newspaper in the United States.

The Literary Club, an informal discussion group, established in London; members, including Samuel Johnson, Sir Joshua Reynolds, Edmund Burke, Oliver Goldsmith, David Garrick, Charles James Fox, and James Boswell, gather at the Turk's Head, a tavern in Gerard Street, Soho.

Claire Francoise Lespinasse and Susanne Curchod Necker establish in Paris literary salons as centers for the major literary figures of the day; Madame Necker was the wife of the French minister of finance and the mother of Anne Louise Germaine de Stael, the writer of political and literary criticism.

1765

DEATHS

Edward Young (b. 1683). English poet who took Holy Orders; engendered enthusiasm for the idea of the dignity and the power of the human will; he provided one of the last contributions to the eighteenth-century debate on the ancients versus the moderns.

PUBLICATIONS

Sir William Blackstone, *Commentaries on the Laws of England*—a tract by the English jurist that not only earned him a fortune, but became the most influential exposition of English law in point of style and accuracy; a comprehensive picture of English law and the English constitution existing as a single organic structure; English law is compared with Roman law and the civil law of the European continent; to 1769.

Michel Jean Sedaine, *Le Philosophe sans le Savoir* (The Duel)—a five-act play by the French playwright and poet, still in the repertory of the Comedie Francaise; attempts to restore dignity to philosophers after their public ridicule in *Les Philosophes* (1760) by Charles Palissot (1730-1814).

Anne Robert Jacques Turgot, *Reflexions sur la Formation et la Distribution des Richesses*—the principal prose tract by the French economist and statesman, a product of the "Physiocrat School" anticipating the work of the Scottish economist and philosopher Adam Smith (1723-1790); among the author's theories are the pronouncements that society should be governed according to an inherent natural order, that the earth exists as the only source of wealth and thus the only proper object of taxation, and that security of property and freedom of industry and exchange must remain the highest of societal priorities.

EVENTS

Christoph Friedrich Nicolai (1733-1811), German author, publisher, and bookseller, begins to edit the *Allgemeine Deutsche Bibliothek* in Berlin, a periodical series for popular philosophy; 106 volumes until 1792.

1766

BIRTHS

Nikolai Mikhailovich Karamzin (d. 1826). Russian historian and novelist; he will have a considerable influence upon his nation's literature and will modernize the Russian literary language by introducing Western idioms.

Anne Louis Germaine de Stael (d. 1817). One of the most significant female authors of France; her Paris salon will become the center of political discussions.

DEATHS

Johann Christoph Gottsched (b. 1700). German writer and critic; professor of philosophy and poetry at Leipzig; attempted to improve the German language as a literary vehicle, as well as to reform German drama by eliminating absurdities in style and tone.

PUBLICATIONS

Heinrich Wilhelm von Gerstenberg, *Briefe uber Merkwurdigkeiten der Literatur* (Letters Concerning the Strange Occurrences in Literature)—a tract by the German writer that formulates the principles of *Sturm und Drang* (Storm and Stress); promotes the revolt of youthful genius against accepted standards of the day.

Oliver Goldsmith, *The Vicar of Wakefield*—a novel by the Irish-born writer, begun as early as 1761 or 1762; a kindly and charitable vicar, devoid of worldly wisdom, bears a series of misfortunes with fortitude and resignation: the degradation of a daughter, the loss of practically all of his worldly goods, imprisonment in the county jail; the Vicar holds steadfast to the idea that the sufferings of the poor are compensated for in the hereafter; the parish functions as a form of political republic, consisting of the family, the parish, and the prison.

Gotthold Ephraim Lessing, *Laokoon*—a critical treatise by the German playwright and essayist, written while he served as secretary to the governor of Breslau; the piece defines the limits of poetry and the so-called "plastic arts"; it also argues against the theories of ancient architecture set forth by Johann Joachim Winckelmann (1717-1768).

Tobias George Smollett, *Travels through France and Italy*—a narrative by the Scottish-born writer, written during the height of British insular self-satisfaction; one of the most entertaining and perceptive English travel accounts.

Christoph Martin Wieland, *Agathon*—one of the earliest examples of the *Bildungsroman,* a novel of psychological development.

EVENTS

James Christie opens his auction house in London, where it will prosper as a major world establishment for the disposal of literary and artistic valuables.

George Steevens, English Shakespearean commentator, publishes his reprint of the *Twenty Plays of Shakespeare*; that project will, in 1773, bring him into collaboration with Samuel Johnson on a noteworthy edition of Shakespeare's works.

The second series of *The Virginia Gazette*, an influential Williamsburg newspaper, begins publication; until 1773.

1767

BIRTHS

Henri Benjamin Constant de Rebecque (d. 1830). French Huguenot writer and politician who will write and speak in favor of constitutional freedom; his literary reputation will rest on his psychological novel, *Adolphe.*

Maria Edgeworth (d. 1849). English novelist and, in conjunction with her father, author of tracts on social reform and education; she will mainly be remembered for her didactic, witty, and realistic fiction.

August Wilhelm von Schlegel (d. 1845). German poet and critic; he will gain recognition for his translations of seventeen plays by William Shakespeare.

DEATHS

Emmerich de Vattel (b. 1714). Swiss jurist, diplomat, and writer; he systematized the doctrines of Hugo Grotius (1583-1645), Samuel Freiherr von Puffendorf (1632-1694), and Johann Christian von Wolff (1679-1754).

PUBLICATIONS

Pierre Augustin Beaumarchais, *Eugenie*—a play by the French dramatist and essayist;

written according to the theories of the "Drame Bourgeois" as set forth by Denis Diderot (1713-1784); thus, the central character is an essentially good person, but one misled by social prejudice; specifically directed toward middle-class audiences.

Gotthold Ephraim Lessing, *Minna von Barnhelm; oder, Das Soldatengluck* (Minna von Barnhelm; or, The Soldier's Fortune)—a comic drama by the German playwright; initiates a new stage in German comedy in which the outwardly comic characters suffer from their eccentricities.

Francois Marie Voltaire, *L'Ingenu* (The Unsophisticated)—a novel by the French dramatist, critic, poet, and prose writer; criticizes French society from the viewpoint of a savage Huron Indian.

EVENTS

The Pennsylvania Chronicle begins publication at Philadelphia; a generally impartial newspaper, although it did publish, during 1767-1768, *Letters from a Pennsylvania Farmer*, by John Dickinson, a leading conservative opponent of English policy toward the American colonies; to 1773.

Jean Jacques Rousseau, the Swiss-born French political philosopher, essayist, and novelist, settles in England at the invitation of David Hume; at Wooton Hall, near Ashbourne, he writes the major portion of his *Confessions* (1781), and he receives a pension from King George III; he will return to Paris in 1770.

1768

BIRTHS

Francois Rene de Chateaubriand (d. 1848). French writer and politician; he will become one of the most important French writers of his day and will help found the Romantic movement in French literature.

Friedrich Ernst Daniel Schleiermacher (d. 1834). German theologian and philosopher; he will rise to become an eminent translator and preacher; he will teach that religion, philosophy, and science are not contradictory.

Friedrich Ludwig Zacharias Werner (d. 1823). German Romantic playwright and religious poet; his mother believed that she had given birth to a messiah; his work will reflect his lifelong interest in religious mysticism.

DEATHS

Carlo Innocenzo Frugoni (b. 1692). Italian poet; he entered and then asked to leave a monastic order to become court poet at Parma; experimented with a wide variety of poetic forms.

Laurence Sterne (b. 1713). English novelist; known as a master of humorous situation and character; was frequently criticized for the unconventional form and style of his fiction.

Johann Joachim Winckelmann (b. 1717). German antiquarian, archaeologist, and essayist; murdered at Trieste by a male acquaintance; known for his contributions to the history of ancient architecture.

PUBLICATIONS

James Boswell, *An Account of Corsica* —a tract by the Scottish journalist and biographer, prompted by his visit to Corsica; the piece was used to strengthen the Corsicans' struggle for freedom from the French; published in combination with *The Journal of a Tour to That Island* [Corsica] *and Memoirs of Pascal Paoli* (1725-1807); as with his later biography of Samuel Johnson, the unique merit of the piece rests on the writer's closeness to his subject.

Oliver Goldsmith, *The Good Natur'd Man* —a comedy by the Irish-born playwright, his first play; focuses upon the idea that all of a major character's faults "are such that one loves him still the better for them"; an ironic attack against sentimentalism; the hero moves from foolish benevolence to common sense; the work contains amusing action and clever language, but it suffers from a complicated plot.

Michel Jean Sedaine, *La Gageure Imprevue* (The Unexpected Wager)—a one-act comedy by the French poet and playwright; remains in the repertory of the Comedie Francaise but, as is true of the majority of his dramas, no significant English translation exists.

Akinari Ueda, *Ugetsu-Monogatari* (Tales of the Rainy Moon)—a collection by the Japanese novelist of stories from China and Japan.

Horace Walpole, *Historic Doubts on the Life and Reign of King Richard the Third* —a work by the English writer intended to examine the implications of a document that he identifies as "the coronation roll" of Richard III; supposedly, that document proves that the young Prince Edward either walked or had been directed to walk in his uncle's coronation procession; this piece negates an account of the coronation originating from Richard's reign.

——————, *The Mysterious Mother*—a tragedy by the English writer; focuses upon the remorse of a mother over an incestuous act committed in the past; her son, who had been the unwitting partner in the act, prepares to marry the offspring of that incest; the mother then takes her own life.

EVENTS

The Royal Academy of Arts is founded under the patronage of King George III of England for the annual exhibition of works by contemporary artists and for the establishment of a school of art; Sir Joshua Reynolds, the portrait painter, serves as the first president.

1769

BIRTHS

Ernst Moritz Arndt (d. 1860). German poet; his poems and patriotic songs will rouse the spirit of his nation against Napoleon; later, he will become professor of history at Bonn.

Ivan Andreevich Krylov (d. 1844). Russian fabulist; he will write over two hundred fables satirizing human weakness and social custom.

DEATHS

Christian Furchtegott Gellert (b. 1715). German poet and moralist; a prolific writer of stories, fables, and comedies.

PUBLICATIONS

Edmund Burke, *Observations on a Late Publication intitled "The Present State of the Nation"*—the Irish-born Parliamentarian's first controversial political publication; a reply to an anonymous pamphlet in which were set forth Sir George Grenville's (1712-1770) policies on the taxation of the American colonies; defends the repeal of the Stamp Act on the principle that people ought to be governed in a manner "agreeable to their temper and disposition."

Thomas Chatterton, "Elinoure and Juga"—published in *Town and Country Magazine,* and thus the only "Rowleian" poem to appear during the poet's brief lifetime.

Sir Joshua Reynolds, *Fifteen Discourses*—a series of formal addresses by the English portrait painter delivered between 1769 and 1790 to the Royal Academy; the writer sought to encourage history painting as the most noble form of art; reveals the intellectual and rhetorical influences of Samuel Johnson; because the addresses were intended for an audience of young students, the general thesis focuses upon the rigorous intellectual and ethical preparation required of the history painter.

EVENTS

The English actor and stage manager David Garrick initiates his Stratford Jubilee, calling the attention of the world to William Shakespeare's birthplace and to his work; the first annual English Shakespeare festival.

The pseudonymous *Letters of Junius* begin to appear in the London *Public Advertiser,* bitterly attacking such political figures as the Duke of Grafton, Lord Mansfield, and George III; speculation mounts concerning the author's identity, with Sir Philip Francis emerging as a likely candidate because of his governmental associations and political alliance; Junius, defending the Whig point of view, combines shrewd and clear political argumentation with ample personal invective, and demonstrates an understanding of Thomas Hobbes and John Locke.

William Woodfall, a London printer, founds the Whig journal *The Morning Chronicle*; until 1862; significant contributors include Richard Brinsley Sheridan, Charles Lamb, Thomas Moore, John Stuart Mill, Charles Dickens, and William Makepeace Thackeray.

1770

BIRTHS

Georg Wilhelm Friedrich Hegel (d. 1831). German philosopher; he will become an extremely important proponent of German idealism.

Johann Christian Friedrich Holderlin (d. 1843). German poet; although he will not receive recognition during his lifetime, he will be rediscovered by Ranier Maria Rilke (1875-1926) and Stefan George (1868-1933) and will be identified as one of the most prominent German poets.

DEATHS

Mark Akenside (b. 1721). English poet and physician; haughty and pedantic, his best work is his didactic verse.

Thomas Chatterton (b. 1752). English "boy poet" dies a pauper, from poison; the Rowley controversy will keep his name in the public eye for the next eighty years, determining, in the end, that he himself had written the poems, not the fifteenth-century priest Thomas Rowley, whom Chatterton had invented.

PUBLICATIONS

Pierre Beaumarchais, *Les Deux Amis; ou, Le Negociant de Lyons* (The Two Friends; or, The Merchant of Lyons)—the second play by the French dramatic innovator, a comedy directed against the merchant class.

Edmund Burke, *Thoughts on the Present Discontents*—a political treatise by the Irish-born Parliamentarian in which he first set forth his constitutional creed; attacks the cabal known as "the King's friends," a system of government outwardly opposed to the constitution; questions whether trust lies more in the people or the courts; the right of free election and attention to public interests are among the first responsibilities of government.

and attention to public interests are among the first responsibilities of government.

Johannes Ewald, *Rolf Krage*—the first Danish tragedy, in prose; written in the Shakespearean manner.

Oliver Goldsmith, *The Deserted Village*—a poem by the Irish-born writer focusing upon the superiority of agriculture over industrialization as the foundation of a national economy; the poet-narrator visits Auburn, a village wrecked by depopulation, and laments conditions where wealth grows, but people decay; according to James Boswell, Samuel Johnson wrote the last four lines of the poem.

Paul Henri Dietrich d'Holbach, *Systeme de la Nature*—a tract by the French philosopher denying that Nature is guided by any divine purpose or master plan; self-interest is the principal motivation for human beings.

Samuel Johnson, *The False Alarm*—a political pamphlet by the London sage; a defense of the decision of the House of commons to reject the election of John Wilkes (1727-1797) by the voters of Middlesex; Wilkes had been prosecuted for libel and obscenity for a parody of Alexander Pope's *Essay on Man*; the writer cites precedents for the power of Commons to pass upon its own members, while attacking mob rule and the general notion of populism.

EVENTS

The printers and publishers of *The Letters of Junius*, the pseudonymous series of epistolary essays attacking George III and his principal judges and ministers, are tried for seditious libel.

Immanuel Kant, the German philosopher, is appointed professor of logic and metaphysics of Konigsberg University.

Isaiah Thomas, printer and editor of Worcester, Massachusetts, founds *The Massachusetts Spy*, a journal devoted to the cause of the American Revolution; to 1781, when the publisher changed the title to *Thomas's Massachusetts Spy; or, The Worcester Gazette* (to 1785); Michel-Guillaume Jean de Crevecoeur was a principal contributor.

Introduction into England of "visiting cards" or "calling cards."

1771

BIRTHS

Charles Brockden Brown (d. 1810). The first "professional" American writer; he will become known for his romantic Gothic novels.

Louis Lemercier (d. 1840). French playwright; he will become one of the most promising playwrights of his time; he will ignore the classical unities and rely upon familiar language in his dialogues.

Sir Walter Scott (d. 1832). Scottish novelist, poet, literary historian, and biographer; he will be considered the inventor of the historical novel and will frequently rely on traditional Highland themes; the popularity of his novels will be unprecedented for his day.

DEATHS

Thomas Gray (b. 1716). English poet; his conciseness of expression and pure, almost musical tone contributed to making him one of the most significant poets in England.

Christopher Smart (b. 1722). English poet; dies insane.

Tobias George Smollett (b. 1721). Scottish novelist and historian; his fiction rose above pure social criticism, proving that adventure and personal experience could provide the foundation for readable fiction, particularly if a writer could create believable characters and realistic plots.

PUBLICATIONS

James Beattie, *The Minstrel*—a poem by the Scottish poet and philosopher, in Spenserian stanzas; traces the development of a poetic visionary in a primitive age who derives most of his knowledge from his own observations; includes touches of satire; ends with an account of the youthful studies of the minstrel; written to counter theories in his native Scotland concerning original genius and native inspiration.

Benjamin Franklin, *The Autobiography*—memoirs by the American writer, scientist, philosopher, and statesman; stops, incomplete, at 1758, prior to his most significant achievements as a diplomat and public servant; remains a masterpiece of autobiography and a key work of colonial American literature.

Philip Freneau and Hugh Henry Brackenridge, "The Rising Glory of America"—a poem by the two classmates at the College of New Jersey at Princeton, read at the commencement exercise; a long piece in blank verse that tells of new towns rising along the Ohio River and nations along the Mississippi, American poets writing at the banks of the Susquehanna River, and new civilizations springing forth from the Appalachians and the Carolinas; New York becomes the daughter of commerce and Philadelphia emerges as the cultural and intellectual mistress of the new world.

Carlo Goldoni, *Le Bourru Bienfaisant* (The Beneficent Grouch)—a comedy by the Italian playwright, written in French for the Comedie Italienne; representative of the "new" Italian comedy of character emphasizing loosely constructed form and improvised dialogue and action.

Samuel Johnson, *Thoughts on the Late Transactions Respecting Falkland's Islands*—a tract by the London intellectual and literary sage, identified as one of his better polemical works; discusses the shocking ignorance with which humankind views warfare, maintaining that people have no experience with the utter horror and suffering of war: they know only of what they have read in romantic fiction.

Friedrich Gottlieb Klopstock, *Odes*—a collection of lyrics by the German poet, typical of which is the "Ode to God": "Thou feelest it, though, as the Eternal One, / I feel, rejoicing, the high angels whom / Thou mad'st celestial—Thy last image, / The fairest and divinest Love!"

Tobias George Smollett, *The Expedition of Humphry Clinker*—an epistolary novel by the Scottish writer, his last major piece; offers a tolerant view of evangelicalism, also considering such topics as the English gentry, scientific agriculture, manufacturing, and structure of Highlands society; above all, the work was the novelist's last attempt to view his native Scotland, and to underscore the struggle within his own soul: the progressive, outspoken Scot battles with the novelist and cultured scholar who chooses to live and work in London.

EVENTS

Matthias Claudius, German poet, publishes at Wandsbeck his weekly literary periodical, *Der Wandsbecker Bote*; he assumes the name of "Asmus"; contains essays and poems written in pure and simple German.

Jean Antoine Houdon, French classical sculptor, completes his bust of Denis Diderot, then in his fifty-eighth year.

John Dunlop begins publication at Philadelphia of *The Pennsylvania Packet; or, General Advertiser*; begun as a tri-weekly, the paper will become a daily by 1784; Thomas Paine was a regular contributor; until 1795.

1772

BIRTHS

Samuel Taylor Coleridge (d. 1834). English Romantic poet and critic; his poetic output, although not large in terms of quantity, will ascend the heights of inspiration and represent the perfect products of Romantic imagination and verbal harmony.

Novalis (pseudonym of Friedrich von Hardenberg; d. 1801). German poet and novelist who will come to be known as "the prophet of Romanticism"; he will be strongly influenced by the philosophy of Johann Gottlieb Fichte (1762-1814).

Manuel Jose Quintana (d. 1857). Spanish poet and political figure; he will publish tragedies and poems in the classical style and produce ardently patriotic odes.

Karl Wilhelm Friedrich von Schlegel (d. 1829). German philosopher and critic; he will become the most significant critic of the German Romantic movement.

PUBLICATIONS

Gyorgy Bessenyei, *Agis Tragediaja* (The Tragedy of Agis)—a historical drama by the Hungarian playwright; reflects the French influence as well as the author's own Jacobin ideals.

Johann Gottfried von Herder, *Uber den Ursprung der Sprache* (On the Origin of Language)—a tract by the German philosopher and critic that investigates the problems inherent in the study of languages, particularly comparative philology and language history; influenced Johann Wolfgang von Goethe.

Gotthold Ephraim Lessing, *Emilia Galotti*—a tragedy by the German playwright focusing upon social ethics; the title character is the beautiful daughter of a soldier, betrothed to a count; a lecherous prince, engaged to marry a princess, casts his eye on Emilia; then follow assassination, abduction, and Emilia's murder by her father, who would rather she die than compromise her chastity.

Thomas Paine, *The Case of the Officers of Excise*—an essay by the then English officer of excise, entreating Parliament for higher wages; he was dismissed from his post because of the essay; while further petitioning for his cause; he met Benjamin Franklin, and that association aroused his interest in the problems of the American colonies.

Girolamo Tiraboschi, *Storia della Letteratura Italiana* (The History of Italian Literature)— a multivolume historical survey of the subject, from its beginnings until 1700; until 1781; at the time of its publication, the writer served as professor of rhetoric at Milan and as librarian to the Duke of Modena.

EVENTS

The Gottinger Hainbund founded as a society of young patriotic German poets.

The London Morning Post begins publication as a daily newspaper; enlists such English literati as Samuel Taylor Coleridge, Robert Southey, William Wordsworth, and Arthur Young.

1773

BIRTHS

Jakob Friedrich Fries (d. 1843). German philosopher; because of his participation in the democratic disturbances of 1819, he will lose his professorship in philosophy at Jena; he will nonetheless contribute to the discussion of Kantian idealism.

Rene-Charles Guilbert de Pixerecourt (d. 1844). French playwright who will come

to be known as "the Corneille of melodrama"; he will write over 120 plays and enjoy unrivaled popularity in the second-rate theaters of Paris.

Johann Ludwig Tieck (d. 1853). German Romantic critic and poet; he will contribute significantly to Shakespearean scholarship by assisting with translations into German; he will also become an important literary critic.

Wilhelm Heinrich Wackenroder (d. 1798). German writer; he will become an early exponent of Romanticism and a verse-biographer of the saints.

DEATHS

Alexis Piron (b. 1689). French poet, playwright, and wit; though a self-declared "nothing," his plays brought him some degree of popularity and literary respectability.

PUBLICATIONS

Gottfried August Burger, "Lenore"—a celebrated ballad by the German poet, based upon the Scottish ballad "Sweet William's Ghost"; Lenore is carried off on horseback by the spectre of her lover and they marry by the graveside; William Taylor (1765-1836) and Sir Walter Scott (1771-1832) both published translations of the piece in 1797.

Johann Wolfgang von Goethe, *Gotz von Berlichingen*—a play by the German poet and dramatist loosely based upon the life of a German knight (1480-1562); the hero is strongly committed to his own honest concept of justice, but he is unable, in the end, to escape the subtle maneuverings of his political adversaries; written in powerful prose with short scenes and numerous set changes; translated into English by Sir Walter Scott in 1799.

Oliver Goldsmith, *She Stoops to Conquer*—a "laughing" comedy by the Irish-born playwright, originally entitled *The Mistakes of a Night*; the action of the piece goes forward on a series of deceptions and errors, and comedy is achieved through character and situation, rather than wordplay; memorable characters include Marlow, the Hardcastles, Hastings, and Tony Lumpkin.

Johann Gottfried Herder, *Von Deutscher Art und Kunst* (Of German Art)—an essay by the German philosopher and critic that became the manifesto of the *Sturm und Drang* movement; he wishes to free German art from the influences of France and classical antiquity; considers Shakespeare more a lyric poet than a playwright.

Phillis Wheatley, *Poems on Various Subjects, Religious and Moral*—a collection of poems by the African-American writer, published in London; the first book published by an African-American; contains "On Virtue," "On Being Brought from Africa to America," "An Hymn to the Morning," "An Hymn to the Evening," "On Imagination," "To S. M. [Scipio Moorhead] A Young African Painter, on Seeing His Works," and "Recollection"; praised by Benjamin Franklin and Voltaire, her poems generally reflect her social, political, and moral considerations, rather than call attention to her race: " 'Twas mercy brought me from my *Pagan* land, / Taught my benighted soul to understand / That there's a God, that there's a *Saviour* too:"

EVENTS

The Philadelphia Museum founded.

James Rivington begins publication in New York City of a newspaper entitled *Rivington's New-York Gazeteer*; espouses Tory sentiments, and thus enjoys the protection of the British Army; suspended between 1775 and 1777, then revived under the title *Rivington's New-York Loyal Gazette*; the Tory poet-surgeon Jonathan Odell was a principal contributor.

George Steevens published *The Plays of William Shakespeare. In Ten Volumes. With the Corrections of Various Commentators; To Which Are Added Notes by Samuel Johnson and George Steevens*; Johnson also worked on the general introduction and the introduction to the Appendix; a young scholar, Steevens volunteered to help Johnson with the project, not for financial return, but to promote himself among London literary circles.

1774

BIRTHS

Robert Southey (d. 1843). English poet, essayist, historian, and biographer; he will become Poet Laureate of England in 1813; his clear

and easy prose style will contribute to his standing in literary history.

DEATHS

Oliver Goldsmith (b. 1728). Irish-born poet, playwright, and novelist; dies in his chambers of fever; his work reflects his generosity, warm-heartedness, and love and pity for humanity.

Albrecht von Haller (b. 1708). Swiss poet and scientist; wrote political romances, poetry emphasizing lyrical description and didacticism, and scientific bibliographies.

PUBLICATIONS

Edmund Burke, *On American Taxation*—a speech by the Irish-born Parliamentarian focusing upon the taxation of commodities and the general issue of colonial policy; traces for its readers the history of colonial administration, while attempting to devise a method for unifying the complexities of that system; presents character studies of statesmen in power during the recent past, considering the individual behavior of each; attempts to demonstrate how "great men are the guideposts and landmarks in the state . . . [and how] the credit of such men at court, or in the nation, is the sole cause of all the publick measures."

Johann Wolfgang von Goethe, *Clavigo*—a Romantic drama by the German writer based upon the *Memoires* of Pierre Augustin Beaumarchais (1732-1799) and relying upon the Hamlet theme.

————— **, *Die Leiden des jungen Werthers*** (The Sorrows of Young Werther)—a novel inspired by the writer's hopeless love affair with Lotte Buff, the fiancee of a friend; the hero solves the problems of clashing obligations by nobly and romantically taking his own life; in the actual situation, the writer simply fled the scene.

Oliver Goldsmith, *Retaliation*—an unfinished poem by the Irish-born writer; a collection of humorous and critical epitaphs composed in friendly "retaliation" for similar efforts directed toward him by a number of his friends, including Edmund Burke, Sir Joshua Reynolds, and David Garrick; thus, "Here lies our good Edmund, whose genius was such, / We scarcely can praise it or blame it too much. . . ."

Samuel Johnson, *The Patriot*—a political pamphlet by the English writer, composed in a single day; significant because of its plea for religious toleration; the writer defends the Quebec Act of 1774, which American colonists strongly opposed; maintains that the Act attempts to protect the religious and general rights of the French people in Canada.

Thomas Warton the younger, *A History of English Poetry*—a pioneering study by the English poet and scholar, the first literary history of any significant range and depth; the writer pays tribute to the classical poets, but he also expresses admiration for Geoffrey Chaucer, Dante, Edmund Spenser, and the English poets of the fourteenth and fifteenth centuries; unsophisticated in terms of its critical and scholarly method, but nevertheless reveals the critical tastes of the middle and late eighteenth century and hints at the transition from primitivism to Romanticism; three volumes to 1781.

Christoph Martin Wieland, *Die Geschichte der Abderiten* (The Story of the Abderites)—a historical and satirical novel by the German Romantic writer; he draws his source material from Abdera, the flourishing classical Greek city on the coast of Thrace; according to Cicero, "Abderites" was a byword for stupidity, and that forms the basis for the German novelist's satire (although Democritus and Protagoras came from Abdera).

EVENTS

The publication of *Letters to His Son,* by Philip Dormer Stanhope, fourth Earl of Chesterfield; written daily from 1737 onward and directed toward the sensible and practical instruction of his son, Philip Stanhope.

London printer Luke Hansard begins to issue the House of Commons journals; the reports of those proceedings have long been referred to simply as "Hansard," although they have subsequently been printed by a number of other publishers.

Thomas Paine arrives in Philadelphia at the age of thirty-seven; he will remain in America, in Philadelphia and New Rochelle, New York, until 1787.

The Royal American Magazine, a Boston monthly journal for instruction and amusement, begins publication; Paul Revere's political cartoons appear on its pages; until 1775.

John Woolman's *Journal* published; the writer, a New Jersey Quaker preacher, spoke and wrote against slavery; the *Journal* will become a favorite book with Charles Lamb; John Greenleaf Whittier will produce an edition in 1871.

1775

BIRTHS

Jane Austen (d. 1817). English novelist; although her life will be relatively uneventful, she will provide deep psychological insights into the characters and situations of her novels.

Charles Lamb (d. 1834). English essayist and poet; he will, in spite of considerable personal hardships, develop into a profound and imaginative writer and literary critic, known for a style that combined hilarity with serious meditation; he will become a master at blending rhetorical opposites.

Walter Savage Landor (d. 1864). English poet, dramatist, and critic; he will engage in a wide range of literary projects, but his reputation will suffer from accusations of superficiality and artificiality.

Matthew Gregory ("Monk") Lewis (d. 1818). English novelist; he will create many gruesome, "blood-and-thunder" plays, novels, and stories.

Friedrich Wilhelm Joseph Schelling (d. 1854). German philosopher; he will advance the notion of Positive Philosophy, which will come to be identified with the philosophy of mythology and revelation.

PUBLICATIONS

Pierre Augustin Beaumarchais, *Le Barbier de Seville; ou, La Precaution Inutile* (The Barber of Seville; or, The Useless Precaution)—a comedy by the French playwright and essayist based upon the familiar theme of a tyrannical guardian being outwitted in his attempt to marry his beautiful young ward; the gallant young lover and rival receives assistance from a clever, intriguing servant; the biting satirical vitality of the character of Figaro gives ample life to the fast-paced comedy, reduced from five acts to four after its first performance; adapted for opera by Gioacchino Antonio Rossini (1792-1868) in 1816 as *Il Barbiere di Seviglia.*

Edmund Burke, *On Conciliation with the Colonies*—a Parliamentary address by the Irish-born political philosopher; concerns broad policy considerations, particularly the concept of the Empire within the context of constitutional government; best appreciated for the essayist's use of aphorisms—"I do not know the method of drawing up an indictment against a whole people. . . . "—as well as for his use of figures of speech—"Knowledge is the Culture of the mind; and he who rested there, would be just as wise as he who should plough his field without any intention of sowing or reaping."

Samuel Johnson, *A Journey to the Western Islands of Scotland*—a record of the 1773 visit to Scotland of the London sage and James Boswell; the trip provided the writer with the opportunity to observe firsthand conditions in what he considered a remote corner of the world; thus, he conducted an "exploration" for the benefit of his eighteenth-century readers who remained in their sitting-rooms and on their tavern benches.

——————— , *Taxation No Tyranny*—an essay in which the English writer responds to the American Congress with impatience and ingenuity; he fears the threat of quarrels within the British Empire resulting from the deepening division between the Crown and its American colonies; the colonists, according to his reasoning, had the responsibility to help pay for their own defense against rival colonial powers; the writer's last political pamphlet.

Friedrich Maximilian von Klinger, *Die Zwillinge* (The Twins)—a tragedy by the German playwright based upon the Cain and Abel theme.

——————— , *Das Leidende Weib* (The Suffering Woman)—another tragedy in which the German dramatist equates passion with the so-called "life force."

Jakob Michael Reinhold Lenz, *Die Soldaten* (The Soldiers)—a tragicomedy by the German playwright, a man becomes a soldier to avenge the seduction of his fiancee by playboy officers; swift action, frequent changes of scene, strong characterization, and even stronger language.

James Macpherson, *The History of Great Britain from the Restoration to the Accession of the House of Hanover*—a two-volume work by the Scottish poet and historian; emphasizes the writer's respect for what he terms the purity and patriotism of those who brought about the Revolution of 1688; thus, there emerges an overly favorable portrait of William III; much of the work came not from original sources, but from previous research carried on by the English historian Thomas Carte (1686-1754), a suspected Jacobite.

Justus Moser, *Patriotische Phantasien*—a tract by the German historian and miscellaneous writer; a plea for a single, unified Germany.

Richard Brinsley Sheridan, *The Duenna*—a comic opera by the English playwright in which an obstinate father determines that his daughter should marry an odious fellow instead of the man she loves; the daughter changes places with her duenna; thus, the husband selected by the father is fooled into marrying the duenna, while the daughter manages a union with her true lover.

——————— , *The Rivals*—the first of the dramatist's plays, produced when he was only twenty-three; borrows from Shakespeare, Ben Jonson, and the writers of the Restoration, with witty and flashing dialogue; refreshing because of its satire upon the sentimental heroine and its topical references; with Mrs. Malaprop, the aunt and guardian of Lydia Languish, the playwright introduced a linguistic phenomenon to the language: "malapropism" is the misapplication of long words (" . . . headstrong as an allegory on the banks of the Nile.")

——————— , *St. Patrick's Day; or, The Scheming Lieutenant*—another comic opera by the Irish-born playwright; a scheming Irish officer strives to win the affections of a willful young woman; he refuses, in the end, to break allegiance to his country by leaving the army; the hard life of the soldier is treated lightheartedly: a soldier returning from war in America does so with "one leg in Boston, and the other in Chelsea Hospital."

EVENTS

Robert Aitken, Scottish-born printer and publisher, begins publication at Philadelphia of *The Pennsylvania Magazine*, a monthly featuring war news and political tracts, including The Declaration of Independence; Thomas Paine was a principal contributor; until 1776.

Augustus Montague Toplady, minister of the Chapel of the French Calvinists in Leicester

Fields, London, publishes in *The Gospel Magazine* the first version of his noted hymn, "Rock of Ages, cleft for me"; a more complete text will appear in the same journal in 1776.

Thomas Tyrwhitt, fellow of Merton College, Oxford, publishes his edition of Geoffrey Chaucer's *The Canterbury Tales* (1387?).

1776

BIRTHS

Ernest Theodor Wilhelm Hoffman (d. 1822). German poet, philologist, and librarian; he will become known for his folk poems and antiquarian studies.

DEATHS

David Hume (b. 1711). Scottish philosopher and historian; contributed a significant argument on causation and became a foremost exponent of skepticism; in his own lifetime, his reputation as an economist was greater than that of his contemporary Adam Smith (1723-1790); as a historian, he upheld Scottish traditionalism and Tory convictions.

PUBLICATIONS

Vittorio Alfieri, *Antigone*—one of the Italian dramatist's most important tragedies; the plot and characterization, though classical, strongly reflect eighteenth-century Italian nationalism.

Edward Gibbon, *The History of the Decline and Fall of the Roman Empire*—the principal work by the English historian, not completed until 1788; continues to be celebrated for its achievement as both literature and history; the writer's pessimism attempts to calm the enthusiasms of his age, both the pagan enthusiasm of Julian the Apostate and Christian enthusiasm.

Friedrich Maximilian von Klinger, *Der Wirrwarr* (later renamed *Sturm und Drang* [Storm and Stress])—a wild dramatic fantasy by the German playwright in which he attempted to resolve all of the European social and political conflicts concerning revolution-

ary America; written in Shakespearean prose and including a love scene lifted directly from *Romeo and Juliet*; important only because it gave the name "Sturm und Drang" to the period of literary ferment in Germany during the late eighteenth century.

Thomas Paine, *The American Crisis*—a series of sixteen essays by the English-American writer, contributed at irregular intervals between 1776 and 1783 to *The Pennsylvania Journal*; concerns the threatening issues of the Revolutionary War, principally financial chaos, loyalist opposition, military conspiracy, national unity, just settlement, and adequate government: "These are the times that try men's souls. The summer soldier and the sunshine patriot will, in this crisis, shrink from the service of their country; but he that stands it *now* deserves the love and thanks of men and women."

——————, *Common Sense*—a political pamphlet published two years after the writer had come to America; attempts to direct the thoughts of Americans from dependence to independence; the issues of the day had, he maintains, moved from the subtleties of constitutional law to the point where solutions could only be achieved through "man's instincts for truth, decency, and fairness" (in other words, through common sense); over 100,000 copies were published within three months, and the piece circulated throughout America and Europe.

EVENTS

The American Congress adopts The Declaration of Independence, which was almost completely written by Thomas Jefferson (1743-1826); the opening paragraphs, based upon the notion of natural rights, brilliantly state the American ideal of government; combines general political principles and theory with the details of specific grievances and injustices; a significant document in the history of Western civilization.

The Independent Chronicle, a Whig newspaper, begins publication in Boston; supports the cause of the American Revolution; contributors include John Hancock and Samuel Adams.

Jean Baptiste Pigalle, a Paris sculptor, completes his statue of Francois Marie Voltaire, then eighty-two years of age.

Adam Smith, the Scottish economist and philosopher, publishes his *Wealth of Nations*, the first masterpiece of political economy; examines the consequences of economic freedom and attacks medieval mercantile monopolies and the theories of the French physiocrats.

1777

BIRTHS

Heinrich von Kleist (d. 1811). German dramatist, poet, and journalist; only in the twentieth century will he be recognized for his significant contribution to German drama.

Friedrich Heinrich Karl de la Motte-Fouque (d. 1843). German Romantic poet; he will publish romances based upon Old Norse legends and Old French poetry; he will exploit the supernatural and the theatrical instead of traditional literary devices.

DEATHS

Prosper Jolyot de Crebillon the younger (b. 1707). French novelist; acquired considerable popularity with licentious stories that, however, offended those in high governmental and social positions.

PUBLICATIONS

Edmund Burke, *A Letter to John Farr and John Harris, Esqrs, Sheriffs of the City of Bristol, on the Affairs of America*—a tract by the Irish-born Parliamentarian, explaining to his constituents why he had absented himself from Parliament whenever that body enacted punitive measures against the American colonies; calls for unity and harmony and attempts to define the term "freedom", as well as to resolve the conflicting claims of liberty and empire.

Thomas Chatterton, *Poems, Supposed To Have Been Written at Bristol, by Thomas Rowley, and Others, in the Fifteenth Century*—a posthumously published collection of the "Rowley" poems, edited by Thomas Tyrwhitt (1730-1786), who actually believed in their authenticity; Chatterton took the name "Thomas Rowley" from a local churchyard gravestone, adopted it as his pseudonym, and wrote poems as though they had been com-

posed by a fifteenth-century priest, even copying them upon pieces of old parchment; poems include "Bristowe Tragedie; or, The Dethe of Syr Charles Bawdin," "Aella, a Tragycal Enterlude," "An Excelente Ide of Charitie," and "Elinoure and Juga" (the only piece published during the poet's lifetime [1769]).

David Hume, *Of the Origin of Government*—a tract by the Scottish philosopher, published posthumously; abandons his former view that men exist as natural equals and that society has been established by contract; instead, he argues that political society has evolved from the family, and thus it exists for the purpose of administering justice.

Gotthold Ephraim Lessing, *Ernst und Falk*—five dialogues on Freemasonry by the German writer; he pleads for religious toleration and freedom.

Richard Brinsley Sheridan, *The School for Scandal*—a play by the Irish-born English dramatist; long recognized as a significant English comedy of manners; various parings of lovers bring about complications and eventual disentanglements; playwright to be adept at characterization and a master of stagecraft.

EVENTS

Robert Aitken, Scottish printer and publisher who eventually settled in America, publishes in Philadelphia an edition of the New Testament, the first complete English-language edition of Scriptures to appear in America; Aitken also served as printer to Congress.

The Encyclopaedia Britannica appears in a new ten-volume edition, adding history and biography; to 1784.

James Rivington revives his suspended New York City newspaper, *Rivington's New-York Gazeteer*, and retitles it *Rivington's New-York Loyal Gazette*; the sheet serves as a Tory organ and is protected by British troops quartered in the city.

1778

BIRTHS

Clemens Brentano (d. 1842). German poet; he will carry to extremes the principles of the

Romantics, yet his works will display considerable dramatic power.

Ugo Foscolo (d. 1827). Italian poet, translator, playwright, and critic; his criticism and lyric poetry will strongly influence Italian literature of the middle and late nineteenth century.

William Hazlitt (d. 1830). English Romantic critic and essayist; he will become a controversialist, a master of the epigram, and a craftsman of irony and invective.

DEATHS

Jean-Jacques Rousseau (b. 1712). French political philosopher, essayist, and novelist; indirectly formulated the battle cry of the French Revolution and ushered the Western world into the Romantic age.

Francois Marie Voltaire (b. 1694). French writer and the embodiment of the Enlightenment of the eighteenth century; his works and ideas will help to bring about the French Revolution, although he essentially espoused a philosophy of common sense.

PUBLICATIONS

Frances Burney, *Evelina; or, A Young Lady's Entrance into the World*—an English novel concerning an abandoned child raised in seclusion by a guardian; she grows up to be a beautiful girl and falls in love, but is poorly treated by a wicked grandmother; in the end, all rights itself; the heroine inherits what belongs to her and then marries her lover; the novel was praised by the young author's literary contemporaries, among them Samuel Johnson, Henry Fielding, Edmund Burke, Edward Gibbon, Richard Brinsley Sheridan, and Sir Joshua Reynolds, because of its character development, dialogue, and social satire.

Benjamin Franklin, *The Ephemera*—a tract printed at the American writer's private press at Passy, near Paris; a fantasy on the passage of time and philosophic resignation.

——————, *A Notre Dame d'Auteuil*—an autobiographical work written when Madame Helvetius declined the American writer's marriage proposal; he lightheartedly responded by recounting how he had, in a dream, gone to the Elysian Fields, where he had found the

Madame's former husband married to his former wife.

Francois Marie Voltaire, *Irene*—a dramatic tragedy by the French philosopher, playwright, and historian; typical of his work in the sense that tragedy becomes philosophical when circumstances and situations illustrate the effects of ideological positions and prejudices rather than tragic fate; the writer's last tragedy, written and performed during his eighty-fourth year.

1779

BIRTHS

Francis Scott Key (d. 1843). American lawyer; he will witness the British bombardment of Baltimore and become inspired to write what eventually became the national anthem of the United States.

Clement Clarke Moore (d. 1863). American poet and biblical scholar; he will gain recognition for his Christmas Eve poem, which will be recited by and to American children thereafter.

Thomas Moore (d. 1852). Irish poet; he will become the national lyricist of Ireland, as well as an intimate friend of George Gordon, Lord Byron (1788-1824).

Adam Gottlob Oehlenschlager (d. 1850). He will become a foremost Danish poet and will be remembered for his two dozen dramatic tragedies.

PUBLICATIONS

William Cowper and John Newton, *Olney Hymns in Three Books*—a collection of congregational odes by the two evangelical poets; takes its name from Newton's position as curate of Olney.

Edward Gibbon, *A Vindication of Some Passages of the Fifteenth and Sixteenth Chapters of the History of the Decline and Fall of the Roman Empire*—the English historian's response to charges that he was an enemy of Christianity; Gibbon counters that he had not attacked religion, but rather the cruelty and trickery of theologians, clerics, and fanatics;

the two chapters in question had focused upon the growth of Christianity.

Samuel Johnson, *The Lives of the English Poets*—a biographical and critical collection by the English writer, intended to accompany and complement a grand edition of the English poets; includes fifty-two critical biographies, beginning with Abraham Cowley (d. 1667) and ending with Thomas Gray (d. 1771); the essays are addressed to the general reading public; to 1781.

Richard Brinsley Sheridan, *The Critic*—a dramatic burlesque by the Irish-born English playwright satirizing the tedium and artificiality of Restoration drama. "But some complain that, former faults to shun, / The reformation to extremes has run. / The frantick hero's wild delirium past, / Now insipidy succeeds bombast. . . . "

EVENTS

Hugh Henry Brackenridge, Pennsylvania religious poet, publishes and edits *The United States Magazine,* a monthly Philadelphia journal; Philip Freneau is a major contributor; twelve numbers, from January through December.

1780

BIRTHS

Pierre Jean de Beranger (d. 1857). French poet; his lyrics will be informed by his republicanism and Bonapartism; his wit and energy will endear him to the masses.

Charles Nodier (d. 1844). French writer; he will be remembered for his fairy tales and will influence the Romantics of 1830; he will also become librarian of the Bibliotheque de l'Arsenal, Paris.

DEATHS

Sir William Blackstone (b. 1723). English jurist; one of the most noted and influential explicators of English law.

Etienne Bonnot de Condillac (b. 1715). French philosopher and the founder of the

"School of Sensationalism"; based all of knowledge upon the senses.

PUBLICATIONS

Edmund Burke, *Speech at the Guildhall, in Bristol*—a published address by the Irish-born Parliamentarian in defense of his belief in free trade with Ireland and of his commitment to Catholic emancipation; those positions cost him his seat in Commons.

Matthias Claudius, *Lieder fur das Volk* (Songs for the People)—a collection of poems by the German writer characterized by a pure and simple style; genuine folk songs appealing to popular tastes and containing a vein of broad humor approaching the burlesque.

Thomas Paine, *Public Good*—a prose tract by the Anglo-American radical politician; in opposition to the Virginia colony's claims for Western lands, restates his earlier pleas for a strong federal government.

Christoph Martin Wieland, *Oberon*—the poem by which the German writer is best remembered; based upon medieval tales about Huon and Bordeaux.

EVENTS

The American Academy of Arts and Sciences founded at Boston; represents all areas of learning.

Frederick the Great publishes his *De la Litterature Allemande,* a historical survey of German literature.

The Morning Herald, London, begins publication; a special feature will report police cases and will be illustrated by George Cruikshank, the noted nineteenth-century caricaturist; until 1869.

1781

BIRTHS

Ludwig Joachim von Arnim (d. 1831). German writer of fantastic, Romantic fiction; he will publish over twenty volumes of fiction and poetry.

Adelbert von Chamisso (d. 1838). French author and biologist; he will join the circle of Madame de Stael; he will be remembered both for his work as a scientist and for his humorous tales.

DEATHS

Johannes Ewald (b. 1743). Danish poet and dramatist; primarily remembered as the founder of Danish tragic drama, but also praised for his lyrics and odes.

Gotthold Ephraim Lessing (b. 1729). German playwright, theater historian, and literary critic; a leader of the Enlightenment and a founder of modern aesthetics.

Anne Robert Jacques Turgot (b. 1727). French economist and statesman; a disciple of the Physiocratic School whose economic theories were similar to those of Adam Smith (1723-1790).

PUBLICATIONS

George Crabbe, *The Library*—a poem by the English writer, somewhat imitative of Alexander Pope (1688-1744).

Philip Freneau, *The British Prison Ship*—a poem by the American writer reflecting upon his experiences as a captive of the British during the American Revolution; focuses upon two ships: the *HMS Scorpion,* the "prison ship," and the *HMS Hunter,* a hospital ship on which there existed unusual, inhumane treatment.

Immanuel Kant, *Kritik der reinen Vernunft* (Critique of Pure Reason)—a tract by the German philosopher that examines the limitations of human understanding, establishing the relationship of pure experience to transcendental philosophy; objects of perception result not only from the evidence provided by our sensations, but also from our innate cognitive faculties, which order our sense-impressions into intelligible unities; essentially, though all knowledge begins with experience, transcendental knowledge is derived from cognitive processes that are formally independent of experience.

Johann Heinrich Pestalozzi, *Leonard und Gertrude*—a novel by the eminent Swiss educationist that sets forth his pedagogical ideals and aims.

Johann Freidrich von Schiller, *Die Rauber* (The Robbers)—a drama in the *Sturm und Drang* tradition by the German poet and playwright; presents two rebellious titans, one vengefully immoral, the other concerned with justice and freedom; the first commits suicide, while the second surrenders to political authority; the vengeful immoralist was patterned after Richard III of England (by way of Shakespeare) and became a model for Raskolnikov in *Crime and Punishment* (1866), by the Russian writer Fyodor Dostoevsky (1821-1881).

EVENTS

Joseph II, Emperor of Germany, grants a patent of religious toleration and freedom of the press to his Austrian dominions.

1782

BIRTHS

Felicite Robert de Lamennais (d. 1854). French essayist and journalist; he will be influenced by the Revolution of 1830 and the idea of popular liberty.

DEATHS

Henry Home, Lord Kames (b. 1696). Scottish philosopher and jurist; wrote on Scottish jurisprudence, literature, and morality.

Pietro Metastasio (b. 1698). Italian poet and opera libretist; court poet of Vienna; wrote the libretti for twenty-seven operas.

PUBLICATIONS

Edmund Burke, *To a Peer of Ireland on the Penal Laws*—an essay by the Irish-born Parliamentarian revealing his sympathy with the Irish Catholics.

Frances Burney, *Cecelia; or, Memoirs of an Heiress*—a novel by the English author concerning a young lady who will inherit a large fortune, provided that her husband assumes her name; until she comes of age, she must live with one of three guardians: one gambles, one is vulgar and avaricious, and the third is arrogant and proud; she goes with the third and falls in love with his son; after several trials involving attempts to the girl's fortune, the two marry, with the guardian reconciling himself to the inevitable union.

William Cowper, *Poems by William Cowper of the Inner Temple, Esq.*—a collection by the English poet containing delicate satires and didactic poems revealing the influence of Alexander Pope (1688-1744); such figures as Benjamin Franklin (1709-1790) and Samuel Johnson (1709-1784) admired the lofty but gentle moral tone of the poems.

Jean de Crevecoeur, *Letters from an American Farmer*—twelve epistolary essays by the French immigrant in which he provides a sketch of American life during the latter part of the eighteenth century; the most noted portion, Letter III, "What Is an American," contrasts the promise of American life to the decadence of Europe; Letter IX looks upon the issue of slavery as it exists in Charleston, South Carolina; published in London, then reprinted in Germany, Holland, and Ireland.

Pierre Ambroise Francois Choderlos de Laclos, *Les Liaisons dangereuses* (Dangerous Liaisons)—an epistolary novel by the French Romantic revealing the influence of Jean Jacques Rousseau (1712-1778) and Samuel Richardson (1689-1761); a cynical and detached analysis of personal and sexual relationships; Richard Aldington (1892-1962) translated the work in 1924 under the title *Dangerous Acquaintances.*

EVENTS

Royal Irish Academy founded at Dublin; directed toward the promotion of arts and letters.

1783

BIRTHS

Washington Irving (d. 1859). American novelist, essayist, sketch writer, biographer, and scholar; he will create some of the most popular pieces of short fiction in American literature.

Stendhal (pseudonym of Marie Henri Beyle; d. 1842). French novelist, biographer, and cultural historian; his work will not be appreciated during his own lifetime, but it will eventually influence late nineteenth-century European realists.

DEATHS

Johann Jakob Bodmer (b. 1698). Swiss poet and critic; helped to spread the knowledge of early German literature through his editions of various works.

Charles Colle (b. 1709). French satiric poet and playwright.

Louise Florence d'Espinay (b. 1726). French writer who formed a social and literary liaison with Jean Jacques Rousseau (1712-1778); honored by the Academie Francaise for her tracts on educational reform.

Yokai Yagu (b. 1702). Japanese poet; one of the most significant literary figures of eighteenth-century Japan.

PUBLICATIONS

William Blake, *Poetical Sketches*—a series of short poems by the English Pre-Romantic, written between 1769 and 1778; described as "the production of an untutored youth": includes "To Spring," "To Summer," "To Autumn," "To Winter," "To the Evening Star," "To Morning," and the verse play "King Edward the Third."

George Crabbe, *The Village*—a poem by the English writer in which he contrasts the cruel realities of country village life with the poetic ideal of that settings: "Fled are those times, when, in harmonious strains, / The rustic poet praised his native plains: / No shepherds now in smooth alternate verse, / Their country's beauty or their nymphs' rehearse. . . . " Samuel Johnson (1709-1784) assisted the poet in revising the piece prior to publication. as the dedication, leads to the poet's appointments as Poet Laureate of Russia and then as minister of justice (1802).

Samuel Johnson, "On the Death of Dr. Robert Levet"—a poem by the London sage, printed in *The Gentleman's Magazine* for August, 1783; Lovet (1705-1782) has been described as a poor, honest, charitable, and uncouth lay physician, who lived in the writer's house; he treated the neighboring poor either gratis or for trifling fees: "When fainting nature call'd for aid, / And hov'ring death prepar'd the blow, / His vig'rous remedy display'd / The power of art without the show."

Immanuel Kant, *Prolegomena*—the German philosopher's introduction to the practical science of metaphysics; although the existence of God cannot be proved through pure reason alone, three transcendental principles remain to guide human reason: God, freedom, and immortality; practical reason requires us to recognize these principles purely out of moral consideration for ourselves and for others.

Moses Mendelssohn, *Jerusalem*—a tract by the German Jewish philosopher in which he appeals for freedom of the conscience.

Johann Friedrich Schiller, *Die Verschworung des Fiesko zu Genoa* (Fiesco; or, The Conspiracy of Genoa)—the second dramatic work by the German playwright; written while in hiding at Bauerbach; acclaims the virtues of the noble revolutionary hero.

EVENTS

The New York Independent Journal; or, General Advertiser begins publication at New York City; it features a number of "The Federalist" essays; until 1788.

Noah Webster, the Connecticut lexicographer, philologist, and essayist, publishes his *A Grammatical Institute of the English Language,* the first part of which contains his "Spelling Book"; the first serious attempt to standardize, in America, English orthography and grammar; until 1785.

1784

BIRTHS

James Henry Leigh Hunt (d. 1859). English poet and essayist; his significance in literary history will stem from his social and intellectual relationships with his literary contemporaries, rather than from his own work.

DEATHS

Denis Diderot (b. 1713). Prolific French novelist, dramatist, satirist, philosopher, critic, and letter writer; dies of apoplexy.

Samuel Johnson (b. 1709). English lexicographer, critic, poet, essayist, and novelist; one of the most significant intellectual figures of eighteenth-century England.

Phillis Wheatley (b. 1753?). Black slave who had been brought from Africa to Boston; after her purchase by the Wheatleys, she taught herself to read and to write poetry in the neoclassic manner.

PUBLICATIONS

Pierre Beaumarchais, *La Folle Journee; ou, Le Marriage de Figaro* (The Marriage of Figaro; or, The Madness of a Day)—a comedy by the French playwright, probably completed as early as 1778; considers the theme of the nature of love within the context of social upheaval; the title character descends from the long comic tradition of the "picaro" and engages himself in intrigue and political mockery; thus, Figaro plots to fool Count Almaviva into believing that his wife is unfaithful and to expose his attempts to seduce Suzanne; the piece stirs political controversy, since Louis XVI views it as a threat to the ancien régime; Wolfgang Amadeus Mozart created an opera version in 1786, further increasing the popularity of the piece.

William Cowper, *The Task*—an English poem in six books: "The Sofa," "The Time-Piece," "The Garden," "The Winter Evening," "The Winter Morning Walk," and "The Winter Walk at Noon"; a mock-Miltonic narrative on the evolution of the sofa gives way to descriptions of rural sights and sounds and to testaments of the pleasures of gardening and the rural life; also criticizes the clergy, the cruelty of certain sports, and town life.

Gavril Romanovich Derzhavin, "**Ode to God**"—the most noted lyric piece by the Russian poet; written shortly after his appointment as Poet Laureate of Russia; an attempt to introduce innovations into neoclassic poetic form.

Jacques-Henri Bernardine de St. Pierre, *Etudes de la Nature* (Studies in Nature)—a three-volume work by the French writer; reveals the influence of Jean-Jacques Rousseau, particularly in its creation of utopian environments.

Johann Friedrich von Schiller, *Kabale und Liebe* (Cabal and Love)—a play by the German poet and dramatist, unpopular with the public; attacks the corruption of the petty German courts and their disregard for basic human values.

EVENTS

Supporters of Charles James Fox, who oppose the policies of William Pitt the younger, found The Esto Perpetua Club; from their meetings emerge *Criticisms on the Rolliad,* a series of Whig political satires against Pitt; members include Dr. French Laurence, who will become Regius professor of civil law at Oxford; George Ellis, scholar and antiquary; and Lord John Townshend, poet and satirist.

Sir William Jones, the distinguished English orientalist and jurist, after having obtained a judgeship in the Supreme Court of the Judicature of Bengal, establishes the Bengal Asiatic Society; focuses upon the study of Sanskrit.

The Massachusetts Centinel and the Republican Journal, a newspaper, begins publication in Boston; combines news, literary pieces, and political cartoons; John Quincy Adams was a contributor; until 1790.

1785

BIRTHS

Thomas De Quincey (d. 1859). English essayist; he will become friends with Samuel Taylor Coleridge, William Wordsworth, and Robert Southey; he will be known for his erudition and for his chronicle describing his opium addiction.

Jakob Grimm (d. 1863). German folklorist and philologist; the elder of the brothers Grimm; he will collect, with his brother, folktales for children.

Alessandro Manzoni (d. 1873). Italian novelist and poet; he will write the most notable historical novel in nineteenth-century Italian literature.

Thomas Love Peacock (d. 1866). English novelist and poet; he will primarily be remembered for his satirical novels of conversation or ideas.

PUBLICATIONS

James Boswell, *Journal of a Tour of the Hebrides, with Samuel Johnson*—the Scottish biographer's narrative of his 1773 journey to Scotland with Johnson; valuable for its records of conversations and as a summary of Johnson's attitudes toward Scotland, its history, customs, and people.

Samuel Johnson, *Prayers and Meditations*—posthumously published from manuscripts dated as early as 25 April 1752, and as late as 12 August 1784: "My indolence, since my last reception of the Sacrament, has sunk into grosser sluggishness, and my dissipation spread into wilder negligence" (21 April 1764, 3:00 a.m.)

Immanuel Kant, *Grundlegung zur Metaphysik der Sitten* (Groundwork to a Metaphysics of Morals)—contains the German philosopher's ethical theory, based upon the good will, which is described in the "Categorical Imperative": "Act only on that maxim through which you can at the same time will that it should become a universal law"; his opponents criticize that argument as "the good will that wills nothing!"

Noah Webster, *Sketches of American Policy*—a tract by the American lexicographer advancing his Federalist leanings; favors a strong central government, one that will establish copyright legislation for such items as his spelling books and grammars.

EVENTS

The Daily Universal Register begins publication as a London newspaper; will change its name to *The Times* in 1788.

John Trumbull, Timothy Dwight, Joel Barlow, Richard Alsop, and Elihu Hubbard Smith form The Friendly Club, at Hartford, Connecticut; a literary group that met until 1807.

Thomas Warton appointed Poet Laureate of England, succeeding William Whitehead; to 1790.

Rev. James Wilmot, D.D., of Warwickshire, claims that Sir Francis Bacon actually wrote the plays attributed to William Shakespeare.

Thomas's Massachusetts Spy; or, The Worcester Gazette, a news and literary periodical at Worcester, Massachusetts, changes its name to

The Worcester Magazine to avoid paying the stamp tax on newspapers; until 1788.

1786

BIRTHS

Ludwig Borne (d. 1837). German political writer and satirist; his work will incite the German people to revolution and reform.

Wilhelm Karl Grimm (d. 1859). German folklorist and philologist; the younger of the brothers Grimm; will publish, with his brother, collections of folktales for children.

DEATHS

Moses Mendelssohn (b. 1729). German philosopher and grandfather of the composer Jakob Ludwig Felix Mendelssohn; a defender of monotheism and an apostle of deism; a student of John Locke, Lord Shaftesbury, and Alexander Pope.

PUBLICATIONS

Robert Burns, *Poems, Chiefly in the Scottish Dialect*—the "Kilmarnock" edition of the poet's work, his first collection; it gains for him instant fame; includes "Corn Rigs an' Barley Rigs," "To a Mouse," "The Holy Fair," "The Cotter's Saturday Night," "To a Mountain-Daisy," "To a Louse," and "Epistle to J. L*****K, an Old Scotch Bard"; in all, forty-four poems, a preface, and a glossary of the dialect words.

Philip Freneau, *Poems*—the first published collection by the American poet; includes "The Power of Fancy," "A Political Litany," "The House of Night, "On the Emigration to America," and "The Wild Honey Suckle."

Johann Karl August Musaus, *Volksmarchen der Deutschen*—a collection of fairy tales by the German writer; combines satirical humor with a graceful prose style.

Thomas Paine, *Dissertations on Government*—a tract by the Anglo-American essayist, written from New York; an attack upon the issue of paper money and the inflation caused by that instrument.

EVENTS

The Anarchiad, an anthology of mock-heroic political poems, published in *The New Haven Gazette* and *The Connecticut Magazine*; written principally by Joel Barlow, Timothy Dwight, John Trumbull, and David Humphreys—the so-called "Connecticut Wits"; until 1787.

The Columbian Magazine, a monthly literary journal, begins publication at Philadelphia; contains fiction, as well as articles on agriculture and science; Charles Brockden Brown, the American Gothic novelist, is a contributor.

Johann Wolfgang von Goethe begins his Italian tour; results in his preoccupation with poetic form and his intellectual and emotional attachment to classical Italy.

Sir William Jones sets forth his Indo-European language hypothesis; the English orientalist and linguist has become a pioneer in the science of comparative philology.

1787

BIRTHS

Francisco Martinez de la Roas (d. 1862). Spanish playwright, poet, statesman, and historian; he will be significant in the development of Romantic drama in Spain.

Johann Ludwig Uhland (d. 1862). German lyric poet; he will become the leader of the "Swabian School" and one of the most popular German poets of the Romantic period.

DEATHS

St. Alfonso Maria dei Liguori (b. 1696). Italian bishop whose seventy volumes of published works cover a wide range of subjects, including divinity, casuistry, history, canon law, and poetry.

Johann Karl August Musaus (b. 1735). German novelist, satirist, and author of popular tales, which he falsely professed to have recorded directly from the lips of elderly Germans.

PUBLICATIONS

Jacques-Henri Bernardin de St. Pierre, *Paul et Virginie*—a French idyll, very popular among contemporaries, though it was extremely sentimental and didactic; concerns the growth of love between two young people, both untainted by civilization amidst their natural surroundings on the island of Mauritius.

Johann Friedrich von Schiller, *Don Carlos, Infante von Spanien* (Don Carlos, Infant of Spain)—a tragic historical play by the German writer, based upon the life of the son of Philip II of Spain; focuses upon the father-son relationship, the former a domestic tyrant; originally a prose piece, but then rewritten in Shakespearean blank verse, marking the playwright's movement toward classicism.

Royall Tyler, *The Contrast*—the first American comic play to be presented in America (John Street Theater, New York City, 16 April); develops the theme of urban sophistication in opposition to rural naiveté; relates somewhat to America's continued cultural dependence upon England; an English scoundrel contends for the hand of an American girl, while at the same time engaging in a dishonorable campaign for a so-called companion for his wife.

————, *May Day in Town; or, New York in an Uproar*—a satiric farce on contemporary manners by the American playwright; spring housecleaning and moving provides the background for the work.

EVENTS

The American Magazine, a monthly journal edited at New York City by the lexicographer Noah Webster, begins publication; contains essays on education and on issues of interest to women; lasts only one year.

Alexander Hamilton, James Madison, and John Jay begin to issue the *Federalist* in New York City; eighty-five essays in support of the Constitution of the United States; to 1788.

Johann Heinrich Wilhelm Tischbein completes his painting *Goethe on the Ruins of the Roman Campagna.*

1788

BIRTHS

George Gordon, Lord Byron (d. 1824). English Romantic poet; he will make an im-

portant contribution to Romanticism with the introduction of the Byronic hero; however, because of the satiric nature of much of his work, he is difficult to place within the Romantic movement.

Joseph Eichendorff (d. 1857). German Romantic poet, novelist, and critic; he will be best remembered for his Romantic lyrics.

Friedrich Ruckert (d. 1866). German poet; he will become filled with a sense of national pride and fervent patriotism; also, he will translate into German works of Oriental origin.

Arthur Schopenhauer (d. 1860). German pessimistic philosopher; he will develop the idea that reason and feeling exist in perpetual conflict.

DEATHS

Georges Louis Buffon (b. 1707). French naturalist philosopher; gave natural science a certain degree of respectability; anticipated the theory of evolution.

Mather Byles (b. 1707). American poet; the majority of his works focus upon theological considerations; although generally considered "dull," his pieces contain occasional outbursts of eighteenth-century wit.

Johann Georg Hamann (b. 1730). German philosopher and theologian, known as "the Magus of the North"; influenced Johann Gottfried Herder and Johann Wolfgang von Goethe; his essays abound with literary allusions.

PUBLICATIONS

Jean Jacques Barthelemy, *Voyage du jeune Anacharsis en Grece* (The Voyage of the Young Anacharsis into Greece)—a work by the French historian praised for its literary merit; concerns the witty Scythian prince who traveled widely in search of knowledge around 590 B.C.; published in five volumes, with a seven-volume edition in 1799.

Johann Wolfgang von Goethe, *Egmont*—a dramatic tragedy by the German poet and playwright, based upon the downfall of Count Egmont (1522-1568), who suffered execution in connection with the revolt of the Netherlands against Spain; the title character strives for freedom, but cannot survive the political machinery that surrounds him; Ludwig van Beethoven wrote the noted musical overture for this play.

——————, *Iphigenie auf Tauris*—a tragedy focusing upon the traditional family curse; through that curse, however, emerges an ethic that recognizes both the limitations of human life and the value of human responsibility and trust.

Immanuel Kant, *Kritik der praktischen Vernunft* (Critique of Practical Reason)—a treatise by the German metaphysical philosopher in which he sets forth the idea that morality requires belief in the existence of God, freedom, and immortality; his system of ethics centers upon the "categorical imperative"; or absolute moral law.

EVENTS

The Calliopean Society founded in New York City as a debating forum; also involved in literary, social, and educational projects; William Irving, the novelist's eldest brother and a satirist, was one of the principal members.

The third edition of the *Encyclopaedia Britannica* begins publication; 15 vols., to 1797.

Sir James Edward Smith, English botanist, founds the Linnean Society; the organization will honor Carl von Linne, the Swedish naturalist and developer of the science of botany; Smith will compile the 36-volume collection, *English Botany* (1794-1814).

The Times of London begins publication on 1 January, succeeding *The Daily Universal Register* (1785-1788); it will shortly emerge as one of the most significant newspapers in the world.

1789

BIRTHS

James Fenimore Cooper (d. 1851). American novelist; although his numerous works will prove artistically inconsistent, he will emerge as the first major American writer of long fiction.

DEATHS

John Cleland (b. 1709). English novelist and journalist; rose to prominence for his "pornographic" novel (*Fanny Hill*) that enjoyed (and still seems to enjoy) surreptitious publication.

Paul Heinrich Dietrich Hollbach (b. 1723). German-born French philosopher; expounded upon the natural principles of morality, while attempting to promote self-interest as the ruling motive of humankind.

PUBLICATIONS

Jeremy Bentham, *An Introduction to the Principles of Morals and Legislation*—a tract by the English writer on jurisprudence and utilitarian ethics that sets forth the fundamental notion that the greatest happiness of the greatest number of persons should be the object of all conduct and legislation.

William Blake, *The Book of Thel*—a poetic allegory of the unborn spirit visiting the world of generation; Thel rejects the self-sacrificing of experience and flees back to eternity; the symbols of the Lily of the Valley, the Cloud, the Worm, and the Clod of Clay represent idealistic fancy, youth, adolescence, and motherhood.

——————, *Songs of Innocence*—a set of poems that includes "A Dream," "The Little Girl Lost," "The Little Girl Found," "The Lamb," "The Blossom," "The Chimney Sweeper," "The Little Boy Found," and "The Little Black Boy."

——————, *Tiriel*—the earliest of the poet's symbolic works; the prototype of the title character may well have been George III in his madness; other characters (Har, Heva) represent poetry and painting, two arts that did not profit during the reign of George III (1760-1820).

Marie Joseph de Chenier, *Charles IX; ou, La Sainte-Barthelemy*—a French pre-Romantic play that combines dramatic tension with poetic language; appeals to the growing fervor of the Revolution.

Noah Webster, *Dissertations on the English Language*—an essay by the American lexicographer that contains his views on reforming "American" spelling; the piece was encouraged by Benjamin Franklin.

EVENTS

The Annals of Congress, Washington, D.C., begins publication; reports the proceedings of the U.S. Senate and the House of Representatives; until 1824.

Dr. Charles Burney, organist, composer, music historian, and member of Samuel Johnson's London literary circle, publishes his *History of Music*; four volumes, begun in 1776.

John Fenno begins publication of the New York City weekly newspaper, *Gazette of the United States*; it becomes an organ of the Federalists and moves, in 1792, to Philadelphia, where it becomes a daily; until 1847.

Sir William Jones, the distinguished English jurist and Oriental scholar, translates from the Sanskrit the tragedy of Kalidasa (c. 220 A.D.), *Sacontala; or, The Fatal Ring: An Indian Drama.*

1790

BIRTHS

Alphonse Marie Louis Lamartine (d. 1869). French poet, historian, and statesman; the power of his artistry will derive from his ability to draw upon both traditional and contemporary sources.

DEATHS

Benjamin Franklin (b. 1706). American statesman, philosopher, scientist, and writer; the epitome of the eighteenth-century enlightened man.

Thomas Warton (b. 1728). Poet Laureate of England; Professor of Poetry at Oxford; authored burlesque poetry and prose, as well as satire.

PUBLICATIONS

Edmund Burke, *Reflections on the Revolution in France*—a treatise by the Irish-born Parliamentarian; repudiates the constitutional doctrine and asserts the system of hereditary succession; determines that the French revolutionists based their ideals upon extravagant and presumptuous speculations inconsistent with an ordered society and promotive only of poverty and chaos; concludes that the defective institutions of the ancien régime should have been reformed, not destroyed.

Andre Chenier, *Avis au Peuple Francais* (An Opinion to the People of France)—a pamphlet by the French poet and diplomat set against the background of the Revolution that he once supported; alarmed by the excesses of that uprising, he attacks the politics of Robespierre.

Johann Wolfgang von Goethe, *Torquato Tasso*—a dramatic tragedy by the German writer; underscores the problems of the artist in society; based purely upon the dramatist's own experiences while resident poet at Weimar.

Immanuel Kant, *Kritik der Urteilskraft* (Critique of Judgment)—a remarkable treatment of the basic philosophical problems in aesthetics; claims the aesthetic judgment to be independent of personal, psychological, and moral considerations, but still singular and universally valid; the essay completes the "Kantian system."

Nikolai Mikhailovich Karamzin, *Letters of a Russian Traveller*—a narrative composed by the Russian historian and novelist as he toured Western Europe; to 1792.

EVENTS

The Columbian Centinel, a Boston newspaper, succeeds and absorbs *The Massachusetts Centinel and Republican Journal*; until 1840.

The General Advertiser, a Philadelphia anti-Federalist newspaper, begins publication; gives way, in 1794, to the *Aurora*.

The New York Magazine, a monthly literary journal, begins publication in New York City; mainly prints previously published material; Charles Brockden Brown, the American novelist, was a principal contributor of original works; until 1797.

Henry James Pye appointed Poet Laureate of England; until 1813; becomes the constant object of ridicule by his literary contemporaries.

David Williams, an English Dissenting minister, Cavendish Square, London, establishes the Royal Literary Fund.

1791

BIRTHS

Franz Grillparzer (d. 1872). Austrian dramatic poet; he will write out of compulsion, rather than from a strong desire to create; thus, he will not strive for public acclaim.

Johann Ludvig Heiberg (d. 1860). Danish dramatic poet, critic, and director of the National Theater of Denmark; he will become extremely influential in establishing norms of taste in both drama and dramatic criticism, especially as he experiments with the materials and techniques of comedy.

Karl Theodor Korner (d. 1813). German lyric poet who will write emotional, patriotic songs.

Augustin Eugene Scribe (d. 1861). French playwright; he will establish a theater workshop in which numerous "collaborators" will work under his supervision and literally mass-produce plays with similar themes and dialogue; the architect of the French "well-made" play.

DEATHS

Honore Gabriel Riqueti, Comte de Mirabeau (b. 1749). French essayist, orator, and revolutionary; his written work reflects the true art of the politician: it is characterized by a spirit of moderation, compromise, and opportunism.

Christian Friedrich Daniel Schubert (b. 1739). German poet; wrote satirical and religious verse; a strong influence upon Johann Friedrich Schiller.

PUBLICATIONS

William Blake, *The French Revolution*—a work in seven books by the English poet; printed, but not published until 1913; fully develops the writer's contempt for oppressive authority: "The dead brood over Europe, the cloud and vision descends over cheerful France. . . ."

James Boswell, *The Life of Samuel Johnson, L.L.D.*—certainly one of the most noted of all biographies in English; combines biographical narrative with a record of conversations that took place during the more than 270 occasions upon which the Scottish lawyer and man of letters sat in the company of the sage and literary-intellectual sovereign of eighteenth-century London; a close reading of the book reveals it to be the work of a conscious literary artist, natural journalist, and careful researcher.

Edmund Burke, *An Appeal from the New to the Old Whigs*—a tract by the Irish-born Parliamentarian defending himself against charges that his attitudes toward the American colonies and the French Revolution were inconsistent.

Robert Burns, *"Tam O'Shanter"*—a poem by the Scottish bard, a mock-heroic version of folk material; based upon a witch story about Allway Kirk, an old ruin near the poet's house in Ayr; according to William Wordsworth, the piece had considerable moral effect upon its readers, though it was not intended to do so.

Marie Joseph Chenier, *Henry VIII*—a heavy dramatic tragedy by the French legislator; representative of his ardent republicanism.

Johann Gottfried Herder, *Ideen zur Geschichte der Menschheit* (Outlines of the Philosophy of Man)—a tract begun in 1784 by the German poet and critic; develops an evolutionary approach to history, propounding the uniqueness of each historical age; remarkable for its anticipation of evolutionary theories that would develop almost six decades later.

Thomas Paine, *The Rights of Man*—a political tract arguing against Edmund Burke's criticism of the French Revolution; in two parts, to 1792; in the first part, the writer denies the idea that one generation can bind another to a specific form of government; in the second part, he compares the principles of the new American and French constitutions with those of the British forms and sets forth proposals for improving conditions in Europe and England.

Ann Radcliffe, *The Romance of the Forest*—a Gothic novel by the English writer; concerns an aristocrat who, after wasting his resources, falls into evil ways and escapes from Paris in the midst of storm and darkness; he meets a ruffian and a beautiful young girl; a series of journeys takes him to a lonely house, a deserted abbey, and over various darkened and stormy highways; the complexities of plot evolve from secret manuscripts and rivals for the hand of the young lady; fortunately, her virtue triumphs, but not without additional trials.

Marquis Donatien Alphonse Francois de Sade, *Justine*—a French novel that focuses upon sexual gratification; the piece supports the theory that sexual deviation and criminal acts exist in nature, representing natural, psychological thought.

EVENTS

Johann Wolfgang von Goethe named director of the Weimar Court Theater; until 1817.

Thomas Jefferson sponsors *The National Gazette,* a newspaper published at Philadelphia; edited by the American writer Philip Freneau, the periodical serves as an organ of the Democratic Republican Party; until 1793.

The Observer begins publication in London; it will become the oldest Sunday newspaper in Great Britain and pass to the ownership of the Atlantic Richfield Oil Company.

1792

BIRTHS

Gustav Schwab (d. 1850). German writer and philosopher.

Percy Bysshe Shelley (d. 1822). English Romantic poet; he will advance the Platonic notion of the poet as divinely inspired, who thus functions as a legislator to humankind.

Edward John Trelawny (d. 1881). English writer and adventurer; friend of Shelley and Byron.

DEATHS

Jakob Michael Reinhold Lenz (b. 1751). German dramatist and poet; a proponent of the *Sturm und Drang* school, and thus an admirer of Shakespeare; suffers from a mental breakdown while living in poverty in Moscow.

Sir Joshua Reynolds (b. 1723). English portrait painter, essayist, and philosopher; founder of

the literary club that included Samuel Johnson, James Boswell, Edmund Burke, Oliver Goldsmith, and Richard Brinsley Sheridan.

PUBLICATIONS

Nikolai Mikhailovich Karamzin, "Poor Liza"—a short story by the Russian writer, important because it forecasts the novel of social protest.

Claude Joseph Rouget de Lisle, "La Marseillaise"—a poem by the French army officer, with music, that will become the national anthem of France; originally entitled "Chant de l'Armee du Rhin"; imported to Paris by troops from Marseilles: "March on! march on! all hearts resolved / On victory, or death."

Mary Wollstonecraft [Godwin], *Vindication of the Rights of Woman*—a blunt attack by the English writer upon the educational restrictions and ill-founded ideas that confine women to ignorance and slavish dependence; woman's primary function in contemporary society should not be to please others; Horace Walpole refers to the author as "a hyena in petticoats."

Arthur Young, *Travels in France*—a narrative by the English writer, based upon his tour during 1787-1790; the writer calls attention to the deteriorating social and economic conditions on the eve of the Revolution, and he envisions the downfall of the *ancien regime*.

EVENTS

Robert Bailey Thomas of West Boylston, Massachusetts, publishes at Boston the first edition of *The Old Farmer's Almanack*; by 1863, the book will reach sales of 225,000 copies.

1793

BIRTHS

Karl Jonas Ludvig Almqvist (d. 1866). Swedish writer; he will compose stories, plays and poems the style of which will range from romantic to starkly realistic.

Jean Francois Casimir Delavigne (d. 1843). French playwright, satirist, and poet; he will gain popularity from his post-Revolutionary satires.

DEATHS

Charles Bonnet (b. 1720). Swiss philosopher and naturalist; an adherent of the catastrophic theory of evolution, he maintained that the nonexistence of the soul could never be proved.

Nicolas Sebastian Chamfort (b. 1740). French playwright and political wit who came to be known as "La Rouchefoucauld-Chamfort"; dies from wounds self-inflicted prior to his arrest during the Reign of Terror.

Carlo Goldoni (b. 1707). Venetian dramatist; his comedies revolutionized the Italian stage; wrote approximately 250 plays.

PUBLICATIONS

William Blake, *America: A Prophecy*—a poem by the English poet focusing upon the American Revolution; historical events and persons gain mystical significance; Orc, the spirit of revolt, functions as the hero, while the villain emerges as the Guardian Prince of Albion (King George III) and typifies the forces of repression.

——————— , *The Marriage of Heaven and Hell*—a poem that primarily serves as a satire against two works by the Swedish mystic Emmanuel Swedenborg (1688-1772): *Heaven and Hell* and *Memorable Relations*; a series of satirical manifestos and paradoxical aphorisms (Proverbs of Hell); begun as early as 1790.

——————— , *Visions of the Daughters of Albion*—a poem that has been characterized as "a dramatic treatise on the related questions of moral, economic, and sexual freedom"; attacks those political philosophies that separate bodies from souls and reduce women and children, nations and lands, to mere possessions; considers, also, the issue of slavery.

William Wordsworth, *Descriptive Sketches*—written by the English poet during a tour of the Italian and Swiss Alps; the theme is the idea that happiness on earth can be found only among the charms of Nature; also considers such political matters as liberty and slavery.

——————— , *An Evening Walk*—the first serious poetic effort by the English Romantic; an exercise in transferring visual memories into formal couplets; introduces the conventionally picturesque gypsy, an image that will emerge in later, more mature pieces.

EVENTS

The American lexicographer Noah Webster begins publication at New York of *The American Minerva*, a daily journal in support of Federalist attitudes toward the French; until 1797, when the name will change to *The Commercial Advertiser*.

Isaiah Thomas, Massachusetts publisher and editor, publishes at Walpole, New Hampshire, *The Farmer's Weekly Museum*, a newspaper and quasi-literary journal; to 1810.

1794

BIRTHS

William Cullen Bryant (d. 1878). American poet and journalist; he will become one of the earliest of American theorists on poetry, as well as a principal translator of Homer.

DEATHS

Cesare Beccaria-Bonesana (b. 1738?). Italian philanthropic and political writer; attacked capital punishment and torture and advocated elimination of crime through early education.

Gottfried August Burger (b. 1747). German lyric poet; his major work was translated into English by Sir Walter Scott.

Andre Chenier (b. 1762). French poet whose idylls reflect his classical studies; executed on the guillotine six days before the end of the Reign of Terror.

Marie Jean Antoine Nicolas Caritat, Marquis de Condorcet (b. 1743). French mathematician and politician; most of his tracts concerned popular but radical issues.

Jean Baptiste de Cloots (b. 1755). Prussian-French revolutionist who considered himself the "orator of the human race"; known for his sometimes absurd prose; guillotined in Paris.

Ramon de la Cruz (b. 1731). Spanish dramatist who wrote over 450 one-act comedies about middle- and lower-class life; freed Spanish drama from foreign influences.

Edward Gibbon (b. 1737). English historian who demonstrated that history could serve and function as literature without sacrificing accuracy and scholarly research.

Girolamo Tiraboschi (b. 1731). Italian scholar, rhetorician, and librarian; accurately surveyed the history of Italian literature.

PUBLICATIONS

William Blake, *The First Book of Urizen*—a series of poems by the English pre-Romantic; concerned with the creation of the material world and of humankind; Urizen, the God of Reason, resembles the Hebrew Jehovah and exists as the Creator; Urizen eventually establishes religion, and humankind entangles itself in the web of religion as civilization emerges in Egypt; Los, the poetic genius and representative of Time, comes in contact with Urizen, since Reason cannot exist without Imagination; from their union comes Orc, the spirit of revolution.

——————, *Europe: A Prophecy*—a historical parable in verse; begins with the Christian era and ends with the French Revolution, also taking into consideration England's preparations for war; the story focuses upon the separation of Enitharmon (Inspiration) from her eternal partner, Los (the spirit of Poetry); the coming of war, with its horrors, results from the imposition of Enitharmon's feminine will upon the world.

——————, *Songs of Experience*—a set of short poems governed by a sense of gloom and mystery, with references to the power of evil; includes "Earth's Answer," "The Clod and the Pebble," "Holy Thursday," "The Chimney Sweeper," "The Fly," "The Tyger," "The Garden of Love," and "London."

Johann Fichte, *Grundlage der Gesamten Wissenschaftslehre* (Foundations of the Whole Theory of Science)—a tract by the German philosopher in which the Ego affirms itself, simply and unconditionally, as the primitive act of consciousness; in opposition to that exists the Non-Ego, or the objective world; herein one finds the rudiments of existentialism; the philosopher departs from Kantian transcendentalism by replacing God with an absolute mind ("Ur-Ich"), or what he terms "a Primeval Self."

Thomas Paine, *The Age of Reason*—a treatise by the English writer, composed during his stay in Paris at the height of the French Revolution; emphasizes the writer's belief in one God, but rejects Christianity and the Bible; a plea for religious toleration; to 1795.

Ann Radcliffe, *The Mysteries of Udolpho*—a novel by the English writer; the main character, carried off by a villainous uncle to a remote mountain castle, lives in fear of supernatural terrors; she finally escapes and is united with her lover; serves as the basis for Jane Austen's *Northanger Abbey* (1818).

Johann Paul Friedrich Richter, *Hesperus*—a romantic novel that brought the German writer literary fame; concerned with the paradoxes rooted within the universe.

EVENTS

The anti-Federalist newspaper *Aurora* begins publication in Philadelphia, espousing pro-French and anti-Washington sentiments; the reason for the passage in Congress of the various Alien and Sedition Acts; to 1822; revived during 1834, but ceased publication the following year.

1795

BIRTHS

Thomas Carlyle (d. 1881). Scottish essayist, translator, and literary historian; he will exert considerable cultural and intellectual influence upon nineteenth-century British letters.

Aleksandr Sergeyevich Griboyedov (d. 1829). Russian playwright and diplomat; he will become a satirist of contemporary Moscow society.

John Keats (d. 1821). English Romantic poet; his odes will exhibit a highly delicate and sensitive imagination.

Leopold von Ranke (d. 1886). German historian; his strength will be in the development of historiography from the political point of view.

Jacques Nicolas Augustin Thierry (d. 1856). French historian who will rely on original documents and present history with an emphasis upon the dramatic.

DEATHS

Jean Jacques Barthelemy (b. 1716). French cleric and antiquary; best known for his editions of classical travel literature.

Karl Michael Bellmann (b. 1740). Swedish poet; his verses convey the detail and humor of Swedish life and include portraits of friends and drinking companions.

PUBLICATIONS

William Blake, *The Book of Ahania*—a series of English poems continuing the myth of Urizen from prehistoric to biblical times; relates the story of the flight of the Israelites from Egypt, the imposition of Mosaic law, settlement in Asia, and the crucifixion of Jesus; Fuzon (Passion) revolts against Urizen; the latter casts out Ahania (Pleasure); in exile, Ahania becomes Sin, and her laments ends the work.

——————— , *The Book of Los*—a series of poems repeating the prehistoric history of the primeval Los and his struggle against Urizen; Los creates the Sun as a creature of system, to which he binds Urizen and compels him to begin the process of material creation by forming earth and man; Los, representing poetic imagination, forces a definition of "reason" so that he can overcome error.

——————— , **"The Song of Los"**—a poem containing two parts, "Africa" and "Asia," though those names seem not to hold considerable significance; Urizen decrees religion and philosophy (repressive laws); Har and Heva (the pleasures of the imagination) flee, while war and lust flourish; they wait for Orc to usher in the Last Judgment and release man from the bonds of mortality and materialism.

Edmund Burke, *Letters on a Regicide Peace*— a series of epistolary essays by the English political philosopher on the necessity of eliminating the Jacobin government in France, which he describes as a "vast tremendous unformed spectre"; he defines Jacobinism as the revolt of the enterprising talents of a nation against its own propriety, particularly dedicated to the destruction of traditional laws and institutions.

Samuel Taylor Coleridge, "The Eolian Harp"—a poem by the English Romantic, the first of the so-called "conversation poems"; the harp of Eolus (god of the winds) serves as the Romantics' symbol of the creative process.

Marie Jean Antoine Nicolas Caritat, Marquis de Condorcet, *Esquisse d'un tableau historique de progres de l'espirit humain* (Outlines of an Historical View of the Progress of the Human Mind) —the French philosopher, politician, and mathematician traces human development through nine epochs to the French Revolution; he predicts a tenth epoch for the ultimate perfection of the human race; insists upon the justice and necessity of establishing a perfect equality of civil and political rights between individuals of both sexes; written while the author was in hiding; published the year after his death.

Immanuel Kant, *Zum ewigen Frieden* (On Perpetual Peace)—an essay by the German idealist philosopher in which he advocates a world federation of free states.

Johann Heinrich Voss, *Luise*—an epic idyll by the German poet and translator, considered his best work.

William Wordsworth, *The Borderers*—a verse drama by the English poet, set during the reign of Henry III (1216-1272); the villain causes the death of a blind old baron, whose daughter he loves; she believes that her father had planned to sell her into infamy.

EVENTS

L'Institut National de France created by the National Convention at Paris to replace the existing "academies," which had been closed since 1791.

1796

BIRTHS

Thomas Chandler Haliburton (d. 1865). Canadian-American writer, lawyer, and jurist; he will create a series of popular newspaper sketches focusing upon a character by the name of "Sam Slick, Yankee peddler."

Karl Leberecht Immermann (d. 1840). German dramatist and novelist noted for his short stories and satire.

Charles-Auguste von Platen (d. 1835). German lyric poet.

John Richardson (d. 1852). Canadian novelist; he will be the first author of his nation to write novels in English.

DEATHS

Robert Burns (b. 1759). Scottish poet; best remembered for a great number of beautiful, passionate, and tender songs that could easily be adapted to Scottish airs; dies of endocarditis induced by rheumatism; closely allied to the Scottish national folk tradition and generally recognized as the national poet of Scotland.

James Macpherson (b. 1736). Scottish poet and translator of the Ossianic poems, most of which were actually products of his own imagination; buried, at his own expense, in Westminster Abbey.

PUBLICATIONS

Louis Gabriel de Bonald, *Theorie du Pouvoir Politique et Religieux* (The Theory of Power, Politics, and Religion)—a tract by the French writer advocating the system of monarchy and predicting the return of the Bourbon dynasty.

Edmund Burke, *Letter to a Noble Lord on the Attacks Made upon Him and His Pension in the House of Lords by the Duke of Bedford and the Earl of Lauderdale*—the English writer's defense of his government pension upon his retirement from Parliament in 1794; the reply, one of the real masterpieces of irony in the English language, compares the writer's own government services with those of his principal attacker, the Duke of Bedford.

Fanny Burney, *Camilla; or, A Picture of Youth*—a novel by the English writer concerning young persons on their journey from love to marriage.

Jean Jacques Cambaceres, *Projet de Code civil*—an essay by the French diplomat that serves as the basis for the Napoleonic Code.

Maria Edgeworth, *The Parent's Assistant*—a collection of popular, didactic stories for children; to 1800.

Edward Gibbon, *The Memoirs of the Life of Edward Gibbon, with Various Observations and Excursions by Himself*—the *Life* in addition to a number of separate essays found in manuscript; published after the English historian's death by John Baker Holroyd, Lord Sheffield; the memoirs were acclaimed by contemporaries as superior examples of autobiography.

Matthew Gregory Lewis, *The Monk*—a Gothic novel by the English writer concerning a fiendish character who invades a monastery, pursues one of the penitents, and murders him; caught by the Inquisition, the "hero" faces death and conducts negotiations with the Devil for his freedom; a grand blend of the supernatural, the horrible, and the indecent; the piece is central to any discussion of the late eighteenth-century Gothic novel.

Joseph de Maistre, *Considerations sur la France* (Considerations upon France)—a tract by the French political philosopher offering arguments against the Revolution of 1789; denounces liberalism and the Republic as enemies of religion, monarchy, and common sense; sees the entire episode within the context of the fall of Man; eighteenth-century man remains a creature of sin, guided by the natural laws of violence, blood-shed, and destruction; thus, the ideas of the Enlightenment represent criminal lunacy.

Thomas Paine, *Letter to George Washington*—an essay by the English-American radical writer; an attack upon the U.S. President and Gouverneur Morris (1752-1816), U.S. minister to France, accusing them of a plot to keep him in a French prison; the piece also considers the various political factions that formed in defense of and opposition to his *The Rights of Man* (1791-1792).

EVENTS

Friedrich Arnold Brockhaus, founder of the Leipzig publishing firm bearing his name, begins publication of *Konversations-Lexikon* (to 1811), the initial edition of the noted German encyclopaedia; the first illustrated edition will appear in 1892; and the *Grosse Brockhaus* will begin in 1928.

France achieves freedom of the press.

1797

BIRTHS

Annette Elisabeth Droste-Hulshoff (d. 1848). German poet, who will become recognized as her nation's most significant woman writer; she will be known for her restrained and classical style.

Jeremias Gotthelf (also known as Albert Bitzius; d. 1854). Swiss writer, pastor, and author of novels depicting Swiss village life.

Heinrich Heine (d. 1856). German poet and essayist, best known for his lyrical verse; he will also be remembered as one of the first important poets to consistently adopt a humorous, ironic tone, seen in his poetry, as well as in his essays on politics, literature, art, history, and society.

Mary Wollstonecraft Shelley (d. 1851). English Gothic novelist; she will be remembered for introducing the Frankenstein monster to the English reading public.

Alfred Victor Vigny (d. 1863). French Romantic writer; his work will generally reflect his own life, that of the congenital misfit who bears his loneliness with dignity.

DEATHS

Edmund Burke (b. 1729). Irish-born English statesman and philosopher; known for his superior rhetoric; defended sound constitutional statesmanship against prevailing incompetence in government; one of the foremost political thinkers in the history of Great Britain.

Michel Jean Sedaine (b. 1719). French poet and playwright; member of the Academie Francaise; his work exhibits the characteristics of the "drame bourgeois," serious, often sentimental plays in which humankind is portrayed as essentially good but misled by social prejudice.

Horace Walpole, fourth Earl of Orford (b. 1717). English writer of letters, novels, and essays; proprietor of his own press; a major intellectual figure of the middle and late eighteenth century.

Mary Wollstonecraft [Godwin] (b. 1759). English-Irish writer, perhaps the earliest of the feminist intellectuals in Great Britain; her essays serve as the doctrines of the feminist movement.

PUBLICATIONS

William Blake, *The Four Zoas: The Torment of Love and Jealousy in the Death and Judgment of Albion*—an extremely complicated and highly symbolic poem by the English poet; through the story of the dream of Albion, the poet recounts the fall of man and his redemption through Christ, the "perfect" man; the poet also relates the psychic struggle of every human being and the destiny of humankind throughout history; the vitality and creativity of the mind play an important role.

Francois Rene de Chateaubriand, *Essai historique, politique et moral, sur les revolutions anciennes et modernes*—a tract by the French writer occasioned by the French Revolution and written during the period of his exile in England; the son of nobility is not really concerned with the elimination of his aristocratic rights, but with the realization that the Revolution has created the spectacle of political murder in the streets; in America, he had learned about democracy and the advantages of Nature; ultimately, he sees a connection between the invasion of France by counter-revolutionary armies, the Reign of Terror, and the upsurge of energy that saved the Republic from defeat; the *ancien regime had caused its own death.*

Samuel Taylor Coleridge, *Osorio*—a tragedy by the English poet, produced at Drury Lane Theater, London, in 1813, under the title *Remorse;* set in Granada during the Spanish Inquisition (beginning 1478), the play depicts the moral deterioration of the title character.

Johann Wolfgang von Goethe, *Hermann und Dorothea*—an epic-idyll by the German poet and dramatist; based upon the expulsion, in 1732, of the Protestants by the Archbishop of Salzburg; the scene shifts to France during the Revolution.

Johann Christian Freidrich Holderlin, *Hyperion*—a novel by the German writer in which he condemns the commercial philistinism of the rising middle class; highly philosophical in tone and substance; to 1799.

Ann Radcliffe, *The Italian*—the last Gothic novel by the English writer, concerning events of the Inquisition; various devices are used to maintain the artificial suspense, but the dialogue is realistic, representative of the writer's ability to cater to the public taste.

Johann Ludwig Tieck, *Der Blonde Ekbert* (The Blond Eckbert)—an immature Romantic novel by the German writer, almost a fairy tale; nonetheless, the piece heralds the transition from *Sturm und Drang* to Romanticism in German fiction.

Royall Tyler, *The Algerine Captive; or, The Life and Adventures of Dr. Updike Underhill*—a picaresque novel by the American dramatist, in the form of fictional autobiography; attacks New England undergraduate education and the medical profession; the author also considers the issue of slavery.

——————, *The Georgia Spec; or, Land in the Moon*—a satire by the American playwright on the land speculation that followed the scandalous Yazoo Purchase in Georgia in 1795.

Wilhelm Heinrich Wackenroder and Johann Ludwig Tieck, *Herzensergiessungen eines kunstliebenden Klosterbruders* (Outpourings of the Heart of an Art-loving Lay Brother)—a collection of Romantic and religious essays derived from a collaboration between two of the early proponents of *Sturm und Drang*.

EVENTS

Noah Webster changes the name of his New York City political journal, *The American Minerva,* to *The Commercial Advertiser*; until 1905.

The *Encyclopaedia Britannica* completes publication of its third edition; fifteen volumes, begun in 1788.

William Cobbett, British journalist who escaped to the United States in 1792 to avoid "problems" from accusations of fraud within the Royal Army, begins publication at Philadelphia of *Porcupine's Gazette and Daily Advertiser,* a pro-British daily newspaper; to 1799.

1798

BIRTHS

Wilibald Alexis (pseudonym of Georg Wilhelm Heinrich Haring; d. 1871). German novelist, playwright, and writer of travel sketches; will attempt to pass off one of his fictional efforts as the work of Sir Walter Scott.

John Banim (d. 1842). Irish novelist; together with his brother Michael, he will write novels that accurately portray humble Irish folk.

Auguste Comte (d. 1857). French philosopher and sociologist; he will emerge as the founder of Positivism, freeing himself from the influence of existing social and religious theories.

Giacomo Leopardi (d. 1837). Italian poet; his lifelong feelings of anguish, despair, and melancholy will form the basis for his profoundly pessimistic philosophy, which he articulated in both his prose and poetry and for which he is best known.

Jules Michelet (d. 1874). French historian who will become Professor of History at the College de France; his refusal to swear allegiance to Napoleon I will adversely affect his contemporary reputation, but not his lasting significance as a historian.

Adam Mickiewicz (d. 1855). Polish patriotic poet; he will provide brilliant delineations of Lithuanian scenery, manners, and beliefs.

DEATHS

Giovanni Jacopo Casanova (b. 1725). Italian adventurer and clever cynic; the manuscript of his *Memoirs* survives the wars of both Napoleon I and Adolf Hitler.

Wilhelm Heinrich Wackenroder (b. 1773). German writer and early adherent of Romanticism.

PUBLICATIONS

Charles Brockden Brown, *Alcuin: A Dialogue on the Rights of Women*—a prose tract by the American writer that demonstrates the influence of the English novelist and political writer William Godwin (1756-1836) and his wife, Mary Wollstonecraft Godwin (1759-1797).

——————, *Wieland; or, The Transformation*—an epistolary Gothic novel based upon an actual murder committed during a hallucination; set in and around Philadelphia, where Theodore Wieland has lived serenely with his wife and sister; Wieland becomes a victim of religious melancholy and hears voices that command him to slay his wife and children.

Samuel Taylor Coleridge, "France: An Ode"—a poem that comments upon "the dire array": Prussia and Austria going to war against France (1792), with England and Holland joining the alliance a year later; the poet's retraction of his faith in the revolutionary movement: "Forgive me, Freedom! O forgive those dreams!"

—————————, *The Rime of the Ancient Mariner*—originally a poem in collaboration with William Wordsworth, who withdrew from the project after contributing only six lines; the story of a seaman who kills an albatross, the poem is religiously symbolic, depicting a spiritual pilgrimage from guilt and doubt to renewal and redemption.

Ugo Foscolo, *Ultime lettere di Jacopo Ortis* (The Last Letters of Jacopo Ortis)—a fictional work expressing the Italian writer's political disillusionment with Napoleon Bonaparte upon the ceding of Venice to Austria; to 1802.

Charles Lamb, "The Old Familiar Faces"—the best of the English essayist's poems, written after he had decided verse was not his strength; reflects his loneliness and sense of failure: "All, all are gone, the old familiar faces."

—————————, *The Tale of Rosamund Gray and Old Blind Margaret*—a simple, tragic story of a young girl who becomes the victim of an undeserved misfortune; she meets a fate worse than death, then confronts death itself; echoes the novels of Samuel Richardson and Henry Mackenzie.

Walter Savage Landor, *Gebir*—an epic poem by the English writer concerning an Iberian prince who invades Egypt, then falls in love with a young queen, which complicates military activities; the treachery of the queen's nurses causes his death, as well as that of his ambitious brother; the poet originally wrote parts of the work in Latin, then published a version entirely in that language under the title *Gebirus.*

Matthew Gregory Lewis, *The Castle Spectre*—a melodrama by the English novelist; proceeds upon a series of shocking incidents.

Johann Friedrich Schiller, *Wallensteins Lager* (Wallenstein's Camp)—the first work in the German poet's dramatic trilogy, based upon the Bohemian general of the Thirty Years' War, Count Albrecht von Wallenstein (1583-1634); an early example of the poet's realism and talent for characterization.

William Wordsworth, "Lines Composed a Few Miles above Tintern Abbey"—an English poem composed near Tintern Abbey, a picturesque ruin in Monmouthshire; an organized meditation in which the poet reviews his past, evaluates the present, and anticipates the future.

—————————, and Samuel Taylor Coleridge, *Lyrical Ballads*—a collection of poems by the two English Romantics; three editions through 1802; Coleridge's poems focus upon supernatural and Romantic characters, Wordsworth's focus upon the charm and novelty of everyday objects; the entire collection was intended as a revolt against the artificial literature of the times, emphasizing simplicity of subject and language.

EVENTS

Johann Friedrich, Freiherr Cotta von Cottendorf (1762-1832), who succeeds to the prominent Leipzig publishing firm operated by his family, begins publication of two German literary periodicals: *Allgemeine Zeitung* and *Almanach fur Damen.*

The Ulster County Gazette begins publication in New York City; a Federalist sponsored newspaper, it will claim notice for printing an account of President George Washington's funeral (4 January 1800); until 1822.

1799

BIRTHS

Honore de Balzac (d. 1850). French novelist; he will author eighty-five novels within a space of twenty years.

Thomas Hood (d. 1845). English poet and humorist; he will gain notice for his burlesque pieces and for inventing what will be termed "picture puns."

Aleksandr Sergeyevich Pushkin (d. 1837). Russian poet and author of novels in verse; certainly Russia's greatest Romantic versifier.

DEATHS

Maria Gaetana Agnesi (b. 1718). Italian linguist, philosopher, mathematician, and theologian;

replaced her father as professor of mathematics at Bologna.

Pierre Augustin Beaumarchais (b. 1732). French playwright; next to Moliere, he made perhaps the most significant contribution to French comic drama; becomes deaf, dies in Paris of apoplexy.

Georg Christoph Lichtenberg (b. 1742). German satirist and physicist; an admirer of David Garrick and William Hogarth.

Giuseppe Parini (b. 1729). Italian poet and priest.

PUBLICATIONS

Charles Brockden Brown, *Arthur Merwyn*—an American novel concerning humanitarian reform, with an emphasis upon civic responsibility; also a study of the problem of yellow fever, which the novelist had observed in epidemic proportions in Philadelphia; to 1800.

——————, *Edgar Huntley*—may well be the first American detective novel; contains a number of thrilling scenes but, overall, the plot suffers from the novelist's interest in morbid curiosity and its relationship to crime; both Edgar Allan Poe and James Fenimore Cooper "borrowed" from certain of its episodes.

——————, *Ormond*—a novel primarily concerned with philosophic anarchism; presents a glamorous, extremely intelligent, and superhuman villain who strongly dislikes middle-class notions of good and evil; thus, he scoffs at the social conventions of marriage, religion, and private property; the hero, on the other hand, appears as an almost perfect combination of the real and the ideal.

Robert Burns, "Holy Willie's Prayer"—a satire by the Scottish poet in the form of a dramatic monologue; adapted from the portrait of an actual self-righteous elder in the parish of Mauchline and directed against a basic tenet of the Scottish Kirk: the title character believes himself to be one of God's elect, predestined for grace, no matter what he does.

——————, *The Jolly Beggars: A Cantata*—a miniature comic opera in three parts: an overture (the maimed veteran and the camp follower), an action (the rivalry between the fiddler and the tinker for the favors of the widowed pickpocket, the bard providing the resolution by relinquishing one of his three women to the disappointed lover), and a finale (the bard's second, climactic song); after the veteran begins the poem, each character comes forward, for dramatic reasons, to sing a song, and each expresses a different view of life.

William Cowper, *The Castaway*—an English poem based upon an incident in *A Voyage Round the World* (1748), compiled by Richard Walter, chaplain to Baron George Anson (1724-1762); the poet depicts the suffering of a seaman swept overboard and about to drown.

Philip Freneau, *Letters on Various Interesting and Important Subjects*—a collection of essays by the American essayist and poet; unpretentious pieces covering a wide range of American political and social subjects.

Johann Gottfried von Herder, *Metakritik*—the German philosopher's attack upon Immanuel Kant and Johann Gottlieb Fichte.

Novalis, *Heinrich von Otterdingen*—an incomplete philosophical romance by the German writer; describes in highly symbolic terms the artist's romantic search for a "blue flower"; overburdened by a complex combination of religious, mystical, and secular symbolism.

Johann Friedrich von Schiller, *Die Piccolomini* (The Piccolomini)—the second dramatic piece of the German playwright's "Wallenstein trilogy"; the hero never actually intends to commit treason, but the idea intrigues him, and he begins to correspond with the Swedish enemy.

——————, *Wallensteins Tod* (Wallenstein's Death)—the third dramatic piece in the "Wallenstein trilogy"; the title character's correspondence with the Swedish enemy is discovered and the Emperor outlaws him; Wallenstein flees, but one of his generals murders him.

Karl Wilhelm Freidrich von Schlegel, *Lucinde*—a romance by the German Romantic writer; based upon his abduction of the daughter of Moses Mendelssohn; contemporaries referred to it as a novel of "questionable character."

——————, *Geschichte der Poesie der Griechen und Romer* (The History of Greek and Roman Poetry)—the result of the German writer's studies at Gottingen and Leipzig (1797-1798); an attempt to refine his classical criticism.

Richard Brinsley Sheridan, *Pizarro*—a tragedy by the English playwright, based upon the Spanish conqueror of Peru and adapted from a similar piece by the German dramatist August Friedrich von Kotzebue, *Die Spanier in Peru.*

William Wordsworth, "Lucy Gray; or, Solitude"—a poem written while the author toured Germany; based upon a true account of a young girl who drowned when she lost her way in a snowstorm; an attempt to color ordinary events with the images of his own imagination: "—Yet some maintain that to this day / She is a living child. . . . "

——————, *The Prelude; or, Growth of a Poet's Mind. An Autobiographical Poem*—the poet presents the events of his life not as they seemed to him when they occurred, but reinterpreted in tranquillity; the protagonist of the piece comes to represent the poet's mind, his creative imagination: "Oh there is blessing in this gentle breeze, / A visitant that while it fans my cheek / Doth seem half-conscious of the joy it brings / From the green fields, and from yon azure sky."

EVENTS

The Monthly Magazine and American Review begins publication in New York City; Charles Brockden Brown serves as its editor, and it includes both scientific and literary pieces; to 1801.

1800

BIRTHS

Thomas Babington Macaulay (d. 1859). English essayist and historian who will gain favor because of his narrative and rhetorical skills, but who will be criticized for his "loose" scholarship and political bias.

Mihaly Vorosmarty (d. 1855). Hungarian poet who will, in 1848, gain a seat in his country's National Assembly; he will also write eleven plays.

DEATHS

William Cowper (b. 1731). English poet; the bard of the eighteenth-century evangelical revival, as well as the precursor of William Wordsworth as a poet of Nature.

Joseph Warton (b. 1722). English poet and literary critic; associated with the London literary gatherings headed by Samuel Johnson; attempted to distinguish between the poetry of reason and the poetry of fancy.

PUBLICATIONS

Johann Gottlieb Fichte, *Die Bestimmung des Menschen* (The Vocation of Man)—a tract by the German philosopher in which he develops a transcendental idealism that considers the individual ego as the source of experience; everything derives from the moral will of the universe, or an absolute ego.

Arnold Hermann Heeren, *Handbuch der Geschichte des Europaischen Staatensystems und seiner Colonien* (A Manual of the History of the Political System of Europe and Its Colonies)—a political history of Europe from the late fifteenth century to the fall of Napoleon.

Johann Friedrich Richter, *Titan*—a novel by the German writer, one that he himself considered among his best; a tale that displays the full potential of the writer's imagination, transporting the reader, with powerful language, through the secrets of Space, Time, Life, and Annihilation.

Friedrich von Schelling, *System des Tranzendentalen Idealismus* (Transcendental Idealism)—a tract by the German philosopher revealing two fundamental and complementary sciences: transcendental philosophy and speculative physics; his so-called "positive philosophy" assumes the forms of mythology and Revelation.

Johann Friedrich Schiller, *Maria Stuart*—a historical drama by the German writer and a remarkable psychological study of Elizabeth I and Mary Queen of Scots; Mary, by her death, gains the moral victory; the playwright takes considerable liberty with historical fact.

Madame de Stael, *Litterature et ses Rapports avec les Institutions Sociales* (On Literature and Its Relationship with the Social Institutions)—an essay by the French writer and intellectual in which she develops the theory that the progress of human reason conforms to the progress of the national organism; the first piece of criticism to consider literature as the outgrowth of social history and environment.

William Wordsworth, *Michael: A Pastoral
Poem*—the English poet based this long piece
upon the actual misfortunes of a family at
Grasmere; a man suffers from two of the
most powerful affections of the human heart:
parental love and love of landed property;
for the poet, the term "pastoral" means the
tragic suffering of people who live the "humble life."

EVENTS

The Congress of the United States appropriates $5000 to purchase 900 books and to
establish the Library of Congress at Washington, D.C.; the Library will remain in the Capitol until 1897.

*The National Intelligencer and Washington Ad-
vertiser* begins publication at Washington,
D.C. as a tri-weekly newspaper; principally a
political periodical that records the debates
and general proceedings of Congress; will become a daily newspaper in 1813; until 1870.

Zachariah Poulson purchases *Claypoole's Ameri-
can Daily Advertiser* and renames it *Poulson's
American Daily Advertiser;* remains a major
Philadelphia newspaper until 1839.

1801

BIRTHS

William Barnes (d. 1886). Perhaps the purest
of all the English poets; he will write idyllic
verse in the dialect of his native Dorset.

Christian Dietrich Grabbe (d. 1836). German
dramatist whose work, particularly his powerful tragedies about historical figures, anticipated Realism.

Johann Nestroy (d. 1862). Austrian playwright
and director of the Vienna Carl Theater; revolutionary in his views on the drama, he will
ridicule theatrical sentimentality with deft
plays on words; influenced the philosopher
Ludwig Josef Wittgenstein.

John Henry Newman (d. 1890). English poet,
essayist, and theologian; he will leave the
Church of England and convert to Roman
Catholicism, ultimately receiving the cardinal's hat.

DEATHS

Novalis (pseudonym of Friedrich von Hardenberg; b. 1772). German poet and writer of
philosophical romances; known as "the
Prophet of Romanticism;" dies from consumption.

PUBLICATIONS

Charles Brockden Brown, *Clara Howard*—a
love story emphasizing an ethical dilemma
and surrounded by a Gothic atmosphere imitative of Samuel Richardson and Ann Radcliffe.

——————, *Jane Talbot*—a novel in which a
sensitive young lady enters into a loveless
marriage, even though she has previously become enamored of another man; relatively
free from the author's traditional Gothicism.

Francois Rene de Chateaubriand, *Atala*—a
novel about American Indian life by the
French writer, sometimes labeled a prose
poem; Atala and her lover represent more
than children of Nature because they find
themselves in conflict with the traditions, customs, and prejudices of their tribe; unable to
solve the conflict, they must suffer and die,
thus illustrating the disappearance of a race.

Jean de Crevecoeur, *Voyage dans la haute
Pennsylvanie et dans l'etat de New York*
(Journey into Northern Pennsylvania and the
State of New York)—a three-volume travel
narrative by the French-American writer,
published in France for the benefit of a
French audience; based upon what he had
seen during the early 1760s, when he had
worked as a surveyor and Indian trader.

Maria Edgeworth, *Belinda*—a novel by the
Irish writer depicting society toward the end
of the eighteenth century; praised by Jane
Austen in her novel *Northanger Abbey.*

——————, *Castle Rackrent*—a novel by the
Irish writer; a steward relates the history of
the title family, whose experiences present a
vivid picture of the reckless living that caused
a number of careless eighteenth-century Irish
landlords to find themselves in ruin.

August von Kotzebue, *Die Beiden Klingsberg*
(The Two Klingsbergs)—perhaps the most
successful stage piece by the German dramatist, playing for more than 170 performances
and as late as 1951; appeals to strong emo-

tion and capitalizes upon middle-class expectations and attitudes.

Thomas Moore, *Poetical Works*—a collection by the Irish poet, issued under the pseudonym "Thomas Little"; contains mostly juvenile poems, including "Fragments of College Exercises," "Anacreontic," "The Sale of Loves," "Elegiac Stanzas," "The Philosopher Aristippus to a Lamp," "A Vision of Philosophers," and "The Devil among the Scholars"; the volume was satirized by Lord Byron.

Johann Friedrich Schiller, *Die Jungfrau von Orleans* (The Maid of Orleans)—a verse drama by the German poet and playwright focusing upon the story of Joan of Arc; yet another of the writer's successful attempts to dramatize history.

Robert Southey, *Thalaba the Destroyer*—a long poem by the English writer; the title character has been directed to destroy the race of magicians whose seminary lies under the roots of the sea; murder, vengeance, and a quest end in Thalba's death, but he finds his beloved wife in Paradise.

EVENTS

The *Encyclopaedia Britannica* publishes its fourth edition; twenty vols.; to 1810.

George Friedrich Hegel and Friedrich von Schelling publish their journal, *Kritische Journal der Philosophie* (Critical Journal of Philosophy), to 1803; in it, Hegel will outline his system of philosophy, which emphasizes reason rather than Romantic intuition.

The New York Evening Post begins publication in New York City as a newspaper in support of Federalist politics; William Cullen Bryant will become one of its early literary staff writers and editors.

Joseph Dennie, a writer of political satire and poetry, publishes at Philadelphia *The Port Folio*, a weekly literary journal; its contributors will include the Irish poet Thomas Moore and the American poet and playwright Royall Tyler; until 1827.

1802

BIRTHS

Alexandre Dumas the elder (d. 1870). French novelist and playwright; a prolific writer and story teller who will "borrow" freely and liberally from other authors.

Victor Marie Hugo (d. 1885). French novelist, playwright, and poet; a creative genius and a master of words, but his works will be almost devoid of humor.

Nikolaus Lenau (d. 1850). Austrian poet best known for his short lyrics; all of his works will be infused with his morbid sensibility.

PUBLICATIONS

Samuel Taylor Coleridge, "Dejection: An Ode"—originally a letter in verse written to Sara Hutchinson, 338 lines in which the poet describes his domestic misery, in contrast to William Wordsworth's happiness; the published version extended to 139 lines, in which the poet announced the loss of his "shaping spirit of imagination"; however, the poem was one of his best.

Washington Irving, *The Letters of Jonathan Oldstyle, Gent.*—a collection of satires on dramatic criticism and New York society by the young American writer; the work belongs to his "juvenile" period, but brings him recognition.

Charles Lamb, *John Woodvil*—a tragedy by the English writer, originally titled *Pride's Cure;* highly imitative of the Elizabethan playwrights.

Sir Walter Scott, *Minstrelsy of the Scottish Border*—a three-volume collection by the Scottish writer, containing historical, romantic, and traditional ballads; a separate section contains imitations of those forms and types; to 1803.

Madame de Stael, *Delphine*—an epistolary novel by the French writer; reflects the frustrations and conflicts of the writer's own personal life, but nonetheless offers to her contemporaries a new image of an active and intellectual woman.

William Wordsworth, "My Heart Leaps Up When I Behold"—a short piece by the English poet in which he affirms his continuing responsiveness to the miracle of ordinary occurrences; that response becomes the religious sentiment that binds the poet's maturity to his childhood: "The Child is the father of the Man. . . . "

——————— , **"Ode: Intimations of Immortality from Recollections of Early Childhood"**—a poem based upon Plato's doctrine of the soul as immortal and existing separately from the body, both before and after birth; the poem, however, proposes that the soul only gradually loses its "vision splendid" after birth.

—————, **"Resolution and Independence"**—a poem loosely based on the poet's personal encounter with an old man from Grasmere; the old man changes into a sequence of figures, not all of whom are entirely human; the poem combines the themes of the haunted wanderer and "natural supernaturalism."

EVENTS

William Cobbett, the Troy journalist, publishes at London *Cobbett's Political Register,* a weekly newspaper that can be identified as the first "cheap" periodical; an uncompromising champion of radicalism and extremely popular; to 1835.

1803

BIRTHS

Edward George Bulwer-Lytton (d. 1873). English novelist, essayist, poet, playwright, and politician.

Ralph Waldo Emerson (d. 1882). American poet and essayist; his work, especially the poetry, will combine the best qualities of nineteenth-century American philosophical and moral thought.

Jose Maria Heredia (d. 1839). Cuban-born poet who will be exiled to the United States for his antigovernment activities.

Prosper Merimee (d. 1870). French novelist and government minister; his literary work will be characterized by his learning, observation, humor, and fluid style.

DEATHS

Vittorio Alfieri (b. 1749). Italian poet and dramatist; published twenty-one tragedies and six comedies; contributed to the rise of Italian nationalism.

James Beattie (b. 1735). Scottish poet and essayist; a forerunner of Romanticism.

Johann Wilhelm Ludwig Gleim (b. 1719). German poet; contributed to the body of militant verse written during the age of Frederick the Great.

Johann Wilhelm Heinse (b. 1749?). German poet and romance writer.

Johann Gottfried von Herder (b. 1744). German poet and critic; exerted a significant influence upon German Romanticism and the work of Johann Wolfgang von Goethe.

Friedrich Gottlieb Klopstock (b. 1724). A significant German religious poet of the eighteenth century, known for his lyrics and odes.

Pierre Ambrose Francois Choderlos de Laclos (b. 1741). French novelist and politician who spent practically all of his adult life in the army; influenced Jean-Jacques Rousseau and Samuel Richardson.

Jean Francois de Saint Lambert (b. 1716). French poet; influenced, in the descriptive detail of his works, by the Greco-Roman classicists and his Swiss-German contemporaries.

PUBLICATIONS

Heinrich von Kleist, *Die Familie Schroffenstein* (The Feud of the Schroffensteins)—a German play cast in the Romeo and Juliet motif, against a Gothic background; mistaken identities increase the pathos of a story of two families who seem unwittingly determined to destroy their own children; however, the playwright sacrifices the quality of true dramatic passion to achieve a number of horrific effects.

Johann Friedrich von Schiller, *Die Braut von Messina* (The Bride of Messina)—a tragedy by the German dramatist that portrays the relentless feud between two hostile brothers.

Zacharias Werner, *Die Sohne des Tals* (The Sons of the Valley)—the first play by the German religious dramatist; divided into two parts: *Die Templar auf Cypern* (The Templars on Cyprus) and *Die Kreuzbruder* (The Brothers of the Cross); both parts focus upon the tragic defeat of the Crusaders.

EVENTS

The Literary Magazine and American Register begins publication at Philadelphia; edited by Charles Brockden Brown, who was also its major contributor; the monthly publishes literary and scientific articles; until 1807.

1804

BIRTHS

Ludwig Andreas Feuerbach (d. 1872). German philosopher; an influence upon Karl Marx; George Eliot will translate his major work.

Francesco Domenico Guerrazzi (d. 1873). Italian writer of fiction and a politician; his work will reflect his patriotism; he will spend time in exile on Corsica.

Nathaniel Hawthorne (d. 1864). American novelist and writer of short fiction; the master of a strong, clear prose style.

Eduard Morike (d. 1875). German poet and novelist; he will develop a deceptively simple poetic style, somewhat akin to that of Heinrich Heine.

Charles Augustin Saint-Beuve (d. 1869). French writer; he will become one of the most significant literary critics of his time.

George Sand (pseudonym of Amandine Aurore Lucie Dupin; d. 1876). French novelist; she will become noted almost as much for her personal associations with Alfred de Musset and Frederic Chopin as for her fiction.

Marie Joseph Eugene Sue (d. 1857). French novelist who will strongly influence the major prose works of Victor Hugo.

DEATHS

Immanuel Kant (b. 1724). German philosopher; the most significant among the idealists.

PUBLICATIONS

Maria Edgeworth, *Popular Tales*—a collection of stories for children by the Irish novelist.

Johann Friedrich von Schiller, *Wilhelm Tell* (William Tell)—the German play based upon the fifteenth-century legend of a fourteenth-century Swiss hero who, with his crossbow, shoots an apple from the head of his young son; it serves as a dramatic manifesto for political freedom.

William Wordsworth, "I Wandered Lonely As a Cloud"—a poem based upon a personal experience in April 1802, while the poet and his sister toured the Lake District of England: "I gazed—and gazed—but little thought / What wealth the show to me had brought. . . ."

——————, *Ode to Duty*—a poem based upon Thomas Gray's "Ode to Adversity" (itself modeled after Horace's "Ode to Fortune"); duty exists as "a light to guide, a rod / To check the erring, and reprove. . . . "

——————, **"She Was a Phantom of Delight"**—a poem written about the poet's own wife, Mary Hutchinson Wordsworth: "A lovely apparition, sent / To be a moment's ornament. . . . "

EVENTS

George Rapp leads his six hundred German pietist settlers to New Harmony, in western Pennsylvania; there they form the New Harmony Society.

Lindley Murray, a Quaker minister who had moved to England from Pennsylvania, publishes his *English Spelling Book,* a text that will have a lasting influence upon English orthography.

1805

BIRTHS

Hans Christian Andersen (d. 1875). Danish author and one of the most significant storytellers of all.

Esteban Echeverria (d. 1851). Argentine poet, novelist, and revolutionary; he will introduce Romanticism into Argentina.

Adalbert Stifter (d. 1868). Austrian novelist and painter; a humanist who expressed a deep love for traditional values.

Alexis Charles Henri Clerel de Tocqueville (d. 1859). the French historian and magistrate; an advocate of centralized government.

DEATHS

Johann Christoph Friedrich von Schiller (b. 1759). German historical dramatist, poet, and historian.

PUBLICATIONS

Francois Rene de Chateaubriand, *Rene*—a novel by the French writer; exemplifies the melancholy, poetic style that becomes typical of the fiction of the age; the story of a young European (the author, himself?) devoured by a secret sorrow, who flees to the solitudes of the New World.

Sir Walter Scott, *The Lay of the Last Minstrel*—a poem in six cantos by the Scottish writer, his first significant work; a metrical romance narrated by the last person of his race; set in the middle of the sixteenth century, the piece takes its theme from an old Scottish border legend concerning a goblin by the name of Gilpin Horner.

Robert Southey, *Madoc*—a poem by the English Romantic writer; the title character is the youngest son of Owen Gwyneth, King of Wales (d. 1169), who has traveled the world in search of adventure; returning to Wales for fresh supplies, he tells his tales, then engages in more adventure.

William Wordsworth, "The Solitary Reaper"—a poem by the English Romantic; one of the rare poems not based upon the bard's own experiences; suggested to him by a passage in a travel book, Thomas Wilkinson's *Tour of Scotland*, in which the traveler passes by a young girl working in the fields: "Behold her, single in the field, / Yon solitary Highland lass!"

EVENTS

The Boston Athenaeum founded, an organization of literati from Boston; a significant influence upon the literary activity of the age, and it continues to be so.

Sir Roger Newdigate, English Parliamentarian, establishes the Newdigate Prize for English poetry at Oxford University.

1806

BIRTHS

Elizabeth Barrett Browning (d. 1861). English poet and wife of Robert Browning.

Heinrich Laube (d. 1884). German playwright and theater manager; a leader of the "Young Germany" movement and editor of its periodical, *Die Elegante Welt*.

John Stuart Mill (d. 1873). English philosopher and advocate of reform; changed the intellectual climate of Victorian England and exerted a significant influence upon the political reformers of his age.

William Gilmore Simms (d. 1870). American novelist of the South who promoted the culture (including slavery) of his region.

DEATHS

Johann Christoph Adelung (b. 1732). German linguist and lexicographer; chief librarian of Dresden.

Charles Augustin de Coulomb (b. 1736). French physicist and philosopher.

Carlo Gozzi (b. 1720). Italian writer of satirical poems and comic dramas.

PUBLICATIONS

Johann Christoph Adelung, *Mithridates, A History of Languages and Dialects*—the principal work by the German philologist and linguistic historian, focusing upon language history and its application to literature.

Heinrich von Kleist, *Der Zerbrochene Krug*—a so-called "village comedy" by the German playwright and journalist.

Charles Lamb, *Mr. H*— a dramatic farce by the English essayist that proved a complete failure at Drury Lane Theatre.

Zacharias Werner, *Das Kreuz an der Ostee* (The Cross on the Baltic Sea)—a drama by the German playwright that focuses upon the defeat of the Crusaders.

EVENTS

Ludwig Joachim von Arnim and his brother-in-law, Clemens Brentano, publish their *Des Knaben Wunderhorn* (The Youth's Cornucopia), a collection of German folktales.

L'Institut de France created by combining the Academie Francaise with other artistic and scientific academies.

Jane and Ann Taylor publish their extremely popular *Rhymes for the Nursery*, an English collection for children that includes "Twinkle twinkle, little star."

Noah Webster, the American lexicographer and philologist, publishes the first version of his major dictionary project and entitled it *A Compendious Dictionary of the English Language.*

1807

BIRTHS

Henry Wadsworth Longfellow (d. 1882). American poet and Professor of Modern Languages and Literature, Harvard College; the simplicity of his poems, as well as their narrative and Romantic elements, will make him one of the most popular American authors of the nineteenth century.

John Greenleaf Whittier (d. 1892). American poet, known for his commitment to his Quaker faith and to the abolition of slavery.

PUBLICATIONS

George Gordon, Lord Byron, *Hours of Idleness*—the first book of poems published by the English Romantic; includes "On the Death of a Young Lady," "The First Kiss of Love," "To the Sighing Strephon," "Elegy on Newstead Abbey," " 'I would I were as a careless child,' " and "Lines Written beneath an Elm in the Churchyard at Harrow."

George Crabbe, *The Parish Register*—a poem in which a country parson relates the memories that come to him as he glances through the registers of births, marriages, and deaths.

————, *Sir Eustace Grey*—a poetic account, in eight-line stanzas, set forth by a patient in a madhouse and concerned with his decline from the heights of happiness and prosperity.

Ugo Foscolo, *Dei Sepolcri* (Of Sepulchres)—the best poem by the Italian writer, one that exercised a strong influence upon Italian literature.

Georg Friedrich Hegel, *Phanomenologie des Geistes* (Phenomenology of the Mind)—the German idealist philosopher outlines his system of thought, as based upon reason rather than Romantic intuition; that system encompasses ethics, aesthetics, history, politics, and religion.

Washington Irving, *Salmagundi; or, The Whim-Whams and Opinions of Launcelot Langstaff, Esq., and Others*—a collection of satirical poems and essays by the American writer; imitative, in form and style, of the *Spectator* papers of Joseph Addison and Sir Richard Steele (1711-1712, 1714); written in collaboration with William Irving and James K. Paulding.

Charles and Mary Lamb, *Tales from Shakespeare*—a successful attempt by the two English writers to transform Shakespeare from verse drama to prose fiction so that the sense of the Elizabethan playwright might be understood and appreciated by children.

Adam Oehlenschlager, *Hakon Jarl*—a tragedy by the Danish playwright that relies heavily upon Scandinavian folklore and mythology; the piece evidences the influence of Friedrich von Schiller; in turn, it will have a significant effect upon the work of August Strindberg.

Robert Southey, *Letters of Espriella*—a prose piece by the English writer, supposedly the letters of a Spanish youth residing in England at the outset of the nineteenth century; the epistles are light in tone and accurately depict life in England during the period.

————, *Palmerin of England*—a revised translation by the English essayist and poet of a chivalric romance, attributed (with extreme hesitation) to either the Portuguese Francisco de Moraes (1500?-1572) or to the Spaniard Luis Hurtado (1530-1579?); consists of eight books and concerns the exploits and loves of Palmerin de Oliva, the emperor of Constantinople, as well as various of his descendants.

Madame de Stael, *Corinne*—a Romantic novel by the French writer; depicts the frustrations and conflicts present in her own life.

Zacharias Werner, *Martin Luther; oder, Die Weihe der Kraft* (Martin Luther; or, The Consecration of Strength)—a German play reflecting the writer's interest in Lutheranism; defends the Protestant religion, underscoring the idea of destiny; Luther, the priest, and Katharina von Bora, a nun, come together because of a force greater than both of them; Katharina sees Luther as a messiah; he sees her as a guardian angel; in the end, they renounce Catholic dogma for a new creed of faith and humanity.

EVENTS

The American Register begins publication in Philadelphia as a semi-annual almanac of national events.

Henry and Sealy Fourdrinier, English paper manufacturers, patent a machine that can produce, from wood pulp, a continuous sheet of paper in any desired size.

1808

BIRTHS

Jose de Espronceda (d. 1842). Spanish poet and revolutionist; his Romantic poems will be patterned after those of Lord Byron.

Jean Baptiste Alphone Karr (d. 1890). French novelist and editor of the journal *Figaro*.

Abraham ben Jekutiel Mapu (d. 1867). Lithuanian Jewish novelist who fashioned a new form of historical romance, the biblical novel.

Gerard de Nerval (d. 1855). French translator and writer of prose and verse.

Henrik Arnold Wergeland (d. 1845). Norwegian poet, playwright, and patriot; a lyric writer who championed the cause of Norwegian nationalism.

PUBLICATIONS

Francois Rene de Chateaubriand, *Les Aventures du Dernier Abencerage*—a work of fiction set in sixteenth-century Spain; not in print until 1826.

Karl Freidrich Eichhorn, *Deutsche Staats-und Rechtsgeschichte*—the German jurist's monumental history of German consitutional law.

Johann Wolfgang von Goethe, *Faust, Part I*—a dramatic tragedy by the German poet and playwright; the story of the old scholar's bargain with the Devil: if Mephistopheles can grant Faust one moment of complete contentment, a moment that will seem as though an eternity, Faust will give his soul to the Devil; the old man becomes rejuvenated by it all, although he fails to discover the world of personal feeling and experience.

Heinrich von Kleist, *Das Kathchen von Heilbronn; oder, Die Feuerprobe* (Cathy from Heilbronn; or, The Trial by Fire)—a German play concerning a world about to disintegrate; only a noble and supreme effort by the principal characters can prevent that from happening; an averted romantic tragedy dramatically transformed into a fairy tale, complete with witches.

——————— , *Robert Guiskard*—an unfinished drama in which a Norman duke is on the verge of conquering Byzantium when the plague infects both him and his army; Guiskard strives desperately to maintain order as panic sweeps through his camp.

Charles Lamb, *The Adventures of Ulysses*—the English essayist's attempt to recreate the Homeric epic into stories that children could easily comprehend; certainly no less successful than he and his sister's *Tales From Shakespeare*, also intended for children.

——————— , *Specimens of English Dramatic Poets Who Lived about the Time of Shakespear*—commends the plays to lovers of poetry, as though they constitute a large anthology of "new" verse; presents entire scenes from plays to support his assertion that more than a third of the plays of the period had been appreciated as literature, rather than as dramatic productions.

Karl Wilhelm Friedrich von Schlegel, *Von der Sprache und Weisheit der Indier* (On the Language and Wisdom of India)—a significant tract by the German philosopher and critic, a pioneer effort in the study of Sanskrit in Europe.

Sir Walter Scott, *The Life of John Dryden*—a biography of the Restoration poet and playwright by the Scottish writer, who assumed that little or no new biographical information remained to be uncovered; however, it is still a worthwhile effort because of its significant contribution to the general literary history of the period; accompanied by an edition of Dryden's works.

——————— , *Marmion, a Tale of Flodden Field*—a poem in six cantos set in the year 1513; a favorite of Henry VIII, the title character is noble, yet treacherous; treason, intrigue, and the usual knightly adventures lead the reader to the battle of Flodden Field, where Marmion meets his end; includes two songs of merit: "Where shall the lover rest" and "Lochinvar."

Zacharias Werner, *Attila, Koenig der Hunnen* (Attila, King of the Huns)—a play by the German writer in which the historical background serves to underscore the question (a personal one with the writer) of the relationship between faith and mysticism; dogma must be replaced by a new creed of faith and humanity.

Vasily Andreyevich Zhukovsky, *Lyudmila*—a ballad by the Russian poet adopted from the *Leonore* of Gottfried August Burger (1747-1794), written in 1773; the poem signals the beginnings of "modern" Russian poetry.

EVENTS

John Hunt and his brother Leigh Hunt begin publication of *The Examiner,* a weekly periodical concerned with literature and politics; significant in its contribution to the development of English journalism; until 1880.

Johann Wolfgang von Goethe meets Napoleon Bonaparte at Erfurt, and identifies the Emperor of the French as the salvation of European civilization.

Henry Crabb Robinson, English lawyer and diarist, becomes the first war correspondent; *The Times* of London sends him to Spain to report on the Peninsular War; afterward (1828) he will become one of the founders of London University.

1809

BIRTHS

Charles Robert Darwin (d. 1882). English naturalist and essayist and the discoverer of natural selection.

Edward Fitzgerald (d. 1883). English translator, poet, and scholar; best known as the translator of the *Rubaiyat,* a work by the eleventh-century Persian poet and astronomer Omar Khayyam.

Nikolai Vasilievich Gogol (d. 1852). Russian novelist and playwright; a powerful satirist of Russian society.

Heinrich Hoffman (d. 1894). German author, illustrator, and physician.

Oliver Wendell Holmes (d. 1894). American physician, poet, essayist, and novelist.

Edgar Allan Poe (d. 1849). American poet, writer of fiction, and literary critic; the "pioneer" of the American detective story.

Juljusz Slowacki (d. 1849). Polish Romantic poet, influenced by Lord Byron.

Alfred, Lord Tennyson (d. 1892). English poet; a major figure of Victorian England; succeeded William Wordsworth as Poet Laureate of England.

DEATHS

Thomas Paine (b. 1737). English-American writer, champion of American independence; a Deist and a radical.

PUBLICATIONS

George Gordon, Lord Byron, *English Bards and Scotch Reviewers*—a satirical poem, in heroic couplets, by the English Romantic; an attack upon the editor of *The Edinburgh Review,* Lord Francis Jeffrey, and Robert Southey, Sir Walter Scott, William Wordsworth, and Samuel Taylor Coleridge; at the same time a defense of the traditional English writers of the classical school, particularly John Dryden and Alexander Pope.

Francois Rene de Chateaubriand, *Les Martyrs*—a prose epic by the French writer and politician focusing upon the persecutions of the Roman emperor Diocletian (245-313) and the problems of the early Christians.

Philip Freneau, *Collected Poems*—a two-volume edition of the American writer's verse; includes "To Sir Toby," "To an Author," "On Mr. Paine's *Rights of Man*," and "On a Honey Bee."

Johann Wolfgang von Goethe, *Die Wahlverwandtschaften* (The Elective Affinities)—a German novel that expresses the writer's dislike for the German Romantics' enthusiasm for the French Revolution, particularly as reflected in their disregard for style; a psychological novel of sorts focusing upon the "elective affinities" of a married couple for two other persons.

Washington Irving, *A History of New York, from the Beginning of the World to the End of the Dutch Dynasty, by Diedrich Knickerbocker*—a satire of contemporary historiography by the American writer, revised on three occasions, 1812, 1819, and 1848; perhaps the first significant piece of comic literature by an American writer.

Charles and Mary Lamb, *Mrs. Leicester's School*—a collection of ten stories by the English writers; reminiscences of their childhood experiences at Hertfordshire school; contains autobiographical details.

August von Schlegel, *Lectures on Dramatic Art and Literature*—lectures by the German essayist promoting his radically Romantic points of view.

Royall Tyler, *Yankee in London*—a series of letters by the American lawyer and dramatist; depicts the reactions of an American resident in London to the sights and activities within the English capital.

William Wordsworth, *Concerning the Relations of Great Britain, Spain, and Portugal . . . as Affected by the Convention of Cintra*—a prose piece by the English Romantic in which he attacks the spiritlessness of British policy and calls for the government's active engagement in the Peninsular War against Napoleon.

EVENTS

The Balance and New York Journal begins publication at Albany, New York; a newspaper that attacks the politics of Thomas Jefferson and serves as an organ of the Federalists.

The Literary Gazette, a Philadelphia journal, begins publication; for a time edited by Washington Irving; until 1831.

John Murray, London publisher, founds *The Quarterly Review,* a London literary and political journal intended to compete with *The Edinburgh Review;* Sir Walter Scott was a sponsor and key contributor.

1810

BIRTHS

Elizabeth Cleghorn Gaskell (d. 1865). English novelist who was particularly interested in the working classes.

Karel Hynek Macha (d. 1836). Czech lyric poet and novelist.

Alfred de Musset (d. 1857). French poet and playwright whose works are unique for their intensity, originality, wit, and variety.

Alexandros Rizos Rangabe (d. 1892). Greek scholar, playwright, and diplomat.

Fritz Reuter (d. 1874). German humorist and poet who wrote works in the Plattdeutsch language.

DEATHS

Charles Brockden Brown (b. 1771). American novelist; known as the first "professional" American writer; specialized in Gothic romances.

PUBLICATIONS

Lazare Hippolyte Carnot, *De la Defense des places fortes*—a tract by the French revolutionary describing his plan for organizing the Republican armies and for masterminding a successful strategy for the French revolutionary wars.

George Crabbe, *The Borough*—an English epistolary poem; twenty-four letters describing life in the Suffolk town of Aldeburgh, his birthplace and where his father served as collector of the salt duties.

Heinrich von Kleist, *Uber das Marionettentheater* (On the Marionette Theater)—an important essay by the German playwright in which he postulated that only self-awareness leads to knowledge of the outside world; without a full understanding of its inner drives and needs, humankind will never comprehend the universe; the governance of man relates clearly to a puppet show, in that one's own inner principles must force him to master his own mechanisms before he can function in the world.

Joseph de Maistre, *Essay on the Generation of Political Constitutions*—a tract by the French political philosopher attacking the idea that the will of the monarch is responsible for everything; human power creates its own limits and destroys itself by the very efforts it makes to extend itself.

Sir Walter Scott, *The Lady of the Lake*—a poem in six cantos by the Scottish writer; a knight falls in love with the daughter of an outlawed lord; she is also pursued by other suitors, which results in a number of armed conflicts; reconciliation leads to marriage; includes several lyrical songs such as "He is gone on the mountain" and "Soldier, rest, thy warfare o'er".

Percy Bysshe Shelley, *St. Irvyne, or, The Rosicrucian*—a juvenile romance by the English poet patterned after the works of the Gothic novelist Matthew (Monk) Lewis.

Robert Southey, *The History of Brazil*—a valuable historical study by the English writer, though the reviewers for *Blackwood's Magazine* termed the project generally "unreadable."

Anne Louise Germaine de Stael, *De l'Allemagne* (On Germany)—the principal work by the French-Swiss woman of letters; introduced German Romanticism to French literature and significantly influenced European thought and letters.

Zacharias Werner, *Der 24. Februar* (The Twenty-fourth of February)—a drama by the German playwright and preacher, his most significant play on the subject of destiny; a simple peasant family struggles against a curse that causes various members of the family to kill one another on 24 February.

William Wordsworth, *A Description of the Lakes in the North of England*—a prose piece by the English poet, written as an introduction to Thomas Wilkinson's *Select Views on Cumberland;* a highly imaginative account of the country and its inhabitants; republished and enlarged in 1822.

1811

BIRTHS

Theophile Gautier (d. 1872). French poet and novelist; a zealous Romantic.

Karl Ferdinand Gutzkow (d. 1878). German journalist and dramatist; influenced by the French Revolution of 1830.

Jules Sandeau (d. 1883). French novelist and playwright; focuses upon the social conflicts in France during his own time.

Harriet Elizabeth Beecher Stowe (d. 1896). American novelist who contributed significantly to the antislavery movement.

William Makepeace Thackeray (d. 1863). English novelist and critic of contemporary English class structures.

DEATHS

Gyorgy Berzenyei (b. 1747). Hungarian lyric poet.

Marie Joseph Chenier (b. 1764). French satirist and playwright; member of the Legislative Assembly.

Heinrich von Kleist (b. 1777). German dramatist and poet; takes his own life on 21 November, after shooting his friend, Henrietta Vogel.

Christoph Friedrich Nicolai (b. 1733). German author, bookseller, publisher, and editor.

Thomas Percy (b. 1729). English poet, antiquary, and churchman; a friend of Samuel Johnson and a member of the London sage's literary circle.

PUBLICATIONS

Jane Austen, *Sense and Sensibility*—an English novel focusing upon a number of complex love affairs, complete with broken engagements and inconsistent attractions; one character directs her attention toward a gentleman of means and honor, while another, her reason clouded from reading sentimental novels, excites herself over an unworthy fellow; the theme of the novel is that "sense" rather than "sensibility" must guide the English lady in her quest for money, position, and proper marriage; selection of the correct male partner must take precedence over the emotions of love and affection.

Johann Wolfgang von Goethe, *Aus Meinem Leben: Dichtung und Wahrheit* (Poetry and Truth)—the autobiography of the German writer, with emphasis upon his happy childhood and those of his experiences that greatly influenced his literary development.

Heinrich von Kleist, *Die Hermansschlacht* (The Battle of Herman)—a German drama in which the playwright attempts to draw a parallel between the occupied Germany of Roman times and that of his own day; a historical piece intended to arouse German patriotism; the German princes unite under Arminius, prince of the Cherusci, and drive the Romans from their land.

——————, *Prinz Friedrich von Homburg* (The Prince of Homburg)—a German Romantic drama in blank verse concerning the question of whether one can equate selfmastery with self-denial; the dreams and the uncontrolled idealism of a prince cause him to endanger his forces in battle; interweaves military battle scenes with key psychological struggles.

Charles Lamb, *On the Genius and Character of Hogarth*—an English essay that explains the writer's early consciousness of the relationship between literature and painting; reminds the reader of the high reputation of William Hogarth (1697–1764) during the early decades of the nineteenth century.

————————, *On the Tragedies of Shakespeare*—the most elaborate piece of literary criticism by the English essayist; those aspects of Shakespeare most important to Lamb appear to be the poetry and the characters; the Elizabethan stage, he believes, provided an inferior medium for Shakespearean drama.

Friedrich de la Motte-Fouque, *Undine*—the most popular work of fiction by the German writer, a romance based upon a combination of Old Norse legend and Old French poetry; the heroine of the title belongs to a race that has no other means of obtaining a soul than by forming a most intimate union of love; the piece went through thirty editions during the nineteenth century.

EVENTS

The French Press Agency, later to become the Agence Havas, founded at Paris.

Hezekiah Niles begins publication at Baltimore, Maryland, of *Niles' Weekly Register;* becomes significant because of its accurate recordings of historical events.

1812

BIRTHS

Robert Browning (d. 1889). English poet and the one nineteenth-century figure to provide poetic substance and form to the dramatic monologue.

Hendrik Conscience (d. 1883). Flemish novelist who concentrated on portraying Flemish life, somewhat after the model of Sir Walter Scott.

Charles Dickens (d. 1870). English novelist who masterfully depicted the thin line between the social tragedies and comedies within English life.

John Forster (d. 1876). English biographer, historian, and journalist; the most artistic Victorian biographer.

Ivan Alexandrovich Goncharov (d. 1891). Russian novelist known for his graphic depictions of the harsh realities of Russian life.

Zygmunt Krasinski (d. 1859). Polish Romantic poet.

Josef Ignacy Kraszewski (d. 1887). Polish historical novelist and poet; author of over three hundred published volumes.

Edward Lear (d. 1888). English writer and artist; author of humorous "nonsense" pieces and a master of the limerick.

DEATHS

Joel Barlow (b. 1754). American poet and diplomat and a member of the "Connecticut Wits."

PUBLICATIONS

George Gordon, Lord Byron, *Childe Harold's Pilgrimage*—an English poem in Spenserian stanzas; cantos i–ii appeared in 1812, iii in 1816, and iv in 1819; the travels of a pilgrim who, after a life of dissipation, seeks something better in foreign climes; the historical significance of the places the speaker visits is emphasized, particularly in terms of their intellectual and cultural contributions; the later sections of the poem become extremely personal in terms of the poet's own experiences and travels.

Maria Edgeworth, *The Absentee*—an English novel that focuses upon one of the social evils in early nineteenth-century Ireland: absentee landlordism; the landlord lives in London with his extravagant wife, who is ashamed of her Irish origins; however, the son familiarizes himself with the effects of the system, and the piece ends with a promise of better days for all concerned.

Jakob and Wilhelm Grimm, *Kinder- und Hausmarchen* (Grimm's Fairy Tales)—the first work in the three-volume collection by the German folklorists and philologists; a work that formed a foundation for the discipline of comparative folklore studies; includes "Tom Thumb," "Little Red Riding Hood," "Bluebeard," "Puss 'n Boots," "Snow

White," "Goldilocks," "Sleeping Beauty," and "Cinderella."

Georg Wilhelm Friedrich Hegel, *Wissenschaft der Logik* (The Science of Logic)— the second significant work by the German idealist philosopher; two volumes, to 1816; the explication of the writer's dialectical logic of thesis-antithesis-synthesis; at the center of the universe there exists an enveloping absolute spirit that guides all reality, including human reason.

Walter Savage Landor, *Count Julian*—a verse tragedy by the English writer; focuses upon the vengeance of the title character, a Spanish nobleman, against King Roderigo, who has dishonored the Count's daughter.

EVENTS

Isaiah Thomas (1749-1831), the Worcester, Massachusetts, printer, publisher, and editor, founds at Worcester the American Antiquarian Society; it will become the foremost repository for early Americana.

Johann Wolfgang von Goethe meets Ludwig van Beethoven (1770-1827) at Teplitz (northern Bohemia); the musician expresses disappointment at the poet's outward respect for social conventions.

The New England Journal of Medicine and Surgery begins publication at Boston.

John Nichols, London printer and writer, publishes the first of his nine volumes of *Literary Anecdotes of the Eighteenth Century;* a significant collection of biographical and bibliographical information; to 1815.

1813

BIRTHS

Georg Buchner (d. 1837). German poet inspired by his revolutionary politics.

Friedrich Hebbel (d. 1863). German playwright and poet whose theory of tragedy opposes the optimistic classical ideal.

Soren Aabye Kierkegaard (d. 1855). Danish philosopher and theologian who will establish modern existentialism.

Otto Ludwig (d. 1865). German playwright and writer of fiction; unsuccessfully attempted to compete with Friedrich Hebbel.

DEATHS

Michel-Guillaume Jean de Crevecouer (b. 1735). French-born writer who became a naturalized American in 1765; changed his name to J. Hector St. John.

Karl Theodor Korner (b. 1791). German lyric poet and writer of patriotic songs; died in battle.

Christoph Martin Wieland (b. 1733). German writer of fiction and poetry; the first German translator of Shakespeare.

PUBLICATIONS

Jane Austen, *Pride and Prejudice*—a novel by the English writer focusing upon a Hertfordshire family with five daughters, but no male heir; the emphasis, within a complicated series of marital matches and mismatches, remains with Elizabeth Bennet and Fitzwilliam Darcy, who lead all characters in the identification of various levels and degrees of pride and prejudice.

George Gordon, Lord Byron, *The Bride of Abydos*—a poem by the English Romantic writer; a bride grieves over being forced to marry by her father's order; a brother-cousin-pirate (all the same person) attempts to convince her to join him, but the intended bridegroom bursts in and kills him; the maiden dies of grief.

—————, *The Giaour*—a poem on the topic of reproach, as applied by Turks to Christians; a Turkish lord kills his unfaithful female slave; the maid's lover avenges the act by killing the lord; eight editions of the piece within the year, increasing in length from 685 lines to 1334.

Albrecht von Chamisso, *Peter Schlemihl*—a quaint and humorous story by the French-born German writer; concerns a man who sold his shadow to the devil, a thin elderly man in a grey coat, in exchange for a purse of Fortunatus; Schlemihl, in spite of his new wealth, discovers himself cast out of society.

John Keats, *Imitation of Spenser*—the first extant poem by the English Romantic.

Alessandro Manzoni, *Inni Sacri*—a collection of poems by the Italian Romantic writer, published shortly after he declared himself totally committed to Roman Catholicism; the poems concern the Nativity, the Passion, the Resurrection, the Pentecost, and the Name of Mary.

Thomas Moore, *The Twopenny Post Bag*—a collection of satiric poems by the Irish writer, directed against the Regency (1811-1820) of George, Prince of Wales: "Since the time of horse-consuls (now long out of date), / No nags ever made such a stir in the state"; fourteen editions between March 1813 and April 1814.

Arthur Schopenhauer, *Uber die Vierfache Wurzel des Satzes vom zureichenden Grunde* (On the Fourfold Root of the Principle of Sufficient Reason)—the first tract by the German philosopher, establishing the perpetual conflict between feeling and reason.

Sir Walter Scott, *The Bridal of Triermain*—a poem by the Scottish writer on the romance of love and magic; a lord's quest for the daughter of King Arthur ends in a rescue from Merlin's spell.

———————— , *Rokeby*—a poem in six cantos set in Yorkshire in the mid-seventeenth century; concerns a conspiracy to murder in order to obtain land and fortune; includes the songs "A weary lot is thine, fair maid" and the well-known "Brignal Banks."

Percy Bysshe Shelley, *Queen Mab*—a juvenile poem by the English poet, published surreptitiously; the fairy Queen Mab carries off the spirit of the maid Ianthe and shows her the past history of the world and its miserable condition; the fairy reveals a regenerate world, where all things have been re-created.

Robert Southey, *The Life of Horatio Nelson*—the English writer's biography of the British admiral; an enlargement of a smaller sketch (1808) contributed to *The Quarterly Review;* for the biographer, Nelson remains "the hero in the hour of victory" and a name to inspire forever the youth of England.

Johann David Wyss, *Der Schweizerisch Robinson* (The Swiss Family Robinson)—the children's classic work of fiction by the Swiss writer, based upon Daniel Defoe's *Robinson Crusoe* (1719); the writer's son, Johann Rudolf Wyss (1781-1830), published the work from his father's manuscripts.

EVENTS

The appearance of *A Collection of Letters, Written by Eminent Persons in the Seventeenth and Eighteenth Centuries, to which are added Hearne's Journies to Reading, and to Whaddon Hall; also Lives of Eminent Men* (3 vols.); the last item identifies the first publication of the *Lives*, by the English antiquarian and writer John Aubrey, who had deposited his manuscripts in the Ashmolean Museum in 1693; the sketches are firsthand, anecdotal portraits of an age.

The Boston Daily Advertiser, the first successful daily newspaper in New England, begins publication; until 1929.

The Christian Disciple begins publication at Boston as a monthly religious review; essentially the voice of American Unitarianism; until 1823.

Robert Southey succeeds Henry James Pye as Poet Laureate of England; until 1843.

1814

BIRTHS

Mikhail Yurevich Lermontov (d. 1841). Russian poet of Scottish extraction for whom literary recognition will not come until after his death.

Taras Shevchenko (d. 1861). Ukranian poet and prose writer whose collections will appear in the Ukranian language.

DEATHS

Johann Gottlieb Fichte (b. 1762). German philosopher and an ardent disciple of Immanuel Kant.

Donatien Alphonse Francois, Marquis de Sade (b. 1740). The French writer from whose name comes the word "sadism," describing the type of sexual perversion from which he suffered.

Jacques Henri Bernardin de Saint-Pierre (b. 1737). French writer strongly influenced by Jean-Jacques Rousseau who was primarily interested in portraying Nature.

PUBLICATIONS

Jane Austen, *Mansfield Park*—an English novel in which a nine-year-old girl becomes an indispensable part of a household; as she matures and develops, she serves as a moral buffer against the extravagant escapades of various family members; in the end, she finds love and marriage.

Fanny Burney, *The Wanderer; or, Female Difficulties*—a novel by the English writer that achieved more financial success than literary recognition; suggests that the writer had exhausted her creativity, particularly in view of her unnecessarily complex prose style.

George Gordon, Lord Byron, *The Corsair*—an English poem in heroic couplets; concerns an unscrupulous pirate who does, however, possess a strong notion of chivalry; a complicated love arrangement and conspiracy provide the narrative vehicles.

——————, *Lara*—another poem in heroic couplets and sequel to *The Corsair*—it contains the same character, but with a name change; supposedly, the piece portrays the Romantic poet's own conception of himself.

Francois Rene de Chateaubriand, *De Buonaparte et les Bourbons*—a tract by the French writer and diplomat that reemphasizes Napoleon's role as the knight-errant of the Bourbon dynasty; nonetheless, he realized fully the new era of democracy, science, and industry that would emerge from the chaos of revolution.

Ernst Hoffman, *Phantasiestucke in Callots Manier*—the largest collection of the German writer's Gothic tales of the insane, grotesque, and supernatural; it contains the greatest number of the so-called "Tales of Hoffman" that have been adapted to the operatic stage; 4 vols. to 1815.

John Keats, *To Byron*—an early sonnet by the English poet; an imitative work heavily reliant upon stock poetic phrases and forced diction and syntax.

Francis Scott Key, *The Star-Spangled Banner*—a poem by the American journalist, composed during a British bombardment of Fort McHenry, outside Baltimore; appeared in *The Baltimore Patriot* under the title "The Defence of Fort M'Henry"; will not become the American national anthem until 1931.

Rene-Charles Guilbert de Pixerecourt, *Le Chien de Montargis; ou, La Foret de Bundy* (The Dog of Montargis; or, The Forest of Bundy)—a melodrama by the French playwright; a blind boy, falsely condemned for murder, finds himself rescued from the scaffold by a dog who recognizes the murderer; thus, suffering innocence and virtue triumph.

Friedrich Karl von Savigny, *The History of Roman Law in the Middle Ages*—the most significant work by the Alsatian jurist and historian; to 1831.

Sir Walter Scott, *Waverely*—the first novel by the Scottish writer, set against the background of the 1745 uprising by the Jacobites; intrigue, mutiny, battle, adventure, and love abound; imprisonment, rescue, and heroism lead to marriage for two characters, treason and execution for another, and retirement to a convent for a third.

——————, *The Works of Jonathan Swift*—an edition of the eighteenth-century writer's work, published almost simultaneously with *Waverley;* a "pioneer" effort, since little work had been done on the Irish satirist prior to this; valuable because it added to the published canon thirty poems, sixteen small prose pieces, and between sixty to seventy of Swift's letters, including twenty-eight written to "Vanessa"; the editorial notes revealed the scholar's knowledge of the people and politics during the reign of Queen Anne (1702-1714).

Robert Southey, *Roderick, the Last of the Goths*—a poem about revenge and penitence by the English writer; a Visigoth king, driven from his throne, becomes a monk and leads a Christian army to victory against the Moors.

William Wordsworth, *The Excursion*—a philosophical poem by the English writer concerning the state of man, nature, and human life; the wanderer suffers from a lack of religious faith and an inability to recognize virtue in his contemporaries; the poet also concerns himself with the problems arising from industrial expansion in the early nineteenth century, particularly its degrading effects upon the lower classes; contains "The Ruined Cottage."

EVENTS

British troops burn the United States Capitol at Washington, D.C., including the Library of Congress; only the most valuable government records and papers can be saved.

The New Monthly Magazine, a London literary journal founded to compete with the *Monthly*

Magazine, begins publication; William Hazlitt is a principal contributor; to 1884.

The United States Congress votes to appropriate $23,700 to acquire the private library (approximately 6500 volumes) of Thomas Jefferson.

1815

BIRTHS

Emanuel von Geibel (d. 1884). German poet and professor of aesthetics at Munich.

Anthony Trollope (d. 1882). English novelist; noted for the Barsetshire series.

DEATHS

Matthias Claudius (b. 1740). German poet and prose writer; an advocate of the return to simplicity in lyric poetry.

PUBLICATIONS

Jane Austen, *Emma*—an English novel that focuses upon a clever and certainly self-satisfied young lady who schemes for the social advancement of a new-found friend; such plans only contribute to her humiliation, from which she must disentangle herself.

Pierre Jean de Beranger, *Chansons* (Songs)—a collection of lyrics by the French poet that became popular because of its wit, vivacity, and satire; reflects the poet's politics, a curious blend of republicanism and Bonapartism.

George Gordon, Lord Byron, *Hebrew Melodies*—a collection of short poems by the English Romantic; most focus upon subjects and themes from the Old Testament, but a number consider, simply, the general theme of love: "She walks in Beauty, like the night / Of cloudless climes and starry skies."

Ernst Hoffman, *Elixiere des Teufels* (The Devil's Elixir)—a collection of tales by the German Romantic novelist.

Aleksandr Sergeyevich Griboyedov, *Malodye Suprugi* (The Newlyweds)—the first dramatic effort by the Russian playwright; a one-act comedy written in alexandrines.

Sir Walter Scott, *Guy Mannering*—a novel of travel, adventure, and love by the Scottish writer, set in the eighteenth century and focusing upon the son of a Scots laird, kidnapped as a child and taken to Holland; the entire affair results from the scheming of a rascal lawyer who hopes to gain the laird's estate; however, the young man manages to gain what rightfully belongs to him.

———————, *Lord of the Isles*—a poem in six cantos; focuses upon the return of Robert Bruce to Scotland in 1307 and moves to the Battle of Bannockburn; against that background unfolds the love story of Edith of Lorn for Lord Ronald, who does not immediately return the affection.

Johann Ludwig Uhland, *Gedichte* (Songs)—a collection of poems by the German lyricist; such pieces as "The Minstrel's Curse" and "The Good Comrade" make him one of the more popular poets of the German Romantic period.

EVENTS

The North American Review begins publication at Boston; a literary, critical, and historical monthly patterned after the major London journals; Ralph Waldo Emerson, Henry Wadsworth Longfellow, Washington Irving, Oliver Wendell Holmes, and Walt Whitman are among the major contributors; to 1939.

1816

BIRTHS

Charlotte Bronte (d. 1865). English novelist; the eldest of the three literary sisters from Yorkshire.

Gustav Freytag (d. 1895). German novelist and playwright.

Joseph Arthur de Gobineau (d. 1882). French Orientalist, diplomat, and philosopher; termed the intellectual parent of Friedrich Wilhelm Nietzsche and the original developer of the ideas of the "superman" and "super-morality."

DEATHS

Gavril Romanovich Derzhavin (b. 1743). Russian poet and diplomat; Poet Laureate of Russia.

Richard Brinsley Sheridan (b. 1751). Irish dramatist.

PUBLICATIONS

George Gordon, Lord Byron, *The Dream*—a visionary poem in blank verse by the English Romantic, inspired by his love for Mary Chaworth.

—————, *Parisi'na*—a poem focusing upon a domestic tragedy; a marquis discovers the incestuous loves of his wife and illegitimate son; he beheads both of them.

—————, *The Siege of Corinth*—a poem founded upon an actual military engagement in 1715 between the Turks and the Venetians; also involves a love relationship.

Samuel Taylor Coleridge, *Kubla Khan, a Vision in a Dream*—a poem by the English Romantic, supposedly composed during a dream; however, he was interrupted during the stage of conscious composition, and thus forgot most of what he had imagined; what remained became a prime representation of exotic poetry and Romantic imagery.

—————, *Christabel*—an unfinished poem; an innocent maiden sees through the disguise of a malignant and supernaturalcreature, but is forced to silence by a spell; called by some the most "beautiful" poem in English.

Henri Benjamin Constant de Rebecque, *Adolphe*—a semiautobiographical, psychological novel by the French-Swiss writer; first published in London; focuses upon his intellectual but passionate relationships with women, particularly Madame de Stael (1766-1817).

Leigh Hunt, *The Story of Rimini*—the chief poetical work of the English Romantic writer; based upon the story of Paolo and Francesca, in which a woman forced into marriage falls in love with her husband's brother; the lovers then suffer death.

Nikolai Karamzin, *The History of Russia*—the most significant work by the Russian historian and novelist; eleven vols. through 1824, but never finished; covers the period from the beginnings to 1613.

John Keats, *On First Looking into Chapman's Homer*—a sonnet by the English poet, his first poem of significance; the writer appears totally invigorated by the translation of Homer by the Elizabethan poet George Chapman (1559?-1634?): "Yet did I never breathe its pure serene / Till I heard Chapman speak out loud and bold."

Felicite de Lamennais, *Essai sur l'Indifference en Maitre de Religion*—a magnificent though paradoxical denunciation of private judgment and toleration by the French priest; favorably received by the Church at Rome.

Giacomo Leopardi, *Canti* (Songs)—Italian poems composed between 1816 and 1836; lyrical, lofty, and pessimistic; patriotic, yet contemptuous of Italian rulers.

Jose Joaquin Fernandez de Lizardi, *The Itching Parrot*—a picaresque satire by the Mexican writer, considered to have been the first Spanish-American novel; to 1830.

Thomas Love Peacock, *Headlong Hall*—a novel by the English writer largely comprised of conversations between an optimist, a pessimist, and an advocate of the status quo; contains a number of lively characters and songs.

Sir Walter Scott, *The Antiquary*—a novel by the Scottish writer in which a young officer, with the stain of illegitimacy, falls in love with a woman who rebuffs him; he follows her to Scotland under an assumed name; in actuality, the young man has more than sufficient claims to legitimacy, and thus all turns out blissful in the end; the novelist draws a character of himself and includes it in the piece.

—————, *The Black Dwarf*—a novel concerning an extremely ugly, but extraordinarily strong, dwarf who resides in eighteenth-century Scotland; he exerts a beneficent influence upon the neighboring communitites; in the end, the dwarf reveals himself to be a noble lord long supposed dead.

—————, *Old Mortality*—a novel based upon a late eighteenth-century figure who roamed about Scotland and cleaned and repaired the tombs of a strict sect of Scots Presbyterians, the Covenanters; religious and political animosities, acts of generosity, and love serve to advance the plot; appears to be an attack upon extreme religious enthusiasm.

Percy Bysshe Shelley, *Alastor; or, The Spirit of Solitude*—a poem by the English Romantic, his first significant piece; an allegory depicting the happy idealist contemplating lofty thoughts and visions of beauty; however, frustrations enter the scene, representing the poet's condemnation of self-centered idealism.

——————, *Hymn to Intellectual Beauty*—a poem in which the word "intellectual" assumes the qualities of the ideal, an abstract sense in opposition to the material qualities of property; the poet adopts the Platonic definition of "ideal beauty," which exists neither on earth nor in heaven, but can be found uniformly and consistently in all places and at all times.

——————, *Mont Blanc*—a presentation of the poet's philosophic position, descriptive of deep and powerful feelings; the poet himself viewed the piece as an undisciplined overflowing of his soul, "the gleams of a remoter world / That visit the soul in sleep. . . ."

Johann Ludwig Uhland, *Vaterlandische Gedichte* (Songs of the Fatherland)— a collection by the German lyric poet in which the well-known ballad "The Good Comrade" again appears.

EVENTS

The Delphian Club, a literary discussion group, founded in Baltimore; members include Francis Scott Key; begins to publish *The Portico,* a monthly literary magazine dedicated to the promotion of all things American.

1817

BIRTHS

Janos Arany (d. 1882). Hungarian poet; a leader, with Sandor Petofi, of the popular national school of Hungarian literature.

William Kirby (d. 1906). English-born Canadian writer.

Theodor Woldsen Storm (d. 1888). German poet and writer of tales.

Tom Taylor (d. 1880). Sottish dramatist, editor, and translator.

Henry David Thoreau (d. 1862) American essayist, poet, and nonconformist ("the hermit of Walden").

Jose Zorilla y Moral (d. 1893). Spanish poet and dramatist.

DEATHS

Jane Austen (b. 1775). English novelist.

Jean Andre Deluc (b. 1727). Swiss geologist, meteorologist, and physicist; attempted to prove that biblical creation was consistent with science.

Anne Louise Germaine Necker de Stael (b. 1766). French playwright, novelist, and essayist; one of the most significant French female writers.

PUBLICATIONS

Jane Austen, *Sanditon*—an unfinished novel by the English writer, not published until 1925; a mediocre man of boundless enthusiasm attempts to create a large and fashionable resort from an insignificant town; an unexpectedly humorous piece.

William Cullen Bryant, *Thanatopsis*—The American writer's most noted piece, a poem in blank verse; a meditation upon death, it reveals the poet's rejection of orthodox Christianity and move toward Unitarianism; the editors of *The North American Review* doubted that such a noble poem could come from the heart and mind of an American writer.

George Gordon, Lord Byron, *The Lament of Tasso*—a poem by the English Romantic based upon the legend of the love of the Italian Torquato Tasso (1544-1595) for Leonora d'Este, for which the epic poet suffered imprisonment.

——————, *Manfred*—a dramatic poem detailing the torture and remorse of the title character, who has been proven guilty of an unidentified crime; he seeks only oblivion and dies after denying the summons of demons.

Samuel Taylor Coleridge, *Biographia Literaria*—a philosophical and critical "autobiography" by the English Romantic poet; in reality, an analysis of the philosophy of Immanuel Kant (1724-1804), Johann Gottlieb Fichte (1762-1814), and Friedrich Wilhelm Josef von Schelling (1775-1854); the writer also discusses criticism of the poetry of William Wordsworth (1770-1850).

——————, *Zapolya*—a dramatic poem reminiscent of Shakespeare's *The Winter's Tale;* a usurper, Emerick, drives the dowager queen of Illyria, Zapolya, from her throne, but, following a twenty-year struggle, she regains her seat.

Maria Edgeworth, *Ormond*—a novel by the Irish writer; a story of Irish life interwoven with commentary upon fashionable society in eighteenth-century Paris; the plot of the piece centers on scheming and unprincipled characters designing a complicated love affair.

Franz Grillparzer, *Die Ahnfrau*—a tragic drama by the Austrian poet and playwright expressing his own personal torment and underscoring the need for the delicate soul to totally withdraw from society; the central female character manifests those problems and desires.

William Hazlitt, *Characters of Shakespeare's Plays*—a collection of essays by the English writer intended to "humanize" Shakespeare's characters; the reader must see these characters as human beings that lived and functioned in the society of that age; then, the characters become parts of the reader's own life; the study is the first to discern psychological elements in Shakespeare's plays.

Georg Friedrich Hegel, *Enzyklopadie der Philosophischen Wissenschaften* (Encyclopaedia of the Philosophical Sciences)—the German idealist philosopher sets forth his tripartite system of logic and philosophy of nature and of mind, complete with lecture notes for his students; written in Heidelberg and republished in 1821; includes theories of ethics, aesthetics, history, politics, and religion.

Joseph de Maistre, *Du Pape*—a tract by the French diplomat and political philosopher maintaining the Pope as the source and center of all earthly authority; thus, an ordered theocracy exists as the only protection from social and religious anarchy.

Thomas Moore, *Lalla Rookh*—a series of Oriental tales by the Irish writer, unified by the journey of the daughter of the Emperor Aurungzebe on her way to be married; includes "The Veiled Prophet of Khorassan," "Paradise and the Peri," "The Fire-Worshippers," and "The Light of the Harem"; the opening piece is written in heroic couplets, with the remainder in stanzas of varied form.

Thomas Love Peacock, *Melincourt; or, Sir Oran Haut-ton*—an English novel concerned with the attempts of various suitors to win the hand of a wealthy woman; those attempts bring togehter a variety of characters who discuss prevailing political and philosophical issues: slavery, the Lake poets, "rotten" boroughs.

Sir Walter Scott, *Harold the Dauntless*—a poem by the Scottish writer concerning the son of a Danish Viking who has been converted to Christianity after having been granted lands in northern England.

——————, *Rob Roy*—a novel set immediately preceding the Jacobite uprising of 1715; misfortune and injustice have embittered the central character and transformed him into a powerful and dangerous outlaw who can outfight and outwit the agents of government; nonetheless, that same outlaw can engage in acts of justice and proves capable of generosity.

Robert Southey, *Wat Tyler*—a drama by the youthful essayist, written while at Balliol College, Oxford, in 1794; published without the writer's consent; as a result of the crude political sentiments of the piece, the members of the House of Commons attacked the writer as a "rengado;" Wat Tyler (d. 1381) led the peasant revolt of 1381.

EVENTS

William Blackwood, Scottish publisher, begins publication of *Blackwood's Edinburgh Magazine,* a monthly literary journal, to compete with *The Edinburgh Review.*

James Harper and John Harper establish the firm of J. and J. Harper, Dover Street, New York City; the publishing firm begins as the forerunner of Harper and Brothers, which will be founded in 1833.

William Hazlitt and Leigh Hunt publish their anthology *The Round Table: A Collection of Essays on Literature, Men and Manners;* forty essays by Hazlitt, twelve by Hunt; two vols.; an extremely popular miscellany.

The Scotsman begins publication as a weekly Edinburgh newspaper.

1818

BIRTHS

Emily Jane Bronte (d. 1848). English novelist and poet; the "middle" of the three literary sisters from Yorkshire.

Charles Marie Leconte de Lisle (d. 1894). French poet; headed the Parnassian school of

French poets and succeeded Victor Hugo in the chair of poetry at the Academie Francaise.

Karl Marx (d. 1883). German philosopher; founder of modern international communism.

Ivan Sergeyevich Turgenev (d. 1883). Russian novelist and poet; examined social and political problems in nineteenth-century Russia.

DEATHS

Matthew Gregory (Monk) Lewis (b. 1775)—Leading English Gothic novelist.

Johann David Wyss (b. 1743). Swiss writer and philosopher; best remembered for his children's tales and sketches.

PUBLICATIONS

Jane Austen, *Northanger Abbey*—an English novel, begun as early as 1798, the author's attempt to satirize the Gothic novel, particularly Ann Ward Radcliffe's *The Mysteries of Udolpho* (1794), and to contrast that piece with the realities of English life.

——————— , *Persuasion*—a novel written between 1815 and 1816, but published posthumously; the novelist's last completed work, a satire of the traditional love story; the theme emphasizes the need of contemporary society to provide husbands for marriageable daughters; the strategies of love and marriage become so intricate that the reader loses the train of thought in a complex interplay of characters.

George Gordon, Lord Byron, *Beppo, a Venetian Story*—a poem in mock heroic style; relates with irony the events surrounding a Venetian carnival; a cup of coffee leads to the reconciliation between two lovers.

Franz Grillparzer, *Sappho*—a tragedy in verse by the Austrian poet and playwright; on one level it exists as the story of an artist of high calling who renounces love for the sake of his own art; however, it also serves as the psychological study of a woman who finds herself unable to love a man for whom she feels real affection; there are those critics who believe the play to be a study in "psychosexuality" presented within a nineteenth-century Romantic context.

William Hazlitt, *Lectures on the English Poets*—the English essayist surveys the development of English poetry through five historical periods: Elizabeth I, James I—Charles I, Charles II—Anne, George I—George II, George II—George III; naturally, the writer focuses upon what he believes to be the "romantic" elements in the writers of those periods, and thus leans toward the likes of Geoffrey Chaucer and Andrew Marvell.

——————— , *A View of the English Stage*—a collection of essays focusing upon the general subject of English dramatic criticism; until 1821.

John Keats, *Endymion*—a poem in four books by the English Romantic poet focusing upon the story of a brain-sick shepherd prince with whom Phoebus, the moon goddess, falls in love; after luring him through a cloud of spirits, she bears him away to eternal life; as an allegory, the piece represents the poet in pursuit of ideal perfection, but distracted in his quest by human beauty.

Thomas Moore, *The Fudge Family in Paris*—satirical verses by the Irish poet in the form of letters by and to members of the Fudge family, who visit Paris after the restoration of the Bourbons (1817); an attempt to ridicule those English who, at the time, came in great numbers to Paris.

Thomas Love Peacock, *Nightmare Abbey*—a novel by the English writer; its ultimate purpose is to satirize the poetry and literary criteria of Lord Byron, Samuel Taylor Coleridge, and their transcendentalist-pessimistic colleagues; thus, the reader encounters a thin plot, but meets a host of amusing and entertaining characters: Toobad, Flosky, Cypress, Larynx, Scythrop, Glowry.

Sir Walter Scott, *The Heart of Midlothian*—a novel by the Scottish writer; focuses upon the old Edinburgh Tolbooth prison ("the Heart of Midlothian") and the Porteous riots of 1736, an incident that involved troops firing upon unarmed citizens; onto that historical backdrop the novelist places the complex story of Jeanie and Effie Deans.

Mary Wollstonecraft Shelley, *Frankenstein; or, The Modern Prometheus*—a novel of terror by the English writer; the first appearance of the monstrous creature endowed with supernatural strength who, in a fit of loneliness and remorse, murders his creator's brother and his bride; the scientist who created him pursues the monster in an effort to destroy it, but dies in the attempt.

Percy Bysshe Shelley, "Julian and Maddalo, a Conversation"—a poem by the English Romantic; a conversation between Shelley and Byron on the power of man to control his mind.

——————, **"The Revolt of Islam"**—a poem in Spenserian stanzas; a symbolic tale illustrating the growth and progress of the individual mind seeking excellence, while devoted to the love of all humanity; a reaction to the fall of Napoleon Bonaparte and its effect upon the poor of Europe; the return of tyrants brings misery, famine, and plague.

——————, **"Stanzas Written in Dejection, near Naples"**—a poem easily understood when one considers the circumstances that caused its production: the poet's first wife, Harriet, had drowned herself; Clara, his infant daughter by Mary Shelley, had just died; the poet found himself suffering from ill health, emotional pain, financial problems, and (perhaps worst of all) a sense that he had failed as a poet: "Alas! I have not hope nor health, / Nor peace within nor calm around. . . . "

EVENTS

Yale College professor of chemistry and lawyer Benjamin Silliman begins publication of *The American Journal of Science and the Arts.*

Thomas Bowdler, an Edinburgh physician, publishes in England his ten-volume *The Family Shakespeare; in Which Nothing Is Added to the Original Text; but Those words and Expressions Are Omitted Which Cannot with Propriety Be Read Aloud in a Family;* such editing practice gives way to the term "bowdlerize," to omit offensive words and phrases.

Joseph Dobrovsky, Czech scholar and founder of Slavonic philology, writes his *History of the Czech Language.*

William Bray publishes his edition of the *Diary* of John Evelyn; that private diary, covering the years 1640–1706, reveals the occupations and pleasures of a cultivated English gentleman and focuses upon art, inventions, curiosities, gardening, public affairs, politics, court life, and science; of significant interest are those entries concerning life in and around London, particularly friendships with scholars and writers; perhaps not as exciting as the *Diary* of Samuel Pepys, his contemporary, but certainly no less informative.

Georg Wilhelm Friedrich Hegel receives the appointment to the professorship of philosophy at Berlin, vacant since the death of Johann Gottlieb Fichte; Hegel will now reign, until his death, as virtual dictator of German philosophical thought.

August Wilhelm von Schlegel, German poet and critical scholar, appointed Professor of Literature and Indian Languages at Bonn; he will translate seventeen of Shakespeare's plays.

1819

BIRTHS

Arthur Hugh Clough (d. 1861). English poet; pupil and close friend of Matthew Arnold.

George Eliot (pseudonym of Mary Ann Evans; d. 1880). English novelist who focused upon farmers, tradesmen, and the lower middle class.

Theodor Fontane (d. 1898). German poet and novelist; an influence upon Thomas Mann.

Julia Ward Howe (d. 1910). American poet and suffragette; the first woman member of the American Academy of Arts and Letters.

Gottfried Keller (d. 1890). Swiss poet and novelist; excelled as a writer of short stories.

Charles Kingsley (d. 1875). English poet, essayist, and novelist.

James Russell Lowell (d. 1891). American poet, essayist, and diplomat.

Herman Melville (d. 1891). American novelist; never recognized as a significant contributor to American letters until thirty years after his death.

John Ruskin (d. 1900). English essayist and art critic; one of the major Victorian figures who roused his nation to a sense of responsibility for the negative effects of industrialization upon society.

Philip Schaff (d. 1893). Swiss-born American Presbyterian theologian; church historian and biblical scholar.

Walt Whitman (d. 1892). American poet; responsible for investing poetry with the full dimension of modern life and humanity.

DEATHS

August Friedrich Ferdinand von Kotzebue (b. 1761). German playwright; assassinated, at Mannheim, as a suspected Russian agent.

PUBLICATIONS

George Gordon, Lord Byron, *Don Juan*—an epic satire by the English poet; a charming, handsome, and unprincipled young man takes pleasure in succumbing to the charms of every woman he meets; a lavish social comedy, but also a stinging attack upon social conditions in England and upon certain political and literary figures, including Robert Southey, Samuel Taylor Coleridge, and the Duke of Wellington; to 1824.

——————, *Mazeppa*—a poem concerning a Polish nobleman who relates a tale of romantic intrigue from his early life; as a punishment, an irate husband has him bound naked on a wild horse that carries him on a mad ride throughout the countryside; local peasants eventually rescue him.

Johann Wolfgang von Goethe, *Der Westostlicher Divan* (West Eastern Divan)—a collection of lyrics by the German poet; the poems reflect the writer's study of the Persian poet Hafiz (Shams ed-Din Muhammed; d. 1338?), whose own lyrics focused upon such subjects as love and drink; supposedly inspired by his relationship with Marianne von Willemer.

William Hazlitt, *Lectures on the English Comic Writers*—a collection of essays by the English writer in which he distinguishes between the laughable, the ludicrous, and the ridiculous; states a preference for the Restoration (1660–1685) writers, particularly William Congreve; not confined, however, to English writers, since the essayist considers such figures as Miguel Cervantes, Alain Rene Le Sage, and Michel de Montaigne.

——————, *A Letter to William Gifford*—perhaps the best example of the English essayist's argumentative prose style; he takes issue with Gifford's obstinate adherence to the classical traditions of English literature and to his distrust of "radicals"; sets out to "cure" Gifford of his "ugly trick of saying what is not true of any one you do not like . . . "

Ernst Hoffman, *Die Serapionsbruder* (The Serapion Brothers)—a collection of short, Gothic tales by the German writer; contains such popular pieces as "Nutcracker and the King of Mice," "The Battle," and "The Pyramid Doctor," the last of which introduced the reader to Doctor Splendiano Accoramboni and his cornfield; to 1825.

John Keats, "La Belle Dame sans Merci" (The Lady without Mercy)—a ballad by the English poet; the story of a mortal man destroyed by his love for a supernatural enchantress; unique in terms of its dialogue form and effective metrical patterns; revised in 1820.

——————, *Hyperion*—a poem based upon the classical myth of the creation of the world and the rise of the Olympic hierarchy of gods; intended as an epic, but never really developed; instead, the significance of the piece derives from the power of the poet's blank verse: his imagery, diction, and phrasing.

——————, **"The Eve of St. Agnes"**—a poem derived principally from the *Il Filocolo* of Giovanni Boccaccio (1313-1375); maidens who perform the proper ceremony on the Eve of St. Agnes (21 January), the patron saint of virgins, might be able to dream of the men they will eventually marry.

——————, *Lamia*—an allegorical poem based on *The Anatomy of Melancholy* (1621) by Robert Burton; the tale of a young philosopher's infatuation with the phantom spirit of a fair gentlewoman; the poet dwells upon two serious human inadequacies: the unreal poetry of dreams and the coldness of analytic philosophy; both bring harm to poetry, and thus the poet must seek a more vital grasp of reality than either dreams or philosophy can provide.

——————, **"Ode on Melancholy"**—a poem intended to demonstrate the relationship between melancholy and joy; thus, "She dwells with Beauty—Beauty that must die. . . . "

——————, **"Ode on a Grecian Urn"**—a poem suggested by the Elgin marbles and the Grecian urns in the British Museum; in a world of change and decay, the object of classical art, the urn, remains a friend to humanity, reminding everyone that "Beauty is truth, truth beauty. . . . "

——————, **"Ode to Psyche"**—the poet's first attempt to construct a new lyrical form totally different from the traditional sonnets of Petrarch and Shakespeare; Psyche ("soul"), loved by Cupid and having difficulties with Venus, at last finds herself reunited with her lover and given immortality.

——————, *Ode to a Nightingale*—the first of the poet's highly successful odes written in the established ten-line stanza form; he attempted to combine the virtues of both the Petrarchan and the Shakespearean sonnets; again, there exists the thought of developing a connection between joy and melancholy.

Arthur Schopenhauer, *Die Welt als Wille und Vorstellung* (The World as Will and Representation)—the German philosopher explicates the logic, metaphysics, aesthetics, and ethics of the world as a constant conflict of individual wills; that conflict results, essentially, in frustration and pain; he determined pleasure to be the simple absence of that pain; the tract exercised considerable influence upon the works of Sigmund Freud (1856-1939) and Friedrich Wilhelm Nietzsche (1844-1900).

Sir Walter Scott, *The Bride of Lammermoor*—a novel by the Scottish writer concerning a noble deprived of his lands after the Glorious Revolution of 1688–1689; after the noble's death, his son inherits his hatred for the one who supposedly caused his ruin; however, the son saves his enemy's life; love and intrigue follow; the heroine stabs her husband, which leads to insanity and death; the hero's end occurs in a bog of quicksand.

——————, *Ivanhoe*—the first attempt by the novelist to concentrate on purely "English" subjects; thus he presents his own ideas on the state of antagonism between Saxon and Norman during the reign of King Richard I (1189-1199); tournaments, castle sieges, fair maidens, and Robin Hood's merry men abound to create a lively piece of adventure and entertainment.

——————, *A Legend of Montrose*—a novel set amid the uprisings in 1644 of the Highland clans in support of Charles I and opposed to the conservative Scottish Covenanters; a gloomy tale of barbarous murder, vengeance, romance, revealed identities, and more murder; really a tragedy, complete with a key character, Captain Dugald Dalgetty, to provide the comic relief.

Percy Bysshe Shelley, *The Cenci*—a dramatic tragedy by the English poet; a daughter, hated by her miserable father, involves herself in a plot to kill that tyrant; after the assassination, the family is arrested and sentenced to death; focuses upon the obviously simple thesis that serious consequences await those who attempt to repay hate with even more hate.

——————, *Ode to the West Wind*—a poem conceived and mostly written in a wood skirting the River Arno, near Florence; the wind combines the qualities of mildness and animation, thus serving to change apathy to spiritual renewal, to alter imaginative sterility to creative power; the wind exists as breath, soul, and inspiration.

——————, *To a Skylark*—In this poem the bird, freed from the bonds of earth and lost to all of the physical senses except hearing, becomes the ideal of pure joy, or the nonmaterial spirit.

William Wordsworth, *The Waggoner*—composed in 1805 and dedicated to Charles Lamb; a fanciful poetic tale of a waggoner who almost totally succumbs to the material temptations offered by the Lakeland hills; in the end, the hills lose both Benjamin (the waggoner) and the wain (his wagon).

EVENTS

The English essayist and poet Leigh Hunt begins publication of *The Indicator*, a London literary periodical; until 1821.

Guilian Crommelin Verplanck, a New York City lawyer and politican, begins publication of *The New York American*, a daily newspaper of Whig and National Republican leanings; until 1845.

1820

BIRTHS

Dionysius (Dion) Lardner Boucicault (d. 1890). Irish-born actor and playwright who wrote both in England and the United States; adapted liberally from French drama.

Friedrich Engels (d. 1895). The cofounder, with Karl Marx, of "Scientific Socialism"; German born, but spent most of his life in England.

PUBLICATIONS

Willem Bilderdijk, *The Destruction of the First Creation*—an unfinished epic by the

Dutch poet, heavily Romantic in its interpretation; his major work.

James Fenimore Cooper, *Precaution*—a novel of manners by the American writer, highly imitative of Jane Austen; its lack of success taught the novelist that he should write about America and for an American audience.

William Hazlitt, *Dramatic Literature in the Age of Elizabeth*—the English essayist's clear and penetrating analyses of Elizabethan dramas and dramatists; focuses upon those playwrights outside of Shakespeare and Ben Jonson; his point of view is decidedly Romantic, particularly when discussing Francis Beaumont (1584-1616), John Fletcher (1579-1625), and Philip Massinger (1583-1640).

Alphonse de Lamartine, *Meditations poetiques* (Poetic Meditations)—a collection of poems by the French Romantic writer, based upon both traditional and contemporary sources; includes his well-known poem "Le Lac" (The Lake); the entire collection resounds with musical lyricism and an affinity for Nature.

Henry Wadsworth Longfellow, *The Battle of Lovell's Pond*—sixteen lines by the American poet, then only thirteen years of age; published in the Portland, Maine *Gazette*, 17 November 1820, and signed "Henry."

Alessandro Manzoni, *Il Conte di Carmagnola* (The Count of Carmagnola)—a historical tragedy in verse by the Italian novelist, based upon the idea of the relationship between the oppressed and their oppressors; the writer also focuses upon the role of divine providence in history.

Aleksandr Sergeyevich Pushkin, *Ruslan and Lyudmila*—the first successful Romantic poem by the Russian writer, a long narrative, or epic; the initial attempt by the poet to bring to life people and historical periods.

Sir Walter Scott, *The Abbot*—a novel by the Scottish writer, set during the period of Mary Queen of Scots (1542-1587) and her imprisonment at Lochleven Castle (1567-1568); focuses mainly upon her escape, interwoven with a narrative of romance and political intrigue.

——————, *The Monastery*—a historical novel and a sequel to *The Abbot;* set during the reign of Elizabeth I (1558-1603); two brothers fall in love with the same girl; an English knight complicates matters by antagonizing one of the brothers, who kills him in a duel; the victorious brother flees Scotland, leaving the young lady for his sibling, and becomes a monk; in addition to "live" characters, the novelist adds a number of supernatural spirits.

Percy Bysshe Shelley, *Ode to Liberty*—a Pindaric ode by the English poet; focuses upon the popular uprisings in Spain, Italy, and Greece; the poet equates liberty with intellectual beauty.

——————, *Oedipus Tyrannus; or, Swellfoot the Tyrant*—a dramatic satire in which the poet ridicules the numerous matrimonial affairs of the newly crowned King George IV.

——————, *Prometheus Unbound*—a dramatic poem and a major work of the English Romantic poet; based upon, but severely modified in terms of "modern" language and imagery, the *Prometheus Bound* of Aeschylus, dramatizing the sufferings of Prometheus; the unrepentent champion of humanity steals fire from heaven, and thus, by the power of Zeus, must remain chained to Mt. Caucasus and tortured by a vulture; the poet transforms the theme of the drama to the origin of evil and its elimination.

——————, *The Sensitive Plant*—a poem in which the poet's spirit exists as a mimosa plant in the garden of a lady; that beautiful maiden dies, and Death corrupts the garden; concerns the permanency and reality of beauty.

Robert Southey, *The Life of Wesley and the Rise of Methodism*—a biography of the founder and leader of British Methodism, drawn heavily from earlier biographies, narratives, and memoirs; Methodist loyalists objected to the English essayist's questioning of his subject's motives, particularly inferences to Wesley's ambition as a taint upon the sincerity of his religious movement.

EVENTS

The English pre-Romantic poet William Blake (1757–1827) completes his watercolor illustrations for *The Book of Job*, an edition of a translation from the Hebrew by George Hunt, to be published at Bath by Wood and Cunningham in 1825.

The Charleston [**South Carolina**] *Mercury* begins publication as a voice of the proslavery radicals and the proponents of secession; until 1865.

The London Magazine (not to be confused with the earlier [1732–1785] version) begins publication as a literary journal; major contributors include Charles Lamb, William Hazlitt, and Thomas De Quincey; until 1829.

The Providence [Rhode Island] *Journal* begins publication; totally free of political bias, the newspaper has often been identified as the conscience of the state.

1821

BIRTHS

Charles Baudelaire (d. 1867). French poet and literary and art critic; a major influence upon Western poetry.

Fyodor Mikhailovich Dostoevsky (d. 1881). Russian novelist; the voice of human suffering in nineteenth-century Russian fiction.

Gustave Flaubert (d. 1880). French novelist; combined the most salient aspects of Romanticism and Realism.

Nikolai Alexeievich Nekrasov (d. 1877). Russian lyrical poet; harshly realistic.

DEATHS

John Keats (b. 1795). English poet; dies in Rome from consumption.

Joseph Marie de Maistre (b. 1754). French diplomat and political philosopher.

PUBLICATIONS

William Cullen Bryant, *Poems*—a collection by the American poet that includes such pieces as "Thanatopsis," "The Yellow Violet," "Inscription for the Entrance to a Wood," "To a Waterfowl," and "Green River."

George Gordon, Lord Byron, *Cain: A Mystery*—a dramatic tragedy in verse by the English poet; Cain revolts against the impositions placed upon him by God and becomes a pupil of Lucifer; he then kills Abel, angry because of his brother's devotion to God; after a period of punishment and remorse, he begins his exile.

——————, *Marino Faliero, Doge of Venice*—a historical tragedy set in the mid-fourteenth century; a lampoon upon the haughty doge leads to the writer's punishment; the doge believes the sentence to have been inadequate for the "crime," and thus attempts to overthrow the government; when his plot fails, he is beheaded.

——————, *Sardanapalus*—a tragedy concerning the last king of Assyria (7th century B.C.); after his defeat in a revolt, the amiable, slothful king perishes in a funeral pyre constructed for him and his favorite Greek slave.

——————, *The Two Foscara*—another of the poet's historical tragedies concerning a doge of Venice and his son; the father exiles his son for the third time; the son, anguished because of his love for Venice, dies; the father, realizing that he has been forced to abdicate his position, falls down and dies upon leaving his palace.

James Fenimore Cooper, *The Spy: A Tale of the Neutral Ground*—the American novelist's first success; the patriotic theme of the piece demonstrates the writer's ideal of a democratic society, one that the Europeans did not possess and the Americans did not appreciate; in Harvey Birch, the reader observes a truly original and natural American character who, with utter selflessness, ultimately confronts his leader and his God.

Johann Wolfgang von Goethe, *Wilhelm Meisters Wanderjahre,* **Part II** (Wilhelm Meister's Travels)—the continuaton · of the travels of the stagestruck youth, during which the completion of Wilhelm Meister's education occurs.

Franz Grillparzer, *Das goldene Vliess* (The Golden Fleece)—a trilogy of short dramatic pieces by the Austrian playwright, focusing upon and held together by the character of Medea; in that character, the writer reveals to the world his own personal problems, particularly his incapacity for heterosexual love, his desire to withdraw, and his search for a father figure.

William Hazlitt, *Table Talk; or, Original Essays on Men and Manners*—a collection of essays by the English writer in an animated, conversational style; includes "On Genius and Common Sense," "The Character of Cobbett," "The Indian Jugglers," "On Paradox and Commonplace," and two essays on Sir Joshua Reynolds; to 1822.

Heinrich Heine, *Gedichte*—an early collection by the German poet, published at Berlin.

Ernst Hoffman, *Kater Murr* (Tom-Cat Murr)—a work of fiction by the German Romantic writer, partly autobiographic and representative of his interest in the supernatural; to 1822, but never completed.

Alessandro Manzoni, *Il Cinque Maggio* (The Fifth of May)—a highly acclaimed poem by the Italian writer focusing upon the death of Napoleon Bonaparte.

Friedrich E. D. Schleiermacher, *Der Christliche Glaube* (The Christian Faith)—the major work of the German Protestant theologian; develops systematically his definition of religion as an absolute dependence on a monotheistic God, achieved through intuition and free from dogma; Christianity thus exists as the highest manifestation of religion; to 1822; six editions through 1864.

Sir Walter Scott, *Kenilworth*—a novel by the Scottish writer set during the reign of Elizabeth I (1558-1603); concerns the tragic fate of a beautiful maiden enticed into a secret marriage; then follow more secret intrigues, attempts at seduction, and disguised appearances; as usual, the novelist provides concrete and accurate descriptions of historical characters and events, all of whom play some role in the tragic end of the heroine.

Percy Bysshe Shelley, *Adonais: An Elegy on the Death of John Keats*—an English poem in Spenserian stanzas; laments not only Keats's early and tragic death, but also, in a tone of bitterness, the unduly negative criticism his poetry received; the poet believes that such criticism hastened Keats's death; in the end, the poet proclaims Keats's artistic immortality.

——————— , *A Defence of Poetry*—an essay by the English Romantic poet; argues on behalf of the elements of imagination and love in poetry and proclaims its moral importance; written in response to Thomas Love Peacock's *The Four Ages of Poetry*, which maintained that poetry was a mere anachronism.

——————— , *Epipsychidion*—contains the poet's philosophy of love, expressed in an emotional stream of musical language; such language carries the reader's imagination breathlessly onward.

Robert Southey, *A Vision of Judgment*—a poem in hexameters by the English writer, the preface of which attacks the poetry of Lord Byron; the poem itself concerns a trance in which the poet sees George III (d. 1820) rise from the tomb and proceed to the gates of Heaven; after receiving testimonials from his political allies, the King enters Paradise, followed by his family and friends;

satirized by Byron in his own *Vision of Judgment* (1822).

EVENTS

Jean Francois Champollion, French Egyptologist, deciphers the Rosetta Stone, found by Napoleon's soldiers in 1799; he publishes his work between 1821 and 1828.

The English novel *Fanny Hill; or, Memoirs of a Woman of Pleasure* (1748-1749), by John Cleland, becomes the subject of a Massachusetts obscenity trial.

The Genius of Universal Emancipation, an antislavery newspaper published by Ohio Quaker Benjamin Lundy, begins publication; until 1835, then again from 1838 to 1839; Lundy will eventually have an editorial association with the poet John Greenleaf Whittier.

The Manchester **[England]** *Guardian* begins publication as a weekly newspaper; it will be issued daily beginning in 1859; in 1959, it will be known only as *The Guardian.*

The Saturday Evening Post begins publication at Philadelphia as a weekly magazine designed for "light" reading; until 1969; revived in 1971 as a quarterly; has traditionally published work by leading American writers.

1822

BIRTHS

Matthew Arnold (d. 1888). English poet and critic.

Edmond de Goncourt (d. 1896). French novelist, artist, and art historian.

Thomas Hughes (d. 1896). English Parliamentarian, trade unionist, and writer of semiautobiographical fiction for young boys.

Sandor Petofi (d. 1849). Hungarian poet and writer of revolutionary war songs, responsible for a new epoch in Hungarian literature.

DEATHS

Ernst Theodor Wilhelm [Amadeus] Hoffmann (b. 1776). German writer and composer; known for his fantastic tales.

Percy Bysshe Shelley (b. 1792). English Romantic poet and lyrical dramatist; drowned while sailing near Spezia, in northwest Italy.

PUBLICATIONS

William Blake, *The Ghost of Abel*—a short dramatic dialogue by the English poet attacking the view that Jehovah uttered the curse upon Cain; instead, the poet attributes that act to Satan; the piece bears the explanatory subtitle, "A Revelation in the Visions of Jehovah/ Seen by William Blake."

George Gordon, Lord Byron, *Heaven and Earth*—a drama by the British poet focusing upon the biblical legend of the marriage between angels and the daughters of men; the principal characters emerge as Samiasa (the seraph) and Aholibamah (grandaughter of Cain).

————————, *The Vision of Judgment*—a satirical poem ridiculing Robert Southey's work of the same title (1821), which had attacked Byron's poetry; regards with scorn the position of Poet Laureate, which Southey then held, and the entire process of appointment to that post.

————————, *Werner*—a dramatic tragedy in which the outlawed son of a noble assumes the name of "Werner" and finds himself in the same house as his enemy; that sets the stage for robbery, murder, false accusations, and death.

Thomas De Quincey, *Confessions of an English Opium Eater*—an account of the English essayist's early years, including his travels about Wales; physical suffering and nervous irritation led to his opium habit; then unfolds an account of extreme suffering, particularly during the period of withdrawal; the supposed object of the book appears to be a warning against the dangers of the drug; an enlarged version published in 1856.

Christian Dietrich Grabbe, *Scherz, Satire, Ironie, und Tiefere Bedeutung* (Jest, Satire, Irony, and Deeper Meaning)—a German play in which the hero is a grotesque and humorous form of Satan; the "deeper meaning" represents the idea that the historical forces within nature and society are completely absurd; tragedy exists because the hero finds himself confronted and then overwhelmed by the "blind furies" of history.

Washington Irving, *Bracebridge Hall; or, the Humorists: A Medley*—a collection of fifty-one miscellaneous tales and sketches by the American writer; principal settings include England, France, and Spain.

Thomas Love Peacock, *Maid Marian*—an English novel, a parody of the medieval romance, with the Robin Hood legend as the basis for plot; the writer included a number of his poems as background songs.

Sir Walter Scott, *The Fortunes of Nigel*—a novel by the Scottish writer, set during the reign of James I (1603-1625); a young Scots noble comes to London to recover 40,000 marks from the King, thus hoping to save the loss of his ancestral home; however, English lords covet the estate, and thus treachery begins its work.

Percy Bysshe Shelley, *Hellas*—a lyrical drama by the English poet, inspired by the Greek proclamation of independence (1821) from the Turks; features emotional lyrics from the chorus of Greek captive women.

Stendhal, *De l'Amour* (On Love)—the French writer's psychological analysis of love based upon his own amorous involvements; significant in that it predates the work of Sigmund Freud (1856-1939).

Alfred de Vigny, *Poemes*—an early collection of Romantic verse by the French writer; the pieces emphasize the lonely struggle of the individual in a hostile universe.

William Wordsworth, *Memorials of a Tour on the Continent*—a volume of poems by the English Romantic reflecting his impressions from his tour of 1820; thirty-seven poems, each identifying a specific locale; written between January and November 1821.

EVENTS

James Fenimore Cooper becomes instrumental in the founding of the Bread and Cheese Club, New York City; devoted to informal discussions among men of letters of literary and intellectual matters; until 1827 (?).

William Church of Connecticut patents the first typesetting machine in England.

George Gordon, Lord Byron, and Leigh Hunt begin publication of *The Liberal,* a magazine of prose and poetry; only two numbers published.

Noctes Ambrosianae, a series of seventy-one imaginary conversations, begins to appear in *Blackwood's Edinburgh Magazine;* written principally by John Wilson, James Hogg, William Maginn, and John Gibson Lockhart; ranged radically in subject matter, from literary and political criticism to the raising of poultry; until 1835.

Henry Thomas Colebrook, English official in India and a specialist in Oriental studies, founds the Royal Asiatic Society for the study of Eastern languages.

Henry White begins publication of *The Sunday Times* of London, a weekly newspaper that still exists.

1823

BIRTHS

Aleksandr Ostrovsky (d. 1886). Russian dramatist; possibly the most prolific of Russia's playwrights.

Coventry Patmore (d. 1896). English poet and essayist; a friend of Alfred, Lord Tennyson and John Ruskin.

Charlotte Mary Yonge (d. 1901). English writer of religious and historical fiction.

DEATHS

Ann Ward Radcliffe (b. 1764). English novelist; one of the most significant Gothic novelists of the late eighteenth and early nineteenth centuries.

Friedrich Ludwig Zacharias Werner (b. 1768). German Romantic playwright and religious poet and mystic.

PUBLICATIONS

George Gordon, Lord Byron, *The Island*—an English poem combining satire and romance; focuses upon the mutiny aboard the HMS *Bounty* in 1789; the poet contrasts the mutineers' island paradise with the rules and restrictions of contemporary society.

James Fenimore Cooper, *The Pilot*—a pioneer effort in the historical sea novel; combines a complicated love story with countless adventures on land and sea; contains careful and accurate descriptions of life aboard an ocean vessel during the American Revolution, substantiated by the author's own naval experience; the title character may well represent the American naval hero John Paul Jones (1747-1792).

——————, *The Pioneers; or, The Sources of the Susquehanna*—the American writer's first novel of the frontier; the heroine is rescued from a forest fire by her lover, the grandson of an old military man; an accurate record of the frontier settlements of west-central New York, sprinkled with sufficient dashes of romantic imagination to make it all fairly interesting; the underlying thesis seems to be the promise of new life on the edges of a developing country.

Thomas De Quincey, *On the Knocking at the Gate in "Macbeth"*—an essay by the English writer focusing on Act II, scene 2, ll.57-74, of Shakespeare's play; the author's interpretation of the scene is guided by his Romantic critical criteria.

Heinrich Heine, *Lyrisches Intermezzo*—a second collection of lyrics by the German poet; the pieces illustrate the poet's modernism and his rejection of "pure" classicism and "pure" Romanticism in favor of an absolute artistic freedom guided by the power of his own imagination.

Charles Lamb, *The Essays of Elia*—a collection of miscellaneous essays that originally appeared in *The London Magazine* between 1820 and 1823; a second series in 1833; treats everyday subjects in what is now regarded by some critics as the epitome of the familiar essay style.

Adam Mickiewicz, *Forefathers' Eve*—a drama in verse by the Polish playwright and poet; based upon pagan worship rites among the peasants of Belorussia; various spirits appear during the celebration and contribute to the tale of unrequited love, which ends in suicide; the piece, including an additional but distinct part in 1831, was never staged during the writer's lifetime.

——————, *Grazyna*—a narrative poem by the Polish poet reflecting his early life in Lithuania.

Thomas Moore, *Loves of the Angels*—the Irish writer's final long poem; recounts the lives of three fallen angels whose souls have declined from the pure state because mortal women are the objects of their love.

Sir Walter Scott, *Peveril of the Peak*—a novel by the Scottish writer set during the Popish Plot of 1678; Cavalier and Puritan neighbors express their different religious and political sentiments, which produces open conflict; offspring of the two factions fall in love, thus leading to intrigue; the writer presents accurate details of several key historical figures: Charles II, the Duke of Buckingham, Titus Oates, and Colonel Blood.

——————————, *Quentin Durward*—a novel set in fifteenth-century France, the principal character of which is Louis XI (1423-1483; reigned from 1461), who is engaged in a struggle with Charles the Bold of Burgundy; the title character enters the plot after having been sent on a mission to Burgundy to protect an heiress; he eventually falls in love with her and wins her heart; a series of characters from French history appear throughout the pages.

——————————, *St. Ronan's Well*—a novel set in the Scottish spa town of St. Ronan's Well; a satire upon the idleness of contemporary fashionable society, with characters having such names as Sir Bingo Banks, Lady Penelope Pennyfeather, and Captain McTurk.

Mary Wollstonecraft Shelley, *Valperga; or, The Life and Adventures of Castruccio, Prince of Lucca*—an English Romantic novel set in fourteenth-century Italy; traces the deterioration of the title character, from his beginnings as a generous youth through his development into a Machiavellian tyrant whose spirit is consumed by pride.

Robert Southey, *History of the Peninsular War*—the English essayist's account of the conflict, from 1808 to 1814, between France and England on the Iberian Peninsula during the Napoleonic Wars; historical accuracy is sacrificed to the writer's elaborate prose style; three volumes to 1832.

EVENTS

The Bannantyne Club founded at Edinburgh, with Sir Walter Scott as president, to promote the publication of old Scottish documents; named after George Bannantyne (1545-1608), compiler of collections of Scottish poetry; until 1861.

The Christian Examiner begins publication at Boston; a bimonthly journal of Unitarian thought and opinion; eventually a supporter of the Transcendentalist movement in New England; until 1869.

King George IV (reigned 1820-1830) presents the library of King George III (reigned 1760-

1820) to the British Museum, which significantly expands the collection.

Clement Clark Moore, classical linguist, lexicographer, and Professor of Biblical Learning and Oriental and Greek Literature at the New York General Theological Seminary (Episcopal), publishes his poem "A Visit from St. Nicholas" (or, "'Twas the night before Christmas") in the *Troy* [New York] *Sentinel.*

The New York Mirror, a weekly newspaper focusing on literature and art, begins publication; James Fenimore Cooper, John Greenleaf Whittier, and Washington Irving contribute; until 1842.

Thomas Burgess, Bishop of St. David's, suggests the establishment of The Royal Society of Literature, under the sponsorship of George IV; pensions of one hundred guineas to each of ten Royal Associates, in addition to a payment of one hundred guineas for a prize dissertation; Samuel Taylor Coleridge is among the first ten Associates.

Sir Robert Smirke the younger begins his design of the British Museum, London; to 1847.

1824

BIRTHS

William Wilkie Collins (d. 1889). English novelist.

Alexandre Dumas the younger (d. 1895). French fiction writer and playwright.

DEATHS

George Gordon, Lord Byron (b. 1788). English Romantic poet; dies at Missolonghi, on the Gulf of Patras in Central Greece, from "marsh fever" while fighting with Greek insurgents against the Turks.

Jean Jacques Cambaceres (b. 1753). French statesman and political and legal philosopher.

PUBLICATIONS

George Gordon, Lord Byron, *The Deformed Transformed*—an unfinished drama by the English poet featuring a hideous hunchback who forms a pact with the Devil; the Devil transforms him into Achilles and follows his participation in the sacking of Rome in 1527.

Thomas Carlyle, *Wilhelm Meister's Apprenticeship*—the Scottish writer's translation of the early wanderings and adventures of Goethe's stagestruck youth.

Henri Benjamin Constant de Rebecque, *De la Religion*—an attempt by the French-Swiss political writer to discuss in detail the sources, origins, and development of the major Western world religions; five volumes, to 1831.

Aleksandr Sergeyevich Griboyedov, *Gore ot uma* (Woe from Wit)—a dramatic comedy in rhymed iambics by the Russian writer; satirizes contemporary Moscow society in a powerful vernacular; phrases from the play will find their way into the permanent idiom of the Russian language.

Washington Irving, *Tales of a Traveller*—a collection of thirty-two stories and fragments by the American novelist displaying his curiosity about the supernatural and the Gothic; imitative of Goethe's *Wilhelm Meister* in terms of its reliance upon folktales and legends.

Walter Savage Landor, *Imaginary Conversations*—dialogues between characters from many historical and cultural eras that assume various forms, including drama and satire; the English writer expresses his own views on a multitude of subjects through the conversations, as Dante speaks with Beatrice, Princess Mary with Princess Elizabeth, Aesop with Rhodope, and so on.

Leopold von Ranke, *The History of the Latin and Teutonic Peoples, 1494-1535*—an early project by the German historian demonstrating his commitment to reconstructing periods from the past as they actually existed, rather than presenting them with a view to the present.

Sir Walter Scott, *Redgauntlet*—a novel by the Scottish writer focusing upon an apocryphal return of the Young Pretender, Prince Charles Edward, a number of years after the Rebellion of 1745; the title character attempts to promote the Jacobite movement by kidnapping his young nephew to attain the support of his followers; contains a number of colorful characters, among them the blind fiddler and Wandering Willie.

Robert Southey, *The Book of the Church*—while never openly supportive of the Church of England, the English essayist nonetheless advances the notion that Anglicanism pro-vides the safest bulwark against religious fanaticism, and thus must be defended.

Royall Tyler, *The Chestnut Tree*—a long poem by the American playwright that describes contemporary rural life with an eye cast toward the arrival of industrialization; not published until 1931.

EVENTS

The Athenaeum Club founded in London as an association for literary, artistic, and scientific persons and patrons; Sir Walter Scott and Thomas Moore are among the original founders.

The Cherokee Indian scholar Sequoya (George Guess) perfects a Cherokee language alphabet of eighty-five letters.

Le Globe, Paris, begins publication as a newspaper.

Pierce Egan the elder, London "man about town," publishes his weekly paper, *Pierce Egan's Life in London and Sporting Guide;* until 1859.

Samuel Bowles the elder begins publication of *The Springfield* [Massachusetts] *Republican* as a weekly news periodical; becomes a daily newspaper in 1844.

The posthumous publication of *Bibliotheca Britannica; or, A General Index to British and Foreign Literature,* by Robert Watt; the first significant bibliographic work to be published in Scotland.

Jeremy Bentham and James Mill establish *The Westminster Review* to promote philosophical radicalism.

1825

BIRTHS

Thomas Henry Huxley (d. 1895). English essayist and biologist.

Maurus (Mor) Jokai (d. 1904). Hungarian novelist.

Conrad Ferdinand Meyer (d. 1898). Swiss poet and novelist.

DEATHS

Johann Paul Friedrich Richter (b. 1763). German novelist and humorist; often wrote under the pseudonym "Jean Paul."

Claude Henri Saint-Simon (b. 1760). French political writer and founder of French socialism.

PUBLICATIONS

John Banim, *Tales of the O'Hara Family*—a series of short stories by the Irish novelist, focusing on the characters and lives of the Irish lower classes.

Thomas Carlyle, *Life of Schiller*—the Scottish writer's biography of the German poet and playwright (1759-1805); originally published serially in *The London Magazine,* 1823-1824; the first serious interpretation of the subject by a British writer and intended for a British audience.

Samuel Taylor Coleridge, *Aids to Reflection*—a philosophical treatise by the English poet and critic in the form of aphorisms and comments; an attempt to distinguish between reason and understanding; also focuses upon the distinctions between morality and prudence, reason and conscience.

William Hazlitt, *The Spirit of the Age*—a series of short essays by the English writer; appreciations of his contemporaries synthesizing the intellectual life of the Romantic Age.

Jose Maria Heredia, *Niagara*—a lyric poem reflecting the Cuban poet's romantic melancholy and joy in nature.

Leigh Hunt, *Bacchus in Tuscany*—the English essayist's translation of the Italian dithyrambic poem, *Bacco in Toscana* (1685), by the physician and poet Francesco Redi (1626-1697).

Adam Mickiewicz, *Crimean Sonnets*—a series of poems by the Polish writer, composed during the period of his exile in Russia (1824-1829).

John Stuart Mill, *Treatise upon Evidence*—the English economic philosopher's edition of the tract written by the English political and legal philosopher Jeremy Bentham (1748-1832); prepared while Mill was only twenty years old.

Aleksandr Sergeyevich Pushkin, *Boris Godunov*—a Russian dramatic tragedy, written in Shakespearean iambic pentameter; the story of Tsar Boris, a strong and complex man, who gains the throne by the assassination of Prince Dmitry; set between 1598 and 1604, the play gains strength from its portrayal of actual characters from history; banned by government censors and not produced on the stage until 1870.

Claude Henri Saint-Simon, *Nouveau Christianisme*—a prose tract by the French socialist advocating an industrial order controlled by industrial chiefs; the spiritual direction of the nation should pass from the Church to the men of science.

Sir Walter Scott, *The Talisman*—a novel by the Scottish writer set during the Crusades; amid dissent and jealousies among the English leaders encamped in the Holy Land, Richard Coeur de Lion becomes ill; he is ultimately cured through the efforts of Saladin; romantic involvement and political and personal intrigue abound.

Robert Southey, *A Tale of Paraguay*—an unnecessarily long poem by the English writer demonstrating the contrast between the pleasures of domestic seclusion and the dangers of the outside world.

Esias Tegner, *Frithjofs Saga*—a Swedish epic ballad collection, translated into every European language; Ingeborg, daughter of Bele, King of Sygua-fylke in Norway, loses her mother, and finds refuge and a permanent home with Hilding, who also rears Frithjof; Frithjof and Ingeborg become lovers, but the girl's brothers refuse to recognize the relationship, since they fear the superior valor and fame of Frithjof.

Jacques Nicolas Augustin Thierry, *Conquete de l'Angleterre par les Normands* (The Norman Conquest of England)—the classic work by the French historian; overdramatized, but its historical documentation is complete.

Mihaly Vorosmarty, *Erlan*—a Hungarian national epic poem; combines folklore with nineteenth-century Romanticism.

EVENTS

The Biblical Repitory, a Presbyterian review and literary journal, begins publication at Princeton, New Jersey; until 1878.

Rev. John Smith deciphers the shorthand diary of Samuel Pepys (1633–1703) and Richard, Lord Braybrook, edits *The Diary and Corre-*

spondence of Samuel Pepys, F.R.S.; four volumes; Smith's transcripts covered fifty-four volumes of translations, but the cleric often misread words and phrases and displayed an ignorance of Spanish expressions; then, Braybrook deleted additional text.

The New Harmony Society, the Indiana socialist community, begins publication of *The New Harmony Gazette,* a weekly journal that reported the activities of the colony, founded originally by Robert Owen (1771–1858); until 1835.

The Register of Debates, the second series of reports on proceedings of the United States Senate and House of Representatives, begins publication at Washington, D.C.; until 1837.

1826

BIRTHS

Walter Bagehot (d. 1877). English essayist and scholar.

Carlo Collodi (pseudonym of Carlo Lorenzini; d. 1890). Italian journalist and writer of stories for children.

Mikhail Evgrafovich Saltykov (pseudonym of N. Schedrin; d. 1889). Russian novelist and satirist.

Josef Viktor von Scheffel (d. 1886). German poet and novelist.

DEATHS

Johann Peter Hebel (b. 1760). German poet.

Nikolai Mikhailovich Karamzin (b. 1766). Russian historian and novelist.

Philippe Pinel (b. 1745). French physician and psychologist.

Royall Tyler (b. 1757). American playwright, essayist, and poet.

Johann Heinrich Voss (b. 1751). German poet and translator.

PUBLICATIONS

Andres Bello, *Silva a la Agricultura de la Zona Torrida*—an important descriptive prose tract by the Brazilian writer and statesman.

Elizabeth Barrett Browning, *Essays on Mind; with Other Poems*—an early collection by the English poet, printed at her father's own expense; the title piece is a juvenile imitation of Alexander Pope's *Essay on Man* (1732-1734).

James Fenimore Cooper, *The Last of the Mohicans*—an early masterpiece by the American novelist; a tale of suspense and almost endless pursuit; the strength of the piece lies in the novelist's descriptions and explications of the American Indian's habits and folkways, vices and virtues, loves and hates.

William Hazlitt, *Notes on a Journey Through France and Italy*—describes the English essayist's impressions while on a tour of the continent collecting material for his *Life of Napoleon* (1828-1830); some discussion of arts and letters.

Heinrich Heine, *Reisebilder* I (Pictures of Travel)—a collection of travel sketches in verse by the German poet, published through 1831; reveals his early tendency toward Romanticism.

Oliver Wendell Holmes, *Songs in Many Keys*—a collection of occasional poems by the Boston physican; reissued in 1861.

Alessandro Manzoni, *I Promessi sposi* (The Betrothed)—a romantic historical novel set in seventeenth-century Milan; the most notable piece of fiction in all of Italian literature, one that influenced the development of Italian prose; 118 editions by 1875.

Sir Walter Scott, *Woodstock; or, The Cavalier: A Tale of the Year 1651*—a novel by the Scottish writer principally concerned with the escape of Charles II after the battle of Worcester; the numerous and wide ranging incidents in the novel underscore the antagonism between Puritans and Royalists.

Mary Wollstonecraft Shelley, *The Last Man*—an English novel narrating the gradual destruction of the human race by an epidemic; all but one man perishes.

Robert Southey, *Vindiciae Ecclesiae Anglicanae*—a series of letters by the English writer to Charles Butler, Esq.; comprise essays on Roman Catholicism defending his own *The Book of the Church* (1824).

Alfred Victor de Vigny, *Cinq-mars*—a French historical novel set during the reign of Louis XIII (1610-1643).

EVENTS

John Burke, an Irish genealogist, publishes the first edition of his directory of British baronets and peers, *A Genealogical and Heraldic History of the Peerage and Baronetage of the United Kingdom;* issued annually beginning in 1847.

Hachette et compagnie, French publishing house, founded at Paris by Louis Christophe Francois Hachette; intends to issue books that will elevate the general intelligence.

Nguan Nguan edits the writings of Confucius.

Aloys Senefelder, Bavarian inventor and printer, develops a process for lithography in color.

1827

BIRTHS

Charles de Coster (d. 1879). Belgian poet and storyteller.

Johanna Spyri (d. 1901). Swiss writer of popular tales for children.

Lewis (Lew) Wallace (d. 1905). American writer, soldier, and diplomat.

DEATHS

William Blake (b. 1757). English poet, painter, engraver, and mystic.

Jose Joaquin Fernandez de Lizardi (b. 1776). Mexican prose writer, dramatist, and poet.

Ugo Foscolo (b. 1778). Italian prose writer, novelist, and poet.

Wilhelm Hauff (b. 1802). German novelist and writer of short stories and fairy tales.

Johann Heinrich Pestalozzi (b. 1746). Swiss educationalist.

PUBLICATIONS

Edward G. E. Bulwer-Lytton, *Falkland*—an early novel by the English writer, criticized because of apparent attacks upon contemporary social and moral obligations.

Thomas Carlyle, *Wilhelm Meister's Travels*—a translation by the Scottish essayist of the second part of Johann Wolfgang von Goethe's (1749-1832) novel.

James Fenimore Cooper, *The Prairie*—a novel, one of the most important literary works in creating, for the "Eastern" American mind, a picture of the American West; documented accounts of Indians and white settlers are, however, colored by the writer's romantic imagination.

——————— , *The Red Rover*—another novel, a magnificent drama of sailing ships in combat on the high seas; once more, the writer relies upon secondary sources and his own imagination; the title refers to a pirate who is pursued by a naval officer in disguise.

Thomas De Quincey, *On Murder as One of the Fine Arts*—the first in a series of three essays (the second and third parts oppeared in 1839 and 1854, respectively); grotesque and sinister comedy prevail and the writer is at once humorist and logical essayist.

Heinrich Heine, *Buch der Lieder*—a collection of popular verse by the German poet; contains pieces that will serve as lyrics for numerous song composers.

Victor Hugo, *Cromwell*—a French drama, deemed unstageable; the preface, however, becomes the credo of French Romanticism, arguing for a free and outspoken style of dramatic poetry that would embrace both tragedy and comedy after the manner of Shakespeare.

Charles Lamb, *On an Infant Dying as Soon as Born*—an elegy by the English writer, considered his finest poem.

Thomas Moore, *The Epicurean*—a novel by the Irish writer concerning the Greek philosopher Alciphron; the title character goes, in 257 A.D., to Egypt in search of the secret of eternal life; he finds, instead, Christianity.

Edgar Allan Poe, *Tamerlane and Other Poems*—a collection by the American poet, the title piece reciting the folly of risking love for ambition; that piece and the remaining ten are reminiscent of Lord Byron.

Sir Walter Scott, *The Highland Widow*—a short novel by the Scottish writer; the son of a warrior fallen in the 1745 rebellion refuses to follow his father's militant past; the widowed mother contrives to have the young man murder a sergeant, for which he is executed; the widow lives her remaining years in remorse, the melancholy survivor of a departed age.

———————, *The Life of Napoleon Buonaparte*—a biography by the Scottish novelist and poet, fairly objective in tone and realistic in content.

———————, *The Surgeon's Daughter*—a novel by the Scottish writer concerning a surgeon who adopts an illegitimate child and raises him in his home; the boy falls in love with the surgeon's daughter; however, the boy, when reaching age, runs off to India, where he encounters an unspeakable adventuress and meets death beneath the foot of an elephant.

———————, *The Tales of a Grandfather*—a history of Scotland, from the beginnings to the close of the Rebellion of 1745-1746; to 1829.

———————, *The Two Drovers*—a short story by the Scottish novelist intended to depict the true Highland character; a Highland drover and his Yorkshire counterpart quarrel and then fight, each with his own particular weapon (Yorkshire fists vs. Highland dirk).

Eugene Scribe, *Le Marriage d'argent* (Marriage for Money)—a French comic drama demonstrating that misery attends mercenary marriages.

EVENTS

The Evening Standard, London, begins publication as a newspaper; until 1905.

The Freeman's Journal, New York City, becomes the first black newspaper in the United States.

Samuel Griswold Goodrich begins publication at Boston of *The Token,* a series of "gift books" principally containing poetry and fiction; to 1842.

Timothy Flint begins publication of *The Western Monthly Review,* a literary journal intended to interpret and promote the culture of the American West; to 1830.

1828

BIRTHS

Edmond Francois Valentin About (d. 1885). French writer.

Henrik Ibsen (d. 1906). Norwegian playwright and poet; pioneer of the social drama.

George Meredith (d. 1909). English novelist.

Dante Gabriel Rossetti (d. 1882). English poet and painter.

Leo Nikolayevich Tolstoy (d. 1910). Russian writer, philosopher, moralist, and mystic.

Jules Verne (d. 1905). French novelist.

PUBLICATIONS

Edward G. E. Bulwer-Lytton, *Pelham; or The Adventures of a Gentleman*—an English novel; follows the ambitions of a young dandy, who uncovers the solution to a murder.

Giovanni Jacopo Casanova, *Memoires Ecrits par Lui-Meme*—the clever, cynical, and highly pornographic recollections of the eighteenth-century Italian adventurer; 12 volumes to 1838, edited by the French poet Jules Laforgue, at Leipzig; complete, original text not published until 1960-1961.

James Fenimore Cooper, *Notions of the Americans*—a prose tract by the American novelist in response to English attacks on American social and political customs; an honest but militant reply that pleased neither the English nor the Americans.

Nathaniel Hawthorne, *Fanshawe*—the first novel by the American writer, published anonymously; Gothic and imitative of Sir Walter Scott; underdeveloped characters and overly pretentious dialogue; love, kidnapping, rescue, and marriage comprise the vehicles for the plot.

Washington Irving, *The History of the Life and Voyages of Christopher Columbus*—the American novelist's biography of the great explorer, eighteen books and 123 chapters; more imaginative then factual.

Adam Mickiewicz, *Konrad Wallenrod*—a narrative poem by the Polish writer, composed during his exile in Russia (1824-1829).

Sir Walter Scott, *St. Valentine's Day; or, The Fair Maid of Perth*—a novel by the Scottish writer set at the close of the fourteenth century; a profligate noble attempts to carry off the daughter of an honest townsman; political intrigue and carnage give way to peace, pacifism, and love.

EVENTS

James Silk Buckingham begins publication of *The Athenaeum*, a London literary and artistic journal; until 1921.

The Cherokee Phoenix, the first newspaper for an American Indian tribe, begins publication; until 1835.

Leigh Hunt edits and publishes *The Companion*, a London literary journal; twenty-nine issues.

The Maitland Club, Glasgow, founded for the publication of works focusing upon the literature and antiquities of Scotland.

The Old Corner Bookstore, Washington and School Streets, Boston, established; serves as both a bookshop and a gathering place for men of letters.

The Roxburghe Club, the first of the London book clubs, issues its initial publication, a printing of the early fourteenth-century metrical romance, *The Lay of Havelock the Dane.*

Robert Stephen Rintoul begins publication of *The Spectator,* a London weekly journal devoted to "educated radicalism."

The Southern Review, a quarterly literary journal, begins publication at Charleston, South Carolina; until 1832.

Noah Webster publishes his *An American Dictionary of the English Language*, begun as early as 1800; 2 volumes, 38,000 words; revised in 1840.

1829

BIRTHS

William Michael Rossetti (d. 1919). English writer and translator.

DEATHS

Aleksandr Sergeyevich Griboyedov (b. 1795). Russian playwright.

Karl Wilhelm Friedrich von Schlegel (b. 1772). German Romantic critical philosopher.

PUBLICATIONS

Honore de Balzac, *Les Chouans*—the French writer's first successful novel, as well as his first conscious attempt to develop the novel as a form.

Edward G. E. Bulwer-Lytton, *Deveroux*—an extraordinary number of characters from history stroll through this English novel: Swift, Pope, Addison, Steele, Colley Cibber, Godfrey Kneller, Richard Cromwell, Mary Wortley Montagu, and the Duchess of Marlborough.

——————— , *The Disowned*—an English novel that suffers from disorganization and dull dialogue; a young man's father disowns him because he believes he is not his real son; the two reconcile, but not until they circumvent considerable villainy.

Christian Dietrich Grabbe, *Kaiser Friedrich Barbarossa*—a realistic German dramatic tragedy; emphasizes Frederick I's (1123?-1190) cruelty, love of danger, and ambition.

Thomas Hood, *The Dream of Eugene Aram*—an English poem based upon the story of Eugene Aram, a brilliant and gentle schoolmaster of Knaresborough (Yorkshire), who, in 1759, underwent trial and then execution for the murder of a Yorkshire man named Clarke.

Victor Hugo, *Le Dernier jour d'un condamne*—an early, yet successful, attempt at fiction by the French writer.

——————— , *Marion de Lorme*—the second verse drama by the French writer; not performed until 1831 because of Charles X's restrictions on freedom of speech; the playwright had used Louis XIII (1601-1643) as one of his characters.

Thomas Love Peacock, *The Misfortunes of Elphin*—an English satirical novel; a parody of the Arthurian legends: the title character spends much of his time in captivity because of a dispute with his captor over whose wife possessed the greatest virtue.

Edgar Allan Poe, *Al Aaraaf*—an American allegorical poem, with a prologue dedicated to science; describes a haven of ideal loveliness, the entrance to which appears to have been denied to the hero because of his passion for an earthly creature.

Charles Augustin Sainte-Beuve, *Vie et poesies de Joseph Delorme*—a French poem that reflects the poet's own morbidity; an example of the writer's biographical approach to literature.

―――――――, *Poesies et pensees*—a critical piece by the French writer that helped to promote the Romantic movement in France by tracing its relationship to the poetry of the sixteenth century.

Sir Walter Scott, *Anne of Geierstein; or, The Maiden of the Mist*—a Scottish novel set during the reign of Edward IV (1461-1483); English knights, returning from the war, pass through Switzerland; capture, political intrigue, and delicate negotiations follow; contains vivid scenes (taken from Goethe) of the secret tribunal of the Vehmgericht that existed in Westphalia for the maintenance of public peace and order.

―――――――, *History of Scotland*—a three-volume work by the Scottish writer originally written for his children; to 1830; emphasizes the character of the Scottish people.

Robert Southey, *All for Love; or, A Sinner Well Saved*—an English poem taken from an incident in the life of St. Basil (329?–379?); involves a pact with the Devil and a grand debate between Satan and St. Basil.

―――――――, *Sir Thomas More: Colloquies on the Progress and Prospects of Society*—the English essayist and poet converses with the ghost of More (1478–1535).

Alfred, Lord Tennyson, *Timbuctoo*—an early piece by the English poet, written during his stay at Trinity College, Cambridge; earned the twenty-year-old student the Chancellor's medal for English verse; the spirit of poetry and myth foresees her surrender to the ultimate advance of science.

EVENTS

Karl Baedeker, a German publisher, issues his first travel book, a guide to the city of Coblenz.

William B. Burt, of Detroit, receives the first United States patent on a typewriter; he calls his machine a "typographer."

The Encyclopedia Americana published by the German-American scholar Francis Lieber; 13 volumes by 1831.

The New Harmony Gazette, an organ of the socialist community in Indiana, gives way to *The Free Enquirer*, a periodical devoted to the advancement of socialism and agnosticism; to 1835.

Thomas Hood, the London poet and essayist, publishes *The Gem*, a literary annual; to 1832.

The French Romantic poet, Alphonse de Lamartine elected to the Academie Francaise.

1830

BIRTHS

Emily Dickinson (d. 1886). American poet.

Jules Alfred Huot de Goncourt (d. 1870). French novelist and diarist.

Judah Leon Gordon (d. 1892). Russian-Jewish novelist and poet.

Paul Heyse (d. 1914). German dramatist and novelist; recipient of the Nobel Prize in literature in 1910.

Frederic Mistral (d. 1914). French Provencal poet; awarded the Nobel Prize in 1904.

Christina Rossetti (d. 1894). English poet.

DEATHS

Henri Benjamin Constant de Rebecque (b. 1767). French writer and politician.

Stephanie Felicite de Saint-Aubin, Comtesse de Genlis (b. 1764). French writer.

William Hazlitt (b. 1778). English essayist.

PUBLICATIONS

Edward G. E. Bulwer-Lytton, *Paul Clifford*—an English novel focusing upon the escapades of a philanthropic highwayman; an argument in favor of improving English jails and penal laws; in spite of it all, the hero ends his career in America.

Auguste Comte, *Cours de philosophie positive* (A Course of Positive Philosophy)—six volumes, to 1842; a prose tract by the French philosopher and sociologist that attempts to organize man's knowledge of the world, humanity, and society into a consistent whole.

James Fenimore Cooper, *The Water-Witch*—an American novel that primarily takes place in New York in the seventeenth century, although it contains ample pirate chases on the open seas.

William Hazlitt, *Conversations of James Northcote*—an informal prose piece on art and drama focusing on the English painter James Northcote (1746–1831).

Oliver Wendell Holmes, *Old Ironsides*—the poem that gained national recognition for the twenty-one-year-old Harvard medical school student by helping to save the U.S. frigate *Constitution* from destruction.

Victor Hugo, *Hernani*—the French writer's most famous play, the first to demonstrate his Romantic dramatic· theories, which had been formulated in his earlier preface to the unstageable verse drama *Cromwell;* the production of the play caused a great controversy because of its denial of the rules of classical tragedy.

Alphonse de Lamartine, *Harmonies poetiques et religieuses*—a series of verses by the French poet and statesman.

Charles Lamb, *Album Verses*—a collection of pleasant lyrics and sonnets by the English writer.

Sir Walter Scott, *Auchindrane; or, The Ayrshire Tragedy*—a drama by the Scottish writer based upon the case of Mure of Auchindrane, as set forth in *Ancient Criminal Trials,* by the Scottish writer and antiquary Robert Pitcairn (1793-1855).

Henrik Wergeland, *Creation, Man, and Messiah*—a Norwegian verse drama focusing on religious motifs.

EVENTS

Honore de Balzac, the French writer, announces that he will group forty novels under the heading "La Comedie humaine" to create a complete picture of modern civilization.

The Boston Daily Evening Transcript, a newspaper dedicated to transmitting conservative New England cultural values, begins publication; to 1941.

William Maginn and Hugh Fraser found *Fraser's Magazine,* a London literary journal; to 1882.

Louis Antoine Godey begins publication in Philadelphia of *Godey's Lady's Book,* a monthly collection of literary pieces on fashion and manners; until 1898.

The Illinois Monthly Magazine, founded by James Hall, begins publication as the first literary periodical west of Ohio; until 1832.

1831

BIRTHS

Nikolai Semenovich Leskov (d. 1895). Russian short story writer.

Wilhelm Raabe (d. 1910). German novelist.

Victorien Sardou (d. 1908). French dramatist.

DEATHS

Ludwig Joachim von Arnim (b. 1781). German writer of popular tales, poems, and novels.

Willem Bilderdijk (b. 1756). Dutch poet and philologist.

Georg Wilhelm Friedrich Hegel (b. 1770). German philosopher.

Friedrich Maximilian von Klinger (b. 1752). German playwright and writer of fiction.

PUBLICATIONS

Honore de Balzac, *La Peau de Chagrin*—a French novel, one of the earliest in the "Comedie Humaine" series.

James Fenimore Cooper, *The Bravo*—an American novel concerned with tyranny in Venice during the Renaissance.

———————— , *A Letter to General Lafayette*—an American prose piece that demonstrates the advantages of - republican government over the institution of monarchy.

Christian Friedrich Grabbe, *Napoleon oder die hundert Tage* (Napoleon, or the Hundred Days)—a German historical drama in which the title hero becomes the victim of the uncontrollable forces of history.

Victor Hugo, *Les Feuilles d'automne* (Autumn Leaves)—a collection of poems by the French writer.

———————— , *Notre-Dame de Paris*—a famous French novel that accurately portrays the sufferings of humanity.

Giacomo Leopardi, *I Canti*—a collection of lyrics by the Italian poet, according to some the most beautiful in all Italian literature; written beginning in 1816; lofty and pessimistic, the poems display the writer's contempt for contemporary Italian rulers.

Thomas Love Peacock, *Crotchet Castle*—another satirical "conversational" novel by the English writer; contains a host of amusing characters who embody literary and intellectual trends of the day.

Edgar Allan Poe, *Poems*—a collection by the American poet dedicated to the Corps of Cadets at the United States Military Academy, an institution from which he had recently been dismissed; includes "To Helen," "The Sleeper," and "The City in the Sea"; marks the artistic maturity of the poet.

Sir Walter Scott, *Castle Dangerous*—a novel by the Scottish writer set in the early fourteenth century; the King of England opposes the forces of Sir Robert Bruce.

──────── , *Count Robert of Paris*—a novel by the Scottish writer, the last in the "Waverley" series; set in Constantinople in the early twelfth century during the Crusades.

Stendhal, *Le Rouge et le Noir* (The Red and the Black)—a French novel featuring acute character analyses; records the spiritual history of the writer's youth; the novel is now admired as an early example of psychological realism.

Edward John Trelawny, *The Adventures of a Younger Son*—a partly autobiographic English novel concerning a young, Byronic character whose harsh father has forced him to sea and then into a life of exciting and dangerous encounters.

John Greenleaf Whittier, *Legends of New England in Prose and Verse*—a collection of prose and verse by the American writer; his first published volume evidencing his acute interest in local historical themes; published while the author retained his newspaper position in Hartford, Connecticut.

──────── , *Moll Pitcher*—a poetical narrative by the New England poet on a legendary New England historical and figure.

EVENTS

The Boar's Head Inn, in the Eastcheap section of London, mentioned in Shakespeare's plays as a meeting place for Sir John Falstaff and his merry companions, undergoes demolition to make way for the approaches to London Bridge.

The Garrick Club, principally for actors, intellectuals, and literary persons, founded in King Street, London.

William Lloyd Garrison begins publication at Boston of *The Liberator,* an abolitionist weekly journal; to 1865.

Merriam, Little, and Company founded in Springfield, Massachusetts, by George and Charles Merriam.

William Trotter Porter founds the *Spirit of the Times,* a New York City periodical devoted to sport, theater, and literature; to 1861.

The United States Copyright Law amended: 28 years, renewable for 14 years.

1832

BIRTHS

Louisa May Alcott (d. 1888). American writer of children's literature.

Bjornstjerne Bjornson (d. 1910). Norwegian novelist and playwright; awarded the Nobel Prize in 1908.

Wilhelm Busch (d. 1908). German writer and comic artist.

Lewis Carroll (pseudonym of Charles Lutwidge Dodgson; (d. 1898). English fantasist, parodist, and mathematician.

Jose Echegaray y Eizaguirre (d. 1916). Spanish dramatist; awarded the Nobel Prize in 1904.

Juan Montalvo (d. 1889). Ecuadorean essayist and political writer.

Sir Leslie Stephen (d. 1904). English critic, biographer, philosopher, and literary and cultural historian.

DEATHS

Jeremy Bentham (b. 1748). English writer on jurisprudence and utilitarian ethics.

George Crabbe (b. 1784). English poet.

Philibert Louis Debucourt (b. 1755). French poet.

Philip Freneau (b. 1752). American poet and sailor.

Johann Wolfgang von Goethe (b. 1749). German poet, dramatist, scientist, and court official.

Sir Walter Scott (b. 1771). Scottish novelist, poet, and editor.

PUBLICATIONS

Edward G. E. Bulwer-Lytton, *Eugene Aram*—an English novel based upon a Knaresborough (Yorkshire) schoolmaster who received a sentence of execution in 1759 for the murder of a York man; in the novelist's version, a romantic character has an accomplice carry out the dastardly deed, then prepares to settle down in the country; the accomplice then exposes the fellow, who goes off to the gallows, while his intended bride succumbs to shock.

James Fenimore Cooper, *The Heidenmauer; or, The Benedictines*—an American novel set in sixteenth-century Bavaria; Benedictine monks struggle with a feudal lord for political power; contains the writer's ideas concerning the rigidity of the Roman Church, as opposed to the more liberal controls of Protestantism.

Casimir Delavigne, *Louis XI*—a French drama based partly upon Sir Walter Scott's novel *Quentin Durward* (1823), in which the French king functions as the main character.

Thomas De Quincey, *Klosterheim*—a prose romance of mediocre merit by the English novelist and essayist.

Esteban Echeverria, *Elvira*—an Argentine poem that introduces Romanticism into that nation.

Johann Wolfgang von Goethe, *Faust, Part II*—a continuation of the 1808 German dramatic masterpiece; the title character enters the great world of history, politics, and culture, but fails to discover his wonderful moment; the play develops the writer's ideas on mythology, culture, art, politics, war, courtly life, economics, natural science, and religion.

Washington Irving, *The Alhambra*—referred to as the American writer's Spanish sketchbook.

Nikolaus Lenau, *Gedichte*—a collection of the German poet's melancholy verse.

Mikhail Lermontov, *The Angel*—a Romantic piece by the Russian poet, strongly Byronic in tone.

Eduard Morike, *Maler Nolten*—a rare novel by the German poet.

John Richardson, *Wacousta*—a romantic novel concerned with life on the Canadian frontier.

George Sand, *Indiana*—a French novel set against the Romantic extravagances of the period; records the writer's feminist sentiments.

EVENTS

Chambers's Journal founded in Edinburgh by Robert Chambers.

Merriam, Little, and Company, Springfield, Massachusetts, becomes G. and C. Merriam Company, Publishers.

The Boston Baptist minister Samuel Francis Smith publishes his patriotic song, "America."

1833

BIRTHS

Pedro Antonio de Alarcon (d. 1891). Spanish writer and radical journalist.

Alfred Nobel (d. 1896). Swedish chemist, engineer, and donor of the funds for the Nobel Prize.

PUBLICATIONS

Honore de Balzac, *Eugenie Grandet*—a French novel focusing upon a sentimental country lass who, through acts of simple sincerity, stands as heroic as Joan of Arc.

Elizabeth Barrett Browning, *Miscellaneous Poems*—a collection by the English poet including her important translation of the *Prometheus* of Aeschylus (525 B.C.-426 B.C.)

Robert Browning, *Pauline*—an anonymously published poem, the first of the English poet's to appear; supposedly an expression of his admiration for Percy Bysshe Shelley (1792-1822).

Edward G. E. Bulwer-Lytton, *Godolphin*—an English historical novel focusing upon the political and social climate of the early eighteenth century, particularly the reign of Queen Anne (1702-1714).

James Fenimore Cooper, *The Headman; or, The Abbaye des Vignerons*—an American novel set in eighteenth-century Bern, Switzerland; concerns mistaken identity and love; one half of the romantic duo turns out to be royalty, which allows the match to be completed.

Joseph von Eichendorff, *Die Freier* (The Wooers)—a romantic comedy not performed until 1849.

Henry Wadsworth Longfellow, *Outre-Mer: A Pilgrimage Beyond the Sea*—the American writer's first prose piece; a narrative imitative of Washington Irving (1783-1859).

Alfred de Musset, *Andre del Sarto*—a French prose drama concerning the Italian Renaissance painter; not produced until 1848.

———————— , *Les Caprices de Marianne* (The Follies of Marianne)—another of the French poet-dramatist's plays concerning the inspirational and redemptive power of love; not performed until 1851.

Johann Nestroy, *Der bose Geist Lumpacivagabundus* (The Evil Spirit Lumpazivagabundus)—an Austrian dramatic farce; a socially oriented satire in which spirits and fairies present a realistic picture of Viennese life.

John Henry Newman, *Lead, Kindly Light*—an English poem that has become one of the important pieces of congregational hymnody within the English-speaking world; composed during the time of the writer's religious conversion: "Lead, Kindly Light, amid the encircling gloom, / Lead Thou me on . . . "

Aleksandr Sergeyevich Pushkin, *Eugenii Onegin*—the Russian poet's novel in verse, highly Romantic and even more Byronic; a man rejects the love of a country girl, but later finds her transformed, by marriage, into a princess; in spite of her earlier longing for the fellow, the princess can now refuse his advances and leave him in despair; further transformation will occur in 1892 when Piotr Ilych Tchaikovsky (1840-1893) adapts the piece into an opera with the same title.

George Sand, *Lelia*—a French novel expressing the writer's feminist beliefs about love and marriage; not without a strong dose of moral idealism.

Eugene Scribe, *Bertrand et Raton ou l'art de conspirer* (Bertrand and Raton; or, The Art of Conspiracy)—a French play that satirizes the revolution of 1830 by attacking the stupidity of political conspiracy; comically portrays the vanity and greed of the middle class.

William Gilmore Simms, *Martin Faber*—the American novelist's first prose tale; concerns a brilliant but evil young man whose wicked deeds include desertion and murder; he finally ends up on the gallows; revised in 1837 as *Martin Faber, The Story of a Criminal.*

Robert Southey, *Lives of the British Admirals*—biographical sketches continued to 1840 and constituting a five-volume history of the British Navy.

Alfred, Lord Tennyson, *The Lotos-Eaters*—an English poem in Spenserian stanzas on the subject of the Lotophagi from Homer's *Odyssey.*

———————— , *Oenone*—an English poem that focuses upon the nymph of Mount Ida, who falls in love with Paris, the youthful shepherd.

EVENTS

Franz Bopp publishes his *Vergleichende Grammatik* (A Comparative Grammar of Sanskrit, Zend, Greek, Latin, Lithuanian, Old Slavonic, Gothic, and German), 6 volumes, to 1852; the German philologist had already (1816) demonstrated the common origins of the Indo-European languages.

Edmund Ruffin, a Virginia agriculturalist, edits and publishes the *Farmer's Register.*

The Knickerbocker Magazine, a monthly literary journal, begins publications in New York City; until 1865.

Benjamin H. Day founds the *New York Sun*, a daily newspaper that sells for one cent; to 1966.

August Wilhelm von Schlegel, Dorothea and Johann Ludwig Tieck, and Wolf von Baudissin complete the great German translation of Shakespeare's works begun in 1794.

Tracts for the Times, a series of essays on religious subjects, is begun by the English writers John Henry Newman, John Keble, Richard Hurrell Froude, and Edward Bouverie Pusey; until 1841.

1834

BIRTHS

Julius Sophus Felix Dahn (d. 1912). German novelist and historian.

Jan Neruda (d. 1891). Czech poet and dramatist.

James Thomson (d. 1882). Scottish poet and essayist.

DEATHS

Samuel Taylor Coleridge (b. 1772). English poet and literary critic.

Charles Lamb (b. 1775). English essayist.

Friedrich Ernst Daniel Schleiermacher (b. 1768). German theologian and philosopher.

PUBLICATIONS

Honore de Balzac, *Le Pere Goriot* (Old Goriot)—one of the French writer's novels belonging to his "Comedie Humaine" series; related to the Juvenalian theme that gems and gold can too easily conceal the true horrors of the world.

Georg Buchner, *Der hessiche Landbote* (The Hessian Messenger)—a controversial prose tract by the twenty-year-old German playwright advocating that the peasants of Hesse forcefully rebel to gain their rights.

Edward G. E. Bulwer-Lytton, *The Last Days of Pompeii*—an English novel focusing upon love in the Italian city immediately prior to its destruction; a blind girl saves the lovers when the volcano erupts; noted for its accurate historical detail of both the times and the catastrophe.

James Fenimore Cooper, *A Letter to his Countrymen*—a harsh essay by the American novelist intended to counter attacks upon his novel *The Bravo* (1831); he announces his premature retirement from writing long fiction.

Thomas De Quincey, *Autobiographic Sketches*—English essayist's recollections; continued until 1853.

Victor Hugo, *Claude Gueux*—a French fictional piece best described as pure humanitarian sentimentalism.

——————, *Literature et philosophie melees*—a French collection of prose juvenilia.

Walter Savage Landor, *The Citation and Examination of William Shakespeare Touching Deer-Stealing*—one of several of the English writer's imaginary dialogues or conversations between noted persons on a range of subjects; the substance never rises to the level of the form.

Adam Mickiewicz, *Pan Tadeusz* (Thaddeus)—a Polish epic poem, a brilliant delineation of Lithuanian scenery, manners, and beliefs; also focuses upon the Polish gentry of the period.

Alfred de Musset, *Lorenzaccio*—a historical prose tragedy by the French dramatist set in Renaissance Italy; reveals the futility and sinister consequences of Lorenzo de' Medici's assassination of the evil duke of Florence; also concerned with the corruption and decadence of an enslaved Florence; not performed until 1896.

Aleksandr Pushkin, *Pikovaya dama* (The Queen of Spades)—a Russian short story; adapted as an opera (three acts, seven scenes) of the same title by Peter Ilich Tchaikovsky (1840-1893); the spirit of a dead countess tells a young gambler about three successful cards; he wins on the first two, but loses everything when the final card changes to the queen of spades.

Leopold von Ranke, *Die Romischen Papste* (The Roman Popes)—a German history of the papacy during the sixteenth and seventeenth centuries; until 1837.

William Gilmore Simms, *Guy Rivers*—an American novel, an action tale focusing upon gold mining in the wilds of northern Georgia; the first of the writer's "Border Romances."

EVENTS

The Abbotsford Club founded in England and Scotland for the purpose of publishing work related to the history or literature of any country connected with the writing of Sir Walter Scott.

Robin Carver publishes in Boston his *Book of Sports*, the first American work to consider "baseball" as a subject.

The Congressional Globe, reporting the proceedings of the U.S. Senate and the U.S.

House of Representatives, begins publication in Washington, D.C.; to 1873.

The Ladies' Companion, a monthly literary journal, begins publication in New York City; until 1844.

Leigh Hunt's London Journal begins publication under the editorship of the English essayist and poet; to 1835.

The New Yorker Staats-Zeitung begins publication in New York City as a German-language weekly newspaper.

The Southern Literary Messenger, a literary magazine, begins publication in Richmond, Virginia; until 1864.

1835

BIRTHS

Samuel Butler (d. 1902). English writer and painter.

Giosue Carducci (d. 1907). Italian poet and Nobel Prize winner (1906).

Emile Gaboriau (d. 1873). French writer of detective fiction.

Leopold von Sacher-Masoch (d. 1895). Austrian lawyer and writer of fiction.

Mark Twain (pseudonym of Samuel Langhorne Clemens; d. 1910). American writer.

DEATHS

August von Platen (b. 1796). German poet.

PUBLICATIONS

Hans Christian Andersen, *Eventyr* (Fairy Tales)—a collection by the Danish writer that includes "The Tinderbox," "The Princess on the Pea," "Little Claus and Big Claus," and "Little Ida's Flowers."

—————, *The Improvisatore*—a series of scenes by the Danish writer inspired by his visits to Rome and Naples.

Robert Browning, *Paracelsus*—an English dramatic poem based upon the sixteenth-century magician and alchemist, Philippus Aureolus Theophrastus Bombastus ab Hohenheim

(1493-1541); Paracelsus sets out to find the secrets of the world; he errs by attempting to pursue knowledge while excluding love.

Georg Buchner, *Dantons Tod* (Danton's Death)—a four-act German tragedy reflecting the playwright's dim view of social progress; Danton and Robespierre both realize that the ideals of the French Revolution can never be achieved; hope for freedom does not exist, a point that underscores the writer's overall sense of fatalism.

Edward G. E. Bulwer-Lytton, *Rienzi; or, The Last of the Tribunes*—a historical novel by the English writer focusing upon a fourteenth-century politician who is brought to an unhappy end by his own arrogance and love of display.

James Fenimore Cooper, *The Monikens*—an American novel and allegorical satire in which four monkeys, a sea captain, and a knight visit various parts of the Western world and observe (and attack) various political systems; almost an Americanized *Gulliver's Travels*.

Theophile Gautier, *Mademoiselle de Maupin*—a French novel advocating the idea of art for art's sake and denouncing bourgeois materialistic desires.

Nickolai Gogol, *Mirgorod*—a collection of Russian stories featuring "Taras Bulba," a novella concerning life among the Cossacks of the seventeenth century.

Christian Dietrich Grabbe, *Hannibal*—A German dramatic tragedy based upon the hero of Carthage; the title character, a highly gifted and extraordinary individual, must confront and ultimately rely upon the masses; their strength destroys him.

Leigh Hunt, *Captain Sword and Captain Pen*—an English poem depicting the horrors of war and predicting the ultimate end to such outrageous activities.

Washington Irving, *A Tour on the Prairies*—an American narrative; an extremely detailed, factual record of the writer's expedition across the territories now known as Oklahoma.

Karl Hynek Macha, *Gypsies*—the only novel by the Czech poet; to 1836.

Alfred de Musset, *Le Chandelier* (The Candlestick)—a comic drama by the French playwright, a piece intended to be read rather than performed.

Edgar Allan Poe, *Politian, A Tragedy*—a drama in blank verse by the American writer set in sixteenth-century Rome; love, lust, and intended murder prevail; to 1836, but never finished.

William Gilmore Simms, *The Partisan*—the first of the American novelist's "Revolutionary Romances."

————————, *The Yemassee*—an American novel set in colonial South Carolina; colonists appear threatened when local Indians break a peace treaty and gain aid from the Spaniards.

Juliusz Slowacki, *Horsztynski*—an unfinished Polish dramatic tragedy in the Shakespearean mode based on events in the city of Wilno during Count Kosciuszko's rebellion of 1794.

Alexis Charles de Tocqueville, *La Democratie en Amerique* (Democracy in America)—a record of the French aristocrat's nine-month travels through the eastern and middle-western United States on a commission to study the American penitentiary system; an analysis of the advantages and disadvantages of democracy that is considered a superior cultural, political, and social treatise.

William Wordsworth, *Yarrow Revisited and Other Poems*—a collection of poems, all but two of which the poet composed during a tour to Scotland and the English border in the autumn of 1831; the title poem serves as a memorial of a day passed with Sir Walter Scott and other friends visiting the banks of the River Yarrow.

EVENTS

The German Federal Diet issues an edict banning the books of "Young Germany" writers, particularly Ludwig Borne, Karl Ferdinand Gutzkow and Heinrich Heine.

James Gordon Bennett founds the *New York Herald* as a daily newspaper to sell for one cent; until 1966.

The Southern Literary Journal and Monthly Magazine begins publication in Charleston, South Carolina; advocates slavery and the advancement of Southern culture; until 1838.

The Western Messenger, a monthly religious and literary journal, begins publication in Louisville and Cincinnati; until 1841.

1836

BIRTHS

Gustavo Adolfo Becquer (d. 1870). Spanish romance writer and lyric poet.

Francis Brett Harte (d. 1902). American writer of fiction.

DEATHS

Christian Dietrich Grabbe (b. 1801). German dramatist.

Karel Hynek Macha (b. 1810). Czech poet and novelist.

Claude Jean Rouget de Lisle (b. 1760). French soldier and poet.

Emmanuel Joseph Sieyes (b. 1748). French statesman and pamphleteer.

PUBLICATIONS

Georg Buchner, *Leonce und Lena* (Leonce and Lena)—a German comedy with a fairy-tale quality, but a royal marriage of convenience provides the author with an opportunity to inject his strong political opinions.

Thomas Carlyle, *Sartor Resartus: The Life and Opinions of Herr Teufelsdrockh*—a semisatiric prose piece written by the Scottish essayist under the influence of the German philosopher Jean Paul Richter (1763-1825); clothes serve as the symbols of the temporary states of human institutions, while the writer manages to attack the causes of his own spiritual crisis.

Charles Dickens, *The Posthumous Papers of the Pickwick Club*—a loosely structured English novel held together by correspondence relating to the journeys, observations, and adventures of the Pickwick Club.

————————, *Sketches by Boz*—the English novelist's sketches relating to the life and customs of the times; until 1837.

Ralph Waldo Emerson, *Nature*—an American essay, perhaps the most original and systematic explication of Transcendentalist philosophy.

Nikolai Gogol, *Revizor* (The Inspector General)—a five-act comedy considered the greatest in Russian theater; combines satiric portrayal of bureaucratic corruption with elements of spiritual allegory, vaudevillian farce, and absurdist commentary on human existence.

Oliver Wendell Holmes, *Poems*—a collection of witty and occasional verse by the American physician-poet, the most noted of which is "Poetry: A Metrical Essay."

Karl Leberecht Immermann, *Die Epigonen* (The Descendants)—a German satirical novel.

Walter Savage Landor, *Pericles and Aspasia*—a long English prose piece consisting of imaginary letters relating to the mythological union of the title characters; discussion of artistic, religious, philosophical, and political issues.

Karel Hynek Macha, *May*—an epic poem, considered the finest lyric piece in the Czech language; reveals the poet's fatalism, love of nature, and national pride.

Alfred de Musset, *Confession d'un enfant du siecle* (Confession of a Child of the Century)—a French autobiographical novel based upon the poet's unhappy love affair with George Sand (1804-1876); also examines the influence on his mind of the revolution and unrest at the beginning of the nineteenth century.

Arthur Schopenhauer, *Uber den Willen in der Natur* (On the Will of Nature)—a tract that reiterates the German philosopher's ideas concerning the primacy of the Will; the Will is the active side of human nature, the key to the self and to understanding.

William Gilmore Simms, *Mellichampe, A Legend of the Santee*—an American novel set during the Revolutionary War; Tories, halfbreeds, and patriots vie with one another.

John Greenleaf Whittier, *Mogg Megone*—a poetic narrative of life among the American Indians during the colonial period; the verse is adequate, but the narrative suffers from artificiality and a lack of organization.

EVENTS

Joshua Ballinger Lippincott founds the Philadelphia publishing firm of J. B. Lippincott and Company.

William Holmes McGuffey publishes the initial two volumes of his *Eclectic Readers* for American school children.

The Philadelphia Public Ledger begins publication as that city's first one-cent newspaper; until 1934.

Fritz Reuter, German novelist, condemned to death for high treason; the sentence is commuted to imprisonment for thirty years in a Prussian fortress.

The Toledo **[Ohio]** *Blade* begins publication.

The Transcendental Club, a group of New England intellectuals, begins to meet at the Concord, Massachusetts, home of Ralph Waldo Emerson to discuss literature, philosophy, and theology; until 1844(?).

1837

BIRTHS

Georg Moritz Ebens (d. 1898). German novelist and Egyptologist.

William Dean Howells (d. 1920). American novelist and critic.

Algernon Charles Swinburn (d. 1909). English poet.

DEATHS

Ludwig Borne (b. 1786). German political writer and satirist.

Georg Buchner (d. 1813). German poet and dramatist.

Giacomo Leopardi (b. 1798). Italian poet.

Aleksandr Sergeyevich Pushkin (b. 1799). Russian poet; mortally wounded in a duel.

PUBLICATIONS

Honore de Balzac, *Le Cure de village*—French fiction.

——————, *Illusions perdues*—French fiction.

Bernhard Bolzano, *Wissenschaftslehre* —a logical treatise by the Austrian Catholic theologian, mathematician, and philosopher.

Robert Browning, *Strafford*—a dramatic tragedy by the English poet about a nobleman loyal to his king; that devotion causes his downfall.

George Buchner, *Wozzek*—a German poetical drama; the basis of a 1924 opera of the same title by Austrian composer Alban Berg (1885-1935); in the play, a simple soldier is driven to kill his wife and himself because he cannot cope with the injustices of life.

Edward G. E. Bulwer-Lytton, *Ernest Maltravers*—a wealthy young man stranded on a moor seeks refuge with a cutthroat; a woman saves him from murder and robbery.

Thomas Carlyle, *History of the French Revolution*—relying upon the historical method he had learned from Sir Walter Scott, the Scottish essayist attempts to destroy the bias of England against the Revolution; the writer's impassioned prose style parallels his enthusiasm for his thesis.

Charles Dickens, *Oliver Twist*—an English novel concerned with a product of the workhouse; raised under cruel conditions and forced to survive in an even crueler world ,of London lowlife, the title character meets a host of colorful underworld characters; in the end, he is adopted by a benevolent person who, earlier, had rescued him; to 1838.

Esteban Echeverria, *The Captive*—an Argentine poem that extols the beauty and the people of the Pampas.

Ralph Waldo Emerson, *The American Scholar*—an oration delivered at Harvard College in which the poet-essayist calls for original American creative and scholarly efforts, rather than mere imitation of European models.

——————— , *Concord Hymn*—a short but passionate American poem written at the completion of the monument (4 July 1837) dedicated to the battles at Lexington and Concord (19 April 1775).

Nathaniel Hawthorne, *Twice-Told Tales*—the first collection of short stories by the American writer; another series in 1842.

Washington Irving, *The Adventures of Captain Bonneville, U.S.A.*—focuses upon the life of an American frontier army officer, Benjamin Louis Eulalie de Bonneville (1769-1878); an original contribution based upon documents and conversations with the subject.

Walter Savage Landor, *The Pentameron*—a long prose work by the English writer expressing his enthusiasm for the writing is of Giovanni Boccaccio (1313-1375).

Mikhail Lermontov, *Death of a Poet*—a Russian poem protesting the death of Aleksandr Sergeyevich Pushkin (1799-1837) in a duel; publication leads to the poet's banishment to the Caucasus.

——————— , *A Song About Czar Ivan Vasilyevich, His Young Bodyguard, and the Valiant Merchant Kalashnikov*—a poetic piece set in the Caucasus.

Eugene Scribe, *La Camaraderie* (The Clique)— a French play based upon the theme of socialevil produced by political fraud.

William Makepeace Thackeray, *The Yellowplush Correspondence*—an English piece of fiction in which an illiterate footman, Charles James Yellowplush, relates his social experiences.

Mihaly Vorosmarty, *The Call*—one of several of the Hungarian Romantic Poet's patriotic lyrics.

EVENTS

Arunah S. Abell founds *The Baltimore Sun* and sells copies for one penny each.

Richard Bentley founds the literary series *Bentley's Miscellany*, with Charles Dickens as editor; it specializes in English fiction.

The Gentlemen's Magazine, a popular variety monthly, begins publication in Philadelphia; to 1840.

The Hartford (**Connecticut**) *Daily Courant* begins publication; to 1887.

Charles Coffin Little and James Brown found the Boston publishing firm of Little, Brown and Company.

William Holmes McGuffey publishes the third and fourth of his *McGuffey's Readers*.

The New Orleans Picayune begins publication.

Henry David Thoreau, age nineteen, delivers the commencement address at Harvard College.

The United States Magazine and Democratic Review, a monthly literary and political journal, begins publication at Washington, D.C.

1838

BIRTHS

William Edward Hartpole Lecky (d. 1903). Irish historian and philosopher.

George Otto Trevelyan (d. 1928). English historian and biographer.

Philippe Auguste Villiers de l'Isle Adam (d. 1889). French writer and pioneer of the Symbolist movement.

DEATHS

Adelbert von Chamisso (b. 1781). French lyric poet and biologist.

Lorenzo Da Ponte (b. 1749). Italian poet; writer of libretti for opera.

PUBLICATIONS

Elizabeth Barrett Browning, *The Seraphim and Other Poems*—a collection of poems by the English writer featuring "Cowper's Grave."

Edward G. E. Bulwer-Lytton, *The Lady of Lyons*—a play by the English novelist, a romantic comedy set during the 1790s.

—————, *Richelieu; or, The Conspiracy*—a historical play in blank verse set in the seventeenth century; attempts to overthrow Cardinal Richelieu fail, but a love affair, despite some dishonorable intentions, does not.

James Fenimore Cooper, *The American Democrat; or, Hints on the Social and Civic Relations of the United States of America*—the American writer's critical discussion of the governmental and political systems of his nation; the author dons the role of a political conservative who appears determined to champion the advantages of an aristocracy over a democracy.

—————, *Home as Found*—an American novel in which the writer satirizes his Cooperstown, New York, neighbors, particularly their participation in social affairs and their hypocricy.

Charles Dickens, *Nicholas Nickleby*—a penniless lad of nineteen, with an equally penniless mother and sister, battles his way up the social ladder; after demonstrating his friendship and compassion, he finds love and marriage; to 1839.

Victor Hugo, *Ruy Blas*—a verse rhapsody by the French poet and novelist; a romantic tragedy in which a commoner unwittingly takes part in an attempt to dethrone a virtuous queen, and thus sets in motion an involved plot.

Karl Leberecht Immermann, *Munchausen*—a novel that attacks the mendacious baron.

Edgar Allan Poe, *The Narrative of Arthur Gordon Pym, of Nantucket*—seventy-five thousand words of fiction, the longest piece produced by the American writer; an account of the disasters that overwhelmed a vessel out of Nantucket, bound for the South Seas.

William Gilmore Simms, *Richard Hurdis; or, The Avenger of Blood*—another of the American novelist's "Border Romances," this one concerning a mysterious outlaw band.

John Greenleaf Whittier, *Poems Written during the Progress of the Abolition Question*—a collection of verse that grew out of the poet's experiences as corresponding editor of *The National Era*, an antislavery newspaper in Washington, D.C., and as secretary of the American Anti-Slavery Society (1836).

EVENTS

D. Appleton and Company, a New York City publishing firm, founded by Daniel Appleton and his son, W. H. Appleton.

Orestes Brownson founds and edits *The Boston Quarterly Review*, a religious and political journal.

The New York Herald becomes the first newspaper in the United States to employ European correspondents.

George Sand, the French novelist, begins her nine-year liaison with composer Frederic Chopin, after having abandoned the French playwright Alfred de Musset in 1834.

Cheney Brothers Silk Manufacturing Company, South Manchester, Connecticut, publishes its trade monthly, *Silk Growers*

Manual, which eventually reaches a circulation of 10,000 readers.

The American Philosophical Society, Philadelphia, issues the first number of its *Transactions and Proceedings.*

1839

BIRTHS

Ludwig Anzengruber (d. 1889). Austrian playwright and novelist.

Joacquim Maria Machado de Assis (d. 1908). Brazilian novelist.

Walter Horatio Pater (d. 1894). English essayist and critic.

Rene Francois Armond Sully-Prudhomme (d. 1907). French poet; recipient of the first Noble Prize in literature (1901).

DEATHS

Jose Maria Heredia (b. 1803). Cuban lyric poet, prose writer, and playwright.

PUBLICATIONS

Thomas Carlyle, *Chartism*—the Scottish essayist's attack on sham and corruption in modern society.

James Fenimore Cooper, *A History of the Navy of the United States*—a work of thorough scholarship by the American writer; interesting enough to attract general readers, particularly as it emphasizes American patriotism, courage, and enterprise.

Charles Darwin, *Journal of Researches into the Geology and Natural History of the Various Countries visited by H. M. S. Beagle*—a record of the English naturalist's voyage, in 1831, on a scientific expedition to South America; the *Beagle* returned to England in 1836.

Christian Friederich Hebbel, *Judith*—an early dramatic success by the German playwright; a struggle between old and new values.

Walter Savage Landor, *Andrea of Hungary, Fra Rupert, and Giovanna of Naples*—a dramatic trilogy by the English writer concerning marriage, assassination, and various other forms of intrigue.

Henry Wadsworth Longfellow, *Hyperion*—an American prose romance focusing upon the love of a professor-poet for the daughter of a merchant; the former's academic interests, particularly Romantic legends and general philosophy, interweave with the narrative; in the end, poetry and love give way to social reality.

—————— , *Voices of the Night*—the American poet's first verse collection, including "Hymn to the Night," "A Psalm of Life," and "The Beleaguered City."

Edgar Allan Poe, *The Fall of the House of Usher*—an American short story, one of Poe's tales of horror; an atmosphere of decay, corruption, and evil pervade this story about Roderick Usher and his sister Madeleine, the last survivors of the Usher line.

William Gilmore Simms, *The Damsel of Darien*—an American historical novel focusing upon the adventures of the Spanish explorer Vasco Nunez de Balboa.

Stendhal, *La Chartreuse de Parme* (The Charterhouse of Parma)—another work by the French novelist recognized for the psychological realism of its characterization; the hero's emotionalism and hypersensitivity rescue him from the stupidity and boredom of life.

William Makepeace Thackeray, *Catherine*—an English novel written under the pseudonym "Ikey Solomon, Jr."; an ironic story of criminal life, intended to discredit the common practice of novelists to romanticize criminal elements; based upon an actual crime in which a woman died upon the gallows, in 1726, for the murder of her husband.

EVENTS

Jean Joseph Charles Louis Blanc, a French journalist, founds *Revue de Progres* to promote his socialist doctrines.

Franz Bopp, the German philologist, identifies Celtic as part of the Indo-European language branch.

George Rex Graham purchases *Atkinson's Casket*, a Philadelphia journal of miscellaneous prose, and renames it *Graham's Magazine*; to 1858.

Maria Chapman sponsors *The Liberty Bell*, a Boston "gift" book that publishes antislavery literature; issued periodically until 1858.

1840

BIRTHS

Alphonse Daudet (d. 1897). French naturalistic writer.

Henry Austin Dobson (d. 1921). English poet.

Thomas Hardy (d. 1928). English novelist and poet.

John Addington Symonds (d. 1893). English cultural historian and poet.

Giovanni Verga (d. 1922). Italian novelist.

Emile Zola (d. 1902). French journalist and novelist.

DEATHS

Louis Gabriel Ambroise de Bonald (b. 1754). French political writer.

Frances Burney (b. 1752). English novelist and diarist.

Karl Leberecht Immermann (b. 1796). German dramatist and novelist.

Louis Lemercier (b. 1771). French writer.

PUBLICATIONS

Amos Bronson Alcott, *Orphic Sayings*—a collection of one hundred aphorisms by the American writer, all of which express his mystical idealism.

Robert Browning, *Sordello*—an English poem set in the early thirteenth century; a simple narrative serves as the vehicle for the theme of the development of a soul.

Edward G. E. Bulwer-Lytton, *Money*—an English comic play based on a series of misconceptions that stand in the way of a successful love affair.

James Fenimore Cooper, *Mercedes of Castile*—an American novel that focuses upon the initial voyages of Christopher Columbus.

——————, *The Pathfinder*—an American novel that idealizes the American Indian, one of the "Leatherstocking Tales."

Leigh Hunt, *A Legend of Florence*—the English essayist's venture into drama, a semi-Elizabethan tragedy successfully produced at Covent Garden Theatre, London.

Washington Irving, *Oliver Goldsmith*—an American biography of the Irish poet, playwright, and novelist, a writer the American author admired and considered a master.

Mikhail Lermontov, *Geroi Nashevo Vremeni* (A Hero of Our Times)—a Russian novel about a disenchanted nobleman; a study in psychological realism.

——————, *Mtsyri* (The Novice)—a Russian poem, another piece inspired by scenes during the poet's exile in the Caucasus.

Prosper Merimee, *Colomba*—a short novel illustrating the writer's concise, understated style.

Edgar Allan Poe, *Tales of the Grotesque and Arabesque*—the American writer's first collection of short stories, containing such pieces as "Berenice," "Ligeia," "The Assignation," and "The unparalleled Adventure of One Hans Pfaal."

John Richardson, *The Canadian Brothers*—a Romantic novel of the Canadian frontier and one of the few pieces of Canadian fiction from the period written in English.

Jules Sandeau, *Marianna*—the first successful novel by the French writer; another accurate picture of the social conflicts of the period.

Eugene Scribe, *Le Verre d'Eau; ou, Les Effects et les Causes* (The Glass of Water; or, Causes and Effects)—a French drama that cleverly illustrates a theme borrowed from Voltaire (and, perhaps, even Alexander Pope): that overwhelming consequences follow from trivial origins; thus, a spilled glass of water determines the fate of a nation.

William Makepeace Thackeray, *The Paris Sketch-Book, by Mr. Titmarsh*—a collection of tales and sketches narrated by the English novelist's fictional persona.

——————, *A Shabby Genteel Story*—an English Romantic tale concerned with marriage, desertion, and disreputable villains skilled in blackmail.

Jose Zorrilla y Moral, *El Zapatero Y el Rey* (The Shoemaker and the King)—one of several of the Spanish dramatist's popular pieces on national legends and stories.

EVENTS

Anna, Duchess of Bedford, introduces afternoon tea into England.

Calvin W. Starbuck founds *The Cincinnati Times*.

The New England Transcendentalists found their quarterly journal of literature, philosophy, and religion: *The Dial*, to 1844.

Thomas Carlyle urges the founding of the London Library, at Number 49 Pall Mall.

The American Anti-Slavery Society, New York City, begins publication of the *National Anti-Slavery Standard*; to 1872.

The Percy Society, London, founded for the purpose of publishing Old English lyrics and ballads.

Fritz Reuter, German humorist and poet, a political prisoner since 1833, set free by Prussian general amnesty.

Max Schnechenburger, a merchant of the Swabian section of Prussia, reacts to an anticipated French invasion by writing the poem "Watch on the Rhine"; the piece is set to music in 1854 by Carl Wilhems and becomes a popular patriotic song.

Noah Webster publishes the two-volume revised edition of his *Dictionary of the English Language*.

1841

BIRTHS

Catule Mendes (d. 1909). French novelist and playwright.

DEATHS

Mikhail Yurevich Lermontov (b. 1814). Russian Romantic poet and novelist; killed in a duel.

PUBLICATIONS

Dion Boucicault, *London Assurance*—a successful English play concerning carnal desire.

Robert Browning, *Pippa Passes*—an English dramatic poem focuses upon a day-long out-

ing of a young girl whose songs and spirit reflect God's love and affect a number of persons whom she meets.

Thomas Carlyle, *On Heroes, Hero-Worship, and the Heroic in History*—initially a lecture by the Scottish essayist; a popular recreation of what had already been written about the romantic concept of the hero; however, the writer turns the doctrine of heroism into a political concept.

James Fenimore Cooper, *The Deerslayer*—an American frontier novel emphasizing the title character's loneliness and kinship with nature; although he takes a human life for the first time, he appears to have a firm idea of the spiritual meaning of human existence.

Charles Dickens, *Barnaby Rudge*—an English historical novel set in the context of the Gordon "No-Popery" riots in London during 1780; the vivid description of the riots and the delineation of the characters complement the narrative of love and murder.

————, *The Old Curiosity Shop*—an English novel introducing the reader to "Little Nell" and her struggle with poverty and a profligate relative; in the end, worn out from those conflicts, she dies.

Ralph Waldo Emerson, *Essays, First Series*—Clarifies and expands upon doctrines presented in earlier works, including the idea that Nature is the divine example for inspiration; sentence constructions reflect the influence of Thomas Carlyle.

Ludwig Feuerbach, *Das Wesen Des Christentums* (The Essence of Christianity)—a German philosophical essay on the nature of religion; translated into English by the novelist George Eliot in 1854.

Jeremias Gotthelf, *Uli Der Knecht* (Uli the Farmhand)—a novel of Swiss village life.

Nathaniel Hawthorne, *Famous Old People*—another in the series of biographical sketches by the American writer, intended for children.

————, *Grandfather's Chair*—a children's book.

————, *Liberty Tree*—history and morality for children.

Thomas Hood, *Miss Kilmansegg and Her Precious Leg, a Golden Legend*—a tragic-comic poem, published serially to 1843; the daughter of a wealthy man loses her leg and has it replaced with one made of gold; she marries a mysterious count, leading to an absurd ending.

Mikhail Lermontov, *The Demon*—a narrative poem inspired by the scenery of the Caucasus, where the poet had lived in exile.

Henry Wadsworth Longfellow, *Ballads and Other Poems*—a collection by the American poet that contains a number of fairly vigorous pieces; includes two poetic tales of the sea, "The Wreck of the Hesperus" and "the Skeleton in Armor"; also "Rainy Day," "The Village Blacksmith," and "Excelsior."

James Russell Lowell, *A Year's Life, and Other Poems*—a collection of the American writer's early poetry; illustrates well that the poet could do more than simply imitate the subjects and forms of British poets, and American critics appreciated that quality of originality.

Edgar Allan Poe, *Murders in the Rue Morgue*—an American short story, a "tale of ratiocination" and the beginning of the detective story; the main character, C. Auguste Dupin, solves a murder committed by an ape.

Juliusz Slowacki, *Beniowski*—a Polish poem on the Don Juan theme.

William Makepeace Thackeray, *The Great Hoggarty Diamond*—an English novel based upon the problems of Samuel Titmarsh with a diamond given to him by a stingy old aunt; swindlers lead him to prison, where his wife rescues him.

EVENTS

Henry George Bohn publishes in London his *Guinea Catalogue of Old Books.*

The Transcendentalist Brook Farm Community, West Roxbury, Massachusetts, established for the promotion of human culture; to 1847.

The Brooklyn Eagle, the New York borough daily newspaper, begins publication; to 1956.

The Cincinnati Enquirer begins publication.

The Cleveland Advertiser begins publication.

August Heinrich Hoffman, German poet and philologist, publishes the lyrics to *Deutschland, Deutschland, Uber Alles*; music by Franz Joseph Haydn.

Victor Hugo elected to the Academie Francaise.

The Ladies Repository, a monthly magazine of religion and literature, begins publication in Cincinnati; until 1880.

Horace Greeley founds the *New York Tribune*, a daily newspaper; until 1966.

Punch; or, The London Charivari begins publication in London as an illustrated weekly comic periodical.

1842

BIRTHS

Georg Morris Cohen Brandes (d. 1927). Danish literary critic.

Ambrose Gwinnet Bierce (d. 1914?). American writer and literary sage.

Francois Coppee (d. 1908). French poet.

Sidney Lanier (d. 1881). American poet.

Stephane Mallarme (d. 1898). French poet.

Karl May (d. 1912). Popular German author of tales for boys.

Antero de Quental (d. 1891). Portuguese poet.

DEATHS

John Banim (b. 1798). Irish poet, playwright, and novelist.

Clemens Brentano (b. 1778). German poet.

Jose de Espronceda (b. 1808). Spanish poet and revolutionist.

Arnold Hermann Ludwig Heeren (b. 1760). German historian.

Stendhal (pseudonym of Marie Henri Beyle; b. 1783). French novelist and biographer.

PUBLICATIONS

Robert Browning, *Dramatic Lyrics*—a collection by the English poet that includes "How They Brought the Good News from Ghent to Aix," "Saul," "The Lost Leader," and "The Pied Piper of Hamlin."

Edward G. E. Bulwer-Lytton, *Zanona*—the English novelist's contribution to the fiction of the supernatural.

James Fenimore Cooper, *The Two Admirals*—an American novel concerned with the British navy prior to the American Revolution.

——————, *Wing-and-Wing*—an American historical novel set in and around a number of Mediterranean islands during the Napoleonic period; the vessel of the title engages in a number of exciting sea chases.

Charles Darwin, *Structure and Distribution of Coral Reefs*—an early tract by the English naturalist containing scientific data that would eventually contribute to his theory of evolution.

Charles Dickens, *American Notes*—an English novel based upon the writer's visit to America; the issue of slavery and scenes of poverty contribute to a negative picture of the New World, which, naturally, caused the piece to be criticized by American readers.

Annette Elisabeth Droste-Hulshoff, *Die Judenbuche: Ein Sittergemalde aus dem gebirgichten Westfalen* (The Jew's Beech Tree)—a German novella.

Nikolai Gogol, *Mertvyye Dushi* (Dead Souls), Part I—one of the most significant novels in Western world literature; concerns an attempt by small landowners to swindle the government by purchasing the names of serfs whose deaths were not offically recorded; contains touches of Swift and Dickens; Part II burned by the Russian writer in 1845.

Friedrich Hebbel, *Maria Magdalena*—the German playwright's only "contemporary" drama.

Henry Wadsworth Longfellow, *Poems on Slavery*—a small volume of eight lyrics by the American poet, composed during a stormy return voyage from Europe; his only artistic response to a national issue.

Thomas Babington Macaulay, *Lays of Ancient Rome*—the English writer's attempt to reconstruct into English form the lost ballad poetry of ancient Rome: "Horatius," "The Battle of Lake Regillus," "Virginia," and "The Prophecy of Capys"; another edition in 1848.

Johann Nestroy, *Einen Jux Will er Sich Machen* (He Wants to Have a Lark)—a Viennese farce; Thornton Wilder will borrow from this play for his 1956 comedy, *The Matchmaker*; relies heavily upon local dialect and plays on words, which makes translation almost impossible.

John Henry Newman, *Essay on Miracles*—the English writer's discussion of those miracles recorded in the early ages of ecclesiastical history.

Edgar Allan Poe, *The Masque of the Red Death*—a short story, one of the writer's tales of horror; Prospero the artist pursues the ghoulish figure of the Red Death through seven colored rooms of his twisted imagination.

William Gilmore Simms, *Beauchampe*—an American novel concerned with an áctual murder in Kentucky; the novel was notorious because of its racial topics and direct references to the actual event.

Eugene Sue, *Les Mysteres de Paris* (The Mysteries of Paris)—a novel of social history that reminds one of Victor Hugo's *Les Miserables* (1862); the French writer focuses his attention upon slum life in Paris; to 1843.

Bakin Takizawa, *Nanso Satomi Hakken*—a Japanese novel begun in 1817.

Alfred, Lord Tennyson, *Locksley Hall*—an English poem in the form of a monologue; the speaker revisits the home of his youth and conjures forth youthful visions of a new and progressive world.

——————, *Morte D'Arthur*—a long English poem concerning the late history of King Arthur and his last battles.

——————, *Ulysses*—a poetic dramatic monologue taken from Dante's conception (*Inferno*); based upon the theme of confronting the struggles and adversities of life.

William Makepeace Thackeray, *The Fitzboodle Papers*—the English writer assumes the guise of George Savage Fitzboodle and confesses the elderly clubman's excitement at seeing several German maidens; to 1843.

Walt Whitman, *Franklin Evans; or, The Inebriate: A Tale of the Times*—a tract written by the American poet in support of the temperance movement.

William Wordsworth, *Poems, Chiefly of Early and Late Years*—the English poet's last collection of verse; a number of pieces inspired by his visit to Italy in 1837.

Jose Zorrilla y Moral, *El Zapatero y el Rey* (The Shoemaker and the King), Part II—the second installment of the Spanish playwright's dramatic recreation of a national legend.

EVENTS

William Harrison Ainsworth, the English novelist, begins publication of *Ainsworth's Magazine*; to 1853.

Thomas Babington Macaulay is instrumental in influencing the passage of the Copyright Act of 1842; copyright extended to the period of forty-two years from the date of publication; replaced by the Act of 1911.

Charles Dickens in New York City; finds Broadway swarming with untended pigs.

Adin Ballou is instrumental in founding the Hopedale Community, Milford, Massachusetts; a Universalist commune promoting Christian socialism; disbanded in 1856.

The Illustrated London News begins publication.

Washington Irving appointed United States Ambassador to Spain; to 1845.

Harriet Farley, a factory worker at Lowell, Massachusetts, edits the *Lowell Offering*, a magazine containing writing by women mill workers; to 1845.

The Pittsburgh Post begins publication.

The Southern Quarterly Review, a proslavery journal, begins publication at Charleston, South Carolina; to 1857.

1843

BIRTHS

Edward Dowden (d. 1913). Irish critic and literary scholar.

Henry James (d. 1916). American-born novelist and essayist.

Benito Perez Galdos (d. 1920). Spanish novelist and dramatist.

Peter Rosegger (known also as P.K. [Petri Kettenfeier]; d. 1918). Austrian poet and novelist.

Bertha Kinsky von Suttner (d. 1914). Austrian writer and pacifist.

Carmen Sylva (pseudonym of Princess Elizabeth of Wied, future Queen of Roumania; d. 1916). Roumanian poet.

DEATHS

Jean Francois Casimir Delavigne (b. 1793). French dramatist, satirist, and lyric poet.

Jakob Friedrich Fries (b. 1773). German philosopher.

Johann Christian Friedrich Holderlin (b. 1770). German poet.

Francis Scott Key (b. 1779). American poet.

Friedrich Heinrich Karl de la Motte-Fouque (b. 1777). German writer of Romantic fiction.

Robert Southey (b. 1774). English poet and biographer.

Noah Webster (b. 1758). American lexicographer.

PUBLICATIONS

Robert Browning, *A Blot in the 'Scutcheon*—an English tragic drama in blank verse, produced in this same year; concerns an illicit love affair in an aristocratic household during the eighteenth century.

Edward G. E. Bulwer-Lytton, *The Last of the Barons*—an English historical novel focusing upon the period 1467-1471 and the quarrel between the Earl of Warwick and Edward IV over the marriage of the King's sister, Margaret.

Thomas Carlyle, *Past and Present*—an essay by the Scottish writer focusing upon contemporary political issues, including the present and future of the laboring class and the teachings of political economists and democratic reformers.

James Fenimore Cooper, *Le Mouchoir*—a short American novel focusing upon New York City society and the sharp distinctions between the social classes there.

—————— , *Ned Myers*—the fictionalized biography of a former shipmate of the American writer.

—————— , *Wyandotte*—an American novel set in New York and focusing upon the Revolutionary War.

Charles Dickens, *A Christmas Carol*—a Christmas story by the English novelist concerning the spiritual awakening of an old miser to the true meaning of human love and kindness; does not neglect social class differences and attitudes.

—————, *The Life and Adventures of Martin Chuzzlewit*—an English novel containing complex character and family relationships dictated according to the availability of money; a sub-plot concerns murder and fraud; legion of humorous characters; published serially during 1843-1844.

Heinrich Heine, *Atta Troll*—a German poem that essentially signals the end of Romanticism; largely satirical and keyed by its subtitle, "A Summer Night's Dream."

Thomas Hood, *A Song of the Shirt*—the English poet's protest verse against sweatshop labor conditions; printed in the Christmas number of *Punch.*

Soren Kierkegaard, *Enten-Eller* (Either/ Or)—the Danish philosopher's repudiation of the objective philosophy of the absolute (as set forth by Georg Friedrich Hegel, [1770-1831]); he preaches a religion of acceptance and suffering based upon faith, knowledge, thought, and reality; heralds the beginning of "existentialism."

—————, *Fear and Trembling*—again the Danish philosopher emphasizes the individual's freedom of choice, the psychological "leap of faith" that allows one to confront the condition of fear and dread (the "angst").

Henry Wadsworth Longfellow, *The Spanish Student*—an American poetic drama, a comedy adapted from Cervantes' *La Gitanilla;* concerns the love of a Spanish student for a gypsy girl.

Thomas Babington Macaulay, *Essays Contributed to the "Edinburgh Review," Critical and Historical*—a collection of pieces by the English writer published between 1825 (on John Milton) and 1843 (on William Pitt); a series of biographical, political, and literary surveys, all highly subjective and a number intensely prejudiced.

John Stuart Mill, *A System of Logic, Ratiocinative and Inductive*—a principal work of the English essayist in which he pounds an inductive method of modern science, setting forth procedures for investigating the causal relations of phenomena.

Edgar Allan Poe, *The Pit and the Pendulum*—a horror story emphasizing the physical nature of the individual's sense of fear and terror; the setting of the Spanish Inquisition helps to create the proper atmosphere.

—————, *The Rational of Verse*—an essay by the American poet and writer of fiction setting forth his theories of poetic technique: what constitutes a metrical unit, as well as the differences between natural and unnatural metrical units.

John Ruskin, *Modern Painters*—originally conceived as an effort to rescue the artistic reputation of the English painter Joseph Mallord William Turner (1775-1851) from obscurity and neglect; develops, instead, into a spiritual history of Europe, with emphasis upon morality and artistic taste; to 1860.

John Greenleaf Whittier, *Lays of My Home and Other Poems*—a collection of poems by the American writer, some of the best of which are "The Norseman," "Raphael," and "Massachusetts to Virginia."

EVENTS

Henry Cole, a London museum director, sends the world's first Christmas card: "A Merry Christmas and a Happy New Year!"

Sir James Wilson begins publication of *The Economist,* a weekly London financial paper.

David Macmillan and his brother, Alexander, open a bookshop in Cambridge, England; Macmillan and Company established in 1844.

London publisher George Routledge begins to sell the one-shilling classic works of literature that become known as "The Railway Library."

The Sunday News of the World, London, begins publication.

Charles Thurber, Worcester, Massachusetts, patents a hand printing "chirographer," the prototype of the typewriter.

William Wordsworth appointed Poet Laureate of England; until 1850.

1844

BIRTHS

Robert Bridges (d. 1930). English poet and poetry editor.

Anatole France (pseudonym of Jacques Anatole Thibault; d. 1924). French novelist and critic.

Gerard Manley Hopkins (d. 1889). English poet.

Detlov von Liliencron (d. 1909). German poet and novelist.

Friedrich Wilhelm Nietzsche (d. 1900). German philosopher and critic.

Paul Verlaine (d. 1896). French Poet.

DEATHS

Ivan Andreevich Krylov (b. 1769). Russian writer of fables.

Charles Nodier (b. 1780). French Romantic writer of short stories and fairy tales.

Rene Charles Guilbert de Pixerecourt (b. 1773). French melodramatic playwright.

PUBLICATIONS

Elizabeth Barrett Browning, *Poems*—a collection by the English poet including "The Cry of the Children."

William Cullen Bryant, *The White-Footed Deer and Other Poems*—a collection by the American poet characterized by the typical grace and dignity of his art.

James Fenimore Cooper, *Afloat and Ashore*—an American novel, a social history; the action on the sea goes forward with a rare combination of emotion and suspense.

————————, *Miles Wallingford*—a novel similar to *Afloat and Ashore* in theme and tone but with more social history and a fair portion of autobiography.

Thomas De Quincey, *The Logic of Political Economy*—an English prose tract that focuses upon and supports the political and economic theories of David Ricardo.

Charles Dickens, *The Chimes*—another Christmas piece by the English writer intended to promote the love and happiness of the season.

Alexander Dumas the elder, *Les Trois mousquetaires* (The Three Musketeers)—a highly Romantic novel, and one scorned by contemporary critics; written with the aid of a collaborator, Auguste Maquet.

Heinrich Heine, *Deutschland, ein Wintermarchen* (Germany, a Winter's Tale)—collection of new poems reflecting the poet's reaction, as a German of Jewish descent, to German anti-Semitism.

Leigh Hunt, *Abou Ben Adhem*—an English poem that concerns a vision of an angel writing in a book of gold the names of those who loved God; the theme is to get the title character's name on that list.

————————, *Imagination and Fancy*—selections from English poets; further editions in 1845 and 1852.

Soren Kierkegaard, *Philosophical Fragments*—another attack by the Danish philosopher and theologian upon all philosophical system building; he formulates the thesis that subjectivity is truth.

James Russell Lowell, *Poems*—the second book of verse by the American poet, focusing upon liberal and humanitarian issues.

Karl Marx, *Introduction to a Critique of the Hegelian Philosophy of the Right*—the German political philosopher argues that religion is the opium of the people, the spirit of unspiritual conditions.

Eugene Sue, *Le Juif errant* (The Wandering Jew)—a French novel that begins with the legend of the wandering Jew, condemned to roam the world until Christ's second coming, but actually focuses upon contemporary scenes.

William Makepeace Thackeray, *The Luck of Barry Lyndon, a Romance of the last Century, By Fitzboodle*—an English novel about an impudent Irish rascal who skips about Europe in search of fashion and career; he marries into wealth, squanders the money, and ends in prison; an obvious satire upon the novels of the eighteenth century.

Henrik Wergeland, *English Pilot*—a poem in which the Norwegian nationalist voices his ultimate goal for the liberation of the human mind.

Jose Zorilla y Moral, *Don Juan Tenorio*—a verse drama that recreates the legend of the title; performed annually on All Saints' Day in Spanish-speaking countries.

EVENTS

Amos Bronson Alcott founds Fruitlands, a Utopian commune in northern Massachusetts; lasts but three months.

Bethel Community, a 4000-acre tract in Missouri, established by Germans and Pennsylvania Dutch as an agricultural commune; to 1880.

Orestes Brownson, New England Unitarian turned Roman Catholic, founds *Brownson's Quarterly Review,* a journal that represents his new-found faith; to 1875.

William Cullen Bryant, the American poet, proposes a public park for the borough of Manhattan.

Robert Chambers begins to publish his *Chambers's Cyclopaedia of English Literature*.

The Columbian Lady's and Gentleman's Magazine, a monthly literary journal, begins publication in New York City; to 1849.

The Evening Mirror, a daily literary newspaper, begins publication in New York City; Edgar Allan Poe serves as literary critic; until 1845.

Friedrich Gottlob Keller invents wood-pulp paper.

Eliakim Littel founds *The Living Age*, a weekly literary journal; until 1941.

Karl Marx and Friedrich Engels meet in Brussels.

Moses Yale Beach of the *New York Sun* publishes his *Wealth and Biography of Wealthy Citizens of the City of New York*; 850 New Yorkers worth $100,000 or more.

Young Men's Christian Association (YMCA) founded in London by George Williams.

1845

BIRTHS

George Edward Bateman Saintsbury (d. 1933). English literary critic and literary historian.

Jacinto Verdaguer (d. 1902). Catalan (Spanish) national poet and priest.

Carl Spitteler (d. 1924). Swiss poet, novelist, and prose writer.

DEATHS

Thomas Hood (b. 1799). English editor, poet, and prose writer.

August Wilhelm von Schlegel (b. 1767). German poet and critic.

Henrik Arnold Wergeland (b. 1808). Norwegian poet, dramatist, and patriot.

PUBLICATIONS

Honore de Balzac, *Les Paysans*—a French novel, part of the writer's "Comedie Humaine," but never really finished.

Thomas Carlyle, *Oliver Cromwell's Letters and Speeches*—a work by the Scottish essayist that presented to the public a new view of the subject; the writer intends to uncover the heroic elements in Cromwell's character and displays his own Puritan sympathies.

James Fenimore Cooper, *The Chainbearer*—an American novel concerning the Revolutionary War, spying, Indian relationships, and love; all of these plot elements underscore the novelist's concern for the growing class structure within the relatively young nation.

———— , *Satanstoe*—the first of the American writer's novels known as the "Littlepage Manuscripts"; upstate New York, New York City, and the French and Indian War serve as the background for the usual love and adventure tale.

Alexandre Dumas pere, *Le Comte de Monte-Cristo* (The Count of Monte Cristo)—a highly Romantic French novel that goes forward on the vehicles of mystery, adventure, and vengeance.

———— , *Vingt ans apres* (Twenty Years After)—the second of the French novelist's "d'Artagnan group."

Friedrich Engels, *Die Lage der Arbeitenden Klassen in England* (The Condition of the Working Class in England)—the German political philosopher expounds upon his belief that labor is being exploited by capital.

Margaret Fuller, *Women in the Nineteenth Century*—perhaps the earliest detailed discussion of the feminist position; the American writer approaches her subject from intellectual, social, economic, political, and sexual points of view.

Henrik Hertz, *Kong Rene's Datter* (King Rene's Daughter)—a Danish drama, a significant work in the literature of that nation identifying the playwright as a poet of the highly emotional and sensuous school of romance.

Henry Wadsworth Longfellow, *The Belfry of Bruges and Other Poems*—a collection by the American poet containing, among other pieces, the popular "The Bridge," "The Old Clock on the Stairs," and the sonnet "Mezzo Cammin"; in the last-mentioned piece, the poet surveys his overall poetic achievement.

Prosper Merimee, *Carmen*—the short French novel of gypsy life that formed the basis for Georges Bizet's popular opera of the same title (1875).

John Henry Newman, *Essay on the Development of Christian Doctrine*—written during the period of the English writer's conversion from Anglicanism to Roman Catholicism; drawn from the last sermon that the then-Anglican divine preached from the pulpit at Oriel College, Oxford.

Sandor Petofi, *Janos the Hero*—a Hungarian epic poem relating the fantastic adventures of a peasant soldier.

Edgar Allan Poe, *The Purloined Letter*—an American detective story involving an amateur investigator who uncovers an elaborate blackmail scheme.

——————— **,** *The Raven and Other Poems*—a collection by the American poet that features the titled piece, a haunting narrative containing one of the most remembered series of refrains in all of literature; focuses upon the darkness surrounding the troubled soul.

——————— **,** *Tales by Edgar A. Poe*—a collection of American short fiction including "The Black Cat" and "The Purloined Letter."

William Gilmore Simms, *Helen Halsey; or, The Swamp State of Conelachita*—another of the Southern writer's "Border Romances" focusing upon nineteenth-century life in the American South.

William Makepeace Thackeray, *Jeames's Diary*—a humorous narrative, one of the English writer's contributions to *Punch*.

John Greenleaf Whittier, *The Stranger in Lowell*—a collection of reflective essays by the American poet.

EVENTS

The American Whig Review, a political and literary journal, begins publication; to 1852.

The Broadway Journal, a New York City literary periodical owned by Edgar Allan Poe, begins publication; to 1846.

Theodore Dwight begins publication of *Dwight's American Magazine*; to 1852.

The Harbinger, a weekly journal of the social sciences, politics, literature, and the arts, begins publication as the official periodical of the Brook Farm community (until 1847); journal itself lasts until 1849.

The National Police Gazette begins publication as a weekly magazine intended to expose crime in New York City; to 1937.

John Henry Newman, English poet, essayist, and thinker, joins the Roman Catholic Church.

Scientific American begins publication in New York City, in newspaper format.

William Gilmore Simms begins editing and publishing *The Southern and Western Monthly Magazine and Review*, a periodical published in Charleston, South Carolina, for the promotion of slavery and Southern culture.

1846

BIRTHS

Svatopluk Cech (d. 1908). Czech poet and novelist.

Edmondo De Amicis (d. 1908). Italian novelist.

Jose Maria Eca de Quieroz (d. 1900). Portuguese novelist.

Rudolf Christoph Eucken (d. 1926). German Philosopher.

Henryk Sienkiewicz (d. 1916). Polish novelist and short story writer.

PUBLICATIONS

Hans Christian Andersen, *Fairy Tale of My Life*—the autobiography of the Danish story teller.

Honore de Balzac, *La Cousine Bette*—a French novel belonging to the "Comedie Humaine" series.

Anne, Charlotte, and Emily Bronte, *Poems by Currer, Ellis, and Acton Bell*—a collection of poems by the three sisters, signed by their respective pseudonyms.

Robert Browning, *Bells and Pomegranates*—a series of poems by the English writer originally published between 1841 and 1846; includes "Pippa Passes," "Dramatic Lyrics," "The Return of the Druses," "A Blot in the 'Scutcheon," and "How They Brought the Good News."

James Fenimore Cooper, *Lives of Distinguished American Naval Officers*—a series of biographies intended to complement the American writer's 1839 history of the American navy.

——————— **,** *The Redskins*—the final novel in the writer's trilogy focusing upon the antagonism between those people in New York state with title to property and those without.

Feodor Dostoevsky, *Bednye lyudi* (Poor Folk)—the Russian writer's first piece of fiction; begun in 1844, after the novelist had left military service.

George Eliot, *Life of Jesus*—The English novelist's translation of the gospel history *Leben Jesu* (1835), by the German theologian David Friedrich Strauss.

Gustav Freytag, *Die Valentine*—a German dramatic comedy; the playwright's journalistic ability is evidenced in his attention to specific details.

Nathaniel Hawthorne, *Mosses from an Old Manse*—a collection of American short stories and sketches; focuses upon the Puritan mind and includes such pieces as "Young Goodman Brown," "Rappaccini's Daughter," and "The Birthmark."

Leigh Hunt, *Stories from Italian Poets*—an anthology by the English poet and essayist.

———————, *Wit and Humor*—annotated selections representative of the title from a variety of English poets.

Walter Savage Landor, *The Hellenics*—a collection by the English writer of short tales and dialogues in verse based upon Greek mythical and idyllic subjects; to 1847.

Edward Lear, *The Book of Nonsense*—written by the English author and traveler for his patron, the Earl of Denby; the piece helped to give the limerick recognition as a literary form.

Herman Melville, *Typee*—an American novel admired for its delightful descriptions of Polynesian life and for its adventure and romance.

Jules Michelet, *Le Peuple* (The People)—an historical essay that calls upon the French to unite in eliminating class divisions created by the industrial revolution.

Edgar Allan Poe, *The Cask of Amontillado*—an American short story that takes place during a carnival in an Italian city; a grotesque tale of revenge.

———————, *The Philosophy of Composition*—a critical essay by the American writer; intended to demonstrate the importance of conscious effort, as opposed to intuitive inspiration, in the creation of a work of art.

George Sand, *La Mare du Diable*—a French novel focusing upon the life of retirement; best described as a "rustic idyll."

John Greenleaf Whittier, *Voices of Freedom*—contains the American poet's antislavery verse, featuring "Massachusetts to Virginia;" the poet had read about the proceedings against a fugitive slave, George Latimer, who was seized in Boston without warrant at the request of his supposed master, a James B. Grey of Norfolk, Virginia.

EVENTS

Charles D. Scribner and Isaac D. Baker form the New York publishing firm of Baker and Scribner.

The Boston Herald begins publication.

Fire destroys the central building of Brook Farm, the New England literary commune in West Roxbury, Massachusetts.

James Dunwoody Brownson De Bow begins *De Bow's Review* a magazine of Southern opinion, in New Orleans; to 1880, under different titles.

Charles Dickens founds *The Daily News*, a Liberal newspaper, at London; to 1930.

The Home Journal, a popular weekly magazine, begins publication in New York City; to 1901.

The Pittsburgh Dispatch begins publication.

Smithsonian Institution, Washington, D.C., founded by the U.S. Congress, with a £100,000 bequest from the late James Smithson.

1847

BIRTHS

Jens Peter Jacobsen (d. 1895). Danish naturalistic novelist.

Joseph Pulitzer (d. 1911). Hungarian-born American newspaper publisher; left funds to Columbia University to endow the Pulitzer Prizes.

PUBLICATIONS

Louis Blanc, *Histoire de Revolution* (History of the Revolution)—the French journalist's account of the French Revolution, viewed somewhat from his own socialist perspective; 12 vols., to 1862.

Anne Bronte, *Agnes Grey*—a rector's daughter gains employment as a governess, but is treated poorly by everyone but the local curate, whom she marries; as usual, the English novelist published her work under the pseudonym "Acton Bell."

Charlotte Bronte, *Jane Eyre*—an English novel depicting the experiences of a penniless orphan as she passes through various phases of her life: an unsympathetic aunt, a charity school for orphans, and a position as governess in a strange house owned by an enigmatic master; after a number of terrifying incidents, the heroine marries her employer and everything is restored to its proper order.

Emily Bronte, *Wuthering Heights*—an English novel that brings to the fore a gypsy waif taken into a respectable English home, there to be humiliated and bullied by his new father's own children; the former gypsy grows to be violent and vindictive, which complicates his attraction to his "father's" daughter.

Charles Dickens, *Dealings with the Firm of Dombey and Son*—an English novel relating the tale of a proud and wealthy father who devotes his attention to a new-born son, whose mother died at childbirth; the son dies while at school, and the father neglects his daughter, who has a love affair with one of her father's employees; eventually, the father remarries and his business collapses, but in the end, he and his daughter reconciliate; to 1848.

————, *The Haunted Man and the Ghost's Bargain*—a Christmas story by the English novelist relating the temptation of a learned chemist by an Evil Genius; only the efforts of a Dickensian-type Good Angel free him from a bargain to blot away the good memories of the past.

Ralph Waldo Emerson, *Poems*—the first volume of the American writer's poetry; includes "Threnody," "Each and All," "The Rhodora," "Concord Hymn," "Uriel," "Ode to W. H. Channing," "Hamatreya," and "Give All to Love."

Heinrich Hoffman, *Struwwelpeter* (Shock-Headed Peter)—a German tale written and illustrated by the German physician for the amusement of his children.

Leigh Hunt, *Men, Women, and Books*—two volumes of sketches, essays, and critical memoirs by the English poet and essayist.

Henry Wadsworth Longfellow, *Evangeline, a Tale of Acadie*—a popular long narrative poem by the American author noted for its lyricism and poignance.

Herman Melville, *Omoo, a Narrative of Adventures on the South Seas*—an American novel originating from the writer's adventures on Tahiti; part of it is devoted to criticism of the Protestant missionary stations in the South Seas.

Karl Marx, *Misere de la Philosophie* (The Poverty of Philosophy)—the German philosopher's attack upon the *Philosophe de la Misere* of Pierre Joseph Proudhon (1809-1865), a French socialist.

Leopold von Ranke, *Neun Bucher Preussischer Geschichte*—a general view of Prussian history by the noted German historian, related with his usual objectivity and accuracy; to 1848.

Jules Sandeau, *Mmle. de la Seigliere*—a brilliant French novel concerned with contemporary social conflicts.

Alfred, Lord Tennyson, *The Princess, a Medley*—an English poem, supposedly a tale of fancy composed by some young persons on a summer day's outing; formed the basis for Gilbert and Sullivan's *Princess Ida* (1884).

William Makepeace Thackeray, *Mr. Punch's Prize Novelists*—the English writer's collection of parodies of major novelists of the period: Benjamin Disraeli, Charles James Lever, Edward Bulwer-Lytton, Mrs. Catherine Grace Frances Gore, George Payne Rainsford James, and James Fenimore Cooper; first published in *Punch*, then reissued in 1856.

————, *Vanity Fair*—an English novel published serially until 1848; focuses on the lives of two characters, Becky Sharp, a ruthlessly ambitious young woman of humble origins, and her friend Amelia Sedley, a good-hearted but weak and sentimental daughter of wealthy parents; the author uses the stories of Becky and Amelia to portray a vivid panorama of upper- and middle-class English life, and the novel contains an array of interesting and amusing major and minor characters.

Anthony Trollope, *The Macdermots of Bally-cloran*—the English writer's first serious attempt at a novel.

EVENTS

A new **British Museum** opens in Great Russell Street, London; replaces Montague House.

The Century Association, a New York City men's club for writers and artists, founded.

Chicago (Daily) Tribune founded.

Oliver Wendell Holmes becomes Dean of the Harvard Medical School.

The Literary World, a New York City weekly periodical devoted to society, literature, and art, founded; until 1853.

Gamiliel Baily begins to edit the antislavery periodical *National Era*, in Washington, D.C.; publishes Hawthorne and Whittier, while serializing Harriet Beecher Stowe's *Uncle Tom's Cabin* (1851-1852); to 1860.

Frederick Douglass (1817-1895), the former slave, founds at Rochester, New York, the *North Star*, an antislavery weekly newspaper; to 1864.

1848

BIRTHS

Khristo Botev (d. 1876). Bulgarian socialist poet.

Joel Chandler Harris (d. 1908). American regionalist writer.

DEATHS

Francois Rene de Chateaubriand (b. 1768). French novelist, essayist, and politician.

Annette Elisabeth Droste-Hulshoff (b. 1797). German poet and novelist.

PUBLICATIONS

Emile Augier, *L'aventuriere* (The Adventuress)—a French drama in verse demonstrating how an adventuress can destroy a family.

Dion Boucicault, *The Corsican Brothers*—the Irish-American playwright's melodrama that he adapted from the French.

Anne Bronte, *The Tenant of Wildfell Hall*—an English novel centering upon a widow whose youth, beauty, and seclusion arouse the interest of local gossips; a violent argument between a neighbor and the widow's landlord sets in motion a complex web of love and intrigue.

Edward G. E. Bulwer-Lytton, *Harold, the Last of the Saxon Kings*—an English historical and romantic novel.

Arthur Hugh Clough, *The Bothie of Tober-na-Voulich* (or *Fuosich*)—an English poem described as a long "vacation pastoral"; relates the story of a young Oxford radical on a reading party in Scotland, who falls in love with the daughter of a Highland farmer; the term "bothie" refers to a Scottish hut or cottage.

James Fenimore Cooper, *The Crater*—an American novel, a Utopian allegory on the theme of an honest man trying to exercise the free play of his creative energy.

—————— , *Jack Tier*—an American historical novel.

—————— , *The Oak Openings; or, The Bee Hunter*—an American historical novel set in Michigan during the War of 1812; drunken settlers, Indians, love, and war generate sufficient excitement.

—————— , *The Sea Lions*—the third historical novel by the American writer written within the year.

Alexandre Dumas fils, *La Dame Aux Camelias* (The Lady of the Camelias)—a French novel that portrays the tragic love affair of a courtesan; became a successful play in 1852 that established the realistic comedy of manners; became the basis for Giuseppe Verdi's opera *La Traviata* (1853).

John Forster, *The Life and Adventures of Oliver Goldsmith*—a lively and eloquent biography of the eighteenth-century Irish poet and dramatist; the English biographer's prose style is akin to that of Thomas Carlyle.

Elizabeth Gaskell, *Mary Barton, a Tale of Manchester Life*—an English novel set during the hard economic times of the 1840s; hunger drives characters to join radical trade unions, which instigate riot, murder, and class struggles; the novelist emphasizes the lack of understanding of employers for their workers' social conditions and political principles.

Charles Kingsley, *The Saint's Tragedy*—an English poetic drama focusing upon St. Elizabeth of Hungary, the wife of Lewis of Thuringa; she struggles with her natural affections and the religious duties forced upon her by a domineering monk.

———————, *Yeast*—the English writer's first novel focusing upon specific contemporary religious and social problems, including the conditions of rural laborers, game laws, and the Tractarian movement.

James Russell Lowell, *The Bigelow Papers*—the American writer's satiric miscellany of prose and verse, published anonymously; a second series followed in 1867; the work grew out of the writer's protest of the Mexican War and the spread of slavery; presented as the work of a New England Yankee farmer, "Hosea Bigelow," a rustic poet who had his verse edited by an overly pedantic parson, "The Reverend Homer Wilbur."

———————, *A Fable for Critics*—the American writer's series of witty and frank poetic sketches of American writers, among them Oliver Wendell Holmes, Nathaniel Hawthorne, William Cullen Bryant, Edgar Allan Poe, Washington Irving, and Henry David Thoreau.

———————, *The Vision of Sir Launfal*—an American verse parable based upon the traditional search for the Holy Grail; interwoven with descriptions of Massachusetts scenery in spring and references to the poet's childhood in Cambridge.

John Stuart Mill, *Principles of Political Economy*—the Scottish philosopher's tract anticipating the marginal utility theory, the standard work on the subject throughout the nineteenth century.

Henri Murger, *Scenes de la Vie de Boheme*—the first novel by the French writer; describes life in the Latin Quarter of Paris, the Bohemian section of the city; became the basis for Giacomo Puccini's opera *La Boheme* (1896).

John Henry Newman, *Loss and Gain*—the English Catholic writer's religious novel containing the noteworthy account of an Oxford tutor's breakfast party.

Sandor Petofi, *Rise, Magyar*—a Hungarian poem voicing the ideals of the Hungarian revolution, in which the poet eventually died (1849).

Edgar Allan Poe, *Eureka*—an American prose poem on the material and spiritual universe, addressed to dreamers and those who place faith in dreams as the only reality.

William Makepeace Thackeray, *The History of Pendennis*—an English novel, published serially to 1850; set in contemporary London, the work is a vivid depiction of Victorian society noted for its wide range of humorous and convincing characters; Arthur Pendennis is the narrator in the novel's sequels, *The Newcomes* and *The Adventures of Philip on His Way through the World*.

Anthony Trollope, *The Kellys and The O'Kellys*—the English writer's second novel; noteworthy only for some interesting characters and isolated episodes, which would be of use in the later novels.

EVENTS

The Astor Library, New York City, founded; in 1895 joined with the New York Public Library.

The Independent, a weekly periodical affiliated (until 1863) with the Congregational Church, begins publication in New York City; until 1928.

Karl Marx and Friedrich Engels issue their *Communist Manifesto*, described at the time as a masterpiece of political propaganda and intellectual browbeating.

Otto von Bismarck establishes the periodical *Neue Preussich Zeitung*.

Karl Marx founds the *Neue Rheinische Zeitung* at Cologne.

The New York News Agency begins operation, until 1856.

David van Nostrand begins D. Van Nostrand Publishers in a New York City bookstore.

1849

BIRTHS

Sir Edmund Gosse (d. 1928). English poet, critic, and scholar.

William Ernest Henley (d. 1903). English poet, playwright, critic, and editor.

Alexander Kielland (d. 1906). Norwegian realistic novelist and playwright.

James Whitcomb Riley (d. 1916). American popular poet; "the Hoosier poet."

(Johan) August Strindberg (d. 1912). Swedish novelist, playwright, and poet.

DEATHS

Anne Bronte (b. 1820). English novelist and poet.

Maria Edgeworth (b. 1767). Irish novelist.

Sandor Petofi (b. 1822). Hungarian poet killed in the revolution of 1849.

Edgar Allan Poe (b. 1809). American poet, critic, short story writer, and editor.

Juliusz Slowacki (b. 1809). Polish poet and dramatist.

PUBLICATIONS

Matthew Arnold, *The Strayed Reveller and Other Poems*—the English poet's first volume of poems, containing "The Forsaken Merman," "The Sick King in Bokhara," and the sonnet on Shakespeare.

Francois Rene de Chateaubriand, *Memoirs de'outre-tombe*—the celebrated autobiography of the French politician and writer, undertaken during the reign of Louis-Philippe (beginning 1830); parts published before the writer's death; the entire work, in six volumes, issued in 1902.

Charles Dickens, *David Copperfield*—an English novel, semiautobiographical in terms of the poverty of the writer's family and his father's imprisonment for debt in Marshalsea Prison; as the author traces the course of Copperfield's life through hardship, deceit, fame, and reawakening, the reader comes into contact with certain of the more noted Dickensian character types, including Agnes Wickfield, Dora Spenlow, Uriah Heep, and Little Em'ly; to 1850.

Charlotte Bronte, *Shirley*—an English novel set in Yorkshire during the Napoleonic wars and the Luddite riots; hard times in the sheep industry relate directly to a complex love triangle.

Edward G. E. Bulwer-Lytton *King Arthur*—an English poem on the Arthurian legends, revised in 1870; the piece proves that industry, ambition, and length cannot substitute for poetic inspiration.

Thomas De Quincey, *The English Mail Coach*—three prose pieces by the English Romantic essayist: "The Glory of Motion" presents an account of the fast moving English coaches that carried both passengers and mail; "The Vision of Sudden Death" describes the writer's own experiences in a near accident; and "Dream-Fugue" combines the near-accident experience with the writer's own dream of terror.

Friedrich Hebbel, *Herodes und Marianne* (Herod and Marianne)—a German drama focusing upon the epoch era of the birth of Christ.

Washington Irving, *A Book of the Hudson*—a series of sketches undertaken by the American writer during his period of retirement at "Sunnyside," his home on the Hudson River at Tarrytown, New York.

——————, *Mahomet and His Successors*—two volumes of conventional biographies; to 1850.

Henry Wadsworth Longfellow, *Kavanagh*—one of the American poet's few attempts at prose fiction; a Roman Catholic converts to Protestantism and becomes a pastor at a New England village church; two women vie for his affection: he marries one and the other dies; on the perimeter, a young schoolmaster awaits the inspiration to write the great romantic tale.

——————, *The Seaside and the Fireside*—a collection of poems by the American writer, including "The Building of the Ship," "The Builders," "King Witlaf's Drinking-Horn," and "Pegasus in Pound."

Thomas Babington Macaulay, *History of England, from the Accession of James II*—history from a Whig and Protestant point of view, but history from one of the nineteenth-century's most gifted prose writers; vols. 1-2 in 1849, 3-4 in 1855, and a fifth vol. published posthumously in 1861.

Herman Melville, *Mardi*—an American novel combining realistic sea adventures, fantastic stories of spiritual quest, and philosophical speculation.

——————, *Redburn*—an American novel drawn upon the author's experiences in Liverpool, England, at age nineteen; describes the suffering of a gentleman's son who sails for a brutal captain and sees, for the first time, the dirt and decay of foreign seaports.

Edgar Allan Poe, *Annabel Lee*—the American poet's last poem, published two days after his death; focuses upon the personal loss of a beloved.

——————, *Bells*—the American poem that relies heavily upon phonetic imitation (onomatopoeia) to represent the various effects of the bells upon the creative imagination.

John Ruskin, *The Seven Lamps of Architecture*—a treatise by the English writer and art critic concerning the seven principles of architecture: sacrifice, truth, power, beauty, life, memory, and obedience; the writer defends the Gothic as the noblest architectural style.

Eugene Scribe and Ernest Legouve, *Adrienne Lecouvreur*—the only tragedy written by Scribe; a strained melodramatic piece created specifically for the actress Eliza Felix Rachel.

William Makepeace Thackeray, *The Ballad of Bouillabaisse*—an English poem in which the writer recalls, with sadness, an old familiar corner of a Paris inn, where he and his wife retired to eat the highly seasoned fish stew known as "bouillabaisse."

Henry David Thoreau, *Civil Disobedience*—a lecture by the New England nonconformist, first delivered under the title "Resistance to Civil Government"; argues that individuals must determine what is morally right through an intuitive act of conscience and must act accordingly, regardless of the law.

——————, *A Week on the Concord and Merrimack Rivers*—a travel narrative recounting a boating trip the writer took with his brother John in 1839.

John Greenleaf Wittier, *Poems*—the first volume of collected poems by the Massachusetts poet; dated 1849, but actually published in late 1848; the "Proem" begins, "I love the old melodious lays / Which softly melt the ages through. . . ."

EVENTS

Feodor Dostoevsky sentenced to death for his revolutionary activities; sentence commuted to penal servitude in Siberia, to 1858.

Eliza Cook, the English poet, begins *Eliza Cook's Journal*, a literary magazine; until 1854.

William John Thoms, English writer and antiquarian, begins *Notes and Queries*, a periodical intended to promote the exchange of thought and information among scholars in literature, the art, and the sciences.

Edmund Hamilton Sears, Massachusetts Unitarian minister, sets his poem "It came upon the midnight clear" to music by Richard Storrs Wills.

The Spirit of the Age, a weekly journal dedicated to reform (slavery, education, temperance, pacifism) begins publication in New York City; publishes from February to April 1850.

Who's Who, the English annual biographical dictionary of contemporary men and women, begins publication.

1850

BIRTHS

Mihail Eminescu (d. 1889). The leading Roumanian poet of the nineteenth century.

Lafcadio Hearn (d. 1904). American writer of Ionian birth; partially blind.

Pierre Loti (pseudonym of Julien Viaud; d. 1923). French novelist.

Guy de Maupassant (d. 1893). French author of short stories novels, plays, and travel sketches; went mad in 1891.

Robert Louis Stevenson (d. 1894). Scottish novelist, poet, and essayist; writer of popular fiction and poetry for children.

Ivan Vazov (d. 1921). Bulgarian poet, novelist, and dramatist.

DEATHS

Honore de Balzac (b. 1799). French novelist.

Nikolaus Lenau (b. 1802). Austrian poet.

Gustav Schwab (b. 1792). German writer and philosopher.

William Wordsworth (b. 1770). English Romantic poet.

PUBLICATIONS

Elizabeth Barrett Browning, *Sonnets from the Portuguese*—a series of sonnets inspired by the poet's love for her poet-husband, Robert; the poet's sense of failure and suffering occasionally permeate the dominant celebration of love and happiness.

Robert Browning, *Christmas Eve and Easter Day*—two distinct poems published under a single title; the first concerns a spiritual experience through various religious organizations to discover where the clearest image of God exists; the second piece narrates a dispute between a Christian and sceptic on how one may reach the "Better Land."

William Cullen Bryant, *Letters from a Traveller*—prose accounts of the American poet's travels in the prairie states; a second series in 1859.

Thomas Carlyle, *Latter-Day Pamphlets*—the Scottish essayist's exaggerated attacks upon universal suffrage, cabinet of the wisest men, without regard to class, popularity, or party, under the direction of a dictator; the unemployed would enter the army and engage in public service; the navy would transport undesirables abroad; the nation would adopt universal education.

Wilkie Collins, *Antonina; or, The Fall of Rome*—the English writer's first novel, a historical piece about the fall of the Roman Empire.

James Fenimore Cooper, *The Ways of the Hour*—the American writer's final novel.

Ralph Waldo Emerson, *Representative Men*—American essays on significant historical and literary figures, including Plato, Emanuel Swedenborg, Shakespeare, Napoleon, and Johann Wolfgang von Geothe, the writer fails to uncover a truly "great" man.

Elizabeth Gaskell, *The Moorland Cottage*—an English novella that may best be described as a kind of Christmas book.

Nathaniel Hawthorne, *The Scarlet Letter*—an American classic novel on the theme of human frailty and sorrow in which the writer skillfully fuses his own imagination into the historical actualities of life in seventeenth century New England; however, the reader must also confront the more intellectually complex issue of the novelist's personal inquiry into the causes and effects of evil and isolation.

Aleksandr Ivanovich Herzen, *From Another Shore*—a Russian novel promoting the writer's revolutionary socialist ideals.

Leigh Hunt, *Autobiography*—a lively narrative, much admired by Thomas Carlyle and other contemporaries of the English essayist; an enlarged edition published from manuscript in 1860.

Henrik Ibsen, *Cataline*—the first play by the Norwegian dramatist; an academic effort written toward the end of his service as a druggist's apprentice; rejected for actual production.

Charles Kingsley, *Alton Locke, Tailor and Poet*—an English novel whose title character, a poet with revolutionary political ideals, allows his writings to be stripped of their political content; then follow riots, a prison term, conversion to Christianity, and understanding of the problems of the poor; the tailor-poet sails for America, but dies on the voyage.

Herman Melville, *White Jacket; or, The World in a Man-of-War*—an American novel, semi-autobiographical, focusing upon the various aspects of human experience aboard an American warship; the most dramatic theme concerns the novelist's attempts to expose the injustices of naval law and brute naval authority.

Edgar Allan Poe, *The Poetic Principle*—a critical essay from the American poet's lectures of 1848-1849, published posthumously in *The Union Magazine*; argues that unity determines the framework of a poem, not length; further emphasizes the poem as a work of art, rather than as a didactic vehicle.

Dante Gabriel Rossetti, *The Blessed Damozel*—an English poem in which a maiden, a chorister of God, views the worlds below her and observes the souls rising to God; she prays to be united with her lover, whom she has left on earth.

Alfred, Lord Tennyson, *In Memoriam, A.H.H.*—an English poem in memory of the poet's promising young friend, Arthur Henry Hallam, who had died in Vienna (1833) when he was only twenty-two years old; a series of elegies reflecting the poet's varying moods of regret over his friend's death; in the end, he achieves a sense of spiritual contact with Hallam, as well as a wider love of God and humanity.

William Makepeace Thackeray, *Rebecca and Rowena: A Romance upon Romance*—a mock continuation of Sir Walter Scott's novel *Ivanhoe.*

Ivan Sergeyevich Turgenev, *Mesyats v Derevne* (A Month in the Country)—a Russian dramatic comedy describing the disruption of life on the country estate of a rich landowner after he hires a university student to tutor his son; the comedy erupts when the man's wife and her seventeen-year-old ward fall in love with the tutor.

John Greenleaf Whittier, *Songs of Labor*—sixteen pieces by the American poet, written in various meters and focusing upon various occupations, such as shoemaker, fisherman, lumberman, ship builder, drover, and husker.

EVENTS

A schoolteacher in Salem, Massachusetts, invents the word-building game to be known as "Anagrams."

The Pre-Raphaelite Brotherhood (W. H. Hunt, J. E. Millais, D. G. Rossetti, W. M. Rossetti, Thomas Woolner, F. G. Stephens, James Collinson) publishes *The Germ: Thoughts Towards Nature in Poetry, Literature, and Art*, a periodical that lasts for only four numbers.

The New York City publishing firm of Harper and Brothers publishes *Harper's Monthly Magazine*, soon to become a leading literary periodical.

Charles Dickens begins *Household Words*, a weekly London literary magazine; to 1859.

The International Monthly Magazine of Literature, Art, and Science begins publication in New York City as a competitor to *Harper's Monthly*; the two merge in 1852.

George Henry Lewes and Thornton Leigh Hunt begin their weekly London periodical, *The Leader*; to 1866.

Alfred, Lord Tennyson succeeds William Wordsworth as Poet Laureate of England.

The United States and its territories can claim to publish 240 daily newspapers.

1851

BIRTHS

Kate O'Flaherty Chopin (d. 1904). American novelist and short story writer.

Arne Garborg (d. 1924). Norwegian novelist and poet.

DEATHS

James Fenimore Cooper (b. 1789). First major American novelist.

Esteban Echeverria (b. 1805). Argentine poet, novelist, and revolutionary.

Mary Wollstonecraft Shelley (b. 1797). English novelist; the daughter of William Godwin and the second wife of Percy Bysshe Shelley.

PUBLICATIONS

Dion Boucicault, *Dame de Pique*—adaptation from the French by the Irish-born dramatist.

Thomas Carlyle, *The Life of John Sterling*—the Scottish essayist's biography of his friend (1806-1844), a frequent contributor to the principal periodicals of the early nineteenth century.

Edward FitzGerald, *Euphranor*—a dialogue on the various systems of education set against the background of the English writer's own Cambridge University.

Elizabeth Gaskell, *Cranford*—an English novel, a prose idyll describing the humor and pathos of life in a quiet Cheshire village in the early nineteenth century; published serially until 1853.

Nathaniel Hawthorne, *The House of the Seven Gables*—an American novel that negates the idea of freedom of the will; concerned with the idea of ancestral sin, the writer bases the piece upon the tradition of a curse dating from the Salem witchcraft trials and underscores the notion of the present as moving forward only upon the vehicles of past actions.

——————, *The Snow Image, and other Tales*—contains seventeen short stories by the New England writer, notably "Ethan Brand," "My Kinsman Major Molyneaux," and "The Great Stone Face."

Heinrich Heine, *Romanzero*—a collection of poems by the German poet and essayist.

Gottfried Keller, *Der Grune Heinrich*—a German autobiographical novel focusing upon the writer's experiences as a painter and politician; to 1854.

Eugene Labiche, *Un Chapeau de Paille d' Italie* (An Italian Straw Hat)—a French comedy that proved to be one of the nineteenth-century's most enduring farces.

Herman Melville, *Moby Dick; or, The Whale*—a significant American novel, extremely symbolic in terms of the confrontation between revenge and human fate; overflowing with biblical allusions and references, and contains accurate and graphic accounts of whales and whaling.

George Meredith, *Poems*—a collection of English poems dedicated to Thomas Love Peacock.

John Henry Newman, *Lectures on the Present Position of Roman Catholics*—a fiercely contemptuous reply to the "no-Popery" agitation of the day.

John Ruskin, *The Stones of Venice*—the English essayist glorifies Gothic art and surveys its rise and decline; exposes the "pestilent" art of the Renaissance, attacking it at its central stronghold, Venice; 3 vols., to 1853.

Jules Sandeau, *Sacs et Parchemins*—a brilliant French novel that became a celebrated play (in collaboration with Emile Angier), *Le Gendre de M. Poirier.*

William Gilmore Simms, *Katharine Walton*—still another of the American novelist's Revolutionary romances.

EVENTS

The Great Exhibition, Crystal Palace, Hyde Park, London, opened.

Henry J. Raymond begins, in New York City, publication of the *New York Times.*

Paul Julius von Reuter begins Reuter's News Service between Brussels and Aachen.

The United States Congress appropriates $100,000 to buy new books for and to fireproof the Library of Congress, severely damaged by a fire on 24 December.

The Young Men's Christian Association (YMCA) opens its American offices at Boston and establishes a Canadian branch in Montreal.

1852

BIRTHS

Leopoldo Alas (d. 1901). Spanish writer and law professor.

Paul Bourget (d. 1935). French Catholic novelist, conservative essayist, and poet.

Lady Augusta Gregory (d. 1932). Irish playwright.

George Augustus Moore (d. 1933). Irish novelist who introduced naturalism into the Victorian novel.

Isaac Peretz (d. 1915). Polish Jewish poet, novelist, playwright, and lawyer; wrote in Hebrew and Yiddish.

Emilia Pardo-Bazan (d. 1921). Spanish novelist and critic; ardent feminist; introduced naturalism into Spanish literature.

DEATHS

Nikolai Vasilyevich Gogol (b. 1809). Russian novelist and playwright.

Thomas Moore (b. 1779). Irish poet and novelist.

John Richardson (b. 1796). THe first Canadian novelist to write in English.

PUBLICATIONS

Matthew Arnold, *Empedocles on Etna and Other Poems*—a collection containing the English poet's dramatic poem "Empedocles on Etna," in which the philosopher climbs the mountain, muses on the mediocre lot of man, and speculates upon the soul after death; also includes "Tristram and Iseult," concerning the death of Tristram as he pines for his beloved.

Charles Dickens, *Bleak House*—an English novel on the abuses of the chancery court system and the effect of delays and costs on litigants; to 1853.

Edward FitzGerald, *Polonius*—the English poet's collection of aphorisms.

Gustav Freytag, *Die Journalisten* (The Journalists)—a comic political play by the German author containing vital tensions and problematic Dickensian characters: e.g., "Schmock," the stereotype Grub Street hack who can write almost anything in almost any style.

Theophile Gautier, *Enamels and Cameos*—a collection of French poems, finely crafted and foreshadowing the revolt against Romanticism.

Nathaniel Hawthorne, *The Blithedale Romance*—an American novel based on Hawthorne's own experiences at the Brook Farm Transcendentalist Commune in West Roxbury, Massachusetts; also a psychological study of the novelist's role in society.

——————— , *The Life of Franklin Pierce*—the American novelist's campaign biography.

——————, *A Wonder Book for Girls and Boys*—tales for children adapted from Greek myths.

Christian Friederich Hebbel, *Agnes Bernauer*—a German play; the title character's sin derives from the simple fact of her impressive beauty; unfortunately, that "sin" stands in the way of the normal operation of the state, since she is a commoner who has fallen in love with a prince.

Herman Melville, *Pierre; or, The Ambiguities*—an American novel that pokes fun at the fallen innocence of a country-bred Hamlet-like hero; a fantastic plot results in the death of the hero and his lover, who take poison, while another woman dies of shock; also explores the nature of the creative process.

Gerard de Nerval, *Contes et Faceties*—a series of fantastic short tales by the French writer.

John Henry Newman, *The Scope and Nature of University Education*—lectures delivered by the English writer and churchman prior to his appointment as rector of the new Catholic University of Dublin; a distinguished analysis of the case for liberal arts education.

Leopold von Ranke, *The History of France*—attempts to reconstruct the past in its pure state, without injecting the spirit of the German historian's own times; 5 vols., to 1861.

Harriet Elizabeth Beecher Stowe, *Uncle Tom's Cabin*—an American novel focusing upon the unavoidable evils of slavery, the separation of families by sale, and the sheer brutality attendant upon the escape, pursuit, and recapture of human beings; an example of how a work of fiction can quickly become a symbol of the times from which it emerged.

William Makepeace Thackeray, *The History of Henry Esmond*—an English historical novel of eighteenth-century military and political struggles; an unconventional love theme and ambiguous characterization have contributed to critical interest in the work; 3 vols.

Ivan Sergeyevich Turgenev, *Zapiski Okhotnika* (A Sportsman's Sketches)—a collection of Russian tales focusing upon the peasantry; sympathetic studies that constitute an attack upon the system of serfdom.

EVENTS

The Boston Public Library founded.

The San Francisco *Golden Era*, a newspaper and literary journal, founded; until 1893.

Peter Mark Roget publishes his *Thesaurus of English Words and Phrases*.

Victoria and Albert Museum, South Kensington, London, founded with money from the surplus funds of the Great Exhibition of 1851.

1853

BIRTHS

Sir Thomas Henry Hall Caine (d. 1931). English popular novelist.

Jose Marti (d. 1895). Cuban poet and patriot.

DEATHS

Ludwig Tieck (b. 1773). German Romantic poet, writer of fiction, and translator.

PUBLICATIONS

Matthew Arnold, *Balder Dead*—an English narrative poem, a tale of the Scandinavian god of the summer sun; relates the lament of the gods for the dead Balder and Hermod's journey to Hell to recall Balder to the upper world.

——————, *Poems*—a collection containing "Sohrab and Rustrum," extracts from "The Scholar Gypsy," "Church of Brou," "Requiescat," "Memorial Verses to Wordsworth," and "Stanzas in Memory of the Author of *Obermann*."

——————, *The Scholar Gypsy*—an English pastoral poem based on the legend of the poor Oxford scholar who joins the gypsies to learn of their lore, but who still haunts the Oxford countryside; underscores the faith of the scholar-gypsy and its conflict with "this strange disease of modern life. . . . "

Charlotte Bronte, *Villette*—an English novel reflecting the writer's own experiences; a strong English girl, without money, beauty, or friends, obtains a teaching position and overcomes the unscrupulous tendencies of her mistress.

Edward G. E. Bulwer-Lytton, *My Novel; or, Varieties in English Life*—an English novel focusing upon a self-taught poet of supposedly humble origins who turns out to be the son of a distinguished politician; the reader meets Italian refugees, money-lenders, and a host of unscrupulous minor characters.

Edward FitzGerald, *Six Dramas of Calderon*—a free translations in blank verse and prose.

Elizabeth Gaskell, *Ruth*—an English novel, an exploration of seduction and illegitimacy; a number of ethical problems are addressed and sound moral lessons are conveyed.

Nathaniel Hawthorne, *Tanglewood Tales*—a collection of children's tales by the American author adapted from Greek legends; has achieved worldwide appeal.

Charles Kingsley, *Hypatia; or, New Foes with an Old Face*—an English historical novel of the fifth century and the Western Empire's retreat before the Teutonic advance; the temperance and sanity of Hypatia confront the violence and fanaticism of the Alexandrian monks.

Walter Savage Landor, *Imaginary Conversations of Greeks and Romans*—another prose work by the English writer recording conversations between historical characters, including the writer's contemporaries; among the participants are Dante, Beatrice, Louis XIV, Pere la Chaise, John Calvin, and Melanchthon; the dialogues reflect the author's own opinions.

Charles Reade, *Christie Johnstone*—an English romantic novel focusing on a Scots fishing-girl and her marriage to a weak-willed artist who cannot free himself from his overbearing mother.

——————, *Peg Woffington*—an English novel based upon the life of an Irish actress who attempts to conquer the heart of a man recently married (although she does not know that); the title character manages to bring the man and his wife back together.

John Ruskin, *On Architecture and Painting*—lectures delivered by the English writer at Edinburgh.

William Gilmore Simms, *The Sword and the Distaff*—one of the American writer's "Revolutionary Romances" focusing upon the actions of Southern American Revolutionary war generals.

——————, *Vasconselos*—an American novel concerned with Mexican history.

Harriet Elizabeth Beecher Stowe, *A Key to Uncle Tom's Cabin*—a fictional reference work compiled by the Connecticut writer to substantiate the accuracy of the facts set forth in *Uncle Tom's Cabin* (1852).

William Makepeace Thackeray, *The English Humourists of the Eighteenth Century*—lectures by the Yorkshire novelist delivered in 1851 in England, Scotland, and the United States; the lecture on Henry Fielding remains the most significant.

——————, *The Newcomes*—an English novel, the first of two sequels to *The History of Pendennis*; focuses upon a young man of generous instincts; the boy's father is a simple-minded gentleman guided through life purely by the sentiments of honor and duty; published serially to 1855.

John Greenleaf Whittier, *The Chapel of the Hermits, and Other Poems*—moralistic poems displaying little sensitivity to nature and even less attention to the passions of the intellect.

EVENTS

August Brentano opens a newsstand in front of the New York Hotel, New York City; the mere beginnings of the large bookstore firm that will follow.

Johann Jakob Herzog, Swiss theologian, edits the *Realencyklopadie fur Protestantische Theologie und Kirche* (Encyclopaedia of Protestant Theology); 22 volumes to 1868; abridged edition in English, 3 volumes, 1882-1884.

Putnam's Monthly Magazine, New York, founded; publishes only American writers; until 1857.

1854

BIRTHS

William Henry Drummond (d. 1907). Canadian poet born in Ireland.

Arthur Rimbaud (d. 1891). French Symbolist poet.

Oscar Wilde (d. 1900). Irish novelist, poet, and essayist.

DEATHS

Jeremias Gotthelf (b. 1797 as Albert Bitzius). Swiss writer and clergyman.

PUBLICATIONS

Amiele Angier and Jules Sandeau, *Le Gendre de M. Poirier*—a celebrated French comic play based upon their novel of 1851, *Sacs et Parchemins*.

Charles Dickens, *Hard Times*—an English novel set in an industrial city and emphasizing the inhumanity of Victorian society; contains the usual number of Dickensian minor characters.

George Eliot, *Essence of Christianity*—a translation of Ludwig Andreas Feuerbach's treatise of 1841, *Das Wesen des Christentums*, which focuses upon the nature of religion.

Julia Ward Howe, *Passion Flowers*—An early collection of the Massachusetts abolitionist's poems.

Gottfried Keller, *Der Grune Heinrich* (Green Henry)—an autobiographical novel by the Swiss novelist and poet.

Gerard de Nerval, *Les Filles du Feu*—a fantastic, yet semiautobiographic, series of tales by the gloomy French poet and prose writer.

Coventry Patmore, *Angel in the House*—an English novel in verse, designed to be the apotheosis of married love; includes "The Betrothal," "The Espousal," "Faithful for Ever," and "The Victories of Love"; 4 volumes to 1862.

William Gilmore Simms, *The Scout; or, The Black Riders of the Congaree* originally published in 1841 as *The Kinsmen*, reissued as one of the American novelist's "Revolutionary Romances"; another of the writer's Tory versus rebel motifs; one of the characters is shot by the father of the girl he has seduced.

Harriet Elizabeth Beecher Stowe, *Sunny Memories of Foreign Lands*—a narrative of the American writer's journey to England, where, at the height of her reputation, she enjoyed an enthusiastic reception.

Alfred, Lord Tennyson, *The Charge of the Light Brigade*—the English poem commemorating the death of 274 officers and men of Lord Cardigan's Light Cavalry at the Battle of Balaclava, 26 September 1854.

——————— , *Ode on the Death of the Duke of Wellington*—perhaps the most significant of all poems by the Poet Laureate of England in performance of his official duties, published on the morning of the Duke's funeral; Robert Louis Stevenson referred to the piece as the finest lyrical poem in the English language.

Henry David Thoreau, *Slavery in Massachusetts*—one of the American essayist's speeches in support of the antislavery movement.

——————— , *Walden; or Life in the Woods*—the American essayist's narrative of his experiment in individualism and self-reliance on the shore of Walden Pond, near Concord, between 1845 and 1847; in eighteen essays the American writer describes and defines his idealistic principles.

EVENTS

The Age, Melbourne, Australia, begins publication as a daily newspaper.

Astor Library, New York, opens; located below Astor's Place in Lafayette Street.

The Chicago Times, until 1864 an anti-Lincoln newspaper, beings publication; merges in 1895 with the Chicago *Herald.*

Jacob Grimm publishes the first volumes of his German-language dictionary, *Die Geschichte der Deutschen*.

Le Figaro, Paris, begins publication as a weekly; becomes a daily newspaper in 1866.

Ticknor and Fields Publishing House, Boston, created by reorganization of Ticknor, Reed, and Fields.

United States Magazine, New York City, begins publication; to 1858; edited by Seba Smith.

1855

BIRTHS

Arthur Wing Pinero (d. 1934). English playwright.

Olive Schreiner (d. 1920). South African novelist; her fiction will reflect her rebellious temperament, hatred of her mother, passion for the rights of women, loyalty to the Boers, and extreme patriotism; her early pieces will appear under the pseudonym of "Ralph Iron."

Emile Verhaeren (d. 1916). Belgian poet and critic.

DEATHS

Charlotte Bronte (b. 1816). English novelist and poet.

Soren Kierkegaard (b. 1813). Danish philosopher and religious writer.

Adam Mickiewicz (b. 1798). Polish poet and playwright.

Mihaly Vorosmarty (b. 1800). Hungarian Romantic poet.

PUBLICATIONS

Edmond About, *Tolla*—a French novel for which the writer was charged with plagiarism.

Matthew Arnold, *Poems, Second Series*—the English writer's collection that includes "Balder Dead."

Robert Browning, *Men and Women*—a collection of fifty-one poems by the English writer, published in two volumes and containing pieces written between 1846 and 1854: "Fra Lippo Lippi," "Bishop Blougram's Apology," "Andrea del Sarto," "Cleon," "Love Among the Ruins," "Childe Roland to the Dark Tower Came."

Thomas Bulfinch, *The Age of Fable*—the American scholar's popular explications of myths: classic, Celtic, Oriental, and Scandinavian.

Charles Dickens, *Little Dorrit*—published in monthly parts to 1857; an elaborate mystery and a corps of minor characters complement the theme of the value of love; takes the reader from the Marshalsea Prison for debtors to the peaks of affluence, where all but the main character become arrogant and materialistic.

Alexandre Dumas fils, *Le Demi-Monde*—a French play about women living upon the fringes of respectable society, supported by wealthy lovers.

Gustav Freytag, *Soll und Haben* (Debit and Credit)—a realistic novel of German commercial life; the German writer's most significant literary achievement.

Elizabeth Gaskell, *North and South*—an English novel that contrasts the inhabitants of northern and southern England, as well as the relations existing there between employers and industrialists; suffering, and misfortune abound, but in the end, characters learn the need for understanding and humanity.

Washington Irving, *Life of Washington*—the American writer's five-volume study of the nation's first president published between 1855 and 1859; contemporary reviews applauded the biographer's efforts to humanize his subject; late twentieth-century biographers and historians hardly acknowledge its existence.

——————, *Wolfert's Roost and Miscellanies*—contains nineteen stories and sketches by the American writer, general essays, as well as pieces on Spanish legends and colonial American folklore.

Charles Kingsley, *Glaucus; or The Wonders of the Shore*—a minor work of fiction that displays the English novelist's enthusiasm for natural history.

——————, *Westward Ho!*—the most successful of the English writer's novels; a patriotic story of adventure, religious intrigue, and naval daring during the reign of Elizabeth I.

Henry Wadsworth Longfellow, *The Song of Hiawatha*—an American verse narrative based on the mythology and folklore of North American Indians.

Herman Melville, *Israel Potter: His Fifty-five Years of Exile*—an American novel about a Revolutionary War beggar, which the writer enlarged from a chapter in the subject's autobiography; a pleasant and picturesque tale highlighted by an episode from the sea battle between the *Serapis* and the *Bonhomme Richard*.

William Gilmore Simms, *The Forayers; or, The Raid of the Dog Days*—an American novel set in South Carolina during the later days of the Revolution; the rebel officer-hero does battle with the Tory relatives of his true love, as well as with a Tory or two in his own family.

Alfred, Lord Tennyson, *Maude*—an English monodramatic poem featuring a narrative who voices his morbid and unbalanced feelings upon such occasions as the mysterious death of his father, the ruin of his family, and the development of his love for Maude; he finally reawakens to life by serving his country.

Anthony Trollope, *The Warden*—the first novel in the Barsetshire series; an old church warden finds himself the object of unpleasant publicity and resigns to it rather than contests; in the end, his accuser marries his daughter, and good will prevails.

Walt Whitman, *Leaves of Grass*—the American poet's masterpiece, a work in which he attempted to prove himself to be the poet of democracy and common men and women; twelve poems, the most noted of which is "Song of Myself"; further, revised editions in 1856, 1860-1861, 1867, 1871, 1876, 1881-1882, 1889, 1891-1892.

Charlotte Yonge, *The Lances of Lynwood*—an early, romantic historical novel by the English writer.

EVENTS

John Bartlett, owner of the University Book Store, Cambridge, Massachusetts, publishes his book of *Familiar Quotations*.

The Daily Telegraph, the first London daily newspaper to sell for a penny, begins publication.

The New York Ledger, a combination newspaper and magazine, begins publication; to 1903.

The Saturday Club, Boston, founded; a gathering intended for informal literary discussion; the actual name for the group does not come until 1857.

The Saturday Review, a weekly periodical established in London to promote liberal interests, begins publication.

1856

BIRTHS

Sigmund Freud (d. 1929). Austrian psychologist and the founder of psychoanalysis.

H(enry). Rider Haggard (d. 1925). English novelist.

Frank Harris (d. 1925). British writer and journalist.

George Bernard Shaw (d. 1950). Irish dramatist, essayist, and critic.

DEATHS

Heinrich Heine (b. 1797). German poet and essayist.

PUBLICATIONS

Ralph Waldo Emerson, *English Traits*—the American writer's lectures on thinkers and writers of England.

Gustave Flaubert, *Madame Bovary*—an important French novel, a psychological portrait of a romantic young woman who, married to a dull provincial physician, becomes frustrated and lapses into vice; to 1857.

James Anthony Froude, *History of England from the Fall of Wolsey to the Defeat of the Armada*—a major work by the English historian, but one better as literature than as history because the writer allows his views of historical figures to be colored by his own judgments; 12 volumes, to 1869.

Victor Hugo, *Les Contemplations*—contains the best of the French writer's early poetry; demonstrates his musical powers and highly personal poetic voice.

Gottfried Keller, *Die Leute von Seldwyla*—a principal collection by the Swiss writer that includes one of his more noted short stories, "A Village Romeo and Juliet."

Herman Melville, "Bartleby the Scrivener"—published anonymously in *Putnam's Magazine (1853)* and reprinted in the American writer's collection, *The Piazza Tales* (1856); a highly symbolic short story focusing upon the sterility of the financial district of New York City and the death that comes to those who work in it.

————, "Benito Cereno"—a short story by the American novelist that explores the appearance versus reality theme; an American sea captain comes upon a Spanish slave master, who finds his way into a monastery.

George Meredith, *The Shaving of Shagpot; an Arabian Entertainment*—the English novelist's series of burlesque fantasies based on the premise of an enchanter holding a king and a city under a spell by means of one hair on his head.

Eduard Morike, *Mozard Auf der Reise Nach Prag* (Mozart's Journey from Vienna to Prague)—a novella by the German poet and clergyman; something of a minor masterpiece.

John Lothrop Motley, *The Rise of the Dutch Republic*—the climax of the Boston historian's ten-year study of the triumph of Protestantism, revealing his concept of similarities between the United States and the United Provinces; 3 volumes.

John Henry Newman, *Callista*—one of two novels by the Anglican turned Catholic prelate; describes the persecution and martyrdom of a third-century Christian convert, the sculptor Callista.

Conventry Patmore, *The Espousals*—one of four works in the English poet's long and popular sequence of poems (*The Angel in the House,* 1854-1863) in praise of married love.

Charles Reade, *It is Never too Late to Mend*—an English novel focusing upon abuse and brutality within the English prison system; a secondary theme considers the perils of gold mining in Australia during the gold rush.

Ernest Renan, *Etudes d'Histoire Religieuse* (Studies in the History of Religion)—a collection of essays by the French historian, who treats religion from a historical point of view.

William Gilmore Simms, *Charlemont*—another of the South Carolina novelist's "Border Romances" concerning life in the South; focuses upon a notorious murder in Kentucky.

——————, *Eutaw*—a romantic novel of the American Revolution, revolving around the battle at Eutaw Springs, South Carolina (8 September 1781).

Harriet Elizabeth Beecher Stowe, *Dred: A Tale of the Great Dismal Swamp*—an American novel emphasizing the demoralizing effects of slavery upon slaveowners; also depicts the cruelty inflicted upon slaves by slaveowners; extremely popular in England.

Ivan Turgenev, *Rudin*—the first of a series of novels by the Russian writer in which he relates individual lives to the social, political, and philosophical issues of the day.

John Greenleaf Whittier, *The Panorama and Other Poems*—a collection of American poems that includes "Maude Muller" and "The Barefoot Boy."

Charlotte Yonge, *The Daisy Chain*—an English novel focusing upon contemporary life; the profits from the novel went to build a missionary college in New Zealand.

EVENTS

Frankfurter-Zeitung begins publication at Frankfurt-am-Main.

Pierre Athanase Larousse, French lexicographer, publishes his *Nouveau Dictionnaire de la Langue Francaise.*

Porter's Spirit of the Times, New York popular periodical established by William Trotter Porter and George Wilkes; until 1861(?).

1857

BIRTHS

Joseph Conrad (Teodor Josef Konrad Korzeniowski; d. 1924). Polish-English novelist and short story writer.

George Gissing (d. 1903). English novelist.

Karl Adolf Gjellerup (d. 1919). Danish novelist; cowinner of the 1917 Nobel Prize for literature.

Henrik Pontoppidan (d.1943). Danish novelist; cowinner of the 1917 Nobel Prize for literature.

Hermann Sudermann (d. 1928). German dramatist and novelist.

DEATHS

Auguste Comte (b. 1798). French philosopher and sociologist.

Joseph Eichendorff (b. 1788). German Romantic poet and novelist.

Alfred de Musset (b. 1810). French Romantic poet, novelist, and playwright.

Eugene Sue (b. 1804). French novelist.

PUBLICATIONS

Charles Baudelaire, *Les Fleurs du Mal* (The Flowers of Evil)—a major work of the French Symbolist poet; originally condemned as obscene, but has become recognized as a poetic masterpiece; strong phrasing, imaginative rhythm, and expressive lyrics.

Bjornstjerne Bjornson, *Mellem Slagene* (Between the Battles)—the Norwegian playwright's first successful (and major) play; a historical drama during the reign of King Sverre (1150-1202); explores and celebrates the identity of Norway.

George Borrow, *The Romany Rye*—a fictional version of the English novelist's own wanderings, ornamented with his graphic descriptions of strange characters; the title, translated from the language of the gypsies, means "Gypsy Gentleman."

Dion Boucicault, *The Poor of New York*—the Irish-American playwright's melodrama based upon financial panic in 1857.

Charlotte Bronte, *The Professor*—written in 1846; a novel based upon the English writer's experiences in Brussels; a young man seeks his fortune in the Belgian capital.

Elizabeth Barrett Browning, *Aurora Leigh*—in 11,000 lines of blank verse, the English poet unveils the life of a woman writer; a novel in verse, complete with a melodramatic sub-plot.

George Eliot, *The Sad Fortune of the Rev. Amos Barton*—the sketch of an ordinary village curate who finally earns the respect of his parishioners through a series of his own misfortunes.

————, *Janet's Repentance*—a series of personal sufferings and losses underscores the continual conflict between evangelical religion and irreligion.

————, *Mr. Gilfil's Love-Story*—a country parson's attitudes and actions originate from a tragic love encounter.

[The three preceding tales by the English novelist first appeared in *Blackwood's Magazine* for 1857; published in two volumes as *Scenes of Clerical Life*, 1858]

Elizabeth Gaskell, *The Life of Charlotte Bronte*—this first and most noted biography of the English novelist contained a number of allegedly libellous statements that had to be withdrawn.

Thomas Hughes, *Tom Brown's Schooldays*—a fictional recreation of Rugby School during the English author's own days there; advocates the elimination of the "bullying system" prevalent then and a return to an independent attitude based upon Christian principles, physical courage, and school loyalty.

Francis Scott Key, *Poems*—the posthumously published collection containing the Maryland lawyer's most noted hymn, the "Star-Spangled Banner."

Charles Kingsley, *Two Years Ago*—the last of the English novelist's pieces on the general theme of reform; this one concerns poor sanitary conditions and public apathy, which allow the spread of cholera to a small fishing village in the west of England.

Henry Wadsworth Longfellow, *Santa Filomena*—published in the first number of the *Atlantic Monthly* (November 1857); a poetic tribute to Florence Nightingale and her service to the British troops during the Crimean War.

Herman Melville, *The Confidence Man*—the last novel to be printed during the American writer's lifetime; an unfinished satire upon human nature in a setting where distrust tends to replace confidence.

George Meredith, *Farina, a Legend of Cologne*—a commerically unsuccessful novel that attempted to burlesque German traditions.

John Ruskin, *The Political Economy of Art*—an essay (from a public lecture delivered in Manchester) in which the English art and cultural critic challenged the economic laws that affected his own intellectual and artistic interests.

Adalbert Stifter, *Der Nachsommer*—an Austrian tale underscoring the writer's love for humanity and traditional values.

William Makepeace Thackeray, *The Virginians*—the English novelist continues his story of the Esmond family, focusing upon Esmond's twin grandsons, George and Harry Warrington, and their experiences in England and America; published serially until 1859.

Anthony Trollope, *Barchester Towers*—the second novel in the "Barsetshire Series"; the English novelist records the struggle for control of a diocese; also focuses upon the political antagonisms of the day.

EVENTS

The Atlantic Monthly founded in Boston; focuses upon literature, the arts, and politics.

Crockford's Clerical Directory first published; a reference volume of facts relating to the Church of England and its clergy.

Harper's Weekly, an illustrated political and literary journal, begins publication in New York City; to 1916.

Russell's Magazine, Charleston, South Carolina, begins publication; a regional literary monthly; to 1860.

1858

BIRTHS

Alfred Doblin (d. 1957). German novelist and psychiatrist.

Selma Lagerlof (d. 1940). Swedish novelist; first woman to receive the Nobel Prize in literature (1909).

PUBLICATIONS

Matthew Arnold, *Merope, A Tragedy*—concerns the revenge of Aepytus on Polyphontes, who has killed Cresphontes, king of Messina and the father of Aepytus; Polyphontes, for political purposes, has proposed marriage to Merope, the widowed mother of Aepytus.

Thomas Bulfinch, *The Age of Chivalry*—the Boston scholar's study of Arthurian and Welsh legends.

Thomas Carlyle, *The History of Frederick II, Commonly Called Frederick the Great*—the English essayist's biographical magnum opus, begun in 1851; final volume published in 1865.

Octave Feuillet, *Roman D'un Jeune Homme Pauvre* (The Romance of a Poor Young Man)—a French epistolary novel, characterized by exact description and complex character relationships.

Elizabeth Gaskell, *My Lady Ludlow*—one of the English novelist's more interesting and still readable tales, published in Dickens's *Household Words* and republished in 1859 in the collection *Round the Sofa*.

Henry Gray, *Anatomy of the Human Body, Descriptive and Surgical*—the standard text in its field for more than a century, enhanced by the skilled drawings of a colleague at St. George's Hospital, London, Dr. H. Vandyke Carter.

Oliver Wendell Holmes, *The Autocrat of the Breakfast Table*—fictional conversations by the American writer and physician in which he presented his views on society with wit and wisdom; responsible for the author's literary popularity.

————————, *The Deacon's Masterpiece: The Wonderful One-Hoss Shay*—published first in

The Atlantic Monthly and (also in 1858) in *The Autocrat of the Breakfast Table;* an extended description of the sudden collapse of that century-old vehicle.

Henry Wadsworth Longfellow, *The Courtship of Miles Standish*—the New England poet's verse story, in hexameters, about the early days of the Plymouth, Massachusetts colony.

William Morris, *The Defence of Guenevere and Other Poems*—the collection contains, in addition to the title poem, such pieces as "The Haystack in the Floods," "Concerning Geffray Teste Noire," "Shameful Death," and "Golden Wings"; the poet combines themes of beauty and brutality and uses medieval settings.

Philip Schaff, *History of the Christian Church*— the Swiss-American Presbyterian theologian's attempt to bring American Protestant theology into line with Continental European trends, restoring the faith of the early reformers; enlarged during 1882-1894.

Tom Taylor, *Our American Cousin*—an English comedy focusing on the character of the brainless "Lord Dundreary"; presented at Ford's Theater, Washington, D.C., on the evening of Abraham Lincoln's assassination (14 April 1865).

Edward John Trelawny, *Records of Shelley, Byron, and the Author*—a series of lively and entertaining narratives about the author's relationships with the two English romantic poets; contains considerable inaccuracies.

Anthony Trollope, *Doctor Thorne*—the third in the London novelist's "Barsetshire Series"; focuses upon the then-delicate issues of seduction, illegitimacy, and adoption.

————————, *The Three Clerks*—three clerks marry the daughters of a widow; then follows a web of competition, temptation, arrest, imprisonment, and exile; reflects somewhat on the English novelist's own experiences in the Post Office.

EVENTS

Edward Payson Dutton, only seventeen years old, establishes the Boston publishing firm of E. P. Dutton and Company.

Francis S. Street and Francis Shubael Smith establish in New York Street and Smith Publications; they begin with the *New York Weekly.*

Under the editorship of Henry Clapp, the *Saturday Press* begins publication as a New York

City weekly literary newspaper; ceases publication in 1866.

Henry David Thoreau pleads for nature park reserves.

Alfred Russel Wallace and Charles Darwin present a joint paper before the Linnaean Society of London, Britain's oldest biological society, on the survival of the fittest in the struggle for existence in nature.

The pen name "Artemus Ward" appears in the *Cleveland Plain Dealer;* Charles Ferrar Browne signs that name to a letter to the editor.

1859

BIRTHS

Sir Arthur Conan Doyle (d. 1930). English author; creator of Sherlock Holmes.

Verner von Heidenstam (d. 1940). Swedish lyric poet.

Knut Hamsun (d. 1952). Norwegian novelist; lost popularity because of his Nazi sympathies.

A(lfred). E(dward). Housman (d. 1936). English poet, Oxford dropout, classical scholar, and recluse.

Kostis Palamas (d. 1943). Greek lyric poet and short story writer.

Francis Thompson (d. 1907). English poet and opium addict who suffered from tuberculosis.

DEATHS

Thomas De Quincy (b. 1785). English essayist and journalist.

Henry Hallam (b. 1777). English historian, lawyer, and commissioner of stamps.

Leigh Hunt (b. 1784). English essayist, journalist, and poet.

Washington Irving (b. 1783). American popular essayist, journalist, short story writer, and satirist.

Thomas Babington Macaulay (b. 1800). English historian, essayist, and Parliamentarian.

PUBLICATIONS

Pedro Antonio de Alarcon, *Diary of a Witness in the War in Africa*—Spanish narrative of the radical journalist's adventures in the African campaign of 1859.

William Barnes, *Hwomely Rhymes*—a collection of poems written in the poet's native Dorset dialect, a county on the south-central coast of England.

Dion Boucicault, *The Octoroon; or, Life in Louisiana*—the Irish-born playwright's attempt to confront the issues of slavery and pre-Civil War racial attitudes.

Richard Henry Dana, Jr., *To Cuba and Back*—another of the New England-born sailor-adventurer's narratives about life on board an American ship.

Charles Darwin, *On the Origin of Species by Means of Natural Selection*—the English scientist's earthshaking, controversial treatise; rejected Genesis–based views of the origins of species and proposed a theory of evolutionary descent from an ancestral source through genetic variation and the principle of natural selection.

Charles Dickens, *A Tale of Two Cities*—the English novelist's examination of social and political life in Paris and London at the outset of the French Revolution and during the "Reign of Terror"; an interesting exercise in complex character relationships.

George Eliot, *Adam Bede*—a realistic English novel focusing upon rural life.

Edward FitzGerald, *The Rubaiyat of Omar Khayyam*—the English poet's translation of the twelfth-century Persian poetic monument to the pleasures of the passing moment; FitzGerald's adaptation mocks the transcience of human grandeur and establishes a number of "philosophic" sayings that have endured for more than a century.

Ivan Aleksandrovich Goncharov, *Oblomov*—a satirical novel in which the Russian government official attacks human indolence.

Karl Marx, *Zur Kritik der Politischen Oekonomie* (Critique of Political Economy)—the prelude to the German political philosopher's magnum opus, *Das Kapital;* based upon the British government's economic policies and supported by Friedrich Engles' direct experience with British industry.

George Meredith, *The Ordeal of Richard Feverel*—an English novel that attacks parental tyranny and the artificial system of British private education; contains a series of sickly sentimental love affairs.

John Stuart Mill, *On Liberty*—an essay by the English philosopher arguing for social and political freedom from the tyranny of the majority and from prevailing conventions and opinions.

Leopold von Ranke, *History of England in the Sixteenth and Seventeenth Centuries*—the German historian approaches his subject from a purely political point of view, failing to consider the social aspects of English national development; not completed until 1867.

Ernest Renan, *Essais de Morale et de Critique*—a collection of essays on various moral and critical issues by the French philologist and historian.

John Ruskin, *The Two Paths*—a miscellany of critical lectures by the English essayist and art critic delivered during 1857-1859; the essays focus upon nature versus conventionalism in art; presents the idea of the lordly kingdom open to the architect as sculptor.

George Sand, *Elle et Lui*—concerns the French novelist's relationship with the French poet and dramatist Alfred de Musset (1810-1857).

Harriet Elizabeth Beecher Stowe, *The Minister's Wooing*—a novel set in New England, that attacks the injustices of Calvinism; based partly upon her own sister's life and experiences.

Alfred, Lord Tennyson, *Idylls of the King*—an attempt by the English poet to impose Victorian morality upon the old chivalric traditions; the strength of the piece lies in its descriptive passages; completed in 1885.

Henry David Thoreau, *A Plea for Captain John Brown*—the first of three essays wherein the Concord philosopher-poet eulogized Brown's actions at Harper's Ferry.

Pasquale Villari, *The Life of Savonarola*—the Italian historian's biography of Girolamo Savonarola (1452-1498), the Italian religious reformer.

EVENTS

The Cooper Union for the Advancement of Science and Art opens at Astor Place and Fourth Avenue, New York City.

The Rocky Mountain News, the first newspaper in what will become the Montana Territory, begins publication.

Daniel Decatur Emmett composes "Dixie," the national anthem of the future Confederate States of America.

George Wilkes establishes the popular periodical *The Spirit of the Times,* which runs until 1902.

Vanity Fair, the original humorous weekly, begins publication in New York City; runs through 1863.

Charles Dickens incorporates his weekly periodical *Household Words* into *All the Year Round,* which he edits until his death (1870).

Macmillan's Magazine, one of the first periodicals to print signed articles, begins publication in London; publishes poetry, serialized fiction, political essays, and travel narratives.

Vauxhall Gardens, London (adjoining St. James's Park), laid out in the seventeenth century and described by Samuel Pepys, Joseph Addison, Fanny Burney, and William Makepeace Thackeray, is closed.

1860

BIRTHS

Mirza Sadeq Khan Amiri (d. 1917). Persian poet and journalist; he will become a leading figure in the Iranian national revival; his verse will be classical in style, while its substance will chronicle the national revival, in which traditional culture assumed a modern guise.

Sir James Matthew Barrie (d. 1937). Scottish novelist and playwright; he will gain a reputation as a social satirist, but his association with "Peter Pan" will perhaps overshadow all of his other efforts.

Anton Pavlovich Chekhov (d. 1904). Russian dramatist, novelist, and writer of short fiction; he will become the most significant Russian writer of the generation following Leo Tolstoy and Fyodor Dostoevsky; he will probe deeply into the human condition and emerge as one of the principal writers of short fiction and drama, developing stylistic innovations in those genres.

Simon Dubnow (d. 1941). Russian-born historian and prose writer; his treatises will focus upon the history of Russian Jewry; he will produce a three-volume study of Hasidism, as well as a ten-volume history of the Jewish people.

Gustaf Froding (d. 1911). Swedish lyric poet; his popular collections will include songs, meditations, and poems in praise of nature.

Simeon Samuel Frug (d. 1916). Russian poet; he will write in three languages: Russian, Yiddish, and Hebrew; his folk themes will include expressions of his people's sufferings.

Egzi'abeher Gabra (d. 1914?). Ethiopian poet and government official; he will be the first poet to write in the Amharic language; he will demonstrate his wit by satirizing leading courtiers of King Menelik II; his work will carry on the older traditions of court poetry.

Hannibal Hamlin Garland (d. 1940). American fiction writer; his tales, partly autobiographical, will reflect the difficult life of the Midwest prairie; he will receive the Pulitzer Prize for biography/autobiography in 1922.

Salvatore di Giacomo (d. 1934). Italian poet; he will write songs and lyrics in the Neopolitan dialect, as well as compile historical and bibliographical works; he will become the librarian of the National Library at Naples.

Jules Laforgue (d. 1887). French poet, playwright, essayist, and writer of short fiction; he will become an early experimenter in free verse, a member of the French Symbolist school, and an advocate of abandoning literary conventions; he will advance the notion of art as the expression of the subconscious mind.

Mori Ogai (d. 1922). Japanese poet and translator; he will earn recognition for his translation of the Faust story into Japanese and for his adaptation of pieces by Hans Christian Andersen.

Abdul-halim Sharar (d. 1926). Urdu journalist, novelist, and popular historian; his quasi-historical romances in praise of the past glories of Muslim civilization will generally appear in serial form; he will also attack contemporary Christendom.

John Henderson Soga (d. 1941). South African poet, hymnodist, translator, and cleric; he will translate English religious tracts and sermons into the Xhosa language and compose hymns in that same tongue.

Mankayi Enoch Sontonga (d. 1904). South African poet and song writer; he will compose the national anthem of the Transkei, and in 1925 the African National Congress will adopt that piece as its anthem.

Togolok Moldo (d. 1942). Kirghiz (SSR) poet and folk singer; he will compose moral and didactic pieces, but after the Revolution of 1917, his themes will become politically charged.

DEATHS

Ernst Moritz Arndt (b. 1769). German poet and patriot; professor of history at Greifswald; he attacked serfdom and Napoleon I, while generally arousing the spirit of his nation; rose to become a professor at the new university in Bonn, where he died.

Johann Ludwig Heiberg (b. 1791). Dånish poet and playwright; introduced vaudeville to Danish theater and wrote musical comedy for that "genre"; his major poetic piece focuses on the theme of the search for a suitable afterlife; his literary reputation primarily derives from his experiments with the materials and techniques of comedy.

Arthur Schopenhauer (b. 1788). German philosopher; he failed in his attempt to achieve greater recognition than Georg Wilhelm Freidrich Hegel, but he considered himself the successor to Immanuel Kant; his most important prose focused upon the doctrine of the primacy of the will.

PUBLICATIONS

Charles Baudelaire, *Les Paradis Artificiels: Opium et Haschisch* (On Hashish and Wine as a Means of Expanding Individuality)—a volume by the French poet, critic, and translator documenting his experiments with hallucinogens; the work contains his translation of Thomas De Quincey's *Confessions of an English Opium Eater* and the poet's own "Poeme du Haschisch."

Bjornstjerne Bjornson, *En Glad Gut*—a peasant tale by the Norwegian novelist and playwright; intended to provide an image of Norwegian life that would be both recognizable and at the same time ideal, so as to motivate his readers.

Dion Boucicault, *The Colleen Bawn*—a comedy by the Irish-born playwright and actor; based upon the novel *The Collegians*, by Gerald Griffin, a tale of seduction and murder, one which the playwright further sensationalized.

Wilkie Collins, *The Woman in White*—a novel by the English writer, published serially; the extremely complicated plot of this mystery begins with a midnight encounter on a lonely road with a mysterious and agitated woman dressed in white.

Charles Dickens, *Great Expectations*—a novel by the English writer; concerns the development of the character of Philip Pirrip (or "Pip"), a village boy raised by his shrewish sister, the wife of a gentle, humorous, and kindly blacksmith; the main character learns from and eventually profits by a series of misfortunes; published serially through 1861.

Nikolai Alexandrovich Dobrolyubov, "Kogda zhe Prediot Nastroyaschi den?" (When Will the Day Come?)—an essay by the Russian critic and poet; in this review of Ivan Turgenev's novel *On the Eve* (1860), the writer ridicules the major characters of the work as "toothless squirrels"; he asks when Russia will produce men and women with enough strength to begin a revolution.

George Eliot, *The Mill on the Floss*—a novel by the English writer; a tale of unhappiness and tragedy focusing upon Tom and Maggie, the children of an honest but ignorant and obstinate miller; a number of entertaining and strong-willed characters help to reduce the somberness of the tragic events.

Ralph Waldo Emerson, *The Conduct of Life*— a collection of essays by the American writer exploring pragmatic as well as ideal tests of conduct; the collection is considered by some to be the culmination of the writer's prose work.

Thomas Chandler Haliburton, *The Season-Ticket*—a collection of fictional sketches and letters by the Canadian essayist and short story writer; the characters speak in their own dialects and convey their opinions on nations, social and political institutions, and their acquaintances and neighbors.

Bret Harte, *M'liss*—a novella by the American fiction writer; concerns the adventures of the title character, a young girl in the mining country during the gold rush period; included in several later collections.

Nathaniel Hawthorne, *The Marble Faun*—a novel by the American writer, the last work of fiction published during his lifetime; the story of Miriam, the beloved of Donatello, who carries the mixed blood of humanity and the legendary race of fauns; the writer leaves a number of unresolved mysteries; set in Rome, the work contains lush descriptions of the city and the Italian plains.

Oliver Wendell Holmes, *The Professor at the Breakfast Table*—a collection of vignettes by the American writer and physician, the second work in the "Breakfast Table series"; termed the height of "miscellaneousness," it combines a variety of styles and forms and presents Holmes's views on an equally various range of subjects.

Eugene Labiche, *Le Voyage de M. Perrichon*— a comic adventure drama by the French playwright, one that became a favorite classroom reading exercise; the action occurs in a railroad station, a country inn, and Paris.

Imre Madach, *Az Ember Tragediaja* (The Tragedy of Man)—a verse drama by the Hungarian poet, essayist, and writer of short fiction; a philosophical examination of the struggle between good and evil; structured as a dramatic poem of eleven dream segments; it relates the story of Adam, Eve, and Lucifer through a variety of historical reincarnations.

George Meredith, *Evan Harrington*—a novel by the English poet and writer of fiction; the story of a tailor's son whose sisters wish to establish a good position for him in society through a grand marriage; complications arise because of debt and the insistence of the young man's mother that he follow into the tailoring business.

Multatuli, *Max Havelaar*—a novel by the Dutch novelist, satirist, and government official; protests the abuses of the Dutch colonial system.

Aleksandr Ostrovsky, *Groza* (The Thunderstorm)—a five-act drama by the Russian playwright; depicts the harsh life of a lower-class merchant family dominated by a matriarch; depicts the grim and absurd environment of the Russian lower middle-class, while at the same time showing how the false values of society can tragically destroy a sensitive soul.

Victorien Sardou, *Les Pattes de Mouche* (A Scrap of Paper)—a light comedy of intrigue by the French playwright; focuses upon the mysterious contents of a love letter; the secret becomes exceedingly exaggerated in importance.

Alfred, Lord Tennyson, *Tithonus*—a dramatic monologue by the English poet; laments the unhappy fate of the Trojan prince, whose request for immortality fails to include continued youth and beauty; thus, he soon becomes old and decrepit.

John Greenleaf Whittier, *Home Ballads and Other Poems*—a verse collection by the American poet; includes "Skipper Ireson's Ride" and "Telling the Bees."

EVENTS

The Dial, a monthly literary and philosophical magazine and the organ of the western Transcendentalists, begins publication at Cincinnati, Ohio; Ralph Waldo Emerson, Bronson Alcott, and William Dean Howells are among the contributors.

James Orchard Halliwell-Phillipps, noted English Shakespearean scholar, publishes his *Dictionary of Old English Plays.*

The Northern Press begins publication at Liverpool, England, to 1863; it will change its name to the *Northern Press and Catholic Weekly Times* (1869-1870) before becoming the *Catholic Times* in 1870.

Christopher Latham Scholes, American inventor, devises a primitive model of what will become the typewriter; he will construct a model in 1867 and receive (with two others) a patent in 1868.

Joseph Emerson Worcester, Massachusetts lexicographer and a rival of Noah Webster, publishes his final effort, *A Dictionary of the English Language;* it will be overshadowed by an 1864 revision of Webster.

1861

BIRTHS

Gaston Fernando Deligne (d. 1913). Puerto Rican poet and journalist; he will write lightly melancholic verse in an extremely smooth style.

David Frishman (d. 1922). German Hebrew essayist and short fiction writer known for his satire and humor; he will write a series of essays on contemporary Hebrew literature.

Jose Rizal (d. 1896). Filipino national figure and writer; fluent in a number of European and Oriental languages, he will write principally in Spanish; his verse and his fiction will express the nationalistic feelings of the rising middle class.

Italo Svevo (b. Ettore Schmitz; d. 1928). Italian novelist; he will write psychological, introspective fiction, discovered and brought to the attention of the world by James Joyce.

Sir Rabindranath Tagore (d. 1941). Indian writer and philosopher; he will write fifty plays, one hundred volumes of verse, and forty novels and books of short fiction; he will rely on classical Indian literature for his sources.

Vazha-Pshavela (pseudonym of Luka Razikashvili; d. 1915). Georgian (SSR) poet; his epic poems will pose a tragic view of the world, presenting life as a constant battle between man and nature, the individual and the community, one tribe and another.

Alfred North Whitehead (d. 1947). English mathematician and philosopher; with Bertrand Russell, he will write a landmark study of logic, while his individual inquiries into the structure of science will provide the background for his metaphysical work.

Jurji Zaydan (d. 1914). Lebanese novelist, essayist, journalist, and historian; his work will express his deep pride in the Arab-Islamic cultural heritage; his fiction will place didacticism over characterization.

Grigor Zohrap (d. 1915?). Armenian writer; he will write short stories, novellas, novels, travel sketches, verse, and nonfiction prose (philosophical, critical, and political); he will strive to expose the inhumanity of bourgeois society in their dealings with the poor.

DEATHS

Elizabeth Barrett Browning (b. 1806). English poet; she displayed a gift for lyric poetry and ardently concerned herself with the liberal political causes of the day; her sonnet sequence recorded the stages of her love for her husband, Robert Browning.

Arthur Hugh Clough (b. 1819). English poet; he anticipates the "Angry Young Men" of English literature following World War II, who shared his contempt for class distinction and the capitalistic system.

Nikolai Alexandrovich Dobrolyubov (b. 1836) Russian essayist, poet, and critic; one of the most influential Russian literary critics of the nineteenth century; noted for his contribution to the philosophy of Russian revolutionary socialism; integrated revolutionary political theory into his literary criticism.

Friedrich Karl von Savigny (b. 1779). German jurist and prose writer; he wrote on the Roman law of property and on the legal codes of Prussia, which he helped to revise.

Augustin Eugene Scribe (b. 1791). French playwright and librettist; he wrote 374 separate dramatic pieces, mainly light satires of bourgeois foibles; formulated the intricately precise plot structure of the French "well-made" play; for him, action, suspense, and theatrics became more important than character development.

Taras Shevchenko (b. 1814). Ukranian poet and artist; published Ukranian ballads in Russian; he also wrote verse in opposition to serfdom and autocracy; he dies one week before the proclamation abolishing serfdom.

PUBLICATIONS

George Eliot, *Silas Marner*—a novel by the English writer; concerns the title character, a linen weaver driven from his small religious community by a false charge of theft; he takes refuge in the village of Raveloe, a figure of loneliness amidst a pile of gold; he finds happiness by adopting a stray child, an act that sets in motion the complexities of the plot.

Oliver Wendell Holmes, *Elsie Venner*—the earliest of three novels by the American writer and physician; advances the idea that criminals, vicious persons, and sinners ought not to be held solely responsible for their misdeeds; they should be educated, rather than punished; from another perspective, he set out to test the doctrine of original sin and human responsibility.

John Stuart Mill, *Utilitarianism*—an essay by the English philosopher and radical reformer; explicates the writer's modification of Benthamism; he admits to qualitative differences in pleasures and provides proofs of the two basic utilitarian principals: the intrinsic good of happiness and the right action providing for the happiness of the greatest number.

Charles Augustin Sainte-Beuve, *Chauteaubriand et Son Groupe Litteraire sous l'Empire*—a collection of lectures by the French essayist, poet, and writer of fiction; criticizes the shallowness of Romanticism and attacks such writers as Francois Rene de Chateaubriand and Honore de Balzac; the pieces appear to be exercises in retaliation—perceptive, but highly subjective.

EVENTS

Vladimir Dahl publishes his *Dictionary of the Living Russian Tongue;* to 1866.

The Rev. Sir Henry Williams Baker, vicar of Monksland, near Leominster, edits (with others) *Hymns Ancient and Modern;* the most significant English hymnal of nineteenth-century England in terms of the literary quality of the hymns; unofficially associated with the Church of England; supplements in 1889 and 1916; first major revision in 1950.

1862

BIRTHS

Gurajtada Wenkata Apparaw (d. 1915). Indian (Telugu) poet and playwright; he will write social drama in colloquial language, produce innovative metrical forms, and adapt spoken dialects to serious literary composition; he will be known for his spontaneity and unconventionality, discarding what he believed to be the pedantry of classicism.

Maurice Barres (d. 1923). French novelist and patriot; his work will celebrate nationalism, individualism, and provincial patriotism.

Georges Feydeau (d. 1921). French playwright; he will have a major influence on the development of the French comic theatre; through his manipulation of the key conventions of vaudeville and the bedroom farce.

Gerhart Hauptmann (d. 1946). German playwright and novelist; he will introduce to Germany the new social drama of Henrik Ibsen, Emile Zola, and August Strindberg; he will also introduce a new theatrical phenomenon, the collective hero; his naturalism will be tempered by compassion.

O. Henry (pseudonym of William Sydney Porter; d. 1910). American writer of short fiction; in his work, he will rely on coincidence and manipulated endings; his employment of exaggeration and caricature will be criticized, but those elements will not detract from his overall technical brilliance and boldness.

Maurice Maeterlinck (d. 1949). Belgian playwright and poet; he will become a disciple of the Symbolist movement, creating a number and variety of popular expositions of scientific subjects; he will receive the Nobel Prize for literature in 1911.

Sir Gilbert Parker (d. 1932). Canadian-born English prose writer and novelist; his fiction will reflect a strong interest in historical incidents.

Mirza Alakbar Sabir (d. 1911). Azerbaijan satirical poet; he will write timely satires of various political events in Turkey, Iran, and Azerbaijan.

Arthur Schnitzler (d. 1931). Austrian Jewish playwright and novelist; he will produce highly psychological and often erotic short plays and novels; he will analyze social problems arising out of familiar Viennese scenes.

Edith Newbold Jones Wharton (d. 1937). American writer of fiction; she will gain recognition for her subtle, ironic, and masterfully crafted fictional studies of turn-of-the-century New York society; she will also write travel literature, criticism, and poetry.

DEATHS

Francisco Martinez de la Rosa (b. 1787). Spanish playwright, poet, historian, and statesman; he is remembered for his contributions to Spanish Romantic drama.

Johann Nestroy (b. 1801). Austrian playwright; he wrote in excess of sixty dramatic pieces, most of them elaborate attacks upon theatrical sentimentality; his ability to play on words, thoughts, and afterthoughts revolutionized the Viennese theater.

Henry David Thoreau (b. 1817). American essayist and poet; known as "the hermit of Walden" and the friend of Ralph Waldo Emerson, he is remembered for his solitary reflections on nature; the daily journals he kept of his walks and studies of nature extended to thirty volumes when published.

Johann Ludwig Uhland (b. 1787). German lyric poet and leader of the "Swabian school"; known especially for his popular lyrics and astute literary essays.

PUBLICATIONS

Bjornstjerne Bjornson, *Sigurd Slembe*—a historical play by the Norwegian poet and playwright; the first piece in a trilogy that attempts to recreate, in the form of a dramatic saga, the epic past of Norway.

Fedor Mikhailovich Dostoevski, *Zapiski iz Myortvogo Doma* (The House of the Dead)—a novel by the Russian writer; a documentary of the novelist's imprisonment in Siberia during 1845-1859; reveals a compassion for the Russian lower classes, as well as insight into the issues of crime and guilt.

Gustav Flaubert, *Salammbo*—a novel by the French writer, his second published piece; focuses upon the struggle between Rome and Carthage; extensive in its presentation of archaeological detail.

Friedrich Hebbel, *Die Nibelungen*—a dramatic trilogy by the German playwright focusing upon legendary figures and settings; beneath the surface of the story line, however, runs the more complex theme of the Hegelian conflict between individuality (self-consciousness and beauty) and humanity as a whole.

Julia Ward Howe, "The Battle-Hymn of the Republic"—a poem by the American Unitarian suffragette and versifier; the piece has long been revered as the supreme expression of the evangelical zeal of the North in its war against the South and in its attempts to eliminate the institution of slavery.

Victor Hugo, *Les Miserables*—a novel by the French writer, considered one of the most memorable pieces of nineteenth-century fiction; the hero, a released convict whose bitterness is eased by a kindly churchman, experiences a tragic history of unfair legal penalties and must endure life in the Paris underworld; the work supports the novelist's conviction that existing laws and customs created and fostered social evils; praises the masses and offers the victims of social injustice the hope of redemption; the piece was influential in the movement for legal and social reform in nineteenth-century France.

George Meredith, *Modern Love*—a tragic poetic tale by the English writer; a series of fifty connected poems, each of sixteen lines; based upon the theme of passionate married love giving way to discord, jealousy, and intense unhappiness; in the end, the two separate, the wife meeting her death by poison.

Coventry Patmore, *The Victories of Love*—the last of a four-poem series by the English writer designed to be the apotheosis of married love.

Christina Rossetti, "Goblin Market"—a poem by the English writer, an allegorical fairy tale in verse; the heroine yields to the temptation of fruits offered by the goblins; the fruits represent worldly pleasures, and the lady wants more, but the goblins deny her request; she then falls sick and dies, but her sister braves the goblins' temptations and redeems her departed sibling.

Anthony Trollope, *Orley Farm*—a novel by the English writer; concerns the dispute over the validity of a codicil.

Ivan Turgenev, *Ottzy i Dyeti* (Fathers and Sons)—a novel by the Russian writer; focuses on the confrontation between two generations of Russians, the young liberals and the older generation of conservatives; in the character of Bazarov, the novelist introduces one of the earliest "nihilist" characters.

Philippe Auguste Villiers de l'Isle Adam, *Isis*—a novel by the French writer; a Symbolist piece, but strongly didactic; based upon Hegelian idealism and Wagnerian romanticism.

1863

BIRTHS

Shloime Ansky (pseudonym of Solomon Seinwil Rapoport; d. 1920). Russian Yiddish writer; he will incorporate folk elements into his fiction, specifically stories of peasants and the Hasidim.

Constantine Cavafy (d. 1933). Egyptian-born Greek poet; his poetry will often be set against the background of a mythic, Hellenistic world, populated with historical and imaginary figures; he will also concern himself with the issue of homosexual love.

Louis Couperus (d. 1923). Dutch poet and novelist; he will write a powerful tetralogy focusing upon the study and analysis of the human soul.

Gabriele D'Annunzio (d. 1938). Italian poet, novelist, poet, and soldier; the sensuous imagery of his early poetry will display unrivaled craftsmanship; his fiction, although shallow and theatrical, will demonstrate supreme control of language; he will become an early exponent of fascism, which will tarnish his literary reputation.

Richard Dehmel (d. 1920). German poet; his passionate and impressionistic verse will represent a revolt against naturalism; he will often devote his literary attentions to social problems.

George Santayana (d. 1952). Spanish-born philosopher and writer; his prose tracts will reflect his view that all thoughts and emotions exist in reaction to the physical world; nonetheless, he emphasized the mind's rational and imaginative vision of physical beauty; he also saw religion as an imaginative creation of real value.

DEATHS

Jakob Grimm (b. 1785). German philologist and folklorist; he became a founder of comparative philology, a student of Germanic languages, and a writer on German grammar and mythology; best known for his collection, with his brother, Wilhelm Grimm (1786-1859), of fairy tales.

Christian Friedrich Hebbel (b. 1813). German playwright; known for his tragedies linking romanticism and realism; his plays tend to portray the struggle between old and new values.

William Makepeace Thackeray (b. 1811). English novelist and satirist; his fiction included humorous sketches on social and literary trends, parodies of sentimental fiction, and satirical panoramas of upper and middle-class life.

Alfred Victor de Vigny (b. 1797). French poet, playwright, novelist, and writer of short fiction; a pioneer of the French Romantic movement, highly regarded during the nineteenth century.

PUBLICATIONS

Eugene Fromentin, *Dominique*—a novel by the French writer; relates the story of the title character's love for a young woman slightly older than he; her marriage to another man incites and dooms their passion for each other; the sheer honesty and evocative power of the piece produced a compelling contribution to the development of confessional literature.

Theophile Gautier, *Capitaine Fracasse*—a novel by the French writer of fiction and apostle of Romanticism; the dominant note of the piece focuses upon beauty, the principal motive being the search for it.

Nathaniel Hawthorne, *Our Old Home*—a series of sketches by the American writer; describes his observations, reactions, and experiences during a residence in England.

Henry Wadsworth Longfellow, *Tales of a Wayside Inn*—the first series of narrative poems by the American poet; narrated by New England speakers gathered about the fireplace of a wayside tavern, a form suggested by Geoffrey Chaucer and Giovanni Boccaccio; contains the familiar "Paul Revere's Ride" and the not always known "Saga of King Olaf."

Hippolyte Adolphe Taine, *Histoire de la Litterature Anglaise* (History of English Literature)—a literary history by the French historian and essayist; approaches his subject through a type of scientific objectivity and interdisciplinary analysis, contending that writers and artists are influenced by heredity, physical environment, and historical, social, and political circumstances; four volumes, to 1864.

EVENTS

Abraham Lincoln delivers his "Gettysburg Address" on 19 November, at the dedication of the Civil War cemetery at Gettysburg, Pennsylvania.

The Round Table, a New York City weekly journal of public opinion, begins publication; primarily features literary criticism from an American perspective; ceased publication during 1864-1865, then continued from 1866 to 1869.

1864

BIRTHS

Caetano da Costa Alegre (d. 1890). Black Portuguese poet; his work will be the first Portuguese verse to concern itself with African life and isolation in white society; he will focus upon his African heritage and the nobility of black women.

Hari Narayan Apti (d. 1919). Major Indian novelist and critic; he will look upon the social problems of his times from a moderately reformist point of view; specifically, he will address with sympathetic insight the subservient position of women in Hindu society.

Huseyin Rahmi Gurpinar (d. 1944). Turkish novelist; he will portray the various social classes, thus producing a valuable record of life there during the end of the nineteenth century.

Herman Heijermans (d. 1924). Dutch playwright, essayist, and writer of fiction, he will become the most significant Dutch playwright of the twentieth century; his plays will be meticulous studies of proletarian and middle-class life emphasizing the social inequities and sufferings arising from class conflicts.

Erik Axel Karlfeldt (d. 1931). Swedish poet; he will compose lyrics upon the subjects of nature, love and peasant life; he will be posthumously awarded the 1931 Nobel Prize for literature, a recognition that he had refused during his lifetime.

Sheikh Abdille Hasan Mahammed (d. 1920). Somali poet; he will compose highly alliterative verse, marked by puritanical religious fervor and extreme patriotism; his verse will be pictorial, containing vivid scenes of the desert and arid plains of his country.

Jules Renard (d. 1910). French diarist, novelist, and poet; he will produce one of the most important pieces of modern autobiographical writing, illuminating his own life as well as the literature of his contemporaries; his style will be vivid, succinct, and ironic.

Miguel de Unamuno (d. 1936). Spanish philosopher, poet, and prose writer; his tracts will convey his own highly individualistic sense of existentialism, as based upon one's faith in faith itself.

Frank Wedekind (d. 1918). German dramatist; as a forerunner of expressionism, he will stress in his plays the primal instincts of the human being.

Stefan Zeromski (d. 1925). Polish poet, novelist, and writer of short fiction; he will express a sincere concern for human freedom and social justice.

DEATHS

Nathaniel Hawthorne (b. 1804). American writer of fiction; he examined the gloomy and brooding spirit of New England Puritanism and created highly symbolic fiction that penetrated and explored complex moral and spiritual conflicts; he helped to establish the short story as an art form in America.

Walter Savage Landor (b. 1775). English poet and essayist; he spent much of his life in Italy, where he wrote poetry and a voluminous prose work consisting of imaginary dialogues between ancient and modern notables; his poetry took a number of different forms, ranging from epigram to epic.

Imre Madach (b. 1823). Hungarian playwright, poet, and writer of short fiction; his work undertook a philosophical examination of the struggle between good and evil; he also wrote satires on the Austrian government bureaucracy.

PUBLICATIONS

Robert Browning, *Dramatis Personae*—a collection of poems by the English writer; includes "Abt Vogler," "Prospice," "Rabbi ben Ezra," "A Death in the Desert," "Caliban upon Setebos," "Mr. Sludge," and "The Medium."

Charles Dickens, *Our Mutual Friend*—a novel by the English writer, published serially through 1865; the piece focuses upon what has been termed a "cultureless culture," middle-class parasites who flaunt their wealth and bribe their way into every known level of society; Victorian society, then, emerges as a dust pile, empty of culture, devoid of integrity, and barren of honesty and humanity.

Gustav Freytag, *Die Verlorne Handschrift* (The Lost Manuscript)—a realistic novel by the German playwright and writer of fiction; focuses upon German commercial life and activities.

Edmond and Jules de Goncourt, *Renee Mauperin*—a realistic novel by the French diarists and novelists; the heroine was patterned after a childhood friend of the brothers.

Henrik Ibsen, *Kongsemnerne* (The Pretenders)—a historical play by the Norwegian dramatist; probes the subject of national responsibility through the psychological study of the two principal characters; the limited man of action succeeds, but the visionary who hesitates fails.

George Meredith, *Emilia in England* (later entitled *Sandra Belloni*)—a novel by the English writer; the title character, a simple and hardworking woman, is the daughter of a disreputable Italian musician; she possesses a fine but untrained voice, and her ambition causes her to leave her family; afterwards she confronts speculators, love entanglements, and the loss of her voice.

John Henry Newman, *Apologia Pro Vita Sua*—an autobiographical essay by the English essayist, poet, and churchman; a spiritual history composed in response to Charles Kinglsey's accusation that Newman did not consider truth a necessary virtue.

Alfred, Lord Tennyson, *Enoch Arden*—a poem by the English writer; the title character, happily married, endures a shipwreck and a ten-year absence from his wife; she waits for his return, then reluctantly marries a suitor; Enoch returns, but vows not to disturb his wife's happiness; she will not know of the truth until after his death.

Leo Tolstoy, *Voina i Mir* (War and Peace)—certainly one of the most significant works of fiction in all Western world literature; represents the variousness of life and underscores the notion that the course of history must necessarily be determined by natural laws that guide the collective actions of anonymous masses of individuals (history proceeds, inexorably, to its own ends); vivid realism and acute characterization.

John Greenleaf Whittier, *In War Time and Other Poems*—a collection by the American poet including one of his most remembered pieces, "Barbara Frietchie," and emotional poem focusing upon the issue of country and flag.

EVENTS

Friedrich von Bodenstedt, a Munich professor, founds the Deutsche Shakespeare Gesellschaft, one of the most notable festivals in the history of Shakespearean performances and studies in Germany.

Frederick James Furnivall, English scholar, founds the Early English Text Society for the publication of Early English and Middle English texts. *Neue Frie Presse* founded at Vienna.

The *Oneida Circular*, a periodical of the Oneida religious society in upstate New York, begins publication; a popular weekly until 1876.

The Radical Club, an association of New England clerics and laymen, begins regular meetings; attempts to cast off supernaturalism and to embrace free religion and a general love of humanity; Bronson Alcott was one of its more notable literary members.

1865

BIRTHS

Micah Joseph Berdyczewski (d. 1921). Ukranian Hebrew essayist and novelist; his thinking will parallel that of Friedrich Nietzsche, declaring the Superman of power and will, the merciless man for whose ambition masses of people might proceed to their doom; he will also rebel against the sages of the Talmud; his fiction will bemoan the collapse of the traditional Jewish family.

Ayodhyasimh Upadhyay Hariaudh (d. 1941). Hindi poet and prose writer; he will write the first modern Hindi epic poem, maintaining national struggles to be more important than personal problems; he will also write satirical verse and prose fiction criticizing the system of forced marriages.

Rudyard Kipling (d. 1936). English poet and writer of fiction; his most successful pieces will dramatize the life and times of nineteenth-century Indian colonialism; he will become known as the most vocal and sincere literary voice of English imperialism; his poems and stories for children will become extremely popular.

Dmitry Sergeyevich Merezhkovsky (d. 1941). Russian novelist, essayist, poet, playwright, and biographer; he will become a leader among Russian Symbolist writers and help to initiate the Russian modernist movement at the turn of the century; his work will reflect the development of a neo-Christian philosophy, attempting to combine Orthodox Christianity with ancient Greek paganism; his work will also express the desire for a worldwide religious revolution generating from within Russia.

Janis Rainis (pseudonym of Janis Plieksans; d. 1929). Latvian poet and playwright; his writing will reflect his political activism; his plays, in particular, will be strongly nationalistic, advocating Latvian independence from Russian and German domination.

Arthur Symons (d. 1945). Welsh-born poet, translator, and essayist; he will strive to familiarize the British with the literature of France and Italy, particularly with his translations of Charles Baudelaire and Gabriele D'Annunzio; he will write on Romanticism and Symbolism.

Albert Verwey (d. 1937). Dutch poet; he will become a leader of literary progressivism, producing melodious and evocative verse; his later poetry will be characterized by complexity of substance and dissonance of tone.

William Butler Yeats (d. 1939). Irish poet, playwright, and essayist; he will initiate the Irish Renaissance and receive the Nobel Prize in 1923; the subjects of his work will range from nationalism and transcendentalism to physical realism and the strict polarity between the physical and the spiritual.

DEATHS

Fredrika Bremer (b. 1801). Swedish novelist and narrative writer; considered the first Swedish novelist of manners, she produced fictional accounts of upper-middle-class family life; her work is characterized by an inspirational moral tone and the accurate portrayal of Swedish customs.

Elizabeth Gaskell (b. 1810). English novelist; her fiction focuses upon a variety of social conditions in England, portraying both provincial life and the manufacturing and working classes; she possessed the true artist's sensitivity to economic and social fact.

Thomas Chandler Haliburton (b. 1796). Canadian essayist and writer of short fiction; a pioneer in the development of Canadian and American humorous literature; created the character of "Sam Slick," an irreverent braggart of New England known for his craft as a peddler.

Otto Ludwig (b. 1813). German playwright and writer of fiction; he undermined his literary efforts by unsuccessfully attempting to compete with Friedrich Hebbel and Franz Grillparzer in developing drama from historical and mythical sources; as a critic, however, he succeeded in developing clear theoretical principles on the laws and techniques of the drama.

PUBLICATIONS

Matthew Arnold, *Essays in Criticism*—a prose volume by the English poet and essayist establishing Arnold's belief in the wide range and significance of literary criticism.

Lewis Carroll, *Alice's Adventures in Wonderland*—a children's story and political satire by the English writer and mathematician; concerns a little girl who dreams that she pursues a white rabbit down a rabbit hole; there she meets strange adventures and odd characters (the Cheshire Cat, the Mad Hatter, *et al*); the debate still continues regarding the piece: Did the writer attempt to entertain his readers, or to frighten them? Does the "madness" of his characters represent their lack of sense or their intense anger?

Bankim Chandra Chatterji, *Durgesnandini* (Durgesa Nandini; or, The Chieftain's Daughter)—a novel by the Indian writer, published in the Bengali language; the first Bengali novel in the modern European style, as well as the first product of creative imagination in Bengali prose; a historical romance set in the sixteenth century during the conflict between the Moguls and the Pathans; the writer makes no attempt at historical accuracy.

Abraham Mapu, *Ashmat Shomeron*—a novel by the Jewish Lithuanian writer in the Hebrew language; set in the time of Agaz, King of Judah; the piece contrasts the righteous, enlightened Jerusalemites with the evil idolaters of Samaria; there exists an obvious parallel between the two ancient kingdoms and contemporary proponents of Haskalah and Hassidism; an English translation bears the title *The Guilt of Samaria.*

Autero de Quental, *Odes Modernas*—a collection of poems by the Azores-born Portuguese poet; the pieces reflect the richness and vitality of his ideas (a number of them political), but demonstrate his lack of concern with poetic technique.

Algernon Charles Swinburne, *Atalanta in Calydon*—a verse drama by the English writer; written in the classical Greek form, with choruses that evidence the poet's mastery of melodious verse, particularly the hymn to Artemis.

Walt Whitman, *Drum-Taps*—a collection of poems by the American writer; calling upon his first hand experience of the terrible suffering caused by war; contains apocalyptic visions of Democracy at the head of an energetic and vigorous nation; also includes poems that capture the grief of stricken families and a tribute to Abraham Lincoln.

EVENTS

Isaac Thomas Hecker, New York-born former Transcendentalist and founder of the Paulist Fathers, begins publication of *The Catholic World,* a monthly magazine of philosophy, religion, and literature; it will become the *New Catholic World* in 1971.

The Contemporary Review, a London political, literary, and religious journal, begins publication; it will eventually become a journal devoted to current affairs.

The Fortnightly Review begins publication at London as a journal to promote liberal ideas; it will change from a fortnightly to a monthly periodical, merging with *The Contemporary Review* in 1955; published fiction, poetry, and prose nonfiction by Anthony Trollope, Walter Bagehot, William Makepeace Thackeray, George Eliot, Matthew Arnold, Thomas Huxley, Thomas Hardy, Dante Rossetti, Henry James, Rudyard Kipling, H. G. Wells, James Joyce, and Ezra Pound.

The Nation begins publication in New York City as a weekly journal to promote a number of political and social causes; its influence can be measured by the extent to which preachers, lecturers, and editors throughout the nation "lifted" its ideas and substance; published extensive criticism of American arts and letters.

Frederick Greenwood founds at London The Pall Mall Gazette, combining the features of a newspaper with those of a literary magazine; Anthony Trollope is among its early contributors.

The Radical, the literary organ of The Radical Club, the informal association of New England ministers and laymen, begins publication; until 1872.

The San Francisco Chronicle and ***The San Francisco Examiner*** begin publication.

1866

BIRTHS

Jeppe Aakjaer (d. 1930). Danish poet and novelist; his lyrical pieces will appear between 1906 and 1924; his native Jutland will form the setting and provide the themes for his fiction.

Jacinto Benavente y Martinez (d. 1954). Spanish playwright; his plays will contain strong social satire and introduce a natural and meaningful diction; he will receive the Nobel Prize in literature in 1922.

Joseph Ephraim Casely-Hayford (d. 1930). Ghanian novelist and writer of nonfiction; he will become a pioneering scholar of African studies, an influential nationalist, and a leading political philosopher; his work will promote Pan-Africanism, criticize African colonial society, and recommend cultural advancement throughout Africa.

Benedetto Croce (d. 1952). Italian philosopher, historian, and literary critic; his work will be recognized for its study of modern idealism, extending to such areas as literary criticism, aesthetics, and cultural history.

Euclides Rodrigues da Cunha (d. 1909). Brazilian historian, poet, and essayist; his narratives and historical accounts, drawing upon a wide and diverse range of disciplines, will significantly influence Brazilian fiction; he will attract attention for his clear discussion of the complex composition of the Brazilian population, and for his personal search for a common Brazilian identity.

Hakob Hakobian (d. 1937). Armenian poet and revolutionary; he will depict the difficult lives of Armenian workers and forecast future possibilities for the working class; he will also turn his attention to socialism and industrialization and popularize Armenian proletarian poetry.

Kesavsut (pseudonym of Krsnaji Kesav Damle; d. 1905). Indo-Iranian poet; the first major versifier of modern Marathi; his poems are anguished responses to the ills of humanity, reflecting fierce indignation, melancholy, and despair.

U Lat (d. 1921). Burmese novelist; he will inject elements of classical Burmese drama into fiction and satirize contemporary life; he will also defend traditional culture against foreign influence.

Sigbjorn Obstfelder (d. 1900). Norwegian poet, novelist, essayist, and playwright; his work will be characterized by inventive language, unconventional forms, and mystical symbolism, in combination with a brooding sense of alienation and restlessness; he will strive for unity with society, the universe, and God.

Beatrix Potter (d. 1943). English children's writer and illustrator; her *Adventures of Peter Rabbit* will gain enduring recognition as a pastoral romance and record of initiation and maturity; she will also engage in accurate and meaningful family-role stereotyping.

Romain Rolland (d. 1944). French novelist, biographer, historian, essayist, and playwright; his fiction, in particular, will reveal his ardent pacifism and humanitarianism; he will explore in his work the fundamental unity of all existing objects, while delineating his conception of humanity's proper role in the universal scheme; he will receive the Nobel Prize for literature in 1915.

Joseph Lincoln Steffans (d. 1936). American essayist, novelist, and journalist; he will become prominent as a "muckraker," a group of writers who will expose corruption in government and industry.

Ramon de Valle Inclan (d. 1936). Spanish fiction writer; he will achieve notoriety for his erotic tales and grotesque caricatures of Spanish life; he will attack brutality among the military and the aristocracy.

Herbert George Wells (d. 1946). English novelist, essayist, and historian; developed, with Jules Verne, the literature of science fiction late in the nineteenth century.

Usakligil Halit Ziya (d. 1945). Turkish novelist; he will become the first Turkish writer to inject into his fiction modern colloquial language, having been influenced by the "art for art's sake" movement of Western Europe.

DEATHS

Carl Jonas Almqvist (b. 1793). Swedish writer; his novels, stories, poems, and plays were collected and published between 1832 and 1851; the style of his works ranged from realism to romanticism; accused of forgery and murder, he lived in the United States, then in Germany, where he died.

Thomas Love Peacock (b. 1785). English novelist and poet; satirized the intellectual trends of his day in loosely structured "novels of conversation"; in general, he represented the reasonable man standing in opposition to morbid romance, mechanical politics, unreasonable scientific advancement, and transcendental philosophy.

Friedrich Ruckert (b. 1788). German poet and Oriental scholar; after flirtations with German patriotism and nationalism, he focused his attention upon recasting, in German verse, the major texts of Oriental literatures; in 1902, Gustav Mahler set to music the poet's songs for children (published 1872).

PUBLICATIONS

Fedor Dostoevski, *Prestuplenie i Nakazanie* (Crime and Punishment)—a novel by the Russian writer, one of the most significant pieces of Western fiction; concerns the story of Rodion Raskolnikov, a young and impoverished law student, who determines to commit murder to see if he can circumvent social restrictions and prove himself an extraordinary individual above the law; in the end, guilt overcomes the murderer: he confesses and is convicted and sentenced to Siberia, where he develops humanitarian instincts through his own suffering; an example of human redemption achieved through human suffering.

George Eliot, *Felix Holt the Radical*—a novel by the English writer; the title character is a noble-minded young reformer willing to sacrifice in order to support his political convictions; he chooses the life of a humble artisan to prove to his fellow workers that hope for improvement in their condition lies in education and independent thought, not in following the stilted programs of politicians.

Emile Gaboriau, *L'Affaire Lerouge* (The Widow Lerouge)—a serialized novel by the French writer, based upon a contemporary crime; innovative in its emphasis on the criminal investigation process and on the two detectives who attempt to solve the case; many critics view the work as the first true detective novel.

Nikolai Nekrasov, *Komu na Rusi Zhit Khrosho* (Who Can Be Happy and Free in Russia?)—an unfinished poem by the Russian writer that appeared in a series of installments; concerns a group of peasants engaged in a debate over who can possibly be happy with his lot in life; each argues in favor of a different class of society, from peasant to czar; they then decide to travel throughout Russia to seek the answer: they find few satisfied people, and even less who have escaped any hardship.

Christina Rossetti, *The Prince's Progress*—an allegorical piece by the English poet; a prince, on his way to see his appointed bride, endures a long and arduous journey; he yields to various allurements, finally arriving to discover that his bride has died.

John Ruskin, *The Crown of Wild Olive*—four lectures by the English writer; the subjects concern war, the future of England, work, and buying and selling; the title, originating from the only prize at the Olympic games, represents the thesis of the four lectures: the importance of not striving for a false idea of reward.

Algernon Charles Swinburne, *Poems and Ballads*—a verse collection by the English writer; includes "Laus Veneris," "Dolores," and "A Litany"; the pieces generally repudiate conventions and embrace the spirit of paganism.

John Greenleaf Whittier, *Snow-Bound*—a poetic idyll by the American writer; a quiet tribute to the passing of rural New England life and rural New England dreams; in their place will come the new ways of an emerging urban America.

EVENTS

Every Saturday, a miscellaneous weekly magazine, begins publication at Boston; principally contains reprints of pieces by foreign writers; until 1874.

The Galaxy, a monthly literary magazine, begins publication at New York City; becomes a rival to the *Atlantic Monthly* and will publish works by such writers as Henry James and Walt Whitman; until 1878.

Pierre Athanase Larousse, French lexicographer, publishes his *Grand Dictionnaire Universel du XIX Siecle;* fifteen volumes to 1876.

Juan Montalvo, Ecuadorean essayist and political journalist, begins to publish his political journal, *El Cosmopolita;* the sheet will publish attacks upon the tyrants Garcia Moreno and Veintimilla; until 1869.

The New York World begins publication as a daily religious newspaper; it will not achieve recognition until its purchase in 1883 by Joseph Pulitzer; until 1931.

1867

BIRTHS

Sayyid Shaykh bin Sayyid Ahmad Al-Hadi (d. 1934). Malay novelist and journalist; he will be largely responsible for introducing the novel to peninsular Malay literature, principally through adaptations of Arabic originals with Egyptian or other Middle Eastern settings; he will explore a variety of contemporary social situations and changing mores.

Shio Aragvispireli (d. 1926). Georgian (SSR) writer of short fiction; he will become a leading populist writer with stories of village life describing the misery and helpless despair of simple and honest people.

Arnold Bennett (d. 1931). English novelist and playwright; his realistic fiction will focus upon the industrial Midlands, revealing the influence of Emile Zola and French naturalism; he will offer in-depth analyses of regional life.

Vicente Blasco Ibanez (d. 1928). Spanish novelist; his anti-monarchist sentiments will find their way into his fiction, underlying his realistic focus upon provincial life and social revolution.

Raul Brandao (d. 1930). Portuguese novelist; his work will principally concern itself with the tragic lives of poor people, revealing a nightmarish world of suffering caused by inexplicable forces.

Ruben Dario (d. 1916). Nicaraguan poet and statesman; he will exercise a significant influence upon Spanish-language writers as one of the founders of the "modernismo" movement, which stressed among other elements, elegant form and exotic imagery.

Ernest Christopher Dowson (d. 1900). English poet; he will produce delicate and highly musical verse, becoming a leader of the "decadent school," with emphasis upon the morbid and macabre elements of human emotion.

Tevfik Fikret (d. 1915). Turkish poet and painter; his poetry will attack sultanic rule, welcome the Russian revolution of 1905, and enthusiastically support the Turkish revolution of 1908; technically, he will reject grammatical rhymes and introduce rhymes based upon the sounds of the words.

John Galsworthy (d. 1933). English novelist and playwright; his best fiction will trace three generations of a complacent upper-middle-class family during 1880-1920; his drama, highly successful in its time, will concern itself with key social issues; he will receive the Nobel Prize for literature 1932.

Henry Archibald Hertzberg Lawson (d. 1922). Australian poet and writer of short fiction; he will write stories of the Australian bush country, known for their simplicity of language and style and vivid realism; he will treat the theme of Australian "mateship," the idealized concept of friendship in an extremely rugged part of the world.

Nar-Dos (pseudonym of Mikhayel Hivhannisian; d. 1933). Armenian novelist, poet, and playwright; he will develop the psychological novel, concentrating upon urban intellectuals at the turn of the eighteenth and nineteenth centuries in the major cities of Transcaucasia; his fiction will provide commentary upon social and family relationships, in addition to sharp character analyses.

Phan-boi-Chau (d. 1940). Vietnamese poet, essayist, and political pamphleteer; he will commit himself to the political struggles against France, attempting to influence young revolutionaries through his prose and poetry; his work will appear in both Chinese and Vietnamese languages.

Tawfiq Piramerd (d. 1950). Kurdish poet, essayist, and journalist; his major literary project will be to preserve and popularize Kurdish folk works, an outgrowth of his desire to educate his people through their own literature; he will also strive to retain the purity of the native language, helping to establish the Sulaimani dialect as the literary language.

Luigi Pirandello (d. 1936). Italian playwright, poet, and writer of fiction; he will become one the the most significant dramatists of the twentieth century, skillfully manipulating philosophical themes and experimenting with traditional dramatic structure; his themes will reflect his obsession with the relationship between reality and appearance and between sanity and madness.

Wladyslaw Stanislaw Reymont (d. 1925). Polish novelist and writer of short fiction; he will attack modern industrial society and create a great prose epic of modern Polish village life; he will receive the Nobel Prize for literature in 1924.

Koda Rohan (pseudonym of Koda Shigeyuki; d. 1947). Japanese novelist, short story writer, poet, and essayist; he will reject the prevailing Naturalist and sociopolitical Realist trends in Japanese art, revealing, instead, his devotion to the themes and techniques of Chinese literature; his fiction will be highly idealistic, ornate, and traditional.

George William Russell (d. 1935). Irish poet and essayist who will adopt the signature AE and become a recognized figure of the Irish Renaissance; his verse will express his mysticism.

Mayer Andre Marcel Schwob (d. 1905). French biographer, essayist, short story writer, and translator; he will become an important figure in the French Symbolist Movement and an authority on medieval and classical French literature.

Isaiah Shembe (d. 1935). South African (Zulu) poet and hymnodist; a self-appointed messiah and Christ figure, he will write in excess of 225 hymns expressing his desire for Zulu-Christian integration, teaching a number of them to the children who followed him.

Masaoka Shiki (d. 1902). Japanese poet, essayist, and writer of short fiction; he will be considered responsible for the early twentieth-century revitalization of the haiku and the tanka and he will establish criteria for preserving the essential aspects of the poetic heritage of Japan.

DEATHS

Charles Baudelaire (b. 1821). French poet, essayist, and translator; considered one of the significant lyric poets of Western literature; his art supports his belief that the individual, if left to his own devices, will be damned because of his own inherent evil; thus, only the artificial can be considered absolutely good, and therefore, poetry should exist only to inspire and express beauty; after a lecture tour to Belgium, he suffers a stroke.

Abraham ben Jekutiel Mapu (b. 1808). Lithuanian Jewish novelist, the first to compose novels in the Hebrew language; he blended elements of European Romanticism with the language and themes of the Bible, thus fashioning a new form of historical romance the biblical novel; he will die, in illness and poverty, on Yom Kippur, the Jewish Day of Atonement.

PUBLICATIONS

Matthew Arnold, *New Poems*—a major collection by the English poet and essayist; contains such pieces as "Thyrsis," "Rugby Chapel," "Heine's Grave," "A Southern Night" (a lament on the death of his brother, William Delafield Arnold, Director of Public Instruction in the Punjab), "Dover Beach," "Growing Old," and "Stanzas from the Grande Chartreuse."

Francois Coppee, *Le Reliquaire*—the first collection of poetry by the French writer, received with favor by readers and critics; the pieces exemplify Parnassian ideals of rigid formalism, semantic precision, and objective responses to ideas and objects.

Charles de Coster, *La Legende de Thyl Ulenspiegel*—a prose epic in Old French by the Munich-born Belgian writer and storyteller; he spent ten years writing the piece; an English translation in 1918.

Bret Harte, *Condensed Novels and Other Papers*—a series of humorous sketches by the American writer of short fiction; clever parodies of popular novelists, including Charles Dickens, Alexandre Dumas, Victor Hugo, Washington Irving, and James Fenimore Cooper.

Henrik Ibsen, *Peer Gynt*—a dramatic poem by the Norwegian playwright; focuses upon a picaresque folk hero from the Gudbrandsdal region of Norway who lives in a fused state of reality and fantasy in an effort to discover his identity and purpose; for the Norwegian poet-playwright, the title character stands somewhere between the soaring, romantic aspiration of Faust and the haunting search for self in the modern political world.

Sidney Lanier, *Tiger-Lilies*—a novel by the American poet; primarily written during the writer's tenure in a Confederate army camp, the work recounts his experiences during the Civil War.

Karl Marx and Friedrich Engels, *Das Kapital: Kritik der Politischen Okonomie* (Capital: A Critical Analysis of Capitalistic Production)—a prose tract, principally by Marx, the German philosopher and essayist; details the history of capitalism, its characteristics, and the events the writer believes will lead to its inevitable decline and destruction; three volumes, only one of which was published during Marx's lifetime.

William Morris, *The Life and Death of Jason*—a poem in heroic couplets by the English writer; the tale of Jason and Medea, the Argonauts, and the Golden Fleece.

John Ruskin, *Time and Tide by Weare and Tyne*—a volume of twenty-five letters by the English writer addressed to a working man of Sunderland on the laws of work; thoughts on social reconstruction, conveying the writer's hope for a happier world and for the disappearance of luxury, poverty, greed, and suffering.

Algernon Charles Swinburne, *A Song of Italy*—a poem by the English writer; written during and about the struggle for Italian independence; emphasizes the poet's dislike of kings and priests and his support of the Italian patriot, Guiseppe Mazzini (1805-1872).

Anthony Trollope, *The Last Chronicle of Barset*—the final novel in the Barsetshire series, with all characters having appeared in earlier works; focuses upon the problems of the Rev. Josiah Crawley, the perpetual curate of Hogglestock—his mistakes, his persecution, and the eventual establishment of his innocence.

Ivan Turgenev, *Dym* (Smoke)—a novel by the Russian writer of fiction; principally concerns the Slavophile-Western intellectual and cultural controversy then underway in Russia; for the writer, Russian intellectualism exists as mere "smoke."

Mark Twain, *The Celebrated Jumping Frog of Calaveras County and Other Sketches*—a collection of short fiction by the American writer, his first significant work; he focuses upon creating the highest sense of the comic out of all that he had seen and heard; the majority of the pieces are set in the West; the frog of the title carries the name "Dan'l Webster" and functions as a gambler's pet.

Paul Verlaine, *Poemes Saturnines*—a collection by the French poet, his first volume of verse; characterized by youthful morbidity and criticized for attempting to rival the work of Charles Baudelaire.

John Greenleaf Whittier, *The Tent on the Beach, and Other Poems*—a collection by the American poet, a cycle of verse narratives much in the manner of Henry Wadsworth Longfellow; includes "The Eternal Goodness," a piece emphasizing the poet's faith and love of God.

Emile Zola, *Therese Raquin* (The Devil's Compact)—a naturalistic novel by the French writer; an extremely powerful and detailed depiction of pure remorse.

EVENTS

Harper's Bazar (later *Bazaar*), a weekly political and literary journal for women, begins publication in New York City; it will not assume its "fashion" mode until early in the twentieth century.

Reclams Universal Bibliothek, the first completely paperbound series of books, founded at Leipzig; Johann Wolfgang von Goethe's *Faust*, Part I (published first in 1775) is the initial number.

The Southern Review, Baltimore, Maryland, begins publication; prints prose and poetry to promote the culture of the South; until 1879.

1868

BIRTHS

Gabra Iyasus Afawark (d. 1947). Ethiopian novelist, poet, and prose writer; he will write Italian tracts upon the Amharic language, as well as an early edition of Psalms; generally, his work will reflect a deep consciousness of Italian culture, but will also evidence an equal concern for the preservation of Ethiopian life and thought.

Paul Claudel (d. 1955). French playwright and poet; his written work will complement his mystical Catholicism; his diplomatic experience and the early influence of the Symbolists will add quality and richness to his writings.

Stefan George (d. 1933). German poet; he will come under the influence of Greek classical forms and the French Symbolists; his verse will combine elements of the pure and the esoteric, while attempting to purify the German language.

Maxim Gorky (d. 1936). Russian writer of fiction and poetry; he will illustrate the vigor and nobility of Russian peasants, workers, and vagabonds, eventually developing the prototype of the Russian revolutionary novel; in general, his work will combine elements of realism with a strong poetic strain emphasizing vitality and optimism.

Gaston Leroux (d. 1927). French novelist, playwright, and writer of short fiction; he will achieve recognition for his contributions to the detective novel and the horror story; further, he will learn how to capture the imagination of audiences, providing legitimacy to the character of the "phantom."

Edgar Lee Masters (d. 1950). American poet; he will gain literary acclaim for a series of free-verse epitaphs revealing the personal lives of small-town Americans; in addition, his biographies of Walt Whitman and Abraham Lincoln will prove deserving of recognition.

Gustav Meyrink (d. 1932). Austrian novelist, writer of short fiction, playwright, and translator; he will be recognized for his supernatural fiction; his outline in his novels of the individual's quest for spiritual enlightenment will evidence a variety of influences, including Christian and Jewish mysticism, Eastern philosophy, and occultism.

Edmond Rostand (d. 1918). French poet and playwright; he will awaken and briefly perpetuate the Romantic spirit of French dramatic literature during the height of the Naturalistic period.

Ahmad Shawqi (d. 1932). Egyptian poet and playwright; his literary work will span both the old and the new, both Arabic and Islamic; he will write historical fiction, poetry, and comic historical drama; he will glorify both ancient Egypt and Persia, in addition to the traditions of Muslim Spain.

Mahmud Tarzi (d. 1935). Afghan statesman, poet and prose writer; he generally attempted to focus his literary efforts upon "new" subjects: science, coal, roads, telegraphic communications; he also spent time translating the novels of Jules Verne into his dialect of Persian (Dari).

DEATHS

Adalbert Stifter (b. 1805). Austrian (Bohemian) writer of fiction and folk tales; his tales of the Bohemian Forest became extremely popular because of the writer's view of the harmony between nature and human-kind.

PUBLICATIONS

Louisa May Alcott, *Little Women*—a novel by the American writer, principally intended for girls; a moralistic portrayal of family life, emphasizing domesticity and female solidarity; all problems can be solved by love and mutual support; nonetheless, the commitment to the family does hinder the drive for individuality; a second part in 1869.

Edmondo de Amicis, *La Vita Militre* (The Military Life)—a novel by the Italian writer composed after he became director of the Italia Militare at Florence; reflects his experiences as a soldier.

Matthew Arnold, *Schools and Universities on the Continent*—the result of the English writer's 1865 tour of Europe to study various educational systems; the writer outlines what he believes to be the deficiencies of the English educational system.

Robert Browning, *The Ring and the Book*—twelve dramatic monologues based upon the record of an Italian murder case that the English poet had discovered in Florence.

Wilkie Collins, *The Moonstone*—a novel by the English writer, a pioneer work in the genre of detective fiction; the "moonstone" is as an enormous diamond that had once been set in the forehead of an image of the Indian moon god; at the siege of Seringapatam it comes into the possession of an English officer; then follow attempts at its recovery and its removal from one place to the next.

Alphonse Daudet, *Le Petit Chose*—a novel by the French writer, a sensitive and compassionate semiautobiographical piece describing life at a boarding school.

Comte da Lautreamont, *Les Chants de Maldoro* (The Lay of Maldoro)—a poem in six cantos by the French writer, celebrated for its shocking and repugnant imagery; based upon the theme of rebellion, the hero, represented as half demon, half rebel, part man and part beast, challenges and even attempts to equal God; to 1869.

William Morris, *Earthly Paradise*—a poem by the English writer; consists of a prologue and twenty-four tales, Chaucerian in form and meter; a company of Norsemen, fleeing from the pestilence, set sail for the fabled earthly Paradise; they fail in their quest and return home to feast and tell tales; the tales are interspersed with lyrics expressing the effects of the changing years upon the English landscape.

Alfred, Lord Tennyson, *Lucretius*—a dramatic monologue by the English poet, perhaps one of his most significant pieces on a classical theme.

EVENTS

The Atlanta **[Georgia]** *Constitution* begins publication; Joel Chandler Harris is one of the early contributors.

Frederick James Furnivall, English lexicographer and literary scholar, founds The Chaucer Society for the purpose of collecting materials for the study of Geoffrey Chaucer's life, times, and works.

The Louisville **[Kentucky]** *Daily Journal* and *The Louisville Courier* merge as the *Courier-Journal;* its news and features will, at the outset, reflect the deep political and regional divisions within the state.

Hearth and Home begins publication at Boston as a weekly journal for agriculture and literature; Harriet Beecher Stowe will serve as one of its editors; until 1875.

Lippincott's Magazine, a literary monthly, begins publication at Philadelphia; reprints the fiction of such English writers as Oscar Wilde, Rudyard Kipling, and Sir Arthur Conan Doyle as well as original work by Americans, including Stephen Crane and Bret Harte; to 1916.

Overland Monthly, a literary magazine, begins publication at San Francisco; Bret Harte is an early editor and contributor, while later contributions come from such writers as Jack London and Frank Norris; to 1875, then revived from 1883 to 1935.

Putnam's Magazine, a monthly literary journal, begins publication at New York City; William Dean Howells is a principal contributor; to 1870.

Vanity Fair, a humorous magazine, begins publication as a weekly in New York City; known for its witty contributions by such writers as William Dean Howells and William Winter; ceased publication in 1936, but reissued in 1983.

Joseph Whitaker, London publisher and a former editor of *The Gentleman's Magazine,* publishes *Whitaker's Almanack,* containing information and statistics on a variety of subjects; issued annually.

1869

BIRTHS

Andre Gide (d. 1951). French novelist and prose writer; he will become a leader of French liberal intellectualism, outwardly defending homosexuality; he will embrace and then disavow communism; his fiction will depict individuals seeking their own identity and at odds with prevailing ethical concepts; in 1947, he will receive the Nobel Prize in literature.

Jalil Mammadguluzada (d. 1932). Azerbaijan prose writer, playwright, and translator; he will write satires and create lively characters from the Azerbaijan peasantry and the Czarist bureaucracy.

Martin Anderson Nexo (d. 1954). Danish novelist; he will produce proletarian novels that focus upon the conditions of the poor in Denmark.

Hjalmar Soderberg (d. 1941). Swedish novelist and writer of short fiction; his witty fiction will depict upper-middle-class life in Stockholm at the beginning of the twentieth century.

Suleyman of Stal (d. 1937). Dagestan (SSR) poet; the Congress of Soviet Writers will, in 1934, crown him "the Homer of our epoch"; he will write poetry in the classical Oriental strophic form (the last line of the quatrain serving as the refrain); his verse will abound in colorful Oriental imagery, reflecting the problems and requirements of modern Soviet life.

Stanislaw Wyspianski (d. 1907). Polish poet and playwright; he will be known as the founder of modern Polish drama; his works will contain elements of myth and fantasy, as well as highly symbolic language.

Mehmed Emin Yurdakul (d. 1944). Turkish poet; his work will rely upon the language of simple and natural speech, and thus will be easily understood by the uneducated; he will also appeal to the patriotism of peasants and craftsmen.

DEATHS

Alphonse de Lamartine (b. 1790). French Romantic poet, novelist, and statesman; he relied upon both traditional and contemporary sources; he wrote a history of the Girondists and briefly headed the provisional government following the revolution of February 1848; he dies at Passy in Paris.

Charles Augustine Sainte-Beuve (b. 1804). French essayist, poet, and novelist; one of the most prominent French literary critics of the nineteenth century and a fervent exponent of Romanticism; his critical criteria took into consideration psychological and biographical elements, for he believed that a writer could not be separated from his or her work; he dies at Paris, buried without religious ceremony at his own instructions.

PUBLICATIONS

Matthew Arnold, *Culture and Anarchy*—a collection of essays by the English writer criticizing English social and political life; contains the writer's definitions of Barbarians, Philistines, Hebraists, and Hellenists.

Charles Baudelaire, *Petits Poemes en Prose: Le Spleen de Paris* (Poems in Prose from

Charles Baudelaire)—a collection of prose poems by the French poet and essayist, published posthumously.

Richard Doddridge Blackmore, *Lorna Doone*— a novel by the English writer; set during the period of Charles II and James II (1680-1685); concerns the vengeance of a yeoman against the Doone family for having murdered his father; the situation becomes even more complicated when the yeoman and the title character fall in love.

Arthur Hugh Clough, *Dipsychus*—a posthumously published poem by the English writer in the form of dialogues between the title character and an attendant of the Mephistophelean spirit; represents the conflict between a tender conscience and worldly standard of conduct.

Alphonse Daudet, *Lettres de Mon Moulin* (Letters from My Mill)—a collection of short narratives by the French writer; gentle and natural portrayals of French life in the Provence.

Gustave Flaubert, *L'Education Sentimentale: Histoire d'un Jeune Homme* (Sentimental Education: A Young Man's History)—an autobiographical novel by the French writer of fiction; portrays the manners and mores of contemporary bourgeois society, also focusing upon the circumstances behind the Revolution of 1848 and the reactions that followed it.

Edmond and Jules de Goncourt, *Madame Gervaisais*—a realistic novel by the French diarists and writers of fiction, an account of the conversion to Catholicism of one of the novelists' aunts.

Ludovic Halevy and Henri Meilhac, *Frou-Frou*—a light dramatic comedy by the French playwrights, considered one of the significant theatrical successes of the nineteenth century.

Henry Kendall, *Leaves from Australian Forests*—the second collection of poems by the Australian poet and journalist; describes life in the Australian bush and the clash between the aboriginal and European cultures.

James Russell Lowell, *Under the Willows, and Other Poems*—a collection by the American writer; the majority of the pieces represent the poet's preference for rhymed declamation and long digression within the framework of the familiar verse essay.

Alfred Lord Tennyson, *The Holy Grail*—the seventh piece in the English poet's cycle, *The Idyls of the King;* Sir Percival recounts the quest for the Holy Grail and the success of Galahad.

Mark Twain, *The Innocents Abroad*—a travel narrative by the American writer, in its time the most popular of American travel books; the writer attempts to strip away the romanticism of the guidebooks and to expose his readers to "the truth of the Old World fraud"; in Europe there existed only cruelty and avarice, "poverty, indolence, and everlasting uninspiring worthlessness."

Paul Verlaine, *Fetes Galantes*—a collection by the French poet; the pieces were inspired by eighteenth-century scenes from the paintings of Jean Antoine Watteau (1684-1721):

EVENTS

Charles Edward Cutts Birch Appleton begins publication of *The Academy,* a London journal of literature, science, art, and learning; Matthew Arnold and Thomas Henry Huxley are among its contributors; issued monthly until 1922.

Appleton's Journal begins publication in New York City as a weekly magazine of literature and current affairs; William Cullen Bryant, Julian Hawthorne, and Brander Matthews are among its contributors; until 1881.

Nature, a periodical designed to provide the public with information on science, begins publication at London; Charles Darwin and Thomas Henry Huxley are among its early contributors.

1870

BIRTHS

Hillaire Belloc (d. 1953). French-born English satirist, poet, and essayist; his work will reflect his distaste for modern industrial society and socialism, while revealing a masterful, light prose style.

Solomon Bloomgarden (d. 1927). American Jewish scholar, poet, prose writer, and translator; he will write verse, short stories, and fables in Yiddish, as well as a three-volume account of his travels through and impressions of Palestine; he will also translate the Bible into Yiddish.

Christopher John Brennan (d. 1932). Australian poet and prose writer; he will become his nation's most accomplished poet and also achieve recognition for his classical scholarship; he will strive to develop a poetic system for the expression of humanity's intellectual, emotional, and spiritual quest for truth.

Hafiz Ibrahim (d. 1932). Egyptian poet and director of the literary section of the Egyptian National Library; his verse will reflect his interest in social and political issues and will become known for its expression of fervent patriotism; he will also translate Victor Hugo's *Les Miserables.*

Aleksandr Kuprin (d. 1938). Russian novelist and short story writer; his fictional tales will rank second only to those of Anton Chekhov among the writers of his country.

Amado Nervo (d. 1919). Mexican poet; he will become a leading figure of the "modernismo" movement; his verse will be characterized by simple diction, musical phrasing, and mysticism.

Benjamin Franklin (Frank) Norris (d. 1902). American novelist; his naturalistic fiction will reveal the influence of Emile Zola; he will concern himself with such topics as human greed and the American railroad and wheat industries.

Tom Redcam (pseudonym of Thomas Henry MacDermot; d. 1933). Jamaican poet and novelist, known as "the father of Jamaican literature"; he will explore themes unique to his island-country, particularly its natural beauty, thus attempting to eschew European literary influences.

Saki (pseudonym of Hector Hugh Munro; d. 1916). Burmese-born English novelist and short story writer; his literary reputation will rest on his short stories, which will be described as humorous, macabre, eccentric, and unconventional.

Tran-te-Xuong (d. 1907). Vietnamese poet; he will practice various verse forms, satirically treating the decadent aspects of Vietnamese society during the first phase of French colonization; he will also ridicule Confucian morality and the pursuit of wealth.

DEATHS

Gustavo Adolfo Becquer (b. 1836). Spanish Romantic poet and prose writer; he is known for his troubadour love verses and for a series of legends written, according to one critic, in "a weirdly musical prose."

Charles Dickens (b. 1812). English novelist and one of the most significant writers of fiction in world literature; his work is known for its detailed and complex portrait of bourgeois society, its denunciation of various social evils, and its sharply drawn and often eccentric characters, many of whom have become familiar literary stereotypes; he dies suddenly at Gadshill, near Rochester, and is buried at Westminster Abbey.

Alexandre Dumas pere (b. 1802). French novelist, playwright, and essayist; considered one of the most significant storytellers of Western world literature, he helped to inaugurate and popularize French Romantic drama; he was such a prolific writer that many critics doubted whether he had actually composed all the works attributed to him; he dies at the home of his son at Puys.

Jules de Goncourt (b. 1830). French diarist, novelist, and essayist; he and his younger brother Edmond (1822-1896) are recognized as literary innovators who, as novelists, are remembered for their realistic technique and, as historians, for revitalizing interest in the eighteenth century; their journal is considered one of the most important records of contemporary developments in art and literature; dies from syphillis, which he contracted in 1850.

Henrik Hertz (b. 1798). Danish poet, playwright, and satirist; the majority of his work is concerned with social and political developments in Copenhagen.

Aleksandr Ivanovich Herzen (b. 1812). Russian novelist, essayist, and short story writer; his work is an astute commentary on the intellectual environment in Russia during the mid-nineteenth century; as a revolutionary thinker, he promoted an agrarian socialist philosophy that combined Slavophile and Western ideals; dies at Geneva from pneumonia.

Comte de Lautreamont (pseudonym of Isidore Lucien Ducasse; b. 1846). French poet; although his most noted work shocked many readers because of its repugnant imagery, French Surrealists consider him their principal nineteenth-century forebear; not until the 1920s will scholars call attention to the importance of his poetry; he dies of unknown causes.

Prosper Merimee (b. 1803). French short story writer, playwright, essayist, and translator; his short fiction reveals keen insight into human nature; his most noted story, *Carmen*, inspired Georges Bezet's famous opera; in his longer fiction, he combined a knowledge of history with his talent for narrative.

Charles Rene de Montalembert (b. 1810). French historian and politician; he advanced the cause of freedom of the press, opposed tyranny and the imperial regime, and argued for religious liberty; he dies at Paris, some two weeks after having written a significant epistolary essay on papal infallibility.

PUBLICATIONS

Ludwig Anzengruber, *Der Pfarrer von Kirchfeld* (The Priest of Kirchfield)—a problem play by the Austrian dramatist, actor, and journalist; accurately depicts peasant life in a village of the Austrian Tyrol, focusing upon the conflict between liberalism and dogmatism.

Charles Dickens, *The Mystery of Edwin Drood*—an unfinished novel by the English writer; concerns two orphans, Edwin Drood and Rosa Bud, betrothed to one another by their parents; complications arise when two other men, a sinister choirmaster and a newcomer to town, develop interest in Rosa, and Edwin mysteriously disappears; a host of Dickensian characters give additional interest to the story: Mr. Grewgious, Mr. Crisparkle, Mr. Datchery, Bazzard, Mr. Sapsea, Mr. Honeythunder, and Durdles; scholars have concentrated on attempting to determine how Dickens intended the story to end.

Ralph Waldo Emerson, *Society and Solitude*—a collection of familiar essays by the American writer noted for their charm and eloquence; focuses upon the pleasures of domestic life.

Ivan Goncharov, *The Precipice*—the third novel by the Russian writer; concerns provincial life on the Volga, depicting an old-fashioned household ruled by a benevolent old matriarch.

Bret Harte, *The Luck of Roaring Camp and Other Sketches*—a collection of short stories by the American writer; the title piece is the prototype of all Western local color stories; the collection immediately established the writer's popularity and literary reputation.

James Russell Lowell, *The Cathedral*—a long poem by the American writer, perhaps his most ambitious effort; concerns a quest for religious certainty by an individual influenced by the general disbelief of his age; concludes, in general, that every age discovers its commonplace miracles.

George Meredith, *The Adventures of Harry Richmond*—a novel by the English writer; the father of the title character becomes obsessed with the idea of his royal ancestry and attempts to obtain an exalted position for his son; the father's eccentric schemes are thwarted, while the designs of a rival squire, the title character's grandfather, succeed; the conflict between the two contributes of the comedy of the piece.

John Henry Newman, *The Grammar of Assent*—a philosophical and religious tract by the English writer; maintains that belief is an act of apprehension, subjective in character and, though rational, incapable of logical proof; logic concerns the notional, or abstract, while assent, or belief, concerns the real and the concrete.

Dante Gabriel Rossetti, *Poems by D. G. Rossetti*—a collection by the English writer; the manuscripts were buried with his wife, Eleanor Siddal, in 1862 and then later disinterred; includes "Sister Helen," "Eden Bower," "The Stream's Secret," and "Love's Nocturn."

Mikhail Evgrafovich Saltykov, *Istoriya Odnogo Goroda* (The History of a Town)—a fictional history by the Russian satirist, novelist, and playwright; one of his most popular works, the piece satirically portrays the tyrannical rule of the czarist regime.

Mosen Jacinto Verdaguer , *Idilis y Cants Mistichs* (Mystical Poems and Songs)—a collection of verse by the Spanish Catalan poet; the work is memorable because the poems were set to music and eventually became part of the music of the Catalan church.

Jules Verne, *Vingt Mille Lieues Sous les Meres* (Twenty Thousand Leagues under the Sea)—a science fiction novel by the French writer; introduces the mysterious submarine commander, Captain Nemo ("no one"), a figure reminiscent of the Greek wanderer Odysseus; the work combines the best elements of ancient myth, scientific fantasy, and prophecy.

EVENTS

Rev. Ebenezer Cobham Brewer, English cleric and scholar, publishes *Brewer's Dictionary* of *Phrase and Fable*; contains explanations of English phrases, cant, slang terms, and fictional characters; revised in 1952 and regularly thereafter.

The Literary World, a magazine of literature and social news, begins publication at Boston; until 1904; not to be confused with the New York City weekly of the same title, issued between 1847 and 1853.

Charles Scribner, begins publication at New York City of *Scribner's Monthly,* a literary journal; contributors include Edward Everett Hale, Bret Harte, Julian Hawthorne, Helen Hunt Jackson, and Sidney Lanier.

Victoria Claflin Woodhull, spiritualist and suffragette, and Stephen Pearl Andrews, radical reformer, begin publication at New York City of *Woodhull and Claflin's Weekly*, a journal advocating socialism, free love, birth control, and vegetarianism; prints (1872) the first English translation of the *Communist Manifesto*; until 1876.

1871

BIRTHS

Leonid Nikilayevich Andreyev (d. 1919). Russian writer of fiction and drama; prior to the Russian revolution, he will write realistic studies of everyday life; afterward, he will emphasize mysticism, expressionism, and allegory.

Stephen Crane (d. 1900). American writer of fiction; he will become the first truly "modern" American writer, introducing realism into American fiction with grim (and often unpopular) subjects and themes; he will also produce admired poetry.

Grazia Deledda (d. 1936). Sardinian-born Italian novelist; she will write lyrical and naturalistic fiction and be awarded the Nobel Prize for literature in 1926.

Theodore Herman Albert Dreiser (d. 1945). American novelist; he will be an early contributor to American literary naturalism; his mechanistic view of life will regard human beings as the victims of such ungovernable forces as economics, biology, society, and simple chance.

John Langalibalele Dube (d. 1946). South African (Zulu) novelist and collector of folk tales; he will receive his education in the United States and then become active, as a moderate, in African politics; his fiction will represent the earliest mastery of the written Zulu language, focusing upon both contemporary and historical subjects.

Heinrich Mann (d. 1950). German novelist, referred to as "the German Zola"; his fiction will ruthlessly expose pre-1914 German society, including the proletariat, the bourgeois, and the governing class within the empire of Kaiser Wilhelm II.

Christian Morgenstern (d. 1914). German expressionist poet and translator; his intense poetry will reflect his mysticism and solemnity, revealing the writer as a self-appointed philosopher.

Marcel Proust (d. 1922). French novelist; he will, upon the death of his mother, isolate himself from society and give himself over to introspection; he will analyze the beauties and complexities of experience that tend to escape the superficial responses of ordinary intelligence.

Stijn Streuvels (pseudonym of Frank Lateur; d. 1969); Flemish writer of novels and short fiction; in 1905, he will foresake his vocation as a baker and turn to literature; his novels of peasant life will become masterpieces of Flemish fiction.

John Millington Synge (d. 1909). Irish playwright; he will settle among the people of the Aran Islands, finding ready material for his plays; his characters will aspire to lives of freedom and fantasy, but will often be limited or denied by the realities of the world; nonetheless, they will succeed because of their Irish imagination and language.

Paul Ambroise Vallery (d. 1945). French poet and nonfiction prose writer; his poetry will prove difficult because of the duality of its symbolism: life and death, emotion and reason, being and doing, consciousness and the world of objects and facts; he will also develop a type of poetic shorthand, compressing imagery and ideas.

DEATHS

Willibald Alexis (pseudonym of Georg Wilhelm Heinrich Haring; b. 1798). German novelist; he composed a historical romance that he claimed was the work of Sir Walter Scott, which led to its translation into several languages; other novels, travel books, sketches, and plays received only mild attention.

Charles Paul de Kock (b. 1794). French novelist and playwright; his highly popular portrayals of Parisian life combine humor and sentimentality and contain lively and good-humored characters; his plots focus upon the lives of the urban lower classes.

PUBLICATIONS

Louisa May Alcott, *Little Men*—a novel by the American writer, intended for boys; focuses upon New England family life and serves as a sequel to her earlier work *Little Women* (1868-1869).

Gustavo Adolfo Becquer, *Rimes* (Rhymes)—a posthumously published collection of verse by the Spanish Romantic poet and prose writer; seventy-six complex and original pieces lamenting the impossibility of fulfilling erotic desires.

Robert Browning, *Balaustion's Adventure*—a poem by the English writer; the title character, a Rhodian girl and an admirer of Euripides, recites the Athenian's play, *Alkestis*, to the Syracusans, transforming hostility into friendship; through the title character, the poet comments upon Athenian dramatic poetry.

——————, *Prince Hohenstiel-Schwangau*—a poetic monolog in which Louis Napoleon assumes the name of the title character; the monarch defends his policy of making the best of existing situations and institutions, rather than attempting to reform them.

Charles Darwin, *The Descent of Man*—a prose tract by the English biologist and naturalist; the writer sets out to prove that the human race derived from a hairy quadrumanous animal belonging to the great anthropoid group, related to the progenitors of the orangutan, chimpanzee, and gorilla; he also develops his important supplementary theory of sexual selection.

Esteban Echeverria, *The Abbatoir*—a novel by the Argentine poet, novelist, and revolutionary; attacks the Argentine dictator Juan Manuel de Rosas (1793-1877); composed during the writer's later years in Uruguay and published twenty years after his death.

George Eliot, *Middlemarch, a Study of Provincial Life*—a novel by the English writer, set in the first half of the nineteenth century and in the town of the title; a vast panorama of English provincial life, the work explores a variety of intellectual and moral issues, including the conflict between materialism and idealism, the issue of free will versus determinism, medical reform, and social pretension; to 1872.

Thomas Hardy, *Desperate Remedies*—the first of the English poet and prose writer's published novels; a tale of mystery, entanglement, and "moral obliquity."

Nikolai Alekseevich Nekrasov, *Russkie Zhenshchini* (Russian Woman)—a poem by the Russian writer, published initially in the journal *Otechestvennye Zapiski*; the story of two princesses who travel to Siberia to join their husbands, who were exiled for their roles in the 1825 Decembrist uprising against Czar Nicholas I; the princesses represent individual courage in the face of political oppression; to 1872.

Aleksandr Ostrovsky, *Les* (The Forest)—a dramatic comedy by the Russian playwright; focuses upon the eternal theme of how young people's simple and tender aspirations are crushed by the artificial and hypocritical values of their elders; there exists also the clash between three social classes: the gentry, the greedy peasantry, and the proletarian intelligentsia.

Wilhelm Raabe, *Meister Artur* (Master Arthur)—a novel by the German writer; a generally grim and tragic reaction against nineteenth-century progress; however, traces of Laurence Sterne and Charles Dickens provide some humor.

Arthur Rimbaud, *Le Bateau Ivre* (The Drunken Boat)—a poem by the Belgian writer; the piece has been acclaimed for its verbal eccentricities, daring imagery, and evocative language; composed before the poet had reached the age of seventeen.

John Ruskin, *Fors Clavigera*—a collection of letters by the English essayist and poet; addressed to the workmen and laborers of Great Britain, the writer attempts to uncover the causes of their poverty and misery and to propose a way to remedy them, principally through guilds; to 1884.

Algernon Charles Swinburne, *Songs before Sunrise*—a collection by the English poet, written during the struggle for Italian independence; as a whole, the pieces reveal the poet's antipathy for kings and priests and his support for Giuseppe Mazzini (1805-1872), the Italian Romantic patriot.

Alfred, Lord Tennyson, *The Last Tournament*—a poem by the English laureate, one of his *Idylls of the King*; the weary and dis-illusioned Lancelot presides over the last tournament held at Arthur's court, "The Tournament of the Dead Innocence"; Tristram wins the prize, carrying it not to his wife, but to his paramour, whose husband crushes Tristram's head; Arthur returns to an empty house, his wife Guinevere having fled.

Walt Whitman, *Democratic Vistas*—a prose pamphlet by the American poet and essayist; considers two crises: the Civil War and the threat of economic oligarchy and monopoly; the writer maintains that the function of democratic government is to provide for the free functioning of every individual; such a government must come to rest, ultimately, upon a fraternity of comrades; at present, according to the writer, Nature has become the servant of man, in which case it must either elevate or destroy the human condition.

——————— **,** *Passage to India*—a poem by the American writer; celebrates the completion of the Suez Canal, the transcontinental railroad, and the Atlantic cable; those technical advances represent a regeneration of the human race: the spiritual wisdom of the East has been united with the materialism of the West.

Emile Zola, *La Fortune des Rougon* (The Rougon-Macquart Family)—the first in a long series (to 1893) of novels by the French writer concerning the Rougon-Macquart family; this initial volume introduces the family, sketches its background, and proceeds to outline its fortunes at the outset of the Second Empire.

1872

BIRTHS

Hemcandra Gosvami (d. 1928). Indo-Iranian (Assam) historian, poet, and editor; he will edit and help to preserve works of Assamese classical and folk literature, compiling a major collection.

Zane Grey (d. 1939). American novelist; he will produce more than fifty "westerns," the most popular of which will sell in excess of two million copies; he will rely upon the escapist lure of simple adventure plots and attractive, but authentic, settings.

Krsnaji Prabhakar Khadilkar (d. 1948). Marathi playwright; his dramas will be anti-British propaganda pieces in the struggle for an independent India.

Ahmud Lufti as-Sayyid (d. 1963). Egyptian essayist and political activist; he will articulate the influences upon and the theories of Egyptian nationalism; he will become professor of philosophy at the Egyptian National University.

Jose Enrique Rodo (d. 1917). Uruguayan essayist; his prose will stress the importance of spiritual values over materialism; he will write in traditional Spanish.

Bertrand Russell (d. 1970). English mathematician and philosopher; he will write frequently controversial works on education, philosophy, economics, and politics, most often basing his arguments on practical considerations; his work in mathematical logic will be a definitive contribution to the discipline.

Bhai Vir Singh (d. 1957). Indian (Panjabi) poet, novelist, and pamphleteer; his short novels will glorify the Sikh past, serving as the earliest examples of modern Panjabi prose fiction; he will also write romantic epics in blank verse and brief lyrics reacting to the beauty of nature.

DEATHS

Ludwig Andreas Feuerbach (d. 1804). German philosopher; he rejected the "illusionistic" nature of religion and established a naturalistic-humanistic ethic, advancing the notion that humanity and nature constituted the proper study of philosophy; he was a decided influence upon Karl Marx.

Theophile Gautier (b. 1811). French poet, novelist, and critic; he advanced the idea of art for art's sake, and his poetry foreshadowed the revolt against Romanticism with its emphasis upon faultless technique, precise form, and emotional detachment; he dies at Neuilly.

Franz Grillparzer (b. 1791). Austrian poet and playwright; his works reflect his general unhappiness and dissatisfaction with life, particularly his psychopathic tendencies; interestingly enough, he placed those problems in various of his female characters.

PUBLICATIONS

Theodore de Banville, *Petit Traite Poesie Francaise* (A Short Treatise on French

Poetry)—a prose tract by the French poet, playwright, and essayist; the writer sets forth his poetic theories, considering such topics as the definition and purpose of poetry, the rules of versification, and the entire creative process; for him, rhyme stands as the most important element of verse; urges a return to Renaissance and medieval verse forms, wherein rhyme determines the structure of a poem.

Georg Brandes, *Main Currents in Nineteenth-Century Literature*—a six-volume work (to 1890) by the Danish literary critic; analyzes the doctrines of realism and radicalism, while discussing the views of Ernest Renan, Hippolyte Taine, and John Stuart Mill.

Samuel Butler, *Erewhon*—a satirical utopian novel by the English writer; the narrator has crossed an unexplored mountain chain in New Zealand, coming upon Erewhon (or "nowhere"); the institutions of that place serve as the objects of the writer's satire, representing hypocrisy, compromise, and mental torpor.

Thomas Hardy, *Under the Greenwood Tree*—an idyllic novel by the English writer set in the rustic village of Mellstock; concerns two lovers and their none-too-serious problems on the route from love to marriage; lively language and interesting characters.

Jose Hernandez, *El Gaucho Martin Fierro* (The Departure of Martin Fierro)—the first of a two-part epic poem by the Argentine poet and journalist; a realistic depiction of the gauchos' vices and redeeming qualities; in 2,325 lines, the gaucho-bard mournfully sings of his conscription into the army, the abuse he received there, his desertion and lawless life, and his ultimate decision to live among his enemies.

Oliver Wendell Holmes, *The Poet at the Breakfast Table*—a collection of essays by the American writer and physician; intended both to amuse and instruct through the writer's witty raillery and vivid pictures of New England life, characters, and scenes.

William Dean Howells, *Their Wedding Journey*—a novel by the American poet and prose writer; based upon the writer's actual travels, the strength of the work derives from its descriptions of the American scene; represents the writer's concept of realism: the avoidance of the heroic or the dramatic, and a reliance upon native honesty and beauty.

Arthur Rimbaud, *Les Illuminations*—a collection of prose and verse poems by the Belgian poet; the pieces clearly establish his poetic doctrine, revealing him as a precursor of Symbolism; he relies heavily upon dreams and mystical images to express his dissatisfaction with the material world and his longing for the spiritual.

Christina Rossetti, *Sing-Song*—a collection of nursery rhymes by the English poet; contains illustrations by Arthur Hughes.

Alfred, Lord Tennyson, *Gareth and Lynette*—a poem by the English laureate, one of his *Idylls of the King;* depicts Arthur's court in its early period of innocence and promise.

Mark Twain, *Roughing It*—an autobiographical narrative by the American writer and humorist; concerns the nineteen-day journey in July 1861 of the writer and his brother across the plains and Rockies to Carson City; a mixture of fact and humorous invention.

John Greenleaf Whittier, *The Pennsylvania Pilgrim and Other Poems*—a collection by the American poet; the title piece is an account of the pious German community established by Francis Daniel Pastorius (1652-1720?) near William Penn's newly settled Quaker colony; the poem emphasizes the community's early protests against slavery, while lauding its attempt to establish an ideal existence.

EVENTS

Publishers Weekly, an early trade journal for publishers and booksellers, established at New York; emphasis upon recent publications and current trends in the industry.

1873

BIRTHS

Mariano Azuela (d. 1952). Mexican novelist; he will write about social conflicts in twentieth-century Mexico, as well as his own experiences as a surgeon with the revolutionary forces of Pancho Villa.

Chaim Nachman Bialik (d. 1934). Ukranian (SSR) poet and writer of short fiction; he will be regarded as one of the significant Hebrew poets of the twentieth century, contributing to the modernization of Hebrew language and literature; his work will reflect the personal suffering of his childhood, as well as the hardships endured by Jews in exile from their ancient homeland.

Henri Barbusse (d. 1935). French novelist; his major fiction will be inspired by his experiences during World War I and will be characterized by powerful realism and sincere concern for human suffering.

Sidonie Gabrielle Colette (d. 1954). French journalist and writer of fiction; she will gain recognition as one of the most significant novelists of twentieth-century France, principally because of her keen observation of nature and the lyrical beauty of her prose; she will confront the issue of the reconciliation of women's struggle for independence with the insistent demands of physical passion.

Walter De la Mare (d. 1956) English poet and novelist; he will write important poetry and fiction and contribute significantly to children's literature; his best work will be characterized by rhythmic invention and fusion of the worlds of the sinister and the innocent.

Ford Madox Ford (originally Ford Madox Hueffer; d. 1939). English essayist, poet, and writer of fiction; he will write five major novels, travel books, poetry, and literary criticism; his work will reflect his romanticism, radicalism, Catholicism, and, above all, his general unhappiness with life.

Muhammad Iqbal (d. 1938). Indian poet, essayist, and philosopher; he will become one of the leading Muslim intellectual figures during the first half of the twentieth century; his innovative poetry, written in Persian, will proclaim the revitalization of Islam through the development of the individual personality; politically, he will be celebrated as the spiritual founder of Pakistan.

Johannes Vilhelm Jensen (d. 1950). Danish novelist, essayist, and poet; his work will describe his native people and their land, as well as his extensive travels to the Far East and America; he will receive the Nobel Prize for literature in 1944.

N. Kumaran Asan (d. 1924). Indian (Malayalam) poet; his work will range from erotic verse to devotional odes and will contribute significantly to the Malayalam Romantic movement of the early twentieth century; he will also write short narrative poems on the general theme of love.

George Edward Moore (d. 1958). English philosopher and essayist; his classification of goodness as a simple, non-natural quality will deeply influence such writers of the period as Leonard Woolf, Lowes Dickinson, John Maynard Keynes, and E. M. Forster (the Bloomsbury circle).

Jose Martinez Ruiz (d. 1967). Spanish essayist, novelist, and writer of short fiction; he will write about Spain in a conventional manner, content to recapture the literary traditions of the sixteenth and seventeenth centuries.

Jakob Wassermann (d. 1934). German novelist, biographer, and short story writer; a Jewish liberal, he will spend most of his life in Austria, there working on and publishing his autobiography; his fiction will reveal him to be a humanitarian concerned with the destruction of innocence by the social and political systems of the world.

DEATHS

Edward George Bulwer-Lytton (b. 1803). English novelist; known principally for his popular and authentic historical novels; he also wrote novels of manners and successful plays; he served in Parliament and as colonial secretary; he dies at Torquay in southwest England and is buried in Westminster Abbey.

Emile Gaboriau (b. 1835?). French novelist and journalist; he has been credited with the invention of the detective novel; he introduced into his popular and highly sensational crime novels narrative methods and detective techniques that have since become stock features of that form; scholars have discussed the links between his fiction and that of Edgar Allan Poe and Sir Arthur Conan Doyle.

Francesco Domenico Guerrazzi (b. 1804). Italian writer and politician; his fiction is based upon his political involvements and reveals his patriotism.

Joseph Sheridan Le Fanu (b. 1814). Irish novelist, poet, and short story writer; contributed significantly to the Gothic literature of the Victorian age; his work is characterized by evocative descriptions of physical settings, foreboding atmosphere, and elements of the supernatural; he also emphasized the psychological aspects of his finely drawn characters.

Alessandro Manzoni (b. 1785). Italian novelist and poet; his romantic novel of seventeenth-century Milan went through 118 editions between 1826 and 1875; he also wrote a celebrated poem on the death of Napoleon I.

John Stuart Mill (b. 1806). English philosopher, economist, and essayist; his work reveals his interest in socialism, his strong advocacy of women's rights, and his support for such social reforms as proportional representation, labor unions, and farm cooperatives; he formulated rules for the process of inductive reasoning and postulated the empirical method as the source of all knowledge; buried at Avignon.

PUBLICATIONS

Matthew Arnold, *Literature and Dogma*—a prose tract by the English poet and essayist, a study of the interpretation of the Bible.

Alexandre Dumas pere, *La Femme de Claude* (The Wife of Claude)—a posthumously produced drama by the French essayist, novelist, and playwright; a propagandistic "thesis play" setting forth the writer's arguments in favor of legalizing divorce and presenting suicide as the alternative.

Thomas Hardy, *A Pair of Blue Eyes*—a novel by the English poet and writer of fiction, set on the northern coast of Cornwall; a vicar becomes angry when a young commoner, an architect, develops an interest in his daughter; the young man goes to seek his fortune in India and, in his absence, his best friend courts the young lady, but abandons her upon discovering her lack of innocence; the lady in question, unmarried, dies before issues are resolved.

William Dean Howells, *A Chance Acquaintance*—a novel by the American poet and writer of fiction; provides an extremely detailed description of Quebec; a sensitive country girl, ignorant of social differences, is propelled into a far more sophisticated society; she demonstrates the superiority of American simplicity over the conventions of a Europeanized society.

John Henry Newman, *The Idea of a University Defined, Third Series*—a series of lectures by the English poet and essayist; the writer maintains that the focus of a university must be upon instruction rather than research; the institution must train the mind and not simply diffuse useful knowledge; theological instruction and tutorial supervision must remain essential to the university system.

Walter Pater, *Studies in the History of the Renaissance*—a volume of essays by the English essayist and art critic; includes discussions of the works of Johann Jachim Wincklemann (1717-1768), Sandro Botticelli (1445?-1510)), and Leonardo da Vinci (1452-1519); the work had a considerable influence upon undergraduates of the period, including Oscar Wilde.

Arthur Rimbaud, *Une Saison en Enfer* (A Season in Hell)—a prose work by the Belgian poet symbolizing his struggle to break with his past; written following the violent end of his relationship with the French poet Paul Verlaine, with whom he had been living since 1871.

Hippolyte Taine, *Les Origines de la France Contemporaine* (The Origins of Contemporary France)—the most significant prose work by the French essayist, historian, and philosopher; constitutes the strongest attack then launched upon the men and motives of the Revolution; discusses in detail the "ancien régime" and the "régime moderne"; to 1894.

Anthony Trollope, *The Eustace Diamonds*—a novel by the English writer; a wealthy noble gives his wife a valuable diamond necklace; after his death, the noble's wife and the family survivors battle for possession of the jewels; the scheming wife fails in her attempts to retain the necklace and improve her social position.

Jules Verne, *Le Tour du Monde en Quatre-Vingts Jours* (Around the World in Eighty Days)—a novel by the French writer of science fantasy; recounts the extraordinary travels of the Englishman Phileas Fogg and his valet, Passepartout.

EVENTS

St. Nicholas, a monthly magazine for children, begins publication at New York City; contributors include Louisa May Alcott, Mark Twain, Robert Louis Stevenson, Rudyard Kipling, William Dean Howells, and Bret Harte; such writers as E. B. White, Edna St. Vincent Millay, William Faulkner, F. Scott Fitzgerald, and Ring Lardner publish their earliest poetry and fiction here; until 1940.

Woman's Home Companion begins publication at Cleveland, Ohio as a semimonthly magazine; after changing its name to *Ladies' Home Companion,* it moves to New York City; Willa Cather and Edna Ferber are among its literary contributors; to 1957.

1874

BIRTHS

Gilbert Keith Chesterton (d. 1936). English essayist, novelist, and poet; his best essays will be published in the major periodicals of the day, including studies of Robert Browning, Charles Dickens, and Robert Louis Stevenson; he will gain popularity through his detective fiction.

Winston Leonard Spencer Churchill (d. 1965). English statesman and historian; he will be referred to, at the height of his career, as "the greatest living Englishman"; as a historian, he will write in the prose style of an Augustan poet, the sound and the drama of his language paralleling the breadth of his mind and the profoundness of his historical sense.

Mordecai Ze'eb Feierberg (d. 1899). German-born Jewish writer of short fiction; his stories will highlight the individuality of his characters, while describing the innermost problems of the "modernized" Jew.

Robert Lee Frost (d. 1963). American poet; revered as "the voice of New England," Frost emphasized humankind's community with nature and created a new style of folk speech for describing simpler, common experiences; he will receive the Pulitzer Prize for poetry in 1924, 1931, 1937, and 1943.

Ellen Glasgow (d. 1945). American novelist; her realistic fiction will present a history of Virginia since 1850; and in her major novels, she will emphasize the changing social order of the South.

Drmit Gulia (d. 1960). Abkhazian (SSR) poet, playwright, novelist, and journalist; he will be considered the founder of Abkhazian literature in a multiplicity of genres; his best original work will be his lyric poetry; he will also collect and publish Abkhazian folklore and translate works from the Russian.

Hugo von Hofmannsthal (d. 1929). Austrian poet and playwright; his symbolic, neo-Romantic poems will capture the transitory and elusive nature of life, its short-lived pleasures fueling the quest for the world of the spirit; he will abandon poetry and instead write dramas and compose libretti for Richard Strauss.

Joseph Klausner (d. 1958). Lithuanian-born Israeli historian, journalist, and essayist; he will author histories of the second commonwealth period and of Hebrew literature; his work on Jesus and the apostle Paul will trace the growth of Christianity from a Jewish perspective.

Amy Lawrence Lowell (d. 1925). American poet; she will achieve recognition for her imagist poetry, characterized by its free verse or, as she will term it, "unrhymed cadence"; she will also produce studies of French verse, modern American poetry, and John Keats.

Leopoldo Lugones (d. 1938). Argentine poet, historian, and writer of short fiction; an extremely versatile poet, his work will demonstrate his changing politics, from young anarchist to fascist nationalist; his later work (perhaps his best) will reveal the influence of the French Symbolists and treat the Argentine countryside with Utopian idealism.

Manuel Machado (d. 1947). Spanish poet, playwright, and essayist; his work will find its origins in Andalusian popular poetry, but it will eventually resound with passion for the fascist revolution; he will collaborate with his younger brother Antonio (1875-1939) on several plays.

William Somerset Maugham (d. 1965). English novelist, playwright, and writer of short fiction; he will become a master of the short story, espousing the theory that fiction should, principally, relate a story; he will maintain that social or political undercurrents in fiction do nothing more than transform art into propaganda.

Robert William Service (d. 1958). English-born Canadian versifier; his experiences as a reporter, traveler, and ambulance driver in World War I will provide material for his popular, often "sing-song," verse; he will later write several novels.

Gertrude Stein (d. 1946). American poet and prose writer; she will settle in Paris, preside over the world of experimental art and letters there, and host "the lost generation" of post-World War I American writers who came to the French capital; she will, with mixed success, attempt to apply the theories of abstract painting to her written work.

DEATHS

Jules Michelet (b. 1798). French historian and professor of history at the College de France; he wrote a twenty-four volume history of France, seven volumes on the French Revolution, and several works (in collaboration with his wife, Adele Mialaret) on natural subjects; he dies at Hyeres.

Fritz Reuter (b. 1810). German (Plattdeutsch) comic poet; he recast local jokes and tales into Plattdeutsch verse, also writing original poetry and prose narratives; he dies at Eisenach, where he had lived since 1863.

PUBLICATIONS

Pedro Antonio de Alarcon, *Sombrero de Tres Picos* (The Three-Cornered Hat)—a witty and realistic novel by the Spanish poet, journalist, and novelist; the Spanish composer Manuel de Falla (1876-1946) based his ballet of the same title (1919) on this piece.

Marcus Clarke, *His Natural Life*—a novel by the Australian playwright, essayist, and writer of fiction; depicts the penal conditions in Australia during the colonial period of the nineteenth century; recreates in gruesome detail the dehumanizing nature of the prison system; focuses upon the issues of colonial displacement, social and spiritual alienation, and the human capacity for both good and evil.

Gustave Flaubert, *La Tentation de Saint Antoine* (The Temptation of Saint Anthony)—a novel by the French writer of fiction; inspired by a painting by the Flemish artist Pieter Breughel (1520?-1569); the work showcases the writer's lyricism; begun as early as 1849.

Thomas Hardy, *Far from the Madding Crowd*—a novel by the English writer of fiction and poetry; contrasts patient, generous devotion with selfish love dominated by violent passion; two lovers are united only after cruelty, insanity, and murder affect their lives.

Victor Hugo, *Quatre-Vingt-Treize* (Ninety-Three)—a novel by the French writer, his last prose romance; a story of the French Revolution, with attention upon Royalist insurrections in Brittany during that period; published in eight languages.

Algernon Charles Swinburne, *Bothwell, a Tragedy*—a play by the English poet, the second in his trilogy on Mary Queen of Scots.

James Thomson, "The City of Dreadful Night"—a poem by the Scottish-born poet; a powerful and sincere expression of the writer's atheistic and despairing creed; published in *The National Reformer* and republished with other poems in 1880.

Paul Verlaine, *Romances sans Paroles* (Romances without Words)—a collection of verse by the French poet that established his reputation as a Symbolist; written while the poet was confined in Mons prison on charges of immorality; represents well the evocative, rhythmic, and musical qualities of the writer's verse.

EVENTS

Ignatius Donnelly, American novelist, essayist, and politician, begins publication at Minneapolis, Minnesota of the *Anti-Monopolist*; a weekly journal of agricultural and reform interests; to 1879.

The Congressional Record, a series of reports on the proceedings of the U.S. Senate and House of Representatives, begins publication at Washington, D.C.

1875

BIRTHS

Leo Baeck (d. 1956). German Jewish writer and theologian; he will write a standard work on Judaism and Jewish history, identifying the prophets as the true prototypes of Judaism; in addition, his work on the Pharisees will antagonize Christians, since he attempted to prove that the Pharisees were progressives rather than hypocrites.

Jose Santos Chocano (d. 1934). Peruvian poet and revolutionary; his works, emphasizing Indian and native themes, will be characterized by a revolutionary tone; his writing will also reflect his fear of United States imperialism.

Mehmed Ziya Gokalp (d. 1924). Turkish poet, writer of fiction, essayist, and philosopher; his prose and poetry will reflect his belief that the Turkish nations had a significant role in the history of the world; those works will also attempt to contribute to the cultural and economic unification of all Turkish speaking peoples.

Julio Herrera y Reissig (d. 1910). Uruguayan poet; his verse will be influenced by Luis de Gongora y Argote (1561-1627), the major figure of the Spanish golden age, and the French Symbolists.

Carl Gustav Jung (d. 1961). Swiss psychiatrist and writer; he will become the most brilliant of Sigmund Freud's early disciples, serving as the first president of the International Psycho-Analytical Association; eventually, he will deny the central Freudian doctrine of sexuality; he will postulate two dimensions of the unconscious, the personal and the collective.

Antonio Machado (d. 1939). Spanish poet, playwright, and essayist; his poetry will be influenced by his Castillian life and environment and by the death of his wife; he will also write philosophical and literary essays, as well as plays with his brother, Manuel (1874-1947).

Thomas Mann (d. 1955). German novelist; he will write as a nineteenth-century German conservative whose cultural identities appeared to have vanished during World War I; thus, he will be compelled toward a critique of the artistic; his art will reflect a number of dilemmas: the artist with a bourgeois fear of Bohemianism, the apolitical person with political responsibilities, the brilliant storyteller in the classical German tradition whose subject matter signalled the end of that tradition.

Samuel Edward Krune Loliwe Mqhayi (d. 1945). South African (Cape Province) poet, biographer, translator, and writer of fiction; he will be recognized as the leading poet and prose writer in the Xhosa language, known especially for his traditional African lyrical poems; in addition to being hailed as the last of the great tribal bards, he will introduce the Western genre of prose fiction to the Xhosa literature of the early twentieth century.

Yonejiro Noguchi (d. 1947). Japanese poet and critic; he will write in both English and Japanese, helping to stimulate Western interest in numerous Japanese literary artists; his major collection of poems will be written in English (1921).

Rainer Maria Rilke (d. 1926). Austrian lyric poet; the spiritual melancholy of his early verse will transform into a mystical quest for the deity; he will then abandon mysticism for the aesthetic ideal, exalting the poet as the mediator between crude nature and pure

form; his work will extend the range and subtlety of the German language.

Jakob Schaffner (d. 1944). Swiss novelist; his novels will rebel against Swiss bourgeois conventions.

Albert Schweitzer (d. 1965). Alsatian philosopher, theologian, musician, and medical missionary; as an intellectual and moralist, he will rise to become one of the noblest figures of the twentieth century; he will publish an authoritative study of Johann Sebastian Bach, an essay on the design of the organ, a series of Pauline studies, and an account of the differences between his own human and ethical principles and the mores of European civilization in general.

Saul Tchernihowsky (d. 1943). Russian Jewish poet; he will write in Hebrew, emphasizing nature, beauty, hedonism, and protest; his verse will evidence his strong interest in classical Greek literature and Greek paganism.

DEATHS

Hans Christian Andersen (b. 1805). Danish writer of fairy tales, poetry, drama, and travel literature; he revitalized and expanded fairy tales by simplifying their structure from their original oral traditions and employing the language of conversation, making them suitable for children; his wit and whimsy appealed to both young and mature readers; he dies at Copenhagen.

Charles Kingsley (b. 1809). English novelist, churchman, and nonfiction writer; his strikingly original novels focused upon social questions and tended to reflect his own views as a Christian Socialist; his essays also addressed social issues, such as various schemes for improving the condition of the working classes; his complete works extend to twenty-eight volumes; two years before his death he gained appointments as canon of Westminster and chaplain to the Queen.

Eduard Friedrich Morike (b. 1804). German poet, playwright, and writer of fiction; considered a major nineteenth-century German lyricist, his work can be linked to at least three literary traditions: the German Romantic movement, the classical period, and the post-Romantic Biedermeier school; he also wrote a semiautobiographical novel and fairy tales.

PUBLICATIONS

Robert Browning, *Aristophanes' Apology*—a long poem in blank verse by the English writer; a discussion between Aristophanes and Balaustion: Aristophanes defends comedy as the representation of real life and attacks Euripedes as ascetic and unnatural; Balaustion maintains the superiority of the tragic poet.

William Dean Howells, *A Foregone Conclusion*—a novel by the American writer of fiction; the heroine is studied with varying degrees of realism against a romantic background; Florida Vervain comes to Venice, where the watchful young artist and consul, Ferris, protects her from the hopeless love of the priest Don Ippolito.

Alfred, Lord Tennyson, *Queen Mary*—a historical drama by the English laureate; presents principal events during the reign of Mary Tudor: Wyatt's rebellion, the marriage with Philip, the submission of England to Cardinal Pole as the Pope's agent, the death of Thomas Cranmer, the loss of Calais, and the death of the unhappy Mary.

EVENTS

Helena Petrova Hahn Blavatsky, Russian psychic philosopher and traveler, founds at New York City the Theosophical Society; originally based upon its founder's psychic powers.

The Chicago Daily News begins publication.

Stephane Mallarme, French poet, translates Edgar Allan Poe's *The Raven* from English to French.

1876

BIRTHS

Sherwood Anderson (d. 1941). American novelist and writer of short fiction; his experimental and poetic fiction will focus upon the loneliness and frustration of small-town life in America; he will also concern himself with the hindrances encountered by human beings as they attempt to challenge Nature.

Else Lasker-Schuler (d. 1945). German poet; her expressionistic work will reveal her Bohemianism; she will live her last eight years in Jerusalem and be regarded as a national Jewish poet.

John (Jack) Griffith London (d. 1916). American writer of fiction; he will incorporate his experiences as a sailor, tramp, and gold miner into his extremely popular novels and short stories.

Mustafa Lufti al-Manfaluti (d. 1924). Egyptian journalist and writer of narratives and essays; he will publish free adaptations of nineteenth-century French novels, essays on social issues, and emotional narratives focusing upon tragic and pathetic social situations.

Filippo Tommaso Marinetti (d. 1944). Italian poet, novelist, and critic, he will become the founder of the Futurists, who portrayed the dynamic character of twentieth-century life, glorified war and the technological age, and favored the growth of fascism.

Thomas Mokupu Mofolo (d. 1948). Lesothian (Basutoland, South Africa) novelist; he will be considered the first significant author of modern African literature, writing in the Sesotho language and concerning himself with the radical effect of Christian teachings upon traditional African society.

Abdulali Mustaghni (d. 1934). Afghan poet; he will write in both the Pashto and Dari languages; his verse will emphasize the importance of education, work, and perseverance; he will move away from the influence of traditional folk poetry.

Thakhin Kopuijto Hmain (d. 1964). Burmese poet, playwright, essayist, journalist, historian, and politician; he will refuse to compose poems for formal British state occasions, preferring to write rhymed prose in reaction to political and social problems; his more than eighty plays will portray the glories of the Burmese past.

George Macaulay Trevelyan (d. 1962). English historian; he will become Regius Professor of Modern History at Cambridge; his volumes of historical lectures and essays will display his mastery of the English language.

DEATHS

Khristo Botev (b. 1848). Bulgarian poet; he spent his student days in Russia, where he absorbed socialist ideas; he published a volume of patriotic lyrics and ballads; he dies leading a band of rebels against Turkish rule.

Aleksander Fredo (b. 1793). Polish playwright, novelist, and translator; one of the most prominent Polish dramatists of the nineteenth century; his comedies succeeded because of their varied language, complex and skillfully executed plots, and individualized characters.

Eugene Samuel Auguste Fromentin (b. 1820). French novelist, critic, and essayist; he became known for his travel literature, fiction, and art criticism; his sketches drew upon his artistic expeditions to North Africa and his studies of Flemish and Dutch painting; he dies following a sudden illness.

George Sand (pseudonym of Amandine Aurore Lucie Dupin; b. 1804). French novelist; her fiction reflected her unconventional life and strong feminist beliefs; romantic love of nature and moral idealism characterize her work, much of which is autobiographical.

PUBLICATIONS

Robert Bridges, *The Growth of Love*—a sonnet sequence by the English poet; enlarged in 1890; recognized for a certain "charm" not observed in English poetry since the days of Elizabeth I.

George Eliot, *Daniel Deronda*—a novel by the English writer, her last major work of fiction; concerns the marriage of Gwendolen Harleth, a high-spirited, self-confident, and self-centered woman; to Henleigh Mallinger Grandcourt, an arrogant and selfish man of the world; Deronda guides and influences the woman, who relies upon him at the death of her husband; a Jew, Deronda devotes himself to the cause of a national center for the Jewish race.

Jens Peter Jacobsen, *Fru Marie Grubbe*—a historical novel by the Danish writer of fiction; concerns the issue of spiritual regeneration and records the struggle within the writer's mind between dreamy romanticism and harsh, cynical realism.

Stephane Mallarme, *L'Apres-Midi d'un Faune* (The Afternoon of a Faun)—a major poem by the French Symbolist writer, successful largely because of its musical qualities; the language is characteristically obscure and defies traditional syntax.

Herman Melville, *Clarel*—a poem by the American writer deriving from his earlier (1856-1857) journey to the Holy Land and his anguish during the Civil War; written in the form of a pilgrimage, a company of assorted persons journey from Jerusalem to Bethlehem and, much in the style of Geoffrey Chaucer, converse about their former adventures; strong character development in evidence throughout the poem.

William Morris, *The Story of Sigurd the Volsung and the Fall of the Niblungs*—an epic poem by the English writer, in four books and anapaestic couplets; recounts the grim tale of Sigurd's father, then focuses upon Sigurd himself; the final portion of the work narrates the fall of the Niblungs, brought about by avarice, revenge, murder, and suicide; the poet's most significant effort.

Benito Perez Galdos, *Dona Perfecta*—a novel by the Spanish playwright and writer of fiction; the second in a series of forty-six "Novelos espanolas contemporaneas"; the writer looks at the principal social and political conflicts of his day in a forceful but humorous manner.

Mikhail Evgrafovich Saltykov, *Gospoda Golovlyovy* (The Golovlev Family)—a novel by the Russian writer of fiction and drama; focusing upon the general theme of the corruption of Russian society; the work graphically depicts the spiritual and physical decline of three generations of a noble family following the disruption of the feudal system.

Algernon Charles Swinburne, *Erectheus*—a drama in the Greek form by the English poet; concerns the mythical king of Athens, who sacrifices his daughter to assure his victory in battle, but in turn loses his life to the anger of Poseidon.

Alfred, Lord Tennyson, *Harold*—a historical drama by the English poet; concerns the final years of the reign of Edward the Confessor (d. 1066) and the short reign of Harold (d. 1066).

Mark Twain, *The Adventures of Tom Sawyer*—a novel by the American writer in which he introduces one of his most memorable characters; in all that he does, Tom Sawyer stands as a challenge to the world of adult tyranny, his wit and humor being his principal weapons; he steals from and outwits adults, enjoys idleness, and fashions lying into a fine art form.

EVENTS

Henry Carter, English-born American engraver and publisher, establishes at New York City

Frank Leslie's Popular Monthly; a miscellaneous journal of current events and literature; to 1906.

The Library Journal, the organ of the American Library Association, begins publication.

Alexander Bain, Scottish philosopher and professor of logic at Aberdeen, begins publication of *The Mind,* a quarterly review of psychology and philosophy.

1877

BIRTHS

Derenik Demirtchian (d. 1956). Armenian novelist, poet, and playwright; he will write lyrics and historical fiction, encouraging Armenian nationalism during World War II.

Hermann Hesse (d. 1962). German novelist and poet; his themes will focus upon the forces of the modern age that hinder individuals in their quest for unity and harmony of the self; his sensitive and sensuous language will raise him to the level of a true visionary; he will receive the Goethe Prize in 1946 and the Nobel Prize in 1947.

Alfred Kubin (d. 1959). Austrian novelist, poet, and essayist; his fiction will portray life in a "dream kingdom," where the worlds of the spiritual and the material intermingle freely; he will influence Franz Kafka and become a precursor of expressionism, surrealism, and the theater of the absurd.

Aleksey Yeliseyevich Kulakovskiy (d. 1926). Yakut (SSR) poet, essayist, and philosopher; he will become the first important writer of Yakut culture, at the same time creating nationalistic works; he will, in his work, reject the czarist regime and support the Soviet structure; he will write in Russian between 1897 and 1900, but in Yakut thereafter.

Mary Jane Mander (d. 1949). New Zealand novelist, essayist, and journalist; her four major novels will offer vivid and evocative descriptions of New Zealand life, portraying characteristic New Zealanders and their occupations; she will avoid portraying transplanted Britons or natives attempting to mimic British culture; she will also introduce into the literature of her nation frankness and directness in the presentation of sexual situations.

Ullur Paramesvarayyar (d. 1949). Malayalam poet and scholar; he will author a voluminous history of the literature of Kerala and become one of the most prolific Malayalam poets of his day; he will abandon Sanskritic meters and verse forms in favor of Malayalam parallels and inject philosophic content and imagery into his verse.

Alexey Mikhailovich Remizov (d. 1957). Russian novelist, playwright, and folklorist; he will become one of the most prolific, versatile, and innovative writers in Russia during the decade prior to the Revolution; his ornate prose style will influence an entire generation of Russian literary artists.

Raymond Roussel (d. 1933). French novelist, poet, and essayist; his experimental writings will be frequently bizarre and extravagant and will reflect his obsession with language and literary invention.

Hamzat Tsadasa (d. 1951). Dagestan poet; he will write witty Arabic parodies and satires, in addition to translations of European writers; his work will abound with allusions to Oriental traditions.

DEATHS

Walter Bagehot (b. 1826). English essayist; his work focused principally upon economics, politics, history, and literature; he approached those topics with remarkable insight and attention to reform.

Fernan Caballero (pseudonym of Cecilia Bohl de Faber; b. 1796). Spanish novelist and essayist; in her fiction, she advocated traditional Hispanic values, presenting realistic portraits of regional life and customs; she emphasized the picturesque elements of a particular locale and reproduced the speech and mannerisms of Andalusian Spain; she dies in retirement amid humble surroundings.

PUBLICATIONS

Joseph Arthur de Gobineau, *La Renaissance: Savonarole, Cesar Borgia, Jules II, Leon X, Michel-Ange; Scenes Historiques*—a set of historical portraits by the French essayist and historian, written in dialogue form; the writer praises each figure, demonstrating his appreciation for an age in which, according to his view, the most intelligent, daring, capable, energetic, and courageous persons could flourish.

Henrik Ibsen, *Samfundets Stotter* (The Pillars of Society)—the first of the Norwegian dramatist's "problem plays," which eventually led to the social drama of the twentieth century; concerns the relationship of the individual to his or her social environment.

Henry James, *The American*—a novel by the American-born writer of fiction and non-fiction; the theme centers on the victimization of an American by European culture and values.

William Kirby, *The Golden Dog*—a novel by the Canadian writer of fiction, a popular romance concerning Quebec in the seventeenth century; published again in 1884 under the title *Chien d'Or.*

Coventry Patmore, *The Unknown Eros*—a collection of odes by the English poet; he departs from the domestic themes of previous poems and focuses on matters ideal and erudite; includes "The Azalea," "Departure," "A Farewell," and "The Toys."

Theodor Storm, *Aquis Submersus*—a historical novella by the German poet and writer of fiction; contains traces of the nostalgic lyricism and sense of tragedy evident in earlier pieces.

Mosen Jacinto Verdaguer, *La Atlantida*—an epic poem by the Catalan versifier; characterized by beautiful language and imagery, it recasts Iberian myths within the context of romantic nationalism and political radicalism; Manuel de Falla (1876-1946), a Spanish composer, began to adapt the piece as a cantata in 1926, but never finished the project; Ernesto Halffter (b. 1905), a pupil of de Falla, finished the work in 1961.

Emile Zola, *L'Assommoir* (The Dram Shop)—a novel by the French writer, one of the works in the "Rougon-Macquart" cycle; a harsh and realistic piece emphasizing the misery and degradation of the French working class; the novelist sees drunkenness as a serious malady that eats away at the poor people of Paris.

EVENTS

Sir James Thomas Knowles, English editor and founder of the Metaphysical Society, begins publication at London of *The Nineteenth Century*; a monthly review presenting contrasting opinions on politics, literature, philosophy, and current affairs; Thomas Henry Huxley, John Ruskin, William Morris, Oscar Wilde, and Alfred, Lord Tennyson are among its contributors.

Puck, a weekly magazine of humor and satire, begins publication at New York City; the substance of the journal shifted from politics to general humor toward the turn of the century; until 1918.

1878

BIRTHS

Mikhail Petrovich Artsybashev (d. 1927). Russian novelist, playwright, and essayist; his works will depict the disintegration of society, its members succumbing to despair and suicide; he will see anarchism as a response to the human condition and will eventually proclaim the utter futility of human existence.

Sadriuuddin Ayni (d. 1954). Tajik (SSR) poet and prose writer; he will become the founder of modern Soviet Tajik prose and will contribute to the philology and historiography of his region; he will abandon traditional forms and subjects and focus upon the inhumanity of the old regime.

Jean de Bosschere (d. 1953). Belgian novelist, poet, and essayist; his work will contain elements of symbolism, mysticism, imagism, and realism; with subtle irony, he will treat conflicting philosophical and human questions; he will provide illustrations to accompany his texts.

Martin Buber (d. 1965). Austrian Jewish theologian and philosopher; he will become professor of comparative religion at Frankfurt and, later, professor of social philosophy at Jerusalem; he will also be recognized as one of the principal proponents of religious existentialism and the "I-Thou" theme; he will exercise considerable influence upon contemporary Jewish and Christian theology.

Herbert George De Lisser (d. 1944). Jamaican (of Portuguese-Jewish ancestry) novelist, journalist, and editor; his fear of mob rule will influence his approach to social and racial reform in the Caribbean, and his works will represent him as a member of the local establishment during the upheavals of the late 1930s.

Stephen Haweis (d. 1968?). English poet and autobiographical writer; he will spend considerable time in Barbados, and his prose and poetry will express his outrage at the racism and colonial arrogance evident throughout the Caribbean.

Sirek Walda Sellase Heruy (d. 1938). Ethiopian (Amharic) novelist and biographer; he will become the founder of modern Amharic literature, as well as the publisher of the first literary journal of the area; his fiction will contain stern moral and social warnings to Ethiopians.

Georg Kaiser (d. 1945). German expressionist playwright; he will develop the idea of the "new man," based upon the Nietzschean concept of the superman and supported by the notion that art should not exist in and for itself, nor should it stand oblivious to the human condition.

Eino Leino (d. 1926). Finnish poet, playwright, novelist, and critic; he will emerge as the most important Finnish poet of his generation, combining the mysticism and allegorical style of the French Symbolists with the meters and subjects of traditional folk poetry; he will become closely associated with the neo-Romantic cultural movement known as Young Finland.

John Masefield (d. 1967). English poet; he will achieve lasting recognition for his poems about the sea and for his long narratives in verse; he will also write plays in both prose and verse, as well as war sketches and adventure fiction for boys; he will become Poet Laureate of England in 1930.

Ferenc Molnar (d. 1952). Hungarian playwright, novelist, and essayist; his light comedies will be recognized for their charm and technical excellence; his themes will focus on relationships between men and women, with men as victims of their scheming but irresistible partners.

Horacio Sylvestre Quiroga (d. 1937). Uruguayan short story writer, poet, essayist and playwright; he will become one of the significant writers of short fiction in Latin America; his stories will portray conflicts between the individual and the natural hazards of South American jungles, with emphasis upon the single mood or the stunning effect.

Carl August Sandburg (d. 1967). American poet; his verse will depict his experiences as a day laborer, soldier, socialist political worker, and journalist; he will draw his inspiration from America's past and its energetic present, composing vigorous, impressionistic free verse celebrating ordinary people and ordinary events; he will also gain considerable recognition for his biographical cycle in prose

on Abraham Lincoln, for which he will earn the Pulitzer Prize.

Upton Beall Sinclair (d. 1968). American novelist; he will become an ardent socialist deeply involved in politics and social and industrial reform; thus, his more than eighty works will preach the gospel of anti-capitalism and anti-industrialism and expose what he believed to be the arms industry's efforts to maintain aggressive policies toward war; he will receive the Pulitzer Prize in 1943.

Anton Hansen Tammsaare (d. 1940). Estonian novelist; he will become the only modern writer of Estonian fiction whose work possesses "epic sweep," principally as he retells biblical narratives; his major piece will focus upon Estonian peasant life in the latter part of the nineteenth century.

Robert Walser (d. 1956). Swiss-born novelist and writer of short stories; his sense of the nightmarish and his stark simplicity of style may well have influenced Franz Kafka, particularly as his characters move through dream-like worlds; most dramatically, he will be remembered as a writer who could transform the commonplace into the remarkable.

DEATHS

William Cullen Bryant (b. 1794). American poet, editor, scholar, and translator; he will advocate free trade, the abolition of slavery, and labor reforms; he was the earliest theorist on American poetry, and his poetic versions of Homer became standard classroom editions; he dies in New York City.

Karl Ferdinand Gutzkow (b. 1811). German journalist and playwright; he was influenced by the French revolution of 1830 and thus became a member of the "Young Germany" movement.

Nikolai Alekseevich Nekrasov (b. 1821). Russian poet, essayist, novelist, and playwright; one of the significant Russian poets of the mid-nineteenth century; his verse is known for its social realism and topical relevance; his work offers a harshly satirical perspective upon the sources of injustice and oppression in Russian society.

PUBLICATIONS

Thomas Hardy, *The Return of the Native*—a novel by the English writer, set in the countryside of Dorset and concerning an engineer turned publican; the man marries one woman to spite another; in the meantime, a former resident of the area returns from Paris and becomes involved in the love complications; the piece represents the novelist's tendency toward the melodramatic.

Henry James, *Daisy Miller*—a novel by the American-born writer; focuses upon the general theme of the artist pitted against the rest of society; the innocent, loyal, and candid spirit appears at the mercy of the world, but intelligence and moral strength fortify the individual for the conflict.

Jan Neruda, *Stories from Mala Strava*—a collection of fiction by the Czech writer; the pieces generally typify early Czech realism.

Rene Francois Sully-Prudhomme, *La Justice*—a poem by the French writer; a series of poetic dialogues between a protagonist identified as "the Seeker," an intellectual who despairs of finding justice in nature or society, and a "Voice" that assures him that justice can be found within every human soul.

Algernon Charles Swinburne, *Poems and Ballads*—a collection by the English writer; includes "A Forsaken Garden," a poetic lament for Charles Baudlaire and Theophile Gautier, and translations of the "Ballades" of Francois Villon.

Leo Tolstoy, *Anna Karenina*—a novel by the Russian playwright, essayist, and writer of fiction; explores the issues of the importance of family life, the role of social institutions in the lives of individuals, and the destructive force inherent in the passion of love; the novelist considers the subtle interplay between four couples; in the end, the piece revolves around the ancient thesis of good versus evil.

EVENTS

Sir George Grove, English musicologist, biblical scholar, and engineer, publishes the first edition of his definitive *Dictionary of Music and Musicians*; the sixth edition (1980) will extend to twenty volumes.

The Biblical Repertory, a significant journal of Presbyterian thought, changes its name to *The Princeton Review* and attempts to become a literary journal with circulation in New York and New Jersey; suspends publication in 1884.

1879

BIRTHS

Albert Einstein (d. 1955.) German-born mathematician, physicist, humanist, musician, and missionary; his truly "literary" endeavors will take the form of passionate appeals against nuclear weapons and for the cause of world peace.

Edward Morgan Forster (d. 1970). English novelist and literary critic; his experiences in India will provide the inspiration for a significant body of fiction representing life in that part of the world; as a critic, he will develop important criteria on the specific aspects of the novel.

Uri Nissan Gnessin (d. 1913). Russian-born Jewish writer of short fiction; his melancholy world will reflect his constant physical illness and discomfort; thus, his characters will always tend to walk the border between life and death.

Nicholas Vachel Lindsay (d. 1931). American poet; he will literally tramp about America, reciting his musical, jazz-like verse and trading copies for people's hospitality; he captured the irrepressible spirits of Black Africa and American evangelicalism.

U Leti Pantita Maun Tyi (d. 1939). Burmese essayist, poet, and translator; he will write the first Burmese historical novels, eulogies of Burma's past glories serving to stimulate national pride.

Vallottol Narayana Menon (d. 1958). Malayalam poet; he will abandon Dravidian metrical forms for Sanskritic ones, becoming a poet of Indian nationalism during the decades preceding independence from Great Britain; later, he will employ his poetry in the struggles for economic and social justice.

Lope K. Santos (d. 1963). Philippine writer of fiction; his novels will concern themselves with the theme of social justice; he will write in the language known as Tagalog.

Wallace Stevens (d. 1955). American poet; he will write elegant, philosophic verse focusing upon the necessity for creating order out of chaos; that theme will also be an important aspect of his drama and nonfiction.

Leon Davidovich Trotsky (d. 1940). Russian political philosopher, historian, and essayist;

he will become the principal strategist and political theorist of the Russian revolution; his essays, letters, and political tracts will form the basis of Marxist literature.

DEATHS

Charles de Coster (b. 1927). German-born Belgian poet and storyteller; his reputation derives from his prose epic in Old French, *Tyl Ulenspiegel,* which took him ten years to write.

PUBLICATIONS

William Dean Howells, *The Lady of the Aroostook*—a novel by the American writer; focuses upon the conflict between three cultures: the central character emerges from her home north of Boston, sails for Italy, and meets cultivated Yankees aboard ship; at Venice, she is shocked by such activities as Sunday opera and by the general immorality of the place; the title of the piece originates from the name of the ship bound for Italy.

Henrik Ibsen, *Et Dukkeehjem* (A Doll's House) —a realistic drama by the Norwegian playwright and poet; a pampered wife commits forgery to save her husband's life; she must endure the threats of a blackmailer before her "crime" comes to her husband's attention; his indignation intensifies because he believes that the marriage has been built upon false premises; the wife leaves her husband and children to find her real identity in the world outside "the doll's house."

George Meredith, *The Egoist*—a novel by the English writer; the central figure is a selfish and conceited man possessing wealth and position; a series of complex romantic relationships results in his humiliation but, through sheer persistence, he wins the hand of the reluctant lady whom he has pursued; the strength of the work lies in its sharply compressed dialogue.

August Strindberg, *Roda Rummet* (The Red Room)—a novel by the Swedish playwright and writer of fiction, his first literary success; based upon the writer's experiences, the work is an episodic satire upon the bohemian circle in Stockholm containing impressions of the artists, journalists, and intellectuals of the period; written in a vivid prose style.

EVENTS

The governors of the British Museum, London, grant unrestricted admission to the general public.

1880

BIRTHS

Muuse Abdillaahi (d.   ?). Somali poet; essentially an oral poet, he will become known for his didactic and occasional verse; he will also be remembered as a folk philosopher, particularly for sayings and maxims summarizing the common wisdom of the people.

Guillaume Apollinaire (d. 1918). French poet (born in Rome of Polish descent); he will become a leader in the movement to reject poetic traditions in attitude, rhythm, and language; thus, his work will resemble that of the cubist school of painters, who revolted against the sensual, emotional art of previous eras; he will become one of the first poets to attempt to produce dislocation and simultaneity.

Sholem Asch (d. 1966). Polish-born American novelist, playwright, and essayist; he will become one of the leading Jewish writers of the twentieth century; he will write principally in Yiddish, portraying small Jewish communities with compassion and shrewdness.

Andrei Bely (pseudonym of Boris Nikolayevich Bugayev; d. 1934). Russian poet and novelist; he will become a leading figure of the symbolist school, at one point attempting to fuse all of the arts into a single poetic work; he will experiment with fiction by following James Joyce's modes and forms.

Alexander Alexandrovich Blok (d. 1921). Russian poet; his mysticism will take the form of a vision of reality where ideal womanhood embodies truth; he will embark upon a symbolic sequence of revolutionary themes that will represent the artistic achievements of Soviet Russia.

Mikheil Javakhisvili (d. 1937). Georgian (SSR) novelist and satirist; he will satirize various aspects of the Georgian national character; in addition, his fiction will treat the conflict between life in the city and life in the village.

Henry Louis Mencken (d. 1956). American essayist, satirist, journalist, and editor; his satirical and highly individual style will exercise a considerable influence on the literary, intellectual, and political climate of post-World War I America; he will also produce a classic work on the American language.

Robert Musil (d. 1942). Austrian novelist; his fiction will be characterized by subtle psychological analyses; stylistically, he will be compared with Marcel Proust.

Alfred Noyes (d. 1958). English poet; his work will focus upon the sea, recalling the days of Elizabeth I; he will receive a visiting professorship of poetry at Princeton University.

Sean O'Casey (d. 1964). Irish playwright and essayist; his early drama will be characterized by an antiheroic view of life and will reveal a chaotic and tragic world, one in which characters resort to ironic and comic defenses for survival; his later pieces will be prophetic morality plays.

Ramon Perez de Ayala (d. 1962). Spanish novelist, essayist, and poet; his fiction will combine realism with an ideal concept of beauty; in general, he will portray reality from a distorted and satirical point of view; in the 1920s, he will turn his attention to experimentation and innovation, creating works of extreme vitality.

Premchand (d. 1936). Indian novelist, short fiction writer, essayist, and playwright; he will become a major figure in twentieth-century Indian literature and the first writer in the Hindi language to employ the themes and techniques of literary realism developed by European writers; he will create realistic representations of Indian life during his own time, thus emphasizing social and political upheaval.

Gershon Schoffman (d. 1971). German-born Jewish novelist and short story writer; he will conduct psychological examinations of his characters' personalities, especially portraying the deep loneliness of young persons uprooted by war and related calamities.

Johann Sigurjonsson (d. 1919). Icelandic playwright and poet; he will become one of the leading figures of modern Icelandic drama and make a significant contribution to the early twentieth-century renaissance in Icelandic literature; his subjects and characters will come from national folk literature, but he will depict them with modern psychological and philosophical insights.

Oswald Spengler (d. 1936). German philosopher and essayist; he will write a treatise on the philosophy of history that will become one of the most important and influential books of the twentieth century; his theories will focus upon the unique identities of separate cultures, yet he will emphasize that each undergoes similar processes of birth, growth, decay, and death.

DEATHS

George Eliot (pseudonym of Mary Ann Evans; b. 1819). English novelist; her fiction focuses upon rural life, revealing her gift for penetrating psychological analysis and insight into moral and philosophical issues; she dies at Cheyne Walk, Chelsea, and her body lies in Highgate Cemetery.

Ludwig Andreas Feuerbach (b. 1829). German philosopher and essayist; as a follower of Georg Wilhelm Friedrich Hegel, he abandoned idealism for materialism; he later established a naturalistic-humanistic ethic.

Gustave Flaubert (b. 1821). French novelist and writer of short fiction; a scrupulous technician and master of realistic fiction, he strived to achieve complete objectivity in both character and theme; he focused upon small-town bourgeois life and the uneventful existence of the Paris middle class; he devoted special care to form, style, and authenticity; he dies at the family home at Croisset.

Tom Taylor (b. 1817). Scottish playwright and editor; he wrote and adapted over one hundred pieces for the stage, but his name has been retained in American history for *Our American Cousin* (1858), the play viewed by Abraham Lincoln when shot by John Wilkes Booth.

PUBLICATIONS

Fedor Dostoevsky, *The Brothers Karamazov*—a novel by the Russian writer of fiction, his last major work before his death; with delicate psychological and philosophical insight, the novelist probed the depth and complexities of the human soul; praised as one of the finest novels ever written, the work is a synthesis of the writer's mature vision; a key issue concerns the denunciation of the alienated radicalism that characterized contemporary Russia.

William Dean Howells, *The Undiscovered Country*—a novel by the American writer, a love story set in the Shakers' religious community.

Jens Jacobsen, *Niels Lynne*—the second of two novels by the Danish poet and writer of fiction; records the author's own mental struggle between dreamy romanticism and harsh, cynical realism.

Henry James, *Washington Square*—a novel by the American-born writer; reworks the theme of the innocent, loyal, and candid spirit at the mercy of the world: in this instance, the central character lacks the intelligence to compensate for her innocence, and she can neither reject nor assent to her gradual exile from society at the hands of an egocentric father and a casual mercenary lover; essentially, the novel is a version of Gustave Flaubert's *Madame Bovary* in reverse.

Sidney Lanier, *The Science of English Verse*—a critical tract by the American poet; a mature recapitulation of the writer's years of experimenting with poetry and his attempts to relate the genre to other creative arts; considers the organic principles of music and poetry as identical, with the concept of sound essential to both, particularly in terms of duration, intensity, pitch, and tonality.

Pierre Loti, *Rarahu*—a novel by the French writer of fiction; semiautobiographical, the piece is set among the Coral seas and relates the story of the love of an Englishman for a Tahitian girl; extremely popular, the work emerged again in 1882 under the title *Le Mariage de Loti.*

Guy de Maupassant, *Boule de Suif*—a work of fiction by the French writer, his first literary success; exposes the hypocrisy, prudery, and ingratitude of the bourgeois in the face of a heroic gesture by a woman of the streets.

George Meredith, *The Tragic Comedians*—a novel by the English writer; based upon Helene von Donniges's account of her tragic love affair with the German Socialist Ferdinand Lassalle; in the fictional version, the daughter of a noble house falls in love, preparing to defy her family by marrying; in the end, that union is only achieved when the man fights a duel with the woman's father and kills him.

Juan Montalvo, *Catilinarias*—a collection of essays by the Ecuadorean essayist and political writer; written during his exile in France and in opposition to the tyrannical regime of Garcia Moreno.

Johanna Spyri, *Heidi*—a children's novel by the Swiss writer, set in the Alps; the piece has retained its popularity.

Alfred, Lord Tennyson, *Ballads and Other Poems*—a collection by the English laureate; includes such pieces as "The Voyage of Maeldune," "Rizpah," "The Revenge," and "The Defense of Lucknow."

Mark Twain, *A Tramp Abroad*—another of the American writer's irreverent, anecdotal travel books; the work attacks and reacts to such aspects of Europe as its languages, guide books, and art criticism; as always, the writer does not hide his own prejudices against the likes of porters, shopkeepers, and authorities.

Giovanni Verga, *Cavalleria Rusticana*—a novella by the Italian writer of fiction; most remembered as the source for an opera of the same title (1890) by Pietro Mascagni.

Lew(is) Wallace, *Ben Hur: A Tale of the Christ*—a novel by the American writer, soldier, and diplomat; a religious piece focusing upon the conversion of a Jewish patrician temporarily turned Roman officer; he rescues his mother and sister, whom Jesus Christ cures of leprosy; the most dramatic segment of the novel occurs during the chariot race; the work became a stage play and then an early film, attesting to its popularity.

Emile Zola, *Nana*—a novel by the French journalist and writer of fiction; narrates the rise and fall of the precociously licentious daughter of an industrious laundress; she becomes the leading Parisian courtesan and symbolizes the ruin of Parisian society.

EVENTS

The Chautauqua (New York) Society, a Methodist Episcopal organization, begins publication of its journal, *The Chautauquan*; it publishes the lectures of a number of leading American scholars; until 1914.

The Dial begins publication at Chicago as a monthly journal of literary criticism; it moves to New York City in 1918; during its final decade, contributors included Thomas Mann and T. S. Eliot; until 1929.

1881

BIRTHS

George Bacovia (pseudonym of Gheorghe Vasiliu; d. 1957). Romanian poet; he will become one of his nation's most significant versifiers, identifying himself with the French Symbolists; his work will also demonstrate close ties with the Expressionists and the Existentialists; the depressed tone and mood of his poetry will reflect his own miserable existence.

Jacob Cohen (d. 1960). Russian-born Israeli poet; he will study philosophy in Switzerland and there organize a circle of intellectuals known for their fervent Zionism; a poet of balanced phrase and measured word, his poetry will be characterized by its harmony, melodious tone, and highly technical style.

Roger Martin du Gard (d. 1958). French novelist and playwright; his training as a historian will lead him to consider phenomena in terms of their broad context; he will strive to create in his fiction and drama a comprehensive and transcendent vision of human existence; he will receive the Nobel Prize for literature in 1937.

Juan Ramon Jiminez (d. 1958). Spanish (Andalusian) poet; through his poetry, he will seek to uncover the language of reality and to relearn the meaning of words; his later pieces will be combinations of the highly abstract and the deliberately humanized; he will receive the Nobel Prize for literature in 1956.

Mordecai Menahem Kaplan (d. 1983). Lithuanian-born American scholar, philosopher, and Hebrew theologian; he will write profound studies of Judaism and become the founder of the religious movement known as Reconstructionism; his works will reflect his intent to reconcile traditional Judaism with current scientific concepts.

Alfonso Henrique de Lima Barreto (d. 1922). Brazilian novelist, essayist, writer of short fiction, and journalist; deeply affected by prejudice and discrimination, he will become the first novelist to examine the problems of black and mulatto Brazilians.

Emil Ludwig (d. 1948). German biographer and playwright; he will write vivid and creative biographies of Johann Wolfgang von Goethe, Napoleon I, and Otto von Bismarck.

Gregorio Martinez Sierra (d. 1947). Spanish novelist and playwright; a number of his plays will become popular in England and America, principally because of their feminist themes.

Giovanni Papini (d. 1956). Italian essayist and biographer; the leader of young radicals and intellectuals anxious to revolutionize Italian letters, arts, and social thought, he will influence modern Italian culture during the early years of the twentieth century.

Lu Xun (d. 1936). Chinese critic; he will lecture at various universities, becoming a founding member of the Left Wing Writers and launching an anticommunist campaign; he will attempt, through his prose, to ignite the militant spirit of the Chinese patriots.

Stefan Zweig (d. 1942). Austrian biographer, fiction writer, and essayist; he will write popular biographies and novellas, both influenced by analytic psychology; his works will support the idea of a Europe undivided by political borders.

DEATHS

Thomas Carlyle (b. 1795). Scottish-born poet, essayist, and historian; he gained attention as an interpreter of German Romanticism; criticizing the materialism of his age and attacking laissez-faire theory and parliamentary democracy, he emphasized his beliefs in strong government and great men (heroes); he dies at his house in Chelsea and is buried in the churchyard of Ecclefechan, Dumfriesshire (Scotland), beside his family.

Marcus Andrew Hislop Clarke (b. 1846). Australian novelist, essayist, and playwright; he wrote one of the first works of Australian fiction to gain attention abroad, principally because of its attention to the specifics of the Australian penal system; the novel's strength derives from its powerful and graphic depiction of the themes of Colonial displacement and alienation.

Fedor Mikhailovich Dostoevsky (b. 1821). Russian novelist and short story writer; his fiction reveals a profound insight into character, a preoccupation with abnormal psychology, and a recognition of the absurd; through his religious and sociological themes, he advanced his own mystical view of Russian Christianity as an antidote to rationalism and socialism.

Sidney Lanier (b. 1842). American poet and essayist; taking a scientific approach to poetry, he broke from traditional metrical techniques and attempted to relate poetry to musical composition.

Edward John Trelawny (b. 1792). English narrative writer and adventurer; remembered for his close friendship with Percy Bysshe Shelley and for his narratives recording his association with that poet, as well as Lord Byron.

PUBLICATIONS

Anatole France, *Le Crime de Sylvestre Bonnard* (The Crime of Sylvestre Bonnard)—the first novel by the French writer of fiction; relates the tale of an old man who seeks after pleasure, capturing, for himself, the daughter of a former mistress.

Thomas Hardy, *A Laodicean*—a novel by the English writer; concerns the daughter of a successful railway contractor whose vacillating and lukewarm character initiates a series of romantic and adventurous trials.

Joel Chandler Harris, *Uncle Remus: His Songs and His Sayings*—the first book-length publication by the American writer; a collection of Negro lore, plantation songs, and country anecdotes; revealed to the American readership the literary potential of life among black Americans; the title character is a composite picture of the Georgia plantation workers whose stories the writer had recorded.

William Dean Howells, *Dr. Breen's Practice*—a novel by the American writer; the strength of the work derives from its shockingly accurate representation of the trivial and malicious nature of the conversations between residents at a Seaside hotel; the key issue of the novel, however, is the question of whether medicine is a suitable profession for women.

Henry James, *The Portrait of a Lady*—a novel by the American writer of fiction; again the writer concerns himself with an American character who is victimized by European Society; in this work, Isabel Archer refuses one marriage to an English peer, but marries another gentleman to whom she remains loyal, despite his vile character; most assuredly, in James's view, the American transplanted into a European environment requires considerable strength of character.

Antoine Louis Camille Lemonnier, *Un Male* (A Male)—a novel by the Belgian writer; the work portrays the idyllic existence of a man who lives unfettered by social restraints in the primeval forest setting, which is portrayed as the proper environment for human beings.

Joacquim Maria Machado de Assis, *Epitaph for a Small Winner*—a novel by the Brazilian writer; combines the writer's keen philosophical insight and his pessimistic vision; a parody of the picaresque and all of the so-called "philosophies," particularly positivism.

Guy de Maupassant, *La Maison Tellier*—a volume of short stories by the French writer; the title piece relates, with penetrating satire and humor, the story of an outing for inmates of a house of ill repute.

Anthony Trollope, *Ayala's Angel*—a novel by the English writer; focuses on a brother and sister who, raised in a luxurious home, find themselves orphans; difficulties arise when they become members of two different households with greatly divergent incomes.

————— , *Dr. Wortle's School*—a novel by the English writer; focuses upon the proprietor of a highly successful private school patronized by the nobility; the title character defends, and eventually proves correct in supporting, an assistant master.

Giovanni Verga, *I Malavoglia* (The House by the Medlar Tree)—a novel by the Sicilian writer; concerns the impact of malign fate upon Sicilian fisherman; attempts to explore the effects of human progress, particularly as it influences the Italian concept of "honor."

EVENTS

The Century Illustrated Monthly Magazine begins publication in New York City as a continuation of *Scribner's Monthly* (begun 1870); contains narratives of the Civil War, publishes pieces by Joel Chandler Harris, and serializes novels by such authors as William Dean Howells, Henry James, and Jack London; until 1930.

The Critic begins publication in New York City as a weekly literary magazine with book reviews; publishes works by Walt Whitman, Joel Chandler Harris, Julia Ward Howe, and Edward Everett Hale; until 1906.

Freedom of the press established in France.

The Vatican archives in Rome are opened to scholars of all nations.

1882

BIRTHS

Mirza Abolqasem Quazvini Aref (d. 1934). Iranian poet; his poetry will reflect his total commitment to the Iranian national revival and to the modernization of his nation.

Jean Giraudoux (d. 1944). French poet, playwright, and writer of fiction; his work will be steeped in symbolism and considerably influenced by then current psychoanalytic theories; his literary style will parallel the techniques of the impressionist painters.

Susan Glaspell (d. 1948). American novelist, playwright, and writer of short stories; she will gain recognition as the founder of the Provincetown Players (1915); in her fiction and drama, she will emphasize the psychological aspects of her characters.

James Augustine Aloysius Joyce (d. 1941). Irish novelist, poet, essayist, and writer of short fiction; his prose fiction will challenge the conventions of the genre: time, for him, will become elastic, as consciousness dominates and dictates the sequence of events; plot and character will emerge in a stream of association, the language so constructed that the sound supersedes the sense and words become almost like music; in one sense, he will translate to the art of fiction the conception and technique of musical composition.

Jacques Maritain (d. 1972). French Roman Catholic philosopher; his critiques will focus upon art, politics, and history.

Cuppiramaniyam Ci. Parati (d. 1921). Indian (Tamil) poet and essayist; his work will display the influence of classical Tamil poetry, with echoes of John Keats, Percy Bysshe Shelley, and Ralph Waldo Emerson; he will attack the social evils of Hindu society with passionately radical songs designed to inspire a national movement within Tamiol India.

Sigrid Undset (d. 1949). Danish-born Norwegian novelist; her fiction will reflect a concern for the problems of young middle-class women, but her best work will be her graphic and authentic recreations of the Middle Ages in Norway; she will receive the Nobel Prize for literature in 1928.

Hendrik Willem Van Loon (d. 1944). Dutch-born American popular historian; his illus-trated history of mankind will become a "best-seller," as will his biographies and studies of sea explorations.

Virginia Woolf (d. 1941). English novelist; her fiction will be marked by an evasive and impressionistic style, a development of the stream of consciousness technique; this, in combination with her psychological penetration, will endow her prose with a quality more associated with poetry than with fiction.

DEATHS

Janos Arany (b. 1817). Hungarian poet; his ballads and epic trilogy have achieved recognition for a powerful and simple style reminiscent of the folk song; he also published successful translations of Shakespeare and Aristophanes.

Richard Henry Dana, Jr. (b. 1815). American writer and lawyer; his classic narrative of the days of the sailing ships was based on his experiences as a sailor and helped to improve the seaman's lot; he also wrote a manual of maritime law.

Charles Robert Darwin (b. 1809). English naturalist and essayist; he firmly established the theory of organic evolution, spending his entire career accumulating and assimilating data to formulate that concept; he dies suddenly, his body taken to Westminster Abbey for burial.

Ralph Waldo Emerson (b. 1803). American poet and essayist; one of the nation's most influential writers and thinkers, he is associated with transcendentalism and its emphasis upon the mystical unity of nature; his philosophy displays the influence of Thomas Carlyle, Samuel Taylor Coleridge, William Wordsworth, Plato, and Emanuel Swedenborg; in religion, he advanced the notion that the soul of each individual stands as the supreme judge over spiritual concerns.

Joseph Arthur de Gobineau (b. 1816). French essayist, historian, poet, and writer of short fiction; one of the earliest writers to promote Aryan superiority as a scientific theory; he dies of apoplexy at Turin.

Henry Kendall (b. 1839). Australian poet and journalist; considered one of the most important Australian poets of the nineteenth century and a significant influence on the development of that nation's literature; his work is known for its nature imagery, its detailed descriptions of the Australian landscape and coast, its praise of the country's beauty, and its highly lyrical quality; he dies from tuberculosis.

Henry Wadsworth Longfellow (b. 1807). American poet and professor of modern languages; he created a body of romantic American legends with his long poetic narratives; his verse, often sentimental and moralizing, has a unique metrical quality due to his use of unorthodox and antiquated rhythms; he dies at his home in Cambridge, Massachusetts.

Dante Gabriel Rossetti (b. 1828). English poet and artist; his poetry, as well as his painting, is marked by pictorial effects and an atmosphere of luxurious beauty; with W. Holman Hunt and John Everett Millais, he founded the Pre-Raphaelite Brotherhood in protest against current standards in British art, which advocated a traditional, stylized approach; they sought, instead, to create beauty and simplicity through the symbolism and imagery of the medieval world.

James Thomson (b. 1834). Scottish poet and essayist; his major poetic piece has gained recognition as a compelling expression of religious despair in Victorian society; in general, his poetry reflects his total negation of Christian faith and idealism; he also translated and analyzed the works of the nineteenth-century Italian poet Giacomo Leopardi; he dies of internal hemorrhaging brought about by years of chronic alcoholism.

Anthony Trollope (b. 1815). English novelist; he produced approximately fifty volumes of fiction, nearly all of them focusing upon the "usual" activities and occurrences of life; he created the fictional county of "Barsetshire," a symbol of ordinary English existence.

PUBLICATIONS

Henry Becque, *Les Corbeaux* (The Vultures)— a naturalistic drama by the French playwright and critic, begun as early as 1877; the piece contains little action but is, instead, an exercise in the depiction of various emotions, from lighthearted joy to hopeless futility; thus, death cancels the prospects for a happy wedding and creates a condition whereby love must give way to the "business" of marriage.

Bankim Chandra Chatterji, *Ananda Math* (The Abbey of Bliss)—a novel by the Indian writer of fiction; concerns the Indian patriots fighting against the British during the 1773 Sannyasi rebellion in North Bengal; the piece helped to fuel the flames of the Indian nationalist movements prior to World War I.

Theodor Fontane, *La Adultera*—a novel by the German poet and writer of fiction; realistically depicts the moral and social decay of contemporary Berlin society.

Thomas Hardy, *Two on a Tower*—a novel by the English writer; a lady falls in love with a young astronomer during her unkind husband's absence; when her husband dies, she marries the astronomer, at the same time depriving him of a legacy; further problems arise when she learns that her husband had not yet died at the moment of the marriage; the astronomer leaves for Africa and the woman (with his child) marries a bishop, who eventually dies; finally, the woman dies in her old age after the astronomer has returned and promised to marry her.

William Dean Howells, *A Modern Instance*—a novel by the American writer, his only study of married life; the piece concerns an ambitious journalist whose character disintegrates; his wife, on the other hand, rises in moral stature; a love triangle occurs here, but in the end the woman discovers that no man can serve as a refuge from her husband.

Henrik Ibsen, *Ein Folkfiende* (An Enemy of the People)—a realistic drama by the Norwegian poet and playwright; the theme concerns the idea that an individual cannot act without at least a superficial knowledge of society; thus, a community will not accept a truth that denies them, even for a moment, their livelihood; the main character cannot accept the notion that no single scientific truth is valid if separated from human truth.

Henry Wadsworth Longfellow, *In the Harbor*—the last collection of verse by the American poet; contains such pieces as "Becalmed," "The Poet's Calendar," "Victor and Vanquished," "The Children's Crusade," "Hermes Trismegistus," "Mad River," and "The Bells of San Blas."

Freidrich Wilhelm Nietzsche, *Die Frohliche Wissenschaft* (The Joyful Wisdom)—a collection of essays and aphorisms by the German philosopher, essayist, and poet; reflects a change in the writer's interests from art and aesthetics to science and what he termed "the free spirit"; also evidences his belief in the meaninglessness of life and in the decadent origins of religion, particularly Christianity.

Algernon Charles Swinburne, *Tristram of Lyonesse*—a romantic poem by the English versifier; written in rhymed couplets, the piece has long been considered the poet's finest work; the volume also includes a series of sonnets on the Elizabethan playwrights and "Athens, an Ode," which compares the victory of Salamis with the defeat of the Spanish Armada.

Mark Twain, *The Prince and the Pauper*—a novel by the American writer and humorist; primarily a story for children focusing on the traditional plot of transposed identities.

Walt Whitman, *Specimen Days and Collect*—a collection by the American poet, autobiographical prose narratives relating his personal distresses, griefs, and frustrations.

EVENTS

Brander Matthews, American essayist and critic, founds, with others, The Author's Club, a New York City literary society.

The Berliner Tageblatt, an influential newspaper, begins publication at Berlin.

George Smith, London publisher, designs and publishes *The Dictionary of National Biography,* with Sir Leslie Stephen, the English critic and literary scholar, as the first editor; contains biographies of all British notables, from the earliest times; the most recent edition was published in 1970.

The Scottish Texts Society founded at Edinburg; prints and edits texts representative of Scottish language and literature; publishes such works as *The Kingis Quair* (1423-1424), John Barbour's *The Bruce* (1375), the *Basilikon Doron* (1599), the poems of the Scottish Chaucerians (William Dunbar, Robert Henryson, William Drummond of Hawthornden, and Sir David Lyndsay), and poems by Allan Ramsay and Robert Fergusson.

1883

BIRTHS

Hjalmar Fredrik Elgerus Bergman (d. 1931). Swedish novelist, playwright, and writer of short fiction; he will become the outstanding Swedish writer of the early twentieth century, often compared with August Strindberg; mel-

ancholic and fundamentally expressionist, he will take refuge in his own world of blindness, poor health, and depression.

Fyodor Vasilyevich Gladkov (d. 1958). Russian novelist, essayist, and playwright; his major fiction will document the changes in Russia following the 1917 revolution; as a member of the Communist Party, he will, in his work, strongly support the new regime and endorse with enthusiasm governmental plans for reorganizing Russian society.

Jibran Khalil Jibran (d. 1931). Lebanese-born American poet and critic; his literary labors will reflect the dilemma of a Christian living in a Western environment who is nostalgically attached to his Arab homeland; he will advance the ideals of universal love and communion with Nature.

Franz Kafka (d. 1924). Czech-born Austrian novelist, essayist, and writer of short fiction; he will be recognized for his clear and precise prose that presents a world both real and dreamlike; in his fiction, modern persons, burdened with guilt, isolation, and anxiety, undertake futile searches for personal salvation.

Nikos Kazantzakis (d. 1957). Greek poet and novelist (born on Crete); his work will reveal an intensely poetic and religious nature; he will reflect on the teachings of Buddha, Jesus Christ, Friedrich Wilhelm Nietzsche, and Vladimir Lenin in his poetic exploration of the world.

John Maynard Keynes (d. 1946). English economist and essayist; he will write important treatises on money, interest, and employment, arguing that government could indeed solve unemployment problems; he will have considerable influence upon the New Deal of Franklin Delano Roosevelt.

Jose Ortego y Gassett (d. 1955). Spanish humanist and essayist; he will introduce the works of James Joyce and Marcel Proust into Spain, and his literary criticism will earn him a reputation throughout the nation; he will outline the national symbols of Spanish literature.

Mutaliyar Tiruvarur V. Kaliyanacuntaram (d. 1953). Indian (Tamil) essayist and philosopher; his essays, literary criticism, and speeches will strongly influence modern Tamil literary, cultural, and linguistic development; he will abandon his adherence to Gandhi and adopt a combination of Marxism and Tamil nationalism.

Henry Masila Ndawo (d. 1949). South African (Xhosa) novelist and poet; his poetry will be highly respected by the Bungani people; he will also write the first Xhosa novel and publish two collections of folk tales.

Pi Mounin (d. 1940). Burmese essayist, novelist, and writer of short fiction; his work will demonstrate a constant preoccupation with the individual: the effects of freedom and choice and responsibility for one's own prosperity are two of his favorite themes; he will also demonstrate an interest in the psychology of character.

Katharine Susanna Prichard (d. 1969). Fijian-born Australian novelist, short fiction writer, poet, essayist, and playwright; she will insist upon a truly national literature based on Australian subject matter; thus, she will travel throughout the nation to authenticate the various settings for her fiction: the bush country of Victoria, the opal fields of northern New South Wales, the karri forests of the southwest, the cattle stations of the west.

Alexey Nikolayevich Tolstoy (d. 1945). Russian novelist, writer of short fiction, playwright, poet, and essayist; he will become one of the most prominent Russian writers of the post-revolutionary era; his novels will depict Russian history in conformity with official Soviet ideology; thus, he will strongly influence the development of the Soviet historical novel.

Federigo Tozzi (d. 1920). Italian novelist, writer of short fiction, poet, essayist, and playwright; he will become one of Italy's most distinctive novelists of the early twentieth century; he will write in colloquial language and discard formal narrative structure; he will focus upon the lower-class life of his native Tuscany.

William Carlos Williams (d. 1963). American poet; an acute observer of American life, he will develop a lucid, vital style, relying upon idiomatic speech and an attention to the ordinary sights and sounds that he experienced.

DEATHS

Hendrik Conscience (b. 1812). Flemish novelist; often considered the founder of modern Flemish literature; produced romantic historical novels in the tradition of Sir Walter Scott.

Edward Fitzgerald (b. 1809). English poet and translator; his translation from the Persian of the *Rubaiyat of Omar Khayyam* established his reputation; he also wrote a dialogue on educational systems, published a collection of aphorisms, and translated Pedro Calderon de la Barca.

Karl Marx (b. 1818). German philosopher and essayist; regarded as one of the significant figures in the history of ideas, he has received credit for the establishment of modern communism; his prose tracts provided the ideological basis for the majority of communist and socialist forms of government and profoundly influenced world politics during the twentieth century; he dies at London, his health having failed after years of poverty and strenuous research.

Cyprian Kamil Norwid (b. 1821). Polish poet, playwright, essayist, and writer of fiction; one of the more innovative of nineteenth-century Polish poets, he ignored the conventions of Romantic poetry and formulated consciously difficult stylistic techniques and methods of construction to express his artistic and philosophic beliefs; the idiosyncratic nature of his literary work gained him only ridicule from his contemporaries; he dies at a home in Paris for poor and elderly Polish emigres.

Jules Sandeau (b. 1811). French novelist and playwright; his work presented an accurate picture of the social conflicts of nineteenth-century France; an academician and librarian as well as a writer.

Ivan Sergeyevich Turgenev (b. 1818). Russian novelist, playwright, and writer of short fiction; his early work contributed to the emancipation of the Russian serfs by the czar; his mature works also closely analyze political and social conditions in Russia; he initiated the term "nihilist."

PUBLICATIONS

Bjornstjerne Bjornson, *Over Aevne* (Beyond Human Endurance)—a play by the Norwegian novelist and dramatist; focuses upon the themes of sexual equality and the social aspects of religion; specifically, a clergyman, capable of working miracles, cannot respond to his wife's love.

Robert Browning, *Jocoseria*—a collection by the English poet; contains the well-received dramatic monologue "Christina and Monaldeschi."

Carlo Collodi, *Pinocchio: The Story of a Puppet*—a work of didactic fiction intended for children by the Italian novelist and journalist.

Arne Garbourg, *Bondestudentar* (Peasant Students)—a novel by the Norwegian writer; an indictment of the circumstances under which young men had to acquire their educations.

Jan Neruda, *Plain Themes*—a collection of poetry by the Czech versifier; the pieces resemble, in style and form, the works of Heinrich Heine.

Friedrich Wilhelm Nietzsche, *Also Sprach Zarathustra: Ein Buch fur Alle und Keinen* (Thus Spake Zarathurstra: a Book for All and None)—the initial presentation of the German philosopher and essayist's mature philosophy; here he introduces his concepts of the will to power, the "Ubermensch" (superman), and the eternal return; all of the writer's subsequent ideas evolve from this work; 4 volumes, to 1885.

Olive Schreiner, *The Story of a South African Farm*—a novel by the South African (Basutoland) writer; the first sustained, imaginative work of fiction to come from Africa; the piece was published under the pseudonym of "Ralph Iron," and it was George Meredith who accepted the work for publication.

Robert Louis Stevenson, *Treasure Island*—a novel by the English poet and writer of fiction; a youngster, the narrator of the piece, gains a treasure map, hands it to a squire, and accompanies him in search of the hidden booty; pirates attempt to seize their vessel, but the youngster discovers the plot and eventually joins in the discovery of the treasure; a work that belongs within the sub-genre of adolescent literature.

Mark Twain, *Life on the Mississippi*—an autobiographical narrative by the American writer; a rich and realistic illustration of the human comedy and tragedy of life against the backdrop of the Mississippi river.

Emile Verhaeren, *Les Flemandes* (The Flemish)—the first collection of verse by the Belgian poet, an exuberant celebration of modern pagan man.

Philippe Auguste Villiers de l'Isle Adam, *Contes Cruels*—a collection of short stories by the French writer of fiction; composed in the manner of Edgar Allan Poe.

EVENTS

Francis James Child, American scholar at Harvard College, publishes his important collection, *English and Scottish Popular Ballads*; five volumes, to 1898.

Cyrus Hermann Kotczaschmar Curtis, New York publisher, founds *The Ladies' Home Journal,* a monthly magazine of popular literature; its later editorial policy will promote social reform.

Life Magazine, a weekly journal of humor, begins publication at New York City; from 1926 to 1972, it will function as an illustrated popular magazine of current events; it will be revived as a monthly in 1978.

Alfred Austin, William John Courthope, and L. J. Maxse found *The National Review,* a London journal of politics and literature.

1884

BIRTHS

Aleksandre Abasheli (d. 1954). Georgian (SSR) poet, novelist, and film writer; he will write in standard Russian and Georgian, both meditative and nature lyrics.

Gaddiel Robert Acquah (d. 1954). Ghana novelist, poet, and scholar; he will compose didactic poems, hymns for children, and one posthumous novel.

Halide Edib Adivar (d. 1964). Turkish novelist and critic; with techniques displaying Western sophistication, she will attempt to interpret traditional Turkish heritage for Western readers.

Yahya Kemal Beyatli (d. 1958). Turkish poet; relying upon traditional poetic meters, he will be considered the last classical poet of Turkey.

Georges Duhamel (d. 1966). French novelist, poet, and essayist; he will study medicine and become an army surgeon, but he will also produce fifty volumes of vigorous and skillful prose.

Lion Feuchtwanger (d. 1958). German novelist, satirist, and translator; his eighteenth-century historical novels will present an elaborate picture of Jews in central Europe, their sufferings and weaknesses; he will also satirize Adolf Hitler's successes in the Munich putsch.

Abdurrauf Fitrat (d. 1947?). Tajik and Uzbek (SSR) satirist and writer of fiction; he will attack the lack of culture and education in Central Asia and emphasize nationalism;

the language of his prose will be simple and easily comprehensible.

Romulo Gallegos (d. 1969). Venezuelan novelist and political leader; he will explore life within his nation, concentrating upon its landscape and customs.

Omer Seyfettin (d. 1920). Turkish writer of fiction; he will become one of the most significant innovators in Turkish literature, relying upon the simple, broken language of the lower classes; he will fight for the modernization of his nation, but without undue reliance upon the West.

Sri (pseudonym of B. M. Srikanthayya; d. 1946). Indian (Kannada) poet and translator; his translations of English Romantic lyrics will inspire a renaissance in Kannada poetry, as he introduces Percy Bysshe Shelley, William Wordsworth, and Robert Burns to his Indian readers.

Su Man-shu (pseudonym of Su Chin; d. 1918). Chinese poet, translator, and writer of fiction; he will be remembered for his translations of English Romantic literature, his autobiographical fiction, and his attempts to create a broader awareness within his nation of Western verse; he will also be recognized as a central figure in the development of modern Chinese poetry.

Daniel Varuzhan (d. 1915). Armenian poet; his poetry will be inspired by the oppressed conditions of minority life in Turkey; it will also reflect his knowledge of the political and cultural trends of Europe.

DEATHS

Emanuel von Geibel (b. 1815). German poet; he published translations from Greek, Spanish, and Italian writers; with Paul Johann von Heyse, he founded the Munich school of poetry, which emphasized harmony and form; he also wrote two dramatic tragedies.

Heinrich Laube (b. 1806). German playwright; a leader of the Young Germany movement and editor of its literary organ; he wrote historical drama, fiction, and biography; he dies at Vienna.

PUBLICATIONS

Leopoldo Alas y Urena, *La Regenta* (The Regentess)—a novel by the Spanish writer; recognized as the most complex and sensitive social analysis written in Spain during the nineteenth century; 2 volumes, to 1885.

Paul Bourget, *L'Irreparable*—the first novel by the French essayist and writer of fiction; depicts cynical and selfish characters, wretches who live at the mercy of their own sensations.

Isabella Valancy Crawford, *Old Spookses' Pass, Malcolm Katie, and Other Poems*—a collection of verse by the Irish-born Canadian poet and writer of fiction; the only volume of her poetry to be published during her lifetime; the two title pieces reflect the influence of Alfred, Lord Tennyson; the first portrays the life and adventures of cattle ranchers in the Rocky Mountains, while the second is a pastoral romance; the other pieces include short lyrics, songs about native Indians, and patriotic verses set against Norse, classical, and oriental backgrounds.

Gabriele D'Annunzio, *L'Intermezzo di Rime* (Intermezzo of Poems)—a collection of verse by the Italian poet, playwright, and writer of fiction; the pieces demonstrate the poet's narrative craft and extraordinary command of language.

Alphonse Daudet, *Sapho* (Sappho)—a work of fiction by the French poet, novelist, and narrative writer, a tale about the infatuation of a young man for a courtesan.

Henrik Ibsen, *Vildanden* (The Wild Duck)—a tragicomedy by the Norwegian playwright; combines naturalistic minuteness of detail with complex symbolism; an attack upon rigid, narrow-minded interpretations of truth, the "wild duck" of the title, a pet, represents an escape from reality on the part of a musician and inventor who cannot easily abandon his world of illusions and confront reality.

Henryk Sienkiewicz, *With Fire and Sword*—a historical novel by the Polish writer of fiction; describes the revolts and struggles of Cossacks, Ukraine Tartars, and Turks against the Polish Commonwealth; also concerns the submerging of Poland and Lithuania by the armies of Sweden in 1655.

August Strindberg, *Giftas* (Married)—a collection of short stories by the Swedish playwright and novelist; most remembered because flippant references in the work to the sacrament of marriage caused the writer to be tried for blasphemy; to 1885.

Alfred, Lord Tennyson, *Becket*—a dramatic tragedy by the English laureate; concerns the bitter quarrel between King Henry II and

Thomas à Becket over the latter's appointment as Archbishop of Canterbury; the king authorizes Becket's murder; also includes the issue of Henry's love for Fair Rosamund and the attempts of Queen Eleanor to eliminate her.

Mark Twain, *The Adventures of Huckleberry Finn*—a novel by the American writer and humorist, the successor to *Tom Sawyer* (1876); the title character, the narrator, represents the skeptic who has risen from a terribly hard environment and developed common sense and a firm idea of reality; at the same time, however, Huck remains faithful to those he comes to know and love, especially the underdogs of life; thus, he instinctively turns upon bullies and serves, essentially, as a true representative of the American democratic character; a classic of world literature.

Paul Verlaine, *Jadis et Naguere*—a collection of lyric poems by the French writer of verse; written during one of his periods of repentance from his generally alcoholic existence; considered his finest lyrics.

EVENTS

The Grolier Club founded at New York City for the study of the art of book production; it has sponsored the publication and exhibition of fine volumes of original and classic works.

Josef Ignacy Kraszewski, the Polish poet and novelist, imprisoned at Magdeburg for treason.

Le Matin, a French periodical, begins publication at Paris.

The first part of *The Oxford English Dictionary* (OED) published by Oxford University Press; completed edition in 1928; supplements in 1933, 1972, 1976, 1982, 1986; new edition in 1989; 414,825 words with 1,827,306 literary examples; based upon historical principles, the meanings and forms of words have been traced from their earliest appearances to their present forms and meanings.

1885

BIRTHS

Dino Campana (d. 1932). Italian poet and prose writer; his lyrics will combine elements of Futurism (reaction against late nineteenth-century Romanticism) with influences from various nineteenth-century Italian and foreign poets, including Giosue Carducci, Walt Whitman, and Arthur Rimbaud; the largest portion of his work will be distinguished by its broad European perspective rather than an exclusively Italian one.

Isak Dinesen (pseudonym of Karen, Baroness Blixen; d. 1962). Danish novelist and short fiction writer; renowned for her gifts as a storyteller, she will also achieve recognition for her epic wisdom, expressions of profound feminine sorrow, and accurate accounts of personal experiences.

Ahmet Hasim (d. 1933). Turkish poet; he will spend most of his life as a professor at Istanbul; he will produce verse that is perfect in form and expression and representative of the poet of delicate feeling; his best poetry will be his impressionistic landscape descriptions.

Ho-bieu-Chanh (pseudonym of Ho-van-Trung; d. 1958). Vietnamese novelist and short fiction writer; he will produce more than sixty novels, written in a lively style and clearly influenced by Hector Malot and Victor Hugo.

Velimir Vladimirovich Khlebnikov (d. 1922). Russian poet, playwright, essayist, and writer of fiction; he will found and become a leading member of Russian Futurism, attempting to revitalize poetry by rejecting traditional aesthetic principles; he will conduct poetic experiments exploring the relationship between sound and meaning.

David Herbert Lawrence (d. 1930). English novelist and poet; with his sensitive spirit, he will have difficulty responding to constant charges that his fiction is obscene; he will challenge the young intellectuals of his day with his attempts to interpret human emotion on a level of consciousness much deeper than theirs; he will become known as one of the most imaginative writers of his generation.

Harry Sinclair Lewis (d. 1951). American novelist; his fiction will satirize the empty and useless materialism of his times, as well as the general prejudice against life in small-town America; he will become the first American to receive the Nobel Prize for literature (1930), having earned a Pulitzer Prize in 1926.

Andre Maurois (pseudonym of Emile Herzog; d. 1967). French novelist and biographer; his work will reflect a shrewd but affectionate observation of the human character; he will gain recognition for his biographies of Percy Bysshe Shelley, Benjamin Disraeli, Lord Byron, Marcel Proust, and George Sand.

Francois Mauriac (d. 1970). French novelist, playwright, and essayist; his characters will appear to be chained to prosperous bourgeois conventions, to religion, and to their own human frailties; he will receive the Nobel Prize for literature in 1952.

Lekhnath Pandyal (d. 1965). Nepali poet; his verse will contain veiled allusions to his desire to be free from his role as court poet at Kathmandu; the style and vocabulary of his poetry will be influenced by Sanskrit.

Ezra Weston Loomis Pound (d. 1972). American-born poet; his literary and personal reputation will suffer when he comes under the influence of fascism and presents antidemocracy radio broadcasts during the early stages of World War II; nonetheless, he will become a major poet and a motivating force behind the emergence of modern poetry; he will also write criticism on literature, music, art, and economics, while publishing translations of Italian, French, Japanese, and Chinese writers.

Liviu Rebreanu (d. 1944). Roumanian novelist, writer of short fiction, playwright, and essayist; he will become the major Roumanian writer of the post-World War I period; his fiction will document, comprehensively and realistically, the turbulent nature of Roumanian life during the early twentieth century.

Sanatizade Kermani (d. ?). Iranian novelist; he will become one of the first Iranians to write historical novels, drawing upon both the ancient history of Iran and its more recent times; he will rely upon Western models, particularly from the French.

Vahan Terian (pseudonym of Ter-Grigorian; d. 1920). Armenian poet; his verse, containing elements of both Russian and French symbolism, will convey the depressing social atmosphere in Russia after the failure of the 1905 revolution, as well as the plight of the Armenian minority in Turkey.

Anzia Yezierska (d. 1970). Russian-born American novelist, writer of short fiction, and essayist; her fiction will reveal in detail the experiences of the Jewish immigrant in the United States during the early twentieth century; thus, her characters will search for the "American dream" while, at the same time, contend with a new and often hostile environment.

DEATHS

Edmund Francois Valentin About (b. 1828). French novelist; his farcical tales gained him both popularity and fame, essentially because they afforded free and wide range to his wit, fancy, and vivacity.

Victor Hugo (b. 1802). French novelist, poet, playwright, and critic; nineteenth-century France's leading literary figure; his fiction portrays the suffering of humanity with considerable passion and power, while reflecting his political shift from monarchist to ardent republican; he dies in Paris.

Susanna Strickland Moodie (b. 1803). English-born Canadian short story writer, poet, and novelist; termed one of the finest Canadian immigrant writers of the nineteenth century, her autobiographical sketches and poems are noted for their humor, vivid descriptions of scenery, and realistic portrayal of life on the Canadian frontier; she dies impoverished in Toronto.

PUBLICATIONS

Henry Becque, *La Parisienne* (Woman of Paris)—a cynical comedy by the French playwright and critic; a parody of Parisian marital relations, a cuckold trusts his wife and allows her lover to remain in his home; the heroine may be obsessed with maintaining a respectable appearance, but she has the sense to recognize and regret the results of her own folly.

William Dean Howells, *The Rise of Silas Lapham*—a novel by the American writer reflecting his attitude toward Boston society; depicts a new American, a self-made millionaire who has risen from humble, rural origins; he has inherited physical strength from generations of workers but he has also dedicated himself to speed and business; his wife, from similar stock, must devote considerable time to the direction of her daughters' social lives.

Guy de Maupassant, *Bel Ami*—a novel by the French writer of fiction; the piece aroused a storm of negative criticism, principally because it presented its readers with the worst possible phase of Parisian life, even though the writer treated his subject with skill.

George Meredith, *Diana of the Crossways*—a novel by the English writer; a beautiful and witty Irish girl marries a stupid official; she engages in innocent indiscretions, which serve only to arouse his jealousy; he attempts to divorce her but fails, and the two live apart; a number of affairs transpire, but when the husband finally dies, Diana finds a faithful lover.

Juan Montalvo, *Chapters Forgotten by Cervantes*—a comic prose piece by the Ecuadorean essayist and political writer; a witty sequel, with political overtones, to Cervantes' *Don Quixote.*

Walter Horatio Pater, *Marius the Epicurean*— a philosophical romance by the English writer; concerns the life of a young Roman during the time of the Antonines; the writer traces the reactions of his character to the various spiritual influences with which he comes into contact: Apuleius, Heraclitus, Aristippus the Cyrenaic, and Marcus Aurelius; he must also wrestle with the contrasts between the ancient Roman religion, the horrors of the Roman ampitheatre, and the quiet courage and enthusiasm of the Christian community.

John Ruskin, *Praeterita, Outlines of Scenes and Thoughts*—an autobiography by the English writer and art critic, published at intervals until 1889, but never completed; relates the influences upon the writer, his childhood, his first visit to the Alps ("the Gates of the Hills"), his travels in France and Italy, and his relationships with friends.

Mikhail Saltykov, *Skazki* (Fables)—a collection of animal stories by the Russian novelist and satirist; as a comment on society, the fables represent the theme of the eventual triumph of the downtrodden masses through revolution.

Robert Louis Stevenson, *Child's Garden of Verses*—a collection of verse for juveniles by the English writer, dedicated to his faithful nurse, Alison Cunningham; the pieces literally radiate with the joys of childhood; underlying all, one finds the poet's characteristic urge to explore, to discover all that is new in the world.

Algernon Charles Swinburne, *Marino Faliero, Doge of Venice*—a historical dramatic tragedy by the English poet; a repetition of the same theme and subject as Lord Byron's effort (1821); focuses upon a conspiracy by a number of discontented individuals to overturn the Venetian constitution and take vengeance upon the government; the plot proves unsuccessful, and the title character loses his head.

Alfred, Lord Tennyson, *Balin and Balan*—a poem by the English laureate; concerns a knight's humble devotion to Queen Guinevere; he and his brother fight when he discovers the Queen's infidelity.

Philippe Auguste Villiers de L'Isle-Adam, *Axel*—a Symbolist play by the French writer; a loose, sprawling, and discursive piece, with lengthy monologues and dialogues; a mystical vision of the human being's place in the universe; the playwright repudiates the claims of material existence and concrete experience; thus, the title character lives in solitude and self-imposed exile in his Black Forest castle, seeking spiritual perfection.

Emile Zola, *Germinal*—a novel by the French writer, concerned with the misery and degradation of the French working class; the principal character becomes the socialist leader of an impoverished mining community and becomes involved in strikes and riots; as usual, the piece gathers strength from its writer's attention to the stark reality of the situation.

EVENTS

The Revised Text of the Authorized Version (King James, 1611) of the Old Testament published at Oxford; revisions carried out by a committee appointed by the Convocation of Canterbury (1870).

The Selborne Society founded at London; dedicated to the preservation of birds and plants; established in memory of Gilbert White, curate of Selborne, Hampshire, the English naturalist who authored tracts and journals on natural history and antiquity.

1886

BIRTHS

Mohammad Taqi Bahar (d. 1950). Iranian poet and historian; he will become the last significant Iranian poet to rely upon the classical forms; thus, he will revive the Khorasan style and use the strophe forms; his popular lyrics will be set within political and social contexts.

Gottfried Benn (d. 1956). German poet and essayist; will shift from expressionistic writings to realistic reflections upon the conflicts during the Nazi era.

Hermann Broch (d. 1951). Austrian writer of fiction, playwright, and essayist; he will contribute significantly to the development of the twentieth-century novel, being influenced by such philosophers as Immanuel Kant and Georg Wilhelm Friedrich Hegel; he will coin the term "epistemological novel," identifying those works of fiction that advanced his metaphysical theories.

Fernand Crommelynck (d. 1970). Belgian playwright; his work will treat a variety of conflicts: between youth and old age, love and sterility, violence and vision, morality and sin; those same plays will also display the writer's expert theatrical craftsmanship and lyric power.

Ricardo Guiraldes (d. 1927). Argentine novelist and short fiction writer; his major fiction will celebrate the life of the Argentine gaucho; early in his career, he will be influenced by the European symbolists, but he will eventually abandon those models to concentrate on depicting the history of his own nation.

Maithilsaran Gupta (d. 1964). Hindi poet; his work will capture the spirit of Hindu nationalism; he will become the first generally accepted poet to write in modern Hindi, and he will strive to transmit Gandhi's philosophy to the Hindi speaking world.

Misak Metsarents (d. 1908). Armenian poet; he will write nature and love lyrics, relying upon medieval Armenian lyric poetry for his style; he will represent those West Armenian poets whose work reflected the extremely difficult conditions of life for the Armenian minority in Turkey.

Franz Rosenzweig (d. 1929). German Jewish narrative writer and translator; he will express the longings of the inspired man who, having lived his faith, stands face to face with God; he will collaborate with Martin Buber in translating the Hebrew Bible into German.

Siegfried Louvaine Sassoon (d. 1967). English poet and novelist; his poetry will reflect his hatred of war, particularly its brutality and utter wastefulness; his novels will include a semiautobiographical trilogy.

Anempodist Ivanovich Sofronov (d. 1935). Yakutsk (SSR) essayist and playwright; he will sharply criticize village life in his homeland and, with his drama, attempt to arouse public opinion against the inhumanity of the pre-Revolutionary patriarchal feudal society of Yakutsk.

Wilbur Daniel Steele (d. 1970). American writer of short fiction; he will place his stories in New England and South Carolina, and his plots and characters will be viewed through the social and religious symbols of those areas.

Tanizaki Junichiro (d. 1965). Japanese novelist and essayist; he will oppose the adoption of Western manners, presenting, instead, characters and themes depicting life in Japan prior to World War II.

Gabdulla Tukay (d. 1913). Turkish (Tartar) poet; his early work will reflect the influence of classical Turkish poetry; however, he will later shift his attention to Russian and European poets and bring a new poetic language to Tartar literature.

DEATHS

Emily Elizabeth Dickinson (b. 1830). American poet; she spent all of her life in Amherst, Massachusetts, gradually withdrawing from social activities and relationships and becoming a recluse in her father's house; she composed over one thousand unique lyrics concerning love, religion, nature, death, and immortality; her poems were not published until after her death (1890, 1891, 1894, 1958); her bold and startling imagery had a significant effect upon twentieth-century American poetry.

Jose Hernandez (b. 1834). Argentine poet and journalist; his major epic poem is a classic representation of the Argentinian gauchos, their political and economic struggles during the nineteenth century; he dies at Buenos Aires from a heart attack.

Alexander Ostrovsky (b. 1823). Russian playwright; the author of more than eighty dramatic pieces; he presented a stark and sarcastic view of the world that he knew, realistically depicting characters in the prosaic, mostly lower-class setting of nineteenth-century Russia; his dominant theme appears to be the conflict between the ardent aspirations of a pure heart and the false values imposed by the environment.

Leopold von Ranke (b. 1795). German historian; generally recognized as the founder of the modern objective school of history; his studies of the sixteenth, seventeenth, and eighteenth centuries demonstrate his aim to reconstruct periods of the past as they actually existed; he sought to avoid injecting the history of the past with the spirit of the present; he dies at Berlin.

Josef Viktor von Scheffel (b. 1826). German poet and novelist; he wrote his major works at Capri and at his estate on the borders of Lake Constance; he also published a collection of student songs and humorous verse.

PUBLICATIONS

Edmondo de Amicis, *Cuore* (Heart of a Boy)— a series of sketches by the Italian novelist; concerns a boy at school, his relationships with his teachers and other pupils; the piece remains a classic of sentimentalism.

Paul Bourget, *Nouveaux Essais de Psychologie Contemporaine* (Recent Essays on Contemporary Psychology)—a collection of essays by the French critic and novelist; the writer examines various leading literary figures, among them Charles Baudelaire and Stendhal, for flaws in their characters that led to the pessimism he observed all about him; he employed the same methods as had Hippolyte Taine.

Benito Perez Galdos, *Fortunata y Jacinta*—a novel by the Spanish writer of fiction, playwright, and essayist; the writer explores the fierce rivalry between two women from radically different social backgrounds; they share the same man, one being his wife, and the other his mistress and the mother of his son; the work provides a comprehensive and realistic portrait of the manners and customs of nineteenth-century Madrid.

George Gissing, *Demos*—a novel by the English writer; illustrates the degrading effects of poverty upon the human character.

Thomas Hardy, *The Mayor of Casterbridge*—a novel by the English writer; a hay-tresser, while drunk at a fair, sells his wife and child to a sailor; he then takes the pledge for twenty years and subsequently becomes wealthy and the mayor of Casterbridge; the wife returns after eighteen years, and then follow quarrels, death, ruin, and a return to drink; the mayor dies in a hut, lonely wretched, and desolate.

William Dean Howells, *Indian Summer*— a novel by the American writer; focuses upon cultivated Midwestern women living in Florence, Italy; the middle-aged hero falls in love with a widow he has known for years, and also develops an attraction for her young protégée; he finally proposes to the widow, who initially refuses his offer; however, she almost immediately reverses that response and accepts.

Thomas Henry Huxley, *Science and Morals*— a prose tract by the English natural scientist and essayist; the writer defines the relation of science to philosophical and religious speculation.

Henrik Ibsen, *Rosmersholm*—a play by the Norwegian poet and dramatist; almost confessional in nature and form, the work appears to cast aside elements of realism and to focus upon psychological symbolism; the playwright adopts a close approximation to the methods of the Greek tragedy; thus, there transpires the gradual revelation, through conflicting characters, of events prior to the opening scene; dramatic action occurs when the characters react, spiritually, to that revelation.

Henry James, *The Bostonians*—a novel by the American-born writer; the work focuses upon the infatuation of a grown woman for a young girl; radical feminism and the suffragette movement are important aspects of the novel.

——————, *The Princess Casamassima*— the second novel published this year by the American-born writer; concerns the title character's disastrous infatuation for the bookbinder's clerk.

Rudyard Kipling, *Departmental Ditties*—a collection of mildly satiric verse by the English novelist and poet; essentially concerns white civilian life in India; the major piece, "One Viceroy Resigns," depicts an English aristocrat who looks down upon his middle-class subjects.

Pierre Loti, *Pecheur d'Islande* (An Island Fisherman)—a novel by the French writer of fiction, an impressionistic description of Breton fishermen, the Brittany countryside, and the sea.

Friedrich Wilhelm Nietzsche, *Jenseits von Gut und Boise: Vorspiel Einer Philosophie der Zukunft* (Beyond Good and Evil: Prelude to a Philosophy of the Future)—a collection of essays and aphorisms by the German philosopher, essayist, and poet; generally repeats the concept that the will to power serves as the essence of all beings.

Robert Louis Stevenson, *Kidnapped*—a novel by the Scottish-born writer of fiction and poetry; concerns the abduction of a young man by his uncle, who has him carried off to the Carolinas; however, when the ship wrecks off the coast of Mull, the youngster witnesses the murder of Colin Campbell at Ardshiel and becomes a suspect; after a journey across the Highlands, the young man manages to retrieve his estate from his villainous uncle.

———————, *The Strange Case of Dr. Jekyll and Mr. Hyde*—the second novel published this year by the Scottish-born writer; a sinister tale depicting the dual aspects of human nature; an upstanding physician, Dr. Henry Jekyll, swallows a potion he has created in his laboratory, changing into an evil creature named Edward Hyde; at first, Jekyll can control the metamorphosis, but eventually Hyde begins to take over and Jekyll kills himself.

August Strindberg, *Transtekvinnans Son* (The Son of a Servant)—a novel by the Swedish playwright and writer of fiction; the novelist portrays himself as the unwanted product of a union between an impoverished aristocrat and a servant.

Philipp Auguste Villiers de L'Isle Adam, *L'Eve Future*—a satiric novel by the French Symbolist writer; attacks the materialism of modern science.

William Butler Yeats, *Mosada*—the earliest volume of verse by the Irish poet, playwright, and essayist; the importance of the work lies in the fact that, at this point in his career, the poet relied upon Greek, rather than Irish, mythology for his symbols.

EVENTS

Cosmopolitan, a monthly magazine intended for general family reading, begins publication at Rochester, New York; it will move to New York City in 1887; noted contributors have included Mark Twain, Henry James, Rudyard Kipling, and Sir Arthur Conan Doyle.

The Forum, a monthly magazine focusing upon contemporary issues, begins publication at New York City; until 1950.

The New Princeton Review, a learned literary magazine, begins publication at Princeton; contributors will include Charles Dudley Warner, Theodore Roosevelt, and Woodrow Wilson.

1887

BIRTHS

Rupert Chawner Brooke (d. 1915). English poet; his poetry will be characterized by youthful and self-probing honesty, fresh perception, gentle lyricism, and a tendency toward the comic; his handsome appearance and untimely death will cause him to be a favorite poet among the young people of the "between the wars" period.

Edna Ferber (d. 1968). American novelist; her colorful novels of American life and her plays and short stories concern a variety of subjects: the American business woman, the sacrifices of women farmers, Polish immigrants in Connecticut, the social conditions in modern Alaska.

Pierre Jean Jouve (d. 1976). French poet, novelist, playwright, and essayist; he will achieve recognition for his poetry, an integration of Christian and Freudian beliefs.

Francis Ledwige (d. 1917). Irish poet; he will become one of the most talented traditional poets of the twentieth century to emerge from the Irish peasantry; he will write pastoral, romantic verse, characterized by its simplicity, spontaneity, and original phrasing.

Reme Maran (d. 1960). Martinique novelist, poet, biographer, and essayist; he will severely criticize colonialism and the assumed racial superiority of whites, provoking a violent reaction among readers to the horrors of colonialism.

Marianne Craig Moore (d. 1972). American poet; her verse will be described as witty, crisp, intellectual, and satirical; she will also publish translations and prose essays.

Samuel Eliot Morison (d. 1976). American historian; he will become the official historian of Harvard College; his work will include a general survey of the United States and histories of naval operations during World War II, as well as the European discovery of America, he will receive Pulitzer Prizes in 1942 and 1959.

Salama Musa (d. 1958). Egyptian prose writer; he will attempt to persuade Egyptians to disassociate themselves, culturally and intellectually, from Asia and awaken to European ideals; his prose, in Arabic, will reveal his life-long love of England.

St. John Perse (pseudonym of Marie-Rene-Auguste Alexis Saint-Leger; d. 1975). French poet; his verse will reveal his belief that humanity has universally subjected itself to alienation; thus, he will focus upon human despair, though he will recognize positive aspects of existence.

Dame Edith Sitwell (d. 1964). English poet; she will set out to refresh the exhausted rhythms of traditional poetry by introducing the rhythms of jazz and popular dance music to the poetic genre; she will also become indignant over the evils within society, countering those with Christian symbolism.

Georg Trakl (d. 1914). Austrian poet; he will produce a body of verse known for its absolute integrity; he will achieve recognition as a visionary poet driven deep into himself by a world that he finds totally intolerable.

Arnold Zweig (d. 1968). German-Jewish essayist and novelist; his work will reveal his socialistic point of view and interest in Zionism; thus, he will seek refuge in Palestine when exiled by the Nazis in 1934.

DEATHS

Isabella Valancy Crawford (b. 1850). Canadian poet and writer of fiction; considered one of the outstanding Canadian poets of the nineteenth century, she depicted the culture, scenery, and character types of the Canadian frontier; she dies suddenly of a heart attack while at work upon a serial novel.

Edward Douwes Dekker (b. 1820); Dutch government official, novelist, and satirist; he wrote under the pseudonym of "Multatuli"; his fiction and satire protested against the abuses of the Dutch colonial system.

Joseph Ignatius Kraszewski (b. 1812). Polish historical novelist and poet; a prolific writer, he produced over three hundred pieces of poetry and prose; imprisoned at Magdeburg for treason in 1884.

Jules Laforgue (b. 1860). French poet, essayist, playwright, and writer of fiction; an early experimenter in free verse and a member of the French Symbolist group; he advocated abandoning popular literary conventions, maintaining that art should be the expression of the subconscious mind; poor in health, he dies from the opiates administered for his illness, which left him too weak to eat or work.

PUBLICATIONS

Sir Arthur Conan Doyle, *A Study in Scarlet*— the first published work of fiction by the English detective novelist, a "Sherlock Holmes story."

William Dean Howells, *The Minister's Charge; or, The Apprenticeship of Lemuel Barker*— a novel by the American writer; focuses upon moral problems, particularly the issue of complicity and the responsibility shared by everyone in society for the actions of everyone else; the writer depicts poor factory girls realistically and without any sentimentality: they wallow in their present existence because they are where they wish to be.

Herman Melville, *Billy Budd, Foretopman*— a novella by the American writer of fiction and poetry; a major work of literature whose power derives from the writer's exploration of the mysteries of sin.

George Meredith, *Ballads and Poems of Tragic Life*— a collection of verse by the English writer; contains the noted ode about the Franco-Prussian War, "France, December 1870."

Emilia Pardo Bazan, *La Madre Naturaleza* (Mother Nature)—a novel by the Spanish critic and writer of fiction; one of the works in which she introduced naturalism into Spanish literature and sought to illustrate the plight of the lower classes.

Jose Rizal, *Noli Me Tangere*— the first novel by the Philippine writer, important for its fervent nationalism.

Victorien Sardou, *La Tosca*— a spectacular melodrama by the French playwright; written specifically for the French-born actress, Sarah Bernhardt (1844-1923); adapted as an opera (with the same title) in 1900 by the Italian composer Giacomo Puccine (1858-1924).

August Strindberg, *Fadren* (The Father)—a drama by the Swedish writer; a modern tragedy containing melodramatic elements; an army captain discovers himself in a death-like struggle with his wife over the education of their only child, a daughter.

Hermann Sudermann, *Frau Sorge* (Dame Care)—a novel by the German playwright and writer of fiction; proved immensely popular because of its psychological insight and social criticism.

EVENTS

The Hartford Daily Courant changes its name to the *Hartford Courant*; it remains the oldest continuously published paper in the United States.

The Newberry Library, a reference and rare book library, is established with funds bequeathed by Walter Loomis Newberry, a Chicago banker.

Charles Scribner the younger, American publisher, founds *Scribner's Magazine,* a monthly literary journal; Robert Louis Stevenson, Henry James, William James, Bret Harte, Rudyard Kipling, Edith Wharton, and Stephen Crane are among the contributors; until 1939.

Frederic William Maitland, English lawyer and Downing Professor of English Law at Cambridge, founds the Selden Society, an organization dedicated to the publication of ancient legal records.

Lazarus Ludwig Zamenhof, Polish Jewish oculist, develops the international language system known as Esperanto.

1888

BIRTHS

Samuel Yosef Agnon (d. 1970). Polish-born Israeli writer of fiction; he will be considered the most significant modern writer of fiction in Hebrew, sharing the Nobel Prize for literature in 1966; his fiction will explore the various aspects of Jewish life.

Mark Aleksandrovich Aldanov (pseudonym of Mark Aleksandrovich Landau; d. 1957). Russian novelist, writer of short fiction, and essayist; he will become known for his historical fiction, some of which focuses upon the revolution of 1917.

Maxwell Anderson (d. 1959). American playwright; he will write more than thirty dramas in which he will generally focus upon serious subjects, reducing complex issues to a series of struggles between good and evil.

Dan Andersson (d. 1920). Swedish poet and novelist; he will focus upon religious and metaphysical themes involving the proletariat (although he will not adopt Marxism).

Georges Bernanos (d. 1948). French novelist and narrative writer; his fiction will reflect his mystical, Catholic beliefs, while his narratives will present accurate pictures of his own times, including his experiences in the Spanish Civil War.

Arthur Joyce Lunel Cary (d. 1957). Irish novelist, writer of short fiction, essayist, and poet; his novels will combine the best elements of eighteenth-century fiction and the modern tendency to provide a sense of immediacy.

Thomas Stearns Eliot (d. 1965). American-born English poet and critic; he will become one of the most important and influential literary figures of the twentieth century; in 1927, he will attain British citizenship and embrace Anglo-Catholicism; his work will generally express the anguish and barrenness of modern life, while gathering its origins from the seventeenth-century English metaphysical poets, Jacobean drama, and the French Symbolists; he will receive the Nobel Prize for literature in 1948.

Mohammad Husayn Haykal (d. 1956). Egyptian journalist, novelist, and critic; he will write one of the earliest novels to appear in modern Arabic; he will combine idealistic romanticism with sociological commentary.

Ghulam Ahmad Mahjur (d. 1952). Iranian (Kashmiri) poet; he will write verse in Urdu, marking the replacement of classical Persian models with modern Urdu influences; his work will display the bombastic tone characteristic of Urdu poetry composed between the wars.

Katherine Mansfield (d. 1923). New Zealand-born English writer of fiction; through the short story, she will demonstrate an ability to adapt the form and style of Anton Chekhov to English prose fiction; her work will prove both simple in form and evocative in substance.

Paul Morand (d. 1976). French short story writer, novelist, poet, and essayist; he will become one of the most noted French writers during the period between the wars, evoking the cosmopolitan atmosphere and energetic social life of the day; he will also create psychological portraits of hedonistic and often disillusioned characters.

Eugene Gladstone O'Neill (d. 1953). American playwright; he will become America's foremost dramatist, earning the Nobel Prize for literature in 1936 and Pulitzer Prizes for drama in 1920, 1922, and 1928.

Fernando Antonio Nogueira Pessoa (d. 1935). Portuguese poet and essayist; he will gain recognition as the most significant Portuguese poet since Luis Vaz de Camoens (1524-1580); his works will epitomize the themes and techniques of twentieth-century literature, specifically by confronting the chaotic plurality of modern life and experimenting with poetic composition; further, he will explore the unstable nature of personal identity.

John Crowe Ransom (d. 1974). American poet and critic; he will achieve recognition as a significant poetic stylist, creating elegant and impersonal verse; he will also become one of the major exponents of "new criticism."

Alan Seeger (d. 1916). American poet; the most significant products of his brief literary career will focus upon his reactions to his experiences during World War I.

Frans Eemil Sillanpaa (d. 1964). Finnish novelist; he will make a significant contribution to the literary history of his nation, concerning himself with such issues as the collapse of old social and cultural values and the failure of the Finnish civil war; he will receive the Nobel Prize for literature in 1939.

Tan-Da (pseudonym of Nguyen-khac-Hieu; d. 1939). Vietnamese poet, novelist, playwright, and essayist; he will defend the rules of classical verse against the criticism of the "new poetry school"; thus, his work will be intensely patriotic and will focus on the themes of sorrow, anxiety, dreams, and escape.

Giuseppe Ungaretti (d. 1970). Egyptian-born Italian poet; he will become professor of Italian poetry at Sao Paulo, Brazil; his verse will gain notice for its symbolism, compressed imagery, and contemporary structure.

DEATHS

Louisa May Alcott (b. 1832). American narrative writer and novelist; her early work demonstrates the influence of Ralph Waldo Emerson and Henry David Thoreau; she owes her literary reputation to her novels for juveniles that portray Victorian American life and values; she dies at Concord, Massachusetts.

Matthew Arnold (b. 1822). English poet and critic; his poetry tends to reflect his loneliness, pessimism, and classicism; his prose stresses the necessity for objectivity, while advocating a culture based upon the best that has been said and thought in the world; he dies suddenly at Liverpool, and is buried at Laleham, near Staines (Surrey).

Eugene Labiche (b. 1815). French playwright; he wrote over one hundred comedies, farces, and vaudevilles; a favorite dramatist of the French bourgeoisie, particularly as he developed unworldly and psychologically shallow characters and then placed them in baffling circumstances; in 1880 he gained election to the Academie Francaise; he dies at Paris.

Theodor Storm (b. 1817). German poet and novelist; his early works demonstrate a sense of nostalgic lyricism, while his later fiction tends to focus on tragic themes.

PUBLICATIONS

Maurice Barres, *Le Culte du Moi* (The Cult of the Self)—a trilogy by the French novelist, completed in 1891; focuses upon a young man (perhaps the novelist himself) who cannot recognize any reality but that of self.

Peter Rosegger, *Jakob der Letzte*—a novel by the Austrian poet and writer of fiction; the piece vividly portrays the writer's native district of Styria, particularly the peasant towns there, and its people.

August Strindberg, *Froken Julie* (Miss Julie)—a one-act tragedy by the Swedish playwright and novelist, the first naturalistic play in Scandinavia; in the preface, the playwright summarizes the naturalist's theory of character and anticipates the doctrines of expressionistic theater; the piece concerns a sexual encounter between the title character, from a noble family, and a footman, who aspires to a better way of life; the emotional direction of the play suggests that ritual and psychological examination may be more important to the playwright than the sociological conflict between the classes.

Rene Francois Sully-Prudhomme, *Le Bonheur* (Happiness)—a poem by the French popular poet; the piece follows the adventures of Faustus and Stella, two lovers who pass through death and the afterlife in pursuit of knowledge and happiness.

Paul Verlaine, *Amour*—a poem by the French writer of verse; occasioned by the death from typhus of the poet's pupil and supposed lover, Lucien Letinois.

EVENTS

The American Folklore Society founded: initially formed to study the lore of the American Indian and early American folk ballads and folk stories.

Peter F. Collier begins publication at New York City of *Collier's*, a weekly magazine originally intended to publicize and promote books issued by the founder's publishing concern; the journal then developed into an illustrated literary magazine covering popular social issues; until 1957.

The London Financial Guide, after publishing issues in January and February, changes its name to *The London Financial Times.*

1889

BIRTHS

Conrad Potter Aiken (d. 1973). American poet, novelist, and essayist; his literary efforts will focus upon the quest for self-knowledge; he will receive a Pulitzer Prize for literature in 1929.

Anna Akhmatova (pseudonym of Anna Andreyevna Gorenkjo; d. 1966). Russian poet; her brief but highly emotional lyrics will combine simplicity with musicality; she will write four major poetic pieces between 1914 and 1966.

Jean Maurice Eugene Clement Cocteau (d. 1963). French playwright, novelist, and essayist; he will rank among the most versatile, innovative, and prolific literary figures of the twentieth century; his dramas will utilize myth and tragedy in modern contexts, thus shocking and surprising audiences and readers; no matter what the genre, he will identify himself as a poet and refer to all of his works as poetry.

Gunnar Gunnarsson (d. 1975). Icelandic novelist; his early work, written in Danish, will help to arouse European interest in Icelandic culture; in general, he will focus his attention upon convincing Western Europeans that life in rural Iceland could provide source material for imaginative and artistic fiction.

Martin Heidegger (d. 1976). German philosopher; he will come under the influence of Soren Kierkegaard, Wilhelm Dilthey, and Friedrich Wilhelm Nietzsche; his analyses of the concepts of care, mood, and the individual's relationship to death will be a significant contribution to the literature on the anguish of modern society.

Yakup Kadri Karaosmanoglu (d. ?). Turkish novelist, essayist, and writer of short fiction; he will become the most representative Turkish writer during the period of the Greco-Turkish war and the early Turkish republic.

George Simon Kaufman (d. 1961). American playwright; he will become one of the most influential figures in the American theater, as a writer, director, and dramatic editor; he will write a number of works in collaboration with other playwrights, proving himself able to adapt his style to each of them; he will also become one of the best satirists of the American theater.

Ibrahim Abdalqadir al-Mazini (d. 1949). Egyptian novelist, poet, and critical essayist; he will write poetry based upon personal feelings and experiences, principally pessimistic in mood.

Claude McKay (d. 1948). Jamaican-born American poet, novelist, and essayist; he will become the first prominent writer of the Harlem Renaissance, and his work will be valued for reclaiming the African heritage and creativity in an alien world.

Sarah Gertrude Millin (d. 1968). South African novelist, essayist, and writer of short fiction; she will be considered among the most significant South African writers of the first half of the twentieth century; she will set her novels in the settlements, farms, small towns, and cities of South Africa, portraying conflicts among European settlers and their relationships with native groups.

Gabriela Mistral (pseudonym of Lucila Godoy de Alcayaga; d. 1957). Chilean poet and prose writer; her literary efforts will be inspired by her vocation as a teacher, her religious sentiments, and her romantic preoccupation with sorrow; she will receive the Nobel Prize for literature in 1945.

John Middleton Murry (d. 1957). English writer and critic; his literary criticism will considerably influence the young intellectuals of the 1920s; he will become a pacifist and, after World War II, develop an interest in agriculture.

Murah Rusli (d. 1968). Indonesian novelist; he will compose the first original novel in the Indonesian language; generally, his fiction will describe the conflict between traditionalism and modernism in Indonesian life.

Taha Husayn (d. 1973). Egyptian poet and prose writer; he will publish critical explications, autobiographical pieces, novels, short narratives, and critical and historical essays; in all, he will create intimate pictures of rural and provincial life.

Vrndavanhal Varma (d. 1969). Indian (Hindi) novelist and writer of short fiction; his work will reflect the influence of Sir Walter Scott, particularly in terms of the popular recreation of history through fiction.

Ben Ames Williams (d. 1953). American novelist and writer of popular short stories; he will attempt to profile life in America, particularly the traditional conflicts between North and South.

DEATHS

Ludivig Anzengruber (b. 1839). Austrian playwright and novelist; known for his nationalistic works focusing upon Austrian peasant life.

Robert Browning (b. 1812). English poet; his psychological character portrayals, experiments in diction and rhythm, and mastery of the dramatic monologue made him an important influence upon twentieth-century poetry..

William Wilkie Collins (b. 1824). English novelist; he wrote over thirty novels, one of which is considered by some critics to be the first full-length detective novel in English; he tended to focus upon intricacy of plot rather than on graphic description or subtle dileneation of character, and his style is known for its simplicity, clarity, and lack of ornamentation.

Mihail Eminscu (b. 1850). Roumanian poet; considered the leading Roumanian poet of the twentieth century; his work extols nature and the simple peasant life and is marked by lyricism and revolutionary zeal.

Gerard Manley Hopkins (b. 1844). English poet; he experimented with forms of prosody, and thus profoundly influenced poets of the twentieth century; his poems and letters demonstrate an inner conflict and deep dissatisfaction with himself as both a poet and a servant of God; his work was published posthumously in 1918.

Juan Montalvo (b. 1832). Ecuadorean essayist; an ardent liberal and master of invective; his prose works reflect his opposition to political tyranny.

Mikhail Saltykov (b. 1826). Russian novelist, playwright, and satirist; a major nineteenth-century Russian satirist, considered a leader of the radical intelligentsia; he contributed numerous sketches to the progressive journals, attacking various aspects of czarist Russia; he continued to write until almost the moment of his death.

Philippe de Villiers de L'Isle Adam (b. 1838). French playwright and writer of short fiction; he was an effective prose stylist, much in the manner of Edgar Allan Poe; his work alsoreflects the influence of Georg Wilhelm Friedrich Hegel's idealism and Richard Wagner's romanticism; after living with the monks of Solesmes, he dies of cancer in a Paris hospital.

PUBLICATIONS

Henri Bergson, *Essai sur les Donnees Immediates de la Conscience* (Time and Freewill)—a prose tract by the French philosopher; he argues that change constitutes the essence of reality.

Robert Browning, *Asolando*—a collection of last poems by the English versifier, published on the very day of his death; contains a number of the writer's best and most beautiful pieces: a series of love lyrics, a group of anecdotal poems and long narratives, and a group of meditative dramatic monologues; the finest piece, "Beatrice Signorini," is last of the writer's significant poems about Italian painters.

Karl Adolf Gjellerup, *Minna*—a novel by the Danish writer of fiction; the work has been described as a sickly song of triumph to the teutonic ideal, as exemplified by the writer's wife.

Gerhart Hauptmann, *Vor Sonnenaufgang* (Before Dawn)—a social play by the German playwright and writer of fiction; in still another example of the writer's dramatic and theatrical formula, an idealistic socialist attempts to stimulate change in a morally corrupt community; his attempts fail, resulting in confusion and then catastrophe.

Lafcadio Hearn, *Chita: A Memory of Last Island*—a long narrative by the American writer of fiction; recalls the writer's journey to the West Indies, and combines descriptions of local color with passages of exoticism; generally characterized by the writer's intenseness of expression.

William Dean Howells, *Annie Kilburn*—a novel by the American writer of fiction; teaches the moral that money is useless without the sympathy that comes from suffering; the heroine learns that the prosperous, as agents of the system that creates poverty, cannot really help the poor.

Maurice Maeterlinck, *Serres Chaudes* (Hothouses)—the first collection of verse by the Belgian poet and playwright; most of the pieces are in free verse and display the influence of Walt Whitman.

Walter Horatio Pater, *Appreciations*—a prose collection by the English poet and essayist; contains his critical reactions to William Shakespeare, Samuel Taylor Coleridge, and other English writers; also includes an essay on prose style.

Robert Louis Stevenson, *The Master of Ballantrae*—a novel by the English poet and writer of fiction; concerns a lifelong feud between two brothers with totally different personalities; set against the background of the Jacobite uprising of 1745.

Hermann Sudermann, *Die Ehre* (Honor)—a dramatic work by the German playwright and novelist; the writer combines new ideas with a masterly grasp of old-fashioned stage technique; thus, a bourgeois sense of honor tends to be both materialistic and flexible.

Bertha von Suttner, *Die Waffen Nieder* (Lay Down Your Arms)—a novel by the Austrian writer of fiction; the piece demonstrates her pacifism and contributed significantly to the spread of antiwar sentiment.

Alfred, Lord Tennyson, *Demeter and Other Poems*—a collection by the English laureate; includes, in addition to the title piece, "Merlin and the Gleam," the lines "To Virgil," and "Crossing the Bar."

Mark Twain, *A Connecticut Yankee in King Arthur's Court*—a realistic but satirical fantasy by the American writer and humorist; depicts the adventures of an ingenious Yankee, a mechanic transplanted to Arthurian Camelot; he transforms medieval England into a land of steam and electric energy; essentially, though, the work is a commentary upon modern American government, true democracy gives way to benign dictatorship.

Giovanni Verga, *Mastro-don Gesualdo*—a novel by the Italian (Sicilian) writer of fiction; the study of a peasant who acquires wealth, but his relatives literally suck him dry, and he dies in total disappointment; known for the brilliance of its detail.

William Butler Yeats, *The Wanderings of Ossian*—a poem by the Irish playwright, essayist, and versifier; based upon the Middle Irish dialogues of St. Patrick and Ossian; however, the events of the poem supposedly occurred within an indefinite period and have been described in folk tales.

EVENTS

The Arena, a monthly literary journal, begins publication at Boston; focuses upon social and economic reform, as well as artistic realism; Hannibal Hamlin Garland is one of its principal contributors; until 1909.

Laksminath Bezbarua, Indian (Assamese) poet, essayist, and journalist, founds the magazine *Jonaki* (Firefly) the journal becomes a means of propagating the romantic and patriotic ideas of the Assamese intelligentsia.

Andre Gide, French novelist, essayist, and narrative writer, begins to record his journals, which he maintains until 1949.

Murray Guthrie founds at Cambridge University the undergraduate periodical *The Granta*; the articles range from political essays and satire to serious poetry and fiction; Sylvia Plath and Ted Hughes may be numbered among its contributors; by 1983, it began to publish works by "young" British novelists.

Frank A. Munsey begins publication at New York City of *Munsey's*, a weekly magazine featuring illustrations and articles of popular interest; becomes a monthly in 1891; until 1929.

Jose Zorilla y Moral, Spanish Romantic playwright and poet, "crowned" Prince of Spanish Poets at Granada before a throng of 16,000 persons.

1890

BIRTHS

Iliya Abu Madi (d. 1957). Syrian-American poet and journalist; his deeply introspective verse will dwell upon individual episodes of romantic doubt and confusion and evince a strong sense of nostalgia.

Karel Capek (d. 1938). Czech playwright and writer of fiction; his work will be characterized by political and social satire, often reminding the reader of H. G. Wells and George Orwell in its anticipation of totalitarianism; he will also write stories on crime and scientific experiments, in addition to a number of travel books.

Walter Hasenclever (d. 1940). German playwright and poet; he will write lyrical verse and pioneer German dramatic expressionism; his work will also reflect his strong sense of pacifism.

Paul Hazoume (d. ?). West African (Dahomey) novelist and biographer; he will attempt to recapture Dahomeyan life of the mid-nineteenth century; he will seek to convince his French readers that despite corruption and barbarism, his people could take comfort in their past heroism and humanity.

Klabund (pseudonym of Alfred Henschke; d. 1928). German poet, novelist, playwright, and writer of short fiction; he will write serious historical novels, while his oriental adaptations will be brilliant constructions of exquisite alien worlds; generally, he will be regarded as a typical expressionist.

Ho Chi Minh (d. 1969). Vietnamese statesman and prose writer; his patriotic prose will recall the splendors of the Vietnamese past, while promoting revolutionary communist ideas; he will use direct and simple language, transmitting ideas in a clear and original style; he will also publish a volume of poetry, written in classical Chinese.

Jigar Muradabadi (d. 1960). Urdu poet; his romantic lyrics will place him mid-way between classicism and modernism; his simple and conventional love poems will contain rich, spiritual imagery and celebrate the agreeable aspects of life.

Boris Leonidovich Pasternak (d. 1960). Russian lyric poet, novelist, and translator; he will become the official translator of Shakespeare's works into Russian; his major fiction will describe the impact of the Russian revolution of 1917 upon sensitive, creative individuals; he will represent those Communists who expressed their disappointment that historical events did not conform to their idealistic visions of the world; he will decline the Nobel Prize for literature in 1958.

Katherine Anne Porter (d. 1980). American writer of fiction and nonfiction; she will study how changes in the Southern United States effected the inhabitants of the region at various stages of their lives; her fiction will be an imaginative quest in search of her self identity, particularly as it was molded by her Southern heritage.

Jean Rhys (d. 1979). West Indian-born English novelist and writer of short fiction; drawing on her personal experience, and with emotional and psychological insight, she will examine the nature of relationships between the sexes; she will create complex, intelligent, and sensitive women dominated and sometimes victimized by men.

Franz Werfel (d. 1945). Czechoslovakian-born Austrian Jewish poet and playwright; his early poems and plays will be expressionistic and more successful than his attempts at fiction; he will be able to blend the ideas of modern commercialism with typical Judaeo-Christian sentiments.

Stephen Zorian (d. 1967) Armenian novelist; his early work, influenced by Anton Chekhov and Ivan Turgenev, will reflect provincial life; he will then write one of the first autobiographical novels in Soviet Armenian-literature.

DEATHS

Dion Boucicault (b. 1822). Irish-born actor and playwright; he spent the last eighteen years of his life in the United States; he authored more than 100 plays, the majority being adaptions of popular European dramas, novels, and events of the nineteenth century; his fast-moving plots tended to arouse laughter, tears, and anticipation; he dies at New York City.

Carlo Collodi (b. 1826). Italian journalist and writer of fiction; his fame will derive from a didactic tale for children, *Pinocchio* (1883), the story of a puppet.

Caetano da Costa Alegre (b. 1864). Portuguese African poet; his verse focuses upon Africans and their isolation from white society; he dies at Lisbon.

Gottfried Keller (b. 1819). Swiss novelist, poet, and writer of short fiction; his literary reputation rests on his vital, realistic, and purposeful fiction; he displayed the ability to characterize, describe, and convey humor.

John Henry Cardinal Newman (b. 1801). English prose writer, poet, and Roman Catholic priest; he helped to form the Oxford Movement, eventually becoming one of the most influential among intellectual English Roman Catholics; his literary contributions include his spiritual autobiography, his sermons, and his expressions of Christian doctrine and faith; he dies at Edgbaston.

PUBLICATIONS

Emily Dickinson, *Poems*—the first verse collection by the American poet, published almost four years after her death; includes "I never lost as much but twice," "These are the days when Birds come back," "A Wounded Deer leaps highest," "I taste a liquor never brewed," "I reason, Earth is short," "The Soul selects her own Society," "Much Madness is divinest Sense," "I died for Beauty—but was scarce," "The Brain, within its Groove," "I cannot live with You," "Pain has an Element of Blank," and "Because I could not stop for Death."

Knut Hamsun, *Sult* (Hunger)—the first novel by the Norwegian writer of fiction, one based upon his own experiences; a brutal and egocentric account of the mental perceptions of its hero, a friendless wanderer; the work was condemned as repulsive, but equally praised for its power.

William Dean Howells, *A Boy's Town*—a novel by the American writer, a reminiscence of adolescent experience.

——————, *A Hazard of New Fortunes*—a novel set in New York City; in panoramic dimensions, the writer attempts to explicate the ideas and ideals of all groups involved in the class struggle, ranging from the established aristocracy to the poor of the lower East Side; the focus is upon the poor, who the writer examines with compassion and realism.

Henrik Ibsen, *Hedda Gabler*—a play by the Norwegian poet and dramatist; concerns a woman recently married to a scholar she does not love; accustomed to the luxury of her father's house, she cannot adjust to middle-class life; she becomes destructive, and eventually commits suicide; a social portrayal of the emergent "new" woman, who has developed capacities for little more than the destruction of others.

Henry James, *The Tragic Muse*—a novel by the American-born writer; a woman possessing beauty, intelligence, and an artistic vocation, becomes engaged in the perpetual battle between the artist and society.

William James, *The Principles of Psychology*—a prose tract by the American psychologist and pragmatic philosopher; strongly establishes the writer's belief that psychology rests upon a firm physiological foundation; the book encouraged the practice of psychological experimentation at Harvard College.

Rudyard Kipling, *The Light That Failed*—a novel by the English writer of poetry and fiction; essentially a decadent tale, with death as the outcome; depicts the idealized world of men existing in a bachelor society, and problems of Victorian sexual divisions, and the dilemma of the expatriate.

Jules Laforgue, *Les Derniers vers de Jules Laforgue*—a volume of poetry by the French writer of verse and fiction, published three years after his death; a twelve-part poem in which intricate structure complements sensitive insight into the uncertainty and anguish of the speaker's struggle to overcome his alienation from society.

William Morris, *News from Nowhere*—a novel by the English poet and prose writer; a response to Edward Bellamy's *Looking Backward* (1888), Morris rejects Bellamy's mechanized society in favor of a system based on small, agricultural communes.

Leo Tolstoy, *Kreitserova Sonata* (The Kreutzer Sonata)—a novel by the Russian writer; a story of romantic passion and violent death, brought about by an adulterous woman who ruins both her husband and her lover; the writer portrays the man as the sympathetic figure.

EVENTS

Sir James George Frazer, fellow of Trinity College, Cambridge, publishes the first volume of his *The Golden Bough*, the definitive comparative study of the beliefs and institutions of mankind; twelve volumes to 1915, a single-volume edition in 1922, a supplement in 1936; the work will influence such writers as D. H. Lawrence, T. S. Eliot, and Ezra Pound.

William Morris (1834-1896), English poet, artist, and printer, founds the Kelmscott Press, at Hammersmith; he designs the founts of type and ornamental letters and borders; from those he issues fifty-three volumes arranged in three categories; his own works, reprints of English classics, and a variety of small volumes by others.

The Literary Digest begins publication at New York City; a weekly collection of newspaper and magazine comments on current affairs; until 1938.

William D'Alton Mann, New York City publisher, begins publication of *The Smart Set*, a monthly social magazine that soon becomes a literary periodical; its contributors include H. L. Mencken, D. H. Lawrence, James Joyce, Ford Madox Ford, Eugene O'Neill, and F. Scott Fitzgerald; until 1930.

1891

BIRTHS

Mikhail Afanasevich Bulgakov (d. 1940). Russian novelist, playwright, biographer, essayist, translator, and writer of short fiction; he will be considered one of the foremost satirists of post revolutionary Russia; his works will examine the adjustment of the Russian intellectual class to life under Communist rule.

Ilya Ehrenburg (d. 1967). Russian journalist and novelist; his works will satirize the outcome of World War I and comment upon the events surrounding World War II; he will receive the Lenin Prize for literature in 1944.

Konstantine Gamsakhurdia (d. 1975). Georgian (SSR) novelist and translator; his fiction will exhibit intricate and well-developed themes, containing literary and historical allusions and relying upon archaic language; he will pay significant attention to formal structure and to the development of ideas, often interspersing the plot with philosophical meditations.

Sidney Coe Howard (d. 1939). American playwright; his plays will focus upon the problems of marriage and family strife; his plots will frequently tend to be melodramatic, but his firm social thesis will contribute dimension to the action; he will receive the Pulitzer Prize for drama in 1925.

Par Lagerkvist (d. 1974). Swedish poet, playwright, and novelist; he will write expressionist poetry, emphasizing the catastrophe of war; his drama and fiction will expose those who would advocate the destruction of social and political systems; he will receive the Nobel Prize for literature in 1951.

Osip Mandelstam (d. 1938). Russian poet; denounced Joseph Stalin, earning for himself persecution and exile; his poetry will reveal a steady progression from classicism, to surrealism, to cubism, a development that reflects the disintegration of his health and hopes.

Henry Miller (d. 1980). American-born novelist and narrative writer; his satires and reminiscences will record the wanderings of an adventurous life, one in opposition to the conventions of modern society; his books, published in Paris, will be banned in England and America.

Pedro Salinas (d. 1951). Spanish poet, playwright, essayist, translator, and writer of short fiction; he will be recognized as one of the outstanding poets of twentieth-century Spain; his themes will reflect the conflicts between being and nothingness, between internal and external reality.

DEATHS

Pedro Antonio de Alarcon (b. 1833). Spanish diplomat and novelist; his novels tend to be both witty and realistic; he also published a war diary, travel notes and a volume of poems.

Theodore Faullain de Banville (b. 1832). French poet, playwright, essayist, and writer of fiction; his poetry reflects the principles of "art for art's sake"; thus, he attempted to create objective and technically perfect verse that would rival the plastic arts in its emphasis upon form.

Ivan Aleksandrovich Goncharov (b. 1812). Russian novelist and government official; his satiric work offers a study of indolence and typifies Russian realism.

James Russell Lowell (b. 1819). American poet and essayist; his poetry ranges from the didactic to the satiric to the critical; hisscholarly works helped to increase European respect for American letters and institutions; his speeches on democracy, published in England, represent his best prose style.

Herman Melville (b. 1819). American novelist, poet, and writer of short fiction; his popular fictional romances were largely based on his experiences at sea, particularly aboard whaling vessels; his fiction generally failed to gain attention, and he dies in New York City in poverty and obscurity; not until the early 1920s does his work begin to receive careful critical attention.

Jan Neruda (b. 1834). Czechoslovakian poet, writer of short fiction and nonfiction, and playwright; his stories represent the early modes of realism in Czech literature, while his lyric poetry reflects the influence of Heinrich Heine; he became known as the foremost classical poet in modern Czech literature.

Antero Tarquínio de Quental (b. 1842). Portuguese poet; in addition to being considered a principal contributor to modern Portuguese verse, he also helped to organize the Portuguese Socialist Party; ill health leads to his suicide.

Arthur Rimbaud (b. 1854). French poet; his dreamlike verse anticipated the French Symbolists and reflects his stormy relationship with Paul Verlaine; he ceased to write poetry after age nineteen, instead wandering throughout Europe and Africa; he dies at Marseilles from complications of a leg amputation.

PUBLICATIONS

Ambrose Bierce, *Tales of Soldier and Civilians*—a collection of short stories by the American fiction writer; includes "An Occurrence at Owl Creek Bridge" and "The Horseman in the Sky."

Sir Arthur Conan Doyle, *The Adventures of Sherlock Holmes*—a collection of stories by the English physician and writer of detective fiction; contains the escapades of the brilliantly deductive title character and his stolid companion, Dr. Watson, who solve a wide variety of crimes.

Arne Garbourg, *Trette Men* (Tired Men)—a novel by the Norwegian writer of fiction; a reaction against the ultrarealism of his times; an indictment of the circumstances under which young men had to acquire both education and vocational skill.

George Gissing, *New Grub Street*—a novel by the English writer; the work depicts the jealousies and intrigues of the literary world of the late nineteenth century and the effects of poverty upon the artistic venture; contrasts the career of a clever and selfish reviewer to those possessed of legitimate artistic temperaments; the end of the piece reveals the triumph of self-advancement over true artistic temperament.

Thomas Hardy, *Tess of the D'Urbervilles, a Pure Woman*—a novel by the English poet and writer of fiction; focuses upon the daughter of a poor and foolish villager, who becomes vain upon learning of his relation-

ship to an ancient family; the title character is besieged by suffering: seduction, illegitimate birth, abandonment; the work ends with her arrest, trial, and death by hanging; in the end, she has become the victim of a form of justice that has done little beyond making sport of her misfortune.

Selma Lagerlof, *Gösta Berlings Saga* (The Story of Gosta Berling)—the first novel by the Swedish writer of fiction; actually a series of short episodes connected by the central character, a defrocked priest who is a womanizer, a drunkard, and a poet.

Joaquim Maria Machado de Assis, *Quincas Borba* (Philosopher or Dog?)—the sixth novel by the Brazilian writer of fiction, devoted to the mad philosopher Quincas Borba; a tragic novel that concerns the thoughts and doings of Borba, his dog, and a schoolmaster, Rubiao.

George Meredith, *One of Our Conquerors*—a novel by the English writer; concerns a young man married to a rich, elderly widow; he falls in love with one of her companions and they have a daughter, who eventually becomes aware of her illegitimacy; the mother dies, the father succumbs to insanity, and the daughter finally finds a proper and understanding mate.

Jose Rizal, *El Filibusterismo*—a novel by the Philippine poet and fiction writer; important as a nationalistic work sharply critical of foreign colonists.

Koda Rohan, "Goju no To" ("The Fire-Storied Pagoda")—a short story by the Japanese writer of fiction, poet, and essayist; concerns the conflict between two artisans that allows each to rise to a new level of virtue; one relinquishes a coveted commission for the benefit of a colleague, while the other advantageously strives for perfection in his craft; the writer's most recognized work.

Frank Wedekind, *Frühlings Erwachen* (Spring's Awakening)—a drama by the German playwright; depicts the tragedy of two teenage lovers brought together by the awakening of a mutual physical and emotional attraction; their natural, uninhibited feelings fall victim to the inflexible moral code of bourgeois society.

Oscar Wilde, *The Picture of Dorian Gray*—a novel by the Irish-born writer; a Gothic melodrama that aroused intense protest; a young man becomes corrupted by sensual indulgence and moral indifference.

EVENTS

The Review of Reviews begins publication in New York City; a monthly magazine with commentaries on current events and reprints of leading essays from other journals; until 1937.

George John Romanes, Canadian-born English scientist, establishes the Romanes Lectures at Oxford University; the lectures focus on subjects relating to science, art, and literature.

1892

BIRTHS

Ahmad Zaki Abu Shadi (d. 1955). Egyptian poet and translator; he will begin to publish poetry at age eighteen, experimenting with various forms; he will also write scripts for operas, translate European writers, and act as primary influence on young writers and artists.

Ryunosuke Akutagawa (d. 1927). Japanese writer of short fiction; he will become a master of the short story during the early twentieth century, and he will strive to anchor Japanese fiction to its native roots.

Richard Aldington (d. 1962). English poet, novelist, and biographer; he will become a member of the "imagist" school, relying upon the power of his own emotions; generally, his work will reveal the pain of the frustrated and failing artist.

Ivo Andric (d. 1975). Yugoslavian novelist; Serbian nationalism will form the core of his fiction, realized through epic themes based upon human isolation and feelings of insignificance in the face of history; he will receive the Nobel Prize for literature in 1961.

Ugo Betti (d. 1953). Italian playwright and poet; he will become a judge by profession; in general, his literary endeavors will focus upon the hypocrisy within society, including his own calling; his plays will be exercises in symbolism.

Pearl S. Buck (d. 1973). American novelist; much of her early fiction will originate from her experiences in China, although her later efforts will focus upon life in the United States; she will receive the Nobel Prize for literature in 1938.

Ivy Compton-Burnett (d. 1969). English novelist; her fiction will be composed almost entirely of dialogue; she will produce more than twenty novels, perceptively exploring the theme of evil.

Bakary Diallo (d. ?). Senegal novelist and poet; his early fiction will reveal a willingness to accept French superiority and African naiveté; nonetheless, he will also recognize and record the brutalities of the colonial period.

Janet Flanner (d. 1978). American novelist, essayist, and narrative writer; as "Genet" she will contribute a number of short pieces to *The New Yorker*, relating her experiences in Paris prior to World War II and revealing herself to be a polished stylist and perceptive observer of the European scene.

Leon Laleau (d. ?). Haitian poet, playwright, and novelist; his literary efforts will concentrate upon the natural beauties of Haiti and his early experiences in France and Italy; in his verse, he will advance the concept of African nationalism and its importance to his nation.

Hugh MacDiarmid (pseudonym of Christopher Murray Grieve; d. 1978). Scottish poet and critic; he will become known as a pioneer of the Scottish literary renaissance; his lyrical verse will establish him as a new prophetic voice of Scotland by containing political, metaphysical, and nationalistic reflections upon the Scottish cultural and intellectual predicament.

Archibald MacLeish (d. 1982). American poet, dramatist, and administrator, his work will reflect the influence of T. S. Eliot and Ezra Pound; his verse will be sincere and unpretentious, creating a link between the poet and the politician; he will receive the Pulitzer Prize for poetry in 1933 and 1953, and for drama in 1959.

Endalkacaw Makonnen (d. 1963). Ethiopian novelist and playwright; his literary efforts will be traditional, moralistic, and didactic, reflecting upon the past culture of his nation and on the activities of the Christian church there.

Edna St. Vincent Millay (d. 1950). American poet; her verse will be characterized by descriptive precision; she will receive the Pulitzer Prize for poetry in 1923.

Konstantin Georgievich Paustovsky (d. 1968). Russian autobiographer, novelist, playwright, and writer of children's books; his work, particularly his multi-volume autobiography, will establish him as a link between classical Russian literature and the creative efforts within the modern Soviet state; he will focus on the Russian working class and celebrate the Russian landscape.

Pham-Quynh (d. 1945). Vietnamese scholar, translator, and journalist; he will write in Chinese, Vietnamese, and French; his translations of Pierre Loti, Rene Descartes, Jean Jacques Rousseau, Auguste Comte, Voltaire, and Anatole France will become important contributions to Vietnamese culture.

Elmer Rice (originally Elmer Reizenstein; d. 1967). American playwright; he will become one of the earliest American playwrights to experiment with dramatic forms and theatrical techniques, including flashback, "jackknife" set, and expressionism; he will receive the Pulitzer Prize for drama in 1929.

W. Abraham Silva (d. 1957). Ceylonese (Sinhalese) novelist and short story writer; he will become the first writer of his nation to gain wide popularity, largely because of his reliance upon ordinary conversational language.

Edith Sodergran (d. 1923). Finnish poet; her works will combine German expressionism and Russian symbolism with aggressively frank language and subjects that reflect her own idiosyncrasies; thus, her innovative verse will be considered a distinguished achievement in modern Finnish literature.

J. R. R. Tolkien (d. 1973). South African-born English novelist, short fiction writer, poet, and scholar; he will become a leading Anglo-Saxon scholar at Oxford, where he will attempt to revive the medieval romance and the fairy tale; he will gain considerable recognition for his fantasy-romance trilogy of novels exploring the timeless cosmic struggle between good and evil.

Rusen Esref Unaydin (d. 1959). Turkish journalist and prose poet; he will become known for his insightful interviews with artists, and for a volume of poems in prose.

Dame Rebecca West (adopted name of Cecily Isabel Fairfield; d. 1983). English novelist and journalist; her fiction will be characterized by strong and unconventional heroines and be noted for its fine craftsmanship.

DEATHS

Judah Leon Gordon (b. 1830). Russian Jewish novelist and poet, born in Lithuania; a leader of the renaissance of progressive culture among Russian Jews, writing in both Russian and Hebrew; his verse tended to be historical, while his fiction satirized traditional Judaism.

Alexandros Rangabe (b. 1810). Greek scholar, playwright, and diplomat; he held a prominent place in the Greek classical revival.

Alfred, Lord Tennyson (b. 1809). English poet; he became a spokesman for the values of the Victorian Age, as well as its most noted poet, appointed Poet Laureate of England in 1850.

Walt Whitman (b. 1819). American poet; known for his innovation with rhythmical free verse and celebrations of sexuality; his *Leaves of Grass* has proved one of the most influential volumes of poetry in American literary history; he suffered a stroke in 1873, and lived as a semi-invalid until his death at Camden, New Jersey.

John Greenleaf Whittier (b. 1807). American poet; a Quaker and a vigorous and politically powerful abolitionist writer; he celebrated the common man and depicted the life, history, and legends of New England; one of the most popular poets of his day, he also wrote over one hundred congregational hymns.

PUBLICATIONS

Hari Narayan Apte, *Yasvantrav Khare*—an unfinished novel by the Indian (Marathi) writer of fiction; provides an extremely vivid and realistic picture of the education and development of a group of young people, indicating how their upbringing has conditioned their attitudes toward life.

Ambrose Bierce, *The Monk and the Hangman's Daughter*—a medieval romance by the American writer of fiction; known for its brilliant irony.

Arne Garbourg, *Fred* (Peace)—a novel by the Norwegian writer of fiction; the hero kills himself after he extends a hand in the direction of practical Christianity; attempts to strike a balance between fatherly approval and disapproval.

Knut Hamsun, *Mysterier* (Mysteries)—a novel by the Norwegian writer of fiction and drama; a young man spends a summer at a resort and events there lead to his self-destruction; the title indicates the mysteries of his contact with others, through whom he searches for himself and his own motives.

Gerhart Hauptmann, *Die Weber* (The Weavers)—a drama by the German playwright and novelist; considered the first socialist play in German literature; depicts the sufferings of the Silesian weavers and the failure of their revolt in 1844 against those who exploited them; the writer replaces the individual hero with a collective one who represents the masses.

Maurice Maeterlinck, *Pelleas et Melisande*—a drama by the Belgian-born French playwright, essayist, and poet; parallel with the medieval tale of Paolo and Francesca and the Arthurian romance of Tristan and Isolde; a naive girl, tricked into marriage, finds her true lover: thus the question of whether she should remain faithful to her husband and follow social law rather than nature.

Sigbjorn Obstfelder, "Navnlos" (Nameless)—a poem by the Norwegian writer of verse, fiction, and drama; identified as the most human of the writer's poems; the poet wanders, at night, across a city park and finds a fallen woman sitting upon a bench; they sit in silence and weep together.

Henrik Pontoppidan, *Det Forjoettede Land* (The Promised Land)—a novel by the Danish writer of fiction and drama; the writer depicts the rural people as a cunning faction of society, making considerable demands on the aid supplied by the church; the people abuse what they view as hypocritical charity, dispensed solely to gain political advantage.

Masaoka Shiki, *Dassai Shooku Haiwa*—a volume of literary criticism by the Japanese poet, short story writer, and essayist; contains the writer's call for reform of the Japanese haiku; he stresses the potential of haiku as a viable art form, and criticizes past haiku poets, whose stale and unimaginative work brought about the debased state of the art.

William Butler Yeats, *The Countess Cathleen*—a historical drama by the Irish poet, playwright, and essayist; set in Ireland during a period of famine, when people sell their souls to the devil for food; the countess strives to relieve their needs, but demons steal her wealth and she must sell her own soul to them; in the end, however, she achieves forgiveness because of her good intentions.

EVENTS

The Bibliography Society founded at London; it will publish monographs and book catalogues, as well as issue (beginning 1893) its *Transactions*.

Godey's Magazine begins publication in New York City; it will primarily publish short novels; until 1898.

Jerome K. Jerome, English novelist and playwright, and Robert Barr begin publication at London of *The Idler*, a popular monthly magazine of general literature; to 1911.

William Peterfield Trent, then professor of English at the University of the South, Sewanee, Tennessee, founds *The Sewanee Review*, the first critical and literary quarterly journal in the United States; its emphasis has tended toward contemporary literature.

1893

BIRTHS

Faith Baldwin (d. 1978). American novelist and poet; her fiction, particularly, will become popular among American women, principally for its romantic themes and simplicity and directness of language and style.

Frank A. Collymore (d. 1980). Barbadian poet; he will make a significant contribution to the literature of the West Indies, particularly through his six volumes of poems and a tract on the dialect of Barbados; his verse will range from couplets to longer pieces on a variety of contemporary topics.

Pierre Drieu La Rochelle (d. 1945). French novelist, poet, and essayist; his work will reflect fascist ideas developed between the world wars; he will bemoan the decay of traditional French values and advocate the formation of a martial state based upon moral vigor and physical fitness; intellectually, he will develop an existentialist philosophy.

Carlo Emilio Gadda (d. 1973). Italian novelist; his satiric pieces, especially, will reveal his innovative sense of humor, a rich mixture of colloquialisms, obsolete, foreign, and technical language; he will write candidly about modern Italian society without moralizing.

Jorge Guillén (d. 1984). Spanish poet who will spend considerable periods of time in the United States; he will strive to achieve poetic purity, in his works, turning away, for the most part, from social or political themes.

Vicente Huidobro (d. 1948). Chilean poet, novelist, essayist, and playwright; a proponent of "Creationism," he will become a leading twentieth-century poet; thus, he will attempt to "create" a new world of images that extend beyond the confines of ordinary experiences.

Nur Sutan Iskandar (d. ?). Indonesian novelist and philologist; his work will follow traditional Malay literary forms, and he will rely upon an archaic language; he will, however, oppose conservative social traditions within his culture.

Sergo Kldiashvili (d. ?). Georgian (SSR) writer of fiction and drama; his work will concentrate on traditional tales from Georgia and offer commentary upon the negative effects of World War I.

Miroslav Krleza (d. 1981). Yugoslavian playwright and novelist; his work will evidence his dedication to Croatian Marxism, his love of European culture, and his hatred of the decaying Austrian empire; he will write poetry in a modernist style.

John Phillips Marquand (d. 1960). American writer of fiction and narrative; he will earn recognition for his detective fiction and social satire, setting a number of works in the Orient; he will receive the Pulitzer Prize for fiction in 1938.

Vladimir Mayakovsky (d. 1930). Russian poet, playwright, and essayist; he will become the central figure of the Russian Futurist movement; thus his work will advocate violent social upheaval and the overthrow of the czarist regime, in combination with the destruction of traditional literary forms and conventions; he will also become the artistic voice of the 1917 Bolshevik Revolution.

Wilfred Owen (d. 1918). English poet; he will begin to experiment with verse forms at an early age; he will write his work from combat in France during World War I, his subjects being war and the pity of war.

Dorothy Parker (d. 1967). American poet, short fiction writer, and critic; she will gain literary prominence through collections of verse and short stories that reflect her satirical humor.

I. A. Richards (d. 1979). English critic and poet; he will maintain that a general insensitivity to poetry reveals a paucity of imaginative thought; his critical work will attack vagueness, sentimentality, and laziness on the parts of poets and readers; essentially, his reputation as a literary critic will develop from his notion of the text as the main line of defense against the evils of critical generalization.

Ernst Toller (d. 1939). German Jewish playwright and novelist; he will write expressionist plays and poetry that is largely autobiographical.

DEATHS

Guy de Maupassant (b. 1850). French dramatist and writer of fiction; best known for his short stories, written in a simple and objective style, reminding one of Gustave Flaubert; themes of psychological realism permeate more than three hundred of his stories; he becomes insane in 1891 and dies in a sanitarium.

Philip Schaff (b. 1819). Swiss-born American Presbyterian theologian and historical writer; he founded the American branch of the Evangelical Alliance and presided over the American Old Testament Revision Committee; he wrote a history of the Christian Church and compiled a dictionary of the Bible.

John Addington Symonds (b. 1840). English poet, intellectual historian, essayist, and translator; he wrote a history of the Italian Renaissance, translated the autobiography of Benvenuto Cellini, wrote studies of Greek and Italian poets, and published biographies of English and European writers; he suffered long periods of ill-health and spent his later years in Italy.

Hippolyte Adolphe Taine (b. 1828). French literary critic, historian, and essayist; known as one of the most accomplished, original, and versatile French scholars of the late nineteenth century; he influenced the development of literary and historical criticism, insisting that critical commentary should be based upon scientific principles that would produce objective conclusions.

Jose Zorilla y Moral (b. 1817). Spanish playwright, poet, and novelist; his drama will represent Spanish Romanticism at its best; he remains important in the literary history of his nation because of his masterful descriptions and overall dramatic power; following his death, the Spanish Academy sponsored a magnificent funeral as a final tribute to his literary endeavors.

PUBLICATIONS

Hari Narayan Apte, *Mi* (I)—a novel by the Indian (Marathi) writer of fiction; presented as an autobiography of a saintly social worker who chooses celibacy so as to be free to devote himself to the poor.

Ambrose Bierce, *Can Such Things Be?*—a collection of short stories by the American writer of fiction; the pieces represent the writer's technique of building suspense toward dramatic crises.

Georges Courteline, *Bouborouche*—a farce by the French playwright; noted for its development of the archetypal cuckold figure modeled after the manner of Ben Jonson's *Every Man in His Humour.*

Stephen Crane, *Maggie: A Girl of the Streets*—a novella by the American writer of fiction and poetry; a story set in the Bowery of New York City that constitutes an impressionistic study of shame.

Max Halbe, *Die Jugend* (When Love Is Young)—a play by the German dramatist; originates in conflicts of the playwright's own youth; a tragedy of adolescent love presented in highly poetic language.

Gerhart Hauptmann, *Der Biberpelz* (The Beaver Coat)—a lively dramatic comedy by the German playwright, novelist and poet; a caricature of authority: a thieving and cunning washerwoman stands in perfect contrast to an absurd bureaucratic official.

William Dean Howells, *The World of Chance*—an autobiographical novel by the American fiction writer; the hero, an Ohio newspaperman, arrives in New York with the manuscript of his romantic novel, which succeeds only because a reviewer takes it home by mistake.

Thomas Henry Huxley, *Ethics and Evolution*—a collection of lectures by the English scientist and philosopher; he finds no basis for morality in the evolutionary struggle.

B. R. Rajam Aiyar, *Kamalampal; or, The Fatal Rumour*—a novel by the Indian (Tamil) lawyer and writer of fiction; published serially between 1893 and 1895; an interesting narrative laced with humor and containing subtley drawn characterizations.

Victorien Sardou and Emile Moreau, *Mme. Sans-Gene* (Madame Devil-May-Care)—a play by the French dramatists; relates the story of a spirited washerwoman who becomes the duchess of Danzig; years later, upon being asked to retire from court, she presents Napoleon with an unpaid laundry bill.

Francis Thompson, "The Hound of Heaven"—a poem by the English poet and essayist; describes the poet's flight from God, who pursues and overtakes the artist.

Ivan Vazov, *Pod Igoto* (Under the Yoke)—a novel by the Bulgarian poet and writer of fiction; depicts the tragedy of the unsuccessful April Rising of 1876; the characters represent those Bulgarians whose names remain unrecorded in the accounts of the revolution, but who nevertheless contributed significantly to the cause of the nation's freedom from the Turks.

Oscar Wilde, *Salome*—a decadent and melodramatic play by the Irish-born poet and playwright; written in French and performed in Paris; Richard Strauss produced an opera with the same title from the text in 1905.

EVENTS

S. S. McClure, Irish-born American newspaper publisher, establishes *McClure's Magazine* in New York City; a monthly magazine of literature and current affairs that later became advocated social and political reform; contributors include O. Henry, Jack London, Ida Tarbell, and Lincoln Steffens; until 1929.

The Outlook begins publication in New York City; a magazine of literature and political commentary; contributors include Theodore Roosevelt, and Booker T. Washington; until 1935.

1894

BIRTHS

Isaac Babel (d. 1941). Russian Jewish writer of fiction; his reputation and creative genius will derive from his Jewish heritage and upbringing; he will manage to capture the Russian Revolution in all of its glory and cruelty.

Bibhutibhusan Bandyopadhyay (d. 1950). Bengali writer of fiction and essays; he will write over fifty volumes of fiction, autobiography, and travel essays; he will display a warm affection for the rural poor and the beauties of nature.

Louis-Ferdinand Celine (pseudonym of Dr. Louis-Ferdinand Destouches; d. 1961). French novelist, playwright, and essayist; he will become a principal stylistic innovator of the twentieth century; specifically, he will receive credit for freeing French literature from the rigid and formalized language of nineteenth-century fiction by introducing a hallucinatory prose style that emphasizes emotion over reality.

E. E. Cummings (d. 1962). American poet; his verse will be composed in a completely modern style, employing unorthodox rhythmic and linguistic devices, including the omission of upper case letters.

Aldous Huxley (d. 1963). English novelist and essayist; his most significant fiction will warn readers of the dangers of moral anarchy within a scientific age; he will challenge the notion of a Utopia where Platonic harmony may be achieved through scientific conditioning and breeding.

Berdi Kerbabayev (d. ?). Turkmen (SSR) novelist and translator; his fiction will focus upon Soviet and pre-revolutionary themes; he will also translate Russian classical works into his native dialect.

John Ebenezer Clare McFarlane (d. 1962). Jamaican poet and essayist; he will produce the first anthology of Jamaican poetry; essentially, his own verse will echo the nineteenth-century English Romantics.

Ngo-tat-To (d. 1954). Vietnamese translator, journalist, and narrative writer; his work will provide an accurate view of poverty in the villages of his country, as well as realistic descriptions of village life and customs.

Boris Pilnyak (pseudonym of Boris Andreyevich Vogau; d. 1937?). Russian novelist and writer of short fiction; considered one of the most representative literary figures of the period following the 1917 Russian Revolution, he will explore in his fiction the relationship between the Russian Revolution and Russian society.

J. B. Priestley (d. 1984). English novelist and writer of narratives and travel books; his work will reveal his various intellectual sympathies: patriot, man of culture, reactionary, and social reformer; he will become a spokesman for "the common sense of the common man."

Abdullo Quodiriy (d. 1939). Uzbek (SSR) satirist journalist, and fiction writer; he will write historical fiction and describe the changes in Uzbek village life during the collectivization of the countryside.

Ye Shengtao (d. ?). Chinese novelist and writer of stories for children; he will become deeply committed to progressive social issues and will explore, without sensationalism, the quiet sufferings of such common people as teachers, mothers, and children.

Mahamud Taymur (d. 1973). Egyptian fiction writer and playwright; he will be influenced by such French story writers as Guy de Maupassant, although his fiction will focus primarily upon twentieth-century Egyptian life.

James Thurber (d. 1961). American journalist, playwright, and writer of fiction; he will write comic and satirical stories, complemented by his own illustrations; his fiction, especially, will capture the desires and imagination of frustrated Americans.

DEATHS

Bankim Chandra Chatterji (b. 1838). Indian novelist, essayist, and poet; he exerted considerable influence on Indian literature and culture, especially in the development of modern Indian fiction; he also helped to inspire the nationalist movement that eventually led to his country emerging as a sovereign nation.

Oliver Wendell Holmes (b. 1809). American poet, essayist, novelist, and physician; a professor of medicine at Harvard and the author of a number of significant medical tracts; his poems, witty narrative sketches, and psychological novels were extremely popular.

Charles Marie Rene Leconte de Lisle (b. 1818). French poet; the leading Parnassian, he strived for faultless workmanship, precise poetic form, and emotional detachment; as an anti-Christian and pessimist, he saw death as the only reality.

Walter Horatio Pater (b. 1839). English essayist and critic; be believed that the ideal life consisted of cultivating an appreciation for the beautiful and the profound; he developed a precise, subtle, and refined prose style.

Christina Georgina Rossetti (b. 1830). English poet; her work reflected her deep spiritual convictions and her feelings of isolation; thus, her verse tended to be both melancholy and religious, often revealing the influence of the eighteenth-century hymnodists.

Robert Louis Stevenson (b. 1850). Scottish novelist, poet, and essayist; his literary reputation derives from his lively and highly imaginative adventure tales for young readers, as well as from his poems for children; he wrote, however, a number of novels with psychological depth; he dies in Samoa from tuberculosis.

PUBLICATIONS

Kate Chopin, *Bayou Folk*—a collection of short stories by the American poet and fiction writer; set in Louisiana, the pieces include "A No-Account Creole," "Desiree's Baby," and "La Belle Zoraide"; characters range from white aristocrats to black slaves.

Knut Hamsun, *Pan*—a novel by the Norwegian writer of fiction; explores the issue of self-destruction; the style of the piece is highly lyrical, underscoring the writer's interest in irrational forces.

Gerhart Hauptmann, *Hanneles Himmelfahrt* (The Assumption of Hanneles)—a drama by the German playwright and writer of fiction; concerns the frustrated protagonist's attempts to escape from a bleak environment to the realm of vision and fantasy.

William Dean Howells, *A Traveler from Altruria*—a novel by the American writer; the writer develops the idea of a cooperative commonwealth (not quite a utopia) wherein inequality and competition give way to what appears to be an uneventful, serene existence.

Rudyard Kipling, *The Jungle Book*—a collection of stories by the English poet and writer of fiction; relates how the child Mowgli is reared under the guidance of wolves, a bear, and a black panther; he learns the laws and the business of the jungle; a second volume followed in 1895.

George Meredith, *Lord Ormont and His Aminta*—a novel by the English writer; concerns a distinguished cavalry commander who has retired from the service, but who bears grievance against the East India Company and the British public in general; he marries a beautiful, and considerably younger, woman of inferior birth; the piece centers upon the husband's refusal to allow his wife a place in London society.

George Moore, *Esther Waters*—a novel by the Anglo-Irish writer of fiction and drama; relates the sufferings and hardships of a young religious girl, a Plymouth Sister, who is driven from her home into service by a drunken stepfather.

Marcel Schwob, *Le Livre de Monelle* (The Book of Monelle)—a biographical study by the French historian, biographer, and short fiction writer; concerns the writer's young mistress, who had recently died; he records the moods and personal characteristics of his subject, emphasizing her kindness, compassion, and gentleness; in three sections of dream-like prose poetry, he reveals insights into her philosophy of life.

Mark Twain, *The Tragedy of Pudd'nhead Wilson*—the American novelist's last notable book about American life; the title character is a nonconformist who appears too witty and wise for the backwoods community in which he lives; the work also examines the delicate area of miscegenation.

William Butler Yeats, *The Land of Heart's Desire*—a play in verse by the Irish poet, playwright, and essayist; a one-act fantasy concerning a newly married peasant girl who has become disillusioned with the plodding world of reality; she tries to escape by reading a wonder book of Celtic legends about ancient heroes; she finally gains freedom in death.

EVENTS

The Chap Book, a semi-monthly literary magazine, is established by the Cambridge, Massachusetts, publishing firm of Stone and Kimball; within the year it moves to Chicago; contributors include Henry James, Hamlin Garland, H. G. Wells, Robert Louis Stevenson, William Ernest Henley, and William Butler Yeats; until 1898.

The Yellow Book, a quarterly illustrated literary magazine, begins publication at London; Aubrey Beardsley, Henry James, Max Beerbohm, Edmund Gosse and Oscar Wilde are among the major contributors; until 1897.

1895

BIRTHS

Umar Fakhuri (d. 1946). Lebanese journalist and essayist; he will become one of the most active propagators of progressive antifascist views in Arab culture and literature; he will advance stimulating ideas on the theoretical aspects of literature and its realationship to reality and aesthetics.

Jean Giono (d. 1970). French novelist; his fiction will offer an interesting combination of moods and techniques, bleakness, ecstasy, tragedy, symbolism, love for the peasantry; his experiences during World War I will lead to his pacifism and the elements of that ideal that appear in his novels; after World War II, he will emerge principally as a historical novelist.

Gilbert Gratiant (d.   ?). Martiniquan poet, novelist, and essayist; a mulatto, he will become one of the earliest Martiniquians to record his pride in his African heritage; in his work, he will argue for a cultural synthesis of both European and African racial strains; he will eventually become a communist and produce poetry that reflects his pacifist inclinations.

Robert Graves (d. 1985). English poet, essayist, and writer of fiction; his work will, at the outset, reflect the new freedom and passionate disillusion of the post-World War I generation; in his later efforts, principally his poetry, he will develop a personal mythology, avoiding identification with any school or movement; he will serve as professor of poetry at Oxford from 1961 to 1966.

Mohammad Ali Jamalzade (d.   ?). Iranian writer of short stories and essays; he will present a realistic picture of life in Iran, relying heavily upon real-life situations and characters; he will also become a respected translator of European prose, particularly of works by Friedrich von Schiller, Oscar Wilde, and Anatole France.

David Jones (d. 1974). English poet; through his father, he will develop a strong literary and cultural identity with Wales; his experiences during World War I will contribute to his fascination with warfare as a subject for his poems and drawings; in addition, he will combine poetry with prose to produce pieces of epic length and substance.

Ernst Jünger (d.   ?). German novelist and essayist; he will gain a literary reputation as a fascinating writer, one known for his vulgarity and his impulse to create violent and dangerous action within a world that will never change.

F. R. Leavis (d. 1978). English scholar and critic; he will attempt to preserve the cultural and intellectual continuity of English life and literature against the threats imposed by technology, the mass media, and advertising; he will strive to introduce a new seriousness into the discipline of English studies.

Kavalam Madhava Panikkar (d. 1963). Indian historian, political writer, poet, and novelist; his fiction will generally reflect his interest in history, and most of his works will be written in the Malayalam dialect.

Titsian Tabisze (d. 1937). Georgian (SSR) poet; his early verse will be imitative of Oscar Wilde, vehement and provocative; later, he will write poetry in praise of the Soviet system.

Cesar Vallejo (d. 1938). Peruvian poet, one of the principal Latin American poets of the twentieth century; his verse will reflect his political passion, and, in general, he will agonize over war and its human casualties; his poetry will essentially consist of a series of abstract components transformed into purely human and compassionate feeling.

Edmund Wilson (d. 1972). American literary and social critic; he will respond to the symbolist movement and comment upon key social issues of his day; he will also write poetry, drama, and travel narratives.

Sergey Aleksandrovich Yesenin (d. 1925). Russian poet; he will, at first, produce simple lyrics concerning peasant life and nature; those pieces will, eventually, give way to highly imagist verse.

Mari Ziyada (d. 1941). Lebanese-born Egyptian critic and translator; she will publish sensitive reviews of contemporary Arabic poetry; her original essays will evidence an ardent patriotism and a sincere compassion for the poor and the unfortunate.

DEATHS

Alexandar Dumas fils (b. 1824). French playwright, poet, novelist, and essayist; considered one of the foremost French playwrights of the nineteenth century; he proclaimed himself a social reformer, focusing upon such subjects as adultery and divorce in his "thesis plays"; he dies at Mary-le-Roi.

Friedrich Engels (b. 1820). German social philosopher and revolutionary; with Karl Marx, he wrote prose tracts that predicted the inevitable triumph of the working class; his literary efforts exercised considerable influence on the theories of Marxism and dialectical materialism; he dies at London.

Gustav Freytag (b. 1816). German novelist and playwright; he is best remembered for realistic fiction about German commercial life, from the time of the Romans to the Napoleonic wars; he dies at Wiesbaden.

Thomas Henry Huxley (b. 1825). English biologist, educator, and essayist; he became an influential publicist for the scientific method; thus, he doubted those notions that could not immediately be challenged by logical analysis and scientific verification; he also believed that civilization could progress by placing human ethics outside the scope of materialistic evolutionary processes.

Jens Peter Jacobsen (b. 1847). Danish novelist and essayist; he developed a sharp and direct prose style that contributed significantly to the rise of naturalism in fiction; his major historical romances concern issues related to spiritual degeneration; he dies from tuberculosis contracted while in Italy.

Jose Marti (b. 1853). Cuban poet and revolutionary; he achieved recognition through his modernist verse, significant for its advocacy of political freedom and human independence; he is killed at the beginning of the final Cuban insurrection against Spain.

Hugh Andrew Johnstone Munro (b. 1819). English Latin scholar; he produced a significant critical edition of Lucretius, with a translation into English prose, as well as an equally noted critical tract on Catullus.

Leopold von Sacher-Masoch (b. 1835). Austrian novelist and jurist; in general, his fiction depicts the lives of small-town Polish Jews; the term "masochism" derives from his name and applies to the form of eroticism described in his later fiction.

PUBLICATIONS

Stephen Crane, *The Red Badge of Courage*—a novel by the American poet and writer of fiction; an imaginative analysis of a boy's initial, traumatic battle experiences during the American Civil War; a study of fear and the failure of courage in action.

George Meredith, *The Amazing Marriage*—a novel by the English writer of fiction; a young boy and girl, left destitute upon the death of their father, find themselves at the mercy of a miserly old uncle; the girl marries an old nobleman, who abandons her prior to the birth of their child; she then accompanies her brother to an insurrection against Spain, while the husband becomes a Roman Catholic monk.

Henryk Sienkiewicz, *Quo Vadis?*—a novel by the Polish writer of fiction; an extremely artful re-creation of Nero's Rome, focusing upon the emperor's bestial paganism as it contrasts with Christian nobility; known for its stylistic vitality, which accounted in part for its appeal as a motion picture.

Amalie Bertha Skram, *Pa St. Jorgen*—a novel by the Norwegian writer of fiction and drama; describes her own treatment for nervous disorders and criticizes the care of the insane.

Oscar Wilde, *The Importance of Being Earnest*—a dramatic farce by the Irish-born English playwright and poet, considered one of the most outstanding and significant comedies of the nineteenth century; focuses upon two couples enroute to inevitable marriages; also a satiric commentary upon various customs and institutions held in high regard by late Victorian society: church, politics, marriage, moral earnestness; includes obvious parodies of popular contemporary techniques.

EVENTS

The American Historical Review, the scholarly organ of the American Historical Society, begins publication at Washington, D.C.

The Bookman, a monthly journal of literature and literary criticism, begins publication at New York City; contains contributions by a variety of American and English writers; emphasizes modern trends in literature; until 1933.

The New York Public Library established in New York City in an effort to combine smaller libraries and collections; essentially state supported, with large endowments from John Jacob Astor, James Lenox, and Samuel Jones Tilden; has become one of the most significant libraries of the world.

Oscar Wilde, Irish-born English writer, completes his unsuccessful libel suit against the Marquis of Queensbury, who had objected to the writer's association with his son, Lord Alfred Douglas; the trial reveals Wilde's homosexual practices, for which he is imprisoned.

1896

BIRTHS

Edmund Blunden (d. 1974). English poet and critic; his work will generally reflect his love of the English countryside and his admiration for early nineteenth-century English writers; thus, his poetry will often focus on nature, and his critical essays and biographies will treat such writers as John Keats, Leigh Hunt, Percy Bysshe Shelley, Charles Lamb, and William Collins.

Andre Breton (d. 1966). French poet and critic; he will experiment with "automatic writing," publish a Surrealist manifesto, and join the Communist Party; he will spend the period of World War II in the United States.

John Dos Passos (d. 1970). American novelist and playwright; his most important work of fiction will be a trilogy of American life, written between 1930 and 1936; his fiction will serve as conscious, moral, and progressive criticism of American communal habits.

F. Scott Fitzgerald (d. 1940). American writer of fiction; his prose will capture the spirit of the 1920s, realistically depicting the illusions and failures of the "Jazz Age" and the emptiness and crass materialism of the American Dream.

Vahe Haik (pseudonym of Vahe Tinchian; d. ?). Armenian novelist, poet, and essayist; he will help to organize an Armenian press in France and the United States; most important, he will translate classical Armenian literary works into English for American Armenians.

Guiseppe Tomasi, Prince of di Lampedusa (d. 1957). Italian novelist; he will draw upon his heritage as an Italian prince and upon Italian history; his best fiction will depict the demise of an aristocratic nineteenth-century society following the unification of Italy.

Eugenio Montale (d. 1981). Italian poet; he will become the leading writer of verse within the modern Italian "hermetic" school; his work will focus upon language and meaning.

Henri de Montherlant (d. 1972). French novelist and playwright; in his novels and plays, he will advocate vigorous action as an antidote to the conflicts of life, thus attacking bourgeois complacency; he will be remembered for his masterful prose style, and his works will tend to be autobiographical.

Said Nafisi (d. 1966). Iranian writer of fiction and critical essays; his short stories will represent life in Iran following modernization, utilizing patriotic themes; he will also produce critical and satirical novels based upon contemporary Iranian life.

Marjorie Kinnan Rawlings (d. 1953). American writer of fiction; her work will focus on the life and customs of isolated regions of Florida, where she resided.

Robert E. Sherwood (d. 1955). American playwright and biographer; he will produce polished, light comedies and violent melodramas, exploring the relationships between reason, power, and civilized and uncivilized behavior.

Tristan Tzara (pseudonym of Samuel Rosenfeld; d. 1963). Romanian-born French poet, playwright, and essayist; he will become a leader in the movement advocating intentional irrationality, urging artists to repudiate traditional artistic, historical, and religious values; he will seek to establish a new style in which random associations serve to evoke a vitality free from the restraints of logic and grammar.

Rashid Yasami (d. 1951). Iranian historian, translator, and poet; he will write on cultural subjects and literary history; he will also produce verse translations from European poets and write original poetic works of his own.

Carl Zuckmayer (d. 1977). German playwright, poet, and writer of fiction; he will work within the traditions of the realistic theater with an instinct for moral decency; he will achieve dramatic success in the 1920s by providing the German public with a degree of cheer when it needed it the most; he will emigrate to the United States.

DEATHS

Edmond de Goncourt (b. 1822). French diarist, novelist, historian, playwright, and essayist; with his brother Jules (1830-1870), he became a literary innovator, noted for his diverse contributions to letters; they revitalized interest in the eighteenth century with intimate social histories based upon seemingly obscure documentation, were early proponents of realism in fiction, and created a diary that is considered a valuable document of nineteenth-century literary and cultural history.

Thomas Hughes (b. 1822). English novelist; he achieved everlasting fame with his novel of school life, *Tom Brown's School Days,* idealizing the head of Rugby School, Dr. Thomas Arnold (1795-1842); he also wrote biographical and social commentary.

William Morris (b. 1834). English poet, essayist, artist, and designer; his poetry is a reaction to industrialization, complementing his attempts to revitalize the splendor of medieval decorative arts; for him, art serves as the expression of joy in labor, rather than in luxury; he founded the Kelmscott Press, Hammersmith, in 1890, for which he designed type, page borders, and bindings for fine books.

Alfred Bernhard Nobel (b. 1833). Swedish chemist and inventor; he established a fund to provide annual awards (Nobel Prize) in the sciences, literature, and the promotion of international peace; the first literature prize was awarded in 1901.

Coventry Patmore (b. 1823). English poet and essayist; his verse focused upon such subjects as the apotheosis of married love and other domestic themes; after his conversion to Roman Catholicism in 1864, the substance of his verse became more profound, and he wrote essays and meditations upon religious subjects.

Jose Rizal (b. 1861). Filipino poet and writer of fiction; his early verse praised the Spanish conquerors of his island, but later he began to express the rising nationalistic sentiments of the middle class; his anticolonial views helped to encourage the revolutionary movement of 1898; he wrote principally in Spanish.

Harriet Beecher Stowe (b. 1811). American novelist and advocate of woman's suffrage; her fiction became influential in spreading the abolitionist sentiment in the northern United States; she also became involved in the temperance movement.

Paul Verlaine (b. 1844). French poet; his symbolist verse possessed a rare musical quality; his life was marked by drunkenness and debauchery, and he had a tempestuous liaison with the poet Arthur Rimbaud; he dies impoverished at Paris.

PUBLICATIONS

Anton Chekhov, *Chayka* (The Seagull)—a drama by the Russian playwright and writer of fiction; concerns a young artist who, disgusted by imitative methods in the drama, seeks new forms and modes of expression.

Ernest Dowson, *Verses*—a collection of poems by the English poet, the first of his two published volumes; includes his most noted piece, "Non Sum Qualis Eram," popularly known as "Cynara."

Paul Laurence Dunbar, *Lyrics of Lowly Life*—a collection of verse by the black American poet and writer of fiction; the volume established the writer's preeminence among black poets and his reputation as the representative of the "folk"; collectively, the pieces develop the idea that humor and pathos are the essentials of dialect.

Remy de Gourmont, *Le Livre de Masques* (The Book of Masques)—a volume of criticism by the French essayist, poet, and writer of fiction; the essayist examines the works of the major symbolist writers of his era; he also identifies the principles of symbolist art, defining symbolism as individualism in literature and liberty in art.

Thomas Hardy, *Jude the Obscure*—a novel by the English writer of fiction and poetry; set in the rough countryside of the writer's native Dorsetshire, the work considers the theme of a deadly war waged with "Apostolic desperation" between the flesh and the spirit.

A. E. Housman, *A Shropshire Lad*—a poetic cycle by the English writer of verse; a series of sixty-three nostalgic poems based largely upon ballad forms; the pieces tend to be addressed to or spoken by a farm boy, a representative of pure innocence; the volume was published at the poet's own expense.

Mark Twain, *The Personal Recollections of Joan of Arc*—a romantic narrative by the American Prose writer and humorist; reveals spiritual forces in conflict with materialism and organized society; characteristically, the writer attacks power politics, imperialism, excessive wealth, and hypocrisy in morality and religion.

H. G. Wells, *The Island of Dr. Moreau*—a novel by the English essayist and writer of fiction; described as an evolutionary fantasy, the work tells the story of a shipwrecked naturalist who involves himself in an experiment to humanize animals through a surgical process.

EVENTS

Alfred Austin appointed Poet Laureate of England, succeeding Alfred, Lord Tennyson; until 1913.

Alfred Charles William Harmsworth (1865-1922), Irish-born English publisher, founds *The Daily Mail* in London; that newspaper, with its "snappy" American-style composition and news format, changes the appearance and philosophy of English journalism.

The estate of Alfred Nobel, the Swedish inventor and manufacturer, establishes five annual prizes for those who, during each preceding year, shall have conferred the greatest benefits upon mankind in the areas of physics, physiology and medicine, chemistry, literature, and peace.

Charles Ricketts, English illustrator, designer, and painter, establishes a private publishing house known as The Vale Press, at Chelsea; one of the most significant among the private presses, printing classical works of literature on elaborately designed woodcut borders.

1897

BIRTHS

Mukhtar Auezov (d. 1961). Kazakh (SSR) playwright and writer of fiction; his plays and fiction will rely upon the historical drama surrounding his homeland; he will also draw upon traditional folk stories.

Nirod C. Chaudhuri (d. ?). Indian historian and autobiographer; he will write principally in English, concerning himself with the origin; and development of the Indian effort to create a modern humanistic culture based upon an East-West cultural synthesis.

William Faulkner (d. 1962). American writer of fiction; his fiction will focus upon the mythology of the American South, including the

social and racial problems of that region; stylistically he will experiment in the manner of James Joyce; he will receive the Nobel Prize for literature in 1949 and the Pulitzer Prize for fiction in 1955 and (posthumously) 1963.

Valentin Petrovich Katayev (d. 1986). Russian poet, playwright, and writer of fiction; his drama will satirize Soviet economic conditions, while in his fiction he will attempt to depict Russian life from the end of the Russo-Japanese War (1905) to the beginnings of World War II.

Alfred H. Mendes (d. ?). Trinidadian writer of fiction and poetry; in frank, direct, and often vulgar language, he will attempt to describe events that altered the attitude of West Indian people toward their lives and manners; his style will capture the essence of West Indian creativity.

Erich Maria Remarque (d. 1970). German novelist; his fiction will capture the utter horror and futility of war and also depict the comedy and tragedy of life in the German nation following World War I.

Sacheverell Sitwell (d. 1988). English poet and art critic; his persistent praise of the baroque mode in art and literature will contribute to the popularity of that period in the twentieth century; for him, poetry and art will forever be united; as a poet, he will create graceful variations upon Alexander Pope and his contemporaries.

Yeghishe Tcharents (d. 1937?). Armenian poet; his earliest published lyrics will be influenced by the symbolist movement, but then he will write verse based upon his war experiences; eventually, he will seek new aesthetic principles to express the revolutionary nature of his times.

Thornton Wilder (d. 1975). American playwright and writer of fiction; his fiction, especially, will be characterized by an exceedingly calm atmosphere of sophistication and detached irony; he will receive Pulitzer Prizes for fiction in 1928 and for drama in 1938 and 1943.

Nima Yushij (d. 1960). Iranian poet; his upbringing in the countryside and his deep love of nature will become important elements in his verse; his work will be strong, influenced by French literature, particularly Romanticism; he will pioneer the employment of free verse in Persian poetry.

DEATHS

Alphonse Daudet (b. 1840). French writer of fiction; noted for his natural portrayals of French life, particularly in his Provence-inspired collections of short stories.

PUBLICATIONS

Gurajtada Wenkata Apparaw, *Kanyasulkam* (Bride Price)—a full-length social drama by the Indian (Telugu) poet and playwright; written in colloquial language, the work powerfully exposes such contemporary social evils as child marriage, the sale of brides, religious bigotry, the caste system, and prostitution; its humor, free from malice, cuts without causing pain.

Leon Bloy, *La Femme Pauvre* (The Woman Who Was Poor)—a novel by the French writer of fiction and nonfiction; depicts a woman who retains her faith and goodness despite strenuous trials; presents a portrait of true Christian behavior that transcends the influence of an increasingly powerless Church.

Kate Chopin, *A Night in Acadie*—a collection of stories by the American writer of fiction; she describes the Acadians in the mid-Louisiana parishes of Natchitoches and Avoyelles; the majority of the pieces focus upon incidents of social rebellion.

Joseph Conrad, *The Nigger of the "Narcissus"*—a novel by the Polish-born English writer of fiction; concerns the voyage of *Narcissus* during a ferocious gale and unsuccessful attempts to incite mutiny; presents a detailed picture of the sea and sea life, and tends to be regarded as the writer's finest work.

William Henry Drummond, *The Habitant, and Other French-Canadian Poems*—a collection of verse by the Irish-born Canadian poet; the poems celebrate the rural life that had been abandoned and stresses the need to return to it.

Stefan George, *Das Jahr der Seele* (The Year of the Soul)—a collection of poems by the German writer of verse; influenced strongly by the work of Paul Verlaine; a self portrait in which the heart of the homosexual appears dead.

William Dean Howells, *The Landlord at Lion's Head*—a novel by the American writer, considered one of his best efforts; a bleak picture of New England life focusing on a tubercular and lonely New Hampshire farm family; an artist comes and suggests the possibility of a summer hotel, which creates serious problems.

Henry James, *The Spoils of Poynton*—a novel by the American writer of fiction; a melodramatic fable that attempts to analyze English character with extreme subtlety.

—————— , *What Masie Knew*—a novel by the American writer; the novelist attempts to determine what will happen to a little girl exposed to a series of marriage failures and shabby divorces.

W. Somerset Maugham, *Liza of Lambeth*—the first novel by the English writer of fiction; classified as belonging to the "new realist" school of George Augustus Moore; originates from the novelist's experience of slums and Cockney life while an obstetric clerk at St. Thomas's Hospital, London.

Edwin Arlington Robinson, *The Children of the Night*—a verse collection by the American poet; focuses upon disillusioned individuals who are representative of various aspects of spiritual and materialistic human existence; includes "Richard Cory" and "Cliff Klingenhagen."

Edmond Rostand, *Cyrano de Bergerac*—a drama by the French poet and playwright; based loosely upon the life of the poet, soldier, and philosopher (1619-1655); an idealized dramatization of the heroic spirit faced with disillusioning reality.

Bram Stoker, *Dracula*—a novel by the Irish lawyer and writer of fiction; a classic horror tale focusing upon the fiendish activities of the title character, a vampire, and the struggles of young and beautiful women to escape Dracula's blood lusts.

August Strindberg, *Inferno*—an autobiographical narrative by the Swedish poet, playwright, and novelist; describes the writer's "inferno" period in Paris during the 1890s, concentrating upon his experiments with alchemy and the occult.

Mark Twain, *Following the Equator*—a travel narrative by the American writer of fiction and humor; recounts the writer's lecture tour in Australia and India.

H. G. Wells, *The Invisible Man*—a science fiction novel by the English writer of fiction and history; concerns a scientist who fatally stumbles upon the age-old secret of invisibility; events produce a tragic outcome.

EVENTS

The Survey Graphic begins publication at New York City as an organ of the New York Charity Organization Society; after 1912 it will function as a liberal political and literary journal, featuring such writers as Ida M. Tarbell, William A. White, Stuart Chase, and Dorothy Thompson; until 1944.

1898

BIRTHS

Vicente Aleixandre (d. 1984). Spanish poet; he will be considered the spiritual father of the younger generations of poets in Spain; he will develop a finely cadenced free verse form; generally, his poems will prove difficult, anguished, and extremely private.

Damaso Alonso (d. 1990). Spanish poet and philologist; he will become a professor of romance philology at Madrid, becoming an authority on the life and works of Don Luis de Gongora y Argote (1561-1627); he will write powerfully emotional religious poetry.

Stephen Vincent Benet (d. 1943). American poet; his verse will reflect his deep interest in the American scene and its historical background; his best ballads will combine American folklore and humor; he will receive the Pulitzer Prize for poetry in 1929 and (posthumously) 1944.

Bertolt Brecht (d. 1956). German poet and playwright; he will come to the forefront of the bourgeois theater, striving to make audiences think; he will attempt to create an alien world so that people can better understand themselves; he will seek depth and complexity from the experiences of discovery and realization; as both a playwright and a stage director, he will strive to rework everything from lighting to costumes, from music to acting.

Harindranath Chattopadhyay (d. ?). Indian (Bengali) prose writer and playwright; writing principally in English, he will create realistic and didactic works revealing his social consciousness.

Malcolm Cowley (d. 1989). American critic, narrative writer, and poet; he will recount the lives and the activities of members of the "Lost Generation" from the 1920s.

Federico Garcia Lorca (d. 1936). Spanish poet and playwright; his gypsy-song poetry will reveal his classical control of imagery, rhythm, and emotion; his intensely personal dramas will lament the death of liberty and creative imagination in Spain after the fall of the Spanish Republic.

Michel de Ghelderode (d. 1962). Belgian (Flemish) poet and playwright; he will inject a number of expressionist techniques into his drama, some of the originating from Flemish folklore and the traditions of the Belgian puppet theater.

Tawfiq al-Hakim (d. 1987). Egyptian playwright and novelist; he will combine plain description and allegory to produce graphic accounts of the life of the middle class and peasants in Egypt and their involvements in the nationalistic struggles following World War I.

Masuji Ibuse (d. ?). Japanese novelist; he will be admired for his acute and humorous observations of human nature; he will, however, shock his readers by writing about the extremely painful realities of Japan in the aftermath of World War II, basing his works upon the actual records of war victims.

C. S. Lewis (d. 1963). English literary scholar and writer on religion and morality he will treat such various subjects as love, literary history, and science fiction; he will also write a spiritual autobiography and produce stories for children.

Vilhelm Moberg (d. 1973). Swedish novelist; he will contribute to the "proletarian literature" of his region; his work will depict Swedish social and economic problems of his day, as well as focus upon Swedish immigrants to the United States during the nineteenth century.

Luis Pales Matos (d. 1959). Puerto Rican poet and novelist; he will become one of Puerto Rico's most significant poets, particularly because of his reliance upon African themes and styles in his works; he will attempt a difficult synthesis of his social and personal experiences as a black and the white cultural values of the United States, especially those imposed upon the island-commonwealth.

Simon Vesldijk (d. 1971). Dutch novelist; he will be considered one of the most important Dutch writers of fiction during the first part of the twentieth century; he will also achieve considerable renown for his poetry, particularly its attention to historical traditions.

Alexander Raban Waugh (d. 1981). English novelist and travel writer; his fiction will focus upon such "scandalous" subjects as public school homosexuality and interracial associations; his autobiographical efforts will cast light upon an important English literary family.

DEATHS

Lewis Carroll (pseudonym of Charles Lutwidge Dodgson; b. 1832). English mathematician and writer of fiction; his fantasy novels originated from stories he related to children during his days as a lecturer at Oxford; his fiction introduced logical problems into the nursery.

Georg Moritz Ebers (b. 1837). German novelist and Egyptologist; professor of Egyptology at Leipzig; his historical work focused upon Goshen, Sinai, and Egypt, while his fiction tended to be historical and closely related to his scholarly interests.

Theodor Fontane (b. 1819). German poet and novelist; achieved recognition for his ballads and for his realistic fiction depicting the decay of contemporary Berlin.

Stephane Mallarme (b. 1842). French poet; the principal forebear of the symbolist poets, he believed that poetry should be transcendental, approaching the abstractions of music; thus his language defies traditional syntax and tends to be complex and obscure.

Conrad Ferdinand Meyer (b. 1825). Swiss poet and novelist; his historical fiction tended to concentrate upon themes from the Renaissance; he displayed keen psychological insight and an interest in ethical problems.

PUBLICATIONS

Stephen Crane, "The Open Boat"—a short story by the American poet and writer of fiction; a correspondent and three companions find themselves adrift following a shipwreck; the portrayal of their despair is a masterpiece of understatement.

Thomas Hardy, *Wessex Poems*—the initial verse collection by the English novelist and poet; early experiments with rhythm, stress, and verse form.

Henry James, *The Turn of the Screw*—a novella by the American-born writer of fiction, recognized as a masterpiece of mystery; an atmosphere of evil permeates a country house, and the reader must, in the end, determine if the "spirits" actually exist, or if they are really the hysterical fantasies of the narrator, a young governess.

Sir Arthur Wing Pinero, *Trelawney of the "Wells"*—a drama by the English playwright; highly representative of the "play of sentiment" popular during the 1890s; attempts to portray life in the most detailed manner possible and to fashion a hero from an actual dull, ordinary person.

Henrik Pontoppidan, *Lykke-Per* (Lucky Peter)—an eight-volume novel (to 1904) by the Danish writer of fiction; the central character is skeptical, restless, and isolated; at the end, he leaves his family for the life of a hermit, there to record (rather than to achieve) his final and positive conclusions about his own existence.

George Bernard Shaw, *Arms and the Man*—a comedy by the Irish-born dramatist and social critic; often misunderstood as an attack upon the military, the piece actually serves to ridicule morals.

H. G. Wells, *The War of the Worlds*—a science fiction novel by the English writer; describes the arrival, at Woking, of Martians, having been driven from their own planet by the need to seek warmth; emphasizes the dull-witted reactions of the English commoners to the destructive intelligence of the invaders; they devastate the countryside before eventually falling victim to earthly bacteria.

Oscar Wilde, *The Ballad of Reading Gaol*—a poem by the Irish-born playwright, novelist, and writer of verse; composed in France after the poet's release from prison for homosexual offenses; best remembered for its final verse of

> And all men kill the thing they love,
>   By all let this be heard,
> Some do it with a bitter look,
>   Some do it with a flattering word,
> The coward does it with a kiss,
>   The brave man with a sword!

EVENTS

The National Institute of Arts and Letters chartered by the United States Congress; based upon the concept of the French Academy, honoring individuals in art, literature, and music; Mark Twain, Henry James, and

William Dean Howells are among the early members; becomes, in 1976, the American Academy and Institute of Arts and Letters.

Emile Zola, French novelist, essayist, and journalist, publishes in the Paris journal *L'Aurore* (January 1898) his open letter to the President of France, "J'Accuse . . . !"; follows the conviction for treason of Captain Alfred Dreyfus.

1899

BIRTHS

Miguel Angel Asturias (d. 1974). Guatemalan writer of fiction and poetry; his political novels will transmit his Gothic vision of Latin America, particularly in terms of the evils of tyranny; he will also consider the exploitation of Guatemalan banana plantations by the United States; he will receive the Nobel Prize for literature in 1967.

Jacques Audiberti (d. 1965). French playwright, poet, novelist, and essayist; his literary efforts will be characterized by passionate, flamboyant language, combined with a strong sense of the melodramatic and the absurd; he will produce complicated and obscure fiction, as well as formal and extravagant poetry.

Aksel Bakunts (pseudonym of Aleksandr Tevosian; d. 1937). Armenian novelist and essayist; he will describe the rural people of Armenia during patriarchal and post-revolutionary times, depicting the conflicts arising from the changing modes of life.

Jorge Luis Borges (d. 1986) Argentinian writer of fiction and poetry; he will become recognized as one of the most prominent literary figures writing in Spanish; in his esoteric short stories, he will blend fantasy with reality, addressing complex philosophical problems; time, infinity, identity, and memory will become his major thematic motifs.

Noel Coward (d. 1973). English playwright and actor; he will write dramas about witty and stylish people who act in accordance with unconventional morals; a major evaluation of his drama will conclude that in his plays, groups of people have difficulty living together, but they experience even more difficulty living apart from one another; simultaneously, his characters will accept and defy social convention.

Hart Crane (d. 1932). American poet; his verse will evidence his indebtedness to Walt Whitman; he will focus his attention upon New York City in an attempt to develop a mythology of America.

Ernest Hemingway (d. 1961). American writer of fiction; his novels and short stories will reveal a keen but narrow vision of humankind and a supreme gift for dialogue and description; he will associate physical courage with moral dignity; he will receive a Pulitzer Prize for fiction in 1953 and the Nobel Prize for literature in 1954.

Jafar Jabbarly (d. 1934). Azerbaijan poet, essayist, and playwright; his early work will be influenced by Persian literature and the ideal of pan-Turkish unity; he will, however, turn his attention to depicting the Azerbaijan national awakening and the new life within the Soviet Socialist Republic.

Erich Kastner (d. 1974). German novelist, playwright, and poet; he will write fiction for children, becoming one of the most outstanding writers of that genre; his drama will reflect his attempts to capture the human and political horror of his times.

Yasunari Kawabata (d. 1972). Japanese novelist; his fiction will focus upon traditional Japanese culture, although his pieces will have contemporary settings and will concern a nation undergoing modernization; he will become Japan's first Nobel laureate, earning the prize for literature in 1968.

R. Kirusnamurtti (d. 1954). Indian (Tamil) novelist and journalist; he will write historical novels and short stories with contemporary themes and settings; his fiction will evidence his commitment to the Indian independence movement of the 1940s.

Dame Edith Ngaio Marsh (d. 1982). New Zealand writer of fiction; she will gain considerable popularity with her detective stories.

Vladimir Nabokov (d. 1977). Russian-born American novelist, poet, essayist, and writer of short fiction; he will gain a reputation as one of the principal literary stylists of the twentieth century, investigating the illusory nature of reality and the literary artist's relationship to his or her craft; he will always emphasize style over such elements as social or moral considerations.

Nazrul Islam (d. 1976). Indian (Bengali) poet; he will write a number of lyrics that contain both Persian and Urdu; he will become one of the most colorful, exuberant, and rebellious poets of the Bengal region.

Payrav (pseudonym of Otajon Sulaymoni; d. 1933). Tajik (SSR) poet; his verse will demonstrate his knowledge of classical forms; he will write about the spread of education and the emancipation of women, becoming, in addition, one of the first poets of his land to depict and explain international events.

Benjamin Peret (d. 1959). French poet, essayist, and writer of short fiction; he will emerge as a central figure of the surrealist movement; his highly original poetry will be characterized by surprising imagery and irrationality, displaying a contempt for social and religious institutions.

Allen Tate (d. 1979). American poet and critic; as a critic, he will become one of the leading forces of the "New Criticism" and will support regionalism in American literature to counter the negativism of abstraction.

Theippam Maun Wa (d. 1942). Burmese playwright, critic, and writer of fiction; he will become known as an innovator of prose style and his short fiction will providing a realistic picture of rural Burmese life; he will describe uneducated and backward villagers, pointing to the need for reform.

Wen I-to (d. 1946). Chinese poet and critic; he will blend Eastern and Western images, symbols, and themes; he will advocate a return from formless, free verse to structured patterns with rhyme.

E. B. White (d. 1985). American essayist, journalist, and fiction writer; with irony and simplicity, he will discuss Nature, which, for him, counterbalances the noise of the city; critical commentators will refer to him as a "sophisticated" Henry David Thoreau; he will also author the popular children's books *Charlotte's Web* and *Stuart Little*.

DEATHS

Mordecai Ze'eb Feirberg (b. 1874). German-born Jewish writer of fiction; he created individualized stories that described the innermost problems of the modern Jew; he wrote to promote cultural Zionism; he dies, prematurely, at age twenty-four.

Guido Gezelle (b. 1830). Belgian poet and a Roman Catholic priest; a forerunner of the Flemish literary revival, his works combine love of nature, intense religious feeling, and patriotism.

PUBLICATIONS

Kate Chopin, *The Awakening*—a novel by the American writer of fiction; relates the torrid story of one Edna Pontellier, who fails in love but succeeds in lust; in the end, she kills herself, completing the cycle of tragic events.

Stephen Crane, *Active Service*—a novel by the American poet and writer of fiction; concerns the Greco-Turkish War of 1898-1899 and those war correspondents who supposedly reported the action.

Georges Feydeau, *La dame de Chez Maxim* (The Lady from Maxim's)—a humorous dramatic piece by the French playwright; the comedy results from the desire of people to practice what they perceive as correct social behavior, no matter how ludicrous that behavior might be; primarily focuses upon male-female relationships.

Jean Moreas, *Les Stances*—a collection of verse by the Greek-born French poet, essayist, playwright, and writer of fiction; the pieces convey a sense of emotional trauma, relying upon powerful symbols (bleeding wounds and fire), simple language, and a carefully modulated tone; 7 volumes, to 1920.

Frank Norris, *McTeague*—a novel by the American writer of fiction; the title character possesses all of the physical and mental characteristics of a brute, but his harmless, childish acceptance of life appears most admirable; unfortunately, poverty contributes to the degeneration of him and his family; the writer examines the issues of ruthless power, the ugliness of life, and the duality of human nature.

Arthur Schnitzler, *Reigen* (Merry-Go-Round)—a play by the Austrian Jewish poet and dramatist; a sexually cynical piece revealing the influence of his relationship with Sigmund Freud.

EVENTS

The Wanamaker's Department Store, Philadelphia, publishes *Everybody's*, a house organ that (in 1903) becomes an independent magazine in support of radical social reform; Upton Sinclair and Lincoln Steffens are among the more noted of its literary contributors; until 1928.

The Gideon Society, dedicated to promoting biblical reading, founded at Janesville, Wisconsin, by the Christian Commercial Men's Association of America; beginning November 1908, the group will place a Bible in hotel rooms throughout the United States.

Karl Kraus, German writer, begins publication at Vienna of a satirical news sheet, *Die Fackel* (The Torch); he will be its principal writer; until 1936.

Pearson's Magazine, a monthly journal of literature, politics, and the arts, begins publication at New York City; contributors include Frank Harris, Upton Sinclair, and George Bernard Shaw; thus, the journal takes on a socialist viewpoint; until 1925.

1900

BIRTHS

Roberto Godofredo Christopherson Arlt (d. 1942). Argentine writer of fiction and essayist; he will earn recognition for his fiction portraying the metaphysical anguish of the alienated individual in twentieth-century society.

Reuben Tolakele Caluza (d. 1965). South African (Zulu) poet and lyricist; he will compose the first secular lyrics ever to be published in the Zulu language; his work will appeal to the increasingly detribalized Zulus working in the large mines of the Rand and performing factory work in the cities.

Robert Desnos (d. 1945). French poet, writer of fiction, playwright, and essayist; he will become one of the original members of the surrealist movement; initially he will experiment with verse forming but eventually he will turn to the more traditional and structured Alexandrine and sonnet; thematically, he will celebrate ecstatic love.

Julien Green (d. ?). French novelist of American parentage; his fiction will focus primarily upon vice and madness.

Mohammad Hejazi (d. ?). Iranian novelist and essayist; his fiction will emphasize erotic themes, while his tone will be unmistakably moral.

Muhammas Mahdi al-Jawahiri (d. ?). Iraqi poet; he will earn recognition as the best contemporary Iraqi poet writing in the traditional manner; he will be classified as a progressive poet, deeply committed to the struggle against foreign domination, feudalism and political reaction.

Eyvind Johnson (d. 1976). Swedish writer of narrative and fiction; he will develop a subtle approach to literature, becoming extremely aware of contemporary mental stress; he will constantly experiment with fiction, but never lose his stylistic coherence.

Aniceti Kitereza (d. ?). Tanzanian novelist and folklorist; he will collect the stories and poetry of his region; he will seek to preserve the ancient values of the mixed population of the island of his birth, Bukerebe, particularly the conflicting customs of the Silangi, Jita, Kara, and Subuma peoples.

Maha Hswei (d. 1953). Burmese writer of fiction and journalist; he will produce over six hundred stories and sixty novels, most of which will contribute to the strength of the Burmese nationalist movement.

Guruprasad Mainali (d. 1971). Nepali writer of short fiction; his best fiction will describe the tragic aspects of Nepali village life; he will develop a style free from artificiality.

Sean O'Faolain. Irish writer of fiction and biography; his popular short fiction will concentrate upon frustrated individuals; missed opportunities, and characters restricted by their surroundings.

Antoine de Saint-Exupery (d. 1944). French writer of narratives, fiction, and children's fables; he will become a commercial airline pilot and war reconnaissance airman; his literary endeavors will reflect his philosophy of heroic action.

George Seferis (d. 1971). Greek poet; his verse will be characterized by clarity, precision, and dignity; he will receive the Nobel Prize for literature in 1963.

Ignazio Silone (d. 1978). Italian writer of fiction; he will respond heatedly to fascism in his work and idealize the Abruzzi peasants.

Tu-Mo (pseudonym of Ho-Trong-Hieu; d. ?). Vietnamese poet; he will gain considerable popularity as a humorist and satirist; he will be active in the anticolonial war on the side of the Communists (DRV) while living and writing in Hanoi.

Thomas Clayton Wolfe (d. 1938). American novelist; he will reflect the strong wave of Southern emotionalism, confronting directly the dimensions of the future; he will become, through his fiction, the central spokesman for American artistic opinions during the 1920s;

he will regenerate the entire tradition of American realism.

Neguse Yoftahe (d. 1949?). Ethiopian playwright and poet; he will produce allegorical drama that will have important political meaning at the Ethiopian court; he will also write nationalistic poetry and moralistic essays.

Nairi Zarian (pseudonym of Hayastan Yeghiazarian; d. 1969). Armenian (SSR) poet and writer of travel books; his poetry will record the building of the socialist state and the collectivization of Armenian village life.

DEATHS

R. D. Blackmore (b. 1825). English novelist; his pastoral tales stir the imagination; he achieved an artistic reputation from his ability to describe, in the most intimate manner, climate, wildlife, and vegetation.

Stephen Crane (b. 1871). American novelist and writer of short fiction; considered the first "modern" American writer, principally because he introduced realism in fiction; he also achieved some degree of literary recognition as a war correspondent.

Ernest Christopher Dowson (b. 1867). English poet; he became one of the best known among the Decadent writers, striving to express the morbid and macabre elements of human emotion; he wrote delicate and highly musical poems, the most noted containing the line, "I have been faithful to thee, Cynara! in my fashion."

Friedrich Wilhelm Neitzsche (b. 1844). German philosopher known as an individual moralist rather than as a systematic philosopher; he passionately rejected what he termed "the slave morality" of Christianity for a new heroic morality that would affirm life; a form of "superman" would lead the new society, one composed of people whose "will to power" would set them apart from inferior humanity; after eleven years of insanity, he dies at Weimar.

Sigbjorn Obstfelder (b. 1866). Norwegian poet, playwright, essayist, and writer of fiction; considered the principal representative of the *fin de siècle* in Norwegian poetry; his work succeeds because of its inventive language, unconventional forms, mysticism, and idiosyncratic symbolism; he dies of tuberculosis.

Jose Maria Eca de Queiroz (b. 1846?). Portugese novelist and statesman; he combined satire and elements of naturalism in his major works of fiction; he established Portugese realism and described the vices of nineteenth-century Portugal, pointing to government, education, and the bourgeoise.

John Ruskin (b. 1819). English art critic and social theorist; he developed the idea of art as a universal language based upon national and individual integrity and morality; he also attacked the ugliness and waste of modern industrial England, proposing a number of social reforms; in 1870 he received the appointment as Slade Professor at Oxford University, the first professorship of art in England.

Oscar Wilde (b. 1854). English poet, playwright, and writer of fiction; he glorified beauty for its own sake, expressing himself in a number of sensitive and witty plays; his fiction focused upon the theme of youth corrupted by sensual indulgence and moral indifference; he dies in exile in Paris.

PUBLICATIONS

Anton Chekhov, *Dyadya Vanya* (Uncle Vanya)—a four-act drama by the Russian playwright and writer of fiction; the title character gives his share of an inheritance to his sister; she, in turn, marries a pompous and dull professor; then follow complex family relationships.

Joseph Conrad, *Lord Jim*—a novel by the Polish-born English writer of fiction; develops the tale of a young Englishman who in a moment of panic deserts his apparently sinking ship; he loses his honor, but retrieves it through an honorable death.

Stephen Crane, *Whilomville Stories*—the last work by the American writer of fiction and poetry; a selection of stories that sharply and vividly convey the fears of the human soul; composed when the writer was suffering from ill health.

Theodore Dreiser, *Sister Carrie*—a novel by the American writer of fiction; concerns a sensitive young girl who escapes poverty by forming a liaison with a man of superior financial and social position; the starkly realistic piece was intensely criticized for so-called immorality.

Sigmund Freud, *Die Traumdeutung* (The Interpretation of Dreams)—an exhaustive study of dreams by the Austrian founder of pyschoanalysis; documents the writer's own dreams, which according to Freud, demonstrate that dreams, like neuroses, are disguised manifestations of repressed wishes of sexual origin; repression differs from conscious suppression.

Herman Heijermans, *Op Hoop van Zegen* (The Good Hope)—a drama by the Dutch playwright and essayist; portrays life in a poor fishing community and the corrupt practices of the fishing industry, criticizing the exploitation of workers and insufficient care of the aged; the piece is instrumental in bringing about legislative reform in the industry.

Henrik Ibsen, *Nar vi Dode Vagner* (When We Dead Awaken)—concerns a sculptor who has subordinated his personal life to his religious mission; he perishes in an avalanche in an ecstatic attempt to capture what he has denied himself; the theme concerns the search for the self within the context of conflicting social demands.

Aleksey Yeliseyevich Kulakovskiy, *Bayanay Algyha* (The Enchantment of Bayana)—a poem by the Yakut (SSR) versifier and essayist; the first literary work ever to be written in the Yakut language by a Yakut writer; becomes the foundation of the region's national literature.

Jack London, *The Son of the Wolf*—the first collection of stories by the American writer of fiction and narrative.

Joaquim Maria Machado de Assis, *Don Casmurro*—a novel by the Brazilian writer; an account of a man who is cuckolded by his best friend; the title character is dehumanized and indulges in self-pity.

Isaac Leib Peretz, *Stories and Pictures*—a collection of stories by the Polish Hebrew writer; combines Jewish nationalism with social realism.

Edmond Rostand, *L'Aiglon* (The Eaglet)—a drama by the French playwright and poet; dramatizes the conflict between ambition and conscience in the Duke of Reichstadt, Napoleon's son by his Austrian wife; his demise comes about after having seen, in a vision, the victims of his father's conquests.

H. G. Wells, *Love and Mrs. Lewisham*—a novel by the English writer of fiction and social history; comically depicts the world of the lower middle class in England at the time of the writer's youth; focuses upon the life of a struggling teacher.

EVENTS

Sir Cyril Arthur Pearson, London publisher and newspaper magnate, founds *The Daily Express,* one of the most significant newspapers in the English capital.

Harper's Monthly, the New York City miscellaneous literary magazine, changes its title to *Harper's New Monthly Magazine;* until 1925.

Sir Arthur Thomas Quiller-Couch, English scholar, edits *The Oxford Book of English Verse,* a collection of poems that exercises considerable influence upon future anthologies and collections.

Walter Hines Page, American journalist, founds *World's Work,* a monthly magazine that focuses upon American values and modes of life; until 1932.

The Chinese *Yung Lo Tai Tien,* perhaps the largest encyclopedia ever written (but never printed), dating from approximately 1403, almost totally destroyed in a fire in the Han-lin College, Peking; the complete manuscript totalled over 500,000 pages.

1901

BIRTHS

Kjeld Abell (d. 1961). Danish playwright; he will become active in the resistance movement during World War II, and his political beliefs will appear in his drama; he will emphasize cinematic and impressionistic techniques.

Gomar Bashirov. Tartar (SSR) novelist and essayist; his fictional themes will be based on events during World War II and the development of collective farms.

Dashti Ali. Iranian essayist and writer of fiction; his nonfiction will offer original views upon modern life and its problems; he will also consider East-West relations and the contrast between autocracy and democracy; his fiction will focus upon the elegant society of Teheran, portraying its women as lovely and capricious and their men as ideal companions and seducers.

Rolfus Reginald Raymond Dhlomo. South African (Zulu) novelist and journalist; in his fiction, he will concentrate upon important aspects of Zulu history and concentrate upon important aspects of Zulu history and simple country people.

Marielouise Fleisser (d. 1974). German playwright; her work will reflect her own personal conflicts, principally her alternating desires to feel protected and to be independent; her plays will not receive attention until the 1960s, when they will be adapted for films.

Cyril Lionel Robert James. Trinidadian novelist, essayist and historian; he will make his major literary contributions in the areas of historical and political thought, with works revealing a strong ideology and considerable intellectual independence; he will also demonstrate the West Indian passion for the sport of cricket as an art form.

Andre Malraux (d. 1976). French novelist and essayist; he will produce fiction based upon revolutionary themes and achieve a significant reputation as a critic and historian of art.

Prince Modupe Paris. Guinean autobiographer and novelist; he will be educated in the United States, living in Los Angeles during the 1950s and 1960s; his autobiography will express a sense of loss and nostalgia for his native land, particularly village life and native customs.

Salvatore Quasimodo (d. 1968). Italian poet; he will become a professor of literature at the Conservatory of Music, Milan; his poetry will reflect his interest in the fate of Italy, and he will complement his striking poetic language with both Christian and mythological allusions; he will receive the Nobel Prize for literature in 1959.

Jean-Joseph Rabearivelo (d. 1937). Madagascar poet; he will be considered the founder of modern poetry in Madagascar, writing in French; he will, however, combine French with local forms and rhythms, creating a ballad-like verse form.

G. Sankara Karuppu. Indian (Malayalam) poet; his work will develop social and political themes and consider the implications of the advance of scientific knowledge; he will also be inspired by the work of Mohandas K. Ghandi to direct his poetry toward serving the movement for Indian independence.

Jaroslav Seifert (d. 1986). Czechoslovakian poet; his work will evidence a variety of phases: he will begin with surrealism, move to patriotism during the Nazi occupation of his nation, and conclude with a meditative, philosophical period.

DEATHS

Leopoldo Alas y Urena (b. 1852). Spanish writer of fiction, essayist, and playwright; he achieved recognition for his astute critical commentary upon Spanish fiction during the middle and late nineteenth century; largely influenced by Realism and Naturalism, his best fiction will contain elements of satire; in both fiction and literary criticism, he sought to raise the intellectual and literary standards of his nation; he dies, at age forty-nine, after suffering for several years from ill health.

Johanna Spyri (b. 1827). Swiss writer of fiction; she has achieved lasting literary recognition for her popular children's stories set in the Swiss Alps, principally *Heidi* (1880).

Charlotte Mary Yonge (b. 1823). English novelist; she explored the positive relationships among members of large families, supporting description with realistic dialogue and narrative; these novels cast light upon the social, ecclesiastical, and educational history of her time and were of interest principally to female readers.

PUBLICATIONS

Rudyard Kipling, *Kim*—a novel by the English poet and writer of fiction; the title character, Kimball O'Hara, the orphaned son of a sergeant of an Irish regiment, spends his childhood as a vagabond; he meets an old lama from Tibet and travels with him until he is discovered by members of his father's old regiment, who send him off to school; the piece abounds with graphic accounts of life in India.

Henry Lawson, *Joe Wilson and His Mates*—a collection of short stories by the Australian writer of fiction and poetry; the stories probe deeply into complex human emotions and relationships, specifically courtship, marriage, hardship, the loss of affection, and tentative reconciliation; the collection includes "Joe Wilson's Courtship," "Brighten's Sister-in-Law," "Water Them Geraniums," and "A Double Buggy at Lahey's Creek."

Thomas Mann, *Buddenbrooks*—a novel by the German writer of fiction, presenting the saga of a family (the writer's own?); the novelist traces its decline through four generations, as business acumen gives way to artistic sensitivities; the piece establishes the writer's literary reputation.

Dmitry Sergeyevich Merezhkovsky, *Voskesshie Bogi: Leonardo da Vinchi* (The Romance of Leonardo da Vinci, the Forerunner)—a novel by the Russian writer of fiction, essayist, and poet; presents the noted Renaissance artist and inventor as torn between Christian devotion and pagan sensuality; the second novel in the trilogy entitled *Khristos i Antikhrist* (Christ and Antichrist).

Frank Norris, *The Octopus*—a novel by the American writer of fiction; concerns the decline of one Magnus Derrick, the master of Los Muertos; wheat growers oppose the railroads in what was the most ambitious fictional project of the period, as the writer studies degeneration through greed in high places.

George Bernard Shaw, *Caesar and Cleopatra*—a play by the Irish dramatist; presents an unromantic relationship between the two title characters, with Caesar being a paternal figure who attempts to train the young Egyptian queen in the responsibilities of government and leadership; the playwright also portrays Caesar as a representative of greatness, one who reveals his vision for the world through the frankness of his statements and the directness of his actions.

August Strindberg, *Pask* (Easter)—a morality play by the Swedish playwright and novelist; Eleanora, a mentally unstable girl, exists as a fusion of Christ, Robert Browning's "Pippa," one of the playwright's sisters, and Honore de Balzac's "Seraphita."

Frank Wedekind, *Der Marquis von Keith*—a play by the German dramatist; a panorama of low life; adventurers, confidence men, artists, prostitutes, and fools march across the stage; the piece celebrates the special talents of a confidence man in cynical but jovial fashion.

Stefan Zweig, *Silberne Saiten*—the first collection of poems by the Austrian biographer and writer of fiction, published at age nineteen; demonstrates the influence of the "Young Vienna" group: Hugo von Hofmannsthal, Rainer Maria Rilke, Arthur Schnitzler.

EVENTS

Rene Francois Armand Sully-Prudhomme, French poet, presented with the first Nobel Prize for literature.

The Home Journal, the weekly New York City magazine, becomes *Town and Country;* the jour-

nal shifts its emphasis from social news and light essays and verse to become a sophisticated society magazine.

Thomas Franklin Grant Richards, English publisher and narrative writer, begins at Oxford The World's Classics, a series of inexpensive reprints of literary standards; Oxford University Press purchases the series in 1905, pocket editions are published in 1907, and in 1980 the volumes become strictly paperbound editions.

1902

BIRTHS

Jorge Barbosa. Cape Verde poet; his early free verse will rely upon the local vernacular of Portuguese, prominent among the Brazilian poets of his day; later, he will develop the local color and vernacular potential of "Caboverdean" literature, focusing upon poverty and suffering among his fellow islanders.

Tembot Charasha. Circassian (SSR) translator and writer of fiction; his short stories will principally function as political propaganda, describing changing village life as Soviet power establishes itself and agriculture becomes collectivized.

Svimon Chikovani. Georgian (SSR) poet; he will seek his creative models in classical Georgian literature, gaining recognition as an accomplished lyric poet; after World War II, he will write of the essential values in international cultural contacts.

Nicolas Guillen. Cuban poet and journalist; his poetry will record the turbulent social and political history of his island; he will also become one of the first poets to celebrate the black Cuban experience, relying upon his African and Spanish heritage; thus, he will combine the colloquialisms and rhythms of Havana's black districts with the formal structure and language of traditional Spanish verse; in 1961, Fidel Castro will identify him as the National Poet of Cuba.

Nazim Hikmet Ran (d. 1963). Turkish poet, playwright, and writer of fiction; he will gain recognition for challenging traditional principles of Turkish poetry; he will write principally in free verse, replacing conventional stanza forms and rhyme patterns with broken lines, irregular stanzas, and internal rhyme.

Kota Sivarama Karanta. Kannada novelist and encyclopaedist; he will record details of the South Kanara region with affection and realism.

Haldor Laxness (pseudonym of Halldor Kiljan Gudyonsson). Icelandic writer of fiction; he will travel widely and absorb several cultural influences (German, Catholic, French, American, communist); his lyrical and satirical fiction will focus upon the contemporary Icelandic scene; he will receive the Nobel Prize for literature in 1955.

Ghabit Musrepov. Kazakh (SSR) essayist and novelist; his themes will concern the social and economic changes in Kazakhstan after the 1917 revolution and during World War II; he also will adapt folk legends into plays, presenting revolutionary moments in the history of the Kazakhs.

Ogden Nash (d. 1971). American popular poet; his comic verse will be aimed directly at a middle-class audience; his poetry will be criticized as banal and irritating, but his volumes will achieve high sales.

Ramon Sender (d. 1982). Spanish-born American novelist; he will leave Spain after the Civil War; his fiction will be direct and realistic, a product of the conflict between his individualism and his sense of the necessity of communal existence; his novels will abound with illustrations of inhumanity and human violence.

Stevie Smith (Florence Margaret Smith; d. 1971). English poet and novelist; she will write three major pieces of fiction, but her literary reputation will rest upon her witty verse, often accompanied by her own comic sketches.

Christina Ellen Stead (d. 1983). Australian novelist; she will spend considerable time traveling about the world; her fiction will provide realistic and detailed considerations of such issues as the Sidney docks, the struggling American family, and husbands who drive their wives to suicide.

John Ernst Steinbeck (d. 1968). American writer of fiction; his success as a novelist will arise from a journalistic grasp of significant detail, underscored by a photographic sense of language; his novels are powerful appeals for consideration of human values and justice; he will receive a Pulitzer Prize for fiction in 1940.

Ali Mahmud Taha (d. 1949). Egyptian poet; his work will be strongly influenced by Western poetic traditions, particularly French Romantic poetry; he will also compose verse-impressions of his travels throughout Europe.

DEATHS

Samuel Butler (b. 1835). English novelist; his major piece of fiction satirizes social and economic injustice in Victorian England.

Francis Brett Harte (b. 1836). American writer of fiction and poetry; he achieved enduring literary recognition for stories and poems concerning life in the Far West; after serving as United States consul in Germany and Scotland, he spent his remaining years in England.

Benjamin Franklin Norris (b. 1870). American novelist; he came under the influence of the Naturalists, principally Emile Zola; his fiction attacks greed, the American railroads, and the wheat industry; his untimely death follows an appendix operation.

Masaoka Shiki (b. 1867). Japanese poet, essayist, and writer of short fiction; he has been considered responsible for the revitalization, in the early twentieth century, of two traditional Japanese verse forms, the haiku and the tanka; he established guidelines for preserving the essential elements of the Japanese poetic heritage; his final literary work was a diary that included poems reflecting his battle with death.

Jacinto Verdaguer (b. 1845). Spanish (Catalan) poet; his major literary contribution is an epic poem concerned principally with Iberian myths; he wrote with considerable energy and attention to poetic technique.

Emile Zola (b. 1840). French novelist and journalist; he became the leading figure among the nineteenth-century Naturalists, depicting French society under the Second Empire in minute and often sordid detail; he became a zealous social reformer, championing such unpopular causes as the Alfred Dreyfus affair; he dies at Paris, accidentally suffocating from charcoal fumes.

PUBLICATIONS

Hilaire Belloc, *The Path to Rome*—a travel work by the French-born English essayist, poet, and writer of fiction and biography; describes a journey, mostly on foot, from Toul (in the north of France), through Switzerland

and northern Italy, to Rome; includes digressions on countless subjects and in the form of anecdotes, reflections, and dialogues.

Arnold Bennett, *Anna of the Five Towns*—a work of fiction by the English novelist; a realistic account of a miser's daughter; the writer guides his reader through the sordid English pottery industry.

Anton Chekhov, *Tri Sestry* (The Three Sisters)—a four-act drama by the Russian playwright and writer of fiction; concerns the three daughters of a dead general who sit in a provincial garrison town trying to determine how they can get back to Moscow; the sisters possess different dreams and ambitions, which leads to complicated affairs of the heart; for the playwright, the lives of his characters are sterile, empty, and completely uneventful; frustration emerges as a major theme of the piece, with migratory birds (the transitory force that keeps people alive and on the move) as the dominant image.

Joseph Conrad, *Heart of Darkness*—a novella by the English writer of fiction; the narrator, Marlowe, relates a tale underscoring his disgust over the greed of African ivory traders; he seeks a successful company agent, Kurtz, who lives "in the heart of darkness" and reigns over "a dark kingdom."

————— , *Typhoon*—another novella by the English writer; asea captain sails his ship through a violentstorm, managing, in the midst of it, to confiscate money from his two hundred Chinese passengers; however, that action, combined with the captain's skill as a sailor, saves the ship, and the mate takes on a different opinion of his master.

Andre Gide, *L'Immoraliste* (The Immoralist)—a novel by the French writer of fiction, drama, and nonfiction; presents a depraved hero who has, in the Calvinist tradition, been damned; he takes his bride to North Africa, contracts and recovers from tuberculosis, and discovers his homosexuality; his bride eventually dies from tuberculosis.

Henry James, *The Wings of the Dove*—a novel by the American-born writer of fiction and essayist; the central theme of the piece focuses upon the passion of human love; the heroines and the men they pursue try unsuccessfully to mix money with love.

William James, *The Varieties of Religious Experience*—a collection of Edinburgh Gifford lectures by the American psychologist and philosopher; the result of the writer's reflections on the conflict between free will and determinism; advances the position that any item of religious faith exists as true for any individual for whom it provides emotional satisfaction.

Maurice Maeterlinck, *Monna Vanna*—a verse drama by the Belgian-born French playwright, poet, and essayist; concerns a woman who sacrifices her honor for her people; suggests, initially, the biblical account of Judith and Holofernes; however, the title character comes to love her would-be seducer and abandons her husband.

Beatrix Potter, *The Tale of Peter Rabbit*—the classic children's tale by the English writer and illustrator of juvenile fiction; the piece was originally written in 1893 as a letter to a little boy; private printing and sale followed in 1900, with the work in its present form published in this year.

Euclides Rodrigues de Cunha, *Os Sertoes* (Rebellion in the Backlands)—a historical study by the Brazilian historian, essayist, and poet; the piece is considered by a number of scholars to be the most significant contribution to Brazilian letters; an account of the rebellion led by the religious mystic Antonio Conselheiro against the Brazilian government in 1896; the first section ("The Backlands") describes in detail the geography, geology, and prehistory of Brazil; the second part ("The Rebellion") relates the process by which the rebellion failed.

August Strindberg, *Ett Dromspel* (A Dream Play)—an episodic play by the Swedish dramatist and novelist; an allegory concerning an Indian deity who visits Earth to prove that misery must have some meaning in the universal scheme; the piece liberated the theater from its restrictions of time and place; the extraordinary technical demands of the work created production problems that became solvable with technical advances.

William Butler Yeats, *Cathleen ni Houlihan*—a play in verse by the Irish poet, playwright, and essayist; the writer's most nationalistic play, written for Maude Gonne, who played the title role; a one-act patriotic allegory set in a peasant village at the time of the ill-fated rebellion of 1798; the playwright attempted to recreate the peasant dialect of the times, with assistance from Lady Augusta Gregory; the title character stands as the traditional symbol of Ireland.

EVENTS

Theodor Mommsen, German historian, awarded the Nobel Prize for literature.

John Spencer Bassett, professor of American history at Trinity College, Durham, North Carolina, founds *The South Atlantic Quarterly,* a journal for scholarly criticism and commentary.

The Times Literary Supplement begins publication at London; a weekly review of literature and scholarship; such writers as Virginia Woolf, T. S. Eliot, John Middleton Murry, and Edmund Blunden wrote for *TLS;* until 1914, it appeared as part of the *Times;* since then, it has existed as a separate publication.

1903

BIRTHS

Raphael Alberti. Spanish poet; his poetry will consider a variety of themes and subjects: love, death, the sea, the past, bullfighting, the poet's friends; his early work will display structural unity, a feature absent from his later collections; a master craftsman, he will skillfully blend the visual and the musical.

Hans Christian Branner (d. 1966). Danish novelist and writer of short fiction; he will gain recognition for his simple style and for his skilled psychological analysis of such themes as fear and solitude.

Morley Edward Callaghan. Canadian novelist, writer of short fiction, and playwright; he will become known for his allegorical fiction, injecting complex moral, psychological, and religious elements into his depictions of ordinary human relationships; he will develop themes based upon redemption and salvation and the conflicts between illusion and reality and materialism and spiritualism.

Alejandro Casona (d. 1965). Spanish playwright, poet, and essayist; he will depict the conflict between illusion and reality, achieving international recognition and popularity for his ability to use such elements as folklore and the supernatural, in the creation of dramas rich in fantasy, symbolism, and moral meaning.

James Gould Cozzens (d. 1978). American novelist and writer of short fiction; he will ap-

peal to the common reader and will be praised as a technician of fiction; his irony will help to conceal his cold objectivity, but he will nonetheless be criticized for his indifference and insensitivity; he will receive the Pulitzer Prize for fiction in 1948.

Herbert Isaac Ernest Dhlomo (d. 1956). South African (Zulu) novelist, playwright, and poet; he will become a prolific playwright, concentrating on such subjects as Zulu history; he will also write occasional poetry in both English and Zulu, all of it sounding his anger at the plight of native South Africans.

Sadeq Hedayat (d. 1951). Iranian writer of fiction, playwright, essayist, and translator; he will come to be known as "the father of modern Persian fiction"; he will rely upon Western literary forms, thus providing the earliest significant models of narrative prose in a literature previously dominated by verse; he will develop a highly individualistic voice, displaying both scholarly erudition and poetic imagination.

Amado V. Hernandez (d. 1970). Philippine (Tagalog) poet, novelist, and playwright; his literary efforts will accurately reflect his experiences among the lowest social classes in Manila; he will begin to write before World War II, but his best work will be composed during the 1960s.

Jasimuddin. Bengali poet; his traditional poetry, composed in simple language, will be similar to local folk ballads; the substance of those pieces will focus upon life in the small villages of Bengal.

Gurgen Mahari (d. 1969). Armenian (SSR) poet and writer of short fiction; he will write lyrics relating to the sorrows of his orphaned childhood, followed by emotional pieces on the rise and development of socialism; his short fiction will combine elements of the lyric and the epic.

Eduardo Mallea (d. 1982?). Argentinian novelist; he will depict characters in anguish who struggle to achieve an authentic existence, demonstrating his sympathy with the poor, the oppressed, and the exploited.

Alio Mirtskhulava. Georgian (SSR) poet; he will principally write meditative lyrics; he will also translate classical Russian poetry into Georgian.

Nguyen-Cong-Hoan. Vietnamese novelist and writer of short fiction; he will produce tales and novels that satirize the upper classes of Vietnamese society under French rule; through his realistic fiction, he will attempt to combat such social evils as promiscuity, prostitution, the arrogance and snobbery of the middle classes, the bigotry of the old mandarins, and economic depression and educational backwardness among the peasantry and working classes.

Anais Nin (d. 1977). French-born American essayist and writer of fiction; of Cuban-Spanish background, she will come to the United States in 1914; in addition to her critical essays and novels, she will achieve literary recognition for six volumes of diaries, in which she will record her psychological and artistic development.

George Orwell (pseudonym of Eric Arthur Blair; d. 1950). English novelist and essayist; he will achieve recognition for his biting satire on communism and his prophecy for mankind in a scientifically perfected but servile state; he will also be known for his intellectual honesty and highly crafted prose style.

Alan Stewart Paton. South African novelist; his fiction will demonstrate his deep concern for racial problems in South Africa; he will also author political essays advancing the liberal point of view.

Raymond Queneau (d. 1976). French novelist, poet, playwright, and essayist; he will introduce contemporary French vernacular into the written language in an attempt to break away from seventeenth-century prose forms; he will parody traditional literary form and devices by spelling words, phrases and even sentences phonetically, reflecting their contemporary usage and pronunciation.

Raymond Radiguet (d. 1923). French writer of fiction, poetry, drama, and nonfiction; he will write two novels before reaching the age of twenty; he will be praised for his ability to relate to the psychology and actions of his characters in a direct and unadorned style; his portrayal of adolescent psychology will become the most insightful in modern literature.

Emile Roumer. Haitian poet and critic; in his poetry, he will exploit local traditions and ancient African customs, covering numerous aspects of typical Haitian life; his poems will generally have a sad and melancholy tone.

Georges Jacques Christian Simenon. Belgian-born French novelist, writer of short fiction, and essayist; he will produce in excess of five hundred titles, with translations into more than forty languages; he will achieve popularity as a writer of detective fiction, introducing to that genre the exploration of character as

the principal means for solving a crime; his protagonists will drive themselves to commit crimes because of psychological crises.

Bhogavaticaran Varma. Indian (Hindi) novelist, poet, and writer of short fiction; in his novels and short stories he will discuss ascetic and lay morals in Hindu surroundings; his short stories and socially committed poetry will be published in both Hindi and Urdu.

Evelyn Arthur St. John Waugh (d. 1966). English novelist; his early fiction will be witty conversation pieces lightheartedly mocking the follies of social life in the 1920s and early 1930s; his later efforts demonstrate a more serious tone, dominated by a sardonic wit.

Muhammad Yamin (d. 1962). Indonesian poet and novelist; he will become one of the pioneers of modern poetry in Indonesia; his verse will sing the praises of his native Sumatra, reverberating with his ardent patriotism.

Yaspal. Indian (Hindi) novelist and writer of short fiction; his stories and novels will focus upon urban middle-class life, attacking all forms of social injustice, superstition, and prejudice; he will concentrate upon burning social issues before 1960 and then turn to intimate personal themes.

Marguerite Yourcenar (originally Marguerite de Crayencour; d. 1987). Belgian-born American poet, essayist, writer of short fiction, and playwright; her themes concern the European past and rely heavily upon her knowledge of philosophy, history, and myth; although she will write in French, she will not depict contemporary French society; in 1981 she will become the first woman to gain election to the Academie Francaise.

DEATHS

George Gissing (b. 1857). English novelist; influenced by Charles Dickens, he wrote grim treatments of social issues that reflected his own unhappy life; he appears at his best when he focuses upon the plight of the poor, alienated artist.

William Ernest Henley (b. 1849). English poet and critic, he produced considerable miscellaneous work for literary and cultural periodicals; he has been remembered for two poems, "Invictus" and "England, my England"; the former contains the often-quoted lines,

>   It matters not how strait the gate,
>   How charged with punishments the
>   scroll,

> I am the master of my fate:
> I am the captain of my soul.

Eugenio Maria Hostos y Bonilla (b. 1839). Puerto Rican essayist and journalist; his prose tracts in support of human rights contributed to his reputation as an important literary figure and social thinker; his complete works fill twenty volumes and include tracts on sociology, social morality, and ethics.

PUBLICATIONS

Chaim Nachman Bialik, "The City of Slaughter"—a poem by the Ukranian Hebrew writer of fiction and poetry; written following the 1903 Kishinev pogrom; the poet denounces the cowardice of acquiescent Jews who failed to defend themselves or their property.

Samuel Butler, *The Way of All Flesh*—a novel by the English writer of fiction, published posthumously; studies the relations between parents and their children, tracing the idiosyncrasies of the Pontifex family through several generations; although clad in gloom and irony, the piece does feature "pleasant" portraits of family members and their friends, most of whom have been drawn from the writer's own experiences.

Grazia Deledda, *Elias Portulu*—a novel by the Italian writer of fiction; establishes a love relationship between the title character and his brother's fiancee; then follow periods of denial of emotion and submission to social expectations; in the end, duty triumphs over passion.

William E. B. DuBois, *The Souls of Black Folk*—a collection of essays by the black American educator and civil rights pioneer; includes a study of Booker T. Washington and sketches of black life in the agricultural South, with pieces on black religion and music.

Joseph Furphy, *Such Is Life*—a novel by the Australian writer of fiction and poetry, written in 1897 under the pseudonym "Tom Collins"; supposedly a random selection of diary entries by the fictional Collins, a government worker in the bush country; contains a series of loosely connected minor episodes that focus upon the romance of two principal characters; underscores the writer's ideas about the accidental and arbitrary nature of life.

George Gissing, *The Private Papers of Henry Ryecroft*—a work of fiction by the English novelist; the imaginary journal of a recluse who submerges himself in his books, memories, and reflections as a release from his concerns and problems; the piece reflects the novelist's own aspirations.

Thomas Hardy, *The Dynasts, an Epic Drama of the War with Napoleon*—a play by the English novelist and poet, written principally in blank verse, but also containing a variety of other meters and passages in prose; in three parts, nineteen acts, and 130 scenes, and completed in 1908; the first part concerns the threatened invasion of England by Napoleon; the second begins with the battle of Jena and ends with Napoleon's divorce of Josephine and marriage to Maria Louise; the final part begins with the invasion of Russia and concludes with Waterloo.

Hugo von Hofmannsthal, *Elektra*—a one-act verse drama by the Austrian poet and playwright, adapted freely from Sophocles' version; the writer attempts to remove from the piece all social, ethical, and moral concerns and to recast it in a mold of psychosexual symbolism; thus, his Elektra derives her motives for murder from her own psychosis, and the play occurs in her distorted, perverted, and morbid mind.

Henry James, *The Ambassadors*—a novel by the American-born writer of fiction; with delicacy and humor, the novelist develops the reactions of various American types to their European environments; a Massachusetts mother dispatches ambassadors to Europe to rescue her wealthy son from romantic entanglements; another example of how the writer subordinates plot to his far greater interest, the delineation of character.

Jack London, *The Call of the Wild*—a novel by the American writer of fiction; a dog breaks with the codes of civilization and reverts to its wolf origins; through the love of dog and man, the writer looks closely at the relationships between man and woman; he also searches for the social significance behind the rejection or acceptance of civilization by the primitive individual.

——————, *The People of the Abyss*—a narrative by the American writer; a study of economic depression in England; the writer records his own observations of poverty and crime in London's East End.

George Moore, *Untitled Field*—a collection of short stories by the Irish writer of fiction, strongly influenced by Ivan Turgenev and Fedor Dostoevsky.

George Bernard Shaw, *Man and Superman*—a dramatic comedy by the Irish playwright, not performed until 1905; the principal female character, the embodiment of the so-called "Life-Force," manipulates all of the other characters in her attempts to gain a spouse; focuses upon the archetypal struggle between man and woman, considering those conflicts that result in the emergence of the "superman."

John Millington Synge, *In the Shadow of the Glen*—a one-act play by the Irish dramatist; recreates the common folk tale concerning the jealous old husband who feigns death in hopes of trapping his young wife; in the end, the Irish playwright's young wife forsakes her loveless marriage to an old farmer and goes off with a poet and idealistic tramp, a young man who embodies the notion of freedom and beauty on the road.

William Butler Yeats, *In the Seven Woods*—a collection of poems by the Irish poet, playwright, and essayist; the title refers to the estate of Lady Augusta Gregory, but the majority of the pieces concern the poet's disappointment over Maude Gonne's marriage in this year; includes the poem "Adam's Curse" and the first of the five plays of the Cuchulain cycle, "On Baile's Strand."

EVENTS

Bjornstjerne Bjornson, Norwegian novelist and playwright, receives the Nobel Prize for literature.

Ilanga Lase Natal (The Natal Sun), the first Zulu language newspaper, founded by John Langalibalele Dube, South African (Zulu) novelist, and Ngazana Luthuli, a leading Zulu journalist.

1904

BIRTHS

Bozorg Alavi. Iranian writer of fiction; he will make a significant contribution to the development of modern Iranian prose, particularly with his lyrical depictions of provincial life; he will also present abnormal, perverted characters as the heroes of his short fictional pieces; a Freudian interpretation of character

and human relationships tends to underlie plot and action.

Osvaldo Alcantara (pseudonym of Balthasar Lopes de Silva). Cape Verde Island novelist and poet; he will become interested in the literary potential of his native language; his verse will rely on images similar to those found in T. S. Eliot's *The Waste Land:* sterility, drought, and rain signify spiritual exile and physical isolation.

Alejo Carpentier y Valmont (d. 1980). Cuban novelist, poet, and essayist; he will become a significant and influential figure in the development of modern Latin American fiction; his stories and novels will contain abundant references to music, history, politics, science, art, and mythology: his novels will reach their heights of complexity and detail when he strives to describe the lush settings and exotic cultures of Latin America.

Gladys May Casely-Hayford (d. 1950). West African poet; the piety and parochialism of the old colonial period will form the basis of her verse; nonetheless, she will attempt to capture the Africa of her personal vision, revealing her sympathy for the lives of ordinary men and women.

Cecil Day-Lewis (d. 1972). Irish-born English poet; he will bring new life to English poetry with the infusion of contemporary symbols and ideas; he will become professor of poetry at Oxford (1951-1956), finding time to write detective stories and to translate the *Aeneid*.

Richard Ghormley Eberhart. American poet; he will be known for his experimentation with poetic technique, and his verse will range from the metaphysical, to the allegorical, to the descriptive-romantic; he will protest against the anonymity of a "system" that "pseudo-orders" the lives of human beings; he will be criticized for the substantive and technical unevenness of his poetry.

Elley (pseudonym of Seraphim Aramaanbys Kulaas'kar). Yakut (SSR) poet; he will publish in excess of twenty volumes of verse, basing his themes upon heroes who built new towns, fur hunters, and collective farmers from the frozen north of Yakut; the majority of his poems will become songs of the Yakut people.

James Thomas Farrell (d. 1979). American novelist, writer of short fiction, and critic; the messages of his fiction will offer little hope to the poor or underprivileged; for him, the American city (Chicago) exists as a poisoned place that corrupts fundamental human decency.

Hayashi Fumiko (d. 1951). Japanese novelist, writer of short fiction, essayist, and poet; she will become the most popular female writer in Japan, depicting the lives of the poor and the dispossessed; in her post-World War II fiction, she will underscore the plight of the poor during that period and skillfully create female characters who rely for economic survival upon improvident and unreliable men.

Witold Gombrowicz (d. 1969). Polish novelist, writer of short fiction, playwright and essayist; he will earn a reputation as an irreverent satirist and early proponent of existentialism; his fiction and drama will be constructed upon themes relative to human beings existing without "independent essence"; thus, the individual's only identity is a combination of responses determined by the actions of others; he will identify that interdependence of human beings as "the interhuman church."

Henry Graham Greene. English novelist and playwright; his religious fiction will contain a strong Catholic message concerning his central concept of the "appalling strangeness of the mercy of God"; he will also devote time to the more popular genres of the spy story and the detective thriller.

Christopher William Bradshaw Isherwood (d. 1986). English novelist; with themes based upon his experiences in Berlin between 1929 and 1933, he will vividly portray Germany at the outset of Adolf Hitler's rise to power; he will collaborate with W. H. Auden, become an American citizen, and develop an interest in Hindu philosophy and Vedanta.

Andrzej Kusniewicz. Polish poet and novelist; he will write poetic novels, highly symbolic and devoid of dialogue; his personal experiences—his arrest by the Gestapo in 1943 and two-year term in the concentration camp at Mauthausen, as well as his journalistic career—will be essential to an understanding of his literary style and themes.

Ding Ling (d. 1986). Chinese writer of fiction; she will become the foremost female Chinese writer of the twentieth century; her fiction will recount her unfortunate political involvements, beginning with her house arrest by the Nationalists (1933-1936) and her expulsion from the Communist Party in 1957; she will frankly discuss the sexual feelings of women and their contempt for conventional social views.

Harry Martinson (d. 1978). Swedish novelist and poet; he will gain international renown and popularity for his proletarian fiction; he will champion the essential goodness of humankind and its eminent victory in the proletarian struggle; nonetheless, he will also cling steadfastly to his belief in the validity of the individual's search for freedom; he will share the Nobel Prize for literature in 1974 with a fellow Swede, Eyvind Johnson.

Pablo Neruda (pseudonym of Neftali Ricardo Reyes; d. 1973). Chilean poet; his work will evoke the teeming natural mysteries of South America, as well as his sense of toughness and amorous point of view; his style will suggest the poetry of disintegration and fragmentation, although in the late 1930s he will focus his efforts sharply upon the fight for Spain against fascism; he will receive the Nobel Prize for literature in 1971.

Hamid Olimjon (d. 1944). Uzbek (SSR) poet, essayist, and translator; as a poet, he will develop a mature voice during World War II, and as a critic, he will attempt to establish clear criteria for Uzbek literature; he will also produce translations of the Russian classical writers.

K. V. Puttapu. Indian (Kannada) poet; he will produce in excess of fifty volumes of poetry, stories, and plays in verse, focusing on the themes of love, nature, idealism, and a yearning for the deity; he will be influenced by Dante, Milton, and the Sanskrit and Kannada literary traditions.

William Lawrence Shirer. American journalist and World War II correspondent; he will achieve literary recognition for his narratives of the rise, reign, and fall of Adolf Hitler's Third Reich; he will also write novels with international and political flavor.

Isaac Bashevis Singer. Polish-born American writer of fiction; he will be recognized as the foremost contemporary Yiddish writer; he will rarely write in English, focusing his scenes and plots on Polish Jewish villages; above all, his literary reputation will rest on his abilities as a storyteller; he will receive the Nobel Prize for literature in 1978.

DEATHS

Anton Pavlovich Chekhov (b. 1860). Russian writer of fiction and drama; the style of his stories, novels, and plays emphasized the internal drama of a situation, its characters and its mood; plot, for him, was a secondary consideration; he also concerned himself with the tragicomic aspects of mundane and banal events; he dies, most likely from tuberculosis, at Badenweiler, at the height of his creative powers and literary reputation.

Kate O'Flaherty Chopin (b. 1851). American writer of fiction; she wrote nearly one hundred short stories, the most noteworthy describing the Acadians in the central Louisiana parishes of Natchitoches and Avoyelles; she frequently described rebellious women struggling against social conventions.

Lafcadio Hearn (b. 1850). American writer of fiction; born on the Ionian Islands, he came to America in 1869; his partial blindness and morbid discontent certainly had effects upon his fiction, which tended toward the macabre and the exotic; he became a citizen of Japan after 1890, and there wrote a dozen volumes in an attempt to understand and interpret the nation's culture.

Mor Jokai (b. 1825). Hungarian novelist; his fiction has been compared with that of Charles Dickens and Sir Walter Scott; he participated in the Hungarian revolt of 1848, an event described in his novels; a jubilee edition of his fiction, plays, and essays, reaching one hundred volumes, appeared in 1894.

Mankayi Enoch Sontonga (b. 1860?). South African (Xhosa) poet and song writer; few of his works were published, but he will be remembered for the composition of a single piece, the 1899 poem "Nkosi Sikel' i-Africa" (God Bless Africa), the national anthem of the Transkei; in 1925, the African National Congress adopted the piece for its anthem; it remains the most famous song in South Africa, a number of the more recent African states having changed the words to fit local contexts.

PUBLICATIONS

James Matthew Barrie, *Peter Pan; or, The Boy Who Wouldn't Grow Up*—a dramatic fantasy by the Scottish novelist and playwright; concerns three children being taken away to "Never-Never Land" by the motherless Peter Pan and the fairy Tinker Bell; they encounter Indians and pirates, the most notable being Captain Hook; the piece has become an internationally famous play for children.

Anton Chekhov, *Vishnevy Sad* (The Cherry Orchard)—a comic drama by the Russian playwright and writer of fiction; a nostalgic parable on the passing of an older order in Russian history in which ignorance and vulgarity triumph over the traditions of elegance

and nobility; the tragedy of life results from the drab and uneventful nature of human existence.

G. K. Chesterton, *The Napoleon of Notting Hill*—the first novel by the English writer of fiction, poetry, and nonfiction; a fantasy set in the London of the future; the color and romance of the "Merry England" of medieval times have been restored, while big business and technology are sternly attacked by the writer.

Joseph Conrad, *Nostromo*—a novel by the Polish-born English writer of fiction; occurs in an imaginary South American nation and concerns the importance of a silver mine on the local economy and its role during a local rebellion; the title character serves as the manifestation of heroism, but he is tempted by love and material possessions; essentially, the piece focuses upon the individual's miserable subjection to his obsession for tangible goods.

Lady Augusta Gregory, *Spreading the News*—a one-act play by the Irish dramatist; concerns, in the playwright's own words, "the Irishman's incorrigible genius for myth-making;" also concerns the hilarious repercussions of half-understood gossip that spreads through a small Galway town.

Lafcadio Hearn, *Kwaiden*—a work of fiction by the American writer, composed during his Japanese period; represents his belief that ghosts exist as manifestations of ancestral experiences; unfortunately, according to the writer, those experiences have been banished by technological advancements.

Hermann Hesse, *Peter Camenzind*—a novel by the German poet and writer of fiction; a charming, idealistic, and derivative piece, steeped in Romanticism; a Swiss peasant becomes an established writer; he renounces the decadent city where he established his reputation and returns to his native countryside; the work seemingly predicts the writer's own experiences.

Jack London, *The Sea Wolf*—a novel by the American writer of fiction and narrative; depicts the failure of the amoral superman, the captain of a sealing schooner; he practices the primitive laws of survival through predatory ruthlessness, relying upon his shrewd intelligence and brute power.

William Vaughan Moody, *The Fire Bringer*—a drama by the American poet and playwright; relates the classical story of Prometheus, but with a messianic interpretation;

through suffering, human beings learn a religion of rebellion that dictates that they struggle against anything that prevents them from helping one another.

Romain Rolland, *Jean Christophe*—a long novel (to 1912) by the French writer of drama poetry, and fiction, for which he earned the Nobel Prize (1915); the study of a musician of genius, whose sterility derives from evil; however, the principal character eventually achieves a form of nobility.

John Millington Synge, *Riders to the Sea*—a drama by the Irish playwright; a single-act, elegiac tragedy set on one of the Aran Islands; establishes the conflict between a brave old peasant woman and the natural foe, the sea; the woman has already lost one husband and five sons to the sea and appears helpless to prevent the death of her youngest son; the prophetic vision of death soon becomes reality; the woman nonetheless endures, stoic in tragedy, heroic in defeat, realistic in her fate.

Ida Minerva Tarbell, *The History of the Standard Oil Company*—a prose tract by the American reform writer; the "muckraker" openly exposes the malpractices of the Standard Oil Company; 2 volumes.

EVENTS

American Academy of Arts and Letters founded; later chartered by the United States Congress; intended to promote the arts and literature by honoring persons in those disciplines.

The Bibliographical Society of America founded at the University of Chicago; intended to promote the study of American bibliography.

Jean Jaures, French Socialist leader and writer, issues his Socialist newspaper, *L'Humanite,* at Paris.

Helen Adams Keller, American writer and lecturer, blind and deaf from the age of two, graduates with honors from Radcliffe College.

Frederic Mistral, French Provencal poet, and Jose Echegaray y Eizaguirre, Spanish Basque playwright, share the Nobel Prize for literature.

1905

BIRTHS

Elias Canetti. Bulgarian-born German novelist and playwright; he will compose sociological and psychological studies of the human conditions; in 1939 he will emigrate to London and there establish his literary base; he will receive the Nobel Prize for literature in 1981.

Fumiko Enchi (d. 1986). Japanese novelist and narrative writer; she will be highly praised for her skills as a storyteller; her themes will focus upon social issues concerning women; essentially, she will depict the glories of an idealized love that cannot exist in a modern world.

Vasily Semenovich Grossman (d. 1964). Russian novelist, poet, and playwright; following World War II, he will harshly criticize the Soviet system, and his works will be suppressed, the strength of his writings will result from his unconditional attachment to intellectual and artistic freedom.

Yahya Haqqi. Egyptian essayist and writer of fiction; his major fiction will emphasize the notion that modern science and culture can only establish themselves in Egypt if native traditions and culture continue to be respected.

Anandilal Jainendrakumar. Indian (Hindi) essayist and writer of fiction; his fiction will focus upon the problems of the Indian middle class, combining psychological analysis with Gandhian political and philosophical views.

Attila Jozsef (d. 1937). Hungarian poet and essayist; he will be deeply influenced by Karl Marx and Sigmund Freud; his poems will explore the ills of society and the human psyche; referred to as the poet of the proletariat, he will become known for verse containing vivid depictions of the misery of the working class.

P. Kesava Dev. Malayalam playwright and writer of fiction; his drama will emphasize political issues, while his fiction will primarily concern social themes, particularly reform.

Emmanuel H. A. Made. South African (Zulu) poet, novelist, and biographer; he will become one of the most significant contemporary Zulu poets; his poems will celebrate the past, consider the future with bitterness, and elegize his close friends.

Roger Mais (d. 1955). Jamaican novelist, poet, and playwright; his imprisonment for his political writings and his life among the poor will provide the inspiration for key themes in his works; he demonstrates a thorough knowledge of West Indian rural and urban people, as well as of the West Indian ethos.

Dehati Mohammad Mas'ud (d. 1948). Iranian novelist and journalist; he will criticize social conditions, analyzing the problems tormenting the young post-war generation of Iran; his fiction, particularly, will survey the attitudes of these young persons and their inability to find a place in society.

Ayn Rand (d. 1982). Russian-born American novelist; she will come to the United States at age twenty-one; her controversial fiction will reflect her fierce political and intellectual independence, as well as her deep sense of bitterness; both her life and her fiction will manifest a completely rationalist philosophy.

Kenneth Rexroth (d. 1982). American poet and critic; his poetry and prose, while reflecting his wide knowledge, will imitate the works of the major literary figures of his time; his poetic style will be bold and assertive.

Jean-Paul Sartre (d. 1980). French philosopher, playwright, essayist, and writer of fiction; he will have a significant impact on world literature in the twentieth century; a leading proponent of the philosophical concept of existentialism, he will emphasize that existence precedes essence and that human beings live in a godless and meaningless universe; thus, he will charge human beings with responsibility for their own actions.

Mikhail Aleksandrovich Sholokhov (d. 1984). Russian (Cossack) writer of fiction; he will attempt to create a form of psychological realism, analyzing his characters in terms of their appearance and inner motivation; he will treat anticommunists objectively; in 1965, he will receive the Nobel Prize for literature.

Charles Percy Snow (d. 1980). English scientist and novelist; his fictional settings will be scientific and academic environments, and his characters will tend to be manifestations of his own self.

Lionel Trilling (d. 1975). American literary and social critic and scholar; he will explore liberal arts theory and its implications for the conduct of life; his thorough understanding of psychoanalysis will add to the depth of his study of ideas and literature.

Erico Lopes Verissimo (d. 1975). Brazilian novelist and essayist; he will begin to write fiction in 1935, producing a major trilogy between 1949 and 1962; from 1953 to 1956 he will serve as Director of the Department of Cultural Affairs of the Pan American Union.

Robert Penn Warren (d. 1989). American novelist, poet, and critic; his work will be strongly regional in character, often drawing its inspiration from the land, people, and history of the South; yet, he transcends the local to comment in universal and symbolic terms on the human condition; as a critic, he will be associated with two movements, the Agrarians and the New Critics; he will receive the Pulitzer Prize for fiction in 1947 and for poetry in 1979.

George Emlyn Williams (d. 1987). Welsh playwright; his dramatic pieces will be governed by his interest in psychological terror; he will, generally, play the lead roles in his own dramas.

DEATHS

Kesavsut (pseudonym of Krsnaji Kesav Damale; b. 1866). Marathi poet; his anguished and despairing verse represents the writer's response to the ills of human existence.

Mayer Andre Marcel Schwab (b. 1867). French short fiction writer, biographer, essayist, historian, and translator; an authority on medieval and classical literature; he wrote short fiction and biographical pieces evoking the distant past and portraying human tragedy and perversity; he dies of pneumonia at Paris.

Amalie Bertha Skram (b. 1847). Norwegian novelist, playwright, and writer of short fiction; she followed the principles of late nineteenth-century literary Naturalism, focusing upon social issues and employing a direct narrative style; her themes emphasized the despair of loveless marriage, the degrading poverty of the lower classes, and the victimizing of the mentally unstable; the epitaph upon her tombstone reads "Danish citizen, Danish subject and Danish author."

Jules Verne (b. 1828). French novelist; he has earned the title of the founder of modern science fiction.

Lewis Wallace (b. 1827). American novelist; his reputation rests on his popular and highly successful religious novel, *Ben Hur* (1880); there have been at least three film versions of the piece.

PUBLICATIONS

Edmondo de Amicis, *L'Idioma Gentile* (The Gentle Language)—a novel by the Italian writer of fiction; advances the writer's views on the purification of the Italian language.

Richard Beer-Hofmann, *Der Graf von Charolais* (The Count of Charolais)—the first play by the Austrian Jewish playwright, novelist, and poet; an adaptation of the English Elizabethan play *The Fatal Dowry,* by John Ford and Philip Massinger; a professional seducer transforms a proper lady into a lustful tart; all characters in the piece appear to be driven by an uncontrollable destiny.

E. M. Forster, *Where Angels Fear to Tread*—a novel by the English critic and writer of fiction; a tragicomedy describing the attraction of an impulsive young widow for an Italian dentist, whom she meets while on tour in Tuscany; the young lady's mother-in-law dispatches her young son to prevent their marriage, but he arrives too late; the woman dies during childbirth, and the father struggles to retain possession of his son; then follow kidnapping of the child and his accidental death.

Sigmund Freud, *Drei Abhandlungen zur Sexualtheorie* (Three Contributions to the Theory of Sex)—a prose tract by the Austrian psychologist and essayist; the work sets forth the hypothesis that the symptoms of hysterical patients, directly traceable to apparently forgotten psychic traumas in early life, represent unreleased sexual energy.

Hermann Hesse, *Interm Rad* (The Prodigy)—a novel by the German critic, poet, and writer of fiction; the writer recreates his early years, particularly his flight from theological school.

Vachel Lindsay, *The Tree of Laughing Bells*—a collection of verse by the American poet, a series of visionary poems.

Heinrich Mann, *Professor Unrat* (The Blue Angel)—a novel by the German writer of fiction and essays; the writer depicts the lack of compassion on the part of villagers toward a schoolmaster who has fallen for a nightclub singer; the professor avenges himself by manipulating the lady into leading his judges into the same humiliating situation; the professor represents "filth," and as such becomes responsible for the downfall of the entire community.

Baroness Emma Orczy (Mrs. Montague Barstow), *The Scarlet Pimpernel*—a novel by the Hungarian-born English writer of fiction; the story of a group known as the League of the Scarlet Pimpernel, a band of English dedicated to the rescue of the innocent victims of the French Reign of Terror; the leader's courage and ingenious disguises outwit his French opponents.

George Santayana, *The Life of Reason*—a five-volume prose tract by the Spanish-born American philosopher (to 1906); promotes the idea that matter is all that truly exists, while thought and feeling are byproducts of the human body; reason consists of judicious control and harmonization of animal impulses so as to secure peace and satisfaction; thus, "Everything ideal has a natural basis and everything natural an ideal development."

H. G. Wells, *Kipps*—a novel by the English essayist, historian, and writer of fiction; focuses upon the lower middle-class world of the writer's youth; relates the tale of an aspiring draper's assistant who meets tragedy in the form of an unexpected inheritance; specifically, the problems of gaining a social education prove far more than the title character can handle; real happiness begins only when Kipps loses his fortune and again begins his life as a shopkeeper.

Edith Wharton, *The House of Mirth*—a novel by the American writer of fiction; concerns the tragedy of a beautiful but poor young woman who lives in a society where money is the only guarantee of security.

Oscar Wilde, *De Profundis*—the prose apologia of the Irish playwright and poet, written during his imprisonment for homosexual offenses and published posthumously; an apology for his conduct, in which he asserts that he stood "in symbolic relation to the art and culture of his age."

EVENTS

Henryk Sienkiewicz, Polish novelist, receives the Nobel Prize for literature.

Sime Silverman, New York City journalist and publisher, begins *Variety,* a theatrical trade journal.

1906

BIRTHS

Amma Achchygyya (pseudonym of Nijukulay Jogyorebis Muordinov). Yakut (SSR) writer of fiction, poetry, and drama; his stories will describe the changes in Yakut life after the 1917 Revolution, as well as the growing political consciousness of the working people.

Sabahattin Ali (d. 1948). Turkish novelist and writer of short fiction; his writing will reflect his two years in Germany (1928-1930), displaying a knowledge of the language and a familiarity with the culture; his awareness of social problems in his own nation, particularly in the rural areas, will also form a key aspect of his writings.

Samuel Barclay Beckett. (d. 1989). Irish-born poet, writer of fiction, and playwright; although his style and substance will be associated with the literature of Ireland, he will write in French; a principal theme of his works will be the anguish and anxiety of theological speculation; his characters will meditate without halt upon their approaching extinction; they will also contemplate language, in their hands a useless weapon.

John Betjeman (d. 1984). English poet; he will earn high marks as a poet of true feeling, being careful to maintain his middle-class outlook; he will compose witty, urbane, satiric, and light poetry; he will receive the appointment as Poet Laureate of England in 1972.

Bhabhani Bhattacharya. Indian novelist, journalist, and translator; he will write novels in English that focus upon the social problems of his nation.

William Empson (d. 1984). English poet and critic; his prose and verse will be richly lyrical, betraying the intensity of his feelings, both personal and political; his poetry will prove extremely difficult, relying upon analytical argument and imagery drawn from modern physics and mathematics.

Masud Farazad. Iranian poet and translator; his lyrics will follow classic Persian forms but will be modern in substance, principally expressing his pessimism and melancholy.

Archibald Campbell Jordan (d. 1968). South African (Cape Province) poet and writer of fiction; his fiction will reflect the sorrows and oppression of the African people; his poems will tend to be militant in tone and substance.

Malai Chuphinit (d. 1963). Thai writer of fiction; his work will reflect his Bhuddist inclinations, advocating sensitivity to the beauty of nature and life in the country.

Klaus Mann (d. 1949). German novelist, essayist, and playwright; he will portray the younger generation as fostering a sickly cult of decadent romanticism and homosexuality; son of Thomas Mann.

Rasipuram Krishnaswami Narayan. Indian writer of fiction and essayist; he will become noted for his creation of a fictitious village in southern India, considered a combination of Mysore and Madras; he will develop a straightforward style derived from the oral and literary traditions of India.

Nhat-Linh (b. Nguyen-tuong-Tam; d. 1963). Vietnamese novelist; his fiction will criticize traditional Vietnamese society, proclaiming the right of the individual to develop his own land and benefit from its profits.

Putumaippittan (d. 1948). Indian (Tamil) novelist and poet; he will write more than two hundred short stories and a number of poems and prose essays; he will concern himself with the failings of modern Hindu society, which he will describe with critical realism.

Leopold Sedar Senghor. Senegal poet and critic; his nostalgic verse will idealize the African past and its people, and lament the black man's suffering under colonialism; he will also write essays on literary, cultural, and political issues.

Benedict Wallet Bambatha Vilakazi (d. 1947). South African (Zulu) poet and novelist; he will publish collections of early Zulu songs, as well as the first works of fiction written in Zulu to consider "modern" subjects; in 1946, he will receive the first doctorate in literature awarded to an African.

Samad Vurghun (d. 1956). Azerbaijan poet and playwright; he will compose short love poems and verse on social themes; he will replace the traditional figure of woman with the image of the working woman (the "fighter"); his verse drama will provide a broad picture of eighteenth-century Azerbaijan.

Vernon Phillips Watkins (d. 1967). Welsh poet, translator, and writer of nonfiction; he will explore metaphysical themes in his verse, evoking the Welsh landscape and combining Christian and Welsh myth.

DEATHS

Paul Laurence Dunbar (b. 1872). Black American poet and writer of fiction; his poetry, especially, relies upon black American folk materials and dialects; his novels and short stories reflect life among Southern blacks.

Henrik Ibsen (b. 1828). Norwegian playwright; one of the most influential figures in modern theater; well known for his social drama rebelling against the sterile and restrictive conventions of his time.

Alexander Lange Kielland (b. 1849). Norwegian writer of fiction and drama; he wrote novels, short stories, and plays focusing upon social reform and representing the realistic school of literature.

William Kirby (b. 1817). English-born Canadian writer of fiction; he wrote fictional romances of life in seventeenth-century Quebec.

Jose Maria de Pereda (b. 1833). Spanish writer of fiction, essayist, poet, and playwright; he is often considered an important figure in the development of the nineteenth-century Spanish novel; his fiction focused upon the rustic life of his home province of Santander in northern Spain, portraying rural characters and settings in a realistic manner; he dies in Santander following a steady decline in his health.

PUBLICATIONS

Gerhart Hauptmann, *Und Pippa Tanzt* (And Pippa Dances)—a fairy tale play by the German dramatist and writer of fiction; an example of the writer's symbolist drama, as well as of his dialectical vision; the title character personifies ephemeral beauty; she finds herself surrounded by creatures who destroy her because they admire and covet her delicate beauty.

Selma Lagerlof, *Nils Holgerssons underbara resa genom Sverige* —a work of children's fiction by the Swedish novelist; essentially a geographical portrait of Sweden as seen from the back of a goose; considered one of the most significant educational books ever written.

Jack London, *White Fang*—a novel by the American writer of fiction and narrative; a dog, part wolf, gradually becomes weaned from its native wild habitat and assumes his place in the world of his "man-god"; for the writer, the man-dog relationship becomes a simpler substitute for the complications arising from the association between men and women in society.

Lope K. Santos, *Banaag at Sikat* (Rays and Sunrise)—a social novel by the Philippine writer of fiction, the first in the Tagalog dialect.

Albert Schweitzer, *Von Reimarus zu Wrede* (The Quest for the Historical Jesus)—a religious tract by the German (Alsatian-born) theologian, missionary, philosopher, mathematician, and musician; a revolutionary work in terms of New Testament criticism; the writer repudiates liberal theology, with its emphasis upon the role of Christ as ethical teacher; develops, instead, the notion of Christ as the herald of God's kingdom at hand, with the short period of the ethical teachings reduced to minor consideration.

Upton Sinclair, *The Jungle*—a novel by the American writer and reformer; through the depiction of the destruction of a Lithuanian immigrant family, the writer develops his thesis that human beings are innocent victims of business and industry; in the end, socialism is the salvation of the central character; referred to by Jack London as "the *Uncle Tom's Cabin* of wage slavery."

Daniel Varuzhan, *Sarsurner* (Frights)—a volume of lyric poetry by the Armenian writer of verse; inspired by the tragedy of minority life in Turkey, the poems emphasize religious and political oppression, as well a the constant insecurity of being isolated from the eastern branch of Armenia; the writer's first poetic collection.

EVENTS

Al-Imam, the first Islamic reform journal in Southeast Asia, begins publication at Singapore.

Frank Leslie's Popular Monthly, a New York City illustrated magazine of popular events, purchased by Ida M. Tarbell, Lincoln Steffens, and other "muckrakers"; the title is changed to *The American Magazine* and the journal combines radical reform issues with regular features; until 1956.

Giosue Carducci, Italian poet, essayist, and literary scholar, claims the Nobel Prize for literature.

The English Association founded at Oxford and London; promotes studies in English language and literature.

Joseph Malaby Dent, London publisher, begins publication of "Everyman's Library"; a reprinting of the classics of world literatures, in addition to some volumes of original reference works.

Upton Sinclair, American "muckraker" novelist and narrative writer, founds with some of his literary associates Helicon Home Colony in Englewood, New Jersey; a commune of young married writers; fire will destroy the colony in 1907.

Sir Walter Wilson Greg, English scholar and bibliographer, founds the Malone Society (after Edmund Malone, English literary critic and Shakespearean scholar); intended for the exact reproduction of English plays and dramatic documents prior to 1640.

Publication of the complete *Journal* (14 vols.) of the American essayist, poet, and narrative writer Henry David Thoreau.

1907

BIRTHS

W. H. Auden (d. 1973). English-born poet; he will be well known for his poetry written in the early 1930s, in which he will express the resentment of middle-class youth at the erosion of a generation through war and unemployment; he will then turn his attention toward international problems, revealing his humanistic view of the human condition; he will receive appointment to the chair of poetry at Oxford, followed by the Pulitzer Prize for poetry in 1948.

Jacques Martin Barzun. French-born American intellectual critic and essayist; his commentaries will focus upon art, science, philosophy, education, and history; he will argue against absolute and fixed systems of belief that claim to explain and define particular facets of nature and human conduct; rather, he will advance forms of intellectual analysis that will offer varied and evolving methods for the understanding of existence and intellect.

Rachel Carson (d. 1964). American zoologist and essayist; she will become a pioneer in the field of ecology, known for her popular prose discussions on subjects of general scientific interest; she will also compose strong and emotional arguments against indiscriminate destruction and defacing of the environment.

Daphne du Maurier (d. 1989). English novelist; she will produce a large quantity of popular fiction, particularly period romances set in the West Country of England.

Gunnar Ekelof (d. 1968). Swedish poet; he will become a philosophical and mystical writer who will live most of his life in seclusion; for him, thought and inner feeling will constitute experience.

Christopher Harris Fry. English playwright; he will emerge as one of the few dramatists of the twentieth century to employ verse successfully in his plays; he will write mystical and religious drama, as well as exuberant and highly popular comedies.

Alec Derwent Hope. Australian poet and critic; he will be considered a romantic classicist, celebrating the virtues of nature, beauty, love, and sexuality; he will also expose what he views as the cultural degeneration of the twentieth century and humanity's capacity for corruption.

Robert Anson Heinlein (d. 1988). American writer of fiction; he will produce a large number of popular science fiction novels; those pieces will consider everything from martians to utopian societies.

Khalilullah Khalili. Afghan poet and historian; he will write lyrics on philosophical themes, particularly upon the ephemeral nature of life and its burdens.

Helen Clark MacInnes (d. 1985). Scottish-born American novelist and playwright; she will become known as "the queen of international espionage fiction," writing at least twenty-one novels belonging to that category; she will set her stories against backgrounds of important world events and openly attack authoritarian governments; her work will sell more than twenty-three million copies in the United States and Canada.

Hugh MacLennan. Canadian novelist; he will present Canadian life as a paradigm of the human condition.

Louis MacNeice (d. 1963). Irish poet; he will gain recognition in the 1930s for his verses reflecting the fears, hopes, and anxieties of the middle class.

Muhammad Mandur (d. 1965). Egyptian critic; he will undertake scholarly studies of the methods of classical Arab literary critics; he will initially emphasize personal impressions as a criteria for judging literature, but he will later stress the need for rational analysis as the basis for objective conclusions.

Bal Sitaram Mardhekar (d. 1956). Indian (Marathi) poet; his verse will revolutionize the post-World War II poetry of his nation; an innovator and experimentalist influenced by Ezra Pound and T. S. Eliot, his style will be both condensed and impersonal.

James Albert Michener. American novelist; he will become an extremely popular writer, composing lengthy novels on such varied topics as World War II, the Korean War, the South Pacific, Hawaii, the Middle East, and American history and politics; he will win the Pulitzer Prize for fiction in 1948.

Alberto Moravia. Italian novelist and writer of short fiction; his work will develop the theme of men indulging in sex because they cannot love; those same men enjoy the company of prostitutes because, through them, they can make contact with other bored, frustrated, and guilty men; his fiction will reveal him to be a man of deep feeling and an astute observer of human behavior.

U Nu. Burmese novelist, playwright, and translator; he will become an ardent Buddhist and pacifist; he will translate fiction and political prose tracts; his own fiction will attack the British judicial system and criticize hypocrisy in social and sexual relations.

Jacques Roumain (d. 1944). Haitian poet, essayist, and writer of fiction; during the late 1920s and 1930s, he will become the leader of the young Haitian intellectuals, who will seek an end to the American military occupation of Haiti.

The-Lu. Vietnamese poet; he will become a leader of the "new school" of his nation's poetry, writing lyrics in clear and popular language and rejecting classical forms of Vietnamese poetry in favor of free verse and modern French poetic techniques.

Zodji (pseudonym of U Thein Han). Burmese poet, translator, playwright, and essayist; he will emerge as a leading historian and literary critic; he will confront the conflict between the old literary traditions of Burma and the needs of the modern literary audience; he will write realistic and romantic fiction, and mystical poetry of formal perfection.

DEATHS

Giosue Carducci (b. 1835). Italian poet, essayist, and scholar; professor of literature at the University of Bologna, 1860-1904; he received the Nobel Prize for literature in 1906.

William Henry Drummond (b. 1854). Canadian poet; his verse portrays the inhabitants of rural Quebec, reproducing their own English dialects; he dies suddenly of a cerebral hemorrhage.

Rene Sully-Prudhomme (b. 1839). French poet, philosopher, and essayist; he became one of the most highly respected French poets of the late nineteenth century, as well as the first recipient of the Nobel Prize for literature (1901); he lived as a recluse during the final years of his life, a victim of paralysis, but nonetheless remained devoted to philosophy and literature.

Francis Thompson (b. 1859). English poet and critic; the substance of his most important verse evidences the influence of the seventeenth-century poet Richard Crashaw, and thus it describes his observations of nature and his deep physical and mental suffering; he will be criticized for a derivate style, imitative of Percy Bysshe Shelley.

Tran-te-Xuong (b. 1870). Vietnamese poet; he wrote a large quantity of verse in a variety of poetic forms; he presents a satirical picture of the decadence of old Vietnamese society during the initial phase of French colonization; he also ridicules the impotence of Confucian morality and the senseless pursuit of wealth.

Stanislaw Wyspianski (b. 1869). Polish playwright, poet, and painter; he has been called the founder of modern Polish drama; his plays, written mainly in verse, contain elements of myth, fantasy, and symbolism.

PUBLICATIONS

Mikhail Artsybashev, *Sanin* (Sanine)—a novel by the Russian writer of fiction, drama, and essays; the title character believes that only through self-willed activity can one experience the fullness of life; thus, he desires to lead a "natural" life free from social and moral restraints; he considers those characters constrained by authority as vulgar and stupid.

Jacinto Benavente, *Los Intereses Creados* (The Bonds of Interest)—a comic drama by the Spanish playwright; a masquerade wherein modern society is presented as a puppet show and humans function only as they can be moved by the strings of passion, selfishness, and ambition.

Joseph Conrad, *The Secret Agent*—a novel by the Polish-born English writer of fiction; the title character is a spy for a foreign embassy and an informer for Scotland Yard; the spy's shop in Soho serves as the stage upon which the writer parades a host of political fanatics from a variety of nations; revolutionary plots and murder soon follow, all contributing to the writer's attack upon anarchy.

E. M. Forster, *The Longest Journey*—an autobiographical novel by the English writer of fiction and criticism; concerns a sensitive and congenitally lame young man, orphaned at age fifteen; he escapes from the misery of suburban life and the bullying of public school to Cambridge; there he discovers sympathetic friends and the opportunity to pursue his literary aspirations; emphasizes the tragedies of the artistic life.

Maxim Gorky, *Mother*—a novel by the Russian writer of fiction; the piece was regarded by Vladimir Ilyich Lenin as a model of socialist literature; a sentimental and didactic story of the radicalization of an uneducated woman.

Edmund Gosse, *Fathers and Sons*—an autobiographical piece by the English poet and literary critic; an early twentieth-century examination of the spiritual crisis of youth; describes a child's fanatical submission to his father and his eventual, agonizing break with parental authority.

Henry James, *The American Scene*—a novel by the American-born writer of fiction and essays; a record of the writer's visit to the United States in 1904, his first in over twenty years.

William James, *Pragmatism: A New Name for Some Old Ways of Thinking*—a prose tract by the American philosopher, developed from a series of lectures; the writer considers philosophical theories not as answers to specific problems, but as instruments for achieving truth.

George Bernard Shaw, *Major Barbara*—a play by the Irish essayist, social critic, and dramatist; focuses upon the conflict between religious ideals and the power of materialism; the playwright creates a remarkable "superman" who manipulates his vast power to create an ideal community for his workers; the playwright's thesis focuses on the notion that money and power, not meekness and humility, can save humanity.

August Strindberg, *Spoksonaten* (The Ghost Sonata)—an expressionistic fantasy by the Swedish playwright and novelist; a mysterious invalid confined to a wheelchair hires a young student to watch over his bastard daughter; the atmosphere of the piece is horrible and grotesque, emphasizing the disparity between appearance and reality; the work belongs to what has become known as "the theater of cruelty," a precursor of "the theater of the absurd."

Rabindranath Thakur, *Gora*—a novel by the Indian (Bengali) poet, dramatist, and writer of fiction; demonstrates the untenability of orthodox Hinduism in the modern world; the piece also underscores the weakness of narrow-minded sectarianism.

William Butler Yeats, *Deirdre*—a heroic tragedy in the Greek manner by the Irish poet, playwright, and essayist; an Irish version of the story of Helen of Troy.

EVENTS

Cambridge University Press begins publication of the *Cambridge History of English Literature;* until 1927.

Charles Hamilton, English writer and publisher of children's works, begins to issue, at London, *The Gem,* a weekly paper for boys; until 1939.

Rudyard Kipling, English poet, novelist, and writer of juvenile fiction and verse, receives the Nobel Prize for literature.

1908

BIRTHS

Martin Adan (pseudonym of Rafael de al Fuente Benavides; d. 1985). Peruvian writer of fiction and poetry; he will become a literary innovator, constructing stories with minimal plot elements and relying upon a stream of images, wordplays, and refurbished clichés.

Agusti Bartra (d. 1982). Spanish (Catalan) writer of fiction; most of his novels and short stories will be written prior to General Francisco Franco's military victories that brought an end to the Spanish Civil War; his later pieces will be permeated by an existentialist vision of the world, with Kafkaesque characters who sense condemnation without knowing the reasons.

Simone de Beauvoir (d. 1986). French existentialist writer of fiction; her works will be noted for their careful analysis, commitment to human and national freedom, vivid characterization, and convincing action.

Paul Hamilton Engle. American poet; his verse will praise the joys of the simple life of the American midwest, at the same time protesting against the American spirit of materialism; he will play an important role in the establishment of the creative writing school at the University of Iowa.

Ian Lancaster Fleming (d. 1964). English journalist and writer of sensationalist fiction; he will create the character of the master intelligence agent James Bond.

Arthur Nuthall Fula. South African (Afrikaans) novelist and poet; his fiction will focus upon the corruption of young village men by big-city life.

Tommaso Landolfi (d. 1979). Italian writer of fiction, poet, and playwright; he will become one of the most innovative stylists in modern Italian fiction, creating nightmarish tales displaying his preoccupation with language.

Claude Levi-Strauss. Belgian-born French anthropologist and theoretical essayist; he will be identified as the founder of structuralism and one of France's foremost intellectuals; he will study structural anthropology and develop ideas from such varied disciplines as linguistics, sociology, philosophy, psychology, and mathematics; he will seek to expose the structures underlying human thought and reveal their universality.

Pashaoghly Mir Jalal. Iranian (Azerbaijan) writer of fiction and essays; his fiction will describe the changes in village life brought about by Soviet rule; he will also concern himself with the rise of the new intelligentsia and the heroism of the people during World War II.

Armijn Pane (d. 1970). Indonesian scholar, grammarian, short story writer, and playwright; he will be regarded as a pioneer in modern Indonesian fiction, particularly because he will abandon the familiar themes of East-West conflict in favor of contemporary social problems.

Cesare Pavese (d. 1950). Italian novelist, poet, and translator; he will emerge as a "neorealist," his narrative work producing an entire poetic and symbolic system; essentially, he will maintain the position that life is not worth living unless it is for the sake of other persons.

Rajo Rao. Indian novelist and short story writer; he will be considered one of India's most outstanding English-language novelists; his fiction will reveal him to be a product of the Gandhian social rebellion of the 1930s, especially as it concerns accounts of nonviolent actions in Indian villages and small towns; he will set his short stories in rural southern India and reflect upon the impact of the Gandhian campaign; he will also explore communism as an ideological misunderstanding of human beings' ultimate aims.

Theodore Roethke (d. 1963). American poet; his themes will focus upon the state of his being as it comes into contact with reality; his work will be influenced by William Blake, William Butler Yeats, T. S. Eliot, W. H. Auden, Dylan Thomas, and Leonie Adams.

William Saroyan (d. 1981). American writer of fiction and drama; a sentimental writer who will continually pursue the glories of an ideal dream.

Mark Schorer (d. 1977). American novelist, literary scholar, and biographer; he will write periodical fiction, novels set in the Midwest, and scholarly studies and biographies of William Blake and Sinclair Lewis; he will teach literature at the University of California at Berkeley.

Jose Garcia Villa. Philippine poet; he will write his verse in English, winning literary prizes both in the United States and the Philippines; he will develop "comma poems," which will be extremely personal and abstract in both language and substance.

Elio Vittorini (d. 1966). Sicilian-born Italian novelist; he will become known for his attention to social realism; his later work will suffer somewhat from his interest in experimentation; he will also write poetry and literary criticism, as well as translate American and English novelists.

Richard Nathaniel Wright (d. 1960). Black American writer of fiction, narrative, and autobiography; he will base his work on historical fact and personal experience, describing with power and passion the predicaments of the black man and the artist.

DEATHS

Joaquin Maria Machado de Assis (b. 1839). Brazilian novelist, considered his nation's most significant writer; his subtly ironic novels display his keen psychological insight and pessimistic vision.

Wilhelm Busch (b. 1832). German caricaturist and poet; he became known for his nonsense verse.

Svatpluk Cech (b. 1846). Czech poet and novelist; his work expresses democratic and reformist ideals.

Francois Coppee (b. 1842). French poet, playwright, and writer of fiction; he developed distinctly Romantic tendencies; his popularity derived from his sympathetic treatment of the poor; and he gained the title "poet of the humble"; his later works display his Roman Catholic faith.

Edmondo De Amicis (b. 1846). Italian writer of fiction and travel narrative; he focused in his fiction upon the plight of illiterate immigrants, openly declaring his sympathies with socialism.

Holger Drachmann (b. 1846). Danish poet; became the principal traditional versifier of his generation, a genuine Bohemian and proponent of genteel values; he celebrated the socialist movement because of its potential for individual anarchy; he also wrote plays, libretti for operettas, and one long novel.

Joel Chandler Harris (b. 1848). American writer of fiction; his popular tales attempted to authentically capture the life, humor, and dialect of Southern blacks; principally remembered for creating the character of the former black slave "Uncle Remus."

Bronson Crocker Howard (b. 1842). American playwright; the first American to rely on the writing of drama as his sole profession; he wrote twenty-one plays, all theatrical successes; he combined sentiment with farce to become a pioneer of American social drama; he founded the American Dramatists Club (1891) and led the way in securing copyright protection for playwrights.

Misak Metsarents (b. 1886). Armenian poet; he wrote nature and love lyrics, relying for form and style upon medieval Armenian lyric verse; one of several West Armenian poets who depicted the extremely difficult social and economic conditions of the Armenian minority in Turkey; the tragedy of their situation drove them to seek escape in nature and in ideal love.

Victorien Sardou (b. 1831). French playwright; he authored more than seventy dramatic pieces, ranging from light comedy to historical melodrama; he became noted for the ingenious construction of his plots ("the well-made play") and the brilliance of his stage effects.

PUBLICATIONS

Gabra Iyasus Afawark, *Wallad Tarik* (A Fictional Story)—a novel by the Ethiopian writer of fiction and poetry; one of the earliest pieces of fiction to reach print in any African language, and the first to be published in Amharic; presents the ideal of Ethiopian existence within the context of the complex, devotional tradition of ancient Ge'ez Church literature.

Arnold Bennett, *The Old Wives' Tale*—a novel by the English writer of fiction; chronicles the lives of two sisters from girlhood to death; one sister chooses a drab life, marrying an insignificant draper; the other allows herself to be dragged through the social mud by an unprincipled blackguard; in the end, the two sisters unite, spending their last years together in the draper's shop.

G. K. Chesterton, *The Man Who Was Thursday*—a novel by the English writer of fiction and literary criticism; a shocking but extremely amusing fantasy set against a surreal, anarchist background; in general attacks the pessimism of his own times.

E. M. Forster, *A Room With a View*—a novel by the English writer of fiction and literary criticism; a satire of English people living abroad (in this instance, in Italy), attacking their sterility, snobbery, and pseudo-intellectualism; thus, the novelist parades before his reader the residents of the Pensione Bertolini in Florence, and in so doing develops a form of comedy of manners as well as a social satire.

Taomaq Gaediaty, *Akchaestony Fystytae* (Writings of a Prisoner)—a verse cycle by the Ossetian (SSR) poet and literary critic; describes the hardships and longings of an imprisoned revolutionary, calling for social liberation and freedom from Siberian exile; until 1909.

Kenneth Grahame, *The Wind in the Willows*—a work of juvenile fiction by the Scottish-born writer; based principally on bedtime stories and letters to the writer's son, and thus never really intended for publication; eventually, the stories of Rat, Mole, Badger, and Toad, as well as their adventures by the river, became classics of children's literature.

Ezra Pound, *A Lumo Spento*—the first published volume of verse by the American-born poet; one hundred copies printed in Venice; highly adorned with images and symbols from medieval literature, set in Provencal and Italian verse forms.

Jules Romains, *La Vie Unanime* (The Unanimous Life)—a verse collection by the French poet and writer of fiction; the poet derives his consciousness from the sights, sounds, and people of the street.

Arthur Schnitzer, *Der Wag ins Freie* (The Road to the Open)—a novel by the Austrian Jewish novelist and playwright; a broad and lengthy panorama of the contemporary social scene, deriving strength from the writer's objective treatment of his fellow Jews.

Hermann Sudermann, *Das Hohe Lied* (The Song of Songs)—a novel by the German (East Prussian) writer of drama and fiction; concerns a loathsome aristocratic German general and his corruption of a young girl; built upon the thesis that a high society that does not function morally must, by nature, be corrupt; thus the piece spoke directly to its intended bourgeois audience.

Vahan Terian, *Mt'nsaga Anurjner* (Dreams in the Twilight)—a collection of verse by the Armenian poet; evidences the influences of French and Russian symbolism; focuses upon the depressing social atmosphere in Russia following the defeat of the 1905 revolution, as well as upon the tragedy of the Armenian minority in Turkey.

EVENTS

Mary Baker Eddy, the founder of the Christian Science, begins publication at Boston of *The Christian Science Monitor;* the daily newspaper is initially a reaction against sensational journalism; contains news and cultural-literary contributions, not attempting to promote the theology of its founder's religious organization.

The English Review, a London literary journal, begins publication; Joseph Conrad, H. G. Wells, and Ford Madox Ford are among its founders; it will merge with *The National Review* after 1923.

Rudolf Christoph Eucken, German philosopher, receives the Nobel Prize for literature.

The fountain pen emerges as a popular writing instrument.

Charles Harold St. John Hamilton, writer of fiction for boys, founds *The Magnet,* a weekly paper for boys; Hamilton writes under the name "Frank Richards"; until 1940.

Alfred Charles William Harmsworth, Viscount Northcliffe, English journalist and newspaper magnate, purchases *The Times,* London; he will, in 1914, reduce the price of the paper to a single penny.

1909

BIRTHS

James Agee (d. 1955). American poet, screenwriter, and novelist; he will write autobiographical fiction celebrating the American family; his financial success will come from adapting other writers' fiction to screenplays; he will also write some poetry.

Nelson Algren (d. 1981). American writer of fiction; the majority of his novels will be set in Chicago and will focus on the poverty that he experienced as a youth; he will write naturalistic fiction depicting an urban society composed of tramps, petty criminals, hustlers, prostitutes, and barflies.

Jean Fernand Brierre. Haitian poet, playwright, novelist, and biographer; one of Haiti's most prolific writers, he will concern himself with the folkloric and Afro-Caribbean aspects of the culture of his country; he will also celebrate the poor and downtrodden black people throughout the world.

Osamu Dazai (d. 1948). Japanese writer of fiction; he will become one of the most significant writers of twentieth-century Japan; his personal problems (drug and alcohol addiction, and suicidal tendencies) will be reflected in his fiction, which will also be characterized by irony and self-mockery.

Laxmiprasad Devkota (d. 1959). Nepali poet, playwright, and writer of short fiction; he will become the most significant poet of modern Nepal; he will merge the themes and techniques of classical Sanskrit literature with elements from modern Nepal culture; his work will also display traces of the European Romantic movement.

Resat Enis (d. 1982). Turkish writer of fiction; his fiction will focus upon the large landowners of the Shukur-Ova region, as well as upon the problems of the impoverished peasantry of that region.

Maun Htin. Burmese playwright, translator, and writer of fiction; his stories will present realistic pictures of Burmese village life, particularly during the difficult years of the Japanese occupation in World War II.

Mahti Husain (d. 1965). Azerbaijan writer of fiction, drama, and history; he will publish short fiction about village life during the collectivization campaign; his novels will focus upon Azerbaijan village life during the civil wars and World War II.

Jalol Ikromi. Tajik writer of fiction and drama; his translations of the works of Anton Chekhov will help him to learn the craft of fiction; his fiction will reflect various problems of his day: agricultural reform, postwar village life, love and ethics within the village family.

Elia Kazan. Turkish-born American playwright, novelist, and stage and film director; although his reputation will derive from his work in Hollywood and the New York theater, he will manage to produce several novels on popular and contemporary subjects, including political escape, assassination, love, and the theatrical career.

Clarence Malcolm Lowry (d. 1957). English novelist; his fiction will reflect the influences of Herman Melville, Eugene O'Neill, Joseph Conrad, and Jack London; his characters will lack self-discipline and will become victims (as did their creator) of alcoholism; however, that very affliction will provide them with intensive insight into the anguish and courage of the terror-haunted mind.

Edgar Mittelholzer (d. 1965). Guyana novelist, playwright, and poet; he will become one of the most significant modern Caribbean writers; he will consider, as subjects for his work, East Indian women and their relations with their fathers, husbands, and boyfriends, the various races and classes among his society, and the entire issue of tensions among members of colonial society; his work will also emphasize the concept of the sins of the father being visited upon the children.

Vladimir Neff (d. 1983). Czech novelist; a skilled storyteller whose fiction will focus principally upon historical characters, both real and fictional; the locale of his work will be limited to the writer's native country; he will rely heavily upon social satire and irony.

Elder James Olson. American poet and literary critic; he will become a professor of literature and criticism at the University of Chicago, and there assume leadership of what will be-

come the "neo-Aristotelian" school of criticism; essentially, his criteria will originate from Aristotle's *Poetics*.

Andre Pieyre de Mandiargues. French writer of fiction, poetry, drama, and nonfiction; he will write allegorical fantasies reflecting the influence of surrealism; his work will combine the appealing and the terrifying, the erotic and the grotesque, and will evoke a bizarre, dreamlike world in which characters seek the correlations between flesh and spirit and between sexuality and death.

Oscar Bento Ribas (d. 1961). Angolan writer of fiction, drama, and poetry; he will lose his eyesight shortly after his twenty-first year; his work will focus principally upon the Kimbundu people, their religion and their culture; he will also derive stories and plots from Angolan folklore.

Shaaban Robert (d. 1962). Tanzanian (Swahili) poet, novelist, essayist, and biographer; he will be considered the most distinguished of all East African writers, particularly since he will introduce the essay into Swahili literature; as a fervent Muslim and African patriot, he will take up the theme of protest against subjugation to European colonialism.

Abul-Qasim ash-Shabbi (d. 1934). Tunisian poet and critic; he will come under the influence of Alphonse Lamartine and Johann Wolfgang von Goethe, and will make a spirited call for modernism in literature.

Stephen Spender. English poet and critic; he will advocate the treatment of political and moral subjects in literature, emphasizing the public and social responsibilities of the writer; nonetheless, he will also write poetry of a highly personal nature.

Wallace Earle Stegner. American writer of fiction; his work will concentrate upon the American West; he will receive the Pulitzer Prize for fiction in 1972.

Thach-Lam (d. 1943). Vietnamese novelist and writer of short fiction; in his fiction he will attempt to combat social evils existing among the peasantry and middle class, including promiscuity, prostitution, snobbery, and bigotry.

Simone Adolphine Weil (d. 1943). French philosopher, essayist, playwright, and poet; she will become one of the most brilliant and enigmatic Christian thinkers of the twentieth century; her aesthetic life and ambivalence toward the Roman Catholic Church will dominate her written work; she will also reveal an intense compassion for the sufferings of other human beings.

Eudora Welty. American writer of fiction; she will gain renown for her stories of the American South and her accurate and skillful manipulation of dialect; her fiction will abound with portrayals of the eccentric, comic, and vital inhabitants of rural Mississippi; she will receive the Pulitzer Prize for fiction in 1973.

Komil Yashin. Uzbek (SSR) poet, playwright, and critic; his poetic and dramatic themes will be based upon the civil war and the early years of postwar socialism; he will also concern himself with collectivization and women's struggle for equality.

DEATHS

Euclides Rodrigues da Cunha (b. 1866). Brazilian writer of narrative and fiction; he became the first writer in Brazil to treat social problems with death and imagination, often combining fact and fiction; the publication of his *Rebellion in the Backlands* in 1902 was the important event in Brazilian literature prior to 1922.

Sarah Orne Jewett (b. 1849). American writer of fiction; her perceptive and humorous studies of small-town New England life became extremely popular.

Detlev von Liliencron (b. 1844). German poet, playwright, and writer of fiction; he became one of the foremost lyric poets of late nineteenth-century Germany, noted particularly for his stylistic innovations; a soldier by profession, he relied upon the themes of war, death, and love; he dies from pneumonia contracted while on tour of the battlefields around Metz.

Cesare Lombroso (b. 1836). Italian psychologist, criminologist, surgeon, and essayist; the founder of the science of criminology, he wrote prose tracts outlining his theories on how a criminal type could be distinguished from a normal human being.

Catule Mendes (b. 1841). French novelist, playwright, and poet; a member of the so-called "Parnassian Poets."

George Meredith (b. 1828). English novelist and poet; his fiction, especially, contains penetrating analyses of individual characters and

social institutions, written in a witty and oblique style; he wrote a series of fifty poems that traced the dissolution of a marriage.

John Millington Synge (b. 1871). Irish playwright and poet; he depicted the harshness of rural Irish life; in 1904, with William Butler Yeats and Lady Augusta Gregory, he founded the Abbey Theatre in Dublin, where he later presented his comedies; he dies, after a prolonged illness, from Hodgkin's disease.

Algernon Charles Swinburne (b. 1837). English poet, playwright, and critic; his work reflects his supreme talent for creating musical, sensuous language; his poetry was an outlet for his enthusiasm for Italian unification and figures from English history.

PUBLICATIONS

Alfonso Henrique de Lima Barreto, *Recordacoes do Escrivao Isaias Caminha*—a novel by the Brazilian essayist and writer of fiction; set in Rio de Janeiro, the work accurately recreates the topography and mores of the capital during the early part of the twentieth century; the title character, a mulatto and a writer, narrates the causes of his internal anguish: racial sensitivity, insecurity, and the pain of the creative process.

John Galsworthy, *The Silver Box*—a social drama by the English playwright and novelist; contrasts two forms of social justice administered to two drunken ne'er-do-wells: a poor man steals a silver cigarette box and goes to prison, while a rich man steals a woman's purse and settles the issue privately.

Hakob Hakobian, *Nor Aravot* (New Morning)—a volume of lyrics by the Armenian poet; portrays the hard lives of the Armenian workers and the future of the working class.

William James, *A Pluralistic Universe*—a prose collection by the American psychologist and pragmatic philosopher; the writer's Oxford Hibbert lectures, in which he comments upon Georg Wilhelm Friedrich Hegel, Gustav Theodor Fechner, and Henri Bergson.

Alfred Kubin, *Die Andere Seite* (The Other Side)—a novel by the Austrian writer of fiction, poet, and essayist; an adventure tale depicting a Central Asian kingdom inhabited by physically and psychologically abnormal individuals; its ruler exercises mysterious psychic control, but psychic forces released by the arrival of a challenger eventually destroy him.

N. Kumaran Asan, *Vina Puuvu* (Fallen Flower)—a poem by the Malayalam versifier; the first significant poem of the Malayalam Romantic movement; reflects the influences of both Bengali and British literature.

Maurice Maeterlinck, *L'Oiseau Bleu* (The Bluebird)—an especially optimistic drama by the Belgian-born French playwright, essayist, and poet; a fairy tale with allegorical significance; focuses upon the myopic quest for the elusive bluebird of happiness and the failure of humankind to realize that happiness may be found most easily at home; usually performed, as a fantasy for children.

Ferenc Molnar, *Liliom*—a play by the Hungarian dramatist, writer of fiction, and essayist; combines the theme of love with elements of the supernatural; the rough exterior of a carnival barker conceals his gentle heart; nonetheless, he cannot refrain from inflicting pain upon his loved ones; the piece will gain recognition from the Richard Rodgers and Oscar Hammerstein adaptation as the musical *Carousel.*

Ezra Pound, *Personae*—a volume of poems by the American-born writer of verse; the title suggests an attempt at a fusion of medieval and modern poetry; the pieces support the attitude that the poet must objectify his emotions by discovering his "anti-Self"; demonstrates the influence of the dramatic monologues of Robert Browning.

Robert Walser, *Jakob von Gunten*—a novel by the Swiss writer of fiction, poetry, and essays; the piece had a profound effect upon the short fiction of Franz Kafka; the title character attends a school where there exists only a single repeated lesson: one must learn the school rules by heart, with tasks limited to sweeping and scrubbing; all pupils will become valets, and thus no hope for the future exists.

H. G. Wells, *Ann Veronica*—a novel by the English writer of fiction and social history; a feminist tract that focuses upon the "new woman"; a young girl defies her father and conventional morality by running away with the man she loves.

————————, *Tono-Bungay*—a highly successful novel by the English writer; a panorama of society in dissolution; describes the rise of a new class of wealthy individuals, embodied in the person of George Ponderevo's uncle, an entrepreneur who peddles a worthless patent medicine ("quap").

EVENTS

Selma Lagerlof, Swedish novelist, receives the Nobel Prize for literature, the first woman to achieve that honor.

Twentieth-Century Magazine, a monthly journal concerned with social reform, begins publication at Boston; Hamlin Garland is one of its principal contributors; until 1913.

1910

BIRTHS

Jean Marie Lucien Pierre Anouilh (d. 1987). French playwright, translator, and writer of fiction; he will become one of the foremost dramatists in France, writing over forty plays in a wide variety of literary modes; he will adopt a skeptical and generally bitter view of the human condition, reacting with despair to the cruelty of life.

Kemal Bilbasar. Turkish writer of fiction; he will view life in the country as the specific province of Turkish literature; he will become a realist with a strong sense of local color.

Chief Daniel Olorunfemi Fagunwa (d. 1963). West Nigerian (Yoruba) novelist; he will develop his fiction from Yoruba folk legends, presenting them as popular, vernacular tales; he will reveal himself to be a highly imaginative moralist.

Jean Genet (d. 1986). French playwright, novelist, and poet; he will become one of the most innovative and controversial post-World War II French writers; he will achieve recognition particularly for his surreal poetic dramas, in which the stage will become an arena for the enactment of bizarre fantasies; he will focus upon dominance and submission, sex, and death.

Julien Gracq (pseudonym of Louis Poirier). French writer of fiction, drama, poetry, and literary criticism; he will explore, particularly in his fiction, such ideas as humanity's search for meaning, the importance of myth in interpreting experience, and the supremacy of the imagination; he will also explore the dialectics of death and resurrection, salvation and condemnation, and dream and reality.

Abdulhay Habibi. Afghan poet and literary scholar; his verse will remain uncollected; his essays will focus upon philosophy, literary history, Afghan writers, and general history; he will also edit Afghan literary classics.

U Luhtu Hla. Burmese journalist and writer of fiction; his stories will reflect his experiences in prison for political activities, recording the histories of his fellow prisoners with sympathetic realism, while at the same time drawing attention to the acute problems within Burmese society.

Bernard Kangro. Estonian poet who will, in 1944, take up residence in Sweden; his verse will be marked by freshness and imagination; he will attempt to lighten the gloom of the present with glimpses into a brighter world (thus, blowing sand forms a dune upon which a forest will grow).

Nicholas John Turney Monsarrat (d. 1979). English novelist; he will gain recognition for his popular books describing his wartime experiences at sea, both with the merchant marine and the Royal Navy; he will also concern himself with the struggle for independence of various African states.

Wright Morris. American writer of fiction; in his novels he will focus upon various aspects of the American experience, particularly in the Midwest and West; his fiction will also reflect his interest in photography: the literary craftsman who relies upon narrative to unite a stream of extremely graphic descriptions.

Vaikkam Muhammad Basir. Malayalam novelist; the majority of his stories focus upon Kerala Muslims, revealing the writer's sense of humor and ability to depict the subtleties of human emotions; his style will be marked by strict attentiveness to the economy of language.

Gul Khan Nasir. Pakistani (Baluchi) poet and essayist; his verse will combine a sense of national consciousness with a strong defense of Islamic ideals; thus, he will convey a spirit of patriotism while attempting to initiate a social awakening of the Baluchi intelligentsia.

Gwendolyn Margaret Pharis Ringwood (d. 1984). American-born Canadian playwright, poet, essayist, and writer of fiction; she will be remembered for her folk plays set in the western provinces of Alberta and British Columbia; her work will reveal her knowledge of classical tragedy, comedy, farce, and the musical stage; she will also develop characters from the common people of the farm and prairie, as well as from folk heroes and noted figures from history.

Rasul Rza. Azerbaijan poet, playwright, and writer of fiction; he will become known for his poetry, which will record the changing life of the villagers of Azerbaijan, the struggles of the peoples of the East against imperialism, and his impressions from the front during World War II.

Abdoulaye Sadji (d. 1961). Senegalese writer of fiction; his stories will focus upon the world of the hybrid society of Dakar and the old port city of Saint-Louis; in a mild, warm style, he will create characters (mostly women) who dominate their societies; his fiction will reveal his personal fascination with the new cities of Africa, contrasting the simple values of the people of the country with the complexities of urban life.

Fakhroddin Shadman (d. 1971). Iranian essayist and novelist; the principal theme of his works will be the issue of cultural relations between Iran and the West; in his view, Iranian culture was gradually deteriorating and being engulfed by Western ideas.

Srirangam Sriniwasaraw. Indian (Telugu) poet; will herald the beginning of a new school of progressive poetry in Telugu literature during the mid-1950s; in short and suggestive poems of considerable beauty and vigor, he will advance the cause of the downtrodden; although a devoted Marxist, he will consciously attempt to transcend the limits of political propaganda.

Kemal Tahir (d. 1973). Turkish novelist; his fiction will analyze the customs and traditions of peasant life; he will also produce historical novels; the majority of his fiction will be published in French.

Cahit Sitki Taranci (d. 1956). Turkish poet; his poems will represent the finest achievement of modern Turkish poetry in syllabic-rhymed verse; he will write of death and its terrors, of old age and solitude, of the search for a lost god and momentary joys, of unfulfilled love; his poetic style will be marked by simplicity and spontaneity.

DEATHS

Bjornstjerne Bjornson (b. 1832). Norwegian poet, playwright, and novelist; a lifelong champion of liberal and reform causes, he sought to free the Norwegian theater from

Danish influence and to revive Norwegian as a literary language; he recreated the epic past of Norway upon the Norwegian stage, and also became the national poet; he received the Nobel Prize in literature in 1903.

Julio Herrera y Reissig (b. 1875). Uruguayan poet; the leader of the Uruguayan "modernismo" school, characterized by elegant form, exotic imagery, and subtle word music; his poetry was influenced by Luis de Gongora y Argote and the French Symbolists.

Julia Ward Howe (b. 1819). American poet, essayist, and reform journalist; her literary reputation is based almost solely upon her ode to human freedom and American unity, "The Battle Hymn of the Republic" (1861).

William James (b. 1842). American philosopher and psychologist; he became the initial proponent of pragmatism, stating that the truth of a proposition must be judged by its practical outcomes; through radical empiricism, he rejected all transcendental principles; he maintained a lifelong interest in religion and psychical research, producing prose tracts of literary merit.

Kalman Mikszath (b. 1847). Hungarian writer of fiction and political journalist; he wrote lighthearted, anecdotal narratives in the manner of Mark Twain, satirizing contemporary social and political institutions; he became the most important Hungarian writer of fiction during the late nineteenth and early twentieth centuries.

William Vaughan Moody (b. 1869). American poet and playwright; his poetic dramas display skilled dramatic technique, intellectual power, and philosophical depth; his themes generally focused upon human beings' relations with God, the problems of free will, and the presence of evil in a God-created world.

Jean Moreas (pseudonym of Johannes Papadiamantopoulos; b. 1856). Greek-born French poet, essayist, playwright, and writer of fiction; he advanced the cause of an emerging generation of Symbolist writers in his poetry and prose; eventually, however, he rejected symbolism in favor of a poetic theory based upon classical ideals; he dies, after prolonged suffering, from a degenerative disease.

William Sydney Porter ("O. Henry"; b. 1862). American writer of short fiction; he achieved popularity with short, simple stories noted for their careful attention to plot, ironic coincidences, and surprise conclusions; he wrote approximately three hundred pieces of short fiction.

Wilhelm Raabe (b. 1831). German writer of fiction; he wrote humorous novels of village life that demonstrate the influence of Laurence Sterne and Charles Dickens.

Jules Renard (b. 1864). French diarist, poet, and writer of fiction; he achieved a niche in literary history with his five-volume collection of journals, which cast light upon both the man and his times; essentially, he sought truth in both the trivial and crucial events of human existence; his death is the result of arteriosclerosis.

Leo Nikolaevich Tolstoy (b. 1828). Russian writer of fiction, essayist, and playwright; ranks as one of the most important figures in modern literary history; if he had written nothing else beyond *War and Peace*, he would be deserving of Marcel Proust's declaration that he stands as "a serene God" of literature; he believed that literature must take the form of simple works, easily assimilated by the toiling masses (such as biblical parables); he will catch a chill in early November and die in a siding of the Astapovo railway station.

Mark Twain (pseudonym of Samuel Langhorne Clemens; b. 1835). American writer of fiction, narrative, nonfiction, and humor; he created at least two of the most memorable characters in American literary history, Tom Sawyer and Huck Finn, while painting a realistic mural of nineteenth-century life; he also revolutionized American fiction by his manipulation of vernacular language; his later works tend to be somber, pessimistic, and misanthropic.

PUBLICATIONS

Sir James Matthew Barrie, *The Twelve-Pound Note*—a play by the Scottish-born dramatist and novelist; the writer bases his theme upon the exposure of a pompous egoist.

E. M. Forster, *Howards End*—a novel by the English writer of fiction and criticism; essentially concerns conflicting values; one group of characters dedicates itself to civilized living, music, literature, and conversations with friends; the other group cares only about the business of life, distrusting emotions and imagination; the title refers to the house where the novel begins and ends.

John Galsworthy, *Justice*—a play by the English novelist and dramatist; a social tragedy that presents a defense for the thief who steals out of weakness of character and suffers and dies for his crime; the play also attacks the prison system; in fact, Winston Churchill, then home secretary, attended a performance and, as a result, initiated reforms.

Henry James, *The Finer Grain*—a collection of short stories by the American writer of fiction and nonfiction; in these pieces, the writer begins to demonstrate, through the poetry of his language, a remote intimacy with the preoccupations of ordinary men and women.

Krsnaji Prabhakar Khadilkar, *Kicakavadha* (The Slaying of Kicak)—a play by the Indian (Maratha) dramatist; the most striking example of the writer's habit of manipulating the stage for the purpose of covertly propagating anti-British propaganda.

Gaston Leroux, *La Fantome de l'Opera* (The Phantom of the Opera)—a novel by the French writer of fiction and playwright; a horror tale that captured (and continues to do so) the popular imagination; a melodramatic piece that relies upon the recognizable plot of a hideously ugly protagonist falling in love with a beautiful young woman, whom he abducts; underneath the brooding horror of the piece lies the writer's graphic picture of life in the Paris Opera.

John Masefield, *Ballads and Poems*—a verse collection by the English poet and writer of fiction; contains the major poem "Cargoes."

Isaac Leib Peretz, *Die Golden Keit* (The Golden Chain)—a mystical play by the Polish-born Yiddish writer of fiction, drama, and nonfiction; examines the struggle between realistic and romantic thought; the spiritual chain linking several generations of a pious family breaks, as the ancestral home gradually becomes a symbol for repression of free thought.

Ezra Pound, *The Spirit of Romance*—a volume of criticism by the American-born poet; focuses upon works by Arnaut Daniel and Guido Cavalcanti; the writer calls for a new form of literary scholarship that will praise beauty and art, rather than history; also demonstrates that the poet had been profoundly affected by the Pre-Raphaelites and English aestheticism.

Edwin Arlington Robinson, *The Town Down the River*—a verse collection by the American poet; contains "Miniver Cheevy" and "How Annandale Went Out"; the poet enlarges upon his gallery of inarticulate characters with tragic problems.

Raymond Roussel, *Impressions d'Afrique* (Impressions of Africa)—a novel by the French writer of fiction, poetry, and nonfiction; demonstrates the stylistic device known as the "procede," whereby each section begins with a pair of nouns, each with more than a single meaning; the novel itself concerns a group of shipwrecked actors, their capture by an African chieftain, and their performance of an elaborate pageant in his honor.

Bertrand Russell and Alfred North Whitehead, *Principia Mathematica*—a treatise by the two English philosophers and mathematicians; termed the most significant single contribution to logic since Aristotle; attempts to resolve current controversies and contradictions concerning symbolic logic by presenting the Russellian theory of types (or classes); until 1913.

John Millington Synge, *Deirdre of the Sorrows*—a tragic drama by the Irish playwright, who died (1909) before he could complete the final revisions; a three-act tragedy of love and betrayal, based upon Irish legend and written in the poetic idiom of the Irish peasantry; the playwright's Deirdre exists as a wild and instinctive creature of nature, proud and passionate; her intuitive wisdom allows her to realize that old age and death must inevitably come, and thus lovers can shape their own destinies before their lives end.

William Butler Yeats, *The Green Hamlet and Other Poems*—a collection by the Irish poet, playwright, and essayist; the pieces reflect a difficult time in the poet's life, particularly his ill-fated love for Maud Gonne; nonetheless, he continues to celebrate the beauty of his former lover; other poems reveal an increasing interest in public life and a concern about age.

EVENTS

The Baltimore Evening Sun, an extension of the daily *Sun,* begins publication.

Cambridge University acquires the *Encyclopaedia Britannica* and issues the noted eleventh edition; 28 volumes, to 1911.

Charles William Elliot, having recently (1909) ended his forty-year tenure as president of Harvard College, edits the fifty-volume *Har-*

vard Classics; a collection of the world's best literary works; primarily intended as an exercise in self-education for those persons who had not attended college or university.

Paul Johann von Heyse, German novelist, playwright, poet, and translator, receives the Nobel Prize in literature.

The Mariner's Mirror begins publication at London; the quarterly journal of the Society for Nautical Research; its title derives from a volume published during the reign of Elizabeth I.

Sir Arthur Quiller-Couch, English literary scholar, edits *The Oxford Books of Ballads.*

The Round Table, a quarterly journal reviewing the state of British politics, begins publication at London.

1911

BIRTHS

Jacques N. Bahelele. Zaire (Kikongo) writer of fiction and poetry; his fiction will be based on Kikongo folk materials; he will also write hymns and study local magic practices.

Odysseus Elytis. Greek poet, essayist, and translator; he will become one of the most significant literary figures in Greece during the twentieth century, writing poetry celebrating the splendors of Nature and affirming humanity's ability to embrace hope and cast off despair; his verse will reveal his interest in surrealism.

Max Rudolf Frisch. Swiss novelist, playwright, and diarist; he will become one of Switzerland's most distinguished and versatile writers and one of the finest twentieth-century novelists to write in German; his diaries will be valued by scholars for their insight into the writer's words and creative process and as important documents of literary history.

William Golding. English writer of fiction; his novels will generally focus upon the darker sides of human nature, emphasizing nightmarish ritual; he will tend to depict isolated individuals or small groups in isolation.

Albert Gomes (d. 1978). Trinidad poet and novelist; he will compose loose and spontaneous verse, much of it focusing upon his interest in political independence and the racial

conditions in his native land, which will he will label "a polychromatic maze".

Mirza Ibrahimov. Iranian-Azerbaijan poet, novelist, playwright, and literary critic; he will describe transformation of Azerbaijan women, and life in collective farm villages, and the lives of oil workers in peace and war, particularly their fraternal feelings toward other Soviet peoples and toward Spain in its fight against fascism.

Umasanker Josi. Indian (Gujarati) poet; his early verse will depict the dry district on the Sabarmati River in rocky northern Gujarati; later, his work will become more complex, reflecting an artistic perception of reality involving mythical contradictions; thus, images within a poem, and between poems, will clash and contradict, to be resolved not by logical conclusion, but by the growth and development of a mythic unity.

Asraru'l-haqq Majaz (d. 1955.) Indian (Urdu) lyric poet; his verse will express the moods and aspirations of the young Muslim middle class of India; he will turn from traditional romantic fantasy to social problems.

Achdiat Karta Mihardja. Indonesian writer of fiction; he will write the most significant works of Indonesian fiction of the post-World War II period; his work will focus upon intellectual struggles involving religion, mysticism, and historical materialism.

Czeslaw Milosz. Lithuanian-born Polish poet, novelist, and essayist; the Lithuanian countryside of his youth will provide the sources for his early poetry, as well as for his autobiographical fiction; his verse will tend to be classical in style and form and his nonfiction will emphasize sociopolitical subjects; in 1960 he will move to the United States, and in 1980 he will receive the Nobel Prize for literature.

Flann O'Brien (pseudonym of Brian O'Nuallain; d. 1966). Irish writer of fiction and drama; his work will be steeped in Irish culture, history, and language; it will feature such comic elements as parody, satire, exaggeration, and black humor in reaction to social, artistic, and historical concerns.

Dennis Chukude Osadebay. West Nigerian poet; his verse will principally be written in English, the first original poetry in English to be published in Nigeria; although his poems tend to be derivative, they display force and urgency.

Terence Rattigan (d. 1977). English playwright; he will become associated with the West End group of London dramatists, becoming known, particularly, for his stagecraft; he will direct his drama toward "the average middle-brow matinee attender," and thus a number of his pieces will be labeled "kitchen-sink" drama.

Nuqui Bienvenido Santos. Philippine writer of fiction and poetry; he will write principally in English; his major collection of short fiction will focus upon Filipinos in America and their attempts to survive in an alien culture.

Ousmane Diop Soce. Senegal novelist and poet; his fiction will concern itself with humiliations suffered by Africans at the hands of Europeans; thus, his characters will attempt to be as heroic as their ancestors, but they meet defeat in an Africa no longer in their possession.

K. Surangkhanang (pseudonym of Kanha Khiengsiri). Thai novelist; her fiction will reveal a strong social consciousness, realistically and critically portraying the negative aspects of modern society.

Mirzo Tursunzoda. Iranian (Tajik) poet and playwright; his work will reveal his distaste for the decadence of the old world and his interest in ordinary people; he will be best known for his lyric poetry characterized by simple language and style and an attention to the merits of folk poetry.

Sotim Ulughzoda. Iranian (Tajik) novelist and playwright; he will write historical drama and fiction, focusing upon peasant revolts and heroic defenses of towns and villages; he will also write literary criticism and literary history.

Thomas Lanier (Tennessee) Williams (d. 1983). American playwright; one of the most important dramatists of the post-World II period; the majority of his plays will reveal an obvious preoccupation with persons who stand outside the world (but who see the world clearly) because they are "different"; although these characters will experience pain, the playwright will see them from a somewhat comic point of view.

Qian Zhongshu. Chinese writer of fiction; he will be considered one of the most important practitioners of the classical Chinese literary mode; he will develop an ability to silhouette his characters against the backgrounds of their problems, thus identifying the causes of their difficulties; he will combine humor and satire with uncomplicated plots.

DEATHS

Wilhelm Dilthey (b. 1833). German philosopher; a strict proponent of empiricism, he rejected transcendental considerations and based his philosophy of life upon a foundation of descriptive and analytical psychology; he influenced the work of early sociologists.

Gustaf Froding (b. 1860). Swedish lyrical poet; his most popular verse collections, written between 1891 and 1896, include songs, meditations, and poems in praise of nature.

William Schwenck Gilbert (b. 1836). English playwright and poet; in collaboration with Sir Arthur Seymour Sullivan (as musical composer) he wrote a series of popular, satiric operettas; a metrical craftsman, his lyrics have proven scintillatingly humorous.

Alexandros Papadiamantis (b. 1851). Greek writer of fiction; he has achieved recognition as a chronicler of life on his native island of Skiathos; he wrote over two hundred short stories and at least four major novels, portraying the lives of farmers, sailors, monks, fisherman, housewives, and poor people in general; he combined lyric descriptions of the Greek islands with realistic pictures of the harsh lives of the villagers.

Joseph Pulitzer (b. 1847). Hungarian-born American newspaper publisher; upon his death he left funds to endow the graduate school of journalism at Columbia University, New York, and to establish the Pulitzer Prizes, annual awards (since 1917) for achievements in journalism, letters, and music.

Mirza Alakbar Sabir (b. 1862). Azerbaijan poet; his works are satirical, addressing political issues and attacking the ills of contemporary society; his work was popular in Turkey and Iran, as well as in Azerbaijan.

Freidrich Spielhagen (b. 1829). German novelist; his popular fiction was graphically realistic and outlined his ideas for social reform; also known for his satire of the Nietzschean idea of the superman.

PUBLICATIONS

Max Beerbohm, *Zuleika Dobson*—a work of fiction by the English essayist, critic and caricaturist, his only completed novel; an amusing story relating the devastating effect of a beautiful adventuress upon an Oxford youth.

Ambrose Bierce, *The Devil's Dictionary*—a form of reference work by the American writer of fiction and narratives; an alphabetical compendium of the writer's most potent witticisms and philosophical epigrams; the volume has remained popular.

Joseph Ephraim Casely-Hayford, *Ethiopia Unbound*—a novel by the Ghanian writer of fiction and nonfiction; a synthesis of the writer's religious and political ideas: urges his readers not to imitate Europeans and to instead take pride in their own African heritage.

Joseph Conrad, *Under Western Eyes*—a novel by the Polish-born English writer of fiction; set in Switzerland and Russia, the work focuses upon the tragedy of a student named Razumov, who is engulfed in the treachery of violence and revolution.

Hugo von Hofmannsthal, *Jedermann* (Everyman)—a one-act morality play in verse by the Austrian writer of drama, poetry, and fiction; Faith and Good Deeds rescue the title character from his materialistic life.

Avetikh Isahakian, *Abdulala Mahari*—an epic poem by the Armenian poet and writer of fiction; one of the most significant lyrical epics in modern East Armenian literature; expresses the poet's rejection of contemporary social norms and institutions; offers a solution to the conflicting values of the individual and society.

Johann Sigurjonsson, *Bjoerg-Ejvind og Hans Hustru* (Eyvind of the Hills)—a play by the Icelandic writer of drama and poetry; based upon the story by a legendary eighteenth-century outlaw and his wife; the couple, pursued into exile in a mountainous region of Iceland, must test their love against a series of physical and psychological hardships, including starvation and isolation from society.

Carl Sternheim, *Die Hose* (The Pants)— a play by the German Jewish dramatist; the first of a trilogy concerning the Maske family; a Prussian petty official beats his wife because she has threatened his position; in fact, while she watched the passing of the Kaiser in the Zoological Gardens, her knickers fell to her ankles and halted the royal progress.

George Macaulay Trevelyan, *Garibaldi and the Making of Italy*—the last of three remarkable historical and biographical studies by the English scholar; the vividness of the narrative partly results from the writer's tracing, on foot, every mile of the Italian patriot's campaigns.

Richard Wagner, *Mein Leben*—the German composer's autobiography, posthumously published.

H. G. Wells, *The Country of the Blind*—the fifth collection of short stories by the English writer of fiction and history; contains, in addition to the title piece (published 1904), the well-known "The Door in the Wall" (1906).

——————— , *The New Machiavelli*—a novel by the English writer, concerns a politician involved in a sexual scandal; although popular, critics viewed the work as a signal of the writer's declining creativity.

Edith Wharton, *Ethan Frome*—a novel by the American writer of fiction; praised for its perfect craftsmanship; set in the harsh New England hills, the work concerns the infidelities of the title character.

EVENTS

Maurice Maeterlinck, Belgian-French poet and playwright, receives the Nobel Prize for literature.

The Masses, a Socialist weekly journal of news and social criticism, begins publication in New York City; the magazine endures several suspensions from the Federal government, particularly after it affiliates with the American Communist Party; until 1953.

1912

BIRTHS

Ahmed Ali. Pakistini writer of fiction; his work will be written both in Urdu and English; he will present realistic pictures of Muslim life in old Delhi and Lucknow, emphasizing the traditions of Muslim culture.

Jorge Amado. Brazilian writer of fiction; his novels will be translated into more than forty languages; the majority of them will be set in the Bahia region of northeastern Brazil, and his themes will be based upon the physical, cultural and social milieu of the area; his works reveal his fascination with the rich mixture of heritages among the inhabitants of Bahia: European, African, native Indian.

Said Aql. Lebanese poet, playwright, and writer of fiction; his work will recast themes from classical antiquity and introduce classical tragedy into Arabic literature; termed "the poet of joy," he will publish lyrics in the Lebanese dialect and attempt to raise the colloquial language to a literary level.

Roussan Camille (d. 1961). Haitian poet and journalist; his work will reflect the influence of Langston Hughes and the Cuban poet Nicolas Guillen; he will develop a personal and a "black-conscious" verse, emphasizing political and social protest; his poetry will also recognize the blessings bestowed upon humanity and the black person's fulfillment of that promise.

Jose Luis Cano. Spanish poet; his poems will range from measured sonnets to free verse, describing scenes from his childhood and the motifs of daily life; he will make his most important contributions to Spanish literature, however, as an editor of verse anthologies and as a critic.

John Cheever (d. 1982). American writer of fiction; his sophisticated and ironic fictional pieces, published principally in American popular literary magazines, will satirize affluent suburban New England life.

Leon Gontran Damas (d. 1978). Guyanan poet; his work will reflect his Socialist and anticolonial militancy; his verse will employ the repetitive, circular pattern of African dance and song, emphasizing staccato rhythms and duplicating and repeating sounds.

Lawrence George Durrell. English poet and novelist; he will generally write in an ornate, lyrical, and sensual style; his extensive travels will lend considerably to his fiction, which will contain images, themes, and settings from the Middle East.

Nikos Gatsos (d. 1985). Greek poet; his work will combine surrealism with folk song and will speak of the past, yet will not be overly nostalgic.

Eugene Ionesco. Romanian-born French playwright, essayist, and writer of fiction; the thematic context and techniques of his plays will connect him to the Theater of the Absurd; he will create darkly comic portraits of the human condition by exploring such themes as alienation, the impossibility of true communication, and the destructive forces of modern social pressures.

John Robin Jenkins. Scottish writer of fiction; he will gain recognition for novels that examine the moral, religious, and social conflicts within his native land; he will combine realistic details with fantastical and symbolic characterization, exploring the inherent humor and irony of the human condition.

Abbe Alexis Kagame. Rwanda poet and historian; a number of his works will focus upon the Christianization of Rwanda; he will also explore the history, culture, and literature of his people.

Qiyamuddin Khadim. Afghan poet; his work will resound with patriotism and religious feeling; he will praise learning and science, declaring that literature must seek "new" subjects.

Najib Mahfuz. Egyptian writer of fiction and drama; he will become recognized as the leading literary figure of modern Egypt; in his novels, he will create psychological portraits of characters whose personal struggles reflect the social, political, and cultural turmoil within his native land; he will receive the Nobel Prize for literature in 1988.

Saadat Hasan Manto (d. 1955). Indian (Urdu) playwright and essayist; his work will focus upon the hypocrisy of the Indian middle class, particularly its loose sexual morality; he will select characters from the urban underworld, never romanticizing them.

Mary Therese McCarthy (d. 1989). American essayist and writer of fiction and narrative; her literary reputation will rest on her abilities as a journalist and narrative writer, and she will compose compassionate commentaries upon social history; she will often attack the cultured and intellectual ranks of society for their ignorance.

Mirsaid Mirshakar. Iranian (Tajik) poet and playwright; he will compose his work in simple language and on subjects appealing to his Tajik readers; he will include dialogue in his poetry, especially writing in praise of the heroism of the Soviet peoples.

Istvan Orkeny. Hungarian playwright; his major literary efforts will date from the 1960s and 1970s, the period of Hungarian liberalization; his plays will take place in grotesque environments, reflecting a generally dark view of reality.

William Sansom (d. 1976). English writer of fiction and travel narrative; his short stories will originate from his experiences with the National Fire Service in London during World War II; London, Germany, Scandinavia, and the Mediterranean will comprise the principal settings for his fiction and travelogues.

Siddhicaran Srestha. Nepali poet; the first Nepali to attempt poetic realism, he will write in simple and colloquial language; he will spend five years in jail for the revolutionary ideals contained in his verse.

Erwin Strithmatter. East German writer of fiction; his characters will tend to be single dimensional, inflated somewhat by the writer's own pretensions to intellectualism; his prose will generally be of a "homespun" quality, appreciated by readers of the early post-World War II period.

Barbara Wertheim Tuchman (d. 1989). American historian; she will achieve recognition for the literary quality of her historical narratives devoted to World War I, World War II, and the Renaissance; she will receive the Pulitzer Prize for history in 1962 and 1971.

Tugelbay Sydykbekov. Kirghiz (SSR) poet and novellist; his work will concentrate upon the collectivization of Kirghiz agriculture upon farmers and their work.

Mu. Varataracan. Indian (Tamil) literary scholar, playwright, and writer of fiction; his works will generally be set in Madras, providing fascinating glimpses of life in that city.

Vu-trong-Phung (d. 1939). Vietnamese translator, playwright, and writer of fiction; his fiction will emphasize the tragic aspects of life and will underscore the influence of Freudian ideas upon his thinking.

Patrick White. London-born Australian novelist; his fiction will be written in a hypnotically descriptive style and its themes will concentrate on the sufferings of extraordinary people; in 1973, he will receive the Nobel Prize for literature.

Terence de Vere White. Irish writer of fiction and biography; his novels will satirize the conventions of the Irish gentility, combining social and political commentary with sophisticated humor; he will write comedies of manners that will explore the decline of the Protestant aristocracy within Ireland.

DEATHS

Joseph Furphy (b. 1843). Australian writer of fiction, poetry, and nonfiction; his fiction expresses nationalistic sentiments, socialist ideals, and a profound understanding of life in the Australian bush during the late nineteenth century; he tended to reject romantic conventions of fiction and instead composed realistic and humorous accounts of provincial life; he dies in Western Australia after suffering a cerebral hemorrhage.

Johan August Strindberg (b. 1849). Swedish playwright, essayist, poet, and writer of fiction; he made a significant contribution to the literary language of Sweden and was an influential innovator in dramatic and literary forms; the most characteristic of his more than seventy plays are naturalistic free verse dramas revealing his derogatory view of women, adoption of Swedenborgian mysticism, and experimental and expressionistic techniques.

PUBLICATIONS

Arnold Bennett, *The Matador of the Five Towns*—a collection of short stories by the English writer of fiction; set in the now federated borough of Stoke-on-Trent: Tunstall, Burslem, Hanley, Stoke-on-Trent, and Longton; the fictional five towns become Turnhill, Bursely, Hanbridge, Knype, and Longshaw.

Paul Claudel, *L'Annonce Faite a Marie* (The Tidings Brought to Mary)—a poetic drama by the French poet and playwright; a revision of a piece written initially in 1892, then revised for the stage in 1948; the idea comes from an old German folk tale, in which a woman miraculously revives a dead child by feeding it from her breast; concerns two completely different sisters: the good one represents Christian charity, the other jealousy; in the end, the evil one murders her sister, but also brings her dead infant back to life; the piece essentially represents the physical-spiritual cycle of birth, death, and rebirth.

Tevfik Fikret, *Halukun Defteri* (Haluk's Notebook)—a collection of poems for children by the Turkish writer of verse; deeply patriotic in tone, the verses reflect the idea that the children will bring to fulfillment the humanistic dreams of their forefathers.

Maithilisaran Gupta, *Bharatbharati*—a long poem by the Indian (Hindi) writer of verse; the piece earned for him the title of National Poet ("rastrakavi").

Robinson Jeffers, *Flagons and Apples*—a volume of verse by the American poet, his first published collection; the pieces tend to be conventionally romantic, registering little or no response to the poetic movements of the first decade of the twentieth century.

Carl Gustav Jung, *The Theory of Psychoanalysis*—a prose tract by the Swedish psychiatrist, the result of his differences with Sigmund Freud; repudiates central Freudian doctrine of sexuality and interprets neurosis as a manifestation of current maladjustment, denying that it arises from infancy.

Su Man-shu, *Tuan-hung Ling-yen Chi* (The Lone Swan)—an autobiographical novel by the Chinese poet, translator, and writer of fiction; a young Japanese man becomes a monk to escape the pain of his existence; however, he experiences considerable difficulty severing his ties to material existence, particularly women; thus, romantic love conflicts with religious and social duty.

Alexandros Papadiamantis, *He Phonissa* (The Murderess)—a novel by the Greek writer of fiction, published in the year following his death; examines the issue of the subservient position of women in Greece; thus, a woman murders young girls in an attempt to save them from the harsh futures awaiting them as wives and mothers.

Giovanni Papini, *Un Uomo Finito* (A Man—Finished)—the autobiography of the Italian essayist, poet, and writer of fiction; a pessimistic and defeatist tome ("I am nothing because I tried to be everything!") describing the inward search for purpose on the part of a young intellectual.

Vahan Terian, *Banastegcut'yunner* (Verses)—a collection of lyrics by the Armenian poet; the poems are written in a "pure" language free from dialect and are noted for their musical quality; the volume raised Armenian lyric poetry to its highest level of achievement.

EVENTS

The Authors League of America founded for the protection of copyrighted material, as well as to advance the legal interests of writers.

Gerhart Hauptmann, German playwright, poet, and novelist, receives the Nobel Prize for literature.

James Loeb, American banker, provides funds for the publication at New York City of the Loeb Classic Library; English translations of Latin and Greek texts.

Poetry: A Magazine of Verse begins publication at Chicago; the poet Harriet Monroe is the founder and first editor; Amy Lowell,

Carl Sandburg, T. S. Eliot, Robert Frost, Vachel Lindsay, Hart Crane, and Ezra Pound are among the early and more noteworthy contributors.

The Poetry Society, London, establishes its journal, *Poetry Review,* as the successor to *Poetry Gazette.*

Sir Arthur Quiller-Couch, English essayist, scholar, and writer of fiction, edits *The Oxford Book of the Victorian Verse.*

1913

BIRTHS

Grigol Abashidze. Georgian (SSR) poet, journalist, and translator; the glorious moments of his country's past will inspire his meditative and nature poetry.

Raphael Ernest Grail Glikpo Armattoe (d. 1953). Ghanian (British Togoland) poet and historian, born in Germany; his poetry will describe the sufferings of Africans under colonial rule and will be readily appreciated by the audiences of the 1930s and 1940s; his verse will not be extremely passionate, but will instead be characterized by a prosaic tone.

Abdurrauf Benawa. Afghan poet, playwright, and historian; he will become one of the leading poets in the effort to modernize verse; he will experiment with new meters and free verse, while stressing the themes of love for country, the simplicity of the people, anger in the face of oppression, and the struggle against backwardness.

Albert Camus (d. 1960). Algerian-born French essayist, novelist, and playwright; he will become a writer of "the left," condemning Stalin's Russia and Franco's Spain and advancing "the politics of the possible"; he will ask human beings to accept the fact that they live in an absurd universe and that they have responsibilities for attaining "good faith."

Aime Fernand Cesaire. Martinique poet and playwright; he will abandon the writing of poetry in the "French mold" and concentrate upon issues on his own island: physical decay, poverty, hunger, and resignation; he will contribute significantly to what will become the "litterature negro-africaine."

William Robertson Davies. Canadian novelist, essayist, playwright, and writer of short fiction; his fiction will be densely plotted and well crafted; he will direct his satirical humor at Canadian provincialism, which he will perceive as a hindrance to the cultural development of his nation.

Gyorgy Faludy. Hungarian-born Canadian poet, biographer, translator, and novelist; he will produce free translations of Francois Villon and Heinrich Heine; his poems ranging from simple love pieces to vehement political attacks against the evils of capitalism, totalitarianism, and imperialism, will contain sensual imagery, irony, metaphor, and satire; his noted autobiography will record persecution under both Nazi and Communist regimes.

Gertrud Fussenegger. German writer of fiction; she will produce a steady stream of short fiction between 1936 and 1986, much of which will be translated into more than ten languages; she will examine the various facets of human existence, demonstrating a keen sensitivity to the complexities of human nature.

Robert Earl Hayden (d. 1980). American poet; he will experiment with free verse forms and inject into his poetry material from the black experience.

Stefan Heym (originally Hellmuth Flieg). East German writer of fiction and poetry; he will write anti-Nazi war novels during the 1940s and early 1950s; his later fiction will comment upon modern political circumstances in Soviet bloc nations; he will receive, in 1959, the German Democratic Republic National Prize, yet his written work will be considered too controversial for publication in East Germany.

William Inge (d. 1973). American playwright; he will concentrate his drama upon Midwestern people and places, relying upon such common but successful devices as bringing strangers together to confront a common problem; in general, he will produce "well-made" and realistic drama.

George Benson Johnston. Canadian poet and translator; he will write "serio-comic" verse, lightly controversial in tone and restrained in style; he will employ conventional poetic structures, particularly variations upon traditional rhyme schemes and stanzaic forms; he will also rely on rhythmic patterns derived from Anglo-Saxon and Norse literatures; his work will emphasize simplicity, social consciousness, and morality.

Kersti Merilaas (d. 1986). Estonian poet; she will begin to publish her work shortly after the death of Josef Stalin, and thus her verse will evidence a combination of boldness and subservience; her later works will express the latent nationalism of all Estonians; she will also write several narratives and at least two plays.

Sripad Narayan Pendse. Indian (Marathi) novelist; he will become the leading Marathi novelist of the post-World War II era; his own Konkan region of Maharashtra will provide the inspiration for his work.

Jean-Jacques Rabemanajara. Malagasy poet and playwright; his work will reflect his patriotism and celebrate the songs and scenery of his own land; he will compose in the grand style of the older French poets (the Romantics and the Parnassians), but he will also rely on popular ballad forms from his own land.

Victor Stafford Reid. Jamaican novelist, playwright, and short story writer; his prose style will take advantage of Jamaican cadences, and his works will be characterized by logical structure and a carefully conceived symbolism; he will discuss the plight of "children" being dragged into battle by older and supposedly wiser adults.

Delmore Schwartz (d. 1966). American poet and critic; he will combine the tradition of the Brooklyn, New York, Jew with the philosophy of the learned academy, his Marxist political inclinations with his poetic imagination; his work will reveal the mind of the philosopher attempting to observe life and to discover an outlet for his Jewish consciousness.

Karl Jay Shapiro. American poet, novelist, and critic; his poems will speak out sharply against war and injustice; his criticism will vigorously attack the excessive intellectualism of the modernist movement; he will receive the Pulitzer Prize for poetry in 1945.

Irwin Shaw (d. 1984). American playwright and writer of fiction; he will tend to dramatize, in both his novels and plays, sensitive conflicts between pairs and small groups of characters; his work will also reflect his deep social conscience.

Ronald Stuart Thomas. Welsh poet and essayist; he will be considered one of the most important Welsh poets writing in English; his work will evidence an attention to detail and an unsentimental approach to the Welsh people and landscape; his poetic themes will relate to the nationalism of his land and to his personal search for modern empirical proof of the existence of God; thus, he will rely upon religious allusions and references to his calling as a priest of the Anglican Church.

Igor Torkar (pseudonym of Boris Fakin.) Yugoslavian (Slovene) novelist; his work will generally focus upon his activities in the pre-World War II Communist Party, resistance against the Nazis during the war, and trials during the period of the establishment of Yugoslavian communism; he will gain a literary reputation for his powerful descriptions and for his ability to integrate dialogue and narrative.

Sandor Weores. Hungarian poet; he will be recognized for his versatility and his verses will range from philosophical poems to nursery rhymes and folk songs; he will illustrate his poems with his own drawings; his longer pieces will reveal him to be on the side of the environment against the "industrial megalomania" of the twentieth century.

Angus Frank Johnstone Wilson. English writer of fiction; his fiction will reveal his brilliant satiric wit, keen social observations and attraction for the strange and the farcical; his work will depict a society corrupt in both its public and private aspects.

DEATHS

Ambrose Gwinett Bierce (b. 1842). American short story writer and satirist; his work is marked by satire, crisp and precise language, and a well-developed sense of humor; he disappears while in Mexico.

Gaston Fernando Deligne (b. 1861). Dominican Republic poet and novelist; his verse expressed his patriotism and nationalism; his interest in character, combined with his extreme sensitivity, led him to develop a type of psychological poetry; he contracts leprosy and dies by suicide.

Edward Dowden (b. 1843). English scholar, literary critic, and biographer; he became professor of English literature at Trinity College, Dublin, and published critical tracts on Shakespeare; he also edited plays from the seventeenth and eighteenth centuries and wrote biographies of Percy Bysshe Shelley, Robert Southey, Robert Browning, and Michel Montaigne.

Uri Nissan Gnessin (b. 1879). Russian-born Jewish writer of short fiction; his work abounds with melancholy themes and characters, most of whom are children of the "twilight" on the edge between life and death.

Antoine Louis Camille Lemonnier (b. 1844). Belgian writer of fiction; his novels and short stories celebrate the spirit of the Belgian people and the beauty of their homeland; realistically sensuous in the manner of the noted Flemish painter, his literary style clearly reveals his interest in the accurate depiction of objects and the communication of physical impressions.

Gabdulla Tukay (b. 1886). Turkish (Tatar) poet; his early poetry evidences the influences of classical Turkish verse; later, he will pattern his work after Russian and European poets, principally Aleksander Pushkin, Mikhail Lermontov, and Lord Byron.

PUBLICATIONS

Willa Cather, *O Pioneers!*—a novel by the American writer of fiction; a chronicle of love and passion in the midst of a rugged environment, the unconquered American West; the principal characters embody honorable ideals: the will to tame the American land for the future and the drive for life in the face of harsh nature.

Joseph Conrad, *Chance*—a novel by the Polish-born English writer of fiction, his first popular success; concerns the lonely daughter of a disreputable financier; the writer combines a nautical background with the theme of romantic love; the one fictional piece in which he dwells upon female interests.

Robert Frost, *A Boy's Will*—a collection of verse by the American poet, written during a stay in England; focuses upon New England and appears remarkably original for a first book.

John Galsworthy, *The Fugitive*—a dramatic piece by the English novelist and playwright; a clergyman's daughter, bored by an unhappy marriage, leaves her husband and attempts to earn her own way in the world; she lives with a poor artist, resorts to prostitution, and finally takes her own life.

D. H. Lawrence, *Sons and Lovers*—an autobiographical novel by the English writer of fiction and poetry; concerns the relationship between a miner and his wife, his intellectual superior; the marriage erupts into a violent struggle, with the wife turning her attention to her children and attempting to keep the family respectable; her two sons both become ill and one dies; in the end, she develops cancer and her remaining son and his sister poi-

son her to end her suffering; one of the earliest English novels set against a truly
working-class background.

**Vachel Lindsay, *General William Booth Enters
into Heaven and Other Poems*—**the first published collection by the American poet; the
writer introduces to the nation what will become known as his "apocalyptic verse."

Thomas Mann, *Der Tod in Venedig* (Death in
Venice)—a novel by the German writer of fiction and essayist; depicts a protagonist whose
orderly life is transformed by disease and repressed passion; the forces of perverse beauty
function freely and powerfully in this short
piece, as the novelist explains in the work how
creativity affects the writer.

EVENTS

Robert Bridges named Poet Laureate of England, succeeding Alfred Austin; until 1930.

The New Statesman, a weekly journal of poli-
tics, arts, and letters, begins publication at
London as an organ of the socialist Fabian
Society; George Bernard Shaw, Virginia
Woolf, and J. B. Priestley are among the early
contributors.

John Singer Sargent, American painter, completes his portrait of Henry James.

The Society for Pure English founded at Oxford, England; Robert Bridges, the poet and
critic, among its major sponsors; it published,
between 1919 and 1966, sixty-six prose tracts
relative to questions on grammar, pronunciation, etymology, and vocabulary.

Rabindranath Thakur, Indian (Bengali) poet,
becomes the first Asian writer of verse to be
awarded the Nobel Prize for literature.

1914

BIRTHS

Khvaja Ahmad Abbas. Indian (Urdu) writer of
fiction; he will begin writing in 1937, producing novels and short stories based upon the
Indian middle and working classes; he will express his political and social views and portray
the love experiences and frustrations of the
younger generation.

Aziz Ahmad. Indian (Urdu) novelist, critic, and
translator; his well-crafted novels will discuss
hitherto forbidden subjects concerning personal relationships and politics.

Tsunao Aida. Japanese poet; he will become associated with several Tokyo publishing
houses; his verse collection *A Lagoon* will earn
the first Kotaro Takamura Poetry prize.

John Berryman (d. 1972). American poet; he
will earn the epithet of "the confessional poet
par excellence"; thus, his poetry will reflect his
own problems, and will tend to be obscure
and private.

William Seward Burroughs. American-born
writer of fiction and prose narrative; he will
be recognized for his profound social commentary and will develop an uncompromising
vision of forms of control in a modern totalitarian state.

Krishan Chandar. Indian (Urdu) writer of fiction; he will concern himself with patriarchal
village life, but he will also recognize the evils
of Indian society and enter into the battle for
democracy against fascism; in addition he will
focus upon the hardships of life among the
lower strata of Indian society.

Julio Cortazar (d. 1984). Belgian-born Argentine writer of fiction; he will become an exponent of surrealism, often depicting life as a
maze and expressing his contempt for philosophical abstraction; he will assume residence
in France.

Marguerite Duras (b. Marguerite Donnadieu).
French writer of fiction, drama, and fiction,
she will depict desire as a force more powerful than death and the effect of time upon
memory and love; she will also portray the
acute sense of isolation that results from longing and loneliness.

Ralph Waldo Ellison. American writer of fiction and prose narrative; he will concern
himself with the struggles of black people in a
hostile society.

Randall Jarrell (d. 1965). American poet,
critic, and writer of fiction; the subjects
and themes of his verse will concern humankind's doomed quest for decency and goodness; he will write about childhood and
innocence and will also compose poetry,
which will be praised for its combination of
irony and compassion.

Orhan Veli Kanik (d. 1950). Turkish poet; he
will reject traditional forms and literary
cliches in his verse and will focus upon the

everyday lives of common people, generally conveying his sentiments in colloquial language.

Orhan Kemal (pseudonym of Mehmet Rasit Kemali Ogutcu; d. 1970). Turkish poet and writer of fiction; his prose will be characterized by accuracy and an ease of expression, which convinces the reader that he has experienced everything he writes about; his characterizations will truthfully recreate manners and speech.

Cannanpuza Krsna Pilla (d. 1948). Indian (Malayalam) poet; he will adopt the romanticism of earlier generations, at the same time introducing a new note of personal frankness into his poems; he will write despairing love lyrics, as well as pieces advocating the social revolution of his day.

Paul Lomami-Tshibamba. Congolese novelist and journalist; his journalistic essays will call for independence for the Belgian Congo; he will write and publish the first novel in French by a Congolese (1948).

Bernard Malamud (d. 1986). American writer of fiction; he will combine humor with compassion in depicting the suffering of protagonists, often Jewish, who struggle through the hardships of modern existence; he will become a leading American author and be praised for his humanistic concerns.

Foteh Niyozi. Iranian (Tajik) poet and writer of fiction; his fiction will focus upon themes relative to World War II; he will emphasize the roles played by Tajik soldiers, noting the friendships among soldiers of all nationalities in the Soviet Army; he will also explore, in a more general sense, the dangers of deeply rooted prejudices and superstitions.

Octavio Paz. Mexican poet, essayist, and playwright; he will seek, in his writing, to reconcile divisive and opposing forces within humanity; thus, he will emphasize that language and love can provide the means for attaining unity; he will rely upon the history, myths, and landscape of Mexico and his works will display his interest in surrealism, existentialism, and romanticism.

Oktay Rifat. Turkish poet; his mature poetry will become somewhat abstract, based upon verbal association; he will create unusual combinations of words, declaring them to be viable approaches to reality.

Yoshiko Shibaki. Japanese writer of fiction; she will produce a steady stream of novels and short stories, beginning in 1946; her work will concentrate upon the historical and cultural traditions of her nation, demonstrating how art can and must be preserved in a technologically oriented society; her fictional style will be direct and easily understood.

Hovhannes Shiraz. Soviet Armenian poet; his lyrics will be characterized by their spontaneity and sincerity; his style will be simple, enhanced by folk and colloquial elements; he will become one of the most popular poets in Armenia.

Takazi Sivasankara Pilla. Indian (Malayalam) novelist and writer of short fiction; he will be committed to social reform, and his work will reveal the influence of the French realist school; the majority of his pieces will take place within the economically depressed sections of Kerala society, particularly focusing on poor coastal fishermen.

William Edgar Stafford. American poet; regarded as the last voice of American transcendentalism; his poems will concern the capacity of the imagination to derive meaning and awe from the world; he will also regard the natural world as a potential model for human behavior.

Thein Pe Myint. Burmese writer of fiction; his short stories and novels will reflect his close involvement with political and social issues; he will choose to shock, persuade, and convince, rather than simply to entertain.

Dylan Thomas (d. 1953). Welsh poet; he will write extremely vital verse, powerful in language and imagery, but with a tendency toward the obscure; he will significantly influence the younger poets of his generation, while at the same time arouse controversy among literary critics.

DEATHS

Egzi'abekar Gabra (b. 1860?) Ethiopian (Amharic) poet; considered possibly the first poet to write in the tradition of older court poetry, satirizing leading courtiers; he dies in relative obscurity.

Paul Heyse (b. 1830). German novelist and playwright; he produced 120 novellas, fifty plays, and six novels, most of them extremely realistic; he received the Nobel Prize for literature in 1910.

Frederic Mistral (b. 1830). French Provencal poet; he led the Felibrige movement to promote Provencal as a literary language, and he became the leading writer of verse in that language; in 1904, he shared the Nobel Prize for literature with Jose Echegaray of Spain.

Christian Morgenstern (b. 1876). German poet and translator; he came under the influence of Friedrich Wilhelm Nietzsche and Rudolph Steiner and believed that philosophical poetry should be his major contribution to literature; he contracted consumption in his early teens and dies prematurely from it.

Bertha Suttner (b. 1843). Austrian novelist; known principally for her strong sense of pacifism, she wrote fiction that had a significant social impact; she became, in 1905, the first woman to receive the Nobel Prize for peace.

Georg Trakl (b. 1887). Austrian poet; the gloom of his tragic and short life pervades his poetry, which develops themes of suicide, incest, and schizophrenia; interestingly enough, that sense of gloom arises from the poet's consciousness of joy, and thus his poetry tends to be ambiguous; he dies from an overdose of cocaine.

PUBLICATIONS

Clive Bell, *Art*—a prose tract by the English critic of art and literature; in this essay, he advances the theory that form, independent of subject, should determine the essential quality of a work of art.

Christopher John Brennan, *Poems 1913*—a collection by the Australian poet, critic, and philosopher; a group of highly symbolic and philosophical pieces, heavily influenced by Alfred, Lord Tennyson, Algernon Charles Swinburne, and Coventry Patmore; the poems contain unorthodox syntax and represent a variety of styles.

Dino Campana, *Canti Orfici* (Orphic Songs)—a collection of lyrics by the Italian poet, personal reflections on the writer's spiritual confusion; contains pieces characterized by repetition, broken syntax, and irregular punctuation—all qualities of Futurist poetry.

Robert Frost, *North of Boston*—a verse collection by the American poet; all of the pieces concern New England themes; the first appearance of the poet's long dramatic monologues, as in "The Mountain."

Ayodhyasimh Upadhyay Hariaudh, *Priyapravas* (The Beloved's Exile)—a poem by the Indian (Hindi) writer of fiction and poetry; the first modern Hindi epic poem, composed in Sanskrit meters; the writer points out that the national cause must transcend personal troubles, and thus his central figure is a brave, self-sacrificing woman.

Muhammad Husayn Haykal, *Zaynab*—a novel by the Egyptian writer of fiction and criticism; one of the earliest novels to appear in modern Arabic, written during the novelist's residence as a law student in Paris; a highly idealized and romantic picture of life in the Egyptian countryside, yet containing serious sociological comment and criticism.

James Joyce, *Dubliners*—a volume of short stories by the Irish writer of fiction; the pieces describe the Ireland from which the writer had chosen to exile himself; but nonetheless display his love for the city, though he approaches it with an obvious note of irony; the stories reflect an awareness that life consists of moments of continuous sin, to be redeemed by equally continuous moments of joy and blessedness.

Vachel Lindsay, *The Congo and Other Poems*—a verse collection by the American poet; the title piece, especially, establishes the writer's reputation as the herald of the "new poetry": it breaks with the genteel, derivative verse that dominated the nation's poetry, yet continues the heritage of Walt Whitman; the pieces reverberate with music and almost uncontrollable energy.

Elmer Rice, *On Trial*—a dramatic piece by the American playwright, his first produced play; contains a flashback technique and a "jackknife" set, in which the courtroom walls move to reveal scenes from the past, thus explaining the defendant's confession.

Abdul-halim Sharar, *Guzashta Lakhanau* (Past Lucknow)—a historical study by the Indian (Urdu) journalist, novelist, and popular historian; a series of articles comprising a picture of the history and social and cultural life of old Lucknow (in northern India); to 1916.

William Butler Yeats, *Responsibilities, Poems and a Play*—a collection by the Irish poet, playwright, and essayist; the poems reflect his pleasure at the patronage of the courts of the Italian Renaissance, which he compares with the attitude of Ireland's new rich; however, in weighing the new politicians against the old heroes, he finds the former sadly lacking; includes "The Fisherman," "A Coat," "The People," and "The Cold Heaven."

EVENTS

The Egoist (originally *The New Freewoman*) begins publication at London; fortnightly, then monthly, it publishes articles on modern poetry and the arts; Ezra Pound, Richard Aldington, and T. S. Eliot lend their influence and support; James Joyce publishes *Portrait of the Artist As a Young Man* there in 1914-15; until 1919.

Augustus Edwin John, English painter and etcher, completes his painting of the Irish playwright and critic George Bernard Shaw.

The Little Review begins publication at Chicago; it proposes to devote its pages to art; James Joyce, Ezra Pound, Henry James, T.S. Eliot, William Butler Yeats, Ford Madox Ford, Wallace Stevens, Amy Lowell, Sherwood Anderson, and Carl Sandburg are among its major contributors; until 1929.

The New Orleans Picayune (1837) combines with the New Orleans *Times Democrat* to become the *New Orleans Times-Picayune,* one of the most significant daily newspapers in the United States.

The New Republic begins publication at New York City; intended as a weekly journal of opinion and liberal views; Walter Lippmann, Malcolm Cowley, and Joyce Carol Oates are among its editorial contributors.

1915

BIRTHS

Lars Sven Ahlin. Swedish novelist; he will become identified with the proletarian writers of his nation, particularly those who endured the hardships of unemployment during the 1930s; he will be influenced by Fedor Dostoevski, concerning himself with themes arising from the religious impulses of modern men and women.

Rajindar Singh Bedi. Indian (Urdu) writer of fiction and drama; his fiction will achieve recognition and popular acceptance during the late 1930s and 1940s; he will publish three volumes of short stories and two collections of plays; in 1966 he will receive the Sahitya Akademi award for literature.

Rene Belance. Haitian poet; his verse will approach surrealism, in part because of its complex associational qualities; he will reside in the United States in his capacity as a professor of writing at Brown University.

Saul Bellow. Canadian-born American writer of fiction; his novels will be moral in tone, reflecting his concern for the state of the individual in an indifferent society; he will receive the Nobel Prize for literature in 1976.

A. Emile Disengomoko (d. 1965). Congolese novelist, poet, and essayist; his fiction will concern itself with the conflicts arising from the competing demands of acquired Christian and traditional values.

Takla Hawaryat Germacaw. Ethiopian novelist and playwright; his fiction will evidence the traditional moralistic tones of his native Amharic and contain highly descriptive passages of local scenery, with emphasis upon improvements in agriculture; he will be the first Amharic writer to have his work translated into Russian and Chinese.

Kypros Hrysanthis. Greek-Cypriot poet and essayist; between 1942 and 1988, he will publish twenty-nine poetry collections, fourteen volumes of fiction, seven volumes of verse translation, six nonfiction prose monographs, twenty-five plays, and twenty-two books for children.

Mikael Kabbada. Ethiopian playwright and poet; his poems will combine the influences of Western literature and native folk tales; his most important works will be his dramas, which will be austere, philosophical treatments of moral and ethical themes resembling the efforts of Jean Racine and Pedro Calderon.

Alfred Kazin. American critic; his commentary will focus upon American literature; he will call for the application of truly modern critical principles, unfettered by critical prejudices of the past.

P. C. Kuttikkrsnan. Indian (Malayalam) writer of fiction; his novels will focus upon the lives of the middle-class people of Malabar, especially the Muslims of that region; he will attempt to construct single novels from separate but interrelated stories of Malabar life during the first half of the twentieth century.

Roland Glyn Mathias. Welsh poet, essayist, and writer of fiction; his verse will reflect the history and geography of Wales, displaying his concern for preserving the country's identity; he will comment upon the dilemma of the poet who writes in the English language, but who describes his personal experiences and feelings as a Welshman; he will rely upon alliteration, complex syntax, and concrete imagery.

Arthur Miller. American playwright; he will concentrate on political and moral issues, incorporating as a principal theme the issue of guilt and passing judgment; he will receive the Pulitzer Prize for drama in 1949.

Eric M. Roach (d. 1974). Tobago poet, playwright, and essayist; his verse will convey a claustrophobic feeling of having been trapped on his native island; he will exaggerate the West Indian's tragic sense of displacement.

Jean Stafford (d. 1979). American writer of fiction; she will be noted for penetrating the private worlds of her characters without shattering their original images.

Leo Vroman. Dutch-born writer of fiction, poetry, and drama; he will write both in his native language and English; his themes will include his homesickness and affection for his family, his thoughts about science, his awareness of death, his amusements over the ironies of life, and his interest in such causes as human rights and world peace; he will settle in the United States in 1946.

Herman Wouk. American novelist; he will achieve success with his novels devoted to World War II, ranging from naval operations in the Pacific to the Holocaust.

DEATHS

Rupert Chawner Brooke (b. 1887). English poet; his wit, attractiveness, romantic air, and tragic death during World War I transformed his memory into a literary legend; his poems (1911, 1914) generally display a highly romantic view of the world, and of war; he will die of blood poisoning on Scyros while on his way to the Dardanelles campaign.

Tefvik Fikret (b. 1867). Turkish poet; he wrote verse attacking the Sultan, after which he welcomed with enthusiasm the Russian revolution of 1905 and the Young Turk Revolution of 1908, singing the praises of the new freedom and the renewed strength of the Turkish people; he relied upon free forms of classical Turkish and Arabic meters, introducing rhymes based upon the sounds of words.

Remy de Gourmont (b. 1858). French critic, poet, playwright, and writer of fiction; a renowned scholar and a man of letters, he became a leader of the French Symbolist school and one of the first critics to articulate clearly the principles of the Symbolist aesthetic; he suffered from lupus for several years and dies as the result of a stroke.

Isaac Leib Peretz (b. 1852?). Polish-born Yiddish writer of fiction, essayist, poet, and playwright; he received recognition for his short stories based upon Hasidic folklore; he combines traditional Jewish lore with the conventions of Western literature, thus transcending the artistic and linguistic limitations long associated with Yiddish letters.

Daniel Varuzhan (b. 1884). Armenian poet; inspiration for his lyrics came from the tragedy of minority life in Turkey, characterized by religious and political oppression; his verse combines faith in the ultimate unification of his people with bitter despair over their present existence and a hatred of violence.

Grigor Zohrap (b. 1861). Armenian writer of fiction, poetry, and critical essays; his work exposed the inhumanity of bourgeois society, underscoring the conflicts between the urban wealthy and the rural poor (their victims).

PUBLICATIONS

Theodore Dreiser, *The "Genius"*—a novel by the American writer of fiction; the principal character takes from society what he needs for his own satisfaction; an artist, he finds in sex the beauty that he requires for his art; thus, he feeds on women for inspiration.

Ford Madox Ford, *The Good Soldier: A Tale of Passion*—a novel by the English writer, considered his finest technical achievement and his most readable piece of fiction; an American narrator relates the history of a series of relationships that began ten years earlier, focusing on two couples who had met in a hotel.

Muhammad Iqbal, *Asar-e Khudi* (Secrets of the Self)—a long poem by the Indian writer of verse and philosopher; advocates a philosophy of activism to awaken the Muslims from their spiritual slumber.

D. H. Lawrence, *The Rainbow*—a novel by the English writer of fiction and poetry; relates the history of an established family on the Derbyshire-Nottingham border; the novelist allows his various characters to pursue their own inclination; upon publication the work was seized by the police and declared obscene, principally because of its language and frankness about sex.

Edgar Lee Masters, *Spoon River Anthology*— a poetry collection by the American versifier; 214 pieces (thirty new ones were added to the second edition of 1916), free verse epitaphs revealing the secret lives of small-town Americans.

W. Somerset Maugham, *Of Human Bondage*— an autobiographical novel by the English writer of fiction; the work describes the central character's lonely boyhood and his subsequent adventures, complicated by his club foot (a parallel to the novelist's stammer).

Vladimir Mayakovsky, *Oblako v Shtanakh* (A Cloud in Trousers)—a long poem by the Russian writer of verse, drama, and nonfiction; the piece exhibits the riotous form and language characteristic of the poet's work; it also features the first-person poet persona, the "megalomaniacal 'I' " that dominates most of his writings; thus, all action is interpreted from the perspective of the "beloved self," the social critic and prophet of the Revolution who chastises the bourgeoisie for their complacency and predicts the destruction of their world.

Gustav Meyrink, *Der Golem*—a novel by the Austrian writer of fiction and drama; considered a masterpiece of supernatural literature; concerns the gradual revelation of spiritual knowledge to the protagonist through a series of dreamlike visions; he encounters emissaries of a superior order of being; the work sells over 200,000 copies.

Katharine Susannah Prichard, *The Pioneers*—the first novel by the Fijian-born Australian writer of fiction and poetry; set in the bush country during the early nineteenth century, the work traces the paths of immigrants and ex-convicts who settled the region.

Virginia Woolf, *The Voyage Out*—the initial novel by the English writer of fiction and critic; indicative of the lyric intensity of her later works; describes the voyage to South America of a young English woman; concerns her engagement, struggle with, a fever, and eventual death.

EVENTS

Ina Donna Coolbrith, Illinois-born poet, appointed the first Poet Laureate of California; to 1928.

The Midland, a regional literary magazine, begins publication at Iowa City, Iowa; MacKinlay Kantor and Paul Engle are among its early contributors; until 1933.

Romain Rolland, French novelist, biographer, historian, critic, and playwright, receives the Nobel Prize for literature.

1916

BIRTHS

Antonio Buero Vallejo. Spanish playwright; he will contribute significantly to the revitalization of post-World War II Spanish theater; he will write serious and moralistic plays, frequently depicting characters consumed by despair and frustration; his tragedies will, however, affirm the redeeming qualities of hope.

John Ciardi (d. 1986). American poet and critic; his verse will belong to the 1940s, characterized by clear language and substance; he will gain an academic reputation with translations of the classics, principally Dante.

Bernard Binlin Dadie. Ivory Coast novelist, playwright, and poet; his verse will reverberate with his patriotism and devotion to his people; his novels and short stories will concern the day-to-day existence of the young Ivorian at home, as well as the young African coming to grips with his European education and environment.

Charles Edward Eaton. American poet; he will be influenced by Robert Frost and will set most of his poetry in New England, but, he will also look to Brazil, which he will term his "new South"; he will display an intense feeling for landscape as a background for human experience.

Ernst von Heerden. South African poet; he will produce fourteen volumes of verse, strong and secure in its diction; he will focus upon the joy of creation, at the same time recognizing the impossibility of absolute perfection; he will also concentrate on the theme of death.

Wolfgang Hildesheimer. German playwright, writer of fiction, and essayist; he will create drama in the tradition of the theater of the absurd, embracing the absurdist tendencies to emphasize the meaninglessness and futility of existence and to restructure, rather than imitate, reality.

Yoshie Hotta. Japanese writer of fiction; he will gain recognition for his focus upon the Japanese experience with the "bomb"; he will relate that tragedy to his nation's military invasion of China during World War II; thus, the American officer who drops the bomb can enter into a discussion with the Japanese officer who witnessed actions in China as ordered by superior officers.

Revaz Margiani. Georgian (SSR) poet; he will write meditative and nature lyrics in the tradition of folk poetry; he will also display a love of the mountains and their inhabitants.

Amrtlal Nagar. Indian (Hindi) novelist; his work will portray middle-class life in urban areas; he will evoke the atmosphere of his home city, Lucknow, particularly its narrow streets and traditional social activities.

Hubert Ogunde. Nigerian playwright; he will produce in excess of fifteen operatic plays, sketching the basic situations and actions, and allowing the actors to improvise; his works will exploit traditional biblical plays, with elements of the dance, the mask, and the song.

La. Sa. Ramamirtam. Indian (Tamil) writer of fiction; he will be influenced by James Joyce, Leo Tolstoi, and Ernest Hemingway; he will publish over one hundred pieces of fiction, most of which will probe deeply into the inner life of his middle-and lower-class heroes.

Samar Sen. Indian (Bengali) poet; he will write prose-poetry during a period when the form was very popular in Bengali literature; his verse will exhibit a Marxist philosophy; he ceased to write when he reached age thirty, claiming that poetry bored him.

Haldun Taner. Turkish writer of fiction and drama; his realistic fiction will be classical in form; he will provide a sensitive portrayal of human beings in their urban environments.

Peter Ulrich Weiss (d. 1982). German-born Swedish playwright, novelist, and essayist; he will become one of the most important and controversial dramatists of post-World War II Europe; his work will be informed by his life-long commitment to Marxism and his sense of displacement from society.

DEATHS

Sholom Aleichem (pseudonym of Sholom Rabinowitz; b. 1859). Jewish-Russian humorist; he principally wrote novels, short stories, and sketches; on the surface he mocks the lives and activities of Jewish people, but, in reality, he directed his satire against humanity in general; he wrote both in Hebrew and English, intending his themes to speak to all of the peoples of central and eastern Europe.

Ruben Dario (b. 1867). Nicaraguan poet; his first publication heralded the founding of the "modernismo" movement with its elegant form, exotic images, and subtle word music; he exercised considerable influence on Spanish language writers.

Jose Echegaray (b. 1832). Spanish playwright and mathematician; he wrote approximately seventy plays, ranging from romances to melodramatic problem pieces; he shared the 1904 Nobel Prize for literature with Frederic Mistral.

Simeon Samuel Frug (b. 1860). Russian poet; he wrote in three languages: Russian, Yiddish, and Hebrew; he became known, for a time, as the national Jewish poet in Russia; he expressed the sufferings of his people in verses that reflected his interest in folk themes.

Henry James (b. 1843). American-born novelist and critic; he became a British citizen in 1915; his major fiction contrasted the sophistication of Europeans with the naiveté of Americans; he became one of the most noted practitioners of the novel, recognized for his subtle characterization and complex prose style.

John (Jack) Griffith London (b. 1876). American writer of fiction and prose narrative; his romantic, realistic, and often brutal fiction originated from his own experiences as a sailor, gold-seeker, and war correspondent; his socialist views are reflected in his work; beset by financial problems and alcoholism, he commits suicide at age forty.

James Whitcomb Riley (b. 1849). American poet; he became known as the "Hoosier poet"; his verses are noted for their humor, pathos, and sentimentality.

Alan Seeger (b. 1888). American poet; he served in the French Foreign Legion during World War I and died in battle; he will be remembered for his poem "I have a rendezvous with death."

Henryk Sienkiewicz (b. 1846). Polish novelist and writer of short stories; he produced significant historical novels that focused upon Christianity and the fight for Polish independence; he received the Nobel Prize for literature in 1905.

Emile Verhaeren (b. 1855). Belgian poet and critic; he wrote in French and expressed his passion for social reform.

PUBLICATIONS

Henri Barbusse, *Le Feu* (Under Fire)—a novel by the French poet and novelist; the story of a doomed squad of men and their corporal during the perpetual winter in the trenches; the men appear as exploited creatures fighting a war that in no way can benefit them; an example of pacifist expressionism.

Vicente Blasco Ibanez, *Los Cuatro Jinetes del Apocalipsis* (The Four Horsemen of the Apocalypse)—a novel by the Spanish writer of fiction; depicts the horrors of World War I, but the writer takes pains to set his story against a pure Valencian background and to emphasize character conflicts.

Robert Bridges, *The Spirit of Man*—a highly successful anthology of poetry and prose edited by the English poet; especially important because it contains verse by Gerard Manley Hopkins (1844-1889) that had never before appeared in print.

Robert Frost, *Mountain Interval*—a collection of verse by the American poet; most of the pieces are brief meditations prompted by an object, a person, or an episode that seizes the poet's attention and compels his wonder; poems include "The Oven Bird," "An Old Man's Winter Night" and the oft-recited "Birches."

Robert Graves, *Over the Brazier*—the first volume of poems by the English writer of verse; appeared while he served at the front in World War I; published as a result of the encouragement and patronage of Sir Edward Howard Marsh (1872-1953), scholar and promoter of modern poetry.

James Joyce, *A Portrait of the Artist as a Young Man*—an autobiographical novel by the Irish writer of fiction; describes the development of the principal character from his early boyhood, through his adolescent crises of sex and faith, then through student days and a gradual recognition of his own destiny; he becomes poet, patriot, and unbeliever.

George Lyman Kittredge, *Shakespeare*—a critical essay on the English poet and playwright by the American scholar and Harvard professor of English; outlines his criteria for evaluating Shakespeare's poetry and drama.

George Moore, *The Brooke Kerith*—a novel by the Irish-born English novelist; relates the interwoven lives of Christ, St. Paul, and Joseph of Arimathea; in this piece, Christ survives the Cross.

Ezra Pound, *Lustra*—a verse collection by the American-born poet and essayist; the poet devotes more than twelve poems to a discussion of the function and purpose of his own poetic achievement.

Akutagawa Ryunosuke, "Rashomon"—a short story by the Japanese writer of fiction, poetry, and critical commentary; the work gained recognition in 1950 as an award-winning film; set in twelfth-century Kyoto amid the plague, violence and anarchy, the work describes the moral collapse of a man driven to assault and thievery by the horror he witnesses within society.

Carl Sandburg, *Chicago Poems*—the initial volume of verse by the American poet; proclaims the majesty of the poet's city in a completely American voice and from a completely American point of view; one commentator noted that the volume "hit genteel readers the way the butcher's maul hits the steer."

Alan Seeger, *Collected Poems*—published posthumously, the collection includes the American poet's most noted piece, "I have a rendezvous with death."

George Bernard Shaw, *Pygmalion*—a play by the Irish dramatist, one of his most popular, produced in 1913; a professor of phonetics, as part of a wager, helps a young cockney girl transform from a seller of flowers into the passable imitation of a duchess; focuses upon English speech and the class system; in 1957 the piece becomes a musical under the title *My Fair Lady*.

Edith Irene Sodergran, *Dikter*—a poetic collection by the Finnish-Swedish writer of verse; generally recognized as a response to the poet's failed love affair; confessional in tone and unique in expression of feminine longing; contains melancholy lyrics that express erotic disappointment or describe dreamlike landscapes; introduces modern poetic innovations into Finnish-Swedish literature.

EVENTS

Verner von Heidenstam, Swedish lyric poet, receives the Nobel Prize for literature.

The Seven Arts, a monthly magazine dedicated to free expression in the arts, begins publication at New York City; contributors include Van Wyck Brooks, Amy Lowell, Robert Frost, John Dos Passos, Vachel Lindsay, Theodore Dreiser, and H. L. Mencken; twelve issues, until 1917.

Theatre Arts, a quarterly, then monthly, journal of theater activity and criticism, begins publication at New York City; until 1964.

1917

BIRTHS

Louis Stanton Auchincloss. American novelist; he will develop and refine the American novel of manners; his occupation as a lawyer will prompt him to create a world where law, finance, and family intersect; he will display an interest in history and class.

Heinrich Theodor Boll (d. 1985). German writer of fiction, drama, and nonfiction; he will become the best-known novelist in West Germany and the literary conscience of his country; he will receive the Nobel Prize for literature in 1972.

Gwendolyn Brooks. American poet; she will record typical scenes of black American life and chronicle the ugliness and despair of the American city; her poems will gain recognition for their syntactic precision; she will receive the Pulitzer Prize for poetry in 1950, and later become recognized as the poet laureate of Illinois.

Anthony Burgess. English novelist; his talents as a musician, journalist, critic, and linguist will serve him well in the craft of fiction; he will concern himself with his nation's withdrawal as a major world power and influence; he will be highly regarded for his surreal, darkly comic novels, a number of them futuristic.

George Robert Acworth Conquest. English poet, historian, and critic; he will publish four major volumes of verse; in his prose, he will attack obscure and overly metaphorical poetry, advocating instead rational structure and comprehensible language.

Sumner Locke Elliott. Australian novelist and playwright; his fiction will focus upon human relationships; two of his plays will be pro-duced on Broadway, and he will write more than thirty plays for television.

Leslie Aaron Fiedler. American literary critic; he will become known for his Freudian literary analysis of the American novel; he will also write essays on American culture and intellect, as well as short stories and historical studies.

Nicodemus (Nick) Joaquin. Philippine poet, essayist, and journalist; he will write principally in English; his work will reveal his admiration for Spanish culture, as well as his native lyrical ability and mastery of language; the majority of his work will remain scattered throughout a host of periodicals.

Hans Bague Jassin. Indonesian essayist and critic; he will encourage younger critics and strive to promote a development of Indonesian literary history; he will write essays on various aspects of Indonesian literature, studies of individual writers, historical surveys, and introductions to anthologies.

al-Bashir Khraief. Tunisian writer of fiction; he will introduce colloquial Arabic to Tunisian literature, depicting the petty bourgeoisie of Tunis reacting to modernism.

Robert Traill Spence Lowell, Jr. (d. 1977). American poet; he will become one of the most important writers of American verse during the post-World War II era; his lines will reverberate with force and urgency, responding to the spiritual corruptions of his age; he will remain, in his life and in his work, rooted to the Puritan traditions of his family and his past; he will both accept and revolt against those traditions.

Djanetjo Ma Ma Lei. Burmese writer of fiction; her fiction will reflect her progressive political views and reveal her to be an astute observer of human nature; she will depict gifted, independently minded women confronting the problems of life.

James Phillip McAuley (d. 1976). Australian poet and critic; he will achieve clarity and precision with classical poetic forms; he will be compared with John Dryden, Alexander Pope, and Jonathan Swift for his emphasis on the importance of the intellect in ordering poetic inspiration; he will write satirical lyrics and meditative verse.

Carson Smith McCullers (d. 1967). American writer of fiction; she will be concerned with what has become known as "the dilemma of the self in history"; her characters will experience an estrangement that cannot be defined in terms of simple alienation; for her and her characters, self-identity will be almost impossible to achieve.

Nam-Cao (originally Tran-huu-Tri; d. 1951). Vietnamese writer of fiction; his pre-1945 fiction will be censored by the French; as a realistic writer, he will describe lower middle-class intellectuals living in poverty; he will also present a critical, pessimistic view of Vietnamese society under French rule.

Toshio Shimao. Japanese writer of fiction; his stories will be highly autobiographical; thus, he will depict his internal reality in a series of dreamy associations, narrate his wartime experiences as a member of a suicide torpedo boat crew, and describe his life with his mentally deranged wife.

Xuan-Dieu. Vietnamese poet; he will play a significant role in the formation of modern Vietnamese poetry; he will also write short fiction, essays, and periodical reviews.

DEATHS

Mirza Sadeq Khan Amiri (b. 1860). Persian poet and journalist; he became a leading figure in the Iranian national revival; his verse appeared in newspapers and magazines, remaining uncollected until 1933.

Leon Bloy (b. 1846). French novelist, short story writer, diarist, and essayist; he became a key figure in the Catholic Literary Revival, a reaction to the trend toward secularism in nineteenth-century French and English literature; his own religious faith tended to be both devout and obsessive, and thus he sensed a need to write "only for God"; he gained recognition as a creator of the Catholic novel.

Francis Ledwidge (b. 1887). Irish poet; a talented traditional poet who arose from the Irish peasantry, he gained a reputation as the Robert Burns of Ireland; he wrote pastoral romantic verse inspired by his experiences as a farm laborer and road worker in County Meath; his style was simple and spontaneous, with original phrasing; he dies from a shell explosion during the third battle of Ypres.

Jose Enrique Rodo (b. 1872). Uruguayan essayist and philosopher; he will support the "modernismo" movement (elegant form, exotic imagery, subtle word music); he based his philosophy and political views on the notion that Spanish America must retain its spiritual values and not allow itself to become soiled by the materialism of the United States.

Mendele Moicher Seforim (pseudonym of Sholem Jacob Abramovitch; b. 1836). Russian writer of fiction; he wrote in Yiddish and Hebrew, gaining recognition as the "grandfather" of both literatures; his fiction displays his belief in the viability of Jewish life in Russia and realities of Jewish life, combining satire with actuality.

PUBLICATIONS

James Matthew Barrie, *Dear Brutus*—a play by the Scottish-born dramatist and writer of fiction; the playwright permits his characters to see what their lives would be like should they be permitted "a second chance"; only one person, an artist, discovers an essential change: that melancholy figure finds inspiration in his make-believe life when he has a daughter.

Jean de Bosschere, *La Porte Fermee* (The Closed Door)—a verse collection by the Belgian poet, essayist, and writer of fiction; the volume is often cited as an influence on the poetry of T. S. Eliot; contains a number of mystical elements, but also reveals the reality behind appearances and the poet's sensitivity to the essential qualities of characters, objects, and situations.

T. S. Eliot, *Prufrock and Other Observations*—the first published volume of verse by the American-born poet and critic; the title piece, "The Love Song of J. Alfred Prufrock," written during the poet's undergraduate years at Harvard, is a highly technical poem evidencing the poet's ability to control tone and to juxtapose colloquial and literary language; a dramatic monologue in which the speaker builds a mood of social futility and inadequacy.

Muhammad Iqbal, *Rumuz-e Bekhudi* (Mysteries of Selfishness)—a traditional Persian poem by the Pakistani romantic poet and philosopher; the thesis focuses upon determining the duties of the individual in the community.

Edna St. Vincent Millay, *Renascence and Other Poems*—a collection by the American poet; the pieces reveal her innocence and freshness in the face of nature, but also demonstrate the extent of her debt to the nineteenth-century English Romantic poets.

Edwin Arlington Robinson, *Merlin*—a dramatic narrative in blank verse by the American poet; concerns the story of the love of Merlin and Vivian and is based upon the theme that even the most sagacious can be misled by their passions; the strength of the piece lies in the title character's inner struggle between the life of the senses and the intellect.

George Bernard Shaw, *Heartbreak House*—a play by the Irish dramatist and critic; written between 1913 and 1916, produced in 1921; the piece unfolds in a room resembling the interior of an antiquated ship and features an old seafarer; complications stem from the loves and marriages of the old man's two daughters; the work abounds in symbolic overtones and allusions.

Miguel Unamuno, *Abel Sanchez*—a novel by the Spanish (Basque) writer of fiction and poetry; the fullest expression of his various attempts at the Cain and Abel theme; the principal character proves to be morally superior to Abel Sanchez, and his lifelong struggle to control his hate of Abel provides him with a sense of tragic grandeur.

Alec Waugh, *The Loom of Youth*—the first novel by the English writer of fiction and travel narratives; gained notoriety through the writer's colorful suggestions of the presence of homosexual activity in English public schools.

William Butler Yeats, "The Wild Swans at Coole"—a poem by the Irish writer of verse, drama, and nonfiction; concerns the poet's second (and equally vain) attempt to marry Maud Gonne.

EVENTS

The Cambridge History of American Literature, volume one, appears; accompanied by an extensive bibliography covering all literary periods; four volumes, to 1921.

Karl Adolf Gjellerup and Henrik Pontoppidan, Danish novelists, share the Nobel Prize for literature.

Hugo von Hoffmannsthal, Richard Strauss, and Max Reinhart initiate the Salzburg (Austria) Festival; features both music and drama.

Jean Jules Jusserand, former French ambassador to the United States, receives the first Pulitzer Prize in history for his *With Americans of Past and Present Days.*

The Pulitzer Prize expanded to include journalism and letters.

Laura Elizabeth Richards and her sister, Maude Howe Elliott, along with their assistant, Florence H. Hall, receive the Pulitzer Prize in biography for their volume *Julia Ward Howe.*

1918

BIRTHS

Timothy Mofolorunso Aluko. Nigerian novelist; in his fiction, he will satirize the quarreling factions within African villages, providing insight into real people and their problems as they attempt to resolve the confusing clash of cultural values within modern Africa.

William Bronk. American poet; he will disdain the ornamental effects of language, never rhyming his lines, but nonetheless relying on formal stanzas; he will look upon the world with wit and stoicism.

George Campbell. Jamaican playwright and poet; he will focus upon the harsh cultural and political realities of the Caribbean experience; his best work will date from the 1940s.

Elsa Morante (d. 1985). Italian writer of fiction and poetry; she will explore conflicts, during the post-World War II period, between illusion and reality; her prose style will be influenced by surrealism, characterized by lucid presentations of unreal events and emphasizing the value of imagination; her fictional themes will focus upon the psychological implications of exclusion and separation.

Nguyn-Hong. Vietnamese writer of fiction; he will write short stories about poor people who resort to crime; his fiction generally will follow the methods of "socialist realism."

Manuel de Pedrolo. Spanish (Catalan) writer of fiction, drama, and poetry; he will become a prolific author and the most widely read of all Catalan writers; in more than thirty-five novels, he will prove himself to be an effective experimentalist; he will delight in casting characters into situations and conditions that limit their thoughts and actions.

Juan Rulfo (d. 1986). Mexican writer of fiction and narrative; he will focus upon the lives of Mexican peasants and their stoicism in the face of adversity; he will become especially skilled at applying the proper words and expressions to suit his characters and their surroundings.

Srirat Sathapanawat. Thai writer of fiction; he will apply in his fiction his knowledge and understanding of poor people, attempting to arouse in the wealthy and affluent a reaction to the plight of the socially underprivileged.

Bert Schierbeek. Dutch novelist; he will become an early experimenter with Dutch prose, producing novels in a type of free verse that lies halfway between poetry and prose; his works will not contain traditional plots, but rather an assemblage of "different voices" in a collage technique; thus, he will develop what will become "the free-form novel."

Aleksandr Isayevich Solzhenitsyn. Russian novelist and narrative writer; he will publish fiction highly critical of life in Stalinist Russia; he will be deported to West Germany, settle in Switzerland, and then come to the United States; his work will reveal a growing religious orientation, and he will attempt, in his later writings, to retrace the circumstances leading to contemporary Soviet society; he will receive the Nobel Prize for literature in 1970.

Muriel Sarah Spark. Scottish-born writer of fiction, poetry, drama, essays, and biography; she will explore a wide range and variety of themes and topics: free will, psychological motivations, moral issues, Roman Catholicism; her novels will feature an omniscient narrator who will outwardly manipulate plot and characters by introducing strange and supernatural events and actions.

Yusuf al-Khal. Lebanese poet; his verse will be emphatically philosophical and concentrate on religious and ethical subjects; he will become the first Arabic poet to rely upon Christian themes, drawing upon the Bible and looking toward the regeneration of humankind; his poems will reveal the influences of Ezra Pound, T. S. Eliot, and Edith Sitwell.

DEATHS

Guillaume Apollinaire (b. 1880). French poet and critic; an influential innovator, his lyric poems blend modern and traditional verse techniques; he introduced cubism (a revolt against the sensual, emotional art of former eras) to literature and wrote plays that proved to be early examples of surrealism.

John McCrae (b. 1872). Canadian poet and physician; he will become known for a single war poem, "In Flanders Fields" (1915); he dies in battle in World War I.

Wilfred Owen (b. 1893). English poet; his verse reflected the horror and the pity of war, relying upon a form that transfigured traditional meter and diction; he dies on the French front in World War I; Siegfried Sassoon will publish twenty-four of his poems in 1920.

Peter Rosegger (b. 1843). Austrian poet and novelist; he published a volume of poems in his native Styrian dialect; he wrote a number of autobiographical narratives and fiction that portrayed, vividly and realistically, the people and the surroundings of his native district.

Edmond Rostand (b. 1868). French poet and playwright; his dramas tended to be written in the tradition of nineteenth-century Romanticism; his sharp wit on more than one occasion failed to rise above his superficiality and sentimentalism; he attempted to free the theater from its unimaginative conventions.

Su Man-shu (pseudonym of Suu Chin; b. 1884). Chinese poet, translator, and writer of fiction; known principally for his verse and his translations of English Romantic writers; he attempted to enrich Chinese literature by creating a deep awareness of Western verse; in so doing, he became a principal influence on the development of modern Chinese poetry; he wrote in the traditional Chinese form of four seven-word lines and exhibited the characteristic features of classical Buddhist verse: native imagery, linguistic simplicity, and metaphysical speculation.

Frank Wedekind (b. 1864). German playwright; a forerunner of expressionism; he tended to emphasize the primal instincts of human beings.

PUBLICATIONS

Willa Cather, *My Antonia*—a novel by the American writer of fiction; develops the story of a great woman ennobling common actions and struggles by elemental passion; noteworthy for its depiction of Czech and Danish servants and working girls who seek that passion amidst the small-town respectability of the settled Midwest.

Leonhard Frank, *Der Mensch Ist Gut* (Man Is Good)—a collection of short stories by the German novelist and playwright; pacifist in tone, the work graphically focuses upon the suffering caused by war, and thus attempts to influence the German home front.

Gerhart Hauptmann, *Der Ketzer von Soana* (The Heretic of Soana)—a novel by the German playwright, novelist, and poet; the writer presents as his subject a priest converted to sensuality and neo-paganism; demonstrates the writer's personal vacillation between erotic paganism and pious Christianity.

Gerard Manley Hopkins, *Poems* (collected and edited by Robert Bridges)—the first available collection by the Victorian poet and Jesuit priest (1844-1889); demonstrates the dilemma of the poet caught between his duties as a priest and his intense and sensuous joy of nature.

George Kaiser, *Gas I*—a play by the German dramatist, the second piece in a trilogy (*Die Gas Trilogie,* 1917-1920); a billionaire's son rejects the capitalistic system of his father and attempts to raise his workers to the level of "the new man" through social reforms; those fail when the workers assume the attitudes and views of capitalists.

Alfred Kerr, *Die Welt in Drama* (The World of Drama)—a five-volume treatise on German theatrical criticism by the poet and critic; demonstrates the writer's preference for naturalism, as exemplified by the social dramatists of the nineteenth century.

Francis Ledwidge, *Last Songs*—a collection of verse by the Irish poet, published posthumously from manuscripts he sent from the Western Front to Lord Dunsany; nostalgic recollections of the countryside in County Meath.

Thomas Mann, *Betrachtungen Eines Unpolitischen* (Reflections of a Nonpolitical Man)— a collection of prose essays by the German writer of fiction and nonfiction; the writer seeks to defend Germany against its critics, demonstrating the nation's moral and cultural superiority and emphasizing the contrast between the subtleties and profundities of the German Romantic tradition and the shallowness of Western progressive humanism.

Andre Maurois, *Les Silences du Colonel Bramble*—a collection of stories and sketches by the French biographer and novelist; the pieces focus upon activities and persons within an English officers' mess.

Luigi Pirandello, *Cosi 'e—se vi Pare* (Right You Are, If You Think So)—the first significant piece of drama by the Italian novelist and playwright; concerns the relative truth of three different points of view; a dramatization of a short story written in 1915 and based upon characters who attempt to confuse one another as well as those who live in the town where they settle.

Anempodist Ivanovich Sofronov, *Olokh Jeberete* (Game of Life)—a drama by the Yakutsk (SSR) playwright; criticizes the negative effects of the Soviet system upon the nationalism of his state; thus, the piece appears supportive of bourgeois intellectualism in Yakutsk and predates the playwright's "conversion" to the realities of socialism.

Oswald Spengler, *Der Untergang des Abendlandes* (The Decline of the West)—a two-volume (to 1922) treatise on the philosophy of history by the German philosopher and essayist; the writer rejects the theories of historians who explain the history of Western Europe as an unbroken sequence of events from antiquity to modern times; he advocates consideration of other important cultures (Egypt, China, classical Greece and Rome) as distinct spirits reflected in every aspect of life.

Giles Lytton Strachey, *Eminent Victorians*—a collection of biographical sketches by the English biographer and essayist; one of the most significant pieces of biographical writing in English, principally because of the writer's powers of wit and narrative.

Stephen Zorian, *Txur Mardik* (Sad People)—a collection of short stories by the Armenian writer of fiction; the pieces reflect the influence of Anton Chekhov and Ivan Turgenev; in general, the stories focus upon life in the provinces of Soviet Armenia.

EVENTS

William Cabbell Bruce receives the Pulitzer Prize in biography for his *Benjamin Franklin, Self-Revealed.*

Richard Huelsenbeck, German psychiatrist and poet, helps find the political and literary "dada movement" in Germany; essentially a European pacifist movement.

Ernest Poole, American journalist and writer of fiction and nonfiction, receives the Pulitzer Prize in fiction for *His Family.*

James Ford Rhodes receives the Pulitzer Prize in history for *A History of the Civil War.*

The Stars and Stripes, the official newspaper of the U.S. Expeditionary Force (AEF), begins publication in France; moves to the United States in 1919 and continues until 1926;

begins again in 1942, to be published wherever American service personnel have stations.

Authorities at the United States Post Office burn installments of James Joyce's novel *Ulysses,* published in the *Little Review.*

Jesse Lynch Williams, American playwright and novelist, receives the Pulitzer Prize in drama for *Why Marry?*

1919

BIRTHS

Peter Lee Abrahams. South African writer of fiction and poetry; his autobiographical fiction will reflect his childhood experiences in the Transvaal and his wanderings about South Africa; his verse, although not metrically smooth, will reflect the early struggles of blacks in South Africa.

Joan Brossa. Spanish (Catalan) poet; between 1943 and 1959, he will publish seventeen volumes of poetry, thus becoming one of the most significant post-civil war poets of Spain; he will maintain an avant garde position, exhibiting a rationalist anxiety and a hatred for what exists in the world.

Georg Emin (pseudonym of Karlen Karapetian). Armenian (SSR) poet; his early verse will become popular among Russian soldiers during World War II; his later works will meditate on the difficulties of living in a technological society.

Emyr Owen Humphreys. Welsh writer of fiction, playwright, and poet; his principal themes will focus upon individual responsibility in contemporary society; he will emphasize the importance of personal example over ideology; thus, idealism is corruptible, while pragmatism is successful in initiating and maintaining positive change.

Noni Helen Nontando Jabavu. South African novelist; her fiction will describe the impact of the West upon peoples of East and South Africa; she will insert actual words from the Xhosa dialect into the English text as an attraction for her African audience.

Shirley Hardie Jackson (d. 1965). American writer of fiction; she will write stories and novels that alternate stylistically between casual observance of domestic life and psychologically compelling Gothic horror.

Benedict Kiely. Irish writer of fiction and nonfiction; he will become a masterful storyteller, combining fiction with history; he will focus upon the people, cities, villages, and rural landscape of Ireland.

Saburo Kuroda. Japanese poet; after World War II, he will become involved in the agrarian movement, which will adversely affect his health; he will go to Tokyo, write poetry, and eventually receive the H Poetry Prize.

Doris May Taylor Lessing. Persian-born English writer of fiction; she will write on such themes and topics as Africa, communism, women, and global catastrophe; her work will be embraced by the women's movement and heralded as a significant contribution to women's studies.

Primo Levi (d. 1987). Italian writer of fiction, essayist, and poet; he will be remembered for his Holocaust narrative chronicling a survivor's memories of Auschwitz and journey home from that death camp.

Yoshioka Minoru. Japanese poet; he will be influenced by the Japanese modernist movement of the 1920s and will thus seek to recreate in poetry spontaneous images within his own stream of consciousness.

Ezekiel Mphahlele. South African essayist and short story writer; he will become black Africa's leading literary critic in English, well known for his anthologies and commentary on new African writing; he will attempt to provide readers with a guide to styles and themes of African writing in English, French, and Portuguese.

Subhas Mukhopdhay. Indian (Bengali) poet; he will become one of the most talented Bengali poets of the Left, making frequent reference to Soviet Russia and China, the people's war against the Axis (World War II), and the famine and the plight of the people.

Iris Jean Murdoch. Irish-born English novelist and philosopher; her symbolic fiction will offer readers a Kantian substitute for Christianity.

Abdurrahman Pazhwak. Afghan poet, playwright, and writer of fiction; he will write in the tradition of Pashto folk literature, emphasizing local color; his themes will generally come from history.

Sadiqullah Rishtin. Afghan writer of travel narratives and critic; his travel sketches of Kataghan will describe the lives of simple people, preaching love of the native country and the mother language; he will attack imperialism and plead for a free Pashtunistan; he will also write some love poetry.

J. D. Salinger. American writer of fiction; he will depict, with considerable pathos and humor, the individual caught in a banal and restrictive world; he will become a spokesman for what has been termed "disengaged seriousness": a state bordering upon whimsy and mysticism.

DEATHS

Endre (Andrew) Ady (b. 1877). Hungarian writer of verse; a lyric poet noted for his original and creative application of language; he was influenced by the French Symbolists.

Leonid Nikolayevich Andreyev (b. 1871). Russian writer of fiction and drama; his early stories were realistic studies of everyday life; after 1917, he detached himself from the influence of Maxim Gorky and emigrated to Finland; there he turned his attention to mysticism and allegory; his dramas are examples of expressionism.

Hari Narayan Apte (b. 1864). Indian (Marathi) novelist; his fiction confronted the major social problems of the day from a moderately reformist point of view; he also displayed a sympathetic insight into the subservient position of women in Hindu society, particularly the evils of child marriage and widowhood.

Karl Adolf Gjellerup (b. 1857). Danish novelist; he shared the Nobel Prize for literature in 1917 with fellow Danish novelist Henrik Pontoppidan.

Amado Nervo (b. 1870). Mexican poet; a leading exponent of "modernismo" (elegant form, exotic imagery, subtle word music); his poetry is known for its simplicity, musical phrasing, and mysticism.

Ricardo Palma (b. 1833). Peruvian writer of short fiction, playwright, historian, poet, and essayist; he created the literary form of the "tradicion," a type of short story in which he combined fictional elements with historical fact, producing a humorous and often satirical narrative; he focused upon the colonial period of Peru, from the fifteenth through the nineteenth centuries.

William Michael Rossetti (b. 1829). English poet, translator, and essayist; he specialized in art criticism, but also published biographies of poets and translated Dante.

Johann Sigurjonsson (b. 1880). Icelandic playwright and poet; he made a significant contribution to the early twentieth-century renaissance in Icelandic literature; his plays range from grim tragedy to romantic idylls; he dies from tuberculosis.

Narayan Vaman Tilak (b. 1862). Indian (Marathi) poet; he focused upon Nature and also produced Christian devotional verse; collections of his poems appeared in bound volumes after his death; his work may still be found scattered among a number of Christian hymnals.

PUBLICATIONS

Sherwood Anderson, *Winesburg, Ohio*—a collection of twenty-three stories by the American writer of fiction; the works all center upon a single figure, a writer, who identifies the principal traits of each character; the collection reveals human beings as both blessed and cursed by their gift of language as they experience the loneliness and frustration of life in small-town America.

Karl Barth, *Der Romerbrief* (The Epistle to the Romans)—a tract by the Swiss Protestant theologian; marks the beginning of Protestant dialectical theology, or the theology of the word.

T. S. Eliot, *Poems*—a collection by the American-born poet; published at the Hogarth Press in Richmond by Leonard and Virginia Woolf; the pieces sounded a new note for modern poetry in English: satiric, allusive, cosmopolitan, lyric, and elegiac.

Hermann Hesse, *Demian*—the first major novel by the German writer of fiction; a first-person narrative, highly expressionist, in which the principal character, an adolescent, explores the dark world in defiance of his bourgeois parents; the theme focuses upon the quest for individual values, a magical experience influenced by Friedrich Nietzsche, Carl Jung, and Christianity.

Karl Jaspers, *Psychologie der Weltanschauungen* (The Psychological Outlook on Life)—a tract by the German existentialist philosopher; philosophy begins with science, but scientific objectivity can never provide a complete description of the self.

N. Kumaran Asan, *Cintavistay-aya Sita* (Sita's Story)—a poem by the Indian (Malayalam) writer of verse narrative; calls for an end to injustices of the caste system.

W. Somerset Maugham, *The Moon and Sixpence*—novel by the English writer of fiction; he applies his first-hand knowledge of Tahiti (acquired in 1917) in recounting the life of Charles Strickland, a Gauginesque artist who neglects responsibility for art.

H. L. Mencken, *The American Language*—a philological tract, a monumental historical linguistic study by the American essayist, journalist, and humorist; four editions to 1936, with supplements to record the most recent linguistic practices.

Siegfried Sassoon, *War Poems*—a collection of verse by the English poet; depicts the horrors of war and underscores the poet's pacifism.

Federigo Tozzi, *Con Gli Occhi Chiusi* (Ghisola) —a novel by the Italian writer of fiction; focuses upon a mysterious and seductive young peasant woman who fascinates and bewilders the sensitive male protagonist; written in a moving poetic style, the work also chronicles a young man's passage from love to disillusionment.

Virginia Woolf, *Night and Day*—a novel by the English writer of fiction and essayist; a realistic piece set in London, the novel focuses upon the daughter of a famous literary family; their pursuits contrast sharply with the activities of the daughter's friend, who is involved in the women's suffrage movement.

William Butler Yeats, *The Only Jealousy of Emer*—a verse play by the Irish poet and dramatist; based upon the writer's discovery of a fourteenth-century Japanese dramatic form; thus, he employs masks, dances, choruses, and formalized diction.

EVENTS

Henry Brooks Adams' *The Education of Henry Adams* is awarded the Pulitzer Prize for biography and autobiography.

Karl Freidrich Georg Spitteler, Swiss poet and novelist, receives the Nobel Prize for literature.

Newton Booth Tarkington, American novelist, receives the Pulitzer Prize in letters for his novel *The Magnificent Ambersons.*

Louis Untermeyer, American poet, biographer, and anthologist, publishes the initial edition of his critical collection *Modern American Poetry.*

Margaret Widdemer (*Old Road to Paradise*) **and Carl Sandburg** (*Corn Huskers*), American poets, share the annual award of the Poetry Society.

Yale University Press issues the first volume of its annual publication, *The Yale Series of Younger Poets.*

1920

BIRTHS

Iman Abubakar. Nigerian (Hausa) writer of short fiction; he will write travel stories and regional fiction.

Jalal Ale Ahmad (d. 1971). Iranian writer of fiction; his work will focus upon the contemporary problems of Iranian urban and rural life, especially those originating from religious prejudice and conventions; he will also become an authority on folklore and dialects.

Isaac Asimov. American biochemist and writer of fiction and nonfiction; he will gain literary recognition for his science fiction stories and for popular introductions to scientific and social issues.

Nabuo Ayukawa. Japanese poet; he will return from fighting in Sumatra during World War II and join "The Waste Land," one of the most influential groups of poets at the time; he will also write critical essays on modern poetry.

Mallam Amadou Hampate Ba. West African (Mali) scholar and storyteller; he will publish prose tracts on Islamic theology and the religions of the Bambara and Fulani peoples; he will also attempt to compile readable texts from original oral stories and tales.

Mario Benedetti. Uruguayan writer of fiction; he will become known for his realistic portrayals of daily life among the urban lower middle class; he will also seek a deep understanding of human nature and attempt to comprehend the complexities of human relationships and human emotions.

Ray Douglas Bradbury. American writer of fiction; he will concentrate upon popular science fiction stories, but those pieces will reveal his knowledge of traditional literary themes and characters; he will develop the relationship between science fiction and political awareness; he will also write drama and poetry.

Edward Ricardo Braithwaite. Guyanan-born novelist; his fiction will tend to be highly autobiographical and ideological; his major novel *To Sir With Love* will become a successful motion picture.

Charles Bukowski. German-born American poet and writer of fiction; his works will depict the sordid urban environments of the socially downtrodden; he will rely upon emotion and imagination, simple, direct language, violent and sexual imagery, and loose poetic structures.

Joao Cabral de Melo Neto. Brazilian poet and critic; he will belong to the Generation of '45, the successor to the Brazilian modernists of the 1920s and 1930s; his work will thus reveal his dissatisfaction with the rhythmic "untidiness," "compositional disequilibrium," and facile wordplay of those poets who preceded him; his poetry will be characterized by clarity and control.

Andree Chedid. Egyptian playwright, poet, and novelist; she will write in French, becoming the leading woman writer of her nation; her themes will tend to focus on aging and death; in 1979, she will receive the Prix Goncourt de la Nouvelle.

Miguel Delibes. Spanish journalist and writer of fiction; he will depict rural life in his novels and demonstrate a mastery of psychological analysis.

Mohammed Dib. Algerian writer of fiction and poetry; he will write in French; his early works will describe rural poverty and the necessity for revolution; his later writings will be dominated by symbolism and introspection and concern subjects outside the realm of politics; in the 1970s, he will briefly return to patriotic themes.

Dennis Joseph Enright. English poet; he will teach literature in the East for a quarter century, and thus his verse will be set in Japan, Egypt, and Singapore (and also Germany); he will focus upon cultural differences and misunderstandings; he will reassert the poetry of "civility, passion, and order," favoring detachment and irony.

Lawrence Ferlinghetti. American poet; he will become one of the principal members of the Beat Generation, publishing volumes of coloquial verse on countless anti-establishment ideals; his City Lights Bookshop in San Francisco will become a center for Beat writers.

Hazhar (pseudonym of Abdurrahman Sharafkandi). Kurdish poet; patriotic themes will dominate his verse; he will rely on traditional styles, but at times will look to the fable for inspiration, a form that has no tradition in Kurdish literature.

Abdarrahman al-Khamisi. Egyptian poet and writer of fiction; he will initially write romantic verse and then proceed to realistic short stories with psychological emphasis; he will concern himself with the ethics of society and those forces working against natural human happiness.

Alex La Guma. South African writer of fiction; his fiction will focus upon the hard and brutal daily lives of South African blacks; it will reflect the writer's own struggles against apartheid, his lengthy incarceration, and his eventual removal to London.

Benjamin Letholoa Leshoai. South African (Orange Free State) writer of fiction and drama; he will become the first creative writer of his land to write in English; he will freely adapt traditional folk tales concerning legendary lands and their rulers; he will explore native themes, but will also attempt to place his work amidst the dominant trend toward Afro-English literature.

Howard Nemerov. American poet; his early poems will tend to be sophisticated and metaphysical; he will then attempt a reconciliation between poetry and philosophy in an attempt to understand his own imagination; he will also attempt humorous but pessimistic fiction.

Djibril Tamsir Niane. Mali story teller, anthologizer, and playwright; he will collect and retell the old legends of ancient Mali; he will also coauthor a richly illustrated history of West Africa.

Joan Perucho. Spanish (Catalan) poet, novelist, and critic; he will appy his own fertile imagination to sources from oral traditions, commenting upon such topics as ghosts and apparitions, prehistory, imaginary monsters, magic, and chivalry; he will also parody and satirize those traditions, "demythologizing" the land and its people and replacing legend with pure humor.

Abdarrahman ash-Sharqawi. Egyptian playwright, writer of fiction, and journalist; his fiction will outline the popular struggles against pashas and landlords and foreign invaders, as well as against a life of urban and rural poverty; he will stress the need for revolutionary action to bring an end to oppression and exploitation and to rid the land of rulers as well as serfs.

Harvey Swados (d. 1972). American writer of fiction and critic; he will focus upon the American experience, concentrating on the conflict between the hustle of American business and technology and the vital needs of humanity.

To-Hoai (pseudonym of Nguyen-Sen). Vietnamese writer of fiction; as a socialist and a realist, he will describe in detail the lives of the minority mountain people of North Vietnam.

To-Huu (pseudonym of Nguyen-kim-Thanh) —revolutionary Vietnamese poet influenced by Maxim Gorky; for him, poetry will come to mean "a beautiful form of revolutionary action."

Amos Tutuola. Nigerian novelist; he will write fiction depicting the lives of his ancestors and demonstrate a deep knowledge of the mythology of West African tribal life.

DEATHS

Dan Andersson (b. 1888). Swedish poet and novelist; one of the foremost writers of his nation; his works develop religious and metaphysical themes and concern themselves with the proletariat; he wanted to promote the interests of actual poor people, and thus stood apart from the class struggles and other issues associated with Marxism.

Shloime Ansky (originally Solomon Samuel Rappaport; b. 1863). Russian Jewish playwright; his dramatic pieces tended to be classical in structure, and focused upon Yiddish themes.

Richard Dehmel (b. 1863). German poet; his passionate, impressionistic verse represented a revolt against naturalism; he tended to concentrate upon complex social problems; he also experimented with the verse novel.

William Dean Howells (b. 1837). American novelist and critic; a strong advocate for realism in American literature, he sponsored such younger American realists as Stephen Crane and Frank Norris; his essays on realistic European writers helped to form American taste; he also wrote drama, travel literature, and reminiscences.

Sheikh Abdille Hasan Mahammed (b. 1864). Somalian oral poet; he composed alliterative poems that became immediately popular because of their emphasis upon the vernacular; politically inflammatory, his verse reflected his puritanical religious fervor and patriotism; his works are filled with graphic scenes of the desert and the arid plains of his country; he dies from influenza while in political exile in Ethiopia.

Benito Perez Galdos (b. 1843). Spanish novelist, playwright, and essayist; considered the most significant Spanish novelist since Miguel de Cervantes; he applied to Spanish fiction the techniques of the European schools of realism and naturalism, creating a portrait of Spanish society that is both accurate and comprehensive; his fiction is a direct reflection of his political ideals.

Vrthanes Phapazian (b. 1866). Armenian novelist; his works (including some short fiction, verse, and drama) provide a realistic view of Armenian life in Iran and Turkey, particularly in the countryside; he protests against social inequality, calls for individual freedom, and sympathizes with the sufferings of his people; his fictional heroes reflect the tragic existence of the Armenian minority in Turkey.

Olive Schreiner (b. 1885). South African writer of fiction and narrative who, on occasion, published under the pseudonym of Ralph Iron; she deserves recognition for establishing the true South African novel, with its descriptions of the countryside and its social preachings against racial injustice; her most noted work underscores her own transition from Calvinism to atheism.

Omer Seyfettin (b. 1884). Kazakh poet, playwright, and writer of fiction; he abandoned traditional folk forms in his verse and, influenced by Vladimir Mayakovsky, developed themes based on the revolution and modern civilization.

Vahan Terian (b. 1885). Armenian poet; he raised the Armenian lyric to its highest literary level; he was influenced by French and Russian symbolism and wrote in "pure" language, free from dialect and heavily alliterative.

Federigo Tozzi (b. 1883). Italian writer of fiction, poetry, and drama; he used colloquial language and disregarded formal narrative structure; his themes concern lower-class life in his native Tuscany, with episodes from his own emotionally troubled youth; he has occasionally been compared with Franz Kafka and Luigi Pirandello; he dies of pneumonia at age thirty-seven.

PUBLICATIONS

Van Wyck Brooks, *The Ordeal of Mark Twain*—a critical study by the American biographer and essayist; for the writer, Twain is the principal example of the artist in a new and modern universe, yet still an artist indebted to America's moral (Puritan) past; the struggle becomes more complicated because of the conflicting psychological forces that shaped Twain's literary career; the high spirited humorist struggled against the bitter and often tortured satirist.

Arnolt Bronnen. *Vatermord* (Parricide)—a play by the German expressionist; a boy, about to be seduced by his naked mother, kills his father with a coal shovel as he breaks into the bedroom; described as the most shocking treatment of a subject that was especially popular at the time.

T. S. Eliot, *Poems*—a collection by the American-born English poet and critic; includes "Sweeney among the Nightingales," "Sweeney Erect," "The Hippopotamus," "Mr. Eliot's Sunday Morning Service," and "Gerontion."

——————, *The Sacred Wood*—a collection of critical essays that includes the noted critical commentary upon Shakespeare's *Hamlet* and introduces the critical term "objective correlative": a set of objects, a situation, a chain of events to constitute the formula of a particular emotion.

F. Scott Fitzgerald, *This Side of Paradise*—an early novel by the American writer of fiction; an attempt to study post-World War I youth; the writer places his own notion of true love against the corrupting power of money.

Jaroslav Hasek, *The Good Soldier Schweijk*—a novel by the Czech writer of fiction, left unfinished at his death (1923); based upon the writer's experiences in the Austro-Czech army in 1915; the hero, an anarchist who pokes fun at his Austrian masters, despises authority and knows every way to circumvent it.

Georg Kaiser, *Gas II*—the third play in a trilogy (*Die Gas Trilogie*, 1917-1920) by the German dramatist; the great-grandchild of the original billionaire works in the gas factory at the time of the war between the Blues and the Yellows; he urges his coworkers to join him in a campaign of patient and nonviolent endurance; rejecting the invitation, the workers proceed to produce poison gas, at which point the central character destroys the factory and all who work there.

D. H. Lawrence, *Women in Love*—a novel by the English writer of fiction and poetry; two sisters living in a coal town commence relationships with different men; one involvement is tender and happy, while the other is completely destructive and results in the death of the man; as usual, references to and descriptions of sexual liberation anger reviewers, readers, and jurists; the novelist, himself, viewed the work as his best novel.

Sinclair Lewis, *Main Street*—a novel by the American fiction writer; the novel's protagonist, Carol Kennicott, is depicted as a sophisticated idealist; her attempts to address the social, cultural, and aesthetic inadequacy of Gopher Prairie fail because of her naivete and lack of a clear program; the novel is as concerned with the hypocrisy of American ethics as it is with the problem of individualism and freedom of choice personified in Carol.

Jane Mander, *The Story of a New Zealand River*—a novel by the New Zealand writer of fiction; a record of the New Zealand frontier experience, most of it firsthand; focuses upon an English woman married to an Australian pioneer and living in an undeveloped part of New Zealand; the novelist also criticizes the Puritanism, conformity, and snobbery found among the society of the region.

Katherine Mansfield, *Bliss, and Other Stories*—a collection of short stories by the New Zealand-born writer of fiction; the pieces underscore her development as an original and exploratory artist; the stories prove among the earliest in English to demonstrate the influence of Anton Chekhov.

Eugene O'Neill, *Beyond the Horizon*—a play by the American dramatist, his first full-length production; concerns a young man from rural Ireland who yearns for the sea; instead, he marries and finds himself trapped on a farm; ironically, the man's brother, well suited to the farm, instead pursues a life of adventure; for the young married man, only death will allow him to sail "beyond the horizon."

——————, *The Emperor Jones*—an expressionistic drama by the American playwright; concerns the black dictator of an island and his subjugation of the inhabitants; a revolt occurs, and the scenes of the play unfold during the emperor's escape; in the end, after enduring severe psychological trauma from guilt, the emperor dies of fright.

Tom Redcam, *San Gloria*—a verse drama by the Jamaican poet and novelist; a narrative piece relating the poet's vision of the founding of Jamaica; the piece has become the classic folk history of the island.

Federigo Tozzi, *Tre Croci* (Three Crosses)—a novel by the Italian writer of fiction, poetry, and drama; the piece is based upon a news item about three brothers who stooped to forgery to save their bankrupt family business; the writer relates the crime through a detailed psychological profile of each brother; he reveals the stupidity, greed, and incompetence that led to their self-destructive actions.

H. G. Wells, *The Outline of History*—a chronicle of world history by the English writer of fiction and nonfiction; the writer wished simply to sketch the movements of historical fact for "the ordinary citizen in the modern state"; he intends to present the "stuff" of history required for general education; the volume becomes an exceptionally popular work.

Edith Wharton, *The Age of Innocence*—a novel by the American writer of fiction; the heroine of the piece possesses sufficient funds to escape the extremely restrictive social environment of New York; she travels abroad, partaking of the benefits of life among the aristocracy; unfortunately, her lover cannot escape his own traditions; thus, the work is a study of a love that suffers because of adherence to a social code.

William Butler Yeats, *Michael Robartes and the Dancer*—a collection of poems by the Irish writer of verse, drama, and essays; the pieces record the poet's clear perception of what had been achieved by the Easter 1916 uprising.

EVENTS

The Freeman, a weekly magazine of arts and politics, begins publication at New York City; discontinued because of financial problems in 1924; revived during 1930-1931.

The Frontier, a literary magazine, founded at Montana State University as a journal for creative writing and Northwest regional history; merges, in 1933, with *The Midland,* another such journal published at Iowa City, Iowa.

The Grabhorn Press begins operation at San Francisco, principally to reprint original publications of the early American West; until 1968.

Knut Hamsun, Norwegian novelist, receives the Nobel Prize for literature.

Eugene O'Neill receives the Pulitzer Prize for his drama *Beyond the Horizon.*

Time and Tide: An Independent Non-Party Weekly Review founded at London by Margaret Haig Thomas, Vicountess Rhondda; a left wing and feminist publication; contributors include D. H. Lawrence, Virginia Woolf, and Robert Graves; until 1977.

1921

BIRTHS

George Mackay Brown. Scottish poet, writer of fiction, essayist, and playwright; he will incorporate into his work elements from Norse sagas, Scottish ballads, medieval legends, and Roman Catholic ritual; he will employ simple language and syntax, exploring themes that focus upon history, religion, mysticism, and the people and life of his native Orkney Islands.

Friedrich Durrenmatt. German playwright; each of his dramatic works will be characterized by a restless probing of human guilt and justice; such ethical considerations will give them a moral force rivaling the dramatic efforts of Bertolt Brecht.

Cyprian Odiatu Duaka Ekwensi. Nigerian writer of fiction; he will become one of the most skillful writers in Africa, depicting the feelings and dilemmas of rural Africans who have pushed into the developing urban centers.

Ida Fink. Polish writer of fiction; her work will describe how the war ended her first love, music; forced into the Warsaw Ghetto, she will remain in hiding until the end of the war, then (1957) emigrate to Israel; her chronicles of the Holocaust will be published in Polish and translated into Hebrew, German, Dutch, and English.

Margherita Guidacci. Italian poet; she will develop a resistance to abstractions and become especially responsive to the physical world, to the mystery and marvel of life itself; thus, her verse will demonstrate an exceptional sensitivity and openness to life, accounting for the universal appeal of her art; she will become professor of English literature at the University Institute, Rome.

Alex Palmer Haley. American novelist and journalist; in his fiction, he will respond to the passion with which black Americans will come to value their heritage; at the same time, his work will become deeply imbedded in the moral imaginations of white

Americans; most noted for his huge saga of a black family, *Roots* (1976).

Theodore Wilson Harris. Guyanan novelist, poet, and critic; he will develop a form of fiction noted for its emphasis upon landscape; through this fictional background, he will attempt to arouse the human imagination and help people to define themselves.

Idrus. Indonesian writer of fiction and drama; he will be known for his short stories, the most effective of which will be written during the period of Japanese occupation; in 1965, he will emigrate to Australia to teach Indonesian literature at Monash University.

Ti Janakiraman. Indian (Tamil) writer of fiction, drama, and travel narratives; he will derive his themes from everyday life in urban middle-class families; his work will be honest and realistic, devoid of affectation.

James Jones (d. 1977). American novelist; his work will evidence the influence of Jack London, Thomas Wolfe, and Ernest Hemingway; in general, he will confront the powerful injustices of the world; his characters will not be able to endure that world, nor will they ever be able to explain or change it.

Fodeba Keita. Guinean poet and playwright; he will write Marxist and nationalistic poems in support of his homeland's fight for independence.

Stanislaw Lem. Polish writer of fiction, playwright, and essayist; he will be recognized for his contributions to science fiction and speculative literature, concerning himself with the moral and ethical consequences of scientific advancement and the impact of technology upon society.

Gabriel Imomotimi Gbaingbain Okara. Nigerian poet and writer of fiction; he will become one of the leading African poets writing in English; he will lament the loss of the African past, but will do so without being overly nostalgic; he will display a particular sensitivity for language.

Janos Oilinszky (d. 1981). Hungarian poet; he will become one of his nation's leading post-World War II poets; he will be referred to as a Catholic existentialist, and his poetry will be mainly concerned with the mystery of Christ's sacrifice and with the enormity of suffering experienced by human beings in a century known for its tyranny and mass murders.

Ziya Qarzada. Afghan poet; he will become an innovator in verse, embracing new themes and abandoning the traditional system of images; his poetry will focus on such themes and ideas as patriotism, peace, respect for the work of simple people, and equality for women.

Amrt Ray. Indian (Hindi) writer of fiction; his themes will focus upon social conflicts, religious fanaticism, and the struggle against tradition; he will also write short stories with a strong psychological emphasis.

Leonardo Sciascia. Sicilian writer of fiction, essayist, and playwright; he will principally write of the pride, passion, and corruption that characterizes Sicilian society; against a background of Sicilian and Mafia politics, he will explore the struggle of the individual who, in the midst of social inequities and official complicity, seeks justice.

Francisco Jose de Vasques Teneiro (d. 1963). Portuguese poet and writer of fiction; his interests will lie in the general study of African literature, and he will attempt to establish a dialogue between Europe and black Africa; his neo-realistic poems will be considered the first major work of "negritude" by an African writing in Portuguese; his long poetic pieces will attack social injustice, insisting that being black is a positive attribute.

Richard Purdy Wilbur. American poet; he will create skillfully crafted, original, and witty intellectual verse; in 1957, he will receive the Pulitzer Prize for poetry.

DEATHS

Micah Joseph Berdyczewski (b. 1865). Polish Jewish novelist, philosopher, and essayist; influenced by Friedrich Nietzsche, he cast doubts upon everything that had been regarded as positive and certain within the Jewish tradition; as a novelist, he described the collapse of the traditional Jewish family.

Aleksandr Aleksandrovich Blok (b. 1880). Russian poet; he became one of the leading Russian symbolists, influenced heavily by Vladimir Sergeyvich Soloviev.

Henry Austin Dobson (b. 1840). English poet and essayist; he wrote what would be termed "accomplished" verse, most of it light and extremely popular in its time; his wide knowledge of the eighteenth century is reflected in his competent biographies of William Hogarth, Sir Richard Steele, Oliver Goldsmith, Horace Walpole, Samuel Richardson, and Frances Burney.

Georges Feydeau (b. 1862). French playwright; he became a major figure in French comic drama, skillfully manipulating the conventions of vaudeville and the so-called "bedroom farce"; his plays tended to be precisely staged, containing highly unlikely coincidences, misunderstandings, and mistaken identities; he contracted a severe venereal disease, which caused him to become insane (he imagined himself either an animal or an emperor); he dies two years after his family has him institutionalized.

Vladimir Korolenko (b. 1853). Russian writer of fiction; although sensitive to the needs of the poor and downtrodden, his fiction tends to transcend those problems to express a sense of the unity of nature.

U Lat (b. 1866). Burmese writer of fiction; he incorporated elements of Burmese drama into the novel; in general, his work depicts human relations in the divided Burma of the nineteenth century (independent kingdom and British colony), defending traditional culture against foreign influences.

Cuppiramaniyam Ci. Parati (b. 1882). Indian (Tamil) poet; his work reveals the influence of classical Tamil poetry and of Percy Bysshe Shelley, John Keats, and Ralph Waldo Emerson; he attacked the social evils of Hindu society, and his passionately radical songs inspired the national movement in Tamil India; he became the first writer to introduce contemporary political and social themes into Tamil verse, relying upon simple and colloquial language.

Emilia Pardo Bazan (b. 1852). Spanish novelist and critic; she introduced naturalism into Spanish literature and systematically focused on the problems of the lower classes.

Ivan Vazov (b. 1850). Bulgarian poet, writer of fiction, playwright, and essayist; a passionate patriot, he depicted Bulgaria's struggle for independence from the Ottoman Empire during the final decades of the nineteenth century; he dies of heart failure.

PUBLICATIONS

Johan Bojer, *Der Sideste Viking* (The Last of the Vikings)—a novel by the Norwegian writer of fiction, especially popular in France; the piece, which focuses upon the cod fishers of the Lofoten Islands, is an excellent example of psychological regionalism.

John Dos Passos, *Three Soldiers*—a novel by the American writer of fiction; traces the impact of military service upon three men: an optical worker who wants a promotion, a farm laborer who wants only to return home, and an educated musician; each suffers a different form of destruction, illustrating the devastating effects of war.

Aldous Huxley, *Crome Yellow*—a novel by the English poet, essayist, and writer of fiction; characterized as a "country-house satire," the piece earned for the writer a reputation for precocity and cynicism.

Mohammad Ali Jamalzade, *Yeki Bud Va Yeki Nabud* (There Was Once—or Was There?)—a volume of six short stories by the Iranian writer of fiction, the title of which originates from the phrase with which Persian fairy tales begin; significant for its realistic depiction of life in Iran and portrayal of real-life situations and characters; the work continues to be popular.

Velimir Khlebnikov, *Nochnoi Obysk* (The Night Search)—a poem by the Russian writer of verse, fiction, drama, and nonfiction; depicts the search of a bourgeois apartment by Communist soldiers during the Revolution; the piece signifies the poet's growing ambivalence toward the new order.

W. Somerset Maugham, *The Circle*—a novel by the English writer of fiction; relates the story of a young woman who falls in love with a rubber planter from Malaya and elopes with him, despite abundant warnings about the impermanence of pure romance.

Eugene O'Neill, *Anna Christie*—a naturalistic "slice-of-life" drama by the American playwright; a sympathetic portrayal of the title character, a prostitute who eventually reunites with her father, a sea captain who had earlier disowned her; the father blames all of life's problems on the sea, but the daughter discovers it to be a cleansing agent; the author is awarded a Pulitzer Prize for the work in 1922.

Luigi Pirandello, *Sei Personaggi in Cerca d'Autore* (Six Characters in Search of an Author)—a philosophical play by the Italian poet, essayist, writer of fiction, and dramatist; a play about the creative process, about people who came to the writer and asked to be placed in his works; the drama also concerns the function of form in art; the piece constitutes an endless paradoxical debate about the difference between art and life, between acting and actually existing.

Giles Lytton Strachey, *Queen Victoria*—a biography by the English miscellaneous prose writer; an extremely popular and sympathetic treatment of the subject, although not always reverent; the writer combines careful construction, revealing anecdotes, and an elegant style.

Alexey Tolstoy, *Khozhdeniye po Mukam* (The Road to Calvary)—an epic novel by the Russian writer of fiction, essayist, poet, and playwright; depicts Russian history in conformity with official Soviety ideology, focusing on the Revolution and civil war; three volumes, to 1941.

Ludwig Wittgenstein, *Tractatus Logico Philosophicus*—a prose treatise by the Austrian philosopher; advances the notion that all significant assertions can be broken down into compound propositions containing logical constants; those constants become "truth functions" of elementary propositions (one kind of fact).

EVENTS

Association of Poets, Playwrights, Editors, Essayists, and Novelists established in England.

Anatole France, French writer of fiction and essayist, receives the Nobel Prize for literature.

Zona Gale, American writer of fiction, wins the Nobel Prize for drama for the adaptation of her novel, *Miss Lulu Bett* (originally published 1920).

The Nation and Athenaeum, London, begins publication, merging the two literary magazines; until 1931.

Der Querschnitt (The Cross Cut), a German intellectual journal, begins publication at Berlin.

The Reviewer begins publication at Richmond, Virginia; a magazine featuring the leading American writers of the period, with emphasis upon those from the South; until 1925.

Edith Wharton, American writer of fiction, receives the Pulitzer Prize in fiction for her novel *The Age of Innocence* (1920).

1922

BIRTHS

Kingsley Amis. English writer of fiction, poetry, and nonfiction; he will be esteemed for novels portraying realistic characters with cynical, often controversial views on cultural and sexual issues; he will be regarded as one of England's foremost comic novelists for his witty social commentary and command of satire.

Alan Ansen. American poet; he will be influenced by W. H. Auden and be associated with the American Beat movement; in 1954, he will move to Athens, Greece, to teach literature and write poetry.

Chairil Anwar (d. 1949). Indonesian poet and essayist; he will become the first poet to employ the Indonesian language in creating succinct and emotionally powerful Modernist verse; although he will write only about seventy-five poems, those who produce verse during the post-war period in Indonesia will be labeled "Chairil's Generation."

Brendan Behan (d. 1964). Irish playwright; he will begin his literary career after experiences in the IRA and British prisons; he will, through both his personality and his plays, come to embody Irish drama: wild, witty, profane, irreverent, and hard-drinking; his tragic themes will be realized through roistering, racy, and swaggering prose.

Vance Nye Bourjaily. American writer of fiction and nonfiction; his fiction, modeled after that of Ernest Hemingway, will be set in a detailed and natural world, a brawling and tumultuous place where individual effort will prove especially important.

John Gerard Braine (d. 1986). English novelist; he will join, at the outset, the group of England's "angry young men," those social critics of the English way of life as it existed prior to World War II (and beyond); later in his career, he will reverse his position and become critical of his earlier radical views.

Donald Alfred Davie. English poet and critic; his poetic theories will be pronounced in both his verse and prose; he will argue for a return to the formal structures and traditional syntax of the eighteenth-century Augustan poets.

Mavis Gallant (born Mavis de Trafford Young); Canadian writer of fiction; she will spend the years from 1950 to 1983 in France before returning to Canada to teach and to write at the University of Toronto; her best work will be her short stories, and her writings will be most popular in New York City and London; she will, in her fiction, consider the Catholicism of her childhood and the merits of provincialism.

Arpad Goncz. Hungarian playwright; his characters will be both universal and representative of contemporary Hungary; his works will be suppressed by the government, and he will spend time in prison; he will focusupon humanity's eternal struggle against oppression; he will also write several pieces of short fiction.

Jack Kerouac (d. 1969). American writer of fiction; he wil be considered the leader of the Beat Movement in American literature and culture; he will experiment with what he will term "spontaneous prose," loosening the syntax of language and maintaining the natural flow of feelings and perceptions; he will announce a new response to experience and attempt to draw a new vision for the world.

Koichi Kihara. Japanese poet and radio dramatist; like so many of his contemporaries, he will respond to the horror of World War II and to the havoc wreaked upon humanity by the atomic bomb.

Philip Larkin (d. 1985). English poet; he will turn his back upon the poetic traditions of Europe, but his work will nonetheless display the influences of such writers as Thomas Hardy and Robert Graves; his poetic imagination will tend toward the skeptical and ironic.

Alistair Stuart MacLean (d. 1987). Scottish writer of fiction and poetry; he will become one of the most successful writers of adventure fiction in the world, writing more than two dozen novels.

Antonio Agostinka Neto. Angolan poet; he will begin to write poetry while a student in Portugal, becoming a new voice of the African population of Angola; his poems will celebrate African men and women and express the sentiments of blacks for independence; he will become the spokesperson for the oppressed peoples of Africa.

Pier Paola Pasolini (d. 1975). Italian poet and novelist; he will fiercely reject bourgeois values and experiment with form and style; his work will promote a revisionist form of Marxism, but he will, however, remain interested in Christian values and Catholicism; he will reject "literary" language because he will associate it with the ruling classes.

Alain Robbe-Grillet. French novelist and essayist; he will become one of the foremost proponents of the new French novel (le nouveau roman), questioning the validity of traditional novelistic form; thus, in his fiction, he will favor disjointed narratives, characters with vague or shifting identities, "metafictional" situations, and precisely detailed descriptions of inanimate objects (chosisme).

Stanlake J. T. Samkange. Rhodesian novelist; he will publish only a single novel, *On Trial for My Country* (1966), but that piece will be highly influential; the work will concern the struggle of the last of the Matabele kings against the plots and manipulations of Cecil Rhodes; the piece parallels the problems in nineteenth-century America between the whites (government, soldiers, and settlers) and the Indians.

Kurt Vonnegut, Jr. American novelist; he will write science fiction in which the environment, intergalactic space, magnifies the pointlessness of human efforts in any direction; he will develop a pessimism based upon a vision of humanity as doomed by a "programming" they cannot resist or change.

DEATHS

Wilfred Scawen Blunt (b. 1840). English poet and pamphleteer; best known for his love sonnets, but also remembered for his defense of nationalism and independence, specifically with regard to Ireland, India, and Egypt.

David Frishman (b. 1861). German Jewish critic, poet, and writer of short fiction; he dominated European Hebrew literature for almost a half century; his principal work is the series *Notes on the History of Literature*.

Velimir Vladimirovich Khlebnikhov (b. 1885). Russian poet, writer of fiction, playwright, and essayist; one of the founders of Russian Futurism, a literary movement of the early twentieth century that sought to revitalize poetry by rejecting traditional aesthetic principles; he experimented with the relationship between sound and meaning; his later poetry expresses an ambivalence toward the events of 1917; he dies in poverty, most likely from malnutrition.

Henry Archibald Hertzberg Lawson (b. 1867). Australian short fiction writer and poet; he wrote sharply realistic short stories about the Australian bush, while his verse tended to be conventional and ordinary; important themes of his work are friendship and personal loyalty; family problems led him to drink, and he is discovered dead at his home in Sydney.

Alfonso Henrique de Lima Barreto (b. 1881). Brazilian writer of fiction and prose; he became the first novelist to examine the problems of black and mulatto Brazilians; he focused upon themes of social and political injustice in early twentieth-century Brazilian society, placing himself at odds with the literary establishment of his nation; he dies alone and impoverished, ravaged by alcoholism and fits of insanity.

Marcel Proust (b. 1871). French novelist; his work tends to be discursive, but alive with brilliant metaphor and sense imagery; convinced of the need for psychological, philosophical, and sociological understanding, he explored the link between external and internal reality as founded in time and memory; he elevated artistic effort to the status of a religion and viewed the individual as isolated and society as false and ruled by snobbery.

Giovanni Verga (b. 1840). Italian writer of fiction; his early novels of passion were written in the style of the French realists; his later pieces, characterized by simplicity and strict accuracy, prompted the coinage of the term "verismo."

PUBLICATIONS

Bertolt Brecht, *Trommeln in der Nacht* (Drums at Night)—a play by the German dramatist, poet, and dramatic theorist; the piece grew out of the playwright's involvement in and disenchantment with the revolution in Bavaria in 1919, particularly his associations with the Augsburg Soldiers Soviet and the Independent Social Democratic Party; the play receives the Kleist Prize for this year.

T. S. Eliot, "The Waste Land"—a poem by the American-born English writer of verse, drama, and literary criticism; among the most innovative and controversial works to emerge from the Modernist period of literature, the piece synthesizes numerous mythic allusions, poetic voices, settings, and tones to depict the social turmoil and spiritual disillusionment of post-World War I Europe.

John Galsworthy, *The Forsyte Saga*—three novels —*The Man of Property* (1906), *In Chancery* (1920), and *To Let* (1921)—and two interludes—*Indian Summer of a Forsyte* (1918) and "Awakening" (1920)—by the English writer of fiction; published as a single volume; collectively, the pieces trace the fortunes of three generations of the title family, held together by the successful solicitor, Soames Forsyte.

Hermann Hesse, *Siddhartha*—a novel by the German-born writer of fiction, poet, and essayist; inspired by the writer's experiences in India; the hero, the son of a Brahmin, develops from an ascetic into a sensual materialist; he learns nothing, however, until he becomes an assistant to a ferryman, who plies the waters between the two worlds of the spirit and the flesh.

James Joyce, *Ulysses*—a novel by the Irish writer of fiction; concerns the events of a single day in Dublin in June 1904, and focuses upon Stephen Dedalus, Leopold Bloom, and Bloom's wife, Molly; the principal characters wander through Dublin until they meet, with each chapter corresponding, generally, to the wanderings of the ancient Ulysses; the characters range through a public bath, a funeral, a newspaper office, a library, several pubs, a maternity hospital, a brothel; employs stream of consciousness technique; published at Paris, and copies of the first English edition were burned by the U.S. postal authorities in New York after the book was banned due to its alleged pornographic content.

Yakup Kadri Karaosmanoglu, *Kiralik Konak* (Palace To Let)—a novel by the Turkish writer of fiction; concerns the improverishment of an upper-class family, brought about by World War I and the collapse of the Turkish Empire.

D. H. Lawrence, *Aaron's Rod*—a novel by the English writer of fiction and poet; the title character, an amateur flutist, forsakes his wife and menial job for music and adventure in the Bohemian environment of the upper class; he becomes involved in the politics of Florence, Italy, and loses his instrument (the rod) in a bomb explosion.

Sinclair Lewis, *Babbitt*—a novel by the American writer of fiction; attacks middle America through the tragic and pathetic figure of the title character: a morally inconsistent, completely bourgeois man without any self-knowledge; a satiric and realistic look at the corruption and sterility of post-war America, where the fruits of the new science and technology become readily available to mediocre and ignorant people.

Katherine Mansfield, *The Garden Party and Other Stories*—a prose collection by the New Zealand-born writer of fiction; the third and last volume of stories to be published during the writer's lifetime; the pieces demonstrate the writer's ability to manipulate time and her tendency to work through suggestion rather than explicit development.

Roger Martin du Gard, *Les Thibault* (The World of the Thibaults)—a novel by the French novelist and playwright; in this multivolume work, the writer presents a comprehensive statement of his personal world view, a combination of social and biological determinism and the philosophy of humanism; thus, he traces the intellectual development of two brothers, in the company of a large cast of characters, illustrating the impact of biological and environmental factors upon the individual; while one brother commits himself to progress and science, the other follows the path of revolution; eight volumes, to 1940.

W. Somerset Maugham, *East of Suez*—a play by the English writer of fiction and drama; fantastic melodrama in which a proper Englishman exercises poor judgment by marrying an amoral Eurasian woman; the piece was successful mainly because of its spectacular scenes of Peking street activity.

Paul Morand, *Ouvert la Nuit* (Open All Night)—a collection of short stories by the French writer of fiction, essayist, poet, and travel writer; contains six pieces, each set in a different European city and featuring a different female protagonist; the writer creates an impressionistic atmosphere and depicts characters representative of the moral confusion of the post-World War I era.

Eugene O'Neill, *The Hairy Ape*—an expressionist play by the American dramatist; relates the problems of a stoker of a steamship who becomes painfully aware of his social class and failings in an unexpected confrontation with a wealthy passenger; he tries to find a place for himself in the world and to avenge himself upon those whose superiority has destroyed him; seeing that he cannot do either, he finds himself in a zoo, where a gorilla crushes him; thus, he belonged neither to the world of humanity nor to that of brutish beasts.

Boris Pilnyak, *Goly God* (The Naked Year)—a novel by the Russian writer of fiction; considered one of the first works to confront the effects of the Revolution of 1917 upon Russian society; fragmentary and seemingly without plot, the work has been described not as a legitimate novel, but simply as bits and pieces of narrative, short stories, newspaper reports, legal documents, folklore, and reflections; the writer's prose style is equally fragmented and varied; he presents the Revolution as a peasant uprising against the Western-style bureaucracy originating from Peter the Great and developed by his successors.

Luigi Pirandello, *Enrico IV* (Henry IV)—a play by the Italian dramatist; considered the writer's masterpiece, the work had a significant influence upon the development of the modern theater; a philosophical piece based upon a German emperor and the problems that unfold when a young woman does not return the love of a man; concerns in a larger sense the idea of illusion and reality, eliminating the distinction between the two phenomena; on a psychological level, the play can easily be viewed as a realistic study of schizophrenic experience.

Rainer Maria Rilke, *Sonette au Orpheus* (Sonnets to Orpheus)—a collection of fifty-five sonnets by the German poet; written in a sudden spirit of frenzy and addressed to the God of Poetry, who is thought, perhaps, to be an idealized version of the poet himself; the poet conceives his Orpheus as freely giving himself to all beings and objects; the work is sometimes seen as an attempt on the poet's part to disprove charges that he was cold and remote.

Marah Rusli, *Sitti Nurbaja*—a novel by the Indonesian writer of fiction; credited as the first original novel in the Indonesian language; describes the conflict between traditionalism and modernism in Minangkabau life.

Dame Rebecca West, *The Judge*—a novel by the English writer of fiction; honored, at the time of its publication, as the best among the psychoanalytical novels.

Virginia Woolf, *Jacob's Room*—a novel by the English writer of fiction and nonfiction; the principal character's story parallels the life of the writer's own brother, contains a number of "new" fictional elements, particularly indirect narration and poetic impressionism; praised for its innovation, but criticized for a lack of traditional plot structure.

EVENTS

Sir Max Beerbohm, English critic, essayist, and caricaturist, completes his drawings of "Rossetti and His Circle."

Jacinto Benavente y Martinez, Spanish playwright, receives the Nobel Prize for literature.

The Critic, a literary journal containing critical essays and reviews, begins publication at London; founded and edited by T. S. Eliot; until 1939.

The Fugitive, a twice-monthly magazine of poetry and literary criticism, begins publication at Nashville, Tennessee; contributors include John Crowe Ransom, Laura Riding, Allen Tate, and Robert Penn Warren; until 1925.

Hamlin Garland, American writer of fiction, receives the Pulitzer Prize in biography-autobiography for *A Daughter of the Middle Border* (1921), an autobiographical narrative.

Nouvelles Litteraires begins publication at Paris.

Eugene O'Neill, American playwright, receives the Pulitzer Prize in drama for *Anna Christie* (1921).

Emily Price Post, American journalist and authority on manners, publishes the first edition of her best-known work, *Etiquette.*

The Reader's Digest, the monthly magazine of summary, precis, and condensation, begins publication at Pleasantville, New York; it will become one of the most popular and widely circulated magazines of the world.

Edwin Arlington Robinson, American poet, receives the Pulitzer Prize in poetry for his *Collected Poems* (1921).

Booth Tarkington, American writer of fiction, receives the Pulitzer Prize in fiction for his novel *Alice Adams* (1921).

J. R. R. Tolkien, South African-born English writer of fiction and literary scholar at Oxford, publishes his major study, *A Middle English Vocabulary.*

1923

BIRTHS

Daniel Abse. Welsh poet; his verses will be informed by his experiences as a physician.

Mia Berner. Swedish writer of autobiographical prose narratives; in her work, she will seek to formulate metaphors for the class structure of society, as well as for her own existential predicament.

Yves Bonnefoy. French poet, essayist, and translator; his poetry will be essentially classical in form and realistic in content; his verse will exist as a form of exchange between the poet who speaks and the reader who listens and responds.

Italo Calvino (d. 1985). Italian writer of fiction, translator, and essayist; he will develop into a master of allegorical fantasy; his work will reflect his interest in folk tales, chivalric romances, and legends; his fictional characters will defy the malaise of life in the modern world.

Sidney (Paddy) Chayevsky (d. 1981). American playwright; he will begin his career as a television dramatist; when he moves to the "legitimate" stage, he will create highly symbolic plays; he will be known for a dramatic form termed "tape recorder symbolism."

Stig Halvard Dagerman (born Sig Halvard Andersson; d. 1954). Swedish writer of fiction, playwright, essayist, and poet; he will advocate a literature that seeks to improve social conditions in post-World War II Sweden.

James Lafayette Dickey. American poet; his verse will be characterized by its realism and energy; he will write on such subjects as war, love, sex, the Southern experience, hunting, flying, canoeing, birds, and animals.

Nadine Gordimer. South African writer of fiction and critic; in her fiction, she will explore the effects, both political and social, of the apartheid system on the ruling whites and the oppressed blacks.

Joseph Heller. American novelist and playwright; he will become noted for his contributions to the experimental post-war novel, particularly for his comic attack upon the absurdities of the U.S. Army and his treatment of the general problem of human frustration.

Sherif Hetata. Egyptian novelist; his fiction will be autobiographical, reflecting his humanitarianism and political beliefs; the worldview and scheme of his fiction will resemble that found in Greek tragedy.

Elizabeth Jolley. English-born Australian writer of fiction and playwright; she will write darkly humorous experimental fiction, exploring such themes as loneliness, aging, homosexual love, and the relationship between imagination and reality; her characters will tend to be lonely and alienated individuals who have been uprooted from their familiar environments.

Denise Levertov. English-born American poet; her poetry will be characterized by its clarity and brevity and will reflect a wide range of human experience; at first, her works will reflect the rhetorical romanticism that dominated post-war British verse; upon moving to America, however, she will reject poetic convention.

Norman Mailer. American writer of fiction and prose narratives; he will achieve recognition early for his novel of World War II *The Naked and the Dead* (1948); thereafter, he will record his sharp views of American society, chronicling such subjects as the Vietnam War peace march on Washington, D.C., and the treatment of a convicted killer.

William Modisane. South African writer of fiction and poet; he will, in vivid language, depict the plight of blacks in an apartheid society; bitter at the racial policies of South Africa, he will reside in London, continuing to respond to the social and political problems of his native land.

Alvaro Mutis. Colombian poet; he will use a variety of traditional meters, creating elegant and flexible free verse lines; his verse will be ironic, and the theme of death will predominate; beginning in 1956, he will reside in Mexico.

Nazik al-Malaika. Iraqi poet and critical prose writer; she will be recognized for her rational approach to modern free verse, and will see the new forms of verse as essential for interpreting modern life; she will look at life's limitations from a female perspective.

John Ormond. Welsh poet; he will demonstrate, an affinity with the metaphysical poetry of John Donne, drawing philosophical and religious messages from common objects and experiences; he will write in non-rhyming free verse, with a wide variety of stanza lengths.

James Amos Purdy. American novelist; he will compose fiction that will tend toward the savage and the satiric; his language will be viewed as profane and wide ranging in terms of cultural variety; his themes will combine the senses of the tragic and the comic, focusing upon the lives of ordinary people.

Nazir Qabbani. Syrian poet; his verse will express his political frustrations, particularly with ineffectual leadership; his language will be that of everyday speech, often relying upon the colloquial and images from Syrian folklore.

Samuel Selvon. Trinidadian novelist and playwright; he will move to London, focusing his fiction upon immigrants to England and their attempts to cope with life in a strange and hostile environment; he will write in what might be termed a Caribbean version of English.

Ousmane Sembene. Senegalese writer of fiction; he will portray the evolution of modern Africa with its mixture of indigenous and Western technological elements; he will also attempt to reveal to Africans certain of the deplorable conditions under which they exist.

Muhammad Ishaq Shamin. Indian (Baluchi) poet; he will write in Urdu, conveying his strong spirit of nationalism.

Ryuichi Tamura. Japanese poet; in addition to writing verse, he will serve as an editor for a Tokyo publishing house; in 1963, he will receive the Koptaro Takamura Poetry Prize; his verse will be highly personal and consist of a wide range of metrical forms and patterns.

DEATHS

Maurice Barres (b. 1862). French novelist and miscellaneous prose writer; his works will reflect his anti-Semitism, as well as his nationalism, which derived from his belief that the uprooting of persons can only lead to political disaster; much of his work is informed by his bitter experiences as a child during the Franco-Prussian War.

Louis Couperus (b. 1863). Dutch writer of fiction; his cosmopolitanism led him to view human beings as unnecessarily concerned with their own collective fate; his fictional themes, therefore, encourage human beings to resign themselves to their circumstances so that they may eventually achieve peace.

Pierre Loti (pseudonym of Julien Viaud; b. 1850). French novelist; his works will range from tales of Breton fishermen to stories of French Basque peasant life; praised for his sensuous descriptions of foreign lands and cultures, he is regarded as one of the foremost impressionistic writers of nineteenth-century France.

Katherine Mansfield (pseudonym of Kathleen Mansfield Beauchamp; b. 1888). New Zealand-born English writer of fiction; considered a master architect of the short story, she was strongly influenced by Anton Chekhov; her stories tend to be simple in form and evocative in substance.

Raymond Radiguet (b. 1903). French writer of fiction, poet, playwright, and essayist; his fiction, particularly, has been praised for relating the psychology and actions of characters in a direct, austere manner; in an understated style, he portrayed the specifics of adolescent psychology; he dies from a typhoid infection, contracted in the south of France.

Edith Irene Sodergran (b. 1892). Finnish-Swedish poet; her innovative verses, marked by frank language, a confessional tone, and a unique expression of feminine longing, are considered a distinguished achievement in modern Finnish literature; after 1920, her health deteriorates rapidly and she dies at Raivola.

Hovhannes Thumanian (b. 1869). Armenian writer of fiction, poet, and essayist; he wrote social, patriotic, love, and nature lyrics, as well as satire; he also gained a reputation as a writer of tales and fables for children; his best works are lyrical epics revealing the tragedy of life among the patriarchal mountain villagers of Armenia.

PUBLICATIONS

Mark Aldanov, *Myslitel* (The Thinker)—a fictional tetralogy by the Russian novelist, short story writer, and essayist; the four volumes dramatize the history of the French Revolution; an attempt to parallel the events of 1789 with those of 1917 in Russia; completed in 1927.

Arnold Bennett, *Riceyman Steps*—a novel by the English writer of fiction; reveals the writer's sincere concern for obscure and ordinary individuals; focuses upon a miserly second-hand bookseller who lives and works in the drab environment of Clerkenwell.

Martin Buber, *Ich und Du* (I and Thou)—a tract by the Austrian-born Jewish philosopher; sets forth a personal and direct dialogue between God and the individual; the piece will have a significant influence upon contemporary Christian and Jewish philosophies.

Karel Capek, *R.U.R.: Rossum's Universal Robots*— a drama by the Czech playwright, novelist, and essayist; the production will always be known for the employment of robots on stage and for its introduction of the word "robot" (from the Czech "robata," meaning toil or servitude); concerns the dehumanizing effects of modern technological civilization;

thus, the robots seize power and eliminate mankind; however, they cannot reproduce until the occurrence of a biological miracle, love; the ultimate message is that humanity will somehow survive the threat of its own technology.

Willa Cather, *A Lost Lady*—a novel by the American writer of fiction; reflective of the writer's disillusionment with society and politics following World War I.

Robert Frost, *New Hampshire*—a long satirical poem by the American writer of verse; announces the writer's preference for the title state above all others, with the exception of Vermont; the poet also writes about himself and his craft; other pieces included in the volume are "An Empty Threat," "I Will Sing to You One-O," "Stopping by Woods on a Snowy Evening," and "The Need of Being Versed in Country Things."

Hemcandra Gosvami, *Asamiya Sahityar Chaneki; or, Typical Selections from Axsamese Literature*—a work in seven volumes by the Indian historian of Assam and Assamese literature; comprises the best examples of Assamese literature, from the beginnings to the modern period.

N. Kumaran Asan, *Duravastha* (A Tragic State)—a poem by the Indian (Malayalam) writer of verse; calls for the removal of the injustices of the caste system; relates the marriage of a Nambudiri Brahmin girl and a Harijan.

D. H. Lawrence, *Kangaroo*—a novel by the English writer of fiction and verse; based upon the writer's visit to Australia in 1922; the work combines political outbursts and meditations with keen observations of Australian life and landscape; the piece ends in the tragic death of the title character, a Jewish barrister involved in radical politics.

Francois Mauriac, *Genitrix*—a novel by the French writer of fiction and verse; a bleak and pessimistic analysis of a murderously intense maternal possessiveness defeating itself in the moment of its apparent victory; focuses upon the loneliness of a weak man for whom love has been nothing but a complete disaster; set in Bourdeax and the sandy, pine and vine filled countryside that surrounds that area.

Raymond Radiguet, *Le Diable au Corps* (The Devil in the Flesh)—a novel by the French writer of fiction; narrates the details of an affair between a fifteen-year-old boy and the nineteen-year-old wife of a soldier fighting in

World War I; a realistic and intellectually sophisticated portrait of adolescent psychology, focusing upon the insecurity, compulsion, and cruelty of the protagonist; the piece strongly parallels the writer's own experiences.

Elmer Rice, *The Adding Machine*—a play by the American dramatist; presents Mr. Zero, a repressed bookkeeper driven to a single moment of passion when he murders his employer, who has replaced him with a machine; following his execution, Zero moves on to the Elysian Field, from which he is ejected because he again fails to master the machine; the piece is a clear example of dramatic expressionism.

Jules Romains, *Knock; ou, Le Triomphe de la Medicine*—a play by the French poet and dramatist; a doctor sends an entire community to bed with an imaginary sickness.

Albert Schweitzer, *Verfall und Wiederaufbau der Kultur* (The Decay and Restoration of Civilization)—a prose tract by the German (Alsatian) medical missionary, theologian, and philosopher; sets forth the writer's newly discovered ethical principle on "the reverence for Life," a notion fully analyzed in relation to the defects of European civilization.

Wallace Stevens, *Harmonium*—a collection of poems by the American writer of verse; the title of the piece reflects the poet's interest in music; the poems reveal an extraordinary display of linguistic color, a tendency toward the exotic and the gorgeous, and an attraction for elevated language; thus, his images tend to reflect the luxury of the decade from which they emerged.

Leon Trotsky. *Literatura i Revolyutsiya* (Literature and Revolution)—a prose tract by the Russian political philosopher, historian, and essayist; an important piece of literary criticism that surveys prominent Russian writers; refutes the notion of proletarian art, maintaining that such a genre will never exist because it stands in opposition to the idea of a classless society and to the concept of a truly universal culture.

Wen I-to, *Hung-chu* (Red Candle)—a collection of verse by the Chinese poet and essayist; displays the poet's attraction to English Romanticism, particularly in terms of such themes as love, beauty, and death; the poems, written during the poet's residence in America, concern his homesickness and experience with racial discrimination; thus, the volume tends to idealize China in contrast to life in the United States.

William Carlos Williams, *Spring and All*—a collection by the American poet; combines aesthetic theory with such pieces as "The Red Wheelbarrow," "To Elsie," and "At the Ballgame."

Neguse Yoftahe, *Vain Entertainment*—an allegorical drama by the Ethiopian playwright and poet; dramatizes the marriage of Faith and Fortune, as commanded by King Solomon.

EVENTS

Willa Cather, American writer of fiction, receives the Pulitzer Prize for fiction for her novel *One of Ours.* (1922).

The William L. Clements Library of Americana established at the University of Michigan, Ann Arbor.

Owen Davis, American popular playwright, receives the Pulitzer Prize in drama for *Icebound* (1923).

The English Place-Name Society established in London; will survey English place-names under the auspices of the British Academy and publish the results, county by county.

The Gregorian calendar introduced into the U.S.S.R.

Augustus John, English painter, completes his portrait of Thomas Hardy.

The London Radio Times begins publication; it will reach a circulation of nine million by 1950.

Edna St. Vincent Millay, American poet, receives the Pulitzer Prize in poetry for "The Ballad of the Harp Weaver," "A Few Figs from Thistles," and eight sonnets in *Amercian Poetry, 1922, A Miscellany.*

Time, a weekly news magazine, founded at New York City; established by Briton Hadden and Henry Robinson Luce.

William Butler Yeats, Irish poet, playwright, and essayist, receives the Nobel Prize for literature.

1924

BIRTHS

Sheikh Kaluta bin Amri Abedi (d. 1964). Tanzanian (Swahili) poet; although he will devote most of his relatively brief life to politics, rising to become his nation's minister of justice, he will produce one major volume of verse that will include a discussion of the rules of versification.

Jamaluddin Abro. Indian (Sindhi) writer of fiction; his realistic short stories will attempt to introduce solutions to various social problems.

James Baldwin (d. 1987). American writer of fiction; he will base a significant number of his themes on the theory that animosity between whites and blacks intensifies as the result of male-female relationships, but can be alleviated by homosexual associations; he will also write emotionally charged essays in support of black causes.

Dennis Brutus. South African (Rhodesian) poet and essayist; he will be decidedly influenced by John Donne and William Butler Yeats; though he endured mental and physical suffering in exile and in South African political prisons, his works will be compassionate rather than bitter or self-pitying.

Truman Capote (d. 1984). American novelist, playwright, and narrative writer; with great technical skill, he will create a world more dreamlike than real; he will gain considerable recognition for his contribution to the "nonfiction novel" (*In Cold Blood*, 1965).

Iordan Chimet. Romanian poet, essayist, writer of fiction, and screenwriter; although he will earn a degree in law, he will pursue a career as a freelance writer; he will publish, beginning in 1968, verse, fiction, and nonfiction monographs on the western and slapstick film genres; his work will be awarded honors in Romania, Los Angeles, Venice, Barcelona, and Teheran.

Humberto Costantini (d. 1987). Argentinian writer of fiction, playwright, and poet; his fiction will be set in the Argentina of the mid-1970s, and he will employ humor and satire to convey his view of the arbitrariness of fate and the oppression resulting from military dictatorships; he will depict innocent civilians unwittingly trapped in a net of political confusion.

Jose Donoso. Chilean writer of fiction; his work will range from ironically realistic studies of decadent Chilean life to surrealistic portrayals of bizarre subjects; his style will be termed dense and powerful.

Janet Frame. New Zealand writer of fiction and poetry; her novels will tend to be complex and disturbing impressionistic narratives, exploring such problems as alienation and conformity as they contribute to the formation of identity and the creative imagination.

William H. Gass. American writer of fiction and criticism; he will become a professor of philosophy at Washington University; in his fiction, he will use early twentieth-century incidents to create a contemporary sense of exile.

Zbigniew Herbert. Polish poet, essayist, and playwright; he will he recognized as a powerful poet whose work represents a search for strong moral and humanistic values; he will underscore the need for poetry to confront the harsh realities of life; he will employ irony and experimental forms devoid of punctuation, attempting to free poetry from rhetoric and to directly address social, artistic, and metaphysical themes.

Alfred Hutchinson (d. 1972). South African biographer, playwright, and writer of short fiction; he will write the most significant analyses of the experience of living under the racist regimes in South Africa; he will, for almost a decade, live and write in England.

Kamala Markandaya (pseudonym of Kamala Purnaiya Taylor). Indian-born English novelist; she will recreate life in the villages and cities of India, while at the same time examining contemporary social issues; she will focus upon the clash between traditional Indian lifestyles and the challenges of existing in the modern world; thus, her characters will display great cultural differences.

Lisel Mueller. German-born American poet and critic; in her verse, she will combine precise, vivid imagery with a minimalistic style, emphasizing the importance of personal concerns and examining the implications of private and public perception; essentially, she will write about experiences that disturb or excite her.

Abioseh Nicol (pseudonym of Nicol Davidson). Sierra Leone poet and short story writer; his work will be described as "broad and open," essentially universal in theme; he will create fully developed African and English characters who will eventually come to understand one another and resolve their bitterness; he will also strive to provide his African characters with a strong sense of nobility and dignity.

Efua Theodora Sutherland. Ghanan playwright, poet, and essayist; in her work, she will seek to combine the deliberate pace of the storyteller's art with set scenes of dramatized or visualized action; she will become one of the founders of the Writer's Workshop at the Institute of African Studies, University of Ghana.

Leon Uris. American novelist; he will write popular pieces that focus upon the more militant aspects of recent history; his fictional subjects will include World War II, Palestine, and pre-1920 revolutionary Ireland.

Zahrat (pseudonym of Zareh Yaldizchian). Armenian-born Turkish poet; he will rebel against tradition, expressing the sensitivities of urban dwellers and their ironic twists of mind; he will experiment with poetic forms and exercise considerable influence over young Soviet Armenian poets.

DEATHS

Valery Bryusov (b. 1873). Russian poet; an experimentalist, he shocked his reading public with intellectual imitations of French Symbolist verse and eventually became a leader of the Symbolist movement.

Joseph Conrad (pseudonym of Teodor Konrad Wallecz Korzeniowski; b. 1857). Polish-born English writer of fiction; he was an accomplished stylist and a skilled creator of character and atmosphere, accurately portraying individuals suffering from isolation and moral disintegration; he also depicted the clash between primitive cultures and modern civilization.

Anatole France (pseudonym of Jacques Anatole Thibault; b. 1844). French writer of fiction, history, satire, and political allegory; one of the most prominent French writers of his day; his early fiction was charming and subtly ironic; he later shifted to satire, particularly following the affair of Alfred Dreyfus and his support of Emile Zola; he gained election to the French Academy in 1906 and received the Nobel Prize for literature in 1921.

Arne Garbourg (b. 1851). Norwegian novelist and poet; a naturalist, he championed Landsmaal, the language of the country, as a literary language.

Mehmed Ziya Gokalp (b. 1875). Turkish poet, writer of fiction, and essayist; his literary works expressed his fervent belief that Turkish nations would perform a significant role in the history of the world; thus, he spoke for the cultural and economic unification of all the Turkish speaking peoples.

Herman Heijermans (b. 1864). Dutch playwright, essayist, and writer of fiction; he introduced naturalism into the Dutch theater, and sought to portray the individuality of his characters; his work conveyed an optimism, compassion, and humor that transcended the bounds of contemporary literary movements.

Iraj Mirza (b. 1874). Persian poet; he turned away from the nationalist revival in literature and focused instead upon such themes as motherhood and motherly love; he also wrote poems for children, simplifying his idiom and relying upon colloquial words and phrases; he spoke French and Russian well and displayed a thorough knowledge of French literature.

Franz Kafka (b. 1883). Czech-born Jewish German writer of fiction; he wrote in clear and precise prose, presenting a world both real and dreamlike; in his fiction, modern people burdened by feelings of guilt, isolation, and anxiety undertake a futile search for personal salvation; his diaries and volumes of correspondence are recognized for their literary merit.

N. Kumaran Asan (b. 1873). Indian (Malayalam) poet; he wrote the first significant poem of the Malayalam Romantic movement, as well as short narratives on love and a number of philosophical pieces.

Mustafa Lufti al-Manfaluti (b. 1876). Egyptian narrative writer, essayist, and journalist; he wrote adaptations of nineteenth-century French novels, essays on social issues, and narratives that, while depicting pathetic situations, inspired penance and compassion; his prose style tended to be highly emotional.

Carl Friedrich Georg Spitteler (b. 1845). Swiss poet and novelist; he wrote a significant mythological epic, *Der Olympische Fruhling* (1900-1903); he received the Nobel Prize for literature in 1919.

PUBLICATIONS

Maxwell Anderson and Lawrence Stallings, *What Price Glory?*—a play by the American dramatists and journalists; the piece originated from Stallings's experiences in World War I; the writers introduced profane dialogue to the American stage and emphasized the bitterness and destruction resulting from modern war.

E. M. Forster, *A Passage to India*—a novel by the English writer of fiction and literary criticism; presents a view of Indian society under the British Raj emphasizing the prejudices and misunderstandings that eventually produced sharp divisions in Indian and British relations; focuses upon a young Muslim physician whose friendliness and loyalty toward the British turns to bitterness.

Sidney Howard, *They Knew What They Wanted*—a drama by the American playwright; concerns a middle-aged Italian immigrant wine-grower who attracts a bride from San Francisco by sending her a picture of his handsome foreman; the girl then responds to the charms of the foreman and bears his child; in the end, however, she willingly accepts the love of her husband and the security of married life; praised for presenting genuine individuals, rather than stereotypes, the piece received the Pulitzer Prize for drama in 1925.

Muhammad Iqbal, *Bang-e Dara*—a collection of Urdu verse by the Persian poet and philosopher; taken from the symbol of the caravan bell that leads pilgrims toward their goal; the poet advocates developing individual personality to its highest degree and maintains that humans must always remain human, never to be united with God; however, they can cooperate with God to improve their lives and change their destiny.

Mikheil Javakhisvili, *Kvachi Kvachantiradze*— a novel by the Georgian (SSR) writer of fiction; a story about a swindler that satirizes certain aspects of the Georgian national character.

Thomas Mann, *Der Zauberberg* (The Magic Mountain)—a novel by the German writer of fiction; set in a tuberculosis sanitarium, the work describes the intellectual and spiritual maturation of the principal character, a resident of the institution; the sanitarium itself represents diseased and decaying Western society; while the political and philosophical convictions of various characters indicate the intellectual temper of Europe during the period immediately preceding World War I; the writer also explores such themes as the nature of time and the seductiveness of death.

Sarah Gertrude Millin, *God's Stepchildren*—a novel by the South African writer of fiction and essayist; begins in 1821, with an English missionary traveling to South Africa to convert the Hottentots; he marries a woman from the tribe, and thus begins the tragic existence of three generations of that mixed marriage; all suffer the pains of ostracism and self-hatred; a controversial piece often attacked for its racial views.

Eugene O'Neill, *Desire under the Elms*—a tragic drama by the American playwright; concerns the passion between the third wife of a New England farmer and his son (by his deceased second wife); as a criticism of Puritan morality, the play contrasts the passionate nature of the youthful characters with the hardness and lovelessness of the Calvinist way of life; thus, the old farmer has nothing but contempt for sensitive individuals; in the end, the young woman bears her stepson's child and convinces her husband that it belongs to him.

Janis Rainis, *Jazeps un Vina Brali* (The Sons of Jacob)—a play by the Latvian poet and dramatist; based upon the biblical story of Jacob and his brothers and written with psychological insight and intense feeling; the playwright sets out to prove that reconciliation and fulfillment can only be achieved in the mystical beyond, outside the confines of the present.

John Crowe Ransom, *Chills and Fever*—a verse collection by the American poet and critic; the pieces focus on such themes as love, death, and mutability and also concern the dualities of childhood and age, science and faith, and mind and body.

Arthur Schnitzler, "Fraulein Else"—a novella by the Austrian writer of fiction and playwright; concerns a financier who demands, as the price for redeeming a girl's father, that the young lady strip for him in her hotel room at midnight; she performs the act, but in the hotel lobby, and then she kills herself.

Alexander Serafimovic, *The Iron Flood*—a novel by the Russian writer of fiction; concerns the retreat of the Red Cossacks through the Northern Caucasus in 1918; the masses become the hero of the piece, solid communists united by party discipline and doctrine; the novel can best be described as "pseudo-impressionistic."

George Bernard Shaw, *Saint Joan*—a play by the Irish dramatist and critic; focuses upon Joan of Arc and the period 1429-1456; in his title character, the writer creates a superior human being, a young lady who appears wise, magnanimous, and warm; the trial scene makes the piece more than simply a rehash of the traditional melodrama of persecuted innocence.

Junichiro Tanizaki, *Naomi*—a novel by the Japanese writer of fiction; as usual for this writer, the female character is central to the piece; thus, he draws a skillful portrait of the archetypal modern girl of the Tokyo dance halls of the 1920s; she is a flamboyant, Westernized woman who dominates her man, the writer himself demonstrating the heavy autobiographical element of the work.

Virginia Woolf, "Mr. Bennett and Mrs. Brown"—a critical essay by the English writer of fiction; attacks the realism of Arnold Bennett and advocates a fluid, internal approach to the problem of characterization; the piece establishes the writer as a leading exponent of modernism and the literature of psychology.

Percival Christopher Wren, *Beau Geste*—a novel by the English writer of fiction, the first volume of a trilogy; a highly romantic piece about the adventures of two brothers and a friend who run off to the French Foreign Legion.

EVENTS

The American Mercury, founded by H. L. Mencken and George Jean Nathan, begins publication at New York City; attempts to portray all aspects of the American cultural scene by publishing criticism as well as fiction; contributors include Theodore Dreiser, Eugene O'Neill, Sherwood Anderson, Carl Sandburg, Sinclair Lewis, and Edgar Lee Masters.

The Commonweal, a weekly Catholic periodical of current news and creative works (literature and the visual arts), begins publication at New York City.

Henry Watson Fowler, English lexicographer and grammarian, publishes his *The Pocket Oxford Dictionary.*

Robert Lee Frost, American poet, receives the Pulitzer Prize in poetry for *New Hampshire: A Poem with Notes and Grace Notes* (1923).

Hatcher Hughes, American playwright, receives the Pulitzer Prize in drama for *Hell-Bent for Heaven.*

The Pierpont Morgan Library, New York City, opens its doors to the public and becomes a significant research institution.

The New York Herald Tribune becomes a daily New York City newspaper as a result of a merger between the *Herald* and the *New-York Tribune;* until 1966; generally supportive of the Republican party.

Wladyslaw Stanislaw Reymont, Polish writer of fiction, receives the Nobel Prize for literature.

The Saturday Review of Literature, a weekly journal of literary commentary, begins publication at New York City; becomes *The Saturday Review* in 1952, then ceases publication in 1982.

The Transatlantic Review, edited and published from Paris by Ford Madox Ford, established as a periodical of general literature; Ford, James Joyce, and E. E. Cummings are among the contributors; until 1925; revived in 1959.

The Tsukiji Little Theater opens in Tokyo, thus beginning the modern theater movement in Japan.

Margaret Wilhemina Wilson, American novelist, receives the Pulitzer Prize in fiction for *The Able McLaughlins* (1923).

1925

BIRTHS

Garnik Addarian. Armenian poet; he will become one of the most popular writers of verse for Armenians in the Near East; his poem on pain and recompense will earn him the principal literary prize awarded on the fiftieth anniversary of the Armenian genocide.

Ali Mohammad Afghani. Iranian novelist; his social fiction will focus upon family relationships, particularly polygamy, among the craftsmen of small Iranian towns, as well as upon general relationships among young people; he will be tried for treason and sentenced to death, but his sentence will be commuted to life imprisonment, and he will finally be pardoned.

Thea Beatrice May Astley. Australian writer of fiction; her well-crafted and perceptive novels will be both poetic and harshly realistic; thematically, she will expose the sterility of human relationships, particularly focusing on the pettiness that contributes to human cruelty.

Eddy J. Bruma. Surinamese playwright, poet, and writer of fiction; through his work, he will attempt to encourage independence of spirit and pride in the local Sranan-Tongo language; in his drama, he will introduce complex themes, scenes, and structures, seeking to fuse past and present native cultures.

Jan Rynveld Carew. Guyanan novelist, playwright, and poet; his energetic literary products will concern the theme of "flights from origins and quests for roots"; he will also confront the problems of racial discrimination and misunderstanding.

Jose Durand. Peruvian essayist, literary commentator and historian, and writer of fiction; he will reside in Mexico between 1947 and 1953, and there write stories whose interest derives from the development of human tensions rather than from plot; his skill with language will become his principal literary contribution.

Frantz Fanon. Martinique essayist; he will become a practicing psychiatrist, as well as a humanist and a revolutionary; his works will concern the identity problems of blacks, the redemptive power of violence in the African struggle for liberation, and the role of violence in effecting historical change; his prose will be powerful and intellectually compelling.

Khalil Hawi. Lebanese poet; his verse will reflect the influences of Arabic and European poetry; he will draw, both for substance and style, upon Percy Bysshe Shelley, Ezra Pound, T. S. Eliot, Jean-Paul Sartre, and Friedrich Nietzsche; he will also rely upon the symbol of the sailor (Sinbad) in search of truth.

Donald Rodney Justice. American poet; his lyrics, sonnets, and sestinas will be stylistically graceful; when the substance of his verse is personal, he will embrace an allusive style and a slightly archaic poetic diction; he will attempt to rejuvenate, rather than to reject, poetic tradition, believing that "tradition thrives principally on the talents of its practitioners."

Clarice Lispector (d. 1977). Ukranian-born Brazilian writer of fiction; she will help to introduce into Brazilian fiction modernist techniques; thus, she will widen the range of her nation's literature by focusing on the subjective nature of reality; her intensely lyrical prose style will be rich in symbolism and metaphor, and she will examine the role of language in shaping and expressing identity.

Lars Lundvist. Swedish poet; his most significant contribution to modern Swedish literature will be his highly innovative and personal application of Lapland themes and imagery to verse; nonetheless, his works will transcend regional interest through their modernist characteristics.

Jon Mirande (d. 1972). French-Basque poet and novelist; he will develop a type of poetic prose that will inject new life into Basque literature; he will become one of the first writers of Basque prose and poetry to exhibit modern tendencies.

Flannery O'Connor (d. 1964). American writer of fiction; she will be recognized for her contribution to the "Southern Gothic," relying upon grotesque humor and complicated symbolism; her Roman Catholic upbringing and beliefs, as well as her creation of grotesque characters, will cause her fiction to be far different from that of the majority of Southern writers; nonetheless, she will present Southern Protestant primitivism as an authentic form of Christianity.

Kerima Polotan-Tuvera. Philippine writer of fiction; he will write in English and publish his stories principally in magazines; he will also write a critical study of Imelda Romualdez Marcos (1969), the wife of the then-president of the Philippines.

Mohan Rakes. Indian (Hindi) writer of fiction; he will write psychological stories and novels concerned with urban middle-class life, emphasizing themes of gradual or sudden disillusionment.

Ras Dizzy. Jamaican poet and essayist; he will become a practicing painter, and he will pen and attach verses to the backs of his canvasses; his poems will tend to be somewhat disconnected, with little discernible rhythm, and stand as commentaries upon his paintings.

Bernardo Santareno (pseudonym of Antonio Martinho do Rosario; d. 1980). Portuguese playwright; as a medical doctor working aboard fishing vessels, he will develop an intimate knowledge of the world of Portuguese fishermen, and those experiences will be reflected in his dramas; laboring under the restrictions of the Salazar regime, he will also write plays of social and political protest, embracing the causes of the simple and the oppressed against the rich and the powerful.

William Styron. American writer of fiction; his powerful novels will emotionally affect readers, primarily because of their themes and the poetic quality of their language; his fiction will generally depict anxious and desperate characters who seek to preserve their identity in the face of alienation.

Yuri Valentinovich Trifonov (d. 1981). Russian writer of fiction; he will earn the reputation as perhaps the finest nondissident Russian writer of the post-World War II era; he will chronicle the lives of the Moscow intelligentsia, concentrating upon the complexity of personal relationships and the stressful nature of the urban Soviet lifestyle.

Pramudya Ananta Tur. Indonesian writer of fiction; he will be identified with the communist movement; thus, the majority of his fictional themes concern his country's revolutionary struggles against the Dutch, British, and Japanese; his heroes, even when defeated, emerge as moral victors: they never lose their human dignity.

Gore Vidal. American novelist, playwright, and critic; he will become an acute and acerbic observer of the American scene, satirizing subjects ranging from United States history to American social life.

John Barrington Wain. English poet, writer of fiction, and critic; his earliest work will fit easily into the mold of the "angry young men" of post-World War II poetry and fiction; his short stories will prove to be his best work, demonstrating the full range of his sensitivity and feeling.

Dieter Wellershoff. German novelist, playwright, and essayist; he will help to form the Kolner Schule, a group of influential West German writers who will employ the methods of new realism to create works in the style of the so-called "anti-novel"; thus, he will abandon conventional forms of logic and order; he will interpret reality as a series of risks, concerning himself with characters confronted by feelings of alienation and aimlessness.

Ru Zhijuan. Chinese writer of fiction; she will be influenced by traditional Chinese novels, Russian classics of the eighteenth and nineteenth centuries, and Soviet wartime fiction; her works will reflect qualities of socialist fiction in their deliberately simple plots and moralistic tone.

DEATHS

Amy Lawrence Lowell (b. 1874). American poet; she began as a writer of conventional verse, but, following a tour of England (1913), she adopted the principles of the imagists; thus, her poems became noted for their sensuous imagery; she also wrote perceptive literary criticism and a biographical study of John Keats; her volume *What's O'Clock* earns a Pulitzer Prize for poetry in 1926.

Wladyslaw Stanislaw Reymont (b. 1867). Polish writer of fiction; in his novels, particularly, he attacked modern industrial society and praised the purity of Polish village life; in 1924, he received the Nobel Prize for literature.

Sergei Aleksandrovich Yesenin (b. 1895). Russian poet; his early works were simple lyrics of peasant life and Nature; later, he attached himself to the imagists; his alcoholism, disillusionment with the results of the Russian Revolution of 1917, and failed marriages to Isadora Duncan and Sophia Tolstoy were factors in his decision to commit suicide.

Stefan Zeromski (b. 1864). Polish writer of fiction and poet; he expressed a deep and sincere concern for freedom and social justice.

PUBLICATIONS

Ivan Bunin, *Mitya's Love*—a novel by the Russian writer of fiction and poetry; written during the novelist's period in exile, the piece concerns an idealistic boy who experiences an unwise and unfortunate love affair.

John Dos Passos, *Manhattan Transfer*—a novel by the American writer of fiction; presents a vast panorama of urban culture, introducing a number of the writer's standard techniques and devices, including newspaper headlines, popular songs, the speech of the common people, political speeches, and actual political and national figures.

Theodore Dreiser, *An American Tragedy*—a novel by the American writer of fiction and social criticism; a naturalistic work indicting the gulf between the American dream of success and the provisions made available for its realization; thus, the destruction of the title character, Claude Griffiths, a weak-willed individual who aspires to wealth and power, is attributed to the American system.

T. S. Eliot, "The Hollow Men"—a poem by the American born-writer of verse and literary criticism; traces the poet's path toward his own individual form of High Anglicanism.

F. Scott Fitzgerald, *The Great Gatsby*—a novel by the American writer of fiction; examines the Jazz-Age generation's elusive search for the American dream, principally through the title character, Jay Gatsby, a farmer's son turned racketeer, whose ill-gotten wealth is acquired solely to gain acceptance into the sophisticated, moneyed world of the woman he loves, Daisy Buchanan; Gatsby's romantic illusions are interwoven with episodes that depict the callousness and moral irresponsibility of the affluent American society of the 1920s.

Fydor Gladkhov, *Tsement* (Cement)—a proletarian novel by the Russian writer of fiction, essayist, and playwright; the novelist documents the changes that occurred in Russia following the Revolution of 1917; a realistic and inspiring account of the rise of the new socialist society from the chaos of war and revolution; describes the collectivization of Russian industry and the transformation of traditional social and cultural values.

Ellen Glasgow, *Barren Ground*—a novel by the American writer of fiction; based upon the notion that the spirit of fortitude will triumph over one's sense of futility; thus, the principal character is defeated by love, but she transforms her father's barren ground into a prosperous farm, relying heavily upon her own determination to succeed.

Maxim Gorky, *Delo Artamonovykh* (The Artamonov Business)—a novel by the Russian writer of fiction and essayist; analyzes the decline of a mercantile family until, in the end, the Soviets even take over the veteran businessman's villa.

Sirek Walda Sellase Heruy, *The New World*—a novel by the Ethiopian writer of fiction; a French-trained young man returns to a backward part of his country; defying custom, he celebrates, with modesty, both the funeral of his father and his marriage to a woman of his own choosing; the piece comes to a close with a utopian vision of a national church council deciding upon certain long-needed social and religious reforms.

Du Bose Heyward, *Porgy*—a novel by the American writer of fiction and playwright; depicts the activities of blacks in Charleston, South Carolina; best known for the 1927 dramatic adaptation by the writer's wife, Dorothy, and for George Gershwin's recreation of the work as a folk opera in 1935.

Robinson Jeffers, *Roan Stallion, Tamar, and Other Poems*—a collection by the American poet; the narrative "Roan Stallion" describes a woman's passionate adoration of a horse, relying heavily upon myth; the combination of myth and forbidden passions (incest, patricide, love of human being for beast) permeates the volume, as does the poet's acute sense of locale.

Franz Kafka, *Der Prozess* (The Trial)—an unfinished novel by the Czech-born Austrian writer of fiction; the narrative relates the arrest of "Joseph K." by warders from a mysterious court; his trial goes on for a year, but he cannot determine the crime of which he has been accused; in the end, he is executed; essentially, the work announces the total disintegration of traditional beliefs and values in the twentieth century.

Sinclair Lewis, *Arrowsmith*—a novel by the American writer of fiction; the writer turns his sharp eye upon the medical profession, also creating his first female character with depth and the ability to play the same hard games as her male counterpart; essentially, medical research and social status vie with ethics and morality; awarded the Pulitzer Prize in fiction.

Thomas Mokopu Mofolo, *Chaka* (Charles: An Historical Romance)—a novel by the Basutoland (Lesotho) writer of fiction; focuses upon the rise and decline of an early nineteenth-century Zulu monarch, who systematically conquered Natal and, by 1824, rules over 50,000 subjects; in the end, his ego and bloodlust prompt a reign of terror, culminating in his murder by his half-brothers.

Sean O'Casey, *Juno and the Paycock*—a tragicomedy by the Irish playwright; concerns a Dublin family caught in the civil war of 1922 in which the newly formed Free State government stood in opposition to the Irish Republican Army; the family suffers destruction by a combination of their own folly and the brutality of war; betrayal, cowardice, vanity, and drunkenness play important roles in that destruction; the comic elements derive from the writer's satiric attacks upon a host of political and paramilitary characters.

Jules Renard, *Journal Inedit* (The Journal of Jules Renard)—an autobiographical narrative by the French diarist, poet, and writer of fiction; offers details about the writer's childhood and his strange relationship with his parents, also providing insight into the peasants of his village and the fashionable social and literary circles of Paris; five volumes, to 1927.

Pauline Urmson Smith, *The Little Karoo*—a collection of stories by the South African writer of fiction, playwright, and poet; the pieces portray Afrikaner men and women isolated from one another by their own preoccupations and sufferings.

Alfred North Whitehead, *Science and the Modern World*—a prose tract by the English philosopher and mathematician; beginning with the sixteenth century, the writer analyzes the patterns of cultural development within Western society; the aesthetic and scientific preoccupations of past ages have shaped the writer's own philosophy of organism.

William Carlos Williams, *In the American Grain*—a volume of criticism by the American poet, essayist, playwright, and writer of fiction; impressionistic essays about significant Western historical and literary figures, all concerned with the rise and development of the United States.

Virginia Woolf, *The Common Reader*—a two-volume collection of essays by the English writer of fiction and literary criticism; the writer generally ranks criticism below imaginative writing and the creative impulse; she also argues against realism and naturalism, preferring the inner exploration of the truth of experience; to 1932.

——————, *Mrs. Dalloway*—a novel by the English writer of fiction; the chimes of Big Ben serve to punctuate the events of a single day in central London; a complex personality study of a fifty-one-year-old woman of affluence and position; the stream of consciousness technique is used to present an interior monologue by the title character, as she reminisces about friends, family, and past suitors.

William Butler Yeats, *A Vision*—a prose exposition by the Irish writer of verse, playwright, and essayist; sets forth the writer's system of symbolism; he envisions life to be patterned after "The Great Wheel," with its twenty-eight phases of the lunar month; revised in 1937.

Anzia Yezierska, *Bread Givers*—a novel by the Russian-born writer of fiction and essayist; traces the efforts of the principal character to free herself from the restrictive religious doctrines of her father and to find a place for herself in America; as an American, the girl learns to accept and to incorporate old world values into her American life; parallels the writer's own struggles for independence.

EVENTS

Edna Ferber, American writer of fiction, receives the Pulitzer Prize in fiction for her novel *So Big* (1924).

Harper's New Monthly Magazine, the New York City illustrated literary and political periodical, changes its name to *Harper's Magazine;* later, *Harper's* is simply placed on the cover.

Sidney Howard, American playwright, receives the Pulitzer Prize in drama for *They Knew What They Wanted* (1924).

The London Bible Society distributes 10.5 million Bibles in 566 languages.

The New Yorker, founded by Harold Ross, begins publication in New York City; a weekly magazine featuring regular columns that highlight aspects of the sophisticated life; carries such contributors as E. B. White, John Updike, John Hersey, Donald Barthelme, and James Thurber; contains poetry, short fiction, and intellectual and humorous cartoons and fillers, particularly linguistic and syntactical "goofs" from magazines and newspapers across the nation.

Sir Arthur Quiller-Couch, English miscellaneous writer and scholar, publishes *The Oxford Book of English Prose.*

Review of English Studies, a scholarly journal devoted to literary and linguistic subjects, begins publication at Oxford; a "new series" commences in 1950.

Edwin Arlington Robinson, American poet, receives the Pulitzer Prize in poetry for his dramatic narrative *The Man Who Died Twice* (1924).

George Bernard Shaw, Irish playwright and critic, receives the Nobel Prize in literature.

The Virginia Quarterly Review, a journal of social and economic commentary, literary criticism, and original poetry and fiction, begins publication at the University of Virginia, Charlottesville; contributors include Allen Tate, Robert Frost, Sherwood Anderson, Thomas Wolfe, T. S. Eliot, and Edwin Arlington Robinson.

1926

BIRTHS

Abd al-Wahhab al-Bayati. Egyptian poet; a leader of the socialist Left, he will spend periods of exile in several East European countries; thus, his poetry will reveal his knowledge of that part of the world, as well as his wide reading on, among other subjects, mythology, the Bible, and history; his themes will include exile, alienation, industrialization and urbanization, deprivation, depersonalization, and spiritual anguish.

Paul Blackburn (d. 1971). American poet; he will combine experiments with verse structure and colloquial speech, creating rhythmic, conversational poetry.

Michel Butor. French writer of fiction; his experimental novels will employ shifting time sequences and interior monologue; he will write three major novels between 1954 and 1977.

Driss Chraibi. Moroccan writer of fiction; he will publish his work in French; his fiction will attack traditional Islam, colonialism, and the impact of French culture upon North Africa; he will also express disillusionment with conditions in independent Morocco.

Robert White Creeley. American poet; his style will exist as "an instrument of exclusion," relying upon exceedingly brief lines (sometimes only one or two words) to trace the immediacy of the poet's feelings.

Rene Depestre. Haitian poet, essayist, and writer of fiction; he will become, at age nineteen, the leading poet of the young radical generation; he will attempt to demonstrate that poetry and revolution develop from a common ground; further, he will free his poems from traditional French rhythms.

James Patrick Dunleavy. American-born Irish playwright and writer of fiction and miscellaneous prose; in his fiction, he will develop a rhapsodic, staccato style, intended to represent the distorted minds of his narrators; he will also adopt the distinctively Irish comic strain prevalent in the works of such writers as James Joyce and Samuel Beckett; the majority of his themes will concern the emotional and psychological changes brought about by the loss of loved ones.

Alda de Espirito Santo. Sao Tome poet; her verse most of which has been published in Portuguese, will describe atrocities committed by whites in black Africa; she will also express her sympathies for the black day laborers toiling on the large Portuguese plantations.

John Robert Fowles. English writer of fiction and poet; he will develop an interest in manipulating the form of the novel, particularly concerning himself with psychological relationships between the historical past and the present; mythology will also become an element of his fiction.

Memet Fuat. Turkish literary critic and writer of fiction; he will publish reviews of literature and art, initiate a series of literary anthologies, and annually survey and evaluate Turkish literature; he will also write short fiction and translate American short stories and plays.

Allen Ginsberg. American poet; he will become a leading figure of the "Beat Generation"; his reputation will come to rest upon *Howl,* a long poem attacking American values that became the manifesto of the Beat movement.

Choku Kanai. Japanese poet; his work will focus upon such themes as love, death, suspicion, and innocence; his volume *Hunger, an Inordinate Ambition* will receive the H Poetry Prize, the highest poetry award in Japan.

Zareh Khrakhuni (real name Artho Tchiumpiushian). Turkish-born Armenian poet; he will write verse that follows the conventions of traditional West Armenian poetry; he will also translate Western classical literature into Armenian and adapt Armenian classics for children.

John Knowles. American writer of fiction; although he will produce several novels and a collection of short stories, his literary reputation will come to rest upon his initial effort, *A Separate Peace* (1960), a novel that will be compared with J. D. Salinger's *The Catcher in the Rye* (1951).

Jean Margaret Wemyss Laurence (d. 1987). Canadian writer of fiction; she will become known for her novels of character depicting individuals that people from all walks of life can recognize; she will also write short stories, essays, and commentaries upon African literature.

James Merrill. American poet; he will represent life as a comedy to be observed and incorporate specifics from American popular culture into his poetry; his work will earn him two National Books Awards, the Bollingen Prize in Poetry (1973), the Pulitzer Prize (1977), and the Book Critics Circle Award.

Alfonso Sastre. Spanish playwright; his controversial dramatic pieces, written from a Marxist and existentialist perspective, will concern such subjects as injustice, alienation, and violence.

William DeWitt Snodgrass. American poet; he will develop a style in which dramatic action unfolds through the speaker's intimate disclosures and self-revelations; he will remain a technically conservative poet, writing most of his verse in tightly rhymed patterns and set meters; thematically, he will provide the average middle-class American with a voice.

Ludvik Vaculik. Czech writer of fiction and diarist; he will become known for his self-portraits of the creative artist during the various stages of life; he will interject into his work personal letters and commentaries concerning his own youthful flights of intellectual, creative, and moral fancies; he will convey his impressions upon what has come to be known as a "life/literature line."

DEATHS

Shio Aragvispireli (b. 1867). Georgian (SSR) writer of fiction; his stories of village life describe the misery and despair of simple, honest people, attacking the debauched and decadent rich.

Rudolf Christoph Eucken (b. 1846). German philosopher; his activist philosophy sought spiritual control of life and approached the ethical idealism of Immanuel Kant and Johann Fichte; he received the Nobel Prize for literature in 1908.

Aleksey Yeliseyevich Kulakovskiy (b. 1877). Yakut poet and scholar; he became a philologist, ethnographer, and tireless promoter of culture among his people; his poem *Bayanay Algyha* (The Enchantment of Bayanay, 1900) became the first literary work written in the Yakut language, thus laying the foundation for the literature of his nation; between 1897 and 1900, he wrote in Russian, but afterwards his works appeared in Yakut.

Eino Leino (pseudonym of Armas Eino Leopold Lonnbohm; b. 1878). Finnish poet, dramatist, and writer of fiction; he effectively combined the mysticism and allegorical style of the French Symbolists with the meters and subjects of traditional Finnish folk poetry; he employed legendary characters and plots, while reflecting upon modern social and political issues; he spent the years immediately preceding his death drinking heavily and engaging in highly publicized love affairs.

Jean Richepin (b. 1849). Algerian-born French poet, writer of fiction, and playwright; his revolutionary volume of poems, *La Chanson des Gueux* (Songs of the Poor, 1876), caused him to be fined and imprisoned.

Rainer Maria Rilke (b. 1875). Czech-born German poet, dramatist, and writer of fiction; considered the most significant lyric poet of modern Germany; ideas for his sensitive and introspective verse originated from his extensive travels, he developed a rich poetic style characterized by striking imagery and symbolism; his elegies of 1923 contain his highest praise of human existence; his fiction contains elements of philosophy, psychology, and poetry.

Abdul-halim Sharar (b. 1860). Indian (Urdu) journalist, novelist, and popular historian; his fictional works are quasi-historical romances in praise of the past glories of Muslim civilization; he composed a series of essays depicting the history, culture, and society of old Lucknow.

PUBLICATIONS

George Bacovia, *Scintei Galbene* (Yellow Sparks)—a verse collection by the Romanian poet; in these pieces, the writer uses symbolic imagery in an attempt to express emotions and ideas by suggestion; the collection appears somber and pessimistic, and the author creates a macabre atmosphere through the use of colors (white, black, dark purple) and recurring images (dampness, darkness, coldness).

Georges Bernanos, *Sous le Soleil de Satan* (Star of Satan)—the first novel by the French writer of fiction; a priest struggles with Satan (in the guise of a horse trader) for his soul and that of a precocious village girl.

Sidonie-Gabrielle Colette, *La Fin de Cheri* (The Last of Cheri)—a novel by the French writer of fiction; concerns the title character's inability to cope with the responsibilities of life away from his middle-aged lover; thus, he adopts a nihilistic attitude and eventually commits suicide, while the woman withdraws from men and sex and finds internal peace.

Hart Crane, *White Buildings*—a collection of the American poet's first verses; the pieces reveal the extent to which the writer had been affected by the French poets' experiments with language, color, and sound; contains "Wine Menagerie," "Praise for an Urn," and a series of "Voyages" displaying the poet's sensitivity toward Herman Melville and the open sea.

Bakary Diallo, *Force-Bonte* (Good Will)—a novel by the Senegalese writer of fiction and poetry; comprised partly of the writer's account of his experiences in the French territorial army and his suffering in a hospital; at that point in his life, the writer appeared (at least in the novel) willing to accept French superiority; nonetheless, the piece does convey the brutalities endured by blacks during the colonial period.

William Faulkner, *Soldiers Pay*—the first novel by the American writer of fiction, published with the help of Sherwood Anderson; concerns a dying soldier's return home, suffering from blindness and loss of memory.

Andre Gide, *Les Faux-Monnayeurs* (The Counterfeiters)—a novel by the French playwright, writer of fiction, and essayist; the writer concerns himself principally with a group of young men who gather around a novelist, whose work in progress is the title of the piece; the plot tends to be melodramatic, going forward on the premise of the consequences of living a forged life; according to the writer's own critical criteria, the work stands as his only "novel."

Ernest Hemingway, *The Sun Also Rises*—a novel by the American writer of fiction; concerns American expatriates searching for meaning in the wake of postwar disillusionment; the novel's publication made Hemingway a famous writer.

Langston Hughes, *The Weary Blues*—a collection of verse by the American poet, playwright, and writer of fiction and miscellany; the pieces obviously incorporate blues stanzas, but each poem has a larger structure deriving from jazz, made more complicated by the writer's experimentation with both form and substance.

Franz Kafka, *Das Schloss* (The Castle)—an unfinished novel by the Czech-born writer of fiction, published posthumously; a nightmarish story of alienation set in a dreamworld that operates according to cryptic and undiscoverable laws; the protagonist, "K," embarks on a quest consisting of a series of frustrations without ultimate resolution; important in establishing the writer's reputation.

D. H. Lawrence, *The Plumed Serpent*—a novel by the English fiction writer, poet, and playwright; a forty-year-old Irish widow arrives in Mexico, where she struggles with deliverance and awaits a mystical rebirth; she meets a mystic and a revolutionary and gains introduction to a cult; ultimately, she accepts subjugation and loss of the self.

H. L. Mencken, *Notes on Democracy*—a volume of social and political criticism by the American journalist and miscellaneous writer; a damning analysis of American political and social assumptions, particularly the notion that the people can effectively govern themselves without reliance upon a civilized aristocracy.

A. A. Milne, *Winnie the Pooh*—a work of juvenile fiction by the English writer of drama, fiction, poetry, and nonfiction; the popularity of the work, as well as its longevity among the classics of literature, have overshadowed everything else produced by this writer.

Henri de Montherlant, *Les Bestiaires* (The Bullfighters)—a novel by the French writer of fiction; reflects the author's actual experiences in the bullring; a number of critics have placed the piece far above anything on the subject written by Ernest Hemingway.

Sean O'Casey, *The Plough and the Stars*—a play by the Irish dramatist; set during the 1916 Easter uprising against the British, the work concentrates upon the poor people struggling and dying in the slums of Dublin; opposite them, British soldiers also struggle and die in the same streets, thus creating a series of tragicomic ironies; the principal characters spend most of their time attacking one another, creating scenes of hilarity and bitterness.

Eugene O'Neill, *The Great God Brown*—an expressionist drama by the American playwright; focuses upon the inner torment of an artist, who becomes a drunken neurotic because his sensitivities are offended by the materialistic world; in contrast stands the title character, who lacks creativity but manipulates the artist and takes credit for his architectural achievements; the play's complexity derives from the playwright's introduction of masks to symbolize aspects of his characters' personalities.

Horacio Quiroga, *Los Desterrados*—a collection of short stories by the Uruguayan writer of fiction, essayist, poet, and playwright; comprised of objective portraits of exiles of the Argentine jungle: pioneers, drunkards, derelicts, day laborers, and general eccentrics; the stories also contain acid social commentary upon the overall exploitation of contract laborers in South America.

Sri, *Inglis Gitagalu* (English Poems)—a collection of English poems translated into the Kannada language by the Indian scholar and writer of prose poems; through this volume, the editor and translator introduced works by William Wordsworth, Percy Bysshe Shelley, and Robert Burns.

Anton Hamsen Tammsaare, *Tode ja Oigus* (Truth and Justice)—a novel by the Estonian writer of fiction, playwright, and essayist; a comprehensive and realistic view of rural Estonians, revealing both their strengths and weaknesses; the writer combines elements of psychological realism and social satire, five volumes, to 1933.

EVENTS

The Book-of-the-Month Club becomes the first of the American literary "discount" clubs, selling volumes produced by various publishers to subscribers at discounted prices.

Grazia Deledda, Italian writer of fiction, receives the Nobel Prize for literature, becoming the first (and only) Italian woman to attain that honor.

Henry Watson Fowler, English lexicographer and grammarian, publishes the initial edition of *A Dictionary of Modern English Usage.*

George Edward Kelly, American playwright, receives the Pulitzer Prize in drama for *Craig's Wife* (1925).

Sinclair Lewis, American writer of fiction, receives the Pulitzer Prize in fiction for *Arrowsmith* (1925); he refuses to accept the $1000 award.

Amy Lawrence Lowell, American writer of imagist verse, posthumously awarded the Pulitzer Prize in poetry for *What's O'Clock* (1925).

1927

BIRTHS

Gunter Wilhelm Grass. German novelist, poet, essayist, and playwright; he will, particularly in his fiction, capture the reactions of German citizens to the rise of Nazism, the horrors of war, and the guilt prevalent in the aftermath of Hitler's ascension to power; he will be influenced by surrealism, German expressionism, and a variety of writers, including Herman Melville, Bertolt Brecht, and Alfred Doblin.

Malek Haddad. Algerian poet and writer of fiction; he will depict the lives of Algerian exiles in France, concentrating upon their personal problems; in introductions to his collections of verse, he will discuss such issues as why Arabs publish their works in French, as opposed to their native languages.

Yusuf Idris. Egyptian writer of fiction and playwright; his short fiction will focus upon ordinary people and their concerns, and will also criticize the bureaucracy and social injustice; his plays will develop the theme of the individuals social responsibility and will address the conflict between egoism and the moral duty of the patriotic person.

Ivar Ivask. Estonian-born American poet and critic; he will undertake critical studies of Gottfried Benn, Hugo von Hofmannsthal, and Austrian literature; he will publish poetry in German, English, and Estonian, complementing a number of the volumes with his own illustrations; he will become a professor of modern languages and literatures at the University of Oklahoma.

Bertene Juminer. Guyanese writer of fiction, playwright, and essayist; his fiction will concern itself with the problem of cultural identity, exploring the anguish of the educated black elite who have been assimilated into French culture, but who have remained responsive to their black cultural heritage; a practicing physician, he will publish more than one hundred essays on medical and scientific subjects.

George Lamming. Barbadian novelist, poet, and critic; he will become committed to the politics of Africa and will explore the question of what happens when those people who have struggled for independence begin to govern and control.

Vyankates Digambar Madgulkar. Indian (Mirathi) writer of fiction; the plots of his short stories and novels will be based on the village life of his own region.

Harry Kurt Victor Mulisch. Dutch writer of fiction, poet, and essayist; his fiction will be realistic in style, with mythic, historic, and symbolic overtones; his work will be especially recognized for his psychological probing and keen awareness of the cruel aspects of human nature.

Richard Murphy. Irish poet and essayist; he will document the lives of both the Catholics and the Anglo-Irish Protestants; he will use clear and direct language and traditional poetic forms.

Nayantara Pandit Sahgal. Indian writer of fiction and miscellany; she will provide insightful analyses of life in post-colonial India, as well as sharp and accurate perspectives on her nation's political leaders; thus, a number of her fictional characters will resemble actual politicians; her close relationship with those leaders and her privileged social status will accord her works an interesting perspective.

Rafael Sanchez Ferlosio. Italian-born Spanish novelist; his work will reveal him to be a skillful manipulator of the Spanish language and an exponent of the nonutilitarian view of literature; his fiction will frequently be poetic, with accurately rendered and interesting dialogue.

DEATHS

Ryunosuke Akutagawa (b. 1892). Japanese writer of fiction, poet, essayist, and translator; his work contributed significantly to his generation's thoughtful consideration of such issues as the function and merit of various literary genres and the artist's role in contemporary society; he was also influential in freeing Japanese literature from the gossip and didacticism that had characterized it prior to 1868; he relied upon elements of both Eastern and Western literary forms, thus creating a distinctive form of Japanese literature; he poisons himself following the mental breakdown of a friend.

Mikhail Petrovich Artsybashev (b. 1878). Russian writer of fiction, playwright, and essayist; his work reveals his preoccupation with sex, death, and the stultification of individual free expression by social convention; in his fiction and drama, society crumbles as its members succumb to despair and suicide, he dies at Warsaw of tuberculosis.

Solomon Bloomgarden (b. 1870). American Jewish scholar, writer, and biblical translator; he wrote verse, short fiction, essays, and fables in Yiddish; his three-volume *The Feet of the Messenger* describes his visit in 1914 with his family to Palestine; his major project was a translation of the Bible into Yiddish; in 1900, he entered a sanitarium for the treatment of tuberculosis.

Georg Morris Cohen Brandes (b. 1842). Danish literary historian and critic; he exposed Scandinavia to contemporary European thought; as a disciple of the French critic and historian Hippolyte Adolphe Taine (1828-1893), he helped to direct Scandinavian literature away from romanticism toward realism and social consciousness.

Ricardo Guiraldes (b. 1886). Argentine writer of fiction; in his principal novels and short stories, he celebrated the life of the Argentine gaucho; rejecting the social and literary models of Europe, he turned in his work to what has been termed the "intrahistory" of his own country, depicting Argentine characters fully equipped to develop and mature within the confines of their own local environments.

Maximilian Harden (b. 1861). German political essayist and journalist; he founded at Berlin the weekly *Die Zukunft*, through which he communicated his fearless criticism of court scandals and political injustice; the government silenced him in 1917 by drafting him into the army as a clerk.

Gaston Leroux (b. 1868). French writer of fiction and playwright; he has been recognized for his original contributions to the detective novel and the horror story; he created classic figures in the annals of crime and detective fiction, and he developed what has become known as the "locked room" mystery.

Matilde Serao (b. 1856). Greek-born Italian writer of fiction; she focused almost entirely upon Neapolitan life, communicating its color and its teeming activity; careful reading of her work reveals that she transcended the age of politeness in the European novel.

PUBLICATIONS

Sadriddin Ayni, *Dokhunda* (The Mountain Villager)—a novel by the Iranian writer of fiction, the first to be written in the Tajik language; relates the rough conditions endured by people in the mountains and their struggles to change their lives.

Willa Cather, *Death Comes for the Archbishop*—a novel by the American writer of fiction; sets during the mid-nineteenth century, the work records the lives of two missionaries, focusing upon the organization of the New Mexico diocese and detailing events from the viewpoints of both the Catholic Church and the Indians.

Jean Cocteau, *Oedipus-Rex*—the first of several dramatic adaptations of the Oedipal myth by the French playwright and poet; an opera-oratorio, with music by Igor Stravinsky.

——————, *Opera: Oevres Poetiques, 1925-1927*—a verse collection by the French poet and playwright; the pieces blend elements of paganism and Christianity, all proceeding from the writer's thesis: "I am the lie that always tells the truth."

Alexander Fadeyev, *Razgrom* (The Rout)—a novel by the Russian writer of fiction; follows the stylistic and psychological methods found in the fiction of Leo Tolstoi; concerns the civil war in Siberia, where the communist guerrillas fight both whites and Japanese; the leader of the guerrillas, a Jew, transforms his dissident band into a united fighting body, emerging, however, as the only true communist among the lot.

E. M. Forster, *Aspects of the Novel*—a critical tract by the English writer of fiction; the essayist examines and then rejects the notion that the writer of fiction must avoid, at all costs, presenting his own point of view, arguing in favor of the omniscient narrator.

Martin Heidegger, *Sein und Zeit* (Being and Time)—a prose tract by the German philosopher; analyzes the concepts of care, mood, and the individual's relationship with death; the writer relates authenticity of being, as well as the anguish of modern society, to the individual's confrontation with his or her own temporality.

Ernest Hemingway, *Men without Women*—a collection of fourteen short stories by the American writer of fiction; includes "The Undefeated," "The Killers," "Fifty Grand," "Today is Friday," "In Another Country," "A Pursuit Race," "Banal Story," "Now I Lay Me," and "Hills Like White Elephants."

Hermann Hesse, *Der Steppenwolf*—a novel by the German-born writer of fiction, poet, and critic; concerns a forty-eight-year-old man who has prepared to commit suicide at age fifty, but who finds a more meaningful solution at the entrance to the "magic theater"; focuses upon the traditional conflict between Nature and Spirit, resolved when the principal character determines to seek a new beginning to his life.

Robinson Jeffers, *The Women at Point Sur*—a long narrative poem by the American writer of verse; a renegade Christian minister completely rejects the principles of traditional morality; the piece is harshly realistic, the poet having abandoned his earlier reliance upon myth and symbol.

Franz Kafka, *Amerika*—a novel by the Czech-born writer of fiction; written between 1911 and 1914 and published posthumously; a harshly realistic account of a condemned man whose family sends him to America; there, he attempts to throw off his sense of exile and isolation, engaging in a futile search for personal salvation.

Sinclair Lewis, *Elmer Gantry*—a novel by the American writer of fiction; considered his harshest attack upon American institutions, in this instance, the evangelical church; the title character applies the ideology of big business to religion, thus exploiting his calling; the work caused a furor among readers.

Charles Lindbergh, *We*—a highly popular narrative by the American aviator; concerns the events of the writer's solo, nonstop transatlantic flight from New York City to Paris, where he landed on 31 May 1927; the title refers to the pilot and his plane, "The Spirit of St. Louis."

Francois Mauriac, *Therese Desqueyroux*—a novel by the French novelist and playwright; the title character, bored with her marriage, allows herself to be tempted into sin, standing ready and willing to poison her husband.

Saluma Musa, *Al-Yawm Wa'l-Ghad* (Today and Tomorrow)—a collection of prose pieces by the Egyptian essayist; written in Arabic, the pieces attempt to synthesize Western thought and popularize it by means of concrete examples; the volume causes a furor because the writer, a Copt, dared to lecture Muslims about modernization.

Vernon Louis Parrington, *Main Currents in American Thought*—a historical and critical survey of literature and thought in the United States by the American literary scholar; the writer attempts to evaluate the entire American tradition in political, social and economic terms; though modern scholars disagree with many of his conclusions, the work is considered a significant first attempt at fashioning an intellectual history of America based on a broad interpretive basis; three volumes, to 1930; the final volume was left incomplete at the writer's death in 1929.

Marcel Proust, *A la Recherche du Temps Perdu* (Remembrance of Things Past)—a cyclic novel by the French writer of fiction, published in installments between 1913 and 1927; focuses upon a neurotic, sensitive, and asthmatic narrator; praised for its artistic construction, this masterpiece is often appreciated for presenting within one work a social historian's chronicle of turn-of-the-century Paris society, a philosopher's reflections on the nature of time and consciousness, and a psychologist's insight into a tangled network of personalities.

Edwin Arlington Robinson, *Tristram*—a long poem by the American writer of verse; one of his Arthurian pieces, the poem is awarded a Pulitzer Prize in 1928.

Upton Sinclair, *Oil!*—a novel by the American writer of fiction; focuses on the son of a large California oil developer, his education in love and business; he disregards his social status to aid the workers; the writer interweaves into this narrative key elements of scandal and corruption during the 1920s.

Thornton Wilder, *The Bridge of San Luis Rey*—a novel by the American writer of fiction and playwright; traces the fortunes of a number of people who are killed when a bridge in South America collapses; the piece will be awarded a Pulitzer Prize for fiction in 1928.

Virginia Woolf, *To the Lighthouse*—a novel by the English writer of fiction and literary criticism; treats the writer's favorite themes of marriage, time, and death; as evidence of the maturation of her subjective mode, plot is abandoned, with unity and coherence provided instead by imagery, symbolism, and poetic elements; establishes a conflict between a gracious and much-admired woman and her husband, a self-centered and self-pitying philosopher.

Arnold Zweig, *Der Streit um den Sergeanten Grischa* (The Case of Sergeant Grischa)—a novel by the German writer of fiction; acclaimed as a significant contribution to the war novel; the writer traces the pitiless nature of bureaucracy as it relates to a Russian prisoner who has been executed not because he was guilty, but because the system demands a victim; by its very nature, according to the writer, war is a great injustice.

EVENTS

The American Caravan, a yearly anthology of American literature, begins publication; Ernest Hemingway, John Dos Passos, Eugene O'Neill, and Gertrude Stein are among its early contributors; until 1936.

Henri Bergson, French philosopher and essayist, receives the Nobel Prize for literature.

Louis Bromfield, American writer of fiction, receives the Pulitzer Prize in fiction for his novel *Early Autumn* (1926).

Paul Eliot Green, American playwright, receives the Pulitzer Prize in drama for *In Abraham's Bosom* (1927).

Emory Holloway, American biographer and literary scholar, receives the Pulitzer Prize in biography/autobiography for *Whitman: An Interpretation in Narrative* (1926).

Hound and Horn, a literary magazine, begins publication at Harvard University in Cambridge, Massachusetts; it will move its offices to New York City in 1928; contributors include Katharine Ann Porter, Allen Tate, Gertrude Stein, Ezra Pound, and T. S. Eliot; until 1934.

The Literary Guild, a subscription discount book club, founded at New York City.

The Prairie Schooner, a literary journal with emphasis upon poetry, begins publication at the University of Nebraska, Lincoln.

Leonora Speyer, American writer of verse, receives the Pulitzer Prize in poetry for *Fiddler's Farewell* (1926).

1928

BIRTHS

Edward Franklin Albee. American playwright; he will produce clever and satiric one-act dramas; his more serious longer plays will focus upon the "existential present," where characters view life in terms of loss, measure love by its failure, and confront contact with absence; he will receive the Pulitzer Prize for drama in 1967 and 1975.

Maya Angelou (pseudonym of Marguerite Johnson). American poet and essayist; in addition to her four collections of verse, she will produce original plays for television and four volumes of autobiographical prose; she will, in her literary efforts and professional activities, stress the importance of African-Americans' cultural contributions.

Chingiz Aytmanov. Kirghiz (SSR) writer of fiction; he will write realistic short stories and novels and translate the works of Kirghiz writers into Russian; he will receive his formal training at the Gorky Literary Institute.

Shawqi Baghdadi. Syrian writer of fiction; his stories will analyze the psychological states of lonely people alienated from their environment, work, or family; he will frequently employ the stream of consciousness technique, often forcing readers to supply for themselves the framework of facts and circumstances.

Uwe Berger. East German poet; he will write classical sonnets, recalling the apocalyptic terror during the collapse of the Third Reich; he will also include in his collections poetic travel impressions of Soviet cities.

Osborne Henry Kwesi Brew. Ghanaian poet and short story writer; in a departure from traditional themes of African poetry, he will consider the value of the individual in contrast to the society in which he or she lives;

his style will tend to be lyrical, utilizing brief lines and broken phrases.

Edip Cansever. Turkish poet; he will constantly change his themes and stylistic techniques, essentially, however, always describing an alienated, drab, and despairing world from which human beings seek refuge in their subconscious; he will view people in their global context: naked, helpless, and incapable of transcending their human limitations.

Don Coles. Canadian poet and critic; in his verse, he will examine such traditional lyric themes as romantic love, beauty, and morality; he will also emphasize the nature and effects of time; his work will be mature and written in a confident, controlled style.

Raymond Federman. French-born American writer of fiction, poet, translator, and critic; he will practice and advocate the theories of "surfiction," a form of writing that does not imitate reality, but exposes the "fictionality" of reality; his work will demonstrate the influence of Samuel Beckett: stylistic innovation, syntactical experimentation, and abandonment of such fictional conventions as plot, character, and chronological development.

Carlos Fuentes. Mexican writer of fiction, playwright, and critic; he will attempt through his fiction to establish a viable Mexican identity; myth, legend, and history will be intertwined throughout his work, and he will examine the heritage of his nation to discover the essence of modern Mexican society.

Gabriel Jose Garcia Marquez. Colombian writer of fiction and critic; his fiction will blend elements of history, politics, social realism, and pure fantasy; he will embellish his works with surreal events and fantastic imagery to obscure the distinctions between illusion and reality and to define human existence; he will receive the Nobel Prize for literature in 1982.

Edouard Glissant. Martinique poet; he will attempt to harmonize his literary modernism with his political concerns, producing highly symbolic pieces; for him, a small collection of people (poets, smiths, the lame and the blind, prostitutes, "earth mothers") will represent the pathos of his island nation; for the blacks of this region, the traumas of colonialism and slavery will deplete their creative energies.

Thomas Kinsella. Irish poet and translator; he will attempt to extend the limits of his own

imagination and creative processes and will discuss such themes as cognition and perception, struggling to achieve, if only temporarily, some degree of creative order; he will employ traditional and formal logic and structure, strong narrative elements, and rich description.

Camara Laye (d. 1980). Guinean writer of fiction and autobiography; he will direct his work to an international audience; although concerned with spirituality and the vibrance of traditional African culture, his fiction will also confront such universal modern themes as alienation and the search for identity; his own exile from his home country (1965) will serve as a chronicle of the plight of the exile and the problems of adapting to change and cultural dislocation.

Hermann Schurrer. German poet; his work will reflect his own life experiences: alcoholic, unemployed, homeless, and banned from coffee houses and public institutions; he will emerge in his verse as socially nonconformist, highly sensitive, and intelligent; his poetry will be as complex and unconventional as his life, and it will not always be understood.

Alan Sillitoe. English writer of fiction and critic; his novels and short stories will reverberate with emotional intensity, attacking social injustice, hypocrisy, and exploitation.

Awang Usman (pseudonym of Tongkat Warrant). Malay poet and writer of fiction; his verse will be noted for its passionate concern for the freedom of his people, peace, and social justice; he will express himself in simple and direct language.

DEATHS

Vicente Blasco Ibanez (b. 1867). Spanish novelist; his political associations and realistic techniques led him to be termed "the Spanish Zola"; his fiction focuses upon a variety of subjects, including bullfighting, landlords and farmers, the horrors of World War I, and religious fanaticism; he spent his last years in exile at Menton, in southeastern France.

Sir Edmund Gosse (b. 1849). English novelist, biographer, and literary scholar; in addition to his *Father and Son* (1907), a spiritual autobiography upon which his reputation rests, he wrote critical biographies of Thomas Gray,

William Congreve, John Donne, and Algernon Charles Swinburne; as a critic, he is known as a popularizer who vividly and entertainingly conveyed a wide range of information to his readers.

Hemcandra Gosvami (b. 1872). Indian literary historian, editor, and poet; he helped to preserve and edit numerous works of Assamese classical and folk literature, offering with them erudite critical commentary; he compiled (1923-1929) a seven-volume anthology of such works, thus helping to provide a basis for an Assamese literary identity.

Thomas Hardy (b. 1840). English novelist and poet; regarded as one of the greatest novelists in the English language; depicted human existence as a tragedy determined by powers beyond the individual's control; his desire to reveal the underlying forces directing his characters' lives led him to realistically examine love and sexuality; he lies buried in Westminster Abbey.

Klabund (pseudonym of Alfred Henschke; b. 1890). German poet, writer of fiction, and playwright; he wrote historical novels that appealed to the middle classes and created in his poetry exquisite Oriental and alien worlds; he dies at age thirty-eight from consumption.

Hermann Sudermann (b. 1857). German playwright and novelist; used contemporary social themes and realistic dialogue, with conventional plotting and staging; early regarded as Germany's foremost exponent of Ibsenian Naturalism, but later judged as belonging to a middle ground between Realism and Romanticism.

Italo Svevo (pseudonym of Ettore Schmitz; b. 1861). Italian writer of fiction; his work tended to be psychological and introspective, remaining virtually unknown until its discovery by James Joyce; in a sophisticated style, he portrayed characters adept at psychoanalyzing themselves, but unable to succeed in their ambitions.

PUBLICATIONS

Stephen Vincent Benet, *John Brown's Body*—a long poem by the American writer of verse; an energetic portrayal of the personalities of the Civil War, the piece has been described both as the national poem of the United States and as a full-length novel in a variety of verse forms; it stands as a monument to the poet's technical facility.

Edmund Blunden, *Undertones of War*—an autobiographical prose work by the English poet and miscellaneous writer; an expression of the writer's antiwar sentiments, it describes with emotion the double destruction of man and nature in Flanders during World War I.

Rolfus Reginald Raymond Dhlomo, *An African Tragedy*—the first work by the African (Zulu) writer of fiction; a rambling account in which the writer describes the effects of the large city on the morals of simple country people; the first book published in English by an African.

Robert Frost, *West-Running Brook*—a volume of verse by the American poet; the pieces take their theme from the significant contrast of the title; the speaker of the title piece will proceed through life in a series of contrary movements.

Jean Giraudoux, *Sigfried*—a play by the French writer of fiction and drama; based upon the writer's novel *Siegfried et le Limousin* (My Friend from Limousin, 1922); the principal character loses his memory in the war and then becomes a leading figure in German politics; a woman attempts to rescue him and return him to his "Frenchness," but the man remains "German-minded."

Nazim Hikmet Ran, *Gunesi Icenlerin Turkusu* (The Song of Those Who Drink the Sun)—a volume of verse by the Turkish poet and playwright; the poet reacts to the poverty in which the villagers of Anatolia live; their call for national independence must correspond with their struggle for social justice; thus, the poet sings the praises of work in a free society.

Aldous Huxley, *Point Counter Point*—a novel by the English writer of fiction; the author demonstrates his sensitivity toward those persons who do not aspire to significance, but simply endure life; thus, the principal character, a novelist, finds himself wandering in his own private void, forced to compete with another, highly motivated writer.

Muhammad Iqbal, *Lectures on the Reconstruction of Religious Thought in Islam*—a collection of six academic lectures by the Indian poet, philosopher, and essayist; the writer describes the ascent of man through the spheres, with highly illuminating political and theological illustrations and explications; republished in 1934.

D. H. Lawrence, *Lady Chatterley's Lover*—a novel by the English writer of fiction, poet, and critic; the title character, married to an invalid, engages in a number of adulterous affairs and becomes pregnant by her husband's gamekeeper; after a trip to Venice, the lady returns, tells her husband of the affair, and, with her lover, awaits the outcome of their divorces; the writer's detailed and poetic descriptions of sexual intimacy, as well as his use of base language, caused a great controversy, and the work was privately printed in Florence in this year, followed by an expurgated London edition in 1930 and the issuance of the complete text at London in 1960.

Frederico Garcia Lorca, *Romancero Gitano* (Gipsy Ballads)—a verse collection by the Spanish poet and playwright, written between 1921 and 1924; the poet invents an unreal and fantastic world of Gipsies in conflict with their brutal oppressors, the civil guards.

Niko Lortkipanidze, *Bilikebidan Liandagze* (From Footpath to Railway Line)—a novel by the Georgian (SSR) writer of fiction and poet; describes village life in western Georgia during the revolutionary year of 1905.

Eugene O'Neill, *Strange Interlude*—a nine-act play by the American dramatist; portrays a modern woman who is driven by a strange, inner love force; after seeking out several unconventional relationships, peace descends upon her at the end of "the strange interlude" of her "premenopausal life history"; the playwright has relied heavily upon Freudian psychology and the details of society life in the United States during the 1920s; the piece earns the Pulitzer Prize in drama for this year.

Evelyn Waugh, *Decline and Fall*—the first novel by the English writer of fiction; the principal character has been sent down from Oxford for indecent behavior, forcing him to abandon a career in the church and to become a schoolmaster; on the verge of his marriage to a woman of disrepute, he is hauled off to prison on a charge related to his lover's activities in the white slave trade; the woman helps him to escape, after which he returns to Oxford and resumes his preparations for a clerical career.

Virginia Woolf, *Orlando*—a biographical fantasy by the English writer of fiction and essayist; the writer traces the life of the beautiful, aristocratic, and youthful Orlando through four centuries; the author provides both male and female accounts of her subject.

William Butler Yeats, *The Tower*—a collection of verse by the Irish poet, playwright, and essayist; the pieces evidence a sense of maturity on the writer's part; the poems generally reflect the richness of his life: marriage, family, political position within the Irish Free State, the Nobel Prize (1923), his Anglo-Irish ancestry; the poet also considers, such problems as world war, age, ruin, and decay; the volume includes "The Tower," "Sailing to Byzantium," "1916," "Leda and the Swan," "Among School Children," "The Three Monuments," and "A Man Young and Old"; the tower reminds the author that glory can vanish, while Byzantium stands in contrast to the realities of living in a country of the young.

EVENTS

The Dictionary of American Biography begins publication, the project having been sponsored by the American Council of Learned Societies; twenty volumes to 1936, with supplements issued periodically.

The Encyclopaedia of Judaica, new edition, published; to 1934.

The English Language Institute of America established.

The Mercury and Weekly News begins publication at Newport, Rhode Island; the newspaper is the result of mergers of newspapers and news sheets that date from 1758.

The New England Quarterly begins publication at Boston, Massachusetts; a scholarly journal of history and literature, with emphasis upon the Northeast.

Eugene Gladstone O'Neill, American playwright, receives the Pulitzer Prize in drama for *Strange Interlude* (1928).

Vernon Louis Parrington, American literary scholar and historian, receives the Pulitzer Prize in United States history for *Main Currents in American Thought*, vols. 1-2 (1927-1928).

Edwin Arlington Robinson, American poet, receives the Pulitzer Prize in poetry for *Tristram* (1927).

Sigrid Undset, Norwegian writer of fiction, receives the Nobel Prize for literature.

Thornton Niven Wilder, American writer of fiction and playwright, receives the Pulitzer Prize in fiction for *The Bridge of San Luis Rey* (1927).

1929

BIRTHS

Yuz Aleshkovsky. Russian novelist; he will publish four novels in the Soviet Union between 1963 and 1973; he will receive significant recognition for his popular songs and books for children; in 1975, he will emigrate to the United States.

Brigid Antonia Brophy. English novelist and miscellaneous writer; her fiction will study the true identities of individuals, while her nonfiction will reflect her interests in music and the visual arts.

Guillermo Cabrera Infante. Cuban-born writer of fiction, essayist, and miscellaneous writer; most of his fiction will be set in Havana, detailing the repressive and violent social and political climate during the period immediately preceding the Castro revolution; he will rely on the playful manipulation of language, abandoning traditional literary forms in favor of loose structure and slight plot; he will leave Cuba for Europe in 1965, eventually settling in London.

Gerard Chenet. Haitian playwright and poet; he will become a militant writer, seeking to understand the African heritage of Haiti and relay to Africans everywhere the message to "fight on"; he will leave Haiti and reside in Dakar, Senegal.

Hans Magnus Enzensberger. West German poet, essayist, translator, and playwright; a socialist, he will gain recognition for the social, political, and cultural criticism contained in his poetry and nonfiction; his essays will focus upon popular culture, German society, and international politics.

Brian Friel. Irish playwright and writer of fiction; he will be praised for his handling of dialogue and for his concern with how language can function to shape and distort reality; he will set his plays in and around the rural village of Ballybeg, depicting the effects of Irish social and cultural problems upon various individuals; his themes will include love, authority, and truth versus illusion.

Thomson William (Thom) Gunn. English poet; in 1960, he will assume permanent residence in San Francisco; his verse, often violent, will focus on active men and popular heroes; he will generally use colloquial language.

Fazil Abdulovich Iskander. Abkhazian (SSR) writer of fiction and poet; his short stories will introduce the people and customs of his native republic to readers in the general area of the Black Sea; his work will tend to be autobiographical, complemented by colorful descriptions of scenery and characters and written in an anecdotal narrative style; he will sarcastically ridicule Soviet policy.

Yacine Kateb. Algerian playwright, poet, and writer of narrative sketches; he will write primarily in French and his themes will be linked to the symbol of Nadjma, the motherland and the beloved one; his work will be highly symbolic and complicated, reflecting his belief that writers needn't concern themselves with order.

Milan Kundera. Czech writer of fiction, poet, and playwright; he will be one of the first writers of his generation to react sharply against the political repression of the Stalinist years; he will satirize those opportunists who attempt to thrive amidst the restrictions of communism; his fiction will bring him into official disfavor in Prague; unable to publish his works in his native country, he will establish residence in France.

Ephraim Alfred Shadrack Lesoro. South African (Orange Free State) writer of fiction, poet, and playwright; in addition to his novels and plays, he will write drama for the radio and translate several Shakespearean plays into the Sotho language; his poetry will include a collection of children's nursery rhymes.

Paule Marshall. Barbadian-born American writer of fiction; in her fiction, she will attempt to arrive at a synthesis of the universal and the particular by revealing to her readers the rich texture of West Indian life; she will receive the Langston Hughes Award medallion (1986) and the New York State Governor's Art Award for Literature (1987).

John Patrick Montague. American-born Irish poet and short story writer; his work will focus upon personal and social conerns, exploring such various subjects as love, death, family life, and the disintegration of traditional Western culture; he will also reveal an interest in the history and myth of Ireland, blending Irish colloquialisms with the forms and patterns of Gaelic verse.

John Munonye. Eastern Nigerian novelist; with sympathy and pathos, he will depict the clash of cultures, specifically African youths seeking Western educations; he will also confront the problem of rural Africans attempting to adjust to village life after periods of residence in the cities.

John James Osborne. English playwright; he will be identified as the original "angry young man," the voice in opposition to the old social order; throughout his literary career, he will not change that voice, but merely alter the targets of his attack, remaining free from allegiance to any particular group; structurally, he will employ such forms as the "old fashioned play," the chronicle play, the musical comedy, and the Jacobean revenge tragedy.

Milorad Pavic. Yugoslav poet and novelist; his work will be broad in scope, witty, inventive, and intellectual; his fiction, particularly, will be complex, intricate, and idiosyncratic; his folktale-like style will be characterized by pungent aphorisms and similes; he will engage in impressive inquiries into the nature of language, time, history, and faith.

A. K. Ramanujan. Indian poet; he will publish in English; his work as professor of Dravidian studies and linguistics at the University of Chicago will lead him to research and publish works on linguistics, folklore, mythology, and comparative literature; most importantly, he will translate literary texts from Kannada, Tamil, and Malayalam languages into English.

Badr Shakir as-Sayyab (d. 1964). Iraqi poet; he will become one of the first exponents of modern poetry and free verse in Iraq; his verse will illustrate his ideological development from communism and Arab nationalism to progressive humanism; his style will be complex, paralleling the intricacy of the questions raised in his verse.

Gilbert Sorrentino. American writer of fiction, poet, and literary critic; he will write almost two dozen volumes of fiction, poetry, and criticism, and he will become a professor of English at Stanford University; he will publish a major trilogy (*Odd Number, Rose,* and *Misterioso*) concerning a myriad of characters all vaguely connected with "the arts."

Rajendra Yadav. Indian (Hindi) writer of fiction and translator; his fiction will be realistic, employing themes from urban middle-class life; he will translate works by Anton Chekhov, Ivan Turgenyev, and Albert Camus.

DEATHS

William Bliss Carman (b. 1861). Canadian-born poet; his verse tends to be emotional and impressionistic, yet has been described as "carefree"; he delivered and published lectures on the history of Canadian literature; his best poetry came after Confederation and emphasized the national conscience of Canada.

Hugo von Hofmannsthal (b. 1874). Austrian poet, playwright, essayist, and writer of short fiction; from his profound, beautiful, and highly formal lyric poetry, he developed the "lyrisch Dramen" (lyrical plays)—intensely personal dramas focusing upon the relation of the poet to life; he also spent considerable time reviving older dramatic pieces, such as Greek classics and plays by the Elizabethans and the Spanish; he enjoyed a successful collaboration with the composer Richard Strauss.

Arno Holz (b. 1863). German essayist and literary critic; one of the leading figures of German naturalism, he wrote a collection of conventional lyrics that considered social and sexual themes; influenced by Walt Whitman, he advocated free verse rhythms.

Hamza Hakimzoda Niyoziy (b. 1889). Uzbek (SSR) poet and playwright; considered the founder of Soviet Uzbek literature; his work generally drew upon the traditions of folk art, but he also attacked all manifestations of inequality; he greeted the October 1917 revolution with enthusiastic verse that spread throughout Central Asia.

Janis Rainis (pseudonym of Janis Plieksans; b. 1865). Latvian poet, playwright, and translator; a romantic writer, his hatred of oppression formed the principal theme of his works; thus, he came under attack by both tsarist Russians and Soviet supporters of Stalin; his poems tend to reflect his own personal feelings and his dilemma over whether to devote his energies to art or politics.

Franz Rosenzweig (b. 1886). German-Jewish scholar, translator, and narrative writer; for him, Scripture affirmed a set of new combinations: God and Creation, humanity and Revelation, the world and Redemption; he will collaborate with Martin Buber in translating the Hebrew Bible into German, attempting to capture the sound and cadence of the original Hebrew; he dies before the project is completed.

PUBLICATIONS

Sayyid Al-Hadi, *Puteri al-Ain* (Princess Nur al-Ain)—a novel by the Malay writer of fiction; in this story of love, a variety of contemporary social situations and changing mores are explored, with obvious didactic intent.

Bibhutibhusan Bandyopadhyay, *Pater Pancali* (Song of the Road)—a novel by the Indian (Bengali) writer of fiction and essayist; the work displays the writer's warm sympathy for the rural poor, as well as his appreciation for the beauties of nature; the work also deserves recognition for its psychological analysis of its child characters.

Robert Bridges, *The Testament of Beauty*—a long poem in four books by the English writer of verse; a philosophical piece attempting to prove the goodness of the natural order.

Tembot Charasha, *Attack*—a novel by the Circassian (SSR) writer of fiction; describes changing Circassian village life during the assertion of Soviet power and the collectivization of agriculture; the piece has been praised for its "fresh directness" toward the subject.

Jean Cocteau, *Les Enfants Terribles* (The Holy Terrors)—a novel by the French poet, novelist, and playwright; a rather sinister study of four young bourgeois who create their own world, with disastrous results, the writer creates a film version in 1950.

Alfred Doblin, *Berlin Alexanderplatz*—a novel by the German writer of fiction; often compared with James Joyce's *Ulysses,* the work focuses upon the life of a Berlin worker; the simple-minded proletarian and victim of the system represents one hero, while the teeming city of Berlin represents another; the writer relies upon such devices (similar to those employed by John Dos Passos) as interior monologue, advertisements, popular songs, radio announcements, and mythological parallels.

William Faulkner, *Sartoris*—a novel by the American writer of fiction; based upon the author's family history, particularly his great-grandfather, who had been shot by a rival eight years before Faulkner's birth; introduces the mythical Yoknapatawpha County and its seat, Jefferson; the reader sees the decline of a family, from the Civil War to shortly after World War I.

————————, *The Sound and the Fury*—a novel by the American writer of fiction; tells the story of the disintegration of a Southern family, the Compsons, through the eyes of four charactors, one of them an idiot; the writing moves backward and forward in time and reveals the "stream of consciousness" and interior monologues of the characters; this kind of writing, realized through long sentences packed with images and detail, forces the reader to enter actively into the imagined world of the story.

Robert Graves, *Goodbye to All That*—an autobiography by the English poet, novelist, critic and miscellaneous writer; a powerful description of his unhappy days at school, the horrors of the trenches during World War I, and the breakdown of his first marriage; also describes the disillusionment and the new freedom of the post-World War I generation.

Graham Greene, *The Man Within*—the first novel by the English writer of fiction; evidences the influence of both Robert Louis Stevenson and Joseph Conrad; the hero rises, through acceptance of guilt for past actions, to a state of grace; the piece is an obvious reflection of the writer's recent conversion to Roman Catholicism.

Ernest Hemingway, *A Farewell to Arms*—a novel by the American writer of fiction; a highly successful World War I love story; the strength of the work lies in its commentary upon the futility of war, its graphic battle scenes, and its examination of the hero's spiritual state.

Vicente Huidobro, *Mio Cid Campeador* (Portrait of a Paladin)—a novel by the Chilean poet, novelist, essayist, and playwright; the writer updates the story of *El Cid,* including a variety of slightly altered borrowings from familiar literary sources; the work supports the writer's contention that the novel is an artistic retelling of something that has already occured; the writer also incorporates into the work a number of conventions from the cinema, including daring heroics, and the piece was dedicated to Douglas Fairbanks.

Sinclair Lewis, *Doddsworth*—a novel by the American writer of fiction; the title character, a fairly sensitive and highly intelligent man, escapes from the clutches of a sophisticated and ruthless woman, who has determined to conquer the soul of man; the writer also attacks the notion that Americans must go to Europe to be properly educated.

Samuel Edward Krune Loliwe Mqhayi, *U-Don Jade*—a novel by the South African (Cape Province) poet, biographer, and writer of fiction; described as a Bantu utopian work that looks toward an ideal world of social justice and the elimination of racism; in three parts, the last of which earned the writer the May Esther Bedford Prize (1935).

Katharine Susannah Prichard, *Coonardoo: The Well in the Shadow*—a novel by the Fijian-born Australian writer of fiction and miscellany, poet, and playwright; the first sympathetic study of an aborigine woman in Australian literature; she loves the son of the cattle station owner for whom she works, but he holds to his white tradition, and rejects her; a powerful piece of social documentation, often described as the Australian version of *Uncle Tom's Cabin.*

J. B. Priestley, *The Good Companions*—a novel by the English writer of fiction and playwright; an account of the theatrical adventures of a group at a concert party; its strength lies in its characterization, accurate settings, and intelligent humor.

Erich Maria Remarque, *Im Westen Nichts Neues* (All Quiet on the Western Front)—a novel by the German-born writer of fiction; a war story seen through the eyes of an ordinary soldier; war is portrayed as completely unheroic, with young lives sacrificed for the political ends of the old order.

Elmer Rice, *Street Scene*—a play by the American dramatist; the scene is a shabby brownstone apartment house, where tenants enter and exit, sit on the steps, or lean out of their windows; they gossip, laugh, scold, quarrel; a husband discovers his wife's infidelity and murders her lover; the piece represents still another example of the writer's desire to experiment with theatrical substance and form.

I. A. Richards, *Practical Criticism: A Study of Literary Judgment*—a prose tact by the English poet and critic; the work revolutionizes the study and teaching of literature; the writer had issued to his students at Cambridge unsigned poems, asking for their written observations and reactions; the majority of the responses attacked the traditional English poets and praised the works of literary nonentities; the writer, in turn, attacks readers' general insensitivity and inattentiveness to poetry.

Edwin Arlington Robinson, *Cavender's House* —a poem by the American writer of verse; a dialogue between a man and his dead wife focusing upon such topics as guilt and jealousy.

Antoine de Saint-Exupery, *Courrier-Sud* (Southern Mail)—a novel by the French writer of fiction; an adventure story based upon the novelist's own experiences as a pioneer of commercial aviation; contains graphic descriptions of actual flight.

Alexey Tolstoy, *Pyotr I* (Peter the Great)—a novel by the Russian writer of fiction, essayist, poet, and playwright; depicts a portion of Russian history in conformity with official Soviet ideology; as one of the first government-approved works of historical fiction of the post-Revolutionary era, it strongly influenced the development of the Soviet novel; the writer emphasizes those aspects of the Petrine era that suggest obvious Soviet parallels: the need for drastic social reforms, brutal and repressive measures to achieve those reforms, widespread misery and suffering, and threats from outside aggressors; three vols., to 1945.

Thomas Wolfe, *Look Homeward, Angel*—an autobiographical novel by the American writer of fiction; concerns the early life of Eugene Gant, a sensitive young man from a southern mountain city; possesses an epic quality—every thought, feeling, and action is depicted as of monumental importance—and an all encompassing empathy for humanity, inspired by the writer's desire to experience all; introduces Wolfe's Wordsworthian vision of life as a lonely search for a sign that will reawaken his subconscious and reveal a world of joy and purpose left behind at birth.

Muhammad Yamin, *Indonesia, Toempah Darahku* (Indonesia, Land of My Birth)—a collection of poems by the Indonesian writer of verse and fiction; ardently patriotic pieces that rely upon new literary forms and mark the poet as a pioneer in modern Indonesian verse.

EVENTS

Stephen Vincent Benet, American poet, receives the Pulitzer Prize in poetry for *John Brown's Body* (1928).

The fourteenth edition of the *Encyclopaedia Britannica* published in London and New York.

Thomas Mann, German writer of fiction and essayist, receives the Nobel Prize for literature.

Julia Mood Peterkin, American novelist, receives the Pulitzer Prize in fiction for *Sister Mary* (1928).

Elmer Rice, American playwright, receives the Pulitzer Prize in drama for *Street Scene* (1929).

1930

BIRTHS

Albert Chinualumogu Achebe. Nigerian (Ibo) writer of fiction, poet, and essayist; his novels will chronicle the colonization and independence of Nigeria; his themes will focus upon the social and psychological conflicts created by the incursion of white culture into the African society and consciousness.

Adonis (pseudonym of Ali Ahmad Said). Syrian poet; his philosophic knowledge will be combined with the esoteric doctrines of Islam, ancient myths of the Near East, and the influence of modern trends in French poetry, including existentialism; his verse will be highly intellectual and metaphysical, but it will also concern social issues.

John Simmons Barth. American writer of fiction; he will emerge as an academic writing nonacademic novels, displaying a talent for the amusing, the inventive, and the manipulative; he will rely upon pun, slang, and parody, particularly as he focuses upon a form and context for education; for him, the universe exists as the principal "institution" of education.

L. Edward Braithwaite. Barbadian poet, critic, and historian; a poet of international reputation, his works will display his knowledge of jazz and history and his interest in the function and operation of language; he will also attempt to identify the main Caribbean cultural experience as it relates to Africa.

Elaine Feinstein. English novelist, poet, and translator; her fiction will develop from the experimental to the naturalistic; she will write a saga of a Jewish immigrant family in Liverpool and also translate poems by the Russian poet and essayist Marina Ivanovna Tsvetaeva (1892-1941).

Roy Fisher. English poet; he will become a member of the Department of American Studies, University of Keele, Staffordshire; he will publish in excess of seventeen collections of verse and two volumes of prose poems; his verse will concern the general issue of immediate experience, and he will be concerned with life and communication, not with isolation; in general terms, his poetry will be sensuous and intellectual.

Edward James (Ted) Hughes. English poet; he will be recognized early as a poet of "power"; he will become aware of both the brute force and the beauty of the natural world and will be obsessed with animals; he will develop an interest in topographical poetry and the relationship between verse and visual art.

Koichi Iijima. Japanese poet and critic; his work will focus upon antiwar themes, and he will be an early critic, in his verse, of U.S. involvement in Vietnam; he will also write essays on surrealism and the collection *Essays on Art for Exorcism.*

Takeshi Kaiko. Japanese writer of fiction; his work will reflect a number of personal and traumatic experiences; the end of World War II, with its dark experiences of hunger, homelessness, and the humiliation of defeat, will stimulate his interest in the Vietnam War; the destruction of traditional Japanese values and the importation of Western views will influence his philosophical and literary development, particularly in terms of the deep divisions between East and West.

Duro Ladipo. Nigerian (Yoruba) playwright; he will strive to bring traditional and adapted dance-drama to the African stage; thus, dance and music will function organically in his plays, serving as a dramatic voice and as a principal "character"; he will also compose Yoruba folk operas.

Condetto Nenekhaly-Camara. Guinean poet and playwright; he will compose plays about the great African warrior chiefs of the past; thus, he will attempt to exploit the epic qualities of his heroes as models for the new heroism of modern Africa.

Christopher Robin Nicole. Guyanese novelist; his first eight novels will focus upon West Indian themes, and then he will turn his attention to those parts of Eastern Europe to which he will travel; he will be at his creative best when he describes the character of the jungle and its relationship to its inhabitants.

Yambo Ouologuem. Mali poet and novelist; his verse and fiction will be historical, attacking eight centuries of prejudice and injustice that had reduced the status of the black man to Negro rabble; his works will be replete with descriptions of slavery, war, torture, and barbarity.

Cosmo George Leopoldt Pieterse. South African poet and playwright; the themes of his work will range from the personal and domestic to the social and political, focusing upon such subjects as war, bribery, deceit, marriage, life in prison, ignorance, and brutality; he will also write reviews for periodicals and edit anthologies for English publishers.

Harold Pinter. English poet and playwright; he will gain recognition for his "comedies of menace," plays in which common occurrences become invested with tension and mystery, often by the employment and manipulation of silence; he will also produce screenplays of high literary merit.

Paavo Rintala. Finnish writer of fiction; his best work will be epistolary in nature and will include animal fables; he will produce a strong indictment, in the manner of Aesop, of the official "peace movement" in Finland; he will, in 1969, be elected chairman of the Finnish Society for the Defense of Peace, a pro-Soviet organization.

James David Rubadiri. Tanzanian novelist and poet; his fiction will focus upon the tensions created by the bureaucracies of corrupt governments; the lives of his characters will represent the confused values of modern African life; for him, there must exist more realistic and humane expectations about the future; in his verse, he will be concerned with being an African in a world only recently emerging from foreign domination.

Carlo Sgorlon. Italian critic and novelist; he will publish commentary on Franz Kafka and Elsa Morante; focusing on the admirable character of proud people, his fiction will reflect his attempt to dramatize historical events; he will receive the Premio Campiello award for fiction in 1973.

Jon Silkin. English poet and critic; he will produce eight major verse collections, as well as a play in verse; he will produce a number of "flower poems," which were inspired by visits to the United States and Israel.

Bernard Slade (originally Bernard Slade Newbound). Canadian-born playwright; he will present various forms of romantic love and familial commitment in his drama; his protagonists will involve themselves in uncommon situations, rendered believable through the playwright's engaging characterizations and language; he will employ pointed jokes and puns, which provide clues to deep truths about the human condition.

Derek Alton Walcott. St. Lucian (West Indies) poet and playwright; his work will be inspired in part by his mixed African and European heritage, and he will explore such themes as racism, the injustices of colonialism, and the collapse of empires; he will also focus upon the individual's quest for personal, cultural, and political identity.

DEATHS

Jeppe Aakjaer (b. 1866). Danish poet and writer of fiction; his fiction concerned the area and people of his native Jutland; he wrote his best poetry in the Jutland dialect, earning him the title "the Danish Burns."

Robert Seymour Bridges (b. 1844). English poet and critic; his verse tended to be philosophical; he wrote two major prose tracts on prosody and published the poems of his friend Gerard Manley Hopkins; he became Poet Laureate of England in 1912, succeeding Alfred Austin.

Joseph Ephraim Casely-Hayford (b. 1866). Ghanian novelist and essayist; known throughout West Africa for his criticism of African colonial society and his recommendations for the cultural advancement of the region; considered one of the most significant contributors to African national literature during the early twentieth century.

Sir Arthur Conan Doyle (b. 1859). English writer of fiction; recognized for his creation of Sherlock Holmes, the most widely acclaimed of all fictional detectives; he also wrote historical romances, a one-act play, and a prose tract on the history of spiritualism.

D. H. Lawrence (b. 1885). English writer of fiction, poet, and critic; he advanced the view that industrial culture dehumanizes the individual, and thus his fiction glorifies union with nature and its corollary, sexual fulfillment; following World War I, he wrote on the subject of a superhuman leader for humankind; his style was sensuous and lyrical, influencing the development of twentieth-century fiction.

Vladimir Vladimirovich Mayakovsky (b. 1893). Russian poet, playwright, and essayist; considered the central figure of the Russian Futurist movement and the principal voice of the 1917 Revolution; he aimed to erase traditional poetic principles by disregarding metonymic and grammatical conventions; he relied in his verse upon bizarre imagery, invented vocabulary, and techniques borrowed from avant-garde painting, irregular type facing, offbeat illustrations, and even his own handwriting; he dies, by his own hand, in a game of Russian roulette.

PUBLICATIONS

Arnold Bennett, *Imperial Palace*—the final novel by the English writer of fiction; a lively and amusing skeptical account of great hotels displaying the writer's attraction to luxury and fantasy.

Jean Fernand Brierre, *"Le Drama de Marchaterre"*—a poem by the Haitian writer of verse, playwright, novelist, and biographer; attempts to capture the outrage that followed the shooting by U.S. Marines in late 1929 of unarmed Haitian peasants, who had been protesting new taxes on tobacco and alcohol; written in the old French alexandrine form.

Paul Claudel, *Le Soulier de Satin* (The Satin Slipper)—a verse drama by the French poet and playwright; attempts to explain the meaning of Providence, focusing upon the temporality of earthly desires, the power of the spirit, and the idea of ultimate salvation.

Marc Connelly, *The Green Pastures*—a drama by the American playwright; the work dramatizes principal events from the Bible as they might be imagined by black children belonging to a rural Louisiana church; it begins with a heavenly fish fry at which God accidentally creates Earth after determining to provide enough firmament for the cooks' custard; God attempts to eliminate humanity's innate corruptibility and learns, at the end, that human beings desire only a loving God, not a wrathful one.

Noel Coward, *Private Lives*—a play by the English dramatist; a man and woman, formerly married to each other, honeymoon with their new mates at the same hotel; each has married a person of opposite personality and interests; the original couple runs off together and resists the efforts of their "leftover" spouses to separate them.

Hart Crane, *The Bridge*—an epic poem by the American writer of verse; a reply to T. S. Eliot's *The Waste Land*, the work was planned to counteract the pessimism of Eliot's poem with an exuberant affirmation of experience; Crane intended to provide a myth for American life and experience; thus, it includes such figures as Christopher Columbus, Rip Van Winkle, Orville and Wilbur Wright, Walt Whitman, Edgar Allan Poe, Emily Dickinson, and Isadora Duncan.

John Dos Passos, *The 42nd Parallel*—a novel by the American writer of fiction, the first of the *U.S.A.* trilogy; the work embraces the notion of social idealism; thus, woven through the narrative of struggle and disillusionment are biographical sketches of such figures from contemporary history as Andrew Carnegie, Eugene V. Debs, Luther Burbank, William Jennings Bryan, Thomas Edison, Robert La Follette, and Charles Steinmetz.

T. S. Eliot, *"Ash Wednesday"*—a poem by the American-born English dramatist and writer of verse and criticism; focuses on the theme of religious conversion; the poem is modern in inspiration and personal without being sentimental.

William Empson, *Seven Types of Ambiguity: A Study of Its Effects on English Verse*—a volume of criticism by the English poet and essayist; in setting forth his theory of ambiguity, the writer declares that double meanings in poetry do not exist as something that intentionally cannot be understood, but represent true doubt in the mind of the poet; revised editions in 1947, 1953, and 1963.

William Faulkner, *As I Lay Dying*—a novel by the American writer of fiction; members of a family (husband, three legitimate sons, one bastard, a pregnant daughter) respond in alternating interior monologues to the death of the mother and their arduous journey, fraught with symbolic natural disasters, to bury her and thus honor her final request.

W. Somerset Maugham, *Cakes and Ale*—a novel by the English writer of fiction; a rather malicious and subtly observed work about writers; the piece contains an extremely humorous caricature of Hugh Walpole ("Alroy Kear") and an equally funny fictionalized presentation of Thomas Hardy.

Robert Musil, *Der Mann ohne Eigenschaften* (The Man without Qualities)—a multivolume novel by the Austrian writer of fiction and playwright, left unfinished at the writer's death in 1942; the principal character is "not godless, but God-free," and has withdrawn from life, paralyzed by his own uncertainty; a plotless but totally realistic work.

Vladimir Nabokov, *Zaschita Luzhina* (The Defense)—a novel by the Russian-born writer of fiction, poet, essayist, and playwright; the principal character, a chessmaster, strives to discover his identity through chess; however, he loses interest in his wife and family as the game becomes an obsession; he removes himself from society, loses his sanity, and commits suicide; his last glimpse of the world reveals a huge chess board, upon which he must play an endless game.

Dorothy Parker, *Laments for the Living*—a series of prose sketches by the American writer of fiction, poet, playwright, and essayist; another skirmish in the 1920s war of the sexes, revealing the writer's wit and her concern for the grief that modern women endure.

Katherine Anne Porter, *Flowering Judas*—a collection of stories by the American writer of fiction; studies the effects of the changes in the South upon the personalities of various characters at different stages of their lives.

J. B. Priestley, *Angel Pavement*—a novel by the English writer of fiction, playwright, and miscellaneous prose writer; grim and self-consciously realistic work focusing upon the specifics of life in contemporary London.

George Macaulay Trevelyan, *England under Queen Anne*—a three-volume study of the period 1702-1714 by the English historian; with the War of the Spanish Succession as the focus, the volumes bear the titles *Blenheim, Ramilles and the Union with Scotland,* and *The Peace and the Protestant Succession.*

Yvor Winters, *The Proof*—a collection of verse by the American poet and critic; the volume demonstrates that at this point in the poet's career, he has moved from free verse to the employment of conventional lines.

Nairi Zarian, *Rusani K'arap* (The Rock of Rushan)—an epic poem by the Turkish-born Soviet Armenian writer of verse and fiction; concerns the collectivization of Armenian village life, as well as the building of the socialist society.

EVENTS

Conrad Potter Aiken, American poet and writer of fiction, receives the Pulitzer Prize in poetry for his *Selected Poems* (1929).

The city council of Boston, Massachusetts, bans the sale of all published works by Leon Trotsky, the Russian revolutionary and prose writer.

Marcus Cook Connelly, American playwright, receives the Pulitzer Prize in drama for *The Green Pastures* (1930).

The Encyclopaedia of the Social Sciences begins publication at New York City; fifteen volumes, to 1935.

Fortune Magazine, a periodical devoted to business, begins publication at New York City; the American poet and playwright Archibald Mac-

Leish is associated with it for a period following his return from five years of residence in Europe.

Oliver Hazard Perry La Farge, American writer of fiction and miscellany, receives the Pulitzer Prize in fiction for his novel *Laughing Boy* (1929).

Sinclair Lewis, American writer of fiction, becomes the first American writer to receive a Nobel Prize for literature.

John Edward Masefield, English poet and novelist, appointed Poet Laureate of England, succeeding Robert Bridges; to 1967.

1931

BIRTHS

Donald Barthelme (d. 1989). American writer of fiction; he will use idiosyncratic language and symbolism in presenting his vision of an absurd reality; his best work will portray frustrated characters who pursue unattainable goals.

Augusto de Campos. Brazilian poet; he will become one of his nation's most innovative writers of verse, uniting the forms of early twentieth-century poetry with his interests in the plastic arts, graphics, and experimental music; he will also become a founder of the Concrete Poetry movement, begun from the Museum of Modern Art, Sao Paulo, in December 1956; he will gain recognition for the tight construction of his verse and its artistic purity.

Cemal Sureya. Turkish poet and critic; he will become a founder of "the Second New Literature School," known for its emphasis on form, personal freedom, and the writer's individuality; the themes of his warm and intimate verse will range from love to social concerns.

Tamaz Chiladze. Georgian (SSR) writer of fiction; he will be associated with the generation of writers who grew up during World War II and focused upon urban themes and the emotional and philosophical problems of the young.

E. L. Doctorow. American novelist; he will blend fiction with historical fact, producing compelling reconstructions of past eras and events in American history, including the

Rosenberg spy case, pre-World War I America, and life in the United States during the Great Depression.

Muhammad Miftah al-Fayturi. Egyptian poet and playwright; his work will reflect a concern with Africanism, as well as the problems of racial discrimination and exploitation; his verse will be characterized by concrete themes, extremely vivid images, and intense emotion.

Jurg F. Federspiel. Swiss writer of fiction, poet, playwright, and essayist; he will explore themes of morality and death as they pertain to Western cultures; his prose style will be terse, and he will rely upon black humor to convey his view of the absurd and arbitrary nature of the fate of humanity.

Juan Goytisolo. Spanish novelist; he will emphasize the cruelty and injustice of war, especially its effects upon innocent children; he will appear obsessed with the anguish of children and young people living in a corrupt and unjust society; he will choose to live and write in Paris.

Rolf Hochhuth. German playwright; he will become the best known among those writers associated with documentary drama as a theater of protest; thus, he will chronicle relations between the Nazis and the Roman Catholic Church and condemn the inhumanity of war; his work will reflect his belief that history is shaped by a small number of personalities who decide the course of events, no matter what their political persuasions or interests.

Ivan Lalic. Yugoslav (Serbian) poet; will become a careful poetic craftsman, applying an intellectual approach and striving to achieve technical perfection; his poems will range widely in terms of geographical locale and thematic focus.

Deidre Levinson. Welsh-born American writer of fiction; she will rely upon her own personal experiences in depicting characters whose lives have been altered by unpleasant circumstances, such as political turmoil in South Africa, disillusionment with revolutionary groups, and the death of friends or their children.

Taghi Modarressi. Iranian-born novelist; he will publish fiction in both Iranian and English; his work will reflect the conflict between modern influences and ancient and revered, but repressive, Persian culture.

Toni Morrison (born Chloe Anthony Wofford). American novelist; she will gain recognition for her concise, poetic language, emotional intensity, and extremely sensitive observation of black American life; she will receive the Pulitzer Prize for fiction in 1988.

Flora Nwapa. Eastern Nigerian novelist; her fiction will provide insights into the circumstances of women in Africa, particularly as they attempt to adjust to simple village life.

J. P. Okot p'Bitek. Northern Ugandan novelist, poet, and essayist; he will experiment with the poetic novel, analyzing the effects of Westernization upon African family life; he will concern himself with the conflict between old African traditions and the fast-moving and changing modern world.

Mordecai Richler. Canadian writer of fiction, essayist, and author of works for children; he will achieve recognition with his darkly humorous novels that examine Canadian society, Jewish culture, the adverse effects of materialism, and relationships between persons of various backgrounds; he will set his fiction either in European locales or in the Jewish section of Montreal, focusing upon alienated and morally disillusioned characters who have difficulty attaining self-knowledge or inner stability.

Richard Rive. South African (Cape Town) writer of fiction and poet; his passionate works will depict the strained relations between blacks and whites in Africa.

Jovan Strezovski. Yugoslav (Macedonian) poet and writer of fiction; he will write more than twenty volumes of poems, short stories, novels, children's books, and television plays; he will receive several important literary awards and will serve as director of the annual poetry festival, "The Struga Poetry Evenings."

Zakaria Tamer. Syrian writer of fiction living in London; his work will reflect his own underprivileged childhood and his attempts at self-education; he will edit several children's magazines and write satirical columns for the Arabic daily press; collections of his short fiction will be published in French, Italian, Spanish, Serbo-Croatian, Bulgarian, and Russian.

Shuntaro Tanikawa. Japanese poet; he will write no less than seventy sonnets and will be attuned to the problems of children in a highly technological society; he will spend 1966-1967 in the United States on a Japanese society fellowship.

Tomas Gosta Transtromer. Swedish poet, translator, and critic; in his verse, he will juxtapose dissimilar images to transform conventional interpretations of reality; he will link artifacts from modern industrial society with natural phenomena in an attempt to evoke a relationship between civilization and nature; his poetry will also be informed by his experiences as a psychologist and world traveler.

Tchicaya Gerard-Felix U'Tam'si (pseudonym of Felix Tchicaya). Congolese poet; he will write avant-garde verse and will be preoccupied with African themes and the idea of cultural loss; his poems will be translated into Czechoslovakian, Polish, and Hungarian.

Janwillem van de Wetering. Dutch writer of fiction, nonfiction, and books for children; he will gain a reputation for his detective novels, as well as for his nonfiction pieces on Zen Buddhism; his detective fiction will engage readers in part through its colorful characterization and vivid descriptions of Dutch locales; he will subordinate plot and action to the attitudes, problems, and desires of his investigators and the persons they encounter.

DEATHS

Enoch Arnold Bennett (b. 1867). English writer of fiction and playwright; he gained a literary reputation from his realistic novels concerning life in the industrial English Midlands; his work reveals the influence of Emile Zola's Naturalism.

Hjalmar Bergman (b. 1883). Swedish writer of fiction and playwright; his popular works are characterized by his insight into the ambivalence of human emotions.

Melvil Dewey (b. 1851). American library scholar and theorist; his most significant contribution was the development of a system by which to catalogue books in libraries, the Dewey Decimal System; he also established the first library school, at Columbia University, New York City, and founded the American Library Association.

Taomaq Gaediaty (b. 1882). Ossetian (SSR) poet, journalist, and literary critic; his early poems called for social liberation, describing the hardships and longings of social revolutionaries; he occasionally wrote free verse and poems in prose.

Hsu-Chi-Mo (b. 1896). Chinese poet; his work reflects his study of English literature and his friendships with H. G. Wells, Katherine Mansfield, and Harold Laski; he attempted to adapt English prose rhythms to Chinese verse; his themes tend to be almost exclusively romantic in substance; he dies in an airplane crash.

Jibran Khalil Jibran (b. 1883). Lebanese-American poet and miscellaneous prose writer; his work reflects the life of a Christian living in a Western environment who is nostalgically attached to his Arab homeland; Christian ideals mingle with the literary influences of Jean-Jacques Rousseau, William Blake, and Friedrich Nietzsche, creating works in which universal love and communion with Nature become primary; his prose has been praised as rising to the majesty and rhythm of biblical language; following his death at New York City, his body is taken back to Lebanon.

Nicholas Vachel Lindsay (b. 1879). American poet; he lived and wrote as a modern-day troubadour, selling his drawings and his poems as he traveled across the country; his best verse, sometimes described as "spoken music," earned for the writer the title of "jazz poet"; he commits suicide, prompting someone to remark, "No other writer will have done so little with so much ability."

Mysost Qamberdiaty (b. 1909). Ossetian (SSR) poet; he published his earliest poems in newspapers, describing the building of a new world, the role of communist education, and the struggles against an outmoded order; known as an innovator of Ossetian poetry.

Arthur Schnitzler (b. 1862). Austrian playwright and novelist; his works gained recognition for their sparkling wit and brilliant style; considered unique for his blending of melancholy and cheerfulness, as well as for his clinical observations of the pathological; in his drama, he tended to study the problems of love and sexual faithfulness.

PUBLICATIONS

Georges Bernanos, *La Grande Peur des Bien-Pensants* (The Great Fear of the Well-Disposed)—a novel by the French writer of fiction; a savage attack upon those unbelievers who approach Catholicism from tradition rather than from faith.

Pearl S. Buck, *The Good Earth*—a novel by the American writer of fiction and missionary to China; a vivid and highly compassionate account of life in China; it will receive the Pulitzer Prize in fiction for 1932.

James Gould Cozzens, *S.S. San Pedro*—a novella by the American writer of fiction; a study of the relationships at sea among men confined to close quarters; decidedly influenced by Joseph Conrad.

William Faulkner, *Sanctuary*—a novel by the American writer of fiction; a young girl attends a party with a drunken escort; on the way home, she wrecks his car, and they find themselves at a bootleggers' den, and subjected to inhuman treatment by the gang there; after being raped, the girl is carried off to a brothel; the incident develops into a murder scenario, complete with trial, lynching, and unwarranted execution.

Ibrahim Abdalqadir al-Mazini, *Ibrahim al-Katib* (Ibrahim the Writer)—an autobiographical novel by the Egyptian writer of fiction, poet, and essayist; portrays the thoughts of a man unable to reconcile his ideals with reality; thus, he fails to confront the decisive moments in his emotional life; although the piece ends on a pessimistic note, the writer does portray human longing for the fullness of life.

Edna St. Vincent Millay, *Fatal Interview*—a sonnet sequence by the American poet; critics tended to associate the pieces with the sonnets of William Shakespeare, particularly the one entitled "O sleep forever in the Latmian cave"; also linked with the sonnets of John Keats.

Thomas Mokopu Mofolo, *Chaka*—a historical novel by the South African writer of fiction; based upon the life and works of Shaka, the most significant of all Zulu chiefs and the organizer of Zulu power in Natal province; although written from a Christian perspective, the piece seeks to depict the atmosphere of Zulu places, as well as their customs, mannerisms, and social organization.

Eugene O'Neill, *Mourning Becomes Electra*—a three-part drama by the American playwright; the classical theme of Aeschylus has been transferred to a New England locale immediately following the Civil War; the issue of the warrior returning home to his unfaithful wife remains the same; a powerful examination of the ways that guilt, jealousy, and sexual passion lead to the downfall of an old New England family.

Payrav, *Takhti Khunin* (The Bloody Throne)—a poem by the Afghan-born writer of verse; in rhymed couplets, the piece exposes the cruelty and decadence that existed during the reign of the Emir of Bukhara.

Anthony Powell, *Afternoon Men*—a novel by the English writer of fiction; portrays the seedy section of pleasure-going and party-loving post-World War I London; the writer makes the best of comedy, irony, and satire.

Elmer Rice, *Counsellor-at-Law*—a drama by the American playwright; a tightly developed and conventional melodrama, quite unlike the writer's usual dramatic experiments; concerns an attorney maliciously accused of unethical behavior.

Joseph Roth, *Radetzkymarsch* (Radetzky March)—a novel by the Austrian writer of fiction; a nostalgic, but not overly sentimental, account of life in Austria during the reign of the Emperor Franz Josef.

Tristan Tzara, *L'Homme Approximatif* (Approximate Man, and Other Writings)—an epic poem by the Romanian-born French versifier, playwright, and critic; considered a landmark of twentieth-century French literature, the piece portrays an unfulfilled wayfarer's search for a universal knowledge and language; in the end, the naked word reveals the naked truth about the world.

Edmund Wilson, *Axel's Castle*—a volume of literary and social criticism by the American writer of miscellaneous prose; a study of Symbolist literature, focusing upon such writers as William Butler Yeats, Paul Valery, Gertrude Stein, and Philippe-Auguste Villiers de L'Isle-Adam; a play by the last-named gave rise to the title of the piece.

Yvor Winters, *The Journey, and Other Poems*—a collection by the American poet and critic; eight pieces written in heroic couplets, reflecting the influence of John Dryden, Alexander Pope, and Charles Churchill; includes "On a View of Pasadena from the Hills," directly influenced by Robert Bridges's "Elegy: The Summer House on the Mound" (1899).

Virginia Woolf, *The Waves*—a novel by the English writer of fiction and essayist; traces the lives of a group of friends from childhood to middle age; Woolf employs the stream-of-consciousness technique, depicting the passage of time through the impressionistic interior monologues of her six characters and attempting coherence through recurrent imagery and symbol.

Carl Zuckmayer, *Der Hauptmann von Kopernick* (The Captain of Kopernick)—a comedy by the German playwright; an attack upon militarism set in Berlin in the early twentieth century; the heartlessness and injustice of the bureaucracy force the hero, a cobbler, to rebel; he cannot obtain a pass without a job, or a job without a pass; in the army, he can obtain either, and thus he masquerades as an officer.

EVENTS

Margaret Ayer Barnes, American writer of fiction and playwright, receives the Pulitzer Prize in fiction for *Years of Grace* (1930).

Robert Frost, American poet, receives the Pulitzer Prize for his *Collected Poems* (1930).

Susan Glaspell, American playwright, receives the Pulitzer Prize in drama for *Alison's House* (1930).

Erik Axel Karlfeldt, Swedish lyric poet, receives the Nobel Prize for literature.

Francis Scott Key's "The Star Spangled Banner" (1814) adopted by the United States Congress as the national anthem of the United States.

The New York World combines with the *New York Telegram* to become the *World-Telegram,* a significant New York City daily newspaper; until 1950.

Story, a monthly literary magazine principally devoted to short fiction, begins publication in Vienna, Austria; moves to New York City in 1933; until 1953.

1932

BIRTHS

Chinua Achebe. Iboland-born Nigerian writer of fiction; he will realistically examine Nigerian life within anthropological and sociological contexts; for him, social and political protest will become a legitimate function of fiction.

Michael Anthony. Trinidad novelist and journalist; his fiction will be written in detailed, precise prose, recalling his experiences as a worker for a rural family and manipulating apparently trivial incidents toward subtle climaxes; as a state official, he will work and write in such diverse places as London and San Fernando, California, and those locales will appear in his work.

Aharon Appelfeld. Romanian-born Israeli writer of fiction, essayist, and poet; he will rely upon symbolism, understatement, and parable to analyze the effects of the Holocaust and anti-Semitism upon European Jews; much of his work will focus upon locales affected by the Nazis immediately prior to World War II; his protagonists will usually minimize their commitment to Judaism so that they might assimilate into European society.

Mongo Beti (pseudonym of Alexandre Biyidi). Cameroon writer of fiction; his fiction will depict the bewilderment and hostility of rural Africans forced into work at industrial sites by European firms; he will look with sympathy upon confused families hurried into a proletarian world that, simultaneously, threatens and attracts them.

Robert Lowell Coover. American writer of fiction; he will gain a reputation as an experimental novelist and will use surrealistic techniques in drawing an exceedingly fine line between reality and nightmare.

Sheila Fugard. English-born South African novelist and poet; in her fiction, she will employ the Gandhian concept of passive resistance to attract attention to the social problems within her nation; she will skillfully render emotion and take historical and surrealistic approaches to the meaning of South African life.

Geoffrey Hill. English poet; he will be concerned with the relationship between the past and modern times and with historical perception; he will also be interested in suffering and death.

Kamalesvar. Indian (Hindi) scholar and script writer; he will write for Indian television and edit literary manuscripts; the themes of his scripts will focus on lower middle-class life in an oppressive atmosphere.

Christopher John Koch. Australian novelist and script writer; he will examine the Australian's continual search for personal identity and for cultural identity in the face of European and Asian influences; he will tend to contrast Australia with his native Tasmania, considering both his yearning for and rejection of life on the mainland; his heroes will generally be young people searching for adventure in foreign lands.

Samuel Asare Konadu. Ghanaian writer of fiction; his work will concern itself with village life in rural Ghana and with local Ghanaian customs; although his English will be termed "unsophisticated," he will appeal to a wide reading public, offering analyses of contemporary problems.

Benjamin Matip. Cameroon novelist, poet, playwright, and biographer; he will attempt to explore the hopes and the fears of leaders of modern Africa; in his view, men of good will may well be thwarted by the tensions existing in the post-colonial African world; in 1961, he will receive the Presence Africaine for excellence in African literature.

Julia O'Faolain. English-born Irish writer of fiction and translator; her work will be set in such locales as Ireland, Italy, France, and the west coast of the United States, and she will explore cultural attitudes in relation to sexuality, male-female relationships, Catholicism, and politics; she will often focus on female characters attempting to establish their identities.

A. Turan Oflazoglu. Turkish playwright; his most significant work will be based upon the major dramatic episodes of the dynastic history of the Ottomans; he will attempt, essentially, to become a Turkish Shakespeare, developing tragedies featuring the lives of such figures as Ibrahim the Mad, Murat IV, Selim III, Mehmed the Conqueror, and Kosem (the wife of Ahmed I and mother of three sultans).

Christopher Okigbo (d. 1967). Nigerian poet; his verse will rely upon local themes and terms and employ the images of his native forests, sacred streams, and shrines; nonetheless, his work will also reflect his admiration for both European and English writers, particularly Ezra Pound and T. S. Eliot.

Lenrie Peters. Gambian writer of fiction and poet; as both a poet and a physician, he will remind his readers of the American writer William Carlos Williams; African motifs will be important in his poems, but they will never dominate, for he will primarily be concerned with modern people residing in urban environments.

Sylvia Plath (d. 1963). American poet; her finely crafted and intensely personal poems will contain sharp and often violent imagery; she will also write an autobiographical novel; she will commit suicide in London.

Jacques Rouband. French mathematician and writer of fiction; he will become professor of mathematics at the University of Paris X Nanterre and produce, between 1987 and 1989, two of the delightful "Hortense" novels; he will also write poems and prose poems.

Arvo Salo. Finnish playwright, poet, and politician; his drama, in particular, reflects the concerns of Finnish writers and intellectuals during the 1860s; his work will generally evidence the influence of Peter Shaffer (*Amadeus*), Pentti Saarkoski, and Tom Stoppard; his most characteristic dramatic themes will deal with political and artistic rivalry.

John Updike. American writer of fiction; he will concern himself with the tensions and tragedies of contemporary middle-class life; his work will prove humorous, entertaining, and highly intelligent; he will discover some degree of sympathy for his middlebrow public (both subject and audience).

Vladimir Nikolaevich Voinovich. Russian writer of fiction, essayist, poet, and playwright; he will revive satire as a mode of expression in Soviet literature and will redefine the Russian hero as an individual concerned with discovering and preserving personal integrity within a totalitarian society.

DEATHS

Rene Bazin (b. 1853). French writer of fiction; his sympathy with the humble and the oppressed has caused his works to be compared with those of Emile Zola; though his staunch Catholic conservatism often limited his range as a writer, he was never dogmatic.

Christopher John Brennan (b. 1870). Australian poet, critic, and philosopher; he patterned his works on those of the French Symbolists and attempted to develop a poetic system to express humankind's emotional, intellectual, and spiritual quest for ultimate truth; he dies of stomach cancer.

Eugene Brieux (b. 1858). French playwright; he enjoyed success in Great Britain and attracted the attention of George Bernard Shaw; he became known as a "problem playwright," focusing his attention upon delicate social issues (such as venereal disease).

Dino Campana (b. 1885). Italian poet and writer of miscellaneous prose; his lyrical verse contains elements of Futurism and is distinguished for its broad European rather than exclusively Italian perspective; he went insane, writing no verse after 1916 and spending the last fourteen years of his life in the Castel Pulci asylum in France.

Hart Crane (b. 1899). American poet; he published only two volumes of verse during his lifetime, but he has been hailed as one of the few truly original American poets; an alcoholic and a homosexual, he was plagued by personal problems that are reflected in his verse; he jumps overboard and drowns on a return trip to the United States from Mexico.

Lady Isabella Augusta Persse Gregory (b. 1859). Irish poet and playwright; she founded and became a principal director of the Abbey Theatre, Dublin; her dramas document the history and development of the Irish Renaissance; she wrote "wonder plays" representative of her rich imagination and knowledge of folk history.

Hafiz Ibrahim (b. 1870). Egyptian poet; his verse reflects his fervent patriotism and passionate concern for social and political justice; he also translated classical pieces from the French.

Jalil Mammadguluzada (b. 1869). Azerbaijan (SSR) writer of fiction and playwright; his stories and plays tend to ridicule religious fanaticism, ignorance, and social backwardness; his characters are often drawn from simple peasants and czarist officials, both ignorant of and isolated from their surroundings.

Gustav Meyrink (b. 1868). Austrian writer of fiction, playwright, and translator; his fiction depicts the individual's quest for spiritual enlightenment; he combines elements of Christian and Jewish mysticism, Eastern philosophy, and occultism; he frequently satirized modern social and political institutions; a debilitating spinal ailment causes his death.

Sir Gilbert Parker (b. 1862). Canadian writer of fiction; he wrote three major novels between 1892 and 1928: *Pierre and His People, The Seats of the Mighty,* and *The Promised Land.*

Ahmad Shawqi (b. 1868). Egyptian poet and playwright; he wrote three historical novels glorifying ancient Egypt and Persia and six historical plays on ancient Egypt, Persia, and Muslim Spain; he patterned his verse upon the aesthetic and artistic values of classical Arabic poetry.

Giles Lytton Strachey (b. 1880). English biographer and essayist; his biographical and critical work captured a large audience because of his wit, satire, and narrative skill; best known as a biographer whose iconoclastic reexaminations of historical figures revolutionized the course of modern biographical writing.

PUBLICATIONS

W. H. Auden, *The Orators*—a verse collection by the English-born poet; critics claimed that the volume combined the influences of Sigmund Freud and Rudyard Kipling, and thus was confusing in substance; revised in 1934 and 1966.

Bertolt Brecht, *Die Heilige Johanna der Schlachthofe* (St. Joan of the Stockyards)—a play by the German dramatist; loosely adapted from George Bernard Shaw's *Major Barbara;* the piece is set in Chicago, where the title character preaches the Gospel to oppressed workers; having caused a general strike to fail, she then attacks all religion, claiming that only radical world changes should be identified as noble.

Erskine Caldwell, *Tobacco Road*—a novel by the American writer of fiction; serves as a chronicle of illiteracy, poverty, and physical and intellectual sterility in the southern United States.

Louis-Ferdinand Celine, *Voyage au Bout de la Nuit* (Journey to the End of the Night)—a novel by the French writer of fiction; described as an "hallucinated account" of the writer's spiritual adventures; the narrator assumes. the role of one Ferdinand Bardamu and his double, Robinson.

John Dos Passos, *1919*—a novel by the American writer of fiction; the second of the *U.S.A.* trilogy; the principal character deserts from the U.S. Navy, wandering around the world and across the United States in search of opportunity; the writer weaves into the piece sketches of such figures as Woodrow Wilson, J. P. Morgan, Joe Hill, and the Unknown Soldier.

T. S. Eliot, *Sweeney Agonistes*—a verse-drama by the American poet and critic; termed an "Aristophanic fragment," the work conveys, in syncopated rhythms, a satiric impression of the sterility of proletarian life; in the first section, two prostitutes entertain cheerful callers; in the second section, they are host to Sweeney, who relates a story of a man who killed a girl.

Hans Fallada, *Kleiner Mann—Was Nun* (Little Man, What Now?)—a novel by the German writer of fiction; a highly popular work that deals frankly and sympathetically with oppressed people confronting serious social problems in Germany following World War I.

James T. Farrell, *Young Lonigan: A Boyhood in Chicago Streets*—a novel by the American writer of fiction; the title character emerges from the social and economic poison of the South Side of Chicago, an area that stifles his sense of right and decency; he also struggles against family pressures and his Catholic background.

William Faulkner, *Light in August*—a novel by the American writer of fiction; the principal character, Joe Christmas, a bastard and possibly part black American (he believes in his black heritage), lives in a strict Calvinist community; the doom and the decline of whites emerge from their inability to treat blacks as human beings; tragedy results because Christmas refuses to give or to accept love, a quality that had been originally denied him.

Dashiell Hammett, *The Thin Man*—a novel by the American writer of detective fiction; significant because the writer introduces a new type of hard-boiled hero whose exploits are set against a seedy urban background; based, in part, on the writer's own experiences as a detective in San Francisco.

Ernest Hemingway, *Death in the Afternoon*—a prose work by the American writer of fiction; describes the bullfight and the traditional events leading up to it (including the raising and training of bulls in Spain); the emphasis throughout tends to be upon ritual and upon the writer's philosophical considerations of life and death.

Aldous Huxley, *Brave New World*—a novel by the English novelist and miscellaneous prose writer; concerns the world in the seventh century "after Ford" (AF), wherein social order depends upon a system controlled by science; essentially a fable, the piece demonstrates that individual freedom cannot exist in a society that relies upon science to remove all doubt and difficulty.

Robinson Jeffers, *Thurso's Landing and Other Poems*—a verse collection by the American poet; set in contemporary California ("Jeffers County") and dominated by mythical overtones; long passages of commentary are interjected into the narratives, suggesting tragic themes "that shine terribly against the dark magnificence of things."

Hugh MacDiarmid, *Scots Unbound and Other Poems*—a verse collection by the Scottish poet; includes such short lyrics as "Milk-Wort and Bog Cotton" and "The Back o'Beyond"; the poems explore the issue of the Scottish dialect and early forms of English.

Archibald MacLeish, *Conquistador*—a long poem by the American writer of verse and playwright; a highly emotional glorification of the Spanish monarchy, the conquest of New Spain, and the Spanish domination of Mexican life and culture; the work earns the poet a Pulitzer Prize in 1933.

Charles Nordoff and James Norman Hall, *Mutiny on the Bounty*—a historical novel by the American writers of fiction; an extremely popular recreation of the April 1789 events concerning the English ship of the title and its captain, William Bligh.

Liviu Rebrenu, *Rascoals* (The Uprising)—a novel by the Romanian writer of fiction, playwright, and essayist; based upon a peasant revolt in 1907, the larger forces that control human destiny and create human conflict stand as background for the accurate narrative account; the work demonstrates the writer's link with such novelists as Thomas Hardy and Emile Zola.

Damon Runyon, *Guys and Dolls*—a collection of short stories by the American journalist and writer of fiction; set in New York City, the pieces relate the adventures of gamblers and characters from the sporting life; highly successful because of its reliance upon semi-illiterate slang and idiom; adapted, in 1950, as an equally successful Broadway musical (and later a motion picture).

William Butler Yeats, *Words for Music, Perhaps, and Other Poems*—a collection of twelve poems by the Irish writer of verse, playwright, and essayist; includes "Crazy Jane and the Bishop," "Crazy Jane Reproved," "Crazy Jane on the Day of Judgment," "Crazy Jane and Jack the Journeyman," "Crazy Jane on God," "Crazy Jane Talks with the Bishop," "Crazy Jane Grown Old Looks at the Dancers," and "The Delphic Oracle upon Plotinus."

EVENTS

The American Scholar, a quarterly journal of education, scholarship, and poetry, begins publication, sponsored by Phi Beta Kappa; the idea for the journal was taken from Ralph Waldo Emerson's 1837 address, "The American Scholar."

Pearl S. Buck, American writer of fiction and missionary to China, receives the Pulitzer Prize in fiction for her novel *The Good Earth* (1931).

Common Sense, a monthly journal of current affairs, begins publication at New York City; essentially liberal in its views, it includes works by John Dos Passos, Archibald MacLeish, and Upton Sinclair; until 1946.

George Dillon, American writer of verse and translator, receives the Pulitzer Prize in poetry for *The Flowering Stone* (1931).

The Folger Shakespeare Memorial Library, Washington, D.C., dedicated; funds for the institution come principally from the estate of Henry Clay Folger, American businessman and president of Standard Oil Company, and his wife; the funds will be administered by Amherst College, Folger's alma mater.

John Galsworthy, English writer of fiction and playwright, receives the Nobel Prize for literature.

Scrutiny, an annual periodical of critical commentary, begins publication at Cambridge, England; essentially an outlet for the views of the new school of literary criticism at Cambridge led by F. R. Leavis; nineteen issues to 1953.

1933

BIRTHS

Michel del Castillo. Spanish-born French writer of fiction; although he will reside in France beginning in 1949, his works will depend upon his native Spain for inspiration, examining, for example, the Spanish Civil War and the slums of Madrid; he will not, in general, complain about his unfortunate past, nor will he appear to have high expectations in life, principally because he will have already experienced extreme physical and emotional suffering.

Augustin-Sonde Coulibaly. North African (Upper Volta) poet and novelist; his musical poetry will be written in French, but its subject matter will concern his African heritage; his racial anger will appear historical and almost abstract, rather than based upon his own grievances; he will spend considerable time collecting the oral literature of his area.

Marian Engel. Canadian novelist; she will introduce elements of feminism into her fiction, producing at least four major novels between 1968 and 1982.

Sulistyautami Iesmaniasita. Javanese poet and writer of fiction; her work will gain recognition for its original style, simple and concise structure, and social themes; her fiction will focus upon contemporary subjects, while her verse will consider ancient Javanese history.

Jerzy Nikodem Kosinski. Polish-born Russian writer of fiction; he will come to the United States in 1957; his most characteristic work will reflect upon the suffering and brutality of World War II; such examinations will give rise to a general study of human vengeance and perversity.

Ian McDonald. Trinidadian novelist and poet; his work will strongly reflect Caribbean culture; in his fiction, he will consider the problems of growing up in a multi-racial society; his novel *The Humming Bird Tree* will be awarded a prize in 1969 by the Royal Society of Literature in London.

Abdul Rahman Mounif. Saudi Arabian novelist; he will be educated in Amman, Baghdad, and Cairo before receiving university training in Yugoslavia; he will experiment in his fiction with such techniques as changing narrators and will present gruesome and disturbingly accurate accounts of cruel conditions in Arab countries; his work will come to the attention of Western readers through French translations.

Philip Roth. American writer of fiction; he will produce witty and ironic pieces focusing upon middle-class Jewish life; he will reveal himself to be an intelligent and serious social critic; with his highly successful *Portnoy's Complaint* (1969), he will introduce the "novel of masturbation" to American literature.

Ahmad Shahnon. Malay writer of fiction; in his short fiction, he will satirize the self-importance of the new Malay; he will also explore religious themes and social and personal relationships among Malay villagers; he will become a member of the faculty at the Australian National University, Canberra.

James Stuart Alexander Simmons. Irish poet, playwright, essayist, biographer, and songwriter; he will become a member of the respected Ulster Poets, those Northern Ireland writers who emerged in the late 1960s; his verse will tend to be personal, lyrical, and colloquial; he will consider such themes as love, marriage, divorce, art, political unrest, and violence.

Susan Sontag. American essayist and writer of fiction; she will be recognized as a brilliant and original thinker; she will argue against literary interpretation based on content or the writer's intentions, instead demanding attention to form in art.

Edwin Thumboo. Singapore (of Chinese and Indian extraction) poet and critic; he will be described as an elegant and humanistic poet, and his work will emphasize the diversity and cultural richness, both past and present, of his land; he will devote his critical attention to Chinese, Malay, and Indian poets who adopt English as their second language; he will become professor of English and dean of the faculty of Arts and Science at the National University of Singapore.

Stephen Vizinczey. Hungarian-born Canadian novelist, essayist, and playwright; he will examine such themes as idealism, avarice, love, and betrayal, relying often upon witty aphorisms; he will come to Canada in 1957, following the Hungarian Revolution of 1956; he will speak little English at first, but will produce a major English-language novel within eight years.

Andrei Andreyevich Voznesensky. Russian poet; he will become a popular writer of verse and will present readings in the Soviet Union and abroad; W. H. Auden will be a principal translator of his works into English.

Yevgeny Alexandrovich Yevtushenko. Russian poet, writer of fiction, playwright, and essayist; he will become known for his dramatic readings of his autobiographical verse; his poetry will be declamatory in tone and will condemn hypocrisy and passivity.

DEATHS

Constantine Cavafy (b. 1863). Egyptian-born Greek poet; he lived most of his life in Alexandria; his poetry presents a mythic, Hellenistic world, populated by historical and imaginary figures; a number of his approximately 150 poems concern the issue of homosexual love.

John Galsworthy (b. 1867). English writer of fiction and playwright; his reputation has come to rest upon his trilogy of novels about three generations of a complacent upper middle-class family, the Forsytes; his successful plays considered various social issues; he received the Nobel Prize for literature in 1932.

Stefan George (b. 1868). German poet; his verse displays the influence of Greek classical forms, the French Symbolist poets, and the philosophy of Friedrich Wilhelm Nietzsche; his aesthetic ideal demanded a controlled humanism; thus, he devoted himself to purifying German language and culture, in the process considerably influencing younger poets; he founded (1892) the literary organ for his circle, *Blatter fur die Kunst.*

Ahmet Hasim (b. 1885). Turkish poet; a leading representative of a generation of Turkish poets who sought to form closer contacts with Western literatures, particularly the poetry of the French Symbolists, and to collaborate with Western literary organizations; thus, he introduced artistic criteria of contemporary Western literatures into Turkish poetry, while his work brought the Turkish poetic idiom closer to that of other world literatures.

Ring Lardner (b. 1885). American writer of short fiction and journalist; originally a sports writer (1907-1929), he became known for his short stories embracing the idiom of the sporting world; his later pieces, although cynical and pessimistic, still retained their humor.

George Augustus Moore (b. 1852). Anglo-Irish writer of fiction; he introduced naturalism into the Victorian novel and attached himself to the Irish literary renaissance; his knowledge of the stage made him integral to the planning of the Irish National Theatre, Dublin.

Nar-Dos (pseudonym of Mikhayel Hovhannisian; b. 1867). Armenian writer of fiction; he wrote psychological novels describing urban intellectuals at the end of the nineteenth century and the beginning of the twentieth century; he commented upon the changes in social and family relationships, attempting careful analyses of his characters.

Payrav (pseudonym of Otajon Sulaymoni; b. 1899). Iranian (Tajik) poet; his work reveals his knowledge of classical European forms; in his verse, he advocated the spread of education, the emancipation of women, and certain international political and military events; he translated works of Russian poets and of other writers, such as Langston Hughes, that had been translated into Russian.

Tom Redcam (pseudonym of Thomas Henry MacDermot; b. 1870). Jamaican poet and novelist; he attempted to cast off European influences and to explore uniquely Jamaican themes in his fiction; similarly, he celebrated the natural beauty of Jamaica in his verse; ill health forced him to move to England in

1923; following his death, the Poetry League of Jamaica conferred upon him the title of Poet Laureate of Jamaica.

Raymond Roussel (b. 1877). French writer of fiction and playwright; an experimental writer who often created works that are wholly removed from the conventions and concerns of realistic literature and that demonstrate his immersion in an unrestricted world of the imagination; thus, he exercised considerable influence upon the surrealists of the late 1920s; addicted to alcohol and barbituates, he commits suicide at Palermo, anguished over his failure to gain critical or popular approval.

George Edward Bateman Saintsbury (b. 1845). English critic, scholar, and literary historian; as a literary critic, he generally based his criteria upon style rather than substance, and thus his work has become antiquated; he became professor of English literature at the University of Edinburgh.

Sara Teasdale (b. 1884). American poet; her lyrics tend to be delicate and highly personal; in total, her work chronicles a woman's emotional development from youthful idealism, through gradual disillusionment, to the final acceptance of death; quite popular in her day, she was awarded a Pulitzer Prize in 1918; she commits suicide at age forty-eight.

PUBLICATIONS

Roberto Arlt, *El Jorobadito* (The Hunchbacks)—a collection of short stories by the Argentine writer of fiction, playwright, and essayist; throughout, the narrators fabricate lies that prove injurious to others or falsely confess to crimes that they did not commit.

Winston Churchill, *Marlborough: His Life and Times*—a multivolume historical and biographical work by the English miscellaneous writer and statesman; focuses upon the writer's ancestor, John Churchill, Duke of Marlborough, and his significant role as commander of the allied forces during the War of the Spanish Succession (1702-1714); to 1938.

James Gould Cozzens, *The Last Adam*—a novel by the American writer of fiction; the principal character dominates life in a small New England town; although he is not a model of complete virtue, his professional competence as a physician and his sense of responsibility serve the town well when required.

Cecil Day Lewis, *The Magnetic Mountain*—a poem by the Irish-born English essayist and writer of verse and fiction; the piece proclaims the voice of a Socialist-Christ, calling upon Britons to forsake their traditional but useless past, to join hands in political and economic brotherhood, and to journey together to the economic "magnetic mountain."

Georges Duhamel, *La Chronique des Pasquier* (Pasquier Chronicle)—a novel by the French poet, playwright, and writer of fiction; a delightfully written work that emphasizes the human condition and parallels the *Forsyte Saga* of John Galsworthy.

Frederico Garcia Lorca, *Bodas de Sangre* (Blood Wedding)—a folk tragedy largely expressionistic in form, by the Spanish poet and playwright; the first play in a trilogy that portrays characters caught in the throes of elemental passions and individuals dominated by a premonition of fate in which dream and reality intermingle; relates the incident of a fatally disrupted wedding that occurs in the hills of Castile.

Tawfiq al-Hakim, *Awdat Ar-Ruh* (The Return of the Spirit)—the first novel by the Egyptian playwright and writer of fiction; describes, within an allegorical context, the lives and problems of the middle class and peasants in Egypt; the writer also concerns himself with the people's involvement in the political uprisings of 1919.

Hans Johst, *Schlageter*—a drama by the German playwright and novelist; a saboteur, executed by the French in the Ruhr in 1923, rises to the status of hero; the piece foreshadows the writer's Nazi and anti-Semitic tendencies.

Archibald MacLeish, *Poems, 1924-1933*—a collection by the American poet, playwright, and miscellaneous writer; includes such major pieces at "Pony Rock," "Unfinished History," and "Lines for an Interment."

Andre Malraux, *La Condition Humaine* (Man's Estate)—a novel by the French writer of fiction and essayist; set against the background of Chiang Kai-Shek's coup, in China in 1927, against the communists; instead of traditional plot, the work consists of a series of scenes, cinematic in technique, that present a lurid drama of deceit and murder; the work bears comparison with the fiction of Joseph Conrad and was one of the earliest political novels in Western literature to contain elements of the spy thriller.

Thomas Mann, *Joseph und Seine Bruder* (Joseph and His Brethren)—a biblical tetralogy by the German writer of fiction; presents the figure of the chosen one as a suffering and regenerated confidence man who reconciles simplicity with sophistication and superstition with skepticism; the work attempts to construct a clear path toward an enlightened democratic German society; until 1943.

Sean O'Casey, *Within the Gates*—a play by the Irish dramatist; a modern morality play set during the depression of the early 1930s; the writer focuses upon the martyrdom of his heroine, who functions as an "everywoman" in this Hyde Park parable; the park, in turn, represents the world of the depression, where everyone suffers spiritually, as well as economically; essentially, the playwright believes that the failure of capitalism relates to the failure of Christianity.

Eugene O'Neill—*Ah, Wilderness!*—a play by the American dramatist; a family comedy set in a small Connecticut city at the outset of the twentieth century; focuses upon adolescence and serene middle age; the piece is unique because it bears no relation to other, more serious themes developed by the playwright.

George Orwell, *Down and Out in Paris and London*—a graphic and realistic narrative by the English writer of fiction and essayist; describes the writer's self-imposed life on the dole during the period when he worked, in Paris and London, at a series of ill-paying jobs.

Ezra Pound, *A Draft of XXX Cantos*—a verse collection by the American-born poet; the first issue of a group of poems upon which he had been working since 1915; the beginnings of what the poet hoped would be a truly modern epic.

Pedro Salinas, *La Voz a ti Debida*—a verse sequence by the Spanish poet, writer of fiction, playwright, essayist, and translator; the volume exists as a single, continuous meditation, with individual pieces not titled or numbered; begins with the discovery of love, proceeds through the loss of love, and ends with hope for the rediscovery of love.

Gertrude Stein, *The Autobiography of Alice B. Toklas*—an autobiographical narrative by the American miscellaneous writer and professional expatriate; a popular work that describes both the writer's Paris salon and her rise to the leadership of the avant-garde literati of the 1920s.

H. G. Wells, *The Shape of Things To Come*—a work of nonfiction by the English writer of fiction and miscellaneous prose; essentially an exercise in scientific and political speculation to confirm the writer's position as a popularizer of current events and an influential voice in terms of the future direction of the world.

EVENTS

The American Review begins publication as a journal for the analysis of contemporary social and economic issues and literature; until 1937.

Maxwell Anderson, American playwright, receives the Pulitzer Prize in drama for *Both Your Houses* (1933).

Ivan Alekseyevich Bunin, Russian writer of fiction, receives the Nobel Prize for literature.

James Joyce's novel *Ulysses* (1922) is permitted into the United States following a court ruling.

Archibald MacLeish, American poet and dramatist, receives the Pultizer Prize in poetry for *Conquistador* (1932).

Nazi Germans burn all books by Jewish and non-Nazi writers.

Thomas Sigismund Stribling, American writer of fiction, receives the Pulitzer Prize in fiction for his novel *The Store* (1932).

1934

BIRTHS

Kareen Fleur Adcock. New Zealand-born English poet; she will write verse in clear, precise language, and her style will be characterized by irony and discipline; her nightmarish imagery will combine elements of both the rational and the fantastic; she will rely on traditional poetic forms.

Mario Antonio (born Mario Antonio de Oliveira). Angolan poet and writer of short fiction; although he will reside in Lisbon, the subject matter of his works will be based upon the folk tales of his native land.

Leonard Norman Cohen. Canadian novelist, poet, and playwright; a self-styled "black romantic," he will blend the themes of love and beauty with a sense of loss and suffering; he will rely upon a combination of sensual and surreal imagery, filtering Judaism, Christianity, and mythology through the conventions of lyric poetry.

Joan Didion. American writer of fiction and essayist; in her work, she will explore what she considers the emptiness of contemporary American life; she will employ "pastiche" and "montage" techniques, setting disparate fictional scenes next to one another; such literary manipulations will attempt to underscore the dislocation of women within contemporary society.

Forugh Farrokhzad (d. 1967). Iranian poet; in her verse, she will attempt to reveal the intimacies of a woman's heart, thus focusing upon subjects never before treated in Persian poetry; she will describe such feelings as passion, fear, melancholy, despair, and tormented longing.

Alasdair Gray. Scottish writer of fiction; an innovator, he will strive for a combination of realism and fantasy; his idiosyncratic style will be noted for its complexity, wit, and energy; thematically, he will explore the oppression of the working class, presenting a dark vision of modern Scottish and British society.

Masuo Ikeda. Japanese writer of fiction; he will gain recognition as a world renowned printmaker, and his work will be purchased by the Museum of Modern Art, New York; his writings will be existential, displaying the influence of Albert Camus and Jean-Paul Sartre; Jean Cocteu and Henry Miller will also contribute to his literary development.

T. Jayakantan. Tamilnad (SSR) writer of fiction; his work, at the outset, will be strongly Marxist in tone, but will later become more humanistic; his short stories and novels will be written in a direct, simple, and forceful prose style and will concern the lives of the workers and middle classes in the towns of Tamilnad.

Uwe Johnson (d. 1984). German writer of fiction, essayist, and translator; his novels will explore the conflicts resulting from a divided Germany, focusing upon the guilt of the collective German consciousness; the Berlin Wall will serve as a microcosm of that divided world; he will receive the Georg Buchner Prize in 1971.

LeRoi Jones (Imamu Amiri Baraka). American poet, playwright, and writer of fiction; his works will, in the emotion of the political moment, express the dislike of black persons for white society; critics have tended to label his poems "assassin's" verse: poems that kill,

shoot guns, and call for the destruction of white America.

Jose Louzeiro. Brazilian writer of adult and juvenile fiction; he will publish over one dozen adult novels and novellas, two children's novels, and two volumes of short stories; his work will generally focus upon the less desirable aspects of his nation's contemporary urban scene: corruption, hypocrisy, social and economic imbalance, poverty, injustice, crime, and violence.

Navarre Scott Momoday. Native American poet and writer of fiction; his literary purpose will be twofold: to describe native ancestral ritual and to explore the American Indian's loss of cultural continuity; he will also write a significant history of Indian migration.

Adolf Muschg. Swiss writer of fiction, playwright, and critic; he will become professor of German literature at the Swiss Institute of Technology at Zurich; his fiction will often be autobiographical and will concern itself with the mentality of the Swiss middle class; a number of his pieces will be set in China and Japan; his work will be translated into at least eight languages.

John Francisco Rechy. American writer of fiction; he will become one of the most significant American novelists to concern himself with the issue of homosexuality; in an eloquent and convincing prose style, he will combine the comic with the tragic as he takes his readers through the hidden world of hustled sex between men.

Akinwande Oluwole Soyinka. Nigerian poet, playwright, novelist, and critic; he will become the first African to win the Nobel Prize in literature; he will write principally in English, although a portion of his work will be composed in Yoruba and Swahili; he will chronicle traditional Yoruban culture and the turbulent history of modern Nigeria; he will consider literature a serious agent of social change and will commit himself to the cause of human rights within Africa.

DEATHS

Murza Abolqasem Qazvini Aref (b. 1882?). Iranian poet; the bard of the Iranian national revival, his poetry describes incidents in the struggle for the modernization of Iran; his favorite poetic form was the ballad of folk origin.

Sayyid Shaykh bin Sayyid Ahmad Al-Hadi (b. 1867). Malay journalist and writer of fiction; he introduced the novel to peninsular Malay literature adapting Arabic originals with Egyptian settings; also known for his vigorously polemic essays.

Bely Andrei (pseudonym of Boris Nikolayevich Bugayev; b. 1880). Russian poet and writer of fiction; he attempted to experiment with fiction in the manner of James Joyce and became interested in the art, music, and poetry of Wolfgang von Goethe; by 1914, he had become the principal theoretician of the symbolists, viewing the 1917 Revolution in terms of the Second Coming.

Chaim Nachman Bialik (b. 1873). Ukrainian poet, writer of short fiction, and essayist; he became one of the most significant poets of the twentieth-century renaissance in Hebrew literature; his verse reflects the personal sufferings of his childhood and the pain of the Jewish people in exile from their homeland; he calls upon Jews to assert their national independence and to take pride in the traditions of their culture.

Jose Santos Chocano (b. 1875). Peruvian poet and political revolutionary; he became an exponent of modernismo (elegant form, exotic imagery, subtle word music) and emphasized Indian and native themes; political opponents murder him in Chile.

Jafar Jabbarly (b. 1899). Azerbaijan (SSR) poet, writer of fiction, and playwright; initially, he was influenced by Turkish literature and the ideal of pan-Turkish unity; later, he depicted the Azerbaijan national awakening and the new life under Soviet influence; considered the founder of Soviet Azerbaijan drama.

Abdulali Mustaghni (b. 1876). Afghan poet; he wrote in both the Pashto and Dari languages; his literary efforts stressed the importance of education, work, and personal endurance; he wrote extensively for the periodicals at Kabul.

Sir Arthur Wing Pinero (b. 1855). English playwright; he achieved success on the English stage with farces and sentimental comedies; also remembered for his social dramas, which advanced the trend toward dramatic realism; because his works reflected continental techniques and trends during an especially stagnant period in the history of the English stage, he is often credited with the revitalization of the English drama.

Joachim Ringelnatz (pseudonym of Hans Botticher; b. 1883). German poet and writer of fiction; he wrote prose poetry and verse that could be easily recited at bars; his fiction relates directly to his war experiences.

Abul-Qasim ash-Shabbi (b. 1909). Tunisian poet and critic; his writings reflect the influence of Alphonse Marie de Lamartine and Johann Wolfgang von Goethe, whose works he read in translation; most of his poems appeared in the periodical press, and he published only one volume of verse during his lifetime; he will represent in his verse the Romantic's zest for life under the shadow of death; he dies from heart disease.

Jakob Wassermann (b. 1873). German-born Jewish novelist; he gained popularity for focusing upon universal humanitarian, rather than strictly German, themes.

PUBLICATIONS

AE, *The House of Titans*—a poem by the English writer of verse; a long and complicated work involved with Celtic mythology.

Bozorg Alavi, *Chamadan* (The Suitcase)—a collection of six short stories by the Iranian writer of fiction; contains a group of unusual and perverted characters who function as heroes: an impotent opium addict, and a father and sons in love with the same girl; demonstrates the writer's Freudian interpretation of character and human relationships.

Louis Aragon, *Les Cloches de Bale* (The Bells of Basel)—a novel by the French writer of fiction; the first in a series of socially and politically realistic novels he composed following his conversion to communism.

Jean Cocteau, *La Machine Infernale* (The Infernal Machine)—a tragic drama by the French poet, novelist, and playwright; an original treatment of the Oedipus theme, focusing upon the machinations and ingeniousness of the Olympian gods.

James Gould Cozzens, *Castaway*—a novella by the American writer of fiction; a fantastic story of a man lost in an empty department store; a parable (in the manner of Franz Kafka) of a mad version of Robinson Crusoe reduced almost to an animal as he fights for life; in the end, the person who threatens him and whom he kills turns out to be himself.

F. Scott Fitzgerald, *Tender Is the Night*—a novel by the American writer of fiction; examines the Jazz-Age generation's search for the elusive American dream of wealth and happiness and scrutinizes the consequences of that generation's adherence to false values; set against the backdrop of expatriate life in Europe in the 1920s, the novel presents the story of a brilliant young psychiatrist, Dick Diver, and his schizophrenic wife, Nicole, who was raped by her father when she was fifteen; Nicole recovers but Diver collapses under the strain of the complex roles he must play as doctor, husband, and father.

Jean Giono, *Le Chant de Monde* (The Song of the World)—a novel by the French writer of fiction; essentially a story of violence and lust; the search for a pair of lovers displays epic grandeur and reveals the writer's reliance upon Homer.

Robert Graves, *I, Claudius*—a historical novel by the English poet and miscellaneous prose writer; reconstructs the grandeur, folly, and sensuality of imperial Rome; the mild Claudius moves unobtrusively among his sinister relatives and records their vile but proud history; the work goes forward upon a string of intriguing and startling events, including poisoning, incest, and black magic.

Hugh MacDiarmid, *Stony Limits*—a collection of meditative poems by the Scottish writer of verse; most noted among the pieces is "On a Raised Beach," a subtle statement of the writer's metaphysical system focusing upon what he termed "beautiful reality."

Henry Miller, *Tropic of Cancer*—an autobiographical work of fiction by the American-born novelist and essayist; published at Paris, the work is a frank, and often vulgar, account of an American artist's adventures in the French capital; banned in Great Britain and the United States until the early 1960s because of its explicit sexual content.

John O'Hara, *Appointment in Samarra*—the first novel by the American writer of fiction; relates the events leading up to a Pennsylvania man's suicide; he insults an individual who might be of help to him, setting the stage for his self-destruction; the writer also undertakes a careful sociological analysis of small-town America.

George Orwell, *Burmese Days*—a novel by the English writer of fiction and essayist; a scathing indictment of British imperial rule, the work presents a bitter and satiric picture of corruption spawned by absolute power.

Fernando Pessoa, *Mensagem* (Message)—a collection of verse by the Portuguese poet and essayist; the pieces depict the legend of King Sebastien's resurrection as the savior of Portugal.

C. P. Snow, *The Search*—a novel by the English writer of fiction and critic; basically concerns the frustrations of a scientist's life; in a number of respects, the piece is similar to Sinclair Lewis's *Arrowsmith* (1925).

Dylan Thomas, *18 Poems*—the first collection by the Welsh poet, playwright, writer of fiction, and miscellaneous prose writer; contains pieces written between July 1931 and November 1934 at Swansea, Wales; often described as incantatory, the collection records Thomas's experimentation with vibrant imagery and with sound as "verbal music."

Arnold Toynbee, *A Study of History*—a prose work by the English cultural and intellectual historian; surveys the principal civilizations of the world; the writer inquires into cycles of creativity and decay, finding evidence for the current fragmentation and decline of Western civilization; the only hope lies in a new universal religion to recapture spirituality; ten vols.; to 1954.

Evelyn Waugh, *A Handful of Dust*—a novel by the English writer of fiction; concerns the infatuation of a titled lady for a young gadfly; when she leaves her husband, he spends the remainder of his life in the Amazon reading Dickens, and she marries someone other than the gadfly; a comic criticism of life in the 1930s, with its unstable values and lack of morality.

Stefan Zweig, *Triumph und Tragik des Erasmus von Rotterdam* (The Triumph and Tragedy of Erasmus Rotterdamus)—a biography by the Austrian writer of fiction, poet, essayist, and biographer; the writer considered the work "a quiet hymn of praise to the antifanatical man," as well as a veiled portrait of himself.

EVENTS

The William Andrews Clark Memorial Library, Los Angeles, California, opens; it will become one of the nation's most significant centers for literary and historical research.

Lazar Goldschmidt completes the twelfth and final volume of his German translation of the Babylonian Talmud, a profject begun in 1893.

Maxim Gorki, Russian writer of fiction and drama, convenes the first Soviet Writers' Congress at Moscow.

Robert Silliman Hillyer, American poet and academician, receives the Pulitzer prize in poetry for his *Collected Verse* (1933).

Sidney Kingsley, American playwright, receives the Pulitzer prize in drama for *Men in White* (1933).

Caroline Miller, American writer of fiction, receives the Pulitzer prize in fiction for her novel *Lamb in His Bosom* (1933).

The Partisan Review, originally a quarterly political and literary journal reflecting communist "partisanship," begins publication at New York City; within four years it loses its political identity and focuses upon artistic criticism and creative literature; noted contributors include W. H. Auden, Saul Bellow, Jacques Barzun, Randall Jarrell, Denise Levertov, Archibald MacLeish, Joyce Carol Oates, Norman Mailer, Philip Roth, Gilbert Sorrentino, Susan Sontag, Lionel Trilling, and Allen Tate.

Luigi Pirandello, Italian poet, essayist, writer of fiction, and playwright, receives the Nobel Prize for literature.

1935

BIRTHS

Ahmud Abralmuti Hijazi. Egyptian poet and critic; his verse will reflect his socialistic attitudes and sympathy for the poor; he will also write critical studies and introductions to anthologies; he will favor, in his critical commentary, those poets of earlier generations who foreshadowed the modern writers of Egyptian verse.

Kofi Awoonor. Ghanaian (Volta Region) poet, novelist, and playwright; he will utilize traditional Ewe songs to lament the neglect of ancient Africa's gods and shrines and the perverting influence of Western culture; other themes will include an awareness of the omnipotence of death.

George Bowering. Canadian poet, writer of fiction, and essayist; he will become a leading innovator in Canadian literature, experimenting with form and technique, while exploring themes related to art, language, and personal identity.

Dollar Brand. South African poet; he will write concise, pictorial verse that relates clearly to his principal vocation, that of professional jazz pianist; thus,

rhythm afrique
joey had the biggest feet
so he played tenor

Richard Brautigan. American writer of fiction and poet; his fiction will warn people to refrain from attempting to recreate traditional American values; humiliation will breed suffering, which will in turn create gentle but terribly cold individuals; from one point of view, he will depict America as a fantastic ruin containing little beyond the remains of technology.

John Pepper Clark. Nigerian poet, playwright, and critic; he will write in English so that he will be able to reach the widest audience possible; African images, themes, settings, and speech patterns will, however, predominate in his work.

Zulfikar Ghose. Pakistani-born writer of fiction, poet, and essayist; he will be raised and educated in India and England, and eventually settle in the United States; thus, his literary works will tend to express the viewpoint of the culturally alienated individual.

Rodney Hall. English-born Australian novelist, poet, biographer, and miscellaneous prose writer; his fiction will develop mythic significance by depicting life in the isolated Australian outback; his expansive and rich prose style will evoke several levels of meaning; his neo-romantic verse will contain witty observations and examine themes relating to love, death, violence, and the role of the artist.

Ramon Hernandez. Spanish novelist; he will become one of his nation's most popular and honored literary figures; he will be concerned with, among other subjects, prison life and adolescents in Madrid.

Thomas Michael Keneally. Australian writer of fiction, playwright, essayist, and author of children's books; he will become known for his novels based upon historical personages and events; he will focus upon individuals struggling with questions of conscience; his subjects will range from the history and people of his native Australia to the military campaigns of the American Confederate Army between 1861 and 1864.

Ken Kesey. American writer of fiction; he will balance totally individualistic and disruptive characters with narrators (or at least narrative voices) who tend to be both reasonable and contemplative; for him, the only possible form of individualism will come through the individual following his or her own advice and listening to his or her own sense of reason.

William Patrick Kinsella. Canadian writer of fiction; he will gain recognition for his short story collections about contemporary Canadian Indians who struggle for survival in a white society, as well as for his novels and stories about baseball, which, for him, exists as a metaphor for imagination, commitment, and individual accomplishment and rejuvenates those who follow it.

Earl Lovelace. Trinidadian writer of fiction, playwright, and poet; he will portray in his fiction the lives of native Trinidadians and examine conflicts arising from the impact of modern culture upon the traditions of their homeland; he will develop a clear and poetic prose style and precisely render his West Indian dialect; he will create characters with whom readers may easily identify despite racial, geographical, and chronological differences.

Thomas Bernard Murphy. Irish playwright; he will examine familial, social, cultural, andreligious pressures that influence the lives of Irish citizens, both at home and in England, as they attempt to establish individual identities; nonetheless, his plays will transcend their localities to depict universal emotions.

Lewis Nkosi. South African (Natal) playwright, essayist, and writer of fiction; he will become a resident of London; his drama will concern young Boer, English, and African students of the early 1960s who try to ignore the racial prejudice around them and the oppressive policies of their government; his prose essays will offer a sensitive and balanced perspective on the plight of the captive millions within South Africa, as well as explore the principal issues of black American poetry.

Kenzaburo Oe. Japanese writer of fiction; his work will be written in an unpretentious, economical style and will display his keen sensitivity to the predicament of the post-war generation in Japan; he will receive recognition for providing that generation with a new type of hero; he will edit an anthology of Japanese short stories that chronicle the impact of the Hiroshima and Nagasaki bombings on the daily lives of peasants, city professionals, artists, children, and families in general.

Francois Sagan (pseudonym of Francois Quoirez). French writer of fiction; her popular works will focus upon bored, shallow, and spoiled people who seek refuge in brief sexual encounters.

Thomas William Shapcott. Australian poet, novelist, and critic; his verse will display his sense of musicality and his ability to manipulate both traditional and experimental prosody; he will concern himself with the contrast between the poet's inner perceptions and the external world, the relationship between time and existence, and the artist's search for self-definition.

Julian Randolph Stow. Australian novelist, poet, and writer of children's books; he will gain favor for his lyrical prose, authentic rendering of dialect, and haunting evocations of Australia's diverse landscapes; his work will tend toward allegory and myth, exploring such themes as the effects of misguided pride and love, the beauty and cruelty of nature, and the individual's alienation from society.

Mats Traat. Estonian writer of fiction and poet; although he will gain stature as a poet, he will primarily be remembered for his fiction, much of which will focus upon contemporary living conditions and reveal the writer's belief that Soviet influence in Estonia has reduced the nation to a third world country.

Luandino Vieira (pseudonym of Jose Vieira Mateus da Graca). Angolan poet, short story writer, and journalist; the child of a Portuguese father and an African mother, he will employ in his work the rich Creole mixture of Portuguese and local Kimbundu; he will occasionally write poetry in the proletariat patois or Pequeno-Portugues, the dialect spoken by the illiterate Africans; he will spend time in prisons on Santiago Island and the Cape Verde Islands because of his support of Angolan independence.

DEATHS

AE (pseudonym of George William Russell; b. 1867). Irish poet and playwright; his literary endeavors reflect his Irish nationalist sentiments; he became a major figure in the Irish literary renaissance, writing mystical and melodious drama and verse.

Henri Barbusse (b. 1873). French writer of fiction and minor poet; he became a successful writer of war fiction, expressing his disillusionment with the military mentality.

Paul Bourget (b. 1852). French writer of fiction and critic; important for his early application of psychological principles in his literary criticism; also one of the foremost psychological novelists of his time.

Fernando Antonio Nogueira Pessoa (b. 1888). Portuguese poet; his four distinct poetic personas—the messianic, the rationalistic, the stoic, and the Nietzschean—reflected his disbelief in the idea of an integrated personality; he wrote sonnets and a collection of *English Poems* (1922).

Edwin Arlington Robinson (b. 1869). American poet; his early verses were probing portraits of residents of a small New England town; his later poems tended to be long psychological narratives and variations upon Arthurian romances; he received the Pulitzer Prize for poetry in 1922 and 1928.

Isaiah Shembe (b. 1867?). South African (Zulu) poet and hymnodist; his work reflects his exposure to fundamentalist Christianity and his knowledge of traditional Zulu beliefs and practices.

Anempodist Ivanovich Sofronov (b. 1886). Yakutsk (SSR) playwright; he attempted to rouse public opinion against the inhumanity of the pre-Revolution patriarchal-feudal society of Yakutsk; by the 1930s he developed into a socialist-realist committed to the Soviet system.

Mahmud Tarzi (b. 1868). Afghan writer of fiction, poet, and essayist; his work brought about a complete change in the literature of his nation; he introduced new subjects to poetry, such as science, coal, roads, and telegraphic communication; he translated fiction by Jules Verne and sought to express the philosophy of the new sciences; he wrote poetry attacking the Japanese invasion of Manchuria and advocated emancipation of women.

PUBLICATIONS

Halide Edib Adivar, *Sinekli Bakkal* (The Clown and His Daughter)—a novel by the Turkish writer of fiction and political essayist; written during the writer's exile from her country and published in England; reflects her interest in interpreting traditional Turkish culture for Western readers.

Maxwell Anderson, *Winterset*—a verse drama by the American playwright; a critically acclaimed sympathetic depiction of the controversial Sacco-Vanzetti murder case.

Enid Bagnold, *National Velvet*—a novel by the English writer of fiction and playwright; concerns a young girl who, disguised as a boy, rides the horse of the title to victory in the Grand National steeplechase; a popular piece that achieved even more recognition as a motion picture.

Jorge Barbosa, *Arquipalago*—a collection of verse by the Cape Verde Island poet; concerns the poverty and suffering of the writer's fellow islanders.

Clarence Day, *Life with Father*—an autobiographical sketch by the American prose writer; concerns life in late nineteenth-century New York City among the affluent and the slightly eccentric; highly successful as a Broadway play, which premiered in 1939.

T. S. Eliot, *Murder in the Cathedral*—a verse play by the American-born English poet, critic, and dramatist; concerns the antagonism between Henry II of England and Thomas à Becket, Archbishop of Canterbury, over the king's attempt to diminish ecclesiastical law and the Archbishop's resolve to defend the power of the Church; the work ends in a celebration of Becket's martyrdom.

William Faulkner, *Pylon*—a novel (his eighth) by the American writer of fiction; the principal character abandons a career in medicine to become a racing pilot; he shares his common-law wife with another man and assumes the paternity of her child who may or may not be his; he loses his life while racing in a defective plane.

Jean Giraudoux, *La Guerre de Troie N'Aura pas Lieu* (Tiger at the Gates)—a dramatic tragedy by the French writer of fiction, essayist, and playwright; concerns the Trojan soldiers, fresh from victory, and their determination to maintain peace; however, war and revolution are portrayed here as inevitable; the work was translated by Christopher Fry in 1955.

Ernest Hemingway, *The Green Hills of Africa*—a narrative by the American writer of fiction; principally focuses upon big game hunting in Africa.

Andre Malraux, *Le Temps du Mepris* (Days of Contempt)—an antiwar novel by the French writer of fiction and miscellaneous prose; focuses upon a communist imprisoned by the Nazis who gains freedom through a comrade's plotting and strategy; thus, he can continue his struggles against totalitarianism.

Clifford Odets, *Waiting for Lefty*—a play by the American dramatist and film writer; demonstrates the writer's sensitivity toward the confusions of young people during the Depression; the piece represents a form of literary and dramatic militancy known as "agitprop": "agitational propaganda" designed in this case to reveal how political and industrial groups manipulate the poor.

Jaysankar Prasad, *Kamayani*—an epic poem by the Indian (Hindi) writer of verse, playwright, and novelist; based upon themes from ancient Indian literature, but concerned, allegorically, with contemporary problems in Indian society.

Abdullo Qodiriy, *Obid Ketman*—a novel by the Uzbek (SSR) satirist and writer of fiction; describes the changes in Uzbek village life during the collectivization of the countryside; contains colorful characterization and a lively rendering of the Uzbek language; until 1936.

George Santayana, *The Last Puritan*—a novel by the Spanish-born American poet, philosopher, and miscellaneous prose writer; satirizes "the genteel tradition" in American society, focusing on the youth in America at the turn of the twentieth century.

Robert Emmet Sherwood, *The Petrified Forest*—a drama by the American playwright and biographer; demonstrates how civilized human beings can easily descend to the level of the savage; a sensitive but morally uncommitted intellectual suffers destruction at the hands of a brutal gangster; behind the melodrama lies a warning concerning the dangers of fascism.

Isaac Bashevis Singer, *Satan in Goray*—a novella by the Polish-born Yiddish-American writer of fiction; describes the acceptance of Eastern European Jews of a false messiah, Sabbatai Zevi; takes place after the Cossack raids of 1648-1649.

Ousmane Diop Soce, *Karimn, Roman Senegalais*—a novel by the Senegalese writer of fiction and poet; the work relates the sad tale of the humiliations suffered by the title character (who symbolizes all Africans) at the hands of Europeans; he and his companions meet defeat in an Africa no longer theirs, a situation their own fathers had previously experienced; republished in 1950.

Stephen Spender, *The Destructive Element: A Study of Modern Writers and Beliefs*—a volume of criticism by the English poet and miscellaneous prose writer; the writer's approach originates from his proclivity for highly personal poetry; thus, he identifies the loss of personal conviction as the cause for England's social, economic, and moral decay.

John Steinbeck, *Tortilla Flat*—a novel by the American writer of fiction; a series of tales about the "paisanos" of the title site, located at the edge of Monterey, California; these people have divorced themselves from society and its values and, although idle and dishonest, they are free from the evils of commerce.

Wallace Stevens, *The Idea of Order at Key West*—a poem by the American playwright and writer of verse and prose; reverses his previous position that nothing exists but individual consciousness, arguing that objective reality does exist, but it lacks any intrinsic purpose except that imposed by human values.

Thomas Wolfe, *Of Time and the River*—a novel by the American writer of fiction; a second autobiographical work about Wolfe's Southern protagonist, Eugene Gant; here, the artist-hero travels north seeking fame.

EVENTS

Zoe Akins, American playwright and novelist, receives the Pulitzer Prize in drama for *The Old Maid* (1935), a dramatic adaptation of a novella by Edith Wharton (1924).

London publisher Victor Gollancz founds the Left Book Club; intended to promote books in opposition to the rise of fascism and Nazism; its circulations include Clifford Odets's *Waiting for Lefty* and George Orwell's *The Road to Wigan Pier;* at its height the club will reach 50,000 members; until 1948.

Josephine Winslow Johnson, American writer of fiction and essayist, receives the Pulitzer Prize in fiction for her novel *Now in November* (1943).

Audrey Wurdemann, American poet, receives the Pulitzer Prize in poetry for her collection *Bright Ambush* (1934).

1936

BIRTHS

Nikolai Baturin. Estonian (SSR) writer of fiction and poet; he will write verse containing hundreds of dialect words and terms and contemplative prose about exotic Central Asian landscapes; his fiction will contain erotic elements and will focus upon the *nouveaux riches,* characteristics that will prevent his works from assuming an important role in "official" Soviet literature; because of his reliance on dialect, he will be at his best when he writes dialogues and soliloquies.

Henryk Grynberg. Polish poet and writer of fiction and nonfiction; his work will reflect his indignation over the Holocaust and will cast light upon the essence of Jewish existence; he will manipulate his native Polish language, proving himself a master of dialogue.

Vaclav Havel. Czech playwright; he will become one of his nation's foremost dissident dramatists and will be in constant conflict with his government, which will, beginning in 1969, banish his work; his drama will present a vivid and terrifying portrait of the artist in a totalitarian state; his arrest, trial, and imprisonment in May 1979 on a charge of subversion will generate widespread international protest among those concerned with freedom of expression and human rights; in 1989, he will become the head of his nation's government.

Jean Ikelle-Matiba. Cameroon novelist, essayist, and poet; he will receive, in 1963, the Grand Prix Litteraire de l'Afrique Noire for fiction for his novel set in the late nineteenth century during the German occupation of parts of Africa; his verse will display the influence of Aime Cesaire, the Martinique poet; thus, he will compose simple poems critical of the "new" Africa and bitter about the colonial past.

Ismail Kadare. Albanian writer of fiction and poet; he will develop such universal themes as traditional values, tyranny, prejudice, and the futility of war, and his works will be translated into more than thirty languages; his surrealistic fiction will become especially popular in France and will blend Albanian history and folklore with elements of realism; in general, his fiction will display his love for his country and its people.

William McIlvanney. Scottish novelist and poet; he will realistically portray conflicts among the social classes of Scotland; his contemporary urban settings will be made more by his depiction of the increasing crime and materialism in Scottish society; he will also rely upon Scottish dialects.

Charles Nokan. Ivory Coast novelist, poet, and playwright; he will combine poetry with prose passages in musical order, attempting to recapture the quality of ancient instruments (tom-toms, for instance); his drama will be melancholy treatments of the African soul.

Nkem Nwankwo. Nigerian novelist and playwright; his work will be characterized by its thematic zest and his reliance upon Ibo words and terms; he will rarely consider European values other than those advanced by aggressive and puritanical Christian villagers; his prose style will tend to be patterned after that of ancient Ibo story tellers.

Marge Piercy. American writer of fiction; her work will describe the problems of people who must go underground to escape the tyrannies of society; she will thus create romances that display a social conscience and announce a future in which human beings, particularly women, can retreat and meet their emotional needs.

Sahle Berhane Mariam Sellassie. Ethiopian writer of fiction; he will write both in Amharic and English; his short novels will dramatize the daily lives of contemporary Ethiopian villagers; he will describe a people adjusting to changes in their lives brought about by new governmental, social, and educational developments.

Jorge Mario Pedro Vargas Llosa. Peruvian writer of fiction, playwright, and critic; he will gain a reputation for his insightful examinations of social and cultural themes; he will rapidly shift narrative perspectives and create disparate but converging story lines to reflect the disorder of human existence.

DEATHS

G. K. Chesterton (b. 1874). English writer of fiction, poet, and essayist; his writings reflect his conservatism and Roman Catholic principles; he produced significant critical studies of Robert Browning and Charles Dickens; he also introduced into detective fiction the character of "Father Brown," an erratic but intuitive solver of crimes.

Grazia Cosima Deledda (b. 1871?). Italian (Sardinian) writer of fiction and playwright; most of her work is set in her native Sardinia, but it transcends its regional limits through its discussion of universal themes; she became one of the most popular Italian romance writers of the early twentieth century, as well as the only Italian woman to receive the Nobel Prize for literature (1926); she dies of breast cancer, after writing an autobiographical novel, *Cosima*, on the subject.

Federico Garcia Lorca (b. 1898). Spanish lyric poet and playwright; his work reflects the spirit of his native Andalusia and his own passionate response to life; he became the most popular Spanish poet of his generation, principally because of his maturity of thought; he dies after being shot by Francisco Franco's soldiers at the outset of the Spanish Civil War.

Maxim Gorky (pseudonym of Aleksey Maximovich Pyeshhkov; b. 1868). Russian writer of fiction, playwright, and essayist; generally, his work is optimistic and vital, combining realism with a strong sense of poetic style; he has been credited with establishing the principles of Soviet realism; prior to the Revolution of 1917, he gained considerable recognition as the literary representative of the nobility of peasants, workers, and vagabonds.

Rudyard Kipling (b. 1865). English poet and writer of fiction; his popular poems and stories depicted the strife and glamor of Indian life; he gave to his reading audience a romantic view of English imperialism, but he also created an accurate portrait of those common English soldiers who built Victoria's empire; in addition, he wrote a significant body of literature that appealed directly to children; he received, in 1907, the Nobel Prize for literature.

Luigi Pirandello (b. 1867). Italian playwright, writer of fiction, critic, and poet; a theatrical innovator who advanced philosophical themes and experimented with dramatic structure; he became obsessed with the relationship of reality to appearance, of sanity to madness; thus, his characters adopted multiple identities (or masks) to reconcile social demands with personal needs; he also combined comedy with tragedy, producing an emotional awareness of both of those aspects of the human condition.

Premchand (pseudonym of Dhanpat Rai Srivastava; b. 1880). Indian writer of fiction, critic, and playwright; the first writer in the Hindi language to employ themes and techniques of literary realism developed by his modern European counterparts, provided an accurate account of the social and political upheaval of contemporary Indian life; a follower of Ghandi, he advocated in his fiction national reforms and expressed a trust in the good of all of the people; he also translated works by Charles Dickens, Leo Tolstoy, and Guy de Maupassant, all of whom were models for his own concept of literary realism.

Oswald Spengler (b. 1880). German philosopher, historian, and essayist; his work, beginning in 1904, advanced the notion that every culture passes through a life cycle from youth through maturity, and from old age to death; following that through to its conclusion, he determined that Western culture, by the end of World War I, had entered a period of decline; he suffered from restrictions placed upon him by the Nazi regime.

Joseph Lincoln Steffans (b. 1866). American writer of fiction and nonfiction; perhaps the most significant of the turn-of-the-century social and political reformers known as "muckrakers" his noted autobiography (1931) casts additional light upon his times, principally the extent of political corruption in early twentieth-century America.

Miguel de Unamuno (b. 1864). Spanish poet, essayist, and novelist; a philosophical writer of Basque descent, he expressed his highly individual form of existentialism, based upon his faith in faith itself.

Ramon de Valle Inclan (b. 1866?). Spanish writer of fiction and poet; he wrote tales that developed the concept of modernismo (highly symbolic, elegant in form, erotic in imagery, subtle in word music) and expressed a symbolist aesthetic; his grotesque caricatures of Spanish life, particularly of aristocratic and military brutality, are reminiscent of the nightmarish etchings of Francisco de Goya.

Lu Xun (b. 1881). Chinese critic; he became a founding member of the League of Left-Wing Writers (1930) after Chiang Kai-shek seized power in 1927; through his prose, he hoped to ignite the spirit of Chinese patriots against the new government; in rational and exceedingly clear language, he attacked aristocratic and reactionary attempts to redefine politics, literary criticism, theater, opera, the role of women, and religious ceremonies; he also attacked the trend of encouraging Chinese to adopt Western modes and Western fashions.

PUBLICATIONS

Jean Anouilh, *Voyageur sans Bagage* (Traveller without Luggage)—a drama by the French playwright; concerns an amnesic former soldier who returns home to discover from his family, who appear uncertain of his identity, that he has been a vicious and cruel individual; thus he carefully avoids his former self and assumes the identity of a more pleasant person.

W. H. Auden and Christopher Isherwood, *The Ascent of F6*—a play by the English writers; concerns a mountaineering expedition on a mysterious and haunted peak; all of the climbers but the leader die before they achieve their objective; the leader dies only after he has reached the top, destroyed by his own self-knowledge and rejection of mystic thoughts; commentary in verse upon the dullness of everyday human existence runs through the dramatic narrative.

Georges Bernanos, *Journal d'un Cure de Campagne* (Diary of a Country Priest)—a novel by the French writer of fiction; the story of a sick and unworldly priest in northern France who attempts to serve the poor, but they, being a vicious lot, abuse him.

Jorge Luis Borges, *Historia de la Eternidad*—a collection of essays by the Argentinian writer of fiction, essayist, poet, and biographer; the writer explores humanity's concept of eternity from ancient times to the present; includes "The Approach to al-Mu'tasim," the writer's review of an imaginary detective novel which he maintains that content exists only in the reader's imagination.

Van Wyck Brooks, *The Flowering of New England*—a volume in the American literary critic's history of the writer in America; concentrates upon the influence of Puritanism on American culture and offers a humanistic interpretation of American literary history; the work receives the Pulitzer Prize for history in 1937.

Louis-Ferdinand Celine, *Mort a Credit* (Death on the Installment Plan)—a novel by the French writer of fiction, essayist, and playwright; concerns the theme of human mortality and the notion that adulthood represents the gradual death of faith and ethics; employs expressionism, grim humor, and fluctuating time frames to depict a rebellious youth's struggle to reject petty middle-class values and family pressures.

John Dos Passos, *The Big Money*—a novel by the American writer of fiction; the final piece of the *U.S.A.* trilogy; set during the 1920s, the work focuses upon America's awakening to its financial power; an aviator returns to the United States after World War I in search of money, the "big time," and love; other characters have similar dreams and desires, and what follows is a mixture of success and destruction.

William Faulkner, *Absalom, Absalom!*—a novel by the American writer of fiction; focuses upon the efforts of a demonic poor white man, Thomas Sutpen, to establish a family dynasty in Mississippi; allusions to biblical and Greek tragedies and issues of racism and sexism, and the decline of the Southern aristoc-

racy feature prominently in this study of the rise and fall of a ruthless, monomaniacal man.

Robert Frost, *A Further Range*—a collection of verse by the American poet; includes "A Lone Striker," "The Gold Hesperidee," and "Two Tramps in Mud Time."

Nazim Hikmet Ram, *Seyh Bedreddin Desatani* (The Epic of Sheik Bedreddin)—a poem by the Turkish writer of verse and playwright; an elegiac historical narrative that relates the events of a medieval uprising led by the title character, an Islamic mystic whose ideals are similar to those of modern communism.

Aldous Huxley, *Eyeless in Gaza*—a novel by the English writer of fiction and essayist; outlines the career of the principal character from early boyhood (and the loss of his mother), through emotional involvements and intellectual guests, to his association with a pacifist movement; covers the period 1902-1935, but also relies on flashbacks; of primary concern is the individual's search for mystical wholeness; the title of the piece is taken from John Milton's *Samson Agonistes* (1671).

John Maynard Keynes, *A General Theory of Employment, Interest, and Money*—a prose tract by the English economist and financial specialist; advocates government intervention in the market; presents a program for governmental activity during periods of recession, to include deficit spending and more lenient monetary policies to stimulate business activity.

C. S. Lewis, *The Allegory of Love*—a prose tract by the Irish-born literary scholar, critic, and novelist; a critical piece that focuses upon the concept of courtly love in European literature.

Archibald MacLeish, *Public Speech: Poems*—a collection by the American poet and playwright; focuses upon such issues as the role of the poet, criticizing those who would urge the writer of verse to concentrate upon social issues; the pieces tend to be highly homiletic in both tone and substance.

Henry Miller, *Black Spring*—an autobiographical narrative by the American-born writer of miscellaneous prose; relates his literary and bohemian life; in typical fashion, he proclaims the man of letters a new being, one for whom sex remains the central focus of all activities.

Margaret Mitchell, *Gone with the Wind*—the only novel by the American writer; an enormously successful work based upon the American Civil War and the ensuing Reconstruction, essentially told from the Southern point of view; the popularity of the motion picture has far exceeded that of the book.

Mohan Singh, *Save Pattar* (Green Leaves)—a collection of verse by the Indian (Sikh) poet; the work has become the most popular book of modern Punjabi poetry.

Henri de Montherlant, *Les Jeunes Filles* (The Girls)—a fictional tetralogy by the French essayist, novelist, and playwright; a comic and ironic study of a brilliant and successful novelist (the writer?) who experiments with women; until 1939.

George Orwell, *Keep the Aphidistra Flying*—a novel by the English writer of fiction and essayist; relates the literary aspirations, financial setbacks, and forced marriage of a bookseller's assistant; the result of the writer's experiences and observations while working in a Hampstead bookstore.

Premchand, *Godan* (The Gift of a Cow)—a novel by the Indian writer of fiction, essayist, and playwright; a realistic depiction of the future of the agricultural community of India; presents a fragmented society without common purposes or goals that must struggle with itself before it can become a nation.

Carl Sandburg, *The People, Yes*—a collection of verse by the American poet, biographer, and miscellaneous prose writer; divided into 107 separate sections and focusing upon such themes as the deaths of those who have departed on behalf of the people; a number of sections are wise utterances of the people on such topics as property, war, justice, and law; there exists (not surprisingly) a section devoted to Abraham Lincoln.

John Steinbeck, *In Dubious Battle*—a novel by the American writer of fiction; concerns a strike by California fruit pickers.

Allen Tate, "Ode to the Confederate Dead"— a poem by the American writer of verse and critic; the poet contrasts the active faith of Southerners of the past with the failure of the contemporary personality to function effectively within nature and society; the piece was highly regarded for the dignity with which the poet approached his subject.

Thein Pe Myint, *Tek Bhountyi* (Modern Monk)—a novel by the Burmese writer of fiction; the piece attacks abuses in the monastic system and urges reform; a popular work that secured the writer's literary reputation.

EVENTS

Robert Peter Tristram Coffin, American writer of verse, receives the Pulitzer Prize in poetry for his *Strange Holiness* (1935).

Harold Lenoir Davis, American writer of fiction, receives the Pulitzer Prize in fiction for his novel *Honey in the Horn* (1935).

Allen Lane, English publisher, founds the Penguin Books series, thus establishing the paperback revolution in British publishing.

Life magazine, a weekly news magazine, begins publication in New York City; until 1972, then reissues in 1978.

New Directions, a thematic periodical dedicated to the promotion of new American writing, begins publication; contributors include Jack Kerouac, Denise Levertov, E. E. Cummings, Henry Miller, James Purdy, Kenneth Rexroth, Gilbert Sorrentino, and Wallace Stevens.

Eugene O'Neill, American playwright, receives the Nobel Prize for literature.

Ralph Barton Perry, American philosopher and historian, receives the Pulitzer Prize in biography and autobiography for *The Thought and Character of William James* (1935), two volumes.

Robert Emmet Sherwood, American playwright, receives the Pulitzer Prize in drama for *Idiot's Delight* (1936).

William Butler Yeats, Irish poet, playwright, and critic, edits *The Oxford Book of Modern Verse;* described as a highly eccentric and personal collection.

1937

BIRTHS

Layla Baalbakki. Lebanese writer of fiction; a Shiite Muslim who will write in Arabic; her fiction will be strongly autobiographical, particularly revealing her revolt against traditionalism; she will portray Lebanese society caught in the throes of change, with emphasis upon the country's youth.

Yitzhak Ben-Ner. Israeli (Hebrew) writer of fiction; his work will be confessional in tone and will employ the first person narrative technique; his prose will be stark and emotional and his themes will be bleak, often associated with death; he will contrast contemporary Israel, with its social and economic problems, with a place such as New Zealand, a land of his dreams.

Maryse Conde. Guadeloupean writer of fiction, playwright, and critic; she will write in French; her work will be political in content and will contain rich historical detail; she will depict individuals in a state of transition, placing them in situations where they must choose between the existing social order of West Africa and the changing cultural order brought about by Western influence.

Cameron Duodu. Ghanaian novelist, poet, and journalist; he will be deeply troubled by the apparent need of modern Africans to establish a culture of their own, neglecting African traditions; he will also focus upon the mental and spiritual frustrations of living in an African state.

Yoshikichi Furui. Japanese writer of fiction; he will receive, in 1970, the Akutagawa Literary Prize; he will explore the inner worlds of ordinary people who lead mundane lives amidst the demands and advancements of modern society; thus, he will become a representative of "naiko no sedai" (the introverted generation); as such, he will comment upon the political and economic changes in Japan during the 1950s and 1960s.

Giris Karnad. Indian (Kannada) playwright; his work will be characterized by linguistic sophistication, spectacle, epic breadth, and an acute sense of theatre; he will experiment by combining contemporary European themes with those of the Kannada folk theater.

Vitauts Ludens. Latvian poet; his lyrics will be strongly nationalistic; he will see himself as the heir to a precious cultural and historical legacy, and thus he will be preoccupied with Latvian and Baltic history.

Patrick McGinley. Irish novelist; he will write darkly comic novels about the Irish in and around the county of Donegal; his intimate knowledge of rural life will be displayed in his explorations of the trivial aspects of life in the insular communities of western Ireland; his dialogue will be extremely accurate, particularly as he records the conversations at the local pubs.

Nelida Pinon. Brazilian writer of fiction; she will publish seven novels and three collections of short stories; she will gain a reputation as a story teller with strong dramatic abilities.

Thomas Pynchon. American writer of fiction; he will gain recognition for his sense of humor and imagination; he will create, in his novels, a wild, dark, and labyrinthine world; he will describe the values of his generation and its belief that the reduction of one's involvement in the affairs of life will, in turn, reduce one's anger and pain.

Henrik Stangerup. Danish writer of fiction; he will rely upon biographical details in novels that offer a combined sense of the realistic and the surrealistic; he will express his contempt for the narrow-mindedness of his nation and will dream of "the evil and magic poetry and prose of a new time," a time dominated by the culture and literature of Latin America.

Tom Stoppard. Czech-born English playwright; he will create brilliant, provocative, off-beat, and verbally fascinating dramatic pieces; nonetheless, his work will maintain a certain continuity with those who, before him, mastered "civilized" English humor: William Congreve, Charles Dickens, George Bernard Shaw, and Lewis Carroll.

Hannelies Taschau. German writer of fiction and poet; through the observations of her traumatized narrators, she will criticize the pettiness of contemporary German Society; her Germany of the 1970s and 1980s will still suffer from the legacy of the Hitler years, particularly from the brutal extinction of individuality.

DEATHS

Sir James Matthew Barrie (b. 1860). Scottish playwright and writer of fiction; he achieved lasting fame with his fantasy *Peter Pan*; the pathos and humor of of his fictional depictions of his native town caused him to be associated with the Kailyard School of Scottish writers, which was noted for is sentimentality.

John Drinkwater (b. 1882). English poet, playwright, and critic; he gained recognition from several historical plays that focused upon such figures as Abraham Lincoln, Mary Stuart, Oliver Cromwell, and Robert E. Lee; he produced critical studies of William Morris, Algernon Charles Swinburne, Lord Byron, and lyric poetry; as an actor, he became one of the founders of the Pilgrim Players and served as manager of the Birmingham Repertory Theatre.

Hakob Hakobian (b. 1866). Armenian poet; prior to the Russian Revolution of 1917, his work focused upon the hard lives of workers and the future possibilities for the working class; after 1917 his lyrics and epics pointed to the building of the socialist state, the industrialization of Armenia, and the new moral outlook; he became one of the founders of Armenian proletarian poetry.

Paolo Iashvili (b. 1894). Georgian (SSR) poet; most of his verse welcomed Soviet rule, and he secured a position in the government, where he came under attack for his nationalism and for activities opposing the interests of the people; as a result, he committed suicide.

Mikheil Javakhisvili (b. 1880). Georgian (SSR) writer of fiction; he satirized various aspects of the Georgian national character; he considered life in the city as the life of the future and viewed idyllic dreams of village existence as poetic but vain attempts at escape; he is arrested and executed for activities "against the interests of the people."

Atilla Jozsef (b. 1905). Hungarian poet and essayist; his work was influenced by Karl Marx and Sigmund Freud, particularly as he explored the implications of society's ills and the human psyche; he became known as the poet of the proletariat, vividly depicting the misery of the working class, he commits suicide after a brief period in a mental institution.

Boris Pilnyak (pseudonym of Boris Andreyevich Vogau; b. 1894). Russian writer of fiction; his work seeks to explain and interpret the 1917 Revolution; he developed a non-linear narrative form described as "a blizzard of words," symbolic of the chaos of the contemporary social and political environment; he dics suddenly after his arrest on charges of spying for the Japanese; thus, he may well have been executed.

Horacio Sylvestre Quiroga (b. 1878). Uruguayan writer of short fiction, essayist, poet, and playwright; he achieved recognition for short stories portraying the conflicts between the individual and the natural hazards of South American jungles; he came under the influence of Edgar Allan Poe, and thus was fascinated by madness, terror, and death; he commits suicide after discovering he has cancer.

Suleyman of Stal (b. 1869). Dagestan (SSR) poet; he became the national epic poet of Dagestan, writing verse abounding with colorful Oriental imagery; his subjects reflect the problems and requirements of modern Soviet existence.

Titsian Tabidze (b. 1895). Georgian (SSR) poet; he founded the symbolist group ("Blue Horns") of Georgian poets; he wrote vehement and provocative verse in a polished and cultivated style; his later poetry evidenced a deep admiration and respect for the Soviet system; accused of nationalism and of activities against the interests of the people, he dies by execution.

Yeghishe Tcharents (b. 1897). Armenian poet; he initially published highly symbolic lyric verse and pieces reflecting his experiences in World War I; after 1917 and the Revolution, he turned to propaganda poetry, creating the "radio poem" through which to express the political heroics of his times; his death by execution comes after he attempts to "interpret" Armenian history.

Edith Newbold Jones Wharton (b. 1862). American writer of fiction, poet, and critic; in 1913, she settled in France; she gained a reputation for subtle, ironic and finely crafted novels concerning New York City society at the beginning of the twentieth century; her most successful piece, the novella *Ethan Frome* (1911), shifts the scene to New England and the tone to tragedy.

PUBLICATIONS

Amma Achchygyya, *Kepseenner* (Tales)—a collection of short stories by the Yakutsk (SSR) writer of fiction, poet, and playwright; the pieces describe the changes in Yakut life after the 1917 Revolution; they also consider the growing political consciousness of the working people; to 1940.

Sadeq Hedayat, *Buf-e Kur* (The Blind Owl)—a novel by the Iranian writer of fiction, playwright, and essayist; introduces a pathologic narrator, frantically discontent with life in general, but with his existence as an Iranian in particular; privately printed in India; the work does not appear in Iran until 1941, and then in serial form.

Ernest Hemingway, *To Have and to Have Not*—a novel by the American writer of fiction; contains a wide variety of charities: poor, rich, reactionaries, revolutions, revolutionaries; the piece opens in Cuba, but the principal action occurs in and around Key West, Florida; the central character, a tough local, becomes a victim of the Depression and the wealthy, and thus engages in illegal activities; the work seems to have brought out the cynical side of the writer.

Christopher Isherwood, *Sally Bowles*—a novel by the English writer of fiction and miscellany; the title character, a cabaret artist, is beautiful and witty, but lacks talent; thus, she pursues a Bohemian style of life to survive; provides a vivid portrait of Nazi Germany at the outset of Adolf Hitler's rise to power; dramatized in 1951 by John Van Druten under the title *I Am a Camera;* it later becomes the musical *Cabaret* (1968).

David Jones, *In Parenthesis*—the first verse collection by the English poet and essayist; the pieces originate from the writer's experiences as an infantry soldier during World War I; also based upon Sir Thomas Malory's Arthurian legends, the Welsh *Mabinogion,* and the medieval battle epic, *Y Gododdin;* in general, the collection exposes the physical destruction and spiritual outrage of battle; the poet sees war as simply another aspect of the serious decline of Western civilization.

Andre Malraux, *L'Espoir* (Days of Hope)—a novel by the French writer of fiction and essayist; describes the chaos of the Spanish Civil War, its aims, and the overall irony of intellectuals killing one another with bullets; contains an excellent account of the siege of Madrid; considers the conflict the tragic prelude to World War II.

J. P. Marquand, *The Late George Apley*—a novel by the American writer of fiction and humor; a gentle satire upon New England life in the form of a memoir; the piece receives the Pulitzer Prize for fiction in 1938.

Vladimir Nabokov, *Dar* (The Gift)—a novel by the Russian-born writer of fiction, essayist, and dramatist; his last novel written in Russian and contains five distinct stories that do not, on the surface, bear a relationship to one another. While following the protagonist's growing awareness of moral and artistic unity the piece addresses such topics as Russian literature, love, and politics.

George Orwell, *The Road to Wigan Pier*—a narrative by the English writer of fiction and essayist; the result of his travels, in 1936, to the north, where he observed with sympathy and anger life in the industrial sections of England, particularly the sufferings of English coal miners; enraged the Socialist Left Book Club, who had commissioned the work, by examining at length the failure of socialists to address the needs of England's poor.

Luis Pales Matos, *Tuntun de Pasa y Griferia*—a verse collection by the Puerto Rican poet and novelist; the work demonstrates the writer's interest in African themes popular in

Cuba and Haiti during the late 1920s and early 1930s.

Katherine Anne Porter, *Noon Wine*—a long story by the American writer of fiction; a realistic piece in which a man, married to an invalid, unhappily and inefficiently maintains a dairy farm in Texas; a hired hand restores order to the place, but a bounty hunter arrives and claims that the hand had escaped from a lunatic asylum; the owner of the farm shoots the hand, but a jury acquits him of any crime; nonetheless, he cannot live with the guilt and kills himself.

Kenneth Roberts, *Northwest Passage*— a novel by the American writer of historical and regional fiction; an extremely popular work, it describes the expeditions (1758-1763) of an American colonial soldier, Robert Rogers (1731-1795), and his British rangers against French outposts.

Leo Rosten, *The Education of Hyman Kaplan*—a series of sketches by the American humorist and writer of miscellaneous prose; the title character, a Jewish immigrant, is a patriotic American who struggles with the English language in a night school for adults; an entertaining piece that succeeds because of its amiable and amusing hero.

John Steinbeck, *Of Mice and Men*—a novel by the American writer of fiction; the story of two casual laborers, the intelligent but physically weak George and his strong but simpleminded friend, Lennie; constantly on the road, the two acquire work where they can find it, always longing for a permanent home; in the end, Lennie accidentally murders George's wife; the writer dramatizes the work in this same year.

Wallace Stevens, "The Man with the Blue Guitar"—a poem by the American writer of verse; concerns the opposition between bare reality and the ability of the imagination to transform it; taking his cue from Pablo Picasso, Stevens contends that art, even when seeming to distort reality, may actually heighten one's awareness of it.

K. Surangkhanang, *Ying Khon Chua* (The Prostitute)— a novel by the Thai writer of fiction; an observant work portraying the deplorable life of the prostitute; a successful novel that soon became a motion picture.

Tugelbay Sydykbekov, *Ken-Suu* (Up the Mountains)—a novel by the Kirghiz writer of fiction and poet; describes the collectivization of Kirghiz agriculture under the Soviet system; drawn from the writer's own experiences as a farmer, the work has received recognition as the first realistic prose work in Kirghizia.

J. R. R. Tolkien, *The Hobbit; or, There and Back Again*—a novel by the South African-born English writer of fiction, essayist, and literary scholar; beneath this highly entertaining adventure story of Middle-earth lies a quiet anguish for a vanishing past and a precarious future; the hobbits are small, furry-footed creatures possessing human qualities.

Virginia Woolf, *The Years*—a novel by the English writer of fiction and essayist; the piece begins in 1880 and develops the history of a London family; the children wait for the death of their mother and their freedom; in 1936, at the end of the story, they reunite, an event that brings together two generations.

EVENTS

Van Wyck Brooks, American literary biographer, critic, and historian, receives the Pulitzer Prize in United States history for his *The Flowering of New England* (1936).

Robert Lee Frost, American poet, receives the Pulitzer Prize in poetry for *A Further Range* (1936).

Moss Hart and George Simon Kaufman, American playwrights, receive the Pulitzer Prize in drama for *You Can't Take It with You* (1936).

Two major London newspapers, the *Daily Telegraph* and the *Morning Post,* merge.

Roger Martin du Gard, French novelist and playwright, receives the Nobel Prize for literature.

Margaret Mitchell, American writer of fiction and journalist, receives the Pulitzer Prize in fiction for her novel *Gone with the Wind* (1936).

1938

BIRTHS

Ayi Kwei Armah. Ghanaian writer of fiction and poet; he will, in his fiction, attack the corrupt politicians in Ghana, offering little hope that political conditions in his native land will improve; he will blame those leaders for forgetting their origins and for betraying the trust of the masses who had hoped they would guide them toward a new Africa; he will establish residence in Paris.

Daniel Katz. Finnish writer of fiction and humorist; he will be regarded as one of the leading humorists writing in Finnish; although his work will be set in various locales, it will always reflect his Jewish heritage.

Taban Lo Liyong. Ugandan writer of fiction and poet; he will become interested in Lwo vernacular literature, recasting tales from that language; in his verse, he will adapt the old stories into a Lwo-English stanza of swinging free verse: "But for fractionalization it-they manand- / woman again and again / The factors can manwoman in test tubes / tool."

Lya Luft. Brazilian writer of fiction; she will write five major novels concerning brooding females who find themselves physically and spiritually isolated; she will also fashion existential themes from her characters' desperation and hopelessness, focusing upon family emotional complications (from alcoholism to handicapped children).

Dom. Moraes. Indian poet; he will write in English; his verse will be described as being "permeated with a self-destroying exile's nostalgia"; he will also write travel narratives and an autobiography.

Leslie Allan Murray. Australian poet and critic; his verse will be nationalistic, objecting to the pervasive influence of British culture upon Australian society; he will celebrate his nation's wildlife, vegetation, and aboriginal folklore.

James Thiong'o Ngugi. Kenyan writer of fiction and playwright; he will be recognized as the most important writer of East Africa; his work will range in subject matter from the Mau Mau rebellions to the divisions within Kikuyu society brought about by political pressures; in a lyrical and graceful style, he will create characters who bring to life the world of the Kikuyu.

Joyce Carol Oates. American writer of fiction and critic; she will, generally, confront decadence and evil in her work, exploring the psychology of the human character; she will pursue an academic career, obtaining an appointment at Princeton University.

Aleksandar Petrov. Yugoslav poet and critic; his verse will reflect his experiences abroad, particularly in the United States; he will develop into a conscientious poetic craftsman, deliberately building his poems word by word and line by line; thus, he will become one of the leading structuralists in modern Serbian poetry.

Ishmael Scott Reed. American writer of fiction and poet; he will become one of the most humorous and outrageous writers of the American counterculture that flourished during the 1960s and 1970s; primarily known for his novels, although his verse will reveal extreme sharpness of thought and language, combining the real and the surreal, the past and the present.

Charles Simic. Yugoslav-born American poet, translator, and essayist; he will write some of the most inventive verse in contemporary poetry, employing abstract terms to describe common objects; he will, for instance, dissect eating utensils with such intensity that they will rise to existential significance; he will also portray a frightening, mysterious, hostile, and dangerous world, one that will contain various levels of meaning; for that reason, his work will invite comparison with that of Theodore Roethke.

DEATHS

Lascelles Abercrombie (b. 1881). English poet, playwright, and essayist; a leading member of the Georgian school of English poetry who emphasized the philosophical aspects of that genre; he concerned himself with abstract ideas and developed a concise, complex style; his verse reflected his concept that life strives toward a perfect consciousness, achieving ecstasy or exultation manifested by the presence of God.

Karel Capek (b. 1890). Czech playwright, novelist, and essayist; in his early work, he collaborated with his brother Josef (1887-1945); known for his anti-Utopian works warning of the dehumanizing effects of modern technology and satirizing various social, political, and economic systems; these works brought the genre of science-fiction drama into its own; also known for his novels exploring the plurality and relativity of truth.

Gabriele D'Annunzio (b. 1863). Italian poet, novelist, and playwright; his early verse displayed sensuous imagery and unrivaled poetic craftsmanship; his novels, though theatrical, revealed his control of language; though the press reported the romantic scandals of his life and criticized the moral outrages of his works, he was renowned, as one of Italy's leading artists, a consummate stylist who combined the poetic grandeur of Dante and the classical writers with contemporary trends of naturalism, symbolism, and decadence.

Sirek Walda Sellase Heruy (b. 1878). Ethiopian (Amharic) writer of fiction and biographer; he argued for social reforms in his fiction, particularly with regard to marriage and religion; he contributed to the development of literature in Ethiopia with a catalogue of books in Ge'ez and Amharic languages, an anthology of funeral chants, and a collection of extracts from the Bible; he dies in Bath, England, after having followed the Emperor Haile Selassie into exile.

Edmund Husserl (b. 1859). Austrian philosopher and founder of the science of phenomenology; he offered a descriptive study of consciousness for the purpose of discovering the laws by which one gains experience; he questioned whether consciousness exists apart from the objects it considers and whether objects exist outside of consciousness.

Muhammad Iqbal (b. 1873?). Indian poet, essayist, and philosopher; his innovative poetic works, written in Persian, called for the revitalization of Islam through the development of the individual personality; he proposed a sovereign Muslim state in northwest India; Pakistan came into existence ten years after his death.

Aleksandr Ivanovich Kuprin (b. 1870). Russian writer of fiction; his most popular works tended to attack Russian military life and exposed social disgrace (for instance, prostitution); as a purestory teller, he displays the influence of Jack London and Rudyard Kipling; he leaves Russia after the Revolution of 1917, but returns there to die.

Leopoldo Lugones (b. 1874). Argentine poet, writer of short fiction, and historian; he wrote nationalistic verse that was serene in tone and combined the influences of French Symbolism and Japanese simplicity; his later works evidence his interest in fascism; he dies by his own hand.

Osip Emilyevich Mandelstam (b. 1891). Russian poet; he became a leader among the Acmeists: those who reacted against the symbolists and emphasized concreteness of imagery and clarity of expression; he wrote fatalistic and meticulously constructed lyrics; he dies as a political prisoner.

Cesar Vallejo (b. 1892). Peruvian poet of Indian and European ancestry; his verse reflects his dedication to social justice; the intensity of his language represents his agony as Franco, with help from the Nazis and the Italians, ravaged Spain in 1936-1937; after 1923, he lived in Paris, where he embraced Marxism and became the poet of the impoverished and the oppressed.

Thomas Clayton Wolfe (b. 1900). American writer of fiction; his four major autobiographical novels follow a young man from his boyhood in the rural South to a career as a teacher and writer in New York City; his work gained recognition for its lyrical and dramatic intensity; through the writer's seemingly obsessive sense of memory, time, and place, his fiction represents a broad picture of American life; he dies from tuberculosis.

PUBLICATIONS

Abbas Mahmud al-Aqqad, *Sara*—the only novel by the Egyptian poet, critic, literary historian, and writer of fiction; a subtle psychological study of a love affair between two young persons; jealousy and doubt contribute to their eventual separation.

Samuel Beckett, *Murphy*—a novel by the Irish writer of fiction and playwright; a highly entertaining piece, but also one that grimly records London life from an Irish point of view; kept by a prostitute, the title character becomes an assistant male nurse in a lunatic asylum; he achieves happiness, but perishes in a fire accidentally caused by his own hand; another accident causes his ashes to be scattered on the floor of a Dublin pub.

Georges Bernanos, *Les Grands Cimetieres Sous la Lune* (The Diary of My Times)—a narrative by the French writer of fiction; reflects his own experiences in Mallorca in 1936, where he witnessed the fascist atrocities being encouraged by his own church; a significant work of protest.

Cleanth Brooks and Robert Penn Warren, *Understanding Poetry*—a volume of literary criticism by the American writers; presents poetry in terms of the New Criticism, revolutionizing the teaching of poetry in American colleges and universities.

Daphne Du Maurier, *Rebecca*—a novel by the English writer of fiction; a popular piece set in the West of England during the 1930s; the title "character," now dead, had tortured her husband with flagrant infidelities until she drove him to murder her; the husband lives with that guilt; he marries another woman,

and, following a time of suffering for both, he reveals his painful memories to her.

William Faulkner, *The Unvanquished*—a novel by the American writer of fiction; links episodes from previously published short stories; focuses upon the fortunes of the Sartoris family during the Civil War period; the stories involved include "Ambuscade" (1934), "Retreat" (1934), "Raid" (1934), "Skirmish at Sartoris" (1935), "The Unvanquished" (1936), and "An Odor of Verbena" (previously unpublished).

Julien Gracq, *Au Chateau d'Argol* (The Castle of Argol)—the first novel by the French writer of fiction, playwright, poet, and critic; relates the macabre story of three characters engaged in a metaphysical adventure in Brittany, two of whom perish in violent deaths; the writer focuses upon such ideas as the attainment of spiritual regeneration through death, the recovery of lost innocence, and the dialectic methods originating from the work of Georg Wilhelm Friedrich Hegel.

Graham Greene, *Brighton Rock*—a novel by the English writer of fiction; described as "a thriller-as-methaphor"; the writer focuses upon the criminal underworld dominated by gang warfare and protection rackets; a female character, "Rose," introduces the Roman Catholic element that typifies the writer's fiction.

Ernest Hemingway, *The Fifth Column and the First Forty-Nine Stories*— a collection by the American writer of fiction; *The Fifth Column* is a play about a newspaperman in Spain during the civil war there; the stories include such titles as "The Short Happy Life of Francis Macomber," "The Snows of Kilimanjaro," "Soldier's Home," "Big Two-Hearted River" (Parts I-II), "The Undefeated," "In Another Country," "The Killers," "Fifty Grand," "A Clean, Well-Lighted Place," "Now I Lay Me," "The Gambler, the Nun, and the Radio," and "Fathers and Sons."

Richard Hughes, *In Hazard*—a novel by the English poet, radio dramatist, and writer of fiction; concerns a steamship caught in an unexpected hurricane; a highly sophisticated narrative brings to light the true characters of the ship's officers and crew.

Louis MacNeice, *Autumn Journal*—a long verse essay by the Irish-born poet; a personal and political meditation upon the events leading to the Munich crisis of this year.

George Orwell, *Homage to Catalonia*—a narrative by the English writer of fiction and essayist; describes the writer's experiences in Spain during the civil war; he became disillusioned with the Communist Party when he discovered its real intentions: to prevent the revolution from ever succeeding.

Ayn Rand, *Anthem*—a novel by the Russian-born American writer of fiction; presents the story of a man who rediscovers, in his words, the pronoun "I"; the event occurs in the dark ages of the future, in a totally collectivized world; published in England; American edition in 1946.

Raja Rao, *Kanthapura*—the first by the Indian writer of fiction; written in English; an account of a small village in Bombay caught up in the nationalist movement of the early 1930s.

Marjorie Kinnan Rawlings, *The Yearling*—a novel by the American writer of fiction; a sympathetic story of a boy and his attachment to a yearling deer; the boy's father must kill the animal because it destroys his already depleted crops; extremely popular as a novel for juveniles, as well as a highly successful motion picture.

Jean-Paul Sartre, *La Nausee* (Nausea)—the first novel by the French playwright, writer of fiction, essayist, and biographer; considered a classic of existentialist literature and the precursor of the "nouveau roman" (the new novel); in the form of a journal maintained by a historian at work on a biography; he comes to realize the gratuitousness and senselessness of the physical objects around him, and that realization brings on the nausea; the writer concludes that the aesthetic constitutes the only authentic mode of being; the piece published in England as *The Diary of Antoine Roquentin*.

Robert Emmet Sherwood, *Abe Lincoln in Illinois*—a play by the American dramatist and biographer; a highly popular piece that studies the responsibilities of power in the face of impending war; awarded the Pulitzer Prize in drama in 1939.

Richard Wright, *Uncle Tom's Children*—a collection of four long short stories by the American writer of fiction and autobiographical narrative; the pieces focus upon the idea of blacks having absolutely no opportunity in a world dominated by whites; the black characters resolve to become as "hard" as their oppressors and to adopt a firm line of resistance; the collection enlarged in 1940.

Thornton Wilder, *Our Town*—a play by the American dramatist, novelist, and essayist; a celebration of human existence, set in a New Hampshire community at the beginning of the twentieth century; intended to remind audiences that in their hurried journeys through life, they may well miss the various wonders of daily and even mundane events; awarded the Pulitzer Prize (the playwright's second) in drama for this year.

EVENTS

Pearl S. Buck, American writer of fiction and biographer, receives the Nobel Prize for literature.

Dictionary of American English published at the University of Chicago; begun in 1925, the four volumes will appear between this year and 1944; the emphasis focuses upon words and phrases that have originated from the United States and that have become distinctly American in usage.

John Phillips Marquand, American satirist, humorist, and writer of fiction, receives the Pulitzer Prize in fiction for *The Late George Apley* (1937).

The Rocky Mountain Review, a quarterly journal of creative writing, begins publication at Salt Lake City, Utah; it will change its editorial offices first to Lawrence, Kansas, and then to Iowa City, Iowa; contributors will include Walter Van Tilburg Clark, Kenneth Burke, R. V. Cassil, Wallace Stegner, and William Carlos Williams; until 1959.

Twice a Year, a semi-annual journal of literature and the arts, begins publication at New York City; Marcel Proust, Franz Kafka, and Federico Garcia Lorca appear in translation; also features such American writers as Kenneth Patchen, Henry Miller, and William Saroyan; until 1948.

Thornton Niven Wilder, American writer of fiction and playwright, receives the Pulitzer Prize in drama for *Our Town* (1938).

Marya Zaturenska, Russian-born American poet, receives the Pulitzer Prize in poetry for her collection of verse *Cold Morning Sky* (1937).

1939

BIRTHS

Toni Cade Bambara. American writer of fiction; her work as an editor, teacher, critic, and social activist will be integral to her art; her wit will blend well with her use of poetic black English; she will write about women and also confront the complex issue of frustrated black men.

Margaret Drabble. English writer of fiction; she will be identified as "an old fashioned novelist" and compared with such novelists as Henry James and George Eliot; her work will reveal a subtle insight into the dilemmas of modern women; she will also publish scholarly studies of classic English writers and edit the most recent edition of *The Oxford Companion to English Literature* (1985).

Alfredo Bryce Echenique. Peruvian writer of fiction; he will become known for his exuberant, original style; his entertaining, fresh, and humorously self-indulgent work will be translated into fifteen languages.

Gus Edwards. West Indian-born American playwright; his naturalistic plays will vividly depict New York City slums; his characters will generally ignore conventional moral standards, but their creator will endow them with redeeming qualities; his authentic dialogue will complement his realistic settings.

Seamus Heaney. Northern Irish poet and critic; his carefully crafted verse will be informed by his own experiences; he will, however, seek a balance between the personal and the topical; his poems will be extremely provocative, yet readers will find them direct and understandable.

Amos Oz. Israeli novelist; he will write his works in Hebrew, assisting with their translation into English; these novels will be rich in atmosphere, often incorporating elements of fantasy; he will usually focus upon life in contemporary Israel.

Peter K. Palangyo. Tanzanian novelist; he will attend, in the late 1960s, the Writers' Workshop at the University of Iowa; he will set his fiction in post-independent Tanzania and attempt to capture the tensions of life in contemporary Africa; he will also focus on such universal experiences as love, death, pain, and ecstasy.

Dennis C. Scott. Jamaican playwright and poet; he will develop a remarkable facility with verse, particularly an ability to apply a wide range of English usage to various Jamaican topics; he will ally himself with Robert Browning and Ezra Pound by emphasizing the dramatic moment in tone, diction, and structure.

Frederick James Wah. Canadian poet; he will publish, between 1960 and 1985, ten volumes of verse; he will construct poetry from the fabric of his own imagination and rely upon his creative energy to achieve unity; through poetic meditation, he will search for his own racial and cultural heritage.

Gozo Yoshimashu. Japanese poet; he will publish long poems that appear to challenge traditional Japanese forms; he will also write lyrics intended for public reading, to be accompanied by musical instruments; his work will rely upon the visual characteristics of the Japanese language, and he will experiment with syntax and mechanics; thus, he will become the first Japanese poet to employ punctuation at the beginnings of sentences, rather than at the ends.

DEATHS

Henry Havelock Ellis (b. 1859). English prose writer; a psychologist and qualified physician, he devoted his efforts to scientific study and to writing; his seven-volume *Psychology of Sex* (1897-1928) proved a valuable contribution to the study of sex problems, helping to alter public attitudes toward that subject.

Ford Madox Ford (pseudonym of Ford Madox Heuffer; b. 1873). English novelist, poet, critic, and writer of travel narratives; he edited two major artistic and literary journals and wrote important novels that reflected his own unsettled emotional state and eccentricities; contributed significantly to the development of twentieth-century English letters; he dies at Deauville.

Sigmund Freud (b. 1856). Austrian psychiatrist; he gained recognition as the founder of psychoanalysis; he devised the technique of free association, which allowed material repressed in the unconscious to emerge to conscious recognition; he also emphasized infantile sexuality and the Oedipus complex; in 1938, he flees to England to escape Nazi domination, and there he dies.

Zane Grey (b. 1872). American writer of fiction; he achieved enormous popularity with his melodramatic tales of the American West; he chose to romanticize that part of American history, particularly the life and activities of the cowboy.

Alfred Edward Housman (b. 1859). English poet and classical scholar; although he failed as a student at Oxford, he became a leading classicist, editing works of Manilius, Juvenal, and Lucan; also known for his verses focusing on mortality and the inevitable passing of youth.

Sidney Coe Howard (b. 1891). American playwright; his dramas are noted for their accurate representation of the speech of ordinary people; he excelled at portraying the psychology of his characters; he dies from a tractor accident on his California farm.

U Leti Pantita Maun Tyi (b. 1879). Burmese writer of fiction, poet, translator, and dramatist; he wrote the first Burmese historical novels; he also produced commentaries and treatises on Buddhism; he supposedly authored in excess of 500 works and thus had a significant influence on Burmese literature.

Bylatyan Oloksuoyebis Oyuunuskay (pseudonym of Platon Alekseyevich Sleptsov; b. 1893). Yakutsk (SSR) poet; he wrote revolutionary songs and political lyrics; he also produced Yakut folk songs and heroic verse in the tradition of his ancestors; he translated the "Internationale" into Yakut; arrested on political charges, he dies of tuberculosis.

Abdullo Qodiriy (b. 1894). Uzbek (SSR) satirist and writer of fiction; he introduced the novel to modern Uzbek literature; he ignored the traditional legendary narratives in his historical fiction; he described Soviet life and the changes in Uzbek village existence during the collectivization of the countryside; he gained a reputation for his colorful descriptions of the lives of his characters; with others, he produced an Uzbek-Russian dictionary and translated works by classical nineteenth-century Russian writers into Uzbek.

Tan-Da (pseudonym of Nguyen-khac-Hieu; b. 1888). Vietnamese poet, novelist, and playwright; in his verse, he defended the rules of classical Vietnamese poetry against the criticism of the "new school"; explored

themes of patriotism, sorrow, anxiety, dreams, and escape.

Ernst Toller (b. 1893). German playwright; he spent five years in prison for his activities as chairman of the Bavarian Soviet Republican Party; his political passion found an outlet in his drama; considered one of the most significant writers of the German Expressionist movement; he kills himself in New York City, following six years of exile.

Vu-trong-Phung (b. 1912). Vietnamese writer of fiction and playwright; he produced over fifteen volumes of fiction, plays, and translations; his novels contain elements of satire, yet they emphasize the tragic rather than the comic aspects of life; he came under the influence of Freudian ideas; an opium addict, he dies from tuberculosis at age twenty-seven.

William Butler Yeats (b. 1865). Irish poet, playwright, and essayist; considered one of the greatest poets in the English language; his visionary work reveals his fascination with the mysteries of Irish legend and the occult; he became a leader of the Irish Literary Renaissance, revealing an intense nationalism and fervent patriotism; his career evidences remarkable creative development and illustrates his lifelong determination to remake himself into his ideal image of the poet: a sacerdotal figure who assumes the role of mediator between the conflicting forces of the objective and subjective worlds; he received the Nobel Prize for literature in 1923.

PUBLICATIONS

Maxwell Anderson, *Key Largo*—a drama by the American playwright; develops the tragedy of a young American who had deserted his post during the civil war in Spain; yet, he regains his sense of purpose in a struggle against a group of Florida mobsters; the piece was reworked into a successful motion picture.

Sholem Asch, *The Nazarene*—a novel by the Polish-born writer of fiction, essayist, and playwright; focuses upon the life of Jesus Christ; the work aroused Jewish public opinion against him: his critics accused him of failing to convey a true picture of the life and times of Jesus.

Philip Barry, *The Philadelphia Story*—an urbane and entertaining comedy of manners by the American playwright; Satirizes the moral hypocrisy of the privileged class through the story of Tracy Lord; on the eve of her second marriage, however, Tracy is enlightened when she experiences a moral indiscretion of her own and realizes that it is love and people that matter, not position or class; the phenomenally successful play continues to be enjoyed in theatrical revivals and in two film versions.

Stephen Vincent Benet, "The Devil and Daniel Webster"—a short story by the American poet, playwright, and writer of fiction; combines the writer's attraction to fantasy with a reliance upon the tradition of the folk tale; only pure American virtue can emerge victorious in an encounter with the devil.

Roy Campbell, "Flowering Rifle: A Poem from the Battlefield of Spain"—a long satirical poem by the South African writer of verse and nonfiction and translator; the poet sets forth his pro-Franco convictions, as well as his disgust for conventional left-wing political attitudes; the poem demonstrates the extent to which the poet had alienated himself from the main body of Western intellectuals and artists.

Joyce Cary, *Mister Johnson*—a novel by the Irish writer of fiction, essayist, and poet; depicts the cultural and intellectual conflicts arising from the imposition of colonial life on Africa; the work stands as the most highly regarded of the writer's "African novels."

Krishan Chandar, *Shikast* (Defeat)—an autobiographical novel by the Indian (Urdu) writer of fiction, his first published work; concerns the life of the peasants and the efforts of a progressive young Indian intellectual to change their lot.

Raymond Chandler, *The Big Sleep*—a novel by the American writer of detective fiction; the first of his well-plotted and brutally realistic detective novels; introduces Philip Marlowe, the tough but definitely honorable "private eye."

T. S. Eliot, *The Family Reunion*—a verse drama by the American-born English poet and literary critic; focuses upon contemporary life, yet contains parallels with the *Oresteia* of Aeschylus; the son of an English middle-class family appears haunted by guilt over the death of his wife; during the course of events, he uncovers family secrets, which serves to relieve his depression.

Moss Hart and George S. Kaufman, *The Man Who Came to Dinner*—a dramatic farce by

the American playwrights; the piece was suggested by the career of Alexander Woolcott (1887-1943), American drama and literary critic; sets forth in detail the havoc created by the visit, to a conservative household in Ohio, of the principal character: a selfish, bad tempered, and witty radio personality.

Lillian Hellman, *The Little Foxes*—a drama by the American playwright; greed and sibling rivalry destroy a Southern family around the beginning of the twentieth century.

Christopher Isherwood, *Goodbye to Berlin*—a novel by the English writer of fiction and nonfiction; a series of sketches that describe in detail the atmosphere in Berlin during the years immediately preceding the rule of Adolf Hitler; sets forth the views of a neutral political observer, relaxed and demanding little from his times; considered the writer's best piece of fiction.

James Joyce, *Finnegans Wake*—a work of fiction by the Irish novelist; an anguished response to his own daughter's gradual mental deterioration, particularly after he takes her to see Carl Jung; thus, the piece goes forward upon the vehicle of a dream sequence, representing the stream of the main character's unconscious.

Henry Miller, *Tropic of Capricorn*—a fictional narrative by the American-born prose writer; published in France, then in the United States in 1962; the piece combines metaphysical speculation (both theosophy and astrology), surrealistic passages, grotesque comedy, and (above everything else) sexually explicit scenes.

Ngo-tat-To, *Tat den* (When the Light Is Out)—a novel by the Vietnamese writer of fiction; considered the most significant pre-revolutionary work of the Vietnamese realist school; the writer provides a painfully graphic portrait of the lives of poor villagers.

George Orwell, *Coming Up for Air*—a novel by the English writer of fiction and essayist; concerns the treat of impending war; the principal character, an insurance man, suffers from a deep sense of nostalgia for the Georgian period and tries to combat his suburban frustration.

Katherine Anne Porter, *Pale Horse, Pale Rider*—a collection of three long stories by the American writer of fiction; includes "Noon Wine," "Old Mortality," and the title piece, a love story about a young girl and a soldier, who dies during an epidemic during World War I; all of the stories concern the

South and the effects of sociological changes there upon extremely delicate personalities.

Jean Rhys, *Good Morning, Midnight*—a novel by the West Indian-born English writer of fiction; set in Paris prior to the beginning of World War II, the work explores a middle-aged woman's attempts to discover meaning in her life; deserted by husbands and lovers, she becomes involved with a gigolo, who mistakes her for a wealthy woman; she then withdraws, only to become victimized by a salesman, for whom she develops both compassion and revulsion.

Gwen Ringwood, *Still Stands the House*—a folk drama by the American-born Canadian writer of fiction; set in a farmhouse in southern Alberta during the height of the Depression; concerns a man who must decide between his desire to satisfy the material values of his city-bred wife and his hope to continue farming the unproductive land left to him by his father; other complications arise because the man's sister believes he will sell the land and betray her father.

William Saroyan, *The Time of Your Life*—a play by the American dramatist and novelist; set in a San Francisco waterfront saloon; a group of loosely connected stories in which such characters are lovesick clerks and pinball machine addicts experience opportunities to realize their dreams; the central story focuses upon a prostitute and a young man who falls in love with her, an incident that occurs within the shadow of World War II; receives the Pulitzer Prize in drama in 1940.

Stephen Spender, *Still Centre*—a collection of verse by the English poet and critic; the pieces reflect his experiences in Spain during the civil war, during which time he wrote propaganda for the Republican cause.

John Steinbeck, *The Grapes of Wrath*—a novel by the American writer of fiction; concerns the trek of the Okies westward during the Great Depression, from the parched lands of Oklahoma to the new world of California; as much a sociological treatise as a work of fiction, especially as it focuses upon the sharecropper family's efforts to escape the dustbowl and seek a new life in California (even if that new life requires them to deal with inhumane profiteers).

Robert Penn Warren, *Night Rider*—the first novel by the American poet, writer of fiction, and literary critic; concerns the illicit organization of the title, formed to destroy a tobacco farmers' ring; the principal character

joins the group, a threat to small tobacco growers in Kentucky, and becomes corrupted by it.

Tennessee Williams, *American Blues*—a group of one-act plays by the American writer of drama; the pieces, mark the beginning of the playwright's national recognition.

William Butler Yeats, *Last Poems and Two Plays*—the final volume by the Irish poet, playwright, and essayist; includes such pieces as "Under Ben Bulben," "In Tara's Halls," "A Bronze Head," "John Kinsella's Lament," "Cuchulain's Death," and "Purgatory".

EVENTS

John Gould Fletcher, American miscellaneous prose writer and poet, receives the Pulitzer Prize in poetry for his *Selected Poems* (1938).

Publication of the English translation of *Mein Kampf* (*My Struggle*, 2 vols., 1925-1926), by Adolf Hitler.

Horizon, a literary journal established by Cyril Connolly and Stephen Spender, begins publication at London; includes works by such writers as George Orwell, Evelyn Waugh, Angus Wilson, Geoffrey Grigson, and W. H. Auden; until 1950.

The Kenyon Review, a literary journal, begins publication at Gambier, Ohio; includes poetry, fiction, and criticism; until 1970, and then revived in 1979.

Frank Luther Mott, journalist and academician, receives the Pulitzer Prize in United States history for his *A History of American Magazines*, 3 vols., 1930-1938; the fourth and fifth volumes will be published in 1957 and 1958.

Marjorie Kinnan Rawlings, American journalist and writer of fiction, receives the Pulitzer Prize in fiction for her novel *The Yearling* (1938).

The Franklin Delano Roosevelt Library established at Hyde Park, New York.

Robert Emmet Sherwood, American playwright, receives the Pulitzer Prize in drama for *Abe Lincoln in Illinois* (1938).

Frans Emil Sillanpaa, Finnish writer of fiction, receives the Nobel Prize for literature.

Carl Clinton Van Doren, American biographer and historian, receives the Pulitzer Prize in biography/autobiography for *Benjamin Franklin* (1938).

1940

BIRTHS

Muhammed Said Abdulla. Kenyan (Swahili) writer of fiction; he will compose novels modeled after Arthur Conan Doyle's "Sherlock Holmes" detective fiction, but with original plots; his fiction will be among the few contemporary works available in Swahili, and they will not be translated.

Joseph Wilfred Arbuquah. Ghanaian novelist; he will write the first Ghanaian autobiographical novel; another work will focus upon an African school maintained according to Western educational principles.

Peter Bradford Benchley. American writer of fiction; he will gain popularity with a highly adventurous and somewhat fantastical novel, *Jaws* (1974); that work will, in turn, inspire an even more successful series of motion pictures.

Josef Brodsky. Russian poet; he will assume residence in the United States in 1972; his work will receive attention for its formal technique, depth, irony, and wit; he will tend to emphasize the themes of loss and exile.

Razmik Davoyan. Soviet Armenian poet; he will produce two volumes of lyrics and a long poem; his poems will be considered among the most original in Armenia.

David McFadden. Canadian poet, writer of fiction, and journalist; his verse will record his observations of domestic life and daily events in his hometown of Hamilton, Ontario; he will rely upon a conversational narrative style and will utilize traditional and experimental poetic forms; he will view life with a combination of mature exuberance and childlike wonder.

Maxine Hong Kingston. Chinese-American writer of fiction; she will record her upbringing and the Chinese view of American society; she will also describe the struggle to preserve the old ways and to acclimate to the new culture.

Nguyen Mong-Giac. Vietnamese prose writer; he will settle in California after the fall of South Vietnam; he will strive to capture the mood of Vietnamese youth between the coup against the government of Ngo Ninh Diem

(1963) and the sufferings within the Indonesian refugee camps (1982).

Cheik A. Ndao. Senegalese poet and playwright; he will write in French, English, and Wolof; his work will blend ancient Senegalese history with contemporary occurrences, freely recreating events to suit his dramatic, poetic, and polemic purposes; he will also consider the problem of preserving and enhancing African values and black identities in the white dominated American South.

Olawale Rotimi. Western Nigerian (Yorubaland) playwright and scholar; he will employ, in his drama, Yoruba motifs and the oral tradition of his culture; he will also seek to correct the distorted images of tribal chieftains during the nineteenth-century British invasions; in addition, he will compose essays on traditional Nigerian playwrights.

DEATHS

Mikhail Afanasevich Bulgakov (b. 1891). Russian writer of fiction, playwright, biographer, essayist, and translator; he became one of the foremost satirists of post-revolutionary Russia; his work focused upon the adjustment of Russian intellectuals to communist domination; he came under the influence of Nikolai Gogol, and thus combined fantasy with realism and satire and ridiculed modern progressive society, including the Soviet system; he dies from nephrosclerosis.

F. Scott Fitzgerald (b. 1896). American writer of fiction; one of the most significant American writers of the twentieth century; considered the literary representative of the Jazz Age of the 1920s, he depicted an entire generation's elusive search for the American dream of wealth and happiness; he created characters whose unsettled lives reflected his own glittering and dissipated existence, both in New York City and Paris.

Hannibal Hamlin Garland (b. 1860). American writer of fiction and autobiographical narrative; his tales about the difficulties of life on the prairie were inspired by his own Midwestern upbringing; he received a Pulitzer Prize in biography-autobiography in 1922.

Han-mac-Tu (pseudonym of Nguyen-trong-Tri; b. 1912). Vietnamese Catholic poet; his verse abounds with images of anxiety and sorrow, but he also wrote in praise of sensual love; he became one of the few Vietnamese poets to

confess his Christianity; he dies of leprosy following a long illness.

Walter Hasenclever (b. 1890). German poet
and playwright; he became an important
figure in the German Expressionist theater;
which flourished between 1916 and 1930; he
also wrote verse that reflected his sexual
escapades; later turning to film scripts and
musical comedies; he commits suicide in an
internment camp in France, where he had
fled in 1933.

Werner von Heidenstam (b. 1859). Swedish
poet; he composed visual, pagan, and exuberant verse, most of which was influenced by
Johann Wolfgang von Goethe; he initiated a
revival of romanticism during a period when
Strindbergian naturalism dominated the literary scene in Sweden; he also wrote historical
fiction; he receives the Nobel Prize for literature in 1916.

Selma Lagerlof (b. 1858). Swedish writer of fiction; her novels are rooted in the legend, history, and peasantry of her native Varmland;
she also wrote literature for children; in 1909,
she becomes the first woman to receive the
Nobel Prize in literature.

Pi Mounin (b. 1883). Burmese writer of fiction;
his written work reflects his interest in freedom of choice and individual responsibility;
he wrote in a clear, concise prose style, analyzing the psychology of his characters.

Amin ar-Rayhani (b. 1876). Lebanese essayist,
historian, writer of fiction, and poet; he introduced the prose poem to modern Arabic literature; his work reveals an attachment to nature, and he criticizes Western intrusions
upon his own culture.

Anton Hansen Tammsaare (b. 1878). Estonian
writer of fiction; he produced epic novels focusing upon Estonian peasant life during the
late nineteenth and early twentieth centuries;
his works reveal the influence of Fydor Dos-
toyevski and George Bernard Shaw (whose
works he translated).

Leon Davidovich Trotsky (b. 1879). Russian
political philosopher, historian, essayist, and
biographer; as the principal strategist of the
Bolshevik Revolution, he contributed numerous essays, letters, and political tracts to the
literature of Marxism; he possessed a compelling narrative style; he dies at the hand of a
Stalinist assassin.

Nathaniel West (pseudonym of Nathan Wallenstein Weinstein; b. 1903). American writer of
fiction; an innovative author, he wrote bitter

novels revealing the sterility and grotesque-
ness of the American dream.

PUBLICATIONS

Iliya Abu Madi, *al-Khama-il* (Thickets)—a volume of verse by the Syrian-American poet;
contains deeply introspective pieces that dwell
on individual episodes of romantic malaise,
doubt, and confusion; the work displays a
characteristically nostalgic tone; published in
New York City.

Sabahattin Ali, *Icimizdeki Seytan* (The Devil
Within)—a novel by the Turkish writer of fiction and poet; the work describes the problems encountered by Turkish intellectuals in
attempting to reconcile the old culture of the
East with the new culture of the West.

Dhun-Nun Ayyub, *Doktor Ibrahim*—the first
novel by the Iraqi writer of fiction, written in
Arabic, an account of corruption in the upper
levels of the Iraqi civil service; the title character, an agronomist, enriches himself by de-
vious means in Iraq, then emigrates to England to enjoy his fortune.

Rene Balance, *Rhythmes de Mon Coeur*—the
first volume of verse by the Haitian poet;
written in French, the poems recall the past,
the power and the ' attraction of voodoo
drums and dances; the pieces approach surrealism in their complex associational quality.

Walter Van Tilburg Clark, *The Ox-Bow Incident*—a novel by the American writer of fiction; a popular study of mob justice, the work
is set in Nevada in 1885 and concerns an episode of mistaken identity resulting from a cattle theft; although the action occurs in the
American West, the book looks to the rise of
fascism and totalitarianism in Europe as men
of action (and little thought) take the law into
their own hands.

William Empson, *The Gathering Storm*—a collection of verse by the English poet and literary commentator; the pieces concern themselves with social and political conditions
prior to World War II, as well as with the
emotional impact of the impending conflict.

William Faulkner, *The Hamlet*—a work of fiction by the American novelist and short story
writer; the stories that form this loosely connected volume suggest that the Snopes family
will descend on the town of Jefferson like, in
one scholar's words, "a cloud of seven-year lo-
custs"; the volume incorporates revised ver-

sions of "Fool about a Horse" (1936), "The Hound," "Spotted Horses" (1931), and "Lizards in Jamshyd's Courtyards" (1932); parts of the story "Barn Burning" (1939) also appear here.

Graham Greene, *The Power and the Glory*—a novel by the English writer of fiction; concerns a cowardly, whiskey-loving priest who fathers a bastard child.

Ernest Hemingway, *For Whom the Bell Tolls*—a novel by the American writer of fiction; takes place during three days of the Spanish Civil War and concerns a young man who must blow up a bridge in the face of a cowardly guerrilla leader, who fears for his life; the leader's "woman" is a powerful figure who encourages a love affair between the young man and a girl she has protected; the piece ends on a note of idealism concerning the "right" cause for the war.

Archibald Campbell Jordan, *Inggoumbo Yeminyanya* (The Wrath of the Ancestral Spirits)—the first novel by the South African (Cape Province) writer of fiction and poet; considered a classic of modern Xhosa writing; written with the encouragement of white missionary friends, the work describes the tragedies and sorrows of an oppressed people.

Berdi Kerbabayev, *Aigytly Adim* (Determined Step)—a novel by the Turkmen (SSR) writer of fiction and translator; focuses upon the revolutionary years from 1915 to 1920 in Turkmenia; proves the writer to be a classicist in Turkmen literature.

Arthur Koestler, *Darkness at Noon*—a novel by the Hungarian-born English writer of fiction and essayist; concerns the arrest, imprisonment, trial, and execution of a political victim within a totalitarian state; contains obvious parallels with the Stalinist Moscow trials of the 1930s.

Carson McCullers, *The Heart Is a Lonely Hunter*—a novel by the American writer of fiction; the piece unfolds in a small mill town in Georgia where an intelligent deaf mute strongly affects the lives of four alienated people and a twelve-year-old girl who dreams of becoming a composer; despair, social pressures, and failures of love and communication eventually lead to tragedy.

Subhas Mukhopadhay, *Padatik* (Pedestrian)—the first collection of verse by the Indian (Bengali) poet; identified the writer as the most talented among the leftist poets of Bengal; the pieces refer to Soviet Russia and China, to the famine and plight of the people, and to their war against the Axis powers; the writer chides the bourgeoisie and urges street processions of protest.

Sean O'Casey, *Purple Dust*—a comic fantasy by the Irish playwright; a satire of pastoral affectation; focuses upon the stupidity of two Englishmen and their attempts to resurrect a crumbling Tudor mansion in an Irish village; in the end, the villagers destroy the superficial reconstruction, and the Englishmen have, for their efforts, little beyond a heap of purple dust.

Sean O'Faolain, *Come Back to Erin*—a novel by the Irish writer of fiction; concerns the seemingly doomed aspirations of the Irish nationalists.

Robert Emmet Sherwood, *There Shall Be No Night*—a political drama by the American playwright; dramatizes the agonized decision of a Finnish intellectual to join his nation's resistance forces; in so doing, he will risk the almost certain possibility of death.

Upton Sinclair, *World's End*—a novel by the American writer of fiction, social reformer, and political radical; the first of a sequence of seven novels that provide a Marxist view of world events from the beginning of World War I to the middle of World War II; introduces the principal character, Lanny Budd, and follows his development toward sophistication in knowledge, business and love; the real tragedy of the piece concerns the Versailles Conference, which, in the writer's view, failed because leaders lacked intelligence and responsibility.

Dylan Thomas, *Portrait of the Artist as a Young Dog*—a collection of semiautobiographical short stories by the Welsh poet and miscellaneous prose writer; stylistically and thematically similar to James Joyce's *Dubliners* and *Portrait of the Artist as a Young Man.*

Simone Weil, "L'Iliade; ou, Le Poeme de la Force" (The Iliad; or, The Poem of Force)—an essay by the French philosopher, essayist, playwright, and poet; for the writer, Homer's *Iliad* illustrates pacifism by depicting the absolute futility of the Trojan War; argues that violence degrades both the victim and the victor, forcing both to become selfless entities; such selflessness, according to the writer, is the supreme sin, since the self, having once been sacrificed from without, could never be sacrificed to God from within, a sacrifice Weil considered central to atonement and redemption.

Edmund Wilson, *To the Finland Station*—a prose work by the American literary and social critic; traces socialist and revolutionary theory from Jules Michelet (1798-1874) and Robert Owen (1771-1858) to Karl Marx (1818-1883) and Vladimir Lenin (1870-1924).

Thomas Wolfe, *You Can't Go Home Again*—a novel by the American writer of fiction, published posthumously; Eugene Gant appears here in the guise of George "Monk" Webber, whose love affair with Esther Jack forms one of the highlights of the novel; the return visit of the principal character to his rural hometown demonstrates to him that materialism remains alive and well, that the lust for money exists everywhere; the writer's artistic scope expands from the individual's quest for fulfillment to include social concerns, such as the rise of the Nazis in Germany.

Richard Wright, *Native Son*—a novel by the American writer of fiction and miscellany; the piece is often described as the "Negro American Tragedy"; relates the story of a poor, suffering black boy from Chicago who society has transformed into a demonic nihilist; he accidentally kills the daughter of his white employer; after capture and before execution, he renounces both Christianity and communism.

EVENTS

Accent, a quarterly journal of contemporary literature, begins publication at the University of Illinois, Champaign; contributors include Katherine Anne Porter, Kay Boyle, Thomas Mann, Wallace Stevens, Richard P. Blackmur, John Crowe Ransom, and Irwin Shaw; until 1960.

Dictionary of American History published at Boston, in six volumes; begun in 1936, with contributions from almost one thousand American historians; two additional volumes published in 1976.

P.M., a combination newspaper and tabloid magazine, begins publication at New York City; issued five days per week, with a "digest" published on Saturdays; Ben Hecht, Margaret Bourke-White, and Louis Kronenberger are among its contributors; until 1948.

Bertrand Arthur William Russell, English philosopher and logician, appointed to the William James lectureship at Harvard University, Cambridge, Massachusetts.

Carl August Sandburg, American poet and historical biographer, receives the Pulitzer Prize in United States history for *Abraham Lincoln: The War Years*; four volumes, published in 1939.

William Saroyan, American writer of fiction and playwright, receives the Pulitzer Prize in drama for *The Time of Your Life* (1939); he refuses the $1000 award, maintaining that it would compromise his art.

John Steinbeck, American writer of fiction, receives the Pulitzer Prize in fiction for *The Grapes of Wrath* (1939).

Mark Albert Van Doren, American literary scholar, critic, writer of fiction, and poet, receives the Pulitzer Prize in poetry for his *Collected Poems* (1939).

1941

BIRTHS

C. Lindsay Barrett. Jamaican writer of fiction, poet, and playwright; his poetry will be militant and crisp in tone; his work will, in general, confront the issue of racial prejudice; he will leave the West Indies for residence in Nigeria.

Rachid Boudjedra. Algerian writer of fiction; he will create protagonists known for their psychoses and somber revelations of their lives; those same characters will appear overly obsessed with physical matters and sex.

Reubem Mauro Machado. Brazilian writer of fiction; his work will display caustic humor as he attacks capitalistic society and bourgeois values; he will develop an ironic fictional world, often violent and surreal, but he will write in clear, uncomplicated language; his fiction will be strongly autobiographical.

R. Anthony McNeil. Jamaican poet; his verse will focus upon life in the West Indies, and it will also reveal his interest in the theory of writing poetry.

Sergio Sant' Anna. Brazilian poet, playwright, and writer of fiction; his work will be characterized by stylistic experimentation, subtle irony, satire, absurd situations, and credible personae; he will also appeal for radical social change, for a movement away from the social hypocrisy that he believes dominates Brazilian life.

Stanislaw Stratiev. Bulgarian writer of fiction; he will become one of the significant satirists of modern East Europe, developing the ideas for his characters and situations from the narrow streets of Sofia; he will rely upon one of the basic realities of Soviet-style communism: in all societies, one can always find, in a time of need, someone to set the situation right.

DEATHS

Sherwood Anderson (b. 1876). American writer of fiction; he set out to explore the loneliness and frustration of American life; in so doing, he was among the first American authors to explore the effects of the unconscious upon American life.

Isaac Emmanuelovich Babel (b. 1894). Russian writer of fiction and playwright; he became recognized as a brilliant stylist, particularly for his depictions of Jewish ghetto life; he drew upon his experiences during the 1917 Revolution and his knowledge of the illegalities practiced by the peasantry; arrested in 1939, he dies in a Soviet labor camp.

Henri Bergson (b. 1859). French philosopher; he became professor of philosophy at the College de France in 1900; his dualistic philosophy held that the world contains two opposite tendencies, the life force and the resistance of matter to that force; the individual understands matter through intellect, but perceives the life force and the reality of time through intuition; he receives the Nobel Prize for literature in 1927.

Simon Dubnow (b. 1860). Russian narrative writer and historian; he wrote definitive prose tracts on the history of the Jews in Russia; he based his three-volume study of Hasidism on original research and produced a ten-volume history of the Jewish people; generally in his work, he attempted to consider the complex relationship between historical facts and their critical interpretations.

Sir James George Frazer (b. 1854). Scottish-born social anthropologist; he undertook comparative studies of folklore, magic, and religion, demonstrating clear parallels between primitive and Christian cultures; his *The Golden Bough* (1890) considerably influenced twentieth-century intellectual thought and continues to be a standard reference work.

Ayodhyasimh Upadhyay Hariaudh (b. 1865). Indian (Hindi) poet and writer of fiction; he wrote the first modern Hindi epic poem (1914), composed in Sanskrit meters; in his most significant fiction, he criticized the system of forced marriages; he lectured in literature at Banaras University.

James Joyce (b. 1882). Irish writer of fiction; he may well be the most significant literary figure of the twentieth century; his virtuoso experiments in prose both redefined the limits of language and recreated the form of the modern novel; he devoted his life to art, and many critics feel that his verbal felicity equals that of Shakespeare or Milton.

George Lyman Kittredge. (b. 1860). American literary scholar and editor; he taught at Harvard College from 1888 to 1936, acquiring a reputation as one of the nation's most significant teachers and scholars; he published nearly four hundred books and essays, his work ranging from almanacs to studies of witchcraft, Geoffrey Chaucer, Sir Thomas Malory, the English and Scottish ballads, and William Shakespeare.

Dmitry Sergeyevich Merezhkovsky (b. 1865). Russian novelist, critic, playwright, biographer, and philosopher; he became a leader of the Russian symbolists and developed a neo-Christian point of view to synthesize Russian Orthodox Christianity and ancient Greek paganism; he also attempted to weave philosophical speculation into striking portrayals of important historical figures; after imprisonment by the Bolsheviks in 1917, he left Russia and settled in Paris.

Elizabeth Madox Roberts (b. 1886). American writer of fiction and poet; she gained popularity with her novels about the mountain people of Kentucky; specifically, she focused upon the poor whites of that region, capturing both their humor and their pathos.

Hjalmar Soderberg (b. 1869). Swedish writer of fiction; he gained a literary reputation for his witty novels and short stories in which he captured the essence of upper middle class-life in Stockholm; his work reflects his beliefs in Darwinism and fate, as well as his attraction to the psychology of Sigmund Freud.

John Henderson Soga (b. 1860). South African hymn writer, poet, and translator; his most important literary contributions were translations of English tracts and sermons into his native Xhosa, which reflected his work as an ordained minister in the United Presbyterian Church of Scotland; he also concluded his father's translation, into Xhosa, of John Bunyan's *Pilgrim's Progress* (1926); he, his wife, and one son die during a German bombardment of Southampton, England.

Rabindranath Thakur (b. 1861). Indian (Bengali) poet, playwright, essayist, and translator; he became the most significant figure in the history of modern Indian literature; he expressed in his work, particularly in his poetry, the changing ideals of his contemporaries, the patriotic enthusiasm and optimism of the young bourgeoisie class, his enchantment with the beauties of nature, the feelings of love, and his original concept of God as the helper and the lover of human beings.

Ibrahim Tuqan (b. 1905). Palestinian Arab poet; he wrote lyrical verse, favoring short meters and multi-rhyme arrangements; his love poems tended to be pleasing rather than profound, to rely more upon language than upon the imagination; his work also displayed his patriotic zeal as he attempted to arouse his readers against the Zionists.

Virginia Stephen Woolf (b. 1882). English writer of fiction and essayist; her work significantly influenced the twentieth-century English novel, particularly through her stream-of-consciousness technique; her prose style was symbolic, poetic, and extremely visual; she also published letters, diaries, and two feminist prose tracts.

Mari Ziyada (b. 1895). Arab essayist, critic, and translator; she wrote principally about the relationship between society and literature; she translated literary works from French, English, and German into Arabic; she combined, in her original essays, ardent patriotism, compassion for the poor and unfortunate, and a general appreciation for Western humanism.

PUBLICATIONS

James Agee, *Let Us Now Praise Famous Men*— a work of nonfiction by the American writer of miscellaneous prose and verse; originally (1936) commissioned by *Fortune* magazine, but rejected by that periodical; focuses upon the shortcomings of rural life in the American South; it depicts people who are bare and beaten, but nonetheless dignified; the work was given added depth by the photographs of Walker Evans.

Louis Aragon, *Le Creve-Coeur* (Heartbreak)—a poem by the French writer of fiction and verse; intended to encourage its readers to maintain their morale against the Nazis and their French collaborators.

W. H. Auden, *The Double Man*—a long transitional verse epistle by the English poet describing what he terms "the baffling crime" of "two decades of hypocrisy"; thus, he rejects the simplicities of politicians and acknowledges the essential solitude of humanity; the piece ends with a prayer for refuge and illumination for the "muddled heart," reflecting the poet's renewed Christian faith.

William Rose Benet, *The Dust Which Is God*—an autobiographical novel in verse by the American poet, playwright, novelist, and miscellaneous prose writer; the piece displays the poet's range of interests and intellect; also demonstrates his versatility in changing forms and rhythms to capture the diverse and rambling nature of his subject, the birth and growth of the nation; the poet sees America as synonymous with his own life; the piece was awarded the Pulitzer Prize for poetry in 1942.

Bertolt Brecht, *Mutter Courage und Ihre Kinder* (Mother Courage and Her Children)—a chronicle play by the German dramatist, poet, and dramatic theorist; concerns the Thirty Years' War, and goes forward in twelve scenes and nine songs; focuses upon the title character, the mother of three illegitimate children by three different fathers; in her traveling canteen wagon, she follows the Swedish soldiers, selling her goods to them; essentially, she exists as a totally materialistic character, determined to make the most profit from her sales, even though she must sacrifice her children in the process.

James M. Cain, *Mildred Pierce*—a novel by the American writer of fiction; focuses upon a hard-boiled woman, a member of the middle class who is driven to violence in an effort to satisfy her love and ambitions; the piece was transformed into a highly successful motion picture.

Noel Coward, *Blithe Spirit*—a dramatic comedy by the English playwright; a husband has remarried, but he remains haunted by the mischievous ghost of his former wife; a bemuddled medium enters the scene, but serves only to contribute to the comedy of the piece, doing nothing to ease the poor man's condition.

Herbert Isaac Ernest Dhlomo, *The Valley of a Thousand Hills*—a collection of verse by the South African (Zulu) novelist, poet, and playwright; the pieces reflect the poet's anger at the plight of the native South African; thus, in "The Great Question," he asks, "Would you have me as a brother / Or a revengeful beast?"; three editions through 1944.

F. Scott Fitzgerald, *The Last Tycoon*—a novel by the American writer of fiction, unfinished at his death and published posthumously; the closest an American novelist had come to depicting the actual activities of Hollywood; the principal character is a man who rose from the impoverished masses to take his place among the swarming parasites of humanity.

Takla Hawaryat Germacaw, *Ar'aya* (Good Example)—a novel by the Ethiopian (Amharic) writer of fiction and playwright; the piece displays the traditional moralistic tone of Amharic fiction and contains highly descriptive passages of local scenery; the writer emphasizes improved agricultural methods; the first Amharic work translated into Russian and Chinese.

Lillian Hellman, *Watch on the Rhine*—a drama by the American playwright; the characters struggle against fascism; a highly emotional piece that was criticized for its obvious political propaganda.

Rahim Jalil, *Gulru*—a historical novel by the Tajik (SSR) writer of fiction and poet; concerns the 1917 Revolution and its effect upon the Tajiks; also focuses upon the emergence of the Tajik proletariat and the brotherhood formed by Tajiks, Russians, and Uzbeks.

Endalkacaw Makonnen, *The Voice of Blood*—a play by the Ethiopian (Amharic) writer of fiction and dramatist; celebrates the martyrdom of Abuina Petros, head of the Ethiopian church; the Italians killed him during their invasion and eventual occupation (1935-1941).

F. O. Matthiessen, *American Renaissance*—a combination literary history and critical study by the American literary scholar; concerns the relationship between literature and society, as observed in works by Ralph Waldo Emerson, Nathaniel Hawthorne, Herman Melville, Walt Whitman, and Henry David Thoreau; the themes of good, evil, and nature are evaluated by the writer.

Carson McCullers, *Reflections in a Golden Eye*—a novel by the American writer of fiction that stands as an experiment in the macabre and the Gothic genre; the story is set in an army camp in the South before World War II and concerns the spiritual but passionate attachment that exists between a deaf mute and a half-wit.

John Crowe Ransom, *The New Criticism*—a critical tract by the American poet; the writer maintains that human experience can be realized only through art; he sets out to discover the unique nature of poetic discourse, which functions principally to induce imaginative thought.

Delmore Schwartz, *Shenandoah*—a verse play by the American poet and writer of fiction; expresses the writer's experience and understanding of the Jewish family emigrating to the United States; here, human beings feel imprisoned by time and bear the guilt of past generations.

Vernon Watkins, *Ballad of the Mari Lwyd, and Other Poems*—a volume of verse by the Welsh poet, translator, and nonfiction writer; in the title piece, the poet depicts the ancient Welsh New Year's Eve custom in which the bearers of a decorated horse's skull challenge the occupants of a house to a rhyming contest, hopeful of gaining entry; thus there exists the symbolic confrontation between the living and the dead.

Eudora Welty, *A Curtain of Green*—a collection of short stories by the American writer of fiction; the strength of the volume lies in characters who, although they may be described as common, nonetheless evidence depth and complexity; those characters tend to be neurotics, eccentrics, and even psychotics, yet they inject comedy and pathos into their small-town Mississippi existences.

Franz Werfel, *Das Lied der Bernadette* (The Song of Bernadette)— a novel by the Czech-born Austrian writer of verse and fiction; described as a spiritual quest in verse; inspired by his wife, the widow of the composer Gustav Mahler; the piece was transformed into a successful motion picture.

EVENTS

Leonard Bacon, American poet and academician, receives the Pulitzer Prize in poetry for his lyric collection *Sunderland Capture* (1940).

Robert Emmet Sherwood, American playwright, receives the Pulitzer Prize in drama for *There Shall Be No Night* (1940).

Ola Elizabeth Winslow, American literary scholar and academician, receives the Pulitzer

Prize in biography-autobiography for her *Jonathan Edwards* (1940).

1942

BIRTHS

Isabel Allende. Chilean novelist, playwright, and writer of juvenile fiction; her work will be inspired by her own family history and by the political upheaval in Chile; a socialist, she will be forced to leave her native land following the 1973 coup and murder of her uncle, President Salvador Allende; thus, through her fiction, she will try to survive the traumatic experience of exile.

Ataol Behramoglu. Turkish poet; he will publish verse in literary journals and translate Russian literature; he will successfully combine in his verse the aesthetic values of traditional poetry with social conditions and ideals; his work will also dwell upon his dissatisfaction with himself and his surroundings, as well as upon his search for solutions to various social and personal problems.

Ariel Dorfman. Chilean-born writer of prose and fiction and poet; in his work, he will treat such issues as exile, life under totalitarian rule, and the influence of popular literature upon social and political values; he will leave Chile in 1973, following the coup of Augusto Pinochet, living variously in Argentina, France, Holland, and the United States.

Douglas Eaglesham Dunn. Scottish poet, writer of fiction, and critical commentator; his poetry will be richly descriptive in language, displaying wit, humanism, emotional depth, and a focus upon social and personal concerns; he will live most of his life in England, returning to Scotland in 1984.

Peter Handke. Austrian playwright, writer of fiction, essayist, and poet; his drama will evidence the influence of the philosopher Ludwig Wittgenstein in its focus upon the relationship between language and reality; thus, his "sprechstucke" (speak-ins) will lack plot, characterization, and dramatic structure; instead of dialogue, the characters will engage in cliché-ridden, fragmented monologues; the audience, therefore, will become aware of how language can distort reality and prevent authentic expression.

Janette Turner Hospital. Australian-born Canadian writer of fiction; she will gain recognition for her rich prose style and her experiments with narrative forms; she will examine the means by which individuals attempt to interpret reality to conform to personal standards; thus, her characters will tend to flaunt social values and customs as they pursue individual integrity; India, Canada, and the United States will be the principal settings for her work.

Erica Mann Jong. American poet and writer of fiction; she will become popular by skillfully combining sex and psychiatry and generally challenging the conventional views of women.

Garrison Keillor. American narrative writer; he will gain considerable recognition from a weekly "homespun" radio show focusing upon the fictional town of Lake Wobegon and the proverbial heartland of America; his writings will be inspired by those broadcasts, creating an original combination of nostalgia and sentiment; he will, in addition, be a gifted satirist who knows how to manipulate humor and social criticism.

Ali Podrimja. Albanian poet; he will study Albanian language and literature in Belgrade, and those intellectual experiences will measurably shape his own thought and verse; between 1961 and 1988, he will produce more than twelve volumes of poetry, all of them reflecting his tendency toward poetic innovation; thematically, he will display an obsession with the destiny of human beings, focusing upon such issues as myth versus reality and the specific in relation to the general.

Paul-Eerik Rummo. Estonian poet and playwright; his verse will demonstrate his nationalism and his interest in world literature as it relates to his own heritage; he will contribute significantly to the renascence of Estonian poetry that occurred during the 1960s, a vast accomplishment considering the devaluation of art and culture by the totalitarian government under which he will have to labor.

Anthony Rudolf. English poet, playwright, and translator; he will produce highly philosophical verse, as well as pieces that focus upon domestic realities and travel.

DEATHS

Roberto Godofredo Christopherson Arlt (b. 1900). Argentine writer of fiction and essayist; he achieved recognition from works portraying the metaphysical anguish of the alienated individual in twentieth-century society; his fiction and his drama concern the plight of individuals who contend with what he considered the inevitably crumbling social edifice; thus, he depicted social unrest, urban alienation, deviant behavior, sexual maladjustment, and class hostility; he dies suddenly from a heart attack.

Miguel Hernandez (b. 1910). Spanish poet and playwright; he served in the Spanish Civil War as a fervent loyalist, and those political activities appear foremost in his verse; his later work reflects a combination of despair and joy; with linguistic simplicity, he describes the emotions of a man who will never again see his wife or his home; he dies in prison from tuberculosis.

Robert Musil (b. 1880). Austrian writer of fiction; his novels will abound with psychological analysis; stylistically, he will invite comparison with Marcel Proust; essentially, he functioned as an absolute skeptic who recognized the relationships between fiction and psychology and philosophy; he lives the last four years of his life in poverty, which undoubtedly contributed to his premature death.

Theippam Maum Wa (b. 1889). Burmese writer of fiction, playwright, and literary critic; he wrote short fictional works providing a realistic and critical view of Burmese village life; his descriptions of backward and uneducated villagers pointed to the need for social and economic reforms; his plays also criticized the state of Burmese society.

Akiko Yosano (b. 1878). Japanese poet; her verse celebrates her femininity, which she believed had been subdued by conventions that denied her full flowering as a human being; thus, she explores and proclaims the self.

Stefan Zweig (b. 1881). Austrian biographer, writer of fiction, playwright, essayist, and translator; his popular biographies and novellas were among the first to venture into the field of analytic psychology; he sought to promote the works of foreign writers in German-speaking countries, trying to eliminate the barriers of language and culture from the world of letters; he becomes depressed by the state of World War II, and he and his wife take their own lives in Petropolis, Brazil.

PUBLICATIONS

Jean Anouilh, *Antigone*—a dramatic tragedy by the French playwright; he creates an intensely pessimistic and willful character; she rejects hope and comes into direct conflict with the imposing political aims of Creon; their temperaments clash and develop into a psychological battle between man and woman.

Albert Camus, *L'Etranger* (The Stranger)—the first novel by the Algerian-born French essayist, writer of fiction, and playwright; the principal character kills an Arab on a beach for no apparent reason and receives the death sentence; beset by recognition of the senselessness and absurdity of existence, and unable to show contriteness for his act during his trial, the man eventually accepts the imperfections of life and resolves to die with dignity; the novel is often linked with the tenets of existentialism.

James Gould Cozzens, *The Just and the Unjust*—a novel by the American writer of fiction; the principal character is an assistant district attorney who follows his father and grandfather into the legal profession; during his practice, he learns about all aspects of the law and comes to recognize the importance of conscience in relation to technicalities and textbooks.

William Faulkner, *Go Down, Moses*—a volume of seven short stories by the American writer of fiction; a set of variations upon two major themes: the changing relationship, from the frontier days to the present, of blacks and whites in the mythical Yoknapatawpha County, and the relationship of both races to the land they inhabit, which, in but only two or three generations, has been transformed from an abundant wilderness to a severe economic problem; includes, in addition to the title piece, such stories as "The Fire and the Hearth," "The Bear," and "Delta Autumn."

Randall Jarrell, *Blood for a Stranger*—a volume of verse by the American poet; demonstrates his reliance upon such literary figures as Allen Tate, John Crowe Ransom, and W. H. Auden; the poet experiments with such forms as villanelles and sestinas; thematically, the poet cries out in defiance of a world that, politically, appears to be heaving itself toward catastrophe; metaphysical questioning underlies the overall tone of existential loneliness and despair.

Alfred Kazin, *On Native Grounds*—a prose tract by the American literary critic; the work focuses upon prose in America following the generation of William D. Howells; the writer essentially laments the existence of critical orthodoxies that lead, in turn, to critical polarization.

C. S. Lewis, *The Screwtape Letters*—a volume of fictional epistles by the Irish-born scholar, literary critic, and writer of fiction; the title character, a member of Hell's "lowerarchy," writes letters to his nephew, an apprentice demon who has just begun the task of enticing human souls to the infernal cause; the piece abounds in Christian orthodoxy and conventional faith; popular work that went into twenty English and fourteen American printings within three years after its initial publication.

Helen MacInnes, *Assignment in Brittany*—a novel by the Scottish-born American writer of fiction and playwright; a tale of espionage in Nazi-occupied Brittany during the summer of 1940; the work was transformed into a popular motion picture.

Mary McCarthy, *The Company She Keeps*— a novel by the American writer of fiction and essayist; presents a portrait of the "new woman," a bohemian in the intellectual world of New York City; combines the fear of exposure with the need to be in full view of the world; the piece conducts the reader upon an exercise in social observation and self-awareness.

Mirsaid Mirshakar, *Qishloqi Tilloi* (The Golden Qishalq)—a poem by the Tajik (SSR) writer of verse and playwright; based upon an old Pamir legend of a happy land for which generations of the oppressed have longed; the poet accompanies a band of pilgrims searching for the happy land, and finds it at home, where the Soviets dominate.

Sean O'Casey, *Red Roses for Me*—a play by the Irish dramatist; an autobiographical and lyrical piece focusing upon the 1913 general strike in Dublin.

Upton Sinclair, *Dragon's Teeth*—a novel by the American radical novelist; the principal character—Lanny Budd, from Sinclair's earlier novel *World's End* (1940)—negotiates with the Nazis for the release of his friends; because of the fascist threat, the piece demonstrates that American socialism and American capitalism could, at the proper moment, achieve some degree of unity; awarded the Pulitzer Prize in fiction in 1943.

John Steinbeck, *The Moon Is Down*—a short novel by the American writer of fiction; focuses upon the Norwegian resistance fighters during the Nazi occupation of their country; transformed into a successful motion picture and stage play.

Francisco Jose de Vasques Tenreiro, *Ilha de Nome Santo* (The Island of the Holy Name)—a volume of verse by the Sao Tome (West Africa) poet and writer of fiction; the neo-realistic pieces have been considered the first major works of "negritude" by an African writing in Portuguese; the title poem attacks social injustice on the island of Saint Thomas; the poet insists that being black is a positive attribute and denies the idea of white superiority.

Thornton Wilder, *The Skin of Our Teeth*—a play by the American novelist, essayist, and dramatist; a comedy that represents an apparently middle-class American family; however, the members exist on different social, intellectual, and emotional levels, and actually represent all of humankind; the playwright filters his plot through the Adam-Eve-Cain motif and transports the characters upon a journey through the history of Western civilization; this extremely complex piece goes forward upon the notion that for all of the absurdity found in human beings, the race must, at all costs, be preserved.

Stefan Zweig, *Schachnovelle* (The Royal Game)—a novella by the Austrian biographer, writer of fiction, playwright, poet, and essayist; the writer's last work of fiction and also his most controversial; concerns a sensitive intellectual who survives solitary confinement at the hands of the Nazis; simply, he learns to play a chess game against himself, but as a result he becomes a schizophrenic; after his release, doctors warn against further play, but he cannot resist; he loses because he becomes a victim of another's manipulation of his delicate mental condition.

EVENTS

William Rose Benet, American poet, essayist, and writer of fiction, receives the Pulitzer Prize in poetry for *The Dust Which Is God* (1941).

Ellen Glasgow, American writer of fiction, receives the Pulitzer Prize in fiction for her novel *In This Our Life* (1941).

The Carl and Lily Pforzheimer Foundation established for the encouragement of American literary scholarship.

1943

BIRTHS

Reinaldo Arenas. Cuban writer of fiction and poet; his work will be noted for its imaginative recreation of history and reality, reflecting the turbulent political atmosphere within Cuba; he will combine a sense of the real with powerful and sincere emotion, but he will also rely upon surrealistic imagery, satire, and elements of the fantastic; he will leave Cuba in 1980 and settle in the United States.

Peter Carey. Australian writer of fiction; his novels will reveal his inventive mixture of the fantastic and the ordinary, clothed in an exuberant but controlled prose style; he will satirize contemporary social values and employ comedy to explore the illusory nature of reality.

Nikki Giovanni (born Yolande Cornelia Giovanni). Black American poet; the major emphasis in her verse will be upon black women, who will emerge as myths to be honored by all females, both white and black; in her poetry, black women will display extreme pride in their vigor and ability to survive.

Marion Patrick Jones. Trinidadian novelist; she will live, at various times, in Brooklyn, London, and Paris; her fiction will reflect the crises of racial and national identity within Trinidad, as well as the failure, during the 1940s, of middle-class people there to respond to the problems of underdevelopment; she will focus upon both the passion and the sense of defeat among the people.

Philip Michael Ondaatje. Ceylonese-born Canadian poet, novelist, playwright, and essayist; he will examine, in his poetry, the dichotomy between rational intellect and disorderly reality, maintaining that the poet's efforts to render personal experience will, necessarily, result in distortion; he will employ humor, flamboyant imagery, extravagant metaphor, and sudden tonal shifts; he will strive to examine and describe the essential nature of human experience.

Justo Jorge Padron. Spanish poet; his poetic style will change from surrealism to a metaphorical richness not found in Spanish verse

ture will be found in the sea, the central metaphor of his later work and the vital element in opposition to nothingness (or death).

Sam Shepard (born Samuel Shepard Rogers). American playwright and writer of fiction; he will be identified as a product of the 1960s counterculture, combining wild humor, grotesque satire, mythology, and haunting language; his plays, particularly, will rely upon the motifs of Western films to create a subversive pop-art version of America; he will receive the Pulitzer Prize for drama in 1978.

Sasha Sokalov. Russian writer of fiction; his work will be verbally complex and intricately crafted, reminding one of William Faulkner; he will focus upon the lives of the governing oligarchy, portraying seductions, suicides, assassinations, executions, and sexual affairs; he will leave the Soviet Union in 1975.

Stoyan (Steve) Tesich. Yugoslavian-born American playwright and novelist; his themes will relate to the role and viewpoint of the outsider: the inability to communicate with loved ones, the feeling of resentment and alienation toward one's surroundings; he will also achieve recognition for his creation of intriguing characters; his screenplay *Breaking Away* will receive an Academy Award in 1980.

Jose Luis de Tomas Garcia. Spanish writer of fiction; he will become a career police officer, and his knowledge and experience in criminology will be applied to fiction that examines the social problems behind individuals' chemical dependencies.

DEATHS

Stephen Vincent Benet (b. 1898). American poet and fiction writer; he gained a reputation from his vivid literary treatments of themes and subjects from American history and folklore; his long verse narratives and ballads lent themselves to dramatic readings and performances, capturing the promise of American democracy and American growth.

Abdul Rahim bin Salim Kajai (b. 1894). Singapore (Malay) writer of fiction and journalist; his humorous short stories presented an accurate picture of daily life, and he earned recognition for his realistic subject matter and style; more importantly, he became known as "the father of Malay journalism."

Kostis Palamas (b. 1859). Greek poet, playwright, and writer of fiction; his major contri-bution was his sense of the history and modern resurgence of Greece; he remained ever the academic, serving on the faculty at the University of Athens until his seventieth year.

Henrik Pontoppidan (b. 1857). Danish writer of fiction and playwright; he became the most prominent Danish novelist of the late nineteenth century; in his work, he examined the cultural effects of changing class structures and sexual mores; he undertook a serious analysis of the sufferings of the peasantry, attacking the upper classes for their failure to enact economic and educational reforms; in 1917, he received the Nobel Prize for literature; he dies at Copenhagen at age eighty-six.

Helen Beatrix Potter (b. 1866). English writer of children's fiction; she entertained and educated millions of children through such characters as Peter Rabbit, Squirrel Nutkin, Benjamin Bunny, Tom Kitten, and Jemima Puddle-Duck.

Saul Tchernihowsky (b. 1875). Russian-born Hebrew poet; his verse will focus upon nature, beauty, hedonism, and political protest; his love poems reflect his own creative energy, passion, freshness, and joy; his work evidences his strong interest in classical Greek culture and mythology.

Shimazaki Toson (b. 1872). Japanese writer of fiction; he depicts, in meticulous detail, how ordinary people in the remote mountain provinces of Japan existed during the latter half of the nineteenth century; he attempts to place his own heritage, as well as that of his nation, into historical perspective; his fiction generally reflects his belief in the rich cultural traditions of Japan.

Simone Adolphine Weil (b. 1909). French philosopher, essayist, playwright, and poet; she has been identified as among the most brilliant and enigmatic Christian thinkers of the twentieth century; her writings are paradoxical and contradictory and convey her intense compassion for human suffering; she denounces modern nihilism and expresses a longing to be united with God; most of her work was collected and published posthumously from her notebooks; she emigrates to the United States in 1942, then travels to England to attempt to assist the Free French; her death has been attributed to a number of causes: anorexia, suicide, mental illness, self-imposed martyrdom, tuberculosis.

PUBLICATIONS

Jacques Barzun, *Romanticism and the Modern Ego*—a critical study by the French-born historian, critic, and miscellaneous prose writer; explores the Romantic sensibility and elucidates the principal tenets of Romanticism including the desire to create a new society different from the age immediately preceding it; thus, the Romantics dedicate themselves to the acceptance and exploration of an open universe; the writer argues that twentieth-century wars and ideologies have destroyed the aims of Romanticism, leading to widespread confusion in the arts; the work was revised and expanded in 1961 under the title *Classic, Romantic, and Modern.*

Stephen Vincent Benet, *Western Star*—an epic poem by the American writer of verse and fiction; intended to be a major piece related to the expansion of America, but only a single section was completed before the poet's death in this year; the underlying theme of the piece concerns the idealistic notion of every person becoming what God intended him or her to be; receives the Pulitzer Prize in poetry in 1944.

John Cheever, *The Way Some People Live*—a collection of short stories, originally published in *The New Yorker,* by the American writer of fiction; realistic and perceptive studies of upper middle-class suburban life; the tone of the stories varies radically: urbanity, grace, detachment, satire, irony, humor; the locale of the pieces is easily identified with Westchester County, New York.

Cecil Day Lewis, *Word over All*—a collection of verse by the Irish-born poet, writer of fiction, and critic; a reaction to World War II; essentially, Lewis posits that the hope for a socialist revolution and a nobler race of human beings has given way to a confrontation with capitalism that has resulted only in war.

Derenik Demirtchian, *Vardanank* (The Companions of Vardan)—a historical novel by the Armenian writer of fiction; inspired by the fifth-century popular uprising against the Persians; thematically, the writer seeks to encourage nationalism during World War II; Volume 2 appears in 1946, along with a dramatized version; a French translation in 1963.

Robert Desnos, *Le Vin est Tire*—a novel by the French poet, writer of fiction, playwright, and essayist; the writer explores, and ultimately condemns, the individual's reliance upon drugs to survive or to escape.

A. Emile Disengomoko, *Kwenkwenda* (Where Shall I Go?)—the first novel by the Zaire writer of fiction, poet, and essayist; the title character must fashion a life for himself in the midst of the competing demands of his newly acquired Christian values and the traditions of his homeland; the novel receives the Margaret Wrong award for fiction in 1948; four editions published through 1955.

John Dos Passos, *Number One*—a novel by the American writer of fiction; the second volume of a trilogy entitled *District of Columbia* (1952); a study in disillusionment, focusing upon the idea of the democratic ideals of the populist movement giving way to the fascism embodied in demagoguery.

T. S. Eliot, *Four Quartets*—a poem in four parts by the American-born poet and critic; the quarters represent the seasons and the elements as well as landscapes in England and the United States of significance in Eliot's life; the poet meditates on war, the fundamentals of Christian faith, and human experience; two elements, the temporal and the timeless, need to be understood in terms of interpreting the patterns of human experience.

Ellen Glasgow, *A Certain Measure*—a collection of essays by the American writer of fiction that served as prefaces to each of her novels; the writer groups her fiction into three categories: novels of the Commonwealth (Virginia), of the country (the Tidewater region of Virginia), and the city (Richmond); the prefaces help the reader to discover the writer's strengths in terms of her colorful style, impassioned realism, profoundness, subtlety, irony, and criticism.

H. L. Mencken, *Heathen Days: 1890-1936*—a collection of narrative sketches by the American journalist, essayist, and social and political satirist; a series of wide-ranging reminiscences on such subjects as the Baltimore Y.M.C.A., prize fighting, evangelists, education, and politics.

U Nu, *Puhtuzinno Ummatako* (Man Is Insane)—a play by the Burmese writer of fiction and dramatist; a criticism of hypocrisy in both sexual and social relationships.

Ayn Rand, *The Fountainhead*—a novel by the Russian-born American writer of fiction; concerns a brilliant architect who struggles against the standards and conventions of the world; the writer dramatizes the notion that the ego constitutes the "fountainhead" of human progress.

Bharati Sarabhai, *The Well of the People*—a drama by the Indian playwright, written in English; the writer's contribution to the Gandhian social order, arising from her involvement in the Indian National Congress; concerns an old lady who spent her life savings digging a village well for the benefit of the poor.

Jean-Paul Sartre, *L'Etre et le Neant* (Being and Nothingness)—a prose tract by the French critic, playwright, essayist, and novelist; partially written while the writer was a German prisoner of war; concerns the broad issue of human authenticity in an atheist century; he turns to Marxism and advocates violent revolution in place of individualism; however, he will not totally commit himself to that philosophy.

Edith Sitwell, *A Poet's Notebook*—a miscellaneous prose collection by the English poet; reveals the variety of the author's taste in literature, as well as her critical criteria; she explains the reasons for her attraction to a number of English and French writers (both major and minor); provides a useful guide to the creative processes of a poet.

Robert Penn Warren, *At Heaven's Gate*—a novel by the American poet, essayist, and writer of fiction; concerns an actual political murder that occurred in Nashville, Tennessee; the principal character comes to an end by his own hand, after tragically losing his daughter.

EVENTS

Robert Frost, American poet, receives the Pulitzer Prize in poetry for *A Witness Tree* (1942).

The Institute of Early American History and Culture established.

Upton Sinclair, American social reformer, novelist, and miscellaneous prose writer, receives the Pulitzer Prize in fiction for his novel *Dragon's Teeth* (1942).

Thornton Wilder, American playwright and writer of fiction, receives the Pulitzer Prize in drama for *The Skin of Our Teeth* (1942).

1944

BIRTHS

Eavan Aisling Boland. Irish poet and critic; she will express in her verse both political and private concerns, particularly the condition of woman as poet and social outcast; she will also focus upon such issues as female sensuality, domestic necessities, and the spiritual torment of the oppressed; the state of poetry in Ireland and the political violence and unrest there also constitute major themes.

Paul Durcan. Irish poet; his intense and emotionally charged verse will feature an exuberant and playful manipulation of language; with surrealistic imagery and humor, he will satirize social and religious values, while celebrating love and nature; he will display a command of poetic tone and a desire to experiment with form, and both qualities will contribute to the lyrical and visionary dimensions of his verse.

Florence Onye Buchi Emecheta. Nigerian-born novelist; she will address the difficulties of modern African women who find themselves forced into traditional and subservient roles; thus, she will expose such African customs as polygamy, servitude, and arranged marriages as destructive to the individuality of African women; her characters will challenge these restrictions and aspire to social and economic independence; in 1962, she will assume residence in England.

Merle Hodge. Trinidadian novelist and translator; her fiction will focus upon the social caste system of Trinidad and her characters' attempts to cope with it.

Christopher David Tully Hope. South African writer of fiction, poet, and essayist; he will offer witty observations on the social problems within South Africa; his fiction and poetry will underscore his belief that humor is the only way one can cope with the contradictions and absurdities of apartheid; through an ironic narrative tone, he will protest against the South African government and its policies; he will emigrate to England in 1975.

Witi Tame Ihimaera. New Zealand writer of fiction and nonfiction; he will explore in his fiction the traditional familial values of his native Maori tribe, being attentive to the cultural changes that have resulted from European colonization; thus, his themes will concern the social conflicts between natives and whites, the loss of Maori reverence for their own traditions, and the disintegration of cultural identity because of attempts by younger Maoris to assimilate into the affluent and urbanized white society.

Maxime N'Debeka. Congolese poet and playwright; he will bluntly and sarcastically attack the new politicians and bureaucrats of post-independence Africa; he will see greed, inefficiency, and arrogance in ruling circles, as well as a host of political sycophants who will destroy well-meaning governors.

Ismet Ozel. Turkish poet; he will develop into an ardent and sincere writer of revolutionary verse; for him, poetry will exist as an essential part of intellectual and educational revolution within Turkey; in 1970, he will abandon his studies in political science and assume the editorship of a Marxist literary periodical.

Botho Strauss. German playwright, poet, and writer of fiction; he will strive to become an acute observer of contemporary society, and will attempt to write with the utmost economy and precision of language; he will look for dimensions of life behind the various surfaces of daily existence; for him, the ego will exist as the creative drive that will transcend the everyday world.

Alice Walker. American writer of fiction, poet, and essayist; she will be concerned with racism and sexism, particularly as they affect the lives and everyday experiences of women; she will offer a message of hope, asserting that healing, change, and growth will eventually occur, despite periods of bleakness and discouragement; she will receive the Pulitzer Prize for fiction in 1983.

DEATHS

George Ade (b. 1866). American writer of fiction and playwright; he gained recognition for his special form of journalistic humor, which he combined with a type of slang that provided Americans at the end of the nineteenth century with a common speech.

Herbert George De Lisser (b. 1878). Jamaican novelist and journalist; he combined his Portuguese-Jewish heritage with extant African elements, contributing significantly to the literature and culture of the Caribbean he also explicated the complexities of the colonialism-imperialism-neocolonialism debates that preceded independence.

Jean Giraudoux (b. 1882). French playwright and writer of fiction; his highly original dramas are imaginative interpretations of Greek myths; he also undertook bitter satires against the materialism of the twentieth century; drama was, for him, the best forum through which to express his talents for irony and paradox.

Huseyin Rahmi Gurpinar (b. 1864). Turkish novelist; he portrayed Turkish life and ideas through characters from different levels of society; his novels (more than thirty in number) accurately described the atmosphere within Turkey at the end of the nineteenth century, and thus are important historical documents of life during the period; for dialogue, he relied upon colloquial Turkish.

Musa Jalil (b. 1906). Tatar (SSR) poet; his verse celebrated the rise of socialism, and he wrote one volume while in a Berlin prison; he joined the Soviet army in 1941, was wounded and eventually captured by the Germans, and then killed by a firing squad in Berlin.

Niko Lortkipanidze (b. 1880). Georgian (SSR) writer of fiction, poet, and dramatist; he wrote poems and stories of village life based upon Georgian history and critical of traditional Georgian interpretation of that history; his work ranks among the finest products of Georgian literature, and has served as a model for younger generations of Georgian writers.

Flippo Tommaso Marinetti (b. 1876). Italian poet, writer of fiction, and critic; recognized as the founder of Futurism (1909), which stressed the dynamic character of twentieth-century life, glorified war and technology, and advocated the growth of fascism; born in Egypt, he wrote in both French and Italian.

Kaj Munk (b. 1898). Danish playwright and clergyman; his drama concerned ethical issues and eventually led to the Danish dramatic revival of the 1930s; although he wrote hastily and impetuously, he produced intensely dramatic plays and highly emotional theatrical moments; his anti-Nazi views and his association with Danish freedom fighters led to his execution by the Gestapo.

Hamid Olimjon (b. 1904). Uzbek (SSR) poet and critic; he wrote verse in the tradition of Vladimir Mayakovsky and Maxim Gorki, attaining the height of his poetic creativity during World War II; as a critic he sought to establish clear criteria for Uzbek literature.

Sir Arthur Thomas Quiller-Couch (b. 1863). English essayist, poet, writer of fiction, and anthologist; his novels, abounding in romanticism and local color, focused upon his native Cornwall.

Liviu Rebreanu (b. 1885). Romanian writer of fiction, playwright, and essayist; his epic novels are comprehensive and realistic documents of the turbulent nature of life in Romania during the first two decades of the twentieth century; his fiction reflects his upbringing in the poor farming region of Transylvania and his concern for the social, economic, and spiritual problems of the Romanian peasantry; he commits suicide.

Romain Rolland (b. 1866). French novelist, biographer, historian, playwright, and critic; his fiction, particularly, expressed his ardent pacifist and humanist principles; he attempted to explore the fundamental unity of all objects and to advance his notions of humanity's proper role in the universal scheme; thus, he must be considered as much as a philosopher as a novelist or playwright; he received the Nobel Prize for literature in 1915; he dies at his small villa near Clamecy (his birthplace) at the end of the year.

Jacques Roumain (b. 1907). Haitian poet, writer of fiction, and essayist; he belonged to that group of young Haitian intellectuals who, during the late 1920s and 1930s, sought Haitian autonomy and an end to the American military occupation of that country; thus, his literary themes reflect his support of causes for the people; generally, he sought to create literature that would be both universal and in accord with the spirit of his "negritude"; he dies of a heart attack at age thirty-seven.

Antoine de Saint Exupery (b. 1900). French narrative writer and author of fiction; his work reflects his commitment to aviation, his feeling for the open skies, and his love of freedom and action; his highly successful *Little Prince* (1943) has become a classic for both adults and children; he loses his life in action in World War II.

Jacob Schaffner (b. 1875). Swiss writer of fiction; his major novels rebel against the conventions of the Swiss bourgeois.

Ida Minerva Tarbell (b. 1857). American miscellaneous prose writer and social historian; as a member of the radical social reformers known as "muckrakers," she launched biting attacks against the abuses of American industry, most notably by the Standard Oil Company; she also wrote biography.

Mehmed Emin Yurdakul (b. 1869). Turkish poet; he wrote verse in classic Turkish syllabic form, and his language was close to colloquial speech; he directed his poetry toward uneducated peasants, attempting to arouse their sense of patriotism.

PUBLICATIONS

Amma Achchygyya, *Saasky Kem* (Springtime)—a novel by the Yakut (SSR) writer of fiction, poet, and playwright; the work portrays the new Soviet citizens, with their fresh moral and spiritual qualities; the piece was exceedingly popular throughout the Soviet Union.

Said Aql, *Kadmus*—a play by the Lebanese poet and dramatist; the writer recreates themes from classical antiquity, thus introducing into Arabic literature the classical form of tragedy.

Saul Bellow, *The Dangling Man*—the first novel by the Canadian-born American writer of fiction; the writer introduces the initial version of his hero, "Joseph"; that character "dangles" because he has left his job and awaits induction into the military; written in journal form, the work depicts modern humanity as both bored and burdened by temporary freedom, in a state of liberty and alienation.

Catherine Drinker Bowen, *Yankee from Olympus*—a biography by the American writer; historical study of Justice Oliver Wendell Holmes (1841-1935) and his celebrated Massachusetts family.

Albert Camus, *Caligula*—a play by the Algerian-born French writer of fiction and dramatist; the handsome young Roman emperor grieves over the death of his sister, an event that convinces him that life can never be happy; thus, he launches upon an exercise of power that leads to his own tragic end.

Joyce Cary, *The Horse's Mouth*—a novel by the Irish writer of fiction and poet; the third volume of a trilogy, the piece concerns the world of art; the narrator and principal character is a disreputable fellow completely committed to art; essentially, he destroys so that he can create.

Alejandro Casona, *La Dama del Alba* (The Lady of the Dawn)—a play by the Spanish dramatist, poet, and essayist; focuses upon the benevolent intervention of Death, personified by the mysterious and beautiful young woman of the title; a wife attempts to make a fool of her husband; Death then claims her life, leaving the man free to find true love with another woman.

Mary Ellen Chase, *The Bible and the Common Reader*—a historical recreation and explication of Scriptures by the American scholar and writer of fiction; emphasizes the literary quality of the Old and New Testaments: the origins of the King James version, the histories of the "characters" in Scriptures, and the various genres and forms of literature presented therein.

Yahya Haqqi, *Qindil Umm Hashim* (The Lamp of Umm Hashim)—a novel by the Egyptian writer of fiction and essayist; a symbolic piece in which the principal character, an Egyptian intellectual, has assimilated modern scientific ideas and culture while in Europe; returning home, he confronts the problem of how to nurture and value the new, while continuing to live among the old traditions; he concludes that modern science and culture can only take hold in Egypt if the native traditions and heritage continue to be respected.

John Hersey, *A Bell for Adano*—a novel by the American writer of fiction; one of the most popular and successful works of fiction about World War II, later adapted to the stage and screen; focuses upon the American occupation of a small village in Sicily and the attempts to restore order, tradition, and pride among the people there; receives the Pulitzer Prize in fiction for 1945.

Muhammad Mandur, *An-Naqd al-Minhafi 'Inda 'l-Arab*— (Arab Methodical Criticism) —a volume of criticism by the Egyptian essayist; studies the methods of classical Arab critics; the writer emphasizes the reasonableness of criteria and methods based upon personal impressions and cultivated taste.

W. Somerset Maugham, *The Razor's Edge*—a novel by the English writer of fiction and playwright; emphasizes the mysticism of the East; the principal character, an American, journeys to India, resides in an "ashram," and generally embraces the principles and values of "non-attachment."

Arthur Miller, *The Man Who Had All the Luck*—a play by the American dramatist, the first of his pieces to be produced on Broadway; the protagonist feels guilty about his lifelong good fortune; he waits for retribution, and, when it does not come, he proceeds to create his own misfortune.

Alberto Moravia, *Agostino*—a novella by the Italian writer of fiction, essayist, and playwright; concerns an adolescent who loses his innocence when be becomes increasingly aware of both his sexuality and the plight of the lower classes.

Vaikkam Muhammad Basir, *Balyakala Sakhi* (Childhood Friend)—a novel by the Indian (Malayalam) writer of fiction; the events of the piece are based on the writer's early life, though the narrative does not explicitly reveal its autobiographical nature; the work is characterized by the writer's delightful sense of humor.

Oybek, *Navoiy*—a historical biography by the Uzbek (SSR) poet and writer of miscellaneous prose; concerns the Uzbek poet Alishir Navai (1441-1501); the biographer views his subject as poet, thinker, and enlightened humanist.

Katherine Anne Porter, *The Leaning Tower*—a collection of stories by the American writer of fiction; studies the effects of changes in the South upon the personalities of individuals at various stages of their lives.

Jacques Roumaine, *Gouverneurs de la Rosee* (Masters of the Dew)—a novel by the Haitian poet, writer of fiction, and essayist; the plot of this traditional peasant novel is realistic and understandable, but the story gains depth from an intricate system of literary and psychological symbolism; its poetic language contains much nature imagery; drought, barrenness, and hopelessness combine with a lack of cooperation to reduce the quality of feuding families.

William Sansom, *Fireman Flower and Other Stories*—a collection of short stories by the English writer of fiction and travel literature; the stories focus upon the writer's experiences within the National Fire Service in London during World War II.

Jean-Paul Sartre, *Huis clos* (No Exit)—a play by the French philosopher, novelist, dramatist, and essayist; three bickering characters, confined to a small room, gradually realize that they have been condemned to hell; trapped for eternity, the three repeat the sadistic and masochistic patterns of their earthly relationships, demonstrating Sartre's thesis that "hell is other people"; in this inverted model of human existence, the inmates must depend on each other for self-definition and are therefore eternally doomed to roles of tormentor and tormented.

Karl Shapiro, *V-Letter and Other Poems*—a verse collection by the American poet and essayist, based on experiences during World War II; contains social commentary, religious themes, and attacks upon intellectualism; the work includes the title piece, "Elegy for a Dead Soldier," "Troop Train," "The Gun," "Sunday: New Guinea," "Christmas Eve: Australia," "The Jew," and "The Intellectual"; awarded the Pulitzer Prize in poetry in 1945.

Junichiro Tanizaki, *Sasameyuki* (The Makioka Sisters)—a novel by the Japanese writer of fiction; celebrates the traditional Japanese woman; focuses upon the lengthy marriage negotiations and involves a reserved, delicate, but determined central character; literally translated, the title means "Light Snow."

George Macaulay Trevelyan, *English Social History*—an extremely popular account by the English historian of how ordinary English people lived between the Middle Ages and the end of the nineteenth century; an illustrated edition published between 1949 and 1952.

Tennessee Williams, *The Glass Menagerie*—a play by the American dramatist; a "memory play" that relates the story of a character who, at his mother's insistence, brings a young man home to dinner; the mother hopes the guest will become involved with her daughter, but, unfortunately, he turns out to be engaged; the mother's energy and attempts to direct the lives of others appear in stark contrast to the shyness of her slightly crippled daughter, who employs her "glass menagerie" as an escape from the world; narrated by the son, whose memories soften the harshness of events; music, lighting, and suggestive sets contribute significantly to the tone of the work.

EVENTS

Stephen Vincent Benet, American poet, is posthumously awarded the Pulitzer Prize in poetry for *Western Star* (1943).

Merle Eugene Curti, American historian, receives the Pulitzer Prize in history for *The Growth of American Thought* (1943).

Martin Archer Flavin, American playwright and writer of fiction, receives the Pulitzer Prize in fiction for his novel *Journey in the Dark* (1943).

Johannes V. Jensen, Danish writer of fiction, receives the Nobel Prize for literature.

1945

BIRTHS

John Banville. Irish writer of fiction and critic; he will experiment with the forms of fiction, relying upon metaphor, allusion, and elements from other genres to create complex aesthetic effects; he will develop enigmatic and ambiguous narratives, reflecting his belief that existence cannot be mirrored accurately by the conventional realistic novel.

Luiz Berto. Brazilian writer of fiction; his novels and stories, dependent upon history, local settings, and myth, will presume upon the reader's sense and intellectual perception; signs, devices, and "magic moments" will provide his fiction with representations of "magic realism"; his work will be characterized by a strong attention to order and structure.

Annie Dillard. American poet and essayist; her prose will focus upon ecological subjects and problems, particularly upon the preservation of the natural environment; her verse will go forward upon her sensitivity to what she observes and believes.

Isaac Goldemberg. Peruvian novelist and poet; he will examine in his fiction the psychological consequences of the Jewish diaspora (Jewish settlements outside Palestine) in his native country; he will investigate his frustrated characters' spiritual rootlessness and loss of personal identity; his prose style will appear subdued, but it will nonetheless incorporate comedy and irony.

Shivadhar Srinivasa Naipaul (d. 1985). Trinidadian writer of fiction; he will gain recognition as one of the most talented and wide-ranging writers of his generation; he will candidly record his observations of the shortcomings of life in the third world; he will eventually assume residence in London.

Gyorgy Petri. Hungarian poet; he will demonstrate that lyric poetry is an important part of the literature of his nation; he will represent the movement among younger Hungarian writers toward a distinctive originality of sensibility, subject matter, and tone; his verse will concern itself with the condition of human beings in a socialist state; his generally concrete and sometimes startling images will detail common existence.

Josep-Lluis Segui. Spanish (Catalan) essayist, poet, playwright, and writer of fiction; he will be an extremely versatile writer, even attempting the mystery novel and the detective story; he will be recognized as a philosophical writer who blends genres as the occasion demands; in his fiction, especially, he will create characters deeply rooted to the world of the theater, where the nature of reality is a significant question.

Adam Zagajewski. Polish poet; he will emerge as a major force in the verse of his nation, belonging to the angry generation of 1968 and satirizing the surreal character of the totalitarian state; he will express the political opposition of his generation through a style totally devoid of metaphor.

DEATHS

Ernst Cassier (b. 1874). German philosopher; a member of the "new School" of Immanuel Kant, he devoted himself to a critical and historical study of the problems of knowledge; he characterized the human being as a symbolic animal, maintaining that all cultural achievements (to include language, art, myth, and science) result from the human ability to conceptualize experience in artful signs or symbols.

Robert Desnos (b. 1900). French poet, writer of fiction, playwright, and essayist; one of the original members of the Surrealist movement, he was proficient at automatic writing and speaking thought while in the midst of a hypnotic sleep; eventually, he rejected the principles of surrealism and turned to traditional and structured verse forms (e.g., the sonnet); irregardless of particular literary influences, his verse achieved unity through his celebration of ecstatic love; he dies in a Nazi concentration camp of typhoid fever, only days after the camp had been liberated by the Allies.

Theodore Dreiser (b. 1871). American writer of fiction; a pioneer of naturalism in American literature, his novels reflected his mechanistic view of life, expressing the idea that human beings are victims of such ungovernable forces as economics, biology, society, and chance; he also wrote short stories, autobiographical works, and prose in reaction to events in both the U.S.S.R. and the United States.

Pierre Drieu La Rochelle (b. 1893). French writer of fiction, poet, and essayist; he joined those French intellectuals who, during the period 1918-1938, advanced the ideals of fascism and eventually collaborated with the Nazis; he believed in the formation of a martial state based upon moral vigor and physical fitness, qualities that would eliminate the spiritual malaise within France; his literary reputation suffered severely because of his politics; in March of this year, he decides to commit suicide rather than stand trial for collaboration with the Germans.

Ellen Glasgow (b. 1873). American writer of fiction; her work will be known for its realism, particularly as it reveals a history of her native state of Virginia from the middle of the nineteenth century to contemporary times; thematically, she emphasized the changing social, economic, and political orders within the South.

Georg Kaiser (b. 1878). German playwright; an expressionist, he early focused upon erotic and psychological themes; in later pieces, he explored social problems and issues, attacking the brutality of the new technology and the negative effects of industrialism upon unsuspecting human beings.

Else Lasker-Schuler (b. 1876). German poet; she became an enthusiastic propagandist of expressionism, known for her statement, "I die of life and breathe again in the image"; she wrote colorful, grotesque, and humorous poems that reflect her obsession with the intellectual nature of her symbols; to prove her commitment to color, she illustrated a number of her own volumes.

Samuel Edward Krune Loliwe Mqhayi (b. 1875). South African (Xhosa) poet, writer of fiction, and biographer; he wrote traditional African lyric poems and introduced Western fiction into Xhosa literature; through his writing, he helped to stabilize and purify the Xhosa language; he dies at his home district of Cape Province.

Pham-Quynh (b. 1892). Vietnamese literary scholar and translator; he wrote in Vietnamese, Chinese, and French; he published translations from French literature and produced critical studies of French writers and philosophers: Pierre Loti, Rene Descartes, Jean-Jacques Rousseau, Auguste Comte, Voltaire, Anatole France; he exercised a significant influence on the vocabulary of modern Vietnamese, introducing a number of words from the Chinese.

Arthur Symons (b. 1865). English poet and literary critic; he became a leading English Symbolist, interpreting the verse of the French Decadents for English readers through his criticism, translations, and poetry.

Alexey Nikolayevich Tolstoy (b. 1883). Russian writer of fiction, playwright, essayist, and poet; he gained a literary reputation for his epic novels depicting Russian history in conformity with official Soviet doctrine; thus, he significantly influenced the Soviet historical novel; he also achieved recognition for his fluent narratives and masterful characterizations; the government proclaims his death an occasion for national mourning.

Paul Valery (b. 1871). French poet and critic; a follower of the symbolists, he became one of the most noted French poets of the twentieth century; he wrote five volumes of essays and four dialogues on subjects ranging from the arts to mathematics.

PUBLICATIONS

Aziz Ahmad, *Gurez* (Flight)—a novel by the Indian (Urdu) writer of fiction, critic, and translator; relates the experiences of an Indian student in London and Paris during the late 1930s; the piece explores with frankness hitherto forbidden aspects of personal relationships.

W. H. Auden, *For the Time Being*—a poem by the English writer of verse, playwright, and essayist; subtitled "A Christmas Oratorio," the piece explicates the poet's conversion to the Christian existentialism of Soren Kierkegaard; thus, human beings must be held responsible for their acts, and they must declare their faith in fear; the poet recreates the Christian myth in contemporary terms, depicting Herod, for instance, as a well-intentioned liberal statesman whose massacre of the innocents was designed for the public good; in the end, the poet views history from the perspective of eternity.

Mohammad Taqi Bahar, *Tarikke Mokhtasare Ahzabe Siyasa, Enqeraze Qajariye* (Brief History of Political Parties, the Fall of the Qajars)—a historical study by the Iranian poet and critic; the work assumes the form of a memoir and constitutes an important source of material for the evaluation of modern Iranian history.

Hermann Broch, *Der Tod des Vergil* (The Death of Virgil)—a novel by the Austrian writer of fiction, essayist, and playwright; focuses upon the end of a cultural epoch, depicting the last day and night in the life of the Roman poet during the declining years of the Roman Empire; Virgil functions as the persona through which the structure of all such end phases of history might be expressed; the novel also incorporates the writer's concern about art as an evasion of reality and ethical responsibility.

Gwendolyn Brooks, *A Street in Bronzeville*—a verse collection by the black American poet; focuses upon typical events in the lives of ordinary black Americans; the pieces evidence a variety of points of view, an emphasis upon reality, and an avoidance of sentimentality; "The Sundays of Satin-Legs Smith" is one of the more interesting poems in the volume.

Stig Dagerman, *Ormen* (The Snake)—the first novel by the Swedish writer of fiction, playwright, essayist, and poet; focuses upon the acute dread of social, emotional, and moral collapse that characterized the post-war Swedish consciousness; the piece shifts from one character to another as the writer attempts to analyze the Swedish social and political climate; underscores the writer's belief that current society tends to by hypocritical, uncaring, and frequently absurd.

Jean Giraudoux, *La Folle de Chaillot* (The Mad Woman of Chaillot)—a play by the French novelist, essayist, and dramatist; a social satire concerning tragic heroes and heroines who willfully separate themselves from humanity and reject the order of the world; the title character, who represents the impoverished people of Paris, leads a crusade against the financiers, creating a world of good against bad; the prevailing spirit of an awakened and responsible France can, eventually, eliminate the spirit of greed.

Hermann Hesse, *Der Glasperlenspiel* (The Glass Bead Game)—a novel by the German writer of fiction, poet, and critic; concerns the quest for perfection; focuses upon an idealized society in the midst of disintegrating because of its commitment to the spirit; the principal character, in a state of despair because he cannot achieve, drowns himself; however, his suicide suggests hope for those who will follow him.

Randall Jarrell, *Little Friend, Little Friend*—a collection of poems by the American writer of verse and essayist; the pieces establish a tone of attraction to death; the poet concerns himself with both the techniques and the psychology of war in the air.

Philip Larkin, *The North Ship*—the first collection of poems by the English writer of verse and fiction; the pieces reveal the decided influence of the work of William Butler Yeats and tend to be highly rhetorical in form and substance; a revised edition in 1966.

Carlo Levi, *Cristo si e Fermato a Eboli* (Christ Stopped at Eboli)—a novel by the Italian writer of fiction; based on the writer's experiences when exiled by the fascists to the remote island of Lucania; focuses upon a village so remote that Christianity has not yet come to it; most importantly, the writer provides an extremely accurate picture of life in the south of Italy.

Sinclair Lewis, *Cass Timberlane*—a novel by the American writer of fiction; the work contains a number of violent attacks upon women, developing the thesis that American men are afraid of their wives; the principal female character, nonetheless, is one of the writer's most engaging creations; the novel contains strong suggestions of sexual relationships but does not remotely approach pornography.

George Orwell, *Animal Farm*—a novel by the English writer of fiction and essayist; essentially a satire upon the Soviet Union and the transformation of communism from a political idea to an exercise in totalitarianism; thus, the animals on the farm revolt against their human masters, drive them out, and establish a tyrannical state in which power corrupts; thus, all animals exist in a state of utter equality, except that certain ones become more equal than others.

Jean-Paul Sartre, *Les Chemins de la Liberte* (The Roads to Freedom)—a novel, the initial volume of a trilogy, by the French writer of fiction, critic, philosopher, and playwright; reflects the writer's philosophical moment of indecision between individualism and collectivism.

Karl Shapiro, *Essay on Rime*—a poem by the American writer of verse and critic; a long piece that constitutes a treatise on the art of poetry; the thirty-two-year-old writer would eagerly proceed to set forth clear guidelines about what poets should and should not attempt; the work was criticized because of the perceived immaturity of the writer.

John Steinbeck, *Cannary Row*—a novel by the American writer of fiction; set in Monterey, California, the work focuses upon a single street at the edge of the Pacific Ocean that represents a careless, lusty, carefree world, where men from the fishing fleets find their entertainment and bars and houses.

Evelyn Waugh, *Brideshead Revisited*—a novel by the English writer of fiction; describes the narrator's relationship with an aristocratic Roman Catholic family whose country home is at the center of the novel's major themes; Waugh's narrative, an unusual blend of satiric wit and genuine nostalgia, explores "the workings of the Divine Purpose in a pagan world," as the author himself stated.

Richard Wright, *Black Boy*—an autobiography by the American writer of fiction; noteworthy for its account of the life and times of black youth; more moderate in tone than his novel *Native Son* (1940), the work was nonetheless shockingly realistic; most importantly, the piece reveals the extent of the writer's horror at the black man's collaboration with white society to keep him in a subservient state.

EVENTS

Mary Coyle Chase, American playwright and writer of books for children, receives the Pulitzer Prize in drama for *Harvey* (1944).

Commentary, a monthly periodical devoted to Jewish cultural advancement and American creativity, begins publication in New York City, succeeding the *Contemporary Jewish Record* (begun 1938); contributors include Alfred Kazin, Bernard Malamud, Norman Mailer, James Baldwin, and Lionel Trilling.

John Richard Hersey, American writer of fiction and nonfiction, receives the Pulitzer Prize in fiction for his novel *A Bell for Adano* (1944).

The Melville Society, an academic scholarly organization devoted to the study of the works of Herman Melville, the American writer of fiction and poet, established.

Gabriela Mistral (pseudonym of Lucila Godoy Alcayaga), Chilean poet, receives the Nobel Prize for literature.

Karl Jay Shapiro, American poet and critic receives the Pulitzer Prize in poetry for *V-Letter and Other Poems* (1944).

The Woodrow Wilson National Fellowship Foundation established for the advancement of academic study and scholarship.

1946

BIRTHS

Octavio Armand. Cuban-born writer of fiction, poet, and translator; he will be concerned little with theme and will instead be preoccupied with the arbitrariness of linguistic forms, with sensory experience, and with the puzzle of identity; he will reveal to readers a sense of playful eccentricity and will create new metaphors.

Andrei Codrescu. Romanian-born American poet; he will compose brief, frank pieces of verse noted for their exacting imagery and playful irreverence; the substance of his poetry will be principally autobiographical, focusing upon recollections of his youth in communist Romania and his experiences as an expatriate in Rome, Paris, and the United States; he will also provide perceptive insights into American culture.

Alexander Kaletski. Russian writer of fiction; after a successful career in Russian theater, dance, film, and television, he will produce highly successful autobiographical fiction reflecting his youth and theatrical apprenticeship in Moscow; most of it will be anti-Soviet; he will emigrate to New York City in 1975.

Franz Xavier Kroetz. German playwright and author of nonfiction; his drama will be characterized by realism and minimal dialogue; his plays will explicitly depict the sexual, cultural, social, and economic conflicts of the rural and urban working class of West Germany; thus, he will manipulate colloquial language and middle-class settings; for him, language will become less meaningful than the gestures and silences of his characters.

Kenji Nakagami. Japanese writer of fiction; his early work will reveal his interests in left wing politics, jazz, and the small theater groups in Tokyo; he will then turn his attention to proletarianism and naturalism; he will eschew the intellectual and introspective influences of his predecessors.

Montserrat Roig. Spanish (Catalan) writer of fiction; his work will be charmingly poetic and deeply symbolic; he will explore complex and often irregular family relationships, doing so by introducing (in a single piece) several narrators with various points of view; for his characters, the processes of life will appear both strange and unnatural.

Irini Spanidou. Greek-born American writer of fiction; she will recreate her own experiences, with emphasis upon her emigration from Thessaly to New York City at age eighteen; she will focus her attention upon her characters' innocence, the mystery and expectation as one begins life in a new world; for her, the world of children is a microcosm of adulthood.

DEATHS

Countee Cullen (b. Countee L. Porter, 1903). American poet and a major figure of the Harlem Renaissance of the 1920s; applied traditional verse forms to black American themes; although his verse was racially inspired, he nonetheless consciously sought to capture the essence of poetic beauty.

Umar Fakhuri (b. 1895). Lebanese essayist and journalist; he became one of the most active propagators of progressive antifascist ideals in Arab culture and literature; he developed stimulating ideas on the theoretical aspects of literature and its relation to reality, on literary techniques, on aesthetics, on the function of art in modern life, and on the place of the writer in society.

Harley Granville-Barker (b. 1877). English theatrical director and producer, playwright, and critic; he gained a literary reputation for his prefaces to Shakespeare's plays, studies presented from the perspective of theatrical producer rather than literary scholar.

Gerhart Hauptmann (b. 1862). German playwright, novelist, and poet; he inaugurated the Naturalist movement in German drama, after which he turned his attention to romantic themes; for three generations, he stood as one of the leading figures of German literature, as well as a sincere humanitarian; in 1905, Oxford university conferred upon him an honorary doctorate in letters, and he received the Nobel Prize for literature in 1912.

John Maynard Keynes (b. 1883). English economist and essayist; his theories are among the most influential economic formulations of the twentieth century; his major publications focused upon the economic consequences of the Treaty of Versailles and the general need for governments to intervene in the market during periods of recession; he also helped to gather support for the formation of a world bank.

Alfred Damon Runyon (b. 1884). American writer of fiction and journalist; he gained a literary reputation for his humorous stories that focused upon the Broadway, sporting, and underworld characters of New York City; he conveyed, through those characters, the slang and idiom of actual life in New York City, a life devoid of affectation.

Sri (pseudonym of B. M. Srikanthayya; b. 1884). Indian (Kannada) translator and critic; he inspired a renaissance in Kannada poetry with his translations of William Wordsworth, Percy Bysshe Shelley, and Robert Burns; he also introduced new meters and poetic diction to a rising generation of poets; in addition, he published a number of his own prose poems.

Gertrude Stein (b. 1874). American-born writer of fiction and narrative, critic, and poet; she spent the years from 1902 until her death living abroad, mostly in Paris; during the 1920s, she established a cultural salon, serving as the patron for such figures as Pablo Picasso, Henri Matisse, Ernest Hemingway, Sherwood Anderson, and F. Scott Fitzgerald; her own writing tended to be innovative and experimental, emphasizing the sounds and the rhythms of words, rather than their meanings; a versatile author, she wrote short stories, narratives, autobiographical and biographical pieces, critical essays, cubist poetry, and even operas.

Booth Tarkington (b. 1869). American writer of fiction and playwright; he gained recognition for novels of small-town Midwestern life; he received the Pulitzer Prize for fiction in 1919.

H. G. Wells (b. 1866). English writer of fiction, essayist, and social historian and philosopher; best known today as one of the forerunners of modern science fiction and as a utopian idealist who foretold an era of chemical warfare, atomic weaponry, and world wars; several of his works are considered classics in the genres of science fiction and science fantasy; his general introduction to world history remained popular until well after his death.

Wen I-to (b. 1899). Chinese poet, essayist, and literary critic; he blended in his work Eastern and Western imagery, symbolism, and themes; his poetry and his prose advocated a return to structured patterns with rhyme, as opposed to formless free verse; he called for a moderate course between pure aestheticism and political propaganda; he died at the hand of a political assassin.

PUBLICATIONS

Peter Lee Abrahams, *Mine Boy*—a novel by the South African writer of fiction and poet; one of the earliest books to dramatize the plight of blacks in South Africa; the second novel by a black South African to be published in English (the first, by Solomon Plaatje, was *Mhudi*, which appeared in 1930); describes the life of a kindly illiterate who endures brutal experiences while working in the mines.

Aziz Ahmad, *Ag* (Fire)—a novel by the Indian (Urdu) writer of fiction and criticism; demonstrates the rise of political consciousness in the area of Kashmir.

Jacques Audiberti, *Quoat-Quoat*—a play by the French dramatist, poet, novelist, and essayist; a satire upon nineteenth-century melodrama; a spy, absurdly condemned to death, gains his release from the captain of a ship; the vessel itself serves as a world at the mercy of primitive forces; the spy commits suicide, for only in death can he determine his own destiny; the captain then destroys the ship, returning the world to its state of nothingness.

Mukhtar Auezov, *Abay Zholy* (Abay's Road)—a biographical novel by the Kazakh (SSR) writer of fiction and playwright; an extremely popular piece that concerns the founder of Kazakh literature; translated into several languages.

Simone de Beauvoir, *Tous les Hommes Sont Mortels* (All Men Are Mortals)—a novel by the French philosopher, writer of fiction, essayist, and playwright; the piece traces, from the fourteenth century to the present, the existence of an Italian who drinks an immortality potion and tries to prove that immortality exists as a meaningless state; in general, an individual that gains eternal life would eventually see the ruin of all of his projects.

Jean Cocteau, *L'Aigle a Deux Tetes* (The Eagle Has Two Heads)—a play by the French dramatist, poet, novelist, essayist; a melodrama in which a young poet allegorically represents the angel of death; he falls in love with a puppet empress and, tragically, attempts to help her regain her power.

Theodore Dreiser, *The Bulwark*—a novel by the American writer of fiction; the moral scruples of a Quaker businessman, Solon Barnes, come up against the reality of American business dealings; as his children drift from him and from Quaker principles, he finds (as a sick and dying old man) consolation in mysticism; in a reversal for Dreiser, Barnes, as the upholder of traditional mores

and values, is portrayed sympathetically and without the usual implied charge of hypocrisy.

Lillian Hellman, *Another Part of the Forest*—a play by the American dramatist; the playwright looks back upon the youth of the Hubbard family and observes the development of their values under the influence of their greedy father and helpless mother; the writer condemns the ethics of materialism, at the same time developing strong dramatic characters.

Philip Larkin, *Jill*—an autobiographical novel by the English poet and writer of fiction; essentially a study of a fragile and lonely young person; set in wartime Oxford, the work describes the undergraduate career of a working-class lad from Lancashire who confronts socially privileged individuals; the title character is the boy's "sister," a product of his imagination.

Carson McCullers, *The Member of the Wedding*—a novel by the American writer of fiction; a brilliant portrayal of an adolescent girl struggling toward individuation, the novel probes issues of sexuality, racial prejudice, and death.

Eugene O'Neill, *The Iceman Cometh*—a play by the American dramatist; a lengthy analysis of human frailty and self-deception in which the exiles and failures of life lead drunken and confusing existences as they attempt to regain their lost status; a principal character forces them to confront the utter uselessness of their hopes; drink and guilt permeate the piece, as well as the attempt to abandon illusion; death becomes the only real hope.

Theodor Plievier, *Stalingrad*—a documentary novel by the German writer of fiction and journalist; highly journalistic and lacking depth of characterization, the work nonetheless conveys a convincing portrait of the collapse of the German military machine during the Russian campaign of World War II.

Dylan Thomas, *Deaths and Entrances*—a collection of verse by the Welsh poet, playwright, and writer of fiction; the volume contains traditional, logical, and controlled narrative pieces; the principal poem, "A Winter's Tale," demonstrates how the poet, as well as every human being, achieves personal salvation through the imagination.

Vrndavanlal Varma, *Jhansi Ki Rani Laksmibai* (Laksmibai, Queen of Jhansi)—a historical novel by the Indian (Hindi) writer of fiction; sets forth a modern view of the Indian Mutiny of 1857 as the initial struggle for the freedom of India.

Robert Penn Warren, *All the King's Men*—a novel by the American poet, writer of fiction, and critic; focuses upon the career of Huey Long and the corrupting power of the prominent politician; the principal character/narrator attempts to comprehend the evil generated by the corrupt politician, and in doing so discovers his own identity; the work is awarded the Pulitzer Prize for fiction in 1947.

Eudora Welty, *Delta Wedding*—a novel by the American writer of fiction; considered a drama of resistance to history, as it relates the story of a single week, in 1923, in the lives of a family; the characters exist in a world that has ceased to represent the reality of the past in the present; thus, the family lives in a fantasy that serves only to expose their loneliness and anxiety; only a single character approaches the real world.

William Carlos Williams, *Paterson*—a long poem by the American playwright and writer of verse and fiction; the work reflects the poet's disillusionment with the American dream; nonetheless, he manages to find ways out of that despair: love, virtue, creativity; the realism of the work derives from the writer's recognition that not all the answers will prove the correct choices; in the end, the poet aspires to a form of modern-day heaven, where the right answers can be attained at least through implication; five vols., to 1958.

Karl Zuckmayer, *Des Teufels General* (The Devil's General)—a play by the German dramatist, writer of fiction, and poet; the piece was suggested by the airplane suicide of Ernst Udet, a World War I fighter pilot; as a quartermaster general of the German air ministry during World War II, he aroused the enmity of the Gestapo; in general, the play depicts with accuracy the domination of Germany by the Nazis, focusing upon the cowardice of those who oppose the regime, but do nothing about it.

EVENTS

The British Arts Council established in London for the advancement of cultural and intellectual activities.

Russel Crouse, American playwright and journalist, and playwright Howard Lindsay receive the Pulitzer Prize in drama for *State of the Union* (1945).

Hermann Hesse, German writer of fiction and poet, receives the Nobel Prize for literature.

The New Bodleian Library, Oxford, completed and opened.

The Rocky Mountain Review, a quarterly journal of general literature, moves its editorial offices to Lawrence, Kansas, and becomes the *Western Review.*

1947

BIRTHS

Patrick Grainville. French writer of fiction; he will write a number of highly regarded novels that, according to one reviewer, will let loose "a flood of lyricism and poetry, but also a torrent of eroticism"; essentially, his fiction will come forth as a sexual carnival; he will become a professor of literature, a frequent contributor to the French literary periodicals, and a recipient of the Prix Goncourt (1976).

Reto Hanny. Swiss writer of fiction; he will produce scathing and grotesque satire; he will assess and condemn the development of Western nations; he will advocate a transcendence of the greedy and trendy society of the twentieth century, but he will come to realize that flight from a corrupted earth will end in nothing but a resounding "crash."

Evan X. Hyde. Belize poet, playwright, and writer of fiction; educated in America, he will, in his early poetry, focus upon such problems in American society as violence and racism; his plays will concern the triumph of love over the privation and isolation of the Caribbean poor.

David Mamet. American playwright; he will develop a flawless gift for reproducing colloquial speech; he will focus upon small-time crooks, real estate salesmen, and the relationships between teachers and their pupils; his work will combine especially harsh dialogue and extraordinary insight into the complexity of human relationships; he will receive the Pulitzer Prize for drama in 1984.

Roi Patursson. Danish (Faeroe Islands) poet; he will become a sailor, then move to Denmark to study philosophy and write; he will become an ardent experimentalist, attempting to control his creative vigor; he will work with different styles and sources of poetic inspiration to produce verse that is both serious and cheerful.

Evelin E. Sullivan. West German writer of fiction; she will develop a form of literary biography; she will parody both the detective novel and the literary life; in 1965, she will settle in the United States and teach at Stanford University.

George F. Walker. Canadian playwright; his work will embrace "black humor," underscoring his resolve not to offer neat resolutions to the troublesome problems of contemporary society; he will set his plays in lower-class urban areas, concerning himself with people who have been bullied and manipulated into associations with groups dedicated to the destruction of law and order.

DEATHS

Gabra Iyasus Afawark (b. 1868). Ethiopian (Amharic) novelist and poet; his work reveals his consciousness of Italian culture, yet he was also a fervent Ethiopian patriot; an early supporter of modernization, he advocated in both his fiction and verse the necessity of change in order for Ethiopia to avoid both domination and disintegration; he died at Jimma, totally blind, at age seventy-nine.

Willa Sibert Cather (b. 1876). American writer of fiction; her fictional themes concerned frontier settlers, the artist's need for freedom from inhibiting influences, and the North American past; she combined history, religion, and extremely attractive characterization; her style—clear, charming, and stately—has been judged among the finest in twentieth-century American fiction.

Hans Fallada (pseudonym of Rudolf Ditzen; b. 1893). German writer of fiction; for his fictional subjects, he focused upon the "little man" and the innocent victim; essentially, his work reflects his lifelong attraction to human survival amidst extremely harsh circumstances; ultimately, he went to prison for stealing, the result of his need to maintain his drug supply.

Abdurrauf Fitrat (b. 1884). Tajik and Uzbek (SSR) writer of fiction, playwright, and essayist; in simple and easily understood prose, he attacked the lack of modernity within Central Asia, specifically in the area of education; his

fiction tends toward the satirical, while his drama emphasizes a nationalistic point of view.

Ricarda Huch (b. 1864). German poet, novelist, critic, and historian; her prose style tended to be lofty, and her subjects appeared aristocratic; she wrote sentimental verse, as well as intelligent detective fiction.

Khai-Hung (originally Tran-khanh-Du; b. 1896). Vietnamese writer of fiction and journalist; a prolific and strongly Buddhist writer; his work demonstrates the characteristics of Vietnamese Romanticism, developing dreamlike and often unrealistic characters; politically, he gained a reputation as an advocate of the Nationalist Party, in direct opposition to Ho-chi-Minh.

Manuel Machado (b. 1874). Spanish playwright and poet; the source of his verse was Andalusian popular poetry; he became a dramatic spokesman for the fascist revolution.

Gregorio Martinez-Sierra (b. 1881). Spanish playwright, novelist, and poet; his work was exceptionally sentimental, and he usually selected women and women's problems for subjects; generally, he emerged as a socially outspoken member of the literati, although his technique tended to be quite subtle.

Yonejiro Noguchi (b. 1875). Japanese poet and critic; he wrote in both Japanese and English; he sought to stimulate Western interest in Japanese art and artists.

Charles Bernard Nordhoff (b. 1887). London-born American writer of historical fiction; he combined efforts with James Norman Hall to produce historical fiction about such subjects as the H.M.S. *Bounty* mutiny and the American flying corps in France during World War I.

Charles Ferdinand Ramuz (b. 1878). Swiss writer of fiction; his work concerns the common people of his native canton of Vaud and reflects their dialect.

Koda Rohan (b. 1867). Japanese writer of fiction, poet, essayist, and historian; he attempted to reject naturalistic and sociopolitical trends, devoting his efforts to themes and techniques of classical Chinese literature; his highly idealistic fiction relies upon ornate and traditional styles; mysticism and supernatural phenomena also play major roles in his fiction, warning of the dangers of straying from the paths of cultural enlightenment.

Benedict Wallet Bambatha Vilakazi (b. 1906). South African (Zulu) poet and novelist; his early Zulu verse reflects Western influence and his Zulu fiction focuses upon modern subject matter; he became a specialist in the area of Bantu language; he eventually joined the faculty of Bantu studies at Pius XII University College at Roma, Lesotho.

Alfred North Whitehead (b. 1861). English philosopher and mathematician; his inquiries into the structure of science provided the background for his work in metaphysics; he created a special vocabulary for the philosophy of organism and viewed the universe as consisting of processes of becoming, God being interdependent with the world and developing from it.

PUBLICATIONS

Nelson Algren, *The Neon Wilderness*—a collection of short stories by the American writer of fiction; the pieces focus, in general, upon the lives of the lower classes in Chicago and Detroit (the backgrounds for most of writer's work).

Maxwell Anderson, *Joan of Lorraine*—a drama by the American playwright; its most significant aspect focuses upon the study of Joan of Arc through the device of a group of actors rehearsing a play about the title character.

Saul Bellow, *The Victim*—a novel by the American writer of fiction; concerns the subject of "Jewishness"; the principal character, a Jewish journalist worries about his position in life; after being persecuted by a mad and drunken antisemite, the journalist finally finds someone *he* can hate; the struggle can end only when he discovers the virtues of human dignity.

Albert Camus, *La Peste* (The Plague)—a novel by the French writer of fiction and playwright; concerns a plague that affects Oran, Algeria, in the 1940s; the rat-carried virus represents despair and leads to total acceptance of absurdity; only the writer's own sense of humanism preserves the order of the piece.

Elley, *Sakha Sarggyta* (The Fortune of Yakutsk)—a ballad by the Yakut (SSR) poet; a poetic vision of the history of the writer's land and its people; contains the principal elements of the poetic folk tale.

Girakhpuri Firaq, *Rup* (Shapes)—a collection of erotic quatrains by the Indian (Urdu) lyric poet; the pieces constitute a synthesis of Western and Islamic culture and gather ancient Hindu and Buddhist motifs; the poet relies upon both Urdu and Sanskrit imagery.

Jean Genet, *Les Bonnes* (The Maids)—a play (his first produced) by the French dramatist, novelist, and poet; based upon the actual murder of an upper-class mistress by her female servants; a ritualistic drama of uncertain identities in which two sisters assume the roles of sadistic employer and submissive servant, each enacting her powers of fantasy and revenge; their attempts to kill their real mistress fail, and thus one sister takes her own life while the other reads a eulogy; the thesis of the piece embraces the notion that all acts are carried forth to completion and assume a "beautiful" end.

Maun Htin, *Nga Bha* (The Peasant Nga Ba)—a novel by the Burmese writer of fiction; a simple but vivid picture of the difficult life of a Burmese peasant; set during the period of the Japanese occupation of the area.

Philip Larkin, *A Girl in Winter*—a novel by the English poet and writer of fiction; concerns one day in the life of a female refugee, a librarian who works in a drab English provincial town; the strength of the work rests upon a lengthy flashback about an abortive adolescent romance with someone with whom she had been corresponding.

Thomas Mann, *Doktor Faustus*—a novel by the German writer of fiction and essayist; the piece, on one level, attacks the expressionist artist as somewhat devilish, since creativity has been bought at the terrible price of disease; on the political level, unbridled expressionism turns to fascism; the artist as criminal can easily be linked to the problems arising from Nazism.

Arthur Miller, *All My Sons*—a drama by the American playwright; concerns a manufacturer who has sold defective parts to the Air Force, causing a number of planes to fail; his partner goes to prison, but the principal character possesses few feelings of guilt; one of his sons, a pilot, seeks death because of his father's guilt, while the other son confronts him concerning his responsibility for the deaths of others; the father comes to realize that all the young men who fought and died in the war had become his "sons," and thus he takes his own life; the work receives the Drama Critics Circle Award for the best American play of the season.

Foteh Niyoza, *Intiqomi Tojik* (Tajik Vengeance)—a prose collection by the Iranian (Tajik) poet and writer of fiction; contains historically valuable stories and narrative accounts from the front during World War II.

Vladimir Nabokov, *Bend Sinister*—a novel in English by the Russian writer of fiction, poet, playwright, and essayist; a political piece that recounts the struggle of a world-renowned philosopher to defend human values against a tyrannical police state that has dedicated itself to eliminating individuality; the philosopher dies attempting to murder the dictator of the nation.

Budd Schulberg, *The Harder They Fall*—a novel by the American writer of fiction; focuses upon the evil and crime arising from prize fighting in the United States; based upon the unfortunate experience of an Argentine boxer named Primo Carnero, who fought a series of "pre-arranged" bouts before being badly mauled in one that could (or would) not be fixed.

Karl Shapiro, *Trial of a Poet, and Other Poems*—a collection by the American writer of verse; important to the poet's development, since the pieces demonstrate that he had transcended the impersonal mode and become strongly confessional; although containing strict and traditional quatrains, the volume reveals the poet's experimentation with what he termed "the prosody of prose"; the piece entitled "Recapitulations" remains one of his finest.

Stephen Spender, *Poems of Dedication*—a collection by the English poet; known particularly for its revelation of personal and private concerns, elements not usually found in his more public and social verse; the volume is essentially a group of elegies dedicated to the poet's sister-in-law.

Mickey Spillane, *I, the Jury*—a novel by the American writer of popular fiction; introduces the tough, hard hitting, and sexually overactive detective-hero Mike Hammer; that character's exploits become more important than the loose strands of mystery and crime that hold the piece together.

John Steinbeck, *The Wayward Bus*—a novel by the American writer of fiction; a group of Americans find themselves stranded on a bus somewhere in rural California; the characters voice their frustrations about life in the United States.

Robert Penn Warren, *The Circus in the Attic*—a collection of short stories by the American writer of fiction, poet, and literary critic; the pieces tend to focus upon the thoughts and emotions of the people from the American South; includes, in addition to the title work, such stories as "Blackberry Winter" and "The Patented Gate and the Mean Hamburger."

Richard Wilbur, *The Beautiful Changes, and Other Poems*—the first collection by the American writer of verse; the poet writes frankly and directly about beauty; he appears totally delighted by the sounds, sights, and movements of the world, which he attempts to recreate; the volume reverberates with the poet's wit, imagination, and playfulness, yet he maintains control over his emotions.

Tennessee Williams, *A Streetcar Named Desire*—a drama by the American playwright; the principal character, a delicate Southern woman, labors under the burdens of sexual desire, preoccupation with death, and guilt over her husband's suicide; she flees to her married sister's home in New Orleans, but she suffers more after being raped by her animal-like brother-in-law; she goes mad; the play receives both a Pulitzer Prize and the Drama Critics Circle Award.

Yvor Winters, *In Defense of Reason*—a volume of criticism by the American poet and critic; the work contains earlier essays—"Primitivism and Decadence" (1937), "Maule's Curse" (1938), and "The Anatomy of Nonsense" (1943); the writer attacks obscurantism and Romanticism; he also includes an essay on Hart Crane.

EVENTS

The Bibliographical Society of the University of Virginia established.

Andre Gide, French writer of fiction, essayist, and playwright, receives the Nobel Prize for literature.

Robert Lowell, American writer of verse, receives the Pulitzer Prize in poetry for *Lord Weary's Castle* (1946).

Robert Penn Warren, American poet, writer of fiction, and critic, receives the Pulitzer Prize in fiction for his novel *All the King's Men* (1946).

1948

BIRTHS

Kathy Acker. American novelist; she will write fiction based upon the trials and adventures of young but "tough" women; hers will be the voice of the brash, feisty, sexy, and smart woman; her novels will blend autobiography, eroticism, violence, and sensuality.

Aldo Busis. Italian writer of fiction; his works will develop strong love-hate relationships between his characters; they will also make use of the writer's varied experiences as substitute teacher, interpreter, and chauffeur; he will translate into Italian various works by German, French, English, and American writers.

Katherine Govier. Canadian writer of fiction; she will portray women undergoing the process of self-discovery and attempt to reconstruct their sense of personal identity; she will develop an interest in the inner lives of serious-minded women who must reveal themselves totally so as to survive and succeed; her work will be rooted in what may be termed "the Canadian experience."

Bodo Kirchhoff. West German writer of fiction; he will become recognized for his exuberant language, through which he will transmit the thoughts and reactions of his characters; those characters, although jaded by their own preoccupations, will, nonetheless, be extremely sympathetic creatures.

Erika Ritter. Canadian playwright and essayist; she will explore in her drama the problems of contemporary women who attempt to assert their individualities and principles while maintaining their careers and romances; for her characters, work will represent individual expression and relationships will stand for sexual expression; she will also manipulate dialogue to underscore the ambiguities within her characters' lives.

Leslie Marmon Silko. American writer of fiction and poet, of native American and Mexican ancestry; she will study law before devoting her energies to teaching and writing; she will rely in her work upon Indian materials and sources, but at the same time attempt to reach a universal audience; she will stress the importance of maintaining the native American community and culture.

George Szirtes. Hungarian-born English poet and critic; his verse will reflect his dual interests in painting and poetry; thus, he will attempt to capture subtle meaning in imaginative and original description; he will also respond to the everyday world, blending intense, and often surreal, imagery with witty observation; the themes of his poems will relate to love, art, and politics.

Michitsuna Takahashi. Japanese writer of fiction and sportswriter; his fiction will focus upon Japanese youth living abroad, as well as upon the ideals, friendships, and budding sexualities of the young; in 1974, he will receive the seventeenth Gunzo New Writers Prize, and four years later the seventy-ninth Akutagawa Prize.

DEATHS

Sabahattin Ali (b. 1906). Turkish writer of fiction; he acquired as a young man, a thorough knowledge of German, German literature, and Western culture; his fiction, informed by these influences, opened a new era in Turkish literature; he gained recognition for his clear style, penetrating psychological observations, and pitiless exposure of social evils; murdered at the height of his literary career.

Georges Bernanos (b. 1888). French writer of fiction; his novels, particularly, reflected his commitment to both Catholicism and mysticism; in his diaries, he condemned the politics of Francisco Franco's fascist Spain.

Osamu Dazai (pseudonym of Tsushima Shuji; b. 1909). Japanese writer of fiction; his work displays an obsession with suicide, ironic and gloomy wit, and intense fantasy; he also concerned himself with the issue of the decline of the Japanese nobility following World War II.

Susan Glaspell (b. 1876). American writer of fiction and playwright; an idealist, she eventually came to question the values and mores of her own Midwestern upbringing; she concerned herself with such themes as illegitimacy, divorce, unionism, socialist politics, evolution, pacifism, women's rights, and the problems arising from small-town life.

Vicente Huidobra (b. 1893). Chilean poet, novelist, essayist, and playwright; through his work, he challenged the conventions and traditions of literary practice; for him, poetry could no longer imitate nature with images of the real world; instead, the poet must create a new world by inventing entirely original images that transcend the confines of ordinary experience; he believed controversy to be a dynamic part and function of literary development; he died from a stroke, partially brought about from a head wound suffered in World War II (he had gone to France in 1944 as a war correspondent).

Alfred Kerr (pseudonym of Alfred Kempner; b. 1867). German poet and critic; his verse and criticism reflected his dedication to naturalism; thus, he imitated and defended the work of Henrik Ibsen and Gerhart Hauptmann; he has been credited with destroying the literary reputation of the German playwright and novelist Hermann Sudermann (1857-1928).

Krsnaji Prabhakar Khadilkar (b. 1872). Indian (Marathi) playwright; he developed a literary reputation in India by relying upon the stage as an outlet for his covert, anti-British political propaganda during the period of intense nationalism.

Cannampuza Krsna Pilla (b. 1914). Indian (Malayalam) poet; his popularity stemmed from his adoption of the romanticism of earlier generations, along with his introduction of frank personal experiences as the themes of his poems; his love poetry focuses upon despair, and he also wrote verse in support of social revolution; he died prematurely from tuberculosis.

Emil Ludwig (b. 1881). German biographer; his work was noted for its literary merit, particularly for its vivid prose; however, he did not always pay careful attention to historical or biographical fact; his principal biographies include those on Johann Wolfgang von Goethe, Napoleon I, and Otto von Bismarck.

Dehati Mohammad Mas'ud (b. 1905?). Persian novelist and journalist; he analyzed in his fiction the problems tormenting the young postwar generation in Iran, particularly their inability to find a place for themselves in society; a skeptic, he tended toward naturalism and coarse expression, yet maintained formal fictional structure; he died at the hand of an assassin.

Claude McKay (b. 1889). Jamaican-born poet, novelist, and literary critic; his work reveals his lifelong involvement in political and religious value conflicts; although he left Jamaica in 1912, his verse displayed his continuing nostalgia for his homeland and demonstrated keen insight into its people; he also carried on, in his writing, a long struggle for racial

justice; he lies buried in the Borough of Queens, New York City.

Thomas Mokopu Mofolo (b. 1876). African (Lesothan) novelist; his fiction focuses upon the radical effect of Christian teachings upon African society; it reveals the influence of African religious tradition, of African and European history, and of such writers as H. Rider Haggard and Marie Corelli.

Putamaippittan (b. 1906). Indian (Tamil) writer of fiction, poet, and essayist; a prolific writer, he will primarily be remembered for his short stories, which number over two hundred; although his fiction tends to be highly imitative of Guy de Maupassant and Anton Chekhov, it nonetheless deserves recognition for its ruthless and frank exposure of the failings of modern Hindu society; his work also contains ample humor, pathos, and satire; he died in extreme poverty, suffering from consumption.

PUBLICATIONS

Maxwell Anderson, *Anne of the Thousand Days*—a play by the American dramatist; a tragicomedy that portrays the relationship between King Henry VIII of England and Anne Boleyn.

W. H. Auden, *The Age of Anxiety: A Baroque Eclogue*—a verse drama by the English poet and essayist; the thesis of the piece concerns the acknowledgment of guilt as the basis for freedom; a reflection of the isolation of humankind, the piece begins at night, in a New York City bar, and concludes at dawn, on the street; produced on the stage in 1954; awarded the Pulitzer Prize in poetry in this year.

Dhun-Nun Ayyub, *al-Yad Wa'l-ard Wa'l-ma* (The Hand, the Earth, and the Water)—a novel in Arabic by the Iraqi writer of fiction; relates the poignant story of a group of Iraqis who, led by a lawyer, attempt to assist landless peasants by renting uncultivated land and forming a cooperative there; the project fails, but the writer hails the attempt itself as a victory for humanity.

Jacques N. Bahelele, *Kinzonzi ye Ntekolo andi Makundu* (Kinzonzi and His Grandson Makundu)—a novel by the Zaire (Kikongo) writer of fiction and poet; the title character, a young man, learns the wisdom of his people by studying some three hundred proverbs and other traditional lore from his grandfather.

John Berryman, *The Dispossessed*—a collection of verse by the American poet, begun while an undergraduate at Princeton; the pieces tend to be traditional in form and meter; demonstrating the influences of W. B. Yeats and W. H. Auden, they focus upon the crises of the times and display an objective tone.

Mongo Betti, *Mission Terminee*—a novel by the Cameroon writer of fiction; a humorous and ironic account of the native hero being manipulated in and out of bizarre situations; ultimately, the work attacks the European educational system, which had unsettled two generations of Africans; that system, according to the writer, alienated natives from their own culture and provided them with only the rudiments of Western learning and tradition; thus, the principal character must rely on humor and irony because he has failed his baccalaureate examinations; the work receives the Sainte-Beuve Prize for this year.

Truman Capote, *Other Voices, Other Rooms*—a novel by the American writer of fiction; the principal character, a boy, enters into a decadent homosexual relationship with a transvestite; during this time, the house of the boy's father, who is paralyzed, gradually sinks into the swamp upon which it was built; essentially, the boy has gone upon a pilgrimage that takes him through a world that has been violated.

James Gould Cozzens, *Guard of Honor*—a novel by the American writer of fiction; a detailed account of three days at a United States Air Corps training base in Florida in 1943; a conservative analysis of routine military life on the home front; awarded the Pulitzer Prize in fiction in 1949.

T. S. Eliot, *Notes towards a Definition of Culture*—a prose tract by the American-born poet and critic; the writer emphasizes the importance of universal culture, as opposed to culture that simply pertains to a group or an individual; manners, knowledge, philosophy, and the arts constitute culture; maintains that culture functions best in a society of classes, rather than in a closed structure with an intellectual elite; finally, sub-cultures prove valuable, since they provide the necessary intellectual tension and stimulus for the imagination.

William Faulkner, *Intruder in the Dust*—a novel by the American writer of fiction; explains how a white boy manages to save a black man from the lynch mob; essentially, the boy has come to understand how human beings should treat each other; the work almost exists as a treatise on race relations and an attempt to construct a reasonable moral system within the framework of an unreasonable society.

Gilbert Gratiant, *Credo des Sang-Mele ou Je Veux Chanter la France*—a volume of verse and essays by the Martiniquan poet, novelist, and critic; written in both French and Creole; the writer argues for a cultural synthesis of European and African racial strains that could remain attached to what he termed the "essential" France of 1789; further editions in 1950 and 1961.

Graham Greene, *The Heart of the Matter*—a novel by the English writer of fiction and playwright; set in West Africa during World War II; concerns the deputy commissioner of police, who must sacrifice his career out of pity for an unhappy wife and then an unhappy mistress; he attempts, through false entries in his diary, to conceal his suicide (a sin for a Roman Catholic) from his wife; a young investigator, in love with the commissioner's wife, had watched his every move and uncovers his suicide.

Shirley Jackson, **"The Lottery"**—a short story by the American writer of fiction; a horrifying fable of ritualistic murder in a small American town; the piece is responsible for the writer's contemporary reputation.

Mikael Kabbada, *Hannibal*—a play by the Ethiopian (Amharic) dramatist and poet; emphasizes the jealousy of the Carthaginian nobles toward Hannibal, which results in the defeat of Carthage by the less divided Romans; the work was performed as early as 1945, during the celebration of the Emperor Haile Selassie's twenty-fifth year in power.

Yacine Kateb, *Nedjma; ou, Le Poeme ou le Couteau* (Nedjma, Poem or Knife)—a poem by the Algerian writer of verse, playwright, and novelist; the symbol of Nedjma, the motherland or the beloved, appears for the first time in his work; the piece serves to advance the nationalist cause with Algeria.

Abolqasem Lahuti, **"Pariye Bakht"** (Fairy Good Fortune)—a poem by the Iranian writer of verse; concerns the prerevolutionary struggle of subjugated peoples against czarist tyranny; the work was condemned as politically dangerous.

F. R. Leavis, *The Great Tradition*—an insightful prose tract by the English critic, discussing the tradition and moral concerns of English fiction.

Paul Lomami-Tshibamba, *N'Gando* (The Crocodile)—a novel by the French Congolese writer of fiction and journalist; the first novel in French by a Congolese; weaves the dream-like qualities of old Congolan myths with fragments of the old and new life along the Congo River; the piece was republished in 1971.

Norman Mailer, *The Naked and the Dead*—the first novel by the American writer of fiction and miscellaneous prose; a realistic piece about World War II, set on a Pacific island and focusing upon two types of proto-fascists; a liberal lieutenant tries to serve as a balance between the tyrants, a general and a sergeant, and attempts to analyze the motivations behind authoritarian minds; considered one of the best of the war novels, yet the piece has always been found to be lacking in character development.

Ezra Pound, *The Pisan Cantos*—a collection by the American poet; the pieces recount the poet's imprisonment by American troops during the Allied invasion of Italy; contains vivid and dramatic imagery.

Terence Rattigan, *The Browning Version*—a play by the English dramatist; focuses upon an English schoolmaster; a repressed and unpopular taskmaster, he finds his life even more dismal because of the activities of his faithless wife.

Theodore Roethke, *The Lost Son, and Other Poems*—a collection by the American writer of verse; contains the much anthologized "My Pap's Waltz" and "Dolor"; the majority of the volume is dedicated to stream-of-consciousness verse exploring the origins of life; the collection was highly praised for Roethke's original blend of traditional poetic elements and such modern concerns as the unconscious and humanity's relation to its evolutionary past.

Jean-Paul Sartre, *Les Mains Sales* (Dirty Hands)—a play by the French dramatist, essayist, and writer of fiction; described as the writer's most "moving" dramatic work, the piece attacks the inhumanity of communist tactics; combines traces of the writer's existentialist and Marxist philosophies.

Delmore Schwartz, *The World Is a Wedding, and Other Stories*—a collection of short fiction by the American poet, philosopher, and writer of fiction; a group of Jewish stories, all marked by social and religious predicaments and highlighted by the writer's intellectual honesty toward his own form of Judaism.

Irwin Shaw, *The Young Lions*—a novel by the American writer of fiction; focuses upon the lives of three soldiers in World War II, two Americans (one Jewish) and a German; the tragedy of war transcends their sociological and religious differences.

Robert Emmet Sherwood, *Roosevelt and Hopkins*—a narrative by the American playwright and biographer; derives from the writer's experiences during World War II in the Office of War Information; describes the relationship between Franklin Delano Roosevelt and his principal advisor, Harry Lloyd Hopkins (1890-1946).

John Steinbeck, *A Russian Journal*—a narrative by the American writer of fiction; an account of a journey to Soviet Russia with the photographer Robert Capa.

Evelyn Waugh, *The Loved One*—a novel by the English writer of fiction; satirizes the Hollywood cult of death and funeral practices in California.

Thornton Wilder, *The Ides of March*—a novel by the American writer of fiction and playwright; termed a "fantasia" on certain events and persons during the final days of the Roman republic; an imaginative account of the last month in the life of Julius Caesar, based on a series of fictitious documents: private letters, entries in journals, reports filed by Caesar's secret police.

Tennessee Williams, *Summer and Smoke*—a drama by the American playwright; another analysis of sexual maladjustment and breakdown, the piece is built upon verbal and visual symbols that indicate the split between body and soul.

EVENTS

W. H. Auden, English poet, receives the Pulitzer Prize in poetry for his long dramatic poem *The Age of Anxiety: A Baroque Eclogue* (1948).

The Bollingen Foundation, financed by the American industrialist Paul Mellon, establishes the Bollingen Prize in poetry; the initial award will go to Ezra Pound.

Books in Print, an annual listing of works published in and available in the United States, presents its initial volume.

T. S. Eliot, American-born poet and critic, receives the Nobel Prize for literature.

The Hudson Review, a quarterly journal of imaginative literature, begins publication at

New York City; contributors include Saul Bellow, T. S. Eliot, W. S. Merwin, Marianne Moore, Ezra Pound, W. D. Snodgrass, Allen Tate, Eudora Welty, Yvor Winters, and R. P. Blackmur.

James Albert Michener, American writer of fiction, receives the Pulitzer Prize in fiction for *Tales of the South Pacific.*

Statistics reveal that 135 million paperbound books have been sold in the United States during this year.

Tennessee Williams, American playwright, receives the Pulitzer Prize in drama for *A Streetcar Named Desire* (1947).

1949

BIRTHS

Peter Ackroyd. English writer of fiction; he will write hilariously comic and entertaining novels; essentially, his work will focus upon the issue of authenticity in both life and art.

Jamaica Kincaid. West Indian-born writer of fiction; born on the island of Antigua, she will eventually settle in the United States; her fiction will focus upon the intense emotional bonds between mothers and daughters, as well as upon the ambivalent reactions resulting from such relationships; she will combine West Indian dialects with American idiom, often imitating the forms and speech patterns of Caribbean folk tales.

Greg Matthews. Australian novelist; his work will display his strong interest in American culture, particularly in the work of Mark Twain; his fictional themes will include the randomness of fate and the destructiveness of the human will (themes found in both Twain and Ernest Hemingway).

Mary Robison. American writer of fiction; her acclaimed short stories will consider small, insignificant events that engage the lives of ordinary persons; she will emphasize characterization, and humor and irony will comprise essential elements of her fiction; she will become a regular contributor to *The New Yorker* magazine.

Patrick Suskind. West German novelist and playwright; he will refuse to accept a literary prize amounting to $5000 from a Frankfurt newspaper, maintaining that he would never accept an award for his work; his narratives will be absorbing and imaginative and will rely upon invention and intrigue rather than realism.

DEATHS

Chairil Anwar (b. 1922). Indonesian poet; his works had a significant impact upon late twentieth-century Indonesian literature, although he wrote only some seventy poems; his verse has gained recognition more from its emotional intensity than from its themes or general substance; he also influenced the development of the modern Indonesian language; he died, at age twenty-seven, from typhus.

Ali ad-Duaji (b. 1909). Tunisian writer of fiction, playwright, and painter; his short fiction is ironic, developing penetrating and paradoxical observations of life in the working class quarters of Tunis; he wrote plays in colloquial Arabic, as well as topical songs and poems.

Vilhelm Ekelund (b. 1880). Swedish poet and prose writer; although his poems and essays were not widely read during his lifetime, he had a decided influence upon Scandinavian modernism.

Maurice Maeterlinck (b. 1862). Belgian writer of fiction, playwright, and essayist; he published more than sixty volumes of prose in French; generally, his work suggested a universal mystery and sense of impending doom, characteristics that appealed to the French Symbolists; in 1911, he received the Nobel Prize for literature.

Mary Jane Mander (b. 1877). New Zealand novelist and essayist; she wrote four major novels set in her native New Zealand, each of which presents accurate and highly descriptive accounts of life in that country; her characters are both native New Zealanders and transplanted Britons; she introduced into the literature of her nation a quality of frankness in focusing upon sexual situations.

Klaus Mann (b. 1906). German playwright and the son of the writer Thomas Mann; generally, his work focuses upon a young generation caught amidst sickly cults, decadent romanticism, and homosexual practices.

Ibrahim Abdalqadir al-Mazini (b. 1889). Egyptian novelist, poet, and critic; he wrote pessimistic verse based upon personal feelings and experience; his criticism strongly attacks sterile traditionalism in modern Arabic poetry and prose; he demonstrated a high level of linguistic competence.

Margaret Mitchell (b. 1900). American writer of fiction; her reputation rests on her enormously popular novel *Gone with the Wind* (1936); she received the Pultizer Prize for fiction in 1937.

Khalil Mutran (b. 1872?). Egyptian poet and journalist; his verse demonstrates versatility and variety, ranging from traditional and occasional poetry to narratives and subjective lyrics; generally, his work concentrates on the emotions and the crises of individual predicaments.

Henry Masila Ndawo (b. 1883). South African (Xhosa) novelist, poet, and collector of folk tales; his verse earned for him the title of "praise poet of the Bungani people," while his fiction focuses upon the educational system of the 1920s; he died after falling from a jolted train platform.

Ullur Paramesvarayyar (b. 1877). Indian (Malayalam) poet and scholar; he wrote a history of Kerala literature and was one of the most prolific Malayalam poets; he gained recognition for the philosophic substance of his verse and for his mastery of imagery.

Ali Mahmud Taha (b. 1902). Egyptian poet; his attraction to French Romantic poetry and his extensive travels throughout Europe are reflected in his work, which is noted for its Western influences; he experimented with the poetic drama in Arabic.

Sigrid Undset (b. 1882). Danish-born Norwegian writer of fiction; a dominant figure among Scandinavian novelists; her most important works are skillfully rendered portrayals of medieval Norwegian life that have been praised as exemplary models of historical fiction; she received the Nobel Prize for literature in 1928.

Neguse Yoftake (b. 1900?). Ethiopian (Amharic) playwright and poet; he wrote allegorical drama that was especially popular when performed at the royal court; he also wrote nationalistic poetry and two thin volumes of moral essays.

PUBLICATIONS

Nelson Algren, *The Man with the Golden Arm*—a novel by the American writer of fic-

tion; an extremely tense and compelling account of drug addiction, one in which compassion takes precedence over moralizing; the principal character possesses good looks, strength, sensitivity, and the ability to deal cards; yet, death claims him at age thirty.

Chairil Anwar, "Aku" (Me)—a poem by the Indonesian writer of verse and essayist; thirteen lines in which the poet advocates a form of ruthless honesty and total disregard for literary and social conventions; reveals the author's awareness of the emotional impact of language.

Antonio Buero Vallejo, *Historia de Una Escalera* (The Story of a Staircase)—a play by the Spanish dramatist; depicts tenement life in Madrid through two generations of a poor family; the principal characters attempt to reconcile their poverty with their economic aspirations; the work was acclaimed for injecting new life into a stagnant Spanish theater.

John Dos Passos, *The Grand Design*—a novel by the American writer of fiction; the last volume in a trilogy entitled *District of Columbia;* focuses on Franklin Delano Roosevelt's New Deal and its suffocation by the red tape and bureaucracy of Washington.

T. S. Eliot, *The Cocktail Party*—a verse drama by the American-born poet and critic; an unconventional psychoanalyst intrudes abruptly into the lives of a husband, his wife, and their lovers; the intruder restores the marriage, sending the husband's lover off to Africa as a nurse to be crucified by a band of rebellious natives; the piece was patterned after Euripides' *Alcestis*, and the analyst was based upon the character of Heracles.

Jean Genet, *Haute Surveillance* (Deathwatch)—a drama by the French playwright, novelist, and poet; essentially a blend of naturalism and fantasy that focuses upon the ritualistic efforts of a petty criminal trapped in a cell with two murderers; his purpose appears to achieve the "saintly" description of killer; unlike his cellmates, however, the petty criminal has never killed without cause or reason, and thus must endure ridicule for his immoral inferiority.

Sidney Kinsgley, *Detective Story*—a play by the American dramatist; an atmospheric piece that gained considerable recognition for its vivid recreation of a police station; contains little in terms of plot or characterization.

Mary McCarthy, *The Oasis*—a novel by the American writer of fiction; the piece brings to the fore her skills as a journalist, as she focuses upon a modern "would-be" utopia.

Achdiat Karta Mihardja, *Atheis* (Atheist)—a novel by the Indonesian writer of fiction; recognized as the most significant novel of post-World War II Indonesia; the writer, a Muslim, attempts to depict the intellectual struggle between various religious concepts, mysticism, and historical materialism.

Arthur Miller, *Death of a Salesman*—a dramatic tragedy by the American playwright; concerns a salesman whose career is no longer successful, principally because of his age, his times, and his own incompetence; he cannot understand how his own sons have inherited his inability to confront the truth and his tendency to be unfaithful; in the end, he takes his own life, which proves the only means out of his dilemma; awarded the Pulitzer Prize for drama this year.

Sean O'Casey, *Cock-a-Doodle-Dandy*—a dramatic comedy by the Irish playwright; the enchanted cock is a merry figure of apocalyptic exuberance, symbolizing the life force; he descends upon a joyless Irish village where the people, committed to and led by their priest, have been taught to fear him as the devil; the semiautobiographical theme of exile becomes the principal conflict of the piece, as the forces of life battle the elements of despair; in the end, original joy carries the day against original sin. ˙

John O'Hara, *A Rage to Live*—a novel by the American writer of fiction; essentially a tragic satire directed at a world in which characters follow their own roads to ruin, here recorded in the torments of a faithless wife who, actually, loves her husband.

George Orwell, *Nineteen Eighty-Four*—a novel by the English writer of fiction and essayist; a grim depiction of one man's struggle to maintain a degree of personal autonomy in a totalitarian society in which privacy, individuality, and intellectual integrity have disappeared; Orwell's narrative asserts the value of history, both personal and cultural, as a means to establish sanity and human identity.

Stephen Spender, "Responsibility: The Pilots Who Destroyed Germany, Spring 1945"—a poem by the English poet and critic; the piece focuses upon the psychic tension brought about by mixed joy; Germany has been destroyed by the Allied bombers, but, at the same time, one group of people has slaughtered another group.

Ilham Notodijo Subagijo, *Gelenging Tekad*—a collection of verse by the Javanese poet and author of short fiction, written in his native tongue; the pieces are primarily concerned with patriotism, the struggle against colonialism, and the ideals of freedom.

Eudora Welty, *The Golden Apples*—a collection of stories by the American writer of fiction; possesses a sense of unity approaching the novel; the theme of the pieces concerns the drama of resistance: family and community confront historical change in the twentieth-century American South.

EVENTS

American Heritage, a journal dedicated to American history, begins publication under the sponsorship of the American Heritage Association for State and Local History.

American Quarterly, a scholarly journal dedicated to American studies, begins publication at the University of Minnesota, Minneapolis; in 1951, its editorial offices move to the University of Pennsylvania at Philadelphia.

The Antiquarian Booksellers Association of America established, principally for the used book dealers of the nation.

Bertolt Brecht, German poet, stage director, and playwright; forms the Berliner Ensemble as a group within the larger organization of the Deutsches Theater; by 1954, the group will have its own building; it becomes the most impressive theatrical ensemble in the Western world.

James Gould Cozzens, American writer of fiction, receives the Pulitzer Prize in fiction for his novel *Guard of Honor* (1948).

William Faulkner, American writer of fiction, receives the Nobel Prize for literature.

Arthur Miller, American playwright, receives the Pulitzer Prize in drama for *Death of a Salesman* (1949).

Graham Sutherland, English painter, completes his noted portrait of the English writer W. Somerset Maugham.

Peter Viereck, American historian and writer of verse, receives the Pulitzer Prize in poetry for *Terror and Decorum* (1948).

1950

BIRTHS

Hedin M. Klein. Danish (Faeroe Islands) poet and translator; his verse will take on a "gloomy-sweetish" quality and concern itself with human life as a contradictory experience; he will also contrast the decadent social life with the proud history and culture of Iceland; additional themes focus on such issues as the threat of nuclear warheads and the need to maintain a peaceful existence in spite of them.

Medbh McGuckian. Irish poet; she will examine themes related to femininity, infusing her language with thick rhythms and erotic imagery; she will transform elements of everyday experience into metaphoric representations of the female psyche; she will rely upon oxymorons to juxtapose concrete and abstract adjectives; her work will, in general, avoid the obvious political issues and problems of twentieth-century Ireland.

Timothy Mo. Hong Kong-born English novelist and critic; he will produce "seriocomic" novels concerning the lives of expatriates; thus, much of his material will derive from his own Chinese heritage, evolving into examinations of problems encountered by immigrants as they adapt to foreign cultures; he will excel as a writer of accurate dialogue and description, as well as a reporter of the cultural clash between Eastern and Western societies.

Tidor Rosic. Yugoslavian (Serbian) writer of fiction; his work will emphasize a cosmopolitan and universal approach to reality; his stories, particularly, will be direct and matter-of-fact; he will develop principal characters from the common folk: housewives, retired professional people, taxi drivers, craftsmen, students, and intellectuals; they will conduct their business in recognizable environments, but beyond them lies a world of fantastic happenings and abnormal behavior.

Stella Voyatzoglou. Greek writer of fiction; her works will be based on her own experiences and recollections; she will create fully dramatized and representative characters; one of her principal themes will focus upon how history has shaped the lives of various generations.

DEATHS

Mohammed Taqi Bahar (b. 1886). Iranian poet, scholar, and historian; the last Iranian poet to hold the title "King of Poets," as well as the last significant poet to rely upon the classical forms of Iranian verse; his work evolved into a revival of the Khorasan style, with unusual stress upon strophe forms; he provided those forms with a new social and political content; his scholarly work is still an important source for the study of modern Iranian history.

Bibhutibhusan Bandyopadhyay (b. 1894). Indian (Bengali) writer of fiction, essays, and travel narratives; his novels, especially, demonstrate a warm sympathy for the rural poor and a feeling for the beauties of nature; he will also gain recognition for his psychological treatment of juvenile characters.

William Rose Benet (b. 1886). American poet and writer of fiction; in his lyrics and ballads, he developed a poetic voice free from ego, bravado, and ornamentation; he achieved his greatest recognition as a reviewer, anthologist, and critic; the elder brother of Stephen Vincent Benet and the husband of the poet Elinor Wylie.

Edgar Rice Burroughs (b. 1875). American writer of fiction; he gained literary recognition and popularity for his stories of Tarzan, the ape-man; those pieces were adapted for movies and comic strips.

Henry Courts-Mahler (b. 1867). German writer of fiction; he wrote in excess of 192 novels, practically all of them popular romances.

Heinrich Mann (b. 1871). German writer of fiction and elder (by four years) brother of Thomas Mann; he published more than fifty volumes of fiction, in addition to plays, essays, memoirs, and anthologies; his work reflects the influence of Stendhal, Guy de Maupassant, Emile Zola, and Gabriele D'Annunzio; he appeared at his best when he wrote political and social satire.

Edgar Lee Masters (b. 1869). American poet and biographer; his literary reputation rests upon a collection of free-verse epitaphs that serve to reveal the lives and secrets of small-town Americans; he also wrote biographies of Abraham Lincoln and Walt Whitman.

Francis Otto Matthiessen (b. 1902). American critic and intellectual historian; he taught

American literature at Harvard (1929-1950) and published important studies upon the American literary renaissance, Henry James, and Theodore Dreiser.

Edna St. Vincent Millay (b. 1892). American poet and writer of verse drama; she gained recognition as much for her bohemian lifestyle as for her verse; she wrote exceptional lyrics and sonnets, relying upon traditional forms and language; the substance of her work focused upon the human being as completely absorbed in human situations and human conditions.

George Orwell (pseudonym of Eric Arthur Blair; b. 1903). English writer of fiction and essayist; his fiction, particularly, tends to be autobiographical and highly socio-political; his most noted fiction concerns the failure of communism and the results of life in a totalitarian world; his literary essays have achieved lasting and broad recognition.

Cesare Pavese (b. 1908). Italian poet, novelist, and translator; he translated several principal American works into Italian, particularly those of Herman Melville, whose fiction influenced his own; his major novels focus upon humankind's search for stability and freedom from isolation.

Tawfiq Piramerd (b. 1867). Kurdish poet, translator, and journalist; he greatly helped to preserve and popularize Kurdish folk works, which he translated and edited; he wrote, published, and translated classical Kurdish poetry, being extremely careful to maintain the purity of the language; he also versified and published 6500 Kurdish proverbs.

George Bernard Shaw (b. 1856). Irish playwright and critic; his dramas of ideas revolutionized the Victorian stage, attacking political, social, and philosophical institutions; a Fabian socialist, he enjoyed popularity as a speaker, as well as a critic of drama and music; he argued, in his drama, against poverty and mocked English class attitudes; he received the Nobel Prize for literature in 1925.

PUBLICATIONS

Ray Bradbury, *The Martian Chronicles*—a novel by the American writer of science fiction; essentially concerned with the universal forces of love, hate, fear, and courage, all of which become unleashed when Earth collides with Mars; the work illustrates the energies and emotions that have historically influenced human beings' behavior in alien, new worlds.

Kenneth Burke, *A Rhetoric of Motives*—a volume of prose by the American critic; he seeks to achieve an ideal, closed system wherein one can move through a variety of terminologies and methods; he creates a critical approach that combines psychoanalysis, theology, new critical theory, and radical political analysis with a heavy reliance upon the principles of structure.

Christopher Fry, *Venus Observed*—a play by the English dramatist; described as a romantic chateau comedy, the piece gains strength from the playwright's fresh optimism following World War II, as well as from his enjoyable wordplay; an aged duke observes the planet Venus and sets in motion a series of romantic events dedicated to the necessity of love and companionship for both the young and the elderly.

Graham Greene, *The Third Man*—a novel by the English writer of fiction, originally intended as a screenplay, and termed by the author himself "an entertainment"; an expressionist adventure/thriller that becomes another contrast between good and evil; as always, his principal character struggles for grace to free humanity from the bondage of sin.

Ernest Hemingway, *Across the River and Into the Trees*—a novel by the American writer of fiction; the work continues the author's attack on those values that the man of action detests; thus, an American writer constantly takes notes and consults his travel guide, but he never experiences what he observes; in contrast, a retired colonel, filled with the pain of emotional and physical wounds, nevertheless has experienced life (even though he has committed mistakes).

Jack Kerouac, *The Town and the City*—a novel by the American writer of fiction and narrative; the theme marks the beginning of his lifelong complaint against the world: ignorance, incoherence, and illiteracy may well be god-like, while crime, drunkenness, and permissiveness constitute sweetness and light.

Vincas Kreve, *Pagunda* (The Temptation)—a satirical novel by the Lithuanian writer of fiction, playwright, poet, and critic; the writer relates a number of his frustrating experiences with the totalitarian Soviet regime; perhaps one of the best portraits of what one must endure to function as a communist official and a communist intellectual within the modern socialist state.

Doris Lessing, *The Grass Is Singing*—the first novel by the Persian-born, Rhodesian-reared English writer; concerns the complex relationship between a white farmer's wife and her black servant; the writer's social and political concerns direct the piece to its violent conclusion.

Mary McCarthy, *Cast a Cold Eye*—a collection of criticism by the American writer of fiction and esssayist; the pieces focus principally upon the American theater and reflect the years spent by the writer composing critical essays and reviews.

Edgar Mittelholzer, *Morning at the Office*—a novel by the Guyanan novelist, playwright, and poet; focuses upon Trinidadian society: its color, class, ethnic and occupational tensions; those problems further relate to metropolitan-colonial tensions in that locale, as well as throughout the Caribbean; the work was eventually translated into French and Italian.

Octavio Paz, *El Laberinto de la Soledad* (The Labyrinth of Solidad)—a volume of nonfiction by the Mexican poet, essayist, playwright, and translator; the writer explores Mexican history, mythology, and social behavior; he advances his belief that modern Mexico and its people suffer from a collective identity crisis; that problem arises from mixed Indian and Spanish heritage, marginal associations with Western cultural traditions, the influence of the United States, and recurring war and isolation; he attempts to define the outrages, violations, and defeats that have become fixtures upon the national personality.

Isaac Bashevis Singer, *The Family Moskat*—a novel by the Polish-born Yiddish writer of fiction; written as early as 1945; set in Poland during the first half of the twentieth century, the work traces the decline and eventual decay of a Jewish family, whose end is brought about by the Holocaust.

Lionel Trilling, *The Liberal Imagination*—an essay by the American literary and intellectual critic; reveals the writer's strong admiration for the liberal imagination of the nineteenth century and his belief that only through integration with society can one define the self.

Robert Penn Warren, *World Enough and Time*—a novel by the American writer of fiction, poet, and critic; the principal character, as usual in his fiction, searches for the American self; in this instance, that character arrives at the source of his guilt, as well as determines what he must do to clear his conscience; based upon an actual criminal case in Kentucky that took place between 1824 and 1826, involving a love affair that prompted attempted murder, murder, corruption, and suicide.

Richard Wilbur, *Ceremony, and Other Poems*—a collection by the American poet; the pieces are noted for their linguistic delicacy, contemplative aestheticism, and technical correctness; contains, in addition to the title work, such poems as "Juggler" and "The Death of the Toad," illustrative of how the poet generates metaphor from experience.

Richard Wright, *The God That Failed*—a novel by the American writer of fiction; the work serves as another example of the brutally realistic portrayal of the black experience; essentially an account of the writer's own disenchantment with communism.

EVENTS

James Boswell's *London Journal, 1762-1763* published for the first time; edited by Professor Frederick A. Pottle of Yale University.

Gwendolyn Brooks, American poet and writer of fiction, receives the Pulitzer Prize in poetry for *Annie Allen* (1949).

Alfred Bertram Guthrie, Jr., American writer of fiction, receives the Pulitzer Prize in fiction for *The Way West* (1949).

Oliver Waterman Larkin, American intellectual historian, receives the Pulitzer Prize in United States history for *Art and Life in America* (1949).

The Library of Congress, Washington, D.C., increases its collection to 8.6 million books, 128,000 yearly newspaper volumes, 11 million manuscripts, 2 million maps, 76,000 microfilms, 2 million musical scores, and 4 million "miscellaneous" items.

The National Book Awards established by the American Book Publishers Council, the American Booksellers Association, and the Book Manufacturers Institute.

Bertrand Russell, third Earl Russell, English mathematician, philosopher, and essayist, receives the Nobel Prize for literature.

1951

BIRTHS

Nedim Gursel. Turkish writer of fiction; his work will help foreign scholars and critics to understand and appreciate the intellectual growing pains of the Islamic world as it awakens from medievalism and confronts the problems of the late twentieth century; he will emigrate to Paris and teach at the Ecole des Langues Orientales.

Drazen Mazur. Yugoslavian (Croatian) poet and writer of fiction; he will present fragments of everyday life in a modern city; his fictional characters will lack the ability to orient themselves to the quagmire of urban existence; his verse will emphasize hyperbole and the grotesque, with a conglomeration of paradox, uproarious incident, and non sequitur; his humor will take advantage of satire, irony, and sarcasm.

Guy Vanderhaeghe. Canadian writer of fiction; he will achieve recognition for his accurate dialogue, precise detail, and skillful character development; he will portray unheroic human beings within the context of their unheroic lives; at his best, he will generate high levels of energy and intensity.

DEATHS

James Bridie (pseudonym of Osborne Henry Mavor; b. 1881). Scottish playwright; his drama, on more than one occasion, takes advantage of his experiences as a physician, particularly the issue of ethics in medicine; his works include biblical plays, experimental symbolic pieces, and verse dramas; he helped to establish, in 1943, the Glasgow Citizens' Theatre, and has received credit for the founding of the first college of drama in Scotland (1950).

Hermann Broch (b. 1886). Austrian writer of fiction, essayist, and playwright; he contributed significantly to the twentieth-century European novel; his work was strongly influenced by the philosophers Immanuel Kant and Georg Wilhelm Freidrich Hegel; he received credit for originating the term "epistemological novel," designating fictional pieces

through which he communicated his metaphysical theories; he emigrated to the United States in 1938, following a three week detention by the Gestapo.

Hayashi Fumiko (b. 1904). Japanese writer of fiction, essayist, and poet; she portrayed the lives of the poor and the dispossessed (her own social class), particularly in her fiction written after World War II; she created female characters who are economically dependent upon immoral and unreliable men; she wrote serial fiction for popular magazines to the time of her death, from a heart attack.

Andre Gide (b. 1869). French writer of fiction and journal narratives, playwright, and critic; a leader of French liberal thought, he became one of the founders of the influential *Nouvelle Revue Francaise;* he encountered criticism because of his frank defense of homosexuality and his initial espousal of communism; his principal novels depict individuals searching for their true selves, which in many cases exist in opposition to prevailing ethical conventions; in 1947, he received the Nobel Prize for literature.

James Norman Hall (b. 1887). American essayist and writer of fiction and narratives; in addition to composing nonfiction based upon his experiences in World War I, he collaborated with Charles Bernard Nordhoff (1887-1947) on several popular historical novels, most notably the trilogy concerning the eighteenth-century mutiny aboard the *H.M.S. Bounty.*

Sadeq Hedayat (b. 1903). Iranian writer of fiction, playwright, essayist, and translator; often regarded as the father of modern Persian fiction, he relied upon Western literary forms of the novel and the story, thus providing the first significant models of narrative prose in a literature previously dominated by verse; a highly individual writer, he displayed in his prose a scholar's erudition, a poet's imagination, and a philosopher's insight; his work reveals an irremediable desolation at the very core of human existence; he takes his own life while at Paris.

Sinclair Lewis (b. 1885). American writer of fiction; a brilliant satirist, he presented harsh pictures of the various aspects of middle-class American life: the small Midwestern town, the destruction brought about by total conformity, the medical profession, and material opportunism in the guise of organized religion; he received a Pulitzer Prize for fiction in 1926, and in 1930 he became the first American to receive the Nobel Prize for literature; he died at Rome.

Nam-Cao (pseudonym of Tran-huu-Tri; b. 1917). Vietnamese writer of fiction; a realistic writer, he was successful at describing lower middle-class intellectuals; he presents a critical, almost pessimistic view of Vietnamese society under French domination; yet, he also praises the strength and tenacity of simple Vietnamese villagers who resist colonialism; he died, during the War of Resistance, while on a mission behind French lines.

Pedro Salinas (b. 1891). Spanish poet, writer of fiction, playwright, essayist, and translator; his work reflects the conflict between being and nothingness, as well as between internal and external reality; he wrote long sequences of poetry that constitute beautiful meditations upon the general theme of romantic love; he spent the last fifteen years of his life in North America, teaching at a number of universities; he died from cancer.

Hamzet Tsadasa (b. 1877). Dagestan (Avar) poet; he wrote witty parodies in Arabic, love poetry, and satire; generally, his verse tends toward the scholarly, abounding in Arabic references and allusions to the Oriental traditions; he translated the works of Aleksandr Pushkin from the Russian and was designated the National Poet of Dagestan.

Ludwig Josef Johan Wittgenstein (b. 1889). Austrian philosopher and critic; he came in contact with logical positivism, declaring the existence of a close, formal relationship between language, thought, and the world; he argues that language and thought were a literal picture of the real world, and that to understand any sentence, one must comprehend the reference of its constituents; his work, which maintains that all philosophical problems arise from the allusions created by the ambiguities of language, came to be termed the ordinary language philosophy.

Rashid Yasami (b. 1896). Iranian historian, translator, and poet; he became professor of pre-Islamic history at the University of Teheran; he wrote tracts on cultural and literary history, translated poems from the French, and wrote original lyric verse on nature and intimate themes.

PUBLICATIONS

Peter Lee Abrahams, *Wild Conquest*—a novel by the South African writer of fiction and poet; one of its principal themes focuses upon the Zulu resistance to the encroaching Boers; contains a number of strong and fully developed native characters representing various levels of Zulu society; issued, also, in New York and London.

Samuel Beckett, *Molloy*—a novel (the first of a trilogy) by the Irish-born playwright and writer of fiction; somewhat philosophical, the work reduces existence to pure thought; at the same time, the writer defines the meaning of being Irish: hopelessness, helplessness, perennial despair, pointless passion; thus, the title character, a cripple, sets off on a bicycle to find his mother, but fails to do so; originally written in French, the work essentially is an interior monologue.

Ray Bradbury, *The Illustrated Man*—a collection of short stories by the American writer of science fiction; the volume contains nineteen pieces that blend strange fantasy and chilling truth; recognized for its deft plots and appealing style.

Truman Capote, *The Grass Harp*—a novel by the American writer of fiction and nonfiction; concerns an eleven-year-old orphan; with one of his elderly aunts and three other persons, he finds himself driven, by the nastiness of the world, to live in a tree house; there they must confront reality, and do so with the help of techniques that remind one of Noah's ark and the raft of Huck Finn.

Nirad C. Chaudhuri, *The Autobiography of an Unknown Indian*—a combination narrative and history by the Indian (Bengali) writer of narrative; the piece demonstrates the writer's sensitivity to death and decay; his principal theme focuses upon the origin and death of the Indian effort to create a modern, humanistic culture from a synthesis of Eastern and Western ideals; he analyzes the life and times of Bengal.

John Dos Passos, *Chosen Country*—a novel by the American writer of fiction; once more advances his belief that the national and personal values so necessary to eighteenth-century America must be applied to contemporary life.

William Faulkner, *Requiem for a Nun*—a novel by the American writer of fiction; Christian history becomes historical reality as the principal character professes to be the bride of Christ, rather than the daughter of humankind; described as a "novel-play," the work links the theme of faith with an exploration of the mythical compulsions of the human imagination.

Hayashi Fumiko, *Ukigumo* (Floating Cloud)—a novel by the Japanese writer of fiction, essayist, and poet; presents a powerful vision of Japan following World War II; two lovers cannot find fulfillment in their relationship, or, for that matter, in any aspect of their bleak lives; their resignation to their state symbolizes the general mood of hopelessness pervading post-war Japan.

Graham Greene, *The End of the Affair*—a novel by the English writer of fiction; concerns a wartime love affair with emphasis upon religious and supernatural elements.

Langston Hughes, *Montage of a Dream Deferred*—a collection of verse by the American poet, playwright, and writer of fiction and miscellaneous prose; the pieces rely upon the varieties in jazz music for both subject and style; the work also contains elements of the black spiritual and the gospel song.

Randall Jarrell, *The Seven-League Crutches*—a collection of verse by the American poet; the pieces reflect fragments of the poet's private life, which he presents in a tone of relaxation; in general, the poems tend to combine a sense of dreaminess with an emphasis upon self-analysis.

James Jones, *From Here to Eternity*—the first novel by the American writer of fiction; set in Hawaii, the work concerns the United States Army during peacetime, prior to World War II; contains two principal characters, outsiders who represent, respectively, cynicism and integrity in a system where the latter quality is totally absent; essentially, both characters turn their backs upon a world devoid of humanism and justice, a world that cannot possibly hope to change.

Kota Sivarama Karanta, *Kudiyara Kusu* (A Child of the Kudiyas)—a novel by the Indian (Kannada) writer of fiction and encyclopaedist; an anthropological work that focuses upon hunting hill tribes; the piece reflects the writer's knowledge of modern science and ethnography, as well as his astute observation and satiric voice.

Thomas Mann, *Der Erwahlte* (The Holy Sinner)—a novel by the German writer of fiction; the principal character marries his sister, who in reality is his mother; he becomes the Pope, which means that his mother can call him "Father"; another of the writer's

projects intended to cast stones at his overly middle class reading audience.

John P. Marquand, *Melville Godwin, U.S.A.*—a novel by the American writer of fiction and playwright; concerns a professional soldier, a man of action, who finds himself totally unable to take action and preoccupied with his memories.

Carson McCullers, "**The Ballad of the Sad Cafe**"—a long short story by the American writer of fiction; concerns a woman, a merchant and a healer, and the theme of estrangement; the work gives the title to a collection of three novellas and six short stories.

Nicholas Monsarrat, *The Cruel Sea*—an extremely popular novel by the English writer of fiction; focuses upon the writer's own experiences at sea during World War II, both with the merchant service and the Royal Navy; the work was transformed into an equally popular motion picture.

Theodore Roethke, *Praise to the End!*—a collection of verse by the American poet; the pieces take full advantage of the lively rhythm and inconsequential surrealism of nursery rhyme and baby talk; the attempt of these poems appears to be the enactment of the birth or rebirth of the scattered psyche from a tangled web of instincts (eating, touching, sniffing, sucking, licking); human identity becomes synonymous with a fall from innocence into disenchantment, allowing the human being to become aware of time and consequence; the tone of the volume takes on the sound of a child who neither expects nor receives answers, awaiting only confirmation of that which actually exists.

J. D. Salinger, *The Catcher in the Rye*—a novel by the American writer of fiction; the writer strives to capture the tone and the flavor of adolescence and alienation in post-World War II America; the principal character, forced to leave prep school, must return to his parents; before doing so, he spends a weekend in New York City, where he comes in contact with every aspect of falsehood and insincerity; essentially, the monologue that constitutes the narrative vehicle of the book functions as the boy's therapy; unfortunately, he cannot solve his (or society's) psychological problems.

Jean-Paul Sartre, *Le Diable et le Bon Dieu* (The Devil and the Good Lord)—a play by the French philosopher, dramatist, writer of fiction, essayist, and biographer; set in Germany during the Reformation, the piece concerns a man who initially pursues absolute evil, and then goes after absolute good; eventually, he discovers the falseness of both routes; the work is viewed as the writer's most determined statement in behalf of atheism.

C. P. Snow, *The Masters*—a novel by the English writer of fiction and critic; a study of the internal politics and the struggle for power within a college at Cambridge; perhaps the writer's most popular and best known piece of fiction.

William Styron, *Lie Down in Darkness*—a novel by the American writer of fiction; indebted stylistically to the works of James Joyce and William Faulkner; the principal character attempts to reclaim her self-identity; she thus kills her nameless self, being tortured in her final moment by her last vestige of identity: her repressed passion for her own father.

Herman Wouk, *The Caine Mutiny*—a novel by the American writer of fiction and playwright; concerns life aboard a U.S. Navy minesweeper during World War II; the captain proves himself capable of cruelty and cowardice, driving his officers to mutiny; the work contains a highly dramatic court martial segment, which the novelist transposed into a successful play in 1954; the fictional version receives a Pulitzer Prize in 1952.

Tennessee Williams, *The Rose Tatoo*—a play by the American dramatist; examines the tension between the spirit and the flesh; the principal characters, a mother and daughter, work through difficulties in their personal lives to ultimately celebrate the life-affirming power of human sexuality.

EVENTS

The American Studies Association, intended to sponsor American literature and general intellectual and cultural projects, established.

Par Fabian Lagerkvist, Swedish novelist, poet, and playwright, receives the Nobel Prize for literature.

Conrad Michael Richter, American writer of novels and short stories, receives the Pulitzer Prize in fiction for *The Town* (1950).

Carl August Sandburg, American poet and historical biographer, receives the Pulitzer Prize in poetry for his *Complete Poems* (1950).

1952

BIRTHS

Antoine Laurent. French novelist; he will achieve recognition for his clever language and inventiveness; thus, within each of his novels, he will ponder over the various ideas about the writing of fiction and develop what commentators will term an "audaciously inventive" narrative; simply, he will intersperse fantastical plots with discourses on the art of fiction.

Ryu Murakami. Japanese writer of fiction; he will become involved with the hippie culture, rock bands, and contemporary musical composition; his fiction will reflect his experiences near a U.S. Air Force base: American airmen and their dependents, Amerasians, bar girls, prostitutes, and pimps; in addition, he will incorporate into his works references to drugs, rock music, and group sex; violence will constitute an essential element of his fiction; he will receive the Guynzo New Writers Prize for 1976 and the Akutagawa Prize for 1976.

Vikram Seth. Indian-born novelist, poet, and travel writer; his fiction will be praised for its technical virtuosity and wit, as well as for its accessible language, which will move from elevated literary allusion to colloquial speech; his work will focus upon such topics as religious guilt, the nuclear arms race, the ethics of occupational choice, sexual politics, love, and death.

Mara Zalite. Soviet Latvian poet; her work will reflect her overall love of the world, and its freshness will be complemented by dramatic tension; she will compose love poetry addressed to the poet's language, to her ancestors, and to the beauty of her native land; she will strive to create imagery representative of the Latvian poetic unconscious, anchoring her lines to a rich folk song tradition.

DEATHS

Mariano Azuela (b. 1873). Mexican writer of fiction; his fiction evolved from his experiences as a surgeon with the revolutionary forces of Pancho Villa; he tended to focus upon the social conflicts within twentieth-century Mexico.

Benedetto Croce (b. 1866). Italian historian, philosopher, and literary critic; his early works on general linguistics and spiritual philosophy were landmarks of modern idealism; he gained recognition for his tracts on literature, aesthetics, cultural history, and historical methodology; politically, he was an ardent anti-fascist.

John Dewey (b. 1859). American educational philosopher; in his prose tracts, he rejected authoritarian teaching methods, promoting a system of education that would enable citizens to integrate their cultures and vocations purposefully; his educational philosophy became identified as a form of pragmatic instrumentalism, advocating truth as an instrument by which human beings could solve most of their problems.

Knut Hamsun (b. 1859). Norwegian writer of fiction; the themes for his novels came from his youthful travels, including visits to the United States; in his work he expressed his interest in irrational forces, his love of nature, and his concern for the effect of material conditions on the individual spirit; he received the Nobel Prize for literature in 1920, but his popularity declined during World War II because of his reputed Nazi sympathies.

Ghulam Ahmad Mahjur (b. 1888). Indian (Kashmiri) poet; he wrote poetry in Urdu, initiating the replacement of classical Persian models with modern Urdu literary influences; his verse contains loving descriptions of Kashmiri scenery and life and emphasizes patriotism.

Ferenc Malnar (originally Ferenc Neumann; b. 1878). Hungarian playwright, writer of fiction, and essayist; he wrote light comedies known for their charm and technical excellence; his plays depicted relationships between men and women, with men the victims of their scheming but irresistible partners; in 1941, he emigrated to the United States; he experienced a massive heart attack in 1943, but finally succumbed to stomach cancer.

George Santayana (b. 1863). Spanish-born American philosopher and novelist; generally, he viewed the mind as being placed in and responsive to a physical, biological context; also emphasized the mind's rational and imaginative vision of physical beauty; for him, religion existed as an imaginative creation of real value, yet it lacked absolute significance.

PUBLICATIONS

Sopalakrishna Adiga, *Nadedu Banda Dari* (The Road We Have Walked)—a collection of verse by the Indian (Kannada) poet; a group of impassioned pieces, highly complex in form and substance and containing abundant irony; also noted for its attentiveness to the harsh aspects of contemporary reality.

Bozorg Alavi, *Chashmhayesh* (Her Eyes)—a novel by the Iranian writer of fiction and documentary prose; concerns a group of intellectuals working against the Iranian dictatorship at home and abroad, striving to bring about a just social order; the piece was translated into Polish and German.

Jean Anouilh, *La Valse des Toreadors* (The Waltz of the Toreadors)—a play by the French dramatist; focuses upon a general's infatuation with a woman he danced with some eighteen years earlier; the general's commitment to his own marriage prevented the consummation of the affair with the dancer; however, when the two meet again, the woman falls in love with a younger man; the theme concerns the disillusionment and pettiness that occur in the aftermath of lost love; further, the device of coincidence highlights the artificiality of theatrical convention.

Isaac Asimov, *Foundation and Empire*—a novel by the Russian-born writer of science fiction; concerns the collapse of the great million-planet galactic empire; the universe sinks into war and chaos, but the Foundation (one world against a galaxy) struggles to save civilization.

Samuel Beckett, *En Attendant Godot* (Waiting for Godot)—a play by the Irish-born French dramatist; two tramps wait by a tree for the arrival of the title character, joined by a master and a slave, and finally a young boy; Godot never comes, the tramps continue their vigil, and the tree (after two days) sprouts leaves; the tree and leaves thus represent the only vestige of order in a totally alienated world; when initially produced in 1953, the piece ran for four hundred performances.

Joyce Cary, *Prisoner of Grace*—a novel by the Irish writer of fiction, essayist, and poet; the initial volume in a trilogy; the work emphasizes the writer's belief that politics is pervasive, existing just as much in family life as in the public sector; the principal character, a Labour Party politician, dances around the question of his being a hypocritical fraud in private life and a conscientious public servant in the open.

Mohammed Dib, *La Grande Maison* (The Big House)—a novel by the Algerian writer of fiction; the work focuses upon the problems of poverty in Algeria and certainly deserves the label of social novel; the initial volume of a trilogy entitled *L'Algerie.*

Lawrence Durrell, *A Key to Modern Poetry*—a prose volume by the English writer of fiction, poet, and essayist; the work casts light upon the entire range of twentieth-century verse, including the writer's own work; he principally considers the impact of the theories of relativity and psychoanalysis upon modern art.

Ralph Ellison, *The Invisible Man*—a novel by the American essayist and writer of fiction and narrative; the piece contains a strong social message, describing the symbolic treatment of blacks in white America; at the same time, however, the writer asserts the universality of human experience; the piece receives the National Book Award for 1953.

Leonhard Franks, *Links Wo das Herz Ist* (Heart on the Left)—an autobiographical novel by the German writer of fiction and playwright; the work has gained recognition because of the writer's utter disregard for "elementary decency," both in terms of substance and language.

Ernest Hemingway, *The Old Man and the Sea*—a novella by the American writer of fiction; the story of an old man who manages to catch and then loses a huge fish; the thesis concerns the futility of life, yet emphasizes that life must go forward with both nobility and courage; a highly symbolic and descriptive work; the writer receives the Pulitzer Prize in fiction for this piece in 1953.

Eugene Ionesco, *Le Chaises* (The Chairs)—a play by the Romanian-born French dramatist, essayist, and writer of fiction; an elderly couple serve as hosts to an audience that assembles to hear an orator deliver a message intended to save the world; the two arrange seating for the group, but the stage becomes inundated with chairs; when the audience appears to be imaginary, the couple commit suicide, while the orator turns out to be a deaf mute; everything in the play exists as a metaphor underscoring the absurdity of life.

Doris Lessing, *Martha Quest*—a novel by the Persian-born Rhodesian-reared English writer of fiction; the first of a quintet entitled *Children of Violence* (1952-1969); traces the history of the title character from her childhood in Rhodesia; also concerns socialism and its complex dilemmas.

Louis MacNeice, *Ten Burnt Offerings*—a collection of ten poetic pieces by the Irish-born writer of verse and playwright; ten medium length poems described by the poet as "experiments in dialectical structure."

Bernard Malamud, *The Natural*—the first novel by the American writer of fiction; a mythological story about baseball and the American hero.

Mouloud Mammeri, *La Colline Oubliee* (Forgotten Hill)—a novel by the Algerian writer of fiction; depicts Kabyle village life during World War II, as well as social conflict on various levels, expressing the author's longing for a new life to replace grim reality; the writer combines his keen sense of observation with his ability to generate mounting tension.

Mary McCarthy, *The Groves of Academe*—a novel by the American writer of fiction; focuses upon supposed political problems that, in reality, tend to be highly personal in nature; thus, a teacher dismissed for incompetence insists that he has, instead, been accused of communist associations.

Gul Khan Nasir, *Gulbang* (Call)—a collection of verse by the Iranian (Baluchi) poet and prose writer; the writer emphasizes the importance of returning to the simplicity and directness of Islamic life and culture.

Dennis Chukude Osadebay, *Africa Sings*—a volume of verse by the West Nigerian poet; the pieces represent the style and the preoccupations of the generation of African writers who continued to search for their own poetic voices; thus, the volume tends to be didactic and derivative of English models, but nonetheless originates from the poet's own emotional reactions.

Kenneth Rexroth, "The Dragon and the Unicorn"—a poem by the American writer of verse; evidences the degree to which the writer emphasized the didactic purpose of poetry; essentially, the piece is a long travelogue poem.

Bharati Sarabhai, *Two Women*—a play by the Indian dramatist, who published her work in English; a realistic piece, written in clipped prose; contains realistic political references associated with the Western world and displays the influence of such writers as T. S. Eliot and William Butler Yeats.

Samuel Selvon, *A Brighter Sun*—the first novel by the Trinidadian writer of fiction and playwright; a humorous and essentially quiet and pleasant piece that attempts to prove to the world that the native can indeed cope with the problems of the large city.

Jean Stafford, *The Catherine Wheel*—a novel by the American writer of fiction; focuses upon the notion that those who choose to function outside the usual conventions must be prepared to confront various forms of disaster; thus, the heroine of the work must perish from fire, realizing that happiness does not function as an automatic quality or entity.

John Steinbeck, *East of Eden*—a novel by the American writer of fiction; an account of an American family that ranges in time from the Civil War to World War I; symbolically transforms the story of Cain and Abel.

Dylan Thomas, *Collected Poems, 1934-1952*—a volume of verse by the Welsh poet; an extremely popular volume that revealed the writer to be a craftsman who labored with both passion and obsession; in describing the pieces, the poet noted in his preface that "these poems, with all their crudities, doubts, and confusions, are written for the love of Man and in Praise of God, and I'd be a damn fool if they weren't."

Evelyn Waugh, *Men at Arms*—a novel by the English writer of fiction; focuses upon a thirty-five-year-old divorced Roman Catholic, who manages to gain a commission at the outbreak of World War II; he becomes involved with a number of strange characters, including his former wife, both in and outside of the army.

E. B. White, *Charlotte's Web*—an extremely popular children's story by the American essayist and miscellaneous prose writer; concerns a spider and a pig, who function as the pets of a little girl; the piece became an equally popular animated film.

Cecil Woodham-Smith, *The Reason Why*—an historical account by the English biographer and historian; the work focuses upon the (in)famous charge of the Light Brigade at the Battle of Balaclava during the Crimean War; the writer argues that the British general staff, trained during the Napoleonic War and deeply mired in the purchase system, evidenced little understanding of warfare at the middle of the nineteenth century and that their deficiencies manifested themselves at Balaclava.

EVENTS

Mortimore Jerome Adler and Robert Maynard Hutchins, American scholars, issue their fifty-four volume classic collection, *Great Books of the Western World;* the works will comprise an essential reading list for American students at all levels of education, and they will become subjects for debate among educationists and social reformers.

Joseph Kramm, American playwright, receives the Pulitzer Prize in drama for *The Shrike* (1952).

Marianne Craig Moore, American poet, receives the Pulitzer Prize in poetry for her *Collected Poems* (1951).

Francois Charles Mauriac, French writer of fiction, playwright, and critic, receives the Nobel Prize for literature.

New World Writing, an anthology of miscellaneous fiction, poetry, drama, and nonfiction, begins publication at New York City; W. H. Auden, James T. Farrell, Dylan Thomas, Robinson Jeffers, Nelson Algren, James Baldwin, Jack Kerouac, and Eugene Ionesco are among the writers whose works appear; until 1959.

The Revised Standard Version of the Bible (RSV), which had been in preparation since 1937 by a group of thirty-two American scholars under the chairmanship of Luther A. Weigle, published for Protestants simultaneously in Toronto, New York, and Edinburgh by the firm of Thomas Nelson and Sons.

Herman Wouk, American writer of fiction and playwright, receives the Pulitzer Prize in fiction for *The Caine Mutiny* (1951).

1953

BIRTHS

Adonis Fostieris. Greek poet and periodical editor; his verse will reveal imagination, sonority, and range; he will write both playful and somber poems, creating brilliant metaphor and quasi-surrealism; however, those same poems will never lose a grasp upon reality.

Rod Jones. Australian writer of fiction; his work will be powerfully intense and imaginative, holding the reader's attention with a mesmerizing force; his lush imagery will evoke exotic physical and psychological landscapes, creating an interplay of psyche and history.

DEATHS

Sir Bheeromal Mehrchand Adwani (b. 1876). Indian (Sindhi) linguist, historian, playwright, and critic; he wrote scholarly essays on literary subjects, produced comic drama, and adapted, among other works, Sir Walter Scott's *Talisman* and Harriet Beecher Stowe's *Uncle Tom's Cabin* to the Sindhi language.

Joseph Hilary Pierre (Hilaire) Belloc (b. 1870). French-born English essayist, novelist, poet, and biographer; he attacked and satirized Edwardian society, advanced the principles of Roman Catholicism, set forth his personal reflections on the intellectual state of the world, and recounted his various travels.

Ugo Betti (b. 1892). Italian playwright and poet; he ranks second only to Luigi Pirandello among twentieth-century Italian dramatists; his plays combine pessimism and morality with Christian optimism and faith; thus, Hell exists as a manifestation of God's will, and human beings must accept it as such.

Jean de Bosschere (b. 1878). Belgian poet, writer of fiction, critic, and diarist; his work contains an abundance of literary elements: symbolism, mysticism, imagism, realism; in addition, it sets forth a number of paradoxes, including beauty and ugliness and simplicity and sophistication; a highly competent illustrator, he provided caricatures for classical works of literature, as well as for his own poems and stories; after spending long periods in London and Paris, he withdrew, in later years, to seclusion in a small town in central France.

Ivan Alekseyevich Bunin (b. 1870). Russian writer of fiction; he gained recognition for his pessimistic novels about peasant life in Russia, as well as for ironic fictional studies of vanity and death; in 1933, he received the Nobel Prize for literature; after 1919, he lived in exile outside Russia.

Douglas Southall Freeman (b. 1886). American historian and newspaper editor; his published work focused upon Robert E. Lee, the American Civil War, and the military men of the Confederacy; his seven-volume biography of George Washington (1949-1957), completed by others following his death, received the Pulitzer Prize for biography in 1958.

Raphael Ernest Grail Glikpo Armattoe (b. 1913). Ghanaian poet and historian; his verse focused upon the dignity and the suffering of Africans under colonialism; he attacked the petty bickering among third-rate chiefs, puppet kings, and politicians who functioned only at the pleasure of their colonial masters; died suddenly, of pneumonia, in a hospital at Hamburg, Germany.

Mutaliyar Tiruvarur V. Kaliyanacuntaram (b. 1883). Indian (Tamil) essayist, journalist, and philosopher; his essays and critical commentary exercised a decided influence upon modern Tamil literary, linguistic, and cultural development; he tended to combine Marxism with Tamil nationalism.

Maha Hswei (b. 1900). Burmese essayist and writer of fiction; he published in excess of six hundred short stories and sixty novels, most of which supported his anti-British point of view and helped to strengthen the growth of the nationalist movement in Burma.

Richard von Mises (b. 1883). Austrian philosopher and mathematician; held professorships at Dresden, Berlin, and Istanbul; his philosophical essays focused upon a frequency theory of probability, which he claimed to be empirical; however, his requirement of "randomness" (or the principle of impossibility of gambling systems), in addition to his reliance upon convergence in an infinite series, raised the question of whether his frequency assertions can be confirmed or falsified by empirical investigations confined to finite series.

Eugene Gladstone O'Neill (b. 1888). American playwright; he rose to become the foremost dramatist in the United States (a position he may continue to occupy); although the quality of his drama may prove uneven and highly experimental, his work abounds in poetry and dramatic genius; he spent his last years burdened by family problems and ill health; he received the Pulitzer Prize for drama in 1920, 1922, 1928, and (posthumously) 1957; in 1936, he received the Nobel Prize for literature.

Marjorie Kinnan Rawlings (b. 1896). American writer of fiction; her work tended to be regional, focusing upon farmers, hunters, trappers, and general family life in her native Florida; she received, in 1939, the Pulitzer Prize for fiction.

Dylan Thomas (b. 1914). Welsh poet and writer of autobiographical prose; he developed a mastery of sound (related, perhaps, to his own resonant voice), combining that with complex and difficult imagery; readers became attracted to his work because of its robust love of life and its sincere humor; he died while on a lecture tour in the United States.

Ben Ames Williams (b. 1889)—American journalist and writer of fiction; his fiction concerned itself with the various historical and social aspects of American life, including his own experiences as a Boston newspaperman; his work found favor more among the general reading public than among literary scholars.

PUBLICATIONS

Lars Ahlin, *Kanelbiten* (Cinnamon-candy)—a novel by the Swedish writer of fiction; the piece concerns a young girl, the title character, who matures in the shadow of a vivacious, egocentric mother; her epic movement ends in tragedy, principally because of her extreme sensitivity.

Phyllis Shand Allfrey, *The Orchid House*—a novel by the Dominican writer of fiction and poet; concerns a black nurse who analyzes, with independence and honesty, the children for whom she cares; the piece in no way considers the usual West Indian themes of political oppression and social deprivation.

Robert Anderson, *Tea and Sympathy*—a play by the American dramatist; the title of the piece offers one definition of adolescent love, while its theme focuses upon the relationship between the understanding wife of a school headmaster and a sensitive student who has doubts about his own masculinity; the drama has often been defined as an exercise in therapeutic sex.

James Baldwin, *Go Tell It on the Mountain*—the first novel by the American writer of fiction and miscellaneous prose, essayist, and playwright; an account of two generations of an American black family.

Simone de Beauvoir, *Le Deuxieme Sexe* (The Second Sex)—a nonfiction sociological study by the French novelist and miscellaneous prose writer; a primer of women's liberation that exercised profound influence upon contemporary feminist thought (although the writer thought of herself more as a Marxist than a feminist).

Samuel Beckett, *L'Innommable* (The Unnamable)—a novel by the Irish-born playwright; the work goes forward upon the device of the interior monologue (soliloquy), with characters in the throes of desolation and obsession; the hero has died, but in that death he cannot find the longed-for annihilation he has been seeking; instead, he discovers only that his anguish has increased.

Saul Bellow, *The Adventures of Augie Marsh*—a novel by the Canadian-born American writer of fiction; the life story of a Jewish version of Huck Finn; the writer traces his movements from the slums of Chicago to the "glitzy" capitals of Europe; the work receives the National Book Award.

Ray Bradbury, *Fahrenheit 451*—a novel by the American writer of science fiction; focuses upon a future in which censorship runs rampant; the new world predicted by this work may appear chilling, but it is, nonetheless, believable.

Paddy Chayevsky, *Marty*—a drama by the American playwright and film writer; written for television and later adapted as a motion picture; an extremely sympathetic and sensitive illustration of what sociologists might term "peer-induced loneliness."

Cecil Day Lewis, *An Italian Visit*—a collection of verse by the English poet and critic; records a journey to Italy with the English poet, publisher, and editor John Lehmann; the poet also portrays his own generation, describing them as an "odd lot," "skeptical yet susceptible," "dour though enthusiastic".

T. S. Eliot, *The Three Voices of Poetry*—a volume of criticism by the American-born poet and essayist; the writer places verse in three categories: lyric—the poet speaks to himself or to no one in particular; nondramatic—the poet addresses a specific audience; and Shakespearean drama—the poet attempts to create a dramatic character speaking in verse.

Roy Fuller, *The Second Curtain*—a novel by the English poet and writer of fiction; focuses upon the timid involvements in crime and punishment of a character named George Carner; he exists as a marginal literary type who finds himself confronting the malevolence of big business.

Mark Harris, *The Southpaw*—a novel by the American writer of fiction and academic; the first of the "Henry Wiggins" novels, in which the principal character pitches his team to the pennant, himself to the most valuable player award; upon its publication, the work was considered the best serious baseball novel ever written.

William Inge, *Picnic*—a play by the American dramatist; concentrates upon an extremely virile drifter and his effect upon a collection of women in a small Kansas town (the writer's state of birth); yet another example of the playwright's ability to construct a strong dramatic piece upon the bases of simple setting and fully realized characters; the play was transformed into a highly successful film; awarded the Pulitzer Prize in drama for this year.

James A. Michener, *The Bridges at Toko-Ri*—a novel by the American writer of popular fiction and miscellaneous prose; a skillfully developed example of war literature that focuses upon the war in Korea (1950-1954).

Arthur Miller, *The Crucible*—a play by the American dramatist; the piece combines a focus upon the Salem witchcraft trials of the seventeenth century with undertones of the anticommunist crusade of Senator Joseph McCarthy during the early 1950s; the central figure of the piece, John Procter, refuses an offer of amnesty in return for naming the witches; he goes off to the gallows to protect his good name.

Amrt Ray, *Bij* (Seed)—a novel by the Indian (Hindi) writer of fiction; relates the story of a young couple, particularly focusing on the woman as she travels the road to sexual and social equality; considered the writer's best literary effort.

Theodore Roethke, *The Waking: Poems, 1933-1953*—a verse collection by the American poet; in this volume, the poet abandons his experimental style for a unification of feeling, especially for sexual unity and the joy to be derived from it; includes such pieces as "Four for Sir John Davies," "The Renewal," "I Knew a Woman Lovely in Her Bones," and "The Pure Fury"; awarded the Pulitzer Prize in poetry in 1954.

J. D. Salinger, *Nine Stories*—a collection by the American writer of fiction; includes "A Perfect Day for Bananafish," "Uncle Wiggily in Connecticut," "Just before the War with the Eskimos," "The Laughing Man," "Down at the Dinghy," "For Esme, with Love and Squalor," "Pretty Mouth and Green My Eyes," "De Daumier-Smith's Blue Period," and "Teddy."

Karl Shapiro, *Poems, 1940-1953*—a collection by the American writer of verse and critic; although the majority of the pieces tend to be brief, the volume does contain a seven-part sequence that relates the story of Adam and Eve; the poet also includes his piece "Israel," on the founding of that nation.

Banmo Tin Aun, *Anjatra Tyekto* (Pauper Tyekto)—a novel by the Burmese writer of fiction and historian; a social novel that draws attention to the miserable existence of a young man from the lowest class of society.

Amos Tutola, *The Palm-Wine Drunkard*—a novel by the Western Nigerian writer of fiction; the work is generally considered the first modern African novel in English; the "Drunkard" undergoes an archetypal journey to the land of the dead; he searches for his tapster, who had fallen from a high palm tree while going after the sap (which becomes palm-wine); he faces a number of adventures, undergoes several punishments and imprisonments, and finally returns to his native village; there he offers abundance to all from his magical egg; however, human beings become greedy, and a quarrelsome crowd breaks the egg, which becomes a large number of whips; the work goes through nine printings in the United States through 1970; the novel has been translated into Czech, Danish, Dutch, Finnish, French, Italian, Magyar, Serbian, and Swedish.

John Wain, *Hurry On Down*—the first novel by the English poet, critic, and writer of fiction; an episodic and picaresque tale of the career of the young Charles Lumley, who leaves the university and rejects his lower middle-class origins by working as a window cleaner, crook, hospital orderly, bar bouncer, and chauffeur; essentially, the work is but another example of the life of the "angry young man" of post-World War II England.

Robert Penn Warren, *Brother to Dragons: A Tale in Verse and Voices*—a combination of verse and fiction by the American poet, writer of fiction, and critic; the principal character, a nephew of Thomas Jefferson, wantonly murders one of his slaves; that crime symbolizes the historical guilt of the United States in terms of an act against humanity, one that originates from the inhumane institution of slavery.

Tennessee Williams, *Camino Real*—a drama by the American playwright; an example of a situation in which the principal character attempts to escape the criticisms of others; in this instance, escape takes the form of a surrealistic dream which offers lyrical, idealistic outpourings of optimism and hope.

Richard Wright, *The Outsider*—a novel by the American writer of fiction and autobiographical narrative; influenced by the writer's contact with the French existentialists; focuses upon a black man's life in Chicago and New York City, as well as his involvement with the Communist Party; in the end, he realizes (before his murder) that the entire social and political system has completely manipulated him.

EVENTS

Sir Winston Churchill, English statesman, historian, and miscellaneous prose writer, receives the Nobel Prize for literature.

Discovery, a literary magazine in paperbound book form, begins publication under the editorship of Vance Bourjaily, the American writer of fiction; contributors include William Faulkner, Nelson Algren, Norman Mailer, and William Styron; six issues through 1955.

Ernest Hemingway, American writer of fiction, receives the Pulitzer Prize in fiction for his novella *The Old Man and the Sea* (1952).

William Inge, American playwright, receives the Pulitzer Prize in drama for *Picnic* (1953).

Archibald MacLeish, American poet and verse dramatist, receives the Pulitzer Prize in poetry for his *Collected Poems, 1917-1952* (1952).

The Paris Review, a quarterly journal of miscellaneous literary productions, begins publication; edited at both Paris and New York City; William Styron is one of its founding editors; the contributors have tended to be American.

1954

BIRTHS

Carlo Ernest Gebler. Irish novelist; he will create authentic portraits of real life, rich in sensation and atmospheric detail; the unpleasant nature of a number of scenes and events produces an unsentimental tone and a fresh approach to the usual rite-of-passage novel; although Irish by birth, he will assume permanent residence in London.

DEATHS

Aleksandre Abasheli (b. 1884). Georgian (SSR) poet; he wrote meditative and nature lyrics;

in collaboration with Grigol Abashisze, he wrote the national anthem of Georgia.

Sait Faik Abasiyanik (b. 1906). Turkish writer of fiction and poet; he gained recognition for his work with the short story; he began by emphasizing plot, but later shifted to a free, lyrical prose form, considerably philosophical in mood; his poetry reflected the life and the people of Istanbul, particularly the fishermen.

Sadriddin Ayni (b. 1878). Tajik (SSR) literary and linguistic scholar, essayist, poet, and writer of fiction and autobiographical narrative; he became known as the founder of modern Soviet Tajik prose; in all of his work, he provides a truthful and fascinating picture of life in his native land: the corruption among officials, the law courts and the military, the trials and the pleasures of student life, and the literature of the region; he held, until his death, the first presidency of the Tajik Academy of Sciences.

Jacinto Benavente y Martinez (b. 1866). Spanish playwright; he gained recognition for his sparkling satires, written in clear and natural prose; in 1922, he received the Nobel Prize for literature.

Sir Edmund Kerchever Chambers (b. 1866). English dramatic historian and Shakespearean scholar; he wrote histories of the medieval stage and the Shakespearean theater, as well as produced an edition of all of Shakespeare's plays; he also wrote full-length studies of Samuel Taylor Coleridge and Matthew Arnold and a volume of the *Oxford History of English Literature* (on the late Middle Ages); in addition, he edited the works of Walter Savage Landor, John Milton, and Henry Vaughan.

Sidonie Gabrielle Colette (b. 1873). French writer of fiction and journalist; she gained critical attention for her warm, subjective style, sharp observations of nature, and lyrical prose; thematically, she concerned herself with the struggle of women for independence, which she reconciled with the insistent demands of physical passion; her characters generally yearn to abandon the conflicts of adulthood and return to the protected innocence of their childhoods; she gained election to the prestigious Academie Royale Belge and to the Academie Goncourt.

Stig Halvard Dagerman (originally Stig Halvard Andersson; b. 1923). Swedish writer of fiction, playwright, essayist, poet, and journalist; his works display a modern temperament and a conscientiousness about the struggles of human existence; essentially, he advocated a literature that sought social improvement, and thus he became known as a model of the socially committed writer in post-war Sweden; after a mental breakdown in 1950, he became convinced that he had failed to realize his potential as a writer and that he had disappointed his nation; after several abortive attempts at suicide, he finally succeeded in asphyxiating himself.

R. Kirusnamurtti (b. 1899). Indian (Tamil) novelist and journalist; he wrote fourteen novels, equally divided between historical and contemporary settings; deeply committed to the movement for Indian independence, he found the novel a worthwhile outlet for the communication of his political beliefs; in addition, he worked hard to reconstruct for his readers the Tamil past, and he achieved popularity through his patriotism, humor, lively dialogue, and ability to inject reality into seemingly improbable events.

Vincas Kreve (Mickevicius; b. 1882). Lithuanian writer of fiction, playwright, poet, and critic; in his fiction, he tended to portray heroic types, ranging from medieval figures to common people of his own times; thus, he dedicated his fiction to expressing the independent spirit of the Lithuanian people as they struggled for political freedom; he left his native land in 1944, emigrating to Austria; in 1947 he came to the United States and accepted a position at the University of Pennsylvania, where he remained until his death.

Martin Andersen Nexo (b. 1869). Danish writer of fiction; he gained recognition for his proletarian novels, pieces that focus upon the conditions of poverty in Denmark between 1905 and 1930.

Ngo-tat-To (b. 1894). North Vietnamese writer of fiction, translator, and journalist; he became the first writer to introduce into Vietnamese literature themes of pain and suffering among the poor villagers; he also translated literature from the Chinese.

PUBLICATIONS

Khvaja Ahmad Abbas, *Inqilab*—a prose piece by the Indian (Urdu) writer of fiction, journalist, and film director; the narrative traces the history of the Indian freedom movement.

Abdalwahhab al-Bayati, *Abariq Muhashshama* (Broken Pitchers)—a volume of verse by the Iraqi poet; collectively, the pieces raise the voice of protest on the part of humanists against the political oppression throughout Iraq.

Kingsley Amis, *Lucky Jim*—a novel by the English writer of fiction and poet; another of the "angry young men" pieces protesting against the ancient traditions that came in the wake of World War II; the title character, a lecturer in history who is striving for academic success, cannot totally obliterate his lower middle-class, radical origins; however, he falls victim to the very establishments that he attempts to subvert.

John Cheever, *The Enormous Radio, and Other Stories*—a collection by the American writer of fiction; the pieces were originally published in *The New Yorker* magazine; the stories focus upon feeling and emotion, rather than upon politics or history; essentially a series of momentary comments upon the suburban world of New York and Connecticut.

Driss Chiraibi, *Le Passe Simple* (The Simple Past)—the first novel by the Moroccan writer of fiction; an exceedingly strong attack upon both traditional Islam and French colonialism; the style of the piece tends toward the dynamic and the emotional.

T. S. Eliot, *The Confidential Clerk*—a dramatic farce in verse by the American-born poet and critic; concerns a financier's quest for the illegitimate son who will be his heir; the search for a vocation sends a character off to seek a new destiny; based upon the *Ion* of Euripides.

William Faulkner, *A Fable*—a novel by the American writer of fiction; an attempt to recreate Christ's Passion against the background of World War I; essentially a bitter work since it displays the novelist's own lack of faith in what he is trying to reenact; begun in 1944, the novel emerged as his largest "non-Yoknapatawpha" fictional project; receives the Pulitzer Prize in fiction in 1955.

Max Frisch, *Stiller* (I'm Not Stiller)—a novel by the Swiss playwright, writer of fiction, and diarist; the theme of self-acceptance and identity is developed through the story and interrogation of a man who may or may not be the vanished sculptor Stiller; the most popular of the writer's novels.

William Golding, *Lord of the Flies*—a novel by the English writer of fiction, poet, and essayist; the story of a group of English boys wrecked on a desert island; they create a savage society dependent upon myth and ritual:

terror assumes absolute rule, a dictator predominates, boys die, and civilization returns only upon their rescue by an officer, who is shocked at what he views.

Thom Gunn, *Fighting Terms*—a verse collection by the English-born poet; the pieces combine technical competence with an Elizabethan elegance of argument; thematically, the rationalist human being seeks an identity so as not to be crippled by intellectualism.

Yusif Idris, *Arkhas Iayali* (The Cheapest Night)—a collection of short stories by the Egyptian writer of fiction and playwright; the pieces describe ordinary people and their concerns, providing illustrations of rural folk life; the writer condemns bureaucracy, social injustice, and prejudices.

Robinson Jeffers, *Hungerfield, and Other Poems*—a collection of verse by the American poet; in the title piece, the poet creates a modern myth that recalls the tale of Heracles.

Jigar Muradabadi, *Atish-e gul* (Fire of Rose)—a collection of verse by the Indian (Urdu) lyric and romantic poet; the volume gained recognition for its delicate sensibility and reflective wisdom; certainly the best known of the poet's published volumes.

P. C. Kuttikkrsnan, *Ummaccu*—a novel by the Indian (Malayalam) writer of fiction; the piece recounts the tragic consequences of the love of two Muslim boys for the same girl.

Camara Laye, *La Regard du Roi* (The Radiance of the King)—a novel by the Guinean writer of fiction; the work focuses upon a white man alone in an African village; to survive, he must adapt to his surroundings; mysticism and the spiritual presence of nature, as related to African tradition, play important roles in the work, particularly since the writer reverses the conventional notion of the black person in an alien culture.

Thomas Mann, *Bekenntnisse des Hochstaplers Felix Krull* (The Confessions of Felix Krull)—a picaresque novel by the German writer of fiction; concerns a "chosen being," a gay criminal amorist and confidence man; the last significant piece of fiction by the writer.

Kamal Markandaya, *Nectar in a Sieve*—a novel in English by the Indian writer of fiction; a story of rural India as it struggles for survival; one of the principal characters, an English missionary, has the dual function of sympathetic observer of the Indian scene and representative of the finer traditions of the West.

W. S. Merwin, *The Dancing Bears*—a collection by the American poet and translator; the pieces evidence the combined influences of Ezra Pound and Robert Graves (the poet tutored Graves' children on Majorca for two years); the poems represent the full range of his literary, linguistic, and intellectual talents; the volume includes "December: Of Aphrodite" and "East of the Sun and West of the Moon," an extended mythological poem.

Henri de Montherlant, *Port Royal*—the eighth play by the French essayist, writer of fiction, and dramatist; the plot of the piece consists of a series of moments of the soul and goes forward upon inner psychological action; set in 1664 and based upon the history of Jansenism, the play outwardly depicts a crisis within a religious community; the influences of the Greek tragic playwrights and of Jean Racine are clearly evident here.

Iris Murdoch, *Under the Net*—the first novel by the Irish-born writer of fiction and philosopher; the work begins with the narrator, a writer, searching in London for a place to live; he proceeds to become involved in a variety of bizarre encounters, both sexual and psychological.

Foteh Niyozi, *Valfo* (Loyalty)—a novel by the Iranian (Tajik) writer of fiction; describes the fate of a Tajik teacher at the front during World War II, and then relates the details of his life after he returns home; described as a mural of the part played by the Tajiks during the war, the work also emphasizes the friendships among Soviet soldiers of all nationalities.

Terence Rattigan, *Separate Tables*—two one-act plays by the English dramatist; the works are set in a hotel and constitute studies of emotional failure and inadequacy.

Abdarrahman ash-Sharqawi, *Al-Ard* (The Earth)—a novel by the Egyptian playwright, essayist, and writer of fiction; a truthful and knowledgeable portrait of Egyptian village life and the peasants' social problems during the 1930s; the writer emphasizes the need for revolutionary action against oppression and exploitation.

C. P. Snow, *The New Men*—a novel by the English writer of fiction and scientist; primarily concerns conflicts during the atomic age between scientists and bureaucrats.

Dylan Thomas, *A Child's Christmas in Wales*—a semifictional, semiautobiographical narrative by the Welsh poet and miscellaneous prose writer; exists, purely and simply, as an evocation of childhood; the work has gained popularity because of the poet's lusty and resonant phonograph recording.

———————, *Under Milkwood*—a verse drama by the Welsh poet, written principally for radio presentation; a literary mood painting of an imaginary town in Wales; behind the facade of Welsh piety and respectability stands an obvious naughtiness, and the poet declares his preference for those who would follow the whimsical forces of life; the work was initially performed by the B.B.C. following the poet's death.

J. R. R. Tolkien, *The Fellowship of the Ring*—a novel by the English writer of fiction, poet, and literary scholar; the first volume of a trilogy (*The Lord of the Rings*); concerns the eight companions chosen by Elrond to accompany the Ring-bearer on the quest of Mount Doom; the fellowship sets out from Rivendell on 25 December, in the year 3019 of the Third Age.

Sotim Ulughzoda, *Subhi Javonii Mo* (The Morning of Our Lives)—an autobiographical novel by the Tajik writer of fiction and playwright; based on the writer's own experiences, describes how Soviet power established itself in the Tajik countryside during the 1920s.

Gore Vidal, *Messiah*—a novel by the American writer of fiction and miscellaneous prose; although, on the surface, the work appears related to the actions and people of Madison Avenue, it actually exists as a fictional exercise in the creation of cult conformity; thus, a religion based upon death reverses the entire concept of Christian mythology and its inherent rituals.

Eudora Welty, *The Ponder Heart*—a novel by the American writer of fiction; focuses upon a wealthy man who has been accused of murdering his seventeen-year-old bride; as usual, the writer sets the piece in a small town in the South; the narrator, Edna Earle Ponder, delivers a monologue upon the foibles of her family in that small town.

Richard Wright, *Black Power*—a narrative by the American-born writer of fiction and miscellaneous prose; the work recounts the writer's travels among the then-emerging independent nations of West Africa.

EVENTS

Ernest Hemingway, American writer of fiction, receives the Nobel Prize for literature.

The London Magazine (the third such periodical to bear that title), a monthly literary journal, begins publication in the English capital with the intent of bringing literature to the common reader; contributors have included Louis MacNeice, Evelyn Waugh, Roy Fuller, W. H. Auden, and Derek Walcott.

John Patrick (pseudonym of John Patrick Goggan), American playwright, receives the Pulitzer Prize in drama for *Teahouse of the August Moon* (1953), an adaptation of a novel by Vernon John Sneider.

The National Book Committee established as the sponsor for the National Book Awards and as a nonprofit American educational organization.

Research reveals that, in this year, 1,768 newspapers in the United States publish fifty-nine million copies each day.

Theodore Huebner Roethke, American poet, receives the Pulitzer Prize in poetry for *The Waking: Poems, 1933-1953* (1953).

1955

BIRTHS

Thomas Bohme. East German poet; his verse will voice the sentiments of the proletariat, but it will also evidence "the gentle soul of the Saxon"; his work will reveal the thoughts and emotions of blue-collar workers in and around Berlin; thus, storefront dwellings will become plagued by malfunctioning laundry equipment, and modernization will appear to be more trouble than it is worth.

Julio Llamazares. Spanish novelist, essayist, and poet; he will publish two volumes of verse, write radio scripts, and receive, in 1982, the Jorge Guillen Prize for prose nonfiction; he will represent human beings as perpetually hunted beasts, but in possession of unexpected survival skills.

Julio Cesar Monteiro Martins. Brazilian writer of fiction; his work will concentrate upon the post-1964 period of his nation's history and the military regime in power; he will write tragicomedies upon the brutality of life in Brazil, ranging in subject matter from the trendy youth roaming the cities to the decimated Indian tribes in the provinces; his prose style will initially emphasize stark realism and satire, but then will shift to a form of poetic prose.

Irina Ratushinskaya. Russian poet; in 1983, she will be arrested for "oral agitation and propaganda," which means that she simply wrote and published her verse; she will write of the Soviet penal system, of the gulags, and of the solidarity among her fellow prisoners; she will gain release from prison in 1987, largely through the efforts of Western writers who protested on her behalf; she will emigrate to the United States and publish her memoirs of life in the Soviet labor camps.

DEATHS

Ahmad Zahi Abu Shadi (b. 1892). Egyptian poet, opera librettist, and translator; his major contribution was his founding, in 1932, of the Apollo Club and its literary organ, *Apollo;* thus, he encouraged young writers and poets and developed a forum for literary discussions; he emigrated to the United States in 1946 and died in Washington, D.C.

James Agee (b. 1909). American author of fiction and script writer; he focused upon the tenant farmers of the Depression era and wrote moving tributes to the strength of the family; he also produced quality critical commentary upon motion picture films; he posthumously received the Pulitzer Prize for fiction in 1958.

Paul Claudel (b. 1868). French playwright and poet; his literary efforts reflect his profound and mystical commitment to the Roman Catholic faith; his versification, based upon lengthy phrases, became known as "verset claudelien"; he exerted a significant influence upon the French poets and playwrights of the succeeding generation; he served the French government at its embassies in Japan, the United States, and Belgium.

Albert Einstein (b. 1879). German-born physicist, mathematician, philosopher, musician, and missionary; his literary efforts included a defense of Zionism, a philosophical discussion of war, and work in the area of musicology.

Roger Mais (b. 1905). Jamaican novelist, poet, and playwright; his knowledge of prisons and the lives of the poor had an important function in his works; he mastered the nuances of the Jamaican dialects and became attracted to the poetic rhythms of the King James Version of the Bible; the substance of his work reveals him to have been a wide reader, one curious

about experience, and a person with a vast capacity for anger and passion.

Asaru'l-haqq Majaz (b. 1911). Indian (Urdu) lyrical poet; his verse expresses the moods and the aspirations of the young Muslim middle class of India; he eventually used his poetry to support the national freedom movement within India; he experiences three bouts with insanity, then died from excessive drinking.

Thomas Mann (b. 1875). German writer of fiction, one of the most significant figures in twentieth-century Western world literature; raised the German novel to an international stature it had not enjoyed since the time of the Romantics; his work reflects his preoccupation with the relationship of creative art to neurosis, with the affinity of genius and disease, and with the problem of artistic values within a bourgeois society; he also studied psychological and mythological elements in the Bible and denounced fascism; in 1929, he received the Nobel prize for literature; he left Germany in 1933, lived in the United States, and moved to Switzerland in 1953.

Saadat Hasan Manto (b. 1912). Indian (Urdu) writer of fiction and playwright; his fiction considers the hypocrisy of the Indian middle class, as well as its sexual morality; attracted to the urban underworld, he found a basis for his characters there, particularly those caught in the excesses of fratricidal feuding; he died from alcoholism.

Jose Ortega y Gasset (b. 1883). Spanish philosopher and essayist; during his tenure as professor of metaphysics at the University of Madrid, he sought to establish the ultimate reality from which everything took root; as early as 1929, he contended that the masses must be directed by an intellectual minority; otherwise, chaos would result for humanity.

Theodor Plievier (b. 1892). German writer of fiction; he believed that literature was an outlet for political expression, and his works walk a fine line between documentary narrative and novel; he went to Russia in 1933, settled in East Germany in 1945, fled to Bavaria in 1947, and finally moved to Switzerland.

Robert Emmet Sherwood (b. 1896). American playwright; his drama ranges from comedy to melodrama to historical biography; he explored the theme of the disintegration of the artist in modern society, as well as the totalitarian influences that affected world politics during the 1930s; he wrote speeches for Franklin Delano Roosevelt and received a Pulitzer Prize in biography-autobiography for his memoirs (1948) of that administration.

Wallace Stevens (b. 1879). American poet; while pursuing a career as an insurance executive, he wrote elegant and philosophical verse principally concerned with creating order out of chaos; he also explored the theme of the purification of the human intellect and sensibility, as applied to both the poet and the reader.

PUBLICATIONS

Sir Tafawa Balewa Abubakar, *Shaihu Umar*—a novel by the Nigerian writer of fiction; a fable concerning a mother and a son carried into slavery at the end of the nineteenth century; after separation, a number of adventures, and extreme suffering, they find each other; considers death and violence, also advancing the idea that virtue is severely tried and only partially rewarded; in addition, the writer observes the court system and the Muslim system of education.

Richard Aldington, *Lawrence of Arabia: A Biographical Inquiry*—a biography by the English novelist and miscellaneous prose writer; a controversial work concerning Thomas Edward Lawrence (1888-1935), the legendary English soldier of fortune known as "Lawrence of Arabia"; the biographer sees his subject as a hysterical homosexual and an "impudent mythomaniac"; despite the efforts of Lawrence's defenders, the work caused the biographer's literary reputation to decline.

W. H. Auden, *The Shield of Achilles*—a collection of verse by the English poet and essayist; includes such major pieces as "Horae Canonicae" and "Bucolics"; the poems are considered among the best of the poet's work.

Enid Bagnold, *The Chalk Garden*—a drama by the English writer of fiction and playwright; theatrically, her most successful dramatic piece.

James Baldwin, *Notes of a Native Son*—a collection of essays and reminiscences by the American writer of fiction and miscellaneous prose; ranges from journalistic pieces to reviews of books and theatrical productions and critiques of various aspects of the American experience (both in and outside of Harlem).

Joyce Cary, *Not Honour More*—a novel by the Irish writer of fiction, essayist, and poet; an examination of politics in which the central character, a revolutionary by the name of Jim Latter, represents the person who rejoices in freedom, destroys order to create, and ignores all priorities but his own.

J. P. Donleavy, *The Ginger Man*—the first novel by the American-born Irish writer of fiction; noted for its rhapsodic, staccato narrative style, which represents the central character's disordered state; considers the outsider in a hostile society; motivated by greed and envy, preoccupied with death, and desperate for love and meaning in his life, he spends most of his time in pursuit of women and alcohol, neglecting his family and his studies; he refuses to compromise his nonconformist nature to gain financial success.

Jean Genet, *Le Balcon* (The Balcony)—a satiric drama by the French playwright and writer of fiction; depicts false dignitaries indulging in erotic fantasies in a brothel, while outside a revolution erupts; eventually, the make-believe incidents are woven into the realities of the revolution; essentially, according to the playwright, the origins of political power lie within the world of erotic fantasy.

Shirley Ann Grau, *The Black Prince, and Other Stories*—a collection by the American writer of fiction; the works focus upon the writer's native South, particularly New Orleans; thus, the volume exists as a series of vividly depicted native scenes.

William Inge, *Bus Stop*—a play by the American dramatist; concerns a group of strangers temporarily stranded in a small cafe; the playwright's dialogue and convincing characterization give the work additional substance; the piece is later transformed into a successful motion picture.

MacKinlay Kantor, *Andersonville*—a historical novel by the American writer of fiction; focuses upon a Confederate prison in Georgia, its tragic commandant, and the 12,000 miserable souls housed there; receives the Pulitzer Prize for fiction in 1956.

Philip Larkin, *The Less Deceived*—a collection of verse by the English poet and writer of fiction; an extremely popular volume that generated immediate critical notice; with this volume, the poet became recognized as the successor to W. H. Auden (much as Alexander Pope had succeeded John Dryden more than two hundred years earlier).

Claude Levi-Strauss, *Tristes Tropiques* (A World on the Wane)—a prose tract by the Belgian-born French anthropologist and essayist; based upon the writer's early field work in Brazil, the volume comes forth as a spiritual, philosophical, and anthropological account of a modern traveler among tribal communities; the writer reflects upon the nature of landscape and the meaning of physical hardship; in essence, the work exists as an intellectual autobiography.

Mahmud al-Mas'adi, *As-Sudd* (The Dam)—an eight-act play by the Tunisian writer of drama and fiction; the writer symbolically treats the conflict between dream and reality; the work evidences the influence of classical Greek tragedy.

Norman Mailer, *The Deer Park*—a novel by the American writer of fiction and miscellaneous prose; an extremely realistic piece focusing upon a young writer who comes of age within the total freedom of a film colony during the 1950s.

Mouloud Mammeri, *Le Sommeil du Juste* (The Sleep of the Just)—a novel by the Algerian writer of fiction; focuses upon a war theme; conveys the trauma of social, national, and religious problems, while at the same time condemning colonialism and the senseless traditions of the old world.

J. P. Marquand, *Sincerely, Willis Wayde*—a novel by the American writer of fiction and journalist; the piece concerns the rise of a businessman to a position of power, a subject about which the writer appears most knowledgeable; as usual, the writer satirizes and indulges, but does not offend.

Mary McCarthy, *A Charmed Life*—a novel by the American writer of fiction; castigates the artists of the world, principally because life among them tends to be more destructive than creative.

Albert Memmi, *Agar*—a novel by the Tunisian writer of fiction and critic; a psychological piece concerning a conflict within an educated young Tunisian whose marriage is crumbling, but who is bound by the traditions of society; the problems, according to the writer, stem from French colonialism and French cultural domination.

Arthur Miller, *A View from the Bridge*—a drama by the American playwright; in its original version, the piece contained a number of passages in verse; a longshoreman refuses to acknowledge his romantic interest in his niece, which ultimately leads to the betrayal of illegal immigrants from Italy, since one of them is also interested in the girl; another of the immigrants kills the longshoreman; the tragedy of the work stems from the

fact that, in actuality, the longshoreman has sought his own death.

Vladimir Nabokov, *Lolita*—a novel in English by the Russian-born writer of fiction, essayist, playwright, and poet; published originally in France, then issued in the United States in 1958; a middle-aged European professor develops a passion for a twelve-year-old girl, whom he pursues to compensate for his own deficiencies during adolescence; the work can also be viewed as a satire on American morals and values.

Flannery O'Connor, *A Good Man Is Hard To Find*—a collection of short stories by the American writer of fiction; the title piece focuses upon an escaped murderer who at one point apologizes to a lady for not wearing his shirt during their conversation; however, he also bears responsibility for the murders, one by one, of the woman's son, daughter-in-law, and grandchildren.

Adrienne Rich, *The Diamond Cutters, and Other Poems*—a verse collection by the American poet; the volume contains referential poems and dramatic monologues that dramatize the inner life of the writer (the poet as wife and mother).

Mordecai Richler, *Son of a Smaller Hero*— an autobiographical novel by the Canadian writer of fiction; depicts the struggle of a young Jew to escape the mental and physical ghetto of his boyhood, as well as to turn away from the alternative WASP world that lies outside.

Jean Paul Sartre, *Nekrassov*—a play by the French writer of fiction, dramatist, essayist, and philosopher; a political piece in which the writer attempts to demonstrate the difficulty of maintaining personal freedom within a society obsessed with the threat of communism.

Stephen Spender, *Collected Poems, 1928-1953*—a collection by the English poet in which the writer attempts both to proclaim collectivist propaganda and to engage in lyric contemplation; the volume includes "The Express," "The Pylons," "Not Palaces, an Era's Crown," "I Think Continually," "Ultima Ratio Regum," "The Double Shame," and "Responsibility: The Pilots Who Destroyed Germany, Spring 1945."

J. R. R. Tolkien, *The Two Towers*—a novel by the English writer of fiction and literary scholar; the second piece of *The Lord of the Rings* trilogy; searching for Drodo and Sam, the Fellowship divides itself; Boromir, repenting of his ill deeds, comes to the aid of the two younger Hobbits, Pippin and Merty, who separated from the others and found themselves lost in the woods; a band of Orcs descends upon them, and Boromir stands against them; his last stand ends in glory, but he falls to his death; thus does the writer set the stage for the transition between the first and final volumes of the trilogy.

Lionel Trilling, *The Opposing Self*—a collection of nine essays by the American literary critic and scholar; includes comments upon Charles Dickens's *Little Dorrit,* Leo Tolstoy's *Anna Karenina,* Henry James's *The Bostonians,* Gustave Flaubert's *Bouvard et Pecuchet,* and Jane Austen's *Mansfield Park.*

Giyorgis Walda Yohannes Walda, *Ag'azi* (I Went Abroad)—a novel by the Ethiopian (Amharic) poet and writer of fiction; a historical and psychological study of a young man who must brave the conservative influence of his family so that he can achieve a foreign education.

Robert Penn Warren, *A Band of Angels*—a novel by the American writer of fiction, poet, and literary critic; through his central character, the writer outlines the American search for the self; reared in luxury as a white girl, the protagonist discovers her mixed blood origin; then, as a slave, she speaks with insight into her true relation with history: history may conquer the self, but the self may eventually remain as an embodiment of an idea from history.

Evelyn Waugh, *Officers and Gentlemen*—a novel by the English writer of fiction; continues the account of Guy Crouchback (from *Men at Arms,* 1952) from his commando training and combat experiences through a series of comic but often painfully truthful encounters; the strength of the piece lies in its characterization and wit.

Tennessee Williams, *Cat on a Hot Tin Roof*—a play by the American dramatist and writer of fiction; concerns the anguishes and frustrations of a Southern family: Big Daddy masks his separateness with an illness, mother Maggie searches for future happiness, and the alcoholic son, Brick, cannot deal with his homosexuality; receives the Pulitzer Prize in drama for this year.

EVENTS

The American Academy of Arts and Sciences establishes the quarterly journal *Daedalus,* containing scholarly and critical essays; each issue will focus upon a specific theme or subject.

William Faulkner receives the Pulitzer Prize in fiction for his novel, *A Fable* (1954).

Halldor Kiljan Laxness, Icelandic writer of fiction, receives the Nobel Prize for literature.

The number of public libraries in the United States listed for this year is 8,420.

Wallace Stevens receives the Pulitzer Prize in poetry for his *Collected Poems* (1954).

The Universal Copyright Convention, established by UNESCO in 1952, takes effect in the United States.

Tennessee Williams, American playwright and writer of fiction, receives the Pulitzer Prize in drama for *Cat on a Hot Tin Roof* (1955).

1956

BIRTHS

Andrea Dworkin. American writer of fiction and miscellaneous prose; her novels will concern woman's search for identity within environments that will tend to outrage and discomfort her readers; in her nonfiction, she will also advance issues related to feminism, such as intercourse serving to enslave women and pornography being a means by which men attempt to possess females.

Amitav Ghosh. Indian novelist; he will write fiction revealing the influence of Herman Melville's sea novels; his language will be described as "arresting," his style as "dazzling"; thus, both main and peripheral episodes will become animated with rich and exotic descriptions, creating a form of magic realism; he will also gain a reputation as a competent storyteller.

DEATHS

Leo Baeck (b. 1875). German-Jewish scholar, theologian, and prose writer; he wrote the standard interpretation of Judaism and Jewish history, and in another work set out to prove that the Pharisees were the most progressive party at the time of the Crucifixion;

he refused to leave Germany during the Nazi regime and spent two years in a concentration camp at Terezin, Czechoslovakia; he died in London.

Gottfried Benn (b. 1886). German poet; his early verse tended toward expressionism, while later poems reflect the conflicts and tragedies of the Nazi era; he also wrote critical essays on aesthetics and politics.

Bertolt Brecht (b. 1898). German poet and playwright; in the late 1920s, he concentrated upon expressionism and began to develop his revolutionary "epic theater," designed to create (with the help of bright lights, films, and mottos displayed on flash cards) a politically conscious distance between the audience and the stage; during the Nazi era, he resided in Denmark, and then settled in the United States; from 1948, he lived in East Berlin, where he directed the state supported Berliner Ensemble; he dies from heart problems.

Ali Akbar Dehkhoda (b. 1879?). Iranian poet, satirist, and philologist; his verse describes the patriotic struggles against the despotic regime; he became a pioneer of nontraditional verse forms, as well as the first writer to develop a modern Persian prose idiom; he also compiled the first modern Persian dictionary.

Walter De la Mare (b. 1873). English poet and writer of fiction; one of modern literature's chief exemplars of the romantic imagination; his works form a sustained treatment of romantic themes: dreams, death, rare states of mind and emotion, fantasy worlds of childhood, and the pursuit of the transcendent; his verse reflects his own sense of wonder at the ordinary sights and sounds of common experiences; in his view, the minutia of life mirror the very nature of the vast and the timeless.

Derenik Demirtchian (b. 1877). Armenian writer of fiction, poet, and playwright; he attempted, during World War II, to arouse the patriotism of his people, writing verse inspired by classical Persian themes and forms; he assisted in establishing the continuity of democratically informed Armenian literature with the mood of the post-revolutionary period.

Herbert Isaac Ernest Dhlomo (b. 1903). South African (Zulu) novelist, poet, and playwright; his drama focused upon such themes and subjects as Zulu heroes, social struggles, and working conditions; he wrote occasional verse in both Zulu and English that expressed his anger at the plight of the native South Afri-

cans; he died in a Durban hospital, where he had spent some months after his most recent heart attack.

Resat Nuri Guntekin (b. 1892). Turkish writer of fiction, playwright, and translator; he will treat, in his fiction, the decadent political figures of the nineteenth century, combining realistic narration and description with simple and clear language; he also considered the themes of love and fidelity, treating those with controlled sentiment and delicate humor; he generally translated French works; he died in London.

Muhammad Husaym Haykal (b. 1888). Egyptian novelist, critic, and journalist; he authored one of the earliest novels (*Zaynab*, 1914) to appear in modern Arabic, written while he was a law student in Paris; he attempted serious sociological commentary and criticism, both in his fiction and nonfiction.

Bal Sitaram Mardhekar (b. 1907). Indian (Marathi) poet; his verse revolutionized Indian poetry following World War II; those pieces appeared in two collections, published in 1947 and 1951; his essay demonstrating the relationship between artists and their art appeared (in English) in 1960.

H. L. Mencken (b. 1880). American essayist, narrative writer, reviewer, journalist, and editor; he produced outspoken essays, attacking the mental and intellectual complacency of the American middle class and their equally complacent political and social systems; he produced a significant reference work on American English, one that went through four editions and a supplement.

Giovanni Papini (b. 1881). Italian essayist, biographer, writer of fiction, and poet; in his youth, he led the attempts to revolutionize Italian culture and social thought by introducing the literatures, philosophies, and arts of other nations into his own country; he considered and then discarded such ideas and theories as pragmatism, futurism, and atheism before embracing Roman Catholicism.

David Shimonowitz (b. 1886). Israeli poet; his verse reflected his attraction to landscape; thus, he emerged as a true son of nature and the major idyllic poet of Israel; his work transmits the peaceful tone and melodious rhythm of the true wayfarer.

Cahit Sitki Taranci (b. 1910). Turkish poet; his work represents one of the highest achievements of modern Turkish poetry in syllabic-rhymed verse; he wrote of death and its terrors, of old age and solitude, of the search for a lost god, and of unfulfilled love; his verse is the authentic expression of the intellectual and emotional preoccupations of the intelligent Kemal writer and his generation; he died in a Vienna hospital, where he had been undergoing treatment for a lengthy illness.

Samad Vurghun (b. 1906). Azerbaijan (SSR) poet and playwright; his verse ranges from short love poems to longer pieces on social themes; he replaced the traditional figure of the beautiful woman with the new working-class female; his verse drama provides a panoramic view of eighteenth-century Azerbaijan; he also translated verse and drama from the Russian.

Robert Walser (b. 1878). Swiss writer of fiction, essayist, and poet; his novels and short stories tend to portray people in socially subordinate positions, particularly clerks and servants; the writer praises their simplicity and advocates a rejection of intellectual analysis in favor of a spontaneous way of life; his fiction combines playfulness with gentle irony, and therefore his prose style helps to suggest his vision of life; he died suddenly, on Christmas day, while on a solitary walk.

PUBLICATIONS

James Baldwin, *Giovanni's Room*—the second novel by the American playwright and writer of fiction and miscellaneous prose; focuses upon the desire (principally within the writer himself) to escape to a new world; the piece occurs in Paris and concerns a serious struggle between homosexual and heterosexual love.

John Barth, *The Floating Opera*—a novel by the American writer of fiction; concerns both the decision and indecision of the principal character upon the very day he has determined to take his own life; a lawyer given to obsessive reasoning, he spends his time in declaration and negation, in doing and undoing himself; the exercise requires ten years of the man's life, and the novel stands as the writer's attack upon the process of logic (not totally unlike that seen in Jonathan Swift's *Gulliver's Travels*).

Abdalwahhab al-Bayati, *Al-Majd li'l-Atafal wa z-Zaytun* (Glory to Children and Olives)—a collection of verse by the Iraqi poet; the writer

abandons the traditional Arabic verse forms for new ones; thus, the volume reflects the influence of European poetic theory and the writer's attempt to create a progressive poetic humanism.

Brendan Behan, *The Quare Fellow*—a play by the Irish dramatist, first produced in Dublin in 1954; set in a prison on the night of a scheduled execution, the work explores the effect of that impending occurrence on prisoners and their jailers; despite the pervasive gloom and doom, the writer manages to inject ample ribaldry into the lively speeches of his various characters.

Saul Bellow, *Seize the Day*—a novella by the Canadian-born American writer of fiction; the principal character proves a failure, both as a provider and a son; he recognizes himself as a worthless fool, but nonetheless continues to pay money to an incompetent psychiatrist; the piece ends with the man tearfully confessing his inadequacies at the funeral of a perfect stranger.

Catherine Drinker Bowen, *The Lion and the Throne*—a biography by the American writer; concerns the life of Sir Edward Coke (1552-1634), the English jurist and rival of Sir Francis Bacon; in 1616, James I dismissed him from the King's Bench, an event that created a crisis between king and parliament.

Harindranath Chattopadhyay, *Siddhartha: Man of Peace*—a historical play by the Indian dramatist; an ambitious piece that portrays the main events in the life of the great Buddha.

Leon Gontran Damas, *Black-Label*—a poem by the Guyanean writer of verse, eighty-four pages in length and written in four parts; employs the poet's basic technique of staccato lines and overlapping, repetitive phrases; a complex intellectual structure is produced by leitmotives and recurring images; the poet attempts to reproduce the polyphonic textures of traditional African poems played on the "talking drum" and accompanied by dance and chorus, as well as the prevailing West Indian music.

Friedrich Durrenmatt, *Der Besuch der Alten Dame: Eine Tragische Komodie* (The Visit: A Tragi-Comedy)—a play by the Swiss dramatist, writer of fiction, and essayist; concerns a rich old woman who returns to her impoverished native village and offers one million dollars to the villagers in return for the death of the person who, years earlier, had denied his responsibility for her pregnancy; the people profess righteous indignation and defend the murder as just; in 1959, the play receives the New York Drama Critics Circle Award.

T. S. Eliot, *Essays on Elizabethan Drama*—a collection of criticism on poetry and drama by the American-born English poet and essayist; the writer reevaluates his earlier views, stating that he had dealt justly and accurately with the minor figures of the period, but that his attitude toward William Shakespeare had been "callow"; he argues that critical consistency toward Shakespeare proves the smallness of one's mind, and that the wise critic requires years (a lifetime, perhaps) to develop critical criteria by which to measure his works.

Arthur Nuthall Fula, *Met Erbarming, O Here* (With Pleasure, Dear Sirs)—a novel in Afrikaans by the South African writer of fiction and poet; the principal character, a physician, attempts to overcome the superstitious fears of the poor in the slums of Johannesburg; based upon the writer's own extensive experiences with such conditions.

Allen Ginsberg, *Howl, and Other Poems*—a collection by the American writer of verse; the title poem stands as the trumpet call of the "Beat Generation"; the pieces exist as expressions of anxious indignation or, according to the poet, as his "Angel Ravings"; originally banned by San Francisco authorities on the grounds of lewdness and obscenity.

William Golding, *Pincher Martin*—a novel by the English writer of fiction; concerns the survivor of a torpedoed destroyer; he must call upon all of his internal resources and instincts as he clings to a bare rock in the mid-Atlantic Ocean.

Mark Harris, *Bang the Drum Slowly*—a novel by the American writer of fiction and miscellaneous prose; the second appearance of the writer's baseball hero, Henry Wiggen; in this work, he attaches himself to a dying catcher; transformed into a motion picture.

Khin Hnin Ju, *Myei Ka Ye Thij* (The Earth Is Laughing)—a collection of short stories by the Burmese writer of fiction; the pieces express her Buddhist feelings for nature and its impermanence; throughout the collection, she emphasizes the ephemeral beauties of the landscape, and her descriptions have been praised for their "poetry" of language.

Guiseppe Lampedusa, *Il Gattopardo* (The Leopard)—a novel by the Italian writer of fiction; the work describes the reactions of a noble Sicilian family to the political and social changes brought about by Guiseppe Garibaldi's annexation of Sicily in 1860; the piece exists both as an indictment and a lament.

Meyer Levin, *Compulsion*—a popular novel by the American writer of fiction and autobiographical prose; essentially a psychological study of the principal figures, Nathan Leopold and Richard Loeb, in the 1924 kidnapping and murder of Bobby Franks; the two highly intelligent and well-educated men had selected their victim at random, simply to determine what it would feel like to kill someone; the work contains an extremely dramatic courtroom episode.

Najib Mahfuz, *Bayna al-Qasraym*—a novel by the Egyptian writer of fiction; describes the changes brought about by political and social developments in the lives of three generations of a traditional Muslim family; the piece takes place between 1917 and 1944.

Benjamin Matep, *Afrique Nous T'ignorans* (Africa, We Don't Pay Attention to You)—a novel by the Cameroon writer of fiction, poet, playwright, and biographer; concerns the Cameroons of the 1930s and the turbulence occasioned by the outbreak of World War II; explores the hopes and fears of three representative leaders of modern Africa: the Christian priest, the medical doctor, the village chief; the tensions among the three neighbors and men of good will demonstrate the difficulties of achieving balance in the postcolonial world.

Amrtlal Nagar, *Bund aur Samudr* (The Drop and the Sea)—a novel by the Indian (Hindi) writer of fiction; a portrayal of urban middle-class life in the writer's hometown of Lucknow.

Edwin O'Connor, *The Last Hurrah*—a novel by the American writer of fiction; concerns the demise of an Irish-American political boss; set in the rough and tumble political arena of Boston, Massachusetts, and patterned after the career of one of that city's more colorful mayors of the 1940s and 1950s, James Michael Curley.

Eugene O'Neill, *Long Day's Journey into Night*—an autobiographical drama by the American playwright, published and produced three years after the writer's death; vividly portrays his mother's recurring mental illness and his father's coldness; a naturalistic family drama that goes forward without plot contrivances or artificial intrigues, relying instead on dialogue to convey meaning and emotion; an uncommonly moving revelation of character and human relationships; the work receives the Pulitzer Prize for drama in 1957.

Takazi Sivasankara-Pilla, *Cemmin* (Shrimps)— a novel by the Indian (Malayalam) writer of fiction; concerns the struggles of the poor fishermen from the coast of Kerala; contains passionate but highly accurate descriptive passages.

J. R. R. Tolkien, *The Return of the King*—a novel by the English writer of fiction and literary scholar; the final volume in the trilogy *The Lord of the Rings;* relates the opposing strategies of Gandalf and Sauron that lead to the final catastrophe and to the end of the great darkness; when the ring can be destroyed, Middle-earth's magical beauty and creatures will slowly fade, and a new age will begin in which human beings become dominant.

Richard Wilbur, *Things of This World*—a verse collection by the American poet; the writer extends his range beyond the contemplative aestheticism of earlier volumes; he creates functional and mythical allusions to intelligence, attempting to cast an inner light upon the outward darkness; thus, even with the extension of his substantive range, the poet continues to meditate; receives the Pulitzer Prize in poetry in 1956.

EVENTS

The American "Beat Movement" begins in San Francisco and New York City; a collection of "new barbarian" writers (as well as other artists) who choose the present as the compass of their lives; includes Anatole Broyard, R. V. Cassill, George Mandel, Clellon Holmes, Jack Kerouac, Chandler Brossard, "William Lee," Carl Solomon, and Allen Ginsberg.

The American Society for Theater Research is established to investigate both the literary and performance aspects of drama.

Elizabeth Bishop, American writer of verse, receives the Pulitzer Prize for *Poems: North and South—A Cold Spring* (1955).

Albert Hackett, American actor and playwright, and his wife, Frances Goodrich, receive the Pulitzer Prize in drama for *The Diary of Anne Frank* (1955), an adaptation of the autobiographical narrative published in 1952.

Juan Ramon Jimenez, Spanish poet (and resident of Puerto Rico), receives the Nobel Prize in literature.

MacKinlay Kantor, American writer of historical fiction, receives the Pulitzer Prize in fiction for his novel *Andersonville* (1955).

1957

DEATHS

Iliya Abu Madi (b. 1890?). Lebanese-born poet; he produced deeply introspective verse that dwells upon individual episodes of romantic malaise, doubt, and confusion; he also wrote with a strong sense of nostalgia; he emigrated from Lebanon to Alexandria, Egypt, then in 1912 settled permanently in New York City.

Mark Aleksandrovich Aldanov (pseudonym of Mark Aleksandrovich Landau; b. 1888?). Russian writer of fiction, essayist, and biographer; he gained recognition for his historical novels, a number of which underscore the ideals of the Revolution; he patterned his work after that of Leo Tolstoy, and thus created powerful portraits of historical figures; he became noted for his direct style, intelligent assessment of historical events, scholarly accuracy, and penetrating analysis of human nature; he left Russia after the Revolution for the Ukraine, then lived in both Germany and France; he died, suddenly, in Nice.

Sholem Asch (b. 1880). Polish-born writer of fiction; he wrote almost exclusively in Yiddish; he introduced an element of romanticism into the harsh realism of Hebrew and Yiddish literature; he became noted for his passionate and insightful portrayals of small Jewish communities; he also sought to combine the most positive elements of Jewish and Christian ideals into his later fiction, more for philosophical manipulation than out of his own religious convictions; he became an American citizen in 1920, then moved to Israel and England; he died in London.

George Bacovia (pseudonym of Gheorghe Vasiliu; b. 1881). Romanian poet; his work has been associated with French Symbolism, expressionism, and existentialism, and much of it is based on his own personal suffering: poverty, isolation, alcoholism, and emotional instability; toward the end of his career, Marxist critical commentators praised the social perspective of his verse; he spent most of his later years in a sanitarium where, nonetheless, he continued to produce poetry.

Arthur Joyce Lunel Cary (b. 1888). Irish-born writer of fiction, essayist, and poet; he portrayed complex and memorable characters who embodied his own philosophy: life, although profoundly unfair and arbitrary, can become a magnificent adventure for those resourceful individuals willing to acknowledge no authority higher than their own vital and creative natures; he tended to rely upon a first-person, present-tense narrative form to convey a sense of immediacy.

Alfred Doblin (b. 1858). German writer of fiction; his work reflected his socialist politics, expressionist philosophy, and religious sentiments; he adopted a wide range of fictional techniques and forms (expressionism, fantasy, realism, and even the detective story motif) to achieve his varied purposes; with the rise of Nazism, he left Germany for Russia, Palestine, France, and the United States; following World War II, he returned to West Germany; during his stay in America, he converted from Judaism to Roman Catholicism.

Avetikh Isahakian (b. 1875). Armenian poet; the themes of his verse focus upon folk stories, social problems, and revolutionary ideals; he rejected contemporary social norms, institutions, and relationships and attempted to resolve the eternal conflicts between the hierarchy of values of both the individual and society; he lived and published verse in Paris, Venice, Geneva, and the USSR; historically, his poetry serves as a link between early twentieth-century Armenian literature and that of the Soviet period.

Nikos Kazantzakis (b. 1883). Greek poet and writer of fiction; his work reflects his intensely poetic and religious nature; his fiction tends to be highly realistic, while his poetry probes the major religious and political philosophies of East and West, from Buddha and Jesus Christ to Friedrich Nietzsche and Vladimir Lenin.

Guiseppe Tomasi di Lampedusa (b. 1896). Italian writer of fiction; a member of a Sicilian noble family, he drew upon his knowledge and experience to produce a major novel illustrating the decline of his own social and political class, *The Leopard* (1955-1956).

Clarence Malcolm Lowry (b. 1909). English writer of fiction; he lived and wrote in such diverse locales as Mexico and British Columbia, but eventually returned to England; his novels tend to be classified as "powerful," principally because his heroes appear as desperate and as self-destructive as their creator; an incurable alcoholic, he died in Sussex from a "misadventure."

Curzio Malaparte (b. 1898). Italian writer of fiction; his major novels focus upon World War II and its aftermath; essentially, he concerns himself with demonstrating the demoralization of Italy in the face of foreign invasion, first by the Germans and then by the Americans; he gained critical recognition for drawing, with extravagant detail, the seething activities of cities.

Gabriela Mistral (pseudonym of Lucila Godoy Alcayaga; b. 1889). Chilean poet, educator, and diplomat; her verse reflects her two loves—the Roman Catholic Church and men—as well as the tragedies resulting from personal losses: the unexplained death of a lover, the suicide of her beloved nephew, and the lack of opportunity to become a mother (she never married); thus, she became a poet of moods; in 1945, she achieved the dual honor of being the first woman and the first Latin American to receive the Nobel Prize for literature; she dies of cancer while in the United States.

John Middleton Murry (b. 1889). English critic, editor, and literary biographer; he sought to achieve a personal identification with his subjects by examining their literary accomplishments through their own "inward spirits"; he viewed literature as a proclamation of the self, as something essentially "good" for human beings; he lacked the desire to pursue scholarship on the serious or investigative level, and thus his work, in the years since his death, has received mention rather than extended consideration.

Alexey Mikhailovich Remizov (b. 1877). Russian folklorist, writer of fiction, playwright, and essayist; he earned recognition for his ornate prose style, which influenced a generation of Russian writers; he wrote fiction, mystery plays, religious parables, adaptations of folklore, records of dreams, and experimental narratives that combined historical chronicle, memoir, fiction, and literary criticism; he unified modern literary techniques with elements of the Russian oral tradition and nineteenth-century literary realism; he emigrated to Berlin in 1921 and two years later settled in Paris, where he died.

W. Abraham Silva (b. 1892). Ceylonese (Sinhal) writer of fiction; his novels and short stories gained popularity because of his introduction of ordinary conversational language into Sinhalese literature.

John William Van Druten (b. 1901). Englishborn American playwright and writer of fiction; his plays and novels were most popular on the stage and motion picture screen; he did, however, achieve a lightness and warmth of both language and tone.

Bhai Vir Singh (b. 1872). Indian (Panjabi) writer of fiction and poet; he wrote a trilogy of short novels glorifying the Sikh past, the first examples of Panjabi prose fiction; his romantic epic of 12,000 lines in blank verse and his short mystical lyrics, his most important literary achievement, reveal his finely developed sense of the beauty of nature.

PUBLICATIONS

Abd'ul-Karim, *Dzoley Guluna* (An Armful of Blossoms)—a volume of short stories by the Pakistani (Pashto) writer of fiction; these pieces represent a new direction in Pashto literature, since the heroes of the stories generally come from the lower social classes and constitute individuals with whom the writer sympathized.

James Agee, *A Death in the Family*—a novel by the American screenwriter, poet, and author of fiction; highly autobiographical and unfinished at the writer's death (1955); relates the shattering effect on a happy family in Tennessee of the father's premature death in an automobile accident; its strength lies in its depiction of pure decency in the midst of adversity.

Ray Bradbury, *Dandelion Wine*—a novel by the American writer of science fiction; relates the story of one Douglas Spaulding and his strange twelfth summer; during that time he discovers that the small town in which he lives contains a human time machine and a "wax witch" who possesses the gift of telling the future.

John Braine, *Room at the Top*—the first novel by the English writer of fiction; another in a line of "angry young men" pieces of literature; thus, the central figure, Joe Lampton, emerges as a ruthless opportunist who begins with a position in the town hall, then seduces and marries a wealthy young woman; prior to that, he had been in love with an unhappily married older woman.

Michel del Castillo, *Tanguy: Histoire d'un Enfant d'Aujourd'hui* (A Child of Our Time)—

an autobiographical novel by the Spanishborn French writer of fiction; an account of the suffering endured by the writer as a child during World War II; thus, the central figure of the piece was born in Madrid twenty-five years earlier (and three years prior to the Spanish Civil War) to a French father and a Spanish mother; the father, a bourgeois opportunist, deserts his family and flees to France, while the mother, a journalist, remains behind to fight for the Republican cause; when the Republic falls, she takes her child and moves to France, whereupon her husband denounces her to the authorities; she and her child endure in a French internment camp for political exiles.

John Cheever, *The Wapshot Chronicle*—a novel by the American writer of fiction; a comic but highly elegiac account of the eccentric New England family of the title; an aging matriarch and her heirs are portrayed with subtle irreverence.

James Gould Cozzens, *By Love Possessed*—a novel by the American writer of fiction; focuses upon both the pridefulness and the emptiness of the inhabitants of small American towns; the central character, a lawyer, displays a realistic combination of faults and virtues; all of the action takes place within two days.

Lawrence Durrell, *Justine*—a novel by the English poet and writer of fiction and travel narrative; the first volume of *The Alexandria Quartet;* written by the novelist's supposed alter-ego, the work focuses upon the title character, a Jewess who has suffered from a childhood rape and the kidnapping of her baby daughter from her first marriage; married to a rich Coptic Christian, she spends most of her time searching for the child; about her and her life roam a host of European characters.

T. S. Eliot, *On Poetry and Poets*—a collection of sixteen essays by the English poet and critic; the pieces were written between 1926 and 1956; concerns such issues as the social functions of poetry and its music, the definitions of minor and classical poetry, the voices of poetry, and the frontiers of criticism; the writer discusses Virgil, Sir John Davies, John Milton, Samuel Johnson, Lord Byron, Johann Wolfgang von Goethe, Rudyard Kipling, and William Butler Yeats.

William Faulkner, *The Town*—a novel by the American writer of fiction; incorporates revised versions of "Centaur in Brass" (1932) and "Mule in the Yard" (1934); essentially a story of the Snopes family, related with ample detail and humor; Eula Snopes, the unfaithful wife of Flem Snopes, commits suicide; she does not want her daughter to know that someone other than Flem has fathered her, nor does she want the town to reduce her to the very human status from which she has spent her life attempting to escape.

Thom Gunn, *The Sense of Movement*—a volume of verse by the English-born poet; the work conveys the theme of the rationalist who seeks an existence in which intellectualism will not cripple thought and restrict human action (or movement).

Ted Hughes, *The Hawk in the Rain*—the first collection of verse by the English poet; the poems reveal his obsession with nature, which began during his boyhood in Yorkshire; thus, the volume reflects his love for animals, his sense of the beauty of nature, and his reactions to the violence of the natural world.

William Inge, *The Dark at the Top of the Stairs*—a drama by the American playwright; an extremely somber portrayal of a family haunted by its prejudices, regrets, and unfocused fears; the writer again focuses upon life in small-town America, striving to give form to the deep yearnings and guilts of his unsophisticated characters.

James Jones, *Some Came Running*—a novel by the American writer of fiction; the central character returns to his home in Illinois after a tenure in the army and time spent in California writing fiction; he attempts to regain those sights and thoughts that had escaped him in previous years at home; as usual for this writer, plot gives way to character and human obsessions; thus, the work focuses upon the frustrations of the writer as he struggles between his desire for detachment and the need to be close to the naturalness of life.

Jack Kerouac, *On the Road*—a novel by the American writer of fiction, poetry, and narrative; a principal contribution to the literature of the "Beat Generation"; records the wanderings of three transients; written on a continuous roll of art paper and completed within three weeks.

Al-Bashir Khraief, *Iflas aw Hubbuk Darbani* (Decline; or, Your Love Has Destroyed Me)— an autobiographical novel by the Tunisian writer of fiction; the piece gained popularity because of its reliance upon colloquial Arabic dialogue; the writer depicts the Tunisian

petty bourgeois reacting to the impact of modernism.

Denise Levertov, *Here and Now*—a volume of verse by the English-born American poet; demonstrates the influence of William Carlos Williams; the poet strives to take advantage of her own experiences; for her, prosody exists as the direct expression of the movement of the poet's perception, while sounds imitate the feelings of experience.

Louis MacNeice, *Visitations*—a collection of lyrical poems by the Irish-born poet; the first volume of short pieces published by the poet since his *Holes in the Sky* of 1948.

Bernard Malamud, *The Assistant*—a novel by the American writer of fiction; focuses upon the theme of goodness; a Gentile hoodlum robs a poor Jewish shopkeeper and then, driven out of a sense of pity that he cannot overcome, goes to work for his victim, gradually becoming involved in the Jew's defeated and unsuccessful life; he falls in love with the grocer's daughter, assumes the man's business (and even his inner self) after his death, and finally, through the rite of circumcision, becomes a Jew.

Alberto Moravia, *La Ciociara* (Two Women)— a novel by the Italian writer of fiction, playwright, essayist, and translator; reflects the writer's notion of the redeeming nature of human suffering; a shopkeeper and her daughter endure the brutal effects of war by overcoming their inabilities to experience passion and grief.

Iris Murdoch, *The Sandcastle*—a novel by the Irish-born English writer of fiction; concerns the passion of a married middle-aged man for an artist considerably younger than he; the relationship causes him to become consumed with guilt.

Vladimir Nabokov, *Pnin*—a novel by the Russian-born writer of fiction, poet, essayist, playwright, and translator; considered one of his most complex works; focuses upon the bumbling attempts of an exiled Russian scholar to adapt to life and work at an American university.

John Osborne, *The Entertainer*—a drama by the English playwright, commissioned for the distinguished English actor Sir Laurence Olivier; concerns three generations of a theatrical family who had formerly enjoyed success in the music halls of England; they now find themselves reduced to second-rate billings and half-empty houses; the father, a has-been comic, has little left but a passion for drink and stale jokes; nonetheless, he attempts, with disastrous results, to return his father to the stage, hoping to revitalize the family's fortunes; Olivier also starred in the film version.

——————— , *Look Back in Anger*—a play by the English dramatist (performed in 1956), heralded as the principal dramatic contribution of the generation of "angry young men"; the central character, although educated, sells sweets from a stall, argues with his wife (who leaves him), and takes up with her friend; after losing their child, the wife returns, the friend goes back to her husband, and the reunited couple proceeds to confront the prospect of a considerably bleak future; throughout, the anger of the central character, Jimmy Porter, rarely subsides.

Prince Modupe Paris, *I Was a Savage*—an autobiography by the Guinean writer of fiction and autobiographical narrative; considers the writer's childhood in his Soussou village on the coast of Guinea, the Western and American influences that led to his voyage to the United States, and his journey to America and his experiences there; although written after the prince had spent thirty-six years in the United States, the piece does present nostalgic descriptions of his homeland.

Ayn Rand, *Atlas Shrugged*—a novel by the Russian-born American writer of fiction and miscellaneous prose; the work sets out to demonstrate what will occur in the world when the intellectuals and the persons of ability go on strike; it has been described as a form of mystery story that concerns the murder and rebirth of the human spirit.

Isaac Bashevis Singer, *Gimpel the Fool*—a collection of short stories (originally written in Yiddish) by the Polish-born American writer of fiction; the title character represents various forms of failure and weakness; he has been described as the "ranking schlemiel in contemporary Jewish fiction," a manifestation and an amalgam of defeat, disaster, and righteousness.

Muriel Spark, *The Comforters*—the first novel by the Scottish-born writer of fiction, poet, playwright, essayist, and biographer; the novelist employs a variety of fictional techniques; studying the creative process of art, depicting grotesque and eccentric characters, and introducing supernatural elements into realistic settings.

Robert Penn Warren, *Promises: Poems, 1954-1956*—a collection by the American writer of fiction, poet, and critic; contains verse sequences and a series of lyrics on common themes, ranging from the poet's reminiscences, to his parents, to meditations upon Ralph Waldo Emerson; the volume receives the Pulitzer Prize for poetry in 1958.

Evelyn Waugh, *The Ordeal of Gilbert Pinfold*—a novel by the English writer of fiction; presents a noted fifty-year-old Roman Catholic novelist who drinks, cannot sleep, and generally finds himself out of touch with the modern world; disgusted and bored, he sets off on a cruise for Ceylon; however, he develops severe paranoia, believing that the people there are accusing him of being a Jew, a fascist, an alcoholic, and a blatant social climber; he eventually finds salvation.

Ivor Winters, *The Function of Criticism: Problems and Exercises*—a volume of essays by the American poet and critic; sets forth the writer's critical theories concerning the nature of poetry; essentially, the successful poem is a statement in words about a human experience; verse exists as a precise and rhythmic means for communicating that experience, particularly in terms of conveying human emotion.

EVENTS

Albert Camus, Algerian-born French novelist, playwright, and philosopher, receives the Nobel Prize for literature.

The Evergreen Review, a quarterly magazine of poetry, fiction, drama, literary criticism, and general political and social commentary, begins publication at New York City; until 1973.

The New Cambridge Modern History, Cambridge University Press, publishes its first volume.

Eugene Gladstone O'Neill, American playwright, is posthumously awarded the Pulitzer Prize in drama for *Long Day's Journey into Night* (published and produced in 1956).

The Carl H. Pforzheimer Library, New York City, is established for the encouragement of scholarly research in the arts and sciences.

Richard Purdy Wilbur, American writer of verse, receives the Pulitzer Prize in poetry for *Things of This World* (1956).

1958

BIRTHS

Ulf Eriksson. Swedish critic, poet, and novelist; his verse will represent his most significant literary achievement, particularly as he experiments with simile and metaphor; his poems will be evasive and abstract, complicated by what has been termed "fleeting diction"; his best poetry will accurately reflect the experiences of his childhood, which will be infused with mature impressions.

DEATHS

Johannes R. Becher (b. 1891). German poet; he became a communist in 1918 and spent the years 1933-1945 in Russia before being appointed to the post of Minister of Culture in East Germany; his verse expressed the sense of loneliness experienced by people living in large cities; he also produced a powerful novel, *Abschied* (1948), about the effect of World War I upon the bourgeois youth.

Yahya Kemal Beyatli (b. 1884). Turkish poet; considered the last classical writer of verse in Turkey, he relied upon the traditional meters; his work was influenced by the eighteenth-century Turkish poets and the French Symbolists; his verse concerns the old glory of the Ottoman Empire, as well as Turkish music and the activities in and around Istanbul.

Lion Feuchtwanger (b. 1884). German writer of fiction; his best works are autobiographical; he also attempted to modernize historical subjects (Elizabeth I of England, Nero, the French Revolution), and became known as a writer who exploited history.

Jacob Fichman (b. 1881). Russian-born poet and critic; he settled in Palestine following World War I; his verse depicts the fields, vineyards, and orchards of Bessarabia, in southern Russia; thus, he comes forth as a poet of tranquility, gentility, and prayer; he also directs his poetic voice and imagination toward the men and women of the Old Testament.

Fyodor Vasilyevich Gladkov (b. 1883). Russian writer of fiction, playwright, and essayist; his fiction reflects his politics, particularly his support of the Soviet regime following the Revolution; nonetheless, he also criticized the negative aspects of the new communist world.

Ho-bieu-Chanh (pseudonym of Ho-van-Trung; b. 1885). South Vietnamese writer of fiction; he produced at least sixty novels and an equal number of short stories; he depicted popular themes and subjects in a lively prose style.

Juan Ramon Jimenez (b. 1881). Spanish poet; he identified his work with the modernismo movement (elegant form, exotic imagery, subtle word music) and thus produced distinctive prose poems; later, he adopted a simple, spare style into which he injected the elements of mysticism; he left Spain during the civil war to live first in the United States, then in Puerto Rico; in 1956, he received the Nobel Prize for literature.

Joseph Klausner (b. 1874). Lithuanian-born Israeli scholar, essayist, editor, and encyclopaedist; he became professor of modern Hebrew literature at Hebrew University, Jerusalem; a noted historian, editor, and modernizer of the Hebrew language; he wrote on Jesus and Paul, tracing the growth of Christianity from a Jewish perspective.

Dame Emilie Rose Macaulay (b. 1881). English essayist and writer of fiction and travel narrative; a number of her fictional pieces reflect her return to Anglicanism, a faith that she had left because of her attraction to a married man; she wrote witty satires and what has been identified as "unusual and sad comedy."

Roger Martin du Gard (b. 1881). French novelist and playwright; trained as a historian, he tended to consider phenomena in terms of context and sought to create a comprehensive and transcendent vision of human existence; thus, he depicted characters whose lives had been determined by the interaction of innate qualities and purely environmental factors; his fictional world has been called "the junction of nineteenth-century naturalism and psychological realism on the one hand, and the contemporary social and political novel on the other"; he received, in 1937, the Nobel Prize for literature.

George Edward Moore (b. 1873). English philosopher and essayist; he became interested in critical epistemology and in distinguishing between the acts of consciousness and their possible objects; he directed his attention toward the philosophical implications of linguistic analysis, questioning the definition of reality;

through his work on common sense beliefs, he significantly influenced English and American philosophy.

Salama Musa (b. 1887?). Egyptian essayist writing in Arabic; he developed a lifelong attraction to everything British, pleading with his Arab readers to follow his inclinations; he attempted to synthesize Western thought and to popularize it through concrete examples; he also promoted the idea of ancient Egypt as the glorious period in history, with the Copts being the true descendants of the ancient Egyptians.

Vallattol Narayana-Menon (b. 1879). Indian (Malayalam) poet; he favored Dravidian metrical forms over the Sanskritic; he became the poet of Indian nationalism in the decades preceding Indian independence, later becoming known as a poet who fought for economic and social justice; his verse stresses the spiritual unity of humankind, whatever one's religious or political background.

George Jean Nathan (b. 1882). American editor, essayist, and drama critic; he gained a significant reputation for his erudite and cynical reviews of drama; he proclaimed the modern drama of ideas in a theatrical world dominated by the tastes of one or two major producers; as with his close colleague, H. L. Mencken, he placed "Kulture" above everything.

Alfred Noyes (b. 1880). English poet and biographer; he earned a reputation for popular poetry that gained strength from its reliance upon rhyme and close attention to the general subjects of love and history; although considered a "minor" poet, he published no less than forty-two volumes of verse between 1902 and 1956.

Robert William Service (b. 1874). English-born Canadian poet and writer of fiction; if nothing else, he will remain forever etched in the memories of a certain few for his "The Shooting of Dan McGrew" and "The Cremation of Sam McGee," two narrative poems deeply rooted to the heart and the life of the Yukon; he also recorded in his poetry the attitudes toward patriotism and fear among those who served in World War I.

Abd al-Rahman Shukri (b. 1886). Egyptian poet; his verse reflects a careful and systematic study of English poetry and criticism of the eighteenth and nineteenth centuries; he spent three years, 1909-1912, in Sheffield, England, during which time he refined his interest in the literature of that nation.

PUBLICATIONS

Chinua Achebe, *Things Fall Apart*—the first novel by the Nigerian writer of fiction, poet, and essayist; a realistic and anthropological account of Ibo tribal society before colonization; set in an Ibo village in the late 1880s, when English missionaries and bureaucrats first appeared in the area; the work traces the conflicts between tribal and Western customs through the portrayal of a proud village leader who refuses to adapt to European influence; his stubbornness leads to murder and suicide.

Jalal Ale Ahmad, *Madre Madrase* (The Headmaster)—a novella by the Iranian writer of fiction; a dryly humorous look at incidents within an Iranian village school; the piece gains strength from the writer's own experiences as a teacher.

Jorge Amado, *Gabriela, Cravo e Canela* (Gabriela, Clove and Cinnamon)—a novel by the Brazilian writer of fiction; the work is set in a town on Bahia, after that region has prospered from the cultivation of cacao; the title character, a lovely migrant worker, and a wealthy young man arrive and begin to overturn restrictive social values, freeing the town from domination by wealthy land owners; focuses upon the themes of love, sexuality, and friendship.

Layla Ba'albakki, *Ava Ahya* (I Live)—the second novel by the Lebanese Shiite Muslim writer of fiction; reflects the writer's revolt against tradition and conservatism, relaying with sensitivity the desires of the young for lives of their own; thus, the heroine of the novel despises her mother, and she conveys that dislike through unabashed sensual thoughts; French critics likened the novel to those of Sidonie-Gabrielle Collette.

John Barth, *The End of the Road*—a novel by the American writer of fiction; the principal character comes forth as the prototype of the contemporary human being; he finds himself paralyzed by his aimlessness, principally because "he feels nothing for anything"; in other words, he lacks both motivation and direction, and thus he ceases to exist; in the end, he can only emerge as a parody of that which actually does exist.

Samuel Beckett, *La Derniere Bande* (Krapp's Last Tape)—a play by the Irish-born dramatist; a monologue in which the principal character listens to a former self; he simply exists to pass the time, to forget himself, to engage in meaningless diversions and amusements that represent life.

Brendan Behan, *The Hostage*—a play by the Irish dramatist; first produced in 1956; originally written in Gaelic, and then translated into English by the writer; set in a local brothel, where an English soldier stands as an IRA hostage; his captors hope to prevent the execution of an Irish lad convicted of murder.

Truman Capote, *Breakfast at Tiffany's*—a novella by the American writer of fiction; focuses upon Holly Golightly, a character who, as a backwoods girl, rides the so-called "fast track" in Manhattan; she exists as superficial, "flip," and phoney.

Ali Akbar Dehkhoda, *Charandparand* (Pele-mele)—a collection of short character sketches in verse by the Iranian writer of fiction and poet; the volume was an important contribution to the development of modern literary Persian, especially as it molds a modern Persian prose idiom within a poetic environment.

Marguerite Duras, *Moderato Cantible*—a novel by the French writer of fiction, playwright, and essayist; begins with a duality of structure, in that a music lesson occurs in a woman's apartment at the same time that a murder takes place in the café below; the woman becomes obsessed with the crime, and from that emerges an exploration of human passion and the interconnection between earthly love and death.

Lawrence Durrell, *Balthazar*—a novel by the English poet and writer of fiction and travel narrative; the second of the *Alexandria Quartet;* the title character, a physician, undertakes a linear revision of the first volume, *Justine;* thus, Darley, one of the European novelist-drifters, learns to his surprise that Pursewarden, a novelist he admires, has captured Justine's affections, rather than himself.

Max Rudolf Frisch, *Biedermann und die Brandstifter* (The Firebugs)—a drama by the Swiss writer of fiction and playwright; a warning against the "long littleness of life"; the principal character comes forth as the little man who will never dare to be himself, and thus deserves all that he receives; he accepts into his house two fire raisers, realizing full well their purposes and intentions; he welcomes them, allows them to store drums of fuel in his attic, offers them a banquet, and provides them with the matches to light their fire.

Graham Greene, *Our Man in Havana*—a novel by the English writer of fiction; a touch of irony alleviates the tragic consequences of a vacuum cleaner salesman's unwitting involvement in espionage exercises between two major world powers.

Malek Haddad, *La Derniere Impression* (Last Impression)—a novel by the Algerian writer of fiction and poet; the style of the work is quite poetic; it demonstrates how a young Algerian intellectual awakens to the reality of politics; thus, he participates in the liberation movement.

Aldous Huxley, *Brave New World Revisited*—a work of nonfiction by the English novelist, historian, essayist, and writer of travel narrative; an explicit warning concerning the issue of freedom and those who oppose it; advances the notion that humanity will, in the end, be forced to fight to protect itself.

Sukistyautami Iesmaniasita, *Kidung Wenging Gunung Gamping* (Evening Verses from Gunung Gamping)—a collection of short stories by the Javanese poet and writer of fiction; eight romantic stories that became extremely popular throughout the region; the writer presents her social themes against a background of lyrical moods and idealized personal relationships; Christian mysticism blends well with colloquial Javanese language.

Jalol Ikromi, *Man Gunahgoram* (I Am Guilty)—a psychological novel by the Iranian (Tajik) writer of fiction and playwright; concerns the problems of family life, love, and ethics; considered one of the finest pieces of fiction in all of Tajik literature.

Shirley Jackson, *The Sundial*—a novel by the American writer of fiction; focuses upon the Halloran family; they have been informed that the world will be destroyed and that they alone will survive; thus, they wait in their mansion for the comic and surprising end.

Jack Kerouac, *The Subterraneans*—a novel by the American writer of fiction and poet; set in San Francisco, it captures, with "raw power and awesome beauty," the offbeat and exhilarating experiences of free spirits; the writer concerns himself with the love and despair of the young poets, painters, and jazz musicians of the west coast; according to the writer, there stands a world of terror and exaltation that his generation never created.

Thomas Kinsella, *Another September*—a collection of verse by the Irish poet; the pieces are characterized by traditional and formal logic and structure, active narrative, and rich description; its themes concern married love, romantic ordeal, and the erosion of relationships; a revised version issued in 1962.

Archibald MacLeish, *J. B.*—a verse play by the American poet; a contemporary Job acts out his story in a circus tent; the poet effectively dramatizes the tragedies that surround the title character; he also sets forth a lively debate between a representative of orthodox religion and an agent of pure pragmatism; receives the Pulitzer Prize in drama in 1959.

Bernard Malamud, *The Magic Barrel*—a collection of short stories by the American writer of fiction; the pieces appeal to the individual self and, as usual, rely upon Yiddish dialect and Yiddish points of view; the work receives the National Book Award for 1958.

R. K. Narayan, *The Guide*—a novel by the Indian writer of fiction and essayist; a former convict, mistaken for a holy man upon his arrival in a village, finds himself besieged by the people, who beg him to avert a famine; he cannot convince them of his dishonesty, and thus determines to embrace the role that they have thrust upon him; he dies during a prolonged fast, and the villagers revere him as a saint.

Kenzaburo Oe, *Shisha No Ogori* (Proud Are the Dead)—a collection of short stories by the Japanese writer of fiction; the pieces generally express the feelings of degradation, humiliation, and disorientation brought about by the surrender of Japan and the conditions following World War II; the tone of the collection reflects the writer's own sense of emptiness.

John Osborne and Anthony Creighton, *Epitaph for George Dillon*—a drama by the English playwrights; an imitative, but deeply psychological, study of a playwright who decides to sell his talents to the security offered by the Edwardian music halls.

Boris Pasternak, *Doctor Zhivago*—a novel by the Russian writer of fiction and poet, originally published in Italy; a lyrical piece that encompasses the Revolution of 1917 and the civil strife that followed; a grand story of a Russian physician and poet and his tender love for a beautiful woman; in a larger sense, the work demonstrates how the destinies of human beings become shaped and then changed by history.

Karl Shapiro, *Poems of a Jew*—a collection by the American poet; dedicated to the notion that the Holocaust, if nothing else, served to revive the spiritual image of Jews; thus, the pieces illustrate the results of that experience, the remains of defenseless human beings who have endured the "crushing impersonality of history."

Alan Sillitoe, *Saturday Night and Sunday Morning*—a novel by the English writer of fiction and poet; concerns the life of a dissatisfied Nottingham factory worker; although the central figure differs from the typical "angry young man" in that he does not belong to the rising middle class, he nonetheless seethes under the frustrations brought about by petty victories and defeats.

C. P. Snow, *The Conscience of the Rich*—a novel by the English writer of fiction and essayist; the writer seeks to offer insights into contemporary society and to trace the moral growth of his principal character, who has risen from provincial clerk to upper level civil servant, from vigorous leftist to genteel conservative.

Muriel Spark, *Momento Mori*—a novel by the Scottish-born writer of fiction, poet, playwright, and essayist; essentially an exercise in analyzing a particular aspect of society; several elderly persons receive anonymous phone calls, the message being "Remember you must die"; the statement has varying effects on characters, a number of whom even come to gain a new appreciation for life; others receive reinforcement from their pursuits of self-gratification.

Ronald Stuart Thomas, *Poetry for Supper*—a collection of verse by the Welsh poet and essayist; the writer laments the abandonment of farms by Welsh families who have sought urban employment; he examines the demise of poetry as a mirror of the views of common people.

John Wain, *The Contenders*—a novel by the English writer of fiction and poet; another example of "the angry young man" motif and theme; the narrator and principal character, a journalist, cannot understand the purpose of the violent and competitive spirit embodied in two of his friends, one an artist and the other a businessman.

Tennessee Williams, *Suddenly Last Summer*—a drama by the American playwright; described as a "gothic" piece, it focuses upon the conflicting feelings of a cousin and mother toward a recently deceased homosexual poet and his sizable estate; greed and truth intertwine as the mother seeks to conceal the reality behind the poet's death.

Yospal, *Jhutha Sac* (The Lying Truth)—a novel by the Indian (Hindi) writer of fiction; a broad and vivid portrayal of the partition of India and the first decade of independence from British rule; in two parts, to 1960.

EVENTS

James Agee, American poet and writer of fiction, posthumously awarded the Pulitzer Prize in fiction for the autobiographical novel *A Death in the Family* (1957).

Ketti Frings, American writer of fiction and playwright, receives the Pulitzer Prize in drama for *Look Homeward, Angel* (1957), an adaptation of Thomas Wolfe's 1929 novel.

U Luhtu Hla, Burmese journalist, publisher, and writer of fiction, awarded the UNESCO Prize in literature for his short story collection *Hlauncjain Twin Hma Hngek nge Mja* (Little Birds from a Cage), published this year.

Boris Pasternak, Russian poet and writer of fiction, awarded the Nobel Prize for literature; however, the Soviet government will not permit him to accept it.

The complete works of Count Leo Nikolaevich Tolstoy, Russian writer of fiction and miscellaneous prose, published in the USSR in ninety volumes.

Tri-Quarterly, a general literary journal of critical commentary, begins publication at Northwestern University, Evanston, Illinois.

Robert Penn Warren, American poet, writer of fiction, and critic, receives the Pulitzer Prize in poetry for *Promises: Poems, 1954-1956* (1957).

1959

DEATHS

Maxwell Anderson (b. 1888). American playwright; his dramatic pieces, a number of which he wrote in verse, focus upon social and moral problems, as well as historical subjects; he wrote more than thirty plays, tending to reduce issues to simple struggles between good and evil.

Johan Bojer (b. 1872). Norwegian writer of fiction; he considered social issues from a classical liberal point of view and relied upon conventional realism; although his fictional works are examples of psychological regionalism, he became popular outside of Norway, particularly in France; he also wrote verse and drama.

Laxmiprasad Devkota (b. 1909). Nepali poet, writer of fiction, essayist, and playwright; he combined the themes and techniques of classical Sanskrit literature with elements derived from modern Nepali culture and European Romanticism; he infused his narrative and lyric poetry with a totally modern and highly regional character; for political and economic reasons, little of his work reached publication during his lifetime; his early death was caused by cancer.

Laurence Housman (b. 1865). English essayist and writer of fiction (and younger brother of A. E. Housman); he gained a literary reputation for a dramatic biography of Queen Victoria (1934); he also was an excellent illustrator of books and a competent art critic.

Hans Henny Jahnn (b. 1894). German writer of fiction; described variously as the most significant German prose writer of his time and an artist "who has befouled the image of the human being like no other"; he created perhaps the most profound novel of homosexual love, struggling to produce "two angels who appear in two human figures and nonetheless eat of the flesh down to its last extreme with shyness and majesty"; such was the substance and purpose of his fiction.

Alfred Kubin (b. 1877). Austrian writer of fiction, poet, essayist, and artist; both his fantastic fiction and his graphic art reflected his peculiar vision of the world, with its elements of expressionism, surrealism, and the absurd; he created a dream kingdom, where the material and the spiritual worlds intermingled freely; he spent the last fifty years of his life in isolation in his country home in Zwickledt, Austria.

Abolqasem Lahuti (b. 1887). Persian and Tajik poet and librettist; his verse tended to be bound to his revolutionary activities and thus resounded with patriotic enthusiasm; he also celebrated the victory of the oppressed against political tyranny; he introduced new strophe forms, created new poetic dimensions, and instituted changes in the prosody of Tajik folk poetry; during World War II, his verse focused upon such themes as the brotherhood of nations, resistance to fascism, and the heroism of Soviet soldiers.

Edwin Muir (b. 1887). Scottish poet, writer of fiction, and critic; in his verse, he attempted to reach the center of human life and experience; in addition, he combined dream and myth with a profound comprehension of reality; he wrote in excess of one thousand literary reviews and published volumes of social and literary criticism; in all of his writing, he conducted a thorough search for human values.

Luis Pales Matos (b. 1898). Puerto Rican poet and writer of fiction; he was deeply interested in expressing African themes and styles, principally because of his birth and heritage; in his verse in particular he sought to synthesize his black social and personal experiences and the white cultural values imposed on his island commonwealth by the United States.

Benjamin Peret (b. 1899). French poet, essayist, and writer of fiction; he became a central figure in the Surrealist movement, producing highly original verse; his work contains surprising imagery and displays his obvious contempt for social and religious institutions; he related, in essence, psychoanalytic theory to the creative process in an attempt to enter a world of larger reality; he dies in Paris.

Zalman Schnaiur (b. 1887). Russian writer of fiction and poet; he gave to Hebrew literature a distinct tone of individualism combining arrogance, strength, and sensual joy; he turned away from the spiritual motifs of life and concentrated upon the full expressiveness of the human senses; although a poet of the large city, his fiction reflects his small-town upbringing in its descriptions of simpletons, uncultivated boors, and ill-bred peasants.

Galaktion Tabidze (b. 1892). Georgian (SSR) poet; influenced by the Russian symbolists, whose techniques he adopted, then later simplified; as his work became simpler and more monumental, echoes of classical and folk poetry appeared; in 1933, he became a National Artist of the Georgian Republic.

Rusen Esref Unaydin (b. 1892). Turkish essayist and prose poet; he conducted and then published interviews with literary artists under the title *Diyorlar ki* (They Say, 1918); he also published, in 1929, a volume of prose poems.

PUBLICATIONS

Edward Albee, *The Zoo Story*—a one-act play (his first) by the American dramatist, first performed in German at the experimental branch of the Schiller Theater, the Werkstatt, in West Berlin; two strangers with nothing in common meet on a park bench and encounter extreme difficulty in attempting to communicate with each other; the older person is a moderately successful bourgeois family man, while the younger one emerges as a lonely bohemian rebel; they can only communicate through violence, and the rebel convinces the family man to kill him.

Jacques Barzun, *The House of Intellect*—a prose tract by the French-born American historian, critic, and miscellaneous prose writer; the writer maintains that American intellectuals appear to be undermining their social purpose of exploring and disseminating significant ideas; he questions why artists stress creativity and personal expression while they forsake order, why scientists promote invalid interdisciplinary theories, and why philanthropists reward lavish group efforts rather than modest individual achievements; considered one of the most significant critiques of American culture.

Saul Bellow, *Henderson the Rain King*—a novel by the American writer of fiction; concerns a millionaire who goes to Africa in quest of wisdom; the piece reflects the writer's interest in anthropology; the main character is portrayed as exuberant and intellectually curious.

Charles Bukowski, *Flower, Fist and Bestial Wail*—a volume of verse by the German-born American poet and writer of short fiction; these early poems rely upon a definite surrealist technique, but abandon reference to the first person (the poet's later device to establish unity); the pieces reveal the poet's interest in music, his sense of a desolate and abandoned world, his love of art, and his desire for sexual adventurism and experimentation.

William S. Burroughs, *The Naked Lunch*—a novel by the American writer of fiction and autobiographical narrative; termed "a black satiric masterpiece"; analyzes with uncompromising honesty the horrors of drug addiction; the novel also evidences the writer's meaningful search for true values.

Hayden Carruth, *The Crow and the Heart*—the first collection of verse by the American poet; contains, principally, a group of "near-sonnets," or sequences of fifteen-line stanzas; includes one of his most notable early poems, "The Asylum."

Paddy Chayefsky, *The Tenth Man*—a play by the American dramatist and writer of films;

the work combines an authentic Bronx setting with the traditional Jewish story of the "Dybbuk" (the wandering Jewish soul).

Bernard Binlin Dadie, *Un Negre a Paris*—a novel by the Ivory Coast writer of fiction, poet, and playwright; the first African novel since World War II to place the protagonist in the French capital; thus, the work allows the central character to cast a critical eye upon the French from within the confines of their own territory; the work sets in motion a trend on the part of the writer's fellow African novelists.

Geoffrey Drayton, *Christopher*—the first novel by the Barbadian writer of fiction, poet, and critic; the piece recalls the writer's childhood on a sugar plantation; more generally, it reveals the consciousness of an isolated boy and exposes to the public a number of West Indian cult practices.

Lawrence Durrell, *Mountolive*—a novel by the English writer of fiction, poet, and critic; the third volume of *The Alexandria Quartet;* from the cool heights of Mountolive, the English ambassador to Egypt adds various dimensions and complexities to the relationships between Justine, Balthazar, Darley, Melissa, and Pursewarden; Justine and her husband, Nessim Hosnani, inject anti-British and pro-Zionist sentiments into the account.

Gunter Grass, *Die Blechtrommel* (The Tin Drum)—a novel by the German writer of fiction, essayist, poet, and playwright; the central figure, a precocious dwarf, had intentionally stunted his growth at an early age to protect himself from the chaos and destruction of his times; he vividly recounts the traumas of the Nazi era while playing a tin drum in his cell in a mental institution during the late 1950s; the novel combines fantasy with realism, relying also upon allusions to mythology and the New Testament.

Nicolas Guillen, *La Paloma de Vuelo Popular: Elegias*—a collection of verse by the Cuban poet; the pieces advance the ideals of revolution; the poet praises the activities of such figures as Che Guevara and Fidel Castro; in his view, the triumph of the Cuban revolution signifies the abolition of racial and economic discrimination.

Qurratu'l'ain Haidar, *Ag Ka Darya* (River of Fire)—a novel by the Indian (Urdu) writer of fiction and translator; she relates, through symbol and allegory, the development of Indian history; the work achieved broad popular recognition.

Lorraine Hansberry, *A Raisin in the Sun*—a dramatic comedy by the American playwright; relates the struggles of a black family to escape the dreariness of the Chicago ghetto; the work transcends the issue of racial and economic politics with its theme of the struggle to achieve the American dream; the first play by a black woman to be produced on Broadway; the work receives the New York Drama Critics Circle Award for the 1958-1959 season.

Yusuf Idris, *Al-Haram* (Guilt)—a novella by the Egyptian writer of fiction and playwright; depicts the miserable existence of seasonal agricultural laborers; an exercise in critical realism and an expression of the writer's patriotic and anticolonial ideals.

Jack Kerouac, *Mexico City Blues*—the only book of verse by the American writer of fiction and poet; relies upon the various qualities unique to the jazz idiom; in 242 "choruses," the poet roams wildly across continents and cultures in a restless pursuit for meaning and expression.

Doris Lessing, *A Ripple from the Storm*—a novel by the Persian-born and Rhodesian-raised English writer of fiction; the third volume of the five-volume series *Children of Violence;* the central figure, Martha Quest, recently (volume 2) liberated from an unfortunate marriage, has remarried a member of the Communist Party; she discovers that ideals can be turned to political jargon and to personal advantage.

Denise Levertov, *With Eyes at the Back of Our Heads*—a volume of verse by the English-born American poet; direct and honest personal disclosures in which the poet seeks to grasp a personal identity that underlies the sexual stereotype; "The Goddess" is one of the most representative poems in the collection.

James A. Michener, *Hawaii*—a novel by the American writer of fiction and miscellaneous prose; an extremely popular work that chronicles the history of the state, from its beginnings to the present; the writer strived for faithfulness to the facts and cultural spirit of the islands.

Ezekiel Mphahlele, *Down Second Avenue*—an autobiographical novel by the South African writer of fiction and critic; the work exists as an extremely important expression of what it feels like to grow up black in the slums of South Africa; the writer describes the environment there as "a chamber of horrors" that nonetheless allows one to sense the fortitude of the people; the novel has been translated into French, German, Serbo-Croatian, Bulgarian, Hungarian, Japanese, and Swedish.

Anais Nin, *Cities of the Interior*—a five-volume novel cycle by the French-born American writer of fiction: includes *Ladders to Fire, Children of the Albatross, The Four-Chambered Heart, A Spy in the House of Love*, and *Seduction of the Minotaur*.

Raymond Queneau, *Zazie dans le Metro* (Zazie in the Metro)—a satiric novel by the French writer of fiction and miscellaneous prose, poet, and playwright; concerns an outspoken little girl who visits her uncle in Paris; she causes discomfort for the adults around her because of her pranks and foul language; the theme develops the uncertainty and confusion of conventional social roles.

Mordecai Richler, *The Apprenticeship of Duddy Kravitz*—a novel by the Canadian writer of fiction and essayist; chronicles the title character's rise from a Montreal ghetto dweller to a prominent landowner; driven by greed, he acquires property through ruthless and exploitative means, coming to represent the immoral city and evil of society in general.

Philip Roth, *Goodbye, Columbus*—a novella and five short stories by the American writer of fiction; the title piece, the novella, focuses upon a love affair between a poor boy from Newark, New Jersey, and a rich girl from Radcliffe College; the volume receives the National Book Award for fiction.

Srirat Sathapanawat, *Phrung ni Tong mi Arun Rung* (Tomorrow Will Be Another Sunrise)—a novel by the Thai writer of fiction; demonstrates how the weak position of women is exploited by men (husbands or wealthy protectors); the plot is serious, the mood sad, and the language straightforward and simple.

Paruir Sevak, *Anlreli Zangakatun* (The Never Silent Bells)—a long poem by the Soviet Armenian writer of verse and literary historian; the life story of an Armenian composer, Komitase, into which the author has injected his conception of Armenian national history; the nation need not feel obligated, because of centuries of suffering, to pay tribute to anyone; he seeks a dignified form of existence for the entire nation; the poem aroused profound and widespread soul-searching among Armenians, and thus it has been considered the most important event (at least from a social point of view) in modern Armenian poetry.

Alan Sillitoe, *The Loneliness of the Long-Distance Runner*—a collection of short stories by the English writer of fiction; in the title piece, considered the most significant work in the volume, a rebellious and anarchic Borstal boy presents a first-person portrait of himself and his refusal to particpate (realistically and metaphorically) in the games of the establishment; in general, the work reflects the writer's hatred of injustice, hypocrisy, and exploitation.

Isaac Bashevis Singer, *The Magician of Lubin*—a novel (originally in Yiddish) by the Polish-born writer of fiction; the piece focuses upon a womanizing circus magician and acrobat, set in nineteenth-century Poland; the central character, Yasha Mazur, belongs properly within the tradition of the Yiddish "shlemiel."

W. D. Snodgrass, *Heart's Needle*—a verse collection by the American poet; thematically, the pieces develop a sense of increasingly depersonalized identity as one's social existence becomes excessively rational; thus, the poet concerns himself with the disenchantments of returning World War II veterans, their confusions and their struggles; among the ten poems, the most representative remain "Heart's Needle," "Returned to Frisco, 1946," and "Home Town"; receives the Pulitzer Prize in poetry in 1960.

C. P. Snow, *The Affair*—a novel by the English writer of fiction and essayist; a conflict arises at Cambridge University over the dismissal of a physicist for possible associations with the Communist Party; a cynical compromise resolves the problem.

William Strunk, Jr. and E. B. White, *The Elements of Style*—a reference text by the American prose writers; a classic style manual, brief and direct, that sets forth clear and simple criteria for effective expository writing; several editions through 1990.

John Updike, *The Poorhouse Fair*—the first novel by the American writer of fiction; concerns the revolt of a group of old people in an institution against their liberal director; the piece is set in the distant future during a holiday weekend; the director means well, but he represents abstract solutions in the face of the residents' practical needs.

Bhagavaticaran Varma, *Bhule-Bisre Citr* (Forgotten Pictures)—a novel by the Indian

(Hindi) writer of fiction; the work depicts the lives of four generations of an Indian family; a monumental work that gained almost immediate popularity.

Kurt Vonnegut, Jr., *Sirens of Titan*—a science fiction novel by the American writer; intergalactic space magnifies the uselessness of human effort; thus, a friendly "machine" cannot deliver its message to every planet in the universe because it lacks a single part; the means for delivering that part become mired in an overly complicated plan.

Tennessee Williams, *Sweet Bird of Youth*—a drama by the American playwright; the work focuses upon a faded movie star and her gigolo, who, once a promising young man, eventually pays the price for abandoning his hometown sweetheart.

EVENTS

Stanley Jasspon Kunitz, American poet and compiler of literary reference works, receives the Pulitzer Prize in poetry for *Selected Poems, 1928-1958* (1958).

Archibald MacLeish, American poet, receives the Pulitzer Prize in drama for his verse play *J. B.* (1958).

Salvatore Quasimodo, Italian poet and translator, receives the Nobel Prize in literature.

Arthur Summerfield, Postmaster-General of the United States, bans D. H. Lawrence's *Lady Chatterley's Lover* (1928) from the U.S. mails on the grounds of "obscenity"; in 1960, the U.S. Court of Appeals will reverse that ruling.

Robert Lewis Taylor, American writer of fiction and journalist, receives the Pulitzer Prize in fiction for his novel *The Travels of Jamie McPheeters* (1958).

1960

DEATHS

Albert Camus (b. 1913). Algerian-born French playwright, writer of fiction, and philosopher; he early became attracted to the theater, organizing the avant-garde drama group, Theatre de l'Equipe (1935-1938); his achievements stem from his dual function as polemicist and chronicler; his plays provided

a forum for his philosophic moments of "tragic lucidity" with regard to social and political ideas; he received the Nobel Prize for literature in 1957.

Jozef Ciger-Hronsky (b. 1896). Czechoslovakian writer of fiction; his works will be banned in his nation between 1946 and 1966; he contributed significantly to Slovak literature and decidedly influenced the younger generation of Slovak writers; his themes underscore what has come to be known as "the social reality": inequality, poverty, alcoholism, unemployment, emigration, law, politics, religion; he died in Argentina.

Jacob Cohen (b. 1881). Russian-born Israeli poet and translator; a poet of the balanced phrase and the measured word: his verse displays a melodious tone, a highly technical style, and a deep love for harmony; his work is also profoundly religious; he will reveal a fondness for the folk legend and the ballad; he translated works of classical world literature into Hebrew.

Drmit Gulia (b. 1874). Abkhazian (SSR) poet, playwright, and writer of fiction and nonfiction; he established all of the genres of Abkhazian literature; as a translator, he provided workable texts of Russian, Ukranian, and Georgian writers; he published textbooks for the schools and taught potential writers; his best works are the lyrics he composed after abandoning the notion that poetry should function as a vehicle for political propaganda.

John Philips Marquand (b. 1893). American writer of fiction; he became known for his satirical novels that focused upon the life and attitudes of New England; his work assumed the flavor of popular journalism and the tone of middlebrow comedies of manners; thus, he satirized his own society, but he never offended it; he received the Pulitzer Prize for fiction in 1938.

Jigar Muradabadi (b. 1890). Indian (Urdu) lyric and romantic poet; standing midway between poetic traditionalism and the "new" verse, he wrote simple and fluent conventional love pieces; his work is musical and rich in spiritual imagery, celebrating the most agreeable aspects of human existence; essentially, he expressed the feelings of modern humanity and its relationship to contemporary life.

Sir Lewis Bernstein Namier (b. 1888). Polish-born English historian; in 1931, he became professor of modern history at the University of Manchester; a romantic and an ardent nationalist; he strived to reduce to the utmost conciseness the general propositions and scholarly impressions of his colleagues; he also underscored what he had learned from Sigmund Freud about the important relationship between history and biography.

Boris Leonidovich Pasternak (b. 1890). Russian poet, writer of fiction, and translator; his verse is fresh, lyrical, and passionate; during the 1930s, he devoted his labors to translating the works of William Shakespeare, Johann Wolfgang von Goethe, and other Western writers; he then turned his attention to an epic treatment of the tragic political and social upheavals of twentieth-century Russia; the Soviet government would not allow him to accept the 1958 Nobel Prize for literature; he spent his remaining years at an artists' colony near Moscow.

Richard Nathaniel Wright (b. 1908). American writer of fiction, autobiographical narrative, and miscellaneous prose; he focused his literary energies upon the plight of the blacks in the United States, always keeping in mind his own Mississippi childhood of transience and poverty; in 1947, he settled in Paris.

Nima Yushij (b. 1897). Iranian poet; his rural upbringing inspired in him a deep love of nature, which he combined with an interest in French literature; he turned away from the principles of classical Persian rhetoric and pioneered a new trend in Persian poetry: free verse; thus, he chose rhythm and rhetorical modes according to the general mood of each poem.

PUBLICATIONS

Muhammed Said Abdulla, *Mizmu Wa Watu Wa Kale* (The Home of the Spirits of the Ancestors)—the first novel by the Kenyan (Swahili) writer of fiction; based, strangely enough, upon the Sherlock Holmes stories of Sir Arthur Conan Doyle; however, the plot is set against an authentic Zanzibar background.

Edward Albee, *The Sandbox*—a play by the American dramatist; a short, imagistic piece that depicts the death of an energetic grandmother, an individual who emerges as the only sympathetic person in an extremely tiresome family; commisssioned for the Festival of Two Worlds, in Italy.

W. H. Auden, *Homage to Clio*—a collection of poetry by the English writer of verse; one of the major volumes of his "later" period, the work includes a fairly large proportion of light verse.

Layla Baalbakki, *Al-Alika al-Mamsukha* (The Monster Gods)—a novel by the Lebanese Shiite Muslim writer of fiction; written in Arabic, the piece advances the notion of rebellion against social conservatism and tradition; thus, the novelist concerns herself with the sensual feelings and illicit love of a twenty-one-year-old woman for a forty-year-old married man; the writer draws an interesting picture of Lebanese society in an atmosphere of change; specifically, she concerns herself with the problems of Arab youth.

John Barth, *The Sot-Weed Factor*—a novel by the American writer of fiction; a ribald, picaresque satire of the eighteenth-century hero and novel; essentially, the work may be identified as a "joke book" and as an endless series of humorous barbs; experimental, unconventional, and erudite.

John Betjeman, *Summoned by Bells*—an autobiography in blank verse by the English poet; focuses upon the poet's boyhood and experiences at Oxford.

Olympe Bhely-Quenum, *Un Prege sans Fin* (The Endless Trip)—the first novel by the Benin (Dahomey) writer of fiction; focuses upon the tribulations of being black in Europe and in colonial Africa; the piece was widely acclaimed in France and throughout Europe; published in Paris.

Anthony Burgess, *The Doctor Is Sick*—a novel by the English writer of fiction; concerns a philologist in the throes of marriage; he embarks upon a burlesque quest through the seamy side of London during the 1950s.

William Burroughs, *Exterminator*—a novel by the American writer of fiction; an experimental piece, the work is a fictional mosaic in which espionage, science-fantasy war, racism, corporate capitalism, drug addiction, and a variety of medical and psychiatric horrors play significant roles.

E. L. Doctorow, *Welcome to Hard Times*—the first novel by the American writer of fiction; a small town in the Dakotas is almost totally destroyed by an evil and vicious stranger.

Lawrence Durrell, *Clea*—the concluding volume of the English writer's fictional *Alexandrian Quartet;* in this novel, Darley, one of the European drifters, flees from Alexandria and finds true love with the title character, a beautiful girl with a frustrated talent for painting.

William Faulkner, *The Mansion*—a novel by the American writer of fiction; a tale of vengeance, and the final volume in the Snopes trilogy; contains the most humorous elements of character and language within the writer's "later" canon.

Leslie Fiedler, *Love and Death in the American Novel*—a volume of literary criticism by the American critic, academician, and writer of fiction; essentially, the work summarizes the writer's own literary and intellectual heritage.

Alfred Hutchinson, *Road to Ghana*—an autobiographical work by the South African writer of narrative and fiction and playwright; considered the finest study to date about the experience of living under the racist regime in South Africa; the writer views his life as a series of trials that will result in some form of personal and national salvation.

Eugene Ionesco, *Rhinoceros*—a play by the Romanian-born French dramatist, essayist, and writer of fiction; two characters, talking, observe a rhinoceros charging; eventually, every character but the main one has been transformed into a rhinoceros; the individual questions whether he should also become transformed, but decides he cannot; thus, he determines to fight the beasts and to defend humanity; essentially, the playwright denounces mindless conformity.

Randall Jarrell, *The Woman at the Washington Zoo: Poems and Translations*—a collection by the American writer of verse; the pieces tend to be formal in style and substance; the title poem reflects the poet's concern with aging and loneliness, with transforming a life of emptiness into one of substance and activity.

Jose Antonio Jarvis, *The King's Mandate*—a play in blank verse by the Virgin Island poet, playwright, and miscellaneous prose writer; the title refers to the proclamation declared by the then-governor of the Virgin Islands, in accord with the mandate from the King of Denmark, Christian VIII, that all bondsmen would immediately become free within the Danish Virgin Islands; concerns the liberation of the black slaves in that region.

Jack Kerouac, *Tristessa*—a novel by the American writer of fiction and miscellaneous prose; focuses upon a "strung-out" Mexican prostitute; as usual, the work contains portions related to the writer's own experiences.

John Knowles, *A Separate Peace*—a novel by the American writer of fiction; concerns the coming of age of a group of boys at a preparatory school in New England at the outset of World War II; involved, most importantly, with adolescent friendships.

John Le Carre, *Call for the Dead*—a novel by the English writer of fiction; a conventional "thriller" that introduces George Smiley (who will appear often), the epitome of the mild mannered mastermind, reluctant spy, and secret agent.

Harper Lee, *To Kill a Mockingbird*—a novel by the American writer of fiction; a vivid autobiographical account of growing up in the South; the work receives the Pulitzer Prize for fiction in 1961.

Kamal Markandaya, *A Silence of Desire*—a novel by the Indian writer of fiction; the heroine's husband is a middle-class Indian whose attitude toward life illustrates the influence of the West upon India.

Henry Miller, *The Rosy Crucifixion: Nexus*—the third volume of the American author's autobiographical account of his efforts to become a writer; details his financial, spiritual, and sexual struggles and vividly recalls his years as a down-and-out artist in New York City.

Alberto Moravia, *La Noia* (The Empty Canvas)—a novel by the Italian writer of fiction, essayist, playwright, and translator; emphasizes ideology over narration and plot, presenting a protagonist who suffers intellectual, creative, and sexual crises; the characters' dilemmas resolve themselves through Freudian and phenomenological principles.

Flannery O'Connor, *The Violent Bear It Away*—a novel by the American writer of fiction; a character's great-uncle, a mad prophet and an illicit whiskey distiller, dies; he had instructed his great-nephew to become a prophet and to baptize his cousin; however, the nephew functions under the influence of Satan, who drugs and sodomizes him; the piece focuses upon "the true Church," which must essentially lose itself and its reason so as to save the world; the piece reflects the writer's belief that the Roman Catholic Church had betrayed itself.

Harold Pinter, *The Caretaker*—a drama by the English playwright; the plot develops from the characters' unrelated attitudes toward a shared environment; thus, one character owns a derelict house, and he entrusts it to his brain-damaged brother, who engages a tramp as a caretaker; the tramp changes from a servile character to a greedy aggressor who, eventually, finds himself back on the street; of utmost importance is the playwright's mastery of the poetic comedy of common speech.

Anthony Powell, *Casanova's Chinese Restaurant*—a novel by the English writer of fiction; the central character, Nick, marries into a family named Tolland; amid the confusion of the Spanish Civil War and the abduction of the Spanish monarchy, he recognizes old friends.

Raja Rao, *The Serpent and the Rope*—a novel in English by the Indian writer; considered the most important piece of fiction by an Indian in the twentieth century; written during the space of twenty-nine days, the work is a statement of the writer's understanding of the attitudes and values of India and Europe; reflects pro-Indian sentiment, but successfully blends Indian and Western forms of fiction; concerns an Indian Brahmin who goes to France to conduct historical research; there he meets a French history teacher, whom he marries; the union ends in failure, which reveals to him his own native identity.

Jean-Paul Sartre, *Critique de la Raison Dialectique, Volume I: Theorie des Ensembles Pratiques* (Critique of Dialectical Reason: Theory of Practical Ensembles)—a volume of literary essays by the French philosopher, playwright, essayist, biographer, and writer of fiction; the writer attempts to fuse Marxism and existentialism to provide a new approach to historical analysis; he condemns capitalism and Western democratic institutions, calling for a synthesis of personal freedom and moral duty within a neo-Marxian context; essentially, he wishes to create the foundation for social revolution.

Ousmane Sembene, *Les Bouts de Boise de Dieu* (God's Bits of Wood)—a novel by the Senegalese writer of fiction; focuses upon the independence struggle of French Africa; the writer strives to portray the evolution of modern Africa, with its mixture of indigenous and Western technological elements.

William L. Shirer, *The Rise and Fall of the Third Reich*—a popular and widely read journalistic account by the American correspondent; an accurate and firsthand analysis of how Adolf Hitler came to power and why those who opposed him seemed almost helpless to prevent the rise of the most horrible form of dictatorship that the world had known.

William Stafford, *West of Your City*—the first volume of verse by the American poet; basically, the writer attempts to depict the open spaces; he shuns the streets of the city and strives to journey outside of human life to find himself apart from others.

Louis Untermeyer, *Lives of the Poets*—a collection of biographical sketches by the American poet and anthologizer; a survey beginning with the *Beowulf* poet and ending with the Welsh writer Dylan Thomas.

John Updike, *Rabbit, Run*—a novel by the American writer of fiction; the first part of the writer's continuing saga of a Pennsylvania used car dealer, a former basketball star whose life deteriorated after he graduated from high school; he must, essentially, desert his wife and children and remain on the "run," without purpose or direction.

Rajendra Yadav, *Sara Akas* (The Whole Sky)—a novel by the Indian (Hindi) writer of fiction; the piece depicts the personal lives of members of an orthodox Hindu family; another attempt by the writer to treat themes of urban middle-class existence, with emphasis upon intellectuals.

EVENTS

Allen Stuart Drury, American writer of fiction, receives the Pulitzer Prize in fiction for his novel *Advise and Consent* (1959).

Noble Savage, a biannual literary magazine, begins publication in New York City; contributors include such writers as Ralph Ellison, Saul Bellow, Arthur Miller, and Wright Morris; until 1962.

St.-John Perse (pseudonym of Marie-Rene-Auguste Alexis Saint-Leger Leger; 1887-1975), French poet, receives the Nobel Prize for literature.

William Dewitt Snodgrass, American writer of verse, receives the Pulitzer Prize in poetry for *Heart's Needle* (1959).

1961

DEATHS

Abdul-Karim (b. 1908). Pakistani (Pashto) writer of fiction; he wrote short stories with heroes from the lower social classes and used his works to promote Pashtun independence.

Kjeld Abell (b. 1901). Danish playwright; he became an innovator in terms of stage technique, and his plays focused upon justice and social protest; his so-called "seriocomic theater" was considerably indebted to the efforts of Hans Christian Andersen; his work represented an imaginative extension of the best of the contemporary expressionist heritage; in 1960, he gained election to the Danish Academy.

Mukhtar Auezov (b. 1897). Kazakhstan (SSR) writer of fiction and playwright; he based his work on contemporary themes, the history of his region, and biographical facts concerning the founders of Kazakh literature.

Roussan Camille (b. 1912). Haitian poet and journalist; his work reflects the influence of the American Langston Hughes and the Cuban Nicolas Guillen; thus, he developed a personal and black voice; he also began to consider the anguished history of his own nation; he believed, essentially, that black poets should use verse as an instrument of political and social protest.

Louis-Ferdinand Celine (b. 1894). French writer of fiction, essayist, and playwright; he has been credited with freeing French literature from the rigid, formalized language of nineteenth-century fiction; he introduced an immensely influential hallucinatory prose style that emphasizes emotion over reason; in his fiction, he condemns depravity and violence through what can only be termed "Puritan slum vernacular."

Elmer Diktonius (b. 1896). Finnish writer of fiction and poet; wrote in Swedish; he foreshadowed the rise of modernism in the Western world, becoming, first, a poet of the Left, and then mellowing his political and social position; in effect, he viewed and then reflected Finland during and after the bloody civil strife of 1918.

Ernest Miller Hemingway (b. 1898). American writer of fiction; he pursued the masculine life that he idealized in his novels and short stories; he insisted upon an active and sensuous life and developed a simple, descriptive literary style with crisp, staccato, masculine dialogue; everything, for him, focused upon physical experience, courage, and heroic action; he received the Nobel Prize for literature in 1954; his final years were marked by physical illness and emotional despair, and he committed suicide.

Carl Gustav Jung (b. 1875). Swiss psychiatrist and founder of analytic psychology; his prose

tracts postulated dimensions of the unconscious: the personal (repressed or forgotten content of an individual's mental and material life) and the collective (acts and mental patterns shared either by members of a culture or universally by all human beings); he determined the most significant task for any individual to be the achievement of harmony between the conscious and the unconscious.

Orixie (pseudonym of Nicolas Ormaetxea; b. 1888). Basque writer of fiction and poet; he gained recognition in particular for his epic and religious verse; he acquired a knowledge of several Basque dialects and became known as a competent translator.

Nirala (b. 1898). Indian (Hindi) poet, writer of fiction, and translator; he wrote historical verse overflowing with patriotic emotion, in addition to social and critical poems; he realistically depicted the misery and the poverty of the lower classes.

Oscar Bento Ribas (b. 1909). Angolan writer of fiction, playwright, and poet; his work focuses upon the people of Kimbundu, their religion and culture; he also prepared Portugese versions of Angolan folk literature and compiled a glossary of regional terms and vernacular expressions.

Abdoulaye Sadji (b. 1910). Senegalese writer of fiction; his works focused upon the hybrid society of Dakar and the old port city of Saint-Louis; he created characters (principally women) who dominated their societies; fascinated with the new cities of Africa, he tended to contrast the country people and their simple values with the more complex inhabitants of urban environments; he projected the dual view of the Gallicized African and the Muslim African, as well as the conflicts arising between those two cultures.

James Grover Thurber (b. 1894). American writer of fiction and humorist; his wistful, ironic cartoons and stories express deep psychological insights into human nature; he became a staff member of and principal contributor to *The New Yorker* magazine.

PUBLICATIONS

Grigol Abashidze, *Mogzauroba Sam Droshi* (Wandering through Three Times)—a play by the Georgian (SSR) poet and dramatist; presents a lyrical view of the past, present, and future of Georgia; relies significantly upon the techniques of science fiction; reflects the writer's deep interest in the history of the Georgian Republic.

Ali Mohammad Afghani, *Shouhare Ahu Khanom* (The Husband of Ahu Khanom)—a novel by the Iranian writer of fiction; a social piece focusing upon family relationships, particularly polygamy among the craftsmen of an Iranian town; the work, nine hundred pages in length, assumes a heavily encyclopaedic character; a second edition (1967) was equally lengthy.

Edward Albee, *The American Dream*—a play by the American dramatist; a handsome young man calls upon a family comprised of a domineering mother, an emasculated father, and a rebellious grandmother; the young man identifies himself as the American Dream and proves to be the identical twin of a child previously adopted and destroyed by the mother and father; the writer artistically parodies American "small talk" and the "average" American life; the piece both amuses and offends.

James Baldwin, *Nobody Knows My Name*—a collection of nonfiction by the American writer of fiction and miscellaneous prose; the writer sets out to explore the meaning of the black experience and focuses upon the general themes of race relations and the function of the artist in society; he also traces the development of his views and attitudes from his decade-long stay in France to his return to Harlem.

Samuel Beckett, *Oh! Les Beaux Jours* (Happy Days)—a play by the Irish-born dramatist; the principal character, a woman, lies half buried in a mound of sand and carries on a monologue as she sinks deeper; she confuses the order of time as she tries to recall the events of the past, fearing the silence that will settle over everything if she ceases to speak; thus (as usual), the piece really never comes to an end.

John Pepper Clark, *Song of a Goat*—a drama by the Nigerian playwright, poet, and writer of fiction; concerns an impotent husband, a frustrated wife, and the husband's younger, virile brother; tension, temptation, anger, revenge, and the decay of a household dominate both action and theme; written in blank verse, the play contains ample action, emotional contrast, and dramatic moments (it ends with a murder).

John Dos Passos, *Midcentury*—a novel by the American writer of fiction; the piece details the growth of labor unions in the United States, while focusing upon the loss of integrity among the rank and file membership; the writer's last novel.

Cyprian Odiatu Duaka Ekwensi, *Jagua Nana*—a novel by the Nigerian writer of fiction; concerns the lusty, bright heroine of the title, named after the British automobile, the Jaguar; thus, she exists as expensive, wanted, and ostentatious; she moves through all levels of society, particularly the urban world of country hustlers and city sophisticates.

William Empson, *Milton's God*—a work of criticism by the English poet and critic; argues against the Christian idea of God as presented by John Milton; presents the writer's notion of the Christian God as responsible for all of the evil as well as the good, of the past; a representative example of the writer's belief that literary interpretation must be supported by biographical facts.

Max Frisch, *Andorra*—a play by the Swiss dramatist; depicts neutral Switzerland, a nation smugly aware of its own virtue and confident of its ability to dissuade a neighboring nation from invading it; the central character, a schoolboy, is the bastard son of a schoolmaster and a woman from the neighboring nation; he dies as the result of being the Jewish scapegoat for the murder of his mother by his own countrymen; the title exists as the name of the country supposedly representative of Switzerland, while the writer identifies the other nation as, simply, "the Blacks."

Jean Genet, *Les Paravents* (The Screens)— the last play by the French dramatist, novelist, and poet; the colonialism existing in North Africa functions as a metaphor for the worst traits of humanity; the writer condemns the involvement of France in the Algerian War, but the work does not exist principally to promote revolutionism; the emphasis of the play remains on innovative stage techniques: as the scenes progress, settings become suggestive through camera projections onto a series of folding screens; or, actors sketch those settings on canvases.

Gunter Grass, *Katz und Maus* (Cat and Mouse)—a novella by the West German novelist, poet, playwright, and essayist; concerns a young athlete and hero set apart from his peers by an enormous Adam's apple; ultimately, he manages to gain acceptance by his small-minded friends.

Shirley Ann Grau, *The House on Coliseum Street*—a novel by the American writer of fiction; representative of the Southern point of view, the writer directs her attention to the life of a young girl living in New Orleans; her lonely, loveless existence is contrasted with the life of that city.

Khalil Hawi, *An-Nay Wa'r-Rih* (The Flute and the Wind)—a volume of verse by the Lebanese poet; constructed upon a symbolic character, Sinbad, the sailor in search of truth; although native to the East, the sailor examines both Eastern and Western values: the spiritual values of the East, the philosophy and science of the West; neither can provide humanity with the final solutions to problems; thus, humanity must reject the present for a future renewal of life.

Robert A. Heinlein, *Stranger in a Strange Land*—a novel by the American writer of fiction; examines an alien nation in which the culture anchors itself to the exercise of "grokking"; the work was exceedingly popular among the "hippie" groups of the 1960s.

Joseph Heller, *Catch-22*—a novel by the American writer of fiction; an exceedingly humorous piece set during World War II; the writer captures the absurdities that can result from a rigid system; thus, the Army tries to shut off all means of escape with red tape, and the principal character of the piece tries to find a way out of the system.

Al-Bashir Khraief, *Barq al-Layl*—a novel by the Tunisian writer of fiction; a historical piece that focuses upon Tunis in the sixteenth century; the writer does not aim for a high degree of historical precision, but instead chooses to create a deeply symbolic folk hero.

Stanislaw Lem, *Powrot z Gwiazd* (Return from the Stars)—a novel by the Polish writer of fiction, playwright, and essayist; concerns an astronaut who returns from a mission in space and discovers that Earth has aged 127 years during his short absence; society has achieved peace through a scientific method that eliminates aggression; however, as a result, human beings no longer wish to assume risks, a quality so necessary for their progress and survival.

Robert Lowell, *Imitations*—a collection of verse by the American poet; highly original translations of works by Homer, Sappho, and fifteen other poets from Francois Villon to Eugenio Montale; the language of the poems rises to an intensity that transcends that of the other poets; concentrates upon the works of Charles Baudelaire and Arthur Rimbaud, Symbolist writers for whom poetry functioned as a self-created world.

Louis MacNeice, *Solstices*—a collection of lyrical verse by the Irish-born poet; the final volume published during the writer's lifetime.

Carson McCullers, *Clock Without Hands*—a novel by the American writer of fiction, her last; another exercise in search of the self, focusing on the relationship between blacks and whites in a rural town in Georgia.

Arthur Miller, *The Misfits*—a screenplay by the American playwright; starred his wife, Marilyn Monroe; concerns a group of cowboys who capture wild mustangs for dog food.

Mirsaid Mirshakar, *Dashti Laband* (The Lazy Steppe)—a long poem by the Iranian (Tajik) playwright and writer of verse; concerns the campaign to reclaim the Central Asian steppes; frankly confronts a number of negative aspects of the Stalin cult period.

Iris Murdoch, *A Severed Head*—a novel by the English writer of fiction; a satirical portrait of the adulterous and incestuous liaisons of a social set that represents a typical Bloomsbury group; the work was dramatized in 1963 by J. B. Priestley.

John Osborne, *Luther*—a play by the English dramatist; based upon the life and times of Martin Luther; the playwright places as much emphasis on the title character's physical problems as on his spiritual concerns.

At-Tayyib Salih, *Mawsim al-Hijra ila 'Sh-Shimal* (Time of Migration Northwards)—the first novel by the Sudanese writer of fiction; the writer portrays the impact of two contrasting cultures and mentalities upon a European-educated Sudanese youth.

J. D. Salinger, *Franny and Zooey*—a volume of two short stories by the American writer of fiction; the pieces focus upon the crises, triumphs, and tragedies of the Glass family, the youngest members of which are the title characters.

Muriel Spark, *The Prime of Miss Jean Brodie*—a novel by the Scottish-born writer of fiction, poet, playwright, and essayist; set at a school for girls in Edinburgh during the 1930s; the title character, a teacher, chooses to nurture and guide a select group of girls, to control their lives; one of them eventually complains to the headmistress concerning their teacher's exercise in totalitarianism.

John Steinbeck, *The Winter of Our Discontent*—a novel by the American writer of fiction; focuses upon the demise of an old New

England family, accompanied by the fatal loss of ideals.

Leon Uris, *Mila 18*—a novel by the American writer of popular fiction; concerns an uprising in the Warsaw ghetto during the Holocaust period of World War II.

Kurt Vonnegut, Jr., *Mother Night*—a novel by the American writer of fiction; a satirical analysis of a former American Nazi, who, in fact, has functioned as a counter-intelligence agent; he writes his detailed confessions while awaiting trial for his war crimes; in the cell next to him sits Adolph Eichmann.

Auberon Waugh, *The Foxglove Saga*—a novel by the English writer of fiction; an extremely comic piece about an unintelligent and eccentric, but well meaning, woman and her equally strange family, the Foxgloves; essentially an attack upon "do-gooders" who have little or no purpose and thus bring about more harm than good.

Richard Wright, *Eight Men*—a collection of short stories by the American writer of fiction and miscellaneous prose; each story focuses upon a black man who is beaten down by his cruel surroundings.

EVENTS

Ivo Andric, Yugoslav poet, essayist, and writer of fiction, receives the Nobel Prize for literature.

The Bollingen Poetry Translation Prize established, to be administered by Yale University and the Bollingen Trust.

Floating Bear, a magazine and newsletter in mimeograph for writers of contemporary fiction and verse, begins publication at New York City; William S. Burroughs and Robert Creeley are among the contributors; until 1969.

Harper Lee, American writer of fiction, receives the Pulitzer Prize in fiction for her novel *To Kill a Mockingbird* (1960).

Phyllis McGinley, American poet, receives the Pulitzer Prize in poetry for *Times Three: Selected Verse from Three Decades* (1960).

Tad Mosel (originally George Ault Mosel, Jr.), American playwright, receives the Pulitzer Prize in drama for *All the Way Home* (1960), a dramatic adaptation of James Agee's novel *A Death in the Family* (1957).

The New English Bible. New Testament published in London jointly by the Oxford and Cambridge university presses; a completely new translation from the original texts and rendered into contemporary English.

Renzo Rosselini's Italian opera *Uno Sguardo Dal Ponte,* based upon Arthur Miller's play *A View from the Bridge* (1955), has its first performance.

1962

BIRTHS

Pia Juul. Danish poet; her verse will be soft and introspective; she will create disciplined lines in the manner of the Danish surrealist poets of the 1930s.

DEATHS

Richard Aldington (b. 1892). English poet and writer of fiction; his verse gained recognition for its linguistic and metrical precision; most of his novels are bitter satires.

E. E. Cummings (b. 1894). American writer of verse; known especially for his disregard for upper case letters, he gained a reputation for his lyrical poems and his eccentric language and typography; in 1922, he wrote an exceptional prose account of his internment in France during World War I, *The Enormous Room.*

Isak Dinesen (pseudonym of Baroness Karen Blixen; born 1885). Danish writer of fiction; most of her work was written in English; she achieved literary recognition for her imaginative tales containing romantic and supernatural elements; she also wrote an autobiographical account of her years on a coffee plantation in Kenya.

William Faulkner (b. 1897). American writer of fiction; his celebrated series of "Yoknapatawpha County" stories developed a fictional county in Mississippi where characters, past and present, paraded across the social and economic spectrum of the old and the new South; constantly experimented with technique, employing such devices as stream of consciousness narration and interior monologues; in 1949, he received the Nobel Prize for literature.

Michel de Ghelderode (b. 1898). Belgian playwright; as both a satirist and a poet, he became one of the most original French-language dramatists of the "modern" literary period; medieval morality plays, Flemish painting, puppet theater, commedia dell'arte, and the Elizabethan dramatists all influenced his work.

Abdullah Goran (b. 1904). Kurdish poet; he wrote Romantic lyrics influenced by Percy Bysshe Shelley before adopting a realistic attitude and point of view; he also turned his attention to social and political issues; when he died, he left behind a significant body and variety of work: theatrical plays, novellas, and translations from English and French.

Herman Hesse (b. 1877). German poet and writer of fiction; an ardent pacifist, he became a Swiss citizen following the outbreak of World War I; one of his principal themes, particularly in his symbolic novels, is the spiritual loneliness of the artist; he also expressed a deep interest in the mysticism of the Orient; in 1946, he received the Nobel Prize for literature.

John Robinson Jeffers (b. 1887). American poet; he wrote extremely virile and intense verse, and thus he became known as one of America's most powerful and controversial poets; in both long narratives and short lyrics, he embraced the elements of myth, which he attempted to adapt to realistic settings of twentieth-century America.

John Ebenezer Clare McFarlane (b. 1894). Jamaican poet and essayist; his verse reveals the influence of nineteenth-century English literature, particularly the poetry of William Wordsworth; he founded the Poetry League of Jamaica and compiled anthologies of Jamaican verse.

Ramon Perez d'Ayala (b. 1880?). Spanish writer of fiction, essayist, and poet; his fiction tended to be realistic, although somewhat distorted by his satirical viewpoints; most of his works are set in his home region (Oviedo) and based on his own experiences; his stories are brutal tales of misfits destroyed by a world that reflects their own ugliness.

Shaaban Robert (b. 1909). Tanzanian (Swahili) poet, novelist, essayist, and biographer; he introduced the formal essay into Swahili literature and composed satires on contemporary events in the manner of Jonathan Swift; an ardent Moslem and an African patriot, he protested against subjugation to European colonialism; he achieved recognition as the undisputed poet laureate of the Swahili language.

George Macaulay Trevelyan (b. 1876). English historian; he rose to prominence as the recognized master of the literary school of history and as the leading opponent of the scientific method of historiography; the son of the English historian and politician George Otto Trevelyan (1838-1928).

Mohammad Yamin (b. 1903). Indonesian poet, novelist, and historian; he became one of the pioneers of modern poetry in Indonesia; he wrote ardently patriotic verse and tended to develop new literary forms; a native of Sumatra.

PUBLICATIONS

Edward Albee, *Who's Afraid of Virginia Woolf?*—a drama by the American playwright; his first full-length dramatic piece; concerns a middle-aged history professor and his wife as they "entertain" a young married couple after a faculty party; the older couple quarrel, nag each other, and dredge up painful memories from the past; thus, violence becomes the means for communication and even the means for attempting to maintain their love for one another.

Brian Aldiss, *Hothouse*—a novel by the English writer of popular science fiction; concerns a highly surrealist future that becomes dominated by the plant world.

James Baldwin, *In Another Country*—a novel by the American writer of fiction and miscellaneous prose; men and women, both black and white, strip off their masks of color and gender to reveal elemental passions; the work is a subtle exploration of the complexities of love and, at the same time, a study of the terrifying power of hate.

Rajindar Singh Bedi, *Ek Cadar Mali Si* (A Soiled Sheet)—the first novel by the Indian (Urdu) writer of fiction; concerns a marital tragedy, set in rural Punjab; the piece receives the Sahitya Akademi award for 1966.

John Braine, *Life at the Top*—a novel by the English writer of fiction; the work continues (from *Room at the Top*, 1957) the account of Joe Lampton, the angry young man who finds both success and disillusion.

Anthony Burgess, *A Clockwork Orange*—a novel by the English writer of fiction; violent satire revealing an original vision of a futuristic and highly authoritarian society; adapted for the motion picture screen in 1971.

Alejo Carpentier, *El Siglo de las Luces* (Explosion in a Cathedral)—a novel by the Cuban writer of fiction, poet, and essayist; a historical epic that follows the lives of three characters as they participate in an early nineteenth-century Caribbean revolution; reveals the novelist's reluctance to align himself with a specific ideology.

Driss Chraibi, *Succession Ouverte* (An Unclaimed Inheritance)—a novel in French by the Moroccan writer of fiction; the work reveals a general disillusionment with conditions in independent Morocco, and thus the principal character wishes to leave his country; the writer also expresses disappointment with Moroccan relations with Europe.

Gregory Corso, *Long Live Man*—a collection of verse by the American poet; the pieces reflect the writer's general protest against the times and reveal him as a "word slinger," a dispenser of language in various forms and for various purposes; the influence of Allen Ginsberg appears obvious.

Robert Creeley, *For Loves: Poems, 1959-1960*—a collection by the American writer of verse; termed his most accomplished work, the poems rely upon elementary forms: quatrains, tercets, couplets; includes such pieces as "Ballad of the Despairing Husband," "I Know a Man," "La Noche," and "A Wicker Basket"; drug trips and erotic sensations generally form the substance of the volume.

James Dickey, *Drowning with Others*—a collection by the American writer of fiction and poet; as the title would indicate, images of water, creatures, and transfiguration dominate in the poems; includes such pieces as "Fog Envelops the Animals," "The Heaven of Animals," "The Summons," "For the Nightly Ascent of the Hunter Orion," and "In the Mountain Tent"; the writer strives to fuse dream, fantasy, and allusion.

George Faludy, *My Happy Days in Hell*—an autobiographical narrative by the Hungarian-born Canadian poet, translator, and writer of fiction; presents an account of the writer's life as a literary celebrity turned political dissident; outlines the tragedy of Hungary during the fascist and communist dictatorships; reveals the passion, humor, and dignity of life in the concentration camp; essentially, the work defines the meaning of human persistence in a society ruled by the enemies of humanity.

William Faulkner, *The Reivers: A Reminiscence*—a novel by the American writer of fiction; one of the writer's funniest books, the work is a classic account of an eleven-year-old boy who takes his grandfather's automobile and ventures—in a single day in 1905 and in company with two older friends—from Jefferson, Mississippi, to Memphis, Tennessee; the three "reivers" (those who would take by force or by plunder) embark on a series of adventures and conflicts with the law; the writer's final effort, a Pulitzer Prize winner and eventually a motion picture.

Zbigniew Herbert, *Barbarznca w Ogrodzie* (The Barbarian in the Garden)—a collection of essays by the Polish poet, essayist, and playwright; the pieces principally concern European art and architecture as viewed by the "barbarian" of the title, who exists outside the dominant Western tradition.

Yusuf Idris, *Al-Ayb* (Sin)—a novella by the Egyptian writer of fiction; demonstrates how a woman who decides to leave the home and seek work becomes victimized by the ills of urban society; essentially, the writer sets out to condemn prejudice and to present a positive view of rural folk life and lore.

Jalol Ikromi, *Dukhtari Otash* (Daughter of Fire)—a three-part novel by the Iranian (Tajik) playwright and writer of fiction; provides a vivid picture of life in Bukhara in the early twentieth century, to the beginning of the Russian Revolution in 1917; the work gained literary recognition for its striking portrayal of Tajik women.

Uwe Johnson, *Das Dritte Buch uber Achim* (The Third Book about Achim)—a novel by the German writer of fiction; concerns a West German journalist who attempts to write a biography of an East German champion cyclist; the writer discovers that he cannot portray the cyclist's life without considering his political environment, nor can he reconcile the differences between East and West; he eventually abandons the project, learning that human beings cannot hope to discover themselves amid the uncertainty of common words and phrases.

Ken Kesey, *One Flew over the Cuckoo's Nest*—a novel by the American writer of fiction; the blackly humorous piece, set in a mental institution, is a modern fable pitting good against evil; the principal character appears maniacal because of his eccentricities and disruptive nonconformity; the institution's hospital staff are repressive authority figures who attempt to purge the patients of their individuality.

Doris Lessing, *The Golden Notebook*—a novel by the Persian-born, Rhodesian-raised English writer of fiction; describes the writer's creative problems as she struggles with her domestic and political life; the piece was passionately embraced by feminists, as the central character manifests the entire issue of female fragmentation.

Vladimir Nabokov, *Pale Fire*—a novel by the Russian-born writer of fiction, poet, essayist, and playwright; a playful parody on a long poem about death, immortality, and art; to celebrate authorial judgment and parody critical explication.

Charles Nokan, *Violent Etait le Vent* (Wild Blew the Wind)—a novel (his first) by the Ivory Coast poet, playwright, and writer of fiction; the writer seeks to conform to the aesthetic of his own people, wherein the dance satisfies the ear and the eye; thus, the work combines both prose and verse passages to "recapture" the quality of the "tom-tom"; the principal character represents the past that resists change, while another character carries "the torch of the present."

Sylvia Plath, *The Colossus and Other Poems*—a volume of verse by the American poet; the title poem, addressed to the poet's dead father, displays the extent of her emotional involvement in her work.

Katherine Anne Porter, *Ship of Fools*—a novel by the American writer of fiction; a moral allegory that embraces the theme of the unity of human beings; the North German Lloyd liner *S. A. Vera* is enroute from Veracruz, Mexico, to Bremerhaven, Germany, during August and September of 1931; simply, the vessel of the contemporary world finds itself on a voyage to eternity, its passengers and crew representative of Western civilization in the twentieth century.

Anthony Powell, *The Kindly Ones*—a novel by the English writer of fiction; concerns Nick Jenkins, the principal character of a host of the writer's novels; this work harkens back to scenes from Nick's childhood.

Isaac Bashevis Singer, *The Slave*—a novella by the Polish-born writer of fiction; the volume incorporates several stories from the Old Testament, including the account of the bondage of Joseph and his brethren in Egypt.

Alexandr Solzhenitsyn, *One Day in the Life of Ivan Denisovich*—a novel by the Russian writer of fiction; the work exposes the conditions in one of Josef Stalin's slave labor camps; narrated from the point of view of a traditional Russian peasant, the simplest and most honest of souls; the piece was personally sanctioned by Nikita Khrushchev in 1963.

John Steinbeck, *Travels with Charley in Search of America*—a travel narrative by the American writer of fiction; the novelist rides, with his poodle, in a van by the name of "Rociante" during 1961; as the title indicates, they seek to learn of and identify with their country.

Barbara Tuchman, *The Guns of August*—a historical narrative by the American historian; concerns World War I: specifically, the breakdown of negotiations, the Germans' drive through Belgium and their threat upon Paris, and the view of the beginnings of the war from both fronts; the work receives the Pulitzer Prize for general nonfiction in 1963.

John Wain, *Strike the Father Dead*—a novel by the English writer of fiction, critic, and poet; written in the "angry young man" mold, the piece focuses upon a rebellious young man, the son of a "red-brick" university professor, who runs away from home, school, and his father's expectations to become a jazz pianist.

Thornton Wilder, *Plays for Bleecker Street*—a drama collection by the American playwright, novelist, and essayist; a double series of fourteen plays, seven upon the deadly sins and seven on the ages of humankind; the title of the work identifies the location of the theater in which the work would be performed; titles include *Someone from Assisi, Infancy,* and *Childhood.*

Tennessee Williams, *The Night of the Iguana*—a play by the American writer of fiction and drama; the characters of the piece struggle against what they perceive as a "murderously indifferent" God; to survive their ordeal in a Mexican hotel, they almost embrace theology.

EVENTS

Ci Cu Cellappa, Tamil poet, writer of miscellaneous fiction and nonfiction, and critic, founds the influential critical journal *Eluttu* (Writing).

Alan Dugan, American writer of verse, receives the Pulitzer Prize for poetry for his volume of *Poems* (1961).

Edwin O'Connor, American writer of fiction, receives the Pulitzer Prize for fiction for his novel *The Edge of Sadness* (1961).

John Ernst Steinbeck, American writer of fiction, receives the Nobel Prize for literature.

1963

DEATHS

Van Wyck Brooks (b. 1886). American critic and intellectual historian; his early work focused upon the influence of Puritanism on American culture; he also produced a multivolume analysis and humanistic interpretation of American literary history; he received the Pulitzer Prize for United States history in 1937.

Jean Maurice Eugene Clement Cocteau (b. 1889). French writer of fiction, playwright, and film writer; he stands, almost without rival in the twentieth century, for versatility in the creative arts; he experimented in almost every artistic medium: poetry, fiction, drama, film, ballet, drawing, and operatic libretto; his work is characterized by surrealistic fancy.

William Edward Burghardt DuBois (b. 1868). Black American civil rights leader and essayist, poet, and writer of autobiographical narrative, and miscellaneous prose; after earning his Ph.D. from Harvard, he taught history and economics and became an early advocate of social and racial equality.

Robert Lee Frost (b. 1874). American poet; he celebrated the common people and the landscape of New England; his lyric, dramatic, and deeply symbolic verse, however, transcends regional borders; he received the Pulitzer Prize for his works in 1924, 1931, 1937, and 1943; an edition of his complete poems appeared in 1967.

Ramon Gomez de la Serna (b. 1891). Spanish writer of fiction, playwright, and biographer; his fiction and drama reflect his bohemian life-style; he also produced short, semisurrealistic aphorisms and biographies of John Ruskin, Oscar Wilde, and Ramon Maria del Valle-Inclan; he left Spain during the civil war and spent his remaining years in Buenos Aires.

Nazim Hikmet Ran (b. 1902). Turkish poet, playwright, writer of fiction, and journalist; he set out to challenge the restrictions of traditional Turkish poetry by introducing free verse in place of conventional stanzas and rhyme patterns; a committed communist, he spent fifteen years in jail, where he produced his most significant poems; his verse abounds with political themes, yet he could also be extremely personal and private, writing of his love for family, friends, and nature; after his release from prison in 1951, he settled in the Soviet Union; in 1950, he shared the Soviet Union World Peace Prize with Pablo Neruda.

Aldous Leonard Huxley (b. 1894). English writer of fiction, critic, and poet; his novels depicted social decadence and the nightmarish consequences of so-called utopian societies; as an agnostic, he openly challenged those phenomenon not immediately adaptable to logical analysis or scientific verification; he did, however, place human ethics outside the range of materialistic evolutionary processes, believing that human beings could achieve progress through the control of evolution.

Jose Antonio Jarvis (b. 1902). Virgin Islands poet, playwright, essayist, and historian; he wrote simple and direct poems expressing his concern for nature, life, and religion; he also produced historical narratives about the Virgin Islands, pieces valuable because of his knowledge of the area and its inhabitants; he was praised for his vivid interpretation of the culture throughout the islands.

Oliver la Farge (b. 1901). American writer of nonfiction and fiction and anthropologist; he relied in his novels upon material from his ethnological and archaeological expeditions to authenticate his observations and reactions; he received a Pulitzer Prize for fiction in 1929 for his *Laughing Boy.*

C. S. Lewis (b. 1898). English literary scholar, critic, and writer of religious and moral narratives; he gained recognition as an explicator of Christian tenets, a commentator upon medieval romantic love, and a writer of outerplanetary fantasies with moral overtones.

Ahmad Lufti as-Sayyid (b. 1872). Egyptian philosopher and essayist; from his prose emerged a carefully conceived notion of an Egypt based upon the political ideals of Jean Jacques Rousseau, Auguste Comte, John Stuart Mill, and Herbert Spencer; he became professor of philosophy at the Egyptian University.

Louis MacNeice (b. 1907). Irish poet and literary classicist; his early verse reflected the social protests of the 1930s; later in his career, he wrote ironic poetry that directed itself to the futility of modern life; he also translated works of Aeschylus and Johann Wolfgang von Goethe.

Kavalam Madhava Panikkar (b. 1895). Indian historian, poet, playwright, and writer of fiction; his novels reflected his interests in history and politics.

Endalkacaw Makonnen (b. 1892). Ethiopian (Amharic) writer of fiction, playwright, and autobiographer; thematically, his literary efforts tended to be conservative and traditional, looking back upon the old political and religious practices and institutions; he focused upon the ascendancy of the feudal lords and on what he termed "the good old ways."

Malai Chuphinit (b. 1906). Thai author of fiction who wrote under no less than eighteen pseudonyms; his fiction reflects a sensitivity to the beauties of nature and the country life; throughout, he demonstrates a subtle understanding of humanity.

Nhat-Linh (originally Nguyen-tuong-Tam; b. 1906). Vietnamese writer of fiction; he criticized traditional Vietnamese society and existing social conventions and proclaimed the right of the individual to free development of his or her personality, especially in terms of the emotions.

Sylvia Plath (b. 1932). American poet; she developed finely crafted and intensely personal verse, dominated by sharp, often violent imagery; a major theme of her work concerns juvenile traumas that lie, treacherously, beneath the surface of adult experience; for her personal relationships become predatory, exploitative, and destructive; she commits suicide in London.

John Cowper Powys (b. 1872). English poet, essayist, and writer of fiction; his fiction best demonstrates his greatest strengths as a writer: the ability to develop powerful characters and intense relationships and to portray specific locales; his work became associated with Wales, where he eventually settled.

Theodore Roethke (b. 1908). American poet; his verse combined his love of the Midwest with his intense vision of individual development; the tone of his poems ranges from the sharply witty to the harmonious and simple.

Lope K. Santos (b. 1879). Philippine writer of fiction and poet; his fictional themes focus upon social justice, while his verse tends to be highly sentimental; a specialist in the Tagalog language, he wrote grammar texts and headed the Institute of the National Language during the Japanese occupation.

Francisco Jose de Vasques Tenreiro (b. 1921). Sao Tome poet and writer of fiction; he devoted his relatively brief literary career to scholarship, poetry, and the general study of African literature; his "neo-realist" poems stand as the first major works of "negritude" by an African writing in Portuguese, and they have influenced African writers throughout the former Portuguese colonies.

Tristan Tzara (pseudonym of Samuel Rosenfeld; b. 1896). Romanian-born French poet, playwright, and essayist; a principal proponent of Dadaism, the intellectual movement of the World War I era espousing intentional irrationalism and urging individuals to repudiate traditional artistic, historic, and religious values; he sought to establish a new style in which random associations would serve to evoke a vitality free from the restraints of logic and grammar; his verse achieved unity through his critique of and search for a universal language and cosmic wisdom.

William Carlos Williams (b. 1883). American poet and practicing physician; he became an acute observer of American life, developing a lucid and vital poetic style that reflected idiomatic speech; his poetic view remained faithful to the ordinary objects of sight and sound; he wrote a five-volume philosophical poem, critical essays, short stories, novels, and plays; in this year he receives the Pulitzer Prize for poetry.

PUBLICATIONS

Michael Anthony, *The Games Were Coming*— the first novel by the Trinidadian writer of fiction; concerned with the dedicated preparation of a champion for victory in a fifteen-mile bicycle race; the achievement of that victory takes its personal toll; the work was reissued in Boston in 1968.

James Baldwin, *The Fire Next Time*—a volume of nonfiction by the American writer of fiction and miscellaneous prose; the work takes the form of two letters to his nephew on the one-hundredth anniversary of the emancipation; a series of prophetic warnings about the reality of being black in America; an intensely personal work that also exists as an important historical document.

Ray Bradbury, *Something Wicked This Way Comes*—a novel by the American writer of science fiction and fantasy; a fascinating study of the events that occur in a small town following the showing of "the Pandemonium Shadow Show"; a school teacher becomes transformed into a child, a full-grown man finds himself reduced into the body of a dwarf, and a boy advances to the age of Methuselah.

Anthony Burgess, *Inside Mr. Enderby*—a novel by the English writer of fiction, the first of the "Enderby" novels; an account of a flatulent middle-aged writer who can write only in the lavatory; his life, after marriage, becomes a series of incredible adventures.

Rachel Carson, *Silent Spring*—a work of nonfiction by the American essayist and marine biologist; an extremely popular and influential study of the dangers that insecticides pose to plants, animals, and humans.

Aime Fernand Cesaire, *La Tragedie du Roi Christophe* (The Tragedy of King Christophe)—a drama by the Martinique poet, playwright, and translator; Shakespearean in tone and style, the piece relies upon historical material from the reign of King Henry Christophe, one of Haiti's early leaders; the writer essentially illustrates the problems of independence, combining significant accomplishment and tragic failure, particularly when a leader becomes insensitive to the needs of his people.

J. P. Donleavy, *A Singular Man*—a novel by the American-born Irish writer of fiction; the central character, who resembles the business tycoon Howard Hughes, becomes enthralled with the notion of death; he dedicates his life to the building of a large mausoleum; as he suffers from a number of personal misfortunes, he becomes more withdrawn.

Sumner Locke Elliott, *Careful, He Might Hear You*—a novel by the Australian writer of fiction and playwright; related principally from the viewpoint of an orphaned boy whose aunts fight for custody of him; adapted as a motion picture.

John Fowles, *The Collector*—the first novel by the English writer of fiction; a psychological thriller in which the narrator, a repressed clerk and collector of butterflies, wins a fortune on a football bet; he spends the money on the kidnapping of a female art student;

she dies, and thus he plans to add another specimen to his collection.

Gunter Grass, *Hunderjahre* (Dog Years)—a novel by the German writer of fiction, essayist, poet, and dramatist; the final volume of *The Danzig Trilogy;* through the disparate perspectives of three narrators, the writer describes the forces of German society between 1917 and 1957; there emerges a relationship between a German and his half-Jewish friend; in childhood, the man defends his friend from a gang of ruffians, but as a Nazi stormtrooper, he beats him viciously; after the war, consumed with guilt and vengeance, he stalks the German countryside, infecting the daughters and the wives of former Nazis with venereal disease; the writer also describes how the German language became defiled by the rhetoric of fascism.

Rolf Hochhuth, *Der Stellvertreter* (The Deputy [or, depending upon the translator, The Representative])—a play by the German documentary dramatist; an indictment of Pope Pius XII and the alleged indifference of the Roman Catholic authorities to the plight of the Jews; accuses the pope of failing to denounce Nazi persecution of Jews; a popular work that aroused considerable controversy.

Jean Ikelle-Matiba, *Cette Afrique-la!* (This Particular Africa)—a novel by the Cameroon writer of fiction, essayist, and poet; describes the career of Franz Momha in the late nineteenth century, during the German occupation; published at Paris, with a German edition in 1971; the work received the Grand Prix Litteraire de l'Afrique Noire for this year.

Eugene Ionesco, *Le Roi se Meurt* (Exit the King)—a play by the Romanian-born French dramatist, essayist, and writer of fiction; the principal character, a modern-day Everyman (Berenger, who appears in several of the author's plays), is a king who has been informed that he will soon die.

Noni Helen Nontando Jabavu, *The Ochre People: Scenes from a South African Life*—a novel by the South African (Cape Province) writer of fiction; an autobiographical piece that focuses upon a different geographical area in each of its three sections; written in English, but the novelist relies upon an abundance of words in the Xhosa language.

Ismail Kadare, *Gjenerali i Ushtrise se Vdekur* (The General of the Dead Army)—a novel by the Albanian writer of fiction and poet; an antiwar chronicle, the first Albanian novel to be published in the United States; examines the repercussions of war through the story of an Italian general sent to Albania to bring back the bodies of his countrymen killed in World War II; during his search for the soldiers' remains, the general recognizes his need to discover his own identity; in the end, he goes mad, burdened by the absurdity of his mission and guilt from his participation in war.

Jack Kerouac, *Visions of Gerard*—a novel by the American writer of fiction and miscellaneous prose; presents the early childhood of Ti Jean Duluiz, the writer's alter ego, as reflected in the short life of his brother, Gerard.

John Le Carre, *The Spy Who Came in from the Cold*—a novel by the English writer of fiction; an immensely popular complex study of international espionage; the issues focus upon the Cold War and the Berlin Wall.

Bernard Malamud, *Idiots First*—a collection of short stories by the American writer of fiction; unusual for Malamud because they are set in places outside of Brooklyn, New York.

Mary McCarthy, *The Group*—a novel by the American writer of fiction; concerns six girls from Vassar College, class of 1933; the writer traces the destinies of this group until the early days of World War II, each character representing a facet of American experience; attitudes and emotions become especially important to the portrayal and analysis of these women.

W. S. Merwin, *The Moving Target*—a collection of verse by the American poet and playwright; in each piece, the writer appears to emphasize a disembodied voice; displays surrealistic poetic techniques that the writer adopted from the Spanish writers he was translating.

William Modisane, *Blame Me on History*—an autobiographical novel by the South African poet and writer of fiction; in vivid language, the writer depicts the plight of the black man in the world of apartheid; though bitter about the racial policies of South Africa, the principal character (the novelist) expresses his sense of guilt at fleeing the country.

Sylvia Plath, *The Bell Jar*—a novel by the American poet and writer of fiction; focuses upon the emotional breakdown of the principal character, her unsuccessful suicide attempt, and the ominously successful suicide of her ghostly counterpart; through a successful sexual experience, the nineteen-year-old girl returns to a normal life.

Thomas Pynchon, *V*—a novel by the American writer of fiction; an allegory in which technological imagery shapes religious and erotic sensations; the messiah machine serves as the principal character, possessed of a clock heart and a sponge brain, which he fears will become disassembled; he represents a profane version of Christ who moves too fast to lose his heart or allow anyone to touch his head; the religious allegory becomes more obvious as the work proceeds toward its complex finish.

Adrienne Rich, *Snapshots of a Daughter-in-Law: Poems, 1954-1962*—a collection by the American writer of verse; the poems constitute an attempt to understand the very dynamics of experience; thus, the poet confronts the tension that she sees around her, directing her view toward the world and then toward herself.

Alain Robbe-Grillet, *Pour un Nouveau Roman* (For a New Novel)—a volume of theoretical essays by the French writer of fiction and essayist; the writer questions the validity of traditional forms of the novel, discounting the notion that realism necessarily offers the most accurate reflection of life; he advocates a spontaneous recording of events without imposing subjective interpretation.

J. D. Salinger, *Raise High the Roof-Beam, Carpenters/Seymour: An Introduction*—two collections of short stories (published in a single volume) by the American writer of fiction; the pieces were all previously published in *The New Yorker* magazine; all of the pieces concern the Glass Family, particularly Buddy and Seymour.

Oluwole Soyinka, *The Swamp Dwellers*—a play by the Nigerian dramatist, poet, and writer of fiction; concerns an old woman, her husband, and their son, as well as a beggar from the north and a corrupt priest; the playwright exploits the contrast between younger and older generations, also dramatizing the dangers of the large, Europeanized cities of the new Africa; in the author's view, the role of the traditional African priest has become seriously diminished, and the old tribal village faiths and leaders have failed to provide young people with either spiritual or physical security.

John Updike, *The Centaur*—a novel by the American writer of fiction, poet, playwright, and essayist; a mythological story of a teacher/father and his student/son that loosely parallels that of Chiron (the centaur) and Prometheus (the student); the work receives the National Book Award.

Kurt Vonnegut, Jr., *Cat's Cradle*—a novel by the American writer of fiction; a humorous yet tragic satire upon modern human beings and their madness; the writer masterfully combines satire, realism, and fantasy.

EVENTS

The Center for Editions of American Authors established by the Modern Language Association; devoted to producing accurate texts of significant works by American writers.

Joseph Leon Edel, American academician and literary scholar, receives the Pulitzer Prize for biography/autobiography for two volumes of his five-part biographical study of Henry James: *Henry James: The Conquest of London, 1870-1881* (vol. 2) and *Henry James: The Middle Years, 1881-1895* (vol. 3).

William Faulkner, American writer of fiction, posthumously awarded the Pulitzer Prize for fiction for his novel *The Reivers* (1962).

The New York Review of Books begins publication; results from a printers' strike against the newspapers of New York City.

George Seferis (originally Giorgos Sefiriadis), Greek poet, critic, and diplomat, receives the Nobel Prize for literature.

Barbara Wertheim Tuchman, American historian, receives the Pulitzer Prize for nonfiction for her *Guns of August* (1962), the history of events leading to World War I.

William Carlos Williams, American writer of fiction and verse, critic, and playwright, receives the Pulitzer Prize in poetry for *Pictures from Breughel and Other Poems* (1962).

1964

DEATHS

Sheikh Kaluta bin Amri Abedi (b. 1924). Tanzanian (Swahili) poet; he published a single collection of verse and a critical text on the rules of versification; the poems, published originally in 1954, appeared in an enlarged edition this year; he held, at his death, the position of Tanzanian justice minister.

Halide Edib Adivar (b. 1884). Turkish writer of fiction and essayist; she taught English literature at the University of Istanbul and served in the Turkish National Assembly; her fiction combines personal, feminine emotionalism with a universal theme; the individual overshadowed in importance by history or environment; she viewed her writing as an attempt to interpret, for the Western reader, the traditional Turkish background; through her nineteen novels, she has gained recognition as one of the most representative of Turkish writers of fiction at the end of World War I and during the early period of the Turkish Republic.

Abbas Mahmud al-Aqqad (b. 1889). Egyptian writer of fiction, critic, literary historian, and poet; his work reveals the influence of English literature; thus, he wrote lyrical and contemplative verse in classical Western forms; as a critic, he emphasized the essential unity of a literary work; he regarded poetry as the expression of the poet's personality, feelings, and experiences; his literary biographies follow the principles of analysis set forth by Sigmund Freud.

Konrad Bayer (b. 1932). Austrian poet and writer of fiction; he specialized in nonsensical verse, but also published chansons, sketches, essays, novels, and stories; he wrote a quasi-biographical account of Vitus Bering, the Russian discoverer of the strait that bears his name; he dies by his own hand.

Brendan Behan (b. 1923). Irish playwright; he served in the Irish Republican Army and, as a result, was imprisoned several times; these experiences are reflected in his plays; his swaggering prose characterized by profanity, wit, and irreverence, served well on the stage to counter the pervasiveness of themes related to death in his dramas; excessive drinking leads to his death from diabetes and liver deterioration.

Rachel Louise Carson (b. 1907). American essayist and marine biologist; she wrote an influential study on the danger of insecticides (1962) and appeals to save life in and around the seas (1951, 1954).

Vasily Semenovich Grossman (b. 1905). Russian writer of fiction, playwright, poet, and journalist; he gained recognition for his novels and journalistic accounts of World War II; later, he became an outspoken critic of the Soviet state, particularly in terms of the prevailing anti-Semitism and restrictions upon artistic activity; most of his postwar literary efforts were suppressed during his lifetime.

Maithilisaran Gupta (b. 1886). Indian (Hindi) poet; his verse focused upon Hindu nationalism, depicting, in his longer pieces, the vision of the ideal Hindu society; he became the first generally accepted poet to write in modern Hindi, and later he emerged as the one poet to explain the principles of Mohandas Gandhi to the Hindi speaking world.

Thakhin Koujto Hmain (b. 1876). Burmese poet, writer of fiction, playwright, and historian; he produced verse, rhymed prose, literary commentaries, social criticism, and harsh political attacks upon Burmese Anglophiles; his more than eighty plays tended to portray the glorious past of Burma; after 1948 he drifted toward Marxism and, in 1954, he received the International Stalin Peace Prize.

Sean O'Casey (b. 1880). Irish playwright; his works present a chaotic and tragic world in which characters resort to comedy and irony in order to survive; loose and flexible in structure, his work proceeds from an ensemble of characters, rather than from a principal role; in the end, a sense of antiheroic comedy prevents total human catastrophe; he eventually left Ireland for England, settling finally in Torquay, Devonshire, where he dies from a heart attack.

Flannery O'Connor (b. 1925). American writer of fiction; her short stories, especially, depict a world of estrangement, suffering, and violence, of confusion and contradiction; incidents tend to be bizarre and melodramatic, while characters are lame, blind, and generally handicapped; her unflattering and unpleasant picture of human nature exposes the essential truth about humanity: as spiritual cripples, they drift about in a godless and secular world of their own manufacture; her complete stories, published in 1971, receive the National Book Award.

Badr Shakir as-Sayyab (b. 1929). Iraqi poet; he became one of the first exponents of modern poetry and free verse in Iraq; his style ranged from romanticism to realism; his verse demonstrates the influence of such English poets as T. S. Eliot, Dame Edith Sitwell, Percy Bysshe Shelly, and John Keats.

Frans Eemil Sillanpaa (b. 1888). Finnish writer of fiction; the foremost Finnish writer of his time, he focused his creative attention upon the Finnish civil war and the collapse of traditional Finnish values; in 1939, he received the Nobel Prize for literature.

Dame Edith Sitwell (b. 1887). English poet and critic; known for her eccentric wit, she wrote critical commentaries, biographies, and verse influenced by the French symbolists.

PUBLICATIONS

Ahmed Ali, *Ocean of Night*—a novel in Urdu by the Pakistani writer of fiction; a nostalgic but realistic picture of Muslim life in old Delhi and Lucknow.

Louis Auchincloss, *The Rector of Justin*—a novel by the American writer of fiction and historical narrative; a sharply defined moral portrait of the headmaster of a prestigious preparatory school.

Donald Barthelme, *Come Back, Dr. Caligari*—a collection of short stories by the American writer of fiction; reflects the writer's outrageous imagination, genius for absurd juxtaposition, and perception of the madness of life in contemporary America.

Saul Bellow, *Herzog*—a novel by the American writer of fiction; the title character, Moses Herzog, directly confronts his own personal crisis by compulsively writing erudite and readable letters to both the living and the dead.

John Berryman, *77 Dream Songs*—a series of poems by the American writer of verse; the pieces are controlled and unified by a persona (variously Henry, Pussy-Cat, Mr. Bones), who evokes his daily inner life; he struggles through the routine of teaching, drying out from alcoholism, and writing ambitious books of verse; he simply cannot transcend his "middleness": middle-aged, middle-class, and possessing only average (middle) talent; the work receives the Pulitzer Prize for poetry.

R. P. Blackmur, *Eleven Essays in the European Novel*—a collection of criticism by the American poet and essayist; in broad terms, the writer traces the decline of humanism; literary criticism, he maintains, can support the special status of literature and identify its relationship to other academic disciplines.

William S. Burroughs, *Nova Express*—a novel by the American writer of fiction; the work consists of a series of whistle stops along a train route that represent life speeding toward explosive destruction; the writer ridicules everything that he views as false, primitive, and vicious in current American life.

Jan Rynveld Carew, *Moscow Not My Mecca*—a novel by the Guyanan writer of fiction, playwright, and poet; concerns the impact of a new white society upon a colored observer; the writer refers, prophetically, to the future alignment of the "colored" races against the white superpowers of the West.

John Cheever, *The Wapshot Scandal*—a novel by the American writer of fiction; continues the saga of the Wapshot family (from *The Wapshot Chronicle*, 1957); the work ranges in time from the early twentieth century to the 1960s; in terms of geography, the family members move from a small New England village to New York City, then on to Paris and Italy.

Ralph Ellison, *Shadow and Act*—a collection of essays by the American writer of fiction and critic; autobiographical pieces relating directly to the writer's spiritual and intellectual experiences.

Hans Magnus Enzensberger, *Politik und Verbrechen* (Politics and Crime)—a collection of essays by the German poet, essayist, playwright, and translator; concerns such topics as treason, capitalism, communism, and the interaction of various revolutionary movements in Russia during the nineteenth and early twentieth centuries.

Vasily Grossman, *Vse Techet* (Forever Flowering)—a novel by the Russian writer of fiction, playwright, and poet; the first of the writer's suppressed works to be published outside of Russia; concerns a man who has been freed after spending thirty years in a Siberian work camp for delivering a speech in opposition to official Soviet doctrine; the man travels throughout Russia, meeting former friends and relatives who express guilt and embarrassment over the disparity between their comfortable lifestyles and the suffering that the man endured while in prison.

Ernest Hemingway, *A Moveable Feast*—a memoir by the American writer of fiction, published three years after the writer's death; concerns the writer's life in Paris during the 1920s.

LeRoi Jones (Amiri Baraka), *The Toilet*—a one-act play by the American poet and dramatist; focuses upon a boy who, with reluctance, joins other blacks in beating a white friend.

Silva Kaputikian, *K'Aravanner der K'Aylum En* (Caravans Are Still Marching)—a poem by the Armenian writer of verse; provides an impassioned picture of the lives of Armenian minorities in the Near East.

Doris Lessing, *African Stories*—a collection by the Persian-born and Rhodesian-raised English writer; inspired by the writer's youth in Rhodesia.

Robert Lowell, *For the Union Dead*—a collection of verse by the American poet; contains thirty-five poems that demonstrate the demise of New England life as it has traditionally been known; for example, Boston Common must be plowed under as an example of contemporary American materialism; nuclear war and social upheaval constitute other principal themes.

James Phillip McAuley, *Captain Quiros*—a book-length poem by the Australian writer of verse and essayist, a narrative intended for oral presentation; a Portuguese explorer searches for the "Great South Land" in hopes of discovering a new Jerusalem; physical and spiritual journeys are portrayed through symbolism and metaphor, while characters with good intentions suffer because of inherent human weakness.

Arthur Miller, *After the Fall*—a drama by the American playwright; subjective, autobiographical piece focusing upon a lawyer who, as a child, survived family rivalries and the loss of prosperity; he then suffers because of his involvement in left-wing politics; marriage, divorce, infidelity, and suicide parallel the playwright's own personal experiences.

Iris Murdoch, *The Italian Girl*—a novel by the Irish-born English writer of fiction; a servant girl achieves power over an unhappy family.

Lewis Nkosi, *The Rhythm of Violence*—a play by the South African (Natal) dramatist, critic, and writer of fiction; concerns a groups of young Boer, English, and African students who, in the early 1960s, attempt to ignore the racial prejudice around them and the oppressive atmosphere created by the apartheid policies of their government; plans to bomb public buildings, love, destruction, death, betrayal, and arrest follow.

Hubert Ogunde, *Yoruba Ronu* (Yorubus, You Must Think)—a political play by the Nigerian (Yoruba-land) dramatist; attacks the political abuses of the period prior to the outbreak of violence throughout Nigeria; those events led to the Ibo secession and the outbreak of the Biafran War, and the playwright features the contentious and divided leadership.

Gabriel Imomotimi Gbaingbain Okara, *The Voice*—a novel by the West Nigerian poet and writer of fiction; the work reflects the writer's native Ijaw district; the principal character, intensely interested in language, evaluates people by determining how language relates the meaning of their inner lives.

Eugene O'Neill, *More Stately Mansions*—a drama by the American playwright, produced and published well after his death; an indictment of the growth of materialism in the modern world; the poetic spirit within the soul of the principal character dies, forcing him to become a relentless materialist, but not before his mental deterioration.

Sumitranandan Pant, *Lokayatan* (The House of People)—an epic poem by the Indian (Hindi) writer of verse; focuses upon contemporary problems from a classical-humanistic point of view; the poem receives the Soviet Land Nehru Award.

Konstantin Paustovsky, *Povest' o Zhizni* (The Story of a Life)—a six-volume autobiography by the Russian writer of fiction and nonfiction; the work ranges over fifty years, presenting an intimate account of the writer's personal life set against the social and political atmosphere of early twentieth-century Russia; the entire work reflects the writer's ability to produce forceful and dramatic prose.

Anthony Powell, *The Valley of Bones*—a novel by the English writer of fiction; the central character's wartime service begins in backwater ports in Ireland and Wales; his adventures and experiences go forward amidst a collection of military "oddballs."

Richard Rive, *Emergency*—a novel (his first and only) by the South African writer of fiction and poet; begins with the events leading up to the Sharpeville massacres; the writer then focuses upon the following three days in the life of his protagonist, which end in a proclamation of a state of emergency throughout South Africa; the work culminates in a riot and the burning of an armed personnel carrier; a crowd no longer able to contain its fury frees the wounded protagonist from the police.

Theodore Roethke, *The Far Field*—a posthumous collection of verse by the American poet; a retrospect of the writer's lifelong preoccupations; in these pieces, he acknowledges his debt to those poets who have confronted the mystery of personal extinction: T. S. Eliot, William Butler Yeats, Walt Whitman.

Hubert Selby, Jr., *Last Exit to Brooklyn*—a collection of stories (or episodes) by the American writer of fiction; these interrelated and harshly realistic pieces focus upon life in Brooklyn, New York, especially as they hone in upon the bottom of the heap; its graphic language and imagery caused a profound shock throughout the United States and abroad.

Haldun Taner, *Kesanli Ali Destan* (Destan about Ali of Kesan)—a play by the Turkish dramatist and writer of fiction; the first epic drama to appear on the Turkish stage.

Gore Vidal, *Julian*—a novel by the American writer of fiction; takes the form of a fictional journal of a witty and promiscuous Roman emperor of the fourth century.

Robert Penn Warren, *Flood*—a novel by the American poet, critic, and writer of fiction; the principal character works on a movie script about a town that will soon be abandoned and flooded by a man-made lake; the subject dramatizes the alienation and isolation of the modern South.

Peter Ulrich Weiss, *Die Verfolgung und Ermordung Jean Paul Marats, Dargestellt Durch die Schauspielgruppe des Hospizes zu Charenton unter Anleitung des Hernn de Sade* (The Persecution and Assassination of Jean-Paul Marat, as Performed by the Inmates of the Asylum of Charenton, under the Direction of the Marquis de Sade)—a play by the German-born Swedish dramatist, writer of fiction, essayist, and translator; a documentary drama that emphasizes the writer's pessimistic view of human existence since the end of World War II; the characters of the title represent the duality of humanity: the ideological pre-Marxist intellectual who commits violent acts for the benefit of society (Marat) and the self-indulgent and mindless symbol of anarchy (de Sade).

EVENTS

Walter Jackson Bate, American academician, literary scholar, historian, and biographer, receives the Pulitzer Prize for biography/autobiography for his life of John Keats (1963).

Sumner Chilton Powell, American historical scholar, receives the Pulitzer Prize for United States history for his *Puritan Village: The Formation of a New England Town* (1963).

Jean-Paul Sartre, French philosopher, essayist, playwright, and writer of fiction, declines to accept the Nobel Prize for literature.

The Shakespeare Quatercentenary Exhibition opens at Stratford-upon-Avon, England, and at Edinburgh, Scotland.

Louis Aston Marantz Simpson, Jamaican-born, American writer of verse and critic, receives the Pulitzer Prize for poetry for his collection *At the End of the Open Road* (1963).

1965

BIRTHS

Toni Pascual. Spanish (Catalan) writer of fiction; he will create a mystical atmosphere in his novels and will treat human anxieties and passions; his intense and poetic vision of the world will blend heterogeneous elements into a harmonious whole.

DEATHS

Jacques Audiberti (b. 1899). French playwright, poet, writer of fiction, and essayist; his work became recognized for its flamboyant language and strong sense of the melodramatic and the absurd; his novels are complicated and obscure, while his verse is formal and extravagant; his plays combine absurdist farce with surrealist melodrama.

R. P. Blackmur (b. 1904). American poet and critic; an advocate of the "new school of criticism," he emphasized close reading and explication, as well as the detailed analysis of language and structure.

Martin Buber (b. 1878). Austrian Jewish philosopher; he taught Jewish philosophy and religion in Germany; he left Germany in 1938 and settled in Jerusalem; he came under the influence of the mysticism of the Hasidim and the Christian existentialism of Soren Kierkegaard; he set forth the notion of direct dialogue between God and the individual, which influenced significantly both Christian and Jewish theology.

Reuben Tolakele Caluza (b. 1900). South African (Zulu) poet and writer of songs; his verse appealed directly to the increasingly detribalized Zulus working in the large mines of the Rand and performing factory and domestic work in the large cities; he also appealed to African cultural hybrids experiencing trials of social adjustment.

Alejandro Casona (b. 1903). Spanish playwright, poet, and essayist; he depicted the conflict between illusion and reality and achieved international recognition for injecting into his work such elements as folklore, supernaturalism, and imaginary settings; he strived to create plays rich in fantasy, symbolism, and moral meaning.

A. Emile Disengomoko (b. 1915). Zaire (Kikongo) novelist, poet, and essayist; in addition to his fiction and ethical prose tracts, he wrote fifteen hymns; most of his work focuses upon the need to choose between Christian values and the traditions of tribal Africa.

T. S. Eliot (b. 1888). American-born poet, playwright, and critic; one of the most influential literary figures of the twentieth century; he became an English citizen in 1927, the same year that he embraced Anglo-Catholicism; generally, his verse expressed his own anguish at the sterility of modern life; he broke with the poetic tradition of the nineteenth century and drew his creative strength from the metaphysical poets of the seventeenth century, Dante, Jacobean drama, and the French symbolists; in his work for the stage, he attempted to revitalize the verse drama; he received the Nobel Prize for literature in 1948.

Joseb Grishashvili (originally Joseb Mamulaishvili; b. 1889). Georgian (SSR) poet and literary historian; his verse tends to be meditative and reflects his knowledge of the literary traditions of his native city of Tbilisi; thus, he echoes the work of obscure folk poets; he also wrote excellent scholarly essays on poetry and art.

Lorraine Hansberry (b. 1930). American playwright; her work focuses upon the problems of black families in twentieth-century America as they attempt, in vain, to pursue the great American dream.

Mahti Husain (b. 1909). Azerbaijan writer of fiction, playwright, and literary historian; he began his career with novels about the civil war in Azerbaijan, village life, and the heroes of World War II; he then drifted toward subjects about the oil fields and the history of his country.

Bashir al-Ibrahimi (b. 1889). Algerian philosopher and essayist; his prose displays a brilliant style and poetic improvisation, at the same time revealing him to be a master of subtle humor and irony; he also became one of the significant scholars in the general renaissance of Arabic culture in Algeria.

Shirley Hardie Jackson (b. 1919). American writer of fiction; she relied upon the elements of supernatural terror in creating metaphors for the natural terror within the world; she also wrote stories about everyday reality; further, she created chronicles that depict with humor, affection, and insight the raising of her own perfectly "normal" family.

Randall Jarrell (b. 1914). American poet; his verse displays a sensitive and tragic view of the world; he also wrote books for children, fiction, and critical essays; through prose and verse, he tried to guide his contemporaries toward a definition of twentieth-century art; essentially, he combined mature poetic sophistication with sincere yearnings for the expressions of childhood.

Mohammad Mandur (b. 1907). Egyptian essayist and literary critic; as a critic, he began by stressing the soundness of a method based upon personal impressions; later, he emphasized the need for rational analysis as the basis for objective conclusions; he also explored the important social functions of literature; literary criticism, he maintained, should exist as an independent academic discipline.

William Somerset Maugham (b. 1874). English writer of fiction; he gained a literary reputation as a skilled storyteller, his work punctuated with frequent irony and cynicism; he has been described as the most serious popular prose writer of the twentieth century, combining intelligence with craft and generally avoiding dull formulas.

Edgar Mitteholzer (b. 1909). Guyanan writer of fiction, playwright, and poet; a compulsive and prolific writer, he developed themes relative to the sins of the parents falling upon the children, as well as situations involving odd sexual relationships; his theories of inheritance and of the innate superiority of certain races were also expressed in his work; his fictional themes and nightmares are clearly connected to Guyana and its history; he dies in England.

Lekhnath Pandyal (b. 1885). Nepali poet and writer of fiction; his early verse praises the court at Katmandu, while his later fiction criticizes the hypocrisy in both social and sexual relationships.

Albert Schweitzer (b. 1875). German (Alsatian) theologian, musician, medical missionary, and miscellaneous prose writer; he wrote a biography of Johann Sebastian Bach, coedited his own musical compositions, and explicated his notion of ethical philosophy; in his theological works, he rejected the historical infallibility of Christ, while following him spiritually; in 1952, he received the Nobel Peace Prize.

Giorgi Shalberashvili (b. 1910). Georgian (SSR) writer of fiction, poet, and playwright; his efforts tend to reflect the romantic Georgian tradition; he also attempted to discover, in Georgian history, the answer to the eternal question of the purpose of human life.

Paul Johannes Tillich (b. 1886). German-born American theologian and philosopher; he taught theology in Germany until his opposition to the Nazi regime caused him to be dismissed from that country; he then came to the United States, where he developed in 1933 the concept of the "Protestant Principle," aimed at correlating questions about the human condition and drawing answers from the symbolism of Christian revelation.

PUBLICATIONS

Salah Abdassabur, *The Tragedy of Al-Hallaj*— a play by the Egyptian poet, essayist, and dramatist; provides an interpretation of the Islamic mystic of the title, who was crucified.

Edward Albee, *Tiny Alice*—a play by the American dramatist; a lay brother, summoned to a mysterious house, marries a wealthy but equally mysterious lady he meets there; she and her strange followers desert him; the brother resembles Christ, Job, and Faust, and his martyrdom appears as a cruel cosmic joke, emphasizing the playwright's hostility toward religion and the Church.

Michael Anthony, *The Year in San Fernando*— a novel by the Trinidadian writer of fiction; the work recalls a number of the writer's own early experiences when he worked, at age twelve, for a rural family.

Guillermo Cabrera Infante, *Tres Tristes Tigres* (Three Trapped Tigers)—a novel by the Cuban-born writer of fiction, essayist, and translator; a humorous narrative developed through a series of monologues; the piece chronicles nightlife in Havana on the eve of Batista's overthrow; it contains an abundance of puns, parodies, and wordplay; written in the vernacular of the street and narrated by several characters, the novel depicts a society heading toward physical and spiritual confusion; language becomes grotesque, reshaped by people struggling for new means of communication; the work was eventually banned in Cuba.

Alec Derwent Hope, *The Cave and the Spring: Essays on Poetry*—a collection of prose by the Australian poet and critic; he equates, in the principal theoretical essay, "The Discursive Mode," the demise of the epic, ode, verse satire, and epistle with the decline of the nobility of humanity; he also defends the capacity of poetry to consider, with flexibility and effectiveness, exposition, argument, satire, and narrative.

Ti Janakiraman, *Amma Vantal* (Mother Came)—a novel by the Indian (Tamil) playwright and writer of fiction and travel literature; the work concerns a sinful mother, and the narrative tends to be extremely honest and realistic.

Randall Jarrell, *The Lost World: New Poems*—a collection by the American writer of verse; the pieces are confessional in tone and substance; throughout, the speaker appears filled with a sense of guilt and helplessness, extending forgiveness in numerous directions; a number of the poems contain a female persona, a woman often unfaithful to her lover and cruel (to the point of murder) to people and animals.

Doris Lessing, *Landlocked*—a novel by the Persian-born Rhodesian-raised English writer of fiction; the fourth volume in the quintet *The Children of Violence;* the central figure, Martha Quest, seeks her identity through the competing social and political forces of four decades; the novel is set in England, where Martha's political activism becomes tempered.

Norman Mailer, *An American Dream*—a novel by the American writer of fiction and miscellaneous nonfiction; the central figure, a middle-aged man named Rojack, murders his wife, an heiress, in an act of madness; there exists a strong relationship between the corruption within the man's life and marriage and the decay of society in general.

James A. Michener, *The Source*—a novel by the American writer of popular fiction and nonfiction; concerns the nation of Israel, both past and present; the country is revealed to the reader through the progressive discoveries of a modern archaeological expedition.

Arthur Miller, *Incident at Vichy*—a one-act play by the American dramatist; occurs during World War II in unoccupied France; a number of Jews (and persons suspected of being Jewish) have been readied for transport to a concentration camp; an Austrian nobleman gives up his pass to freedom to save a Jewish psychoanalyst because he believes his need for survival is greater than his own.

Samuel Eliot Morison, *The Oxford History of the American People*—a narrative by the distinguished American historian; he describes it as "a legacy to my countrymen after studying, teaching, and writing the history of the United States for over half a century"; the work was not conceived as a textbook and does not contain the usual scholarly apparatus.

John Osborne, *A Patriot for Me*—a dramatic work by the English playwright; set in Vienna, the play focuses upon the rise and fall of an Austro-Hungarian army officer, a homosexual named Redl; he comes to ruin through blackmail.

Harold Pinter, *The Homecoming*—the first full-length play by the English dramatist; illustrates the ferocity of his characters' sense of territory, as though they are animals jealously guarding their dens; the principal character returns home after having achieved success in America; he must confront his family, whose members prove repugnant to him.

Kathleen Raine, *The Hollow Hill, and Other Poems, 1960-1964*—a collection of verse by the English poet and critic; in general, the pieces tend to be musical in tone and serious in substance; the poet is concerned more with the mysteries of life than with its realities.

La. Sa. Ramamirtam, *Putra* (Son)—a novel by the Indian (Tamil) writer of fiction; written in a haunting prose rhythm, with often difficult syntax; the writer attempts to probe into the inner lives of his principal characters, combining a psychological approach to character analysis with Hindu orthodoxy and traditional views.

May Sarton, *Mrs. Stevens Hears the Mermaids Singing*—a novel by the Belgian-born American poet and writer of fiction; reflects the writer's beliefs concerning the inspiration and commitment necessary for artistic creation; the poet of the title prepares for and engages in an interview about her career; the principal question focuses upon whether a woman can function as a successful artist while maintaining a family; in addition, such issues as what compels a writer to create and the relationship between personal emotion and art are treated.

Ahmad Shahnon, *Rentong* (Burnt to a Cinder)—a novel by the Malay writer of fiction; explores social and personal relationships within a Kedah rice farming village; the central dramatic theme focuses upon the conflict between two young men, representing the traditional and the modern; the village headman intervenes and restores the necessary harmony; the writer was praised for his use of local dialect to depict peasant society.

Wole Soyinka, *The Interpreters*—a novel by the Nigerian playwright, poet, writer of fiction, and critic; an intricate and complex narrative, much in the manner of James Joyce or William Faulkner; the structure of the piece appears chaotic, while characters exist as complicated symbols.

Muriel Spark, *The Mandelbaum Gate*—a novel by the Scottish writer of fiction, playwright, poet, and essayist; concerns a partly Jewish woman, a Catholic convert, who travels to Israel and Jordan on a religious pilgrimage; the work receives the James Tait Black Memorial Prize.

Lionel Trilling, *Beyond Culture*—a collection of essays by the American critic and academician; contains one of his most significant contributions, "On the Teaching of Modern Literature," in which he applies liberal definitions and criteria to the term "modern"; one must, essentially, consider the writer's "social and personal will."

Gabre-Medhin Tsegaye, *Oda Oak Oracle*—a novel in English by the Ethiopian playwright, poet, and writer of fiction; demonstrates the tensions arising from protagonist's tribal fears and his love for his newly Christianized friend; in the midst of this, an oracle proclaims that the friend's first born must be sacrificed; superstition, fear, death, and murder complicate the spiritual forces that vie for control of people's lives.

Stephen Vizinczey, *In Praise of Older Women: The Amorous Recollections of Andras Vajada*—the first novel by the Hungarian-born Canadian writer of fiction, essayist, and playwright; written in English and published by his own company (after rejecting an offer from a major publisher); a picaresque narrative focusing upon the sexual exploits of a young Hungarian, whose life parallels that of the writer; the title character matures during a period of political turmoil and (as did the writer) emigrates to Canada, where he pursues the academic life.

Kurt Vonnegut, Jr., *God Bless You, Mr. Rosewater*—a novel by the American writer of fiction; an hilariously comic piece in which the writer launches an attack against inherited wealth, as well as against the general state of foolishness within society; the title character, the head of his own foundation, rushes about performing absurdly "good" deeds for useless

people; who is mad (Rosewater or the people) remains the principal issue.

EVENTS

John Berryman, American poet, receives the Pulitzer Prize for poetry for *77 Dream Songs* (1964).

Frank Daniel Gilroy, American playwright, receives the Pulitzer Prize for drama for *The Subject Was Roses* (1964).

Shirley Ann Grau, American writer of fiction, receives the Pulitzer Prize for fiction for her novel *The Keepers of the House* (1964).

The National Book Committee establishes the National Medal for Literature, honoring the career of a distinguished contributor to American letters; Thornton Niven Wilder, writer of fiction, playwright, and essayist, receives the first medal.

Salmagundi, a quarterly magazine of literature, begins publication; in 1969, it will become associated with Skidmore College, Saratoga Springs, New York.

Mikhail Aleksandrovich Sholokhov, Russian writer of fiction, receives the Nobel Prize for literature.

1966

DEATHS

Sir Tafawa Balewa Abubakar (b. 1912). Nigerian writer of fiction; his fiction reflects his vision for the destiny of his nation; he fashioned a number of short pieces from Hausa folk tales and institutions of the nineteenth-century (court, slavery, the Muslim system of education); he dies at the hands of an assassin in January, during a military coup.

Anna Akhmatova (pseudonym of Anna Andreyevna Gorenko; b. 1889). Russian poet; she followed the Acmeist school of versifiers that arose in 1912 in reaction to the symbolist poets, emphasizing concreteness of imagery and clarity of expression; she wrote brief, highly emotional lyrics, governed by simplicity and rhythm.

Hans Christian Branner (b. 1903). Danish writer of fiction and playwright; his themes tended to be complex and psychological, focusing upon the problems of fear and solitude; most importantly, he specialized in revealing the child's psyche, with its irrational terrors and its inability to comprehend the adult world.

Andre Breton (b. 1896). French poet and critic; one of the founders of the Surrealist school of writing, he also experimented in "automatic" composition; in 1924, he wrote the initial Surrealist manifesto, followed by two other such declarations in 1930 and 1943; he also worked in the area of surrealist visual art.

Georges Duhamel (b. 1884). French poet, playwright, and writer of fiction; his fiction, in particular, revealed him to be a compassionate writer committed to humanity; a thorough-going idealist, he remained with his family in France during the World War II Nazi occupation, where they experienced suffering; however, his fictional sketches during that period tend not to be overly bitter.

Ghafur Ghulom (b. 1903). Uzbek writer of fiction, poet, and critic; he began his career by publishing humorous verse and satiric fiction in periodicals; he came under the influence of Vladimir Mayakovskiy, and adapted works by Aleksandr Pushkin, Mikhail Lermontov, William Shakespeare, and Pablo Neruda; in turn, Russian writers translated a number of his volumes.

Giorgi Leonidze (b. 1899). Georgian (SSR) poet; his verse tended to be lively and temperamental, and he produced both traditional love lyrics and intricate, reflective pieces; his long poems on Georgian history reveal his talents for the epic, particularly for vivid imagery and symbolic inventions.

Sa'id Nafisi (b. 1896). Iranian writer of fiction and critic; he wrote short stories about life in Iran at the outset of its modernization; he then devoted his attention to historical and patriotic themes; in his novels, he was more concerned with social and political conditions in Iran than with literary considerations.

Flann O'Brien (pseudonym of Brian O'Nuallain; b. 1911). Irish writer of fiction, translator, and playwright; his fiction, especially, gained depth and substance from his knowledge of Irish culture, history, and language; he also took advantage of such light elements as comedy, parody, satire, exaggeration, and black humor; however, he also addressed serious concerns: the relation between life and art and between reality and fiction, the artifi-

ciality of literary conventions, death and the afterlife, the folly of pedantic knowledge.

Delmore Schwartz (b. 1913). American poet, critic, and writer of fiction; his verse accurately portrayed political and historical realities, particularly as he expressed his family's Jewish experiences; for him, human beings appear imprisoned in and by time, bearing the guilt and anxieties of past generations; throughout, however, his language remains vibrant and robust; weakened by alcohol and mental instability, he dies alone in a run-down hotel in New York City.

Lao She (b. 1899). Chinese (Manchu) writer of fiction; his writings reflect the influence of Charles Dickens, whose works he studied while in England during the 1920s; in his short fiction, he revealed himself a satirist, a relentless social critic with bold and incisive strokes of humor; he concerned himself with the daily lives of common persons: policemen, prostitutes, railway stewards; he visited the United States in the late 1940s; he dies at the hands of the Red Guards at the outset of the Cultural Revolution.

Elio Vittorini (b. 1908). Italian writer of fiction; in his novels, he undertook a serious assessment of the fascist experience; he became the leading advocate of social realism in post-World War II Italy; he also produced a significant body of literary criticism.

Arthur David Waley (b. 1899). English scholar and translator; he contributed significantly to the Western world's knowledge of Chinese and Japanese literature with his English translations of such writers as Wu Ch'eng-en and Tao Te Ching; for the serious students of Chinese and Japanese literatures, he provided accurate historical and linguistic contexts in which to understand and appreciate the original texts.

Evelyn Arthur St. John Waugh (b. 1903). English writer of fiction; recognized as the foremost social satirist of his generation; a conservative moralist, he also turned his attention to the spiritual regeneration of English Roman Catholics, both at home during the late 1930s and in the activities of World War II; he proved adept at fictionalizing his own experiences and criticizing his own shortcomings.

PUBLICATIONS

Peter Abrahams, *This Island Now*—a novel by the South African writer of fiction; focuses upon social, political, and racial problems in Africa during the early period of independence; considers the struggles between those who once led the fight for nationalism and those who find themselves in political control.

Chinua Achebe, *Man of the People*—a novel by the Nigerian (Ibo) writer of fiction, poet, and essayist; in addition to conflicts between villagers and inhabitants of the Nigerian capital, the work considers what independent Nigeria has become as a result of greedy and corrupt politicians; essentially, however, the writer indicts all of the people, their cynicism and their apathy.

Edward Albee, *A Delicate Balance*—a play by the American dramatist; concerns a family disrupted by an unexpected visit of two close personal friends; they have been running from a sudden, strange, and indescribable fear ("the terror"); the husband and wife (the "visited") continue to suffer from guilt over the death of their small son and the problems of their frequently divorced daughter; thus, they resent their guests; the wife's sister, who tries to obliterate her problems with drink, also plays an important part; the work receives the Pulitzer Prize for drama in 1967.

Isaac Asimov, *Fantastic Voyage*—a novel by the American writer of science fiction; five people, reduced to microscopic size, journey through the body of a dying man; they attempt to destroy a blood clot and save the man's life.

John Barth, *Giles Goatboy*—a novel by the American writer of fiction; the work supposedly concerns education, but the writer's "university" exists as the entire universe: there, the title character functions as a false messiah and as a student with horns; his purpose appears to be the proclamation of a truly godless world.

Mikhail Bulgakov, *Master i Margarita* (The Master and Margarita)—a novel by the Russian writer of fiction; a fantasy on the devil in modern Moscow; the piece was suppressed because of its obvious anticommunist sentiments; the writer combines fable, satanic fantasy, political satire, and even slapstick comedy to create an ironic parable on power and its corruption, on good and evil, on human frailty and the strength of love.

Truman Capote, *In Cold Blood*—a "nonfiction novel" by the American novelist, playwright, and writer of miscellaneous prose; a detached, yet nonetheless penetrating, account of an actual murder of an entire family; the writer focuses upon the personalities of the two young men who committed the savage crime and were executed for it.

Mbella Sonne Dipoko, *A Few Nights and Days*—the first novel by the Cameroon writer of fiction and poet; a frank treatment of a love affair between an African student and a bourgeois girl; the work is set in Paris; the girl's father forces her to break off the engagement, which causes her to take her own life; in the interim, the young African has impregnated a Swedish girl; the African returns to his native land, chastened and alarmed by his encounters with love and death in Paris.

J. P. Donleavy, *The Saddest Summer of Samuel S*—a novel by the American-born Irish writer of fiction and playwright; the piece is set in Vienna, where the title character, after two years of libertine roaming about Europe, decides to undergo psychoanalysis; he wishes to adjust to the conventions of society, including a wife and children; however, he can only become involved with women who wish nothing to do with marriage; he eventually comes to understand his own despair, a state that can provide him with neither faith nor the desire to change.

Gunter Grass, *Die Plebeier Proben den Aufstand* (The Plebeians Rehearse the Uprising)—a play by the German novelist and dramatist; a sardonic portrait of Bertolt Brecht working with his theater troupe in East Germany.

Graham Greene, *The Comedians*—a novel by the English writer of fiction; an extremely tense story of a group of foreigners caught up in the violence of Haiti during the regime of Francois ("Papa Doc") Duvalier.

Samuel Asare Konadu, *Come Back, Dora!*—a novel by the Ghanaian writer of fiction; focuses upon the intimate confessions of the principal character; concerns pity, duty, and the shattering impact caused by those custodians of African culture who would stop at nothing to see that he has been properly guided through the correct rituals of life.

Iris Murdoch, *The Time of the Angels*—a novel by the Irish-born English writer of fiction; set in the city, the piece concerns a darkened vicarage (both physically and spiritually) and the satanic priest who lords over the place; the atmosphere exists as a wasteland dominated and beset by evil.

Vladimir Nabokov, *Despair*—a novel by the Russian-born writer of fiction, poet, essayist, and playwright; concerns the protagonist as artist, and that character both narrates and controls the flow of the piece.

Flora Nwapa, *Efuru*—a novel by the East Nigerian writer of fiction; provides interesting insight into the woman's world in Africa; a distinguished African woman undergoes considerable trials as she loses two husbands and a child; she cannot fit into the simple life of the villager, nor can she understand how she can lose so much and still retain such a considerable degree of respect.

John Osborne, *A Bond Honoured*—a play by the English dramatist, an adaptation of Lope de Vega's *La Fianza Satisfecha;* the work commissioned by the National Theatre.

J. P. Okot p'Bitek, *Song of Lawino. A Lament*—a "poetic novel" by the Ugandan poet and essayist; the writer, himself, translated the work into English after having first written it in his native Lwo; studies the effects of Westernization upon an African family.

Sylvia Plath, *Ariel*—a verse collection by the American poet and writer of fiction; one of the principal poems, "The Edge," appears to foreshadow the writer's own death ("The woman is perfected. Her dead / Body wears the smile of accomplishment"); her second posthumous volume of verse, edited by her poet-husband, Ted Hughes.

Anthony Powell, *The Soldier's Art*—a novel by the English writer of fiction, a part of the sequence entitled *A Dance to the Music of Time;* Nick Jenkins, the narrator and principal character, finds himself in London, following tours of duty in Ireland and Wales; during the Blitz, he observes Major Widmerpool jockeying for position and status against Hogbourne-Jones.

Thomas Pynchon, *The Crying of Lot 49*—a novel by the American writer of fiction; a fable and a surreal comedy in which the writer satirizes the life-style of California.

Jean Rhys, *Wide Sargasso Sea*—a novel by the West Indian-born English writer of fiction and translator; set in the lush terrain of the West Indies, following the abolition of slavery; the writer "reinterprets" Charlotte Bronte's *Jane Eyre* (1847): in this version, an exotic, passionate, and complex woman becomes attracted to native culture that conflicts decidedly with her colonial upbringing and her husband's English background; the husband restricts his wife's natural yearnings, and thus contributes significantly to her demise; the work also focuses upon such larger issues as the effects of historical events upon individu-

als, the functions of myth and religion, and the connection between the physical and metaphysical worlds.

Stanlake J. T. Samkange, *On Trial for My Country*—a novel by the Zimbabwean writer of fiction; describes the dramatic confrontation of King Lobengula with his father, Mzilikazi, and the elders of the Metabele; they accuse the king, during a long "ghost-trial," of failing to stop the loss of their land to the English; parallel with this event, Cecil John Rhodes and his allies and agents stand trial in a parish church at Bishop's Sortford, England, where Cecil's father, the Rev. Francis William Rhodes, serves as prosecutor.

Isaac Bashevis Singer, *In My Father's Court*—a memoir by the Polish-born writer of fiction, playwright, and translator; relates the writer's earliest experiences and intellectual development, as set against the background of his father's rabbinical court.

Susan Sontag, *Against Interpretation*—a collection of prose by the American intellectual essayist and writer of fiction; includes selections from her early work concerning the arts and contemporary culture, among them "Notes from Camp" and "The Imagination of Disaster."

Tom Stoppard, *Rosencrantz and Gildenstern Are Dead*—a play by the Czech-born English dramatist; a combination of comedy and drama; the playwright places the two attendants from Shakespeare's *Hamlet* in the middle of their original situation as both bewildered witnesses to a significant event and predestined victims; the writer also relies, heavily and successfully, upon Shakespeare's linguistic and dramatic wit.

Martin Walser, *Das Einhorn* (The Unicorn)—a novel by the German writer of fiction, playwright, and critic; an amusing, yet highly psychological, piece that focuses upon the experiences of a man commissioned by a female publisher to write a novel about love; naturally, his "material" emerges from an affair with his publisher.

EVENTS

Shmuel Yosef Agnon (b. Samuel Josef Czaczkes), Polish-born Israeli writer of fiction, and Nelly Sachs, German poet and translator, share the Nobel Prize for literature.

Richard Ghormley Eberhart, American poet and playwright, receives the Pulitzer Prize for poetry for *Selected Poems, 1930-1965* (1965).

The International John Steinbeck Society established; intended to promote study of the writer's work.

Katherine Anne Porter, American writer of fiction, receives the Pulitzer Prize for fiction for her *Collected Stories* (1965).

The Western Literature Association, Colorado State University, begins publication of *Western American Literature,* a quarterly journal devoted to scholarly studies and book reviews of the literature of the western United States.

1967

DEATHS

Ilya Grigoryevich Ehrenburg (b. 1891). Russian writer of fiction and journalist; he lived in Western Europe between 1909 and 1917 and from 1921 to 1941; his fiction focuses on political subjects, ranging from the decay of French society immediately before and during World War II to the specifics of Stalinist repression in the Soviet Union.

Forugh Farrokhzad (b. 1934). Iranian poet; in her verse, she dared to reveal the innermost feelings of a woman's heart, considering subjects that had never before been treated in Persian poetry; her work is characterized by ardent passion, fear, melancholy, despair, and tormented longing; she dies, early this year, in an automobile accident.

James Langston Hughes (b. 1902). American poet, playwright, writer of fiction, and essayist; he became known for his versatility as a writer and for the sheer quantity of the work he produced; he also gained recognition fom his lyric verse, which captures the spirit of the black urban environment, as well as for his fictional sketches, in which he created the character of "Simple," the representative of that environment; he struggled to establish a sense of literary respectability for the black theater, being careful to preserve the dignity of the black character.

Jose Martinez Ruiz (b. 1873?). Spanish essayist and writer of fiction; he achieved recognition for his descriptive essays (*Espana,* 1909; *Castilla,* 1912) and several autobiographical novels; he also published drama and short fiction.

John Edward Masefield (b. 1878). English poet, playwright, writer of fiction, and critic; his verse concerning the sea gained the most popularity; his drama appeared in both verse and prose; he held the title Poet Laureate of England from 1930 until his death.

Andre Maurois (originally Emile Herzog; b. 1885). French biographer and writer of fiction and nonfiction; his biographies of Percy Bysshe Shelley, Lord Byron, Benjamin Disraeli, Francois Rene de Chateaubriand, and George Washington are of high literary quality; he also wrote a popular novel (1918) concerning British military life.

Carson Smith McCullers (b. 1917). American writer of fiction; her work explores the problems of spiritual isolation, relying heavily upon outcasts and misfits as principal characters; she tended to emphasize the loving and beautiful qualitities of these characters, rather than the horror that surrounds them.

Christopher Okigbo (b. 1932). Nigerian poet; his verse reflects the influence of Gerard Manley Hopkins, Herman Melville, Malcolm Cowley, Stephane Mallarme, Rabindranath Tagore, and Federico Garcia Lorca; thus, he combines local African themes and impressions with European (especially English) culture and learning; he dies in August near Nsukka (then the provisional capital of Biafra) from wounds received in the fighting during the Biafran war.

Dorothy Rothschild Parker (b. 1893). American writer of fiction and poet; known for her wit, which found expression in her light, ironic verse; her short fiction tended to be poignant and satirical, and it appeared in the leading popular literary magazines of the period; she became the most talked about woman of her time, and she helped to establish a new style in both life and art.

Elmer Rice (originally Elmer Leopold Reizenstein; b. 1892). American playwright; the shabby apartment houses and streets of New York City, so much a part of his youth, became essential elements of his plays; he became one of the first American playwrights to experiment with dramatic form.

Carl August Sandburg (b. 1878). American poet and historical biographer; his experiences as a day laborer, soldier, socialist political worker, and journalist provided him with the knowledge of American life that informs his verse; he drew his inspiration from the past and present of America, writing vigorous, impressionistic, and free verse that celebrated ordinary people and ordinary objects; he collected folk ballads and songs and wrote a six-volume biography of Abraham Lincoln; he received Pulitzer prizes in 1940 and 1951.

Siegfried Lauvain Sassoon (b. 1886). English poet, novelist, and biographer; his best verse reflects his experiences as an army officer during World War I; he wrote of the brutality and waste of war in grim and forceful language.

Alice B. Toklas (b. 1877). American writer of miscellaneous prose; she gained recognition as the companion to Gertrude Stein, especially during their residence in Paris following World War I; for whatever reasons, her cookbook (1954), with its recipes and reminiscences of the literary life, established her niche in the history of American letters.

Jean Toomer (b. 1894). American writer of fiction; she wrote of black life in Georgia during the twentieth century; in so doing, she expressed the ethos of the black within the Southern environment; her insights into particular problems of her race anticipated questions raised by historians and sociologists.

Vernon Phillips Watkins (b. 1906). English poet, born of Welsh parents; he wrote lyrical and controlled verse that can be associated with symbolism; he developed a close relationship with Dylan Thomas, and thus he became interested in Welsh folklore and mythology.

Stephen Zorian (b. 1890). Armenian writer of fiction and translator; his popular historical novels began a tradition in Soviet Armenian literature; prior to the establishment of Soviet rule, his short fiction concentrated upon provincial life; he also wrote one of the first autobiographical novels in all of Soviet Armenian literature (1935-1939).

PUBLICATIONS

Fleur Adcock, *Tigers*—a volume of verse by the New Zealand-born English poet; the first volume of her work to attract critical attention; describes the familiar objects, scenes, and relationships of domestic life.

Michael Anthony, *Green Days by the River*—a novel by the Trinidadian writer of fiction; an authentic and imaginative piece written in precise and deceptively simple prose; under the writer's skillful control, the narrative moves through apparently trivial incidents toward a subtle climax.

Francis Bebey, *Le Fils d'Agatha Moudio* (Agatha Moudio's Sons)—a novel by the Cameroon writer of fiction; a highly amusing work that focuses upon the complications that arise when a man falls in love with "the wrong woman"; the piece is set in a society that does not move fast enough to allow a man to marry his "true love" without involving the entire village and the man's loving mother; the work was translated into Italian, Dutch, and German; it receives the Grand Prix Litteraire de l'Afrique Noire.

L. Edward Braithwaite, *Rights of Passage*—a collection of verse by the Barbados poet and critic; the pieces in the collection possess a vitality that tends to be associated more with the American poetical tradition than with the English; combines traditional with experimental verse forms.

Cameron Duodo, *The Gab Boys*— a novel by the Ghanaian writer of fiction and poet; the work reflects the writer's own frustrations growing up in an African state; one may be free from England, but the values of England remain; one may be free from tyranny, but there still exist the police, spies, and informers of President Kwame Nkrumah.

Gabriel Garcia Marquez, *Cien Anos de Soledad* (One Hundred Years of Solitude)—a novel by the Colombian writer of fiction and essayist; chronicles the history of Macondo, from its harmonious beginnings under Jose Arcadio Buenida through its chaotic decline under six generations of his descendants; Macondo becomes a microcosm of Colombia, of South America, and of the entire world; thus, the work has gained recognition for its epic scope.

William Golding, *The Pyramid*—a novel by the English writer of fiction and poet; set in a provincial town in 1930, it concerns the Operatic Society's production of *The King of Hearts.*

Thom Gunn, *Touch*—a volume of verse by the English poet; contains the writer's most ambitious poem, "Mistanthropos"; employs the concept of the first man/last man on earth to explore the relationship between mind with body, as well as between the individual and his or her society and environment.

Rolf Hochhuth, *Soldaten* (Soldiers)—a play by the German dramatist; lengthy piece, chaotic in structure and dialogue; nonetheless, the work is a clear condemnation of the inhumanity of war; the thesis focuses on the writer's belief that history tragically expresses itself in one or two personalities who determine events.

Langston Hughes, *The Panther and the Lash: Poems of Our Times*—a collection by the American writer of verse and miscellaneous prose and playwright; as the title would indicate, these poems support the rising sentiment of black militancy; the pieces tend to be wistful, angry, dramatic, and tragic as the poet reacts to the oppression of his people.

Donald Justice, *Night Light*—a collection of verse by the American poet; reflects the writer's concern with poetry as a reflection of the artist's intuition; thus, in this volume, he proceeds toward "a phenomenology of absence" as the self dissolves into its perceptions and intuitions: "certain words, / That will come together to mourn, / Waiting, in their dark clothes, apart."

Alex La Guma, *The Stone Country*—a novel by the South African writer of fiction; concerns daily life in brutal South African jails; the inmates in this jail suffer from dual damnation: as blacks, they are doomed in their struggle against oppression and cruelty, both in and out of prison; the work is dedicated to "the daily average of 70,351 prisoners in South African jails in 1964."

Robert Lowell, *Near the Ocean*—a verse collection by the American poet; the principal pieces are elegies for a generation that suffered through a large part of the Vietnam War and the threat of nuclear extinction; the poems are generally written in strict neoclassic forms, reminding one of the verse of Andrew Marvell; includes "Walking Early Sunday Morning."

Najob Mahfuz, *Miramar*—a novel by the Egyptian writer of fiction and playwright; the writer juxtaposes the observations of several narrators to examine the actions of five male residents of an Alexandrian hotel; a beautiful, naive young woman, hired as a maid, seriously affects their lives.

Bernard Malamud, *The Fixer*—a novel by the American writer of fiction; set in Russia during the regime of the czars, the work concerns an "ordinary man" accused of a ritual murder; the novel receives both the National Book Award and the Pulitzer Prize.

Andre Pieyre de Mandiargues, *La Marge* (The Margin)—a novel by the French writer of fiction, poet, playwright, essayist, and biographer; recounts the fate of a man on a business trip who receives a telegram alluding to his wife's suicide; he refuses to acknowledge the message and takes up temporary residence in a seedy district of Barcelona; the writer may well be suggesting, in part, a perceptive examination of Spain under the rule of Francisco Franco; the work receives the Prix Goncourt.

Cheik A. Ndao, *L'Exil d'Albouri* (The Exile of Albouri)—a play by the Senegalese poet and dramatist; concerns events in the Senegalese (or Djolof) part of the ancient empire of Mali; the writer recreates the times and the actions to suit his dramatic and polemic purposes; the play receives a first prize at the Pan African Cultural Festival at Algiers in 1969.

Philip Roth, *When She Was Good*—a novel by the American writer of fiction; the work centers upon a Madame Bovary type from the Midwest; she sets out to prove that in matters of right and wrong, she will rise to become the ultimate authority.

James David Rubadiri, *No Bride Price*—a novel by the Tanzanian writer of fiction and poet; concerns the tensions experienced by a government bureaucrat, the lover of the village "belle"; a coup topples the government, the woman dies giving birth to the man's child, and the latter finds himself in prison; he must begin life anew, with less scorn for the old values of his lover; essentially, he represents the confused values of life in modern Africa.

Bertrand Russell, *Autobiography, 1872-1914*—an absorbing account by the English philosopher, the principal figure in the evolution of English language philosophy from speculation to analysis; the work is characterized by lucidity and candor, especially as it describes his introduction of a new brevity and precision to the discipline of philosophy.

Ahmad Shahnon, *Menteri* (The Minister)—a novel by the Malay writer of fiction; focuses, in part, upon corruption in politics and the bureaucracy; a bitter satire against Malay leadership, the work contains a section in which one of the characters finds himself in a remarkable dream; there he witnesses Malay subjugation to the Chinese in 1987.

Isaac Bashevis Singer, *The Manor*—a novel by the Polish-born Yiddish writer; set in nineteenth-century Poland, the work develops from the events of the Polish uprising against the Russian czar in 1863.

George Steiner, *Language and Silence: Essays on Language, Literature and the Inhuman*—a volume of literary criticism by the American writer of nonfiction; the volume contains essays about language and politics, language and the future of literature, the pressures on language of "totalitarian lies" and "cultural decay"; the writer also focuses upon language and other modes of meaning: music, translation, mathematics, and even silence.

William Styron, *The Confessions of Nat Turner*—a novel by the American writer of fiction; focuses upon a rebellion by slaves in the American South during 1831; the title character is a chattel slave who has learned to read and write; he has also acquired the complex literary sensibility of the white world; as such, Nat's story becomes the apocalypse of the modern self in the world of romantic existentialism.

Efua Theodora Sutherland, *Edufa*—a play by the Ghanaian dramatist, poet, and essayist; concerns a clever, wealthy, educated merchant who gradually approaches the secret horror in his life; having learned from a sorcerer of his forthcoming death, he pleads for some magic that will save him from his fate; thus, he seeks someone who will trade his or her life for his own; the piece exists as a study of the conflicts between the superstitious world of old Africa and the cynical world of the new, rich, and pro-Western elite.

Gore Vidal, *Washington, D.C.*—a novel by the American writer of fiction and playwright; set in the last years of the Great Depression, the piece traces the parallel lives of a U.S. Senator and a newspaper publisher; the connection focuses upon a startling marriage between the politician's protegé and the publisher's daughter.

Thornton Wilder, *The Eighth Day*—a novel by the American playwright and writer of fiction; the writer directs his attention to murder and its sweeping metaphysical implications; set in a small Illinois mining town in 1902.

EVENTS

Edward Franklin Albee III, American playwright, receives the Pulitzer Prize for drama for *A Delicate Balance* (1966).

Miguel Angel Asturias, Guatemalan writer of fiction and poet, receives the Nobel Prize for literature.

The James Branch Cabell Society founded to promote scholarly study of the American writer of fiction (1879-1958).

Cecil Day-Lewis appointed Poet Laureate of England, succeeding John Masefield; to 1972.

Sir Victor Gollancz, English publisher, dies; he founded his own firm in 1928 and, in 1936, established the Left Book Club.

Justin Kaplan, American scholar and literary historian, receives the Pulitzer Prize for biography/autobiography for his study *Mr. Clemens and Mark Twain* (1966); the work also receives the National Book Award.

Henry Robinson Luce, American publisher and the founder of *Time, Life,* and *Fortune* magazines, dies.

Bernard Malamud, American writer of fiction, receives the Pulitzer Prize for fiction for *The Fixer* (1967); the work also receives the National Book Award.

The National Library, Ottawa, Ontario, established.

Anne Sexton, American writer of verse, receives the Pulitzer Prize in poetry for her collection of lyrics *Live or Die* (1966).

1968

DEATHS

Max Brod (b. 1884). German writer of fiction, playwright, poet, and literary critic; one of the earliest exponents of expressionism and a friend of Franz Kafka, whose works he edited; he developed a strong belief in the possibility of a Jewish state in Palestine, lived there from 1939, and functioned as the director of the Habima Theatre, Tel Aviv.

Gunnar Ekelof (b. 1907). Swedish poet; the most significant writer of verse in Sweden during the twentieth century; his work, philosophical and mystical, reflected his interest in the French symbolist poets and in Oriental literature.

Edna Ferber (b. 1887). American writer of fiction and playwright; she wrote colorful and dramatic novels of American life, as well as plays in collaboration with George S. Kaufmann; in 1925, she received the Pulitzer Prize for fiction for her novel *So Big* (1924).

Tian Han (b. 1898?). Chinese playwright; he became known (at least by Westerners) for his pioneering efforts in introducing Western dramatic realism to the Chinese stage; he played an instrumental role in shaping the history of modern Chinese drama, particularly with reference to the "huo-chu," or spoken drama; he dies, essentially unnoticed, in prison, a victim of one of the vicious purges of literary figures instigated by Jiang Qing and her confederates during the Cultural Revolution.

Stephen Haweis (b. 1878). English-born Dominican autobiographer and poet; his work reflects his outrage at racism and colonial arrogance; in 1966, he went to England to supervise publication of his memoirs; he dies there at age ninety.

Archibald Campbell Jordan (b. 1906). South African (Cape Province) writer of fiction and poet; his fictional works became classics of Xhosa writing, tragically echoing the deep sorrows of an oppressed people; he also wrote historical fiction about the Mpondomise people; he left South Africa in 1962, accepting academic positions at UCLA and the University of Wisconsin; he dies at Madison, Wisconsin, after a lengthy illness.

Sarah Gertrude Millin (b. 1889). South African writer of fiction, biographer, and essayist; she set her novels in the settlements, farms, small towns, and cities of South Africa, portraying conflicts among European settlers and such native groups as Kaffirs and Hottentots; she gained recognition as a vivid interpreter of the history and customs of South Africa.

Oybek (b. 1905). Uzbek (SSR) poet and writer of fiction; his verse is realistic and marked by formal structural perfection; his most significant prose includes historical novels and historical biographies, pieces that underscore his enlightened humanism.

Konstantin Georgievich Paustovsky (b. 1892). Russian autobiographer, writer of fiction, and playwright; his work reflects his survival of the period of Russian history from the Bolshevik Revolution through the end of the Stalin purges; thus, he forms an important link to classical Russian literature; his later work avoids propagandistic communist rhetoric, featuring, instead, lyrical descriptions of the Russian landscape and focusing upon ordinary working people.

Salvatore Quasimodo (b. 1901). Italian poet and translator; his five volumes of verse, published between 1930 and 1938, established him as a leader among Italy's "hermetic" poets, versifiers whose verbal complexities derived from the French symbolists; his later verse became more humanistic in its purpose

and substance; in 1959, he received the Nobel Prize for literature.

Sir Herbert Edward Read (b. 1893). English editor, poet, and critic; his important critical work included studies of William Wordsworth, Thomas Malory, and Laurence Sterne; he produced essays on the visual arts, narratives of life in the trenches during World War I, and a single novel (1935), an allegorical fantasy based upon folk tales.

Conrad Michael Richter (b. 1890). American writer of fiction; his novels focus upon American life and American locales; he favored the East and the period of the American Civil War; his novel *The Town* (1950) receives the Pulitzer Prize for fiction in 1951.

Marah Rusli (b. 1889). Indonesian writer of fiction; he wrote, in 1922, the first original novel in the Indonesian language; he earned a degree in veterinary medicine, practiced on the nearby island of Sumbawa, and recorded his experiences in his fiction.

Upton Beall Sinclair (b. 1878). American writer of fiction; an ardent socialist, he became deeply involved in politics; his interest in social and industrial reform shaped the themes of his eighty novels; he received the Pulitzer Prize for fiction in 1943.

John Ernst Steinbeck (b. 1902). American writer of fiction; he injected into his novels a compassionate understanding of the disinherited of the world: the Dust Bowl survivors, the farmers and migrant laborers of California; in 1962, he received the Nobel Prize for literature.

Arthur Yvor Winters (b. 1900). American poet and critic; he taught literature and criticism at Stanford University (1928-1968), where he wrote controversial criticism that emphasized the moral content of art; his verse ranges from the austere to the lyrical.

Arnold Zweig (b. 1887). German writer of fiction and playwright; he wrote a fictional trilogy based upon World War I (1927-1937), as well as a powerful analysis of life in Germany during the late 1930s; a Zionist, he went to Palestine during the period of the Nazi regime and then, after 1948, emigrated to East Germany.

PUBLICATIONS

Joseph Wilfred Arbuquah, *The Torrent*—a novel by the Ghanian writer of fiction; portrays the difficulties faced by an African boy who has been sent to an African school that operates on Western educational principles.

Ayi Kwei Armah, *The Beautyful Ones Are Not Yet Born*—a novel by the Ghanian writer of fiction and poet; a violent repudiation of the cruelties and corruption of Ghana during the regime of Kwame Nkrumah; the writer attacks postindependence Ghana and the African "Black Colonists" who have replaced the Europeans but who have also taken over the power and arrogance of the whites; the title and its spelling come from a "mammy wagon" (or truck) converted into a bus for the transportation of country people.

James Baldwin, *Let Me Know How Long the Train's Been Gone*—a novel by the American writer of fiction, essayist, and playwright; focuses upon a black actor, who recounts the experiences of his youth and dramatic career while in Harlem; that account becomes, essentially, an evaluation of black life in the United States during the twentieth century.

John Barth, *Lost in the Funhouse*—a collection of fourteen stories by the American writer of fiction; the works are thematically linked by their self-conscious and playful concern with the acts of writing and reading.

Saul Bellow, *Mosby's Memoirs and Other Stories*—a collection of short pieces by the American writer of fiction; the title story portrays the classic disaffected Jewish intellectual; includes "Leaving the Yellow House," "The Old System," "Looking for Mr. Green," "The Gonzaga Manuscripts," and "A Father-to-Be."

Gwendolyn Brooks, *In the Mecca*—a verse collection by the American poet and writer of fiction; the poems reflect the writer's conversion from deep racial pride to harsh militancy, brought about by her exposure to a group of young blacks at Fisk University (Nashville, Tennessee) in 1967; she places emphasis upon what she terms a "black revival."

Dennis Brutus, *Letters to Martha and Other Poems from a South African Prison*—a volume of verse by the Rhodesian poet; reflects his experiences in prison on Robben Island, as well as the pain from his wounds suffered while attempting to escape; the poems constitute actual letters to his sister-in-law, Martha, since he had been forbidden to write anything that might have been of interest to publishers.

Gerard Chenet, *Les Fiancailles Tragiques* (The Tragic Engagement)—a play by the Haitian dramatist and poet; an adaptation of a study of Omar, the Islamic reformer of the Toucouleur people of eastern Senegal, written by Djibril Tamsir Niane.

Robert Coover, *The Universal Baseball Association, Inc., J. Henry Waugh, Prop.*—a novel by the American writer of fiction; a fantasy that relates baseball with life, filtered through the experiences of an accountant; he dreams over his books by day and comes alive at night, maintaining elaborate records of baseball associations that exist only in his imagination; further, the camaraderie of the game contrasts sharply with the loneliness of his real life.

J. P. Donleavy, *The Beastly Beatitudes of Balthazar B*—a novel by the American-born Irish writer of fiction and playwright; concerns the loss of innocence of a young French nobleman; he has lost his loved ones, and thus undergoes emotional and psychological changes; the writer infuses the narrative with ribald episodes and ludicrously comic scenes.

Allen Ginsberg, *Airplane Dreams: Compositions from Journals*—a volume of verse by the American poet; the verses represent the writer's idea of the poem as notation of the spoken voice, or as notation of the process of thought; includes such pieces as "New York to San Fran" and "Portland Coloseum."

Nikki Giovanni, *Black Feeling, Black Talk*—a collection of verse by the American poet; although the pieces in this volume principally concern themselves with the black experience and the attitudes of black militáncy, the writer attempts to provide for *all* people clear directions for "the way to go home."

Bertene Juminer, *La Revanche de Bozambo* (Bozambo's Revenge: Colonialism Inside Out)—a novel by the Guyanean writer of fiction and playwright; a satirical piece in which the writer ridicules the rhetoric and the actions of those who advocate the superiority of one culture or race over another.

Ursula K. Le Guin, *A Wizard of Earthsea*—a novel by the American writer of fiction; the first volume of science fiction series, *The Earthsea Trilogy;* the work has been recognized for its high level of fantasy; magic, mythology, and wizardry remind one of the works by J. R. R. Tolkien.

Norman Mailer, *Miami and the Siege of Chicago*—a prose narrative by the American writer of fiction and nonfiction; concerns the Republican (Miami) and Democratic (Chicago) political conventions of this year, with particular attention upon the protests and riots in the latter city.

Arthur Miller, *The Price*—a drama by the American playwright; concerns two brothers who meet after a lengthy separation to determine what to do with their family's old abandoned furniture; one had gone to college and eventually became a wealthy surgeon; the other left school to support the parents and then became a policeman; focuses on the theme of guilt and responsibility.

Henri de Montherlant, *La Rose de Sable* (The Black Rose)— a novel by the French writer of fiction, playwright, and essayist; a long work about life and events in Africa; the writer finished the piece in 1932, but it reached publication only this year (and then merely in part).

Iris Murdoch, *The Nice and the Good*—a novel by the Irish-born English writer of fiction; a witty, fictional concoction that relies upon science fiction, black magic, and the simple old fashioned "thriller."

Yambo Ouologuem, *Le Devoir de Violence* (The Wages of Violence)—a novel by the Malian poet and writer of fiction, published in Paris; a loose interpretation of African historical events; the work has aroused considerable controversy, particularly since it contains especially close "parallels" with Andre Schwarz-Bart's pseudo-historical novel *Le Dernier des Justes* (1959) and Graham Greene's novel *It's a Battlefield;* nonetheless, the work receives the Prix Renaudot.

Peter K. Palavgyo, *Dying in the Sun*—a novel by the Tanzanian writer of fiction; set in post-independence Tanzania, the work depicts the new tensions of life in contemporary Africa; the principal character, alienated from his father and his fellow villagers, tries to establish a new life after his father's death.

Arabe Shamo, *Dimdim*—a novel by the Kurdish writer of fiction, written in the Kurmmanji dialect; based on a number of Kurdish historical legends, focusing upon the fortress of the title.

John Updike, *Couples*—a novel by the American writer of fiction; concerns itself principally with marriage and adultery in the suburbs; also a frank treatment of the exercise of wife-swapping.

Gore Vidal, *Myra Breckinridge*—a novel by the American writer of fiction, playwright, and essayist; a humorous piece that focuses upon sex and life (in that order) in Hollywood, to include pop culture, pseudo-intellectual ideals, and pornography.

Peter Weiss, *Vietnam Diskurs* (Vietnam Discourse)—a play by the German dramatist; documentary in tone and political in substance; described as a Brechtian political act rather than an imaginative work of dramatic literature.

Marguerite Yourcenar, *L'Oeuvre au Noir* (The Abyss)—a novel by the Belgian-born writer of fiction, poet, playwright, essayist, and translator; concerns a sixteenth-century physician and alchemist; he encounters conflict between the dogmatic beliefs of the Church and his own intellectual questioning.

EVENTS

William James Durant, American intellectual historian, and his wife, Ariel Kaufman Durant, receive the Pulitzer Prize in general nonfiction for their historical study *Rousseau and Revolution* (1967).

Anthony Evan Hecht, American poet, receives the Pulitzer Prize in poetry for *The Hard Hours* (1967).

Yasunari Kawabata, Japanese writer of fiction, becomes the first writer from his nation to receive the Nobel Prize for literature.

Yuri Galanskov, Sergei Pavlovich Dobrovolsky, and Vera Lashkova, Russian writers, sentenced to Soviet prisons for supposedly producing works in opposition to government policies and principles.

The Society for the Study of Literature established to promote American literary scholarship and its eventual publication.

William Clark Styron, American writer of fiction, playwright, and essayist, receives the Pulitzer Prize in fiction for his historical novel *The Confessions of Nat Turner* (1967).

1969

DEATHS

Jalal Al-e Ahmad (b. 1923). Iranian narrative writer and essayist; an intellectual and political philosopher, he joined the Tudeh (Communist) Party in 1944; twenty years later, he undertook the pilgrimage to Mecca, an act incumbent upon all believing Muslims; his work, in general, considers the religious and political dilemmas that confronted Iranian intellectuals between World War II and the Islamic revolution; at the end of his life, he believed religion to be the solution to all of his nation's problems.

Sufi Abdulhaqq Khan Betab (b. 1888). Afghan poet who wrote in the Dari language; he became professor of Persian literature at the University of Kabul and, in 1932, received the title "Malik· ush-shu'ara" (King of Poets); connoisseur and consistent practitioner of the "Indian style" of verse (simplicity of language, philosophical and social in substance, and Persian in influence), he wrote on traditional subjects; yet, he also introduced new poetic themes: electricity, technology, independence and freedom.

Romulo Gallegos (b. 1884). Venezuelan writer of fiction and statesman; his novels explored Venezuelan life, with emphasis upon his nation's customs and landscape; he served as president of Venezuela for eleven months until ousted by a military coup.

Witold Gombrowicz (b. 1904). Polish writer of fiction, playwright, and essayist; through his fiction and drama, he gained a reputation as an irreverent satirist and an early proponent of existentialism; he concerned himself with the interdependence of human beings ("the interhuman church") and with the conflict between humanity's desire to attain maturity and its attraction to youth.

Ho-Chi-Minh (originally Nguyen-tat-Thanh; b. 1890). Vietnamese revolutionary, statesman, and miscellaneous prose writer; his published essays originate from his speeches, letters, and appeals and are patriotic and emotional in tone and subject; he wrote in clear, simple, and "popular" language; in 1964, he published a collection of poems in Chinese.

Karl Jaspers (b. 1883). German philosopher; an adherent of existentialism, he believed that genuine philosophy must originate from the study of a person's individual existence; he viewed that state as enclosed by an all-embracing, transcendental reality that he termed "the encompassing."

Jack Kerouac (b. 1922). American writer of fiction and nonfiction and poet; he became a leader of the "Beat Generation" writers, writing of the frenetic pursuits of new experiences; the poet (and fellow Beat) Allen Gins-

berg viewed him as a "new Buddha of American prose, [who] spit forth intelligence . . . creating a spontaneous bop prosody and original classic literature."

Gurgen Mahari (b. 1903). Soviet Armenian poet and writer of fiction; his early lyrics focused upon the sorrows of his own childhood; he then turned his poetic attention to emotional lines on the building of socialism.

Thomas Merton (b. 1915). American poet (born in France) and writer of miscellaneous prose; he converted to Roman Catholicism, became a Trappist monk (1941), and entered the priesthood; known for his autobiography (1948) and two volumes on Trappist life in Kentucky; he dies in an automobile accident while in Thailand.

Katharine Susannah Prichard (b. 1883). Fijian-born Australian writer of fiction and nonfiction, poet, and playwright; she insisted on the formation of a national literature based on Australian subject matter; thus she sets her work in such locales as Victoria, northern New South Wales, the southwestern forests, and the western cattle stations; her lyrical narratives combine romantic, realistic, and idealistic sentiments.

Stijn Streuvels (pseudonym of Frank Lateur; b. 1871): Belgian (Flemish) writer of fiction; his novels and short stories are moving portraits of everyday life; his works are characterized by fatalism, delicacy of observation, and a poetic sense of the beauty and cruelty of nature.

Vrndavanlal Varma (b. 1889). Indian (Hindi) writer of fiction; he wrote popular historical novels similar to those produced by Sir Walter Scott; he propagated Indian nationalism by depicting hard-working and dutiful characters; he also criticized the evil practices of Hindu society as the results of traditional attitudes of ritualism and apathy.

Nairi Zavian (pseudonym of Hayastan Yeghiazarian; b. 1900); Soviet Armenian poet and writer of travel narratives; he wrote lyrics on the building of socialism, epics on the collectivization of Armenian village life, and historical verse tragedy.

PUBLICATIONS

Samuel Beckett, *Film: A Film Script*—the Irish writer's only venture into the medium of the cinema; this volume is the text of the

1964 film made in New York City, starring Buster Keaton; receives the Film Critics Prize at the 1965 Venice Film Festival, the Special Jury Prize at the 1966 Tours Festival, and the Special Prize at the 1966 Oberthausen Festival.

Brigid Brophy, *In Transit*—a novel by the English writer of fiction and biographer; features a narrator who, while waiting in an airport lounge, explores his (or her?) identity through a series of reflections and verbal fantasies; the writer relies upon typographical "experiments."

John Cheever, *Bullet Park*—a novel by the American writer of fiction; concerns two men engaged in exercises of self-destruction and the violence that stalks them; the two principal characters enjoy the names Hammer and Nailes.

Robert Coover, *Pricksongs and Descants*—a collection of short fictional pieces by the American writer of fiction; the writer draws upon the fables and legends that form the basis of Western culture; he juxtaposes the fabulous and the commonplace, forcing the reader to reassess stereotype concepts of literature.

Robert Creely, *Pieces*—a collection of verse by the American poet; as the title indicates, the poems identify the increasing fragmentation of experience; these "fluid" compositions tend to be lax and include "trivial" details of the poet's own life.

Michael Crichton, *The Andromeda Strain*—a novel by the American writer of fiction and miscellaneous nonfiction prose; an unmanned research satellite returns to earth, mysteriously and lethally contaminated; scientific investigators mobilize their medical and technological resources in a race against time for an antidote; a compelling and reasonably executed piece of fiction.

John Fowles, *The French Lieutenant's Woman*—a novel by the English writer of fiction; on the surface, the work appears as a Victorian romance; in reality, however, the writer has developed a type of narrative ploy as an analogue of the male desire to rationalize and manipulate the enigma of woman.

Antonia Fraser, *Mary, Queen of Scots*—a biography by the English historian and writer of fiction; sets forth the life of the Catholic rival of Elizabeth I, whom the latter put to death in 1587.

Gunter Grass, *Ortlich Betaubt* (Local Anaesthetic)—a novel by the German writer of fiction, essayist, poet, and playwright; the writer sets forth a discourse on the Berlin student uprisings of the 1960's; the dramatic point arises during a confrontation between a teacher and an admired student who threatens to burn, publicly, his pet dachshund to protest the employment of napalm in the Vietnam War; the work illustrates and explores the futility of simplistic solutions to contemporary conflicts.

Ursula K. Le Guin, *The Left Hand of Darkness*—a science fiction novel by the American writer; a tender treatment of the story of a traveler from a planet much like Earth; the person discovers a world in which only a single sex exists, which means that each being has the dual ability to father and to bear children; the father of one child may well be the mother of several others, sexual roles do not exist, nor does there arise the potential inability of people to understand one another because of sexual differences.

Doris Lessing, *The Four-Gated City*—a novel by the Persian-born, Rhodesian-raised English writer of fiction; the fifth and last volume of the series, *Children of Violence;* the work explores the corruptions of post-World War II London, through the observations of the central character of the series, Martha Quest.

Robert Lowell, *Notebook, 1967-1968*—a collection of verse stanzas by the American poet; the poet concerns himself with contemporary events, which he alternates with notations on historical types and analogues; thus, he presents poems on such subjects as Allah, Attila the Hun, Clytemnestra, Roland, Tamerlaine the Great, Richard III of England, Emperor Charles V, the Duc de Nemours, Bishop George Berkeley, Andrew Jackson, and Admiral Onishi.

Bernard Mulamud, *Pictures of Fidelman*—a novel by the American writer of fiction; a picaresque work set in Italy, in which the writer experiments with surrealism; his invention appears comical rather than purely farcical.

Paule Marshall, *The Chosen Place, the Timeless People*—a novel by the American writer of fiction (born of Barbadian parentage); set in the Caribbean, the work focuses upon an American research and developmental group who works with the natives of a small island; the writer portrays both outsiders and natives in terms of the motives of guilt and frustration by which they comprehend their personal lives; she also translates personal drama into general social meaning.

Ian MacDonald, *The Humming Bird Tree*—a novel by the Trinidadian writer of fiction and poet (and international tennis champion); a highly autobiographical piece, the work concerns growing up in Trinidad, which means maturation within a multi-racial society; the writer simply sets forth the specifics of the issue; he does not attempt to offer solutions to the problem; the piece receives a prize by the Royal Society of Literature, London.

N. Scott Momaday, *The Way to Rainy Mountain*—an historical work by the American (native born) writer of fiction and nonfiction prose; concerns the history of the migration of the Kiowa tribe; based upon a combination of legend and fact.

Iris Murdoch, *Bruno's Dream*—a novel by the Anglo-Irish writer of fiction; the grotesque efforts of a dying old man to establish his first bonds of love and affection with the world constitute the principal thrust of this piece.

Ishmael Scott Reed, *Yellow Black Radio Broke Down*—a novel by the American writer of fiction, satirist, and poet; focuses upon a black cowboy and his gang, who wish to liberate the masses and to make certain that all oppressors will meet their ends by hanging from trees.

Philip Roth, *Portnoy's Complaint*—a novel by the American writer of fiction; a comic masterpiece that comes forth with sexual frankness and "devilish" revelation; the piece has been described, generally, as the great "masturbation novel" of America, combined with variations upon the equally "great" Jewish experience.

Tayeb Salih, *Seasons of Migration to the North*—a novel by the Sudanese writer of fiction; the bizarre tale of a sexually talented African scholar who lives in London; he finds himself amid a score of women who lust for exotic sensations; the work exists as a combination of the bitter and the exotic, since every woman who wants the scholar eventually dies; the piece ends in the moral and emotional destruction of the principal character.

Sahle Berhane Mariam Sellassie, *The Afersata*—a novel by the Ethiopian writer of fiction, who wrote in both Amharic and English; depicts the folk "moot court" (or "afersata") in action; that body seeks, through slow, half magical, half common sense procedures, to discover who supposedly has burned one of the villager's houses and stolen the owner's buried money.

Anne Sexton, *Love Poems*—a collection of verse by the American poet; the pieces have been identified as "evocative" and free in form, characterized by the poet's personal honesty and highly delicate imagery.

Ahmad Shahnon, *Perdana* (Premier)—a novel by the Malay writer of fiction; the writer attempts to come to grips with potentially one of the largest themes in contemporary Malay life: the post-World War II national struggle and the achievement of independence; the work exists, actually, as an historical resume of political events.

Susan Sontag, *Styles of Radical Will*—a volume of prose nonfiction by the American critical essayist; details the extent of her intellectual investigations into film, literature, politics, and pornography.

Garth St. Omer, *Nor Any Country*—a novel by the St. Lucian writer of fiction; the central character returns to his native West Indian home from England; he discovers serious changes in his wife, his mother, and the entire country; there exist more demands and less hope; the novel set in a significant social and spiritual climate.

Stephen Vizinczey, *The Rules of Chaos; or, Why Tomorrow Doesn't Work*—a volume of essays by the Hungarian-born Canadian writer of fiction, essayist, and playwright; a collection of prose pieces on such general topics as philosophy, politics, and literature; the writer achieves unity through his belief that the element of chance exerts significant influence upon human life.

Kurt Vonnegut, Jr., *Slaughterhouse Five; or, the Children's Crusade*—a novel by the American writer of fiction; a former American prisoner of war relives the bombing of Dresden, Germany, during World War II; the work especially disturbing because it focuses upon fire bombing and the writer's own experiences in the events described.

Robert Penn Warren, *Audubon: A Vision*—a series of poems by the American writer of fiction and verse; the poet recreates, essentially, the smoldering violence of the American frontier; the title character spends the night in a filthy cabin, in danger of losing his life because an old woman and her sons want his gold watch; three travelers arrive, administer frontier justice to the would-be thieves, and hang the old woman; nonetheless, she earns her dignity by her death.

EVENTS

Samuel Barclay Beckett, Irish-born playwright and writer of fiction, receives the Nobel Prize for literature.

Rene Jules Dubos, French-born American bacteriologist (*So Human and Animal,* 1969), and Norman Mailer, American writer of fiction and miscellaneous prose (*The Armies of the Night,* 1968), share the Pulitzer Prize for prose nonfiction.

Sir Allan Lane (born Allen Lane Williams), English publisher and founder of Penguin Books, retires after almost fifty years in the publishing industry.

Navarre Scott Momaday, native American writer of fiction and nonfiction and poet, receives the Pulitzer Prize in fiction for his novel *House Made of Dawn* (1969).

George Oppen, American writer of verse, receives the Pulitzer Prize in poetry for *Of Being Numerous* (1968).

The Popular Culture Association established at Bowling Green (Ohio) State University; intended to promote interest and study in such areas as folklore, music, literature, and film.

Howard Sackler, American playwright, receives the Pulitzer Prize in drama for *The Great White Hope* (performed 1967, published 1968).

Aleksandr Isayevich Solzhenitsyn, Russian writer of fiction and critic; expelled from the Soviet Writers' Union and from Moscow.

1970

DEATHS

Samuel Joseph Agnon (b. 1888). Israeli writer of fiction; the first Hebrew writer to have received the Nobel Prize for literature (1966); he also received the Bialik Prize in 1937; his work generally portrays Jewish life in eastern Europe, bringing to light an entire gallery of realistic character types; his powerful narratives feature "folksiness," deep sympathy, and a charming naiveté.

Louise Bogan (b. 1897). American writer of verse and critic; her poems tended to be personal, intense, and metaphysical in tone; she generally wrote short pieces in subtly alliterative language, adhering to rhyme and a set meter; she focused upon the themes of love, death, regret, memory, and nature.

Ferdinand Crommelynck (b. 1886). Belgian (Flemish) playwright; his expressionistic dramatic works tend to be distorted and grotesque; his plays reflect his interest in the works of the English playwright Ben Jonson.

John Roderigo Dos Passos (b. 1896). American writer of fiction; he developed a kaleidoscopic technique to portray American life; he combined narration, stream of consciousness, biography, and quotations from newspapers and magazines; he began with decidedly left-wing views, but later became a strict political and social conservative.

Edward Morgan Forster (b. 1879). English writer of fiction, critic, and biographer; with sensitivity, subtlety, and an impeccable style, he brought new dimensions to the English novel of manners; he also spent some time working upon opera libretti.

Jean Giono (b. 1895). French writer of fiction; his novels describe pastoral Provencal life and emphasize his characters' close proximity to nature.

Amado V. Hernandez (b. 1903). Philippine (Tagalog) poet, writer of fiction, and playwright; his best works appeared in the 1960s, particularly as they reflected his experiences among the Manilla poor and as a union leader.

Orhan Kemal (pseudonym of Kemal Sadik Giogceli; b. 1914). Turkish writer of fiction, poet, and essayist; his career as a writer began with his incarceration in the prison at Bursa, where he received encouragement to write prose; he portrayed the dramas of young peasants who attempted to flee their villages and adapt to life in the cities; thus, he sought to document the difficult transition from village existence to life in the industrial centers.

Francis Parkinson Keyes (b. 1885). American writer of fiction; he wrote of subjects both historical and pseudo-historical, depicting individual assertion, excitement, and adventure.

Joseph Wood Krutch (b. 1893). American scholar, critic, literary biographer, and academician; he gained recognition for his critical commentary, ranging in subject from nature and the modern intellectual temper to Samuel Johnson, Henry David Thoreau, Miguel Cervantes, and Samuel Richardson.

Francois Mauriac (b. 1885). French writer of fiction, playwright, and essayist; his works reflect his profound but nonconformist version of Roman Catholicism; in 1952, he received the Nobel Prize for literature.

Yukio Mishima (pseudonym of Kimitake Hiraoka; b. 1925). Japanese writer of fiction, playwright, and essayist; in 1968, he founded and led the Shield Society, a group of men accused by their political opponents of being protofascists; their aim, however, focused upon protecting Japan from leftist uprising; at least five of his novels have been translated into English; he committed suicide in traditional "hara-kiri" fashion, in protest against what he termed the "spinelessness" of Japan's military posture.

Armijn Pane (b. 1908). Indonesian writer of miscellaneous prose and fiction, poet, and playwright; he wrote, in Dutch, a survey of modern Indonesian literature, published a substantial volume of Indonesian grammar, and translated Western writers (for instance, Henrik Ibsen) into Indonesian; through his fiction, he attempted to resolve a number of critical social issues.

Erich Maria Remarque (b. 1897). German-born writer of fiction; he achieved a reputation for his bitter, antiwar novel *All Quiet on the Western Front* (1929); his later works focused upon the grim economic and social conditions in Germany between the wars; he came to the United States in 1939.

Bertrand Arthur William Russell, third Earl Russell (b. 1872). English philosopher, mathematician, social reformer, and essayist; with Alfred North Whitehead, he attempted to demonstrate how the laws of mathematics could be deduced from the basic axioms of logic; his work exercised considerable influence upon twentieth-century symbolic logic; he became deeply convinced of the logical independence of individual facts and the dependence of knowledge upon the data of original experience; he became an ardent pacifist and held liberal views on such issues as marriage, sex, adultery, and homosexuality.

Nelly Sachs (b. 1891). German poet and translator; her verse passionately describes the suffering of the European Jews; after 1940, she lived in Sweden; in 1966, she shared the Nobel Prize for literature with the Polish-born Israeli writer Shmuel Yosef Agnon.

Wilbur Daniel Steele (b. 1886). American writer of fiction and playwright; he devoted the greatest part of his literary labors to short stories set either in the South or in New England; his most-anthologized piece, "How Beautiful with Shoes" (which he also transformed into a play), may appear "folksy," but it conveys serious religious sentiment.

Anzia Yezierska (b. 1885?). Russian-born writer of fiction and critic; she published most of her fiction during the 1920s and 1930s, focusing upon the early twentieth-century Jewish immigrant experience in the United States; her characters search for the American dream, while her women, especially, try to liberate themselves from the orthodoxy of Judaism and its old world traditions; she tried to capture the essence of life on the lower East Side of New York City at the beginning of the twentieth century; she lived in relative obscurity during the last twenty years of her life.

PUBLICATIONS

Timothy Mofolorunso Aluko, *Chief the Honourable Minister*—a novel by the Nigerian writer of fiction; concerns the problems of modern Nigerian officials; the principal character returns to "Afromacoland" from London to become his nation's Minister of Works; the narrative ends in violence, corruption, and the takeover by the military.

Maya Angelou, *I Know Why the Caged Bird Sings*—an autobiographical narrative by the American playwright, poet, writer of fiction, and narrative writer; the writer's moving account of her childhood and adolescence in the South during the Great Depression; she confronts the joys and disappointments of her own life with wonder and dignity.

Sunday Ogbonna Anozi, *Sociologie du Roman Africaine*—a volume of criticism by the Nigerian essayist and scholar; he offers a structuralist analysis of French and English African creative literature, focusing upon the ever-changing political and social climates of African fiction; he also explicates principal works of literature.

Sawako Ariyoshi, *Hanaoka Seishu no Tsuma* (The Doctor's Wife)—a novel by the Japanese writer of fiction; concerns the achievements of Seishu Hanaoka (1760-1835), a late Togukawa period physician who experimented with general anesthesia for surgery;

he administered his anesthetic successfully in 1805, his wife and mother being the subjects of his experiments; the wife (a plain woman) and his mother (extremely beautiful) compete for the doctor's affections.

Donald Barthelme, *City Life*—a collection of short stories by the American writer of fiction; the writer focuses upon the theme of the frustrations resulting from the pursuit of an unattainable goal: consciousness collapses, creative power dissipates, the personality falls apart; includes "The Glass Mountain" and "Brain Damage."

Samuel Beckett, *Lessness*—a short work by the Irish-born playwright, poet, and writer of fiction; described neither as a play nor a novel, neither poetry nor prose; the writer attempts to record, through language, the failure of language to provide a secure artistic refuge; for him, there remains nothing but silence.

Saul Bellow, *Mr. Sammler's Planet*—a novel by the American writer of fiction; the elderly but vivacious title character casts a skeptical eye on the island of Manhattan during the radical period of the 1960s.

John Pepper Clark, *Casualties: Poems, 1966-1968*—a collection of verse by the Nigerian poet, playwright, and critic; with almost journalistic concentration, the poet focuses upon the Nigerian-Biafran conflict and his own support for the Nigerian government; he heavily annotates the volume, detailing his intimate knowledge of the war; the collection considers the role of the artist during war, as both healer and reporter.

Joan Didion, *Play It As It Lays*—a novel by the American writer of fiction; a painful piece about a young Hollywood actress and model; a traumatic abortion, an impending divorce from her film-maker husband, and the hopeless future of her retarded daughter upset the balance of her life; an honest, intelligent, and skillful work.

Gevorg Emin, *XX-rd dar* (Twentieth Century)—a volume of verse by the Soviet Armenian poet; meditations on the conflict between human beings and technical civilization.

Christopher Fry, *A Yard of Sun*—a play by the English dramatist; classified as a "dark comedy," the work combines a medieval horse race with conditions in post-World War II Italy.

Ernest Hemingway, *Islands in the Stream*—a novel by the American writer of fiction, published posthumously; contains a variety of themes and moods: the uncanny sense of life and action characteristic of the writer's early stories, the warmth of past recollections, the rich and relaxed sense of humor, complete with irony and ribaldry; set in the mid-1930s, the work focuses upon a painter on the island of Bimini, in the Gulf Stream; his three young sons come for a vacation, thus breaking the routine discipline of his work; includes episodes in wartime Cuba, then on the painter's improvised "Q-boat," hunting down the survivors of a German submarine.

Merle Hodge, *Crick Crack Monkey*—the first novel by the Trinidadian writer of fiction and translator; depicts a young girl amongst relatives; an aunt remolds the girl's image so that she can cope with the caste system of Trinidad, where shades of darkness and light remain particularly important.

Ted Hughes, *Crow: From the Life and Songs of the Crow*—a volume of verse by the English poet and playwright; the writer offers a grim, sardonic portrait of the world, in which the worst has already occurred; thus, the vision undergoes cold, nihilistic scrutiny, and human beings justify their lust for survival through a flood of language; life denies charity, love, forgiveness, compunction, and remorse.

Eugene Ionesco, *Jeux de Massacre* (The Killing Game)—a play by the Romanian-born French dramatist, essayist, and writer of fiction; focuses upon an epidemic that kills the inhabitants of a village; death represents the absurdist threat of nothingness and the "upsurge of the uncanny."

Fazil Iskander, *Sozvezdie Kozlotura* (The Goat-ibex Constellation)—a novel by the Russian writer of fiction and poet; a subtle political satire that recounts the crossbreeding of a goat and an ibex, which leads to the "goati-bexization" of a farming district; the piece parodies the theories of a Soviet scientist who convinced both Joseph Stalin and Nikita Krushchev that he had disproved existing genetic principles; the writer also ridicules Soviet style propaganda and censorship, by introducing a newspaper that capitalizes on the scientist's foolishness.

Uwe Johnson, *Jahrestage: Aus dem Leben von Gesine Cresspahl* (Anniversaries: From the Life of Gesine Cresspahl)—a four-volume novel (until 1984) by the German writer of fiction and essayist; documents the history of a family from the rise of the Nazi regime to the political tumult of the 1960s in the United States (where the title character has immigrated); the writer draws analogies between German antisemitism and American racism, between German fascism and the American involvement in the Vietnam War; for the writer in this piece, fiction exists as a means of helping the reader to understand the world.

Maxine Kumin, *The Abduction*—a novel by the American poet, essayist, and writer of fiction; presents a black man who sincerely cares about deprived inner city children and their welfare in a government sponsored program; however, when a crisis does develop, only a white woman appears capable of action; she flees the riots following the assassination of Martin Luther King, Jr., taking with her one of her pupils, a black boy, who exists as a symbol of hope for the future.

Mazisi Raymond Kunene, *Zulu Poems*—a collection by the South African poet and playwright, translated (by him) from the original Zulu; the introduction contains explanations about his own poetry and the problems involved with translation; he also sets forth an understanding of specific aspects of the vernacular poetry of the Zulu people; the poems themselves range wide in substance: peace, war, the poet's role in traditional and modern Zulu society, and even Joan Baez (the American folk singer).

Norman Mailer, *Of a Fire on the Moon*—a nonfiction narrative by the American writer of fiction and miscellaneous prose; an account of the voyage of Apollo 11 and its landing on the Moon; combines incisive reporting and sensitive reflection, particularly in terms of forming an image of human energy and purpose.

W. S. Merwin, *The Carriers of Ladders*—a volume of verse by the American poet, playwright, and translator; the writer broods upon such subjects as the overall absence of meaning, death, spiritual transcendence of the objective, and the alien landscape.

Toni Morrison, *The Bluest Eye*—a novel by the American writer of fiction; the writer combines scenes from an underground whose inhabitants suffer from confused social directives, as well as from poverty; the fragmentary form of the work represents the structure (or lack thereof) in that world.

John Munonye, *Oil Man of Obange*—a novel by the Nigerian writer of fiction; a study of the new proletariat in rural Africa; each day, the principal character must carry into town, on his rented, old bicycle, a heavy load of palm oil; he has no other resources through which to support his family; after being robbed of his bicycle and the receipts for his employer, the man loses his mind and dies, in total ruin.

Condetto Nenekhaly-Camara, *Continent-Afrique* (The African Continent)—a play by the Guinean poet and dramatist; concerns an Arab warrior of the sixth century (or first century, according to Moslem chronology) and son of a black African woman; the writer attempts to exploit the epic quality of his hero as a model for the new heroism of modern Africa; thus, the principal character appears as real, rather than as mythological or superhuman.

Michael Ondaatje, *The Collected Works of Billy the Kid: Left Handed Poems*—a volume of verse by the Ceylonese-born Canadian poet, novelist, and playwright; a type of fictionalized biography that probes the psyche of the American outlaw; the writer strives to understand the legend of his title character and to see him as a figure of "modern consciousness"; the book wins a Governor General's Award for literature.

Ezra Pound, *Cantos, No. 1-117, 120*—a collection of verse by the American-born poet, essayist, and translator; begun as early as 1911 and published, from that date, in various versions, editions, and drafts; an epic with various heroes (Odysseus, Sigismundo de Malatesta, Confucius, Thomas Jefferson, John Adams); also includes an account of the poet's imprisonment by American troops during the Allied invasion of Italy in World War II; the poems are a tribute to the poet's vast knowledge of prosody.

Abdarrahman ash-Sharqawi, *Al-Fellah* (The Fellah)—a novel by the Egyptian playwright, journalist, and writer of fiction; describes conflicts that occur during a time of transformation in a modern Egyptian village; a clash occurs between the last remaining feudal and reactionary forces and those people determined to achieve their revolutionary goals (the "fellah"); the piece reflects the writer's knowledge of modern European prose style and technique.

Muriel Spark, *The Driver's Seat*—a novel by the Scottish-born writer of fiction, poet, playwright, and essayist; focuses upon a woman obsessed with controlling her destiny; she devises the method of her own death and searches for a particular type of man to murder her.

Eudora Welty, *Losing Battles*—a novel by the American writer of fiction; concerns the events during a family reunion in rural Mississippi in the 1930s; the writer develops the relation of memory to the structure of community in the South.

EVENTS

Charles Gordone, American playwright, receives the Pulitzer Prize in drama for *No Place To Be Somebody* (1969).

Richard Joseph Howard, American poet, prose writer, editor, and translator, receives the Pulitzer Prize in poetry for *Untitled Subjects* (1969).

Aleksandr Isayevich Solzhenitsyn, Russian writer of fiction and miscellaneous prose, receives the Nobel Prize for literature.

Jean Stafford, American writer of fiction, receives the Pulitzer Prize in fiction for her *Collected Stories* (1969).

1971

DEATHS

Jalal Ale Ahmad (b. 1920?). Iranian writer of fiction, folklorist, and translator; his fiction focused upon the contemporary problems of Iranian rural and urban life that resulted from religious prejudice and social conventions; he translated, from the French, works by Albert Camus and Jean-Paul Sartre.

Paul Blackburn (b. 1926). American poet and translator who blended colloquial and formal language in verse about everyday situations, landscapes, and myth.

Walter Van Tilburg Clark (b. 1909). American writer of fiction; he became one of the most respected writers of Western fiction in the United States; he created a world in which evil exists as an autonomous force that overwhelms human beings' attempts to achieve an ethic of behavior; in his novels, particularly, he called for individual responsibility, individual rights, democratic cooperation, humanitarian legislation, and human recognition of the beauty and indifference of Nature.

Gyorgy Lukacs (b. 1885). Hungarian literary critic, social theorist, and philosopher; a life-long Marxist, he explored relationships between creativity and the social struggle; he wrote concerning class consciousness, realism in European literature, and what he viewed to have been the destruction of reason.

Guruprasad Mainali (b. 1900). Nepali writer of fiction; his work came under the influence of contemporary Hindi writers who, in turn, had been inspired by the European short story; he tended to describe the pathetic aspects of life in the villages of Nepal, writing in a style free from artificiality and with an attitude reflective of the people he portrayed.

Frederick Ogden Nash (b. 1902). American poet; he produced humorous, light verse upon frequently outrageous themes; his pieces violated the rules of symmetry and harmony and expressed, generally, the frustrations of his "plain-spoken" readers over the complexities of contemporary poetry; he wrote about everyday life and clothed his subjects in everyday language.

Gershon Schoffman (b. 1880). German-born Hebrew writer of fiction; the themes of his works focused, generally, upon the loneliness of young people who found themselves uprooted by war and related calamities; he delved into the souls of his characters, into their sorrow and hopelessness, revealing their collective tragedy of having drifted from one shore without ever finding another place.

George Seferis (pseudonym of Giorgos Sefiriadis; b. 1900). Greek poet, critic and diplomat; his surrealistic, highly symbolic verse invokes classical themes and the tragedy of exile; in 1963, he received the Nobel Prize for literature.

Paruir Sevak (originally Paruir Ghazaryan; b. 1924). Soviet Armenian poet, literary historian, and biblical translator; intellectually, his verse proves difficult, as he attempts to probe the roots of the problems of modern life in the second half of the twentieth century; he collaborated in the revised translation of the Bible for the 1970 edition.

Fakhroddin Shadman (b. 1910). Iranian essayist and writer of fiction; he explored the question of cultural relations between Iran and the West; in both his essays and novels, he discussed the problem of native Iranian culture giving way to Western practices and attitudes; he urged Iranians to study thoroughly both native and Western customs, applying their conclusions to their own cultural lives.

Stevie Smith (originally Florence Margaret Smith; b. 1902). English poet and writer of fiction; her verse contains extensive emotional variety, as she demonstrates her adeptness at moving, within the confines of a single poem, from (for example) wild comedy to tragic death; a truly sophisticated artist, she produced verse from nursery rhymes, hymns, and unimaginative songs; she also demonstrated a complex reaction to religion, a subject that both fascinated and repulsed her; she received the Cholmondeley Award (1966) and the Queen's Gold Medal for Poetry (1969).

Simon Vestdijk (b. 1898). Dutch writer of fiction and poet; he became the most significant novelist of his nation during the first half of the twentieth century; he wrote thirty-eight novels, ten volumes of short stories, and twenty-two books of poetry; in addition, he translated such writers as Emily Dickinson and Robert Louis Stevenson; one critic pronounced that he "wrote faster than God can read"; he also found the time to study medicine, psychology, and philosophy, and those disciplines found their ways into his creative efforts.

PUBLICATIONS

Fleur Adcock, *High Tide in the Garden*—a collection of verse by the New Zealand-born English poet and translator; relates familiar objects, scenes, and relationships to domestic life; particularly, the pieces focus upon such topics as dreams and nightmares, love and sex, and the poet's bond with her own children.

Kofi Awooner, *This Earth My Brother*—a novel by the Ghanaian poet, writer of fiction, and playwright; concerns corruption and degradation in African life; the writer views such conditions as the legacy of colonialism, as well as the product of African selfishness and egotism; the work indicts the African political elite as sordid and inefficient; thus, the central character, a lawyer trained in Europe, suffers a nervous breakdown when he confronts the complexities of newly independent Ghana and cannot deal with the bribery and the violence; if a person such as he fails, who, then, will (or can) succeed?

William S. Burroughs, *The Wild Boys*—a novel by the American writer of fiction; described as a bold experiment in fiction, the work exists as a nightmarish journey through time; the writer creates a science fiction vision comprised of nostalgia, violence, and lust.

E. L. Doctorow, *The Book of Daniel*—a novel by the American writer of fiction; concerns the investigation, trial, and sentencing of Ethel and Julius Rosenberg, the American couple executed for revealing secret documents to the Soviets; the title character reviews his life in light of the past actions of his parents.

J. P. Donleavy, *The Onion Eaters*—a novel by the American-born Irish writer of fiction, playwright, and essayist; focuses upon a young man who inherits an Irish manor; he comes in contact with a strange group of guests who create bedlam, bringing ruin to him and to his manor.

Thom Gunn, *Moly*—a volume of verse by the English poet; the writer considers the chaotic dissolution through LSD of San Francisco in the late 1960s; in his own view, the phenomenon relates to Odysseus's meeting with Hermes and his eating of the herb.

Geoffrey Hill, *Mercian Hymns*—a collection of verse by the English poet; through the poet's reliance upon myth, event and sensibility become simultaneous with each other; thus, for instance, the medieval roots of ancient Mercia give way to modern highways and reflections upon the poet's childhood; the hymns appear as prose poems for the purpose of achieving both objectivity and immediacy without destroying chronology.

Evan X. Hyde, *North Amerikkan Blues*—the first collection of verse by the Belizean poet, playwright, and writer of fiction; the pieces focus upon what the writer sees as an American society that "spin the web of whiteness around me"; the work reflects the poet's political involvement in obtaining independence for what was then known as British Honduras.

Giris Karnad, *Hayavadana*—a play by the Indian (Kannada) dramatist; based upon the classical Indian tale of the "transposed heads"; essentially a verse drama, the piece reveals technical sophistication, spectacle, and epic breadth; the playwright relies upon experimental aspects of European theater and the principal elements of Kannada folk theater.

Galway Kinnell, *The Book of Nightmares*—a collection of verse by the American poet, a sequence of ten pieces; focuses upon the writer's intense awareness that growth involves a form of dying, a notion that provides unity to the individual poems.

Doris Lessing, *Briefing for a Descent into Hell*—a novel by the Persian-born, Rhodesian-reared English writer of fiction; the piece exists as a recreation of a nightmare in the form of a medical report; the writer explores the themes of individual and collective breakdown and violence; told from the point of view of a supposed mad man.

Denise Levertov, *To Stay Alive*—a collection of verse by the English-born poet and writer of fiction; the poems represent the writer's increasingly active participation in the principal social and political movements of the late 1950s and the 1960s.

Archibald MacLeish, *Scratch*—a verse drama by the American poet, playwright, and writer of miscellaneous prose; an adaptation of Stephen Vincent Benet's fictional piece *The Devil and Daniel Webster* (1937).

Bernard Malamud, *The Tenants*—a novel by the American writer of fiction; essentially, the writer focuses upon the black-white cultural struggles in New York City as viewed by two inhabitants, both writers, of a tenement house on the lower East Side; emotionalism runs high, and mayhem rules the way of life.

Mary McCarthy, *Birds of America*—a novel by the American writer of fiction; the piece focuses upon an American undergraduate in Paris during the 1960s; from that vantage point the student attempts to understand the problems and values of America.

Iris Murdoch, *An Accidental Man*—a novel by the Irish-born English writer of fiction; thematically, the work serves as a study of the survival of a single person at the expense of others.

Adrienne Rich, *The Will To Change: Poems, 1968-1970*—a collection by the American writer of verse; the poet appears to have found for herself a sense of "wholeness" by which to develop images that respect the integrity of conflicts within and outside herself.

Philip Roth, *Our Gang*—a novel by the American writer of fiction; a satire on President Richard Nixon and his so-called "White House Mafia" responsible for corruption in office.

Jon Silkin, *Amana Gras*—a collection of verse by the English poet; inspired by the poet's visits to Israel and the United States.

Aleksandr Solzhenitsyn, *August 1914*—a novel by the Russian writer of fiction, his first publication after emigrating to the United States; the work offers an alternative view of Soviet history; conceived as the first part of a series of historical novels attempting to find the meaning behind the Bolshevik Revolution of 1917.

Allen Tate, *The Swimmers and Other Selected Poems*—a volume of verse by the American poet, playwright, writer of fiction, and critic; the title piece, especially, sets the poet's experiences with his family and his region (the South) against a background of Christian experience.

John Updike, *Rabbit Redux*—a novel by the American writer of fiction; the writer examines the effect of the uprisings and riots of the 1960s upon a single person; the title character, Rabbit Angstrom, age thirty-six, drifts through the world of social and political conflagration, yet appears sensitive to change.

Derek Walcott, *The Dream on Monkey Mountain*—a play by the West Indian poet and dramatist; concerns a charcoal vendor who comes from his mountain home to sell his wares; jailed for drunkenness, he dreams of becoming the king of a united Africa; dream and reality emphasize the dangers of replacing actual Caribbean cultural diversity with a romanticized version of Africa.

Robert Penn Warren, *Meet Me in the Green Glen*—a novel by the American poet, writer of fiction, and literary critic; the principal character, a lawyer, responds negatively to the idea of identity with other selves; he protests against a world of people "who must mean something."

EVENTS

William Stanley Merwin, American poet and translator, receives the Pulitzer Prize in poetry for *The Carrier of Ladders* (1970).

Pablo Neruda (pseudonym of Neftali Ricardo Reyes Basualto; 1904-1973), Chilean poet and statesman, receives (while serving as ambassador to France) the Nobel Prize for literature.

The Catholic World, a monthly journal of miscellaneous literature founded at New York City in 1865 by Isaac Thomas Hecker, become a bimonthly and changes its name to *The New Catholic World.*

Lawrence Thompson, scholar and librarian at Princeton University, receives the Pulitzer

Prize in biography/autobiography for the second volume of his three-volume study of Robert Frost, *The Years of Triumph, 1915-1938* (1970).

Paul Zindel, American playwright, receives the Pulitzer Prize in drama for *The Effect of Gamma Rays on Man-in-the-Moon Marigolds* (1970).

1972

DEATHS

August Annist (b. 1899). Estonian scholar and literary critic; his literary labors may be placed into three distinct categories: aesthetics and literary theory, essays and articles on Estonian literature, and personal reminiscences; his work reveals him to be a humanist in the traditional sense of the term, acting without undue influence from Soviet politics.

Cecil Day-Lewis (b. 1904). English poet, translator, literary critic, and writer of fiction; his work is didactic, combining social concerns and leftist politics; he translated Virgil's *Aeneid* (1952) and wrote detective fiction under the pseudonym of Nicholas Blake; in 1967, he was appointed Poet Laureate of England.

Alfred Hutchinson (b. 1924). South African autobiographer, playwright, and writer of fiction; his work seems to have been overshadowed by his political activities and problems; he represents a score of black South African writers pursued and antagonized by the authorities; his literary endeavors express his grand lament for the African people; he lived in England for ten years, returned to Nigeria in 1971, and died there of a heart attack.

Yasunari Kawabata (b. 1899). Japanese writer of fiction; he has been described as a truly modern human being, and his fiction focuses upon the contemporary world; at the same time, however, he functioned as a cultural nationalist who sought to preserve the world of tradition in his fiction, lest those traditions vanish forever; in 1968, he became Japan's first Nobel Prize recipient in literature.

Jacques Maritain (b. 1882). French Catholic philosopher and essayist; his principal works focused upon Christian values and education; he also wrote on art, politics, and history.

Jon Mirande (b. 1925). French Basque poet and writer of fiction; his poetic prose, especially as it appears in his novels, brought new life to Basque literature; Basque literary critics considered his *Haur Besoetakoa* (The Godchild; 1970) one of the most significant novels in the history of that area's literature.

Henri de Montherlant (b. 1896). French writer of fiction and playwright; his novels glorify force and masculinity and reflect his decadent and egotistic personality; his drama exhibits his gift for caustic rhetoric and heroic intensity; an extreme political conservative, he consistently opposed modern French democracy.

Marianne Craig Moore (b. 1887). American poet; her verse tends to be witty, crisp, intellectual, and satirical; she stood as a thoroughly American and exclusively modern woman, demonstrating through her verse the possibility of a highly civilized and widely learned mind functioning with discrimination and unsentimental enjoyment; she proved that everything human could serve as material for poetry (including baseball).

Kenneth Patchen (b. 1911). American poet; his verse is the epitome of artistic energy, and he relied, for substance, upon the American experience that comes from the open air and the open road; his language tends to be free ranging, colloquial, and sarcastic.

Ezra Pound (b. 1885). American poet and one of the most influential and controversial figures in twentieth-century literature; he headed the imagist group before founding vorticism (those who sought to simplify artistic forms into machine-like angularity), encouraging such writers as T. S. Eliot and James Joyce; in 1925, he settled in Italy and began to formulate his fascist views; his verse tends to be both brilliant and obscure, weaving together a number of cultural threads in an attempt to reconstruct the history of Western civilization.

Cakkaravartti Rajakopalaccari (b. 1878). Indian writer of fiction and nonfiction; he wrote tracts on aspects of Hinduism, while his short fiction tends to focus upon didactic and social themes; he also rose to become a leading Indian political figure.

Jules Romains (pseudonym of Louis Farigoule; b. 1886). French writer of fiction, playwright, and poet; his work reflects his deep interest in parapsychology; his literary reputation primarily rests on his skill with the "roman fleuve," the novel of sequence; his twenty-seven volume *Les Hommes de Bonne Volonte*

(Men of Good Will; 1932-1947) offers a panorama of French society between 1910 and 1940.

Edmund Wilson (b. 1895). American critic; writer of fiction, and playwright; perhaps the foremost American social and literary critic of the twentieth century; he explored the social, psychological, and political conditions that shape literary ideas; these he filtered through his knowledge of Marxist and Freudian theories; his work reflects his far-ranging interests and concerns, and he wrote on such topics as symbolism, the European literary and revolutionary traditions, and the Great Depression.

Yukio Mishima (b. 1925). Japanese writer of fiction; his novels have achieved recognition because of their paradox and detailed characterization; he committed ritual suicide after haranguing the Japanese army for its powerlessness under the constitution.

PUBLICATIONS

Toni Cade Bambara, *Gorilla, My Love*—the first collection of short stories by the American writer of fiction; composed of realistic portraits of black life, focusing upon proud women and frustrated men.

John Barth, *Chimera*—a volume of short stories by the American fiction writer; the individual pieces achieve unity through the mythic image of the title: the character with a lion's head, a goat's body, and a serpent's tail; the work receives the National Book Award.

Robert Creeley, *A Day Book*—a collection of verse and prose by the American poet, playwright, and writer of fiction; the pieces in the volume tend, generally, to be lax and include considerable detail concerning the writer's daily life.

Franz Xavier Kroetz, *Wunschkonzert* (Request Concert)—a play by the German dramatist and writer of nonfiction; the piece lacks dialogue and conflict, as it depicts an evening in the life of a lonely woman; she maintains a precarious sense of order and purpose through her performance of such common actions as watching television, eating, and cleaning; she commits suicide, which is attributable only to the sterility of her existence.

John Montague, *The Rough Field*—a lengthy poem (eighty pages) by the American-born Irish writer of verse; a poetical analysis of the social and political conditions within Ireland, beginning with the English invasion of Northern Ireland in the seventeenth century; the work details the oppression and exploitation of Ireland, relying upon a variety of traditional and experimental poetic structures; the poet also integrates fragments of historical documents, newspaper accounts, local dialects, and graffiti into his verse narrative.

Sylvia Plath, *Winter Trees*—a collection of verse by the American poet; nearly all of the poems date from the last nine months of the writer's relatively brief life; the poems tend to be personal and confessional; she creates the triple roles of muse, mother, and poet, none of which she, herself, appears capable of filling.

Philip Roth, *The Breast*—a novel by the American writer of fiction; a man awakes to discover that he has become a woman's breast; a tragicomic, sexual-philosophical tale, much in the manner of Franz Kafka.

Olawale Rotimi, *Ovonramwen Nogbaisi*—a play by the Nigerian dramatist and scholar; the writer seeks to correct the distorted image of the maligned Oba chief of the title, who had been blamed for the crushing defeat by the British invading troops who destroyed the Benin empire in 1897.

Helga Schutz, *Vorgeschichten oder Schone Gegend Probstein*—a novel by the East German writer of fiction, her first; the central character has been sent to her grandparents, in Probstein, at the end of World War II; as a third member of the family, she can save them from having to give to the state a third of the pig that they raise; the town abounds in remarkable characters, all of whom seem to belong to a different world, to an idyllic state of enchantment.

Sam Shepard, *The Tooth of Crime*—a play by the American dramatist; a confrontation between a form of "superstar" who gathers to him the images of rock music, firearms, music, and automobiles, and a young man with a totally "new" style; the challenger will replace the older man, supported by the latter's own staff; thematically, the work focuses upon the issue of success, American style.

Alan Sillitoe, *Raw Material*—a novel by the English novelist and poet; semiautobiographical, the piece sets forth a vivid evocation of the writer's own family ancestry; concerns, also, working-class attitudes and reactions to World War I and the Depression that followed.

Lionel Trilling, *Sincerity and Authenticity*—a volume of literary criticism by the American critic, essayist, and academician; the writer focuses upon the notion of how sincerity, defined as being true to the self, came to occupy a place of supreme importance in the moral life; further, he considers how sincerity came to be replaced by the strenuous ideal of authenticity; the writer ranges over the entire sphere of Western world literature.

John Updike, *Museums and Women and Other Stories*—a collection by the American writer of fiction; contains twenty-nine short stories; slight, beautifully written sketches, with little external action; mundane experiences and quiet insights comprise the substance of the pieces; in the end, small losses diminish the existence of daily life.

Eudora Welty, *The Optimist's Daughter*—a novel by the American writer of fiction; focuses upon a daughter's struggle to come to terms with her father's death; the piece received the Pulitzer Prize in fiction for 1973.

EVENTS

John Betjeman, English writer of verse and miscellaneous prose, appointed Poet Laureate of England, succeeding Cecil Day-Lewis; held the post until his death in 1984.

Heinrich Theodor Boll, German writer of fiction, receives the Nobel Prize for literature.

The Center for Southern Folklore, a scholarly society for the study of Southern culture, founded at Memphis, Tennessee.

Clifford and Edith Irving plead guilty to conspiring to defraud McGraw-Hill Book Company, New York, by selling to it a falsified auto-biography of the American capitalist and industrialist Howard Robard Hughes.

The Oxford English Dictionary, Supplement Volume 1 (A-G) is published; the dictionary is based upon historical principles.

The Poe Studies Association founded, dedicated to promoting original scholarship on the American poet, critic, and writer of fiction.

Wallace Earle Stegner, American writer of fiction and nonfiction, receives the Pulitzer Prize in fiction for *Angle of Repose* (1971); the work was adapted as an opera in 1976.

Barbara Tuchman, American historian, receives the Pulitzer Prize in general nonfiction for *Stilwell and the American Experience in China, 1911-1945* (1972).

James Arlington Wright, American writer of verse, receives the Pulitzer Prize in poetry for his *Collected Poems* (1971).

The Yardbird Reader, an anthology of black writers, founded in California by Ishmael Scott Read.

1973

DEATHS

Conrad Potter Aiken (b. 1889). American poet, writer of fiction, and critic; his verse emphasizes the quest for self-knowledge and demonstrates a rich musical quality; he pointed out that it is the somber note "that gives the chord its power"; he received the Pulitzer Prize for poetry in 1930.

W. H. Auden (b. 1907). English-born poet and a major figure in twentieth-century English literature; Auden's finely crafted poems are praised for offering profound investigations of moral, political, and social issues. In 1939, he assumed residency in the United States, becoming an American citizen in 1946; he spent his last years living in England, Austria, Italy, and New York; in 1948, he received the Pulitzer Prize for poetry.

Arna Bontemps (b. 1903). American writer of fiction, essayist, and historian; his novel *God Sends Sunday* (1931) became the basis for the play *St. Louis Woman* (1946); another important piece, *Black Thunder* (1936), focused upon the tragic results of a slave uprising in 1800 at Richmond, Virginia, led by Gabriel Prosser.

Catherine Drinker Bowen (b. 1897). American biographer; her works are noted for their literary merit; the subjects of her pieces included Peter Ilyich Tchaikovsky, Anton and Nicholas Rubenstein, Oliver Wendell Holmes, John Adams, Sir Edward Coke, and Francis Bacon.

Elizabeth Bowen (b. 1900). Irish-born writer of fiction; her novels were highly complex psychological studies, revealing a decided debt to the fiction of Henry James; her descriptions of characters' moods and of specific places tend to be extremely delicate and sensitive.

Pearl Buck (b. 1892). American writer of fiction; her work generally captures her own experiences as a missionary in China, and she gained recognition for her vivid and compassionate novels of life in that country; she published over eighty-five volumes of fiction, children's books, biographies, and prose nonfiction; in 1932 she received the Pulitzer Prize for fiction and, in 1938, the Nobel Prize for literature.

Noel Coward (b. 1899). English playwright (as well as actor, director, producer, and composer of songs); he gained a literary reputation for his wit, sophistication, and unpretentiousness; his work has been characterized as representing the totality of "tolerance and decency."

Carlo Emilio Gadda (b. 1893). Italian writer of fiction; he developed a complex style that combined formal language, slang, dialect, deliberate misspellings, foreign words, and imitations of various prose styles; he wrote satire without becoming a moralist.

Taha Husayn (b. 1889). Egyptian prose writer; he produced numerous critical studies, three volumes of autobiography, short narratives, historical and educational pieces, and social and political essays; the initial volume of his autobiography became the first modern literary work by an Egyptian to attract attention outside the Arab world; throughout his work, he tended to express deep-felt compassion for the underprivileged.

William Inge (b. 1910). American playwright; he wrote realistic dramatic pieces, generally focusing upon small-town life in the American Midwest; his plays gained strength through his development of characters who unknowingly achieve self-revelation; he received the Pulitzer Prize for drama in 1953; his death (on 10 June) suspected as suicide.

Gabriel Marcel (b. 1897). French philosopher; a Roman Catholic existentialist in the manner of Soren Kierkegaard and Karl Jaspers, he repudiated abstraction, generalization, and categorization; instead, he advocated individual authenticity, viewing being as a concept that cannot be analyzed; experience cannot be conceived, but must be lived and explored.

Jacques Maritain (b. 1882). French Roman Catholic philosopher and essayist; his most highly acclaimed and widely read works focused upon Christian values as they applied both to history and to education.

Vilhelm Moberg (b. 1898). Swedish writer of fiction; his work focuses upon rural life; he also devoted his attention to such themes as Swedish emigration to the United States and antitotalitarianism.

Pablo Neruda (pseudonym of Neftali Ricardo Reyes Basualto; b. 1904). Chilean poet (as well as diplomat and communist leader); he achieved recognition through his highly personal verse, evocative pieces with abundant notes of grief and despair; he celebrated the grandeur of the dramatic Chilean landscape and raged against the exploitation of the Indians; his later verse tended to be highly surrealistic; in 1971, he received the Nobel Prize for literature, while serving as his nation's ambassador to France.

Kemal Tahir (b. 1910). Turkish writer of fiction; he trained as a naval officer and, in 1939, received a lengthy sentence in the Cankiri prison for political activities; there he began his literary career; his fiction analyzed the customs and the traditions of Turkish peasant life; he also considered historical subjects for novels, and those proved important contributions to Anatolian literature.

John Ronald Reuel Tolkien (b. 1892). South African-born English writer of fiction, poet, and literary scholar; as an Oxford University professor, he emerged as one of the principal philologists of his time; interest in the medieval romance led him to compose epic fantasies and romances which, during the 1960s and 1970s, established him as a cult hero among the youth of the Western world; he gave to the young an avenue of escape from their disillusionment with war and the threats from contemporary technology; he also produced major prose tracts on Old English and Middle English languages and literature, including studies of the Beowulf poet, Geoffrey Chaucer, and Sir Thomas Malory.

PUBLICATIONS

Brian Aldiss, *Frankenstein Unbound*—a work of fiction by the English writer of fantasy and critic; the "novel" sets out to show that Mary Shelley's *Frankenstein* was the first novel to combine romantic and scientific interests.

Kingsley Amis, *The Riverside Villas Murder*—a novel by the English writer of fiction and poet; essentially an attempt to reconstruct the "classic" detective story.

Arnold Apple, *Son of Guyana*—an autobiography by the Guyanese writer that focuses upon the writer's precarious childhood, his search for education, and his attempts to escape the poverty of his homeland; the writer includes his emigration to England, by way of Genoa and Calais, to begin a new life; he eventually returned to Guyana.

Robert Bly, *Sleepers Joining Hands*— a collection of prose and verse by the American poet; the pieces underscore the writer's notion that society has returned to a matriarchal structure; sensuousness of thought and synthetic reason appear to be replacing the patriarchal emphasis on rationality and analytical thought; contains such poems as "The Teeth Mother Naked at Last" and the Swedenborgian influenced essay "I Come Out of the Mother Naked."

Brigid Brophy, *Prancing Novelist*—a critical biography by the English writer of fiction and miscellaneous prose; concerns the life and work of the English novelist Arthur Annesley Ronald Firbank (1886-1926).

William S. Burroughs, *Exterminator!*—a novel by the American writer of fiction; an extremely experimental piece, the work appears as a mosaic; it includes such elements as espionage, science fiction, fantasy, war, racism, corporate capitalism, drug addiction, and various medical and psychiatric horrors.

Truman Capote, *The Dogs Bark: Public People and Private Places*—a prose miscellany by the American writer of fiction, playwright, and essayist; contains essays, observations, travel pieces, and profiles of notable persons; the writer's style and commentary, as usual, prove subtle, but also sharp and fascinating.

J. P. Donleavy, *A Fairy Tale of New York*—a novel by the American-born Irish writer of fiction and playwright; concerns the brutality and spiritual emptiness of New York City which cause the principal character to feel powerless and depressed; emigration appears as his only form of liberation, but he lacks the money to leave.

Mavis Gallant, *The Pegnitz Junction*—a novella by the Canadian writer of fiction; the writer moves beyond ordinary mental connections into psychic areas where both conversation and recollection have been replaced by strange telepathic awarenesses; incidents and the means by which the visible and audible worlds cut away from the inner world, and then return, remind one of the cutting room of a film company (with which the writer had extensive experience).

Graham Greene, *The Honorary Counsel*—a novel by the English writer of fiction; the principal character, a British derelict, finds himself in Argentina; there, he attempts to maintain at least the appearance of order throughout a period of terrorist activities.

Witi Ihimaera, *Tangi*—a novel by the New Zealand writer of fiction and essayist; the first full-length work of fiction published in English by a Maori writer; concerns the death of a father and its effect on his son, a Maori educated by the "pakeha" society; the narrative alternates between past and present and explores the son's thoughts as he moves between the industrial society and his rural birthplace; in the end, he learns to affirm life in the presence of death and to understand his spiritual inheritance of Maori customs and ideologies.

Marion Patrick Jones, *Pan Beat*—the first novel by the Trinidadian writer of fiction; set in Trinidad in the mid-1960s, the work captures the growing crisis of racial and national identity; the writer relies heavily upon cultural symbolism: the steel band and the pan and fete culture remain fixed within the historical formation and direction of Trinidad and Tabago.

Donald Justice, *Departures*—a collection of verse by the American poet; in these pieces, the writer moves toward what has been termed "a phenomenology of absence"; in that state, the self supposedly dissolves into its various perceptions and intuitions.

Thomas Kinsella, *The Good Fight*—a poem by the Irish writer of verse; an occasional piece for the tenth anniversary of the death of President John F. Kennedy.

Robert Lowell, *The Dolphin*—a sonnet sequence by the American poet; principally concerns the writer's attachment and eventual marriage to the English writer Caroline Blackwood; published simultaneously with two other volumes, *History* and *For Lizzie and Harriet*.

Kamal Markandaya, *Two Virgins*—a novel by the Indian writer of fiction; a clash of values underlies a young girl's maturation into adulthood; the principal character's awareness of the human body grows slowly as she observes her surroundings and listens to older friends talk about matters outside her own sphere of understanding; the process of sexual knowledge goes on "subterraneously"; once she comes to terms with her own sexuality, the girl grasps the mystery of the human body; in addition, her "internal metamorphosis" parallels her understanding of the rapidly changing world around her.

Mervyn Morris, *The Pond*—a collection of verse by the Jamaican poet and critic; the title piece reflects the writer's search into the self; he comes to realize the meanings "beneath the surface," a state that parallels his religious convictions; the collection published both at London and Port of Spain.

Toni Morrison, *Sula*—a novel by the American writer of fiction and poet; focuses upon two women, whose lives take sharply divergent paths; in the end, they reaffirm the bonds of friendship; the piece brings together in the same fictional environment the qualities of love and outrage.

Iris Murdoch, *The Black Prince*—a novel by the Irish-born writer of fiction; described as a type of psychological "whodunit"; the plot of the work concerns an older man's love for a younger woman, followed by a murder; narrated in the first-person, from the male point of view.

Joyce Carol Oates, *Do With Me What You Will*—a novel by the American writer of fiction; a drama that concerns social and personal morality as they relate to the issues of marriage, infidelity, and liberation.

Thomas Pynchon, *Gravity's Rainbow*—a novel by the American writer of fiction; concerns a highly complex and allusive metaphysical quest; the work tends to be almost totally surrealistic, and compulsively elaborate; at the same time it has been described, variously, as silly, obscene, funny, tragic, pastoral, historical, philosophical, poetic, and even dense and dull.

Philip Roth, *The Great American Novel*—a novel by the American writer of fiction; the principal character, Word Smith, the 1959 rookie of the year, narrates a hilarious account of the most inept team in the history of baseball; the political parallels appear most obvious, and thus the piece may easily be characterized as a burlesque work of fiction.

Gore Vidal, *Burr*—a novel by the American writer of fiction and miscellaneous prose; a historical piece that concerns the man who shot Alexander Hamilton; Book I of the five-volume historical fiction series, *The American Chronicle*.

Kurt Vonnegut, Jr., *Breakfast of Champions; or, Goodbye Blue Monday!*—a novel by the American writer of fiction; the author grants unconditional liberty to the literary characters of his previous novels; the entire work

represents the writer's fiftieth-birthday present to himself; the work has been described as a "minutely ordered representation of cosmic chaos."

Derek Walcott, *Another Life*—a volume of verse by the West Indian (St. Lucia) poet and playwright; the work runs to four thousand lines; represents the poet's turbulent meditation on the dilemmas of his time; essentially an autobiographical narrative, the poet's lyrical record of self-assessment.

Alice Walker, *In Love and Trouble*—a collection of short stories by the American writer of fiction and poet; the volume contains thirteen stories about the problems of black women.

Thornton Wilder, *Theophilus North*—a novel by the American writer of fiction and playwright; concerns life among the American wealthy and their servants; set in Newport, Rhode Island, in the 1920s, it presents an extremely entertaining account of American life in a bygone era.

EVENTS

Maxine Winokur Kumin American writer of fiction, poet, and essayist, receives the Pulitzer Prize in poetry for *Up Country: Poems of New England* (1972).

Jason Miller American playwright and actor, receives the Pulitzer Prize in drama for *The Champion Season* (1972).

The USSR agrees to abide by the terms of the Universal Copyright Convention.

Eudora Welty American writer of fiction, receives the Pulitzer Prize in fiction for her novel *The Optimist's Daughter* (1972).

Patrick White (pseudonym of Victor Martindale; b. 1912), Australian writer of fiction, receives the Nobel Prize for literature.

1974

DEATHS

Miguel Angel Asturius (b. 1899). Guatemalan writer of fiction and poet; his novels consider such subjects as dictatorship and worker exploitation in the Caribbean; in 1967, he received the Nobel Prize for literature.

Edmund Charles Blunden (b. 1896). English poet, scholar, and critic; in 1966, he was appointed as professor of poetry at Oxford; memories of his experiences in the trenches during World War I and his guilt at having survived when so many died proved dominant themes in his verse; he combined natural imagery with his own moods and attitudes; his critical and editorial work remain his principal contributions to English literary scholarship.

Marieluise Fleisser (b. 1901). German (Bavarian) playwright; she studied at Munich, where she met the novelist Lion Feuchtwanger and Bertolt Brecht, who staged her plays; early in 1930, she returned to her home town of Ingolstadt, where she married a local tobacconist and suffered nervous breakdowns and temporary losses of memory; her dramas remained obscure until the 1960s, when a group of young writers and filmmakers discovered her work.

David Michael Jones (b. 1895). English poet; his work was influenced by his Welsh ancestry and his experiences in the trenches during World War I; an artist, he attempted to combine his work as an engraver, water color painter, and sketcher with his verse; his most important works focused on war.

Erich Kastner (b. 1899). German writer of fiction, poet, playwright, and author of children's books; his most important literary contribution was his satirical verse; thus, his work has achieved recognition for his irreverent sense of humor, which he employed in recording the horrors of his times; as a moralist, he became one of the most significant writers of children's books in the twentieth century.

Par Fabian Lagerkvist (b. 1891). Swedish writer of fiction, playwright, and poet; his work reflected his concern with the struggle between good and evil, as well as with the search for God; in 1951, he received the Nobel Prize for literature.

St. John Perse (pseudonym of Marie Rene August Alexis Saint Leger Leger; b. 1887). French poet; his verse reflects his perception of humanity as universally subject to alienation; although he focused upon the general theme of despair, he accepted both the positive and negative elements of human existence; he wrote in free verse style, with heavily cadenced, incantatory rhythms; his work reflects the influence of the Old Testament, Paul Claudel, and Walt Whitman; in 1960, he received the Nobel Prize for literature.

John Crowe Ransom (b. 1888). American poet and critic; he wrote elegant and highly impersonal verse, placing considerable emphasis upon style; between 1914 and 1937, he taught at Vanderbilt University, where he helped to establish the periodical *The Fugitive* (1922-1925); at Kenyon College (1937-1958), he founded the influential journal *The Kenyon Review;* he became one of the early proponents of the "new criticism" in literature.

Erich M. Roach (b. 1915). Trinidadian poet, playwright, and critic; his lyrical verse represented the West Indian's tragic sense of displacement; his pieces also reflected his own claustrophobic feeling of being entrapped on the islands, a feeling that biographers and critics believe caused his death.

Anne Harvey Sexton (b. 1928). American poet; she wrote lyrical, ironic, and highly confessional verse that has been praised for its imagery; she underscored the life of the imagination and dealt with religious themes; she committed suicide at age forty-six.

PUBLICATIONS

Fleur Adcock, *The Scenic Route*—a volume of verse by the New Zealand-born English poet and translator; the collection includes poems that focus on an intimate personal realm, as well as observations drawn from the poet's travels through England, Ireland, and Nepal; the poet addresses her connection with New Zealand, the land of her birth and childhood.

Kingsley Amis, *Ending Up*—a novel by the English writer of fiction and poet; a satirical comedy about old age; yet, the point of view tends to be terribly savage.

Maya Angelou, *Gather Together in My Name*—an autobiographical piece by the American writer of narrative, playwright, and poet; the work recounts the writer's life from age sixteen to nineteen, recording her struggles to raise her son and to assume responsibility for her own life.

James Baldwin, *If Beale Street Could Talk*—a novel by the American writer of fiction, essayist, and playwright; a black artist finds himself unjustly imprisoned in the notorious "Tombs" of New York City; then unfolds a moving and painful story, obviously real and vividly personal, yet timeless, as well.

Samuel Beckett, *Not I*—a short play by the Irish-born dramatist, poet, and writer of fiction; a brief, disembodied monologue delivered by an actor whose sex cannot be determined; only the mouth of that person appears.

John Betjeman, *A Nip in the Air*—a collection of verse by the English poet; the poet demonstrates his skill in blank verse, notably in the valediction "On Leaving Wantage," written in 1972; his first major collection following his appointment (1972) as Poet Laureate of England.

Anthony Burgess, *The Clockwork Testament*—a novel by the English writer of fiction; the final volume of the "Enderby" trilogy; traces the amorous, literary, and digestive misfortunes of the principal character (as well as certain of his triumphs) while in England, Rome, Tangiers, and New York City; includes ample satiric social commentary.

Alejo Carpentier, *El Recurso del Metodo*—a novel by the Cuban writer of fiction, poet, and critic; an obvious play on Rene Descartes's *Discours de la Methode;* the work is set in a Mexican-type republic during the period 1912-1927, but the writer incorporates events that occurred throughout Latin America during that time; generally, the novel represents the writer's deep interest in the history of this area.

Chantal Chawaf, *Retable, Reverie*—a two-part novel by the French writer of fiction; the initial section recounts the attempt of a daughter to recreate her mother, who was killed by an explosion as she gave birth to her child during World War II; the writer then describes, solely from the female point of view, the passionate encounter of a man and a woman; the style appears distorted, entangled, and exceedingly intricate.

Graham Greene, *Lord Rochester's Monkey, Being the Life of John Wilmot, Earl of Rochester*—a biography by the English writer of fiction; written in the 1930s, the typescript was stored in the library of the University of Texas before the writer resurrected and revised it; the biographer surveys in depth the social and literary background of the Restoration period.

Zbigniew Herbert, *Pan Cogito*—a series of poems by the Polish writer of verse, essayist, and playwright; the writer follows the exploits of a Mr. Cogito, a tragicomic character in search of moral certainties; he meditates on history, on his personal past, and then contemplates such subjects as hell, nature, magic, and ethics.

Edvard Hoem, *The Ferry Crossing*—a novel by the Norwegian writer of fiction and poet; focuses upon the problems of a small island community threatened with forced depopulation because the Labor government cannot maintain it; there comes forth a compelling world that mirrors all of Norwegian society; the piece anticipates, by nearly a decade, the strong trend toward "metafiction" in Norwegian literature; the work receives the Norwegian Literary Critic Prize and, in 1988, the American Scandinavian Foundation award for the best translation of the year.

David Jones, *The Sleeping Lord and Other Fragments*—a collection of fiction by the English prose-poet; the writer examines Welsh life and lore in such pieces as "The Hunt," "The Sleeping Lord," and "The Tutelar of the Place"; other stories in the volume demonstrate the similarities between the last days of the Roman Empire and the decay of twentieth-century political order and society.

Philip Larkin, *High Windows*—a collection of verse by the English poet and writer of fiction; the pieces reveal a preoccupation with death and transience; the poet adapts contemporary speech rhythms and vocabulary to an unobtrusive metrical elegance; includes such works as "The Old Fools," "Annus Mirabilis," and "Posterity."

John Le Carre, *Tinker, Tailor, Soldier, Spy*—a novel by the English writer of adventure and spy fiction; the writer's permanent spy-hero, George Smiley, involves himself in a complex study of betrayal within the heart of the British intelligence network.

Doris Lessing, *The Memoirs of a Survivor*—a novel by the Persian-born, Rhodesian-raised English writer of fiction; the piece conveys visions of a grim and anarchic near future; the work is set in a city where rats and roving gangs terrorize the streets; the writer blends visionary and realistic writing.

James A. Michener, *Centennial*—a novel by the American writer of popular fiction; the work develops the history of the United States, from its prehistoric geological beginnings to the present time.

Elsa Morante, *La Storia* (History: A Novel)—a work of fiction by the Italian novelist and writer of short fiction; the writer realistically depicts the personal suffering within Italy during World War II; focuses upon a lonely, half-Jewish peasant woman, her two sons, a small band of Resistance fighters, and their ghetto environment; portrays the violent and relentless effects of history upon the lives of common people.

Iris Murdoch, *The Sacred and Profane Love Machine*—a novel by the Irish-born English writer of fiction; a man must choose between his wife and his mistress; described as "a whirlwind of deepening surprise" that provokes the intellect and opens the heart.

Vladimir Nabokov, *Look at the Harlequins!*—a novel by the Russian writer of fiction, playwright, and critic; parts of the work function as allegories of the writer's life as an artist; he recapitulates his principal themes of alienation and mortality.

Ishmael Scott Reed, *The Last Days of Louisiana Red*—a novel by the American writer of fiction and poet; set in Berkeley, California, during the 1960s; essentially, the work exists as an attack upon what the writer terms "moocherism": the mode of persons who manipulate the system for their own selfish gains, who ask you to share when they, themselves, have nothing to offer in return.

Augusto Roa Bastos, *Yo, el Supremo* (I, the Supreme)—a novel by the Paraguayan writer of fiction, poet, and critic; a dense, multilayered piece that depicts the evils of despotism; the writer becomes the "Compiler," a character who must gather various government documents to present a panoramic account of nineteenth-century Paraguay under the regime of Dr. Jose Gaspar Rodriquez de Francia ("El Supremo").

Philip Roth, *My Life As a Man*—a novel by the American writer of fiction; a spirited account of a young writer's attempts to free himself from a woman who, simply, will not let him go.

Oluwole Soyinka, *The Metamorphosis of Brother Jero*—a play by the Nigerian dramatist, poet, essayist, and writer of fiction; the work derives its humor from a sardonic attack on right-wing military regimes; the writer denounces the succession of military supported governments that have appeared in Nigeria (as well as in other African nations).

Muriel Spark, *The Abyss of Crew*—a novel by the Scottish-born writer of fiction, poet, and playwright; a satire upon the Watergate scandal in the United States; although primarily the story of a nun who schemes to gain election as abbess of her convent.

Tomas Transtromer, *Ostersjaor* (Baltics)—a volume of verse by the Swedish poet, translator, and critic; the writer relies heavily upon nature imagery and authentic evocations of past ages; he reflects upon family traditions and legacies through the interjection of history, locale, memory, and social history into poems characterized by loose structures and rhythms.

John Wain, *Samuel Johnson*—a biographical and critical study by the English writer of fiction, poetry, and miscellaneous prose; emphasizes the laborious literary activities of the subject, particularly his *Dictionary* and the mature works of the later period; the periods of personal conflict and joy come forth with clear critical balance; the writer demonstrates particular interest in his subject's commitment to the city of London; in the end, the biographer attempts to establish the importance of Samuel Johnson to the intellectual life of England in the eighteenth century.

EVENTS

Eyvind Johnson, Swedish writer of fiction, and Harry Martinson, Swedish poet and writer of fiction, share the Nobel Prize for literature.

Robert Lowell, Jr., American poet, receives the Pulitzer Prize in poetry for *The Dolphin* (1973).

The Nathaniel Hawthorne Society founded for the advancement of scholarship relative to the American writer and his times.

The National Book Critics Circle, comprised of approximately three hundred American editors and critical commentators, established; the group will select, annually, the most "distinguished" books of American fiction, poetry, literary criticism, and prose non-fiction from the preceding year.

Pulitzer Prize in fiction and drama not awarded this year.

Louis Sheaffer, American scholar and biographer, receives the Pulitzer Prize in biography/autobiography for *O'Neill, Son and Artist* (1973), the second volume of his biography of the American playwright.

Aleksandr Isayevich Solzhenitsyn, Russian writer of fiction, loses his Soviet citizenship; arrested and deported to West Germany, he settles in Switzerland, where he will remain for two years before moving to the United States.

1975

DEATHS

Ivo Andric (b. 1892). Yugoslav poet, essayist, and writer of fiction; he gained literary recognition for his epic novels; his themes focus upon the isolation of the human being and the human feeling of insignificance in the face of the panorama of history; his fiction is usually set in Bosnia during the period of Turkish dominance; he received the Nobel Prize for literature in 1961.

Gunar Gunnarsson (b. 1889). Icelandic writer of fiction; his early works, in Danish, helped to generate an interest in Icelandic culture among Europeans; his five-volume *The Church on the Mountain* (1923-1928) concerns rural life in Iceland and demonstrates the writer's rich imagination and poetic skill.

Sir Julian Sorell Huxley (b. 1887). English essayist, poet, and biologist; his verse reflects his respect of and commitment to the natural world; he also manifested that interest in popular essays on animal biology and the science of life; in 1908, he received the Newdigate Prize for poetry.

Erico Lopes Verissimo (b. 1905). Brazilian writer of fiction and literary critic; his novels appeared regularly between 1935 and 1962, and he published, in 1945, his lectures on Brazilian literature; he served for three years (1953-1956) as director of the Department of Cultural Affairs of the Pan American Union.

Pier Paolo Pasolini (b. 1922). Italian novelist, poet, and film director; a confirmed Marxist, he dedicated his works to an exploration of the religious and social consciousness; in his fierce rejection of bourgeois values, he has been compared with such writers as Gunter Grass, but at the same time he held firmly to his interest in Christian principles.

Arnold Joseph Toynbee (b. 1889). English historian and essayist; he expounded upon the problems of history in terms of significant cultural groups and civilizations, rather than emphasizing nationalities; for him, the well being of a civilization depended upon its ability to respond successfully to human and environmental challenges; he identified twenty-six civilizations in history.

Lionel Trilling (b. 1905). American literary and intellectual critic and academician; he wrote upon such subjects as the liberal imagination and the opposing self, combining social, psychological, and political insights with literary criticism and scholarship; he also wrote fiction and biographical analysis.

Thornton Niven Wilder (b. 1897). American playwright and writer of fiction; his works reflect his notion that meaning and beauty can be discovered in ordinary experiences; he tended to be a serious and highly original playwright, employing nonrealistic theatrical techniques; he received the Pulitzer Prize for fiction in 1928, as well as that award for drama in 1938 and 1943.

PUBLICATIONS

Donald Barthelme, *The Dead Father*—a novel by the American writer of fiction; a gruesome tale in which nineteen children drag the body of their father across a city to his death.

Saul Bellow, *Humboldt's Gift*—a novel by the American writer of fiction; a gifted but troubled writer finds himself torn apart by the conflicting demands of artistic purity and commercial success; the American poet Delmore Schwartz supposedly served as the writer's model.

Jorge Luis Borges, *El Libro de Arena* (The Book of Sand)—a collection of short stories by the Argentinian writer of fiction, essayist, poet, translator, and biographer; the pieces generally reflect the writer's interest in the fantastic; thus, in "The Congress," a world organization attempts to incorporate all of the views and ideologies of humanity by obtaining thousands of books; realizing the task to be arbitrary and conjectural, the Congress then recognizes the need to reject limiting, predominating world views and so destroys the books; periodically, the body concludes, "the library of Alexandria must be burned down."

Andree Chedid, *Fraternite de la Parole*—a collection of verse by the Egyptian-born French writer of fiction, poet, playwright, and essayist; the volume represents the writer's principal poetical concerns: rebirth, her strong reactions to violence and destruction, pleas for recognition of the positive qualities of life; includes meditations upon humanity, nature, love, and art; the volume receives the Prix de l'Academie Mallarme.

Michael Crichton, *The Great Train Robbery*—a novel by the American writer of fiction; an extremely accurate recreation of one of the most famous crimes of Victorian England (c. 1854-1855); the writer also focuses upon and analyzes the society that gave rise to the robbery; the piece was transformed into a motion picture.

E. L. Doctorow, *Ragtime*—a novel by the American writer of fiction; essentially a collage of turn-of-the-century America, with guest appearances by noted historical personages (J. P. Morgan and Evelyn Nesbitt are but two examples).

J. P. Donleavy, *The Unexpurgated Code: A Complete Manual of Survival and Manners*—a work of prose by the American-born Irish writer of fiction and nonfiction and playwright; the volume purports to be a guide for those who have suddenly gained wealth and have no idea how to display or demonstrate it.

Max Frisch, *Montauk*—a novel by the Swiss writer of fiction, playwright, and diarist; a fictionalized account of an actual weekend spent by the writer on Long Island, New York, with an amorous young admirer; beneath the details of the occasion, however, lies a thesis on the nature of identity.

Reyner Heppenstall, *Reflections on the Newgate Calendar*—a historical study and analysis by the English novelist, poet, and literary critic; the writer examines English criminal history during the eighteenth century and the first three decades of the nineteenth; the question to be solved concerns the hanging of so many persons for so little cause (particularly smugglers, highwaymen, parricides, and hungry peasants).

Denise Levertov, *The Freeing of the Dust*—a collection of verse by the English-born American poet; the pieces generally focus upon personal themes and demonstrate clear and simple emotions.

Primo Levi, *Il Sistema Periodico* (The Periodic Table)—a collection of short stories by the Italian writer of fiction, poet, and essayist; described as a combination memoir and "chemico-metaphysical lark" and a triumph of the writer's own eccentricity; these twenty-one largely autobiographical stories mirror the historical events of the writer's generation: fascism, resistance to dictatorship, the years following World War II, the people who died, and the people who kept on working; each story bears, as its title, the name of a chemical element.

William McIlvanney, *Docherty*—a novel by the Scottish writer of fiction and poet; the writer examines the differences between two generations of a Scottish mining family at the beginning of the twentieth century; he details the resignation and the hopelessness of life in a Scottish mining town; the family of the title strives unsuccessfully to approach life with sensitivity and intelligence in an environment of hardship and brutality.

Josue Montello, *Os Tambores de Sao Luis*—a novel by the Brazilian writer of fiction; set in the writer's home state of Maranhao, the work recounts the story of a former slave, from his childhood in a backwoods haven for runaway blacks in the 1840s through his return to bondage and his release to study for the priesthood; the writer examines the hardships and racial injustices experienced by his character as a teacher, journalist, abolitionist leader, and (finally) respected civil rights advocate in the Sao Luis of the early twentieth century; structured as a reminiscence, with the character as an old man looking back upon his life during a twenty-four-hour period while awaiting the birth of a great-grandchild.

Iris Murdoch, *A Word Child*—a novel by the Irish-born English writer of fiction; the principal character nurses his guilt and disappointment while engaged in a dull civil service job; he discovers that a man he hurt and betrayed has become his superior.

Joyce Carol Oates, *The Assassins*—a novel by the American writer of fiction and essayist; a shockingly intimate account of a political murder and its aftermath.

Harold Pinter, *No Man's Land*—a play by the English dramatist; all four of the characters inhabit a no-man's land between time present and time remembered, between reality and imagination; within that territory, the playwright conducts his explorations with wit, aggression, and "anarchic sexuality."

Anthony Powell, *Hearing Secret Harmonies*—a novel by the English writer of fiction, the final work in the series *A Dance to the Music of Time;* the piece is set in Britain during the 1960s, a period that appears to have dampened the courage of all of the principal "Old Guard" characters of the series; however, the egregious and ambitious Widmerpool has managed to attach himself to a counterculture hero by the name of Scorpio Murtlock.

Judith Rossner, *Looking for Mr. Goodbar*—a novel by the American writer of fiction; focuses upon a young school teacher who flirts with danger while cruising the singles' bars of New York City.

Sheik M. Sadeek, *Song of the Sugar Canes*—a novel by the Guyanese writer of fiction and playwright; the events of the piece occur during the period 1917-1953, beginning with the last immigrant ship bringing East Indians to Guyana and ending with the British suspending the Constitution of that land.

John Updike, *A Month of Sundays*—a novel by the American writer of fiction, poet, playwright, and essayist; the central character, the Reverend Tom Marshfield, engages in indiscreet behavior with the women of his parish; the pastor comes forth as literate, charming, serious, and totally outrageous.

Vladimir Voinovich, *Zhizn' i Neobychainye Prikliucheniia Soldata Ivana Chonkina* (The Life and Extraordinary Adventures of Private Ivan Chonkin)—a novel by the Russian writer of fiction, essayist, poet, and playwright, published originally in Paris; set during World War II, the piece focuses upon the title character as an amiable bumbler who resists authority and pursues, innocently enough, his personal pleasures; he has been ordered to guard a crashed airplane near a remote collective farm; however, the bureaucracy forgets about him, and he becomes involved with the locals; after a series of comic mishaps, he is charged with treason for arresting a group of secret police, who he had mistaken for Germans; beneath all of the comedy, however, lies the reality of a powerful police state at work, ready and willing to haunt the lives of ordinary people.

Robert Penn Warren, *Or Else: Poem*—a collection of verse by the American writer of fiction, poet, and essayist; a searching, compassionate exploration of experience and memory.

———————— , ***Democracy and Poetry*—**a critical essay by the American poet and writer of fiction; an analysis of American literature as a tradition with historical continuity; the writer views the moral sense of the private self as besieged, isolated, and endangered by the process of historical change; only personal values can withstand the vicissitudes of history.

EVENTS

Edward Franklin Albee III (b. 1928), American playwright, receives the Pulitzer Prize in drama for his two-act play, *Seascape* (1975).

Annie Dillard (b. 1945), American essayist and poet, receives the Pulitzer Prize in nonfiction for *Pilgrim at Tinker Creek* (1974).

Eugenio Montale (1896-1981), Italian poet and critical essayist, receives the Nobel Prize for literature.

Michael Joseph Shaara, Jr. (1929-1988), American writer of fiction and academician, receives the Pulitzer Prize in fiction for his historical novel, *The Killer Angels* (1974).

Gary Sherman Snyder (b. 1930), American poet and essayist, receives the Pulitzer Prize in poetry for his volume of verse and prose, *Turtle Island* (1974).

1976

DEATHS

Dame Agatha Christie (b. 1891). English writer of detective fiction; she wrote more than seventy-five mysteries, the majority of which featured one or the other of her two major detective creations, Jane Marple and Hercule Poirot; she also wrote a highly successful and long running mystery play, *Mousetrap* (1952).

Martin Heidegger (b. 1889). German philosopher and essayist; he succeeded his mentor, Edmund Husserl (1859-1938), as professor of philosophy at Freiburg, and then came under the influence of Soren Kierkegaard, Friedrich Nietzsche, and Wilhelm Dilthey; he analyzed the concepts of care, mood, and the individual's relationship with death, relating authenticity of being and the anguish of modern society with the individual's confrontation with his or her own temporality; he became regarded as a founder of twentieth-century existentialism and influenced the work of Jean-Paul Sartre; his later studies ranged over such topics as poetry and dehumanization within modern society.

Eyvind Johnson (b. 1900). Swedish writer of fiction; he gained recognition for his cycle of four autobiographical novels *The Novel about Olaf* (1934-1937), noted for its overall psychological penetration; in 1974, he shared the Nobel Prize for literature with his fellow Swede, Harry Martinson.

Pierre Jean Jouve (b. 1887). French poet, novelist, essayist, and playwright; he achieved his greatest recognition for his later verse, in which he integrated Christian and Freudian beliefs; his work in general reflects his knowledge and appreciation of international music and literature; his style evolved from free verse to fragmented and abstract techniques through which he examined religious and psychological concerns; his difficult and obscure style has hindered accurate translation of his verse.

Alexander Lernet-Holenia (b. 1897). Austrian writer of fiction; born into a military family, he underwent grim experiences during World War I, which find their way into his fiction; his prose style is highly lyrical.

Andre Malraux (b. 1901). French writer of fiction, historical and literary essayist, and statesman; his social novels claim, as their source, the writer's experiences in the civil wars in China (1925-1927) and Spain (1936-1939); an intellectual with a broad knowledge of archaeology, art history, and anthropology, he wrote tracts on art and civilization; during the presidency of Charles De Gaulle, he served as minister of information (1945) and minister of cultural affairs (1958-1968).

James Phillip McAuley (b. 1917). Australian poet and critic; he relied on classical forms and techniques in an attempt to achieve clarity and precise meaning; thus, he has been compared with John Dryden, Alexander Pope, and Jonathan Swift; however, he transferred his efforts from satirical lyrics to meditative verse following his conversion to Roman Catholicism; symbols from Christian and Greek myth help him to explore universal social and spiritual values.

Paul Morand (b. 1888). French writer of fiction and travel narrative, essayist, and poet; his most popular work reflected the years between the world wars; he combined the specifics of the cosmopolitan atmosphere and energetic social life with psychological portraits of disillusioned characters; his prose style achieved a high quality through witty and fast-paced description, underscored by rich imagery; in 1968 he gained election to the Academie Francaise.

Samuel Eliot Morison (b. 1887). American historian; he taught at Harvard University from 1915 to 1955, becoming the official historian of that institution in 1926; he wrote a history of U.S. naval operations during World War II, as well as a major general history of the United States; his biographical studies include volumes on Christopher Columbus and John Paul Jones; he received Pulitzer Prizes in 1943 and 1960.

Vladimir Vladimirovich Nabokov (b. 1899). Russian writer of fiction, poet, essayist, playwright, translator, and autobiographer; he wrote both in Russian and English, gaining considerable reputation as a prose stylist; in his fiction, particularly, he investigated the illusory nature of reality and the artist's relationship with his "craft"; for him, the imagination remained primary, more important than moral or social considerations; words, for him, stood as significant objects unto themselves, and so he relied upon wordplays, acrostics, and multilingual puns to create complex, labyrinthine narratives.

Raymond Queneau (b. 1903). French writer of fiction and travel narrative, poet, playwright, and essayist; he introduced contemporary French vernacular into the written language in an attempt to reduce the influence of seventeenth-century bourgeois literary formalism; thus, he sought to modernize French prose and to cleanse it of "its various rusts"; he also parodied traditional literary forms and devices by phonetically spelling words, phrases, and sentences to reflect their contemporary usage and pronunciation; James Joyce proved to be one of his principal influences.

William Sansom (b. 1926). English writer of fiction and travel narrative; his fiction reflects the variety of his experiences, both practical and intellectual, during a lifetime spent in London; in addition, Germany, Scandinavia and the Mediterranean serve as important backdrops for his prose fiction.

PUBLICATIONS

Renata Adler, *Speedboat*—the first novel by the American writer of fiction and essayist; a short, episodic piece in which a New York City journalist takes stock of her values and experiences; the work receives the 1976 Ernest Hemingway Award for the best first novel of the year.

Maya Angelou, *Singin' and Swingin' and Gettin' Merry Like Christmas*—an autobiographical account by the American poet and writer of miscellaneous prose; the narrative displays the writer's courage, wit, talent, and charm as she describes in detail her entrance into the world of show business; the third in her autobiographical series.

James Baldwin, *The Devil Finds Work*—an essay by the American writer of fiction and miscellaneous prose, poet, and playwright; the writer surveys, from an extremely personal point of view, the issue of racism in the American film industry, ranging from *The Birth of a Nation* to *The Exorcist.*

John Banville, *Doctor Copernicus*—a historical novel by the Irish writer of fiction and critic; a reconstruction of the life of the Polish astronomer Nicolaus Copernicus and his formulation of the heliocentric theory of the solar system; the writer brings to light the squalor and superstition of fifteenth-century Europe, as well as his subject's struggle to reconcile his theory of the cosmos with those held by prevailing religious authorities; the work receives the James Tait Black Memorial Prize.

James Dickey, *The Zodiac*—a collection of verse by the American poet, playwright, and writer of fiction; the volume comprises "poetic imitations" of the "works" of a drunken Dutch sailor-poet of the 1940s.

Alex Haley, *Roots: The Saga of an American Family*—a historical account by the American writer of nonfiction; a seven-generation odyssey of the writer's own family, tracing his African heritage and describing all of the difficulties confronted by blacks in their attempts to achieve racial and intellectual equality; transformed into a major television production.

Ryu Murakami, *Kagirinaku Tomei ni Chikai Buru* (Almost Transparent Blue)—a novella by the Japanese writer of fiction; based upon the writer's experiences when living in Fussa, near an American airbase; contains harsh scenes focusing upon bar girls, prostitutes, and pimps; heroin, hashish, and marijuana become the substances that drive the central character to insanity, while blood, vomit, rotten food, and decayed bodies permeate each experience; the piece received the Gunzo New Writers Prize (May 1976) and the seventy-fifth Akutagawa Prize (July 1976); the writer was only twenty-four years old and a university student at the time of publication.

Iris Murdoch, *Henry and Cato*—a novel by the Irish-born English writer of fiction; concerns a priest and an art historian; the two meet again, years after they had formed their boyhood friendship.

Kenji Nakagami, *Misaki* (The Promontory)—a novella by the Japanese writer of fiction; focuses upon complex character relationships within a family residing at the mouth of the Kumano River in southern Kishu; arson and

murder play key roles here; the inhabitants easily go mad in a land surrounded by river, mountains, and sea, and baked by the sun; hatred, jealousy, fear, and incest permeate characters' thoughts and actions.

Howard Nemerov, *The Western Approaches: Poems, 1973-1975*—a collection by the American writer of verse; the writer blends the comic, the serious, and the sorrowful into epigrams and lyrics; he strives to record the imaginative observations of an intelligent person of extreme sensitivity.

Joyce Carol Oates, *Childwold*—a novel by the American writer of fiction and critic; concerns a middle-aged man who becomes obsessed with a destitute fourteen-year-old girl.

Jean Rhys, *Sleep It Off Lady*—a collection of short stories by the West Indian-born English writer of fiction; the majority of the pieces are set in the Caribbean; the writer confronts the issues of death and old age, and she does so without wasting words.

Thomas William Shapcott, *Shabbytown Calendar*—a collection of verse by the Australian poet, writer of fiction, and essayist; the book contains what the writer terms "fugues": poems that increase in intensity and create a form of symphonic climax.

Karl Shapiro, *Adult Bookstore*—a volume of poems by the American writer of verse; the collection ranges widely in subject matter: from Petrarch, through Beethoven, to the California suburbs; includes, in addition to the title poem, such pieces as "The Humanities Building," "A Parliament of Poets," "The Heiligenstadt Testament," and "Garage Sale."

Tom Stoppard, *Dirty Linen*—a play by the Czech-born English dramatist and film writer; satirizes political life, and attempts to expose misdemeanors in the English Parliament.

John Updike, *Marry Me: A Romance*—a novel by the American writer of fiction; an examination of the unfulfilled longings of a married man; the main character must eventually determine the fate of his marriage.

Gore Vidal, *1876*—a novel by the American writer of fiction and miscellaneous prose; a historical piece that focuses upon the closest and most corrupt presidential election campaign in the United States; the writer blends, with ease, historical reality with fiction.

Alice Walker, *Meridian*—a novel by the American writer of fiction and poet; focuses upon problems and issues related both to feminism and the American civil rights movement.

EVENTS

The American Academy and Institute of Arts and Letters formed by combining the various specialized departments of the Institute of Arts and Letters (1904); the Academy, chartered by the U.S. Congress, strives to honor prominent American writers, artists, and musicians.

John Lawrence Ashbery, American writer of verse, receives the Pulitzer Prize in poetry for *Self-Portrait in a Convex Mirror* (1975); the work also receives the National Book Award and the National Book Critics Circle Award.

Saul Bellow, Canadian-born American writer of fiction and playwright, receives the Nobel Prize for literature; his novel *Humboldt's Gift* (1975) receives the Pulitzer Prize for fiction.

Richard Warrington Baldwin Lewis, American academician (Yale), intellectual historian, literary scholar, and biographer, receives the Pulitzer Prize in biography/autobiography for *Edith Wharton: A Biography* (1975).

The National Humanities Center established at Washington, D.C.

1977

DEATHS

Edward Dahlberg (b. 1900). American writer of fiction and nonfiction and poet; he contributed to the proletarian movement of the 1930s; later, he proved a significant influence upon the Beat writers of the 1950s; in addition to his novels and poems, he published cultural criticism, parables, and two volumes of letters.

William Alexander Gerhardie (b. 1895). English critic, writer of fiction, and biographer, he produced the first English-language critical analysis of Anton Chekhov (1923); his fiction combined both comedy and tragedy and was principally autobiographical in substance; between 1940 and his death, he lived in isolation, planning fiction but writing almost nothing.

James Jones (b. 1921). American writer of fiction; he produced novels in the tradition of naturalism; he looked to the "knockabout" prototype established by Jack London, wherein authenticity of experience superseded concern for literary style or structure.

MacKinlay Kantor (b. 1904). American writer of fiction; his work focuses upon dramatic incidents in the history of the United States and nearby areas: the Battle of Gettysburg, Confederate prisons, the revolution in Cuba, World War II, the American Indian wars, and Valley Forge.

Clarice Lispector (b. 1925). Ukranian-born Brazilian writer of fiction; she helped to introduce modernistic experimental approaches to the fiction of her nation; she widened the range of Brazilian literature through her focus upon the subjective nature of reality, her intensely lyrical and symbolic prose style, and her examination of the role of language in forming and expressing identity; the effect of society upon individual identity proved one of her principal themes.

Robert Lowell, Jr. (b. 1917). American poet; he produced intense, richly symbolic, and generally autobiographical verse; he also wrote adaptations of classical drama; in 1947, he received the Pulitzer Prize for poetry.

Anais Nin (b. 1903). French-born American critic, diarist, and writer of fiction; her short stories, in particular, tended to be erotic; her work generally evidences clear insights into the heart of human beings; her five-volume novel cycle bears the general title *Cities of the Interior.*

Sir Terence Mervyn Rattigan (b. 1911). English playwright; he directed his work to the average middle-class, matinee theater audience, whom he both praised and ridiculed; his subjects include petty theft, faithless wives, emotional failure, sexual inadequacy, and historical personages; he became known as an especially effective dramatic craftsman.

Mark Schorer (b. 1908). American literary scholar, academician (California/Berkeley), writer of fiction, and biographer; his fiction and a biography of Sinclair Lewis (1961) are recognized as monumental studies of the relationship between literature and social history.

Louis Untermeyer (b. 1885). American poet and literary critic and biographer; he gained recognition for his anthologies and biographies of American and English poets; his original verse tends to be romantic in tone and substance; he also produced paraphrases and translations of the Greek and Roman classics.

Dennis Yates Wheatley (b. 1897). English writer of fiction; his novels focused upon the occult, and his Satanic thrillers and romances proved exceedingly popular over a period of some forty years.

Henry Williamson (b. 1895). English writer of fiction; his experiences in World War I convinced him of the futility of war and the need for understanding among nations; he became an admirer of Adolph Hitler, which led to his internment at the outset of World War II; he produced a cycle of fifteen novels under the general title *A Chronicle of Ancient Sunlight* (1951-1969).

Cecil Blanche Fitzgerald Woodham-Smith (b. 1896). English historian; a gifted prose stylist, she produced popular and accurate accounts of such events as the charge of the Light Brigade at Balaclava during the Crimean War and the famines in Ireland.

Carl Zuckmayer (b. 1896). German playwright; he wrote highly successful comedies, a number of which became equally successful motion picture films; recognized for revealing his antagonistic attitude toward the Nazi regime in his dramas; during World War II, he lived in the United States; he also wrote some verse and fiction, as well as an autobiography.

PUBLICATIONS

Beryl Bainbridge, *Inquiry Time*—a novel by the English writer of fiction; a quiet dinner party becomes headline news when a gang of escaped criminals bursts upon the scene and takes the guests as hostages; in this piece, violence and the absurd join forces.

Walter Jackson Bate, *Samuel Johnson*—a biography by the American literary scholar, biographer, and academician; a thorough narrative on the life, character, and literary productions of the subject; the emphasis is upon Johnson as an influential figure of the English cultural world in the second half of the eighteenth century; the writer demonstrates how "the great man" triumphed over poverty, trials, tragedies, illnesses, and fears.

Morley Callaghan, *Close to the Sun Again*—a novel by the Canadian writer of fiction and playwright; relates the story of a former naval commander who attempts to come to terms with the materialistic and passionless life that he has experienced; an obvious moral vision comes forth in this piece.

John Cheever, *Falconer*—a novel by the American writer of fiction; a college professor finds himself in prison for killing his brother; the novel gradually unfolds the experiences that led him to murder, prison, and a sudden liberation.

Robert Coover, *The Public Burning*—a novel by the American fiction writer; set during the first year of the administration of Dwight D. Eisenhower, the work concerns the Rosenberg spy case of the early 1950s; the thesis of the novel appears to be, simply, the vindictiveness of American politicians.

Joan Didion, *A Book of Common Prayer*—a novel by the American writer of fiction and miscellaneous nonfiction; the writer demonstrates a knowing and sophisticated grasp of realities and unrealities concerning time and place; a California woman moves to Central America and becomes involved with a man twenty years her junior; the problems that follow are socially and politically complex; yet, the writer confronts them positively and "lyrically."

J. P. Donleavy, *The Destinies of Darcy Dancer, Gentleman*—a novel by the American-born Irish writer of fiction and playwright; the work appears, on the surface, to contain qualities of the eighteenth-century picaresque novel; however, the writer places his work in modern Europe, on a country estate; the work presents the humorous and unfortunate travails of the title character, a person who fails to achieve his singular opportunity for love because of his inopportune birth.

Elaine Feinstein, *Some Unease and Angels*—a miscellaneous collection by the English writer of fiction, poet, and translator; the volume contains a number of her own poems, as well as a selection of translations from the verse of the Russian poet and prose writer Marina Ivanova Tsvetaeva (1892-1941).

John Fowles, *Daniel Martin*—a novel by the English writer of fiction; a lengthy work, the piece has been described as self-searching, semi-naturalistic, and semi-experimental; the title character, a screenwriter, contends with Hollywood, capitalism, art, and his own sister-in-law; the novel is set in a variety of locales, from Devonshire and Oxford to Palmyra.

William Sydney Graham, *Implements in Their Places*—a collection of verse by the Scottish poet; evidences the poet's preoccupation with metaphors of the sea and with the English language; the volume represents the poet's embattled struggle with language and artistic creation; for him, language is either "alive" or residing upon "a frozen tundra of the lexicon and the dictionary."

Theodore Wilson Harris, *Da Silva*—a novel by the Guyanaian writer of fiction, poet, and critic; the piece concerns a Brazilian-born, English-educated painter, who struggles with his spirited wife; the two live in London amid a lively community.

Wolfgang Hildesheimer, *Mozart*—a biography by the German playwright, writer of fiction, and critic; the work combines critical explication and biographical analysis, as the writer considers the life and music of his subject from the point of view of his culture.

Erica Jong, *How To Save Your Own Life*—a novel by the American writer of fiction; concerns the sexuality of one Isadora Wing, a novelist who composes under extremely strange circumstances.

James Kirkup, **"The love that dares to speak its name"**—a poem by the English writer of verse and travel narrative and translator; focuses upon the homosexual love of one of the Roman centurions for Jesus Christ; the work became the subject of the first prosecution for blasphemous libel in over half a century; the editor of *Gay News*, the periodical in which the piece initially appeared, received both a fine and a suspended prison sentence.

John Le Carre, *The Honourable Schoolboy*—a novel by the English writer of fiction; another of the George Smiley spy pieces; the work is set in Hong Kong, where Smiley continues to trace the elusive trail of the KGB master spy, Karla.

Robert Lowell, *Day by Day*—an autobiographical collection of verse by the American poet, his last; the subjects of the pieces include middle age, the poet's third marriage, the birth of his third son, his residence in England, his illness and hospitalization, and his return to the United States.

David Mamet, *A Life in the Theatre*—a play by the American dramatist; the piece explores the relationships between teacher and pupil, mentor and disciple; a thorough examination of the rites of passage, as two actors, a professional and a novice, endure a cycle of onstage and backstage roles.

Olivia Manning, *The Danger Tree*—a novel by the English writer of fiction; the first volume of *The Levant Trilogy*, revealing the experiences of the newly married Guy and Harriet Pringle; they find themselves in rumor-filled Romania, surrounded by a veritable battalion of strange and terribly weak-minded characters who prey upon Guy's generosity.

Kamala Markandaya, *Golden Honeycomb*—a novel by the Indian-born English writer of fiction; a historical work that focuses upon life in India from the late nineteenth century to the outset of World War I; the writer blends the exotic with the realistic, as she depicts the social problems of the period.

W. S. Merwin, *The Compass Flower*—a collection of verse by the American poet, playwright, and translator; in these pieces, the commonplace and the ordinary occurrences of life appear with sudden freshness and vitality.

Philip Roth, *The Professor of Desire*—a novel by the American writer of fiction; the central character, David Alan Kepesh, is portrayed as brilliant and lustful; he harbors an abundance of fantasies and yearnings, and, even when he finds fortune, his winnings do not satisfy him.

Leonardo Sciascia, *Candido: Orvero, un Songo Fatto in Sicilia* (Candido, or a Dream Dreamed in Sicily)—a novel by the Italian (Sicilian) writer of fiction, essayist, and playwright; a modern version of Voltaire's *Candide* (1759), the piece chronicles the misadventures of a young Italian whose simplistic honesty and benevolence disrupt the corrupt, established order.

Paul Mark Scott, *Staying On*—the last novel by the English writer of fiction; a husband and wife, social misfits, decide to remain in India after independence; living on small pensions, they attempt to adjust to the attitudes and conditions of the "new India."

Tom Stoppard, *Every Good Day Deserves Favour*—a play by the Czech-born English dramatist; focuses upon the thoughts and actions of a political dissident in a Soviet psychiatric hospital. ·

J. R. R. Tolkien, *The Silmarillion*—a novel by the South African-born English writer of fiction, poet, critic, and literary scholar; begun by the writer during his service in the trenches during World War I; in a heroic manner that brings to mind the Christian myths of the Creation and the Fall, the piece relates the tale of the first age of the Holy Ones and their offspring; chronologically, the action of the novel occurs prior to the time of *The Hobbit* (1937).

Robert Penn Warren, *A Place To Come To*—a novel by the American poet, critic, and writer of fiction; concerns the life of a classic scholar, Jed Tewksbury, who engages in the search for the American self; he is a literary intellectual, a poor white from a small Southern town, an academic who seeks isolation from "the closure of history."

EVENTS

Vicente Aleixandre, Spanish poet, receives the Nobel Prize for literature.

The American Cultural Association founded.

Michael Cristofer, American playwright, receives the Pulitzer Prize in drama for *The Shadow Box* (1977).

James Ingram Merrill, American writer of verse, fiction, and plays receives the Pulitzer Prize in poetry for his verse collection *Divine Comedies* (1976).

The National Women's Studies Association established to promote the study of American feminist literature and works by women writers.

1978

DEATHS

James Gould Cozzens (b. 1903). American writer of fiction; his novels are meticulously crafted; he focuses upon the themes of idealism and compromise; in 1949, he received the Pulitzer Prize for fiction.

Leon Gontran Damas (b. 1912). Guyanese poet, essayist, and writer of fiction; he became known as one of the principal founders of the international cultural movement identified as "negritude"; thus, in his work, he relied upon African motifs from both the Antilles and from Africa itself; for example, his verse employs the repetition and circular pattern of African dance and song; those same pieces also contain duplications and repetitions of sound to advance the sensations of motion and emotion; he dies in Washington, D.C., during a term as lecturer at Georgetown University.

Janet Flanner (b. 1892). American journalist and narrative writer; she developed a polished prose style and became a perceptive observer of the European scene; under the pen name "Genet," she published (1925-1975) a regular column, "Letter from Paris," in *The New Yorker* magazine.

Albert Gomes (b. 1911). Trinidadian poet and writer of fiction; his verse tends to be spontaneous and loose, pugnacious in nature and reflecting his interest in the politics of independence; he became one of the earliest enthusiasts and supporters of the steel bands that developed "pan music" and calypso in the back country of Trinidad; he dies in London.

F. R. Leavis (b. 1895). English literary critic and academician; a proponent of the "new criticism" of the late 1920s and 1930s, he advanced the claims of T. S. Eliot, William Butler Yeats, and Ezra Pound over the merits of the late Victorians; as a teacher and critic, he upheld vigorous intellectual standards intended to preserve the cultural continuity of English literature and life; in the end, he brought to English studies a new seriousness, albeit one that rejected all other critical and intellectual points of view.

Hugh MacDiarmid (pseudonym of Christopher Murray Grieve; b. 1892). Scottish poet and essayist; he gained literary recognition and popularity with short lyrics in his native Scots dialect; his "English" verse tended to focus on political philosophy (*Hymn to Lenin,* for example); these were lengthy pieces that strove for a world view of experience; his unusual range of subject matter sets him apart from his predecessors among Scots versifiers.

Harry Martinson (b. 1904). Swedish poet and writer of fiction; he gained critical and popular recognition with his innovative, psychologically complex verse that draws upon his extensive travels as a seaman; in 1974, he shared the Nobel Prize for literature with fellow countryman Eyvind Johnson.

Paul Mark Scott (b. 1920). English writer of fiction; he achieved literary recognition for his series of novels labeled the *Raj Quartet;* set in India after World War I, the pieces focus on personal, political, racial, and religious issues; a television series served to increase the popularity of the writer's works after his death.

Ignazio Silone (b. 1900). Italian writer of fiction and journalist; an antifascist, he lived in exile from 1931 to 1944, devoting his literary efforts to promoting socialism without sacrificing human or literary values.

Sylvia Townsend Warner (b. 1893). English biographer, writer of fiction, and poet; her passionate interest in early music is reflected in her fiction; she also developed pieces from supernatural tales and classical sources.

PUBLICATIONS

Isaiah Berlin, *Russian Thinkers*—a collection of essays by the English philosopher, scholar, and intellectual historian; the pieces focus upon the intelligentsia of nineteenth-century Russia; one piece, "The Hedgehog and the Fox," concerns Leo Tolstoy and the tension generated between the monist and pluralist versions of world history.

Dennis Brutus, *Stubborn Hope: New Poems and Selections from China Poems and Strains*—a collection of verse by the Rhodesian-born South African poet and essayist; the pieces reflect the writer's prison experiences and the inhumanity of apartheid; endurance and hope rise as dominant strains, and the poet extends his concern with the oppressive conditions of his homeland to a universal scale; thus, he assumes the role of the voice and conscience of all suffering people.

Antonia Susan Byatt, *The Virgin in the Garden*—a novel by the English writer of fiction and critic; the piece principally takes place during the coronation year of 1953; thus, the work celebrates the second Elizabethan "Golden Age" by a performance, at a country house in Yorkshire, of a new verse drama by a public school master in which a schoolgirl plays the role of "the Virgin Queen"; the writer combines allegorical allusions with the realities of provincial English life during the 1950s.

Robert Creeley, *Hello: A Journal*—a collection of verse by the American poet; the writer intended to develop parallels between his emotional expressions and the Buddhist meditations of Allan Ginsberg.

James Gordon Farrell, *The Singapore Grip*—a novel by the English writer of fiction; the novelist blends real and fictitious characters in describing the fall of Singapore to the Japanese during World War II; the event, in the writer's view, constitutes the death of the British Empire.

Graham Greene, *The Human Factor*—a novel by the English writer of fiction; an ironic tale of espionage, based upon life in the "Secret Service"; English, African, Russian, and Polish agents engage in what the writer labels "Operation Uncle Remus."

Masuo Ikeda, *Egekai ni Sasagu* (To the Aegean Sea)—a novella by the Manchurian-born writer of fiction and printmaker; the piece resembles a one-act drama with four characters; the influences of Jean Cocteau and Albert Camus are clearly evident.

John Robin Jenkins, *A Would-Be Saint*—a novel by the Scottish writer of fiction; a modern and realistic work detailing the life of a devout Presbyterian who renounces modern society; that act leads to his isolation in a remote Scottish forest.

Doris Lessing, *Collected Stories*—a two-volume collection by the Persian-born, Rhodesian-reared English writer of fiction; the pieces demonstrate a wide range of subject matter, from feminism ("One of the Short List") to meditations on the material and spiritual life ("The Temptation of Jack Orkney"); the collection also includes a popular piece of childhood bravado, "Through the Tunnel."

Clarice Lispector, *A Hora de Estrela* (The Hour of the Star)—a novella by the Ukranian-born Brazilian writer of fiction; concerns a young woman who moves from an isolated rural locale to Rio de Janeiro; the narrator, a man, relates her experiences and comments upon how he will present them in fictional form; the work reflects the writer's views on art and language, as well as her interests in social issues; essentially, the female character struggles to establish herself in a male dominated society.

Olivia Manning, *The Battle Lost and Won*—a novel by the English writer of fiction; one of the various works that reflect the writer's experiences during World War II while traveling with her husband, a BBC producer; the work is noted for its dramatic recreation of the Battle of Alamein.

James A. Michener, *Chesapeake*—a novel by the American writer of fiction and miscellaneous prose; a historical piece that focuses upon the lives of six families; the characters symbolize the conflicts, horrors, and violence that accompanied the development of the American nation; the writer also details the natural resources of the Chesapeake region.

Iris Murdoch, *The Sea, the Sea*—a novel by the Irish-born English writer of fiction; focuses upon the life of a theater director and his childhood love; the piece is reminiscent of William Shakespeare's *The Tempest;* receives, in this year, the Booker McConnell Prize for Fiction for the best full-length novel published within the previous twelve months.

Joyce Carol Oates, *Son of the Morning*—a novel by the American writer of fiction; concerns the activities of an evangelist whose inordinate pride leads to his downfall.

Erika Ritter, *The Splits*—a play by the Canadian dramatist and essayist; the principal female character has written a novel that the Canadian Broadcasting Corporation wishes to adapt to a situation comedy series for television; the writer refuses the offer, since she does not wish to abandon her relationships with her husband and lover; in the end, she forsakes the financial advantages of television for a new life and the continuation of her efforts to write serious fiction.

Sam Shepard, *Buried Child*—a drama by the American playwright; focuses upon a family in Illinois and the altogether strange and eerie events they encounter; the piece receives the Pulitzer Prize for drama in 1979.

Isaac Bashevis Singer, *Shosha*—a novel by the Polish-born American writer of fiction; the title character represents one of the novelist's innocent figures who symbolizes a return to the uncomplicated world of childhood; at the same time, the narrator, who yields to worldly pleasure, represents the moral disintegration of modern life.

Bernard Slade, *Tribute*—a play by the Canadian-born dramatist; the writer addresses the subject of death and the importance of familial relationships; the principal character, an unsuccessful scriptwriter and Hollywood public relations man, can charm everyone except his own son; upon learning of his approaching death from leukemia, his friends rent a theater to pay tribute to him; at the same time, he strives hard to win his son's love.

Tom Stoppard, *Night and Day*—a play by the Czech-born dramatist; concerns the dangers of the "closed shop" as it exists in the journalism profession.

Michitsuna Takahashi, *Kugatsu no Sora* (The Sky of September)—a novel by the Japanese writer of fiction and sportswriter; focuses upon the ideals, friendships, and budding sexuality of boys; the characters tend to value friendship more than the love of women; thus, the member of a high school fencing team becomes offended when a new girl joins the group; after she has some success on the team, he becomes more tolerant of her.

William Trevor, *Lovers of Their Time*—a novel by the Irish writer of fiction; emphasizes the events surrounding the romance of a middle-aged couple; the principal activities occur in a bathroom in a London hotel.

Yuri Trifonov, *Starik* (The Old Man)—a novel by the Russian writer of fiction; essentially an analysis of the nature of truth and the influence of the past upon the present; through the character of a war veteran, the writer employs historical allusions to suggest that contemporary Russians need to understand the nation's recent history and civil war; the veteran searches for the truth about an incident that resulted in the trial and murder of a supposed revolutionary against whom he had testified.

Barbara Tuchman, *A Distant Mirror: The Calamitous Fourteenth Century*—a historical account by the American scholar and journalist; an especially lucid and interesting narrative of events in fourteenth-century Europe, complete with maps, illustrations, and a thorough bibliography of primary and secondary sources; the piece receives the American Book Award for history.

EVENTS

Walter Jackson Bate, American literary scholar and biographer, receives the Pulitzer Prize in biography/autobiography for *Samuel Johnson* (1977).

Donald Lee Coburn, American playwright, receives the Pulitzer Prize in drama for *The Gin Game* (1976), his first play.

Howard Nemerov, American poet and writer of fiction, receives the Pulitzer Prize in poetry for his *Collected Poems* (1977).

James Alan McPherson, American short story writer, receives the Pulitzer Prize in fiction for his collection, *Elbow Room* (1977).

Carl Edward Sagan, American astronomer and writer of popular science nonfiction, receives the Pulitzer Prize in nonfiction for *The Dragons of Eden* (1977).

Isaac Bashevis Singer, Polish-born Yiddish writer of fiction, playwright, translator, and writer of books for children, receives the Nobel Prize for literature.

The 1909 United States Copyright law undergoes first major revision, effective on 1 January.

1979

DEATHS

James Gordon Farrell (b. 1935). English writer of fiction; the settings of his novels range from France, through Ireland, to India and Singapore; his historical pieces represent the falling away of the traditional British Empire and focus upon characters who refuse to accept the eventualities of history; death comes from accidental drowning shortly after he moves from England to Ireland.

James Thomas Farrell (b. 1904). American writer of fiction; he gained a literary reputation in the 1930's with his novel of Studs Lonigan and Danny O'Neill, characters reflecting his own Chicago Catholic experiences; his work belongs within the tradition of American naturalism.

Tommaso Landolfi (b. 1908). Italian writer of fiction, poet, playwright, critical essayist, and translator; he achieved recognition as a literary stylist in the mold of Edgar Allan Poe, Franz Kafka, and Jorge Luis Borges; his excessively imaginative tales rely upon nightmare, fantasy, and experimentation with language; his characters, infused with irony and macabre humor, cannot communicate effectively or discover love, faith, or spiritual grace; the writer, himself, believed that his work could be understood only by intellectuals.

Nicholas John Turney Monsarrat (b. 1910). English writer of fiction; his experiences during World War II included service in both the merchant marines and the Royal Navy, and a number of incidents from this period find their way into his popular fiction about ships and the sea; he also fictionalized a number of events relative to African independence.

Jean Rhys (originally Ella Gwendolen Rees Williams; b. 1890). West Indian-born (Dominica, Lesser Antilles) English writer of fiction, writer of autobiographical narrative, and translator; she combines, in her fiction, personal experiences with emotional and psychological insights into the nature of relationships between the sexes; thus, she created complex, intelligent, and sensitive women dominated and victimized by men and society; her literary career gained, in Paris during the 1920's, the support and sponsorship of Ford Madox Ford.

I. A. Richards (b. 1893). English literary critic, literary scholar, and poet; during his tenure at Harvard, he investigated linguistics, which led, in turn, to his interest in "Basic English," a system by which one could say or write anything for "everyday" purposes by relying upon only 850 words; his critical studies included practical literary criticism, scientific and emotive language in poetry, and the practices and procedures of literary study.

Allen Tate (b. 1899). American poet and literary critic; in addition to establishing and editing a number of literary magazines (including *Fugitive* [1922-1925] and *The Sewanee Review* [1944-1946]), he wrote on the limits and limitations of poetry and the relationship between the literary artist and modern society; his own highly skillful poetry is frequently marked by bitter imagery.

Nikolai Tikhonov (b. 1896). Russian poet; his earliest verse dates from 1910; as a cavalry soldier in World War I, he maintained a verse diary and he also commented poetically upon the 1917 Revolution; his mature work relates his poetic impressions of the civil war period (1919-1923), as well as his various travels throughout Europe and the Soviet Union; his verse lauded the efforts of Soviet industrialization, and he eventually became the principal poetic voice of the Soviet Union and the Soviet point of view.

Antonia White (b. 1899). English writer of fiction and translator; her novels reflect her experiences in a convent, as an actress in provincial repertory theatre, as a free-lance copywriter, and her attempts at serious writing; they also reflect her relationship with her possessive father, as well as her illness and confinement in a mental institution; she also translated novels by the French writer, Colette (1873-1954).

PUBLICATIONS

Fleur Adcock, *The Inner Harbour*—a volume of verse by the New Zealand-born English poet and translator; the writer's attraction to the land of her birth permeates these poems; in addition, she details the experiences of dreams, sickness, death, and self-discovery; the poet's quiet, rational voice is frequently punctuated by startling images rooted in the emotions.

Kingsley Amis, *Jake's Thing*—a novel by the English writer of fiction; the principal character of the title, an Oxford don, searches for a renewed libido; he is aided in this search by an astonishing variety of sex therapies.

John Berger, *Pig Earth*—a miscellaneous collection by the English writer of fiction and critical essayist; the stories, essays, and poems relative to French peasant life dramatize the struggle between the people of the soil and heartless bureaucrats; the initial volume of a projected trilogy entitled *Into Their Labours*.

J. P. Donleavy, *Schultz*—a novel by the American-born Irish writer of fiction and playwright; one of the writer's few "orthodox" pieces, it concerns the escapades of a Jewish-American theatrical impresario who attempts to produce a vulgar farce in London; the work is characterized by lewd language and a parade of sexual escapades.

Odysseus Elytis, *Maria Nefeli*—a poem by the Greek writer of verse, essayist, and translator; the work consists of a series of antiphonal passages between a liberated woman, who symbolizes the individual in contemporary society, and an intelligent and mature poetic persona; the thesis of the work is the ability of humanity to attain harmony amid the chaos of the modern world; considered the poet's major work of the 1970's.

Buchi Emecheta, *The Joys of Motherhood*—a novel by the Nigerian-born writer of fiction, autobiographical narrative, and children's books; the writer condemns the practice of polygamy, the stigma of barrenness, and the pressures placed upon African women to produce male offspring; focuses upon two women married to the same man and who compete to bear children for him; one turns out to be sterile, while the second becomes reduced to servitude after bearing several children in rapid succession.

Hans Magnus Enzensberger, *Der Untergang de Titanic* (The Sinking of the Titanic)—a poem by the German writer of verse, essayist, playwright, and translator; contains thirty-three cantos upon the sinking of the ill-fated luxury liner (14-15 April 1912); the vessel exists as a metaphor for society, as the poet comments upon the differences between the conditions and fates of poor and wealthy passengers; he also considers the events from several perspectives, invoking a variety of historical and personal references.

John Fuller, *Lies and Secrets*—a volume of verse by the English poet and writer of fiction; includes his most significant piece, "The Most Difficult Position," concerning the refusal of two nineteenth-century chess masters to confront each other in a game.

Ted Hughes, *Remains of Elmet* (with photographs by Fay Godwin)—a volume of description and verse by the English poet; the writer celebrates the landscapes of his youth in the Calder Valley; he describes that area as "the last ditch of Elmet, the last British kingdom to fall to the Angles."

Elizabeth Jennings, *Moments of Grace*—a collection of verse by the English poet; the pieces are open, quiet, and sensitively controlled; they reflect the writer's own suffering, loneliness, friendships, and commitment to Roman Catholicism.

Doris Lessing, *Canopus in Argus: Archives*—a cycle of novels by the Persian-born, Rhodesian-raised English writer of fiction; a series of futuristic allegories constituting a radical departure in style and substance from the novelist's earlier work; the powerful and benign Canopus receives reports from agents throughout the universe; each novel illuminates a specific aspect of current political and emotional problems; up to 1983 the cycle includes *Shikasta, Re: Colonized Planet 5-Shikasta, The Marriages between Zones Three, Four, and Five, The Sirian Experiments, The Making of the Representative for Planet Eight,* and *Documents Relating to the Sentimental Agents in the Volyen Empire*.

Norman Mailer, *The Executioner's Song*—a work of fiction by the American novelist and writer of miscellaneous prose; actually two short novels in one: the first concerns the brutal life and death of convicted killer Gary Gilmore; the second focuses upon the no less savage struggle on the part of the news media to gain control of the story rights; described as a book that has discovered the true voices of the American culture.

Mary McCarthy, *Cannibals and Missionaries*—a novel by the American writer of fiction; focuses upon complex relationships between terrorists and their hostages.

Brian Moore, *The Mangan Inheritance*—a novel by the English writer of fiction; an American journalist searches for his Irish heritage, which relates to the tragic career of the impoverished and drunken Irish poet, Charles Mangan (1803-1849).

Adolph Muschg, *Noch Ein Wunsch* (Yet Another Wish)—a novel by the Swiss writer of fiction, playwright, and critical essayist; focuses upon the central character's private life and experiences, and reveals a person tragically flawed and in a state of retreat; resignation, frustration, and loneliness pervade the narrative; communication appears almost impossible and desperation rises to dangerous heights; nonetheless, with all of the psychological complications, the writer conveys his narrative in clear, precise, and evenly flowing sentences.

V. S. Naipaul, *A Bend in the River*—a novel by the Trinidadian-born English writer of fiction; an emotionally powerful piece set in a fictitious African nation; the writer focuses upon the damage inflicted by Western influence and control on the Third World; the narrator is a Muslim store keeper from the east coast of Africa; he buys a small business in a town in a French-speaking African state; there exist in this work echoes of Joseph Conrad's *Heart of Darkness*.

Shiva Naipaul, *North of South*—a nonfiction narrative by the Trinidadian-born English writer of fiction, journalist, and essayist; describes an African journey through Kenya, Tanzania, and Zambia, and includes the writer's reactions to hapless encounters with immigration officials and persons whom he identifies as racists; he underscores the view that independence has principally benefitted a black elite who crave the materialism of the West.

F. T. Prince, *Collected Poems*—a volume of verse by the South African-born poet; contains dramatic monologues and long meditations on literary figures and characters from literature; includes, also, experiments with a variety of obscure poetic forms.

John Rechy, *Rushes*—a novel by the American writer of fiction; establishes a dramatic confrontation among the different factions of the male gay world; with "passionate honesty," the writer sifts through the actions and experiences of that world, coming to grips with difficult moral questions and rejecting simple answers.

Alain Robbe-Grillet, *Le Rendez-vous*—a novel by the French writer of fiction and essayist; an experimental piece intended by the writer as a vehicle for teaching French to Americans; the work shifts between first-person and third-person narrative; with each shift in point of view, the details of the narration are altered and reshuffled.

Philip Roth, *The Ghost Writer*—a novel by the American writer of fiction, the first work of "the Zuckerman trilogy"; a young writer believes that he has met and fallen in love with Anne Frank, the young Jewish girl who recorded her experiences of the Nazi occupation of Holland during World War II; a variation on the theme of the artist as a young man.

Peter Shaffer, *Amadeus*—a play by the English dramatist; the work presents an account of the career of Wolfgang Amadeus Mozart (1756-1791); the account is presented from the point of view of the rival musician and composer, Antonio Salieri (1750-1825); the play was transformed into a highly successful motion picture.

Gilbert Sorrentino, *Mulligan Stew*—a novel by the American writer of fiction and poet; a wildly imaginative and comic piece in which an avant-garde novelist struggles with "a new wave murder mystery"; in the process, he becomes insane; as his personal life deteriorates into hopeless frustration, his novel, which unfolds before the reader, becomes increasingly obsessive, erotic, and hilarious.

William Styron, *Sophie's Choice*—a novel by the American writer of fiction; a 1940s immigrant comes to New York City and reveals her terrible secrets and personal experiences relative to the Nazi concentration camp at Auschwitz; the narrative is pervaded by the incomprehensible atrocities that took place there.

D. M. Thomas, *The Flute Player*—a novel by the English writer of fiction and translator of Russian works; the piece exists as a fantasy based on the lives and works of Osip Emilyevich Mandelstam (1891-1938?), Boris Leonidovich Pasternak (1890-1960), Anna Akhmatova (1889-1966), and Marina Ivanova Tsvetaeva (1892-1941); of equal importance and focus is the question of the survival of poetry, love, and humanity in an imaginary city that bears a sharp resemblance to Leningrad.

John Updike, *Too Far To Go*—a collection of stories by the American writer of fiction; the pieces achieve unity through the writer's own notion that "all things end under heaven, and if temporality is held to be invalidating, then nothing real succeeds"; specifically, the stories focus upon the Maple family and trace the gradual decline of the principal characters' marriage.

Kurt Vonnegut, Jr., *Jailbird*—a novel by the American writer of fiction; the work reflects an angry man's penetrating look at the

United States of the late 1970's; the principal character attempts to humanize the capitalistic system and prove that personal values can coexist with corporate goals.

Patrick White, *The Twyborn Affair*—a novel by the English-born Australian writer of fiction; described as "a baroque novel with an international canvas"; the dramatic moment of the piece occurs in the midst of the London blitz in World War II.

EVENTS

John Cheever, American writer of fiction, receives the Pulitzer Prize in fiction for *The Stories of John Cheever* (1978).

Odysseus Elytis, Greek poet, essayist, and translator, receives the Nobel Prize for literature.

The Henry James Society founded, at New York City, to promote scholarly activities related to the life and works of the American-born writer.

The Library of America begins publication of new editions of the principal works of major American writers.

The London Review of Books begins publication at University College, London; a literary and cultural review of books, as well as an organ for critical essays and scholarly commentary by major writers and commentators of the day.

Sam Shepard (originally Samuel Shepard Rogers, Jr.), American playwright, receives the Pulitzer Prize in drama for *Buried Child* (1978).

Robert Penn Warren, American writer of fiction, poet, and literary critic, receives the Pulitzer Prize in poetry for *Now and Then: Poems, 1976-1978* (1978).

1980

DEATHS

Alejo Carpentier (b. 1904). Cuban writer of fiction and critic; he achieved recognition as the first Caribbean writer to consider that entire region in his work; he wrote several of his fictional pieces in French, which enabled him to depart from his strictly native focus; he became one of the first writers to exploit black themes, although he later repudiated these early treatments of African subjects and considerations.

Marc Connelly (b. 1890). American playwright; he gained a literary and theatrical reputation through his collaborations with George S. Kaufman, most of which were adaptations and satires of fictional pieces; he received a Pulitzer Prize in 1930.

Robert Hayden (b. 1930). American poet and academic; although he achieved acclaim as a major black poet, his work transcends racial motifs and focuses on a wide range of universal human experience.

Camara Laye (b. 1928). Guinean writer of fiction; his work confronted such modern dilemmas as alienation and the search for identity; he had to leave his native land in 1965 because of his opposition to its government; thus, he lived in Senegal during the last fifteen years of his life; generally, his writing chronicles the plight of the exile and the problems of adapting to change and cultural dislocation.

Olivia Manning (b. 1908). English writer of fiction; she traveled with her husband, a British Council lecturer and a BBC producer, during World War II, and their experiences in Greece, Egypt, and Jerusalem became the sources for her novels; essentially, she grasped the tragedy and comedy of war, its effects upon civilian life, and its role in the history of the world.

David Mercer (b. 1928). English playwright; he became known for his television trilogy focusing upon Yorkshire politics and the various social conflicts existing in that region; his principal themes included mental disturbance, alienation, class conflict, the differences between the working class and educated members of society, and the significance of Marxism to various classes and political entities.

Henry Miller (b. 1891). American essayist, dramatist, and writer of fiction, travel literature, and autobiographical narrative; he lived in New York City, moved to Paris, and eventually settled in the Big Sur region of California; his controversial fiction combined frank sexual description, autobiographical details, philosophical speculation, and commentary upon literature and society; his major pieces did not appear in the United States until the 1960s, although they date from the 1930s.

Katherine Anne Porter (b. 1890). American writer of fiction; she became known for her masterful short stories, highly accomplished in language, form, and style; she produced insightful fictional studies of the psychology of human relationships, relying on myth and symbol to illuminate her themes; she received a Pulitzer Prize in 1965.

Muriel Rukeyser (b. 1913). American poet; her extremely passionate verse portrayed the individual contending with a constantly changing world; she found the solution to individual problems by placing faith in the ideals of social justice.

Bernardo Santareno (pseudonym of Antonio Martinho do Rosario; b. 1925). Portuguese playwright; the majority of his work can be classified as social protest; thus, he championed the cause of the simple and the oppressed against the wealthy and the powerful; his plays focus on factory workers, peasants, and fishermen as they stand against the church and the state.

Jean-Paul Sartre (b. 1905). French philosopher, writer of fiction, and essayist; he has long been acknowledged as one of the leading proponents of existentialism; in his view, existence preceded essence, while human beings existed alone in a godless and meaningless state; further, while individuals may remain free, they stand morally responsible for their actions; in 1964, the Nobel Prize committee awarded him its citation for literature, which he refused to accept.

C. P. Snow (b. 1905). English physicist and writer of fiction; his major contribution to letters was his eleven-volume novel cycle *Strangers and Brothers* (1940-1970), an analysis of power and the relation between science and the community; those pieces also delineated the changes in English life during the twentieth century.

Benjamin Travers (b. 1886). English writer of fiction and playwright; he achieved recognition for a series of plays written and produced during the 1920s and known as "the Aldwych farces."

Kenneth Tynan (b. 1927). English dramatic critic; he helped shift the focus of popular theater from the drawing-room comedy and verse drama of such writers as T.S. Eliot and Christopher Fry to theatrical naturalism and working-class drama; he was a principal force in the formation of the National Theatre.

PUBLICATIONS

Eavan Boland, *In Her Own Image*—a collection of verse by the Irish poet and critic; the style of the pieces tends to be terse, the lines short, the diction "striking," and the syntax "abrupt"; the poems focus on humanist and feminist concerns; the poet challenges traditional notions of femininity and rages against the social forces that imprison people in constricted lives.

Anthony Burgess, *Earthly Powers*—a novel by the English writer of fiction; written in the first person and narrated by a successful octogenarian and homosexual writer; real and fictitious characters mingle to produce "an international panorama of the twentieth century."

Truman Capote, *Music for Chameleons: New Writings*—a miscellaneous collection by the American writer of fiction and nonfiction; the volume includes stories, interviews, and sketches on a wide variety of subjects; the thirteen "conversational portraits" range from the writer's early childhood memories of New Orleans and its lush Garden District to a pensive twilight with Marilyn Monroe and a raucous afternoon spent trailing a New York City cleaning lady on her appointed rounds.

E.L. Doctorow, *Loon Lake*—a novel by the American writer of fiction; the work is set in the 1930s, during the Great Depression, and details the experiences of a young man from Patterson, New Jersey, who leaves home to find his fortune; on a cold and lonely night in the Adirondack Mountains he discovers a vision of life so different from his own that it changes his destiny.

Brian Friel, *Translations*—a play by the Irish dramatist and writer of fiction; set in nineteenth-century Ireland as British troops arrive to survey the Ballybeg landscape and to "Anglicize" Gaelic place names; the playwright examines a number of themes related to translating, including the means by which human beings interpret reality through language and action; considered one of the writer's most important pieces.

John Fuller, *The Illusionists*—a volume of verse by the English poet and writer of fiction; a satiric narrative in stanza form, focusing upon contemporary people and experiences.

Roy Fuller, *The Reign of Sparrows*—a collection of verse by the English poet and writer of fiction; the writer concerns himself with developing the highest poetic forms and techniques; in terms of substance, the pieces tend to be strongly personal, particularly as the poet reflects upon old age and the aging process.

William Golding, *Rites of Passage*—a novel by the English writer of fiction; presented as the journal of a voyage to the Antipodes during the Napoleonic era; includes vivid and accurate descriptions of life aboard ship; the work receives the Booker McConnell Prize for fiction as the best full-length novel published during the past twelve months.

Robert A. Heinlein, *The Number of the Beast*—a novel by the American science fiction writer; a science fiction and fantasy piece in which four travelers in time and space escape California in search of a new world, a place free from hostile aliens.

Zhang Jie, *Leaden Wings*—a novel by the Chinese writer of fiction; the writer presents a frank and generally critical view of heavy industry in modern China; the work also exists as a portrait of heroic idealism, altruism, and integrity, balanced by cowardice, selfishness, and ambition; the thesis of the piece focuses upon the notion that for China to become truly modern, democracy and respect for ideas must assume precedence over dogmatism and narrow-minded party loyalty.

Erica Jong, *Fanny: Being the True History of the Adventures of Fanny Hackabout-Jones*—a novel by the American writer of fiction; in form and style, the piece is a picaresque novel in the eighteenth-century mold of Daniel Defoe and Henry Fielding; rather than a parody, however, the work is a reflection of the writer's fascination with the eighteenth-century novel.

John Knowles, *Peace Breaks Out*—a novel by the American writer of fiction; a "companion piece" to *A Separate Peace* (1960); the scene returns to Devon School, focusing upon the restless post-World War II students; the writer combines routine events with remarkable experiences.

John Le Carre, *Smiley's People*—a novel by the English writer of spy and adventure fiction; in this piece, the title character, a British agent, comes into direct confrontation with his KGB enemy, Karla; the writer combines grim and realistic detail with "Byzantine elaboration of plot."

Shirley Lim, *No Man's Grove*—the first volume of verse by the Singapore poet; contains seventy-five poems or short sequences that prove perceptive, intelligent, and enjoyable; three groups of poems are unified by the theme of personal maturation as a woman, a poet, and a Chinese-Malaysian immigrant in the United States; the poet seeks to grasp her various heritages and resolve the struggle between order and anarchy; the work receives the British Commonwealth Prize for poetry.

David Lodge, *How Far Can You Go?*—a novel by the English writer of fiction and critic; the piece analyzes the responses, submitted over twenty years, of an interconnected group of Roman Catholics to moral and sociological change.

Olivia Manning, *The Sum of Things*—a novel by the English writer of fiction; the final volume of *The Levant Trilogy;* a tragicomedy of war and its overall effect upon the lives of civilians; the work provides a sharp and accurate sense of time and period.

Joyce Carol Oates, *Bellefleur*—a novel by the American writer of fiction; an account of six generations of an aristocratic family in the Adirondack Mountains.

Julia O'Faolain, *No Country for Young Men*—a novel by the English-born writer of fiction and translator; the writer confronts the issue of Irish nationalism to explain to her readers the destructive, cyclical pattern of Irish history; the work depicts murder, mystery, the oppression of women in Ireland, and the misconception of values in the name of patriotism; the plot weaves through three generations of a family involved in "the troubles."

Marge Piercy, *Vida*—a novel by the American writer of fiction; focuses upon a fugitive from the 1960s who remains "on the run" some ten years later; the writer captures the optimism of the 1960s when thousands of people belonged to the organization "Students Against the War"; the title character, Vida Asch, a political star of the anti-Vietnam War movement, lives underground for almost a decade.

James Simmons, *Constantly Singing*—a collection of verse by the Irish poet, critic, and playwright; the pieces tend, generally, to reveal the poet's celebratory spirit, although he does focus upon such negative issues as divorce and political upheaval; the writer evokes images of the Irish countryside and anchors his themes to middle age.

Steve Tesich, *Division Street*—a play by the Yugoslav-born American dramatist and writer of fiction; in this farce, the playwright portrays a group of 1960s radicals as they search, in the spiritless world of the 1980s, for a cause to support.

Anthony Thwaite, *Victorian Voices*—a volume of verse by the English poet and critic; the work contains fourteen dramatic monologues that focus upon a number of obscure figures from the Victorian Age, such as Philip Henry Gosse and John Churton Collins.

Angus Wilson, *Setting the World on Fire*—a novel by the South African-born English writer of fiction and biographer; the piece presents a contrast of character and purpose between two brothers; one, a theater director, gravitates toward artistic daring; the other, a lawyer, cannot confidently confront disorder or approaching chaos.

EVENTS

The Hemingway Society established; dedicated to promoting scholarly studies of the life and works of the American writer of fiction.

Donald Rodney Justice, American poet, receives the Pulitzer Prize in poetry for his *Selected Poems* (1979).

Norman Mailer, American writer of fiction and miscellaneous prose, receives the Pulitzer Prize in fiction for his *The Executioner's Song* (1979).

Czeslaw Milosz, Polish poet, writer of fiction, and essayist, receives the Nobel Prize for literature.

Lanford Wilson, American playwright, receives the Pulitzer Prize in drama for *Talley's Folly* (1979).

1981

DEATHS

Nelson Algren (b. 1909). American writer of fiction; his novels, particularly, reflect his experiences as a youngster raised amidst poverty in the slums of Chicago; his technique tended to be realistic, and he used fiction as a vehicle for social protest; in general, his characters' frustration leads to tragedy.

Enid Bagnold (b. 1889). English writer of fiction and playwright; her traditional, conser-

vative pieces are unrelated to the artistic, bohemian existence she led during the 1920s and 1930s.

Paddy Chayevsky (b. 1923). American playwright and film writer; his dramatic and realistic works have adapted well to motion picture and television screens; his characters are generally ordinary human beings whom anyone might meet at any time and place.

David Garnett (b. 1892). English writer of fiction and critic; he wrote fables related to the postwar world of the 1920s; he also produced biographies, and edited the letters of T. E. Lawrence and the novels of Thomas Love Peacock.

Miroslav Krleza (b. 1893). Croatian writer of fiction, playwright, and poet; in his work, he captured the concerns of a revolutionary era in Yugoslavia, particularly in a trilogy of social dramas (1928-1932) that focus upon a single family and in a multi-volume fictional saga (1932-1963) of the Croatian bourgeoise set in the early twentieth century.

Eugenio Montale (b. 1896). Italian poet and critic; his verse tends to be highly complex and extremely pessimistic; in 1975, he received the Nobel Prize for literature, based upon four major verse collections published between 1925 and 1977.

Janos Pilinszky (b. 1921). Hungarian poet; he became one of the leading post-World War II poets of his nation; identified as a "Catholic existentialist," he produced verse that focused upon the mystery of Christ's sacrifice, as well as upon the enormity of suffering experienced by human beings in a century characterized by tyranny and mass murder.

William Saroyan (b. 1908). American playwright, biographer, and writer of fiction; his work generally combined optimism, sentimentality, and nationalism; in 1940, he received a Pulitzer Prize in drama.

Yaakov Shabtai (b. 1934). Israeli writer of fiction and playwright; during his relatively brief career, he focused upon questions related to ethics and to the human condition; in his work, the past becomes part of the present and relates to the breadth of human experience; he attempts to confront the meaning of death, not as a remote possibility, but as an ever-present reality.

Yuri Valentinovich Trifonov (b. 1925). Russian writer of fiction; his work chronicles the lives of the Moscow intelligentsia, analyzing the stress of living in Soviet Russia; the writer addresses what he perceives as the transformation from spiritual and ideological ethics to egoistic values brought on by the pressures of life under the Soviet system; thus, his characters must compromise their moral principles so that they can live in comfort.

Alexander Raban (Alec) Waugh (b. 1898). English writer of fiction and travel narratives; he achieved a temporary claim to literary fame with a fictional piece concerning public school homosexuality; a brother of the more famous Evelyn Waugh.

Dame Francis Amelia Yates (b. 1899). English Renaissance literary scholar; she concerned herself principally with Neoplatonism and the Rosicrucian traditions in Renaissance thought, particularly their relationship to literature and the drama of the period.

PUBLICATIONS

Maya Angelou, *The Heart of a Woman*—a narrative by the American playwright, poet, and writer of miscellaneous prose; the fourth work in an autobiographical cycle; describes the writer's transformation in her early thirties from nightclub singer and dancer to writer and political activist.

Edward Bond, *Restoration*—a play by the English dramatist; an ambitious historical work cast in the mold of drama by Bertolt Brecht.

Gus Edwards, *Weep Not for Me*—a play by the West Indian-born dramatist; the piece centers upon a family in the South Bronx area of New York City; their decadent lifestyle metaphorically relates to the deteriorating neighborhood in which they live and try to survive.

Alasdair Gray, *Lanark: A Life in Four Books*—the first novel by the Scottish writer of fiction; a disjointed narrative emphasizes the surreal and dreamlike qualities of the piece; the writer creates a stark and prophetic vision of a society where the governing elite depend upon and perpetuate the gradual dehumanization and moral decay of ordinary citizens; combines realistic depiction of contemporary Glasgow with a nightmarish account of its decadent future.

Josephine Jacobsen, *The Chinese Insomniacs*—a collection of verse by the Canadian-born American poet, writer of fiction, and essayist; the poet examines the role of language in creating and maintaining human relationships and a sense of community; she relies upon a detached tone and minimal poetic structure to emphasize her themes.

David Lodge, *Working with Structuralism*—a critical essay by the English writer of fiction and prose; the author introduces and explicates Continental literary theory to Britons, maintaining, all the while, his profound faith in the future of realistic fiction.

Toni Morrison, *Tar Baby*—a novel by the American writer of fiction and poet; described as a stunning and eloquent contemporary love story; the writer sets out to dramatize the dilemma of black identity.

Minoru Oda, *Hiroshima*—a novel by the Japanese writer of fiction; a wide-ranging work that concerns events from Pearl Harbor to the bombing of Hiroshima; the characters include an American soldier and a uranium mine worker who develops cancer; considers the problems within the American army associated with the atomic bomb and uranium.

Philip Roth, *Zuckerman Unbound*—a novel by the American writer of fiction; the second volume of the "Zuckerman trilogy"; the title character, Nathan Zuckerman, struggles with the wealth, fame, intrusions, and estrangements that follow the enormous success of his fourth novel; the work abounds in comic diatribes: the conflicts between id and superego, between Jew and gentile, between artistic honesty and human decency.

D. M. Thomas, *The White Hotel*—a novel by the English writer of fiction, poet, and translator; a fictional recreation of the case history of one of Sigmund Freud's patients; a Russian-Jewish woman has erotic and nightmarish fantasies that she expresses in prose and verse; she relates her career as an opera singer and divulges the secrets of her subsequent marriages; she and her stepson drift toward a dream-foreseen death in the 1941 massacre at Babi Yar.

John Updike, *Rabbit Is Rich*—a novel by the American writer of fiction and essayist; continues the story of the mid-life crisis of the title character, Harry "Rabbit" Angstrom; the work receives the Pulitzer Prize, the National Book Critics Circle Award, and The American Book Award.

Gore Vidal, *Creation*—a novel by the American writer of fiction and miscellaneous prose; the work presents a panoramic view of ancient Persia, India, China, and Greece during the time of the great Buddha, Confucius, Socrates, and the great kings of the Persian Empire.

Patrick White, *Flaws in the Glass: A Self-Portrait*—an autobiographical work by the

Australian writer of fiction; the piece contains a brief but revealing account of the writer's allegedly ungracious reception of the 1973 Nobel Prize for literature; specifically, the writer persuaded his friend, the artist Sidney Nolan, to accept the award on his behalf.

EVENTS

Elias Canetti, Bulgarian-born German writer of fiction and playwright, receives the Nobel Prize for literature.

Elizabeth Becker Henley, American playwright, receives the Pulitzer Prize in drama for *Crimes of the Heart* (1979).

The National Humanities Alliance founded in Washington, D.C.; intended to support projects in the various humanities disciplines.

James Marcus Schuyler, American poet and writer of fiction, receives the Pulitzer Prize in poetry for his collection *The Morning of the Poem* (1980).

John Kennedy Toole, American writer of fiction, posthumously awarded the Pulitzer Prize in fiction for his novel *A Confederacy of Dunces,* (published, also posthumously, in 1980).

Marguerite Yourcenar, Belgian-born novelist, becomes the first woman elected to the Academie Francaise.

1982

DEATHS

Agusti Bartra (b. 1908). Spanish (Catalan) writer of fiction and playwright; after the Spanish Civil War, he spent time in Mexico and the United States before returning to Barcelona in 1970; his work reflects an existentialist and Heideggerian vision of the world, complete with Kafkaesque characters who feel condemned without knowing why; in his short pieces, in particular, he experimented with a range of techniques and tempos, particularly with the device of the same characters appearing frequently.

John Cheever (b. 1912). American writer of fiction; a moralist whose works were either comic or surreal; his characters and settings reflected life in the affluent suburbs of the United States, symbolizing what came to be called *The New Yorker* school of sophisticated fiction; in 1979 he received a Pulitzer Prize for his short story collection.

Babette Deutsch (b. 1895). American poet and essayist; she explored social problems in her verse, which tended to be sensitive, "intellectual," and emotional; she also reacted against the poetic values of nineteenth-century women poets.

Resat Enis (b. 1909). Turkish writer of fiction; his work revealed his extensive knowledge of the values and practices of the large landowners of the Shukur-Ova region, as well as of the problems of the impoverished peasants of that area.

Richard Franklin Hugo (b. 1923). American poet and essayist; he concentrated upon the deterioration of towns in the American West; his work tended to be autobiographical.

Geoffrey Langdon Keynes (b. 1887). English surgeon, scholar, and bibliographer; he compiled bibliographies of John Donne, John Evelyn, and William Blake; his most significant contributions to literature, however, are his editions and critical studies of Blake's works (1925-1966).

Eduardo Mallea (b. 1903). Argentinian writer of fiction; his novels, particularly, concentrate upon the theme of alienation; he also produced (1935) a significant critical work entitled *History of an Argentine Passion.*

Dame Ngaio Edith Marsh (b. 1899). New Zealand-born writer of fiction; her reputation rests on her detective novels, works praised for their characterization and style; her principal "hero" bears the name Chief Detective Inspector Roderick Alleyn.

Archibald MacLeish (b. 1892). American poet; his early verse ranges from expressions of post-World War I disillusionment to long narratives related to historical events; during the 1930s he expressed concern over the rise of fascism, and at that time developed his skill in the verse drama; during the administration of Franklin Delano Roosevelt, he served as Librarian of Congress (1939-1944) and undersecretary of state (1944-1945); he received the Pulitzer Prize in 1933, 1953, and 1959.

Ayn Rand (b. 1905). Russian-born American writer of fiction; she emigrated to the United States in 1926; her fiction, highly autobiographical and personal, reveals her independent spirit, a quality that appeared to have negatively affected her literary popularity and reputation; according to one view, "the Atlas that was Ayn Rand never shrugged"; she rarely found, during her lifetime, a suitable audience for her fiction.

Kenneth Rexroth (b. 1905). American poet; he became a leader of the San Francisco literary revival and, for a brief period, associated himself with the "Beat Generation"; his poems tend to be philosophical, lyrical, erotic, and "economical"; he also wrote critical essays and translated Oriental verse.

Edgell Rickword (b. 1898). English poet and critic; his literary reputation emerges from his association with a number of English literary periodicals: *The Calendar of Modern Letters, Scrutiny, The Left Review, Our Time.*

Ramon Jose Sender (b. 1902). Spanish writer of fiction, playwright, poet, and critic; he left Spain following the civil war in 1939 and eventually settled in the United States; his novels principally concern the issue of social injustice; he saw fiction more as a means for depicting the harshness of reality than as a highly intricate art form.

Frank Swinnerton (b. 1884). English writer of fiction and critic; he set his novels in contemporary London, which he described and observed with specificity and accuracy; his knowledge of the literary life and his friendships with the prominent literary figures of the day (principally Arnold Bennett and John Galsworthy) provided material for volumes of reminiscences; he continued to write and publish well past his 90th year.

Peter Ulrich Weiss (b. 1916). German-born Swedish playwright, writer of fiction, essayist, and translator; he always viewed drama as an instrument for self-discovery and political debate; thus, his lifelong commitment to Marxism found its way into all of his work, as did his sense of displacement from society and his guilt over having escaped the horrors of the Nazis and the Holocaust; his dramatic themes focus upon alienation, the "mechanisms of history," and the conflicts between individualism and collectivism and reality and illusion; he became a Swedish citizen after joining a commune of German-speaking artists and refugees in Stockholm (1938-1939).

PUBLICATIONS

Isabel Allende, *La Casa de los Espiritus* (The House of the Spirits)—the first novel by the Chilean writer of fiction and playwright; the writer's family history and the political upheaval in modern Chile serve as the primary sources for this work; the work gathers the recollections of its three main characters, beginning in the early part of the twentieth century, and blends dramatic events with subtle political messages.

Reinaldo Arenas, *Otra vez el Mar* (Farewell to the Sea: A Novel of Cuba)—the first novel by the Cuban writer of fiction and poet; the two parts of this work focus upon a husband and wife who, with their eight-month-old baby, leave Havana for a short vacation at the seashore; the wife relates her frustrated love for her husband and her confusion over his depressed state; the second part, presented as a long rambling poem, reveals the husband's alienation, disillusionment, and homosexuality; the novelist was forced to rewrite the piece twice from memory after Cuban authorities confiscated his manuscripts.

Saul Bellow, *The Dean's December*—a novel by the American writer of fiction; the principal character, the dean of men at a Chicago college, is married to a Romanian astronomer; he accompanies his wife to her homeland to visit her dying mother; the communist authorities deny them visiting rights; back home, the dean must confront the problems of a campus revolt and racism; thus, injustice exists in both a democratic society as well as in a totalitarian state.

Alan Bennett, *An Englishman Abroad*—a broadcast drama by the English playwright; concerns the theme of exile, as developed through the story of the life of an English spy in the Soviet Union; also focuses upon an affair between the spy and an actress.

John Cheever, *Oh What a Paradise It Seems*—a novel by the American writer of fiction; relates the story of an elegant but elderly man caught in an unlikely series of circumstances; those events reflect his despair at growing old, and thus he seeks renewal through love; the last significant work by the writer.

Dan Coles, *The Prinzhorn Collection*—a volume of verse by the Canadian poet and critic; reveals the poet's preoccupation with time, and thus the poems become meditations upon loss and aging; the poet relies upon his extensive travels through Europe and his interest in European history and culture; the title piece concerns a collection of writings and artworks produced by inmates of a German insane asylum in the late twentieth century; another poem, "Landslides," has been identified as one of the poet's finest achievements.

Noel Coward, *The Noel Coward Diaries*—published almost ten years after the writer's death, this edition of his diaries constitutes an entertaining volume of theatrical gossip, criticism of fellow playwrights, and comments upon members of the English royal family.

Li Cunbao, *The Wreath at the Foot of the Mountain*—a novel by the Chinese writer of fiction; the work created a sensation in China, principally because it concerns the brief war between that nation and Vietnam in 1979; the writer counters the propaganda demanded by the Cultural Revolution with realism; thus, he depicts military life as harsh and unromantic, while boldly exposing political corruption and inefficiency; the piece was transformed into a successful motion picture, thus offering an even closer look into the daily lives of Chinese soldiers and common people.

Jurg F. Federspiel, *Die Ballade von der Typhoid Mary* (The Ballad of Typhoid Mary)—a novel by the Swiss writer of fiction, poet, playwright, and essayist; an allegorical work based upon the history of the infamous carrier of typhus; the writer contrasts the optimism of late nineteenth-century America to the fate of the people who come in contact with the title character; from another view, he has conjured forth "a penitential vision of Western prosperity as the incubating phase of a moral illness."

Elaine Feinstein, *The Survivors*—a novel by the English writer of fiction, poet, and translator; the piece focuses upon a Jewish immigrant family thrust into an alien existence in Liverpool, England.

Max Frisch, *Blaubart* (Bluebeard: A Tale)—a short novel by the Swiss playwright, diarist, and writer of fiction; the title antihero engages in lengthy reflections on the theme of public guilt versus private guilt, injecting into his ruminations accounts of sexual promiscuity with his seven wives; there appears no real attempt on the part of the writer to draw strong parallels between his character and the original fairy tale or emotional opera of the same title.

John Fowles, *Mantissa*—a novel by the English writer of fiction; described as "a stunning exercise in literary invention"; the writer relies upon a confrontation between a writer and his Muse as the vehicle for exploring the nature of imagination, illusion, eroticism, and the modern novel.

Carlos Fuentes, *Una Familia Lejana* (Distant Relations)—a novel by the Mexican writer of fiction, playwright, and essayist; concerns a Mexican archaeologist and his son, who meet relatives in France; the theme of the piece directs itself toward the interaction between Mexican and European cultures; structurally, an old man relates the tale to a man named Carlos Fuentes, who, in turn, transmits the account to the reader; the writer includes ghosts and mysterious characters, thrusting fantastic events into the midst of realistic settings (a device termed "magic realism").

Thom Gunn, *The Occasion of Poetry: Essays in Criticism and Autobiography*—a collection by the English poet and essayist; a prose miscellany collected over twenty years; the writer discusses those older modern poets he most admires, such as William Carlos Williams and Thomas Hardy; he also writes about favorite contemporary poets, including Gary Snyder and Robert Duncan; the autobiographical pieces indicate how the poet became one the of "Americanized" English writers of verse who chose "a trans-Atlantic identity."

Mitsuaki Inoue, *Asu* (Tomorrow)—a novel by the Japanese writer of fiction; the work describes in detail the daily lives of "average" people in Nagasaki the day before the atomic bomb attack: a young female factory worker thinks of the man who made her pregnant and then fled, another woman anticipates her wedding, and a streetcar driver comments upon the scene; no one can even conceive that "tomorrow" will bring the ultimate in death and destruction.

Thomas Keneally, *Schindler's Ark*—a novel by the Australian writer of fiction, playwright, and essayist; the title character, a German industrialist, actually saved more than one thousand Jews from Nazi persecution; thus, the work filters history through fiction, since the writer interviewed Holocaust survivors who knew Oskar Schindler personally; the work receives the Booker Prize for fiction.

William Patrick Kinsella, *Shoeless Joe*—a novel by the Canadian writer of fiction; an Iowa farmer obsessed with baseball builds a ballpark in his cornfield; where baseball stars from the past magically appear, including Shoeless Joe Jackson, who was banned from the sport for his part in the 1919 "Black Sox" Scandal; the farmer kidnaps a reclusive writer and baseball fan named J. D. Salinger; the two men find renewed love for the game, and the farmer is offered an opportunity for reconciliation with his dead father; the novel was adapted into a popular Film—*Field of Dreams*— in 1988.

Primo Levi, *Se Non Ora, Quando?* (If Not Now, When?)—a novel by the Italian writer of fiction, memoirist, poet, and essayist; the writer reconstructs the historical odyssey of a group of Jewish partisans from Eastern Europe during World War II.

Earl Lovelace, *The Wine of Astonishment*—a novel by the Trinidadian writer of fiction, playwright, and poet; the writer details, through the perspective of a peasant woman, an actual historical incident; members of the Spiritual Baptist Church, denied the right of worship by government authorities, stage a revolt and restore their religious freedom; however, in the process, they lose their cultural spirit and must hope for renewal of their faith through the ardency of the younger generation.

Bernard Malamud, *God's Grace*—a novel by the American writer of fiction; a prophetic piece in which the writer forces his characters to examine the dreams and failures of humanity.

Julian Mitchell, *Another Country*—a play by the English writer of fiction and dramatist; set in an English public school, the work identifies the pressures and conflicts that caused a number of intellectuals during the 1930s to espouse Marxism and to commit acts of espionage against their own nation; the play produced in the year preceding its publication.

Harry Mulisch, *De Aanslag* (The Assault)—a novel by the Dutch writer of fiction, poet, and essayist; written in a realistic style, but with mythic, historic, and symbolic overtones; a Dutch anesthesiologist tries to distance himself from the childhood memory of the murder, by the Nazis during World War II, of his parents and brother; he encounters, by chance, a number of people who witnessed or were involved in the event; those confrontations force him to meditate upon the tragedy and cause him considerable grief.

Heberto Padilla, *En Mi Jardin Pastan Los Heroes* (Heroes Are Grazing in My Garden)—a novel by the Cuban poet, writer of fiction, and translator; the work focuses upon two characters: one, a writer, struggles with alcoholism, apathy, and constraints upon his work; the other finds that his work as a translator for his repressive government has left him disillusioned; the piece reflects the writer's mounting fear as revolutionary fervor hardens into dogma and people's private lives are restricted by politics.

Marge Piercy, *Circles on the Water: Selected Poems*—a collection of verse by the American writer of fiction and poet; contains more than 150 pieces collected from the writer's seven volumes of verse between 1963 and 1982.

Ishmael Scott Reed, *The Terrible Twos*—a novel by the American writer of fiction and poet; an elderly gentleman by the name of St. Nicholas and a dwarf identified as Black Peter wreak havoc in the White House oval office and on Wall Street.

Carlos Rojas, *El Sueno de Sarajevo* (The Dream of Sarajevo)—a novel by the Spanish writer of fiction; set in a private clinic high in the Pyrenees Mountains, the work goes forward upon various conversations between the patients; personalities, memories, and value systems all come into play here, against the background of impeccably white walls; the combination of fantasy and history becomes oppressive, and the reader may even question his or her own definition of sanity; the novel contains interesting parallels with Thomas Manns's *The Magic Mountain* and works by Franz Kafka.

Isaac Bashevis Singer, *Collected Stories*—the dominant motif of these pieces by the Polish-born Yiddish writer of fiction and playwright concerns the notion of human beings as defenseless and unprotected in the face of powerful, callous, and malevolent forces.

Tom Stoppard, *The Real Thing*—a play by the Czech-born English dramatist and writer of fiction; essentially a tragicomedy about love and marriage.

Guy Vanderhaeghe, *Man Descending*—the first collection of short stories by the Canadian writer of fiction; the majority of the twelve stories focus upon despondent, aimless, and unsuccessful characters; they represent the ability of the hopeless to comfort one another, which, in turn, offers them the only way out of their situations; the volume was awarded the Governor General's Literary Award for fiction.

Yevgeny Yevtushenko, *A Dove in Santiago: A Novella in Verse*—a "poem" by the Russian writer of verse and fiction, playwright, and essayist; the writer combines blank and free verse to describe the tragic experience of a young art student living in Chile; the piece is set during the presidency of Salvador Allende and focuses upon the universal issue of life and death.

EVENTS

Charles H. Fuller, Jr. American playwright, receives the Pulitzer Prize in drama for *A Soldier's Play* (1981).

Gabriel Jose Garcia Marquez, Columbian writer of fiction, receives the Nobel Prize for literature.

Sylvia Plath, American writer of fiction and poet, posthumously awarded the Pulitzer Prize in poetry for *The Collected Poems* (1981).

John Hoyer Updike, American writer of fiction, poet, and essayist, receives the Pulitzer Prize in fiction for his novel *Rabbit is Rich* (1981).

1983

DEATHS

Fedor Aleksandrovich Abramov (b. 1920). Russian writer of fiction; his work fused the tonal qualities of tragedy, bittersweet humor, and irony; thematically, he focused upon the extremes of human nature, the family, the strengthening qualities of hardships, the devastating effects of war, and the disappointment of failed lives; he wrote a number of his short pieces in the "earthy" dialects of simple country folk.

Eric Hoffer (b. 1902). American essayist and writer of prose narrative; in terms of social and political thought, he represented the working class, he having been a laborer and a longshoreman.

Frances Hooker Horovitz (b. 1938). English poet; she wrote lyrical descriptions of and emotive reactions to the countryside around Gloucestershire and Northumberland, the two principal places she lived; she died in Northumberland from cancer.

Mordecai Menahem Kaplan (b. 1881). Lithuanian-born scholar, philosopher, theologian, and essayist; he wrote profound works on Judaism and became the founder of a religious movement known as Reconstructionism; his thought and work evolved from the conflict within his own mind between traditional religious beliefs and modern conceptions nurtured by science; thus, for him, Judaism became more than simply a religion: he tended to view it as a civilization.

Arthur Koestler (b. 1905). Hungarian-born writer of fiction, essayist, and philosopher; in the 1930s he embraced communism, but left the party during the Stalin purge trials; he then became a prominent voice of the noncommunist Left, combining a brilliant journalistic prose style with an obvious sense of commitment; in 1940, he settled in England.

Vladimir Neff (b. 1909). Czech writer of fiction; his work principally concerns itself with real and fictional historical characters and is set against the background of his own nation; a skilled storyteller who displayed a strong sense of social satire and irony; he published steadily between 1933 and 1981, receiving, in 1979, the title of National Artist.

Merce Rodoreda (b. 1909). Spanish (Catalan) writer of fiction; she created a number of moods in her work, from the starkly realistic to the surreal or fantastic, and an equal variety of character types from different social classes; her work focuses upon brutal life in a shanty town, retarded and abused maidservants, and love frustrated by timidity; admirers of her fiction have referred to her as "the greatest contemporary Catalan novelist and possibly the best Mediterranean woman author since Sappho."

Christina Ellen Stead (b. 1902). Australian writer of fiction; without undue reliance upon sentimentalism, she wrote about the problems of human obsession and evil; her work was influenced by Emile Zola, and she embraced such contemporary movements as feminism; her wandering lifestyle and left-wing views hindered her productivity and popularity.

Dame Rebecca West (originally Cecily Isabel Fairfield; b. 1892). Irish-born English writer of fiction and journalist; her novels tend to be highly reportorial in tone, but contain insightful psychological analyses of characters; she developed strong and unconventional female characters and demonstrated skill in structuring her fiction; she continued to write almost to the moment of her death, at age ninety.

Tennessee Williams (b. 1914). American playwright; his highly poetic pieces, filled with dramatic tension and literary dialogue, explore the passions and frustrations of society, particularly in the American South; he also wrote short fiction, two novels, and memoirs.

PUBLICATIONS

Maya Angelou, *Shaker, Why Don't You Sing?*— a collection of verse by the American poet and writer of fiction and autobiographical narrative; these "deceptively light and graceful" pieces tend to be lyrical, emotional, and melancholy in tone, drawing the reader toward a sense of both history and myth and exposing the contrasts within black and white tensions; contains such poems as "Family Affairs" and "Caged Bird."

Jacques Barzun, *A Stroll with William James*—a work of nonfiction by the French-born American historian and critic; the writer blends biographical details with analysis and explanation of James's philosophy.

Malcolm Stanley Bradbury, *Rates of Exchange*—a novel by the English writer of fiction and critic; a realistic account of an English academic in Eastern Europe; the writer blends the picaresque with the political, as the professor discovers, in his wandering, confusion, anxiety, and unlikely romance.

Ariel Dorfman, *Widows*—a novel by the Chilean-born writer of nonfiction and fiction and poet; focuses upon the struggle between an autocratic government and thirty-seven women who suspect that their missing husbands have been abducted and murdered by the authorities; the work is set in Greece during the 1940s, but only to avoid the Chilean censors; the writer draws sensitive portraits of the wives, but does not ignore those young men pressured to execute the commands of a repressive regime.

Maureen Duffy, *Londoners*—a novel by the English poet, playwright, and writer of fiction; concerns, on one level, the writer's own situation in the contemporary cosmopolitan section of Earl's Court, London; although the narrator bears the name "Al," the writer clothes the sex of that character in intentional ambiguity; in typical fashion, she confronts the issue of homosexuality with directness and honesty.

John Fuller, *Flying to Nowhere*—a novel by the English poet and writer of fiction; the work is set on an island off Wales and exists as a fantasy about a sixteenth-century abbot; that character believes that he has discovered, through surgical dissection, the source of the human soul.

Geoffrey Hill, *The Mystery of the Charity of Charles Peguy*—a poem by the English writer of verse; a complex piece that exists as a med-itation on the life, faith, poetry, political career, and death of the French writer.

Francis King, *Act of Darkness*—a novel by the Swiss-born English writer of fiction and critic; a psychological "thriller" set in India; a study in perverse and pathological behavior, the work focuses on the murder of a small boy and the possible involvement in that act of his father, sister, and governess.

John Le Carre, *The Little Drummer Girl*—a novel by the English writer of fiction; Israeli intelligence agents manipulate a leftist-leaning British actress; through her, they attempt to penetrate a Palestinian cell.

Norman Mailer, *Ancient Evenings*—a fantasy by the American writer of fiction and miscellaneous prose; presents a portrait of Ramses II and life and events within ancient Egypt; underneath the surface of the piece lies a definite parallel with contemporary occurrences in the United States.

Kamal Markandaya, *Shalimar*—a novel by the Indian writer of fiction; set in post-independence India, the work concerns the collision between primitive innocence and technological sophistication; missionaries of a South Indian fishing village educate an orphan; an Englishman builds a luxury pleasure complex, thus disturbing the pastoral serenity of the community; ultimately, the conflict arises when the orphan, now grown, drifts toward the life of the Englishman and his corporate world; in the end, the novelist appears to have accepted the modernization that must necessarily come to her nation.

Roland Glyn Mathias, *Burning Brambles: Selected Poems, 1944-1979*—a collection by the Welsh poet; writer of fiction, essayist, and biographer; the volume brings together the most important works of the writer, skillful, resonant pieces that transcend the particulars of place and history.

John Montague, *The Dead Kingdom*—a poem cycle by the American-born Irish writer of verse and fiction, critic, and translator; the poet recounts his travels from the Irish Republic to Northern Ireland for his mother's funeral; during the journey, he reflects upon his life and family, mourning the secular and religious divisions in Ireland.

R. K. Narayan, *A Tiger for Malgudi*—a novel by the Indian writer of fiction, essayist, and memoirist; the writer relies upon Indian legends and folk tales to suggest that beasts may be as capable of thought and feeling as human beings; a tiger serves as the narrator, tracing his spiritual development in overcoming his potential for violence; thus, a creature may attain spiritual maturity without having to assume human form.

Kanzaburo Oe, *Atarashii Hito Yo Mezameyo* (Rise Up, O Young Men of the New Age)—a collection of short stories by the Japanese writer of fiction and essayist; these seven pieces derive their individual titles from the verse of William Blake; in this volume, the writer confronts the themes of madness, fear of death, and infanticide.

Philip Roth, *The Anatomy Lesson*—a novel by the American writer of fiction; the final volume of the "Zuckerman trilogy"; a hilariously funny piece, yet not without its dark moments; Nathan Zuckerman endures his own self-doubt and guilt as he searches for the meaning of the angst that plagues twentieth-century humanity.

A. J. P. Taylor, *A Personal History*—an autobiographical narrative by the eminent English historian; comments upon his colleagues and acquaintances; more importantly, the work traces the writer's political sympathies, from his support of labor in the General Strike to his alliance with the Campaign for Nuclear Disarmament.

Gore Vidal, *Duluth*—a novel by the American writer of fiction and miscellaneous prose; described as an Orwellian tragedy set in a grotesque version of a typical American town.

Alice Walker, *The Color Purple*—a novel by the American writer of fiction, poet, and essayist; an epistolary work that traces thirteen years in the life of Celie, a poor Southern black woman who is victimized physically and emotionally by both her stepfather and her husband; eventually she finds strength and solace in her friendships with other women and gains the courage to leave her loveless marriage; the work was awarded both the Pulitzer Prize for fiction and the American Book Award.

Dieter Wellershoff, *Der Sieger Nimmt Alles* (Winner Takes All)—a novel by the German writer of fiction, playwright, and essayist; the piece relates how a man's passion for money and power leads to his demise; the writer focuses upon the psyche of his principal character, but at the same time comment upon present-day West Germany: the means and the motivation behind the nation's economic recovery following World War II.

EVENTS

William Gerald Golding, English writer of fiction, poet, and essayist, receives the Nobel Prize for literature.

Galway Kinnell, American writer of verse, receives the Pulitzer Prize in poetry for *Selected Poems* (1982).

Marsha Norman, American playwright, receives the Pulitzer Prize in drama, for *'Night, Mother* (1982).

Alice Malsenior Walker, American writer of fiction, poet, and essayist, receives the Pulitzer Prize in fiction for her novel *The Color Purple* (1983).

1984

DEATHS

Vicente Aleixandre y Meilo (b. 1898). Spanish poet; his verse was surrealistic in form and substance; in 1977, he received the Nobel Prize for literature.

Justin Brooks Atkinson (b. 1894). American drama critic; he dominated the New York City drama scene as early as the late 1920s; he also wrote essays and biographical studies on American literature; he served as a feature news correspondent during World War II, receiving a Pulitzer Prize in journalism for his efforts.

John Betjeman (b. 1906). English poet and critic; his verse combined witty appraisal of contemporary events with an obvious sense of nostalgia for the Victorian era; in 1972, he received the appointment as Poet Laureate of England.

Truman Capote (b. 1924). American writer of fiction and miscellaneous prose; his novels and stories reflected a world of grotesque and strangely innocent individuals; he also displayed extreme skill in transforming topics of exceptionally popular interest into the "non-fiction novel."

Julio Cortazar (b. 1914). Belgian-born Argentinian writer of prose fiction; he proved an exponent of surrealism, and thus tended to depict life as a complex labyrinth; his novels reached the height of their popularity during the 1960s.

William Empson (b. 1906). English poet and literary critic; he gained literary recognition for the witty substance and tone of his verse, as well as for his critical prose tract *Seven Types of Ambiguity,* a classic work of modern literary commentary.

Jorge Guillen (b. 1893). Spanish poet and essayist; his verse tended to be classical in form, yet proved exceedingly difficult because of the complexity of its symbolism; he settled in the United States in 1939 and produced a valuable bilingual anthology of verse in 1968.

Uwe Johnson (b. 1934). German writer of fiction and translator; his novels explore the conflict of a divided Germany and focus upon the guilt of the collective German consciousness; thus the Berlin Wall appears on numerous occasions in his work as a symbol of a divided world; born in East Germany, he crossed over to the West in 1959, specifically so that he could publish his work; in 1971, he received the Georg Buchner Prize.

William Denis Johnston (b. 1901). Irish playwright and critic; in addition to producing, between 1924 and 1958, a series of mildly successful plays, he became director of the Dublin Gate Theater; he engaged in the study of mystical philosophy, while also writing drama for radio and television.

Richmond Alexander Lattimore (b. 1906). American literary scholar, poet, and translator; he served on the English faculty at Bryn Mawr between 1935 and 1971; he gained a distinguished reputation as a translator of the classics: Pindar, Homer, Aeschylus, Aristophanes, Euripides; he wrote verse steadily during his tenure at Bryn Mawr.

Liam O'Flaherty (b. 1897). Irish writer of fiction; his realistic stories and novels focused upon the conditions and situations of ordinary human beings; between 1928 and 1946, he concentrated his interest upon nineteenth-century Ireland.

John Boynton Priestley (b. 1894). English writer of fiction, critic, poet, playwright, and miscellaneous prose writer; the quantity and variety of his literary output almost defies summary; he wrote novels, short fiction, social and experimental drama, history, literary and social criticism, and mystery fiction; one of his major lifelong projects focused upon his attempt to "define the Englishness of English."

Gwendolyn Margaret Pharis Ringwood (b. 1910). American-born Canadian playwright, writer of fiction, poet, and essayist; she gained literary recognition for her folk dramas set in the western provinces of Alberta and British Columbia; she relied, in her work, upon a variety of dramatic forms: classical tragedy, farce, comedy, and the musical; her characters range from the common people of the farm and prairie to folk heroes and famous historical figures; she presented accurate and realistic pictures of the people, landscapes, and conditions of the Canadian West.

Irwin Shaw (b. 1913). American writer of fiction and playwright; his fiction, particularly, concerns itself with the contemporary world: business, war, Hollywood, romance, and white-collar crime; the ability to sustain high levels of intensity and a concern for realistic situations proved the principal reasons for his popularity among readers.

Mikhail Aleksandrovich Sholokhov (b. 1905). Russian writer of fiction; he depicted the effects of Russian life of World War I, the Revolution on 1917, and the civil war that followed; other themes involved the Cossacks and agricultural collectivization; in 1965, he received the Nobel Prize for literature.

Jesse Hilton Stuart (b. 1907). American poet and writer of fiction and autobiographical narrative; representative of the typical regionalist writer, he tended to develop themes and characters from his native Kentucky, as well as descriptions of the countryside there; he produced a steady stream of verse and prose between 1934 and 1979.

PUBLICATIONS

Risto Ahti, *Loistana Yksinaisyys* (Shining Solitude)—the eleventh collection of verse by the Finnish poet; the poems demonstrate a clear relationship between the romanticism of the eighteenth-century English poet William Blake and that of late twentieth-century Finnish verse; thus, the writer searches for meaning in life and for a key to human survival; at the same time, however, the poet does not abandon his humor: a taxi driver too shy to receive passengers, a hunter carrying his gun upside down, a swimmer with an anchor tied to his ankle; human beings go forward in their "blindness," creating impasses for themselves, but remaining confident in their abilities to reason.

Abd-al-Wahhab al-Bayati, *Qamar Shiraz* (The Moon of Shiraz)—a collection of poetry in free verse by the Egyptian poet; the pieces reflect the turmoil, change, and quest for stability and meaning characteristic of the recent history of Arab nations; the themes of this collection focus on exile and alienation, the impact of industrialization and growing urbanization, deprivation in the midst of plenty, depersonalization of human values, and general spiritual anguish.

J. G. Ballard, *Empire of the Sun*—a novel by the Shanghai-born writer of science fiction; highly autobiographical, the piece is based on the writer's capture and imprisonment by the Japanese following the fall of Shanghai early in World War II; the work becomes the basis for a motion picture by Steven Spielberg.

S. S. Bhoosnurmath, *Bhavya Manava* (The Grand Man)—a poem by the Indian writer of verse; epic in form and scope, the work appears in six cantos ("kandas") and depicts the evolution of the entire human race, from the five elements to the divine human being; written in free-verse narrative, the piece sustains the high level of drama necessary for depicting the cosmic drama of the world; the reader will immediately see its debt to and parallels with John Milton's *Paradise Lost*.

George Mackay Brown, *Time in a Red Coat*—the third novel by the Scottish poet, writer of fiction, essayist, and playwright; a fable that chronicles the experiences of a young Eastern princess; she journeys through distant countries and flees the devastation of her homeland by marauders; a representation of innocence, she begins her travels with a white coat that gradually turns red as she encounters human folly and injustice.

Andree Chedid, *Echec a la Reine* (The Queen's Defeat)—a play by the Egyptian-born French writer of fiction, poet, playwright, and essayist; the work is set in a palace and focuses upon the interaction between a lonely queen and a clown, her constant companion; the height of the piece comes during a confrontation involving the queen, the clown, and the queen's runaway son.

Annalisa Cima, *Ipotesi d'Amore*—a collection of verse by the Italian poet; the writer addresses the thirty-six pieces to Cherubino, the young character from Wolfgang Amadeus Mozart's opera *Nozze di Figaro* (The Marriage of Figaro); Cherubino appears as a "jolly god," a playful cupid who can still cast arrows and induce people toward love; in addition, he appears as "the interior musicality" that the poet finds within herself; the poet also directs her thoughts to "the interior musicality"

within other writers of verse, particularly the lyric poets of the rich Italian tradition.

Leonard Cohen, *Book of Mercy*—a volume of verse by the Canadian poet, playwright, songwriter, and writer of fiction; the poet focuses upon spiritual themes and patterns pieces after traditional Hebrew prayers for forgiveness.

Humberto Costantini, *La Larga Noche de Francisco Sanctis* (The Long Night of Francisco Sanctis)—a novel by the Argentinian writer of fiction, playwright, and poet; the title character questions whether he should remain a passive citizen of a fascist regime or deliver information that could save the lives of two enemies of the government.

Paul Durcan, *Jumping the Train Tracks with Angela*—a collection of verse by the Irish poet; the pieces evidence the poet's characteristic scorn of repressive social and religious practices in Northern Ireland, as well as his hatred of the violence in that part of the country; the pieces also display his whimsical humor on such themes as love and social relationships.

Jan Drzezdzon, *Twarz Boga* (God's Face)—a volume of miscellaneous pieces by the Polish writer of fiction, essayist, and academician (Gdansk University); an extremely personal and reflective collection that reveals the writer's acute awareness of self and his continuous need for self-assessment; the reflections range through a variety of subjects; political and historical influences, the Warsaw literary establishment, "dialogues" with Christ, the nature of time and the disappearance of civilizations; the book has two distinct parts: "God's Face" represents a series of diary entries (7 January 1981-1 February 1981), while "Noah" serves as a collection of vignettes or "metaphysical parables."

William Empson, *Using Biography*—a collection of essays by the English poet and critic, published posthumously; the pieces published between 1958 and 1982; the writer attacks the New Critics (of which the writer, himself, had been a distinct part) for their neglect of biographical details.

Louise Erdrich, *Jacklight*—the first volume of verse by the native American poet and novelist; the forty-four pieces focus upon the theme suggested by the title, a "jacklight" being a usually illegal light to lure game when hunting at night; set in the Turtle Mountain Chippewa reservation in North Dakota; she writes of the Chippewa, Cree, French, English, Scottish, and German legacies of the people there; they stand in the midst of degradation, but reject self-pity and improvise their strength from whatever surrounds them.

Nguyen Mong Giac, *Ngu'a Na'n Chan Bon* (A Tired Horse Trots On)—a collection of short stories by the Vietnamese writer of fiction; the thirteen pieces were composed during the writer's terms in refugee camps in Indonesia, as he waited to be resettled in the United States; the stories tend to be philosophical in theme and form, focusing upon such issues as death and religion, reenforced by statements on human bondage, emotion, and suffering.

Allen Ginsberg, *Collected Poems, 1947-1980*— a volume by the American writer of verse, for which he wrote the preface; the work draws from over ten books of the writer's verse and includes a manual for readers, a large section of notes to the poems, and an index of proper names; the pieces themselves tend to be highly autobiographical and reveal the degree of spontaneity that has long characterized the poet's work.

Natalia Ginzburg, *La Citta e la Casa*—an epistolary novel by the Italian writer of fiction; the principal letter writer is as a middle-aged man who leaves his home and position at a Rome newspaper to live with his brother in Princeton, New Jersey; he abandons his former friends and becomes lonely and alienated, the other characters of the piece lead equally unhappy existences, all seeming to support the writer's contention of life as a "mysterious deadlock."

William Golding, *The Paper Men*—a novel by the English writer of fiction; an English novelist declines into drink and self-pity; nonetheless, he manages to turn the tables on a young American academician who aspires to become his biographer; a satire upon the entire literary establishment.

Gyorgy Gomori, *Nyugtalan Koranmyar* (Restless Early Summer)—a volume of verse by the Hungarian poet, published at Washington, D.C.; the poet assesses his own life, principally the rigors and failures of middle age and the invigorating possibilities of a new beginning.

Francisco Gonzalez Ledesma, *Cronica Sentimental en Rojo*—a murder mystery by the Spanish writer of fiction; the novel contains a street-wise police officer and the traditional elements of murder, suspense and motive; the writer also provides insights into both high and low life in Barcelona, offering realistic local color and inside views into the news media (the results of the writer's experiences as a reporter); depicts life among prostitutes, transvestites, and drug dealers; the work receives the Planeta Prize for fiction.

Michael Hartnett, *Collected Poems*—a volume of verse by the Irish poet; the poems continue the writer's intellectual struggle with the past and evidence the tension between a romantic ideal and the real world; further, the pieces evidence the writer's almost lifelong creative battle with the Anglo-Irish traditions of William Butler Yeats.

Stefan Heym, *The Wandering Jew*—a novel by the East German writer of fiction, poet, and translator; a complex piece of theological satire set, concurrently, in the sixteenth century, the present, and an eternal and timeless region; concerns the efforts of the title character to persuade a latter-day Jesus Christ to assume responsibility for the world and to avert human misery, as opposed to directing the wrath of God against innocent people.

Christopher Hope, *Kruger's Alp*—a novel by the South African-born English writer of fiction, poet, and critic; essentially a "slapstick" parody of John Bunyan's *Pilgrim's Progress;* with allegory, myth, and dreamlike imagery, the writer describes the adventures of a former priest's search for a legendary city of gold, supposedly built in 1901 near Geneva, Switzerland, by the exiled Boer revolutionary leader Paul Kruger; the writer combines metaphor with South African history.

F. Sionil Jose, *Po-on*—a novel by the Philippine writer of fiction; the fifth and final volume of a cycle begun in 1962 and entitled *The Pretenders;* the piece occurs between 1880 and 1900 and concerns the migration of the principal character from the Ilocos to central Luzon, settling on lands adjoining the hacienda of a Spanish family.

Jaan Kaplinski, *Tule Tagasi Helmemand* (Return, Pinus Succinifera)—the seventh collection of verse by the Estonian poet; the title signifies a call for the reappearance of a tree that became extinct at the beginning of the Ice Age, and it also parallels the poet's return to the earliest stages of his own poetic creativity; the mood of the poems tends to be lyrical and the themes philosophical; the poet calls for universal harmony, inviting the reader to look inward, to contemplate the universe, to discover peace in the simple activities of daily existence.

Jamaica Kincaid, *At the Bottom of the River*— a collection of short stories by the West Indian-born American writer of fiction; her prose style in these pieces achieves a poetic lyricism that evokes the surrealistic qualities of ordinary objects and events; the majority of the stories rely upon repetition of phrases and images that reinforces themes of individuality, identity, and purpose.

Deirdre Levinson, *Modus Vivendi*—a novel by the Welsh-born American writer of fiction; the principal character, Queenie Quesky, mourns the loss of her infant son; she may well have contributed to his death by relying upon amphetamines during her pregnancy; she must endure her loss by earning a living as a teacher, raising her daughter, and attempting to save her marriage to a professor addicted to drugs; the entire "hallowed halls of ivy" have become a living nightmare.

David Lodge, *Small World*—a novel by the English critic and writer of fiction; the American academician Martin Zapp and his English colleague, Philip Swallow (both from earlier novels), engage in a series of "highjinks" on the jet-set international academic conference circuit.

Norman Mailer, *Tough Guys Don't Dance*—a novel by the American writer of fiction and miscellaneous prose; a "thriller" set on the east coast of the United States, the work concerns a man who cannot remember whether he has actually murdered a girl.

Medbh McGuckian, *Venus and the Rain*—a volume of verse by the Irish poet; she employs the dramatic monologues of an indeterminate persona to focus upon such themes as love, sex, and relationships between females of different generations; the elements of fantasy emerge here.

Leslie Allan Murray, *The People's Other World*—a poetry collection by the Australian writer of verse and fiction and critic; the poet relies upon metaphor and allusion to comment upon spiritual concerns, which he contrasts with the material world; the strength of these pieces derives from the poet's ability to clothe philosophical and theological ideas in concrete images.

Marge Piercy, *Fly Away Home*—a novel by the American writer of fiction and poet; focuses upon a successful writer who manages to reconstruct her life after a devastating divorce.

Viktoras Pivonas, *Der Himmel des Humoristen*—a novel by the Lithuanian-born German writer of fiction; develops the character of an entrepreneur and his establishment of a non-profit charitable organization to aid the homeless and the hungry of Third World nations; however, the organization expands to become a financial empire, with only a small portion of its receipts filtering down to those who need help; simply, the novel serves as a brutal piece of social satire, directed against the institutionalization of charity.

Kenneth Rexroth, *Selected Poems*—a volume of verse by the American poet and critic, issued two years following his death; collects "representative" works covering sixty years of the poet's creative productivity, with the pieces arranged chronologically; four major themes emerge from these poems: philosophical meditation, nature experience complemented by universal and mystical concepts, socially conscious outcries against human beings' inhumanity to one another, and the general topic of love.

Moshe Shamir, *Hinumat Kala* (Bridal Veil)—a novel by the Israeli writer of fiction; focuses on the "throbbing" Jewish world of czarist Russia at the beginning of the twentieth century; the central character, a daughter of the middle class, becomes active in the radical politics of the Jewish intelligentsia; she survives a cruel prison experience, endures harassment from the police, and manages to smuggle herself out of the country with the aid of her comrades; after an uninspired affair with a man out of her past, she devotes the remainder of her life to others, thus determining to abandon hope of all personal happiness.

Muriel Spark, *The Only Problem*—a novel by the Scottish-born writer of fiction, poet, playwright, essayist, and biographer; the work exists as a version of the biblical story of Job; the principal character continues to write a monograph on the Book of Job despite a number of personal problems: the disintegration of his marriage and the knowledge that his former wife functions as a terrorist; finding his life to parallel that of Job, he realizes that only through suffering can the individual approach a true appreciation of the meaning of being alive.

Terje Stigen, *Baldershavn*—a novel by the Norwegian writer of fiction; set on a small imaginary island west of Lofoten during the early period of the Renaissance and the reign of Christian VII of Denmark; the place of the title houses a penal colony, governed by an all-powerful tyrant; the plot of the piece goes forward upon the themes of political corruption, autocratic governance, and cruel exploitation of unfortunate and innocent people.

Tom Stoppard, *Squaring the Circle*—a political play by the Czech-born English dramatist; originally aired on London television in May of this year; presents the history of the Solidarity movement in Poland; the piece is unique to the writer because of its documentary style.

Randolph Stow, *The Suburbs of Hell*—a novel by the Australian writer of fiction; the novelist manipulates the conventions of crime fiction to comment upon modern humanity's fascination with horror and misfortune; thus, he relies upon epigraphs from Elizabethan and Jacobite plays to complement his tale of a seaside English village plagued by several grisly murders.

Ibrahim Tahir, *The Last Imam*—a novel by the Nigerian writer of fiction; in this piece, the writer provides a view of the workings and functions of the court of an emir; he also considers, the reactions of worshipers to their imam's sermons; a "tour" of kitchens and bedrooms provides an intimate look at domestic and sexual crises in the life of the eminent but flawed protagonist of the title.

Antonio Torrado, *De Vitor ao Xadres*—a volume of short fiction by the Portuguese poet and writer of fiction; the pieces present a world of fantasy and distortion through a host of subjective speakers, narrators, and characters who dream and hallucinate; the stories range widely in inventiveness and tone, while the writer's style comes forth as "clean and concise"; the thirty-two stories subvert the rational and ordered unity of cotemporary society.

John Updike, *The Witches of Eastwick*—a novel by the American writer of fiction; focuses upon the revelry and mystery of three Rhode Island witches; these free-spirited women, in the aftermath of their failed marriages, rejoice together in their newly found supernatural powers.

Derek Walcott, *Midsummer*—a fifty-four poem sequence by the West Indian writer of verse and playwright; the author relies upon detailed visual imagery, repetition, a loose rhyme scheme, and a firm narrative structure; the theme of the work concerns divided allegiance.

Alice Walker, *Horses Make a Landscape Look More Beautiful*—a volume of poems by the American writer of fiction and verse; the collection contains seventy poems upon the themes of racial oppression and personal fulfillment; includes "Well," "Family Of," "Killers," "The Diamonds on Liz's Bosom," and "Listen."

George F. Walker, *Criminals in Love*—the eleventh play by the Canadian dramatist; the piece represents the writer's characteristic black humor; the action occurs in a low-class urban area, where two teenage lovers find themselves bullied and manipulated into joining a terrorist conspiracy organized by the boy's disreputable relatives; the work receives the Governor General's Literary Award for drama.

Theodore Weiss, *A Slow Fuse*—a collection of poems by the American poet and critic; the forty poems have been divided into five sections, the first and the last dedicated to Hannah Arendt and Heinrich Blucher; generally, the pieces reveal the writer as a poet of nature and of "the dark and lonely seasons of the heart"; in addition, as a technician, he proves himself a master of the schemes of embellishment: chiasmus, anadiplosis, familiar figures of sound, and the juxtaposition of decorative figures with plain English.

Yevgeny Yevtushenko, *Ardobiola*—a novel by the Russian poet, writer of fiction, playwright, and essayist; the work consists of chapters written in diverse styles, each combining elements from a variety of genres; the central character, a humanist Soviet scientist, crosses an insect with a plant to create the title of the piece, a hybrid that cures cancer; the work also satirizes Soviet culture and government and considers the influence of American materialism upon Russian youth.

EVENTS

Edward James (Ted) Hughes, English poet, critic, and biographer, appointed Poet Laureate of England, succeeding Sir John Betjeman.

William Kennedy, American writer of fiction, receives the Pulitzer Prize in fiction for *Ironweed* (1983).

Mary Oliver, American writer of verse, receives the Pulitzer Prize in poetry for *American Primitive* (1983).

Otto Oliveira, Cuban critic and literary scholar, publishes (in the United States) his *Bibliografia de la Literatura Domminicana (1960-1982)*, a bibliography of 1181 entries emphasizing the creative literature of the Dominican Republic, Cuba, and Puerto Rico.

Jaroslav Seifert, Czech poet, receives the Nobel Prize for literature.

Yar Slavutych, Ukrainian (SSR) literary scholar, compiles and publishes his *An Annotated Bibliography of Ukrainian Literature in Canada; Book Publications 1908-1983;* refers to 328 writers and 2200 works published in Ukrainian and English.

1985

DEATHS

Martin Adan (pseudonym of Raphael de la Fuente Benavides; b. 1908). Peruvian writer of fiction and poet; he began writing at age sixteen, while still a student at the Lima Deutsche Schule; a literary innovator, he created streams of images, wordplays, refurbished clichés, and "lexical surprises"; generally, his work requires an extreme imaginative commitment from readers.

Heinrich Theodor Boll (b. 1917). German writer of fiction, essayist, playwright, and translator; he became known as the literary conscience of Germany for his involvement in practically every stage of his nation's post-World War II literary development; he wrote more than forty novels, short stories, and pieces of nonfiction, almost all of which reveal his strong social conscience and hatred of war, totalitarianism, and militarism; in 1972, he received the Nobel Prize for literature.

Janet Taylor Caldwell (b. 1900). English-born writer of fiction; her novels tend to focus upon the popular and dramatic aspects of history, ranging from the Mongolian empire to Nazi Germany, from sixteenth-century France to the great American dream of the early twentieth century.

Italo Calvino (b. 1923). Italian writer of fiction, essayist, and translator; he achieved a reputation as a master of allegorical fantasy, rising to become one of the leading contemporary novelists in Italy; he developed his narratives from traditional folk tales and legends, while his characters "defied the malaise of daily life in the modern world"; he died at a hospital in Siena, Italy, from the effects of a stroke suffered two weeks previously.

Nikos Gatsos (b. 1912). Greek poet, playwright, and translator; he combined in his verse elements of surrealism and the traditional folk song, which gave to his work an unmistakably Greek quality.

Robert Rank Graves (b. 1895). English poet, writer of fiction, critic, and translator; he produced a number of pieces rooted in Roman history and Greek mythology; he also developed a "personal mythology" that permeated his poetry and caused problems for readers; nonetheless, the astute reader cannot fail to grasp the emotionalism of his love poetry, where he combined cynicism and passion with the romantic and the erotic; between 1961 and 1966, he held the chair of poetry at Oxford.

Susanne Katherina Langer (b. 1895). American philosopher, essayist, and academician (Columbia); her works considered such topics as symbolic logic, aesthetics, various art forms, and critical methodology.

Philip Arthur Larkin (b. 1922). English poet and critic; his verse relies heavily upon his subtle wit and his sensitivity toward the truly and ordinary "English" way of life; he also wrote a novel and a series of essays related to jazz criticism.

Helen Clark MacInnes (b. 1907). Scottish-born American writer of fiction and playwright; she gained a popular reputation as a "spy novelist" and her books have sold more than twenty-three million copies in the United States alone; four of those works became motion pictures; her works have been translated into some twenty-two languages; in 1952, she and her husband, the literary critic and scholar Gilbert Highet, became citizens of the United States.

Elsa Morante (b. 1918). Italian writer of fiction, poet, and translator; in her work, she explored conflicts between illusion and reality, relying heavily upon elements of fantasy; her prose style was surrealistic, characterized by a lucid presentation of unreal events; her principal themes included the psychological implications of exclusion and separation, the common person's struggle against the institutions and ideologies of society, the relationships between human beings and their external world, and the encroachment of reality upon dream and memory.

Shivadhar Srinivasa Naipaul (b. 1945). Trinidadian writer of fiction and essayist; his journalistic and travel narratives report with frankness what he viewed as the failings of life in the Third World; he argued that African independence principally benefited a black elite, emphasizing that the African continent continued to crave and demand material goods from the West; he died in London, at age forty, of a heart attack.

Elwyn Brooks White (b. 1899). American essayist, poet, and writer of nonfiction and children's literature; he emerged as a witty, satiric observer of the contemporary American scene, gaining a literary reputation through his regular contributions to *The New Yorker* magazine; he also wrote light, humorous verse.

PUBLICATIONS

Aase Foss Abrahamsen, *Fuglen og den Hvite Duken* (The Bird and the White Tablecloth)—a novel by the Norwegian writer of fiction; concerns a teenage girl in Nazi-occupied Norway in the early 1940s; the writer concerns himself with the unsung heroes of war who must endure on the home front; essentially, he attempts to reconcile the privations of war with loyalties to national principles.

Brian Aldiss, *Helliconia Winter*—a novel by the English writer of fiction; the final volume of an epic trilogy that describes the evolution of an entire planetary system, one in which a season lasts for hundreds of years.

Homero Aridjis, *1492: Vida y Tiempso de Juan Cabezon de Castilla*—a historical novel by the Mexican writer of fiction and poet; the work focuses upon the life and times of Moorish-Judeo-Christian Spain, combining the traditional structure of the picaresque novel with a prose style that tends to be highly lyrical; the writer transports his reader through a shameful and traumatic period of Spanish history: the persecution of Jews that began in 1391 with the assault upon the Jewish section of Seville, the creation of the Inquisition, and the finale of 1492 that witnessed the infamous Edict of Expulsion.

Bach-Mai, *D'ivoire et d'Opium*—a novel by the Vietnamese writer of fiction; a documentary piece resulting from the writer's experiences in Thailand in 1981 as a bilingual writer for a Canadian Broadcasting Corporation group; the writer relates her exciting journey in the jungles of Southeast Asia, where she observed elephants (thus, the reason for the "d'ivoire" of the title) and encountered mountain tribesmen dealing in narcotics ("d'opium").

Tahar Ben Jelloun, *L'Enfant de Sable*—a novel by the Moroccan poet, writer of fiction, and journalist; an episodic Oriental tale related by a traditional storyteller, as well as a disquieting journal of a solitary soul in distress; a Moroccan father of seven daughters attempts to control destiny, determining that his next child will be male; when the child, a female, is born, the father decides that she will be raised to join the patriarchy; during the child's adolescence, her female body comes in conflict with the father's obsession; she binds her breasts and treats her mother and sisters cruelly; simply, the child's ambiguous sexual identity represents the plight of those who experience loss of identity, be it spiritual or physical.

Heinrich Boll, *Frauen vor Flusblandschaft*—the last novel by the German writer of fiction, essayist, playwright, and translator, published posthumously; written entirely in monologues and dialogues; the twelve chapters concern themselves with a single day during the summer on the outskirts of Bonn; a variety of episodes link several political leaders and their families; characters range from former Nazis to Cuban socialist leaders.

Carl-Martin Borgen, *Uretten* (Injustice)—a novel by the Norwegian writer of fiction; the work, in thirty-six chapters, advances the theme of imprisonment and the tyranny that it produces; it asks the question of what destroys one's sense of morality and transforms a peace-loving humanist into a murderer; unfortunately, there appears no clear answer to the question.

Jorge Luis Borges, *Los Conjurados*—a collection of verse by the Argentinian writer of fiction, essayist, poet, and translator; the title piece foretells the eventual domination of Earth by Switzerland; other pieces set forth ideas controlled by mythology; the poet relies upon his own experiences, universal expressions of the physical world, and an overall sense of historical dread.

Willem Brakman, *De Bekentenis vau de Heer K.* (The Confession of Mr. K.)—the fifteenth novel by the Dutch writer of fiction; the piece exists as a variation on a theme by Franz Kafka: a character's frustrating quest to discover the nature of the charges against him and to provide for his defense.

Anthony Burgess, *Flame into Being: The Life and Works of D. H. Lawrence*—a biographical study by the English writer of fiction; the biographer looks upon his subject as a modern pagan saint; he also emphasizes the writer's class prejudices and pretensions.

Peter Carey, ***Illywhacker***—a novel by the Australian writer of fiction; a comic piece that relates the adventures of a man who claims to be 139 years old; the work takes its cue from the title, translated variously as "taleteller," "trickster," "con man," and "liar"; the central focus of the work involves the deception so necessary to the principal character's survival.

Carlos Coutinho, ***O Que Agora Me Inquieta***—a novel by the Portuguese writer of fiction; in this piece, the writer attempts to explain the mulitnational trauma brought about by the wars for the independence of colonial Portuguese Guinea, Angola, and Mozambique; particularly, the novel concerns the suspicious death of a committed guerrilla fighter and an officer's effort to ascertain the role of the principal character of the piece in that incident.

William Robertson Davies, ***What's Bred in the Bone***—a novel by the Canadian writer of fiction; the writer develops his principal character's pursuit of self-discovery; supernatural, psychological, and religious elements complement such intellectual interests as art, embalming, and astrology.

Sven Delblanc, ***Maria Ensam*** (Maria Alone)—a novel by the Swedish writer of fiction; the last volume of a tetralogy, the first volume of which appeared in 1981; the writer derives the name of the title character from his mother; trained as a teacher, she abandoned her independence and financial security when she married a man who, although physically attractive, proved impetuous, uncommunicative, and brutal; she gradually loses her will to endure, her marriage having ended in a bitter divorce and her family failing to provide her with emotional support; overcome by depression, she takes her own life.

E. L. Doctorow, ***World's Fair***—a novel by the American writer of fiction; the work exposes the reader to the world of the 1930s, as seen through the eyes of a child; a combination suspense thriller and exotic adventure; a recipient of the American Book Award for fiction.

Sergei Dovlatov, ***Remeslo*** (The Craft)—an autobiographical novel by the Russian writer of fiction; the work outlines the "unmaking" of a Soviet writer and his birth as a Russian writer in America; he struggles not only with his art, but, as an immigrant, the problems of survival and the search for an audience for his work; thus, the piece reflects the writer's attempt to come to terms with himself and the entire phenomenon of emigration.

Lawrence Durrell, ***Quinx; or, The Ripper's Tale***—a novel by the English writer of fiction, poet, and essayist; the title reflects a sluggish train that bores its passengers; the principal character, a novelist within the novel, begins by throwing his major work out of the window, but he manages to recover the pages; the final work of the *Avignon Quartet* (1975-1985); it contains a parade of fascinating characters who spend most of their time engaged in intellectual exercises (complete with French and Latin quotations).

Anestis Evangelou, ***To Xenodhohio he to Spiti, he Alla Peza*** (The Hotel and the House and Other Pieces)—a collection of short stories (his tenth book since 1960) by the Greek writer of fiction and poet; the writer appears caught up in his own nostalgia for the past, particularly recollections of family life in Salonika during the early years of the period between the two world wars; memories combine with imagination and fantasy to produce dreamlike images and situations.

George Faludy, ***Selected Poems, 1933-1980***—a collection by the Hungarian-born Canadian poet, biographer, translator, and writer of fiction; in these pieces, the poet warns of the dangerous effects of capitalism on the West, but also condemns the totalitarian regimes of Eastern Europe; the poems reflect his humanist beliefs and his impatience with poverty, cruelty, and ignorance.

Raymond Federman, ***Smiles on Washington Square***—a novel by the French-born American writer of fiction, essayist, and translator; exploring the relation between fiction and reality, the writer obscures the details of a love affair, considering the possibilities rather than the facts; the work receives the American Book Award for fiction.

Jeanette Ferreira, ***Sitate om 'n Revolusie*** (Citations about a Revolution)—a novel by the South African poet and writer of fiction; the writer confronts the realities of conditions in South Africa, specifically the chasm between blacks and whites created by the system of apartheid; the piece takes place in 1974 and is set on the campus of a black university in one of the self-governing homelands; the year has witnessed an upsurge of riot and unrest, and the principal character, a white lecturer in Afrikaans, encounters racism and hostility from both black students and white colleagues; her personal life becomes as sterile and as fruitless as those very policies enforced by the government.

John Fowles, *A Maggot*—a novel by the English writer of fiction; set in the early eighteenth century, the work concerns mysterious events surrounding a journey undertaken by five unrelated but nonetheless interconnected individuals; an investigation goes forward after one character has been found hanging from a tree and another simply vanishes; the title takes its cue from the archaic context of "an obsession."

Carlos Fuentes, *Gringo Viejo* (The Old Gringo)—a novel by the Mexican writer of fiction, playwright, and essayist; essentially a study of Mexican-American relations; the writer creates an imaginative scenario of the fate that befell the American journalist and writer of fiction Ambrose Bierce (1842-1914?) after his disappearance in Mexico.

Mavis Gallant, *Home Truths*—a collection of short stories by the Canadian writer of fiction; her characters tend to reflect the conflict of cultural assimilation and the difficulty of being Canadian during and shortly following World War II; indifference serves only to conceal wounds endured by hopeless and futureless emigrants or by mediocre bureaucrats who save to buy their sons a "good, Protestant education"; the majority of her characters represent "by-products of narrow-mindedness."

Isaac Goldemberg, *Tiempo al Tiempo* (Play by Play)—the second novel by the Peruvian writer of fiction and poet; concerns the fatal search for identity of an alienated Peruvian youth; after spending years with his gentile mother, he comes to live with his Orthodox Jewish father; the boy's story is told through the device of a surrealistic soccer match, during which a maniac broadcaster transmits a play-by-play account of the youth's life and eventual suicide.

Alasdair Gray, *The Fall of Kelvin Walker: A Fable in the Sixties*—a novel by the Scottish writer of fiction; concerns the adventures of a man raised in a strict religious environment who begins an odyssey in London in search of fame and fortune; the piece abounds in social commentary.

Michael S. Harper, *Healing Song for the Inner Ear*—a volume of verse by the American poet; the pieces are arranged into such sections as "Re Persons I Knew," "Ends of Autobiography," "My Book on Trane"; contains such poems as "Chronicles," "Stepto's Veils,"

"The Hawk Tradition," "In Hayden's Collage," "Egyptology," and "The View from Mount Saint Helen's."

Josef Haslinger, *Der Tod des Kleinhauslers Ignaz Hajek* (The Death of the Tenant Farmer, Ignaz Hajek)—a novel by the Austrian writer of fiction; set in rural Austria, the work relates the story of a man's problematic relationship with his Czech father, whose recent suicide and funeral cause a revelation of the dead man's past by friends and relatives; thus, the son can reconstruct the account of his birth and early childhood that had formerly been concealed from him.

Seamus Heaney, *Station Island*—a collection of verse by the Irish poet; the title refers to a pilgrimage to an ancient place of penance, there to encounter the shades of former Irish writers, friends and relatives; they criticize the poet's behavior and offer him advice for the future.

Ernest Hemingway, *The Dangerous Summer*—a narrative, commissioned by *Life* magazine in 1959, but not published until this year; the American writer reflects upon his Spanish experiences, particularly bullfighting; emphasizes the ritual, grace, beauty, pain, dignity, and courage of the bullring; also contains recollections of the 1950s and a form of heroic vision that came from the period between the two world wars.

Lance Henson, *Selected Poems, 1970-1983*—a collection of verse by the Cheyenne native American poet; these brief poems depend upon their images and the ability of the writer to realize language as an "original magic"; thus, the poet believes that words possess their most potent power when they can function free from conventional poetic interference; the individual poems are deeply rooted to the writer's birthplace of Oklahoma and the traditions of the Cheyenne forebearers.

Linda Hogan, *Seeing through the Sun*—a collection of verse by the native American poet; the writer has been identified as one who "happens to be Indian," rather than as a writer of strictly "Indian" verse; thus, in this collection, she produces poems that bridge the gap between her Chickasaw mixed ancestry and the universal condition of which all human beings find themselves a part.

Janette Turner Hospital, *Borderline*—the third novel by the Australian-born Canadian writer of fiction; the work concerns two Canadians who discover a Salvadorian refugee attempting to enter Canada from the United States; the writer explores the motivations of her characters while integrating themes about politics and personal freedom with philosophical speculation on the nature of art and reality.

Alexander Kaletski, *Metro: A Novel of the Moscow Underground*—a novel by the Russian writer of fiction; a fictionalized memoir of the writer's days as a young actor in the Soviet Union; the work transports the reader from the principal character's apprenticeship at the Moscow Theater and Film Institute to his final departure from Russia; although obviously anti-Soviet in tone, the novel does present a fairly positive and lighthearted portrayal of life among those who struggle for food and money in contemporary Russia.

Bernard Kangro, *Tuiskliiv/Talvereis* (Blowing Sand/A Winter Journey)—the thirteenth collection of verse by the Estonian writer of fiction, poet, and literary historian; published in Sweden, where the writer settled in 1944; the poems reflect a number of journeys leading both backward to the land of the poet's youth and forward to a dimly perceived and mysterious future; the pieces suggest travel and develop themes on the general subject of wandering.

Garrison Keillor, *Lake Wobegon Days*—a novel by the American writer of fiction and nonfiction; an incisive portrait of small-town American life that combines sarcastic wit and affectionate respect, evoking both the character of Midwestern people and the tradition of such American humorists as Mark Twain and James Thurber.

Jamaica Kincaid, *Annie John*—a collection of short stories by the West Indian-born American writer of fiction; the pieces were originally published in the *New Yorker* magazine; the stories are unified by their focus upon the life of the title character, a precocious woman who struggles to achieve individuality and to escape the influence of a domineering and possessive mother; eventually, a fierce love-hate relationship develops between mother and daughter.

Ivan Klima, *Moje Prvni Lasky* (My First Loves)—a volume of short stories by the Czech writer of fiction and playwright; the collection leaves the reader with the impression of the writer as a bemused observer who mocks his own attempts to cope with the absurdities of a harsh world; detachment and ironic humor mark all of the stories as char-

acters strive to provide meaning to fascinating and frightening realities.

Fumiko Kometami, *Sugikoshi no Matsuri* (Passover)—two novellas by the Japanese writer of fiction; both works share the same central character: a Japanese woman struggling with a teenaged, brain-damaged son and her pathologically tempermental Jewish-American husband; the title piece receives the Akutagawa Prize and the Shincho Shinjin Prize, while the second novella, *Enrai no Kyaku* (A Guest Who Came from Afar), earns the Bungakukai Shinjin Prize.

Doris Lessing, *The Good Terrorist*—the nineteenth novel by the Persian-born and Rhodesian-raised English writer of fiction; a political piece focusing upon an educated defector from the upper middle class; at age thirty-six, she has done little more than renovate condemned houses as "squats" for loosely organized communes; for basic income she depends upon welfare, but for larger expenses she steals from her parents; through various episodes, she proves herself to be neither a do-gooder nor a terrorist, since the leftist underground serves also as her refuge from a bourgeois existence.

Julio Llamazares, *Luno de Lobos*—a novel by the Spanish writer of fiction; the writer has divided the work into four parts covering the years 1937-1946, with the focus upon the civil war (1936-1939) and the repressions of the Franco regime that followed; a group of Republican partisans must find refuge in the mountains near their villages once the region has been recaptured by the nationalist troops.

Lars Lundkvist, *Korn*—a collection of verse by the Swedish poet; the volume reflects the writer's fascination with the elements of Lapp culture; the tone of the volume is relaxed, showing the poet to be open to everything that presents itself and cognizant of the fact that nothing in this universe can be dismissed as trivial.

James Merrill, *Late Settings*—a collection of poems by the American writer of verse; the thesis of these pieces concerns the notion of life as a comedy to be observed: there simply exists no room for tragedy; the volume also reveals the extent of the poet's debt to popular culture.

Slavko Mihalic, *Tihe Lomace* (Quiet Fires)—a collection of free verse by the Yugoslav poet; essentially, the poet projects a world of isolation and pain, of yearning for the unattainable; simply, the pieces seek to ascertain the meaning of life, the ultimate purpose of which remains, for the writer, a mystery.

Abdul Rahman Mounif, *A l'Est de la Mediterranee* (To the East of the Mediterranean)—a novel by the Saudi Arabian writer of fiction; the piece focuses upon two narrators: one has been imprisoned in a country "east of the Mediterranean," and the other, his sister, attempts to take care of her brother following their mother's death; both attempt to transcend the overwhelming atmosphere of state-sponsored terror.

Richard Murphy, *The Price of Stone and Earlier Poems*—a volume of fifty sonnets by the Irish poet and essayist; the majority of the poems tend to be metaphorically centered upon the building of the poet's house and other structures; additional pieces concern the birth of the poet's son and meditate upon the deaths of fellow writers (Tony White and Mary Ure).

Kurt Narvesen, *Ved Bredden* (On the Brink)— the sixth collection of verse by the Norwegian poet; the poems are generally metaphysical in nature and reflect poet's concern for the soul, the corruption of the modern world, and the theme of love; the modern world seems possessed more by Satan than by God, particularly in light of threatening nuclear disasters; in essence, we appear to be denying our humanity.

Monika van Paemel, *De Vermaledijde Vaders* (The Damned Fathers)—the fourth novel by the Dutch writer of fiction; the various parts of the work implement different narrative forms and techniques, and the work ranges from a form of a fairy tale to a strictly factual account of the German invasion of Belgium in 1940; the action begins with the birth of the principal character in 1945 (VE Day) and then shifts back into the early years of the twentieth century; finally, it drifts forward to the year 2023.

Grace Paley, *Later the Same Day*—a collection of short stories by the American writer of fiction; each piece considers the varieties of human motivation and action; themes range from old friends to aging to love; other concerns focus upon the effects of change and loss.

Gyorgy Petri, *Azt Hiszik* (They Think So)—a collection of verse by the Hungarian poet; the first section concerns such private preoccupations as the poet's fear of aging and death; the second section features short epigrammatic pieces on political and philosophical issues (for instance, the sentimental uttering of Vladimir Lenin or the execution of Nikolai Bukharin).

Yannis Ritsos, *O Yerontas Me Tous Hartaetous* (The Old Man with the Kites)—a novel by the Greek writer of fiction; a respectable old man, a professional writer, spends his time composing a form of fictional diary; he also has a passion for kites (a child's hobby), which he makes and stores, but must hide hurriedly whenever someone comes to visit; he pretends and thinks about immature trivialities, which relate to his preoccupation with his art.

Elisabeth Rynell, *Sorgvingesang* (Songs from the Wings of Sorrow)—a volume of verse by the Swedish poet; generally interpreted as a defiant attempt to counter isolation and despair by means of artistic expression; however, language fails, and words become messengers of impotence and destruction; images of winter landscapes of ice and frigidity dominate the poems.

Francoise Sagan, *De Guerre Lasse*—a novel by the French writer of fiction; set against the background of a defeated France, in May 1942; the principal character, the owner of a small shoe factory, does not like war, particularly since it might interfere with his agreeable life in the as yet unoccupied zone of France; in addition, he spends his leisure time satisfying his "unbridled passion of women."

Nayantara Sahgal, *Plans for Departure*—a novel by the Indian writer of fiction and essayist; the work involves the conflict between the old and the new, as set in a remote Himalayan village during 1914; the principal character, a free-thinking Danish woman, arrives from England to work for an Indian professor; she soon becomes involved in a mystery that develops around a reticent district magistrate and his absent wife.

Jesus Fernandez Santos, *El Griego*—a novel by the Spanish writer of fiction; based upon the life of the painter Domenikos Theotokopoulos (1541-1614), "El Greco."

Isaac Bashevis Singer, *The Image, and Other Stories*—a collection by the Polish-born Yiddish writer of fiction; most of the pieces are set in "shtetl" Europe, but a few occur in the New World, in areas populated by immigrants; the writer focuses upon the religious Jews of Eastern Europe, people who struggle to integrate their spiritual values with their desires for love, success, and material comforts.

Antonio Skarmeta, *Ardiente Paciencia*—a novel by the Chilean writer of fiction; a moving homage to the Nobel laureate of Chile, Pablo Neruda; the novel covers the period 1969-1973 and concerns a character who comes to learn about love and emotional and aesthetic development; the world of literature and ideas come to him through the inspiration of Neruda.

Iain Crichton Smith, *The Tenement*—a novel by the English poet and writer of fiction; concerns a multi-dwelling structure in a Scottish town; the building has shaped and survived its inhabitants; burst water pipes, chipped paint, and names written upon bedroom walls symbolize the movement in and out of six flats and lead to a series of dramatic crises for the characters.

Aleksandr Solzhenitsyn, *Krasnoe Kolesev. 2 Octiabr' Sheslnadsatogo*—a novel by the Russian writer of fiction and miscellaneous prose; the work takes place in October 1916 on the eve of the Russian Revolution, the last period of reasonableness in Russian history; the piece traces the path of Lenin into Russia that leads to the eventual downfall of a world and an idea.

Muriel Spark, *The Stories of Muriel Spark*—a collection of twenty-seven stories by the Scottish writer of fiction; a number of the pieces are set in Africa, treating racial questions that merge with the writer's interest in Roman Catholicism; semimagical and metaphysical events also contribute to the stories: ghosts as narrators and babies' points of view.

Tom Stoppard, *Rough Crossing*—a drama by the English playwright, described as an "entertainingly lunatic" adaptation of Ferenc Molnar's *Play at the Castle,* concerned about a playwright thinking about writing a play; the English dramatist's propensity for puns enlarges upon the formulaic conventions of the boulevard comedy: a love triangle, overheard conversations, and misunderstandings.

Jose Luis de Tomas Garcia, *La Otra Orilla de la Droga*—a novel by the Spanish writer of fiction; focuses upon drug addiction, particularly the traumatic, chemical dependency that lies beyond the illusion of pleasure; set in Valencia, the rich and varied action concerns the tragic decline of two heroin addicts, a man and his lover, a high class prostitute.

Mario Vargas Llosa, *Historia de Mayta* (The Real Life of Alejandro Mayta)—a novel by the Peruvian writer of fiction, essayist, and playwright; the writer conducts a journalistic investigation into the life of the title character, a Trotskyite who led an abortive rebellion against the Peruvian government in the late 1950s, then faded from public view.

Vladimir Voinovich, *Antisovetskii Soventskii Soiuz* (The Anti-Soviet Soviet Union)—a collection of essays and miscellaneous prose pieces by the Russian writer of fiction, essayist, poet, and playwright; concerns such topics as the writer's expulsion from the Soviet Union and the means by which ordinary citizens resist government control in contemporary Russia; relies on the elements of satire.

Kurt Vonnegut, Jr., *Galapagos*—a novel by the American writer of fiction; the writer goes back one million years to the beginning of the human race; he then follows the descendants of an ill-fated cruise to the Galapagos Islands; the narrator of the piece concludes that Charles Darwin's theory of evolution must be correct.

Frederick James Wah, *Waiting for Saskatchewan*—a collection of verse by the Canadian poet; the volume is arranged into four sections: (1) a selection from the poet's long piece "Breathin' My Name with a Sigh," in traditional form; (2) a poetic diary of the writer's journey to China, his father's homeland, in 1982; (3) short prose paragraphs that reflect the poet's memories of his childhood and his father; (4) another set of prose poems, each closing with a traditional Japanese haiku line and meditating upon life in the present; the sections are linked by the common theme of the writer's search for his own racial and cultural heritage; more importantly, the poems reflect the poet's attempt to understand his own father and their relationship.

Eudora Welty, *One Writer's Beginnings*—a volume of autobiographical musings by the American writer of fiction; the author presents her life as though it existed within one of her fictional environments, with emphasis upon the relationship between the artist's work and her experience.

Rebecca West, *Cousin Rosamund*—a novel by the English writer of fiction, published posthumously; the third volume in the writer's saga of the Aubrey family; two sisters, both concert pianists, perform in the capitals of the world during the 1920s; the sister's social standing emerges as important as their art.

Marguerite Yourcenar, *Un Homme Obscur*—a novella by the Belgian-born writer of fiction, playwright, and essayist; relates the life and death of the principal character, Nathanael, in seventeenth-century Holland; throughout his short life, he engages in a number of occupations and experiences that expose him to various environments, and he travels to Greenland, England and the New World; he dies alone of consumption at age twenty-seven, having at least achieved a degree of spiritual harmony.

EVENTS

Jurgen Berndt edits *Bi-Lexiokon: Ostasiatische Literaturen*, an East German (Leipzig) literary journal devoted to works by Chinese, Japanese, Korean, Mongolian, and Vietnamese writers.

Carolyn Ashley Kizer, American writer of verse, receives the Pulitzer Prize in Poetry for *Yin: New Poems* (1984).

Allison Lurie, American writer of fiction, receives the Pulitzer Prize in fiction for her novel *Foreign Affairs* (1984).

President Ronald Reagan signs into law a bill empowering the Librarian of Congress to annually name a Poet Laureate/Consultant in Poetry.

Kenneth Silverman receives the Pulitzer Prize in biography/autobiography for his *The Life and Times of Cotton Mather* (1984).

Claude Simon, French writer of fiction, receives the Nobel Prize for literature.

Stephen Joshua Sondheim and James Elliot Lapine receive the Pulitzer Prize in drama for *Sunday in the Park with George* (1984).

Studs Louis Turkel, American writer of miscellaneous prose, receives the Pulitzer Prize in nonfiction prose for *The Good War: An Oral History of World War II* (1984).

1986

DEATHS

Simone Lucie Ernestine Marie Bertrand de Beauvoir (b. 1908). French philosopher, writer of fiction, essayist, and autobiographer; although in recent years embraced by the feminist movement, she considered herself more of a Marxist; a leading exponent of ex-

istentialism, she became associated with Jean-Paul Sartre, whose influence appears in those of her novels concerned with interpreting the existentialist dilemma; she analyzed the status of women, and commented upon society's treatment of the elderly; she died in a Paris hospital from circulation problems.

Jorge Luis Borges (b. 1899). Argentinian writer of fiction, essayist, poet, and translator; he wrote esoteric short stories that blended fantasy and realism to address complex philosophical problems; with paradox and oxymoron, he combined such seemingly contradictory concepts as universality and particularity, illusion and reality; a hereditary disease seriously affected his sight in the late 1950s, thus limiting his productivity to poetry, lectures, and translations.

John Gerard Braine (b. 1922). English novelist; his fiction contributed significantly to the "angry young man" movement of the late 1950s and early 1960s, particularly in terms of developing characters from the lower middle class and the provinces who attempted to take advantage of every possible opportunity for social advancement; in his later efforts, the writer himself challenged the radicalism with which he had once been identified.

Sid Chaplin (b. 1916). English writer of fiction; a "working-class" novelist from northeast England whose work focused upon the lives of working-class youth in Newcastle-upon-Tyne; he tended to blend, in totally unconventional manner, main plot and subplot, attempting to create a series of "symbolic counterpoints"; realistic and melodramatic modes become the means by which his characters move from one social and psychic structure to another; his novels have been adapted to the motion picture screen.

John Anthony Ciardi (b. 1916). American poet, critic, and classical translator; although his own verse has faded with the frail poetic conventions of the 1940s and 1950s, he achieved recognition as poetry editor of *The Saturday Review* (1956-1972), as well as for his skillful translations of Dante.

Fumiko Enchi (b. 1905). Japanese writer of fiction; a skilled storyteller, whose narratives focus on various social issues relating to women; her work is also distinguished for the atmosphere of horror and spirit-possession that it invokes; simply, she weaves a grim tapestry of the sorry fate of Japanese women.

Hans J. Frohlich (b. 1932). German writer of fiction; his work develops the themes of loss and of the reciprocal relationships of fathers and sons; further, he explored and exposed modern human beings as existing in moral vacuums; he died from a chronic heart condition.

Jean Genet (b. 1910). French playwright, writer of fiction, and poet; his literary reputation rests on his poetic dramas, bizarre fantasies involving dominance and submission, sex and death; he created a universe in which to sin against the bourgeois moral order through theft, rape, or murder meant the infliction of moral censure upon the self; exotic imagery, metaphor, French argot, and scatological language dominate his fiction.

Laura Zametkin Hobson (b. 1900). American writer of fiction; she produced extremely popular pieces that concerned such subjects as antisemitism and homosexual experiences.

Christopher Isherwood (b. 1906). English playwright and writer of fiction and nonfiction; his experiences in Germany provided the substance of his fiction; he formed a relationship with W. H. Auden, with whom he wrote three dramatic pieces; in 1939, he moved to the United States.

Valentin Petrovich Katayev (b. 1897). Russian writer of fiction, playwright, and poet; he satirized economic conditions in the Soviet Union, attempted to draw varying portraits of Russian life from 1905 through World War II, and wrote two volumes of memoirs between 1966 and 1972.

Ding Ling (b. 1904). Chinese writer of fiction; her short stories reflect her outspoken individualism on such issues as women's sexual feelings, the rejection of traditional roles played by virtuous wives and mothers, and the means by which the demands of revolution affect women's emotional and sexual relationships; the Chinese Nationalist government kept her under house arrest for three years (1933-1936); the Communist Party expelled her in 1957, forced her to endure persecution and imprisonment, and recanted its position in 1979; in 1981, she attended the University of Iowa International Writer's Program.

Bernard Malamud (b. 1914). American writer of fiction; in his best work, depicted Jewish traditions and the effects of American urban existence upon Jewish characters; he combined comedy and pathos, fantasy and realism, exploring the full range of possibilities available to contemporary human beings: success, failure, suffering, redemption.

Kersti Merilaas (b. 1913). Estonian poet; her early verse consists of simple, well-rhymed stanzas, with emphasis upon the general topic of humanism; during the Stalin regime in the Soviet Union, she recorded her instinctive emotional reactions to world events; her later poems express the latent nationalism of all Estonians, and she became a popular "mother" figure to young Estonian poets.

Juan Rulfo (b. 1918). Mexican writer of fiction and nonfiction; his work displays stylistic and dramatic force; in his fiction, he focused upon the lives of Mexican peasants and their stoicism in the face of adversity; for background and setting, he relied generally upon his native state of Jalisco, where lives become caught in the eternal cycle of poverty, death hovers near, and existence has little value; in 1970, he received the Mexican Premio Nacional de Literaturia award, and in 1983 the Premio Principle de Asturias from Spain.

Jaroslav Seifert (b. 1901). Czech poet; his work reflects the shifts in his attitude toward the function of poetry; the work he composed during the 1920s appears "ebullient," while in the 1930s he embraced surrealism; during the Nazi occupation, he became a vehement patriot, and then, toward the end of his long life, his verse evidenced qualities of "a meditative, philosophical sage"; in 1984, he received the Nobel Prize for literature; he died in a Prague hospital from an apparent heart attack.

PUBLICATIONS

Fleur Adcock, *The Incident Book*—a volume of verse by the New Zealand-born poet and translator; these highly imaginative pieces reflect the poet's quiet, dry, and sharp sense of humor, perhaps the main reason for the popularity of the volume; the poet shares with the reader her own common experiences, at the same time protesting against the negative social aspects of life in England.

Yuz Aleshkovsky, *Kangaroo*—a novel (his first published in English) by the Russian writer of fiction, written as early as 1975; essentially the account of a small-time criminal whose forced confession to the rape and murder of an elderly kangaroo results in a surreal journey through the Soviet penal system; a satire against the "show trials" of the Stalin regime; narrated in the first person with emphasis upon the main character's profane and criminal-associated language.

Aharon Appelfeld, *To the Land of the Cattails*—a novel by the Romanian-born Israeli writter of fiction, essayist, and poet; a woman rejects her Jewish heritage to marry a gentile; she later journeys to her home with her son in an attempt to reconcile her doubts about Judaism; after experiencing anti-Semitic attitudes during the trip, the two become separated; the son joins a group of Jews by the railroad tracks and awaits an unknown destination.

Maya Angelou, *All God's Children Need Traveling Shoes*—an autobiographical narrative by the American writer of narrative, poet, and playwright; the fifth volume of her autobiography; outlines the search of black Americans for an African home during the 1960s.

Alan Ayckbourn, *A Chorus of Disapproval*—a play by the English dramatist; focuses upon a group of actors whose personal and theatrical experiences become farcically entangled; John Gay's *Beggar's Opera* serves as the unifying element, as a principal character advances his way through a contingent of bored local wives to the leading role; in the end, his personal successes parallel his triumphs on the amateur theatrical stage; the piece exists as an obvious satire upon provincial life and its two principal elements: sex and money.

John Banville, *Mefisto*—a novel by the Irish writer of fiction and critic; the writer examines evil and its relationship to language and memory; a character recounts his lonely childhood, during which he sought order and form through mathematics; he also sought harmony, despite the influence of a satanic mentor he believed may have been his deceased twin brother; the work reflects the influence of Samuel Beckett.

Edward Kamau Braithwaite, *Roots*—a volume of cultural history by the Barbados historian and critic; the work exists as a challenge to Eurocentric theories of West Indian history, religion, art, politics, and music; from another view, the eight essays serve as a statement of the writer's views on the philosophy of black Caribbean culture; of prime importance stands the promotion of "nation language": its rhythms, its collective forms, its ridicule of individualism, its singing of the praises of eccentricity.

Guillermo Cabera Infante, *Holy Smoke*—a work of nonfiction by the Cuban-born writer of fiction and essayist, his first book written in English; a factual account of the history of the cigar; the volume includes an anthology of famous smoking scenes from literature

and film; the piece abounds with puns and wordplay.

Maryse Conde, *Moi, Titubo, Sorciere, Noire de Salem*—a fictionalized biography by the Guadeloupean writer of fiction, playwright, and essayist; the title refers to Tituba, a Barbadian slave executed for practicing witchcraft in colonial Massachusetts; she exists, in this work, as a mystic and healer whose gifts had been misunderstood and feared by her Puritan masters.

Elio Fiore, *In Purissimo Azzurro*—a collection of verse by the Italian poet; the writer emphasizes his own spiritual relationships with poets from the past and the present; thus, the titles of the majority of his poems come from verses by Saba, Ungaretti, Vergil, Luzi, Gatto, Neruda, Aleramao, Garcia Lorca, and Dante; he also dedicates five poetical compositions to Rafael Alberti; Christian doctrine and historical events form additional sources of inspiration for the poet.

William Gaddis, *Carpenter's Gothic*—the third novel by the American writer of fiction; the work consists almost entirely of dialogues and monologues; develops a series of divergent plots focusing on a "never-seen" television evangelist with political connections and aspirations, a geologist and probable intelligence operative in Africa and the Far East, and a scarred Vietnam war veteran turned small-time media consultant; the "carpenter's Gothic house" along the Hudson River serves as the setting for the entire piece.

Amitav Ghosh, *The Circle of Reason*—the first novel by the Indian writer of fiction; the work contains a multitude of characters and events that detail the diverse adventures of the guileless central character; in three sections the author describes the traditional East Bengal village of the protagonist's youth, (with his adoption and apprenticeship), his escape after the murder of his family to the hastily modernized city of al-Ghazira, and his subsequent travels throughout Algeria.

Gunter Grass, *Die Rattin* (The Rat)—a novel by the German writer of fiction, essayist, poet, and playwright; the narrator endures apocalyptic dreams in which a talking rodent (she-rat) documents the history of political and ecological ignorance that has led to the demise of humanity; described as "a disturbing modern-day book of Revelations written in dream language."

David Grossman, *Hiyuch Ha-gedi* (Smile of the Lamb)—a novel by the Israeli writer of fiction; a political piece that concerns the dilemma of the Israeli as a conqueror; it also exists as a moral and philosophic critique of a military government under which a million and a half Arabs must live, allowing the Israeli nation to function "within a plausible state of security"; such a condition can and does produce entanglement, pain, and tragedy.

Ernest Hemingway, *The Garden of Eden*—a novel by the American writer of fiction, published posthumously; in form, "a story within a story"; concerns a newlywed couple that becomes involved with another woman; while attempting to adjust to that relationship, the husband composes a brilliant essay about an elephant hunt; written during the period (late 1950s) of the writer's failing health and deteriorating confidence in his craft.

Witi Ihimaera, *The Matriarch*—a novel by the New Zealand writer of fiction; relates the attempts of the principal character to understand the tribal inheritance assigned to him by his grandmother, the matriarch of his "whanau"; the narrative alternates between past and present, blending expository prose, polemics, and historical record; the woman details her prominent ancestors and manages to reconcile family and tribal rivalries through her mysterious charismatic powers.

Robert Lalonde, *Une Belle Journee d'Avance*—a novel by the French Canadian writer of fiction who publishes his work in France; the writer begins this complex piece with a child not yet born, a novel not yet written, and a day that has not yet dawned; then follow fragmentary stories told in short narrative segments, each one interpreting the other; the narrative constantly shifts between the present and various stages of the past, usually without warning; topics of the piece range from love, to various characters in a small Quebec town, to base human sins.

Aonghas MacNeacail, *An Seachnadh Agus Dain Eile* (The Avoiding and Other Poems)—the fifth volume of verse by the Scottish poet; the pieces lack capitalization, while the writer almost totally disdains punctuation; includes Gaelic originals with English translations, in addition to another fifteen Gaelic poems without benefit of their English parallels; the principal poem focuses upon the harshness of the Scottish countryside and the place of the human being within it; the volume is especially valuable in terms of its linguistic phenomena.

Greg Matthews, *Heart of the Country*—the second novel by the Australian writer of fiction, researched and written in the United States; the piece is set in nineteenth-century Kansas and relates the frontier adventures of an illegitimate half-breed; the principal themes involve the random nature of fate and the destructiveness of the human will.

Timothy Mo, *An Insular Passion*—a novel by the Hong Kong-born English writer of fiction and essayist; a historical piece set during the First Opium War between China and England; two young American journalists campaign to put an end to the British sponsored importation of opium into China; the writer achieves authenticity through the insertion of actual letters, diaries, and newspaper clippings.

Taghi Modarressi, *The Book of Absent People*—a novel by the Iranian-born writer of fiction; the piece is set in the 1960s during the final years of the Shah's regime; the narrator, an artist, searches for his long-absent half brother, a revolutionary, discovering along the way an intricate web of relations within his own aristocratic family; essentially, the family represents the entire nation of Iran.

Marianne Moore, *The Complete Prose*—a collection of pieces by the American poet and essayist, published fourteen years after her death; the volume contains more than four hundred essays, reviews, and short stories published between 1907 and 1968; most significant are the essays focusing upon the art and craft of poetry.

Percy Mtwa, *Bopha!*—the second play by the South African dramatist; the writer explores the predicament of black township police officers who antagonize and alienate fellow blacks by serving the white South African government; for principal characters, he develops the roles of two brothers: one is a career police sergeant, while the other enlists in the police force because he can find no other employment; the younger one leaves the force after being reprimanded for arresting a white lawbreaker, and the career officer resigns after angry blacks burn his house and his son has been sent to prison for involvement with student activists.

Thomas Murphy, *Bailegangaire*—a drama by the Irish playwright; a young woman cares for her demanding and ill-tempered grandmother; as such, she serves as a metaphor for the ambivalent relationship between contemporary Ireland and its ancient traditions.

Lewis Nkosi, *Mating Birds*—the first novel by the South African writer of fiction, essayist, and playwright; the piece explores the ramifications of miscegenation under apartheid, as portrayed through the story of a young Zulu student about to be hanged for allegedly raping a white woman; awaiting his execution in a South African prison, he vividly details the events that led to his arrest and death sentence.

Joyce Carol Oates, *Marya: A Life*—a novel by the American writer of fiction; traces the life and experiences of an intellectual, from her childhood to her middle thirties.

Ariosto Augusto de Oliveira, *A Noite do Galo Doido* (The Night of the Mad Cock)—a collection of short stories by the Brazilian writer of fiction; the nine tales in this volume range in length from two to twelve pages; they focus, collectively, upon the personal minutaie surrounding the daily struggle of the city dweller for survival; the characters reflect the proverbial amorality of Sao Paulo's capitalistic jungle, performing a wide range of illegal acts, most of which underscore their own inferiority complexes.

Agistino Richelmy, *La Lettrice di Isasca*—a volume of verse by the Italian poet; lyric pieces on the subjects of love and nature; the poems reveal the influences of Petrarch, Metastasio, Foscolo, Leopardi, Saba, and Montale; thus, the poet focuses upon the theme of desire, with its attendant longing and melancholy; displays rigorous attention to formal rhythm and versification.

Dominique Rolin, *L'Enfant-Roi*—a novel by the French writer of fiction; concerns a seven-year-old child with the perspicacity of Henry James, the literary style of James Joyce, and the perverse curiosity of Marcel Proust; he maintains a diary for Sunday, 14 August 1984, a fairly typical day for his nuclear family; they engage in a sacrificial rite of visiting with the retarded member of the family, as well as a celebrative rite of a dinner party; the child shares his dreams, his fantasies, and his memories with the reader.

Vikram Seth, *The Golden Gate*—a verse novel by the Indian-born writer of fiction and poet; a series of sonnets through which the narrator relates and comments upon the adventures of several characters; in iambic tetrameter and nearly six hundred stanzas, the writer examines the intertwined romantic lives of five young Californians in the early 1980s; the work was modeled after Alexander Pushkin's *Eugene Onegin*.

Endo Shusaku, *Sukyanduru* (Scandal)—a novel by the Japanese writer of fiction; identified as a psychological mystery story, the piece focuses upon a sixty-five-year-old Catholic novelist (the writer?) comfortably fixed in the literary establishment and at the height of his career; at an award ceremony, he spies a look-alike who watches the proceedings with a derisive smile; later, rumors circulate that the writer has been frequenting a Tokyo red-light district, which causes the man to search out this look-alike imposter and to try to clear his name.

Irini Spanidou, *God's Snake*—a novel by the Greek-born American writer of fiction; the work assumes the form of short story-like chapters in which the narrator's memory moves back and forth in time; she discounts chronological order as she recounts her experiences; those vivid and stark recollections focus upon her childhood in Greece during the aftermath of World War II.

George Szirtes, *The Photographer in Winter*—a collection of poems by the Hungarian-born English writer of verse; the pieces are unified by the poet's visit to Hungary in the early 1980s, and thus he explores such themes as tyranny and exile; the title piece describes his parents' lives in Budapest, evoking an atmosphere of terror and totalitarian surveillance.

Wolfgang Trampe, *Tanzstunde*—a collection of short fiction and travel prose by the East German poet and writer of fiction; the stories constitute vignettes of Berlin life in the 1950s; the travel narratives describe three journeys to Prague, Italy, and Cologne.

Derek Walcott, *Collected Poems, 1948-1984*—a volume of representative verse by the Trinidadian poet; the pieces represent the cultural and racial plurality of the West Indies, countering all simplified visions of the culture of that area; the strength of the volume rests on the poet's obviously public voice.

EVENTS

Elizabeth Frank receives the Pulitzer Prize in biography/autobiography for her *Louise Bogan: A Portrait* (1985).

Larry Jeff McMurtry, American writer of fiction, receives the Pulitzer Prize in fiction for *Lonesome Dove* (1985).

Akinwande Oluwole (Wole) Soyinka, Nigerian playwright, poet, writer of fiction, and autobiographer, receives the Nobel Prize for literature.

Henry Splawn Taylor, American writer of verse, receives the Pulitzer Prize in poetry for *The Flying Change* (1985).

Robert Penn Warren, American writer of fiction, poet, and critic, named the first Poet Laureate of the United States.

1987

DEATHS

Jean Marie Lucien Pierre Anouilh (b. 1910). French playwright, translator, and writer of fiction; his plays reveal a skeptical and bitter attitude toward the human condition; for him, pessimism results when sensitive individuals are confronted by the general cruelty of life; human beings despair because they are never able to discover their true selves; his strength as a dramatist arose from his mastery of stagecraft: simply, he could entertain while investigating serious and intellectual themes.

James Baldwin (b. 1924). American writer of fiction, playwright, and essayist; his works focus upon African-Americans and the various (and most often unsuccessful) relationships between the races; he sought to discover a common ground where racial differences could be stripped of their power to block human communication.

James Alonzo (Jim) Bishop (b. 1907). American journalist, biographer, and miscellaneous prose writer; he gained recognition and achieved popularity for his detailed accounts of the deaths of Jesus Christ, Abraham Lincoln, and John Fitzgerald Kennedy.

Erskine Preston Caldwell (b. 1903). American writer of fiction; he wrote highly popular, extremely realistic novels of life among the "lesser" classes in the American South; labeled "a master illusionist," he could easily create the impression of absolute authenticity; for him, the more shiftless and lazy the people, the better the substance for his short stories and novels.

Humberto Costantini (b. 1924?). Argentinian writer of fiction, playwright, and poet; his works are generally set in the Argentina of the 1970s; through humor and satire, the writer conveys his view of the arbitrariness of fate and the oppression brought about by military dictatorships; he depicted innocent civilians unwittingly involved in political misery and chaos.

Jean Margaret Wemyss Laurence (b. 1926). Canadian writer of fiction and essayist; she focused upon such issues as the vulnerability of childhood, forced solitude, the problems within suburbia, the female's search for meaning, and the source of the impulsive nature.

Primo Levi (b. 1919). Italian memoirist, writer of fiction, poet, and essayist; he gained a reputation for his fiction that focused upon Jewish resistance against the Nazis during World War II; similarly, his verse considered the horrors of the Holocaust and the ability of human beings to survive in the face of utmost horror and tragedy.

Alistair Stuart MacLean (b. 1922). Scottish writer of fiction and poet; he wrote more than two dozen volumes, the majority of which are war adventures and thrillers; the action of those pieces ranges from one continent to the next, occurring in airplanes, ships, and nuclear submarines; his novels sold millions of copies in both Britain and the United States; he died of heart failure while on a visit to Munich, West Germany.

Truman Nelson (b. 1911). American writer of fiction and essayist; his literary endeavors reflect his labors as a social activist; he is remembered today as an authentic voice of radical politics during the middle and late 1960s, a strong voice against hatred and racism.

Lasgush Poradeci (b. 1899). Albanian poet; he lived the final years of his long life in Pogradec, Yugoslavia, on Lake Ohrid, near the border with Albania; intent upon studying the ever-changing moods of that body of water, he injected into his verse the rhythmic and gentle sound of the lapping of the waves; commentators have remarked that he embraced the sensations of romanticism, the thoughts of classicism, and the spiritual loneliness of symbolism; his work evidenced a type of "stylistic finesse" that significantly contributed to the enrichment and diversification of Albanian poetry.

George Emlyn Williams (b. 1905). Welsh playwright; his dramas were fairly popular among those who could associate with their locales; essentially, he intertwined a seriousness of purpose with a tendency toward psychological terror; an excellent actor, he tended to cast himself into the lead roles of his own plays.

Marguerite Yourcenar (originally Marguerite de Crayencour; b. 1903). Belgian-born writer of fiction, poet, essayist, and translator; although she wrote in French, her work has little to do with contemporary French society; rather, she focused upon the overall European past, emphasizing the historical and academic natures of events; philosophy, history, and myth play key roles in her work, helping to link past with present and to provide a thorough understanding of the general human condition; in 1981, she became the first woman to be elected the Academie Francaise in the more than three-hundred-year history of that body.

PUBLICATIONS

Chinua Achebe, *Anthills of the Savannah*—a novel by the Nigerian writer of fiction, poet, and essayist; the piece, set in the imaginary West African nation of Kangan, focuses upon three childhood friends who become leaders in the government of their nation: editor-in-chief of the state owned newspaper, military leader who becomes president, and minister of information; their friendship ends in tragedy when the president fails to achieve a life-long term and ruthlessly begins to oppress his opposition.

Chingiz Aitmatov, *Plakha* (The Block)—a novel by the Russian writer of fiction; the piece represents the first occasion on which a Soviet writer commented upon the hitherto forbidden topics of narcotics trafficking and drug abuse within the Soviet borders; from that issue emerges an even more important point relative to the need for God on the part of Soviet citizens; the principal character of the novel probes deeply into the woes of contemporary Soviet society, challenging the materialistic ideology upon which it has been founded.

Kingsley Amis, *The Old Devils*—a novel by the English writer of fiction; set in Wales, the piece emerges as a combination utopian novel and science fiction narrative; further, the writer creates a slightly distorted but nonetheless believable panorama of London; from another view, the work is an accurate analysis of the history of cities and their complex roles in the development of human culture.

A. R. Ammons, *Sumerian Vistas*—a collection of verse by the American poet; contains, in addition to a sequence of meditations, twenty-nine short lyrics under the title "Tombstones"; the free verse of these pieces lacks clear beginning, end, or full stops; the title represents language written in cuneiform characters and preserved on rocks and clay tablets, all dating from an early period in history; the poems, themselves, lie upon the page as artifacts relating to human order.

Jean Arasanayagam, *Trial by Terror: Sri Lankan Poems*—a collection of verse by the Sri Lankan poet, begun in 1983; the pieces record, with apparent objective detail, the scenes of terrorism, conflict, and degradation that marked the deterioration of life in Sri Lanka through civil and external strife; the poet probes the minds of refugees, examining their fear and agony over confinement, displacement, and loss of dignity and hope; the pieces are enraged cries of frustration in the face of irrational and unwarranted violence that Sri Lankans have brought upon themselves.

Ingmar Bergman, *Laterna Magica*—a volume of memoirs by the Swedish playwright, screenwriter, and film director; in an engaging, candid, and honest style, the writer attempts to equate his life with the wonders of the cinema (the "magic lantern" of the title); he suggests a strong relationship between life and art, each possessing its own set of marvels and mysteries.

George Bowring, *Caprice*—a novel by the Canadian poet, writer of fiction, and essayist; the writer parodies the motif of the Old West revenge tale, depicting a "larger-than-life" female who sets out to avenge the murder of her brother.

Iosif Brodskii, *Uraniia*—a volume of verse by the Russian poet; the collection includes three poetic cycles, all focusing upon the perceptions of time and space, distance and accessibility, limits and limitlessness, matter and spirit; the goddess Urania, for the poet, defines bodies in space, as well as the notion of space itself; in almost every piece, the writer shifts from person, to finite object, to person.

Bruce Chatwin, *Songlines*—a prose narrative by the Australian writer; the piece combines observations and ancedotes of aboriginal life with aboriginal history and a discussion of the means by which these people relate to the earth, to their ancestry, and to one another.

Lucille Clifton, *Next: New Poems*—a collection by the American poet; the pieces focus upon the writer's dreams, her daughters and sons, her illness, her husband, and her experiences in white America; essentially, she senses "the reverberations / of myself / in white america / a black cat / in the belfry / hanging / and / ringing."

William Conton, *The Flights*—a novel by the Nigerian writer of fiction; the author reacts against the Western imperialistic practices of fellow blacks in the fictitious African nation of Songhai; the piece has been labeled "a thriller" that combines action with the issue of an oppressive land-tenure act; the protagonist, an illiterate, finds himself in London in search of the proverbial "golden fleece."

James Dickey, *Alnilam*—a novel by the American poet and writer of fiction, a project that he began before 1957; concerns an estranged father's efforts to explain his son's death in a mysterious training camp accident; blinded by diabetes and having had no contact with his son since his birth, the father nonetheless sets out, in company with a seeing-eye dog, to investigate his son's death; that exercise becomes the only contribution by the father to his son's existence (or, in this case, memory).

Margaret Drabble, *The Radiant Way*—the tenth novel by the English writer of fiction and essayist; the "group plot" focuses on three women friends: a wealthy professional and socialite, an art historian, and an English teacher who supports "good" causes; events weave together their husbands, difficult children, and elderly parents.

Robert Duncan, *Ground Work II: In the Dark*—a collection of verse by the American poet; the pieces are set in such locales as the Pacific basin and San Francisco (where one looks toward the Orient as a source of inspiration); in terms of substance, the poems touch upon the spiritual dilemmas of the twentieth century.

Sumner Locke Elliott, *Waiting for Childhood*—the ninth novel by the Australian writer of fiction and playwright; set in Australia, the work focuses upon the fortunes of a family, beginning in 1912 and extending to the Depression years; the piece starts and ends with the scrutiny of a family photograph taken in Melbourne on a hot summer day in 1912, shortly before the head of the family dies of a heart attack; the novel then follows, for twenty years, the life of each of the children (six girls and one boy).

Carlos Fuentes, *Cristobal Nonato*—a novel by the Mexican writer of fiction; the piece is set in Mexico, between 6 January and 12 October 1992, the gestation period of the central character; as the title might suggest, that charac-

ter will be named for Christopher Columbus on the five-hundredth anniversary of the founding of the New World; the unborn Cristobal not only describes his own formation, but observes his mother and father; those details constitute the significant substance of the piece.

William Golding, *Close Quarters*—a novel by the English writer of fiction; the work continues (from *Rites of Passage*, 1980) a voyage to Australia on a ship that represents class-conscious England in 1810; the vessel finds itself near collapse and in danger of sinking; the narrator promises that he will not perish, for he must remain to relate (in the future) the third installment of the series; the strength of the novel lies in its writer's vivid recreations of life on board a British vessel in the early nineteenth century.

Paula Gomes, *Het Kind met de Clownspop* (The Child with the Clown Doll)—a novel by the Dutch writer of fiction; concerns the Japanese occupation of Indonesia during World War II, as well as the effects of that experience upon the narrator, a young girl of mixed Dutch and Indonesian extraction; the title comes from a doll the narrator received at age five.

Nadine Gordimer, *A Sport of Nature*—a novel by the South African writer of fiction and essayist; the piece reflects the writer's belief that the existing social order of South Africa will be destroyed; the title refers to a botanical phenomenon in which a plant suddenly deviates from its parent stock; thus, the heroine, as a mutated offspring, represents both social and political change in that part of the world, particularly in terms of her experiences (since age seventeen) throughout Africa, the United States, and Europe.

Christiane Grosz, *Die Tochter*—a novel by the East German writer of fiction; the piece begins with the breakdown of the mature protagonist, who does not have the courage to insist upon a divorce; then follows an account of that character's childhood, leading into the marital entrapment into which she eventually falls; although the work does not necessarily feature dramatic and traumatic events, it does emphasize a series of small, significant episodes: a thunderstorm, a rat in the basement, a grandmother's frightening account of her own upsetting childhood.

Henryk Grynberg, *Kadisz*—a novel by the Polish-born American writer of fiction and poet; the title takes its cue from the Jewish prayer for the dead ("Kaddish"), and thus the narrator journeys from Virginia to Los Angeles to witness his mother die from cancer; the essence of the piece concerns his sorrow and frustration as he mourns for his mother in the company of his half brother, a true double-dealer, and his stepfather, who is greedy and deceitful.

Rodney Hall, *Captivity Captive*—an epic novel by the Australian writer of fiction; a fictionalized recreation of the events that culminated in the horrible and unsolved murders of three members of an Australian family in 1898; an eighty-eight-year-old narrator details his family's history and their struggle to fashion a self-reliant existence in an extremely harsh environment.

Omar P. Halldorsson, *Blindflug* (Flying Blind)—the third novel by the Icelandic writer of fiction; an unnamed young woman travels in a small chartered plane from Reykjavik to the eastern fjords of Iceland; she had allowed herself, after the regularly scheduled flight been canceled because of bad weather, to be persuaded to join others in hiring the small craft; the flight allows the young woman to wander back and forth over the events of her life, as she travels homeward to "find herself"; all turns out to be, seemingly, a dream.

Porsteinn fra Hamri, *Urdargaldur*—a volume of verse by the Icelandic poet; the pieces combine the poetic traditions of Iceland with an extremely modern set of preoccupations and outlooks; the specifics of the poems concern the enigmas of illusion, reality, and time; the poet asks such questions as "Who are we? Where are we? Have we lost our way? Are things really what they seem to be?"

Lance Hensen, *Another Song for America*—a collection of verse by the native American poet; the writer frankly suggests that America does not appear to be moving in forward social direction; to that end, he creates striking images relating to the history and wisdom of his Cheyenne forbears, whose traditions are a source of enrichment for his people.

Rolf Hochhuth, *Alan Turing*—a novel by the German playwright and writer of fiction; he depicts the life of his title character, a British mathematician, particularly his achievements in deciphering a code employed by the German military forces during World War II; the tale is complicated by repeating shifts in point of view from that of an omniscient narrator to excerpts of a chronicle purportedly written by a fictitious assistant of the title character;

the writer also includes passages from the mathematician's travel diaries.

Christopher Hope, *Black Swan*—a novel by the South African writer of fiction, poet, and essayist; an ironic tale of a mentally retarded black South African boy whose disability allows him to diffuse the grim political realities within his nation; the government regards him as subversive, imprisons him, and sentences him to death; in the end, he remains totally unaware of his condition.

Dai Houying, *Etincelles dans les Tenebres*—a novel by the Chinese writer of fiction, translated and published at Paris; each chapter begins with a statement by one of the characters of his or her views on a particular problem or situation; the chapter itself then goes forward in a protracted monologue that reviews past conversations, anguished moments, and traumatic ideas; each topic (divorce, love, work) exists as a scene in a play, with proper dialogue, decor, lighting, and characters.

Paula Jacques, *L'Heritage de Tante Carlotta*—the third novel by the French writer of fiction; the work continues the writer's exploration of Middle Eastern Jewry; most of the action is set in Cairo (her birthplace) during 1976-1977, one of the more difficult periods in the regime of Anwar Sadat; the principal character, the Egyptian in her twenties, comes from a Jewish family; the plot goes forward when she learns that her aunt, once a well-known dancer and film star, has died in a Jewish nursing home in Cairo; she returns to that city, and encounters humor, suffering, and loneliness.

Svava Jakobsdottir, *Gunnladar Saga*—a novel by the Icelandic writer of fiction and playwright; described as a tale of imagination and reality; an Icelandic girl happens to be caught ("red-handed") in the Danish National Museum, Copenhagen, standing before a broken display case with an invaluable prehistoric golden bowl in her hands; then follows an irrational account of herself, combined with a tale of a mythical daughter of a giant, the latter being the mythical keeper of the mead of poetry.

Rod Jones, *Julia Paradise*—a novel by the Australian writer of fiction; the writer injects the motifs of Freudian analysis into a story of political and historical upheaval; the work is set in Shanghai during the period of Chiang Kai-shek's nationalist attack on communists; then follows a disturbing psychological study of a young Australian woman suffering from hallucinations and hysteria; revolution forms the background of the piece, complemented by an investigation into the relationship between public and private exploitation.

Jonas Juskaitis, *Anapus Gaiso: Eilerasciai*—a collection of verse by the Lithuanian poet; the volume comprises poems written between 1976 and 1986, and in each piece the writer seeks a sense of simplicity that corresponds with his liberation from recognized conventions of art.

Daniel Katz, *Antti Kaplerin Lait* (Antti Kepler's Laws)—a comic novel by the Finnish writer of fiction; concerns a Finnish screenwriter (the title character) preparing to shoot a film in Cairo based upon the life of a fictional Orientalist; the writer comes into contact with Egyptian locals, engages in street riots, and participates in a convention of Egyptian poets; essentially, he exists as a prototype of the wandering Jew, rejected by Arabs, Christians, and even Israelis.

Thomas Keneally, *The Playmaker*—a novel by the Australian writer of fiction, essayist, and playwright; a historical piece, published to coincide with the bicentennial of Australia; the narrative focuses upon the idealism and moral innocence of the central character, who struggles to express, through the medium of a stage play, the "balances" of art and reality; the novel exists as a melodramatic morality play containing strong psychological undertones and intended to redeem human nature from utter damnation.

Maurice Kenny, *Between Two Rivers: Selected Poems, 1956-1984*—a collection by the native American (Mohawk) poet; the writer emphasizes the notion that poetry, before it represents anything else, functions as an oral art; the poet reveals his wide knowledge of native American cultures, as well as an emotional commitment to the conditions endured by Indian people everywhere; he also addresses painful experiences in his own life that apply to human beings in general and thus transcend ethnic issues.

Eva Kilpi, *Animalia*—a collection of poems by the Finnish writer of verse; the pieces underscore the writer's defense of nature and her argument against cruelty to animals; she serves as an advocate for those who have no voice (poetic or otherwise), thus, the eight sections of the volume recognize the "silent voices."

Okinba Launko, *Minted Coins*—a collection of verse by the Nigerian poet and playwright; the volume contains forty pieces, a series of powerful love songs; within the context of the theme of love, the poet addresses the fate of Africa and Nigeria, commenting upon the significant cultural and economic cost of both colonialism and mismanagement by indigenous moguls; he also expresses sadness at the impotence of contemporary Nigerians in an environment that fails to serve them and functions solely for the advantage of the ruling classes.

Antoine Laurent, *Cuisine Novella*—a novel by the French writer of fiction; the work combines a fantastical plot with outright discourses on the art of fiction; on a train bound from Paris to Nice, a fashion designer receives an education in the interconnected arts of cuisine and storytelling, taught to her by a mysterious marquis (himself a master chef).

Halldor Laxness, *Dager hja Munkum* (Days with Monks)—a combination diary and set of reminiscences by the Icelandic writer of fiction; the diary was maintained during a six-month period when the writer converted to Roman Catholicism in the Luxembourgian abbey of Saint Maurice de Clervaux in 1922-23; the reminiscences, based upon old letters, refer to the period when, at age twenty, the writer roamed about Europe, writing, reading, and always searching for his next meal; in general, the work reveals a young man's excitement over his devotion to the Catholic Church.

Vitants Ludens, *Savas Majas: Dzejoli un Poemas* (In My Own Home)—a collection of verse by the Latvian poet; a selection of lyrics written between 1966 and 1986, all capturing the essential "Latvianness" of the writer's view of the world; thus, he intertwines his own identity with his national consciousness, declaring that "To Latvia I am held by bonds / That have been fashioned from my very life."

Eva Mattsson, *Groucho i Gront* (Groucho in Green)—a collection of short stories by the Swedish writer of fiction; in each story, the writer introduces a different aspect of irrationality, placing it against a background of mundane human existence; the complexity of the pieces emerges through the fact that each character appears, on the surface, to be disturbingly sane and well adjusted; the settings of the stories range geographically from Sweden to France to Italy; chronologically, they move from the eighteenth century to the present.

Shankar Mokashi-Punekar, *Avadhaheswari*—a novel by the Indian writer of fiction; a historical piece that focuses upon the political life of the kingdom of Avadh in Vedic times (c. 1000-500 B.C.) and encompasses three generations linked by political heritage; essentially, the issues involve the rivalries among different exponents of Vedas, the problems of surrogate fatherhood and its psychological and political consequences, racial clashes between Arians and Greeks, and power politics among individual kings.

Raphael Humberto Moreno-Dorani, *Los Felinos del Canciller*—the fourth novel by the Colombian writer of fiction; describes the elegant, elitist culture of Colombia's aristocracy during the first half of the twentieth century; their collective lifestyle comes to an end in 1949; in that year, the central character of the piece finds himself in New York City, meditating upon the past, particularly his family's activities in diplomatic circles during the period 1920-1949; essentially, while the diplomats defend the national honor, the novelist satirizes the traditional institutions of the nation.

Toni Morrison, *Beloved*—the fifth novel by the American writer of fiction; the work concerns an escaped slave in post-Civil War Ohio, who had attempted to kill all of her children prior to the moment of her recapture; however, she managed only to take the life of her baby, whose gravestone reads "Beloved"; the spirit of the dead child haunts the house, particularly since "nothing ever dies"; the spirit then comes out of the water as a live being, establishing a relationship with its mother and sister and driving away a man who had come to live with the former; on a larger, more significant level, the piece details memory, history, and language from the view of black Americans; the work received the Pulitzer Prize for fiction in 1988.

Haruki Murakami, *Noruwei no Mori* (Norwegian Wood)—a novel (in two volumes) by the Japanese writer of fiction; the title, derived from a song by the Beatles, relates to the writer's attempt to define the culture of the 1960s for modernized nations; the characters, although distinctly Japanese, work and play in a decidedly Western environment and atmosphere: they frequent coffee shops, play jazz, inject English phrases into their speech, eat spaghetti and pizza, read books by Western writers, and sing Western popular songs to their own accompaniments; in such an atmosphere, the narrator must come of age and confront the puzzling problems of love and death.

Iris Murdoch, *The Book and Brotherhood*—a novel by the English writer of fiction; a group of middle-aged English intellectuals live in their own world of knowledge and secret passions, each motivated by a burning desire for another member of the group; the central character, the object of a number of those passions, is an enigmatic antihero who both fascinates and catalyzes the group; the failure to create, suicide, and murder constitute the principal activities of the piece, with the underlying thesis focusing upon the power of ideas to unite human beings in both love and hate.

Henrik Nordbrandt, *Under Mausolaeet*—a collection of verse by the Danish poet; with considerable beauty and philosophical subtlety, the poet considers such problems as death, instability, loss, and inconsistency; in considering the whole of humankind, the poet alternates, in substance and tone, between brutal observation and disillusionment.

Joyce Carol Oates, *You Must Remember This*—a novel by the American writer of fiction and critic; the writer places a conventional lower middle-class family against the events and the tensions of the 1950s; in unmasking her characters' respectability, she develops the issue of an incestuous love affair between the youngest daughter and her uncle, which ends in suicide; thus, the errors of the world pull one toward death; from another view, the work is a gothic piece that restates the traditional theme of the release of the captive maiden.

Michael Ondaatje, *In the Skin of a Lion*—a novel by the Ceylonese-born Canadian poet, writer of fiction, essayist, and playwright; the work chronicles the oppressed lives of immigrant workers who helped expand and modernize the city of Toronto, Ontario, early in the twentieth century; the central character represents a growing social awareness that the writer develops through a surreal and collage-like narrative.

Anne Philipe, *Le Regard de Vincent*—a novel by the French writer of fiction; the principal character loses her husband to a young girl; the narrator, a friend of both the woman and her husband, tries to be objective about each; thus, the narrator observes in the affair a phenomenon of nature, an overwhelming passion on the part of one partner and an immense pain experienced by the other; in the end, an harmonious relationship develops between all parties concerned (excepting the husband, who has died).

Nelida Pinon, *A Doce de Caetana*—the eighth novel by the Brazilian writer of fiction; the title character, an unsuccessful actress, returns to Trinidad after an absence of twenty years to star in a production of *La Traviata*, a project doomed from the beginning; through the complexity of plot and action, the work emerges as a broad satire offering a light-hearted and entertaining interpretation of conventional existential dilemmas.

Dennis Quiring, *L'Arbre de Reve*—a novel by the French writer of fiction; focuses upon a young German soldier who returns home from a Russian prisoner-of-war camp and finds ruin and devastation; he suffers from recurring nightmares and images of barbarism that he witnessed and in which he participated; further complicating his problems is his mixed French and German heritage; his guilt forces him to seek explanations and justifications for his actions.

Jovan Radulovic, *Braca po Materi* (Half Brothers)—a novel by the Yugoslavian writer of fiction and playwright; the piece begins with a murder, followed by eight letters containing reflections upon past and present events relative to two half brothers; those letters also relate to the animosities between Yugoslavia's two largest nationalities, Serbs and Croats; thus, the novel really stands as a political and philosophical message on the ethnic complexities of the nation.

Klaus Rifbjerg, *Engel*—a novel by the Danish writer of fiction; a middle-aged couple journey to southern Europe, partly to repeat the trip they made prior to their marriage; a young Dane who joins them attempts suicide, but the wife saves him; then they meet a woman from their first journey, and she strikes up a relationship with the young Dane; the wife, whose first name is Angel, indeed serves the role; the travel motif emphasizes the need to find a common ground between past and present and to satisfy the curiosity.

Tidor Rosic, *Jarac Koji se ne da Uzjahati* (A Goat Who Wouldn't Be Mounted)—a collection of short stories by the Yugoslavian writer of fiction; the nineteen pieces concern everyday life in the large city, related in a matter-of-fact fashion; however, the writer actually unveils in these stories a world bursting with fantastic occurrences and abnormal behavior, a world in which mundane events produce shocking results; the nightmarish consequences clearly resemble those produced by such writers as Karel Capek.

Simone Schwarze-Bart, *Ton Beau Capitaine*—the first play by the Guadeloupcan writer of fiction and dramatist; a migrant agricultural worker from Haiti lives in a shack in Guadeloupe; he holds cassette-taped conversations with his wife, whom he left in Haiti; essentially, he represents the sufferings of the wretched of the earth; from such a context emerges the larger issue of the loss of culture, community, and identity resulting from labor pools.

Thomas Shapcott, *Travel Dice*—a volume of verse by the Australian writer of fiction, poet, and essayist; the pieces record a mid-life journey to such cities as Toronto, New York, London, Rome, Venice, and Naples and to such countries as Hungary, Yugoslavia, Turkey, and Greece; the poet visits museums, parks, zoos, tombs, and historical sites; in the end, he never forgets the relationship between the words "travel" and "travail."

Karl Shapiro, *New and Selected Poems, 1940-1986*—a collection of verse by the American poet; the volume shows the writer's craft undergoing continual formal challenges established by the poet himself.

Yoshiko Shibaki, *Yuki-Mai* (The Snow Dance)—a novel by the Japanese writer of fiction; concerns the life of a woman born into a family of traditional Japanese dangers; although she lives in modern Japan, she works in an expensive traditional Japanese restaurant and dances for its customers; the piece reveals a variety of customs and conventions peculiar to the esoteric world of art, at the same time explaining how a traditional performing art can be preserved within a technologically oriented twentieth-century society.

Terje Stigen, *Katedralen*—a novel by the Norwegian writer of fiction; concerns a group of Germans at the end of World War II; they take refuge in a cathedral that has, miraculously, escaped destruction; the young narrator, who has lost his family in the bombings, shares the building with a deserter and his homosexual partner (an organist), a teacher, and an old woman and her granddaughter; danger, principally in the form of unexploded bombs, lies everywhere about them.

Wilma Stockenstrom, *Kaapse Rekwisiete* (Cape Town Theatrical Props)—a novel by the South African writer of fiction and poet; concerns a group of irrelevant, superficial characters, members of a state theatrical company in Cape Town; these people, in their insignificance, represent the helplessness and alienation of the white South African in the 1980s; cynicism reigns supreme here, and no one appears to care about anything; throughout, the tragedy brought about by apartheid prevails.

Emilio Tadini, *La Lunga Notte*—a novel by the Italian writer of fiction; the title refers to a long night in which a woman tells her story to the narrator and his friends; focuses upon World War II and the difficult months following the liberation of Italy; although the woman serves as the protagonist, the Italy of 1943 turns out to be the principal concern of the piece; the thesis clearly directs itself to the issue of human survival and prosperity amid the difficulties and the deprivations of the times.

Peter Taylor, *A Summons to Memphis*—a novel by the American writer of fiction; a subtle tale of family betrayal, revenge, and reconciliation; a strong-willed Southern patriarch deliberately undermines his son's first engagement, as he had done earlier with each of his two daughters; the abnormal family relationships come forth as the central character, the son, struggles to understand the personality of his father.

Fulvio Tomizza, *Quando Dio Usci di Chiesa: Vita e Fede in un Borgio Istriano del Cinquecento*—a collection of stories by the Italian writer of fiction; based upon actual historical incidents involving several people accused of heresy during the sixteenth century; takes places on the peninsula of Istria, when both the kingdoms of Venice and Austria ruled the territory; a number of the inhabitants have come under the influence of Martin Luther, and thus the religious and political powers look upon them as heretics.

Manuel Veiga, *Oju d'Agu* (The Water's Eye)—a novel by the Cape Verdean writer of fiction, written in the Creole language of that area; a tale of contemporary Cape Verdean families barely able to endure during the transition from Portuguese rule to independence.

Derek Walcott, *The Arkansas Treatment*—a collection of poems by the West Indian-born writer of verse and playwright; the poems focus upon the American South, upon instances and situations that call forth the poet's identity as a black man.

Lothar Walsdorf, *Uber Berge Kam Ich*—a collection of verse by the East German poet; the theme of the volume concerns time, identi-

fied as the nemesis of poets and philosophers; essentially, the poet wishes to cause everything to occur simultaneously, and he sets out to create that illusion; however, he also recognizes that time prevents everything from happening at once; over three-quarters of the poems refer, in the title or first line, to the "time."

Ian Wedde, *Driving into the Storm: Selected Poems*—a collection by the New Zealand writer of verse, written between the 1960s and the early 1980s; a number of poems reveal the influence of the American postmodernists and thus counter Romantic and Georgian traditions; the poet seeks to celebrate the diversity of objects rather than their unity.

Theodore Weiss, *From Princeton One Autumn Afternoon: Collected Poems, 1950-1986*—a collection by the American scholar, editor, and writer of verse; the pieces reflect ease and control of language and vary radically in style and voice; the poet appears at his best when the poems are topical and ironic, when his mood is intimate and frank.

Sandor Weores, *Kutzbanezo* (Gazing into a Well)—a volume of verse by the Hungarian poet, illustrated with his own drawings; includes short meditations on nature, as well as reflections (in the first person singular) upon the unpleasantness of old age and the proximity of death; the poet also considers the "goodness" and "badness" of nature, as he stands on the side of the natural environment and against the industrial megalomania of the twentieth century.

Terence de Vere White, *Chat Show*—a novel by the Irish writer of fiction, biographer, and essayist; a fictional investigation of the British television industry, revealing the ephemeral nature of fame and wealth.

Alki Zei, *I Arravoniastikia tou Achillea* (Achilleas's Fiancee)—a novel by the Greek writer of fiction; relates the story of a woman who lives in Paris during the period (1967-1974) of Greek dictatorship; she recalls the resistance years of World War II, the Greek civil war, and her subsequent journey to Russia in 1960; the writer alternates her narrative between first and third persons, and the work tends to be strongly autobiographical; the title character represents a myth, a legendary captain of the communist guerrillas of the late 1940s, a person the woman hardly ever comes to know.

EVENTS

Iosif Alexandrovich Brodsky, Russian-born writer of verse (living in the United States since 1972), receives the Nobel Prize for literature.

Rita Frances Dove, American poet, receives the Pulitzer Prize in poetry for *Thomas and Beulah* (1986).

Peter Hillsman Taylor, American writer of fiction, receives the Pulitzer Prize in fiction for his novel *A Summons to Memphis* (1987).

Richard Purdy Wilbur, American poet, essayist, and translator, appointed Poet Laureate of the United States for 1987-1988, succeeding Robert Penn Warren.

August Wilson, American playwright, receives the Pulitzer Prize in drama for *Fences* (1986).

1988

DEATHS

Raymond Carver (b. 1938). American writer of fiction, poet, and essayist; he attracted critical attention for his short stories, the majority of which appeared initially in periodicals; these pieces abound in excitement, mystery, danger, and the possibilities of life; he emphasized reality, complemented by his compassion and honesty toward his subjects and characters.

Edward Chodorov (b. 1904). American playwright; he produced his major works prior to the end of World War II, including such pieces as *Wonder Boy* (1932), *Kind Lady* (1935), and *Those Endearing Young Charms* (1943).

Robert Anson Heinlein (b. 1907). American writer of fiction; he achieved recognition as a popular writer of science fiction and fantasy literature; his pieces cast his characters into apocalyptic contexts that force them to observe the resurrection of traditional and conventional concepts; thus, future worlds of chaotic ferocity and intrigues tend not to be too far removed from what the twentieth century recognizes and identifies as reality.

Alan Stewart Paton (b. 1903). South African writer of fiction; his work identified and defined a form of liberalism emphasizing generosity of spirit, tolerance of others, commitment to the rule of law, recognition of the dignity of human beings, repugnance of authoritarianism, and love of freedom.

Miguel Antonio Gomez Pinero (b. 1946). American poet and playwright; his verse tends to be harsh and realistic, combining ghetto invective, feverish sentimentality, and machismo swagger; his most powerful plays focus upon the "anti-universe" of prison life, much in the manner of Jean Genet.

Michael Joseph Shaara, Jr. (b. 1929). American writer of fiction; he gained recognition for his novel *The Killer Angels* (1974), which concerns the four-day Civil War battle at Gettysburg, as seen through dispatches written by General Robert E. Lee and his lieutenant; in 1975, he received the Pulitzer Prize for fiction.

PUBLICATIONS

Alan Ansen, *Contact Highs: Selected Poems, 1957-1987*—a collection by the American writer of verse; the pieces reflect the writer's past associations with the Beats and the New York City school of poets; thus, he fuses Beat sensibility with formalist discipline and rigor; the influence of W. H. Auden can also be recognized here.

Aharon Appelfeld, *The Immortal Bartfuss*—a novel by the Romanian-born Israeli writer of fiction, poet, and essayist; the piece chronicles the quiet anguish of a Holocaust survivor, now age fifty and married, with two grown daughters; he turns inward, isolating himself from everyone, including those he continues to love; he finds comfort only in his "treasures": three gold bars, three thousand dollars, and photographs of his parents.

Wayne C. Booth, *The Company We Keep: An Ethics of Fiction*—a volume of literary and moral commentary by the American essayist and critic; the writer takes his thesis from the notion that although people may not be specialists in art, they know that the power of a book or a painting generates both good and evil; the substance of the discussion rests upon a host of novels, stories, poems and even advertising jingles that need to be observed from an ethical point of view.

Anthony Burgess, *Any Old Iron*—a novel by the English writer of fiction; the writer combines erudition and historical lore: Celtic legends, discourses on etymology, quotations from Ovid, William Blake, and T. S. Eliot, and digressions on Arthur Schopenhauer and the history of Benedictine monasteries; the plot of the work ranges far: the decks of the doomed H.M.S. *Titanic,* the trenches of Verdun in World War I, Petrograd in the midst of the Russian Revolution, the Italian beachheads of World War II, the prison camps of Poland and Gibraltar, contemporary New York City, and embattled Israel.

Andree Chedid, *Mondes Miroirs Magies* (Worlds, Mirrors, Magics)—a collection of short stories by the Egyptian-born French writer of fiction, poet, playwright, and essayist; the volume is divided into three sections, each containing seven stories; section one includes episodes set in Cairo, Paris, Beyreuth, and Florida; section two is comprised of sketches and personal reflections on the writer's childhood; section three consists of fantasies that span a period of time ranging from the biblical Fall to the Egypt of three thousand years ago to the technological age of the present century.

Miriam Cooke, *War's Other Voices: Women Writers on the Lebanese Civil War*—a critical study by the English writer; focuses upon the "Beirut Decentrists," women who have written about the civil strife in Lebanon; their novels, poetry, essays, and short stories, written from the feminist perspective, separate them from the large corpus of general war literature; their principal theme appears to be the dilemma faced by the Lebanese people during these times: to leave or to remain; the men want to emigrate, but the women dare to stay, which involves a moral decision and an act of commitment; remaining represents the acid test of an unmistakable Lebanese identity and exists as a part of the feminine process.

Robertson Davies, *The Lyre of Orpheus*—a novel by the Canadian writer of fiction, essayist, and playwright; essentially a biting satire upon the artistic muse, as portrayed through the experiences of a menagerie of comic, dried-up university intellectuals; the writer also attacks the narrowness of special interest groups, the pretentiousness of the learned, the philistinism of societies hostile to individuality, and the stultifying effects of conformity (particularly among women).

Ellen Douglas, *Can't Quit You, Baby*—the sixth novel by the American writer of fiction; the piece is set in the American South in the 1960s, where everything that has been racially and culturally preserved stands upon the brink of change; focuses upon the growing uncertainty of a relationship between a white upper-class woman and her black domestic servant.

Vladimir Dudintsev, *Belye Odezhdy* (White Robes)—a novel by the Russian writer of fiction; the writer details a sinister struggle during the late 1940s between committed geneticists and the followers of Trofim Lysenko, who achieved notoriety through his irresponsible and unscientific schemes to reform Soviet agriculture; on a more general level, the writer attempts to analyze the development of conscience and to study the dilemma of intellectual responsibility.

Josep Palau i Fabre, *Amb Noms de Dona* (With Women's Names)—a collection of short stories by the Spanish (Catalan) poet, playwright, and writer of fiction; the volume contains ten concise, straightforward tales in which women and the element of eroticism stand in the foreground; all of the women portrayed appear human, liberated, and "earthy," and they collectively represent the writer's attempts to interpret the nature and psychological complexities of woman.

Nadine Gordimer, *The Essential Gesture*—a collection of essays by the South African writer of fiction and nonfiction; the writer functions as a traveler here, recording and shaping an intellectual and artistic journey from the realm of early talent to the realm of mastery and moral responsibility; she anchors her observations and ideas to South African culture and society; that nation represents a crucible in which the artist must discover the means to respond to the conscience and to produce art; in terms of racial differences, those two impulses may well have to contradict each other.

Margita Gutmane, *Ta Pati Diena* (The Very Same Day)—a fictional narrative by the Latvian writer; a difficult piece, first because it appears as prose, yet contains rhythmic and syntactic patterns akin to verse; secondly, the narrator often changes identities; on one level the reader observes a child looking at the world, then that level shifts to a caged animal or an insect trapped in a sink; the piece receives the Janis Jaunsudrabins prize for prose.

Rodney Hall, *Kisses of the Enemy*—a novel by the English-born Australian writer of fiction, poet, biographer, and essayist; the work concerns the degradation of Australia resulting from an American Star Wars conspiracy; set in 1992, with Australia in the midst of mobocracy and conspiracy; the wealthy and the secretive who control the country select a fifty-three-year-old businessman to run for president of the newly formed republic.

Alamgir Hashmi, *Inland and Other Poems*— the sixth collection of verse by the Pakistani poet; the work reveals the personal and artistic struggles of an English-educated post-colonial with the contemporary issues of identity and alienation; surrealistic imagery contributes to the tone of bitterness, self-pity, and discontent.

Raphael Juarez, *Fabula de Fuentes*—the fourth collection of verse by the Spanish poet; twenty-two short poems that strive to recreate the traditional Andalusian song form; rather than relying upon adjectives for description, the poet emphasizes repetition, contrasts, and intellectual suggestion; the poet creates a lonely voice comparable to the melancholy tone of the lyric ballad.

Alfred Kazin, *A Writer's America: Landscape in Literature*—a combination critical essay and autobiography by the American literary critic and memoirist; on one level the writer addresses the issue of the relationship between humankind and nature, on another level, he filters environmentalist history and speculation through the literature of the United States: Henry Adams's Washington, Hart Crane's New York, Robert Lowell's Boston, Joan Didion's Los Angeles; in the end, he produces a positive discussion, one generally praising his nation's landscape and its literature.

Doris Lessing, *The Fifth Child*—a novella by the Persian-born Rhodesian-raised English writer of fiction; described as a moral fable that emphasizes the fragility of a materialistic, self-centered culture and society; a man and woman meet, marry, and pursue happiness; her pregnancy with their fifth child becomes a hellish experience: the newcomer wrestles within her womb and bursts forth as an unwanted monster; the child dominates and then destroys the loving family; essentially, he represents one-fifth of Britain's young: inarticulate, uneducable, alienated, and amoral; he comes from the womb of a sick society that appears suicidally obsessed with happiness at any cost.

Francois Mallet-Joris, *La Tristesse du Cerf-Volant* (The Sadness of the Kite)—a novel by the French writer of fiction; the work traces the lives of three generations of a Flemish family of mill owners in the town of Kerkhove, on the outskirts of Lille; begins with the founding of the firm at the outset of

the twentieth century and extends to the 1970s; the theme focuses upon the search for an absolute; thus, one character spends years painting a fresco in the stairwell of the tower of the family chateau; strange little men all try, without success, to catch the string of an invisible kite; human beings pursue an ideal that they will never catch.

Eduardo Mendoza, *The City of Marvels*—a novel by the Spanish writer of fiction; the writer outlines the anarchic growth of Barcelona at the height of its industrial expansion; from one point of view, the piece functions as an essay in social history, presenting the vibrant coastal city cast in the political shadow of Madrid; Barcelona exists as a case study of the effects of social and economic modernization; a large cast of historical characters allow the reader to visualize why the "second city" of Spain deserves recognition (with Paris and Vienna) as a center of international modernism in the arts.

Arthur Miller, *Danger Memory! Two Plays*— two one-act plays by the American dramatist: *I Can't Remember Anything* and *Clara;* each piece carries the powerful emotional charge and social perceptions associated with the writer; in *I Can't Remember Anything,* a work suffused with comedy and affection, an elderly couple shares and disputes their recollections; in *Clara,* recollection takes the form of a dialogue between a young woman's father and the detective investigating her murder; both plays originally produced in New York City in January 1987.

Patrick Modiano, *Remise de Peine*—a novel by the French writer of fiction; the narrator, now an adult, writes of a time when, as a child, he and his brother had been sent off to live with a friend of his mother in a small town outside Paris; he knows that his knowledge of his life at that time cannot be complete; as a boy, he had little or no comprehension of the actions of adults; further, his memory tends to be imperfect: thus, what the narrator does not know and cannot remember serves to intensify the mysterious quality of the work.

Jose Ferrater Mora, *El Juego de la Verdad* (The Elusiveness of Truth)—a novel by the Spanish philosopher and writer of fiction; concerns the subject of truth: what is and what seems to be; the owner of an escort service sets down three testimonies: the original, the retraction, and the retraction of the retraction; the original testimony implicates a wealthy industrialist in a murder plot against his beautiful socialite wife; the retraction blames the wife and other characters for trying to frame the industrialist; the retraction of the retraction asserts the innocence of the wife and places blame upon the husband; before the truth can be determined, someone discovers the owners of the escort service floating face down in a lily pond; the writer, in addition to wrestling with the issue of truth, reveals a threatening world of AIDS, drug trafficking, child prostitution, and white collar crime.

Joyce Carol Oates, *American Appetites*—a novel by the American writer of fiction; a respected middle-aged man, married and comfortably settled, finds his life shattered; his wife dies under strange circumstances, he discovers she has had an affair, and he suffers from guilt because he had desired (but never even touched) a young woman he had given money to for an abortion; the title refers both to the novel and to a cookbook that the man's wife had been writing at the time of her death; essentially, the appetites of these characters (whether food, power, or sex) have absolutely no foundations.

Gieve Patel, *Mister Behram*—the third play by the Indian dramatist the piece is set during the days of the British Empire and contains several themes: the self-deception of liberals, the mistreatment of women, the cunning of the underdog, the sexual drives that achieve expression in social and political attitudes; the title character, a highly educated and successful lawyer, raises a young tribesman as a member of his own family; he becomes obsessed with the youth, and that leads to the destruction of his reputation.

Milorad Pavic, *Hazarski Recnik* (Dictionary of the Kharzars)—A novel by the Yugoslavian poet, writer of fiction and academician; a complex piece written in the form of a three-part dictionary or encyclopedia; devoted to the history and culture of the Khazars, a powerful group that flourished during the Middle Ages between the Black Sea and the Caspian Sea (now part of the Soviet Union); central to the novel is a debate, held in the late ninth century, between a Christian monk, a Jewish rabbi, and a Moslem dervish; the subject focuses upon a vision of the kaghan (the Khazar ruler) in which an angel said, "The lord is happy with your intentions, but not with your deeds."

Ali Podrimja, *Fund i Gezuar* (Happy Ending)—a collection of verse by the Albanian poet; the poet appears obsessed with the destiny of humankind, and, with unceasing irony, he strives to grasp the essence of a number of dichotomies: past versus present, myth versus reality, specific verses the abstract; the collection contains fifty-four poems divided into five cycles.

Salman Rushdie, *The Satanic Verses*—the fourth novel by the Indian writer of fiction; a Moslem fairy tale that focuses upon an Indian movie star and a British television celebrity; they find themselves aboard a London-bound Air India 747 and hijacked by Sikh terrorists; after months of time at a number of airports, the plane heads for London, but authorities refuse permission to land there; a female terrorist then destroys the craft, and the two celebrities survive, reborn into archangel and devil; the piece was banned in India and a number of Middle East countries, and the writer was forced to seek asylum in Britain to protect himself from an Iranian death threat.

Karl Shapiro, *The Younger Son*—the first volume of an autobiographical trilogy by the American poet and critic; writing from the third person point of view, the poet clearly relates the story of his audacious life in literature, particularly his experiences as poet, editor, and teacher; the writer finds it hard to classify himself among his artistic contemporaries, particularly because of his honesty, resoluteness in avoiding identification with cliques, and determination to change his mind whenever he believes appropriate; the volume supports his contention that "All truths are paired contradictions."

Bapsi Sidhwa, *Ice-Candy-Man*—the third novel by the Pakistani writer of fiction; the mode of the narrative tends to be realistic, and the work emerges as a product of acute intelligence, integrity, and imagination; the novel represents an imaginative response to the traumatic events of the 1947 partition of India; surrealistic techniques prove an effective vehicle for portraying the effect of external events upon human beings; from another view, the work emerges as a complicated and abstract love story.

Isaac Bashevis Singer, *The Death of Methuselah and Other Stories*—a collection by the Yiddish writer of fiction; the pieces reflect his distrust of socio-political causes and systems, as he derides their cocky yet pitiful certainty and their willingness to mortgage a relatively certain present for a promised but dubiously better future.

Susan Sontag, *AIDS and Its Metaphors*—an essay by the American philosopher, critic, and novelist; an attempt to demistify the metaphors of AIDS, principally ancient notions about plagues; the belief that illness serves as a punishment for moral laxity feeds upon the AIDS epidemic, she believes, standing in the way of treatment and cure.

Richard Wagner, *Ausreiseantrag* (The Exile)—a novel by the German writer of fiction; the theme of the piece focuses upon the loss of home; the writer specifically focuses upon Romania, where the government exerted extreme pressure on the German minority to leave the country.

Richard Wilbur, *New and Collected Poems*—a volume by the American poet commemorating his election as Poet Laureate of the United States for 1987-1988; the pieces reveal, in particular, the poet's ability to turn almost any occasion into a civilized poetic commentary; thus, five of the poems comprise a cantata entitled "On Freedom's Ground," a collaboration with the composer William Schuman; the writer performs such public service with wit and feeling, and the poems read well even without the music.

Charles Wright, *Zone Journals*—a collection of verse by the American poet; ten poems ranging in length from one page to forty-seven pages; the language and tone of the volume tend to be direct, informal, and colloquial; the pieces focus upon the poet himself: his self-awareness as man and artist.

EVENTS

David Herbert Donald, American critic and biographer, receives the Pulitzer Prize in biography/autobiography for *Look Homeward Angel: A Life of Thomas Wolfe* (1987).

William Morris Meredith, American writer of verse, receives the Pulitzer Prize in poetry for *New and Selected Poems* (1987).

Toni Morrison, American writer of fiction and editor, receives the Pulitzer Prize in fiction for her novel *Beloved* (1987).

Alfred Uhry, American playwright, receives the Pulitzer Prize in drama for *Driving Miss Daisy* (1987).

1989

DEATHS

Donald Barthelme (b. 1931). American writer of fiction and essayist; he became known, particularly, for his short stories, most of which tended to be experimental and surrealistic; the substance of those pieces ranges widely, reflecting the writer's urbanity, verbal humor, and inclination toward innovative designs in typography; he directed the Houston (Texas) Contemporary Art Museum; managing editor of *Location*, a New York City art and literary review, and regular contributor to the fiction section of *The New Yorker* magazine.

Samuel Barclay Beckett (b. 1906). Irish-born playwright and writer of fiction; he portrayed, in his fiction, the individual's entrapment by grotesque situations in an apparently normal world; writing within the tradition of the theater of the absurd, he combined poignant humor with the development of his characters' overwhelming sense of anguish and loss; in 1969, he received the Nobel Prize for literature.

Malcolm Cowley (b. 1898). American critic; writer of narrative, and poet; he achieved recognition for his recollections of those "lost generation" writers he knew in Paris during the 1920s; his critical commentaries related the literature of the past to the literature of the present, reflecting the general consciousness of contemporary sensibility.

Daphne Du Maurier (b. 1907). English writer of fiction; she has claimed a significant niche in the history of popular fiction with her novels and period romances; she produced her best work when she placed her plots and characters in the West Country of England, an area in which she spent a considerable portion of her life.

Owen Lattimore (b. 1900). American writer of travel narrative, historian, and academician (Johns Hopkins, Leeds [England] University); his travel pieces range through Turkestan, China, Manchuria, and Mongolia; his historical works focus upon Asia and the conflicts between nationalism and revolution; in the early 1950s he came under attack because of his views toward and interest in the political climate in China.

Irving Stone (b. 1903). American writer of fiction; his principal claim to literary recognition focuses upon the popularization of the biographical novel; thus, he wrote novels on Vincent Van Gogh, Jack London, Eugene V. Debs, Mary Todd Lincoln, Michelangelo, Rachel Jackson, and Charles Darwin; a number of those pieces became, in turn, fairly successful motion pictures.

Barbara Wertheim Tuchman (b. 1912). American historian; an extremely gifted writer, as well as an accomplished historical scholar, she produced highly readable discussions and analyses of World War I, General Joseph Stilwell, the fourteenth century, and the entire issue of historiography; she received the Pulitzer Prize for nonfiction in 1963 and 1972.

Robert Penn Warren (b. 1905). American writer of fiction, poet, and critic; as one of the Southern agrarian poets associated with *The Fugitive* magazine (1922-1925), he achieved early praise for poetry that reflected the influence of the English metaphysical poets; his later verse tended toward the simple and the regional; in his fiction, he concerned himself with the moral dilemmas of the modern world; he combined, with Cleanth Brooks, to produce important critical and textual works on the understanding of poetry and the comprehension of modern rhetorical schemes and devices; he received the Pulitzer Prize in 1947 (fiction) and 1958 (poetry).

PUBLICATIONS

Alice Adams, *After You've Gone*—the fourth collection of short stories by the American writer of fiction; the majority of the pieces concern broken love affairs; in general the male characters prove unappealing, while their female counterparts constitute positive forces within this universe.

Aharon Appelfeld, *For Every Sin*—a novel by the Romanian-born Israeli writer of fiction, essayist, and poet; the piece has been described as a poem of love for the survivors of the concentration camps; the writer attempts to extract some meaning from the historic moment when the West crossed the line into the Holocaust era; set in an abandoned, surrealistic landscape somewhere in Germany after World War II; the area is littered with the remains of a German retreat and populated only by Jewish survivors of the concentration camps, shadowy wanderers who never will be able to return to their homes.

Isaac Asimov, *Nemesis*—a novel by the Russian-born American biochemist and writer of fiction and nonfiction; the work is set in the year 2236, when Earth and its space colonies have become overcrowded and socially eroded; hidden in a remote corner of a galaxy, a renegade colony seeks to establish a new utopia, a society purer than and superior to the one left behind.

Maria Bellonci, *Private Renaissance*—a novel by the Italian writer of fiction; a historical piece set during the Italian Renaissance; in a time when males considered women nothing but commodities, the principal character reveals her fierce independence, indomitable courage, and extraordinary intelligence; thus, she will fashion a niche for herself in the history of the world.

Saul Bellow, *The Bellarosa Connection*—a novella by the Canadian-born American writer of fiction; the writer questions (as he had in earlier works) the meaning of being an American, especially if one happens to be Jewish; the old, rich, and unnamed narrator has earned a fortune as founder of the Mnemosyne Institute, which trains VIP's in the art of memory; the longest portion of the piece concerns a flashback to the 1940s, when the narrator was an intellectual roustabout hanging out in Greenwich Village; in his own words, he stood "at the bar of paternal judgment again, charged with American puerility."

Peter Benchley, *Rummies*—a novel by the American writer of fiction; a wildly comic and insightful work that proves the existence of strange creatures lurking in American drug and alcohol rehabilitation centers; the principal character, within a single week, has two double vodkas for breakfast, finds himself in an alcohol rehab center (placed there by his wife), observes the disappearance of a number of fellow patients, and finally becomes a detective.

Benazir Bhutto, *Daughter of Destiny*—an autobiography by the Pakistani politician; the piece emphasizes the education of a future prime minister while, literally, upon the knees of her father; the drama of the story concerns her years in prison and exile, with emphasis upon her emotion and courage; behind all of the events stands the question of personal drive and ambition and the determination required by a Western-educated woman to govern an Islamic nation.

Neil Bissoondath, *A Casual Brutality*—a novel by the Trinidadian writer of fiction (and nephew of V. S. Naipaul); the ancestors of the central character migrated to a fictional Caribbean island as indentured servants; orphaned in childhood, he lives with his grandparents, then moves on to Toronto, with hopes of becoming a doctor; his principal achievement, however, appears limited to marrying a waitress, who miscarries each time he impregnates her.

Breyten Breytenbach, *Memory of Snow and of Dust*—a novel by the South African writer of fiction; the writer extends the scope and purpose of his works beyond South Africa and the African continent; he concerns himself with the bitter dialogue currently developing between the Third World and the West, between the American North and South, between black and white; the piece achieves meaning not through plot and characterization, but through the writer's moral conscience, his clear understanding of Third World realities, and his extraordinarily fertile imagination.

Annie Dillard, *The Writing Life*—a collection of essays by the American writer of nonfiction and poet; essentially, the volume functions as a glimpse into the trials and satisfactions of the life of an author; from another view, it exists as a warm and rambling conversation with a stimulating and extraordinarily talented writer.

E. L. Doctorow, *Billy Bathgate*—the seventh novel by the American writer of fiction; a youth in his teens allows himself to be apprenticed to an outlaw; after the outlaw's death, he acquires his power and his women; the work is set in the 1930s and clearly relates to the mobster "Dutch" Schultz.

Margaret Drabble, *A Natural Curiosity*—a novel by the English writer of fiction and literary scholar; the principal character of the piece appears drawn to danger and risk, to the irresistible lure of the unnatural; she and her friends, although in their early fifties and seemingly settled into middle age, retain an admirable openness to new experiences.

Antonia Fraser, *The Warrior Queens*—a historical study by the English biographer and writer of fiction; the writer focuses upon the warrior queens of history, contradictions to the notion of woman as a pacifying influence upon history: Queen Elizabeth I of England, Catherine the Great of Russia, Boadicea, the Celtic queen of Iceni, Isabella of Castile, Maria Theresa of Austria, Louise of Prussia, Jinga of Angola, Tamara of Georgia, Rani of Jhansi, Uraca of Aragon, Matilda of Tuscany.

Mavis Gallant, *In Transit*—a collection of short stories by the Canadian-born writer of fiction; twenty pieces that originally appeared in *The New Yorker* magazine; each concerns, as the title would indicate, characters traveling or living in countries other than those of their births; the majority of the central figures tend to be Anglophones: Canadians, Americans, English, Irish; each experiences a "foreignness" abroad that appears rooted to the insularity of their common language.

William Golding, *Fire Down Below*—a novel by the English writer of fiction, the final volume in a trilogy; traces the journey of one Edmund Talbot from England to Australia in 1814; the piece is set on board an eighteenth-century fighting ship converted at the end of the Napoleonic wars to transport cargo and passengers; Talbot, a complacent, well-meaning, slightly arrogant but educable Englishman, embarks upon the voyage under the patronage of his rich, aristocratic grandfather, for whom he has promised to maintain a journal of his life at sea; he will tell all and keep nothing from anyone.

Gunter Grass, *Zunge Zeigen* (Show Your Tongue)—a journal narrative by the German writer of fiction, poet, essayist, and playwright; concerns the writer's six months in Calcutta, complemented by a collection of drawings done in that region; the writer appears both appalled by the Indian city and in love with it; however, his strongest emotional reaction focuses upon shame (the title being a Bengali gesture signifying shame: he reacts to the deprivation and complacence of both the middle class and the ruling communists; further, the West appears totally ignorant of the area, a fact that increases the writer's frustration and distaste.

David Grossman, *See Under: Love*—a novel by the Israeli writer of fiction; produced in the style known as "magical realism," begun by Franz Kafka and then perfected by such writers as Jorge Luis Borges, J. G. Ballard, Gabriel Garcia Marquez, and Salman Rushdie; a fantasy about the Holocaust, with an omniscient narrator whose parents and great-uncle survived the concentration camps; he grows up in Jerusalem, but remains obsessed by the events of World War II, wishing only to tame the Nazi beast, to make it good, and to persuade it to change its ways and stop torturing people.

Shusha Guppy, *The Blindfold Horse: Memories of a Persian Childhood*—a narrative by the Iranian writer of nonfiction; essentially a collection of family anecdotes that describes an Iran in troubled transition from the old world that had prevailed for centuries to the turmoil of the present; thus, there exist tales of the bonesetter who also functions as the potter, of the social life in the "hammam" (or community) bath house, of gardens that delight the Persian soul, of opium pipes that delight the Persian body.

Hella S. Haase, *In a Dark Wood Wandering*—a novel by the Dutch writer of fiction; an epic novel of fifteenth-century France and a fictionalized biography of Charles, Duc d'Orleans, the feudal lord and poet; the writer draws specific parallels between the fifteenth century and Europe during and following World War II; the background focuses upon the bloody Hundred Years' War, begun in 1337 by Edward III, King of England, a struggle that, in the end, brought new nations to life.

John Irving, *A Prayer for Owen Meany*—a novel by the American writer of fiction; the work covers a period of thirty-four years, tracing the friendship of two boys from a fictional town in New Hampshire; the narrator, well-bred but illegitimate, has a beautiful and fiercely independent mother who refuses to disclose his father's identity; his best friend proves to be the son of the owner of a hardscrabble granite quarry and his lunatic wife; both labor under their fear of a secret, "unspeakable outrage" connected with the Catholic Church.

Kazuo Ishiguro, *The Remains of the Day*—a novel by the Japanese-born and British-raised writer of fiction; the piece focuses upon the butler, a consummate imperial Englishman who finds himself on the brink of extinction; he serves as the psychological profile of England just past its peak of greatness; he finds himself in the employ of an American gentleman who suggests, unexpectedly, that his dedicated servant spend a week's holiday on an automobile trip in his former employer's splendidly antique Ford.

A. Norman Jeffares, *W. B. Yeats: A New Biography*—a study by the American literary critic; essentially a revision of the writer's 1949 effort; a chronological narrative of the continuous link between the life and the work of the subject.

Erica Jong, *Any Woman's Blues*—a novel by the American writer of fiction; the piece is narrated by a painter enmeshed in aesthetic, cultural, and moral melancholia; throughout, she wrestles with the problems of alcoholism, sexism, addiction, and female dependence; in the end, she wins every one of those battles, withstanding betrayal by the man whom she both loves and supports.

Garrison Keillor, *We Are Still Married*—a miscellaneous collection by the American writer and entertainer; the volume contains stories, poems, essays, and letters "written at the time of President Reagan"; includes ruminations on religion and baseball, instructions for writing letters and post cards, political editorializing, and poetry and fictional sketches relative to Lake Wobegon and its surroundings.

Philip Larkin, *Collected Poems*—a posthumous collection of verse by the English poet and writer of fiction; the poems tend to be bleak, depicting a life devoid of the consolations of religion or romantic love; in that life, communal rites have degenerated to polite routines; nonetheless, the writer remains a visionary of everyday experiences and activities.

John Le Carre, *The Russia House*—a novel by the English writer of fiction; focuses upon the usual games played by the British intelligence services to determine Russian intelligence activities; however, the rules of the game have been altered by "glastnost"; English, Americans, and Russians must all determine if what they know is actually the truth, or mere deceptive "chaff" from the Moscow propaganda machine; further, there emerges a key question: whether truth or falsity any longer assumes legitimate strategic difference.

Brad Leithauser, *Hence*—the second novel by the American writer of fiction, critic, and poet; the work is set four years into the future and focuses upon a chess match between a twenty-one-year-old former champion and a chess-playing computer program; the match, engineered by a giant computer manufacturer, generates public attention and becomes, during a three-week period, a media event of national proportion.

Arkady Lvov, *The Courtyard*—a novel by the Russian writer of fiction; written before the writer emigrated from the Soviet Union in 1976, with a microfilm copy of the manuscript hidden in a shoeshine kit; the work remains unpublished in the Soviet Union; examines the lives of several families and individuals and adheres rigorously to a single setting: an apartment house in Odessa, spanning the period 1936-1956; the characters note the various national and international events that affect their country: the promulgation of the so-called Stalin constitution, the Japanese attack upon Mongolia, the occupation of the Baltic countries, the Nazi invasion of the Soviet Union, and currency reform; although those events are important, they are secondary to character development.

Bernard Malamud, *The People and Uncollected Stories*—an unfinished novel and a collection of stories by the American writer of fiction, published posthumously; in *The People*, the writer introduces a new character, a Jewish peddler who becomes an Indian chief; he stands as an improbably comic hero who represents the writer's ability to transform the ordinary into the heroic; the short stories span the writer's career from the 1940s to the 1980s, providing an overview of his subject matter: from the limited world of the ghetto grocery store to the aristocratic landscape of Kew Gardens to a fictional biography of Virginia Woolf.

David Mamet, *Some Freaks*—the second collection of essays by the American playwright and writer of nonfiction; the title originates from a lecture at Harvard University in 1988 in which the writer described his initial pride and arrogance at being "one of those freaks privileged to live in the world of the arts"; that sensation diminished when he recognized that one does what one does, and thus "you and I are all those freaks"; includes ruminations on politics, aesthetics, and society, as well as recollections of other times and personalized journalistic reports (for instance, commentary upon a soldier of fortune convention).

William Maxwell, *The Outermost Dream*—a collection of essays and reviews by the American writer of fiction and memoirist; the writer composed most of the pieces as "odd jobs" during his forty years as fiction editor of *The New Yorker* magazine; the literary reviews are mainly appreciative, and at least one-fourth of the pieces concern essayists and novelists who had some association with *The New Yorker*.

James A. Michener, *Journey*—a novel by the American writer of fiction; the piece focuses upon twenty-three months in the lives of five men who travel 2,043 miles in an attempt to find an all-British route to the Klondike which happens to be in Canadian territory, but considerably more accessible through Alaska; three of them die along the way, caught in the wilderness and the dark season.

Taghi Modarressi, *The Pilgrim's Rules of Etiquette*—a novel by the Iranian writer of fiction; the piece emphasizes the horrifying conditions within the revolutionary society of Khomeini's regime; a victim of the revolution lives among other such victims, forced into retirement from his teaching post; his neighbors include an army officer (also forced into retirement), the widow of a man executed after the revolution, and a young woman blinded with acid by revolutionary zealots for failing to observe the rules of the clothing standard.

N. Scott Momaday, *The Ancient Child*—the second novel by the native American writer of fiction and narrative; the works concentrate upon a successful artist who lives in California, distanced both physically and emotionally from his Kiowa heritage; when called back to his people for the funeral of an old woman, he suddenly realizes his "sense of connectedness"; after the funeral, he returns immediately to the security of his artistic life, but he cannot escape from the power of tradition.

Harry Mulisch, *Last Call*—the fourth novel by the Dutch writer of fiction; a retired variety "artiste" spends his last days in a shabby house shared with a shrewish sister on the outskirts of Amsterdam; a letter arrives, inviting the old man to join the cast of a new play; he will have the role of a great turn-of-the-century actor, who will be portrayed in his farewell performance; the play turns on a complicated erotic scheme involving the blackmailing of the actor by his homosexual lover during a rehearsal of Shakespeare's *Tempest*.

Cheng Naishen, *The Piano Tuner*—a collection of fiction by the Chinese writer; the volume contains a novella and three stories motivated by a thesis on the cultural revolution; in the writer's own words, "to step into maturity China sacrificed a full generation of its youth"; thus, she depicts social conflicts between the modern Chinese proletariat and members of "declassed" families with financial ties to prerevolutionary China.

Ben Okri, *Stars of the New Curfew*—a collection of short stories by the Nigerian writer of fiction; the first volume of his work to be published in the United States; in poetically feverish language, the writer creates extended hallucinations and startling realizations; after mysteriously losing his job and suffering through a severe rainstorm, the narrator of these pieces drives miles into the jungle and finds himself a captive of a tribe whose feet face backward and who live in huts surrounding a "blinded skyscraper."

V. S. Pritchett, *At Home and Abroad*—a collection of travel essays by the English writer of fiction and critic; a series of portraits displaying the writer's penchant for indulging in comparative geography; he contrasts and compares humerous aspects of various cities; architecture, clothing, manners, and food.

Joao Ubaldo Ribeiro, *An Invincible Memory*— a novel by the Peruvian writer of fiction, playwright, and critic; the work chronicles the history and legends of Brazil; the writer begins with the settlement of the area in the seventeenth century, extends through its independence from Portugal and its founding as a republic in the nineteenth century, and ends with the present.

Adrienne Rich, *Time's Power*—a volume of verse by the American poet and essayist; the lyrics reflect the writer's "controlled outrage" over political and social injustices, but also address concerns; titles include "Letters in the Family," "One Life," "Divisions of Labor," "Turnings," "Harper's Ferry," and "Living Memory."

Simon Schama, *Citizens: A Chronicle of the French Revolution*—an historical study and analysis by the English-born historian and academician (Oxford, Harvard); more than a narrative, the work constitutes a discussion of the transformation that permanently altered the history of Europe: the passing of the subject and emergence of the citizen; the new order, according to the writer, emerged from an infatuation with modernity on the part of the eighteenth-century ruling class; thus, the writer focuses his discussion upon the highest levels of French society and attempts to prove that the seeds of revolution came from the social elite and their differences on how best to energize the state.

Budd Schulberg, *Love, Action, Laughter, and Other Sad Tales*—a collection of sixteen stories by the American writer of fiction; two stories focus upon the motion picture industry, while two others are set in Hollywood; the "sad tales" are wide ranging, from an Indian who travels, for the first time, from his mountain village to Mexico City to a young woman who gives birth without the presence of her husband, who has been called away to war; the pieces also depict an uneducated warehouse laborer, a wandering Jewish painter in Europe during the 1930s, an Irish longshoreman on the docks of New York, an English farmer-carpenter who finds himself aboard the *Mayflower,* and a hard corps of "movie types."

Wole Soyinka, *Isara: A Voyage Round "Essay"*—a memoir by the Nigerian poet, playwright, writer of fiction, and essayist; the second volume of the writer's imaginative reconstruction of his personal and familial history; the writer focuses upon the generation of his father (known as "Essay"), young men who have left their home village of Isara for various parts of Nigeria; they remain intent upon shaping their own futures and the future of the nation that ultimately will be born into independence.

Mickey Spillane, *The Killing Man*—a novel by the American writer of fiction, his first book in nineteen years; the twelfth "Mike Hammer" novel; the central character has not altered significantly: he remains tough, violent, oversexed, and above all independent; he finds himself engaged in a deadly "cat-and-mouse game" with a terrorist referred to by the CIA as a digital butcher; simply, he cuts the fingers from his victims, the first of whom Hammer finds behind the desk of his own office.

Jeanne Tai (compiler and editor), *Spring Bamboo: A Collection of Contemporary Chinese Short Stories*—the volume contains ten new stories from the People's Republic of China, all devoid of politics and propaganda; the writers seek, instead, to restore continuity with their own lost culture; they create fictional contexts characterized by remoteness and eeriness, developing stories that evoke a mythic quest for meaning; the writers revive and reexamine the discarded and destroyed traditions of China; the editor is a Chinese-American lawyer and scholar.

Mario Vargas Llosa, *The Storyteller*—a novel by the Peruvian writer of fiction, playwright, essayist, and literary scholar; two contemporary Peruvian men undergo change through contact with the prehistoric world of the Machiguena Indians, an Amazonian tribe; one, a Peruvian writer, has traveled to Florence for several months of solitude and to read the Italian classics; the other, his friend and former classmate, has a purple birthmark that covers half of his face and that inspires him with a burning passion for the "marginal beings" of this world; the key question of the piece concerns how modern human beings can enter the reality (and thus "tell the story") of a culture innocent of the technology and history of the twentieth century.

John Updike, *Just Looking: Essays on Art*—a collection of essays on art by the American writer of fiction; the author begins with the works of Baziotes, Dubuffet, and Tchelitchew and moves to the older artists he really admires: Cezanne and Matisse; he also considers Sargent, Renoir, and Degas.

Alice Walker, *The Temple of My Familiar*—a novel by the American writer of fiction and essayist; "an ambitious post-modern romance" in which stylized lovers, remembrances of past events, bold flights of fantasy, and visions of a brave new world of cultural diversity and cosmic harmony both challenge and celebrate "the kinship of all things."

Marianne Wiggins, *John Dollar*—a novel by the American writer of fiction; the central figure, a young woman widowed during World War I, finds herself, without love, powerless and joyless; she journeys to Burma to teach young girls at a school in Rangoon; she slowly returns to life, falls in love with the beauty of Burma and also the title character, an Englishman of the sea; then follows a strange tale of a sea voyage, a shipwreck, cannibalism, and what appears to be a reconstruction of the world by eight schoolgirls.

A. N. Wilson, *Incline Our Hearts*—a novel by the English writer of fiction, biographer, and essayist; the central character, a war orphan, lives with his uncle and aunt in a Norfolk village; he grows to maturity, his life punctuated by encounters with a mysterious and increasingly sinister character; the latter leaves misery and disgrace in his wake as he gathers material for a biography; the subject of the biography, a faded man of letters, has also been the lifelong interest of the central character's uncle, and therein lies the complexity of all the various connections.

EVENTS

Richard Ellmann, American literary historian, scholar and biographer, receives the Pulitzer Prize in biography/autobiography for his biographical study *Oscar Wilde* (1988).

Anne Tyler, American writer of fiction, receives the Pulitzer Prize in fiction for her novel *Breathing Lessons* (1988).

Wendy Wasserstein, American playwright, receives the Pulitzer Prize in drama for *The Heidi Chronicles* (1988).

Richard Purdy Wilbur, American writer of verse, receives the Pulitzer Prize in poetry for *New and Collected Poems* (1988).

Index